Microsoft® Office 365™
WORD 2016

COMPREHENSIVE

Microsoft® Office 365™
WORD 2016

COMPREHENSIVE

Misty E. Vermaat

CENGAGE
Learning®

SHELLY CASHMAN SERIES®

Australia • Brazil • Japan • Korea • Mexico • Singapore • Spain • United Kingdom • United States

Office 365 & Microsoft Word 2016: Comprehensive
Misty E. Vermaat

SVP, General Manager: Balraj S. Kalsi

Product Director: Kathleen McMahon

Senior Product Team Manager: Lauren Murphy

Product Team Manager: Andrea Topping

Senior Director, Development: Julia Caballero

Product Development Manager: Leigh Hefferon

Managing Content Developer: Emma F. Newsom

Developmental Editor: Lyn Markowicz

Product Assistant: Erica Chapman

Manuscript Quality Assurance:
Jeffrey Schwartz, John Freitas,
Serge Palladino, Susan Pedicini,
Danielle Shaw, Chris Scriver

Production Director: Patty Stephan

Senior Content Project Manager: Jim Zayicek

Manufacturing Planner: Julio Esperas

Designer: Diana Graham

Text Design: Joel Sadagursky

Cover Template Designer: Diana Graham

Cover image(s): Piotr Zajc/Shutterstock.com;
Mrs. Opossum/Shutterstock.com

Compositor: Lumina Datamatics, Inc.

Vice President, Marketing: Brian Joyner

Marketing Director: Michele McTighe

Marketing Manager: Stephanie Albracht

For product information and technology assistance, contact us at
Cengage Learning Customer & Sales Support, 1-800-354-9706

For permission to use material from this text or product,
submit all requests online at **www.cengage.com/permissions**.
Further permissions questions can be e-mailed to
permissionrequest@cengage.com

Library of Congress Control Number: 2016945904

Soft-cover Edition
ISBN: 978-1-305-87101-4

Loose-leaf Edition
ISBN: 978-1-337-25119-8

Cengage Learning
20 Channel Center Street
Boston, MA 02210
USA

Cengage Learning is a leading provider of customized learning solutions with employees residing in nearly 40 different countries and sales in more than 125 countries around the world. Find your local representative at **www.cengage.com**.

Cengage Learning products are represented in Canada by Nelson Education, Ltd.

To learn more about Cengage Learning, visit **www.cengage.com**
Purchase any of our products at your local college store or at our preferred online store **www.cengagebrain.com**

Printed in the United States of America
Print Number: 02   Print Year: 2017

Microsoft® Office 365™
WORD 2016

COMPREHENSIVE

Contents

Microsoft **Office 365 & Word 2016**

MODULE ONE

Creating, Formatting, and Editing a Word Document with a Picture

MODULE TWO

Creating a Research Paper with References and Sources

Productivity Apps for School and Work

Corinne Hoisington

OneNote
Sway
Office Mix
Edge

Lochlan keeps track of his class notes, football plays, and internship meetings with OneNote.

Zoe is using the annotation features of Microsoft Edge to take and save web notes for her research paper.

Nori is creating a Sway site to highlight this year's activities for the Student Government Association.

Hunter is adding interactive videos and screen recordings to his PowerPoint resume.

© Rawpixel/Shutterstock.com

Being computer literate no longer means mastery of only Word, Excel, PowerPoint, Outlook, and Access. To become technology power users, Hunter, Nori, Zoe, and Lochlan are exploring Microsoft OneNote, Sway, Mix, and Edge in Office 2016 and Windows 10.

Learn to use productivity apps!
Links to companion **Sways**, featuring **videos** with hands-on instructions, are located on www.cengagebrain.com.

Introduction to OneNote 2016

notebook | section tab | To Do tag | screen clipping | note | template | Microsoft OneNote Mobile app | sync | drawing canvas | inked handwriting | Ink to Text

Bottom Line
- OneNote is a note-taking app for your academic and professional life.
- Use OneNote to get organized by gathering your ideas, sketches, webpages, photos, videos, and notes in one place.

As you glance around any classroom, you invariably see paper notebooks and notepads on each desk. Because deciphering and sharing handwritten notes can be a challenge, Microsoft OneNote 2016 replaces physical notebooks, binders, and paper notes with a searchable, digital notebook. OneNote captures your ideas and schoolwork on any device so you can stay organized, share notes, and work with others on projects. Whether you are a student taking class notes as shown in **Figure 1** or an employee taking notes in company meetings, OneNote is the one place to keep notes for all of your projects.

Figure 1: OneNote 2016 notebook

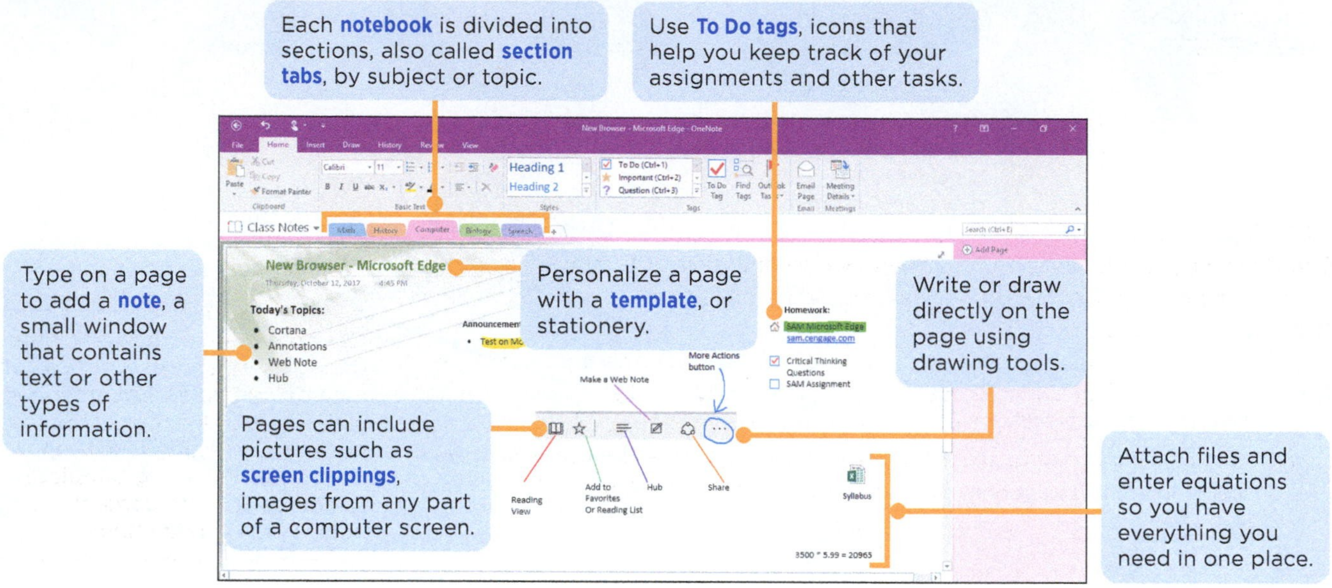

Each **notebook** is divided into sections, also called **section tabs**, by subject or topic.

Use **To Do tags**, icons that help you keep track of your assignments and other tasks.

Type on a page to add a **note**, a small window that contains text or other types of information.

Personalize a page with a **template**, or stationery.

Write or draw directly on the page using drawing tools.

Pages can include pictures such as **screen clippings**, images from any part of a computer screen.

Attach files and enter equations so you have everything you need in one place.

Creating a OneNote Notebook

OneNote is divided into sections similar to those in a spiral-bound notebook. Each OneNote notebook contains sections, pages, and other notebooks. You can use One-Note for school, business, and personal projects. Store information for each type of project in different notebooks to keep your tasks separate, or use any other organization that suits you. OneNote is flexible enough to adapt to the way you want to work.

When you create a notebook, it contains a blank page with a plain white background by default, though you can use templates, or stationery, to apply designs in categories such as Academic, Business, Decorative, and Planners. Start typing or use the buttons on the Insert tab to insert notes, which are small resizable windows that can contain text, equations, tables, on-screen writing, images, audio and video recordings, to-do lists, file attachments, and file printouts. Add as many notes as you need to each page.

Learn to use OneNote!
Links to companion **Sways**, featuring **videos** with hands-on instructions, are located on www.cengagebrain.com.

Syncing a Notebook to the Cloud

OneNote saves your notes every time you make a change in a notebook. To make sure you can access your notebooks with a laptop, tablet, or smartphone wherever you are, OneNote uses cloud-based storage, such as OneDrive or SharePoint. **Microsoft OneNote Mobile app**, a lightweight version of OneNote 2016 shown in **Figure 2**, is available for free in the Windows Store, Google Play for Android devices, and the AppStore for iOS devices.

If you have a Microsoft account, OneNote saves your notes on OneDrive automatically for all your mobile devices and computers, which is called **syncing**. For example, you can use OneNote to take notes on your laptop during class, and then open OneNote on your phone to study later. To use a notebook stored on your computer with your OneNote Mobile app, move the notebook to OneDrive. You can quickly share notebook content with other people using OneDrive.

Figure 2: Microsoft OneNote Mobile app

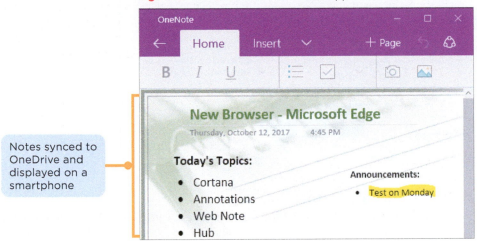

Notes synced to OneDrive and displayed on a smartphone

Taking Notes

Use OneNote pages to organize your notes by class and topic or lecture. Beyond simple typed notes, OneNote stores drawings, converts handwriting to searchable text and mathematical sketches to equations, and records audio and video.

OneNote includes drawing tools that let you sketch freehand drawings such as biological cell diagrams and financial supply-and-demand charts. As shown in **Figure 3**, the Draw tab on the ribbon provides these drawing tools along with shapes so you can insert diagrams and other illustrations to represent your ideas. When you draw on a page, OneNote creates a **drawing canvas**, which is a container for shapes and lines.

On the Job Now

OneNote is ideal for taking notes during meetings, whether you are recording minutes, documenting a discussion, sketching product diagrams, or listing follow-up items. Use a meeting template to add pages with content appropriate for meetings.

Figure 3: Tools on the Draw tab

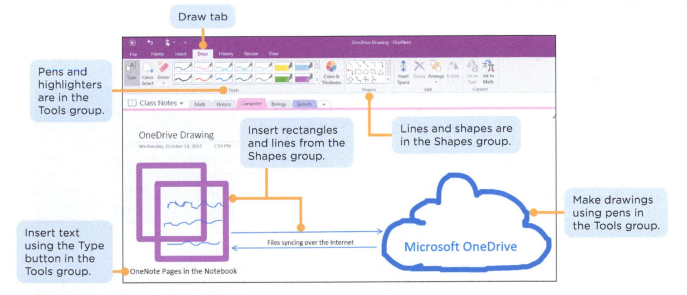

Draw tab

Pens and highlighters are in the Tools group.

Insert rectangles and lines from the Shapes group.

Lines and shapes are in the Shapes group.

Make drawings using pens in the Tools group.

Insert text using the Type button in the Tools group.

Converting Handwriting to Text

When you use a pen tool to write on a notebook page, the text you enter is called **inked handwriting**. OneNote can convert inked handwriting to typed text when you use the **Ink to Text** button in the Convert group on the Draw tab, as shown in **Figure 4**. After OneNote converts the handwriting to text, you can use the Search box to find terms in the converted text or any other note in your notebooks.

Figure 4: Converting handwriting to text

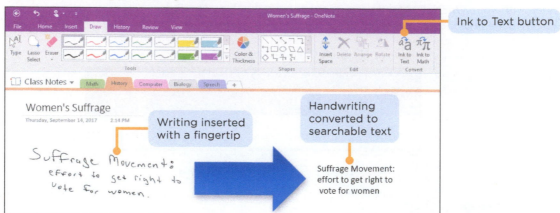

On the Job Now

Use OneNote as a place to brainstorm ongoing work projects. If a notebook contains sensitive material, you can password-protect some or all of the notebook so that only certain people can open it.

Recording a Lecture

If your computer or mobile device has a microphone or camera, OneNote can record the audio or video from a lecture or business meeting as shown in **Figure 5**. When you record a lecture (with your instructor's permission), you can follow along, take regular notes at your own pace, and review the video recording later. You can control the start, pause, and stop motions of the recording when you play back the recording of your notes.

Figure 5: Video inserted in a notebook

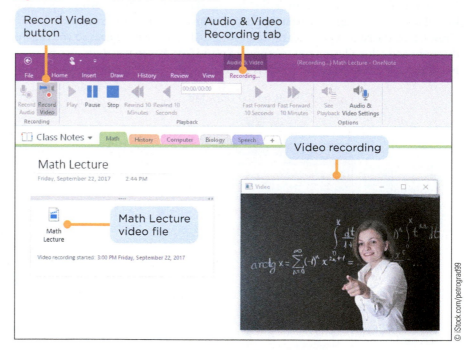

© iStock.com/petrograd99

Try This Now

1: Taking Notes for a Week

As a student, you can get organized by using OneNote to take detailed notes in your classes. Perform the following tasks:

a. Create a new OneNote notebook on your Microsoft OneDrive account (the default location for new notebooks). Name the notebook with your first name followed by "Notes," as in **Caleb Notes**.
b. Create four section tabs, each with a different class name.
c. Take detailed notes in those classes for one week. Be sure to include notes, drawings, and other types of content.
d. Sync your notes with your OneDrive. Submit your assignment in the format specified by your instructor.

2: Using OneNote to Organize a Research Paper

You have a research paper due on the topic of three habits of successful students. Use OneNote to organize your research. Perform the following tasks:

a. Create a new OneNote notebook on your Microsoft OneDrive account. Name the notebook **Success Research**.
b. Create three section tabs with the following names:

- **Take Detailed Notes**
- **Be Respectful in Class**
- **Come to Class Prepared**

c. On the web, research the topics and find three sources for each section. Copy a sentence from each source and paste the sentence into the appropriate section. When you paste the sentence, OneNote inserts it in a note with a link to the source.
d. Sync your notes with your OneDrive. Submit your assignment in the format specified by your instructor.

3: Planning Your Career

Note: This activity requires a webcam or built-in video camera on any type of device.

Consider an occupation that interests you. Using OneNote, examine the responsibilities, education requirements, potential salary, and employment outlook of a specific career. Perform the following tasks:

a. Create a new OneNote notebook on your Microsoft OneDrive account. Name the notebook with your first name followed by a career title, such as **Kara - App Developer**.
b. Create four section tabs with the names **Responsibilities, Education Requirements, Median Salary**, and **Employment Outlook**.
c. Research the responsibilities of your career path. Using OneNote, record a short video (approximately 30 seconds) of yourself explaining the responsibilities of your career path. Place the video in the Responsibilities section.
d. On the web, research the educational requirements for your career path and find two appropriate sources. Copy a paragraph from each source and paste them into the appropriate section. When you paste a paragraph, OneNote inserts it in a note with a link to the source.
e. Research the median salary for a single year for this career. Create a mathematical equation in the Median Salary section that multiplies the amount of the median salary times 20 years to calculate how much you will possibly earn.
f. For the Employment Outlook section, research the outlook for your career path. Take at least four notes about what you find when researching the topic.
g. Sync your notes with your OneDrive. Submit your assignment in the format specified by your instructor.

Introduction to Sway

Sway site | responsive design | Storyline | card | Creative Commons license | animation emphasis effects | Docs.com

Expressing your ideas in a presentation typically means creating PowerPoint slides or a Word document. Microsoft Sway gives you another way to engage an audience. Sway is a free Microsoft tool available at Sway.com or as an app in Office 365. Using Sway, you can combine text, images, videos, and social media in a website called a **Sway site** that you can share and display on any device. To get started, you create a digital story on a web-based canvas without borders, slides, cells, or page breaks. A Sway site organizes the text, images, and video into a **responsive design**, which means your content adapts perfectly to any screen size as shown in **Figure 6**. You store a Sway site in the cloud on OneDrive using a free Microsoft account.

Figure 6: Sway site with responsive design

You can display a Sway presentation in a web browser.

Sway uses responsive design to make sure pages fit perfectly on any device.

© iStock.com/marinello, © iStock.com/marekuliasz

Creating a Sway Presentation

You can use Sway to build a digital flyer, a club newsletter, a vacation blog, an informational site, a digital art portfolio, or a new product rollout. After you select your topic and sign into Sway with your Microsoft account, a **Storyline** opens, providing tools and a work area for composing your digital story. See **Figure 7**. Each story can include text, images, and videos. You create a Sway by adding text and media content into a Storyline section, or **card**. To add pictures, videos, or documents, select a card in the left pane and then select the Insert Content button. The first card in a Sway presentation contains a title and background image.

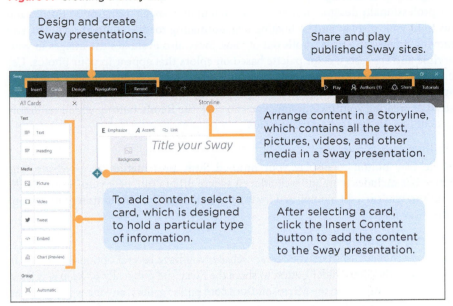

Adding Content to Build a Story

As you work, Sway searches the Internet to help you find relevant images, videos, tweets, and other content from online sources such as Bing, YouTube, Twitter, and Facebook. You can drag content from the search results right into the Storyline. In addition, you can upload your own images and videos directly in the presentation. For example, if you are creating a Sway presentation about the market for commercial drones, Sway suggests content to incorporate into the presentation by displaying it in the left pane as search results. The search results include drone images tagged with a **Creative Commons license** at online sources as shown in **Figure 8**. A Creative Commons license is a public copyright license that allows the free distribution of an otherwise copyrighted work. In addition, you can specify the source of the media. For example, you can add your own Facebook or OneNote pictures and videos in Sway without leaving the app.

On the Job Now

If you have a Microsoft Word document containing an outline of your business content, drag the outline into Sway to create a card for each topic.

Figure 8: Images in Sway search results

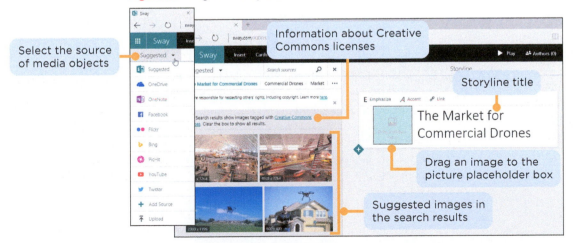

Designing a Sway

Sway professionally designs your Storyline content by resizing background images and fonts to fit your display, and by floating text, animating media, embedding video, and removing images as a page scrolls out of view. Sway also evaluates the images in your Storyline and suggests a color palette based on colors that appear in your photos. Use the Design button to display tools including color palettes, font choices, **animation emphasis effects**, and style templates to provide a personality for a Sway presentation. Instead of creating your own design, you can click the Remix button, which randomly selects unique designs for your Sway site.

Publishing a Sway

Use the Play button to display your finished Sway presentation as a website. The Address bar includes a unique web address where others can view your Sway site. As the author, you can edit a published Sway site by clicking the Edit button (pencil icon) on the Sway toolbar.

Sharing a Sway

When you are ready to share your Sway website, you have several options as shown in **Figure 9**. Use the Share slider button to share the Sway site publically or keep it private. If you add the Sway site to the Microsoft **Docs.com** public gallery, anyone worldwide can use Bing, Google, or other search engines to find, view, and share your Sway site. You can also share your Sway site using Facebook, Twitter, Google+, Yammer, and other social media sites. Link your presentation to any webpage or email the link to your audience. Sway can also generate a code for embedding the link within another webpage.

Figure 9: Sharing a Sway site

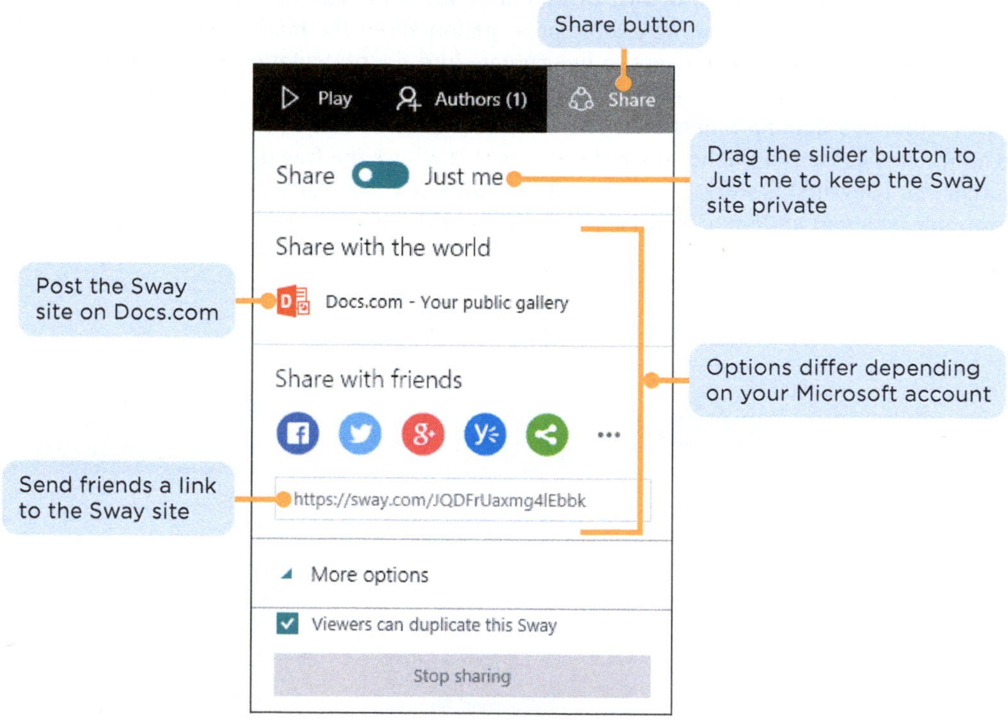

Share button

Play   Authors (1)   Share

Share ⬤ Just me

Drag the slider button to Just me to keep the Sway site private

Share with the world

Post the Sway site on Docs.com

Docs.com - Your public gallery

Share with friends

Options differ depending on your Microsoft account

Send friends a link to the Sway site

https://sway.com/JQDFrUaxmg4lEbbk

More options

✔ Viewers can duplicate this Sway

Stop sharing

Try This Now

Learn to use Sway!
Links to companion **Sways**, featuring **videos** with hands-on instructions, are located on www.cengagebrain.com.

PA-9

1: Creating a Sway Resume

Sway is a digital storytelling app. Create a Sway resume to share the skills, job experiences, and achievements you have that match the requirements of a future job interest. Perform the following tasks:

a. Create a new presentation in Sway to use as a digital resume. Title the Sway Storyline with your full name and then select a background image.
b. Create three separate sections titled **Academic Background, Work Experience**, and **Skills**, and insert text, a picture, and a paragraph or bulleted points in each section. Be sure to include your own picture.
c. Add a fourth section that includes a video about your school that you find online.
d. Customize the design of your presentation.
e. Submit your assignment link in the format specified by your instructor.

2: Creating an Online Sway Newsletter

Newsletters are designed to capture the attention of their target audience. Using Sway, create a newsletter for a club, organization, or your favorite music group. Perform the following tasks:

a. Create a new presentation in Sway to use as a digital newsletter for a club, organization, or your favorite music group. Provide a title for the Sway Storyline and select an appropriate background image.
b. Select three separate sections with appropriate titles, such as Upcoming Events. In each section, insert text, a picture, and a paragraph or bulleted points.
c. Add a fourth section that includes a video about your selected topic.
d. Customize the design of your presentation.
e. Submit your assignment link in the format specified by your instructor.

3: Creating and Sharing a Technology Presentation

To place a Sway presentation in the hands of your entire audience, you can share a link to the Sway presentation. Create a Sway presentation on a new technology and share it with your class. Perform the following tasks:

a. Create a new presentation in Sway about a cutting-edge technology topic. Provide a title for the Sway Storyline and select a background image.
b. Create four separate sections about your topic, and include text, a picture, and a paragraph in each section.
c. Add a fifth section that includes a video about your topic.
d. Customize the design of your presentation.
e. Share the link to your Sway with your classmates and submit your assignment link in the format specified by your instructor.

Introduction to Office Mix

add-in | clip | slide recording | Slide Notes | screen recording | free-response quiz

To enliven business meetings and lectures, Microsoft adds a new dimension to presentations with a powerful toolset called Office Mix, a free add-in for PowerPoint. (An **add-in** is software that works with an installed app to extend its features.) Using Office Mix, you can record yourself on video, capture still and moving images on your desktop, and insert interactive elements such as quizzes and live webpages directly into PowerPoint slides. When you post the finished presentation to OneDrive, Office Mix provides a link you can share with friends and colleagues. Anyone with an Internet connection and a web browser can watch a published Office Mix presentation, such as the one in **Figure 10**, on a computer or mobile device.

Figure 10: Office Mix presentation

Adding Office Mix to PowerPoint

To get started, you create an Office Mix account at the website mix.office.com using an email address or a Facebook or Google account. Next, you download and install the Office Mix add-in (see **Figure 11**). Office Mix appears as a new tab named Mix on the PowerPoint ribbon in versions of Office 2013 and Office 2016 running on personal computers (PCs).

Figure 11: Getting started with Office Mix

Capturing Video Clips

A **clip** is a short segment of audio, such as music, or video. After finishing the content on a PowerPoint slide, you can use Office Mix to add a video clip to animate or illustrate the content. Office Mix creates video clips in two ways: by recording live action on a webcam and by capturing screen images and movements. If your computer has a webcam, you can record yourself and annotate the slide to create a **slide recording** as shown in **Figure 12**.

On the Job Now

Companies are using Office Mix to train employees about new products, to explain benefit packages to new workers, and to educate interns about office procedures.

Figure 12: Making a slide recording

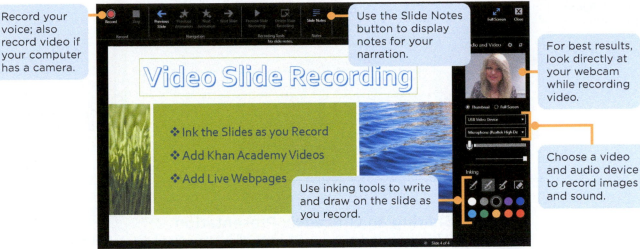

Record your voice; also record video if your computer has a camera.

Use the Slide Notes button to display notes for your narration.

For best results, look directly at your webcam while recording video.

Choose a video and audio device to record images and sound.

Use inking tools to write and draw on the slide as you record.

When you are making a slide recording, you can record your spoken narration at the same time. The **Slide Notes** feature works like a teleprompter to help you focus on your presentation content instead of memorizing your narration. Use the Inking tools to make annotations or add highlighting using different pen types and colors. After finishing a recording, edit the video in PowerPoint to trim the length or set playback options.

The second way to create a video is to capture on-screen images and actions with or without a voiceover. This method is ideal if you want to show how to use your favorite website or demonstrate an app such as OneNote. To share your screen with an audience, select the part of the screen you want to show in the video. Office Mix captures everything that happens in that area to create a **screen recording**, as shown in **Figure 13**. Office Mix inserts the screen recording as a video in the slide.

On the Job Now

To make your video recordings accessible to people with hearing impairments, use the Office Mix closed-captioning tools. You can also use closed captions to supplement audio that is difficult to understand and to provide an aid for those learning to read.

Figure 13: Making a screen recording

Record the action on the screen within the red dashed outline.

Record audio while capturing your on-screen actions.

Select Area button

Inserting Quizzes, Live Webpages, and Apps

To enhance and assess audience understanding, make your slides interactive by adding quizzes, live webpages, and apps. Quizzes give immediate feedback to the user as shown in **Figure 14**. Office Mix supports several quiz formats, including a **free-response quiz** similar to a short answer quiz, and true/false, multiple-choice, and multiple-response formats.

Figure 14: Creating an interactive quiz

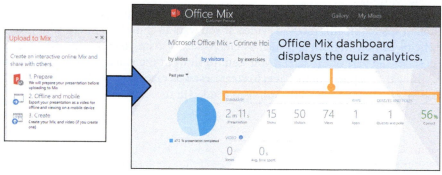

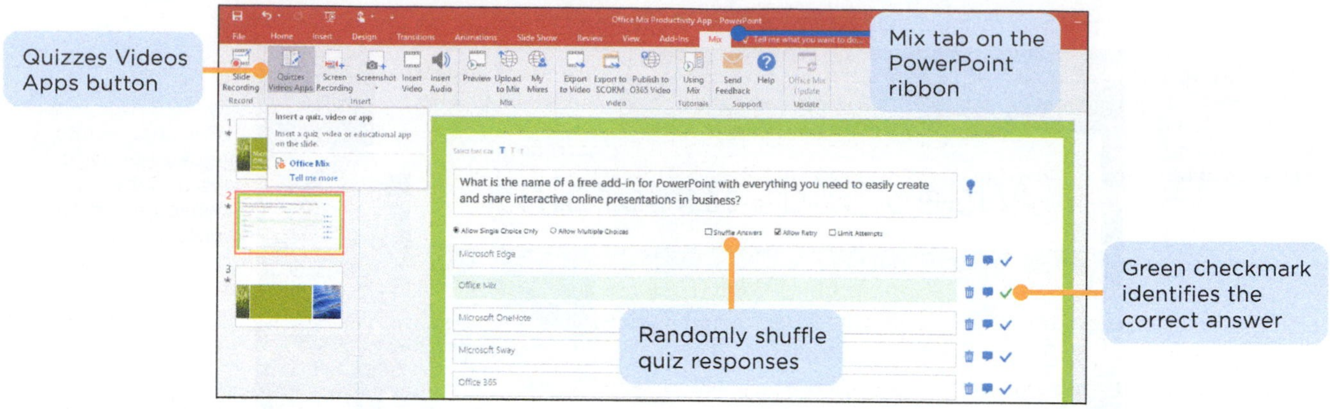
Quizzes Videos Apps button
Mix tab on the PowerPoint ribbon
What is the name of a free add-in for PowerPoint with everything you need to easily create and share interactive online presentations in business?
Green checkmark identifies the correct answer
Randomly shuffle quiz responses

Sharing an Office Mix Presentation

When you complete your work with Office Mix, upload the presentation to your personal Office Mix dashboard as shown in **Figure 15**. Users of PCs, Macs, iOS devices, and Android devices can access and play Office Mix presentations. The Office Mix dashboard displays built-in analytics that include the quiz results and how much time viewers spent on each slide. You can play completed Office Mix presentations online or download them as movies.

Figure 15: Sharing an Office Mix presentation

Upload to Mix
Create an interactive online Mix and share with others
1. Prepare
2. Offline and mobile
3. Create
Office Mix
Microsoft Office Mix - Corinne Hoi
Office Mix dashboard displays the quiz analytics.

Try This Now

1: Creating an Office Mix Tutorial for OneNote

Note: This activity requires a microphone on your computer.

Office Mix makes it easy to record screens and their contents. Create PowerPoint slides with an Office Mix screen recording to show OneNote 2016 features. Perform the following tasks:

Office Mix makes it easy to record screens and their contents. Create PowerPoint slides with an Office Mix screen recording to show OneNote 2016 features. Perform the following tasks:

a. Create a PowerPoint presentation with the Ion Boardroom template. Create an opening slide with the title **My Favorite OneNote Features** and enter your name in the subtitle.

b. Create three additional slides, each titled with a new feature of OneNote. Open OneNote and use the Mix tab in PowerPoint to capture three separate screen recordings that teach your favorite features.

c. Add a fifth slide that quizzes the user with a multiple-choice question about OneNote and includes four responses. Be sure to insert a checkmark indicating the correct response.

d. Upload the completed presentation to your Office Mix dashboard and share the link with your instructor.

e. Submit your assignment link in the format specified by your instructor.

2: Teaching Augmented Reality with Office Mix

Note: This activity requires a webcam or built-in video camera on your computer.

A local elementary school has asked you to teach augmented reality to its students using Office Mix. Perform the following tasks:

a. Research augmented reality using your favorite online search tools.

b. Create a PowerPoint presentation with the Frame template. Create an opening slide with the title **Augmented Reality** and enter your name in the subtitle.

c. Create a slide with four bullets summarizing your research of augmented reality. Create a 20-second slide recording of yourself providing a quick overview of augmented reality.

d. Create another slide with a 30-second screen recording of a video about augmented reality from a site such as YouTube or another video-sharing site.

e. Add a final slide that quizzes the user with a true/false question about augmented reality. Be sure to insert a checkmark indicating the correct response.

f. Upload the completed presentation to your Office Mix dashboard and share the link with your instructor.

g. Submit your assignment link in the format specified by your instructor.

3: Marketing a Travel Destination with Office Mix

Note: This activity requires a webcam or built-in video camera on your computer.

To convince your audience to travel to a particular city, create a slide presentation marketing any city in the world using a slide recording, screen recording, and a quiz. Perform the following tasks:

a. Create a PowerPoint presentation with any template. Create an opening slide with the title of the city you are marketing as a travel destination and your name in the subtitle.

b. Create a slide with four bullets about the featured city. Create a 30-second slide recording of yourself explaining why this city is the perfect vacation destination.

c. Create another slide with a 20-second screen recording of a travel video about the city from a site such as YouTube or another video-sharing site.

d. Add a final slide that quizzes the user with a multiple-choice question about the featured city with five responses. Be sure to include a checkmark indicating the correct response.

e. Upload the completed presentation to your Office Mix dashboard and share your link with your instructor.

f. Submit your assignment link in the format specified by your instructor.

Introduction to Microsoft Edge

Reading view | Hub | Cortana | Web Note | Inking | sandbox

Microsoft Edge is the default web browser developed for the Windows 10 operating system as a replacement for Internet Explorer. Unlike its predecessor, Edge lets you write on webpages, read webpages without advertisements and other distractions, and search for information using a virtual personal assistant. The Edge interface is clean and basic, as shown in **Figure 16**, meaning you can pay more attention to the webpage content.

Figure 16: Microsoft Edge tools

Forward button • New tab button • Web address in the Address bar • Add to favorites or reading list button • Back button • Reading view button • More button • Refresh (F5) button • Hub (Favorites, reading list, history, and downloads) button • Share Web Note button • Make a Web Note button

Browsing the Web with Microsoft Edge

One of the fastest browsers available, Edge allows you to type search text directly in the Address bar. As you view the resulting webpage, you can switch to **Reading view**, which is available for most news and research sites, to eliminate distracting advertisements. For example, if you are catching up on technology news online, the webpage might be difficult to read due to a busy layout cluttered with ads. Switch to Reading view to refresh the page and remove the original page formatting, ads, and menu sidebars to read the article distraction-free.

Consider the **Hub** in Microsoft Edge as providing one-stop access to all the things you collect on the web, such as your favorite websites, reading list, surfing history, and downloaded files.

Locating Information with Cortana

Cortana, the Windows 10 virtual assistant, plays an important role in Microsoft Edge. After you turn on Cortana, it appears as an animated circle in the Address bar when you might need assistance, as shown in the restaurant website in **Figure 17**. When you click the Cortana icon, a pane slides in from the right of the browser window to display detailed information about the restaurant, including maps and reviews. Cortana can also assist you in defining words, finding the weather, suggesting coupons for shopping, updating stock market information, and calculating math.

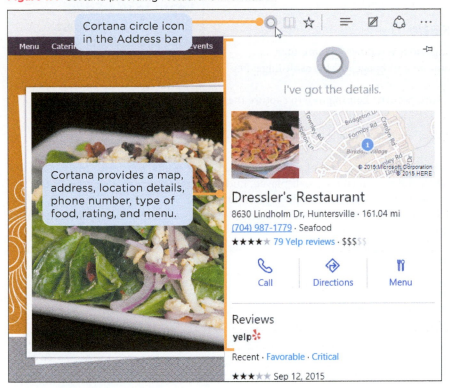

Annotating Webpages

One of the most impressive Microsoft Edge features are the **Web Note** tools, which you use to write on a webpage or to highlight text. When you click the Make a Web Note button, an **Inking** toolbar appears, as shown in **Figure 18**, that provides writing and drawing tools. These tools include an eraser, a pen, and a highlighter with different colors. You can also insert a typed note and copy a screen image (called a screen clipping). You can draw with a pointing device, fingertip, or stylus using different pen colors. Whether you add notes to a recipe, annotate sources for a research paper, or select a product while shopping online, the Web Note tools can enhance your productivity. After you complete your notes, click the Save button to save the annotations to OneNote, your Favorites list, or your Reading list. You can share the inked page with others using the Share Web Note button.

On the Job Now

To enhance security, Microsoft Edge runs in a partial sandbox, an arrangement that prevents attackers from gaining control of your computer. Browsing within the **sandbox** protects computer resources and information from hackers.

Figure 18: Web Note tools in Microsoft Edge

Try This Now

1: Using Cortana in Microsoft Edge

Learn to use Edge!

Links to companion **Sways**, featuring **videos** with hands-on instructions, are located on www.cengagebrain.com.

Note: This activity requires using Microsoft Edge on a Windows 10 computer.

Cortana can assist you in finding information on a webpage in Microsoft Edge. Perform the following tasks:

a. Create a Word document using the Word Screen Clipping tool to capture the following screenshots.

- Screenshot A—Using Microsoft Edge, open a webpage with a technology news article. Right-click a term in the article and ask Cortana to define it.
- Screenshot B—Using Microsoft Edge, open the website of a fancy restaurant in a city near you. Make sure the Cortana circle icon is displayed in the Address bar. (If it's not displayed, find a different restaurant website.) Click the Cortana circle icon to display a pane with information about the restaurant.
- Screenshot C—Using Microsoft Edge, type **10 USD to Euros** in the Address bar without pressing the Enter key. Cortana converts the U.S. dollars to Euros.
- Screenshot D—Using Microsoft Edge, type **Apple stock** in the Address bar without pressing the Enter key. Cortana displays the current stock quote.

b. Submit your assignment in the format specified by your instructor.

2: Viewing Online News with Reading View

Note: This activity requires using Microsoft Edge on a Windows 10 computer.

Reading view in Microsoft Edge can make a webpage less cluttered with ads and other distractions. Perform the following tasks:

a. Create a Word document using the Word Screen Clipping tool to capture the following screenshots.

- Screenshot A—Using Microsoft Edge, open the website **mashable.com**. Open a technology article. Click the Reading view button to display an ad-free page that uses only basic text formatting.
- Screenshot B—Using Microsoft Edge, open the website **bbc.com**. Open any news article. Click the Reading view button to display an ad-free page that uses only basic text formatting.
- Screenshot C—Make three types of annotations (Pen, Highlighter, and Add a typed note) on the BBC article page displayed in Reading view.

b. Submit your assignment in the format specified by your instructor.

3: Inking with Microsoft Edge

Note: This activity requires using Microsoft Edge on a Windows 10 computer.

Microsoft Edge provides many annotation options to record your ideas. Perform the following tasks:

a. Open the website **wolframalpha.com** in the Microsoft Edge browser. Wolfram Alpha is a well-respected academic search engine. Type **US$100 1965 dollars in 2015** in the Wolfram Alpha search text box and press the Enter key.

b. Click the Make a Web Note button to display the Web Note tools. Using the Pen tool, draw a circle around the result on the webpage. Save the page to OneNote.

c. In the Wolfram Alpha search text box, type the name of the city closest to where you live and press the Enter key. Using the Highlighter tool, highlight at least three interesting results. Add a note and then type a sentence about what you learned about this city. Save the page to OneNote. Share your OneNote notebook with your instructor.

d. Submit your assignment link in the format specified by your instructor.

Office 2016 and Windows 10: Essential Concepts and Skills

Objectives

You will have mastered the material in this module when you can:

- Use a touch screen
- Perform basic mouse operations
- Start Windows and sign in to an account
- Identify the objects on the Windows 10 desktop
- Identify the apps in and versions of Microsoft Office 2016
- Run an app
- Identify the components of the Microsoft Office ribbon

- Create folders
- Save files
- Change screen resolution
- Perform basic tasks in Microsoft Office apps
- Manage files
- Use Microsoft Office Help and Windows Help

This introductory module uses Word 2016 to cover features and functions common to Office 2016 apps, as well as the basics of Windows 10.

Roadmap

In this module, you will learn how to perform basic tasks in Windows and Word. The following roadmap identifies general activities you will perform as you progress through this module:

1. **SIGN IN** to an account.
2. **USE WINDOWS.**
3. **USE** features in Word that are common across Office **APPS.**
4. **FILE** and folder **MANAGEMENT.**
5. **SWITCH** between **APPS.**
6. **SAVE** and manage **FILES.**

7. **CHANGE SCREEN RESOLUTION**.

8. **EXIT APPS**.

9. **USE ADDITIONAL** Office **APPS FEATURES**.

10. **USE** Office and Windows **HELP**.

At the beginning of the step instructions throughout each module, you will see an abbreviated form of this roadmap. The abbreviated roadmap uses colors to indicate module progress: gray means the module is beyond that activity, blue means the task being shown is covered in that activity, and black means that activity is yet to be covered. For example, the following abbreviated roadmap indicates the module would be showing a task in the USE APPS activity.

1 SIGN IN | 2 USE WINDOWS | **3 USE APPS** | 4 FILE MANAGEMENT | 5 SWITCH APPS | 6 SAVE FILES
7 CHANGE SCREEN RESOLUTION | 8 EXIT APPS | 9 USE ADDITIONAL APP FEATURES | 10 USE HELP

Use the abbreviated roadmap as a progress guide while you read or step through the instructions in this module.

Introduction to the Windows 10 Operating System

Windows 10 is the newest version of Microsoft Windows, which is a popular and widely used operating system (Figure 1). An **operating system (OS)** is a set of programs that coordinate all the activities among computer or mobile device hardware.

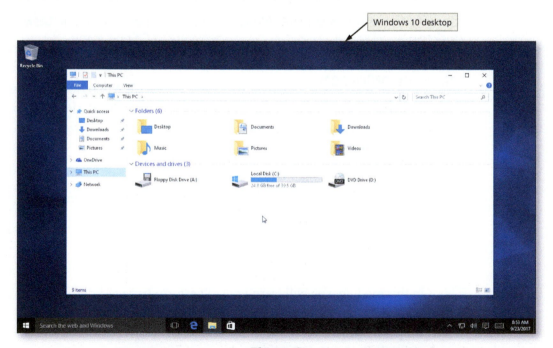

Figure 1

The Windows operating system simplifies the process of working with documents and apps by organizing the manner in which you interact with the computer. Windows is used to run apps. An application, or **app**, consists of programs designed to make users more productive and/or assist them with personal tasks, such as word processing or browsing the web.

Using a Touch Screen and a Mouse

Windows users who have computers or devices with touch screen capability can interact with the screen using gestures. A **gesture** is a motion you make on a touch screen with the tip of one or more fingers or your hand. Touch screens are convenient because they do not require a separate device for input. Table 1 presents common ways to interact with a touch screen.

If you are using your finger on a touch screen and are having difficulty completing the steps in this module, consider using a stylus. Many people find it easier to be precise with a stylus than with a finger. In addition, with a stylus you see the pointer. If you still are having trouble completing the steps with a stylus, try using a mouse.

Table 1 Touch Screen Gestures

Motion	Description	Common Uses	Equivalent Mouse Operation
Tap	Quickly touch and release one finger one time.	Activate a link (built-in connection). Press a button. Run a program or an app.	Click
Double-tap	Quickly touch and release one finger two times.	Run a program or an app. Zoom in (show a smaller area on the screen, so that contents appear larger) at the location of the double-tap.	Double-click
Press and hold	Press and hold one finger to cause an action to occur, or until an action occurs.	Display a shortcut menu (immediate access to allowable actions). Activate a mode enabling you to move an item with one finger to a new location.	Right-click
Drag, or slide	Press and hold one finger on an object and then move the finger to the new location.	Move an item around the screen. Scroll.	Drag
Swipe	Press and hold one finger and then move the finger horizontally or vertically on the screen.	Select an object. Swipe from edge to display a bar such as the Action Center, Apps bar, and Navigation bar (all discussed later).	Drag
Stretch	Move two fingers apart.	Zoom in (show a smaller area on the screen, so that contents appear larger).	None
Pinch	Move two fingers together.	Zoom out (show a larger area on the screen, so that contents appear smaller).	None

© 2015 Cengage Learning

Will the screen look different if you are using a touch screen?
The Windows and Microsoft Office interface varies slightly if you are using a touch screen. For this reason, you might notice that your Windows or Word screens looks slightly different from the screens in this book.

CONSIDER THIS

Windows users who do not have touch screen capabilities typically work with a mouse that has at least two buttons. For a right-handed user, the left button usually is

BTW
Pointer
If you are using a touch screen, the pointer may not appear on the screen as you perform touch gestures. The pointer will reappear when you begin using the mouse.

the primary mouse button, and the right mouse button is the secondary mouse button. Left-handed people, however, can reverse the function of these buttons.

Table 2 explains how to perform a variety of mouse operations. Some apps also use keys in combination with the mouse to perform certain actions. For example, when you hold down the CTRL key while rolling the mouse wheel, text on the screen may become larger or smaller based on the direction you roll the wheel. The function of the mouse buttons and the wheel varies depending on the app.

Table 2 Mouse Operations

Operation	Mouse Action	Example*	Equivalent Touch Gesture
Point	Move the mouse until the pointer on the desktop is positioned on the item of choice.	Position the pointer on the screen.	None
Click	Press and release the primary mouse button, which usually is the left mouse button.	Select or deselect items on the screen or run an app or app feature.	Tap
Right-click	Press and release the secondary mouse button, which usually is the right mouse button.	Display a shortcut menu.	Press and hold
Double-click	Quickly press and release the primary mouse button twice without moving the mouse.	Run an app or app feature.	Double-tap
Triple-click	Quickly press and release the primary mouse button three times without moving the mouse.	Select a paragraph.	Triple-tap
Drag	Point to an item, hold down the primary mouse button, move the item to the desired location on the screen, and then release the mouse button.	Move an object from one location to another or draw pictures.	Drag or slide
Right-drag	Point to an item, hold down the right mouse button, move the item to the desired location on the screen, and then release the right mouse button.	Display a shortcut menu after moving an object from one location to another.	Press and hold, then drag
Rotate wheel	Roll the wheel forward or backward.	Scroll vertically (up and down).	Swipe
Free-spin wheel	Whirl the wheel forward or backward so that it spins freely on its own.	Scroll through many pages in seconds.	Swipe
Press wheel	Press the wheel button while moving the mouse.	Scroll continuously.	None
Tilt wheel	Press the wheel toward the right or left.	Scroll horizontally (left and right).	None
Press thumb button	Press the button on the side of the mouse with your thumb.	Move forward or backward through webpages and/or control media, games, etc.	None

*Note: The examples presented in this column are discussed as they are demonstrated in this module.

© 2015 Cengage Learning

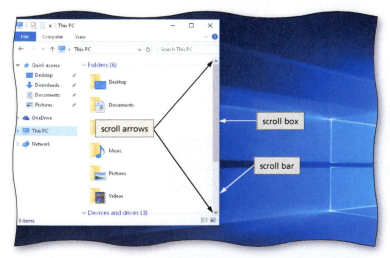

Figure 2

Scrolling

A **scroll bar** is a horizontal or vertical bar that appears when the contents of an area may not be visible completely on the screen (Figure 2). A scroll bar contains **scroll arrows** and a **scroll box** that enable you to view areas that currently cannot be seen on the screen. Clicking the up and down scroll arrows moves the screen content up or down one line. You also can click above or below the scroll box to move up or down a section, or drag the scroll box up or down to move to a specific location.

Keyboard Shortcuts

In many cases, you can use the keyboard instead of the mouse to accomplish a task. To perform tasks using the keyboard, you press one or more keyboard keys, sometimes identified as a **keyboard shortcut**. Some keyboard shortcuts consist of a single key, such as the F1 key. For example, to obtain help in many apps, you can press the F1 key. Other keyboard shortcuts consist of multiple keys, in which case a plus sign separates the key names, such as CTRL+ESC. This notation means to press and hold down the first key listed, press one or more additional keys, and then release all keys. For example, to display the Start menu, press CTRL+ESC, that is, hold down the CTRL key, press the ESC key, and then release both keys.

Starting Windows

It is not unusual for multiple people to use the same computer in a work, educational, recreational, or home setting. Windows enables each user to establish a **user account**, which identifies to Windows the resources, such as apps and storage locations, a user can access when working with the computer.

Each user account has a user name and may have a password and an icon, as well. A **user name** is a unique combination of letters or numbers that identifies a specific user to Windows. A **password** is a private combination of letters, numbers, and special characters associated with the user name that allows access to a user's account resources. An icon is a small image that represents an object; thus, a **user icon** is a picture associated with a user name.

When you turn on a computer, Windows starts and displays a **lock screen** consisting of the time and date (Figure 3). To unlock the screen, click the lock screen. Depending on your computer's settings, Windows may or may not display a sign-in screen that shows the user names and user icons for users who have accounts on the computer. This **sign-in screen** enables you to sign in to your user account and makes the computer available for use. Clicking the user icon begins the process of signing in, also called logging on, to your user account.

BTW

Minimize Wrist Injury
Computer users frequently switch between the keyboard and the mouse during a word processing session; such switching strains the wrist. To help prevent wrist injury, minimize switching. For instance, if your fingers already are on the keyboard, use keyboard keys to scroll. If your hand already is on the mouse, use the mouse to scroll. If your hand is on the touch screen, use touch gestures to scroll.

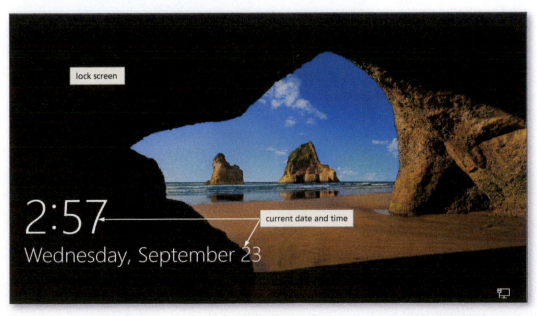

lock screen

2:57
Wednesday, September 23

current date and time

Figure 3

At the bottom of the sign-in screen is the 'Connect to Internet' button, 'Ease of access' button, and a Shut down button. Clicking the 'Connect to Internet' button displays a list of each network connection and its status. You also can connect to or disconnect from a network. Clicking the 'Ease of access' button displays the Ease of access menu, which provides tools to optimize a computer to accommodate the needs of mobility, hearing, and vision impaired users. Clicking the Shut down button displays a menu containing commands related to putting the computer or mobile device in a low-power state, shutting it down, and restarting the computer or mobile device. The commands available on your computer or mobile device may differ.

- The Sleep command saves your work, turns off the computer fans and hard drive, and places the computer in a lower-power state. To wake the computer from sleep mode, press the power button or lift a laptop's cover, and sign in to your account.
- The Shut down command exits running apps, shuts down Windows, and then turns off the computer.
- The Restart command exits running apps, shuts down Windows, and then restarts Windows.

1 SIGN IN | 2 USE WINDOWS | 3 USE APPS | 4 FILE MANAGEMENT | 5 SWITCH APPS | 6 SAVE FILES
7 CHANGE SCREEN RESOLUTION | 8 EXIT APPS | 9 USE ADDITIONAL APP FEATURES | 10 USE HELP

To Sign In to an Account

The following steps, which use SCSeries as the user name, sign in to an account based on a typical Windows installation. *Why? After starting Windows, you might be required to sign in to an account to access the computer or mobile device's resources.* You may need to ask your instructor how to sign in to your account.

- Click the lock screen (shown in Figure 3) to display a sign-in screen.

- Click the user icon (for SCSeries, in this case) on the sign-in screen, which depending on settings, either will display a second sign-in screen that contains a Password text box (Figure 4) or will display the Windows desktop (Figure 5).

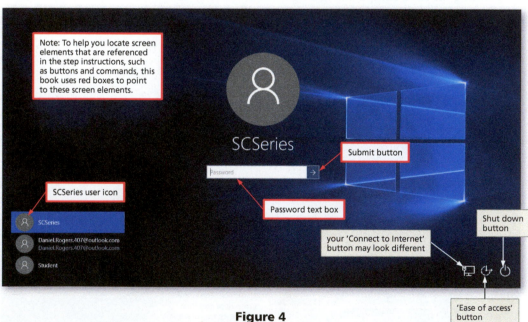

Figure 4

Q&A

Why do I not see a user icon?
Your computer may require you to type a user name instead of clicking an icon.

What is a text box?
A text box is a rectangular box in which you type text.

Why does my screen not show a Password text box?
Your account does not require a password.

- If Windows displays a sign-in screen with a Password text box, type your password in the text box.

2

- Click the Submit button (shown in Figure 4) to sign in to your account and display the Windows desktop (Figure 5).

Q&A

Why does my desktop look different from the one in Figure 5?
The Windows desktop is customizable, and your school or employer may have modified the desktop to meet its needs. Also, your screen resolution, which affects the size of the elements on the screen, may differ from the screen resolution used in this book. Later in this module, you learn how to change screen resolution.

How do I type if my tablet has no keyboard?
You can use your fingers to press keys on a keyboard that appears on the screen, called an on-screen keyboard, or you can purchase a separate physical keyboard that attaches to or wirelessly communicates with the tablet.

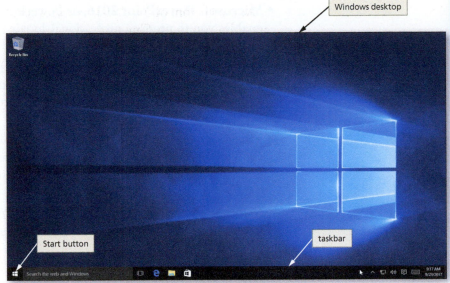

Figure 5

The Windows Desktop

The Windows 10 desktop (shown in Figure 5) and the objects on the desktop emulate a work area in an office. Think of the Windows desktop as an electronic version of the top of your desk. You can perform tasks such as placing objects on the desktop, moving the objects around the desktop, and removing items from the desktop.

When you run an app in Windows 10, it appears on the desktop. Some icons also may be displayed on the desktop. For instance, the icon for the **Recycle Bin**, the location of files that have been deleted, appears on the desktop by default. A **file** is a named unit of storage. Files can contain text, images, audio, and video. You can customize your desktop so that icons representing programs and files you use often appear on your desktop.

Introduction to Microsoft Office 2016

Microsoft Office 2016 is the newest version of Microsoft Office, offering features that provide users with better functionality and easier ways to work with the various files they create. This version of Office also is designed to work more optimally on mobile devices and online.

Microsoft Office 2016 Apps

Microsoft Office 2016 includes a wide variety of apps, such as Word, PowerPoint, Excel, Access, Outlook, Publisher, and OneNote:

- **Microsoft Word 2016**, or Word, is a full-featured word processing app that allows you to create professional-looking documents and revise them easily.

- **Microsoft PowerPoint 2016**, or PowerPoint, is a complete presentation app that enables you to produce professional-looking presentations and then deliver them to an audience.

- **Microsoft Excel 2016**, or Excel, is a powerful spreadsheet app that allows you to organize data, complete calculations, make decisions, graph data, develop professional-looking reports, publish organized data to the web, and access real-time data from websites.

- **Microsoft Access 2016**, or Access, is a database management system that enables you to create a database; add, change, and delete data in the database; ask questions concerning the data in the database; and create forms and reports using the data in the database.

- **Microsoft Outlook 2016**, or Outlook, is a communications and scheduling app that allows you to manage email accounts, calendars, contacts, and access to other Internet content.

- **Microsoft Publisher 2016**, or Publisher, is a desktop publishing app that helps you create professional-quality publications and marketing materials that can be shared easily.

- **Microsoft OneNote 2016**, or OneNote, is a note taking app that allows you to store and share information in notebooks with other people.

Microsoft Office 2016 Suites

A **suite** is a collection of individual apps available together as a unit. Microsoft offers a variety of Office suites, including a stand-alone desktop app, Microsoft Office 365, and Microsoft Office Online. **Microsoft Office 365**, or Office 365, provides plans that allow organizations to use Office in a mobile setting while also being able to communicate and share files, depending upon the type of plan selected by the organization. **Microsoft Office Online** includes apps that allow you to edit and share files on the web using the familiar Office interface.

During the Office 365 installation, you select a plan, and depending on your plan, you receive different apps and services. Office Online apps do not require a local installation and can be accessed through OneDrive and your browser. **OneDrive** is a cloud storage service that provides storage and other services, such as Office Online, to computer and mobile device users.

CONSIDER THIS

How do you sign up for a OneDrive account?

- Use your browser to navigate to onedrive.live.com.

- Create a Microsoft account by clicking the Sign up button and then entering your information to create the account.

- Sign in to OneDrive using your new account or use it in Word to save your files on OneDrive.

Apps in a suite, such as Microsoft Office, typically use a similar interface and share features. Once you are comfortable working with the elements and the interface and performing tasks in one app, the similarity can help you apply the knowledge and skills you have learned to another app(s) in the suite. For example, the process for saving a file in Word is the same in PowerPoint, Excel, and some of the other Office apps. While briefly showing how to use Word, this module illustrates some of the common functions across the Office apps and identifies the characteristics unique to Word.

Running and Using an App

To use an app, you must instruct the operating system to run the app. Windows provides many different ways to run an app, one of which is presented in this section (other ways to run an app are presented throughout this module). After an app is running, you can use it to perform a variety of tasks. The following pages use Word to discuss some elements of the Office interface and to perform tasks that are common to other Office apps.

Word

Word is a full-featured word processing app that allows you to create many types of personal and business documents, including flyers, letters, memos, resumes, reports, fax cover sheets, mailing labels, and newsletters. Word also provides tools that enable you to create webpages and save these webpages directly on a web server. Word has many features designed to simplify the production of documents and add visual appeal. Using Word, you easily can change the shape, size, and color of text. You also can include borders, shading, tables, images, pictures, charts, and web addresses in documents.

To Run an App Using the Start Menu and Create a Blank Document

1 SIGN IN | **2 USE WINDOWS** | 3 USE APPS | 4 FILE MANAGEMENT | 5 SWITCH APPS | 6 SAVE FILES
7 CHANGE SCREEN RESOLUTION | 8 EXIT APPS | 9 USE ADDITIONAL APP FEATURES | 10 USE HELP

Across the bottom of the Windows 10 desktop is the taskbar. The taskbar contains the **Start button**, which you use to access apps, files, folders, and settings. A **folder** is a named location on a storage medium that usually contains related documents.

Clicking the Start button displays the Start menu. The **Start menu** allows you to access programs, folders, and files on the computer or mobile device and contains commands that allow you to start programs, store and search for documents, customize the computer or mobile device, and sign out of a user account or shut down the computer or mobile device. A **menu** is a list of related items, including folders, programs, and commands. Each **command** on a menu performs a specific action, such as saving a file or obtaining help. *Why? When you install an app, for example, the app's name will be added to the All apps list on the Start menu.*

The following steps, which assume Windows is running, use the Start menu to run Word and create a blank document based on a typical installation. You may need to ask your instructor how to run Word on your computer. Although the steps illustrate running the Word app, the steps to run any Office app are similar.

- Click the Start button on the Windows 10 taskbar to display the Start menu (Figure 6).

Figure 6

2

- Click All apps at the bottom of the left pane of the Start menu to display a list of apps installed on the computer or mobile device. If necessary, scroll to display the app you wish to run, Word 2016, in this case (Figure 7).

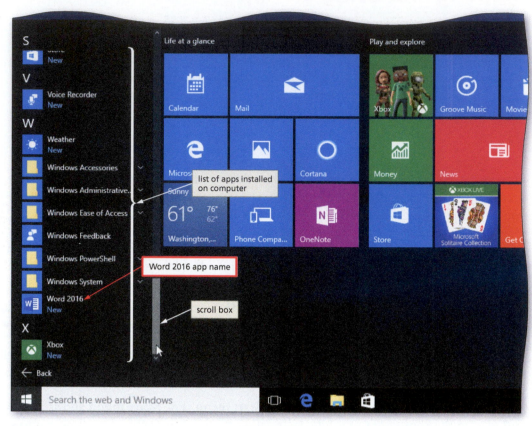

Figure 7

3

- If the app you wish to run is located in a folder, click or scroll to and then click the folder in the All apps list to display a list of the folder's contents.

- Click, or scroll to and then click the app name (Word 2016, in this case) in the list to run the selected app (Figure 8).

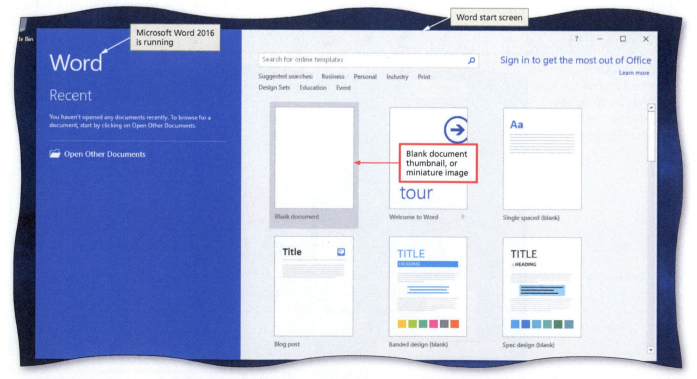

Figure 8

4

- Click the Blank document thumbnail on the Word start screen to create a blank Word document in the Word window (Figure 9).

Q&A

What happens when you run an app?

Some apps provide a means for you to create a blank document, as shown in Figure 8; others immediately display a blank document in an app window, such as the Word window shown in Figure 9. A **window** is a rectangular area that displays data and information. The top of a window has a **title bar**, which is a horizontal space that contains the window's name.

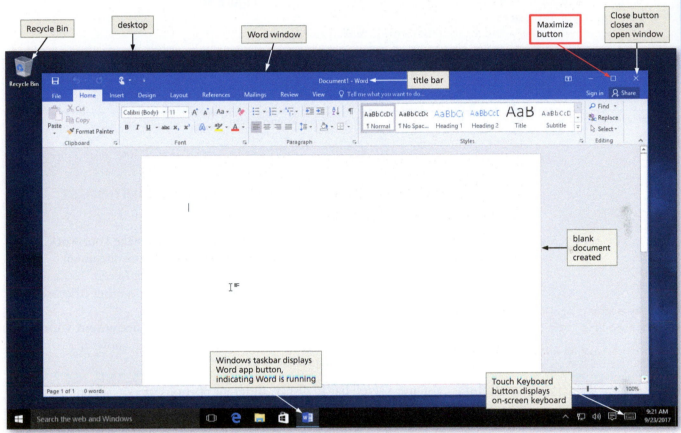

Figure 9

Other Ways

1. Type app name in search box, click app name in results list
2. Double-click file created in app you want to run

1 SIGN IN | 2 USE WINDOWS | 3 USE APPS | 4 FILE MANAGEMENT | 5 SWITCH APPS | 6 SAVE FILES
7 CHANGE SCREEN RESOLUTION | 8 EXIT APPS | 9 USE ADDITIONAL APP FEATURES | 10 USE HELP

To Maximize a Window

Sometimes content is not visible completely in a window. One method of displaying the entire contents of a window is to **maximize** it, or enlarge the window so that it fills the entire screen. The following step maximizes the Word window; however, any Office app's window can be maximized using this step. *Why? A maximized window provides the most space available for using the app.*

● If the Word window is not maximized already, click the Maximize button (shown in Figure 9) next to the Close button on the Word window's title bar to maximize the window (Figure 10).

Figure 10

Q&A

What happened to the Maximize button?
It changed to a Restore Down button, which you can use to return a window to its size and location before you maximized it.

How do I know whether a window is maximized?
A window is maximized if it fills the entire display area and the Restore Down button is displayed on the title bar.

Other Ways

1. Double-click title bar
2. Drag title bar to top of screen

Word Document Window, Ribbon, and Elements Common to Office Apps

The Word window consists of a variety of components to make your work more efficient and documents more professional. These include the document window, ribbon, Tell Me box, mini toolbar, shortcut menus, Quick Access Toolbar, and Microsoft Account area. Most of these components are common to other Microsoft Office apps; others are unique to Word.

You view a portion of a document on the screen through a **document window** (Figure 11). The default (preset) view is **Print Layout view**, which shows the document on a mock sheet of paper in the document window.

Scroll Bars You use a scroll bar to display different portions of a document in the document window. At the right edge of the document window is a vertical scroll bar. If a document is too wide to fit in the document window, a horizontal scroll bar also appears at the bottom of the document window. On a scroll bar, the position of the scroll box reflects the location of the portion of the document that is displayed in the document window.

BTW

Touch Keyboard
To display the on-screen touch keyboard, click the Touch Keyboard button on the Windows taskbar (shown in Figure 9). When finished using the touch keyboard, click the X button on the touch keyboard to close the keyboard.

Status Bar The **status bar**, located at the bottom of the document window above the Windows taskbar, presents information about the document, the progress of current tasks, and the status of certain commands and keys; it also provides controls for viewing the document. As you type text or perform certain tasks, various indicators and buttons may appear on the status bar.

The left side of the status bar in Figure 11 shows the current page followed by the total number of pages in the document, the number of words in the document, and an icon to check spelling and grammar. The right side of the status bar includes buttons and controls you can use to change the view of a document and adjust the size of the displayed document.

Ribbon The ribbon, located near the top of the window below the title bar, is the control center in Word and other Office apps (Figure 12). The ribbon provides easy, central access to the tasks you perform while creating a document. The ribbon consists

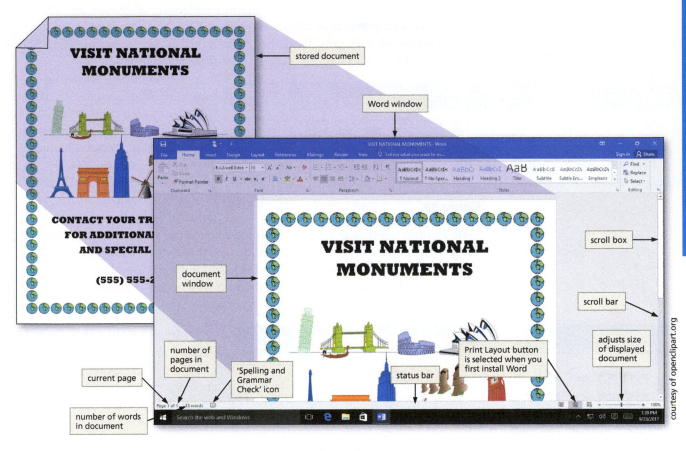

courtesy of openclipart.org

Figure 11

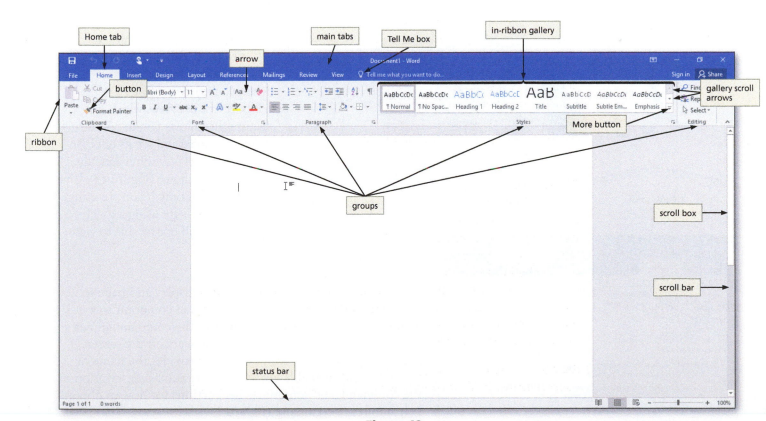

Figure 12

of tabs, groups, and commands. Each **tab** contains a collection of groups, and each **group** contains related commands. When you run an Office app, such as Word, it initially displays several main tabs, also called default or top-level tabs. All Office apps have a Home tab, which contains the more frequently used commands.

Figure 13

In addition to the main tabs, the Office apps display **tool tabs**, also called contextual tabs (Figure 13), when you perform certain tasks or work with objects such as pictures or tables. If you insert a picture in a Word document, for example, the Picture Tools tab and its related subordinate Format tab appear, collectively referred to as the Picture Tools Format tab. When you are finished working with the picture, the Picture Tools Format tab disappears from the ribbon. Word and other Office apps determine when tool tabs should appear and disappear based on tasks you perform. Some tool tabs, such as the Table Tools tab, have more than one related subordinate tab.

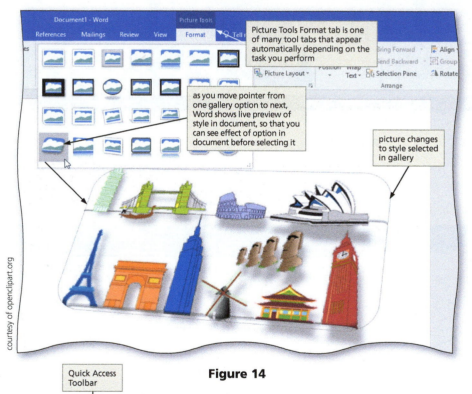

Figure 14

Items on the ribbon include buttons, boxes, and galleries (shown in Figure 12). A **gallery** is a set of choices, often graphical, arranged in a grid or in a list. You can scroll through choices in an in-ribbon gallery by clicking the gallery's scroll arrows. Or, you can click a gallery's More button to view more gallery options on the screen at a time.

Some buttons and boxes have arrows that, when clicked, also display a gallery; others always cause a gallery to be displayed when clicked. Most galleries support **live preview**, which is a feature that allows you to point to a gallery choice and see its effect in the document — without actually selecting the choice (Figure 14). Live preview works only if you are using a mouse; if you are using a touch screen, you will not be able to view live previews.

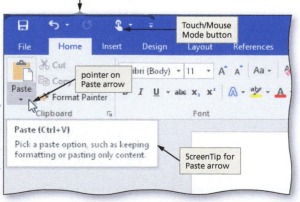

Figure 15

Some commands on the ribbon display an image to help you remember their function. When you point to a command on the ribbon, all or part of the command glows in a shade of gray, and a ScreenTip appears on the screen. A **ScreenTip** is an on-screen note that provides the name of the command, available keyboard shortcut(s), a description of the command, and sometimes instructions for how to obtain help about the command (Figure 15).

Some groups on the ribbon have a small arrow in the lower-right corner, called a **Dialog Box Launcher**, that when clicked, displays a dialog box or a task pane with additional options for the group (Figure 16). When presented with a dialog box, you make selections and must close the dialog box before returning to the document. A **task pane**, in contrast to a dialog box, is a window that can remain open and visible while you work in the document.

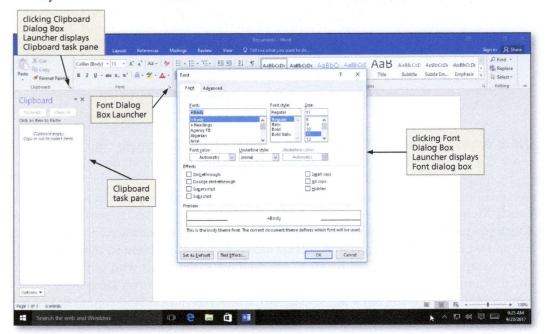

Figure 16

Tell Me Box The **Tell Me box**, which appears to the right of the tabs on the ribbon, is a type of search box that helps you to perform specific tasks in an Office app (Figure 17). As you type in the Tell Me box, the word-wheeling feature displays search results that are refined as you type. For example, if you want to center text in a document, you can type "center" in the Tell Me box and then select the appropriate command. The Tell Me box also lists the last five commands accessed from the box.

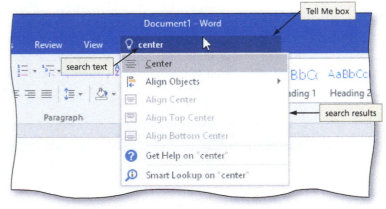

Figure 17

Mini Toolbar The **mini toolbar**, which appears automatically based on tasks you perform, contains commands related to changing the appearance of text in a document (Figure 18). If you do not use the mini toolbar, it disappears from the screen. The buttons, arrows, and boxes on the mini toolbar vary, depending on whether you are using Touch mode versus Mouse mode. If you right-click an item in the document window, Word displays both the mini toolbar and a shortcut menu, which is discussed in a later section in this module.

All commands on the mini toolbar also exist on the ribbon. The purpose of the mini toolbar is to minimize hand or mouse movement.

BTW

Turning Off the Mini Toolbar

If you do not want the mini toolbar to appear, click File on the ribbon to open the Backstage view, click the Options tab in the Backstage view, if necessary, click General (Options dialog box), remove the check mark from the 'Show Mini Toolbar on selection' check box, and then click the OK button.

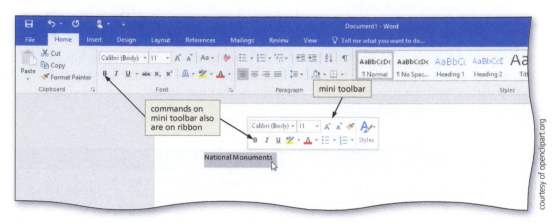

Figure 18

Quick Access Toolbar The **Quick Access Toolbar**, located initially (by default) above the ribbon at the left edge of the title bar, provides convenient, one-click access to frequently used commands (shown in Figure 15). The commands on the Quick Access Toolbar always are available, regardless of the task you are performing. The Touch/Mouse Mode button on the Quick Access Toolbar allows you to switch between Touch mode and Mouse mode. If you primarily are using touch gestures, Touch mode will add more space between commands on menus and on the ribbon so that they are easier to tap. While touch gestures are convenient ways to interact with Office apps, not all features are supported when you are using Touch mode. If you are using a mouse, Mouse mode will not add the extra space between buttons and commands. The Quick Access Toolbar is discussed in more depth later in the module.

KeyTips If you prefer using the keyboard instead of the mouse, you can press the ALT key on the keyboard to display **KeyTips**, or keyboard code icons, for certain commands (Figure 19). To select a command using the keyboard, press the letter or number displayed in the KeyTip, which may cause additional KeyTips related to the selected command to appear. To remove KeyTips from the screen, press the ALT key or the ESC key until all KeyTips disappear, or click anywhere in the app window.

BTW

Touch Mode

The Office and Windows interfaces may vary if you are using Touch mode. For this reason, you might notice that the function or appearance of your touch screen in Word differs slightly from this module's presentation.

Figure 19

Microsoft Account Area In this area, you can use the Sign in link to sign in to your Microsoft account. Once signed in, you will see your account information, as well as a picture if you have included one in your Microsoft account.

To Display a Different Tab on the Ribbon

1 SIGN IN | 2 USE WINDOWS | **3 USE APPS** | 4 FILE MANAGEMENT | 5 SWITCH APPS | 6 SAVE FILES
7 CHANGE SCREEN RESOLUTION | 8 EXIT APPS | 9 USE ADDITIONAL APP FEATURES | 10 USE HELP

When you run Word, the ribbon displays nine main tabs: File, Home, Insert, Design, Layout, References, Mailings, Review, and View. The tab currently displayed is called the **active tab**.

The following step displays the Insert tab, that is, makes it the active tab. **Why?** *When working with an Office app, you may need to switch tabs to access other options for working with a document.*

1

- Click Insert on the ribbon to display the Insert tab (Figure 20).

Experiment

- Click the other tabs on the ribbon to view their contents. When you are finished, click Insert on the ribbon to redisplay the Insert tab.

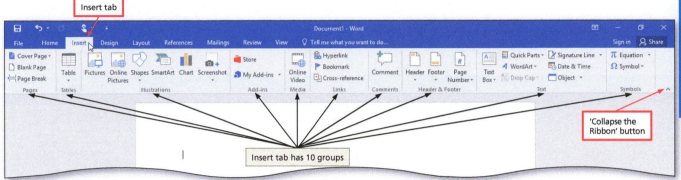

Figure 20

Other Ways

1. Press ALT, press letter corresponding to tab to display   2. Press ALT, press LEFT ARROW or RIGHT ARROW until desired tab is displayed

To Collapse and Expand the Ribbon and Use Full Screen Mode

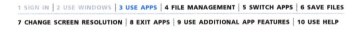

To display more of a document or other item in the window of an Office app, some users prefer to collapse the ribbon, which hides the groups on the ribbon and displays only the main tabs, or to use **Full Screen mode**, which hides all the commands and just displays the document. Each time you run an Office app, such as Word, the ribbon appears the same way it did the last time you used that Office app. The modules in this book, however, begin with the ribbon appearing as it did at the initial installation of Office or Word.

The following steps collapse, expand, and restore the ribbon in Word and then switch to Full Screen mode. **Why?** *If you need more space on the screen to work with your document, you may consider collapsing the ribbon or switching to Full Screen mode to gain additional workspace.*

1

- Click the 'Collapse the Ribbon' button on the ribbon (shown in Figure 20) to collapse the ribbon (Figure 21).

Q&A What happened to the 'Collapse the Ribbon' button?
The 'Pin the ribbon' button replaces the 'Collapse the Ribbon' button when the ribbon is collapsed. You will see the 'Pin the ribbon' button only when you expand a ribbon by clicking a tab.

Figure 21

2

- Click Home on the ribbon to expand the Home tab (Figure 22).

Q&A

Why would I click the Home tab?

If you want to use a command on a collapsed ribbon, click the main tab to display the groups for that tab. After you select a command on the ribbon and resume working in the document, the groups will be collapsed once again. If you decide not to use a command on the ribbon, you can collapse the groups by clicking the same main tab or clicking in the app window.

Experiment

- Click Home on the ribbon to collapse the groups again. Click Home on the ribbon to expand the Home tab.

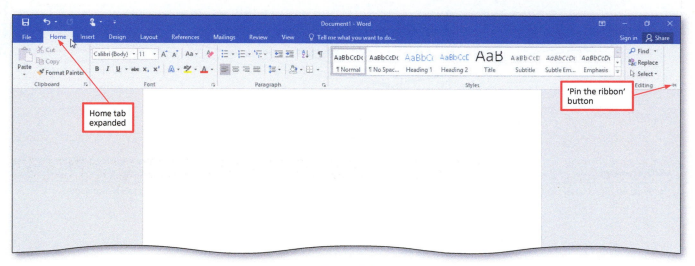

Figure 22

3

- Click the 'Pin the ribbon' button on the expanded Home tab to restore the ribbon.

- Click the 'Ribbon Display Options' button to display the Ribbon Display Options menu (Figure 23).

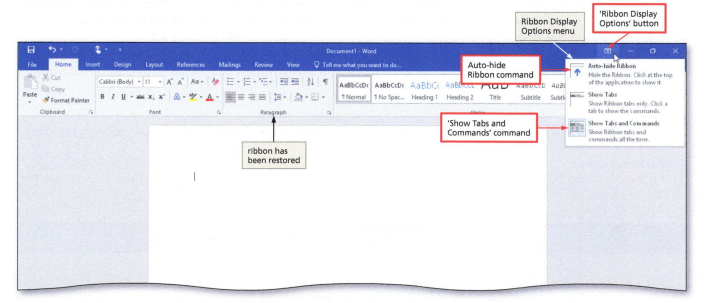

Figure 23

4

- Click Auto-hide Ribbon to use Full Screen mode, which hides all the commands from the screen (Figure 24).

- Click the ellipsis to display the ribbon temporarily.

- Click the 'Ribbon Display Options' button to display the Ribbon Display Options menu (shown in Figure 23).

- Click 'Show Tabs and Commands' on the Ribbon Display Options menu to exit Full Screen mode.

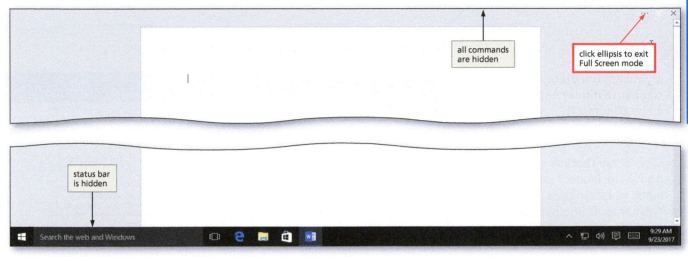

all commands are hidden

click ellipsis to exit Full Screen mode

status bar is hidden

Search the web and Windows

9:29 AM
9/23/2017

Figure 24

Other Ways

1. Double-click a main tab on the ribbon
2. Press CTRL+F1

To Use a Shortcut Menu to Relocate the Quick Access Toolbar

1 SIGN IN | 2 USE WINDOWS | 3 USE APPS | 4 FILE MANAGEMENT | 5 SWITCH APPS | 6 SAVE FILES

7 CHANGE SCREEN RESOLUTION | 8 EXIT APPS | 9 USE ADDITIONAL APP FEATURES | 10 USE HELP

When you right-click certain areas of the Word and other Office app windows, a shortcut menu will appear. A **shortcut menu** is a list of frequently used commands that relate to an object. *Why? You can use shortcut menus to access common commands quickly.* When you right-click the status bar, for example, a shortcut menu appears with commands related to the status bar. When you right-click the Quick Access Toolbar, a shortcut menu appears with commands related to the Quick Access Toolbar. The following steps use a shortcut menu to move the Quick Access Toolbar, which by default is located on the title bar.

1

- Right-click the Quick Access Toolbar to display a shortcut menu that presents a list of commands related to the Quick Access Toolbar (Figure 25).

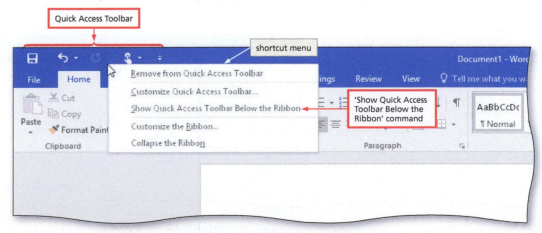

Quick Access Toolbar

shortcut menu

Document1 - Word

Remove from Quick Access Toolbar

Customize Quick Access Toolbar...

Show Quick Access Toolbar Below the Ribbon

Customize the Ribbon...

Collapse the Ribbon

'Show Quick Access Toolbar Below the Ribbon' command

Figure 25

- Click 'Show Quick Access Toolbar Below the Ribbon' on the shortcut menu to display the Quick Access Toolbar below the ribbon (Figure 26).

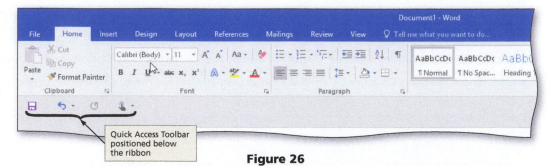

Figure 26

- Right-click the Quick Access Toolbar to display a shortcut menu (Figure 27).

- Click 'Show Quick Access Toolbar Above the Ribbon' on the shortcut menu to return the Quick Access Toolbar to its original position (shown in Figure 25).

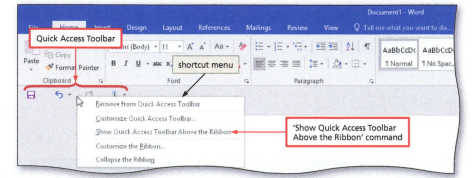

Figure 27

Other Ways

1. Click 'Customize Quick Access Toolbar' button on Quick Access Toolbar, click 'Show Below the Ribbon' or 'Show Above the Ribbon'

To Customize the Quick Access Toolbar

1 SIGN IN | 2 USE WINDOWS | 3 USE APPS | 4 FILE MANAGEMENT | 5 SWITCH APPS | 6 SAVE FILES
7 CHANGE SCREEN RESOLUTION | 8 EXIT APPS | 9 USE ADDITIONAL APP FEATURES | 10 USE HELP

The Quick Access Toolbar provides easy access to some of the more frequently used commands in the Office apps. By default, the Quick Access Toolbar contains buttons for the Save, Undo, and Redo commands. If your computer or mobile device has a touch screen, the Quick Access Toolbar also might display the Touch/Mouse Mode button. You can customize the Quick Access Toolbar by changing its location in the window, as shown in the previous steps, and by adding more buttons to reflect commands you would like to access easily. The following steps add the Quick Print button to the Quick Access Toolbar in the Word window. *Why? Adding the Quick Print button to the Quick Access Toolbar speeds up the process of printing.*

- Click the 'Customize Quick Access Toolbar' button to display the Customize Quick Access Toolbar menu (Figure 28).

Q&A

Which commands are listed on the Customize Quick Access Toolbar menu?

It lists commands that commonly are added to the Quick Access Toolbar.

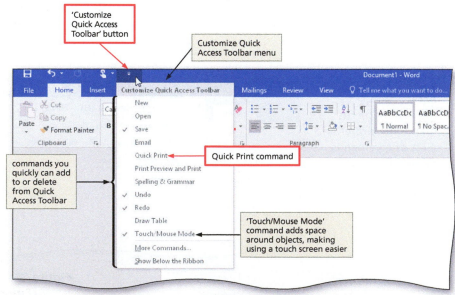

Figure 28

2

- If it is not selected already, click Quick Print on the Customize Quick Access Toolbar menu to add the Quick Print button to the Quick Access Toolbar (Figure 29).

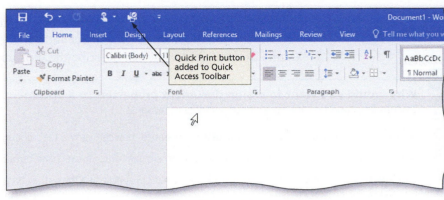

Q&A How would I remove a button from the Quick Access Toolbar?
You would right-click the button you wish to remove and then click 'Remove from Quick Access Toolbar' on the shortcut menu or click the 'Customize Quick Access Toolbar' button on the Quick Access Toolbar and then click the button name in the Customize Quick Access Toolbar menu to remove the check mark.

Figure 29

To Enter Text in a Document

1 SIGN IN | 2 USE WINDOWS | 3 USE APPS | 4 FILE MANAGEMENT | 5 SWITCH APPS | 6 SAVE FILES
7 CHANGE SCREEN RESOLUTION | 8 EXIT APPS | 9 USE ADDITIONAL APP FEATURES | 10 USE HELP

The first step in creating a document is to enter its text by typing on the keyboard. By default, Word positions text at the left margin as you type. The following steps type this first line of a flyer. ***Why?*** *To begin creating a flyer, for example, you type the headline in the document window.*

1

- Type **VISIT NATIONAL MONUMENTS** as the text (Figure 30).

Q&A What is the blinking vertical bar to the right of the text?
The blinking bar is the insertion point, which indicates where text, graphics, and other items will be inserted in the document. As you type, the insertion point moves to the right, and when you reach the end of a line, it moves down to the beginning of the next line.

What if I make an error while typing?
You can press the BACKSPACE key until you have deleted the text in error and then retype the text correctly.

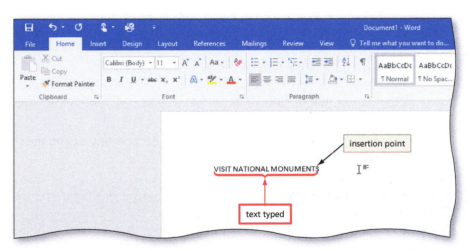

Figure 30

2

- Press the ENTER key to move the insertion point to the beginning of the next line (Figure 31).

Q&A Why did blank space appear between the entered text and the insertion point?
Each time you press the ENTER key, Word creates a new paragraph and inserts blank space between the two paragraphs. Depending on your settings, Word may or may not insert a blank space between the two paragraphs.

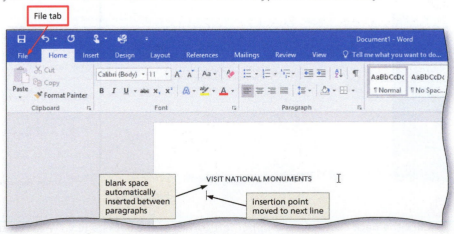

Figure 31

Document Properties

You can organize and identify your files by using **document properties**, which are the details about a file, such as the project author, title, and subject. For example, a class name or document topic can describe the file's purpose or content.

Why would you want to assign document properties to a document?
Document properties are valuable for a variety of reasons:

- Users can save time locating a particular file because they can view a file's document properties without opening the file.

- By creating consistent properties for files having similar content, users can better organize their files.

- Some organizations require users to add document properties so that other employees can view details about these files.

To Change Document Properties

1 SIGN IN | 2 USE WINDOWS | 3 USE APPS | 4 FILE MANAGEMENT | 5 SWITCH APPS | 6 SAVE FILES
7 CHANGE SCREEN RESOLUTION | 8 EXIT APPS | 9 USE ADDITIONAL APP FEATURES | 10 USE HELP

You can change the document properties while working with the file in an Office app. When you save the file, the Office app (Word, in this case) will save the document properties with the file. The following steps change document properties. *Why? Adding document properties will help you identify characteristics of the file without opening it.*

1

- Click File on the ribbon (shown in Figure 31) to open the Backstage view and then, if necessary, click the Info tab in the Backstage view to display the Info gallery.

What is the purpose of the File tab on the ribbon, and what is the Backstage view?
The File tab opens the Backstage view for each Office app, including Word. The **Backstage view** contains a set of commands that enable you to manage documents and provides data about the documents.

What is the purpose of the Info gallery in the Backstage view?
The Info tab, which is selected by default when you click File on the ribbon, displays the Info gallery, where you can protect a document, inspect a document, and manage versions of a document, as well as view all the file properties, such as when the file was created.

- Click to the right of the Comments property in the Properties list and then type **CIS 101 Assignment** in the Comments text box (Figure 32).

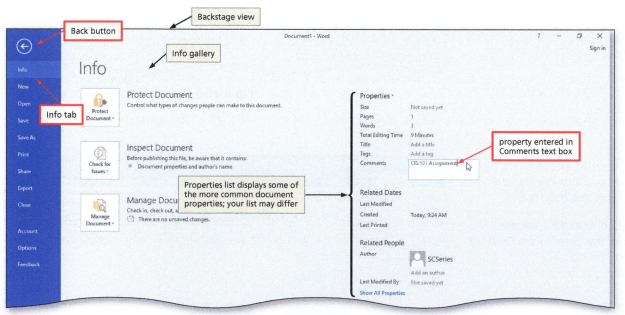

Figure 32

2

- Click the Back button in the upper-left corner of the Backstage view to return to the document window.

Printing, Saving, and Organizing Files

While you are creating a document, the computer or mobile device stores it in memory. When you save a document, the computer or mobile device places it on a storage medium, such as a hard disk, solid state drive (SSD), USB flash drive, or optical disc. The storage medium can be permanent in your computer, may be portable where you remove it from your computer, or may be on a web server you access through a network or the Internet.

A saved document is referred to as a file. A **file name** is the name assigned to a file when it is saved. When saving files, you should organize them so that you easily can find them later. Windows provides tools to help you organize files.

> **BTW**
> **File Type**
> Depending on your Windows settings, the file type .docx may be displayed immediately to the right of the file name after you save the file. The file type .docx is a Word 2016 document.

Printing a Document

After creating a document, you may want to print it. Printing a document enables you to distribute it to others in a form that can be read or viewed but typically not edited.

What is the best method for distributing a document?

The traditional method of distributing a document uses a printer to produce a hard copy. A **hard copy** or **printout** is information that exists on a physical medium, such as paper. Hard copies can be useful for the following reasons:

- Some people prefer proofreading a hard copy of a document rather than viewing it on the screen to check for errors and readability.

- Hard copies can serve as a backup reference if your storage medium is lost or becomes corrupted and you need to recreate the document.

Instead of distributing a hard copy of a document, users can distribute the document as an electronic image that mirrors the original document's appearance. The electronic image of the document can be sent as an email attachment, posted on a website, or copied to a portable storage medium, such as a USB flash drive. Two popular electronic image formats, sometimes called fixed formats, are PDF by Adobe Systems and XPS by Microsoft. In Word, you can create electronic image files through the Save As dialog box and the Export, Share, and Print tabs in the Backstage view. Electronic images of documents, such as PDF and XPS, can be useful for the following reasons:

- Users can view electronic images of documents without the software that created the original document (e.g., Word). For example, to view a PDF file you use a program called Adobe Reader, which can be downloaded free from Adobe's website.

- Sending electronic documents saves paper and printer supplies. Society encourages users to contribute to **green computing**, which involves reducing the electricity consumed and environmental waste generated when using computers, mobile devices, and related technologies.

CONSIDER THIS

1 SIGN IN | 2 USE WINDOWS | 3 USE APPS | 4 FILE MANAGEMENT | 5 SWITCH APPS | 6 SAVE FILES
7 CHANGE SCREEN RESOLUTION | 8 EXIT APPS | 9 USE ADDITIONAL APP FEATURES | 10 USE HELP

To Print a Document

With the document opened, you may want to print it. *Why? Because you want to see how the text will appear on paper, you want to print a hard copy on a printer.* The following steps print a hard copy of the contents of the document.

- Click File on the ribbon to open the Backstage view.
- Click the Print tab in the Backstage view to display the Print gallery (Figure 33).

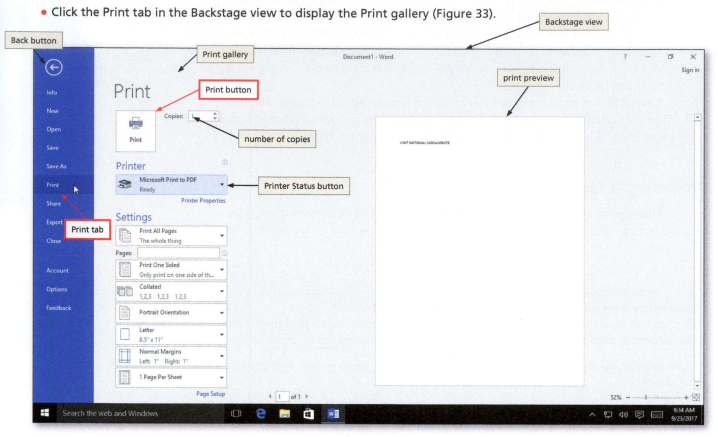

Figure 33

Q&A

How can I print multiple copies of my document?
Increase the number in the Copies box in the Print gallery.

What if I decide not to print the document at this time?
Click the Back button in the upper-left corner of the Backstage view to return to the document window.

- Verify that the selected printer will print a hard copy of the document. If necessary, click the Printer Status button to display a list of available printer options and then click the desired printer to change the currently selected printer.

- Click the Print button in the Print gallery to print the document on the currently selected printer.

- When the printer stops, retrieve the hard copy (Figure 34).

Q&A

What if I want to print an electronic image of a document instead of a hard copy?
You would click the Printer Status button in the Print gallery and then select the desired electronic image option, such as Microsoft XPS Document Writer, which would create an XPS file.

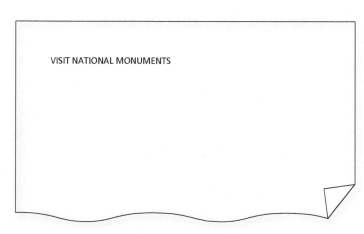

VISIT NATIONAL MONUMENTS

Figure 34

Other Ways

1. Press CTRL+P

Organizing Files and Folders

A file contains data. This data can range from a research paper to an accounting spreadsheet to an electronic math quiz. You should organize and store files in folders to avoid misplacing a file and to help you find a file quickly.

If you are taking an introductory computer class (CIS 101, for example), you may want to design a series of folders for the different subjects covered in the class. To accomplish this, you can arrange the folders in a hierarchy for the class, as shown in Figure 35. The hierarchy contains three levels. The first level contains the storage medium, such as a hard drive. The second level contains the class folder (CIS 101, in this case), and the third level contains seven folders, one each for a different Office app that will be covered in the class (Word, PowerPoint, Excel, Access, Outlook, Publisher, and OneNote).

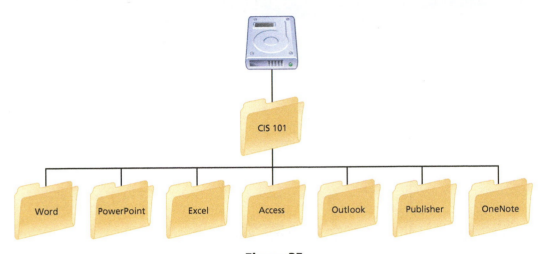

Figure 35

When the hierarchy in Figure 35 is created, the storage medium is said to contain the CIS 101 folder, and the CIS 101 folder is said to contain the separate Office folders (i.e., Word, PowerPoint, Excel, etc.). In addition, this hierarchy easily can be expanded to include folders from other classes taken during additional semesters.

The vertical and horizontal lines in Figure 35 form a pathway that allows you to navigate to a drive or folder on a computer or network. A **path** consists of a drive letter (preceded by a drive name when necessary) and colon, to identify the storage device, and one or more folder names. A hard drive typically has a drive letter of C. Each drive or folder in the hierarchy has a corresponding path.

By default, Windows saves documents in the Documents folder, music in the Music folder, photos in the Pictures folder, videos in the Videos folder, and downloads in the Downloads folder.

The following pages illustrate the steps to organize the folders for this class and save a file in a folder:

1. Create the folder identifying your class.
2. Create the Word folder in the folder identifying your class.
3. Save a file in the Word folder.
4. Verify the location of the saved file.

To Create a Folder

When you create a folder, such as the CIS 101 folder shown in Figure 35, you must name the folder. A folder name should describe the folder and its contents. A folder name can contain spaces and any uppercase or lowercase characters, except a backslash (\), slash (/), colon (:), asterisk (*), question mark (?), quotation marks ("), less than symbol (<), greater than symbol (>), or vertical bar (|). Folder names cannot be CON, AUX, COM1, COM2, COM3, COM4, LPT1, LPT2, LPT3, PRN, or NUL. The same rules for naming folders also apply to naming files.

The following steps create a class folder (CIS 101, in this case) in the Documents folder. *Why? When storing files, you should organize the files so that it will be easier to find them later.*

1

- Click the File Explorer button on the taskbar to run File Explorer.

- If necessary, double-click This PC in the navigation pane to expand the contents of your computer.

- Click the Documents folder in the navigation pane to display the contents of the Documents folder in the file list (Figure 36).

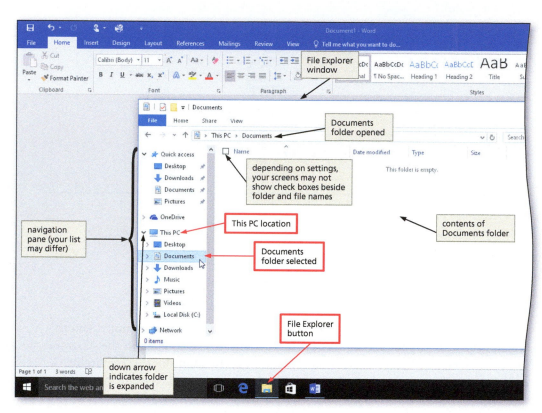

Figure 36

2

- Click the New folder button on the Quick Access Toolbar to create a new folder with the name, New folder, selected in a text box (Figure 37).

Q&A
Why is the folder icon displayed differently on my computer or mobile device?
Windows might be configured to display contents differently on your computer or mobile device.

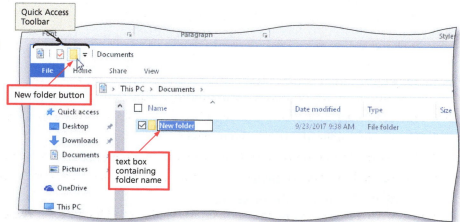

Figure 37

3

- Type **CIS 101** (or your class code) in the text box as the new folder name.

  If requested by your instructor, add your last name to the end of the folder name.

- Press the ENTER key to change the folder name from New folder to a folder name identifying your class (Figure 38).

Q&A

What happens when I press the ENTER key?

The class folder (CIS 101, in this case) is displayed in the file list, which contains the folder name, date modified, type, and size.

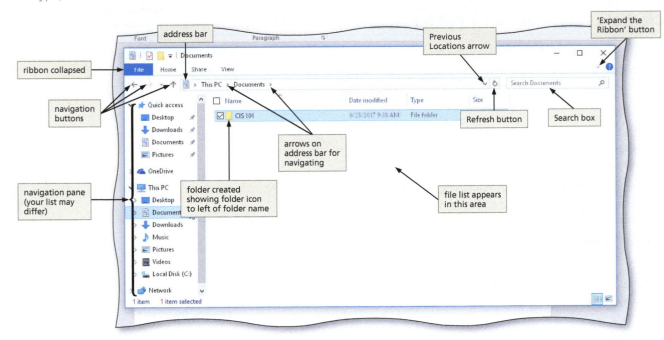

Figure 38

Other Ways

1. Press CTRL+SHIFT+N

2. Click the New folder button (Home tab | New group)

Folder Windows

The File Explorer window (shown in Figure 38) is called a folder window. Recall that a folder is a specific named location on a storage medium that contains related files. Most users rely on **folder windows** for finding, viewing, and managing information on their computers. Folder windows have common design elements, including the following (shown in Figure 38).

- The **address bar** provides quick navigation options. The arrows on the address bar allow you to visit different locations on the computer or mobile device.

- The buttons to the left of the address bar allow you to navigate the contents of the navigation pane and view recent pages.

- The **Previous Locations arrow** displays the locations you have visited.

- The **Refresh button** on the right side of the address bar refreshes the contents of the folder list.

- The **Search box** contains the dimmed words, Search Documents. You can type a term in the search box for a list of files, folders, shortcuts, and elements containing that term within the location you are searching.

- The **ribbon** contains four tabs used to accomplish various tasks on the computer or mobile device related to organizing and managing the contents of the open window. This ribbon works similarly to the ribbon in the Office apps.
- The **navigation pane** on the left contains the Quick access area, the OneDrive area, the This PC area, and the Network area.
- The **Quick access area** shows locations you access frequently. By default, this list contains links only to your Desktop, Downloads, Documents, and Pictures.

To Create a Folder within a Folder

1 SIGN IN | 2 USE WINDOWS | 3 USE APPS | **4 FILE MANAGEMENT** | 5 SWITCH APPS | 6 SAVE FILES
7 CHANGE SCREEN RESOLUTION | 8 EXIT APPS | 9 USE ADDITIONAL APP FEATURES | 10 USE HELP

With the class folder created, you can create folders that will store the files you create using Word. The following step creates a Word folder in the CIS 101 folder (or the folder identifying your class). *Why? To be able to organize your files, you should create a folder structure.*

- Double-click the icon or folder name for the CIS 101 folder (or the folder identifying your class) in the file list to open the folder.
- Click the New folder button on the Quick Access Toolbar to create a new folder with the name, New folder, selected in a text box folder.
- Type **Word** in the text box as the new folder name.
- Press the ENTER key to rename the folder (Figure 39).

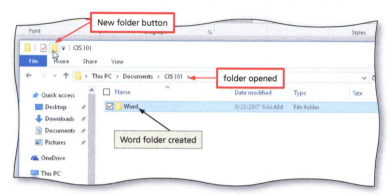

Figure 39

Other Ways	
1. Press CTRL+SHIFT+N	2. Click the New folder button (Home tab | New group)

To Expand a Folder, Scroll through Folder Contents, and Collapse a Folder

1 SIGN IN | 2 USE WINDOWS | 3 USE APPS | **4 FILE MANAGEMENT** | 5 SWITCH APPS | 6 SAVE FILES
7 CHANGE SCREEN RESOLUTION | 8 EXIT APPS | 9 USE ADDITIONAL APP FEATURES | 10 USE HELP

Folder windows display the hierarchy of items and the contents of drives and folders in the file list. You might want to expand a folder in the navigation pane to view its contents, scroll through its contents, and collapse it when you are finished viewing its contents. *Why? When a folder is expanded, you can see all the folders it contains. By contrast, a collapsed folder hides the folders it contains.* The following steps expand, scroll through, and then collapse the folder identifying your class (CIS 101, in this case).

- Double-click the Documents folder in the This PC area of the navigation pane, which expands the folder to display its contents and displays a black down arrow to the left of the Documents folder icon (Figure 40).

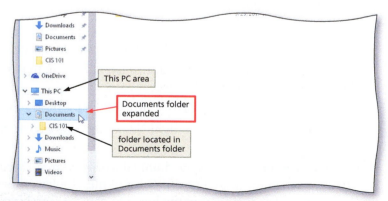

Figure 40

• Double-click the CIS 101 folder, which expands the folder to display its contents and displays a black down arrow to the left of the folder icon (Figure 41).

Experiment

• Drag the scroll box down or click the down scroll arrow on the vertical scroll bar to display additional folders at the bottom of the navigation pane. Drag the scroll box up or click the scroll bar above the scroll box to move the scroll box to the top of the navigation pane. Drag the scroll box down the scroll bar until the scroll box is halfway down the scroll bar.

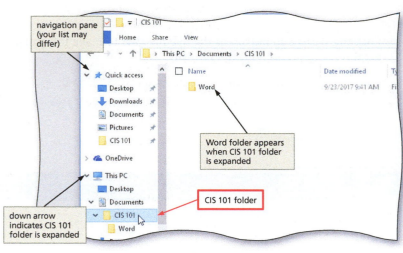

Figure 41

• Double-click the folder identifying your class (CIS 101, in this case) to collapse the folder (Figure 42).

Q&A Why are some folders indented below others?
A folder contains the indented folders below it.

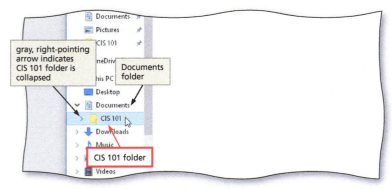

Figure 42

Other Ways

1. Point to display arrows in navigation pane, click arrow to expand or collapse

2. Select folder to expand or collapse using arrow keys, press RIGHT ARROW to expand; press LEFT ARROW to collapse

---

To Switch from One App to Another

1 SIGN IN | 2 USE WINDOWS | 3 USE APPS | 4 FILE MANAGEMENT | **5 SWITCH APPS** | 6 SAVE FILES
7 CHANGE SCREEN RESOLUTION | 8 EXIT APPS | 9 USE ADDITIONAL APP FEATURES | 10 USE HELP

The next step is to save the Word file containing the headline you typed earlier. Word, however, currently is not the active window. You can use the Word app button on the taskbar and live preview to switch to Word and then save the document in the Word document window.

Why? *By clicking the appropriate app button on the taskbar, you can switch to the running app you want to use.* The following steps switch to the Word window; however, the steps are the same for any active Office app currently displayed as a button on the taskbar.

1

• Point to the Word app button on the taskbar to see a live preview of the open document(s) or the window title(s) of the open document(s), depending on your computer's configuration (Figure 43).

Q&A What if I am using a touch screen?
Live preview will not work if you are using a touch screen. If you are using a touch screen and do not have a mouse, proceed to Step 2.

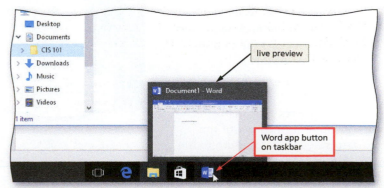

Figure 43

2

- Click the Word app button or the live preview to make the app associated with the app button the active window (Figure 44).

Q&A

What if multiple documents are open in an app?
Click the desired live preview to switch to the window you want to use.

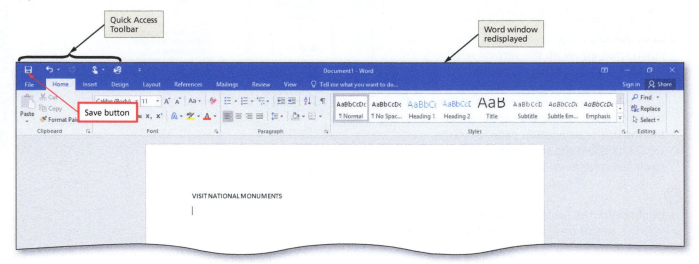

Figure 44

Other Ways

1. Press ALT+TAB until app you wish to display is selected

To Save a File in a Folder

1 SIGN IN | 2 USE WINDOWS | 3 USE APPS | 4 FILE MANAGEMENT | 5 SWITCH APPS | **6 SAVE FILES**
7 CHANGE SCREEN RESOLUTION | 8 EXIT APPS | 9 USE ADDITIONAL APP FEATURES | 10 USE HELP

With the Word folder created, you can save the Word document shown in the document window in the Word folder. *Why? Without saving a file, you may lose all the work you have completed and will be unable to reuse or share it with others later.* The following steps save a file in the Word folder contained in your class folder (CIS 101, in this case) using the file name, National Monuments.

1

- Click the Save button (shown in Figure 44) on the Quick Access Toolbar, which depending on settings, will display either the Save As gallery in the Backstage view (Figure 45) or the Save As dialog box (Figure 46).

Q&A

What if the Save As gallery is not displayed in the Backstage view?
Click the Save As tab to display the Save As gallery.

How do I close the Backstage view?
Click the Back button in the upper-left corner of the Backstage view to return to the Word window.

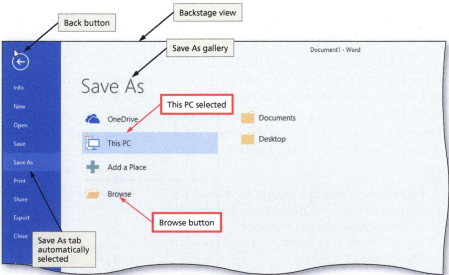

Figure 45

② 2

● If your screen displays the Backstage view, click This PC, if necessary, to display options in the right pane related to saving on your computer or mobile device; if your screen already displays the Save As dialog box, proceed to Step 3.

Q&A What if I wanted to save on OneDrive instead?
You would click OneDrive. Saving on OneDrive is discussed in a later section in this module.

● Click the Browse button in the left pane to display the Save As dialog box (Figure 46).

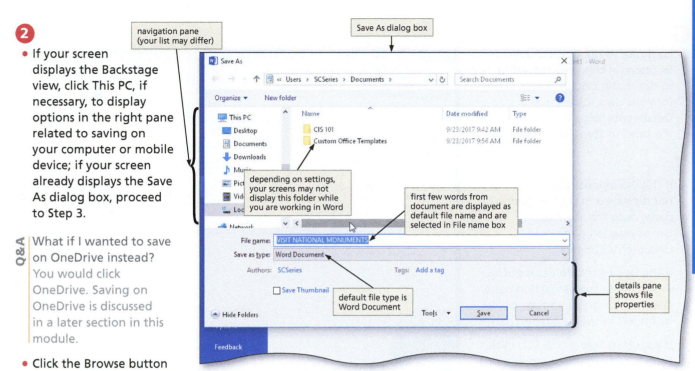

navigation pane (your list may differ)

Save As dialog box

depending on settings, your screens may not display this folder while you are working in Word

first few words from document are displayed as default file name and are selected in File name box

default file type is Word Document

details pane shows file properties

Figure 46

Q&A Why does a file name already appear in the File name box?
Word automatically suggests a file name the first time you save a document. The file name normally consists of the first few words contained in the document. Because the suggested file name is selected, you do not need to delete it; as soon as you begin typing, the new file name replaces the selected text.

③ 3

● Type **National Monuments** in the File name box (Save As dialog box) to change the file name. Do not press the ENTER key after typing the file name because you do not want to close the dialog box at this time (Figure 47).

Q&A What characters can I use in a file name?
The only invalid characters are the backslash (\), slash (/), colon (:), asterisk (*), question mark (?), quotation mark ("), less than symbol (<), greater than symbol (>), and vertical bar (|).

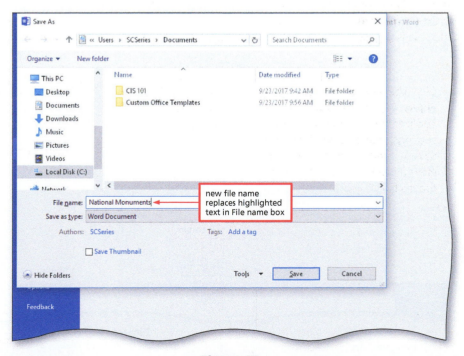

new file name replaces highlighted text in File name box

Figure 47

4

- Navigate to the desired save location (in this case, the Word folder in the CIS 101 folder [or your class folder] in the Documents folder) by performing the tasks in Steps 4a and 4b.

4a

- If the Documents folder is not displayed in the navigation pane, drag the scroll bar in the navigation pane until Documents appears.

- If the Documents folder is not expanded in the navigation pane, double-click Documents to display its folders in the navigation pane.

- If your class folder (CIS 101, in this case) is not expanded, double-click the CIS 101 folder to select the folder and display its contents in the navigation pane (Figure 48).

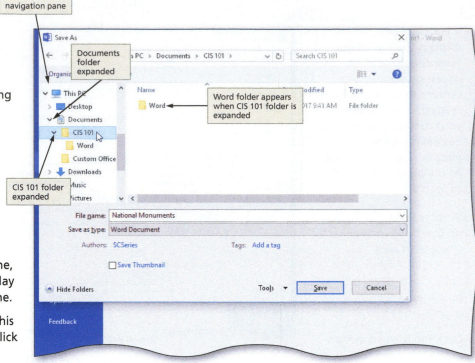

Figure 48

Q&A | What if I do not want to save in a folder?

Although storing files in folders is an effective technique for organizing files, some users prefer not to store files in folders. If you prefer not to save this file in a folder, select the storage device on which you wish to save the file and then proceed to Step 5.

4b

- Click the Word folder in the navigation pane to select it as the new save location and display its contents in the file list (Figure 49).

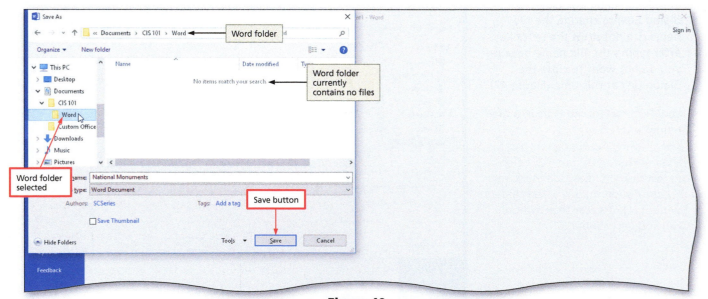

Figure 49

5

- Click the Save button (Save As dialog box) to save the document in the selected folder in the selected location with the entered file name (Figure 50).

Q&A How do I know that the file is saved?

While an Office app such as Word is saving a file, it briefly displays a message on the status bar indicating the amount of the file saved. In addition, the file name appears on the title bar.

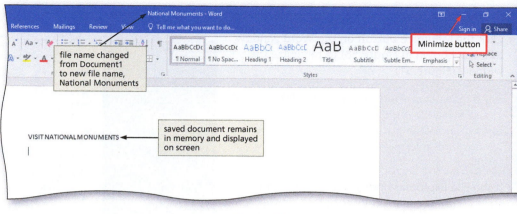

Figure 50

Other Ways

1. Click File on ribbon, click Save As tab in Backstage view, click This PC, click Browse button, type file name (Save As dialog box), navigate to desired save location, click Save button
2. Press F12, type file name (Save As dialog box), navigate to desired save location, click Save button

CONSIDER THIS

How often should you save a document?

It is important to save a document frequently for the following reasons:

- The document in memory might be lost if the computer is turned off or you lose electrical power while an app is running.
- If you run out of time before completing a project, you may finish it at a future time without starting over.

Navigating in Dialog Boxes

Navigating is the process of finding a location on a storage device. While saving the National Monuments file, for example, Steps 4a and 4b navigated to the Word folder located in the CIS 101 folder in the Documents folder. When performing certain functions in Windows apps, such as saving a file, opening a file, or inserting a picture in an existing document, you most likely will have to navigate to the location where you want to save the file or to the folder containing the file you want to open or insert. Most dialog boxes in Windows apps requiring navigation follow a similar procedure; that is, the way you navigate to a folder in one dialog box, such as the Save As dialog box, is similar to how you might navigate in another dialog box, such as the Open dialog box. If you chose to navigate to a specific location in a dialog box, you would follow the instructions in Steps 4a and 4b.

To Minimize and Restore a Window

1 SIGN IN | **2 USE WINDOWS** | 3 USE APPS | 4 FILE MANAGEMENT | 5 SWITCH APPS | 6 SAVE FILES
7 CHANGE SCREEN RESOLUTION | 8 EXIT APPS | 9 USE ADDITIONAL APP FEATURES | 10 USE HELP

Before continuing, you can verify that the Word file was saved properly. To do this, you will minimize the Word window and then open the CIS 101 window so that you can verify the file is stored in the CIS 101 folder on the hard drive. A **minimized window** is an open window that is hidden from view but can be displayed quickly by clicking the window's button on the taskbar.

In the following example, Word is used to illustrate minimizing and restoring windows; however, you would follow the same steps regardless of the Office app you are using. *Why? Before closing an app, you should make sure your file saved correctly so that you can find it later.*

The following steps minimize the Word window, verify that the file is saved, and then restore the minimized window.

1

- Click the Minimize button on the Word window title bar (shown in Figure 50) to minimize the window (Figure 51).

Q&A Is the minimized window still available?
The minimized window, Word in this case, remains available but no longer is the active window. It is minimized as a button on the taskbar.

- If the File Explorer window is not open on the screen, click the File Explorer button on the taskbar to make the File Explorer window the active window.

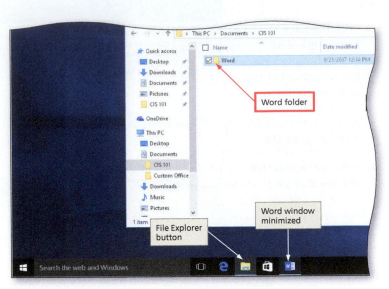

Figure 51

2

- Double-click the Word folder in the file list to select the folder and display its contents (Figure 52).

Q&A Why does the File Explorer button on the taskbar change?
A selected app button indicates that the app is active on the screen. When the button is not selected, the app is running but not active.

3

- After viewing the contents of the selected folder, click the Word app button on the taskbar to restore the minimized window (as shown in Figure 50).

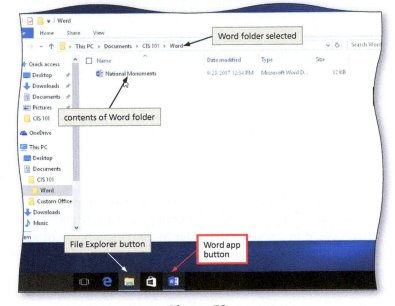

Figure 52

Other Ways

1. Right-click title bar, click Minimize on shortcut menu, click taskbar button in taskbar button area
2. Press WINDOWS+M, press WINDOWS+SHIFT+M
3. Click Word app button on taskbar to minimize window. Click Word app button again to restore window.

1 SIGN IN | 2 USE WINDOWS | 3 USE APPS | 4 FILE MANAGEMENT | 5 SWITCH APPS | 6 SAVE FILES
7 CHANGE SCREEN RESOLUTION | 8 EXIT APPS | 9 USE ADDITIONAL APP FEATURES | 10 USE HELP

To Save a File on OneDrive

One of the features of Office is the capability to save files on OneDrive so that you can use the files on multiple computers or mobile devices without having to use an external storage device, such as a USB flash drive. Storing files on OneDrive also enables you to share files more efficiently with others, such as when using Office Online and Office 365.

In the following example, Word is used to save a file on OneDrive. **Why?** *Storing files on OneDrive provides more portability options than are available from storing files in the Documents folder.*

You can save files directly on OneDrive from within an Office app. The following steps save the current Word file on OneDrive. These steps require that you have a Microsoft account and an Internet connection.

- Click File on the ribbon to open the Backstage view.

- Click the Save As tab in the Backstage view to display the Save As gallery.

- Click OneDrive in the left pane to display OneDrive saving options or a Sign In button, if you are not signed in already to your Microsoft account (Figure 53).

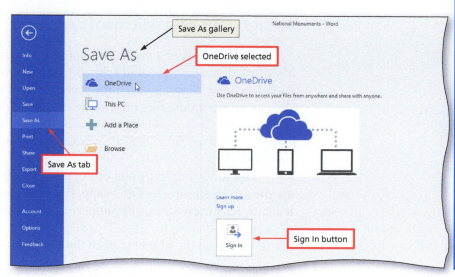

Figure 53

- If your screen displays a Sign In button (shown in Figure 53), click it to display the Sign in dialog box (Figure 54).

Q&A What if the Sign In button does not appear?
If you already are signed into your Microsoft account, the Sign In button will not be displayed. In this case, proceed to Step 3.

- Follow the instructions on the screen to sign in to your Microsoft account.

Figure 54

- If necessary, in the Backstage view, click OneDrive in the left pane in the Save As gallery to select OneDrive as the save location.

- Click the Documents, or similar, folder in the right pane to display the Save As dialog box (Figure 55).

Q&A Why does the path in the OneDrive address bar in the Save As dialog box contain various letters and numbers?
The letters and numbers in the address bar uniquely identify the location of your OneDrive files and folders.

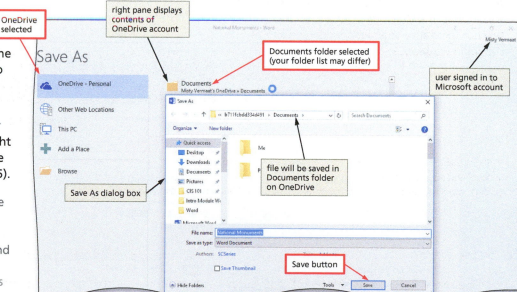

Figure 55

- Click the Save button (Save As dialog box) to save the file on OneDrive.

To Sign Out of a Microsoft Account

If you are using a public computer or otherwise wish to sign out of your Microsoft account, you should sign out of the account from the Accounts gallery in the Backstage view. Signing out of the account is the safest way to make sure that nobody else can access online files or settings stored in your Microsoft account. ***Why?*** *For security reasons, you should sign out of your Microsoft account when you are finished using a public or shared computer. Staying signed in to your Microsoft account might enable others to access your files.*

The following steps sign out of a Microsoft account from Word. You would use the same steps in any Office app. If you do not wish to sign out of your Microsoft account, read these steps without performing them.

1 Click File on the ribbon to open the Backstage view.

2 Click the Account tab to display the Account gallery (Figure 56).

3 Click the Sign out link, which displays the Remove Account dialog box. If a Can't remove Windows accounts dialog box appears instead of the Remove Account dialog box, click the OK button and skip the remaining steps.

> **Q&A** Why does a Can't remove Windows accounts dialog box appear?
> If you signed in to Windows using your Microsoft account, then you also must sign out from Windows, rather than signing out from within Word. When you are finished using Windows, be sure to sign out at that time.

4 Click the Yes button (Remove Account dialog box) to sign out of your Microsoft account on this computer or mobile device.

> **Q&A** Should I sign out of Windows after removing my Microsoft account?
> When you are finished using the computer, you should sign out of Windows for maximum security.

5 Click the Back button in the upper-left corner of the Backstage view to return to the document.

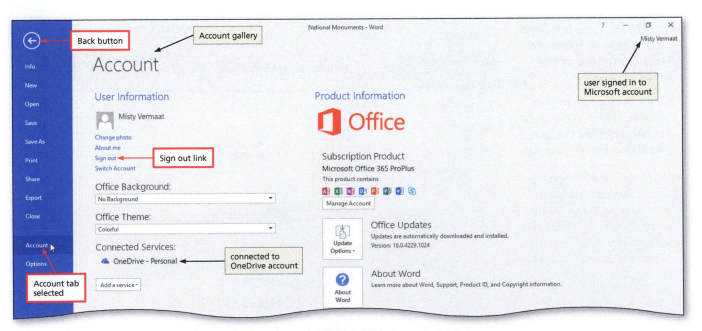

Figure 56

Screen Resolution

Screen resolution indicates the number of pixels (dots) that the computer uses to display the letters, numbers, graphics, and background you see on the screen. When you increase the screen resolution, Windows displays more information on the screen, but the information decreases in size. The reverse also is true: as you decrease the screen resolution, Windows displays less information on the screen, but the information increases in size.

Screen resolution usually is stated as the product of two numbers, such as 1366 × 768 (pronounced "thirteen sixty-six by seven sixty-eight"). A 1366 × 768 screen resolution results in a display of 1366 distinct pixels on each of 768 lines, or about 1,050,624 pixels. Changing the screen resolution affects how the ribbon appears in Office apps and some Windows dialog boxes. Figure 57, for example, shows the Word ribbon at screen resolutions of 1366 × 768 and 1024 × 768. All of the same commands are available regardless of screen resolution. The app (Word, in this case), however, makes changes to the groups and the buttons within the groups to accommodate the various screen resolutions. The result is that certain commands may need to be accessed differently depending on the resolution chosen. A command that is visible on the ribbon and available by clicking a button at one resolution may not be visible and may need to be accessed using its Dialog Box Launcher at a different resolution.

Figure 57 (a) Ribbon at 1366 × 768 Resolution

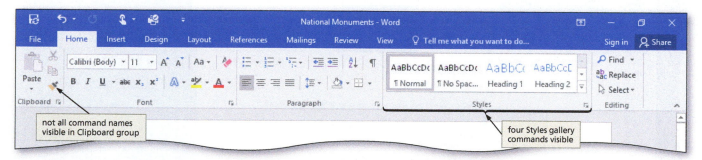

Figure 57 (b) Ribbon at 1024 × 768 Resolution

Comparing the two ribbons in Figure 57, notice the changes in content and layout of the groups and galleries. In some cases, the content of a group is the same in each resolution, but the layout of the group differs. For example, the same gallery and buttons appear in the Styles groups in the two resolutions, but the layouts differ. In other cases, the content and layout are the same across the resolution, but the level of detail differs with the resolution.

To Change the Screen Resolution

If you are using a computer to step through the modules in this book and you want your screen to match the figures, you may need to change your screen's resolution. *Why? The figures in this book use a screen resolution of 1366 × 768.* The following steps change the screen resolution to 1366 × 768. Your computer already may be set to 1366 × 768. Keep in mind that many computer labs prevent users from changing the screen resolution; in that case, read the following steps for illustration purposes.

1

- Click the Show desktop button, which is located at the far-right edge of the taskbar, to display the Windows desktop.

- Right-click an empty area on the Windows desktop to display a shortcut menu that contains a list of commands related to the desktop (Figure 58).

Q&A Why does my shortcut menu display different commands? Depending on your computer's hardware and configuration, different commands might appear on the shortcut menu.

Figure 58

2

- Click Display settings on the shortcut menu to open the Settings app window. If necessary, scroll to display the 'Advanced display settings' link (Figure 59).

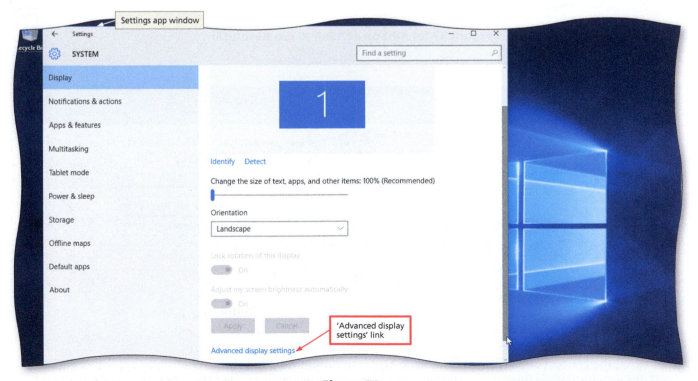

Figure 59

3

- Click 'Advanced display settings' in the Settings app window to display the advanced display settings.

- If necessary, scroll to display the Resolution box (Figure 60).

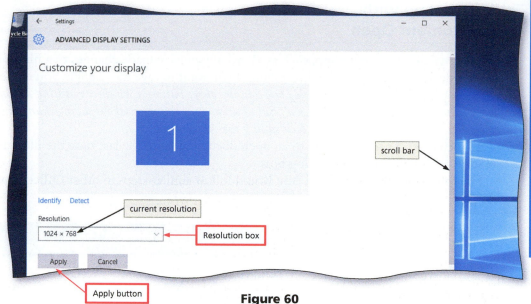

Figure 60

4

- Click the Resolution box to display a list of available screen resolutions (Figure 61).

- If necessary, scroll to and then click 1366 × 768 to select the screen resolution.

Q&A What if my computer does not support the 1366 × 768 resolution?
Some computers do not support the 1366 × 768 resolution. In this case, select a resolution that is close to the 1366 × 768 resolution.

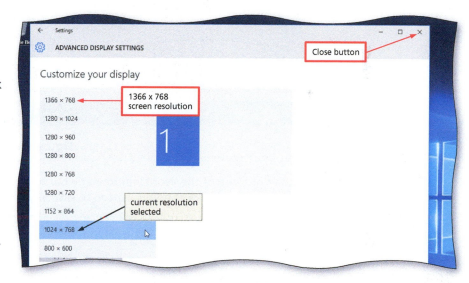

Figure 61

5

- Click the Apply button (Advanced Display Settings window), shown in Figure 60, to change the screen resolution and a confirmation message (Figure 62).

- Click the Keep changes button to accept the new screen resolution.

- Click the Close button (shown in Figure 61) to close the Settings app window.

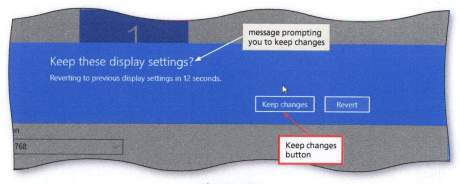

Figure 62

Other Ways

1. Click Start button, click Settings, click System, click Display, click 'Advanced display settings,' select desired resolution in Resolution box, click Apply button, click Keep changes button

2. Type **screen resolution** in search box, click 'Change the screen resolution,' select desired resolution in Resolution box, click Apply button, click Keep changes button

To Exit an App with One Document Open

1 SIGN IN | 2 USE WINDOWS | 3 USE APPS | 4 FILE MANAGEMENT | 5 SWITCH APPS | 6 SAVE FILES
7 CHANGE SCREEN RESOLUTION | **8 EXIT APPS** | 9 USE ADDITIONAL APP FEATURES | 10 USE HELP

When you exit an Office app, such as Word, if you have made changes to a file since the last time the file was saved, the app displays a dialog box asking if you want to save the changes you made to the file before it closes the app window. *Why? The dialog box contains three buttons with these resulting actions: the Save button saves the changes and then exits the app, the Don't Save button exits the app without saving changes, and the Cancel button closes the dialog box and redisplays the file without saving the changes.*

If no changes have been made to an open document since the last time the file was saved, the app will close the window without displaying a dialog box.

The following steps exit Word. You would follow similar steps in other Office apps.

1

- If necessary, click the Word app button on the taskbar to display the Word window on the desktop (Figure 63).

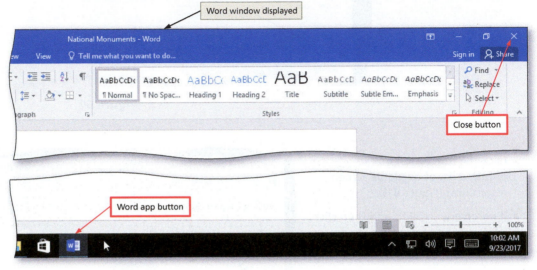

Figure 63

2

- Click the Close button on the right side of the Word window title bar to close the document and exit Word. If a Microsoft Word dialog box appears, click the Save button to save any changes made to the document since the last save.

Q&A What if I have more than one document open in Word?

You could click the Close button for each open document. When you click the last open document's Close button, you also exit Word. As an alternative that is more efficient, you could right-click the Word app button on the taskbar and then click 'Close all windows' on the shortcut menu to close all open documents and exit Word.

Other Ways

1. Right-click the Word app button on Windows taskbar, click 'Close all windows' on shortcut menu
2. Press ALT + F4

To Copy a Folder to OneDrive

1 SIGN IN | 2 USE WINDOWS | 3 USE APPS | **4 FILE MANAGEMENT** | 5 SWITCH APPS | 6 SAVE FILES
7 CHANGE SCREEN RESOLUTION | 8 EXIT APPS | **9 USE ADDITIONAL APP FEATURES** | 10 USE HELP

To back up your files or easily make them available on another computer or mobile device, you can copy them to OneDrive. The following steps copy your CIS 101 folder to OneDrive. If you do not have access to a OneDrive account, read the following steps without performing them. *Why? It often is good practice to have a backup of your files so that they are available in case something happens to your original copies.*

1

- Click the File Explorer button on the taskbar to make the folder window the active window.

- Navigate to the CIS 101 folder (or your class folder) in the Documents folder.

- Click Documents in the This PC area of the navigation pane to display the CIS 101 folder in the file list.

Q&A What if my CIS 101 folder is stored in a different location? Use the navigation pane to navigate to the location of your CIS 101 folder. The CIS 101 folder should be displayed in the file list once you have located it.

- Click the CIS 101 folder in the file list to select it (Figure 64).

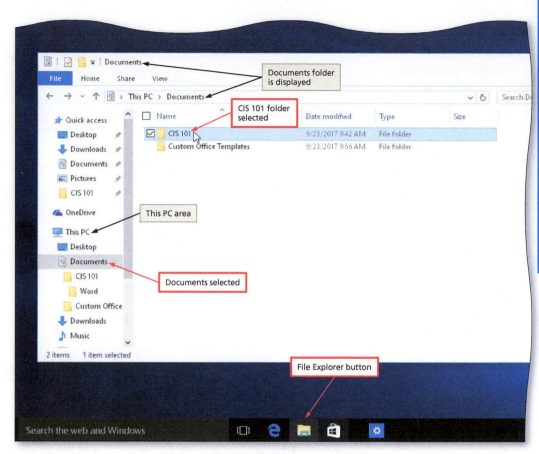

Figure 64

2

- Click Home on the ribbon to display the Home tab.

- Click the Copy to button (Home tab | Organize group) to display the Copy to menu (Figure 65).

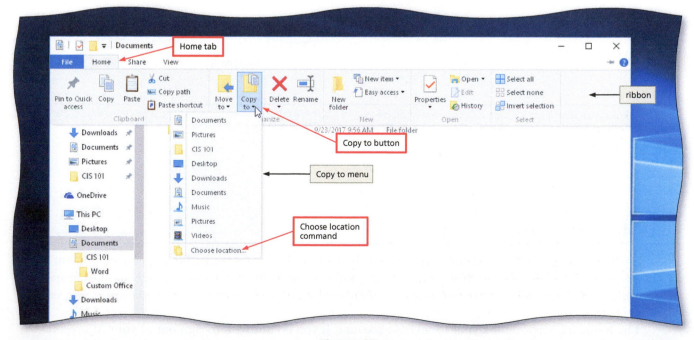

Figure 65

3

- Click Choose location on the Copy to menu to display the Copy Items dialog box.

- Click OneDrive (Copy Items dialog box) to select it (Figure 66).

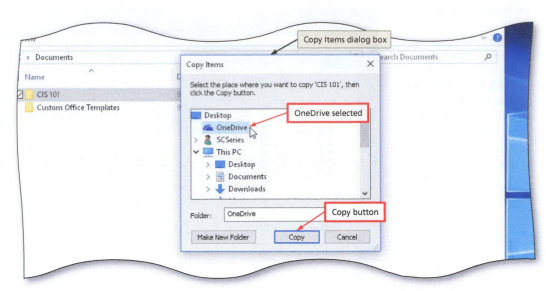

Figure 66

4

- Click the Copy button (Copy Items dialog box) to copy the selected folder to OneDrive.

- Click OneDrive in the navigation pane to verify the CIS 101 folder displays in the file list (Figure 67).

Q&A Why does a Microsoft OneDrive dialog box appear when I click OneDrive in the navigation pane?

If you are not currently signed in to Windows using a Microsoft account, you will manually need to sign in to a Microsoft account to save files to OneDrive. Follow the instructions on the screen to sign in to your Microsoft account.

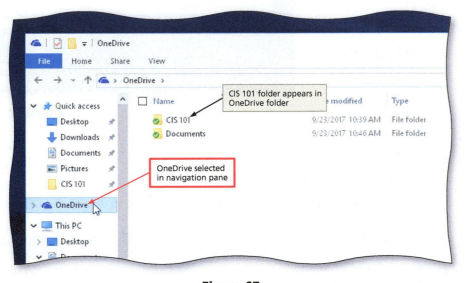

Figure 67

Other Ways

1. In File Explorer, select folder to copy, click Copy button (Home tab | Clipboard group), display contents of OneDrive in file list, click Paste button (Home tab | Clipboard group)

2. In File Explorer, select folder to copy, press CTRL+C, display contents of OneDrive in file list, press CTRL+V

1 SIGN IN | 2 USE WINDOWS | 3 USE APPS | **4 FILE MANAGEMENT** | 5 SWITCH APPS | 6 SAVE FILES
7 CHANGE SCREEN RESOLUTION | 8 EXIT APPS | **9 USE ADDITIONAL APP FEATURES** | 10 USE HELP

To Unlink a OneDrive Account

If you are using a public computer and are not signed in to Windows with a Microsoft account, you should unlink your OneDrive account so that other users cannot access it. **Why?** *If you do not unlink your OneDrive account, other people accessing the same user account on the computer will be able to view, remove, and add to files stored in your OneDrive account.*

The following steps unlink your OneDrive account. If you do not wish to sign out of your Microsoft account, read these steps without performing them.

● Click the 'Show hidden icons' button on the Windows taskbar to show a menu of hidden icons (Figure 68).

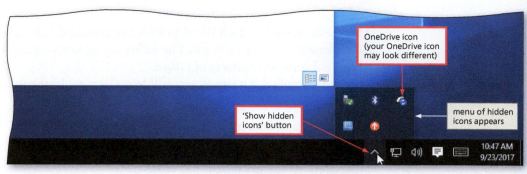

Figure 68

● Right click the OneDrive icon (shown in Figure 68) to display a shortcut menu (Figure 69).

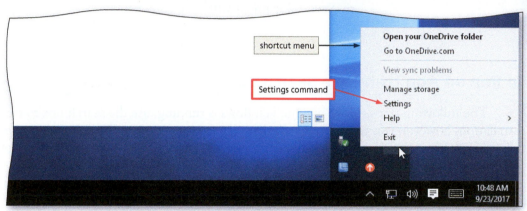

Figure 69

❸

● Click Settings on the shortcut menu to display the Microsoft OneDrive dialog box (Figure 70).

● If necessary, click the Settings tab. (Some versions require you click an Account tab instead.)

● Click the Unlink OneDrive button (Microsoft OneDrive dialog box) to unlink the OneDrive account.

● When the Microsoft OneDrive dialog box appears with a Welcome to OneDrive message, click the Close button.

● Minimize the File Explorer window.

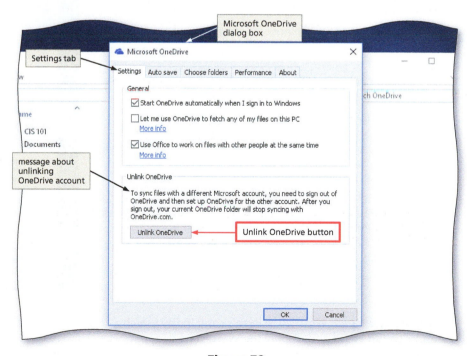

Figure 70

Break Point: If you wish to take a break, this is a good place to do so. To resume at a later time, continue to follow the steps from this location forward.

Additional Common Features of Office Apps

The previous section used Word to illustrate common features of Office and some basic elements unique to Word. The following sections continue to use Word present additional common features of Office.

In the following pages, you will learn how to do the following:

1. Run Word using the search box.
2. Open a document in Word.
3. Close the document.
4. Reopen the document just closed.
5. Create a blank Word document from Windows Explorer and then open the file.
6. Save a document with a new file name.

To Run an App Using the Search Box

1 SIGN IN | **2 USE WINDOWS** | 3 USE APPS | 4 FILE MANAGEMENT | 5 SWITCH APPS | 6 SAVE FILES
7 CHANGE SCREEN RESOLUTION | 8 EXIT APPS | **9 USE ADDITIONAL APP FEATURES** | 10 USE HELP

The following steps, which assume Windows is running, use the search box to run Word based on a typical installation; however, you would follow similar steps to run any app. *Why? Some people prefer to use the search box to locate and run an app, as opposed to searching through a list of all apps on the Start menu.* You may need to ask your instructor how to run Word on your computer.

- Type **Word 2016** as the search text in the search box and watch the search results appear in the search results (Figure 71).

Q&A

Do I need to type the complete app name or use correct capitalization?

No, you need to type just enough characters of the app name for it to appear in the search results. For example, you may be able to type Word or word, instead of Word 2016.

What if the search does not locate the Word app on my computer?

You may need to adjust the Windows search settings. Search for the word, index; click 'Indexing Options Control panel'; click the Modify button (Indexing Options dialog box); expand the Local Disk, if necessary; place a check mark beside all Program Files entries; and then click the OK button. It may take a few minutes for the index to rebuild. If it still does not work, you may need to click the Advanced button (Indexing Options dialog box) and then click the Rebuild button (Advanced Options dialog box).

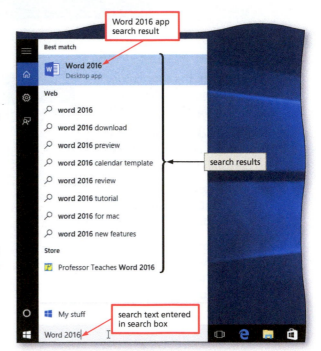

Figure 71

- Click the app name, Word 2016 in this case, in the search results to run Word and display the Word start screen.

- Click the Blank document thumbnail on the Word start screen (shown earlier in this module in Figure 8) to create a blank document and display it in the Word window. If the Word window is not maximized, click the Maximize button on its title bar to maximize the window.

To Open an Existing File

As discussed earlier, the Backstage view contains a set of commands that enable you to manage documents and data about the documents. *Why? From the Backstage view in Word, for example, you can create, open, print, and save documents. You also can share documents, manage versions, set permissions, and modify document properties. In other Office apps, the Backstage view may contain features specific to those apps.* The following steps open a saved file, specifically the National Monuments file, that recently was saved.

- Click File on the ribbon to open the Backstage view and then click the Open tab in the Backstage view to display the Open gallery in the Backstage view.

- Click This PC to display recent folders accessed on your computer.

- Click the Browse button to display the Open dialog box.

- If necessary, navigate to the location of the file to open (Word folder in the CIS 101 folder).

- Click the file to open, National Monuments in this case, to select the file (Figure 72).

- Click the Open button (Open dialog box) to open the file (shown earlier in the module in Figure 50). If necessary, click the Enable Content button.

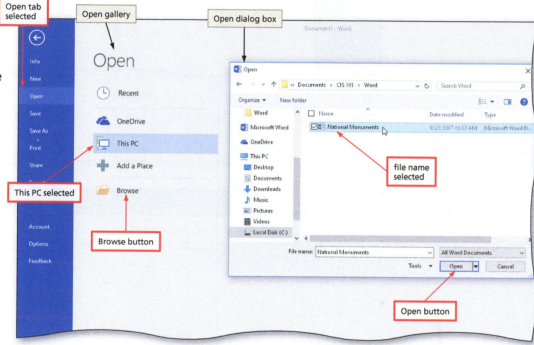

Figure 72

Q&A | Why did a Security Warning appear?
The Security Warning appears when you open an Office file that might contain harmful content. The files you create in this module are not harmful, but you should be cautious when opening files from other people.

Other Ways

1. Press CTRL+O

2. Navigate to file in File Explorer window, double-click file name

To Create a New Document
from the Backstage View

You can open multiple documents in an Office program, such as Word, so that you can work on the documents at the same time. The following steps create a file, a blank document in this case, from the Backstage view. *Why? You want to create a new document while keeping the current document open.*

1

- Click File on the ribbon to open the Backstage view.

- Click the New tab in the Backstage view to display the New gallery (Figure 73).

Q&A

Can I create documents through the Backstage view in other Office apps? Yes. If the Office app has a New tab in the Backstage view, the New gallery displays various options for creating a new file.

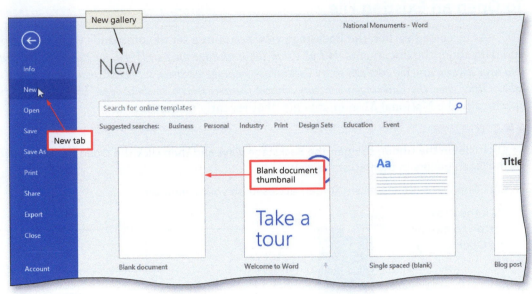

Figure 73

2

- Click the Blank document thumbnail in the New gallery to create a new document (Figure 74).

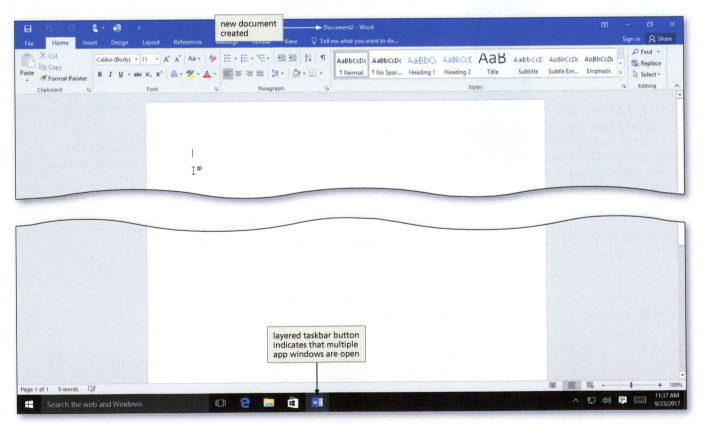

Figure 74

Other Ways

1. Press CTRL+N

To Enter Text in a Document

The following step enters the first line of text in a document.

1 Type **List of Special Rates for National Monuments** and then press the ENTER key (Figure 75).

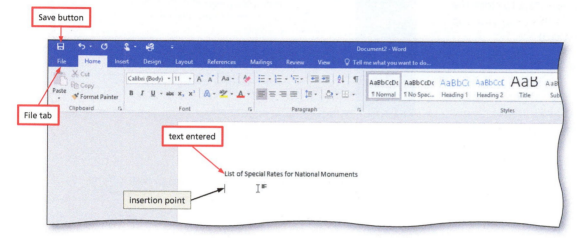

Figure 75

To Save a File in a Folder

The following steps save the second document in the Word folder in the class folder (CIS 101, in this case) in the Documents folder using the file name, Special Rates.

1 Click the Save button on the Quick Access Toolbar, which depending on settings, will display either the Save As gallery in the Backstage view or the Save As dialog box.

2 If your screen displays the Backstage view, click This PC, if necessary, to display options in the right pane related to saving on your computer; if your screen already displays the Save As dialog box, proceed to Step 4.

3 Click the Browse button in the left pane to display the Save As dialog box.

4 If necessary, type **Special Rates** in the File name box (Save As dialog box) to change the file name. Do not press the ENTER key after typing the file name because you do not want to close the dialog box at this time.

5 If necessary, navigate to the desired save location (in this case, the Word folder in the CIS 101 folder [or your class folder] in the Documents folder). For specific instructions, perform the tasks in Steps 4a and 4b in the previous section in this module titled To Save a File in a Folder.

6 Click the Save button (Save As dialog box) to save the document in the selected folder on the selected drive with the entered file name.

To Close a File Using the Backstage View

1 SIGN IN | 2 USE WINDOWS | 3 USE APPS | 4 FILE MANAGEMENT | 5 SWITCH APPS | 6 SAVE FILES
7 CHANGE SCREEN RESOLUTION | 8 EXIT APPS | 9 USE ADDITIONAL APP FEATURES | 10 USE HELP

Sometimes, you may want to close an Office file, such as a Word document, entirely and start over with a new file. You also may want to close a file when you are done working with it. **Why?** *You should close a file when you are done working with it so that you do not make inadvertent changes to it.* The following steps close the current active Word file, that is, the Special Rates document, without exiting Word.

- Click File on the ribbon to open the Backstage view (Figure 76).

- Click Close in the Backstage view to close the open file (Special Rates, in this case) without exiting the active app (Word).

Q&A

What if Word displays a dialog box about saving?

Click the Save button if you want to save the changes, click the Don't Save button if you want to ignore the changes since the last time you saved, and click the Cancel button if you do not want to close the document.

Can I use the Backstage view to close an open file in other Office apps, such as PowerPoint and Excel?

Yes.

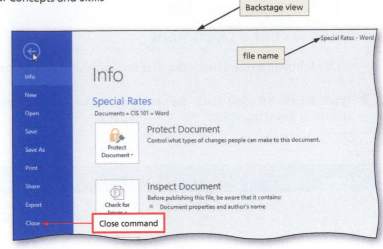

Figure 76

Other Ways

1. Press CTRL+F4

To Open a Recent File Using the Backstage View

1 SIGN IN | 2 USE WINDOWS | 3 USE APPS | 4 FILE MANAGEMENT | 5 SWITCH APPS | 6 SAVE FILES
7 CHANGE SCREEN RESOLUTION | 8 EXIT APPS | 9 USE ADDITIONAL APP FEATURES | 10 USE HELP

You sometimes need to open a file that you recently modified. **Why?** *You may have more changes to make, such as adding more content or correcting errors.* The Backstage view allows you to access recent files easily. The following steps reopen the Special Rates file just closed.

- Click File on the ribbon to open the Backstage view.

- Click the Open tab in the Backstage view to display the Open gallery (Figure 77).

- Click the desired file name in the Recent list, Special Rates in this case, to open the file.

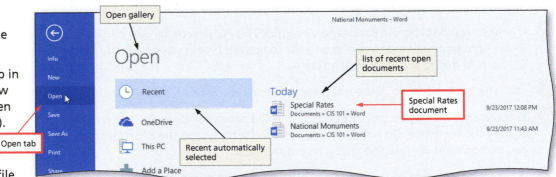

Figure 77

Other Ways

1. Click File on ribbon, click Open tab in Backstage view, click This PC, click Browse button, navigate to file (Open dialog box), click Open button

To Create a New Blank Document from File Explorer

1 SIGN IN | 2 USE WINDOWS | 3 USE APPS | 4 FILE MANAGEMENT | 5 SWITCH APPS | 6 SAVE FILES
7 CHANGE SCREEN RESOLUTION | 8 EXIT APPS | 9 USE ADDITIONAL APP FEATURES | 10 USE HELP

File Explorer provides a means to create a blank Office document without running an Office app. The following steps use File Explorer to create a blank Word document. **Why?** *Sometimes you might need to create a blank document and then return to it later for editing.*

- Click the File Explorer button on the taskbar to make the folder window the active window.

- If necessary, double-click the Documents folder in the navigation pane to expand the Documents folder.

- If necessary, double-click your class folder (CIS 101, in this case) in the navigation pane to expand the folder.

- Click the Word folder in the navigation pane to display its contents in the file list.

- With the Word folder selected, right-click an open area in the file list to display a shortcut menu.

- Point to New on the shortcut menu to display the New submenu (Figure 78).

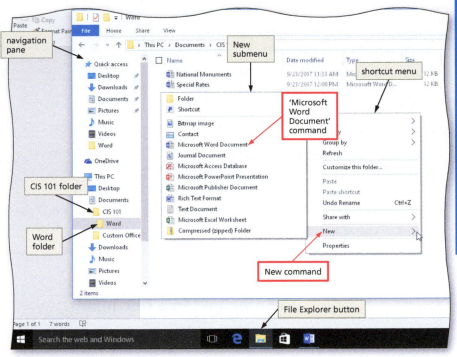

Figure 78

- Click 'Microsoft Word Document' on the New submenu to display an icon and text box for a new file in the current folder window with the file name, New Microsoft Word Document, selected (Figure 79).

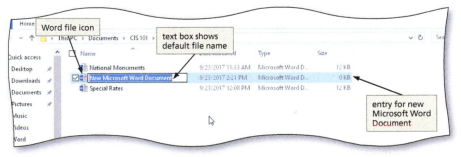

Figure 79

- Type **Recommended Travel Agents** in the text box and then press the ENTER key to assign a new file name to the new file in the current folder (Figure 80).

Figure 80

To Run an App from File Explorer and Open a File

1 SIGN IN | 2 USE WINDOWS | 3 USE APPS | 4 FILE MANAGEMENT | 5 SWITCH APPS | 6 SAVE FILES

7 CHANGE SCREEN RESOLUTION | 8 EXIT APPS | 9 USE ADDITIONAL APP FEATURES | 10 USE HELP

Previously in this module, you learned how to run Word using the Start menu and the search box. The following steps, which assume Windows is running, use File Explorer to run Word based on a typical installation. **Why?** *When you open an existing file from File Explorer, the app in which the file was created runs and then opens the selected file.* You may need to ask your instructor how to run Word for your computer.

1

- If necessary, display the file to open in the folder window in File Explorer.

- Right-click the file icon or file name you want to open (Recommended Travel Agents, in this case) to display a shortcut menu (Figure 81).

2

- Click Open on the shortcut menu to open the selected file in the app used to create the file, Word in this case (shown in Figure 82).

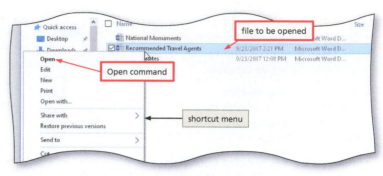

Figure 81

- If the window is not maximized, click the Maximize button on the title bar to maximize the window.

Other Ways

1. Double-click the file name in the file list

To Enter Text in a Document

The following step enters a line of text in the blank Word document.

1 Type **List of Recommended Travel Agents** and then press the ENTER key (shown in Figure 82).

To Save an Existing Office File with the Same File Name

1 SIGN IN | 2 USE WINDOWS | 3 USE APPS | 4 FILE MANAGEMENT | 5 SWITCH APPS | 6 SAVE FILES
7 CHANGE SCREEN RESOLUTION | 8 EXIT APPS | 9 USE ADDITIONAL APP FEATURES | 10 USE HELP

Saving frequently cannot be overemphasized. ***Why?*** *You have made modifications to the file (document) since you created it. Thus, you should save again. You should continue saving files frequently so that you do not lose the changes you have made since the time you last saved the file.* You can use the same file name, such as Recommended Travel Agents, to save the changes made to the document. The following step saves a file again with the same file name.

1

- Click the Save button on the Quick Access Toolbar to overwrite the previously saved file (Recommended Travel Agents, in this case) in the Word folder (Figure 82).

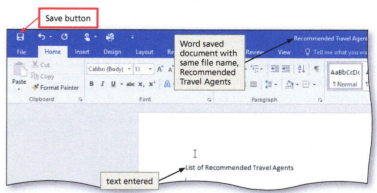

Figure 82

Other Ways

1. Press CTRL+S   2. Press SHIFT+F12

To Save a File with a New File Name

You might want to save a file with a different file name or to a different location. For example, you might start a homework assignment with a data file and then save it with a final file name for submission to your instructor, saving it to a location designated by your instructor. The following steps save a file with a different file name.

1 Click the File tab to open the Backstage view. Click the Save As tab to display the Save As gallery.

2 If necessary, click This PC to display options in the right pane related to saving on your computer. Click the Browse button in the left pane to display the Save As dialog box.

3 Type `Travel Agents` in the File name box (Save As dialog box) to change the file name. Do not press the ENTER key after typing the file name because you do not want to close the dialog box at this time.

4 If necessary, navigate to the desired save location (in this case, the Word folder in the CIS 101 folder [or your class folder] in the Documents folder). For specific instructions, perform the tasks in Steps 4a and 4b in the previous section titled To Save a File in a Folder.

5 Click the Save button (Save As dialog box) to save the document in the selected folder on the selected drive with the entered file name.

To Exit an Office App

You are finished using Word. The following steps exit Word.

1 Because you have multiple Word documents open, right-click the Word app button on the taskbar and then click 'Close all windows' on the shortcut menu to close all open documents and exit Word.

2 If a dialog box appears, click the Save button to save any changes made to the file since the last save.

Renaming, Moving, and Deleting Files

Earlier in this module, you learned how to organize files in folders, which is part of a process known as **file management**. The following sections cover additional file management topics including renaming, moving, and deleting files.

To Rename a File

1 SIGN IN | 2 USE WINDOWS | 3 USE APPS | 4 FILE MANAGEMENT | 5 SWITCH APPS | 6 SAVE FILES
7 CHANGE SCREEN RESOLUTION | 8 EXIT APPS | 9 USE ADDITIONAL APP FEATURES | 10 USE HELP

You may want to change the name of, or rename, a file or a folder. *Why? You may want to distinguish a file in one folder or drive from a copy of a similar file, or you may decide to rename a file to better identify its contents.* The following steps change the name of the National Monuments file in the Word folder to National Monuments Flyer.

1

- If necessary, click the File Explorer button on the taskbar to make the folder window the active window.

- Navigate to the location of the file to be renamed (in this case, the Word folder in the CIS 101 [or your class folder] folder in the Documents folder) to display the file(s) it contains in the file list.

- Click the file to be renamed, the National Monuments icon or file name in the file list in this case, to select it.

- Right-click the selected file to display a shortcut menu that presents a list of commands related to files (Figure 83).

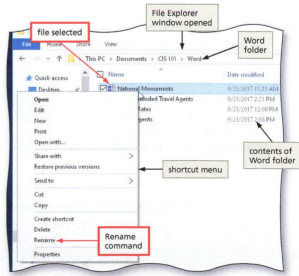

Figure 83

2

- Click Rename on the shortcut menu to place the current file name in a text box.

- Type **National Monuments Flyer** in the text box and then press the ENTER key (Figure 84).

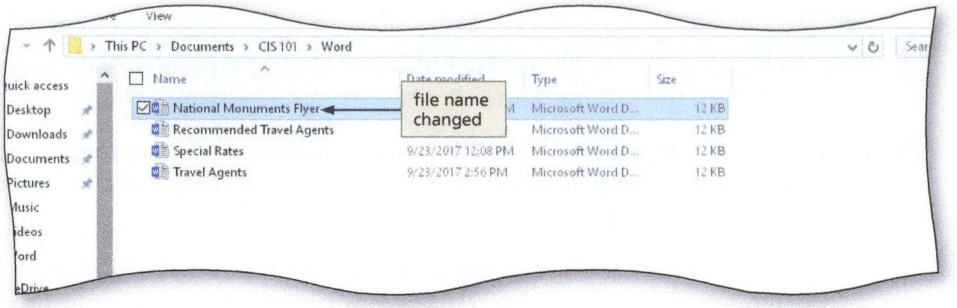

Q&A

Are any risks involved in renaming files that are located on a hard drive?
If you inadvertently rename a file that is associated with certain apps, the apps may not be able to find the file and, therefore, may not run properly. Always use caution when renaming files.

Can I rename a file when it is open?
No, a file must be closed to change the file name.

Figure 84

Other Ways

1. Select file, press F2, type new file name, press ENTER

2. Select file, click Rename (Home tab | Organize group), type new file name, press ENTER

1 SIGN IN | 2 USE WINDOWS | 3 USE APPS | 4 FILE MANAGEMENT | 5 SWITCH APPS | 6 SAVE FILES
7 CHANGE SCREEN RESOLUTION | 8 EXIT APPS | 9 USE ADDITIONAL APP FEATURES | 10 USE HELP

To Move a File

Why? At some time, you may want to move a file from one folder, called the source folder, to another, called the destination folder. When you move a file, it no longer appears in the original folder. If the destination and the source folders are on the same media, you can move a file by dragging it. If the folders are on different media, you will need to right-drag the file and then click Move here on the shortcut menu. The following step moves the Recommended Travel Agents file from the Word folder to the CIS 101 folder.

1

- If necessary, in File Explorer, navigate to the location of the file to be moved (in this case, the Word folder in the CIS 101 folder [or your class folder] in the Documents folder).

- If necessary, click the Word folder in the navigation pane to display the files it contains in the right pane.

- Drag the file to be moved, the Recommended Travel Agents file in the right pane in this case, to the CIS 101 folder in the navigation pane (Figure 85).

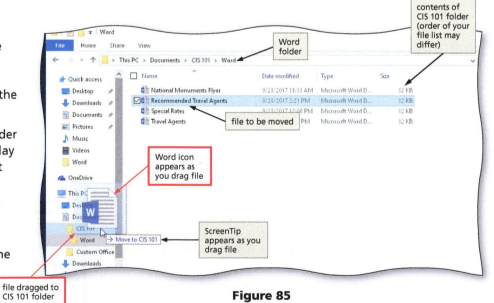

Figure 85

Experiment

- Click the CIS 101 folder in the navigation pane to verify that the file was moved.

Other Ways

1. Right-click file to move, click Cut on shortcut menu, right-click destination folder, click Paste on shortcut menu

2. Select file to move, press CTRL+X, select destination folder, press CTRL+V

To Delete a File

A final task you may want to perform is to delete a file. Exercise extreme caution when deleting a file or files. When you delete a file from a hard drive, the deleted file is stored in the Recycle Bin where you can recover it until you empty the Recycle Bin. If you delete a file from removable media, such as a USB flash drive, the file is deleted permanently. The next steps delete the Recommended Travel Agents file from the CIS 101 folder. *Why? When a file no longer is needed, you can delete it to conserve space on your storage location.*

1
- If necessary, in File Explorer, navigate to the location of the file to be deleted (in this case, the CIS 101 folder [or your class folder] in the Documents folder).

- Click the file to be deleted, the Recommended Travel Agents icon or file name in the right pane in this case, to select the file.

- Right-click the selected file to display a shortcut menu (Figure 86).

2
- Click Delete on the shortcut menu to delete the file.

- If a dialog box appears, click the Yes button to delete the file.

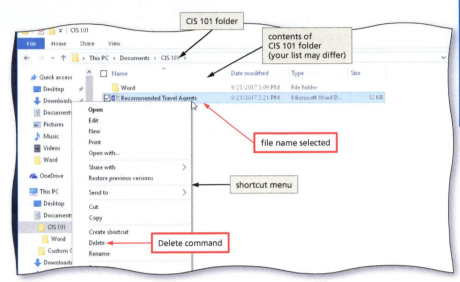

Figure 86

Q&A
Can I use this same technique to delete a folder?
Yes. Right-click the folder and then click Delete on the shortcut menu. When you delete a folder, all of the files and folders contained in the folder you are deleting, together with any files and folders on lower hierarchical levels, are deleted as well. For example, if you delete the CIS 101 folder, you will delete all folders and files inside the CIS 101 folder.

Other Ways

1. Select file, press DELETE

Microsoft Office and Windows Help

At any time while you are using one of the Office apps, such as Word, you can use Office Help to display information about all topics associated with the app. Help in other Office apps operates in a similar fashion.

In Office, Help is presented in a window that has browser-style navigation buttons. Each Office app has its own Help home page, which is the starting Help page that is displayed in the Help window. If your computer is connected to the Internet, the contents of the Help page reflect both the local help files installed on the computer and material from Microsoft's website.

To Open the Help Window in an Office App

1 SIGN IN | 2 USE WINDOWS | 3 USE APPS | 4 FILE MANAGEMENT | 5 SWITCH APPS | 6 SAVE FILES
7 CHANGE SCREEN RESOLUTION | 8 EXIT APPS | 9 USE ADDITIONAL APP FEATURES | 10 USE HELP

The following step opens the Word Help window. *Why? You might not understand how certain commands or operations work in Word, so you can obtain the necessary information using help.*

1

- Run Word.
- Click the Blank document thumbnail to display a blank document.
- Press F1 to open the Word Help window (Figure 87).

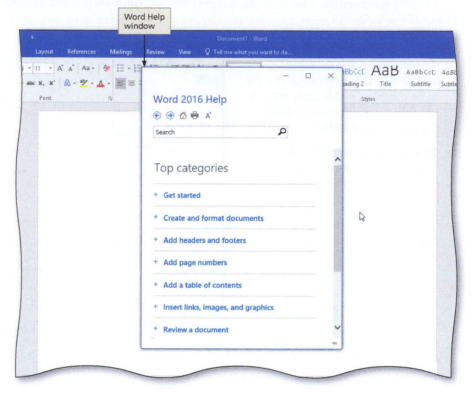

Figure 87

Moving and Resizing Windows

At times, it is useful, or even necessary, to have more than one window open and visible on the screen at the same time. You can resize and move these open windows so that you can view different areas of and elements in the window. In the case of the Help window, for example, it could be covering document text in the Word window that you need to see.

To Move a Window by Dragging

1 SIGN IN | 2 USE WINDOWS | 3 USE APPS | 4 FILE MANAGEMENT | 5 SWITCH APPS | 6 SAVE FILES
7 CHANGE SCREEN RESOLUTION | 8 EXIT APPS | 9 USE ADDITIONAL APP FEATURES | 10 USE HELP

You can move any open window that is not maximized to another location on the desktop by dragging the title bar of the window. *Why? You might want to have a better view of what is behind the window or just want to move the window so that you can see it better.* The following step drags the Word Help window to the upper-left corner of the desktop.

1

- Drag the window title bar (the Word Help window title bar, in this case) so that the window moves to the upper-left corner of the desktop, as shown in Figure 88.

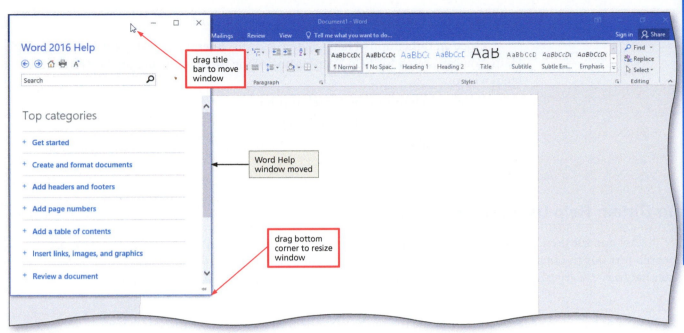

Figure 88

To Resize a Window by Dragging

1 SIGN IN | 2 USE WINDOWS | 3 USE APPS | 4 FILE MANAGEMENT | 5 SWITCH APPS | 6 SAVE FILES
7 CHANGE SCREEN RESOLUTION | 8 EXIT APPS | 9 USE ADDITIONAL APP FEATURES | 10 USE HELP

A method used to change the size of the window is to drag the window borders. The following step changes the size of the Word Help window by dragging its borders. *Why? Sometimes, information is not visible completely in a window, and you want to increase the size of the window.*

- Point to the lower-right corner of the window (the Word Help window, in this case) until the pointer changes to a two-headed arrow.

- Drag the bottom border downward to display more of the active window (Figure 89).

Q&A

Can I drag other borders on the window to enlarge or shrink the window?
Yes, you can drag the left, right, and top borders and any window corner to resize a window.

Will Windows remember the new size of the window after I close it?
Yes. When you reopen the window, Windows will display it at the same size it was when you closed it.

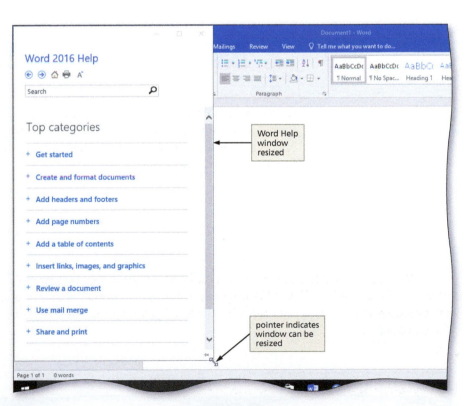

Figure 89

Using Office Help

Once an Office app's Help window is open, several methods exist for navigating Help. You can search for help by using any of the three following methods from the Help window:

1. Enter search text in the Search text box.
2. Click the links in the Help window.
3. Use the Table of Contents.

To Obtain Help Using the Search Text Box

1 SIGN IN | 2 USE WINDOWS | 3 USE APPS | 4 FILE MANAGEMENT | 5 SWITCH APPS | 6 SAVE FILES
7 CHANGE SCREEN RESOLUTION | 8 EXIT APPS | 9 USE ADDITIONAL APP FEATURES | **10 USE HELP**

Assume for the following example that you want to know more about fonts. The following steps use the Search text box to obtain useful information about fonts by entering the word, fonts, as search text. **Why?** *You may not know the exact help topic you are looking to find, so using keywords can help narrow your search.*

- Type `fonts` in the Search text box at the top of the Word Help window to enter the search text.
- Press the ENTER key to display the search results (Figure 90).

Q&A

Why do my search results differ?

If you do not have an Internet connection, your results will reflect only the content of the Help files on your computer. When searching for help online, results also can change as content is added, deleted, and updated on the online Help webpages maintained by Microsoft.

Why were my search results not very helpful?

When initiating a search, be sure to check the spelling of the search text; also, keep your search specific to return the most accurate results.

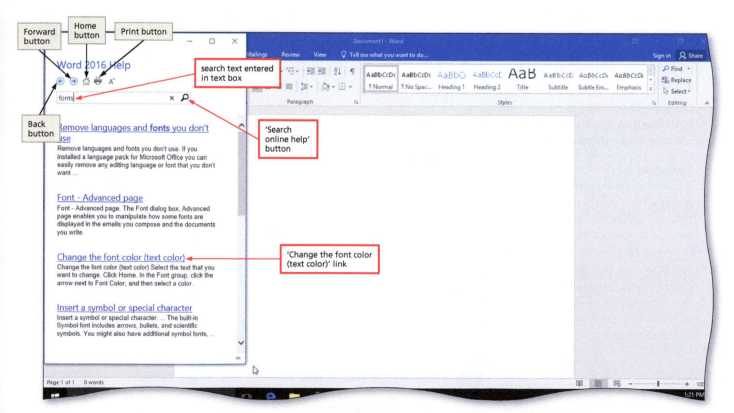

Figure 90

2

- Click the 'Change the font color (text color)', or a similar, link to display the Help information associated with the selected topic (Figure 91).

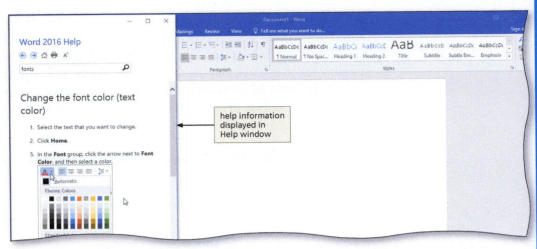

Figure 91

3

- Click the Home button in the Help window to clear the search results and redisplay the Help home page (Figure 92).

- Click the Close button in the Word 2016 Help window to close the window.

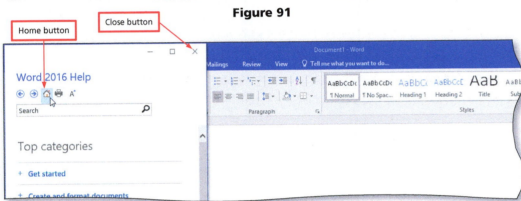

Figure 92

Obtaining Help while Working in an Office App

Help in the Office apps, such as Word, provides you with the ability to obtain help directly, without opening the Help window and initiating a search. For example, you may be unsure about how a particular command works, or you may be presented with a dialog box that you are not sure how to use.

Figure 93 shows one option for obtaining help while working in an Office app. If you want to learn more about a command, point to its button and wait for the ScreenTip to appear. If the Help icon and 'Tell me more' link appear in the ScreenTip, click the 'Tell me more' link or press the F1 key while pointing to the button to open the Help window associated with that command.

BTW

Customizing the Ribbon

In addition to customizing the Quick Access Toolbar, you can add items to and remove items from the ribbon. To customize the ribbon, click File on the ribbon to open the Backstage view, click the Options tab in the Backstage view, and then click Customize Ribbon in the left pane of the Options dialog box. More information about customizing the ribbon is presented in a later module.

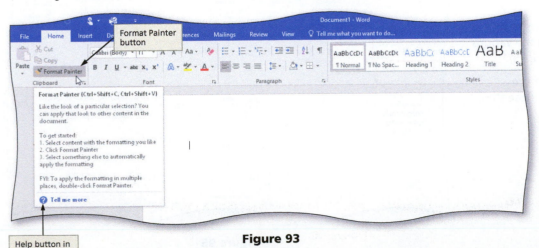

Figure 93

Figure 94 shows a dialog box that contains a Help button. Clicking the Help button or pressing the F1 key while the dialog box is displayed opens a Help window. The Help window contains help about that dialog box, if available. If no help file is available for that particular dialog box, then the main Help window opens.

As mentioned previously, the Tell Me box is available in most Office apps and can perform a variety of functions. One of these functions is to provide easy access to commands by typing a description of the command.

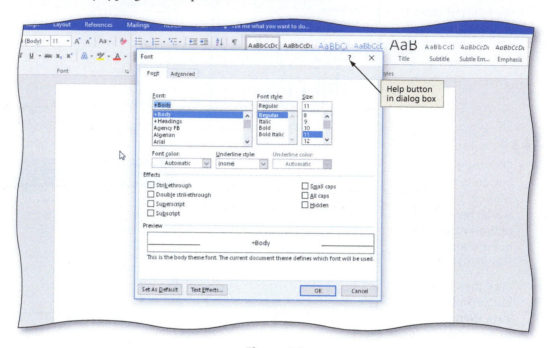

Figure 94

To Obtain Help Using the Tell Me Box

1 SIGN IN | 2 USE WINDOWS | 3 USE APPS | 4 FILE MANAGEMENT | 5 SWITCH APPS | 6 SAVE FILES
7 CHANGE SCREEN RESOLUTION | 8 EXIT APPS | 9 USE ADDITIONAL APP FEATURES | 10 USE HELP

If you are having trouble finding a command in an Office app, you can use the Tell Me box to search for the function you are trying to perform. As you type, the Tell Me box will suggest commands that match the search text you are entering. *Why? You can use the Tell Me box to access commands quickly that you otherwise may be unable to find on the ribbon.* The following steps find information about margins.

1

- Type **margins** in the Tell Me box and watch the search results appear.

- Point to Adjust Margins to display a submenu displaying the various margin settings (Figure 95).

- Click an empty area of the document window to close the search results.

2

- Exit Microsoft Word.

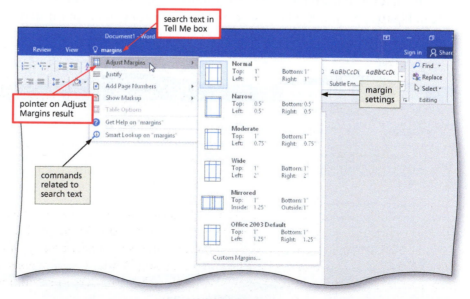

Figure 95

Using the Windows Search Box

One of the more powerful Windows features is the Windows search box. The search box is a central location from where you can type search text and quickly access related Windows commands or web search results. In addition, **Cortana** is a new search tool in Windows that you can access using the search box. It can act as a personal assistant by performing functions such as providing ideas; searching for apps, files, and folders; and setting reminders. In addition to typing search text in the search box, you also can use your computer or mobile device's microphone to give verbal commands.

To Use the Windows Search Box

1 SIGN IN | 2 USE WINDOWS | 3 USE APPS | 4 FILE MANAGEMENT | 5 SWITCH APPS | 6 SAVE FILES
7 CHANGE SCREEN RESOLUTION | 8 EXIT APPS | 9 USE ADDITIONAL APP FEATURES | 10 USE HELP

The following step uses the Windows search box to search for a Windows command. *Why?* *Using the search box to locate apps, settings, folders, and files can be faster than navigating windows and dialog boxes to search for the desired content.*

• Type **notification** in the search box to display the search results. The search results include related Windows settings, Windows Store apps, and web search results (Figure 96).

• Click an empty area of the desktop to close the search results.

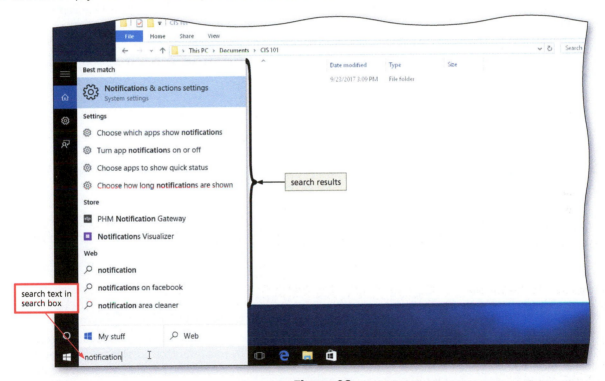

Figure 96

Summary

In this module, you learned how to use the Windows interface, several touch screen and mouse operations, and file and folder management. You also learned some basic features of Word and discovered the common elements that exist among Microsoft Office apps. Topics covered included signing in, using Windows, using apps, file management, switching between apps, saving files, changing screen resolution, exiting apps, using additional app features, and using Help.

CONSIDER THIS: PLAN AHEAD

What guidelines should you follow to plan your projects?

The process of communicating specific information is a learned, rational skill. Computers and software, especially Microsoft Office 2016, can help you develop ideas and present detailed information to a particular audience and minimize much of the laborious work of drafting and revising projects. No matter what method you use to plan a project, it is beneficial to follow some specific guidelines from the onset to arrive at a final product that is informative, relevant, and effective. Use some aspects of these guidelines every time you undertake a project, and others as needed in specific instances.

1. Determine the project's purpose.

   a) Clearly define why you are undertaking this assignment.

   b) Begin to draft ideas of how best to communicate information by handwriting ideas on paper; composing directly on a laptop, tablet, or mobile device; or developing a strategy that fits your particular thinking and writing style.

2. Analyze your audience.

   a) Learn about the people who will read, analyze, or view your work.

   b) Determine their interests and needs so that you can present the information they need to know and omit the information they already possess.

   c) Form a mental picture of these people or find photos of people who fit this profile so that you can develop a project with the audience in mind.

3. Gather possible content.

   a) Locate existing information that may reside in spreadsheets, databases, or other files.

   b) Conduct a web search to find relevant websites.

   c) Read pamphlets, magazine and newspaper articles, and books to gain insights of how others have approached your topic.

   d) Conduct personal interviews to obtain perspectives not available by any other means.

   e) Consider video and audio clips as potential sources for material that might complement or support the factual data you uncover.

4. Determine what content to present to your audience.

   a) Write three or four major ideas you want an audience member to remember after reading or viewing your project.

   b) Envision your project's endpoint, the key fact you wish to emphasize, so that all project elements lead to this final element.

   c) Determine relevant time factors, such as the length of time to develop the project, how long readers will spend reviewing your project, or the amount of time allocated for your speaking engagement.

   d) Decide whether a graph, photo, or artistic element can express or enhance a particular concept.

   e) Be mindful of the order in which you plan to present the content, and place the most important material at the top or bottom of the page, because readers and audience members generally remember the first and last pieces of information they see and hear.

CONSIDER THIS

How should you submit solutions to questions in the assignments identified with a ✳ symbol?

Every assignment in this book contains one or more questions with a ✳ symbol. These questions require you to think beyond the assigned file. Present your solutions to the question in the format required by your instructor. Possible formats may include one or more of these options: write the answer; create a document that contains the answer; present your answer to the class; discuss your answer in a group; record the answer as audio or video using a webcam, smartphone, or portable media player; or post answers on a blog, wiki, or website.

Apply Your Knowledge

Reinforce the skills and apply the concepts you learned in this module.

Creating a Folder and a Document

Instructions: You will create a Word Assignments folder and then create a Word document and save it in the folder.

Perform the following tasks:

1. Open the File Explorer window and then double-click to open the Documents folder.

2. Click the New folder button on the Quick Access Toolbar to display a new folder icon and text box for the folder name.

3. Type **Word Assignments** in the text box to name the folder. Press the ENTER key to create the folder in the Documents folder.

4. Run Word and create a new blank document.

5. Type **Contact Information** and then press then ENTER key to enter a line of text (Figure 97).

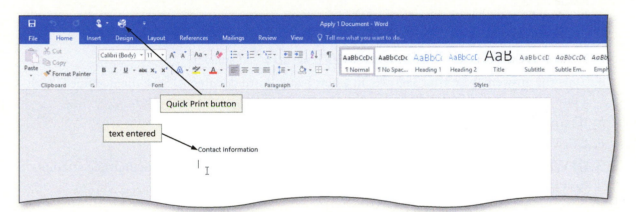

Figure 97

6. If requested by your instructor, enter your name, phone number, and email address in the Word document.

7. Click the Save button on the Quick Access Toolbar. Navigate to the Word Assignments folder in the Documents folder and then save the document using the file name, Apply 1 Document.

8. If your Quick Access Toolbar does not show the Quick Print button, add the Quick Print button to the Quick Access Toolbar. Print the document using the Quick Print button on the Quick Access Toolbar. When you are finished printing, remove the Quick Print button from the Quick Access Toolbar.

9. Submit the printout to your instructor.

10. Exit Word.

11. ✳ What other commands might you find useful to include on the Quick Access Toolbar?

Extend Your Knowledge

Extend the skills you learned in this module and experiment with new skills. You will use Help to complete the assignment.

Continued >

Extend Your Knowledge *continued*

Using Help

Instructions: Use Word Help to perform the following tasks.

Perform the following tasks:

1. Run Word.

2. Press F1 to open the Word Help window (shown in Figure 87).

3. Search Word Help to answer the following questions.

   a. What are three new features of Word 2016?

   b. What type of training is available through Word Help for Word 2016?

   c. What are the steps to customize the ribbon?

   d. What is the purpose of the Office Clipboard?

   e. What is the purpose of Read mode?

   f. Why would you use mail merge?

   g. How do you insert pictures?

   h. How do you change the size of text?

   i. What are the steps to zoom in and out of a document?

   j. What is the purpose of the Insights pane? How do you display it?

4. Type the answers from your searches in a new blank Word document. Save the document with a new file name and then submit it in the format specified by your instructor.

5. If requested by your instructor, enter your name in the Word document.

6. Exit Word.

7. ✹ What search text did you use to perform the searches above? Did it take multiple attempts to search and locate the exact information for which you were searching?

Expand Your World

Create a solution that uses cloud or web technologies by learning and investigating on your own from general guidance.

Creating Folders on OneDrive and Using the Word Online App

Instructions: You will create the folders shown in Figure 98 on OneDrive. Then, you will use the Word Online app to create a small file and save it in a folder on OneDrive.

Perform the following tasks:

1. Sign in to OneDrive in your browser.

2. Use the New button to create the folder structure shown in Figure 98.

Figure 98

3. In the Upcoming Events folder, use the New button to create a Word document with the file name, Expand 1 Task List, that contains the text, Prepare agenda for Tuesday's meeting.

4. If requested by your instructor, add your name to the Word document.

5. Save the document in the Upcoming Events folder and then exit the app.

6. Submit the assignment in the format specified by your instructor.

7. ✸ Based on your current knowledge of OneDrive, do you think you will use it? What about the Word Online app?

In the Labs

Design, create, modify, and/or use files following the guidelines, concepts, and skills presented in this module. Labs 1 and 2, which increase in difficulty, require you to create solutions based on what you learned in the module; Lab 3 requires you to apply your creative thinking and problem-solving skills to design and implement a solution.

Lab 1: **Creating Folders for a Bookstore**

Problem: Your friend works for a local bookstore. He would like to organize his files in relation to the types of books available in the store. He has seven main categories: fiction, biography, children, humor, social science, nonfiction, and medical. You are to create a folder structure similar to Figure 99.

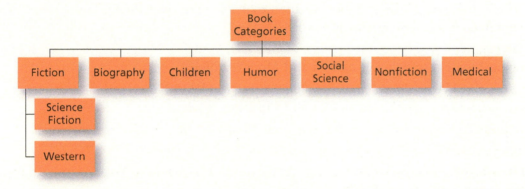

Figure 99

Perform the following tasks:

1. Click the File Explorer button on the taskbar and display the contents of the Documents folder.

2. In the Documents folder, create the main folder and name it Book Categories.

3. Navigate to the Book Categories folder.

4. Within the Book Categories folder, create a folder for each of the following: Fiction, Biography, Children, Humor, Social Science, Nonfiction, and Medical.

5. Within the Fiction folder, create two additional folders, one for Science Fiction and the second for Western.

6. If requested by your instructor, add another folder using your last name as the folder name.

7. Submit the assignment in the format specified by your instructor.

8. ✸ Think about how you use your computer for various tasks (consider personal, professional, and academic reasons). What folders do you think will be required on your computer to store the files you save?

Lab 2: Creating Word Documents and Saving Them in Appropriate Folders

Problem: You are taking a class that requires you to complete three Word modules. You will save the work completed in each module in a different folder (Figure 100).

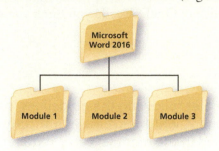

Figure 100

Perform the following tasks:

1. Create the folders shown in Figure 100.

2. Create a Word document containing the text, Module 1 Notes.

3. In the Backstage view, click Save As and then click This PC.

4. Click the Browse button to display the Save As dialog box. Click Documents to open the Documents folder. Navigate to the Module 1 folder and then save the file in the Word folder using the file name, Lab 2 Module 1 Notes.

5. Create another Word document containing the text, Module 2 Notes, and then save it in the Module 2 folder using the file name, Lab 2 Module 2 Notes.

6. Create a third Word document containing the text, Module 3 Notes, and then save it in the Module 3 folder using the file name, Lab 2 Module 3 Notes.

7. If requested by your instructor, add your name to each of the three Word documents.

8. Submit the assignment in the format specified by your instructor.

9. ✳ Based on your current knowledge of Windows and Word, how will you organize folders for assignments in this class? Why?

Lab 3: Consider This: Your Turn

Performing Research about Malware

Problem: You have just installed a new computer with the Windows operating system. Because you want to be sure that it is protected from the threat of malware, you decide to research malware, malware protection, and removing malware.

Perform the following tasks:

Part 1: Research the following three topics: malware, malware protection, and removing malware. Use the concepts and techniques presented in this module to use the search box to find information regarding these topics. Create a Word document that contains steps to safeguard a computer properly from malware, ways to prevent malware, as well as the different ways to remove malware or a virus should your computer become infected. Submit your assignment and the answers to the following critical thinking questions in the format specified by your instructor.

Part 2: ✳ You made several decisions while searching for this assignment. What decisions did you make? What was the rationale behind these decisions? How did you locate the required information about malware?

1 Creating, Formatting, and Editing a Word Document with a Picture

Objectives

You will have mastered the material in this module when you can:

- Enter text in a Word document
- Check spelling as you type
- Format paragraphs
- Format text
- Undo and redo commands or actions
- Change theme colors

- Insert digital pictures in a Word document
- Resize pictures
- Format pictures
- Add a page border
- Adjust spacing
- Correct errors and revise a document

Introduction

To advertise a sale, promote a business, publicize an event, or convey a message to the community, you may want to create a flyer and hand it out in person or post it in a public location. Libraries, schools, community organizations, grocery stores, coffee shops, and other places often provide bulletin boards or windows for flyers. You also see flyers posted on webpages, on social media, or in email messages.

Flyers announce personal items for sale or rent (car, boat, apartment); events, such as garage or block sales; services being offered (animal care, housecleaning, lessons, tours); membership, sponsorship, or donation requests (club, community organization, charity); and other messages, such as a lost or found pet.

Project — Flyer with a Picture

Individuals and businesses create flyers to gain public attention. Flyers, which usually are a single page in length, are an inexpensive means of reaching the community. Many flyers, however, go unnoticed because they are designed poorly.

The project in this module follows general guidelines and uses Word to create the flyer shown in Figure 1–1. This colorful, eye-catching flyer announces surfing lessons. The picture of the surfer riding a wave, taken with a digital camera, entices passersby or viewers to stop and look at the flyer. The headline on the flyer is large and colorful to draw attention into the text. The body copy below the picture briefly describes what is included in the lessons, along with a bulleted list that concisely highlights important information. The signature line of the flyer calls attention to the contact phone number. The word, expert, and the signature line are in a different color so that they stand apart from the rest of the text on the flyer. Finally, the graphical page border nicely frames and complements the contents of the flyer.

Figure 1–1

In this module, you will learn how to create the flyer shown in Figure 1–1. The following roadmap identifies general activities you will perform as you progress through this module:

1. **ENTER TEXT** in a new document.
2. **FORMAT** the **TEXT** in the flyer.
3. **INSERT** a **PICTURE**, called Surfer, in the flyer.
4. **FORMAT** the **PICTURE** in the flyer.
5. **ENHANCE** the **PAGE** with a border and spacing.
6. **CORRECT** errors **AND REVISE** text in the flyer.

To Run Word and Specify Settings

If you are using a computer to step through the project in this module and you want your screens to match the figures in this book, you should change your screen's resolution to 1366 × 768. For information about how to change a computer's resolution, refer to the Office and Windows module at the beginning of this book.

1 Run Word and create a blank document in the Word window.

2 If the Word window is not maximized, click the Maximize button on its title bar to maximize the window.

3 If the Print Layout button on the status bar is not selected (shown in Figure 1–2), click it so that your screen is in Print Layout view.

Q&A What is Print Layout view?
The default (preset) view in Word is **Print Layout view**, which shows the document on a mock sheet of paper in the document window.

4 If Normal (Home tab | Styles group) is not selected in the Styles gallery (shown in Figure 1–2), click it so that your document uses the Normal style.

Q&A What is the Normal style?
When you create a document, Word formats the text using a particular style. The default style in Word is called the **Normal style**, which is discussed later in this book.

What if rulers appear on my screen?
Click View on the ribbon to display the View tab and then remove the check mark from the View Ruler check box (View tab | Show group).

Entering Text

The first step in creating a document is to enter its text. With the projects in this book, you enter text by typing on the keyboard. By default, Word positions text you type at the left margin. In a later section of this module, you will learn how to format, or change the appearance of, the entered text.

For an introduction to Office and instructions about how to perform basic tasks in Office apps, read the Office and Windows module at the beginning of this book, where you can learn how to run an application, use the ribbon, save a file, open a file, print a file, exit an application, use Help, and much more.

For an introduction to Windows and instructions about how to perform basic Windows tasks, read the Office and Windows module at the beginning of this book, where you can learn how to resize windows, change screen resolution, create folders, move and rename files, use Windows Help, and much more.

BTW
The Word Window
The modules in this book begin with the Word window appearing as it did at the initial installation of the software. Your Word window may look different depending on your screen resolution and other Word settings.

To Type Text

To begin creating the flyer in this module, type the headline in the document window. **Why?** *The headline is the first line of text in the Surf Flyer.* The following steps type the first line of text in the document.

1

• Type **Surf's Up!** as the headline (Figure 1–2).

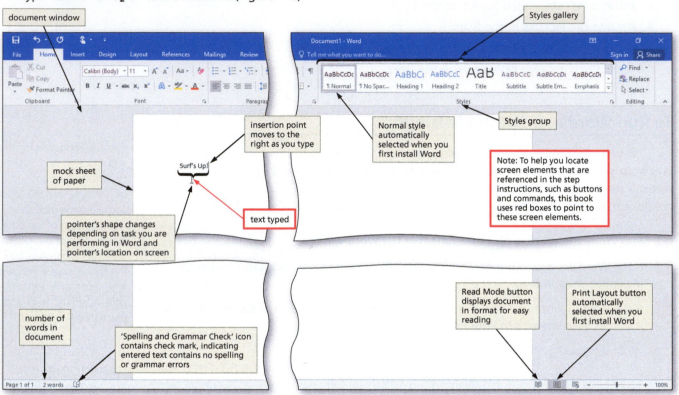

Figure 1–2

Q&A What if I make an error while typing?
You can press the BACKSPACE key until you have deleted the text in error and then retype the text correctly.

What is the purpose of the 'Spelling and Grammar Check' icon on the status bar?
The **'Spelling and Grammar Check' icon** displays either a check mark to indicate the entered text contains no spelling or grammar errors, or an X to indicate that it found potential errors. Word flags potential errors in the document with a red, green, or blue wavy underline. Later in this module, you will learn how to fix flagged errors.

2

• Press the ENTER key to move the insertion point to the beginning of the next line (Figure 1–3).

Q&A Why did blank space appear between the headline and the insertion point?
Each time you press the ENTER key, Word creates a new paragraph and inserts blank space between the two paragraphs. Later in this module, you will learn how to increase and decrease the spacing between paragraphs.

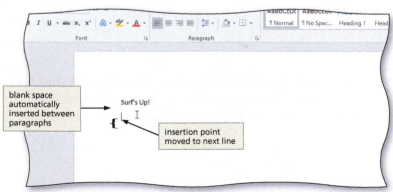

Figure 1–3

How do you use the touch keyboard with a touch screen?

To display the on-screen touch keyboard, tap the Touch Keyboard button on the Windows taskbar as shown in the Office and Windows module at the beginning of this book. When finished using the touch keyboard, tap the X button on the touch keyboard to close the keyboard.

1 ENTER TEXT | 2 FORMAT TEXT | 3 INSERT PICTURE
4 FORMAT PICTURE | 5 ENHANCE PAGE | 6 CORRECT & REVISE

To Display Formatting Marks

You may find it helpful to display formatting marks while working in a document. *Why? Formatting marks indicate where in a document you pressed the* ENTER *key,* SPACEBAR, *and other nonprinting characters.* A **formatting mark** is a character that Word displays on the screen but is not visible on a printed document. For example, the paragraph mark (¶) is a formatting mark that indicates where you pressed the ENTER key. A raised dot (·) shows where you pressed the SPACEBAR. Formatting marks are discussed as they appear on the screen.

Depending on settings made during previous Word sessions, your Word screen already may display formatting marks (Figure 1–4). The following step displays formatting marks, if they do not show already on the screen.

- If the Home tab is not the active tab, click Home on the ribbon to display the Home tab.
- If it is not selected already, click the 'Show/Hide ¶' button (Home tab | Paragraph group) to display formatting marks on the screen (Figure 1–4).

Q&A What if I do not want formatting marks to show on the screen?

You can hide them by clicking the 'Show/Hide ¶' button (Home tab | Paragraph group) again. It is recommended that you display formatting marks so that you visually can identify when you press the ENTER key, SPACEBAR, and other keys associated with nonprinting characters. Most of the document windows presented in this book, therefore, show formatting marks.

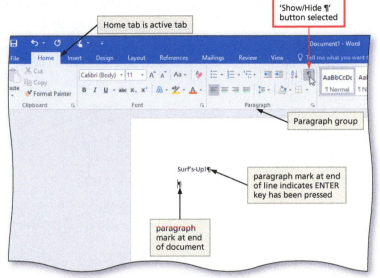

Figure 1–4

Other Ways

1. Press CTRL+SHIFT+*

1 ENTER TEXT | 2 FORMAT TEXT | 3 INSERT PICTURE
4 FORMAT PICTURE | 5 ENHANCE PAGE | 6 CORRECT & REVISE

To Insert a Blank Line

In the flyer, the digital picture of the surfer appears between the headline and body copy. You will not insert this picture, however, until after you enter and format all text. *Why? Although you can format text and insert pictures in any order, for illustration purposes, this module formats all text first before inserting the picture. Thus, you leave a blank line in the document as a placeholder for the picture.*

To enter a blank line in a document, press the ENTER key without typing any text on the line. The following step inserts one blank line below the headline.

- Press the ENTER key to insert a blank line in the document (Figure 1–5).

Figure 1–5

To Zoom Page Width

1 ENTER TEXT | 2 FORMAT TEXT | 3 INSERT PICTURE
4 FORMAT PICTURE | 5 ENHANCE PAGE | 6 CORRECT & REVISE

The next step in creating this flyer is to enlarge the contents that appear on the screen. ***Why?*** *You would like the text on the screen to be larger so that it is easier to read.* The document currently displays at 100% (shown in Figure 1–6). With Word, you can zoom page width, which zooms (enlarges or shrinks) the mock sheet of paper on the screen so that it is the width of the Word window. The following steps zoom page width.

- Click View on the ribbon to display the View tab (Figure 1–6).

Q&A Why did the groups on the ribbon change?

When you switch from one tab to another on the ribbon, the groups on the ribbon change to show commands related to the selected tab.

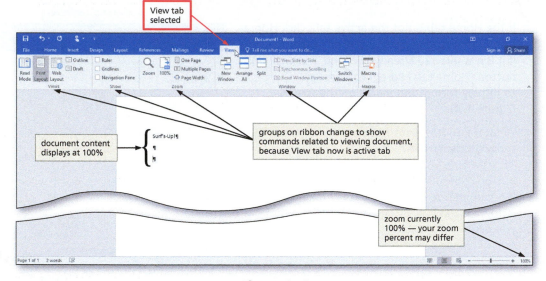

Figure 1–6

- Click the Page Width button (View tab | Zoom group) to display the page the same width as the document window (Figure 1–7).

Q&A If I change the zoom, will the document print differently?

Changing the zoom has no effect on the printed document.

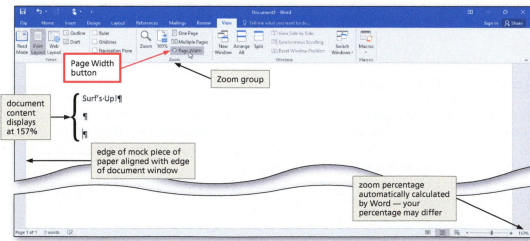

Figure 1–7

Q&A What are the other predefined zoom options?

Through the View tab | Zoom group or the Zoom dialog box (Zoom button in Zoom group), you can zoom to one page (an entire single page appears in the document window), many pages (multiple pages appear at once in the document window), page width, text width, and a variety of set percentages. Whereas page width zoom places the edges of the page at the edges of the document window, text width zoom places the document contents at the edges of the document window.

Other Ways

1. Click Zoom button (View tab | Zoom group), click Page width (Zoom dialog box), click OK button

Wordwrap

Wordwrap allows you to type words in a paragraph continually without pressing the ENTER key at the end of each line. As you type, if a word extends beyond the right margin, Word also automatically positions that word on the next line along with the insertion point.

Word creates a new paragraph each time you press the ENTER key. Thus, as you type text in the document window, do not press the ENTER key when the insertion point reaches the right margin. Instead, press the ENTER key only in these circumstances:

1. To insert a blank line(s) in a document (as shown in previous steps)
2. To begin a new paragraph
3. To terminate a short line of text and advance to the next line
4. To respond to questions or prompts in Word dialog boxes, task panes, and other on-screen objects

> **BTW**
>
> **Zooming**
> If text is too small for you to read on the screen, you can zoom the document by dragging the Zoom slider on the status bar or by clicking the Zoom Out or Zoom In buttons on the status bar. Changing the zoom has no effect on the printed document.

1 ENTER TEXT | 2 FORMAT TEXT | 3 INSERT PICTURE
4 FORMAT PICTURE | 5 ENHANCE PAGE | 6 CORRECT & REVISE

To Wordwrap Text as You Type

The next step in creating the flyer is to type the body copy. **Why?** *In many flyers, the body copy text appears below the headline.* The following steps illustrate how the body copy text wordwraps as you enter it in the document, which means you will not have to press the ENTER key at the end of the line.

1

• Type the first sentence of the body copy: `Learn to surf or improve your form and skills on the waves through expert instruction from our award-winning surf school.`

Q&A Why does my document wrap on different words?

The printer connected to a computer is one factor that can control where wordwrap occurs for each line in a document. Thus, it is possible that the same document could wordwrap differently if printed on different printers.

2

• Press the ENTER key to position the insertion point on the next line in the document (Figure 1–8).

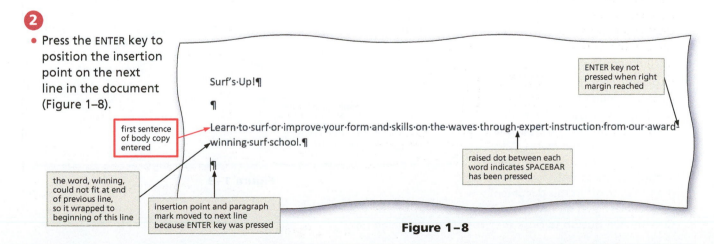

Figure 1–8

Spelling and Grammar Check

As you type text in a document, Word checks your typing for possible spelling and grammar errors. If all of the words you have typed are in Word's dictionary and your grammar is correct, as mentioned earlier, the Spelling and Grammar Check icon on the status bar displays a check mark. Otherwise, the icon shows an X. In this case, Word flags the potential error(s) in the document window with a red, green, or blue wavy underline.

- A red wavy underline means the flagged text is not in Word's dictionary (because it is a proper name or misspelled).

- A green wavy underline indicates the text may be incorrect grammatically.

- A blue wavy underline indicates the text may contain a contextual spelling error, such as the misuse of homophones (words that are pronounced the same but that have different spellings or meanings, such as one and won).

Although you can check the entire document for spelling and grammar errors at once, you also can check flagged errors as they appear on the screen.

A flagged word is not necessarily misspelled. For example, many names, abbreviations, and specialized terms are not in Word's main dictionary. In these cases, you can instruct Word to ignore the flagged word. As you type, Word also detects duplicate words while checking for spelling errors. For example, if your document contains the phrase, to the the store, Word places a red wavy underline below the second occurrence of the word, the.

To Check Spelling and Grammar as You Type

1 ENTER TEXT | 2 FORMAT TEXT | 3 INSERT PICTURE
4 FORMAT PICTURE | 5 ENHANCE PAGE | 6 CORRECT & REVISE

In the following steps, the word, group, has been misspelled intentionally as goup. *Why? These steps illustrate Word's check spelling as you type feature. If you are completing this project on a computer, your flyer may contain different or no misspelled words, depending on the accuracy of your typing.*

1

- Type **Private or goup** and then press the SPACEBAR, so that a red wavy line appears below the misspelled word (Figure 1–9).

What if Word does not flag my spelling and grammar errors with wavy underlines?

To verify that the check spelling and grammar as you type features are enabled, click File on the ribbon to open the Backstage view and then click the Options tab in the Backstage view. When the Word Options dialog box is displayed, click Proofing in the left pane and then ensure the 'Check spelling as you type' and 'Mark grammar errors as you type' check boxes contain check marks. Also ensure the 'Hide spelling errors in this document only' and 'Hide grammar errors in this document only' check boxes do not contain check marks.
Click the OK button to close the Word Options dialog box.

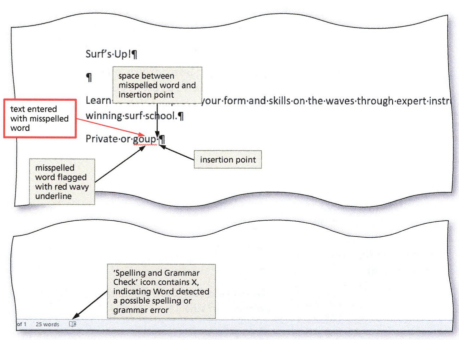

Figure 1–9

● Right-click the flagged word
(goup, in this case) to display a
shortcut menu that presents a list
of suggested spelling corrections
for the flagged word
(Figure 1–10).

Q & A

What if, when I right-click the
misspelled word, my desired
correction is not in the list on
the shortcut menu?
You can click outside the
shortcut menu to close the
shortcut menu and then retype
the correct word.

What if a flagged word actually is,
for example, a proper name and
spelled correctly?
Right-click it and then click Ignore All on the shortcut menu to instruct Word not to flag future occurrences
of the same word in this document.

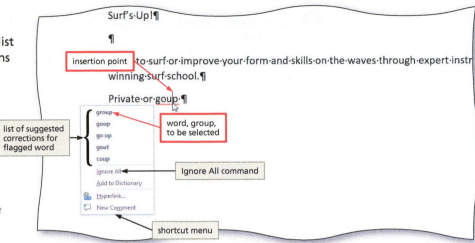

Figure 1–10

3

● Click group on
the shortcut menu
to replace the
misspelled word in
the document with
a correctly spelled
word (Figure 1–11).

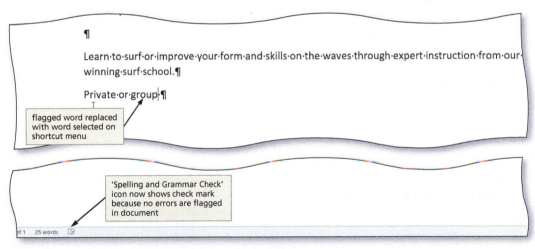

Figure 1–11

Other Ways

1. Click 'Spelling and Grammar Check' icon on status bar, click desired word in Spelling pane, click Change button, click OK button

To Enter More Text

In the flyer, the text yet to be entered includes the remainder of the body copy,
which will be formatted as a bulleted list, and the signature line. The following steps
enter the remainder of text in the flyer.

1 Press the END key to move the insertion point to the end of the current line.

2 Type **lessons** and then press the ENTER key.

3 Type **Photo and video packages available** and then press the ENTER key.

4 Type **Reef shoes and surfboard rental included** and then press the ENTER key.

5 Type the signature line in the flyer (Figure 1–12): **To sign up for a lesson, call 555-SURF!**
If requested by your instructor, enter your phone number instead of 555-SURF in the signature line.

Figure 1–12

Within the figure:
Surf's·Up!¶

¶

Learn·to·surf·or·improve·your·form·and·skills·on·the·waves·through·expert·instructi[]·winning·surf·school.¶

three paragraphs of body copy that will be formatted as a bulleted list entered

Private·or·group·lessons¶

Photo·and·video·packages·available¶

Reef·shoes·and·surfboard·rental·included¶

signature line entered

To·sign·up·for·a·lesson,·call·555-SURF!¶

6 Save the flyer on your hard drive, OneDrive, or other storage location using Surf Flyer as the file name.

Q&A Why should I save the flyer at this time?
You have performed many tasks while creating this flyer and do not want to risk losing work completed thus far. For information about how to save, refer to the Office and Windows module at the beginning of this book.

CONSIDER THIS

How should you organize text in a flyer?
The text in a flyer typically is organized into three areas: headline, body copy, and signature line.

- The **headline** is the first line of text on the flyer. It conveys the product or service being offered (such as a car for sale, lessons, or sightseeing tours) or the benefit that will be gained (such as a convenience, better performance, greater security, higher earnings, or more comfort), or it can contain a message (such as a lost or found pet).

- The **body copy** consists of text between the headline and the signature line. This text highlights the key points of the message in as few words as possible. It should be easy to read and follow. While emphasizing the positive, the body copy must be realistic, truthful, and believable.

- The **signature line**, which is the last line of text on the flyer, contains contact information or identifies a call to action.

Navigating a Document

You view only a portion of a document on the screen through the document window. At some point when you type text or insert graphics, Word probably will **scroll** the top or bottom portion of the document off the screen. Although you cannot see the text and graphics once they scroll off the screen, they remain in the document.

You can use touch gestures, the keyboard, or a mouse to scroll to a different location in a document and/or move the insertion point around a document. If you are using a touch screen, simply use your finger to slide the document up or down to display a different location in the document and then tap to move the insertion point to a new location. When you use the keyboard, the insertion point automatically moves when you press the desired keys. For example, the previous steps used the END key to move the insertion point to the end of the current line. Table 1–1 outlines various techniques to navigate a document using the keyboard.

Table 1–1 Moving the Insertion Point with the Keyboard

Insertion Point Direction	Key(s) to Press	Insertion Point Direction	Key(s) to Press
Left one character	LEFT ARROW	Up one paragraph	CTRL+UP ARROW
Right one character	RIGHT ARROW	Down one paragraph	CTRL+DOWN ARROW
Left one word	CTRL+LEFT ARROW	Up one screen	PAGE UP
Right one word	CTRL+RIGHT ARROW	Down one screen	PAGE DOWN
Up one line	UP ARROW	To top of document window	ALT+CTRL+PAGE UP
Down one line	DOWN ARROW	To bottom of document window	ALT+CTRL+PAGE DOWN
To end of line	END	To beginning of document	CTRL+HOME
To beginning of line	HOME	To end of document	CTRL+END

© 2015 Cengage Learning

With the mouse, you can use the scroll arrows or the scroll box on the scroll bar to display a different portion of the document in the document window and then click the mouse to move the insertion point to that location. Table 1–2 explains various techniques for using the scroll bar to scroll vertically with the mouse.

Table 1–2 Using the Scroll Bar to Scroll Vertically with the Mouse

Scroll Direction	Mouse Action	Scroll Direction	Mouse Action
Up	Drag the scroll box upward.	Down one screen	Click anywhere below the scroll box on the vertical scroll bar.
Down	Drag the scroll box downward.	Up one line	Click the scroll arrow at the top of the vertical scroll bar.
Up one screen	Click anywhere above the scroll box on the vertical scroll bar.	Down one line	Click the scroll arrow at the bottom of the vertical scroll bar.

© 2015 Cengage Learning

Formatting Paragraphs and Characters

With the text for the flyer entered, the next step is to **format**, or change the appearance of, its text. A paragraph encompasses the text from the first character in the paragraph up to and including its paragraph mark (¶). **Paragraph formatting** is the process of changing the appearance of a paragraph. For example, you can center or add bullets to a paragraph. Characters include letters, numbers, punctuation marks, and symbols. **Character formatting** is the process of changing the way characters appear on the screen and in print. You use character formatting to emphasize certain words and improve readability of a document. For example, you can color, italicize, or underline characters. Often, you apply both paragraph and character formatting to the same text. For example, you may center a paragraph (paragraph formatting) and underline some of the characters in the same paragraph (character formatting).

Although you can format paragraphs and characters before you type, many Word users enter text first and then format the existing text. Figure 1–13a shows the flyer in this module before formatting its paragraphs and characters. Figure 1–13b shows the flyer after formatting. As you can see from the two figures, a document that is formatted is easier to read and looks more professional. The following sections discuss how to format the flyer so that it looks like Figure 1–13b.

BTW
Minimize Wrist Injury
Computer users frequently switch among the keyboard, the mouse, and touch gestures during a word processing session; such switching strains the wrist. To help prevent wrist injury, minimize switching. For instance, if your hand already is on the mouse, use the mouse to scroll. If your fingers already are on the keyboard, use keyboard keys to scroll. If your fingertips already are on the screen, use your finger to slide the document to a new location.

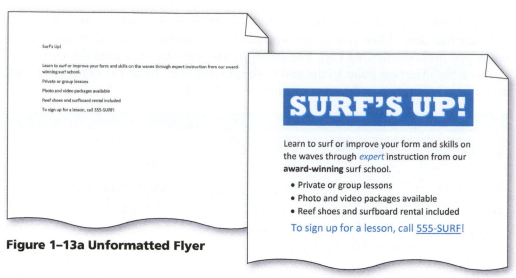

Figure 1–13a Unformatted Flyer

Figure 1–13b Formatted Flyer

Figure 1–13

BTW

Character Widths

Many word processing documents use variable character fonts, where some characters are wider than others; for example, the letter w is wider than the letter i.

Font, Font Sizes, and Themes

Characters that appear on the screen are a specific shape and size. The **font**, or typeface, defines the appearance and shape of the letters, numbers, and special characters. In Word, the default font usually is Calibri (shown in Figure 1–14). You can leave characters in the default font or change them to a different font. **Font size** specifies the size of the characters and is determined by a measurement system called points. A single **point** is about 1/72 of one inch in height. The default font size in Word typically is 11 (Figure 1–14). Thus, a character with a font size of 11 is about 11/72 or a little less than 1/6 of one inch in height. You can increase or decrease the font size of characters in a document.

A document **theme** is a set of unified formats for fonts, colors, and graphics. Word includes a variety of document themes to assist you with coordinating these visual elements in a document. The default theme fonts are Calibri Light for headings and Calibri for body text. By changing the document theme, you quickly can give your document a new look. You also can define your own document themes.

CONSIDER THIS

How do I know which formats to use in a flyer?

In a flyer, consider the following formatting suggestions.

- **Increase the font size of characters.** Flyers usually are posted on a bulletin board or in a window. Thus, the font size should be as large as possible so that passersby easily can read the flyer. To give the headline more impact, its font size should be larger than the font size of the text in the body copy. If possible, make the font size of the signature line larger than the body copy but smaller than the headline.

- **Change the font of characters.** Use fonts that are easy to read. Try to use only two different fonts in a flyer; for example, use one for the headline and the other for all other text. Too many fonts can make the flyer visually confusing.

- **Change the paragraph alignment.** The default alignment for paragraphs in a document is **left-aligned**, that is, flush at the left margin of the document with uneven right edges. Consider changing the alignment of some of the paragraphs to add interest and variety to the flyer.

- **Highlight key paragraphs with bullets.** A bulleted paragraph is a paragraph that begins with a dot or other symbol. Use bulleted paragraphs to highlight important points in a flyer.

- **Emphasize important words.** To call attention to certain words or lines, you can underline them, italicize them, or bold them. Use these formats sparingly, however, because overuse will minimize their effect and make the flyer look too busy.

- **Use color.** Use colors that complement each other and convey the meaning of the flyer. Vary colors in terms of hue and brightness. Headline colors, for example, can be bold and bright. Signature lines should stand out more than body copy but less than headlines. Keep in mind that too many colors can detract from the flyer and make it difficult to read.

To Center a Paragraph

The headline in the flyer currently is left-aligned (shown in Figure 1–14). *Why? Word, by default, left-aligns text, unless you specifically change the alignment.* You want the headline to be **centered**, that is, positioned horizontally between the left and right margins on the page. Recall that Word considers a single short line of text, such as the one-word headline, a paragraph. Thus, you will center the paragraph containing the headline. The following steps center a paragraph.

1
- Click Home on the ribbon to display the Home tab.
- Click somewhere in the paragraph to be centered (in this case, the headline) to position the insertion point in the paragraph to be centered (Figure 1–14).

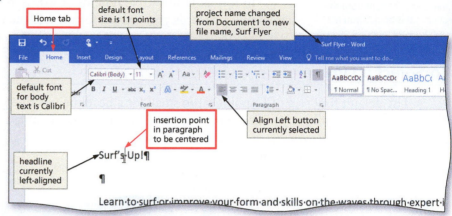

Figure 1–14

2
- Click the Center button (Home tab | Paragraph group) to center the paragraph containing the insertion point (Figure 1–15).

Q&A What if I want to return the paragraph to left-aligned?
You would click the Center button again or click the Align Left button (Home tab | Paragraph group).

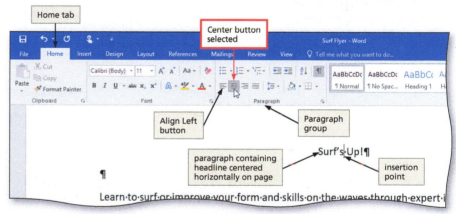

Figure 1–15

Other Ways

1. Right-click paragraph (or if using touch, tap 'Show Context Menu' button on mini toolbar), click Paragraph on shortcut menu, click Indents and Spacing tab (Paragraph dialog box), click Alignment arrow, click Centered, click OK button
2. Click Paragraph Settings Dialog Box Launcher (Home tab or Layout tab | Paragraph group), click Indents and Spacing tab (Paragraph dialog box), click Alignment arrow, click Centered, click OK button
3. Press CTRL+E

To Center Another Paragraph

In the flyer, the signature line is to be centered to match the paragraph alignment of the headline. The following steps center the signature line.

1 Click somewhere in the paragraph to be centered (in this case, the signature line) to position the insertion point in the paragraph to be formatted.

2 Click the Center button (Home tab | Paragraph group) to center the paragraph containing the insertion point (shown in Figure 1–16).

BTW

File Type
Depending on your Windows settings, the file type .docx may be displayed on the title bar immediately to the right of the file name after you save the file. The file type .docx identifies a Word 2016 document.

BTW

The Ribbon and Screen Resolution
Word may change how the groups and buttons within the groups appear on the ribbon, depending on the computer or mobile device's screen resolution. Thus, your ribbon may look different from the ones in this book if you are using a screen resolution other than 1366 × 768.

Formatting Single versus Multiple Paragraphs and Characters

As shown in the previous sections, to format a single paragraph, simply position the insertion point in the paragraph to make it the current paragraph and then format the paragraph. Similarly, to format a single word, position the insertion point in the word to make it the current word, and then format the word.

To format multiple paragraphs or words, however, you first must select the paragraphs or words you want to format and then format the selection.

1 ENTER TEXT | **2 FORMAT TEXT** | 3 INSERT PICTURE
4 FORMAT PICTURE | 5 ENHANCE PAGE | 6 CORRECT & REVISE

To Select a Line

The default font size of 11 point is too small for a headline in a flyer. To increase the font size of the characters in the headline, you first must select the line of text containing the headline. *Why? If you increase the font size of text without selecting any text, Word will increase the font size only of the word containing the insertion point.* The following step selects a line.

• Move the pointer to the left of the line to be selected (in this case, the headline) until the pointer changes to a right-pointing block arrow (Figure 1–16).

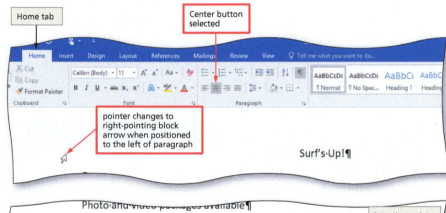

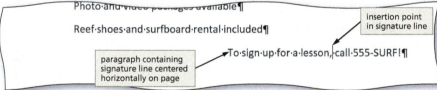

Figure 1–16

2

• While the pointer is a right-pointing block arrow, click the mouse button to select the entire line to the right of the pointer (Figure 1–17).

Q&A

What if I am using a touch screen?
You would double-tap to the left of the line to be selected to select the line.

Why is the selected text shaded gray?
If your screen normally displays dark letters on a light background, which is the default setting in Word, then selected text is displayed with a light shading color, such as gray, on the dark letters. Note that the selection that appears on the text does not print.

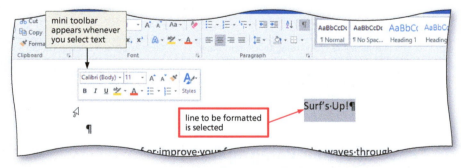

Figure 1–17

Other Ways

1. Drag pointer through line   2. With insertion point at beginning of desired line, press CRTL+SHIFT+DOWN ARROW

To Change the Font Size of Selected Text

The next step is to increase the font size of the characters in the selected headline. ***Why?*** *You would like the headline to be as large as possible and still fit on a single line, which in this case is 72 point.* The following steps increase the font size of the headline from 11 to 72 point.

- With the text selected, click the Font Size arrow (Home tab | Font group) to display the Font Size gallery (Figure 1–18).

Q&A

What is the Font Size arrow?
The Font Size arrow is the arrow to the right of the Font Size box, which is the text box that displays the current font size.

Why are the font sizes in my Font Size gallery different from those in Figure 1–18?
Font sizes may vary depending on the current font and your printer driver.

What happened to the mini toolbar?
The mini toolbar disappears if you do not use it. These steps use the Font Size arrow on the Home tab instead of the Font Size arrow on the mini toolbar.

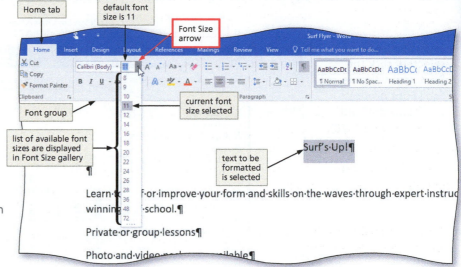

Figure 1–18

- Point to 72 in the Font Size gallery to display a live preview of the selected text at the selected point size (Figure 1–19).

Q&A

What is live preview?
Recall from the Office and Windows module at the beginning of this book that live preview is a feature that allows you to point to a gallery choice and see its effect in the document — without actually selecting the choice.

Can I use live preview on a touch screen?
Live preview is not available on a touch screen.

font size of selected text changes to 72 points, showing live preview of font size to which you are pointing in gallery

selection on text disappears temporarily while you use live preview

pointer on 72

Surf's·Up!¶

Figure 1–19

 **Experiment**

- Point to various font sizes in the Font Size gallery and watch the font size of the selected text change in the document window.

3

- Click 72 in the Font Size gallery to increase the font size of the selected text.

Other Ways

1. Click Font Size arrow on mini toolbar, click desired font size in Font Size gallery

2. Right-click selected text (or, if using touch, tap 'Show Context Menu' button on mini toolbar), click Font on shortcut menu, click Font tab (Font dialog box), select desired font size in Size list, click OK button

3. Click Font Dialog Box Launcher, (Home tab | Font group) click Font tab (Font dialog box), select desired font size in Size list, click OK button

4. Press CTRL+D, click Font tab (Font dialog box), select desired font size in Size list, click OK button

To Change the Font of Selected Text

The default theme font for headings is Calibri Light and for all other text, called body text in Word, is Calibri. Many other fonts are available, however, so that you can add variety to documents.

The following steps change the font of the headline from Calibri to Rockwell Extra Bold. *Why? To draw more attention to the headline, you change its font so that it differs from the font of other text in the flyer.*

1

- With the text selected, click the Font arrow (Home tab | Font group) to display the Font gallery (Figure 1–20).

Q&A Will the fonts in my Font gallery be the same as those in Figure 1–20?
Your list of available fonts may differ, depending on the type of printer you are using and other settings.

What if the text no longer is selected?
Follow the steps described earlier to select a line.

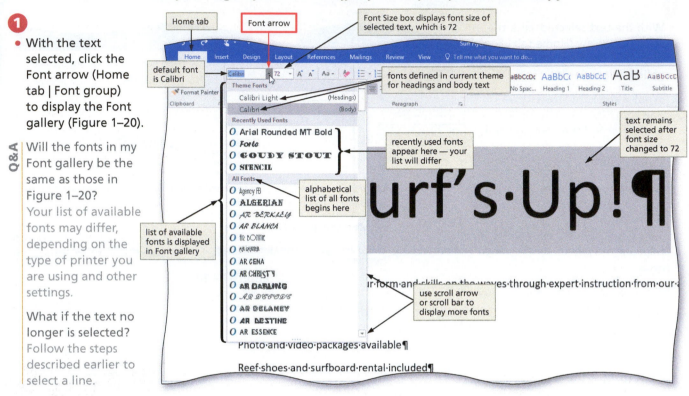

Figure 1–20

2

- If necessary, scroll through the Font gallery to display Rockwell Extra Bold (or a similar font).

- Point to 'Rockwell Extra Bold' (or a similar font) to display a live preview of the selected text in the selected font (Figure 1–21).

🔎 **Experiment**

- Point to various fonts in the Font gallery and watch the font of the selected text change in the document window.

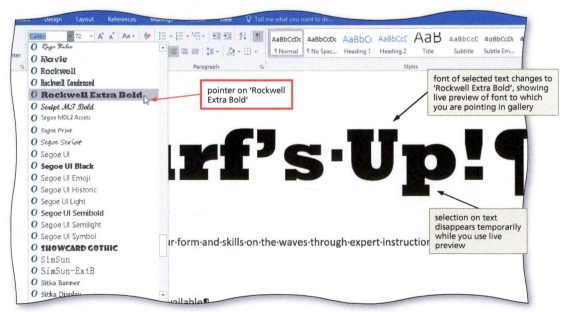

Figure 1–21

3

- Click 'Rockwell Extra Bold' (or a similar font) in the Font gallery to change the font of the selected text.

Q&A If the font I want to use appears in the Recently Used Fonts list in the Font gallery, could I click it there instead?
Yes.

Other Ways

1. Click Font arrow on mini toolbar, click desired font in Font gallery

2. Right-click selected text (or, if using touch, tap 'Show Context Menu' button on mini toolbar), click Font on shortcut menu, click Font tab (Font dialog box), select desired font in Font list, click OK button

3. Click Font Dialog Box Launcher (Home tab | Font group), click Font tab (Font dialog box), select desired font in Font list, click OK button

4. Press CTRL+D, click Font tab (Font dialog box), select desired font in Font list, click OK button

To Change the Case of Selected Text

1 ENTER TEXT | **2 FORMAT TEXT** | 3 INSERT PICTURE
4 FORMAT PICTURE | 5 ENHANCE PAGE | 6 CORRECT & REVISE

The headline currently shows the first letter in each word capitalized, which sometimes is referred to as initial cap. The following steps change the headline to uppercase. **Why?** *To draw more attention to the headline, you would like the entire line of text to be capitalized, or in uppercase letters.*

1

- With the text selected, click the Change Case button (Home tab | Font group) to display the Change Case gallery (Figure 1–22).

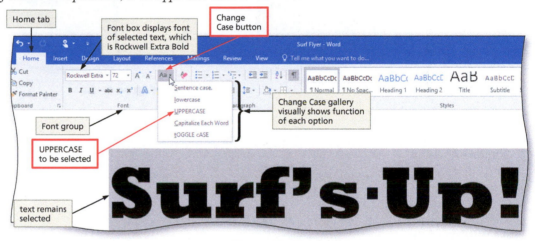

Figure 1–22

2

- Click UPPERCASE in the Change Case gallery to change the case of the selected text (Figure 1–23).

Q&A What if a ruler appears on the screen or the pointer shape changes?
If you are using a mouse, depending on the position of your pointer and locations you click on the screen, a ruler may appear automatically or the pointer's shape may change. Simply move the mouse and the ruler should disappear and/or the pointer shape will change.

Figure 1–23

Other Ways

1. Right-click selected text (or, if using touch, tap 'Show Context Menu' button on mini toolbar), click Font on shortcut menu, click Font tab (Font dialog box), select All caps in Effects area, click OK button

2. Click Font Dialog Box Launcher (Home tab | Font group), click Font tab (Font dialog box), select All caps in Effects area, click OK button

3. Press SHIFT+F3 repeatedly until text is desired case

To Apply a Text Effect to Selected Text

1 ENTER TEXT | **2 FORMAT TEXT** | 3 INSERT PICTURE
4 FORMAT PICTURE | 5 ENHANCE PAGE | 6 CORRECT & REVISE

Word provides many text effects to add interest and variety to text. The following steps apply a text effect to the headline. *Why? You would like the text in the headline to be even more noticeable.*

1

• With the text selected, click the 'Text Effects and Typography' button (Home tab | Font group) to display the Text Effects and Typography gallery (Figure 1–24).

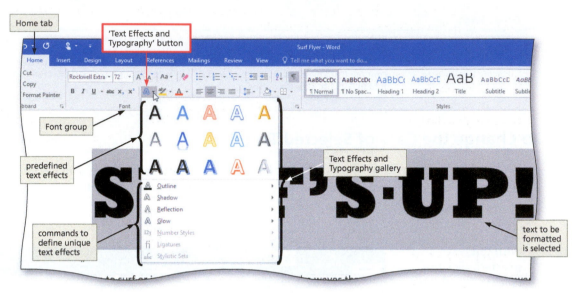

Figure 1–24

2

• Point to 'Fill - White, Outline - Accent 2, Hard Shadow - Accent 2' (fourth text effect in third row) to display a live preview of the selected text with the selected text effect (Figure 1–25).

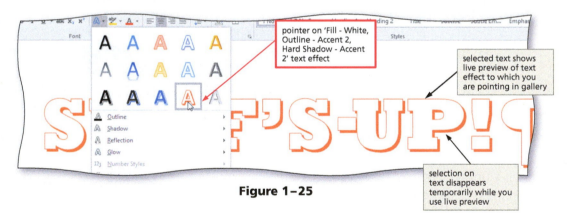

Figure 1–25

 Experiment

• Point to various text effects in the Text Effects and Typography gallery and watch the text effects of the selected text change in the document window.

3

• Click 'Fill - White, Outline - Accent 2, Hard Shadow - Accent 2' to change the text effect of the selected text.

4

• Click anywhere in the document window to remove the selection from the selected text.

Other Ways
1. Right-click selected text (or, if using touch, tap 'Show Context Menu' button on mini toolbar), click Font on shortcut menu, click Font tab (Font dialog box), click Text Effects button, expand Text Fill or Text Outline section and then select the desired text effect(s) (Format Text Effects dialog box), click OK button, click OK button   2. Click Font Dialog Box Launcher (Home tab | Font group), click Font tab (Font dialog box), click Text Effects button, expand Text Fill or Text Outline section and then select desired text effect (Format Text Effects dialog box), click OK button, click OK button

To Shade a Paragraph

When you **shade** text, Word colors the rectangular area behind any text or graphics. If the text to shade is a paragraph, Word shades the area from the left margin to the right margin of the current paragraph. To shade a paragraph, place the insertion point in the paragraph. To shade any other text, you must first select the text to be shaded.

This flyer uses a shading color for the headline. **Why?** *To make the headline of the flyer more eye-catching, you shade it.* The following steps shade a paragraph.

1
- Click somewhere in the paragraph to be shaded (in this case, the headline) to position the insertion point in the paragraph to be formatted.

- Click the Shading arrow (Home tab | Paragraph group) to display the Shading gallery (Figure 1–26).

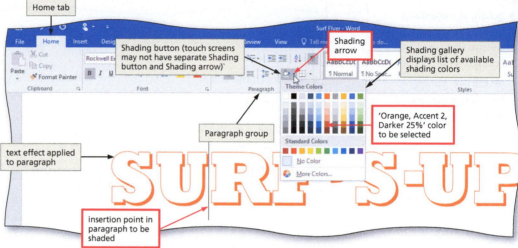

Figure 1–26

Q&A What if I click the Shading button by mistake?
Click the Shading arrow and proceed with Step 2. Note that if you are using a touch screen, you may not have a separate Shading button.

Why does my Shading gallery display different colors?
Your color scheme setting may display colors in a different order or may be different from Office, which is the default color scheme. To change the color scheme, click Design on the ribbon, click the Theme Colors button (Design tab | Document Formatting group), and then click Office in the Theme Colors gallery.

Experiment
- Point to various colors in the Shading gallery and watch the shading color of the current paragraph change.

2
- Click 'Orange, Accent 2, Darker 25%' (sixth color in fifth row) to shade the current paragraph (Figure 1–27).

Figure 1–27

Q&A What if I apply a dark shading color to dark text?
When the font color of text is Automatic, the color usually is black. If you select a dark shading color, Word automatically may change the text color to white so that the shaded text is easier to read.

Other Ways

1. Click Borders arrow (Home tab | Paragraph group), click Borders and Shading, click Shading tab (Borders and Shading dialog box), click Fill arrow, select desired color, click OK button

To Select Multiple Lines

The next formatting step for the flyer is to increase the font size of the characters between the headline and the signature line. *Why? You want this text to be easier to read from a distance.*

To change the font size of the characters in multiple lines, you first must select all the lines to be formatted. The following steps select multiple lines.

● Scroll, if necessary, so that all text below the headline is displayed on the screen.

● Move the pointer to the left of the first paragraph to be selected until the pointer changes to a right-pointing block arrow (Figure 1–28).

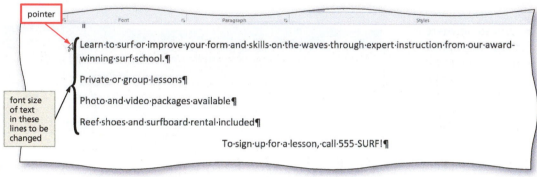

Figure 1–28

◀ **Q&A** What if I am using a touch screen?

You would tap to position the insertion point in the text to select.

● While the pointer is a right-pointing block arrow, drag downward to select all lines that will be formatted (Figure 1–29).

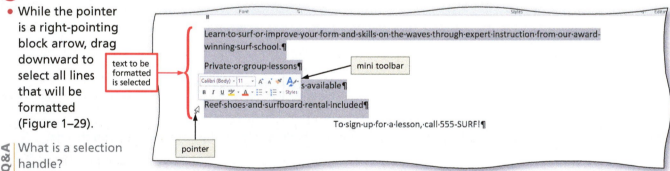

Figure 1–29

◀ **Q&A** What is a selection handle?

When working on a touch screen, a **selection handle** (small circle) appears below the insertion point. Using a fingertip, you drag a selection handle to select text.

Other Ways

1. With insertion point at beginning of desired line, press SHIFT+DOWN ARROW repeatedly until all lines are selected

---

BTW

Formatting Marks

With some fonts, the formatting marks will not be displayed properly on the screen. For example, the raised dot that signifies a blank space between words may be displayed behind a character instead of in the blank space, causing the characters to look incorrect.

To Change the Font Size of Selected Text

The characters between the headline and the signature line in the flyer currently are 11 point. To make them easier to read from a distance, this flyer uses a 24-point font size for these characters. The following steps change the font size of the selected text.

1 With the text selected, click the Font Size arrow (Home tab | Font group) to display the Font Size gallery.

2 Click 24 in the Font Size gallery to increase the font size of the selected text.

3 Click anywhere in the document window to remove the selection from the text.

4 If necessary, scroll so that you can see all the resized text on the screen (Figure 1–30).

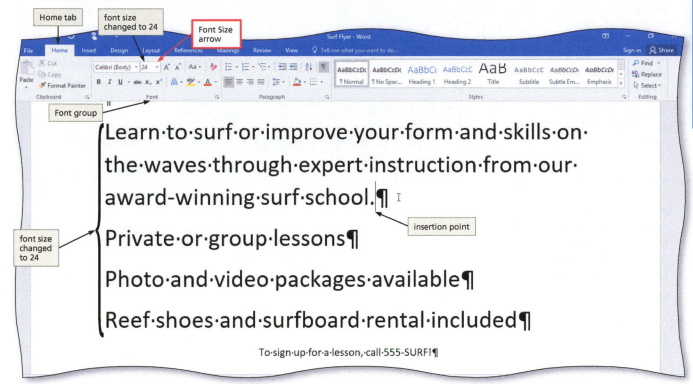

Figure 1–30

To Bullet a List of Paragraphs

1 ENTER TEXT | **2 FORMAT TEXT** | 3 INSERT PICTURE

4 FORMAT PICTURE | 5 ENHANCE PAGE | 6 CORRECT & REVISE

A **bulleted list** is a series of paragraphs, each beginning with a bullet character. The next step is to format the three paragraphs about the lessons that are above the signature line in the flyer as a bulleted list.

To format a list of paragraphs with bullets, you first must select all the lines in the paragraphs. *Why? If you do not select all paragraphs, Word will place a bullet only in the paragraph containing the insertion point.* The following steps bullet a list of paragraphs.

1

- Move the pointer to the left of the first paragraph to be selected until the pointer changes to a right-pointing block arrow.

- Drag downward until all paragraphs that will be formatted with a bullet character are selected (Figure 1–31).

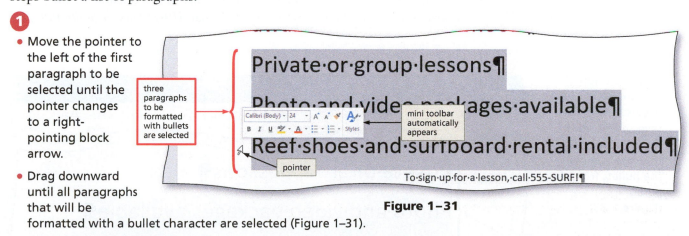

Figure 1–31

Q&A What if I am using a touch screen?

Tap to position the insertion point in the text to select and then drag the selection handle(s) as necessary to select the text that will be formatted.

2

- Click the Bullets button (Home tab | Paragraph group) to place a bullet character at the beginning of each selected paragraph (Figure 1–32).

Q&A

Why does my screen display a Bullets gallery?

If you are using a touch screen, you may not have a separate Bullets button and Bullets arrow. In this case, select the desired bullet style in the Bullets gallery.

What if I accidentally click the Bullets arrow?

Press the ESCAPE key to remove the Bullets gallery from the screen and then repeat Step 2.

How do I remove bullets from a list or paragraph?

Select the list or paragraph and then click the Bullets button again, or click the Bullets arrow and then click None in the Bullet Library.

Other Ways

1. Right-click selected paragraphs, click Bullets button on mini toolbar

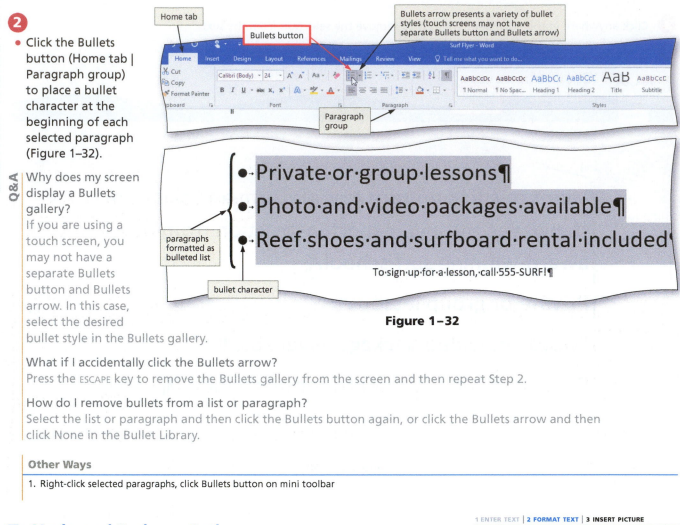

Figure 1–32

1 ENTER TEXT | **2 FORMAT TEXT** | 3 INSERT PICTURE

4 FORMAT PICTURE | 5 ENHANCE PAGE | 6 CORRECT & REVISE

To Undo and Redo an Action

Word provides a means of canceling your recent command(s) or action(s). For example, if you format text incorrectly, you can undo the format and try it again. When you point to the Undo button, Word displays the action you can undo as part of a ScreenTip.

If, after you undo an action, you decide you did not want to perform the undo, you can redo the undone action. Word does not allow you to undo or redo some actions, such as saving or printing a document. The following steps undo the bullet format just applied and then redo the bullet format. *Why? These steps illustrate the undo and redo actions.*

1

- Click the Undo button on the Quick Access Toolbar to reverse your most recent action (in this case, remove the bullets from the paragraphs) (Figure 1–33).

Figure 1–33

• Click the Redo button on the Quick Access Toolbar to reverse your most recent undo (in this case, place a bullet character on the paragraphs again) (shown in Figure 1–32).

Other Ways

1. Press CTRL+Z to undo; press CTRL+Y to redo

To Italicize Text

Italic text has a slanted appearance. The next step is to italicize the word, expert, in the flyer to further emphasize it. As with a single paragraph, if you want to format a single word, you do not need to select it. *Why? To format a single word, you simply position the insertion point somewhere in the word and apply the desired format.* The following step italicizes a word.

• Click somewhere in the word to be italicized (expert, in this case) to position the insertion point in the word to be formatted.

• Click the Italic button (Home tab | Font group) to italicize the word containing the insertion point (Figure 1–34).

Q&A

How would I remove an italic format?
You would click the Italic button a second time, or you immediately could click the Undo button on the Quick Access Toolbar or press CTRL+Z.

How can I tell what formatting has been applied to text?
The selected buttons and boxes on the Home tab show formatting characteristics of the location of the insertion point. With the insertion point in the word, expert, the Home tab shows these formats: 24-point Calibri italic font.

Why did the appearance of the Redo button change?
It changed to a Repeat button. When it is a Repeat button, you can click it to repeat your last action. For example, you can select different text and then click the Repeat button to apply (repeat) the italic format to the selected text.

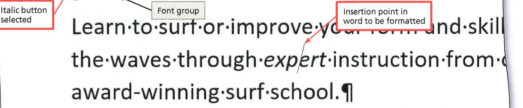

Figure 1–34

Other Ways

1. Click Italic button on mini toolbar

2. Right-click selected text (or, if using touch, tap 'Show Context Menu' button on mini toolbar), click Font on shortcut menu, click Font tab (Font dialog box), click Italic in Font style list, click OK button

3. Click Font Dialog Box Launcher (Home tab | Font group), click Font tab (Font dialog box), click Italic in Font style list, click OK button

4. Press CTRL+I

To Color Text

The following steps change the color of the word, expert. *Why? To emphasize the word even more, you change its color:*

● With the insertion point in the word to format, click the Font Color arrow (Home tab | Font group) to display the Font Color gallery (Figure 1–35).

Q&A What if I click the Font Color button by mistake?
Click the Font Color arrow and then proceed with Step 2. Note that you may not have a separate Font Color button if you are using a touch screen.

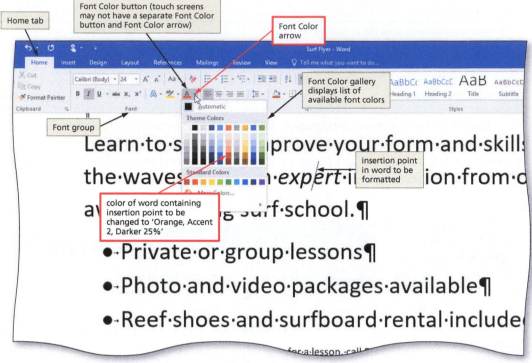

Figure 1–35

🔍 Experiment

● If you are using a mouse, point to various colors in the Font Color gallery and watch the color of the current word change.

● Click 'Orange, Accent 2, Darker 25%' (sixth color in fifth row) to change the color of the text (Figure 1–36).

Q&A How would I change the text color back to black?
You would position the insertion point in the word or select the text, click the Font Color arrow (Home tab | Font group) again, and then click Automatic in the Font Color gallery.

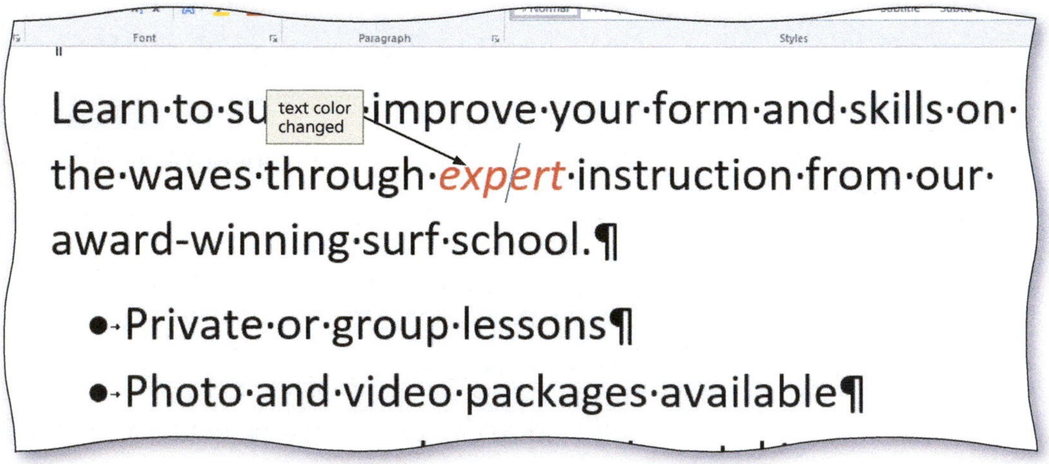

Figure 1–36

Other Ways

1. Click Font Color arrow on mini toolbar, click desired color
2. Right-click selected text (or, if using touch, tap 'Show Context Menu' button on mini toolbar), click Font on shortcut menu, click Font tab (Font dialog box), click Font color arrow, click desired color, click OK button
3. Click Font Dialog Box Launcher (Home tab | Font group), click Font tab (Font dialog box), click Font color arrow, click desired color, click OK button

To Use the Mini Toolbar to Format Text

Recall from the Office and Windows module at the beginning of this book that the mini toolbar automatically appears based on certain tasks you perform. ***Why?*** *Word places commonly used buttons and boxes on the mini toolbar for your convenience. If you do not use the mini toolbar, it disappears from the screen.* All commands on the mini toolbar also exist on the ribbon.

The following steps use the mini toolbar to change the color and font size of text in the signature line of the flyer.

1

- Move the pointer to the left of the line to be selected until the pointer changes to a right-pointing block arrow and then click to select the line and display the mini toolbar (Figure 1–37).

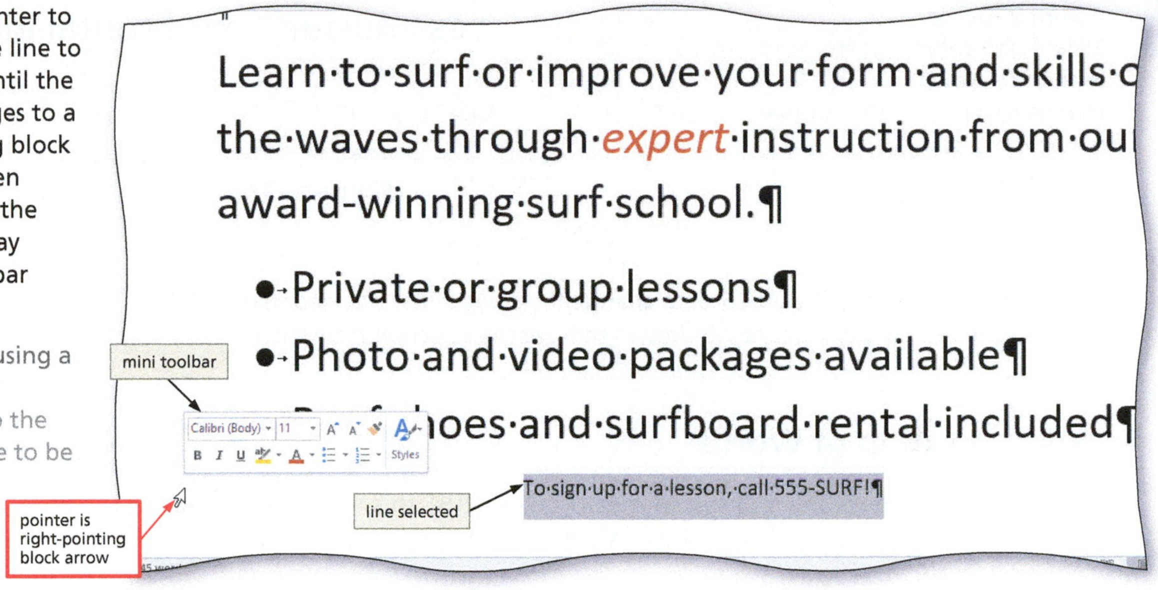

Q&A What if I am using a touch screen?
Double-tap to the left of the line to be selected to select the line and then tap the selection

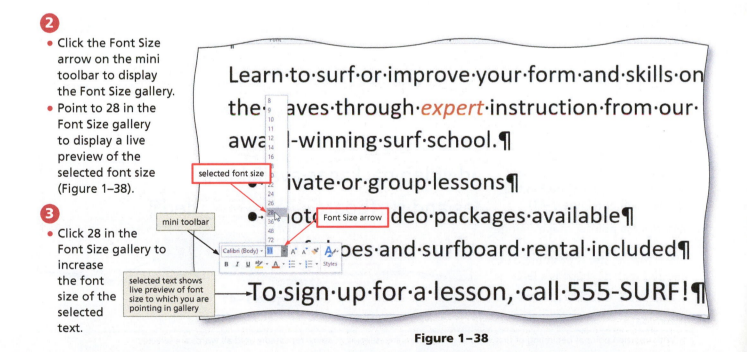

Figure 1–37

to display the mini toolbar. If you are using a touch screen, the buttons and boxes on the mini toolbar differ. For example, it contains a 'Show Context Menu' button at the far-right edge, which you tap to display a shortcut menu.

2

- Click the Font Size arrow on the mini toolbar to display the Font Size gallery.
- Point to 28 in the Font Size gallery to display a live preview of the selected font size (Figure 1–38).

3

- Click 28 in the Font Size gallery to increase the font size of the selected text.

Figure 1–38

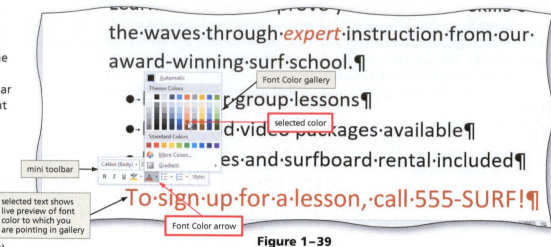

- With the text still selected and the mini toolbar still displayed, click the Font Color arrow on the mini toolbar to display the Font Color gallery.
- Point to 'Orange, Accent 2, Darker 25%' (sixth color in the fifth row) to display a live preview of the selected font color (Figure 1–39).

Figure 1–39

- Click 'Orange, Accent 2, Darker 25%' to change the color of the selected text.
- Click anywhere in the document window to remove the selection from the text.

To Select a Group of Words

1 ENTER TEXT | **2 FORMAT TEXT** | 3 INSERT PICTURE
4 FORMAT PICTURE | 5 ENHANCE PAGE | 6 CORRECT & REVISE

To emphasize the contact phone number (555-SURF), this text is underlined in the flyer. Because the phone number is separated with a hyphen, Word considers it a group of words. To format a group of words, you first must select them. **Why?** *If you underline text without selecting any text first, Word will underline only the word containing the insertion point.* The following steps select a group of words.

- Position the pointer immediately to the left of the first character of the text to be selected, in this case, the 5 in 555 (Figure 1–40).

Q&A Why did the shape of the pointer change?
The pointer's shape is an I-beam when positioned in unselected text in the document window.

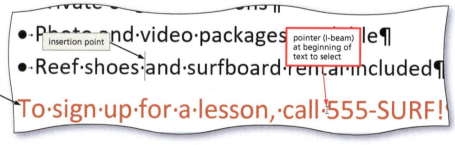

Figure 1–40

- Drag the pointer through the last character of the text to be selected, in this case, the F in the phone number (Figure 1–41).

Q&A Why did the pointer shape change again?
When the pointer is positioned in selected text, its shape is a left-pointing block arrow.

Figure 1–41

Other Ways

1. With insertion point at beginning of first word in group, press CTRL+SHIFT+RIGHT ARROW repeatedly until all words are selected

1 ENTER TEXT | **2 FORMAT TEXT** | 3 INSERT PICTURE

4 FORMAT PICTURE | 5 ENHANCE PAGE | 6 CORRECT & REVISE

To Underline Text

Underlined text prints with an underscore (_) below each character. In the flyer, the contact phone number, 555-SURF, in the signature line is underlined. *Why? Underlines are used to emphasize or draw attention to specific text.* The following step formats selected text with an underline.

1

• With the text selected, click the Underline button (Home tab | Font group) to underline the selected text (Figure 1–42).

Q&A What if my screen displays an Underline gallery? If you are using a touch screen, you may not have a separate Underline button and Underline arrow. In this case, select the desired underline style in the Underline gallery.

If a button exists on the mini toolbar, can I click that instead of using the ribbon? Yes.

How would I remove an underline? You would click the Underline button a second time, or you immediately could click the Undo button on the Quick Access Toolbar.

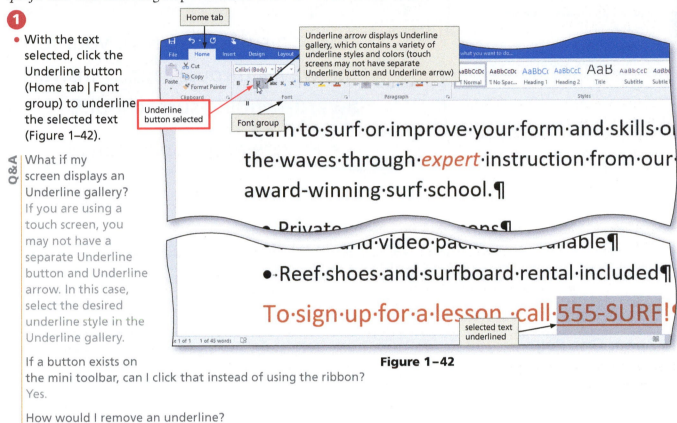

Figure 1–42

Other Ways

1. Click Underline button on mini toolbar	2. Right-click text (or, if using touch, tap 'Show Context Menu' button on mini toolbar), click Font on shortcut menu, click Font tab (Font dialog box), click Underline style box arrow, click desired underline style, click OK button	3. Click Font Dialog Box Launcher (Home tab | Font group), click Font tab (Font dialog box), click Underline style arrow, click desired underline style, click OK button	4. Press CTRL+U

1 ENTER TEXT | **2 FORMAT TEXT** | 3 INSERT PICTURE

4 FORMAT PICTURE | 5 ENHANCE PAGE | 6 CORRECT & REVISE

To Bold Text

Bold characters appear somewhat thicker and darker than those that are not bold. The following steps format the text, award-winning, in bold characters. *Why? To further emphasize this text, it is bold in the flyer.* Recall that if you want to format a single word, you simply position the insertion point in the word and then format the word. To format text that consists of more than one word, as you have learned previously, you select the text first.

1

• Select the text to be formatted (the text, award-winning, in this case); that is, position the pointer immediately to the left of the first character of the text to be selected and then drag the pointer through the last character of the text to be selected.

Q&A What if I am using a touch screen? Tap to position the insertion point in the text you want to select word then drag the selection handle(s) to select the text to be formatted.

2

- With the text selected, click the Bold button (Home tab | Font group) to bold the selected text (Figure 1–43).

Q&A How would I remove a bold format?

You would click the Bold button a second time, or you immediately could click the Undo button on the Quick Access Toolbar.

3

- Click anywhere in the document window to remove the selection from the screen.

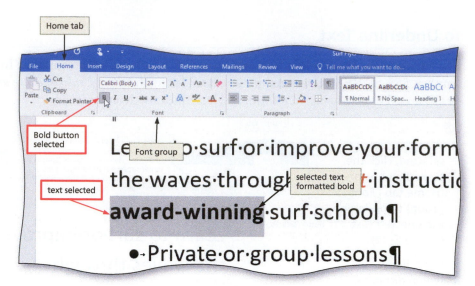

Figure 1–43

Other Ways

1. Click Bold button on mini toolbar	2. Right-click selected text (or, if using touch, tap 'Show Context Menu' button on mini toolbar), click Font on shortcut menu, click Font tab (Font dialog box), click Bold in Font style list, click OK button	3. Click Font Dialog Box Launcher (Home tab | Font group), click Font tab (Font dialog box), click Bold in Font style list, click OK button	4. Press CTRL+B

1 ENTER TEXT | **2 FORMAT TEXT** | 3 INSERT PICTURE

4 FORMAT PICTURE | 5 ENHANCE PAGE | 6 CORRECT & REVISE

To Zoom One Page

Earlier in this module, you changed the zoom to page width so that the text on the screen was larger and easier to read. In the next set of steps, you want to see the entire page (as a mock sheet of paper) on the screen at once. **Why?** *You want be able to see the effect of adjusting colors in the document as a whole.* The next step displays a single page in its entirety in the document window as large as possible.

1

- Click View on the ribbon to display the View tab.
- Click the One Page button (View tab | Zoom group) to display the entire page in the document window as large as possible (Figure 1–44).

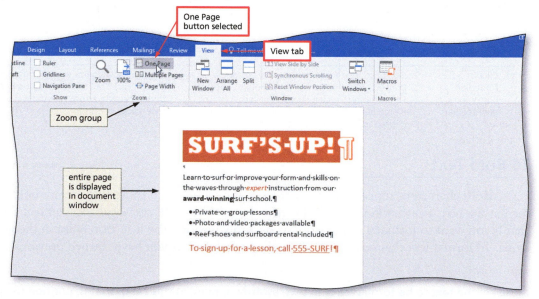

Figure 1–44

Other Ways

1. Click Zoom button (View tab | Zoom group), click Whole page (Zoom dialog box), click OK button

What colors should I choose when creating documents?

When choosing color, associate the meaning of the color with your message:

- Red expresses danger, power, or energy and often is associated with sports or physical exertion.

- Brown represents simplicity, honesty, and dependability.

- Orange denotes success, victory, creativity, and enthusiasm.

- Yellow suggests sunshine, happiness, hope, liveliness, and intelligence.

- Green symbolizes growth, healthiness, harmony, and healing and often is associated with safety or money.

- Blue indicates integrity, trust, importance, confidence, and stability.

- Purple represents wealth, power, comfort, extravagance, magic, mystery, and spirituality.

- White stands for purity, goodness, cleanliness, precision, and perfection.

- Black suggests authority, strength, elegance, power, and prestige.

- Gray conveys neutrality and, thus, often is found in backgrounds and other effects.

To Change Theme Colors

1 ENTER TEXT | 2 FORMAT TEXT | 3 INSERT PICTURE
4 FORMAT PICTURE | 5 ENHANCE PAGE | 6 CORRECT & REVISE

A **color scheme** in Word is a document theme that identifies complementary colors for text, background, accents, and links in a document. With more than 20 predefined color schemes, Word provides a simple way to coordinate colors in a document.

The default color scheme is called Office. In the flyer, you will change the color scheme. *Why? You want the colors in the flyer to represent integrity, trust, confidence, stability, healthiness, harmony, blooming, and safety, which are conveyed by shades of blues and greens. In Word, the Blue color scheme uses these colors.* The following steps change theme colors.

- Click Design on the ribbon to display the Design tab.

- Click the Theme Colors button (Design tab | Document Formatting group) to display the Theme Colors gallery.

- Point to Blue in the Theme Colors gallery to display a live preview of the selected theme color (Figure 1–45).

 **Experiment**

- Point to various color schemes in the Theme Colors gallery and watch the colors change in the document.

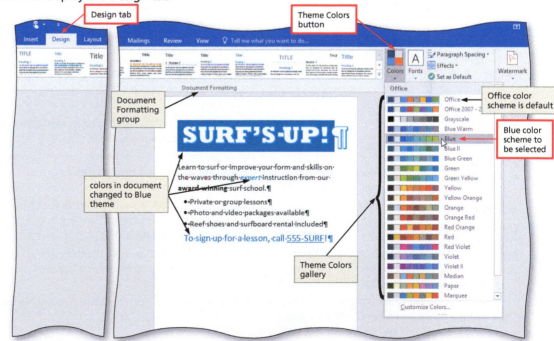

Figure 1–45

- Click Blue in the Theme Colors gallery to change the document theme colors.

Q&A | What if I want to return to the original color scheme?

You would click the Theme Colors button again and then click Office in the Theme Colors gallery.

To Zoom Page Width

Because the document contents are small when displayed on one page, the next steps zoom page width again.

BTW

Selecting Nonadjacent Items
In Word, you can use keyboard keys to select nonadjacent items, that is, items not next to each other. This is helpful when you are applying the same formatting to multiple items. To select nonadjacent items (text or graphics), select the first item, such as a word or paragraph, as usual; then, press and hold down the CTRL key. While holding down the CTRL key, select additional items.

1 Click View on the ribbon to display the View tab.

2 Click the Page Width button (View tab | Zoom group) to display the page the same width as the document window (shown earlier in the module in Figure 1–7).

3 Save the flyer again on the same storage location with the same file name.

Q&A Why should I save the flyer again?
You have made several modifications to the flyer since you last saved it; thus, you should save it again.

Selecting Text

In many of the previous steps, you have selected text. Table 1–3 summarizes the techniques used to select various items.

Table 1–3 Techniques for Selecting Text			
Item to Select	**Touch**	**Mouse**	**Keyboard (where applicable)**
Block of text	Tap to position insertion point in text to select and then drag selection handle(s) to select text.	Click at beginning of selection, scroll to end of selection, position pointer at end of selection, hold down SHIFT key, and then click; or drag through the text.	
Character(s)	Tap to position insertion point in text to select and then drag selection handle(s) to select text.	Drag through character(s).	SHIFT+RIGHT ARROW or SHIFT+LEFT ARROW
Document		Move pointer to left of text until pointer changes to right-pointing block arrow and then triple-click.	CTRL+A
Graphic	Tap the graphic.	Click the graphic.	
Line	Double-tap to left of line to be selected.	Move pointer to left of line until pointer changes to right-pointing block arrow and then click.	HOME, then SHIFT+END or END, then SHIFT+HOME
Lines	Tap to position insertion point in text to select and then drag selection handle(s) to select text.	Move pointer to left of first line until pointer changes to right-pointing block arrow and then drag up or down.	HOME, then SHIFT+DOWN ARROW or END, then SHIFT+UP ARROW
Paragraph	Tap to position insertion point in text to select and then drag selection handle(s) to select text.	Triple-click paragraph; or move pointer to left of paragraph until pointer changes to right-pointing block arrow and then double-click.	CTRL+SHIFT+DOWN ARROW or CTRL+SHIFT+UP ARROW
Paragraphs	Tap to position insertion point in text to select and then drag selection handle(s) to select text.	Move pointer to left of paragraph until pointer changes to right-pointing block arrow, double-click, and then drag up or down.	CTRL+SHIFT+DOWN ARROW or CTRL+SHIFT+UP ARROW repeatedly
Sentence	Tap to position insertion point in text to select and then drag selection handle(s) to select text.	Press and hold down CTRL key and then click sentence.	
Word	Double-tap word.	Double-click word.	CTRL+SHIFT+RIGHT ARROW or CTRL+SHIFT+LEFT ARROW
Words	Tap to position insertion point in text to select and then drag selection handle(s) to select text.	Drag through words.	CTRL+SHIFT+RIGHT ARROW or CTRL+SHIFT+LEFT ARROW repeatedly

Break Point: If you wish to take a break, this is a good place to do so. You can exit Word now. To resume at a later time, run Word, open the file called Surf Flyer, and continue following the steps from this location forward. For a detailed example of exiting Word, running Word, and opening a file, refer to the Office and Windows module at the beginning of the book.

Inserting and Formatting a Picture in a Word Document

With the text formatted in the flyer, the next step is to insert a digital picture in the flyer and format the picture. Flyers usually contain a graphical image(s), such as a picture, to attract the attention of passersby. In the following sections, you will perform these tasks:

1. Insert a digital picture into the flyer.
2. Reduce the size of the picture.
3. Change the look of the picture.

CONSIDER THIS

How do I locate a graphic file to use in a document?

To use a graphic in a Word document, the image must be stored digitally in a file. Files containing graphics are available from a variety of sources:

- The web has images available, some of which are free, while others require a fee.
- You can take a picture with a digital camera or smartphone and **download** it, which is the process of copying the digital picture from the camera or phone to your computer.
- With a scanner, you can convert a printed picture, drawing, or diagram to a digital file.

If you receive a picture from a source other than yourself, do not use the file until you are certain it does not contain a virus. A **virus** is a computer program that can damage files and programs on your computer. Use an antivirus program to verify that any files you use are virus free.

To Center Another Paragraph

In the flyer, the digital picture of a surfer should be centered on the blank line below the headline. The blank paragraph below the headline currently is left-aligned. The following steps center this paragraph.

1 Click Home on the ribbon to display the Home tab.

2 Click somewhere in the paragraph to be centered (in this case, the blank line below the headline) to position the insertion point in the paragraph to be formatted.

3 Click the Center button (Home tab | Paragraph group) to center the paragraph containing the insertion point (shown in Figure 1–46).

To Insert a Picture

1 ENTER TEXT | 2 FORMAT TEXT | **3 INSERT PICTURE**
4 FORMAT PICTURE | 5 ENHANCE PAGE | 6 CORRECT & REVISE

The next step in creating the flyer is to insert a digital picture of a surfer in the flyer on the blank line below the headline. The picture, which was taken with a digital camera, is available on the Data Files. Please contact your instructor for information about accessing Data Files.

The following steps insert a picture, which, in this example, is located in the Module 01 folder in the Data Files folder. ***Why?*** *It is good practice to organize and store files in folders so that you easily can find the files at a later date.*

1

- If necessary, position the insertion point at the location where you want to insert the picture (in this case, on the centered blank paragraph below the headline).

- Click Insert on the ribbon to display the Insert tab (Figure 1–46).

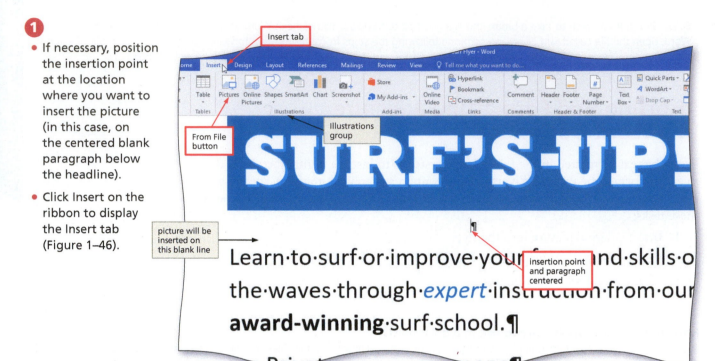

Figure 1–46

2

- Click the From File button (Insert tab | Illustrations group) (shown in Figure 1–46) to display the Insert Picture dialog box (shown in Figure 1–47).

3

- Navigate to the desired picture location (in this case, the Module 01 folder in the Data Files folder). For a detailed example of this procedure, refer to Steps 4a and 4b in the To Save a File in a Folder section in the Office and Windows module at the beginning of this book.

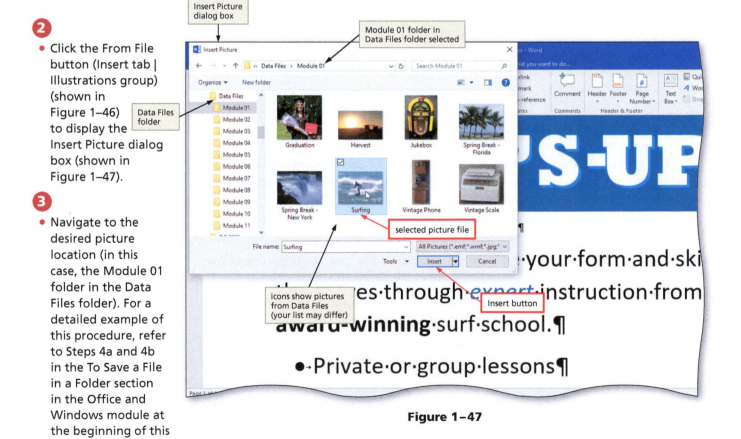

Figure 1–47

- Click Surfing to select the file (Figure 1–47).

4

- Click the Insert button (Insert Picture dialog box) to insert the picture at the location of the insertion point in the document (Figure 1–48).

Q&A What are the symbols around the picture?
A selected graphic appears surrounded by a **selection rectangle**, which has small squares and circles, called **sizing handles**, at each corner and middle location.

What is the purpose of the Layout Options button?
When you click the Layout Options button, Word provides options for changing how the graphic is positioned with text in the document.

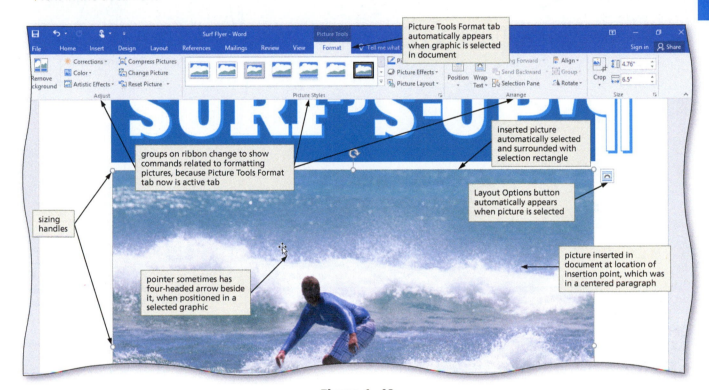

Figure 1–48

How do you know where to position a graphic on a flyer?
The content, size, shape, position, and format of a graphic should capture the interest of passersby, enticing them to stop and read the flyer. Often, the graphic is the center of attention and visually the largest element on a flyer. If you use colors in the graphical image, be sure they are part of the document's color scheme.

1 ENTER TEXT | 2 FORMAT TEXT | 3 INSERT PICTURE
4 FORMAT PICTURE | 5 ENHANCE PAGE | 6 CORRECT & REVISE

CONSIDER THIS

To Zoom the Document

In the steps in the following sections, you will work with the picture just inserted. The next task is to adjust the zoom percentage. *Why? Currently, you can see only a small amount of text with the picture. Seeing more of the document at once helps you determine the appropriate size for the picture.* The following step zooms the document.

1

  Experiment

- Repeatedly click the Zoom Out and Zoom In buttons on the status bar and watch the size of the document change in the document window.

Q&A | What if I am using a touch screen?
Repeatedly pinch (move two fingers together on the screen) and stretch (move two fingers apart on the screen) and watch the size of the document change in the document window.

• Click the Zoom Out or Zoom In button as many times as necessary until the Zoom button on the status bar displays 40% on its face (Figure 1–49).

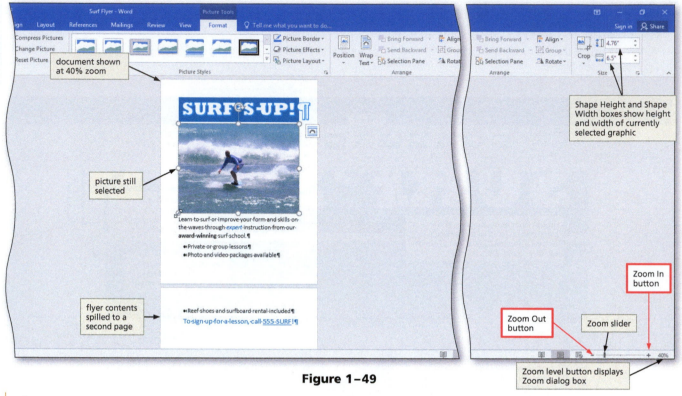

Figure 1–49

Other Ways

1. Drag Zoom slider on status bar	2. Click Zoom level button on status bar, select desired zoom percent or type (Zoom dialog box), click OK button	3. Click Zoom button (View tab | Zoom group), select desired zoom percent or type (Zoom dialog box), click OK button

To Resize a Graphic

1 ENTER TEXT | 2 FORMAT TEXT | 3 INSERT PICTURE
4 FORMAT PICTURE | 5 ENHANCE PAGE | 6 CORRECT & REVISE

Resizing includes both increasing and reducing the size of a graphic. The next step is to resize the picture so that it is smaller in the flyer. **Why?** *You want the graphic and all the text on the flyer to fit on a single sheet of paper.* The following steps resize a selected graphic.

• Be sure the graphic still is selected.

Q&A | What if my graphic (picture) is not selected?
To select a graphic, click it.

• Point to the lower-left corner sizing handle on the picture so that the pointer shape changes to a two-headed arrow (Figure 1–50).

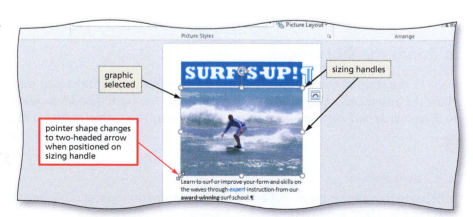

Figure 1–50

2

- Drag the sizing handle diagonally inward until the lower-left corner of the picture is positioned approximately as shown in Figure 1–51. Do not release the mouse button at this point.

Q&A What if I am using a touch screen?
Drag a corner of the graphic, without lifting your finger, until the graphic is the desired size.

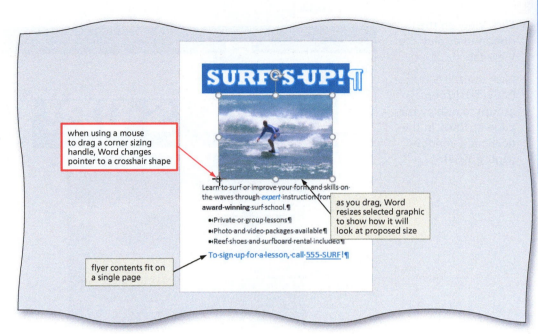

Figure 1–51

3

- Release the mouse button to resize the graphic, which, in this case, should have a height of about 3.7" and a width of about 5.06".

Q&A How can I see the height and width measurements?
Look in the Size group on the Picture Tools Format tab to see the height and width measurements of the currently selected graphic (shown in Figure 1–49).

What if the graphic is the wrong size?
Repeat Steps 1, 2, and 3, or enter the desired height and width values in the Shape Height and Shape Width boxes (Picture Tools Format tab | Size group).

What if I want to return a graphic to its original size and start again?
With the graphic selected, click the Size Dialog Box Launcher (Picture Tools Format tab | Size group), click the Size tab (Layout dialog box), click the Reset button, and then click the OK button.

Other Ways

1. Enter height and width of graphic in Shape Height and Shape Width boxes (Picture Tools Format tab | Size group)

2. Click Advanced Layout: Size Dialog Box Launcher (Picture Tools Format tab | Size group), click Size tab (Layout dialog box), enter desired height and width values in boxes, click OK button

1 ENTER TEXT | 2 FORMAT TEXT | 3 INSERT PICTURE
4 FORMAT PICTURE | 5 ENHANCE PAGE | 6 CORRECT & REVISE

To Zoom 100%

In the next series of steps, you will format the picture. Earlier in this module, you changed the zoom to 40% so that you could see more of the page while resizing the graphic. The following step zooms the screen to 100%. **Why?** *You want the contents of the image to be enlarged a bit, while still seeing some of the text in the document.*

1

- Click View on the ribbon to display the View tab.

- Click the 100% button (View tab | Zoom group) to display the page at 100% in the document window (Figure 1–52).

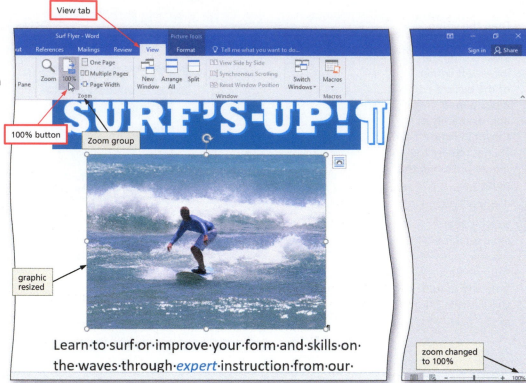

Figure 1–52

Other Ways

1. Click Zoom button (View tab | Zoom group), click 100% (Zoom dialog box), click OK button

To Apply a Picture Style

1 ENTER TEXT | 2 FORMAT TEXT | 3 INSERT PICTURE
4 FORMAT PICTURE | 5 ENHANCE PAGE | 6 CORRECT & REVISE

A **style** is a named group of formatting characteristics. Word provides more than 25 picture styles. **Why?** *Picture styles enable you easily to change a picture's look to a more visually appealing style, including a variety of shapes, angles, borders, and reflections.* The flyer in this module uses a style that applies an oval shape to the picture. The following steps apply a picture style to a picture.

1

- Ensure the graphic still is selected and then click Picture Tools Format on the ribbon to display the Picture Tools Format tab (Figure 1–53).

Q&A

What if my graphic (picture) is not selected?
To select a graphic, click it.

What is the white circle attached to top of the selected graphic?
It is called a rotate handle. When you drag a graphic's **rotate handle**, the graphic moves in either a clockwise or counterclockwise direction.

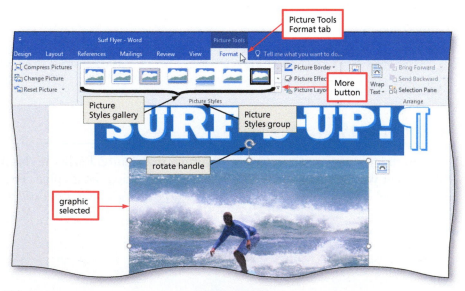

Figure 1–53

2

- Click the More button in the Picture Styles gallery (Picture Tools Format tab | Picture Styles group) (shown in Figure 1–53) to expand the gallery.

- Point to 'Soft Edge Oval' in the Picture Styles gallery to display a live preview of that style applied to the picture in the document (Figure 1–54).

 Experiment

- Point to various picture styles in the Picture Styles gallery and watch the style of the picture change in the document window.

3

- Click 'Soft Edge Oval' in the Picture Styles gallery (sixth style in third row) to apply the style to the selected picture.

Learn·to·surf·or·improve·your·form·and·skills·on·

Figure 1–54

Other Ways

1. Right-click picture, click 'Picture Styles' on mini toolbar, select desired style

---

To Apply Picture Effects

1 ENTER TEXT | 2 FORMAT TEXT | 3 INSERT PICTURE
4 FORMAT PICTURE | 5 ENHANCE PAGE | 6 CORRECT & REVISE

Word provides a variety of picture effects, such as shadows, reflections, glow, soft edges, bevel, and 3-D rotation. The difference between the effects and the styles is that each effect has several options, providing you with more control over the exact look of the image.

In this flyer, the picture has a slight lime green glow effect and beveled edges. The following steps apply picture effects to the selected picture. *Why? Picture effects enable you to further customize a picture.*

1

- With the picture still selected, click the Picture Effects button (Picture Tools Format tab | Picture Styles group) to display the Picture Effects menu.

- Point to Glow on the Picture Effects menu to display the Glow gallery.

- Point to 'Lime, 5 pt glow, Accent color 6' in the Glow Variations area (rightmost glow in first row) to display a live preview of the selected glow effect applied to the picture in the document window (Figure 1–55).

 Experiment

- If you are using a mouse, point to various glow effects in the Glow gallery and watch the picture change in the document window.

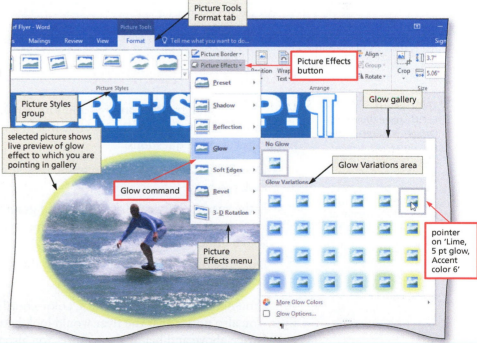

Figure 1–55

2

- Click 'Lime, 5 pt glow, Accent color 6' in the Glow gallery to apply the selected picture effect.

Q&A What if I wanted to discard formatting applied to a picture?
You would click the Reset Picture button (Picture Tools Format tab | Adjust group). To reset formatting and size, you would click the Reset Picture arrow (Picture Tools Format tab | Adjust group) and then click 'Reset Picture & Size' on the Reset Picture menu.

3

- Click the Picture Effects button (Picture Tools Format tab | Picture Styles group) to display the Picture Effects menu again.

- Point to Bevel on the Picture Effects menu to display the Bevel gallery.

- Point to Angle in the Bevel area (first effect in second row) to display a live preview of the selected bevel effect applied to the picture in the document window (Figure 1–56).

🔎 **Experiment**

- If you are using a mouse, point to various bevel effects in the Bevel gallery and watch the picture change in the document window.

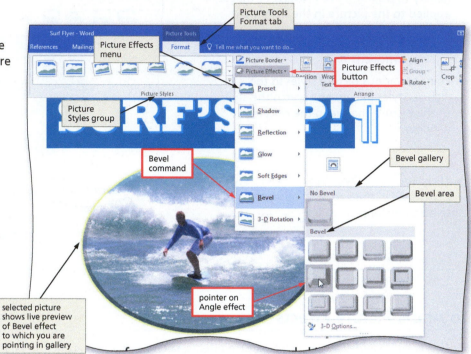

Figure 1–56

4

- Click Angle in the Bevel gallery to apply the selected picture effect.

Other Ways
1. Right-click picture (or, if using touch, tap 'Show Context Menu' button on mini toolbar), click Format Object or Format Picture on shortcut menu, click Effects button (Format Picture task pane), select desired options, click Close button 2. Click Format Shape Dialog Box Launcher (Picture Tools Format tab | Picture Styles group), click Effects button (Format Picture task pane), select desired options, click Close button

Enhancing the Page

With the text and graphics entered and formatted, the next step is to look at the page as a whole and determine if it looks finished in its current state. As you review the page, answer these questions:

- Does it need a page border to frame its contents, or would a page border make it look too busy?

- Is the spacing between paragraphs and graphics on the page adequate? Do any sections of text or graphics look as if they are positioned too closely to the items above or below them?

- Does the flyer have too much space at the top or bottom? Should the contents be centered vertically?

You determine that a graphical, color-coordinated border would enhance the flyer. You also notice that the flyer would look better proportioned if it had a little more space above and below the picture. You also want to ensure that the contents are centered vertically. The following sections make these enhancements to the flyer.

To Add a Page Border

In Word, you can add a border around the perimeter of an entire page. The flyer in this module has a lime border. *Why? This border color complements the color of the flyer contents.* The following steps add a page border.

- Click Design on the ribbon to display the Design tab.

- Click the 'Borders and Shading' button (Design tab | Page Background group) to display the Borders and Shading dialog box (Figure 1–57).

Figure 1–57

- Scroll to, if necessary, and then click the sixth border style in the Style list (Borders and Shading dialog box) to select the style.

- Click the Color arrow to display a Color palette (Figure 1–58).

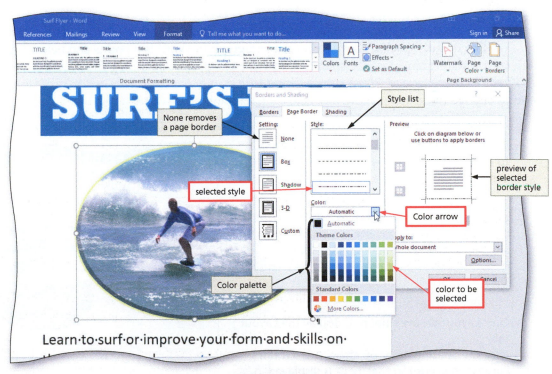

Figure 1–58

3

- Click 'Lime, Accent 6, Lighter 40%' (rightmost color in fourth row) in the Color palette to select the color for the page border.

- Click the Width arrow to display the Width list and then click 4 ½ pt to select the thickness of the page border (Figure 1–59).

4

- Click the OK button to add the border to the page (shown in Figure 1–60).

Q&A What if I wanted to remove the border?
You would click None in the Setting list in the Borders and Shading dialog box.

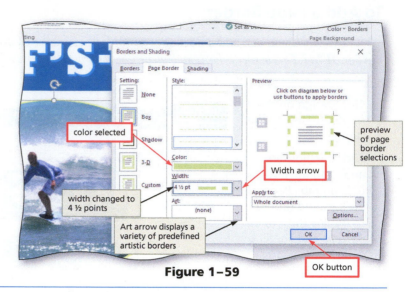

Figure 1–59

To Zoom One Page

The next steps zoom one page so that you can see the entire page on the screen at once.

1 Click View on the ribbon to display the View tab.

2 Click the One Page button (View tab | Zoom group) to display the entire page in the document window as large as possible.

To Change Spacing before and after Paragraphs

1 ENTER TEXT | 2 FORMAT TEXT | 3 INSERT PICTURE
4 FORMAT PICTURE | 5 ENHANCE PAGE | 6 CORRECT & REVISE

The default spacing above (before) a paragraph in Word is 0 points and below (after) is 8 points. In the flyer, you want to increase the spacing below the paragraph containing the headline and above the signature line. *Why? The flyer spacing will look more balanced with spacing increased above and below these paragraphs.* The following steps change the spacing above and below a paragraph.

1

- Position the insertion point in the paragraph to be adjusted, in this case, the paragraph containing the headline.

Q&A What happened to the Picture Tools Format tab?

When you click outside of a graphic or press a key to scroll through a document, Word deselects the graphic and removes the Picture Tools Format tab from the screen. That is, this tab appears only when a graphic is selected.

- Click Layout on the ribbon to display the Layout tab.

- Click the Spacing After up arrow (Layout tab | Paragraph group) so that 12 pt is displayed in the Spacing After box to increase the space below the current paragraph (Figure 1–60).

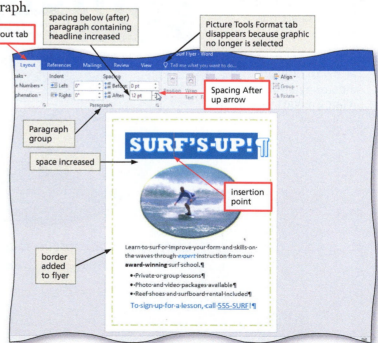

Figure 1–60

• Position the insertion point in the paragraph to be adjusted, in this case, the paragraph containing the signature line.

• Click the Spacing Before up arrow (Layout tab | Paragraph group) as many times as necessary so that 12 pt is displayed in the Spacing Before box to increase the space above the current paragraph (Figure 1–61).

• If the text flows to two pages, reduce the spacing above and below paragraphs as necessary.

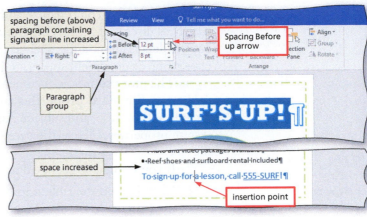

Figure 1–61

Other Ways

1. Right-click paragraph (or, if using touch, tap 'Show Context Menu' button on mini toolbar), click Paragraph on shortcut menu, click Indents and Spacing tab (Paragraph dialog box), enter spacing before and after values, click OK button

2. Click Paragraph Settings Dialog Box Launcher (Home tab or Layout tab | Paragraph group), click Indents and Spacing tab (Paragraph dialog box), enter spacing before and after values, click OK button

---

1 ENTER TEXT | 2 FORMAT TEXT | 3 INSERT PICTURE
4 FORMAT PICTURE | 5 ENHANCE PAGE | 6 CORRECT & REVISE

To Center Page Contents Vertically

In Word, you can center the page contents vertically. *Why? This places the same amount of space at the top and bottom of the page.* The following steps center page contents vertically.

• If necessary, click Layout on the ribbon to display the Layout tab.

• Click the Page Setup Dialog Box Launcher (Layout tab | Page Setup group) to display the Page Setup dialog box.

• Click the Layout tab (Page Setup dialog box) to display the Layout sheet (Figure 1–62).

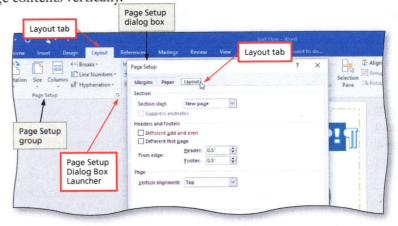

Figure 1–62

❷

• Click the Vertical alignment arrow (Page Setup dialog box) to display the list of alignment options and then click Center in the list (Figure 1–63).

❸

• Click the OK button to center the page contents vertically on the screen (shown in Figure 1–1 at the beginning of this module).

Q&A What if I wanted to change the alignment back?
You would select the Top vertical alignment from the Vertical alignment list in the Layout sheet (Page Setup dialog box).

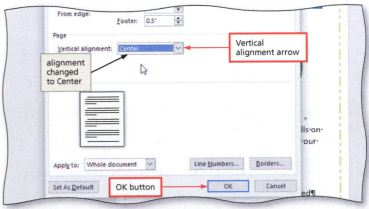

Figure 1–63

TO CHANGE DOCUMENT PROPERTIES

Word helps you organize and identify your files by using **document properties**, which, as discussed in the Office and Windows module at the beginning of this book, are the details about a file, such as the project author, title, and subject. For example, a class name or document topic can describe the file's purpose or content.

The more common document properties are standard and automatically updated properties. **Standard properties** are associated with all Microsoft Office files and include author, title, and subject. **Automatically updated properties** include file system properties, such as the date you create or change a file, and statistics, such as the file size.

If you wanted to change document properties, you would follow these steps.

1. Click File on the ribbon to open the Backstage view and then, if necessary, click the Info tab in the Backstage view to display the Info gallery.

2. If the property you wish to change is displayed in the Properties list in the right pane of the Info gallery, try to click to the right of the property. If a text box appears to the right of the property, type the text for the property in the text box and then click the Back button in the upper-left corner of the Backstage view to return to the Word window. Skip the remaining steps.

3. If the property you wish to change is not displayed in the Properties list in the right pane of the Info gallery or you cannot change it in the Info gallery, click the Properties button in the right pane to display the Properties menu and then click Advanced Properties on the Properties menu to display the Properties dialog box. If necessary, click the Summary tab (Properties dialog box) to display the Summary sheet, fill in the appropriate text boxes, and then click the OK button.

Q&A Why are some of the document properties in the dialog box already filled in?
The person who installed Office 2016 on your computer or network may have set or customized the properties.

BTW
Printing Document Properties
To print document properties, click File on the ribbon to open the Backstage view, click the Print tab in the Backstage view to display the Print gallery, click the first button in the Settings area to display a list of options specifying what you can print, click Document Info in the list to specify you want to print the document properties instead of the actual document, and then click the Print button in the Print gallery to print the document properties on the currently selected printer.

To Save the Document and Exit Word

Although you still need to make some edits to this document, you want to exit Word and resume working on the project at a later time. Thus, the following steps save the document and exit Word. For a detailed example of the procedure summarized below, refer to the Office and Windows module at the beginning of this book.

1 Save the flyer again on the same storage location with the same file name.

2 Close the open document and exit Word.

Break Point: If you wish to take a break, this is a good place to do so. To resume at a later time, continue following the steps from this location forward.

Correcting Errors and Revising a Document

After creating a document, you may need to change it. For example, the document may contain an error, or new circumstances may require you to add text to the document.

Types of Changes Made to Documents

The types of changes made to documents normally fall into one of the three following categories: additions, deletions, or modifications.

Additions Additional words, sentences, or paragraphs may be required in a document. Additions occur when you omit text from a document and want to insert it later. For example, you may want to add your email address to the flyer.

Deletions Sometimes, text in a document is incorrect or no longer is needed. For example, you may discover that the lessons no longer include reef shoes. In this case, you would delete the words, reef shoes, from the flyer.

Modifications If an error is made in a document or changes take place that affect the document, you might have to revise a word(s) in the text. For example, the phone number may change.

To Run Word, Open a Document, and Specify Settings

Once you have created and saved a document, you may need to retrieve it from storage. For example, you might want to revise the document or distribute it. Earlier in this module you saved the flyer using the file name, Surf Flyer. The following steps run Word, open this document, and specify settings. For a detailed example of the procedures summarized below for running Word or opening a document, refer to the Office and Windows module.

1 Run Word.

2 Open the document named Surf Flyer from the Recent list or use the Open dialog box to navigate to the location of the file and then open it in the Word window.

3 If the Word window is not maximized, click the Maximize button on its title bar to maximize the window.

4 Click View on the ribbon to display the View tab and then click the 100% button (View tab | Zoom group) to display the page at 100% in the document window.

BTW

Word Help
At any time while using Word, you can find answers to questions and display information about various topics through Word Help. Used properly, this form of assistance can increase your productivity and reduce your frustrations by minimizing the time you spend learning how to use Word. For instructions about Word Help and exercises that will help you gain confidence in using it, read the Office and Windows module at the beginning of this book.

1 ENTER TEXT | 2 FORMAT TEXT | 3 INSERT PICTURE

4 FORMAT PICTURE | 5 ENHANCE PAGE | **6 CORRECT & REVISE**

To Insert Text in an Existing Document

Word inserts text to the left of the insertion point. The text to the right of the insertion point moves to the right and downward to fit the new text. The following steps insert the word, today, to the left of the word, or, in the flyer. *Why? These steps illustrate the process of inserting text.*

1

- Scroll through the document and then click to the left of the location of text to be inserted (in this case, the o in or) to position the insertion point where text should be inserted (Figure 1–64).

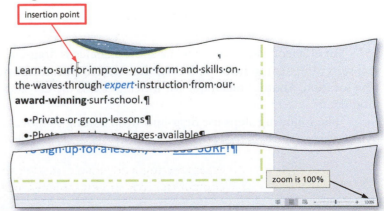

Figure 1–64

2

- Type **today** and then press the SPACEBAR to insert the word to the left of the insertion point (Figure 1–65).

Q&A Why did the text move to the right as I typed? In Word, the default typing mode is **insert mode**, which means as you type a character, Word moves all the characters to the right of the typed character one position to the right.

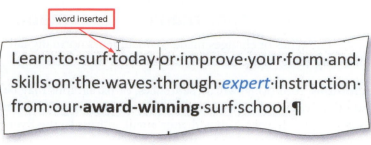

word inserted

Learn·to·surf·today·or·improve·your·form·and· skills·on·the·waves·through·*expert*·instruction· from·our·**award-winning**·surf·school.¶

Figure 1–65

To Delete Text

1 ENTER TEXT | 2 FORMAT TEXT | 3 INSERT PICTURE
4 FORMAT PICTURE | 5 ENHANCE PAGE | **6 CORRECT & REVISE**

It is not unusual to type incorrect characters or words in a document. As discussed earlier in this module, you can click the Undo button on the Quick Access Toolbar to undo a command or action immediately — this includes typing. Word also provides other methods of correcting typing errors.

To delete an incorrect character in a document, simply click next to the incorrect character and then press the BACKSPACE key to erase to the left of the insertion point, or press the DELETE key to erase to the right of the insertion point.

To delete a word or phrase, you first must select the word or phrase. The following steps select the word, today, which was just added in the previous steps, and then delete the selection. *Why? These steps illustrate the process of selecting a word and then deleting selected text.*

1

- Double-click the word to be selected (in this case, today) to select the word (Figure 1–66).

2

- Press the DELETE key to delete the selected text.

Q&A What if I am using a touch screen? Tap the selected text to display the mini toolbar and then tap the Cut button on the mini toolbar to delete the selected text.

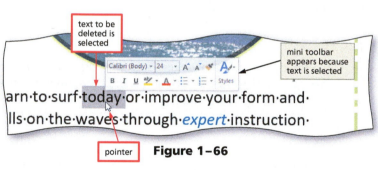

text to be deleted is selected

mini toolbar appears because text is selected

arn·to·surf·today·or·improve·your·form·and· lls·on·the·waves·through·*expert*·instruction·

pointer **Figure 1–66**

Other Ways

1. Right-click selected item, click Cut on shortcut menu
2. Select item, press BACKSPACE to delete to left of insertion point or press DELETE to delete to right of insertion point
3. Select item, press CTRL+X

To Move Text

1 ENTER TEXT | 2 FORMAT TEXT | 3 INSERT PICTURE
4 FORMAT PICTURE | 5 ENHANCE PAGE | **6 CORRECT & REVISE**

An efficient way to move text a short distance is drag-and-drop editing. With **drag-and-drop editing**, you select the item to be moved, drag the selected item to the new location, and then drop, or insert, it in the new location. Another technique for moving text is the cut-and-paste technique, which is discussed in the next module.

The following steps use drag-and-drop editing to move text. *Why? While proofreading the flyer, you realize that the body copy would read better if the last two bulleted paragraphs were reversed.*

1
- Position the pointer in the paragraph to be moved (in this case, the last bulleted item) and then triple-click to select the paragraph.
- With the pointer in the selected text, press and hold down the mouse button, which displays a small dotted box with the pointer (Figure 1–67).

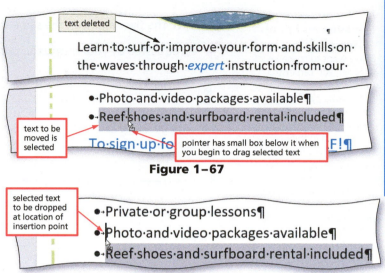

Figure 1–67

2
- Drag the insertion point to the location where the selected text is to be moved, as shown in Figure 1–68.

Figure 1–68

3
- Release the mouse button to move the selected text to the location of the dotted insertion point (Figure 1–69).

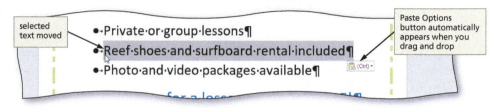

Figure 1–69

Q&A What if I accidentally drag text to the wrong location?
Click the Undo button on the Quick Access Toolbar and try again.

Can I use drag-and-drop editing to move any selected item?
Yes, you can select words, sentences, phrases, and graphics and then use drag-and-drop editing to move them.

What is the purpose of the Paste Options button?
If you click the Paste Options button, a menu appears that allows you to change the format of the item that was moved. The next module discusses the Paste Options menu.

- Click anywhere in the document window to remove the selection from the bulleted item.

Q&A What if I am using a touch screen?
If you have a stylus, you can follow Steps 1 through 3 using the stylus. If you are using your finger, you will need to use the cut-and-paste technique: tap to position the insertion point in the text to be moved and then drag the selection handles as necessary to select the text that you want to move; tap the selection to display the mini toolbar and then tap the Cut button on the mini toolbar to remove the text; tap to position the insertion point at the location where you want to move the text; display the Home tab and then tap the Paste button on the Home tab to place the text at the location of the insertion point. The next module discusses this procedure in more depth.

Other Ways

1. Click Cut button (Home tab | Clipboard group), click where text or object is to be pasted, click Paste button (Home tab | Clipboard group)

2. Right-click selected text, click Cut on mini toolbar or shortcut menu, right-click where text or object is to be pasted, click Paste on mini toolbar or 'Keep Source Formatting' on shortcut menu

3. Press CTRL+X, position insertion point where text or object is to be pasted, press CTRL+V

To Save and Print the Document

It is a good practice to save a document before printing it, in the event you experience difficulties printing. The following steps save and print the document. For a detailed example of the procedure summarized next for saving and printing a document, refer to the Office and Windows module at the beginning of this book.

BTW

Conserving Ink and Toner

If you want to conserve ink or toner, you can instruct Word to print draft quality documents by clicking File on the ribbon to open the Backstage view, clicking the Options tab in the Backstage view to display the Word Options dialog box, clicking Advanced in the left pane (Word Options dialog box), scrolling to the Print area in the right pane, placing a check mark in the 'Use draft quality' check box, and then clicking the OK button. Then, use the Backstage view to print the document as usual.

1 Save the flyer again on the same storage location with the same file name.

2 If requested by your instructor, print the flyer.

Q&A What if one or more of my borders do not print?

Click the Page Borders button (Design tab | Page Background group), click the Options button (Borders and Shading dialog box), click the Measure from arrow and click Text, change the four text boxes to 15 pt, and then click the OK button in each dialog box. Try printing the document again. If the borders still do not print, adjust the boxes in the dialog box to a number smaller than 15 point.

To Switch to Read Mode

1 ENTER TEXT | 2 FORMAT TEXT | 3 INSERT PICTURE
4 FORMAT PICTURE | 5 ENHANCE PAGE | **6 CORRECT & REVISE**

Some users prefer reading a document on-screen instead of on paper. *Why? If you are not composing a document, you can switch to **Read mode**, which hides the ribbon and other writing tools so that more content fits on the screen. Read mode is intended to make it easier to read a document.* The following step switches from Print Layout view to Read mode.

- Click the Read Mode button on the status bar to switch to Read mode (Figure 1–70).

Experiment

- Click the arrows to advance forward and then move backward through the document.

Q&A Besides reading, what can I do in Read mode?

You can zoom, copy text, highlight text, search, add comments, and more.

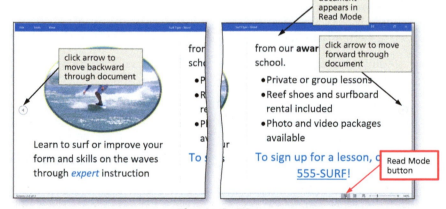

Figure 1–70

Other Ways

1. Click Read Mode button (View tab | Views group)

BTW

Distributing a Document

Instead of printing and distributing a hard copy of a document, you can distribute the document electronically. Options include sending the document via email; posting it on cloud storage (such as OneDrive) and sharing the file with others; posting it on social media, a blog, or other website; and sharing a link associated with an online location of the document. You also can create and share a PDF or XPS image of the document, so that users can view the file in Acrobat Reader or XPS Viewer instead of in Word.

To Switch to Print Layout View

1 ENTER TEXT | 2 FORMAT TEXT | 3 INSERT PICTURE
4 FORMAT PICTURE | 5 ENHANCE PAGE | **6 CORRECT & REVISE**

The next steps switch back to Print Layout view. *Why? If you want to show the document on a mock sheet of paper in the document window, along with the ribbon and other writing tools, you should switch to Print Layout view.* The following step switches to Print Layout view.

- Click the Print Layout button on the status bar to switch to Print Layout view (Figure 1–71).

- Because the project now is complete, you can exit Word.

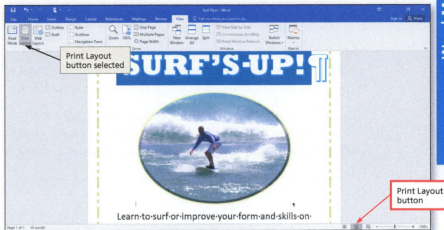

Figure 1–71

Other Ways

1. Click Print Layout button (View tab | Views group)   2. Click View on the ribbon, click Edit Document

---

Summary

In this module, you have learned how to enter text in a document, correct spelling errors as you type, format paragraphs and characters, insert and format a picture, add a page border, adjust paragraph and page spacing, and correct errors and revise a document.

What decisions will you need to make when creating your next flyer?

Use these guidelines as you complete the assignments in this module and create your own flyers outside of this class.

1. Choose the text for the headline, body copy, and signature line — using as few words as possible to make a point.

2. Format various elements of the text.

   a) Select appropriate font sizes for text in the headline, body copy, and signature line.
   b) Select appropriate fonts for text in the headline, body copy, and signature line.
   c) Adjust paragraph alignment, as appropriate.
   d) Highlight key paragraphs with bullets.
   e) Emphasize important words.
   f) Use color to convey meaning and add appeal.

3. Find an eye-catching graphic(s) that conveys the overall message and meaning of the flyer.

4. Establish where to position and how to format the graphical image(s) so that the image grabs the attention of passersby and draws them into reading the flyer.

5. Determine whether the flyer needs enhancements, such as a graphical, color-coordinated border, or spacing adjustments to improve readability or overall appearance.

6. Correct errors and revise the document as necessary.

   a) Post the flyer on a wall and make sure all text and images are legible from a distance.
   b) Ask someone else to read the flyer and give you suggestions for improvements.

7. Determine the best method for distributing the document, such as printing, sending via email, or posting on the web or social media.

CONSIDER THIS: PLAN AHEAD

Apply Your Knowledge

Reinforce the skills and apply the concepts you learned in this module.

Modifying Text and Formatting a Document

Note: To complete this assignment, you will be required to use the Data Files. Please contact your instructor for information about accessing the Data Files.

Instructions: Run Word. Open the document, Apply 1–1 Graduation Flyer Unformatted, which is located in the Data Files. The flyer you open contains an unformatted flyer. You are to modify text, format paragraphs and characters, and insert a picture in the flyer to create the flyer shown in Figure 1–72.

Figure 1–72

Perform the following tasks:

1. Correct each spelling (red wavy underline) and grammar (green and blue wavy underlines) error by right-clicking the flagged text and then clicking the appropriate correction on the shortcut menu.

2. Delete the word, degree, in the sentence below the headline.

3. Insert the word, need, between the words, or directions (so that it reads: Questions or need directions?), in the second to last line of the flyer.

4. Change the word, on, to the word, by, in the last line so that the text reads: Please RSVP by May 18.

5. If requested by your instructor, change the phone number in the flyer to your phone number.

6. Center the headline and the last two paragraphs of the flyer.

7. Select the third, fourth, and fifth paragraphs of text in the flyer and add bullets to the selected paragraphs.

8. Change the theme colors to the Blue II color scheme.

9. Change the font and font size of the headline to 48-point Arial Rounded MT Bold, or a similar font. Change the case of the word, Celebrate, in the headline to uppercase letters. Apply the text effect called Fill - Dark Green, Accent 1, Outline - Background 1, Hard Shadow - Accent 1 to the entire headline. Change the font color of the headline text to Dark Green, Accent 5, Darker 25%.

10. Change the font size of the sentence below the headline, the bulleted list, and the last line of flyer to 26 point.

11. Use the mini toolbar to change the font size of the sentence below the bulleted list to 18 point.

12. Switch the last two bulleted paragraphs. That is, select the '125 Park Court in Condor' bullet and move it so that it is the second bulleted paragraph.

13. Select the words, open house, in the paragraph below the headline and italicize these words. Undo this change and then redo the change.

14. Select the text, Saturday, May 27, in the first bulleted paragraph and bold this text. Change the font color of this same text to Dark Red.

15. Underline the word, and, in the third bulleted paragraph.

16. Bold the text, Please RSVP by May 18., in the last line of the flyer. Shade this same text Dark Green, Accent 5, Darker 50%. If the font color does not automatically change to a lighter color, change its color to White, Background 1.

17. Change the zoom so that the entire page is visible in the document window.

18. Insert the picture of the graduate centered on the blank line below the headline. The picture is called Graduation and is available on the Data Files. Resize the picture so that it is approximately 2.9" × 2.89". Apply the Simple Frame, Black picture style to the inserted picture.

19. Change the spacing before the first bulleted paragraph to 12 points and the spacing after the last bulleted paragraph to 24 points.

20. The entire flyer should fit on a single page. If it flows to two pages, resize the picture or decrease spacing before and after paragraphs until the entire flyer text fits on a single page.

21. Change the zoom to text width, then page width, then 100% and notice the differences.

22. If requested by your instructor, enter the text, Graduation Open House, as the keywords in the document properties. Change the other document properties, as specified by your instructor.

23. Click File on the ribbon and then click Save As. Save the document using the file name, Apply 1–1 Graduation Flyer Formatted.

24. Print the document. Switch to Read Mode and browse pages through the document. Switch to Print Layout view.

25. Submit the revised document, shown in Figure 1–72, in the format specified by your instructor.

26. Exit Word.

27. ✳ If this flyer were announcing a victory parade instead of a graduation, which color scheme would you apply and why?

Extend Your Knowledge

Extend the skills you learned in this module and experiment with new skills. You may need to use Help to complete the assignment.

Modifying Text and Picture Formats and Adding Page Borders

Note: To complete this assignment, you will be required to use the Data Files. Please contact your instructor for information about accessing the Data Files.

Figure 1–73

Instructions: Run Word. Open the document, Extend 1–1 Painting Lessons Flyer Draft, from the Data Files. You will enhance the look of the flyer shown in Figure 1–73. *Hint:* Remember, if you make a mistake while formatting the picture, you can reset it by using the Reset Picture button or Reset Picture arrow (Picture Tools Format tab | Adjust group).

Perform the following tasks:

1. Use Help to learn about the following: remove bullets, grow font, shrink font, art page borders, decorative underline(s), picture bullets, picture border shading, picture border color, shadow picture effects, and color saturation and tone.

2. Remove the bullet from the last paragraph of the flyer.

3. Select the text, Painting Lessons, and use the 'Increase Font Size' button (Home tab | Font group) to increase its font size.

4. Add an art page border to the flyer. If the border is not in color, add color to it if the border supports color.

5. Change the solid underline below the word, all, to a decorative underline. Change the color of the underline.

6. Change the style of the bullets to picture bullet(s). Adjust the hanging indent, if necessary, to align the text in the bulleted list.

7. Change the color of the picture border. Add a shadow picture effect to the picture.

8. Change the color saturation and color tone of the picture.

9. If requested by your instructor, change the name of the art studio (Bakersfield) to your last name.

10. Save the revised document with the file name, Extend 1–1 Painting Lessons Flyer Final, and then submit it in the format specified by your instructor.

11. ✳ In this assignment, you changed the bullets to picture bullets. Which bullet character did you select and why?

Expand Your World

Create a solution that uses cloud or web technologies by learning and investigating on your own from general guidance.

Using Word Online to Create a Flyer with a Picture

Note: To complete this assignment, you will be required to use the Data Files. Please contact your instructor for information about accessing the Data Files.

Instructions: You will use Word Online to prepare a flyer. The text for the unformatted flyer is shown in Figure 1–74. You will enter the text in Word Online and then use its tools to enhance the look of the flyer.

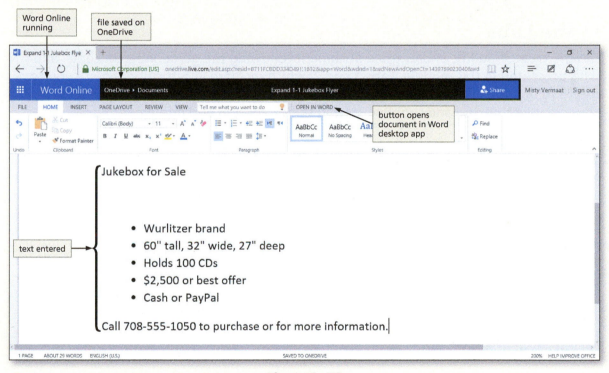

Figure 1–74

Perform the following tasks:

1. Run a browser. Search for the text, Word Online, using a search engine. Visit several websites to learn about Word Online. Navigate to the Office Online website. You will need to sign in to your OneDrive account.

2. Create a new blank Word document using Word Online. Name the document Expand 1–1 Jukebox Flyer.

3. Notice the differences between Word Online and the Word desktop app you used to create the project in this module.

4. Enter the text in the flyer, shown in Figure 1–74, checking spelling as you type.

5. Insert the picture called Jukebox, which is located in the Data Files.

Continued >

Expand Your World *continued*

6. Use the features available in Word Online, along with the concepts and techniques presented in this module, to format this flyer. Be sure to change the font and font size of text, center a paragraph(s), italicize text, color text, underline text, and apply a picture style. Resize the picture. Adjust spacing above and below paragraphs as necessary. The flyer should fit on a single page.

7. If requested by your instructor, replace the phone number in the flyer with your phone number.

8. Save the document again. Click the button to open the document in the Word desktop app. If necessary, sign in to your Microsoft account when prompted. Notice how the document appears in the Word desktop app.

9. Using either Word Online or the Word desktop app, submit the document in the format requested by your instructor. Exit Word Online. If necessary, sign out of your OneDrive account and your Microsoft account in Word.

10. ✳ What is Word Online? Which features that are covered in this module are not available in Word Online? Do you prefer using Word Online or the Word desktop app? Why?

In the Labs

Design, create, modify, and/or use a document following the guidelines, concepts, and skills presented in this module. Labs 1 and 2, which increase in difficulty, require you to create solutions based on what you learned in the module; Lab 3 requires you to apply your creative thinking and problem-solving skills to design and implement a solution.

Lab 1: **Creating a Flyer with a Picture**

Note: To complete this assignment, you will be required to use the Data Files. Please contact your instructor for information about accessing the Data Files.

Problem: Your boss asked you to prepare a flyer that advertises the company's commodity trading seminars. First, you prepare the unformatted flyer shown in Figure 1–75a, and then you format it so that it looks like Figure 1–75b. *Hint:* Remember, if you make a mistake while formatting the flyer, you can use the Undo button on the Quick Access Toolbar to undo your last action.

Commodity Trading?

blank line →

Answer all of your market questions at an expert-led seminar by Jansen Investments!

Agricultural, energy, livestock, and metals commodities

Risk management strategies

Beginning and experienced investors

Located at 1134 Cedar Road in Donner

For more information, visit us on Facebook or call 816-555-7733.

Figure 1–75a Unformatted Text

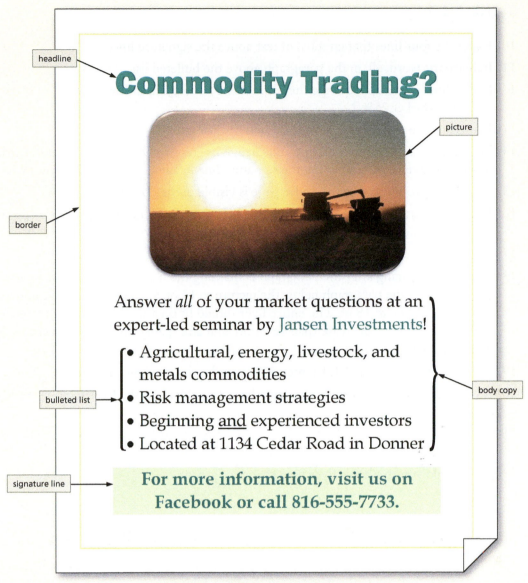

Figure 1–75b Formatted Document

Perform the following tasks:

1. Run Word. Display formatting marks on the screen.

2. Type the flyer text, unformatted, as shown in Figure 1–75a, inserting a blank line between the headline and the body copy. If Word flags any misspelled words as you type, check their spelling and correct them.

3. Save the document using the file name, Lab 1–1 Commodity Trading Flyer.

4. Center the headline and the signature line.

5. Change the theme colors to Green.

6. Change the font size of the headline to 48 point and the font to Franklin Gothic Heavy or a similar font. Apply the text effect called Fill - Dark Teal, Accent 4, Soft Bevel.

7. Change the font size of body copy between the headline and the signature line to 24 point.

8. Change the font size of the signature line to 26 point.

9. Change the font of the body copy and signature line to Book Antiqua.

Continued >

In the Labs *continued*

10. Bullet the four lines (paragraphs) of text above the signature line.

11. Italicize the word, all, in the paragraph above the bulleted list.

12. In the same paragraph, change the color of the words, Jansen Investments, to Dark Teal, Accent 4, Darker 25%.

13. Underline the word, and, in the third bulleted paragraph.

14. Bold the text in the signature line and change its color to Dark Teal, Accent 4, Darker 25%. Shade the paragraph containing the signature line in Lime, Accent 2, Lighter 80%.

15. Change the zoom so that the entire page is visible in the document window.

16. Insert the picture centered on a blank line below the headline. The picture is called Harvest, which is on the Data Files. Reduce the size of the picture to approximately 3.29" × 5.11".

17. Apply the Bevel Rectangle picture style to the inserted picture.

18. Change the spacing after the paragraph containing the headline to 0 pt. Change the spacing above (before) the paragraph below the picture to 12 pt. Change the spacing above (before) the signature line to 18 pt. The entire flyer should fit on a single page. If it flows to two pages, resize the picture or decrease spacing before and after paragraphs until the entire flyer text fits on a single page.

19. Add a ½-pt Lime, Accent 3, Lighter 40% page border, as shown in Figure 1–75b.

20. If requested by your instructor, change the street address in the flyer to your home street address.

21. Save the flyer again with the same file name. Submit the document, shown in Figure 1–75b, in the format specified by your instructor.

22. ✹ Why do you think this flyer used shades of green?

Lab 2: Creating a Flyer with Multiple Pictures

Note: To complete this assignment, you will be required to use the Data Files. Please contact your instructor for information about accessing the Data Files.

Problem: Your boss at Gingham Travel has asked you to prepare a flyer that promotes its business. You prepare the flyer shown in Figure 1–76. *Hint:* Remember, if you make a mistake while formatting the flyer, you can use the Undo button on the Quick Access Toolbar to undo your last action.

Perform the following tasks:

1. Run Word. Type the flyer text, unformatted. If Word flags any misspelled words as you type, check their spelling and correct them.

2. Save the document using the file name, Lab 1–2 Spring Break Flyer.

3. Change the theme colors to the Aspect color scheme.

4. Add bullets to the four paragraphs shown in the figure. Center all paragraphs, except the paragraphs containing the bulleted list.

5. Change the font size of both lines in the headline to 48 point. Change the font of the first line in the headline to Ravie, or a similar font, and the second line in the headline to Arial Rounded MT Bold, or a similar font. Apply this text effect to the first line in the headline: Fill - Dark Purple, Accent 1, Outline - Background 1, Hard Shadow - Accent 1. Shade the second line of the headline to the Dark Green, Accent 4 color, and change the font color to White, Background 1.

Figure 1–76

6. Change the font of all text below the headline to Arial Rounded MT Bold. Change the font size of the company name to 28 point, the company address to 24 point, and the bulleted list and signature line to 22 point.

7. Change the color of the company name and address to Dark Green, Accent 4, Darker 25%. Underline the company name.

8. Italicize the word, and, in the first bulleted paragraph.

9. Bold the word, Discounted, in the second bulleted paragraph. Change the color of this same word to Dark Purple, Accent 5.

10. Shade the signature line to the Dark Green, Accent 4 color, and change the font color to White, Background 1.

11. Change the zoom so that the entire page is visible in the document window.

12. Insert two pictures on the same blank line below the headline. The pictures are called Spring Break - Florida and Spring Break - New York, which are both in the Data Files.

Continued >

In the Labs *continued*

13. Resize the top picture so that it is approximately 2.4" × 3". Apply the Simple Frame, White picture style to both pictures. Apply the Perspective Right 3-D Rotation picture effect to the picture on the left and the Perspective Left 3-D Rotation to the picture on the right. Resize the pictures, if necessary, so that they fit on the same line. Add space as necessary between the two pictures.

14. Change the spacing before and after the paragraph containing the company name to 0 pt, the spacing after the company address to 12 pt, and the spacing before the signature line to 12 pt. The entire flyer should fit on a single page. If it flows to two pages, resize the pictures or decrease spacing before and after paragraphs until the entire flyer text fits on a single page.

15. Add the 6-point page border shown in Figure 1–76, using the color Dark Purple, Accent 5.

16. Center the page contents vertically.

17. If requested by your instructor, change the company name to your last name.

18. Save the flyer again with the same file name. Submit the document, shown in Figure 1–76, in the format specified by your instructor.

19. ✺ Why do you think this flyer used shades of purple and green?

Lab 3: **Consider This: Your Turn**

Design and Create an Antique Store Flyer

Note: To complete this assignment, you will be required to use the Data Files. Please contact your instructor for information about accessing the Data Files.

Problem: Your boss at Antiques Galore has asked you to prepare a flyer that promotes its business.

Perform the following tasks:

Part 1: The flyer should contain two digital pictures appropriately resized; the Data Files contains two pictures called Vintage Phone and Vintage Scale, or you can use your own digital pictures if they are appropriate for the topic of the flyer. The flyer should contain the headline, Antiques Galore, and this signature line: Questions? Call 312-555-2000 or find us on Facebook. The body copy consists of the following text, in any order: We sell all types of vintage items and also buy items individually or as an entire estate. Bring your items in for a free appraisal!; 1,200 square foot shop; Collectibles, costume jewelry, furniture, paintings, pottery, toys, and more!; Affordable items with new inventory daily; Located at 229 Center Street in Snow Hill; Open from 9:00 a.m. to 8:00 p.m. daily.

Use the concepts and techniques presented in this module to create and format this flyer. Be sure to check spelling and grammar. Submit your assignment and answers to the Part 2 critical thinking questions in the format specified by your instructor.

Part 2: ✺ You made several decisions while creating the flyer in this assignment: where to place text, how to format the text (i.e., font, font size, paragraph alignment, bulleted paragraphs, underlines, italics, bold, color, etc.), which graphics to use, where to position the graphics, how to format the graphics, and which page enhancements to add (i.e., borders and spacing). What was the rationale behind each of these decisions? When you proofread the document, what further revisions did you make and why? How would you recommend distributing this flyer?

2 | Creating a Research Paper with References and Sources

Objectives

You will have mastered the material in this module when you can:

- Describe the MLA documentation style for research papers
- Modify a style
- Change line and paragraph spacing in a document
- Use a header to number pages of a document
- Apply formatting using keyboard shortcuts
- Modify paragraph indentation

- Insert and edit citations and their sources
- Add a footnote to a document
- Insert a manual page break
- Create a bibliographical list of sources
- Cut, copy, and paste text
- Find text and replace text
- Find a synonym
- Check spelling and grammar at once
- Look up information

Introduction

In both academic and business environments, you will be asked to write reports. Business reports range from proposals to cost justifications to five-year plans to research findings. Academic reports focus mostly on research findings.

A **research paper** is a document you can use to communicate the results of research findings. To write a research paper, you learn about a particular topic from a variety of sources (research), organize your ideas from the research results, and then present relevant facts and/or opinions that support the topic. Your final research paper combines properly credited outside information along with personal insights. Thus, no two research papers — even if they are about the same topic — will or should be the same.

Project — Research Paper

When preparing a research paper, you should follow a standard documentation style that defines the rules for creating the paper and crediting sources. A variety of documentation styles exists, depending on the nature of the research paper. Each style requires the same basic information; the differences in styles relate to requirements for presenting the information. For example, one documentation style uses the term, bibliography, for the list of sources, whereas another uses the term, references, and yet a third prefers the term, works cited. Two popular documentation styles for research papers are the **Modern Language Association of America** (**MLA**) and **American Psychological Association** (**APA**) styles. This module uses the MLA documentation style because it is used in a wide range of disciplines.

The project in this module follows research paper guidelines and uses Word to create the short research paper shown in Figure 2–1. This paper, which discusses using headphones and earbuds safely, follows the MLA documentation style. Each page contains a page number. The first two pages present the name and course information (student name, instructor name, course name, and paper due date), paper title, an introduction with a thesis statement, details that support the thesis, and a conclusion. This section of the paper also includes references to research sources and a footnote. The third page contains a detailed, alphabetical list of the sources referenced in the research paper. All pages include a header at the upper-right edge of the page.

In this module, you will learn how to create the research paper shown in Figure 2–1. The following roadmap identifies general activities you will perform as you progress through this module:

1. **CHANGE** the **DOCUMENT SETTINGS**.
2. **CREATE** the **HEADER** for each page of the research paper.
3. **TYPE** the **RESEARCH PAPER** text **WITH CITATIONS**.
4. **CREATE** an **ALPHABETICAL WORKS CITED** page.
5. **PROOFREAD AND REVISE** the **RESEARCH PAPER**.

MLA Documentation Style

The research paper in this project follows the guidelines presented by the MLA. To follow the MLA documentation style, use a 12-point Times New Roman or similar font. Double-space text on all pages of the paper using one-inch top, bottom, left, and right margins. Indent the first word of each paragraph one-half inch from the left margin. At the right margin of each page, place a page number one-half inch from the top margin. On each page, precede the page number with your last name.

The MLA documentation style does not require a title page. Instead, place your name and course information in a block at the left margin beginning one inch from the top of the page. Center the title one double-spaced line below your name and course information.

In the text of the paper, place author references in parentheses with the page number(s) of the referenced information. The MLA documentation style uses in-text **parenthetical references** instead of noting each source at the bottom of the page or at the end of the paper. In the MLA documentation style, notes are used only for optional content or bibliographic notes.

If used, content notes elaborate on points discussed in the paper, and bibliographic notes direct the reader to evaluations of statements in a source or provide a means for identifying multiple sources. Use a superscript (raised number) both to signal that a note exists and to sequence the notes (shown in Figure 2–1). Position notes at the bottom of the page as footnotes or at the end of the paper as endnotes. Indent the first line of each note one-half inch from the left margin. Place one space following the superscripted number before beginning the note text. Double-space the note text (shown in Figure 2–1).

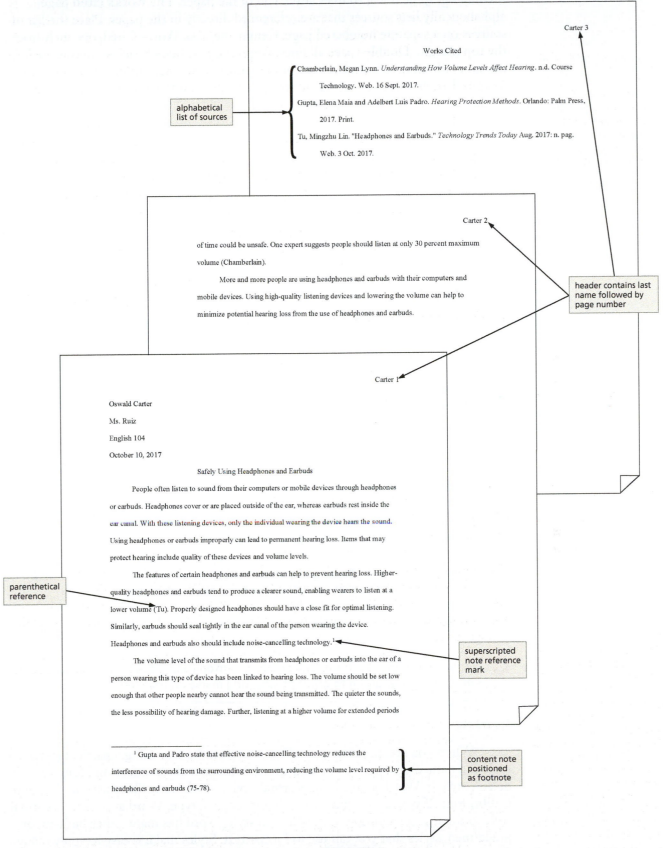

Figure 2–1

The MLA documentation style uses the term, works cited, to refer to the bibliographic list of sources at the end of the paper. The **works cited** page alphabetically lists sources that are referenced directly in the paper. Place the list of sources on a separate numbered page. Center the title, Works Cited, one inch from the top margin. Double-space all lines. Begin the first line of each source at the left margin, indenting subsequent lines of the same source one-half inch from the left margin. List each source by the author's last name or, if the author's name is not available, by the title of the source.

Changing Document Settings

The MLA documentation style defines some global formats that apply to the entire research paper. Some of these formats are the default in Word. For example, the default left, right, top, and bottom margin settings in Word are one inch, which meets the MLA documentation style. You will modify, however, the font, font size, and line and paragraph spacing.

To Run Word and Specify Settings

If you are using a computer to step through the project in this module and you want your screens to match the figures in this book, you should change your screen's resolution to 1366 × 768. For information about how to change a computer's resolution, refer to the Office and Windows module at the beginning of this book.

1 Run Word and create a blank document in the Word window.

2 If the Word window is not maximized, click the Maximize button on its title bar to maximize the window.

3 If the Print Layout button on the status bar is not selected (shown in Figure 2–2), click it so that your screen is in Print Layout view.

4 If Normal (Home tab | Styles group) is not selected in the Styles gallery (shown in Figure 2–2), click it so that your document uses the Normal style.

5 Display the View tab. To display the page the same width as the document window, if necessary, click the Page Width button (View tab | Zoom group).

6 Display the Home tab. If the 'Show/Hide ¶' button (Home tab | Paragraph group) is not selected already, click it to display formatting marks on the screen.

Styles

When you create a document, Word formats the text using a particular style. A **style** is a named group of formatting characteristics, including font and font size. The default style in Word is called the **Normal style**, which most likely uses an 11-point Calibri font. If you do not specify a style for text you type, Word applies the Normal style to the text. In addition to the Normal style, Word has many other built-in, or predefined, styles that you can use to format text. Styles make it easy to apply many formats at once to text. You can modify existing styles and create your own styles. Styles are discussed as they are used in this book.

For an introduction to Office and instructions about how to perform basic tasks in Office apps, read the Office and Windows module at the beginning of this book, where you can learn how to run an application, use the ribbon, save a file, open a file, print a file, exit an application, use Help, and much more.

For an introduction to Windows and instructions about how to perform basic Windows tasks, read the Office and Windows module at the beginning of this book, where you can learn how to resize windows, change screen resolution, create folders, move and rename files, use Windows Help, and much more.

BTW

Style Formats
To see the formats assigned to a particular style in a document, click the Styles Dialog Box Launcher (Home tab | Styles group) and then click the Style Inspector button in the Styles task pane. Position the insertion point in the style in the document and then point to the Paragraph formatting or Text level formatting areas in the Style Inspector task pane to display a ScreenTip describing formats assigned to the location of the insertion point. You also can click the Reveal Formatting button in the Style Inspector task pane or press SHIFT+F1 to display the Reveal Formatting task pane.

To Modify a Style

The MLA documentation style requires that all text in the research paper use a 12-point Times New Roman or similar font. If you change the font and font size using buttons on the ribbon, you will need to make the change many times during the course of creating the paper. *Why? Word formats various areas of a document based on the Normal style, which uses an 11-point Calibri font. For example, body text, headers, and bibliographies all display text based on the Normal style.*

Thus, instead of changing the font and font size for various document elements, a more efficient technique is to change the Normal style for this document to use a 12-point Times New Roman font. *Why? By changing the Normal style, you ensure that all text in the document will use the format required by the MLA.* The following steps change the Normal style.

- Right-click Normal in the Styles gallery (Home tab | Styles group) to display a shortcut menu related to styles (Figure 2–2).

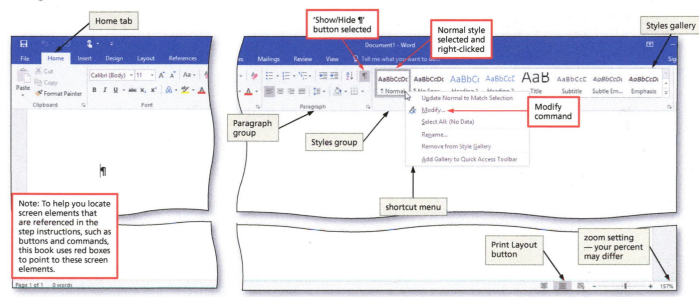

Figure 2–2

- Click Modify on the shortcut menu to display the Modify Style dialog box (Figure 2–3).

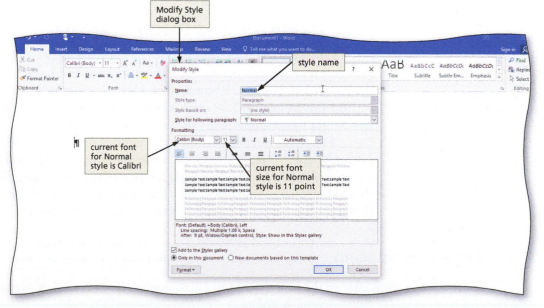

Figure 2–3

- Click the Font arrow (Modify Style dialog box) to display the Font list. Scroll to and then click Times New Roman in the list to change the font for the style being modified.
- Click the Font Size arrow (Modify Style dialog box) and then click 12 in the Font Size list to change the font size for the style being modified.
- Ensure that the 'Only in this document' option button is selected (Figure 2–4).

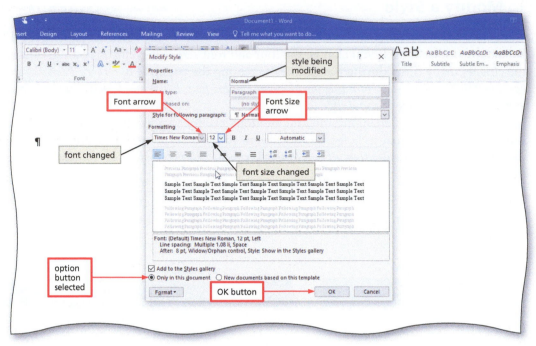

Figure 2–4

Q&A

Will all future documents use the new font and font size?

No, because the 'Only in this document' option button is selected. If you wanted all future documents to use a new setting, you would select the 'New documents based on this template' option button.

- Click the OK button (Modify Style dialog box) to update the Normal style to the specified settings.

Other Ways

1. Click Styles Dialog Box Launcher, click arrow next to style name, click Modify on menu, change settings (Modify Style dialog box), click OK button

2. Press ALT+CTRL+SHIFT+S, click arrow next to style name, click Modify on menu, change settings (Modify Style dialog box), click OK button

---

BTW

Line Spacing

If the top of a set of characters or a graphical image is chopped off, then line spacing may be set to Exactly. To remedy the problem, change line spacing to 1.0, 1.15, 1.5, 2.0, 2.5, 3.0, or At least (in the Paragraph dialog box), all of which accommodate the largest font or image.

Adjusting Line and Paragraph Spacing

Line spacing is the amount of vertical space between lines of text in a paragraph. **Paragraph spacing** is the amount of space above and below a paragraph. By default, the Normal style places 8 points of blank space after each paragraph and inserts a vertical space equal to 1.08 lines between each line of text. It also automatically adjusts line height to accommodate various font sizes and graphics.

The MLA documentation style requires that you double-space the entire research paper. That is, specifying a document use **double-space** means that the amount of vertical space between each line of text and above and below paragraphs should be equal to one blank line. The next sets of steps adjust line spacing and paragraph spacing according to the MLA documentation style.

To Change Line Spacing

1 CHANGE DOCUMENT SETTINGS | 2 CREATE HEADER | 3 TYPE RESEARCH PAPER WITH CITATIONS
4 CREATE ALPHABETICAL WORKS CITED | 5 PROOFREAD & REVISE RESEARCH PAPER

The following steps change the line spacing to 2.0 to double-space lines in a paragraph. *Why? The lines of the research paper should be double-spaced, according to the MLA documentation style.*

1

- Click the 'Line and Paragraph Spacing' button (Home tab | Paragraph group) to display the Line and Paragraph Spacing gallery (Figure 2–5).

What do the numbers in the Line and Paragraph Spacing gallery represent?

The options 1.0, 2.0, and 3.0 set line spacing to single, double, and triple, respectively. Similarly, the 1.15, 1.5, and 2.5 options set line spacing to 1.15, 1.5, and 2.5 lines. All of these options adjust line spacing automatically to accommodate the largest font or graphic on a line.

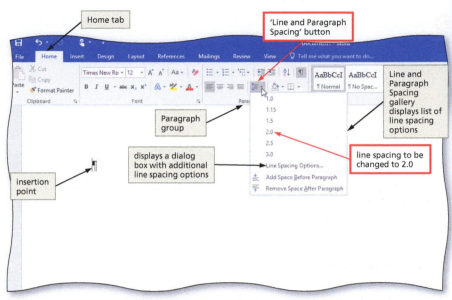

Figure 2–5

2

- Click 2.0 in the Line and Paragraph Spacing gallery to change the line spacing at the location of the insertion point.

Can I change the line spacing of existing text?

Yes. Select the text first and then change the line spacing as described in these steps.

Other Ways

1. Right-click paragraph (or, if using touch, tap 'Show Context Menu' on mini toolbar), click Paragraph on shortcut menu, or click Indents and Spacing tab (Paragraph dialog box), click Line spacing arrow, select desired spacing, click OK button

2. Click Paragraph Settings Dialog Box Launcher (Home tab or Layout tab | Paragraph group), click Indents and Spacing tab (Paragraph dialog box), click Line spacing arrow, select desired spacing, click OK button

3. Press CTRL+2 for double-spacing

To Remove Space after a Paragraph

1 CHANGE DOCUMENT SETTINGS | 2 CREATE HEADER | 3 TYPE RESEARCH PAPER WITH CITATIONS
4 CREATE ALPHABETICAL WORKS CITED | 5 PROOFREAD & REVISE RESEARCH PAPER

The following steps remove space after a paragraph. *Why? The research paper should not have additional blank space after each paragraph, according to the MLA documentation style.*

1

- Click the 'Line and Paragraph Spacing' button (Home tab | Paragraph group) to display the Line and Paragraph Spacing gallery (Figure 2–6).

Why does a check mark appear to the left of 2.0 in the gallery?

The check mark indicates the currently selected line spacing.

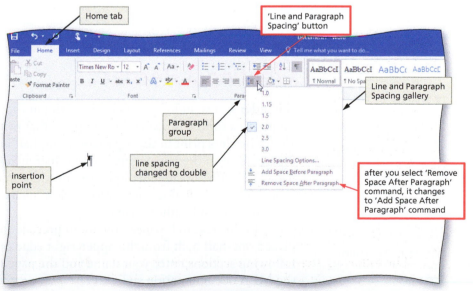

Figure 2–6

- Click 'Remove Space After Paragraph' in the Line and Paragraph Spacing gallery so that no blank space appears after paragraphs.

Q&A Can I remove space after existing paragraphs?
Yes. Select the paragraphs first and then remove the space as described in these steps.

Other Ways

1. Adjust Spacing After arrows (Layout tab | Paragraph group) until 0 pt is displayed

2. Right-click paragraph (or, if using touch, tap 'Show Context Menu' on mini toolbar), click Paragraph on shortcut menu, click Indents and Spacing tab (Paragraph dialog box), adjust After arrows until 0 pt is displayed, click OK button

3. Click Paragraph Settings Dialog Box Launcher (Home tab or Layout tab | Paragraph group), click Indents and Spacing tab (Paragraph dialog box), adjust After arrows until 0 pt is displayed, click OK button

---

To Update a Style to Match a Selection

1 CHANGE DOCUMENT SETTINGS | 2 CREATE HEADER | 3 TYPE RESEARCH PAPER WITH CITATIONS
4 CREATE ALPHABETICAL WORKS CITED | 5 PROOFREAD & REVISE RESEARCH PAPER

To ensure that all paragraphs in the paper will be double-spaced and do not have space after the paragraphs, you want the Normal style to include the line and paragraph spacing changes made in the previous two sets of steps. The following steps update the Normal style. *Why? You can update a style to reflect the settings of the location of the insertion point or selected text. Because no text has been typed in the research paper yet, you do not need to select text prior to updating the Normal style.*

- Right-click Normal in the Styles gallery (Home tab | Styles group) to display a shortcut menu (Figure 2–7).

- Click 'Update Normal to Match Selection' on the shortcut menu to update the selected (or current) style to reflect the settings at the location of the insertion point.

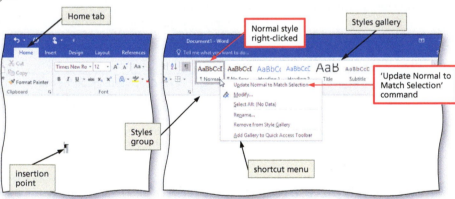

Figure 2–7

Other Ways

1. Click Styles Dialog Box Launcher, click arrow next to style name, click 'Update Normal to Match Selection'

2. Press ALT+CTRL+SHIFT+S, click arrow next to style name in Styles pane, click 'Update Normal to Match Selection'

Creating a Header

BTW
The Ribbon and Screen Resolution
Word may change how the groups and buttons within the groups appear on the ribbon, depending on the computer or mobile device's screen resolution. Thus, your ribbon may look different from the ones in this book if you are using a screen resolution other than 1366 x 768.

A **header** is text and/or graphics that print at the top of each page in a document. Similarly, a **footer** is text and/or graphics that print at the bottom of every page. In Word, headers print in the top margin one-half inch from the top of every page, and footers print in the bottom margin one-half inch from the bottom of each page, which meets the MLA documentation style. In addition to text and graphics, headers and footers can include document information, such as the page number, current date, current time, and author's name.

In this research paper, you are to precede the page number with your last name placed one-half inch from the upper-right edge of each page. The procedures in the following sections enter your name and the page number in the header, as specified by the MLA documentation style.

To Switch to the Header

The following steps switch from editing the document text to editing the header. *Why? To enter text in the header, you instruct Word to edit the header.*

- Click Insert on the ribbon to display the Insert tab.
- Click the 'Add a Header' button (Insert tab | Header & Footer group) to display the Add a Header gallery (Figure 2–8)

🔍 **Experiment**

- Click the down scroll arrow in the Add a Header gallery to see the available built-in headers.

Q&A Can I use a built-in header for this research paper?
None of the built-in headers adheres to the MLA documentation style; thus, you should enter your own header content instead of using a built-in header for this research paper.

How would I remove a header from a document?
You would click Remove Header in the Add a Header gallery. Similarly, to remove a footer, you would click Remove Footer in the Add a Footer gallery.

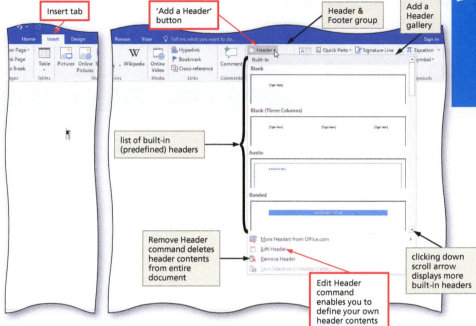

Figure 2–8

- Click Edit Header in the Add a Header gallery to switch from the document text to the header, which allows you to edit the contents of the header (Figure 2–9).

Q&A How do I remove the Header & Footer Tools Design tab from the ribbon?
When you are finished editing the header, you will close it, which removes the Header & Footer Tools Design tab.

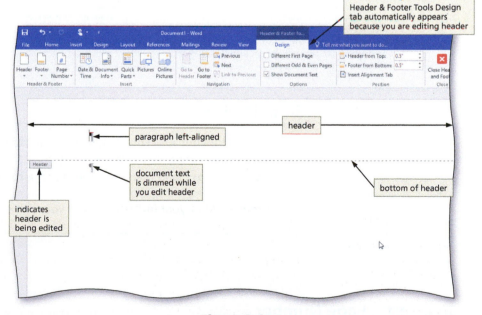

Figure 2–9

Other Ways

1. Double-click dimmed header

2. Right-click header in document, click Edit Header button that appears

To Right-Align a Paragraph

The paragraph in the header currently is left-aligned (shown in Figure 2–9). The following steps right-align this paragraph. *Why? Your last name and the page number should print **right-aligned**; that is, they should print at the right margin, according to the MLA documentation style.*

- Click Home on the ribbon to display the Home tab.

- Click the Align Right button (Home tab | Paragraph group) to right-align the current paragraph (Figure 2–10).

Q&A What if I wanted to return the paragraph to left-aligned? You would click the Align Right button again, or click the Align Left button (Home tab | Paragraph group).

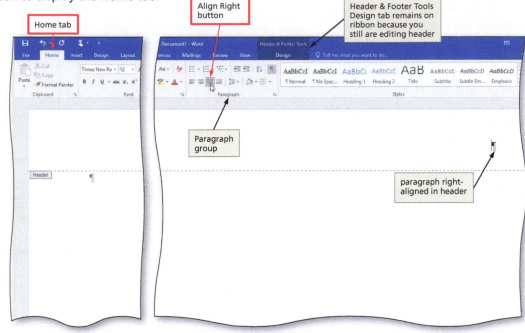

Figure 2–10

Other Ways

1. Right-click paragraph (or, if using touch, tap 'Show Context Menu' button on mini toolbar), click Paragraph on shortcut menu, click Indents and Spacing tab (Paragraph dialog box), click Alignment arrow, click Right, click OK button

2. Click Paragraph Settings Dialog Box Launcher (Home tab or Layout tab | Paragraph group), click Indents and Spacing tab (Paragraph dialog box), click Alignment arrow, click Right, click OK button

3. Press CTRL+R

BTW

Footers
If you wanted to create a footer, you would click the 'Add a Footer' button (Insert tab | Header & Footer group) and then select the desired built-in footer or click Edit Footer in the Add a Footer gallery to create a customized footer; or, you could double-click the dimmed footer.

To Enter Text

The following step enters the last name right-aligned in the header area.

1. Type **Carter** and then press the SPACEBAR to enter the last name in the header.

If requested by your instructor, enter your last name instead of Carter in the header.

To Insert a Page Number

The following steps insert a page number at the location of the insertion point. *Why? The MLA documentation style requires a page number following the last name in the header.*

1

- Click Header & Footer Tools Design on the ribbon to display the Header & Footer Tools Design tab.
- Click the 'Add Page Numbers' button (Header & Footer Tools Design tab | Header & Footer group) to display the Add Page Numbers menu.

Q&A

Why does the button name in the step differ from the name on the face of the button in the figure?

The text that appears on the face of the button may vary, depending on screen resolution. The name that appears in the ScreenTip (when you point to the button), however, never changes. For this reason, this book uses the name that appears in the ScreenTip to identify buttons, boxes, and other on-screen elements.

- Point to Current Position on the Add Page Numbers menu to display the Current Position gallery (Figure 2–11).

Experiment

- Click the down scroll arrow in the Current Position gallery to see the available page number formats.

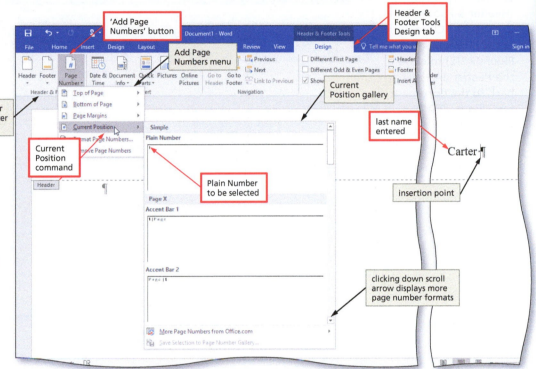

Figure 2–11

2

- If necessary, scroll to the top of the Current Position gallery.
- Click Plain Number in the Current Position gallery to insert an unformatted page number at the location of the insertion point (Figure 2–12).

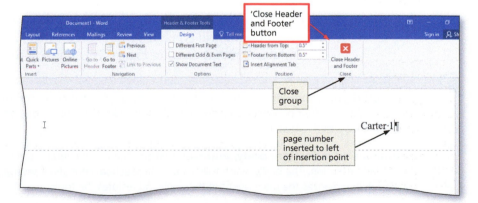

Figure 2–12

Other Ways

1. Click 'Add Page Numbers' button (Insert tab | Header & Footer group)

2. Click 'Explore Quick Parts' button (Insert tab | Text group or Header & Footer Tools Design tab | Insert group), click Field on Explore Quick Parts menu, select Page in Field names list (Field dialog box), select desired format in Format list, click OK button

1 CHANGE DOCUMENT SETTINGS | 2 CREATE HEADER | 3 TYPE RESEARCH PAPER WITH CITATIONS
4 CREATE ALPHABETICAL WORKS CITED | 5 PROOFREAD & REVISE RESEARCH PAPER

To Close the Header

The next task is to switch back to the document text. *Why? You are finished entering text in the header.* The following step closes the header.

- Click the 'Close Header and Footer' button (Header & Footer Tools Design tab | Close group) (shown in Figure 2–12) to close the header and switch back to the document text (Figure 2–13).

Q&A
How do I make changes to existing header text?
Switch to the header using the steps described previously in the section titled To Switch to the Header, edit the header as you would edit text in the document window, and then switch back to the document text.

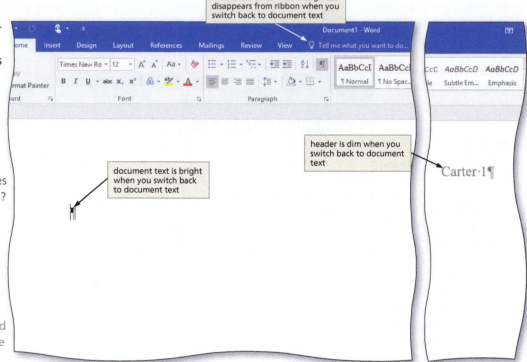

Header & Footer Tools Design tab disappears from ribbon when you switch back to document text

header is dim when you switch back to document text

document text is bright when you switch back to document text

Carter·1¶

Figure 2–13

Other Ways

1. Double-click dimmed document text

Typing the Research Paper Text

The text of the research paper in this module encompasses the first two pages of the paper. You will type the text of the research paper and then modify it later in the module, so that it matches Figure 2–1 shown at the beginning of this module.

What should you consider when writing the first draft of a research paper?
As you write the first draft of a research paper, be sure it includes the proper components, uses credible sources, and does not contain any plagiarized material.

- **Include an introduction, body, and conclusion.** The first paragraph of the paper introduces the topic and captures the reader's attention. The body, which follows the introduction, consists of several paragraphs that support the topic. The conclusion summarizes the main points in the body and restates the topic.

- **Evaluate sources for authority, currency, and accuracy.** Be especially wary of information obtained on the web. Any person, company, or organization can publish a webpage on the Internet. When considering the source, consider the following:

  - Authority: Does a reputable institution or group support the source? Is the information presented without bias? Are the author's credentials listed and verifiable?

  - Currency: Is the information up to date? Are dates of sources listed? What is the last date revised or updated?

  - Accuracy: Is the information free of errors? Is it verifiable? Are the sources clearly identified?

- **Acknowledge all sources of information; do not plagiarize.** Sources of research include books, magazines, newspapers, and the Internet. As you record facts and ideas, list details about the source: title, author, place of publication, publisher, date of publication, etc. When taking notes, be careful not to **plagiarize**. That is, do not use someone else's work and claim it to be your own. If you copy information directly, place it in quotation marks and identify its source. Not only is plagiarism unethical, but it is considered an academic crime that can have severe punishments, such as failing a course or being expelled from school.

When you summarize, paraphrase (rewrite information in your own words), present facts, give statistics, quote exact words, or show a map, chart, or other graphic, you must acknowledge the source. Information that commonly is known or accessible to the audience constitutes common knowledge and does not need to be acknowledged. If, however, you question whether certain information is common knowledge, you should document it — just to be safe.

To Enter Name and Course Information

As discussed earlier in this module, the MLA documentation style does not require a separate title page for research papers. Instead, place your name and course information in a block at the top of the page, below the header, at the left margin. The following steps enter the name and course information in the research paper.

BTW

Date Formats
The MLA style prefers the day-month-year (10 October 2017) or month-day-year (October 10, 2017) format.

1 Type **Oswald Carter** as the student name and then press the ENTER key.

2 Type **Ms. Ruiz** as the instructor name and then press the ENTER key.

3 Type **English 104** as the course name and then press the ENTER key.

4 Type **October 10, 2017** as the paper's due date and then press the ENTER key (Figure 2–14).

If requested by your instructor, enter your name and course information instead of the information shown above.

Q&A Why did the word, October, appear on the screen as I began typing the month name?
Word has an AutoComplete feature, where it predicts some words or phrases as you are typing and displays its prediction in a ScreenTip. If the AutoComplete prediction is correct, you can press the ENTER key (or, if using touch, tap the ScreenTip) to instruct Word to finish your typing with the word or phrase that appears in the ScreenTip.

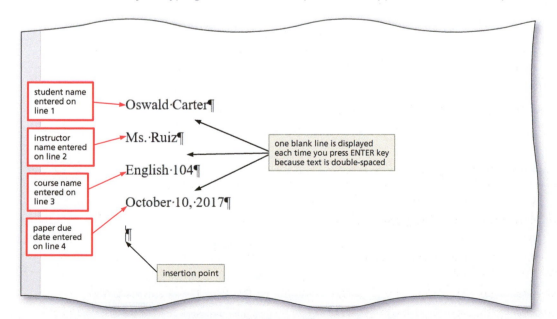

Figure 2–14

To Click and Type

The next task is to enter the title of the research paper centered between the page margins. In Module 1, you used the Center button (Home tab | Paragraph group) to center text and graphics. As an alternative, if you are using a mouse, you can use Word's Click and Type feature to format and enter text, graphics, and other items. ***Why? With Click and Type,*** *you can double-click a blank area of the document window and Word automatically formats the item you type or insert according to the location where you double-clicked.* The following steps use Click and Type to center and then type the title of the research paper.

Experiment

- Move the pointer around the document below the entered name and course information and observe the various icons that appear with the I-beam.

- Position the pointer in the center of the document at the approximate location for the research paper title until a center icon appears below the I-beam (Figure 2–15).

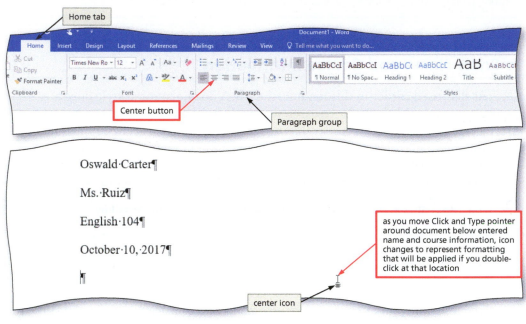

Figure 2–15

What are the other icons that appear in the Click and Type pointer?

A left-align icon appears to the right of the I-beam when the Click and Type pointer is in certain locations on the left side of the document window. A right-align icon appears to the left of the I-beam when the Click and Type pointer is in certain locations on the right side of the document window.

What if I am using a touch screen?

Tap the Center button (Home tab | Paragraph group) and then proceed to Step 3 because the Click and Type feature does not work with a touch screen.

- Double-click to center the paragraph mark and insertion point between the left and right margins.

- Type **Safely Using Headphones and Earbuds** as the paper title and then press the ENTER key to position the insertion point on the next line (Figure 2–16).

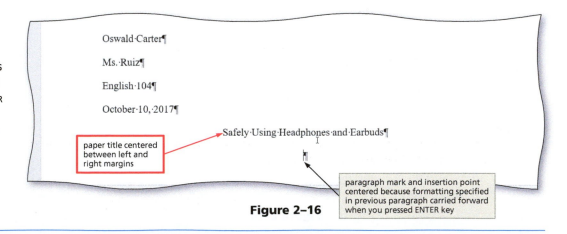

Figure 2–16

Keyboard Shortcuts

Word has many **keyboard shortcuts**, sometimes called shortcut keys or keyboard key combinations, for your convenience while typing. Table 2–1 lists the common keyboard shortcuts for formatting characters. Table 2–2 lists common keyboard shortcuts for formatting paragraphs.

Table 2–1 Keyboard Shortcuts for Formatting Characters

Character Formatting Task	Keyboard Shortcut	Character Formatting Task	Keyboard Shortcut
All capital letters	CTRL+SHIFT+A	Italic	CTRL+I
Bold	CTRL+B	Remove character formatting (plain text)	CTRL+SPACEBAR
Case of letters	SHIFT+F3	Small uppercase letters	CTRL+SHIFT+K
Decrease font size	CTRL+SHIFT+<	Subscript	CTRL+EQUAL SIGN
Decrease font size 1 point	CTRL+[	Superscript	CTRL+SHIFT+PLUS SIGN
Double-underline	CTRL+SHIFT+D	Underline	CTRL+U
Increase font size	CTRL+SHIFT+>	Underline words, not spaces	CTRL+SHIFT+W
Increase font size 1 point	CTRL+]		

© 2015 Cengage Learning

Table 2–2 Keyboard Shortcuts for Formatting Paragraphs

Paragraph Formatting	Keyboard Shortcut	Paragraph Formatting	Keyboard Shortcut
1.5 line spacing	CTRL+5	Justify paragraph	CTRL+J
Add/remove one line above paragraph	CTRL+0 (ZERO)	Left-align paragraph	CTRL+L
Center paragraph	CTRL+E	Remove hanging indent	CTRL+SHIFT+T
Decrease paragraph indent	CTRL+SHIFT+M	Remove paragraph formatting	CTRL+Q
Double-space lines	CTRL+2	Right-align paragraph	CTRL+R
Hanging indent	CTRL+T	Single-space lines	CTRL+1
Increase paragraph indent	CTRL+M		

© 2015 Cengage Learning

To Format Text Using a Keyboard Shortcut

The paragraphs below the paper title should be left-aligned, instead of centered. Thus, the next step is to left-align the paragraph below the paper title. When your fingers already are on the keyboard, you may prefer using keyboard shortcuts to format text as you type it.

The following step left-aligns a paragraph using the keyboard shortcut CTRL+L. (Recall from Module 1 that a notation such as CTRL+L means to press the letter L on the keyboard while holding down the CTRL key.)

1 Press CTRL+L to left-align the current paragraph, that is, the paragraph containing the insertion point (shown in Figure 2–17).

Q&A Why would I use a keyboard shortcut instead of the ribbon to format text?
Switching between the mouse and the keyboard takes time. If your hands are already on the keyboard, use a keyboard shortcut. If your hand is on the mouse, use the ribbon.

2 Save the research paper on your hard drive, OneDrive, or other storage location using the file name, Headphones and Earbuds Paper.

Q&A Why should I save the research paper at this time?
You have performed many tasks while creating this flyer and do not want to risk losing work completed thus far.

BTW

Keyboard Shortcuts
To print a complete list of keyboard shortcuts in Word, press F1 to display the Word Help window, type **keyboard shortcuts** in the Search box in the Word Help window, press the ENTER key, click the Keyboard shortcuts for Microsoft Word link, click the Print button in the Help window, and then click the Print button in the Print dialog box.

To Display the Rulers

According to the MLA documentation style, the first line of each paragraph in the research paper is to be indented one-half inch from the left margin. Although you can use a dialog box to indent paragraphs, Word provides a quicker way through the **horizontal ruler.** This ruler is displayed at the top edge of the document window just below the ribbon. Word also provides a **vertical ruler** that is displayed along the left edge of the Word window. The following step displays the rulers. *Why? You want to use the horizontal ruler to indent paragraphs.*

- If necessary, scroll the document so that the research paper title is at the top of the document window.
- Click View on the ribbon to display the View tab.
- If the rulers are not displayed, click the View Ruler check box (View tab | Show group) to place a check mark in the check box and display the horizontal and vertical rulers on the screen (Figure 2–17).

Q&A What tasks can I accomplish using the rulers?
You can use the rulers to indent paragraphs, set tab stops, change page margins, and adjust column widths.

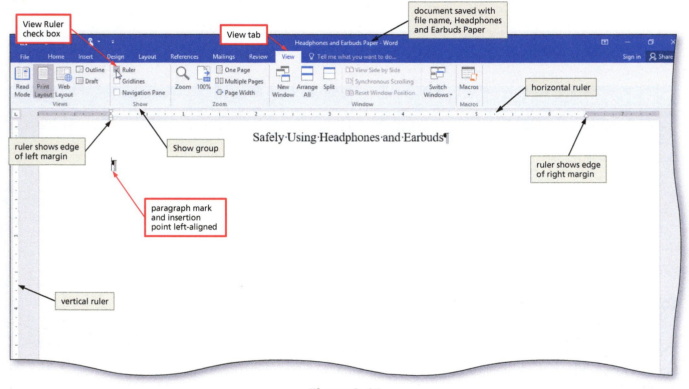

Figure 2–17

To First-Line Indent Paragraphs

If you are using a mouse, you can use the horizontal ruler, usually simply called the **ruler,** to indent just the first line of a paragraph, which is called a **first-line indent.** The left margin on the ruler contains two triangles above a square. The **'First Line Indent' marker** is the top triangle at the 0" mark on the ruler (shown in Figure 2–18). The bottom triangle is discussed later in this module. The small square at the 0" mark is the Left Indent marker. The **Left Indent marker** allows you to change the entire left margin, whereas the 'First Line Indent' marker indents only the first line of the paragraph.

The following steps first-line indent paragraphs in the research paper. *Why? The first line of each paragraph in the research paper is to be indented one-half inch from the left margin, according to the MLA documentation style.*

• With the insertion point on the paragraph mark below the research paper title, point to the 'First Line Indent' marker on the ruler (Figure 2–18).

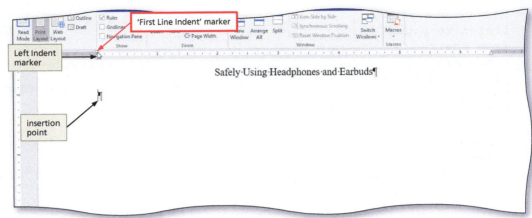

Figure 2–18

• Drag the 'First Line Indent' marker to the .5" mark on the ruler to display a vertical dotted line in the document window, which indicates the proposed indent location of the first line of the paragraph (Figure 2–19).

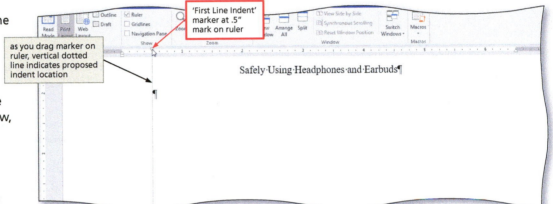

Figure 2–19

• Release the mouse button to place the 'First Line Indent' marker at the .5" mark on the ruler, or one-half inch from the left margin (Figure 2–20).

Q&A What if I am using a touch screen?

If you are using a touch screen, you cannot drag the 'First Line Indent' marker and must follow these steps instead: tap the Paragraph Settings Dialog Box Launcher (Home tab or Layout tab | Paragraph group) to display the Paragraph dialog box, tap the Indents and Spacing tab (Paragraph dialog box), tap the Special arrow, tap First line, and then tap the OK button.

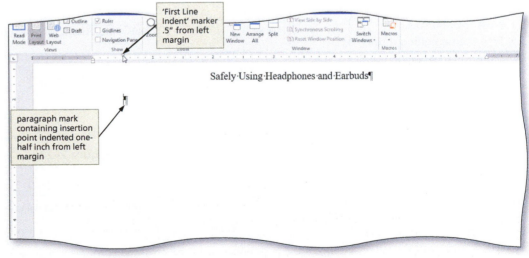

Figure 2–20

4

- Type **People often listen to sound from their computers or portable devices through headphones or earbuds.** and notice that Word automatically indents the first line of the paragraph by one-half inch (Figure 2–21).

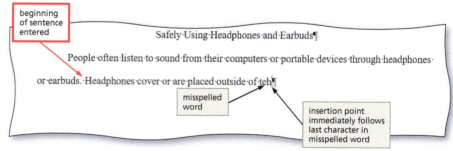

Figure 2–21

Q&A

Will I have to set a first-line indent for each paragraph in the paper?

No. Each time you press the ENTER key, paragraph formatting in the previous paragraph carries forward to the next paragraph. Thus, once you set the first-line indent, its format carries forward automatically to each subsequent paragraph you type.

Other Ways

1. Right-click paragraph (or, if using touch, tap 'Show Context Menu' button on mini toolbar), click Paragraph on shortcut menu, click Indents and Spacing tab (Paragraph dialog box), click Special arrow, click First line, click OK button

2. Click Paragraph Settings Dialog Box Launcher (Home tab or Layout tab | Paragraph group), click Indents and Spacing tab (Paragraph dialog box), click Special arrow, click First line, click OK button

To AutoCorrect as You Type

1 CHANGE DOCUMENT SETTINGS | 2 CREATE HEADER | **3 TYPE RESEARCH PAPER WITH CITATIONS**
4 CREATE ALPHABETICAL WORKS CITED | 5 PROOFREAD & REVISE RESEARCH PAPER

Word has predefined many commonly misspelled words, which it automatically corrects for you. ***Why?*** *As you type, you may make typing, spelling, capitalization, or grammar errors. Word's **AutoCorrect** feature automatically corrects these kinds of errors as you type them in the document. For example, if you type the characters, ahve, Word automatically changes it to the correct spelling, have, when you press the SPACEBAR or a punctuation mark key, such as a period or comma.*

The following steps intentionally misspell the word, the, as teh to illustrate the AutoCorrect feature.

1

- Press the SPACEBAR.
- Type the beginning of the next sentence, misspelling the word, the, as follows: **Headphones cover or are placed outside of teh** (Figure 2–22).

Figure 2–22

2

- Press the SPACEBAR and watch Word automatically correct the misspelled word.
- Type the rest of the sentence (Figure 2–23): **ear, whereas earbuds rest inside the ear canal.**

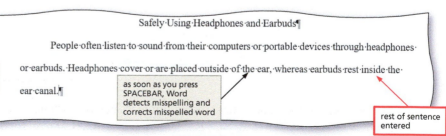

Figure 2–23

To Use the AutoCorrect Options Button

The following steps illustrate the AutoCorrect Options button and menu. *Why? If you are using a mouse, when you position the pointer on text that Word automatically corrected, a small blue box appears below the text. If you point to the small blue box, Word displays the AutoCorrect Options button. When you click the* **AutoCorrect Options button**, *Word displays a menu that allows you to undo a correction or change how Word handles future automatic corrections of this type.*

- Position the pointer in the text automatically corrected by Word (the word, the, in this case) to display a small blue box below the automatically corrected word (Figure 2–24).

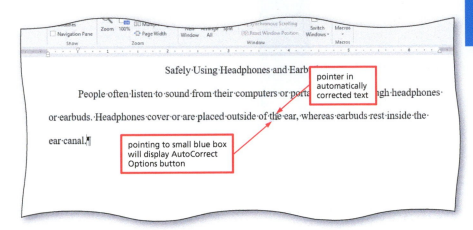

Figure 2–24

- Point to the small blue box to display the AutoCorrect Options button.
- Click the AutoCorrect Options button to display the AutoCorrect Options menu (Figure 2–25).
- Press the ESC key to remove the AutoCorrect Options menu from the screen.

Q&A Do I need to remove the AutoCorrect Options button from the screen?

No. When you move the pointer, the AutoCorrect Options button will disappear from the screen. If, for some reason, you wanted to remove the AutoCorrect Options button from the screen, you could press the ESC key a second time.

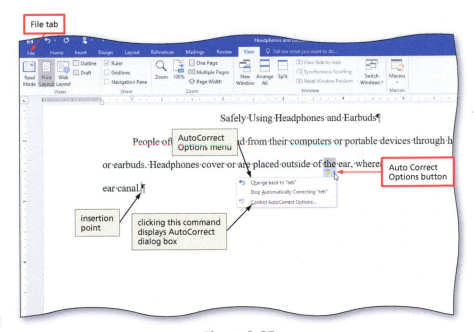

Figure 2–25

To Create an AutoCorrect Entry

The next steps create an AutoCorrect entry. *Why? In addition to the predefined list of AutoCorrect spelling, capitalization, and grammar errors, you can create your own AutoCorrect entries to add to the list. For example, if you tend to mistype the word computer as comptuer, you should create an AutoCorrect entry for it.*

1

- Click File on the ribbon (shown in Figure 2–25) to open the Backstage view (Figure 2–26).

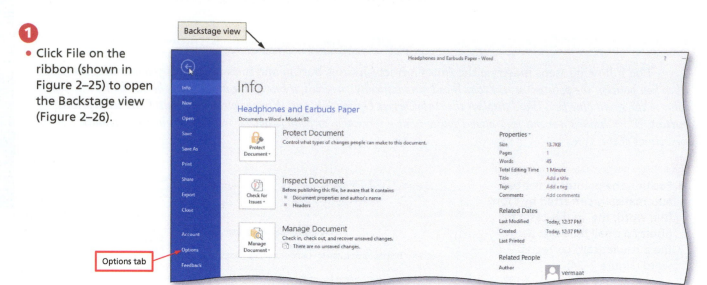

Figure 2–26

2

- Click the Options tab in the Backstage view to display the Word Options dialog box.
- Click Proofing in the left pane (Word Options dialog box) to display proofing options in the right pane.
- Click the AutoCorrect Options button in the right pane to display the AutoCorrect dialog box.
- When Word displays the AutoCorrect dialog box, type **comptuer** in the Replace text box.
- Press the TAB key and then type **computer** in the With text box (Figure 2–27).

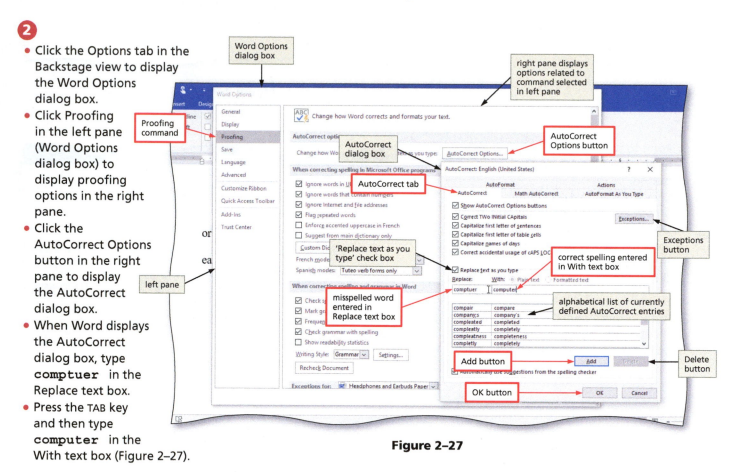

Figure 2–27

3

- Click the Add button (AutoCorrect dialog box) to add the entry alphabetically to the list of words to correct automatically as you type. (If your dialog box displays a Replace button instead, click it and then click the Yes button in the Microsoft Word dialog box to replace the previously defined entry.)
- Click the OK button (AutoCorrect dialog box) to close the dialog box.
- Click the OK button (Word Options dialog box) to close the dialog box.

The AutoCorrect Dialog Box

In addition to creating AutoCorrect entries for words you commonly misspell or mistype, you can create entries for abbreviations, codes, and so on. For example, you could create an AutoCorrect entry for asap, indicating that Word should replace this text with the phrase, as soon as possible.

If, for some reason, you do not want Word to correct automatically as you type, you can turn off the Replace text as you type feature by clicking the Options tab in the Backstage view, clicking Proofing in the left pane (Word Options dialog box), clicking the AutoCorrect Options button in the right pane (shown in Figure 2–27), removing the check mark from the 'Replace text as you type' check box, and then clicking the OK button in each open dialog box.

The AutoCorrect sheet in the AutoCorrect dialog box (Figure 2–27) contains other check boxes that correct capitalization errors if the check boxes are selected:

- If you type two capital letters in a row, such as TH, Word makes the second letter lowercase, Th.
- If you begin a sentence with a lowercase letter, Word capitalizes the first letter of the sentence.
- If you type the name of a day in lowercase letters, such as tuesday, Word capitalizes the first letter in the name of the day, Tuesday.
- If you leave the CAPS LOCK key on and begin a new sentence, such as after, Word corrects the typing, After, and turns off the CAPS LOCK key.

If you do not want Word to perform any of these corrections automatically, simply remove the check mark from the appropriate check box in the AutoCorrect dialog box.

Sometimes, you do not want Word to AutoCorrect a particular word or phrase. For example, you may use the code, WD., in your documents. Because Word automatically capitalizes the first letter of a sentence, the character you enter following the period will be capitalized (in the previous sentence, it would capitalize the letter i in the word, in). To allow the code, WD., to be entered into a document and still leave the AutoCorrect feature turned on, you would set an exception. To set an exception to an AutoCorrect rule, click the Options tab in the Backstage view, click Proofing in the left pane (Word Options dialog box), click the AutoCorrect Options button in the right pane, click the Exceptions button (Figure 2–27), click the appropriate tab in the AutoCorrect Exceptions dialog box, type the exception entry in the text box, click the Add button, click the Close button (AutoCorrect Exceptions dialog box), and then click the OK button in each of the remaining dialog boxes.

To Enter More Text

The next task is to continue typing text in the research paper up to the location of the in-text parenthetical reference. The following steps enter this text.

1 With the insertion point positioned at the end of the first paragraph in the paper, as shown in Figure 2–25, press the SPACEBAR and then type these three sentences, intentionally misspelling the word sound as sould: `With these listening devices, only the individual wearing the device hears the sould. Using headphones or earbuds improperly can lead to permanent hearing loss. Items that may protect hearing include quality of these devices and volume levels.`

Q&A Why is the word, sound, misspelled?
Later in this module, you will use Word's check spelling and grammar at once feature to check the entire document for errors.

BTW

Automatic Corrections

If you do not want to keep a change made automatically by Word and you immediately notice the automatic correction, you can undo the change by clicking the Undo button on the Quick Access Toolbar or pressing CTRL+Z. You also can undo a correction through the AutoCorrect Options button (Word Options dialog box) (shown in Figure 2–27).

BTW

Spacing after Punctuation

Because word processing documents use variable character fonts, it often is difficult to determine in a printed document how many times someone has pressed the SPACEBAR between sentences. Thus, the rule is to press the SPACEBAR only once after periods, colons, and other punctuation marks.

② Press the ENTER key to start a new paragraph.

③ Type `The features of certain headphones and earbuds can help to prevent hearing loss. Higher-quality headphones and earbuds tend to produce a clearer sound, enabling wearers to listen at a lower volume` and then press the SPACEBAR (Figure 2–28).

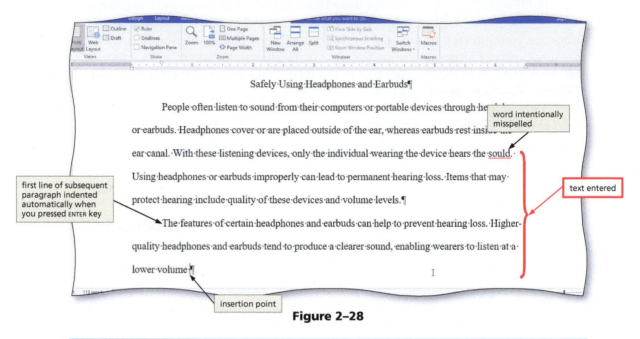

Figure 2–28

Citations

Both the MLA and APA guidelines suggest the use of in-text parenthetical references (placed at the end of a sentence), instead of footnoting each source of material in a paper. These parenthetical references, called citations in Word, guide the reader to the end of the paper for complete information about the source.

Word provides tools to assist you with inserting citations in a paper and later generating a list of sources from the citations. With a documentation style selected, Word automatically formats the citations and list of sources according to that style. The process for adding citations in Word is as follows:

1. Modify the documentation style, if necessary.

2. Insert a citation placeholder.

3. Enter the source information for the citation.

You can combine Steps 2 and 3, where you insert the citation placeholder and enter the source information at once. Or, you can insert the citation placeholder as you write and then enter the source information for the citation at a later time. While creating the research paper in this module, you will use both methods.

To Change the Bibliography Style

1 CHANGE DOCUMENT SETTINGS | 2 CREATE HEADER | **3 TYPE RESEARCH PAPER WITH CITATIONS**
4 CREATE ALPHABETICAL WORKS CITED | 5 PROOFREAD & REVISE RESEARCH PAPER

The first step in inserting a citation is to be sure the citations and sources will be formatted using the correct documentation style, called the bibliography style in Word. **Why?** *You want to ensure that Word is using the MLA documentation style for this paper.* The following steps change the specified documentation style.

- Click References on the ribbon to display the References tab.
- Click the Bibliography Style arrow (References tab | Citations & Bibliography group) to display the Bibliography Style gallery, which lists predefined documentation styles (Figure 2–29).

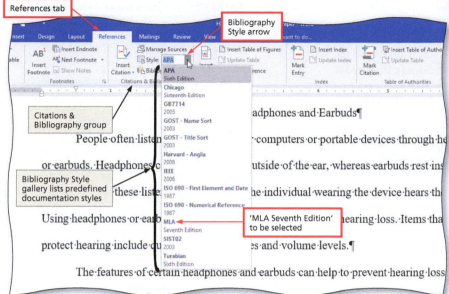

- Click 'MLA Seventh Edition' in the Bibliography Style gallery to change the documentation style to MLA.

Q&A What if I am using a different edition of a documentation style shown in the Bibliography Style gallery?
Select the closest one and then, if necessary, perform necessary edits before submitting the paper.

Figure 2–29

What details are required for sources?

During your research, be sure to record essential publication information about each of your sources. Following is a sample list of types of required information for the MLA documentation style.

- Book: full name of author(s), complete title of book, edition (if available), volume (if available), publication city, publisher name, publication year, and publication medium

- Magazine: full name of author(s), complete title of article, magazine title, issue number (if available), date of magazine, page numbers of article, publication medium, and date viewed (if medium is a website)

- Website: full name of author(s), title of website, website publisher or sponsor (if none, write N.p.), publication date (if none, write n.d.), publication medium, and date viewed

CONSIDER THIS

To Insert a Citation and Create Its Source

1 CHANGE DOCUMENT SETTINGS | 2 CREATE HEADER | **3 TYPE RESEARCH PAPER WITH CITATIONS**
4 CREATE ALPHABETICAL WORKS CITED | 5 PROOFREAD & REVISE RESEARCH PAPER

With the documentation style selected, the next task is to insert a citation at the location of the insertion point and enter the source information for the citation. You can accomplish these steps at once by instructing Word to add a new source. The following steps add a new source for a magazine (periodical) article on the web. **Why?** *The material preceding the insertion point was summarized from an online magazine article.*

- With the insertion point at the location for the citation (as shown in Figure 2–28), click the Insert Citation button (References tab | Citations & Bibliography group) to display the Insert Citation menu (Figure 2–30).

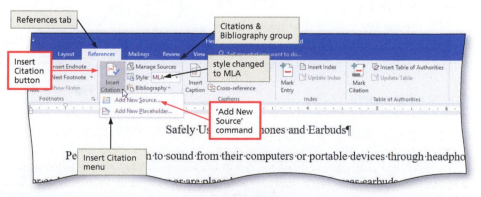

Figure 2–30

2

- Click 'Add New Source' on the Insert Citation menu to display the Create Source dialog box (Figure 2–31).

Q&A What are the Bibliography Fields in the Create Source dialog box?
A **field** is a placeholder for data whose contents can change. You enter data in some fields; Word supplies data for others. In this case, you enter the contents of the fields for a particular source, for example, the author name in the Author field.

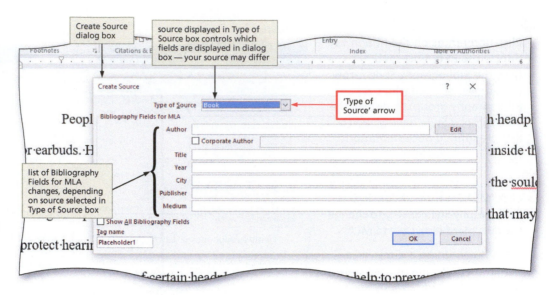

Figure 2–31

🔍 **Experiment**

- Click the 'Type of Source' arrow and then click one of the source types in the list, so that you can see how the list of fields changes to reflect the type of source you selected.

3

- If necessary, click the 'Type of Source' arrow (Create Source dialog box) and then click 'Article in a Periodical', so that the list shows fields required for a magazine (periodical).

- Click the Author text box. Type **Tu, Mingzhu Lin** as the author.

- Click the Title text box. Type **Headphones and Earbuds** as the article title.

- Press the TAB key and then type **Technology and Trends Today** as the periodical title.

- Press the TAB key and then type **2017** as the year.

- Press the TAB key and then type **Aug.** as the month.

- Press the TAB key twice and then type **n. pag.** as the number of pages.

- Press the TAB key and then type **Web** as the medium (Figure 2–32).

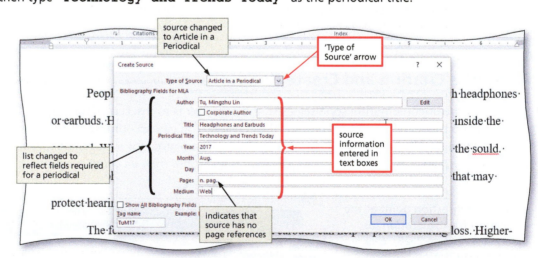

Figure 2–32

Q&A Why is the month abbreviated?
The MLA documentation style abbreviates all months, except May, June, and July, when they appear in a source.

What does the n. pag. entry mean in the Pages text box?
The MLA documentation style uses the abbreviation n. pag. for no pagination, which indicates the source has no page references. This is common for web sources.

4

- Place a check mark in the 'Show All Bibliography Fields' check box so that Word displays all fields available for the selected source, including the date viewed (accessed) fields.

- If necessary, scroll to the bottom of the Bibliography Fields list to display the date viewed (accessed) fields.

- Click the Year Accessed text box. Type `2017` as the year.

- Press the TAB key and then type `Oct.` as the month accessed.

- Press the TAB key and then type `3` as the day accessed (Figure 2–33).

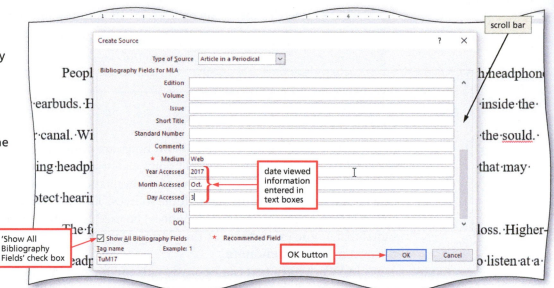

Figure 2–33

Q&A

What if some of the text boxes disappear as I enter the fields?

With the 'Show All Bibliography Fields' check box selected, the dialog box may not be able to display all fields at the same time. In this case, some may scroll up off the screen.

5

- Click the OK button to close the dialog box, create the source, and insert the citation in the document at the location of the insertion point.

- Press the END key to move the insertion point to the end of the line, if necessary, which also deselects the citation.

- Press the PERIOD key to end the sentence (Figure 2–34).

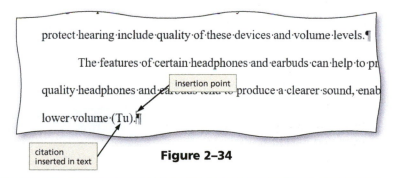

Figure 2–34

To Enter More Text

The next task is to continue typing text in the research paper up to the location of the footnote. The following steps enter this text.

1 Press the SPACEBAR.

2 Type the next sentences (Figure 2–35): **Properly designed headphones**

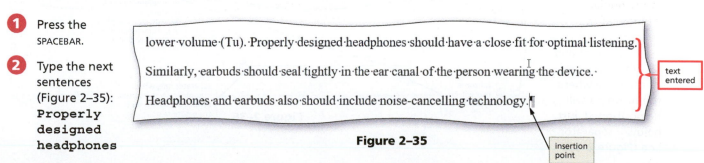

Figure 2–35

should have a close fit for optimal listening. Similarly, earbuds should seal tightly in the ear canal of the person wearing the device. Headphones and earbuds also should include noise-cancelling technology.

3 Save the research paper again on the same storage location with the same file name.

Q&A | Why should I save the research paper again?
You have made several modifications to the research paper since you last saved it; thus, you should save it again.

Footnotes

As discussed earlier in this module, notes are optional in the MLA documentation style. If used, content notes elaborate on points discussed in the paper, and bibliographic notes direct the reader to evaluations of statements in a source or provide a means for identifying multiple sources. The MLA documentation style specifies that a superscript (raised number) be used for a **note reference mark** to signal that a note exists either at the bottom of the page as a **footnote** or at the end of the document as an **endnote**.

In Word, **note text** can be any length and format. Word automatically numbers notes sequentially by placing a note reference mark both in the body of the document and to the left of the note text. If you insert, rearrange, or remove notes, Word renumbers any subsequent note reference marks according to their new sequence in the document.

To Insert a Footnote Reference Mark

1 CHANGE DOCUMENT SETTINGS | 2 CREATE HEADER | 3 TYPE RESEARCH PAPER WITH CITATIONS
4 CREATE ALPHABETICAL WORKS CITED | 5 PROOFREAD & REVISE RESEARCH PAPER

The following step inserts a footnote reference mark in the document at the location of the insertion point and at the location where the footnote text will be typed. *Why? You will insert a content note elaborating on noise-cancelling technology, which you want to position as a footnote.*

1

- With the insertion point positioned as shown in Figure 2–35, click the Insert Footnote button (References tab | Footnotes group) to display a note reference mark (a superscripted 1) in two places: (1) in the document window at the location of the insertion point and (2) at the bottom of the page where the footnote will be positioned, just below a separator line (Figure 2–36).

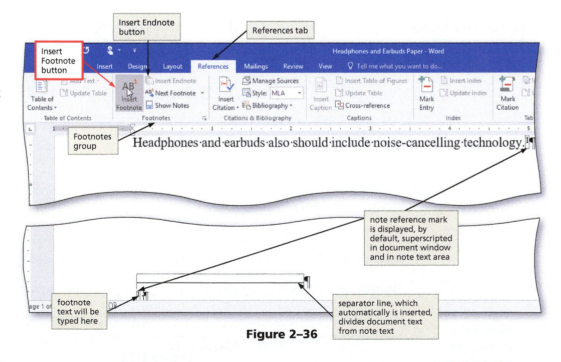

Figure 2–36

What if I wanted notes to be positioned as endnotes instead of as footnotes?

You would click the Insert Endnote button (References tab | Footnotes group), which places the separator line and the endnote text at the end of the document, instead of the bottom of the page containing the reference.

Other Ways

1. Press ALT+CTRL+F

To Enter Footnote Text

The following step types the footnote text to the right of the note reference mark below the separator line.

1 Type the footnote text up to the citation (shown in Figure 2–37): `Gupta and Padro state that effective noise-cancelling technology reduces the interference of sounds from the surrounding environment, reducing the volume level required by headphones and earbuds` and then press the SPACEBAR.

To Insert a Citation Placeholder

Earlier in this module, you inserted a citation and its source at once. In Word, you also can insert a citation without entering the source information. *Why? Sometimes, you may not have the source information readily available and would prefer to enter it at a later time.*

The following steps insert a citation placeholder in the footnote, so that you can enter the source information later.

1

- With the insertion point positioned as shown in Figure 2–37, click the Insert Citation button (References tab | Citations & Bibliography group) to display the Insert Citation menu (Figure 2–37).

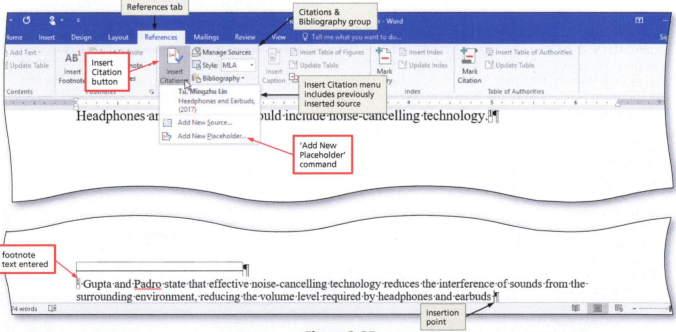

Figure 2–37

- Click 'Add New Placeholder' on the Insert Citation menu to display the Placeholder Name dialog box.
- Type **Gupta** as the tag name for the source (Figure 2–38).

Q&A | What is a tag name?
A tag name is an identifier that links a citation to a source. Word automatically creates a tag name when you enter a source. When you create a citation placeholder, enter a meaningful tag name, which will appear in the citation placeholder until you edit the source.

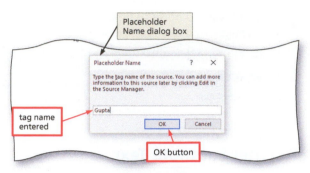

Figure 2–38

3

- Click the OK button (Placeholder Name dialog box) to close the dialog box and insert the entered tag name in the citation placeholder in the document (shown in Figure 2–39).
- Press the PERIOD key to end the sentence.

Q&A | What if the citation is in the wrong location?
Click the citation to select it and then drag the citation tab (on the upper-left corner of the selected citation) to any location in the document.

Footnote Text Style

When you insert a footnote, Word formats it using the Footnote Text style, which does not adhere to the MLA documentation style. For example, notice in Figure 2–37 that the footnote text is single-spaced, left-aligned, and a smaller font size than the text in the research paper. According to the MLA documentation style, notes should be formatted like all other paragraphs in the paper.

You could change the paragraph formatting of the footnote text to first-line indent and double-spacing and then change the font size from 10 to 12 point. If you use this technique, however, you will need to change the format of the footnote text for each footnote you enter into the document.

A more efficient technique is to modify the format of the Footnote Text style so that every footnote you enter in the document will use the formats defined in this style.

1 CHANGE DOCUMENT SETTINGS | 2 CREATE HEADER | 3 TYPE RESEARCH PAPER WITH CITATIONS
4 CREATE ALPHABETICAL WORKS CITED | 5 PROOFREAD & REVISE RESEARCH PAPER

To Modify a Style Using a Shortcut Menu

The Footnote Text style specifies left-aligned single-spaced paragraphs with a 10-point font size for text. The following steps modify the Footnote Text style. **Why?** *To meet MLA documentation style, the footnotes should be double-spaced with a first-line indent and a 12-point font size for text.*

1

- Right-click the note text in the footnote to display a shortcut menu related to footnotes (Figure 2–39).

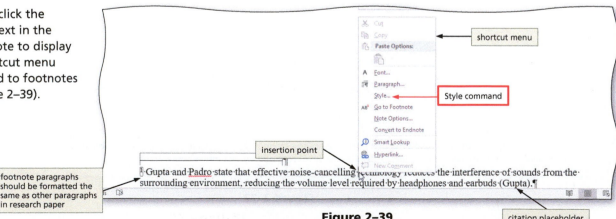
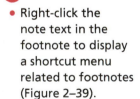

Figure 2–39

• Click Style on the shortcut menu to display the Style dialog box. If necessary, click the Category arrow, click All styles in the Category list, and then click Footnote Text in the Styles list to select the style to modify.

• Click the Modify button (Style dialog box) to display the Modify Style dialog box.

• Click the Font Size arrow (Modify Style dialog box) to display the Font Size list and then click 12 in the Font Size list to change the font size.

• Click the Double Space button to change the line spacing.

• Click the Format button to display the Format menu (Figure 2–40).

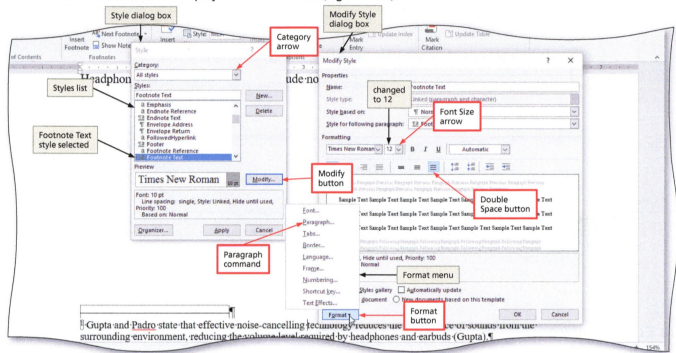

Figure 2–40

3

• Click Paragraph on the Format menu (Modify Style dialog box) to display the Paragraph dialog box.

• Click the Special arrow in the Indentation area (Paragraph dialog box) and then click First line (Figure 2–41).

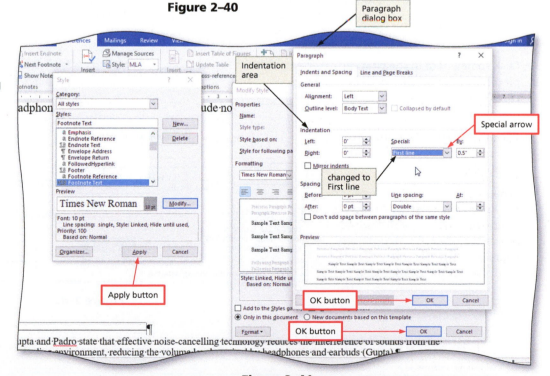

Figure 2–41

4

- Click the OK button (Paragraph dialog box) to close the dialog box.

- Click the OK button (Modify Style dialog box) to close the dialog box.

- Click the Apply button (Style dialog box) to apply the style changes to the footnote text (Figure 2–42).

Q&A Will all footnotes use this modified style?
Yes. Any future footnotes entered in the document will use a 12-point font with the paragraphs first-line indented and double-spaced.

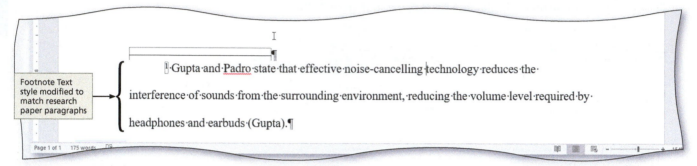

Figure 2–42

Other Ways

1. Click Styles Dialog Box Launcher (Home tab | Styles group), point to style name in list, click style name arrow, click Modify, change settings (Modify Style dialog box), click OK button

2. Click Styles Dialog Box Launcher (Home tab | Styles group), click Manage Styles button in task pane, select style name in list, click Modify button (Manage Styles dialog box), change settings (Modify Style dialog box), click OK button in each dialog box

To Edit a Source

1 CHANGE DOCUMENT SETTINGS | 2 CREATE HEADER | **3 TYPE RESEARCH PAPER WITH CITATIONS**
4 CREATE ALPHABETICAL WORKS CITED | 5 PROOFREAD & REVISE RESEARCH PAPER

When you typed the footnote text for this research paper, you inserted a citation placeholder for the source. The following steps edit a source. **Why?** *Assume you now have the source information and are ready to enter it.*

1

- Click somewhere in the citation placeholder to be edited, in this case (Gupta), to select the citation placeholder.

- Click the Citation Options arrow to display the Citation Options menu (Figure 2–43).

Q&A What is the purpose of the tab to the left of the selected citation?
If, for some reason, you wanted to move a citation to a different location in the document, you would select the citation and then drag the citation tab to the desired location.

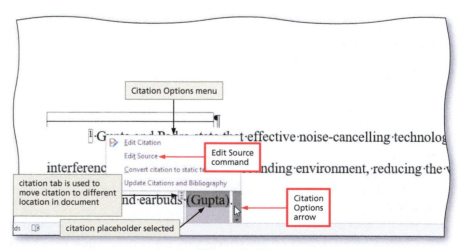

Figure 2–43

2

- Click Edit Source on the Citation Options menu to display the Edit Source dialog box.

- If necessary, click the 'Type of Source' arrow (Edit Source dialog box) and then click Book, so that the list shows fields required for a book.

- Because this source has two authors, click the Edit button to display the Edit Name dialog box, which assists you with entering multiple author names.

- Type **Gupta** as the first author's last name; press the TAB key and then type **Elena** as the first name; press the TAB key and then type **Maia** as the middle name (Figure 2–44).

Q&A What if I already know how to punctuate the author entry properly?
You can enter the name directly in the Author box.

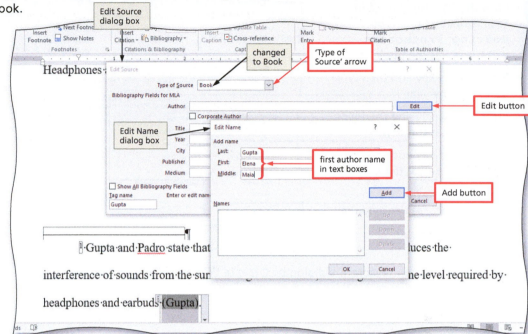

Figure 2–44

3

- Click the Add button (Edit Name dialog box) to add the first author name to the Names list.
- Type **Padro** as the second author's last name; press the TAB key and then type **Adelbert** as the first name; press the TAB key and then type **Luis** as the middle name.
- Click the Add button (Edit Name dialog box) to add the second author name to the Names list (Figure 2–45).

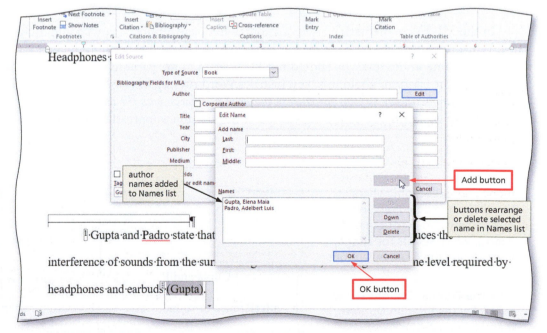

Figure 2–45

4

- Click the OK button (Edit Name dialog box) to add the author names that appear in the Names list to the Author box in the Edit Source dialog box.

- Click the Title text box (Edit Source dialog box). Type **Hearing Protection Methods** as the book title.

- Press the TAB key and then type **2017** as the year.

- Press the TAB key and then type **Orlando** as the city.

- Press the TAB key and then type **Palm Press** as the publisher.

- Press the TAB key and then type **Print** as the medium (Figure 2–46).

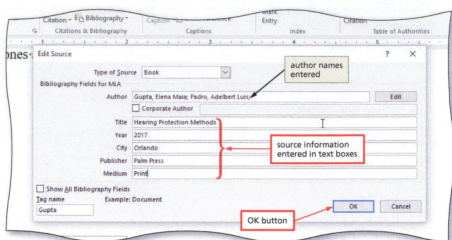

Figure 2–46

5

- Click the OK button to close the dialog box, create the source, and update the citation to display both author last names (shown in Figure 2–47).

Other Ways

1. Click Manage Sources button (References tab | Citations & Bibliography group), click placeholder source in Current List, click Edit button (Source Manager dialog box)

To Edit a Citation

1 CHANGE DOCUMENT SETTINGS | 2 CREATE HEADER | **3 TYPE RESEARCH PAPER WITH CITATIONS**
4 CREATE ALPHABETICAL WORKS CITED | 5 PROOFREAD & REVISE RESEARCH PAPER

In the MLA documentation style, if a source has page numbers, you should include them in the citation. Thus, Word provides a means to enter the page numbers to be displayed in the citation. Also, if you reference the author's name in the text, you should not list it again in the parenthetical citation. Instead, just list the page number(s) in the citation. To do this, you instruct Word to suppress author and title. **Why?** *If you suppress the author, Word automatically displays the title, so you need to suppress both the author and title if you want just the page number(s) to be displayed.* The following steps edit the citation, suppressing the author and title but displaying the page numbers.

1

- If necessary, click somewhere in the citation to be edited, in this case somewhere in (Gupta and Padro), which selects the citation and displays the Citation Options arrow.

- Click the Citation Options arrow to display the Citation Options menu (Figure 2–47).

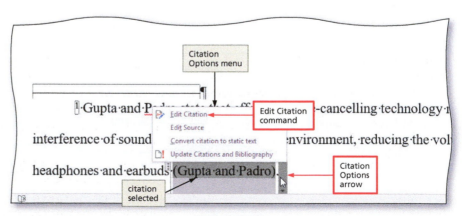

Figure 2–47

2

- Click Edit Citation on the Citation Options menu to display the Edit Citation dialog box.

- Type **75–78** in the Pages text box (Edit Citation dialog box).

- Click the Author check box to place a check mark in it.

- Click the Title check box to place a check mark in it (Figure 2–48).

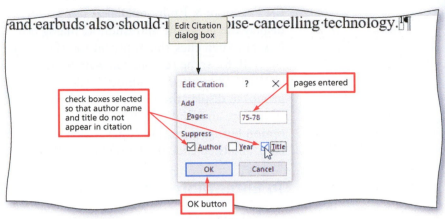

Figure 2–48

3

- Click the OK button to close the dialog box, remove the author names from the citation in the footnote, suppress the title from showing, and add page numbers to the citation.

- Press the END key to move the insertion point to the end of the line, which also deselects the citation (Figure 2–49).

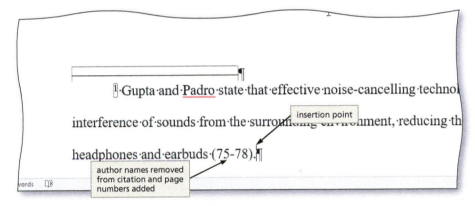

Figure 2–49

Working with Footnotes and Endnotes

You edit footnote text just as you edit any other text in the document. To delete or move a note reference mark, however, the insertion point must be in the document text (not in the footnote text).

To delete a note, select the note reference mark in the document text (not in the footnote text) by dragging through the note reference mark and then click the Cut button (Home tab | Clipboard group). Or, click immediately to the right of the note reference mark in the document text and then press the BACKSPACE key twice, or click immediately to the left of the note reference mark in the document text and then press the DELETE key twice.

To move a note to a different location in a document, select the note reference mark in the document text (not in the footnote text), click the Cut button (Home tab | Clipboard group), click the location where you want to move the note, and then click the Paste button (Home tab | Clipboard group). When you move or delete notes, Word automatically renumbers any remaining notes in the correct sequence.

If you are using a mouse and position the pointer on the note reference mark in the document text, the note text is displayed above the note reference mark as a ScreenTip. To remove the ScreenTip, move the pointer.

If, for some reason, you wanted to change the format of note reference marks in footnotes or endnotes (i.e., from 1, 2, 3 to A, B, C), you would click the Footnote & Endnote Dialog Box Launcher (References tab | Footnotes group) to display the Footnote and Endnote dialog box, click the Number format arrow (Footnote and Endnote dialog box), click the desired number format in the list, and then click the Apply button.

BTW

Footnote and Endnote Location
You can change the location of footnotes from the bottom of the page to the end of the text by clicking the Footnote & Endnote Dialog Box Launcher (References tab | Footnotes group), clicking the Footnotes arrow (Footnote and Endnote dialog box), and then clicking Below text. Similarly, clicking the Endnotes arrow (Footnote and Endnote dialog box) enables you to change the location of endnotes from the end of the document to the end of a section.

If, for some reason, you wanted to change a footnote number, you would click the Footnote & Endnote Dialog Box Launcher (References tab | Footnotes group) to display the Footnote and Endnote dialog box, enter the desired number in the Start at box, and then click the Apply button (Footnote and Endnote dialog box).

If, for some reason, you wanted to convert footnotes to endnotes, you would click the Footnote & Endnote Dialog Box Launcher (References tab | Footnotes group) to display the Footnote and Endnote dialog box, click the Convert button (Footnote and Endnote dialog box), select the 'Convert all footnotes to endnotes' option button (Convert Notes dialog box), click the OK button (Convert Notes dialog box), and then click the Close button (Footnote and Endnote dialog box).

To Enter More Text

The next task is to continue typing text in the body of the research paper. The following steps enter this text.

1 Position the insertion point after the note reference mark in the document and then press the ENTER key.

2 Type the first three sentences in the third paragraph of the research paper (shown in Figure 2–50): `The volume level of the sound that transmits from headphones or earbuds into the ear of a person wearing this type of device has been linked to hearing loss. The volume should be set low enough that other people nearby cannot hear the sound being transmitted. The quieter the sounds, the less possibility of hearing damage.`

To Count Words

1 CHANGE DOCUMENT SETTINGS | 2 CREATE HEADER | **3 TYPE RESEARCH PAPER WITH CITATIONS**
4 CREATE ALPHABETICAL WORKS CITED | 5 PROOFREAD & REVISE RESEARCH PAPER

Often when you write papers, you are required to compose the papers with a minimum number of words. The minimum requirement for the research paper in this module is 275 words. You can look on the status bar and see the total number of words thus far in a document. For example, Figure 2–50 shows the research paper has 231 words, but you are not sure if that count includes the words in your footnote. The following steps display the Word Count dialog box. ***Why?*** *You want to verify that the footnote text is included in the count.*

1

- Click the Word Count indicator on the status bar to display the Word Count dialog box.

- If necessary, place a check mark in the 'Include textboxes, footnotes and endnotes' check box (Word Count dialog box) (Figure 2–50).

Why do the statistics in my Word Count dialog box differ from those in Figure 2–50?
Depending on the accuracy of your typing, your statistics may differ.

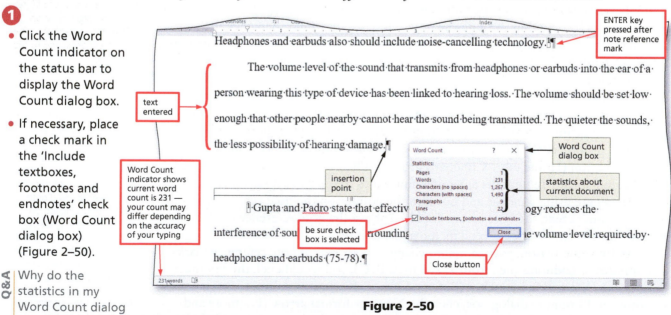

Figure 2–50

2
- Click the Close button (Word Count dialog box) to close the dialog box.

Q&A Can I display statistics for just a section of the document?
Yes. Select the section and then click the Word Count indicator on the status bar to display statistics about the selected text.

Other Ways

1. Click Word Count button (Review tab | Proofing group) 2. Press CTRL+SHIFT+G

Automatic Page Breaks

As you type documents that exceed one page, Word automatically inserts page breaks, called **automatic page breaks** or **soft page breaks**, when it determines the text has filled one page according to paper size, margin settings, line spacing, and other settings. If you add text, delete text, or modify text on a page, Word recalculates the location of automatic page breaks and adjusts them accordingly.

Word performs page recalculation between the keystrokes, that is, in between the pauses in your typing. Thus, Word refers to the automatic page break task as **background repagination**. An automatic page break will occur in the next set of steps.

To Enter More Text and Insert a Citation Placeholder

The next task is to type the remainder of the third paragraph in the body of the research paper. The following steps enter this text and a citation placeholder at the end of the paragraph.

1 With the insertion point positioned at the end of the third sentence in the third paragraph, as shown in Figure 2–50, press the SPACEBAR.

2 Type the rest of the third paragraph: **Further, listening at a higher volume for extended periods of time could be unsafe. One expert suggests people should listen at only 30 percent maximum** and then press the SPACEBAR.

Q&A Why does the text move from the second page to the first page as I am typing?
Word, by default, will not allow the first line of a paragraph to be by itself at the bottom of a page (an **orphan**) or the last line of a paragraph to be by itself at the top of a page (a **widow**). As you type, Word adjusts the placement of the paragraph to avoid orphans and widows.

3 Click the Insert Citation button (References tab | Citations & Bibliography group) to display the Insert Citation menu. Click 'Add New Placeholder' on the Insert Citation menu to display the Placeholder Name dialog box.

4 Type **Chamberlain** as the tag name for the source.

5 Click the OK button (Placeholder Name dialog box) to close the dialog box and insert the tag name in the citation placeholder (shown in Figure 2–51).

6 Press the PERIOD key to end the sentence.

BTW
Page Break Locations
As you type, your page break may occur at different locations depending on Word settings and the type of printer connected to the computer.

To Hide and Show White Space

With the page break and header, it is difficult to see the entire third paragraph at once on the screen. With the screen in Print Layout view, you can hide white space, which is the space that is displayed at the top and bottom of pages (including headers and footers) and also the space between pages. The following steps hide white space, if your screen displays it, and then shows white space. *Why?* *You want to see as much of the third paragraph as possible at once, which spans the bottom of the first page and the top of the second page.*

1

- Position the pointer in the document window in the space between pages so that the pointer changes to a 'Hide White Space' button (Figure 2–51).

Q&A What if I am using a touch screen?
Proceed to step 2.

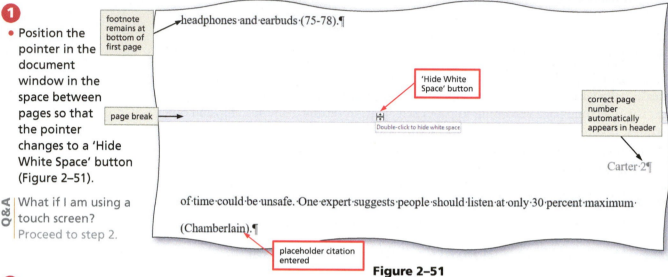

Figure 2–51

2

- Double-click while the pointer is a 'Hide White Space' button to hide white space.

Q&A What if I am using a touch screen?
Double-tap in the space between pages.

Does hiding white space have any effect on the printed document?
No.

3

- Position the pointer in the document window on the page break between pages so that the pointer changes to a 'Show White Space' button (Figure 2–52).

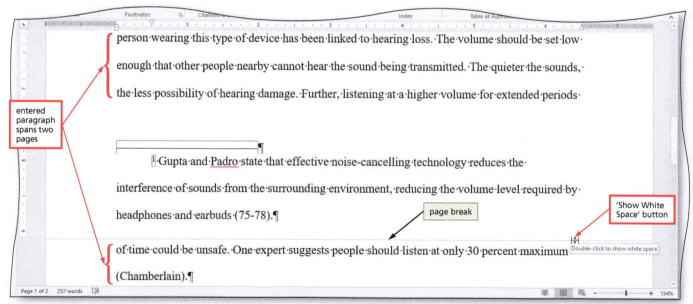

Figure 2–52

4
- Double-click while the pointer is a 'Show White Space' button to show white space.

What if I am using a touch screen?
Double-tap the page break.

Other Ways

1. Click File on ribbon, click Options tab in Backstage view, click Display in left pane (Word Options dialog box), remove or select check mark from 'Show white space between pages in Print Layout view' check box, click OK button

To Edit a Source

When you typed the third paragraph of the research paper, you inserted a citation placeholder, Chamberlain, for the source. You now have the source information, which is for a website, and are ready to enter it. The following steps edit the source for the Chamberlain citation placeholder.

1 Click somewhere in the citation placeholder to be edited, in this case (Chamberlain), to select the citation placeholder.

2 Click the Citation Options arrow to display the Citation Options menu.

3 Click Edit Source on the Citation Options menu to display the Edit Source dialog box.

4 If necessary, click the 'Type of Source' arrow (Edit Source dialog box); scroll to and then click Web site, so that the list shows fields required for a Web site.

5 Place a check mark in the 'Show All Bibliography Fields' check box to display more fields related to Web sites.

6 Click the Author text box. Type **Chamberlain, Megan Lynn** as the author.

7 Click the 'Name of Web Page' text box. Type **Understanding How Volume Levels Affect Hearing** as the webpage name.

8 Click the Production Company text box. Type **Course Technology** as the production company.

9 Click the Year Accessed text box. Type **2017** as the year accessed (Figure 2–53).

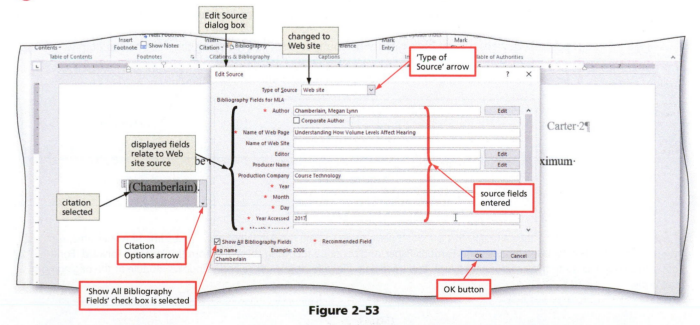

Figure 2–53

10 Press the TAB key and then type **Sept.** as the month accessed.

11 Press the TAB key and then type **16** as the day accessed.

12 Press the TAB key as many times as necessary to move the insertion point to the Medium text box and then type **Web** as the Medium.

◄ Do I need to enter a web address (URL)?
Q&A The latest MLA documentation style update does not require the web address in the source.

13 Click the OK button to close the dialog box and create the source.

BTW

Organizing Files and Folders
You should organize and store files in folders so that you easily can find the files later. For example, if you are taking an introductory technology class called CIS 101, a good practice would be to save all Word files in a Word folder in a CIS 101 folder. For a discussion of folders and detailed examples of creating folders, refer to the Office and Windows module at the beginning of this book.

To Enter More Text

The next task is to type the last paragraph of text in the research paper. The following steps enter this text.

1 Press the END key to position the insertion point at the end of the third paragraph and then press the ENTER key.

2 Type the last paragraph of the research paper (Figure 2–54): **More and more people are using headphones and earbuds with their computers and portable devices. Using high-quality listening devices and lowering the volume can help to lessen potential hearing loss from the use of headphones and earbuds.**

3 Save the research paper again on the same storage location with the same file name.

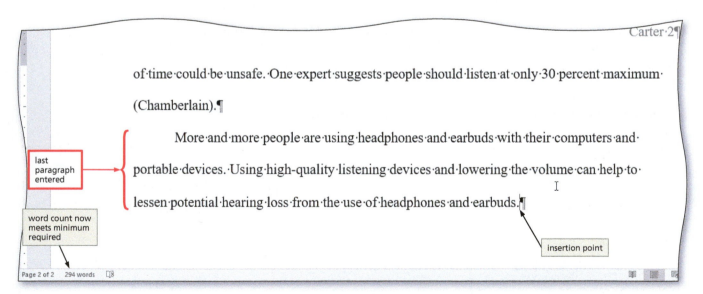

Figure 2–54

Break Point: If you wish to take a break, this is a good place to do so. You can exit Word now. To resume at a later time, run Word, open the file called Headphones and Earbuds Paper, and continue following the steps from this location forward. For a detailed example of exiting Word, running Word, and opening a file, refer to the Office and Windows module at the beginning of the book.

Creating an Alphabetical Works Cited Page

According to the MLA documentation style, the **works cited page** is a list of sources that are referenced directly in a research paper. You place the list on a separate numbered page with the title, Works Cited, centered one inch from the top margin. The works are to be alphabetized by the author's last name or, if the work has no author, by the work's title. The first line of each entry begins at the left margin. Indent subsequent lines of the same entry one-half inch from the left margin.

What is a bibliography?

A **bibliography** is an alphabetical list of sources referenced in a paper. Whereas the text of the research paper contains brief references to the source (the citations), the bibliography lists all publication information about the source. Documentation styles differ significantly in their guidelines for preparing a bibliography. Each style identifies formats for various sources, including books, magazines, pamphlets, newspapers, websites, television programs, paintings, maps, advertisements, letters, memos, and much more. You can find information about various styles and their guidelines in printed style guides and on the web.

To Page Break Manually

1 CHANGE DOCUMENT SETTINGS | 2 CREATE HEADER | 3 TYPE RESEARCH PAPER WITH CITATIONS
4 CREATE ALPHABETICAL WORKS CITED | 5 PROOFREAD & REVISE RESEARCH PAPER

     The next step is to insert a manual page break following the body of the research paper. *Why? According to the MLA documentation style, the works cited are to be displayed on a separate numbered page.*

     A **manual page break**, or **hard page break**, is one that you force into the document at a specific location. Word never moves or adjusts manual page breaks. Word, however, does adjust any automatic page breaks that follow a manual page break. Word inserts manual page breaks immediately above or to the left of the location of the insertion point. The following step inserts a manual page break after the text of the research paper.

- Verify that the insertion point is positioned at the end of the text of the research paper, as shown in Figure 2–54.

- Click Insert on the ribbon to display the Insert tab.

- Click the 'Insert a Page Break' button (Insert tab | Pages group) to insert a manual page break immediately to the left of the insertion point and position the insertion point immediately below the manual page break (Figure 2–55).

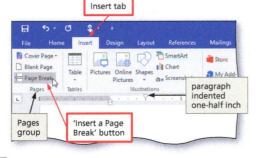

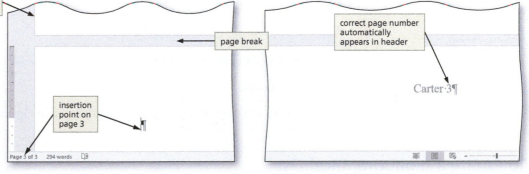

Figure 2–55

Other Ways

1. Press CTRL+ENTER

To Apply a Style

The works cited title is to be centered between the margins of the paper. If you simply issue the Center command, the title will not be centered properly. *Why? It will be to the right of the center point because earlier you set the first-line indent for paragraphs to one-half inch.*

To properly center the title of the works cited page, you could drag the 'First Line Indent' marker back to the left margin before centering the paragraph, or you could apply the Normal style to the location of the insertion point. Recall that you modified the Normal style for this document to 12-point Times New Roman with double-spaced, left-aligned paragraphs that have no space after the paragraphs.

To apply a style to a paragraph, first position the insertion point in the paragraph and then apply the style. The following step applies the modified Normal style to the location of the insertion point.

- Click Home on the ribbon to display the Home tab.

- With the insertion point on the paragraph mark at the top of page 3 (as shown in Figure 2–55) even if Normal is selected, click Normal in the Styles gallery (Home tab | Styles group) to apply the Normal style to the paragraph containing the insertion point (Figure 2–56).

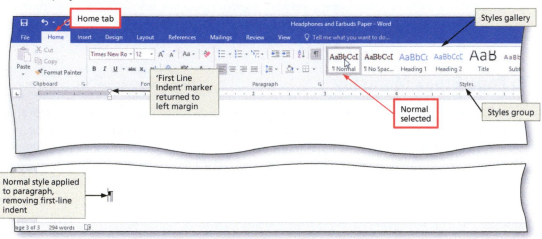

Figure 2–56

Other Ways

1. Click Styles Dialog Box Launcher (Home tab | Styles group), select desired style in Styles task pane

2. Press CTRL+SHIFT+S, click Style Name arrow in Apply Styles task pane, select desired style in list

To Center Text

The next task is to enter the title, Works Cited, centered between the margins of the paper. The following steps use a keyboard shortcut to format the title.

1 Press CTRL+E to center the paragraph mark.

2 Type **Works Cited** as the title.

3 Press the ENTER key.

4 Press CTRL+L to left-align the paragraph mark (shown in Figure 2–57).

To Create a Bibliographical List

While typing the research paper, you created several citations and their sources. The next task is to use Word to format the list of sources and alphabetize them in a **bibliographical list**. *Why? Word can create a bibliographical list with each element of the source placed in its correct position with proper punctuation, according to the specified style, saving you time looking up style guidelines. For example, in this research paper, the book source will list, in* *this order, the author name(s), book title, publisher city, publishing company name, and publication year with the correct punctuation between each element according to the MLA documentation style.* The following steps create an MLA-styled bibliographical list from the sources previously entered.

1

- Click References on the ribbon to display the References tab.
- With the insertion point positioned as shown in Figure 2–57, click the Bibliography button (References tab | Citations & Bibliography group) to display the Bibliography gallery (Figure 2–57).

Q&A Will I select the Works Cited option from the Bibliography gallery?
No. The title it inserts is not formatted according to the MLA documentation style. Thus, you will use the Insert Bibliography command instead.

References tab
Bibliography button
Citations & Bibliography group
Bibliography gallery
Insert Bibliography command
insertion point
title centered and typed
Works Cited

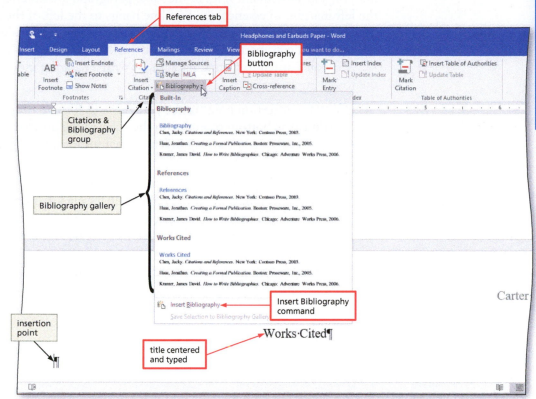

Figure 2–57

2

- Click Insert Bibliography in the Bibliography gallery to insert a list of sources at the location of the insertion point.
- If necessary, scroll to display the entire list of sources in the document window (Figure 2–58).

Q&A What is the n.d. in the first work?
The MLA documentation style uses the abbreviation n.d. for no date (for example, no date appears on the webpage).

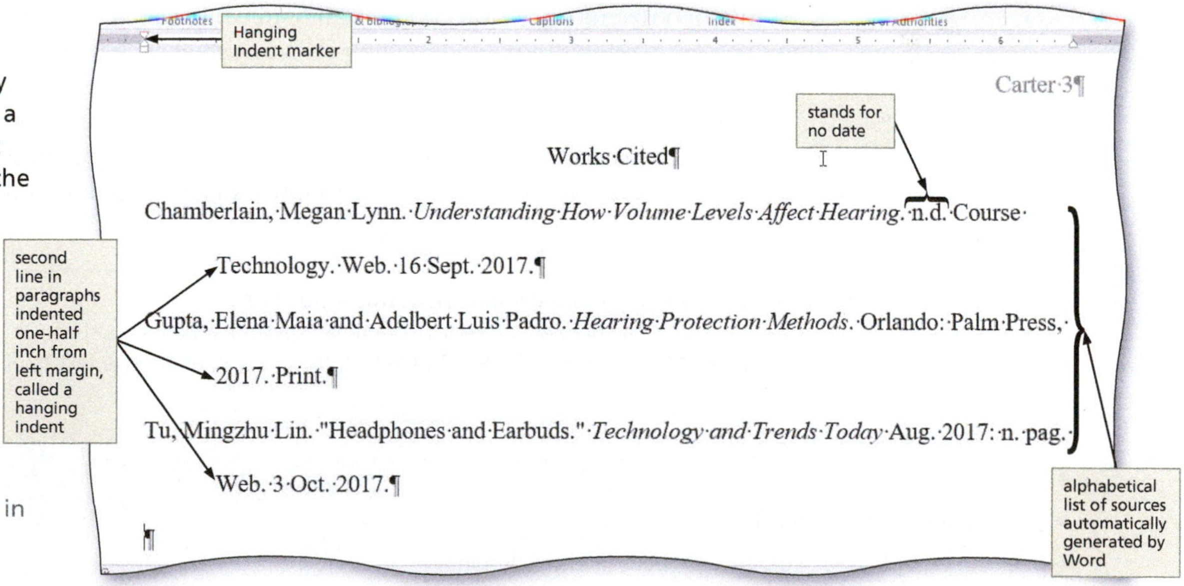

Hanging Indent marker
Carter 3
stands for no date
Works Cited
Chamberlain, Megan Lynn. Understanding How Volume Levels Affect Hearing. n.d. Course Technology. Web. 16 Sept. 2017.
Gupta, Elena Maia and Adelbert Luis Padro. Hearing Protection Methods. Orlando: Palm Press, 2017. Print.
Tu, Mingzhu Lin. "Headphones and Earbuds." Technology and Trends Today Aug. 2017: n. pag. Web. 3 Oct. 2017.
second line in paragraphs indented one-half inch from left margin, called a hanging indent
alphabetical list of sources automatically generated by Word

Figure 2–58

- Save the research paper again on the same storage location with the same file name.

To Format Paragraphs with a Hanging Indent

Notice in Figure 2–58 that the first line of each source entry begins at the left margin, and subsequent lines in the same paragraph are indented one-half inch from the left margin. In essence, the first line hangs to the left of the rest of the paragraph; thus, this type of paragraph formatting is called a **hanging indent**. The Bibliography style in Word automatically formats the works cited paragraphs with a hanging indent.

If you wanted to format paragraphs with a hanging indent, you would use one of the following techniques.

- With the insertion point in the paragraph to format, drag the **Hanging Indent marker** (the bottom triangle) on the ruler to the desired mark on the ruler (i.e., .5") to set the hanging indent at that location from the left margin.

or

- Right-click the paragraph to format (or, if using a touch screen, tap the 'Show Context Menu' button on the mini toolbar), click Paragraph on the shortcut menu, click the Indents and Spacing tab (Paragraph dialog box), click the Special arrow, click Hanging, and then click the OK button.

or

- Click the Paragraph Dialog Box Launcher (Home tab or Layout tab | Paragraph group), click the Indents and Spacing tab (Paragraph dialog box), click the Special arrow, click Hanging, and then click the OK button.

or

- With the insertion point in the paragraph to format, press CTRL+T.

BTW

Conserving Ink and Toner

If you want to conserve ink or toner, you can instruct Word to print draft quality documents by clicking File on the ribbon to open the Backstage view, clicking the Options tab in the Backstage view to display the Word Options dialog box, clicking Advanced in the left pane (Word Options dialog box), scrolling to the Print area in the right pane, placing a check mark in the 'Use draft quality' check box, and then clicking the OK button. Then, use the Backstage view to print the document as usual.

Proofreading and Revising the Research Paper

As discussed in Module 1, once you complete a document, you might find it necessary to make changes to it. Before submitting a paper to be graded, you should proofread it. While **proofreading**, ensure all the source information is correct and look for grammatical, typographical, and spelling errors. Also ensure that transitions between sentences flow smoothly and the sentences themselves make sense.

To assist you with the proofreading effort, Word provides several tools. You can go to a page, copy text, find text, replace text, insert a synonym, check spelling and grammar, and look up information. The following pages discuss these tools.

CONSIDER THIS

What should you consider when proofreading and revising a paper?

As you proofread the paper, look for ways to improve it. Check all grammar, spelling, and punctuation. Be sure the text is logical and transitions are smooth. Where necessary, add text, delete text, reword text, and move text to different locations. Ask yourself these questions:

- Does the title suggest the topic?

- Is the thesis clear?

- Is the purpose of the paper clear?

- Does the paper have an introduction, body, and conclusion?

- Does each paragraph in the body relate to the thesis?

- Is the conclusion effective?

- Are sources acknowledged correctly?

To Modify a Source

While proofreading the paper, you notice an error in the magazine title; specifically, the word, and, should be removed. If you modify the contents of any source, the list of sources automatically updates. *Why? Word automatically updates the contents of fields, and the bibliography is a field.* The following steps delete a word from the title of the magazine article.

- Click the Manage Sources button (References tab | Citations & Bibliography group) to display the Source Manager dialog box.
- Click the source you wish to edit in the Current List, in this case the article by Tu, to select the source.
- Click the Edit button (Source Manager dialog box) to display the Edit Source dialog box.
- In the Periodical Title text box, delete the word, and, from the title (Figure 2–59).

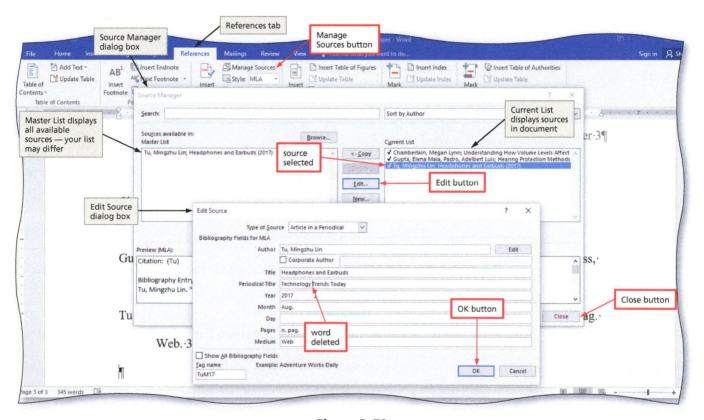

Figure 2–59

- Click the OK button (Edit Source dialog box) to close the dialog box.
- If a Microsoft Word dialog box appears, click its Yes button to update all occurrences of the source.
- Click the Close button (Source Manager dialog box) to update the list of sources and close the dialog box.

To Update a Field

Depending on settings, the bibliography field may not automatically reflect the edited magazine title. Thus, the following steps update the bibliography field. *Why? Because the bibliography is a field, you may need to instruct Word to update its contents.*

1

• Right-click anywhere in the bibliography text to display a shortcut menu related to fields (Figure 2–60).

What if I am using a touch screen?
Press and hold anywhere in the bibliography text and then tap the 'Show Context Menu' button on the mini toolbar.

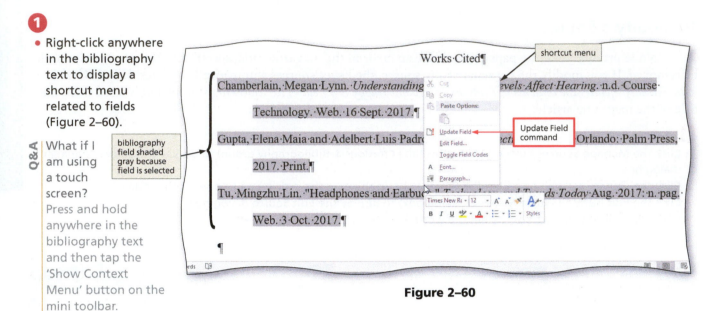

Figure 2–60

Why are all the words in the bibliography shaded gray?
By default, Word shades selected fields gray.

What if the bibliography field is not shaded gray?
Click File on the ribbon to open the Backstage view, click the Options tab in the Backstage view, click Advanced in the left pane (Word Options dialog box), scroll to the 'Show document content' area, click the Field shading arrow, click When selected, and then click the OK button.

2

• Click Update Field on the shortcut menu to update the selected field (Figure 2–61).

Can I update all fields in a document at once?
Yes. Select the entire document and then follow these steps.

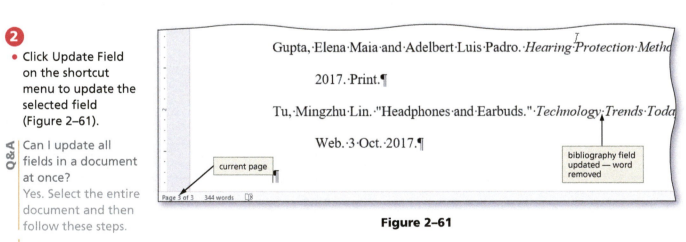

Figure 2–61

Other Ways

1. Select the field, press F9

To Convert a Field to Regular Text

If, for some reason, you wanted to convert a field, such as the bibliography field, to regular text, you would perform the following steps. Keep in mind, though, once you convert the field to regular text, it no longer is a field that can be updated.

1. Click somewhere in the field to select it, in this case, somewhere in the bibliography.

2. Press CTRL+SHIFT+F9 to convert the selected field to regular text.

To Go to a Page

The next task in revising the paper is to modify text on the second page of the document. ***Why?*** *You want to copy text from one location to another on the second page.* You could scroll to the desired location in the document, or you can use the Navigation Pane to browse through pages in a document. The following steps display the top of the second page in the document window and position the insertion point at the beginning of that page.

1

- Click View on the ribbon to display the View tab.

- Place a check mark in the 'Open the Navigation Pane' check box (View tab | Show group) to open the Navigation Pane on the left side of the Word window.

- If necessary, click the Pages tab in the Navigation Pane to display thumbnails of the pages in the document.

- Scroll to, if necessary, and then click the thumbnail of the second page to display the top of the selected page in the top of the document window (Figure 2–62).

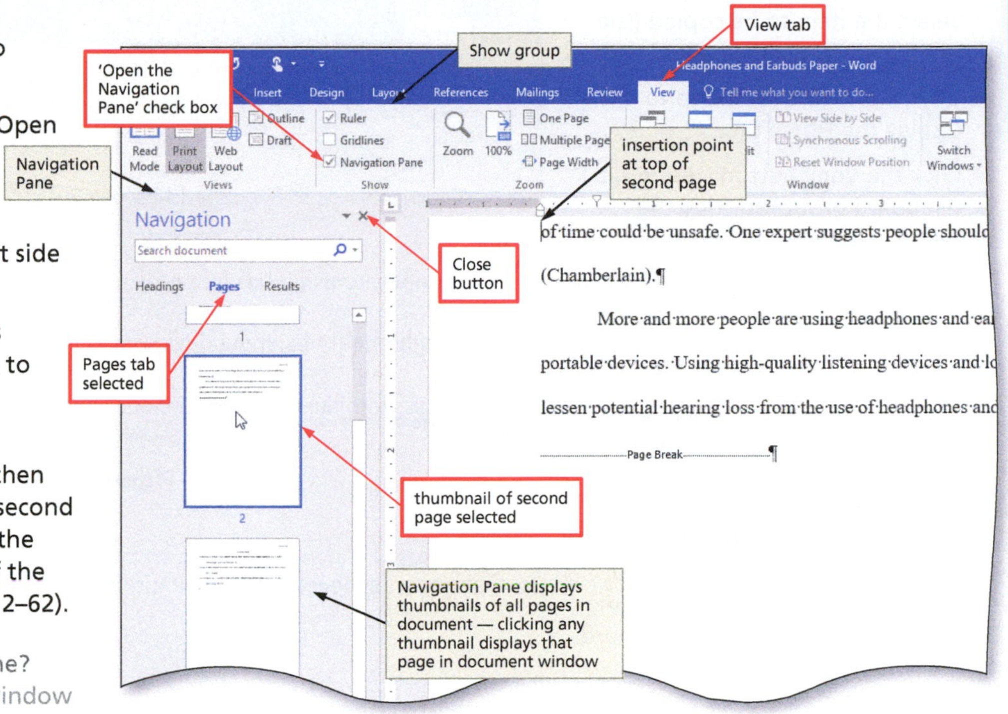

Q&A What is the Navigation Pane?
The Navigation Pane is a window that enables you to browse through headings in a document, browse through pages in a document, or search for text in a document.

Figure 2–62

2

- Click the Close button in the Navigation Pane to close the pane.

Other Ways

1. Click Find arrow (Home tab | Editing group), click Go To on Find menu, click Go To tab (Find and Replace dialog box), enter page number, click Go To button

2. Click Page Number indicator on status bar, click Pages tab in Navigation Pane, click thumbnail of desired page (Navigation Pane)

3. Press CTRL+G, enter page number (Find and Replace dialog box), click Go To button

Copying, Cutting, and Pasting

While proofreading the research paper, you decide it would read better if the word, volume, in the second sentence of the last paragraph also appeared after the word, maximum, in the last sentence of the previous paragraph. You could type the word at the desired location, but you decide to use the Office Clipboard. The **Office Clipboard** is a temporary storage area that holds up to 24 items (text or graphics) copied from any Office program. The Office Clipboard works with the copy, cut, and paste commands:

- **Copying** is the process of placing items on the Office Clipboard, leaving the item in the document.

- **Cutting** removes the item from the document before placing it on the Office Clipboard.

- **Pasting** is the process of copying an item from the Office Clipboard into the document at the location of the insertion point.

To Copy and Paste

In the research paper, you copy a word from one location to another. *Why? The sentence reads better with the word, volume, inserted after the word, maximum.* The following steps copy and paste a word.

- Select the item to be copied (the word, volume, in this case).
- Click Home on the ribbon to display the Home tab.
- Click the Copy button (Home tab | Clipboard group) to copy the selected item in the document to the Office Clipboard (Figure 2–63).

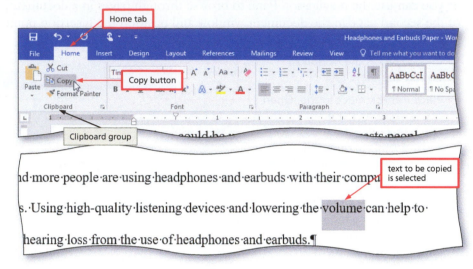

Figure 2–63

- Position the insertion point at the location where the item should be pasted (immediately following the space to the right of the word, maximum, in this case) (Figure 2–64).

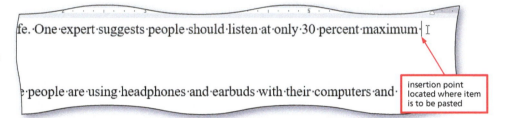

Figure 2–64

③

- Click the Paste button (Home tab | Clipboard group) to paste the copied item in the document at the location of the insertion point (Figure 2–65).

Q&A
What if I click the Paste arrow by mistake?
Click the Paste arrow again to remove the Paste menu and repeat Step 3.

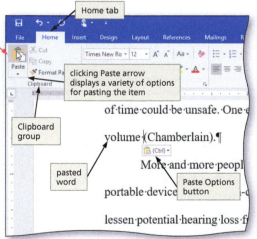
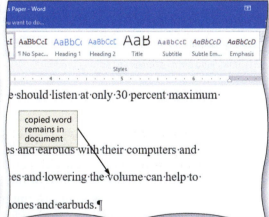

Figure 2–65

Other Ways

1. Click Copy on shortcut menu (or, if using touch, tap Copy on mini toolbar), right-click where item is to be pasted, click 'Keep Source Formatting' in Paste Options area on shortcut menu (or, if using touch, tap Paste on mini toolbar)

2. Select item, press CTRL+C, position insertion point at paste location, press CTRL+V

To Display the Paste Options Menu

1 CHANGE DOCUMENT SETTINGS | 2 CREATE HEADER | 3 TYPE RESEARCH PAPER WITH CITATIONS
4 CREATE ALPHABETICAL WORKS CITED | 5 PROOFREAD & REVISE RESEARCH PAPER

When you paste an item or move an item using drag-and-drop editing, which was discussed in the previous module, Word automatically displays a Paste Options button near the pasted or moved text (shown in Figure 2–65). *Why? The Paste Options button allows you to change the format of a pasted item. For example, you can instruct Word to format the pasted item the same way as where it was copied (the source) or format it the same way as where it is being pasted (the destination).* The following steps display the Paste Options menu.

1
- Click the Paste Options button to display the Paste Options menu (Figure 2–66).

Q&A What are the functions of the buttons on the Paste Options menu?

In general, the left button indicates the pasted item should look the same as it did in its original location (the source). The second button formats the pasted text to match the rest of the item where it was pasted (the destination). The third button removes all formatting from the pasted item. The 'Set Default Paste' command displays the Word Options dialog box. Keep in mind that the buttons shown on a Paste Options menu will vary, depending on the item being pasted.

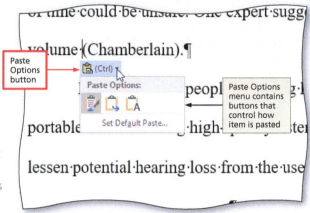

Figure 2–66

2
- Click anywhere to remove the Paste Options menu from the window.

Other Ways

1. CTRL or ESC (to remove the Paste Options menu)

To Find Text

1 CHANGE DOCUMENT SETTINGS | 2 CREATE HEADER | 3 TYPE RESEARCH PAPER WITH CITATIONS
4 CREATE ALPHABETICAL WORKS CITED | 5 PROOFREAD & REVISE RESEARCH PAPER

While proofreading the paper, you would like to locate all occurrences of the word, portable. *Why? You are contemplating changing occurrences of this word to the word, mobile.* The following steps find all occurrences of specific text in a document.

1
- Click the Find button (Home tab | Editing group) to display the Navigation Pane.

Q&A What if I am using a touch screen?

Tap the Find button (Home tab | Editing group) and then tap Find on the menu.

- If necessary, click the Results tab in the Navigation Pane, which displays a Search box where you can type text for which you want to search (Figure 2–67).

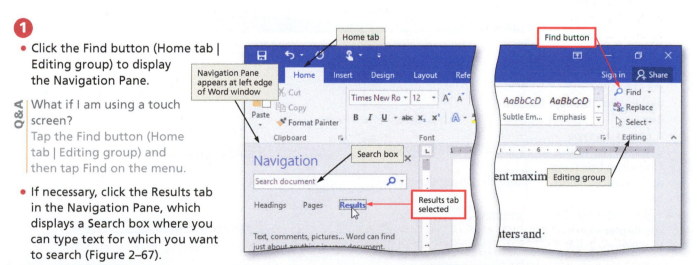

Figure 2–67

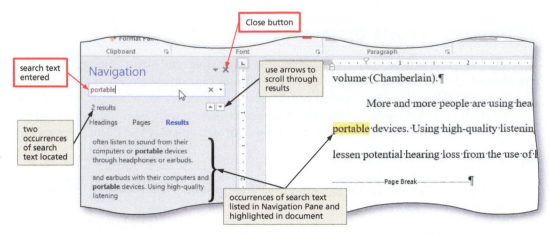

2

- Type **portable** in the Navigation Pane Search box to display all occurrences of the typed text, called the search text, in the Navigation Pane and to highlight the occurrences of the search text in the document window (Figure 2–68).

Figure 2–68

3

 Experiment

- Click both occurrences in the Navigation Pane and watch Word display the associated text in the document window.

Experiment

- Type various search text in the Navigation Pane Search box, and watch Word both list matches in the Navigation Pane and highlight matches in the document window.

- Click the Close button in the Navigation Pane to close the pane.

Other Ways
1. Click Find arrow (Home tab | Editing group), click Find on Find menu, enter search text in Navigation Pane   2. Click Page Number indicator on status bar, enter search text in Navigation Pane   3. Press CTRL+F, enter search text in Navigation Pane

1 CHANGE DOCUMENT SETTINGS | 2 CREATE HEADER | 3 TYPE RESEARCH PAPER WITH CITATIONS
4 CREATE ALPHABETICAL WORKS CITED | 5 PROOFREAD & REVISE RESEARCH PAPER

To Replace Text

You decide to change all occurrences of the word, portable, to the word, mobile. ***Why?*** *The term, mobile devices, is more commonly used than portable devices.* Word's find and replace feature locates each occurrence of a word or phrase and then replaces it with text you specify. The following steps find and replace text.

1

- Click the Replace button (Home tab | Editing group) to display the Replace sheet in the Find and Replace dialog box.

- If necessary, type **portable** in the Find what box (Find and Replace dialog box).

- Type **mobile** in the Replace with box (Figure 2–69).

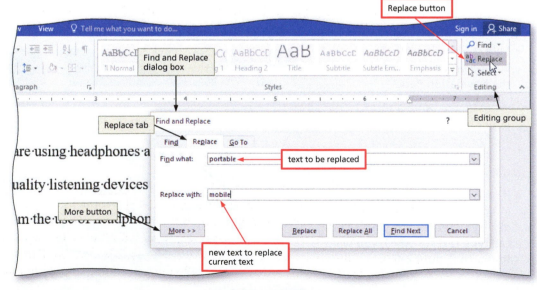

Figure 2–69

2

- Click the Replace All button to instruct Word to replace all occurrences of the Find what text with the Replace with text (Figure 2–70). If Word displays a dialog box asking if you want to continue searching from the beginning of the document, click the Yes button.

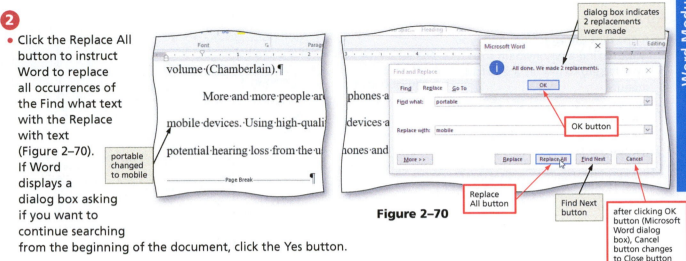

Figure 2–70

Q&A Does Word search the entire document?

If the insertion point is at the beginning of the document, Word searches the entire document; otherwise, Word may search from the location of the insertion point to the end of the document and then display a dialog box asking if you want to continue searching from the beginning. You also can search a section of text by selecting the text before clicking the Replace or Replace All button.

3

- Click the OK button (Microsoft Word dialog box) to close the dialog box.
- Click the Close button (Find and Replace dialog box) to close the dialog box.

Other Ways

1. Press CTRL+H

Find and Replace Dialog Box

The Replace All button (Find and Replace dialog box) replaces all occurrences of the Find what text with the Replace with text. In some cases, you may want to replace only certain occurrences of a word or phrase, not all of them. To instruct Word to confirm each change, click the Find Next button (Find and Replace dialog box) (shown in Figure 2–70), instead of the Replace All button. When Word locates an occurrence of the text, it pauses and waits for you to click either the Replace button or the Find Next button. Clicking the Replace button changes the text; clicking the Find Next button instructs Word to disregard the replacement and look for the next occurrence of the Find what text.

If you accidentally replace the wrong text, you can undo a replacement by clicking the Undo button on the Quick Access Toolbar. If you used the Replace All button, Word undoes all replacements. If you used the Replace button, Word undoes only the most recent replacement.

BTW

Finding Formatting
To search for formatting or a special character, click the More button in the Find and Replace dialog box (shown in Figure 2–69). To find formatting, use the Format button in the Find dialog box. To find a special character, use the Special button.

1 CHANGE DOCUMENT SETTINGS | 2 CREATE HEADER | 3 TYPE RESEARCH PAPER WITH CITATIONS
4 CREATE ALPHABETICAL WORKS CITED | 5 PROOFREAD & REVISE RESEARCH PAPER

To Find and Insert a Synonym

In this project, you would like a synonym for the word, lessen, in the last paragraph of the research paper. **Why?** *When writing, you may discover that you used the same word in multiple locations or that a word you used was not quite appropriate, which is the case here.* In these instances, you will want to look up a **synonym**, or a word similar in meaning, to the duplicate or inappropriate word. A **thesaurus** is a book of synonyms. Word provides synonyms and a thesaurus for your convenience. The following steps find a suitable synonym.

- Right-click the word for which you want to find a synonym (in this case, lessen) to display a shortcut menu.
- Point to Synonyms on the shortcut menu to display a list of synonyms for the word you right-clicked (Figure 2–71).

Q&A What if I am using a touch screen? Press and hold the word for which you want a synonym, tap the 'Show Context Menu' button on the mini toolbar, and then tap Synonyms on the shortcut menu.

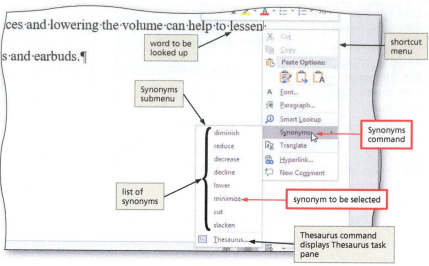

Figure 2–71

- Click the synonym you want (in this case, minimize) on the Synonyms submenu to replace the selected word in the document with the selected synonym (Figure 2–72).

Q&A What if the synonyms list on the shortcut menu does not display a suitable word?
You can display the thesaurus in the Thesaurus task pane by clicking Thesaurus on the Synonyms submenu. The Thesaurus task pane displays a complete thesaurus, in which you can look up synonyms for various meanings of a word. You also can look up an antonym, or word with an opposite meaning.

More and more people are using headphones and earbuds with the mobile devices. Using high-quality listening devices and lowering the vol minimize potential hearing loss from the use of headphones and earbuds.¶

word, lessen, changed to minimize

Figure 2–72

Other Ways

1. Click Thesaurus button (Review tab | Proofing group)
2. Press SHIFT+F7

To Check Spelling and Grammar at Once

1 CHANGE DOCUMENT SETTINGS | 2 CREATE HEADER | 3 TYPE RESEARCH PAPER WITH CITATIONS
4 CREATE ALPHABETICAL WORKS CITED | 5 PROOFREAD & REVISE RESEARCH PAPER

As discussed in Module 1, Word checks spelling and grammar as you type and places a wavy underline below possible spelling or grammar errors. Module 1 illustrated how to check these flagged words immediately. The next steps check spelling and grammar at once. **Why?** *Some users prefer to wait and check their entire document for spelling and grammar errors at once.*

Note: In the following steps, the word, sound, has been misspelled intentionally as sould to illustrate the use of Word's check spelling and grammar at once feature. If you are completing this project on a computer or mobile device, your research paper may contain different misspelled words, depending on the accuracy of your typing.

1

- Press CTRL+HOME because you want the spelling and grammar check to begin from the top of the document.
- Click Review on the ribbon to display the Review tab.

- Click the 'Spelling & Grammar' button (Review tab | Proofing group) to begin the spelling and grammar check at the location of the insertion point, which, in this case, is at the beginning of the document.

- Click the desired word in the list of suggestions in the Spelling task pane (sound, in this case) (Figure 2–73).

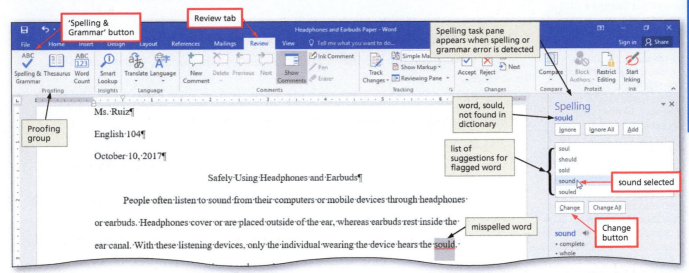

Figure 2–73

2

- With the word, sound, selected in the list of suggestions, click the Change button (Spelling task pane) to change the flagged word to the selected suggestion and then continue the spelling and grammar check until the next error is identified or the end of the document is reached (Figure 2–74).

3

- Because the flagged word is a proper noun and spelled correctly, click the Ignore All button (Spelling task pane) to ignore this and future occurrences of the flagged proper noun and then continue the spelling and grammar check until the next error is identified or the end of the document is reached.

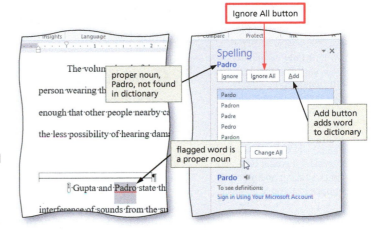

Figure 2–74

4

- When the spelling and grammar check is finished and Word displays a dialog box, click its OK button.

 Can I check spelling of just a section of a document?

Yes, select the text before starting the spelling and grammar check.

Other Ways

1. Click 'Spelling and Grammar Check' icon on status bar
2. Press F7

The Main and Custom Dictionaries

As shown in the previous steps, Word may flag a proper noun as an error because the proper noun is not in its main dictionary. You may want to add some proper nouns that you use repeatedly, such as a company name or employee names, to Word's dictionary. To prevent Word from flagging proper nouns as errors, you can add the proper nouns to the custom dictionary. To add a correctly spelled word to the custom dictionary, click the Add button (Spelling task pane) or right-click the flagged word

BTW

Readability Statistics

You can instruct Word to display readability statistics when it has finished a spelling and grammar check on a document. Three readability statistics presented are the percent of passive sentences, the Flesch Reading Ease score, and the Flesch-Kincaid Grade Level score. The Flesch Reading Ease score uses a 100-point scale to rate the ease with which a reader can understand the text in a document. A higher score means the document is easier to understand. The Flesch-Kincaid Grade Level score rates the text in a document on a U.S. school grade level. For example, a score of 10.0 indicates a student in the tenth grade can understand the material. To show readability statistics when the spelling check is complete, open the Backstage view, click the Options tab in the Backstage view, click Proofing in the left pane (Word Options dialog box), place a check mark in the 'Show readability statistics' check box, and then click the OK button. Readability statistics will be displayed the next time you check spelling and grammar at once in the document.

(or, if using touch, press and hold and then tap 'Show Context Menu' button on the mini toolbar) and then click 'Add to Dictionary' on the shortcut menu. Once you have added a word to the custom dictionary, Word no longer will flag it as an error.

TO VIEW OR MODIFY ENTRIES IN A CUSTOM DICTIONARY

To view or modify the list of words in a custom dictionary, you would follow these steps.

1. Click File on the ribbon and then click the Options tab in the Backstage view.
2. Click Proofing in the left pane (Word Options dialog box).
3. Click the Custom Dictionaries button.
4. When Word displays the Custom Dictionaries dialog box, if necessary, place a check mark next to the dictionary name to view or modify. Click the 'Edit Word List' button (Custom Dictionaries dialog box). (In this dialog box, you can add or delete entries to and from the selected custom dictionary.)
5. When finished viewing and/or modifying the list, click the OK button in the dialog box.
6. Click the OK button (Custom Dictionaries dialog box).
7. If the 'Suggest from main dictionary only' check box is selected in the Word Options dialog box, remove the check mark. Click the OK button (Word Options dialog box).

TO SET THE DEFAULT CUSTOM DICTIONARY

If you have multiple custom dictionaries, you can specify which one Word should use when checking spelling. To set the default custom dictionary, you would follow these steps.

1. Click File on the ribbon and then click the Options tab in the Backstage view.
2. Click Proofing in the left pane (Word Options dialog box).
3. Click the Custom Dictionaries button.
4. When the Custom Dictionaries dialog box is displayed, place a check mark next to the desired dictionary name. Click the Change Default button (Custom Dictionaries dialog box).
5. Click the OK button (Custom Dictionaries dialog box).
6. If the 'Suggest from main dictionary only' check box is selected in the Word Options dialog box, remove the check mark. Click the OK button (Word Options dialog box).

To Look Up Information

1 CHANGE DOCUMENT SETTINGS | 2 CREATE HEADER | 3 TYPE RESEARCH PAPER WITH CITATIONS
4 CREATE ALPHABETICAL WORKS CITED | 5 PROOFREAD & REVISE RESEARCH PAPER

If you are connected to the Internet, you can use the Insights task pane to search through various forms of reference information, including images, on the web and/or look up a definition of a word. The following steps use the Insights task pane to look up a definition of a word. *Why? Assume you want to see some images and know more about the word, headphones.*

1

- Position the insertion point in the word you want to look up (in this case, headphones).
- Click the Smart Lookup button (Review tab | Insights group) to open the Insights task pane (Figure 2–75).

Q&A Why does my Insights task pane look different? Depending on your settings, your Insights task pane may appear different from the figure shown here.

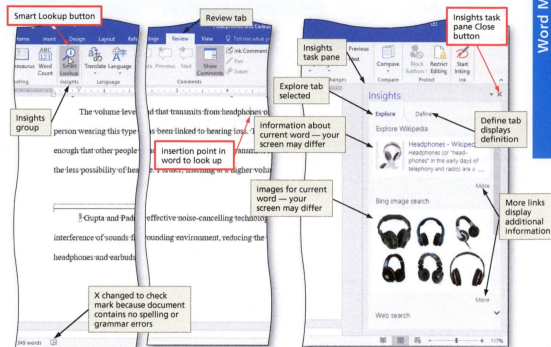

Figure 2–75

Experiment

- With the Explore tab selected in the Insights task pane, scroll through the information and images that appear in the Insights task pane. Click the Define tab in the Insights task pane to see a definition of the current word. Click the Explore tab to redisplay information from the web and images of the current word. Click one of the More links in the Insights task pane to view additional information. Click the Back button at the top of the Insights task pane to return to the previous display.

Q&A Can I copy information from the Insights task pane into my document?
Yes, you can use the Copy and Paste commands. When using Word to insert material from the Insights task pane or any other online reference, however, be careful not to plagiarize.

2

- Click the Close button in the Insights task pane.

Q&A Is the Research task pane from previous Word editions still available?
Yes. While holding down the ALT key, you can click the word you want to look up (such as headphones) to open the Research task pane and display a dictionary entry for the ALT+clicked word.

To Zoom Multiple Pages

1 CHANGE DOCUMENT SETTINGS | 2 CREATE HEADER | 3 TYPE RESEARCH PAPER WITH CITATIONS
4 CREATE ALPHABETICAL WORKS CITED | 5 PROOFREAD & REVISE RESEARCH PAPER

The next steps display multiple pages in the document window at once. **Why?** *You want to be able to see all pages in the research paper on the screen at the same time. You also hide formatting marks and the rulers so that the display is easier to view.*

1

- Click Home on the ribbon to display the Home tab.
- If the 'Show/Hide ¶' button (Home tab | Paragraph group) is selected, click it to hide formatting marks.
- Click View on the ribbon to display the View tab.

- If the rulers are displayed, click the View Ruler check box (View tab | Show group) to remove the check mark from the check box and remove the horizontal and vertical rulers from the screen.

- Click the Multiple Pages button (View tab | Zoom group) to display all three pages at once in the document window (Figure 2–76).

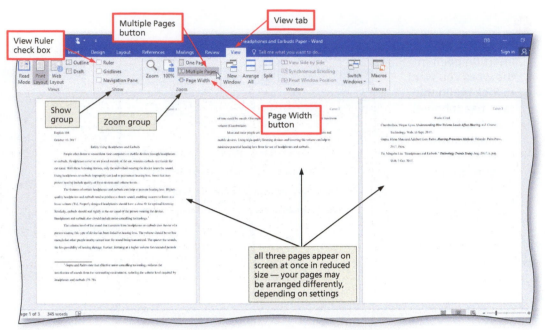

Why do the pages appear differently on my screen? Depending on settings, Word may display all the pages as shown in Figure 2–76 or may show the pages differently.

Figure 2–76

 2

- When finished, click the Page Width button (View tab | Zoom group) to return to the page width zoom.

To Change Read Mode Color

1 CHANGE DOCUMENT SETTINGS | 2 CREATE HEADER | 3 TYPE RESEARCH PAPER WITH CITATIONS
4 CREATE ALPHABETICAL WORKS CITED | **5 PROOFREAD & REVISE RESEARCH PAPER**

You would like to read the entire research paper using Read mode but would like to change the background color of the Read mode screen. *Why? You prefer a different background color for reading on the screen.* The following steps change the color of the screen in Read mode.

 1

- Click the Read Mode button on the status bar to switch to Read mode.

- Click the View tab to display the View menu.

- Point to Page Color on the View menu to display the Page Color submenu (Figure 2–77).

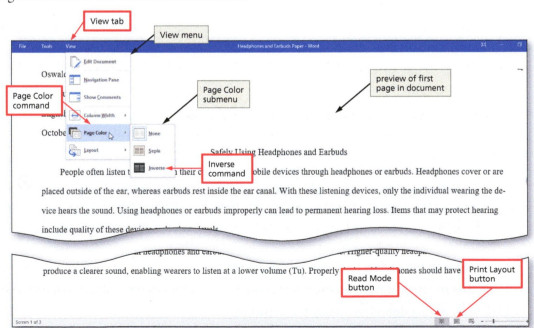

Figure 2–77

2

- Click Inverse on the Page Color submenu to change the color of the Read mode screen to inverse (Figure 2–78).

3

- When finished, click the Print Layout button (shown in Figure 2–77) on the status bar to return to Print Layout view.

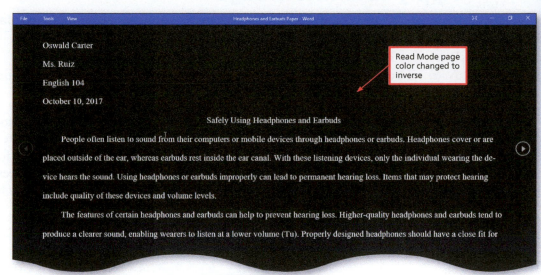

Read Mode page color changed to inverse

Figure 2–78

To Save and Print the Document and Exit Word

The following steps save and print the document and then exit Word. For a detailed example of the procedure summarized below, refer to the Office and Windows module at the beginning of this book.

1 Save the research paper again on the same storage location with the same file name.

2 If requested by your instructor, print the research paper.

3 Exit Word.

Summary

In this module, you have learned how to modify styles, adjust line and paragraph spacing, use headers to number pages, insert and edit citations and their sources, add footnotes, create a bibliographical list of sources, update a field, go to a page, copy and paste text, find and replace text, check spelling and grammar, and look up information.

CONSIDER THIS: PLAN AHEAD

What decisions will you need to make when creating your next research paper?
Use these guidelines as you complete the assignments in this module and create your own research papers outside of this class.

1. Select a topic.
    a) Spend time brainstorming ideas for a topic.
    b) Choose a topic you find interesting.
    c) For shorter papers, narrow the scope of the topic; for longer papers, broaden the scope.
    d) Identify a tentative thesis statement, which is a sentence describing the paper's subject matter.
2. Research the topic and take notes, being careful not to plagiarize.
3. Organize your notes into related concepts, identifying all main ideas and supporting details in an outline.
4. Write the first draft from the outline, referencing all sources of information and following the guidelines identified in the required documentation style.
5. Create the list of sources, using the formats specified in the required documentation style.
6. Proofread and revise the paper.

Apply Your Knowledge

Reinforce the skills and apply the concepts you learned in this module.

Revising Text and Paragraphs in a Document

Note: To complete this assignment, you will be required to use the Data Files. Please contact your instructor for information about accessing the Data Files.

Instructions: Run Word. Open the document, Apply 2-1 3-D Printers Paragraph Draft, which is located in the Data Files. The document you open contains a paragraph of text. You are to revise the document as follows: move a word, move another word and change the format of the moved word, change paragraph indentation, change line spacing, find all occurrences of a word, replace all occurrences of a word with another word, locate a synonym, and edit the header. The modified paragraph is shown in Figure 2–79.

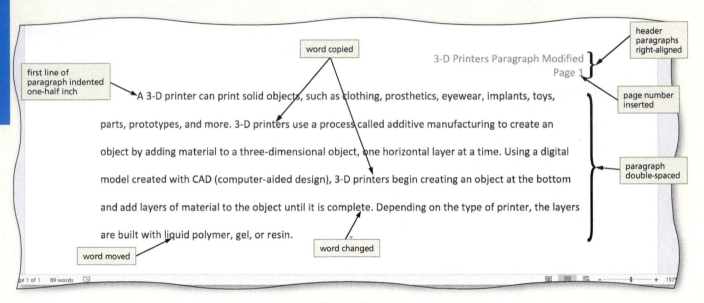

Figure 2–79

Perform the following tasks:

1. Copy the text, printers, from the second sentence and paste it in the third sentence after the underlined word, liquid.

2. Select the underlined word, liquid, in the third sentence. Use drag-and-drop editing to move the selected word, liquid, so that it is before the word, polymer, in the last sentence. (If you are using a touch screen, use the cut and paste commands to move the word.) Click the Paste Options button that displays to the right of the moved word, liquid. Remove the underline format from the moved word by clicking 'Keep Text Only' on the Paste Options menu.

3. Display the ruler, if necessary. Use the ruler to indent the first line of the paragraph one-half inch. (If you are using a touch screen, use the Paragraph dialog box.)

4. Change the line spacing of the paragraph to double.

5. Use the Navigation Pane to find all occurrences of the word, printer. How many are there?

6. Use the Find and Replace dialog box to replace all occurrences of the word, 3D, with the word, 3-D. How many replacements were made?

7. Use the Navigation Pane to find the word, finished. Use Word's thesaurus to change the word, finished, to the word, complete. What other words are in the list of synonyms?

8. Switch to the header so that you can edit it. In the first line of the header, change the word, Draft, to the word, Modified, so that it reads: 3-D Printers Paragraph Modified.

9. In the second line of the header, insert a page number (a plain number with no formatting) one space after the word, Page.

10. Change the alignment of both lines of text in the header from left-aligned to right-aligned. Switch back to the document text.

11. If requested by your instructor, enter your first and last name on a separate line below the page number in the header.

12. Click File on the ribbon and then click Save As. Save the document using the file name, Apply 2-1 3-D Printers Paragraph Modified.

13. Submit the modified document, shown in Figure 2–79, in the format specified by your instructor.

14. Use the Insights task pane to look up the word prosthetics. Click the Explore tab in the Insights task pane. Which web articles appeared? What images appeared? Click the Define tab in the Insights task pane. Which dictionary was used?

15. ✸ Answer the questions posed in #5, #6, #7, and #14. How would you find and replace a special character, such as a paragraph mark?

Extend Your Knowledge

Extend the skills you learned in this module and experiment with new skills. You may need to use Help to complete the assignment.

Working with References and Proofing Tools

Note: To complete this assignment, you will be required to use the Data Files. Please contact your instructor for information about accessing the Data Files.

Instructions: Run Word. Open the document, Extend 2-1 Databases Paper Draft, from the Data Files. You will add another footnote to the paper, convert the footnotes to endnotes, modify the Endnote Text style, change the format of the note reference marks, use Word's readability statistics, translate the document to another language (Figure 2–80), and convert the document from MLA to APA documentation style.

Perform the following tasks:
1. Use Help to learn more about footers, footnotes and endnotes, readability statistics, bibliography styles, AutoCorrect, and Word's translation features.

2. Delete the footer from the document.

3. Insert a second footnote at an appropriate place in the research paper. Use the following footnote text: A data warehouse is a huge database that stores and manages the data required to analyze past and current transactions.

4. Change the location of the footnotes from bottom of page to below text. How did the placement of the footnotes change?

5. Convert the footnotes to endnotes. Where are the endnotes positioned?

6. Modify the Endnote Text style to 12-point Times New Roman font, double-spaced text with a hanging-line indent.

7. Change the format of the note reference marks to capital letters (A, B, etc.).

Continued >

Extend Your Knowledge *continued*

8. Add an AutoCorrect entry that replaces the word, buziness, with the word, business. Type the following sentence as the first sentence in the last paragraph of the paper, misspelling the word, business, as buziness to test the AutoCorrect entry: `Organizations often use a database to manage buziness or other functions.` Delete the AutoCorrect entry that replaces buziness with the word, business.

9. Display the Word Count dialog box. How many words, characters without spaces, characters with spaces, paragraphs, and lines are in the document? Be sure to include footnote and endnote text in the statistics.

10. Check spelling of the document, displaying readability statistics. What are the Flesch-Kincaid Grade Level and the Flesch Reading Ease score? Modify the paper to increase the reading ease score. How did you modify the paper? What are the new statistics?

11. If requested by your instructor, change the student name at the top of the paper to your name, including the last name in the header.

12. Save the revised document with the file name, Extend 2-1 Databases Paper Modified, and then submit it in the format specified by your instructor.

13. If you have an Internet connection, translate the research paper into a language of your choice using the Translate button (Review tab | Language group), as shown in Figure 2–80. Submit the translated document in the format specified by your instructor. Use the Mini Translator to hear how to pronounce three words in your paper.

14. Select the entire document and then change the documentation style from MLA to APA. Save the APA version of the document with a new file name. Compare the APA version to the MLA version. If you have a hard copy of each and your instructor requests it, circle the differences between the two documents.

15. ✳ Answer the questions posed in #4, #5, #9, and #10. Where did you insert the second footnote and why?

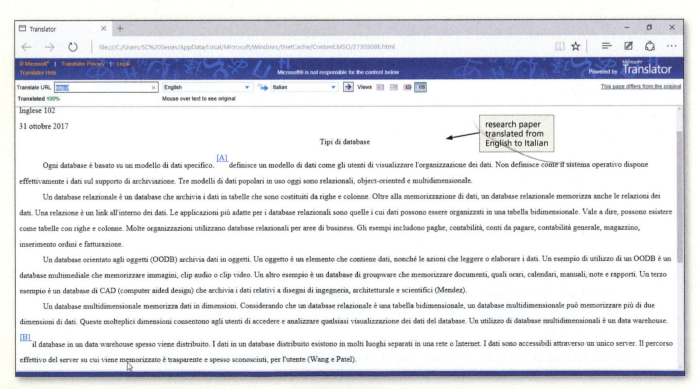

Figure 2–80

Expand Your World

Create a solution that uses cloud or web technologies by learning and investigating on your own from general guidance.

Using an Online Bibliography Tool to Create a List of Sources

Instructions: Assume you are using a computer or mobile device that does not have Word but has Internet access. To make use of time between classes, you use an online bibliography tool to create a list of sources that you can copy and paste into the Works Cited pages of a research paper that is due tomorrow.

Perform the following tasks:

1. Run a browser. Search for the text, online bibliography tool, using a search engine. Visit several of the online bibliography tools and determine which you would like to use to create a list of sources. Navigate to the desired online bibliography tool.

2. Use the online bibliography tool to enter list of sources shown below (Figure 2–81):

    Alverez, Juan and Tracy Marie Wilson. *Radon in the Home*. Chicago: Martin Publishing, 2017. Print.

    Buchalski, Leonard Adam. *Radon and Your Health*. Los Angeles: Coastal Works, 2017. Print.

    Johnson, Shantair Jada. "Radon Facts." *Environment Danger* Aug. 2017. Web. 31 Aug. 2017.

    Slobovnik, Vincent Alexander. *The Radon Guide*. Aug. 2017. Course Technology. Web. 18 Sept. 2017.

    Wakefield, Ginger Lynn and Bethany Olivia Ames. "Radon Removal Systems." *Living Well Today* Aug. 2017. Web. 3 Oct. 2017.

    Zhao, Shen Li. *Radon Testing Procedures*. Sept. 2017. Course Technology. Web. 8 Sept. 2017.

3. If requested by your instructor, replace the name in one of the sources above with your name.

4. Search for another source that discusses radon issues in the home. Add that source.

5. Copy and paste the list of sources into a Word document.

6. Save the document with the file name, Expand 2-1 Radon Issues Sources. Submit the document in the format specified by your instructor.

7. ✺ Which online bibliography tools did you evaluate? Which one did you select to use and why? Do you prefer using the online bibliography tool or Word to create sources? Why? What differences, if any, did you notice between the list of sources created with the online bibliography tool and the lists created when you use Word?

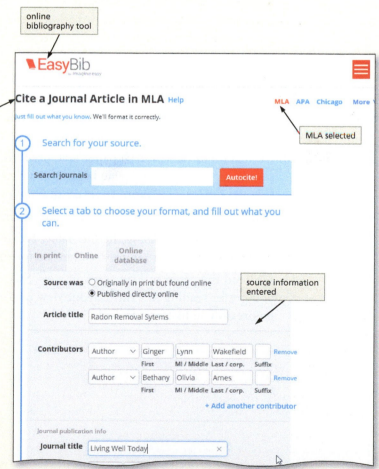

Figure 2–81

In the Labs

Design, create, modify, and/or use a document following the guidelines, concepts, and skills presented in this module. Labs 1 and 2, which increase in difficulty, require you to create solutions based on what you learned in the module; Lab 3 requires you to apply your creative thinking and problem-solving skills to design and implement a solution.

Lab 1: Preparing a Short Research Paper

Problem: You are a college student currently enrolled in an introductory English class. Your assignment is to prepare a short research paper (300–350 words) in any area of interest to you. The requirements are that the paper be presented according to the MLA documentation style and have three references. At least one of the three references must be from the web. You prepare the paper shown in Figure 2–82, which discusses wearable devices.

Perform the following tasks:

1. Run Word. If necessary, display formatting marks on the screen.

2. Modify the Normal style to the 12-point Times New Roman font.

3. Adjust line spacing to double.

4. Remove space below (after) paragraphs.

5. Update the Normal style to reflect the adjusted line and paragraph spacing.

6. Create a header to number pages.

7. Type the name and course information at the left margin. If requested by your instructor, use your name and course information instead of the information shown in Figure 2–82a. Center and type the title.

8. Set a first-line indent to one-half inch for paragraphs in the body of the research paper.

9. Type the research paper as shown in Figures 2–82a and 2–82b. Change the bibliography style to MLA. As you insert citations, enter their source information (shown in Figure 2–82c). Edit the citations so that they are displayed according to Figures 2–82a and 2–82b.

10. At the end of the research paper text, press the ENTER key and then insert a manual page break so that the Works Cited page begins on a new page. Enter and format the works cited title (Figure 2–82c). Use Word to insert the bibliographical list (bibliography).

11. Check the spelling and grammar of the paper at once.

12. Save the document using the file name, Lab 2–1 Wearable Devices Paper. Submit the document, shown in Figure 2–82, in the format specified by your instructor.

13. ✳ Read the paper in Print Layout view. Switch to Read mode and scroll through the pages. Do you prefer reading in Print Layout view or Read mode? Why? In Read mode, which of the page colors do you like best and why?

Hakimi 1

Farrah Iman Hakimi

Mr. Danshov

English 103

November 15, 2017

Wearable Devices

A wearable device or wearable is a small, mobile computing device designed to be worn by a consumer. These devices often communicate with a mobile device or computer using Bluetooth. Three popular types of wearable devices are activity trackers, smartwatches, and smart glasses.

An activity tracker is a wearable device that monitors fitness-related activities such as distance walked, heart rate, pulse, calories consumed, and sleep patterns. These devices typically sync, usually wirelessly, with a web or mobile app on your computer or mobile device to extend the capability of the wearable device (Pappas 32-41).

A smartwatch is a wearable device that, in addition to keeping time, can communicate wirelessly with a smartphone to make and answer phone calls, read and send messages, access the web, play music, work with apps such as fitness trackers and GPS, and more. Most include a touch screen (Carter and Schmidt).

Smart glasses, also called smart eyewear, are wearable head-mounted eyeglass-type devices that enable the user to view information or take photos and videos that are projected to a miniature screen in the user's field of vision. For example, the device wearer could run an app while wearing smart glasses that display flight status information when he or she walks into an airport. Users control the device through voice commands or by touching controls on its frame. Some smart glasses also include mobile apps, such as fitness trackers and GPS (Yazzie).

Figure 2–82a

Continued >

In the Labs *continued*

Hakimi 2

Activity trackers, smartwatches, and smart eyewear are available from a variety of
manufacturers. Before making a purchase, consumers should research costs and features of all
options to determine the device that best suits their requirements.

Figure 2–82b

Hakimi 3

Works Cited

Carter, Calvin J. and Karl Hans Schmidt. "Smartwatch Review." *Technology Trends* Aug. 2017:

n. pag. Web. 12 October 2017.

Pappas, Anastasia Maria. *Activity Trackers and Other Wearable Devices*. Dallas: Western Star

Publishing, 2017. Print.

Yazzie, Nina Tamaya. *Evaluating Today's Smart Glasses*. 25 Aug. 2017. Course Technology.

Web. 25 Sept. 2017.

Figure 2–82c

Lab 2: **Preparing a Research Report with a Footnote**

Problem: You are a college student enrolled in an introductory technology class. Your assignment is
to prepare a short research paper (350–400 words) in any area of interest to you. The requirements are
that the paper be presented according to the MLA documentation style, contain at least one note
positioned as a footnote, and have three references. At least one of the three references must be from
the web. You prepare a paper about two-step verification (Figure 2–83).

Perform the following tasks:
1. Run Word. Modify the Normal style to the 12-point Times New Roman font. Adjust line spacing
   to double and remove space below (after) paragraphs. Update the Normal style to include the
   adjusted line and paragraph spacing. Create a header to number pages. Type the name and
   course information at the left margin. If requested by your instructor, use your name and course
   information instead of the information shown in Figure 2–83a. Center and type the title. Set a
   first-line indent for paragraphs in the body of the research paper.
2. Type the research paper as shown in Figures 2–83a and 2–83b. Insert the footnote as shown in
   Figure 2–83a. Change the Footnote Text style to the format specified in the MLA documentation

Wagner 1

Bryan Wagner

Dr. Rosenberg

Technology 104

October 27, 2017

Two-Step Verification

In an attempt to protect personal data and information from online thieves, many organizations, such as financial institutions or universities, that store sensitive or confidential items use a two-step verification process. With two-step verification, a computer or mobile device uses two separate methods, one after the next, to verify the identity of a user.

ATMs (automated teller machines) usually require a two-step verification. Users first insert their ATM card into the ATM (Step 1) and then enter a PIN, or personal identification number, (Step 2) to access their bank account. If someone steals these cards, the thief must enter the user's PIN to access the account (Tanaka).

Another use of two-step verification requires a mobile phone and a computer or mobile device.[1] When users sign in to an account on a computer or mobile device, they enter a user name and password (Step 1). Next, they are prompted to enter another authentication code (Step 2), which is sent as a text or voice message or via an app on a smartphone. This second code generally is valid for a set time, sometimes only for a few minutes or hours. If users do not sign in during this time limit, they must repeat the process and request another verification code

---

[1] According to Moore and O'Sullivan, users should register an alternate mobile phone number, landline phone number, email address, or other form of contact beyond a mobile phone number so that they still can access their accounts even if they lose their mobile phone (54).

Figure 2–83a

Wagner 2

(Marcy). Microsoft and Google commonly use two-step verification when users sign in to these websites (Moore and O'Sullivan).

Some organizations use two separate methods to verify the identity of users. These two-step verification procedures are designed to protect users' sensitive and confidential items from online thieves.

Figure 2–83b

Continued >

In the Labs *continued*

style. Change the bibliography style to MLA. As you insert citations, use the following source information, entering it according to the MLA style:

a. Type of Source: Article in a Periodical
   Author: Hana Kei Tanaka
   Article Title: Safeguards against Unauthorized Access and Use
   Periodical Title: Technology Today
   Year: 2017
   Month: Sept.
   Pages: no pages used
   Medium: Web
   Year Accessed: 2017
   Month Accessed: Oct.
   Day Accessed: 3

b. Type of Source: Web site
   Author: Fredrick Lee Marcy
   Name of webpage: Two-Step Verification
   Year/Month/Date: none given
   Production Company: Course Technology
   Medium: Web
   Year Accessed: 2017
   Month Accessed: Sept.
   Day Accessed: 18

c. Type of Source: Book
   Author: Aaron Bradley Moore and Brianna Clare O'Sullivan
   Title: Authentication Techniques
   Year: 2017
   City: Detroit
   Publisher: Great Lakes Press
   Medium: Print

3. At the end of the research paper text, press the ENTER key once and insert a manual page break so that the Works Cited page begins on a new page. Enter and format the works cited title. Use Word to insert the bibliographical list.

4. Check the spelling and grammar of the paper.

5. Save the document using the file name, Lab 2–2 Two-Step Verification Paper. Submit the document, shown in Figure 2–83, in the format specified by your instructor.

6. ✸ This paper uses web sources. What factors should you consider when selecting web sources?

Lab 3: Consider This: Your Turn

Create a Research Paper about Wireless Communications

Note: To complete this assignment, you will be required to use the Data Files. Please contact your instructor for information about accessing the Data Files.

Problem: As a student in an introductory computer class, your instructor has assigned a brief research paper that discusses wireless communications.

Perform the following tasks:

Part 1: The source for the text in your research paper is in a file called Lab 2–3 Consider This Your Turn Wireless Communications Notes, which is located in the Data Files. If your instructor requests, use the Insights task pane to obtain information from another source and include that information as a note positioned as a footnote in the paper, along with entering its corresponding source information as appropriate. Add an AutoCorrect entry to correct a word you commonly mistype. If necessary, set the default dictionary. Add one of the source last names to the dictionary.

Using the concepts and techniques presented in this module, organize the notes in the text in the file on the Data Files, rewording as necessary, and then create and format this research paper according to the MLA documentation style. Be sure to check spelling and grammar of the finished paper. Submit your assignment and answers to the critical thinking questions in the format specified by your instructor.

Part 2: ✸ You made several decisions while creating the research paper in this assignment: how to organize the notes, where to place citations, how to format sources, and which source on the web to use for the footnote text (if requested by your instructor). What was the rationale behind each of these decisions? When you proofread the document, what further revisions did you make and why?

3 Creating a Business Letter with a Letterhead and Table

Letter Extra assignments
Tab assignments

Objectives

You will have mastered the material in this module when you can:

- Change margins
- Insert and format a shape
- Change text wrapping
- Insert an online picture and format it
- Insert a symbol
- Add a border to a paragraph
- Clear formatting
- Convert a hyperlink to regular text

- Apply a style
- Set and use tab stops
- Insert the current date
- Create, modify, and insert a building block
- Insert a Word table, enter data in the table, and format the table
- Address and print an envelope

Introduction

In a business environment, people use documents to communicate with others. Business documents can include letters, memos, newsletters, proposals, and resumes. An effective business document clearly and concisely conveys its message and has a professional, organized appearance. You can use your own creative skills to design and compose business documents. Using Word, for example, you can develop the content and decide on the location of each item in a business document.

Project — Business Letter with a Letterhead and Table

At some time, you more than likely will prepare a business letter. Contents of business letters include requests, inquiries, confirmations, acknowledgements, recommendations, notifications, responses, thank you letters, invitations, offers, referrals, complaints, and more.

The project in this module follows generally accepted guidelines for writing letters and uses Word to create the business letter shown in Figure 3–1. This business

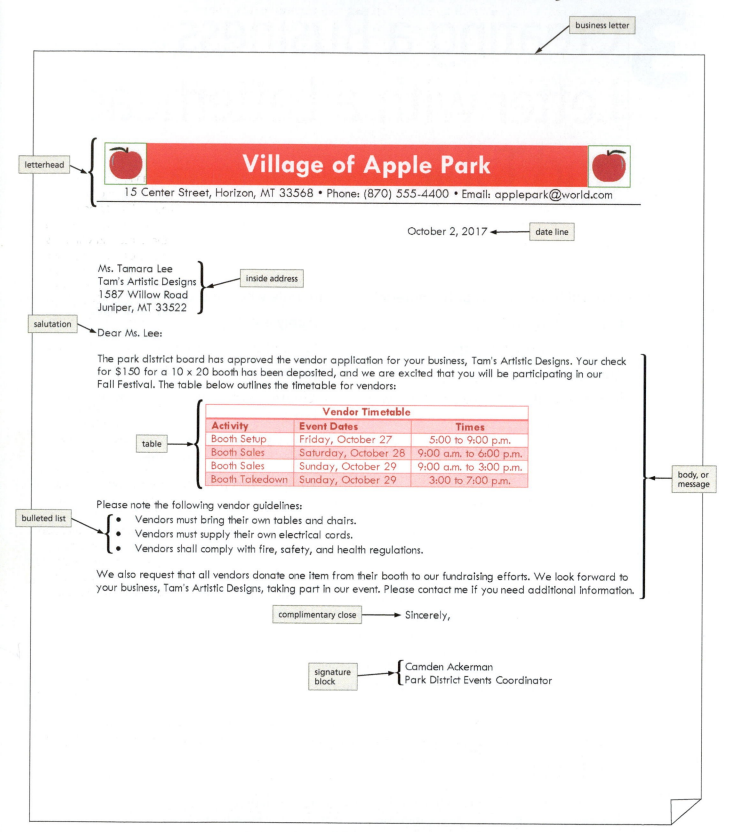

Figure 3–1

letter is a letter from the park district events coordinator at the Village of Apple Park that confirms a vendor application to participate in its community event. The letter includes a custom letterhead, as well as all essential business letter components: date line, inside address, salutation, body, complimentary close, and signature block. To easily present the vendor timetable during the event, the letter shows this information in a table. The vendor guidelines appear in a bulleted list.

In this module, you will learn how to create the letter shown in Figure 3–1. The following roadmap identifies general activities you will perform as you progress through this module:

1. CREATE AND FORMAT a LETTERHEAD WITH GRAPHICS.

2. SPECIFY the LETTER FORMATS according to business letter guidelines.

3. INSERT a TABLE in the letter.

4. FORMAT the TABLE in the letter.

5. INSERT a BULLETED LIST in the letter.

6. ADDRESS an ENVELOPE for the letter.

To Run Word and Change Word Settings

If you are using a computer to step through the project in this module and you want your screens to match the figures in this book, you should change your screen's resolution to 1366 × 768. For information about how to change a computer's resolution, refer to the Office and Windows module at the beginning of this book.

The following steps run Word, display formatting marks, and change the zoom to page width.

1 Run Word and create a blank document in the Word window. If necessary, maximize the Word window.

2 If the Print Layout button on the status bar is not selected (shown in Figure 3–2), click it so that your screen is in Print Layout view.

3 If the 'Show/Hide ¶' button (Home tab | Paragraph group) is not selected already, click it to display formatting marks on the screen.

4 To display the page the same width as the document window, if necessary, click the Page Width button (View tab | Zoom group).

For an introduction to Windows and instructions about how to perform basic Windows tasks, read the Office and Windows module at the beginning of this book, where you can learn how to resize windows, change screen resolution, create folders, move and rename files, use Windows Help, and much more.

For an introduction to Office and instructions about how to perform basic tasks in Office apps, read the Office and Windows module at the beginning of this book, where you can learn how to run an application, use the ribbon, save a file, open a file, print a file, exit an application, use Help, and much more.

To Change Margin Settings

1 CREATE & FORMAT LETTERHEAD WITH GRAPHICS | 2 SPECIFY LETTER FORMATS
3 INSERT TABLE | 4 FORMAT TABLE | 5 INSERT BULLETED LIST | 6 ADDRESS ENVELOPE

Word is preset to use standard 8.5-by-11-inch paper, with 1-inch top, bottom, left, and right margins. The business letter in this module uses .75-inch left and right margins and 1-inch top and bottom margins. *Why? You would like more text to fit from left to right on the page.*

When you change the default (preset) margin settings, the new margin settings affect every page in the document. If you wanted the margins to affect just a portion of the document, you would divide the document into sections (discussed in a later module), which enables you to specify different margin settings for each section. The following steps change margin settings.

1

- Display the Layout tab.

- Click the Adjust Margins button (Layout tab | Page Setup group) to display the Adjust Margins gallery (Figure 3–2).

2

- Click Moderate in the Adjust Margins gallery to change the margins to the specified settings.

Q&A What if the margin settings I want are not in the Adjust Margins gallery?

You can click Custom Margins in the Adjust Margins gallery and then enter your desired margin values in the top, bottom, left, and right boxes in the Page Setup dialog box.

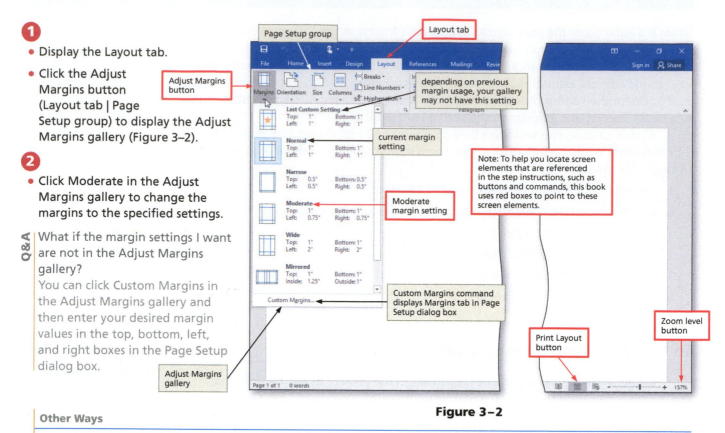

Figure 3–2

Other Ways

1. Position pointer on margin boundary on ruler; when pointer changes to two-headed arrow, drag margin boundary on ruler

Creating a Letterhead

The cost of preprinted letterhead can be high. An alternative is to create your own letterhead and save it in a file. When you want to create a letter at a later time, you can start by using the letterhead file. The following sections create a letterhead and then save it in a file for future use.

What is a letterhead?

A **letterhead** is the section of a letter that identifies an organization or individual. Often, the letterhead appears at the top of a letter. Although you can design and print a letterhead yourself, many businesses pay an outside firm to design and print their letterhead, usually on higher-quality paper. They then use the professionally preprinted paper for external business communications.

If you do not have preprinted letterhead paper, you can design a creative letterhead. It is important the letterhead appropriately represent the essence of the organization or individual (i.e., formal, technical, creative, etc.). That is, it should use text, graphics, formats, and colors that reflect the organization or individual. The letterhead should leave ample room for the contents of the letter.

When designing a letterhead, consider its contents, placement, and appearance.

- **Contents of letterhead.** A letterhead should contain these elements:
  - Complete legal name of the individual, group, or company

  - Complete mailing address: street address including building, room, suite number, or post office box, along with city, state, and postal code

  - Phone number(s) and fax number, if applicable

  - Email address

– Website address, if applicable

– Many letterheads also include a logo or other image; if an image is used, it should express the organization or individual's personality or goals

- **Placement of elements in the letterhead.** Many letterheads center their elements across the top of the page. Others align some or all of the elements with the left or right margins. Sometimes, the elements are split between the top and bottom of the page. For example, a name and logo may be at the top of the page with the address at the bottom of the page.

- **Appearance of letterhead elements.** Use fonts that are easy to read. Give the organization or individual name impact by making its font size larger than the rest of the text in the letterhead. For additional emphasis, consider formatting the name in bold, italic, or a different color. Choose colors that complement each other and convey the goals of the organization or individual.

When finished designing the letterhead, determine if a divider line would help to visually separate the letterhead from the remainder of the letter.

The letterhead for the letter in this module consists of the organization's name, appropriate graphics, postal address, phone number, and email address. The name and graphics are enclosed in a rectangular shape (shown in Figure 3–1), and the contact information is below the shape. You will follow these general steps to create the letterhead in this module:

1. Insert and format a shape.
2. Enter and format the organization name in the shape.
3. Insert, format, and position the images in the shape.
4. Enter the contact information below the shape.
5. Add a border below the contact information.

BTW

The Ribbon and Screen Resolution
Word may change how the groups and buttons within the groups appear on the ribbon, depending on the computer or mobile device's screen resolution. Thus, your ribbon may look different from the ones in this book if you are using a screen resolution other than 1366 x 768.

To Insert a Shape

1 CREATE & FORMAT LETTERHEAD WITH GRAPHICS | 2 SPECIFY LETTER FORMATS
3 INSERT TABLE | 4 FORMAT TABLE | 5 INSERT BULLETED LIST | 6 ADDRESS ENVELOPE

Word has a variety of predefined shapes, which are a type of drawing object, that you can insert in documents. A **drawing object** is a graphic that you create using Word. Examples of shape drawing objects include rectangles, circles, triangles, arrows, flowcharting symbols, stars, banners, and callouts. The following steps insert a rectangle shape in the letterhead. *Why? The organization's name is placed in a rectangle for emphasis and visual appeal.*

- Display the Insert tab.
- Click the 'Draw a Shape' button (Insert tab | Illustrations group) to display the Draw a Shape gallery (Figure 3–3).

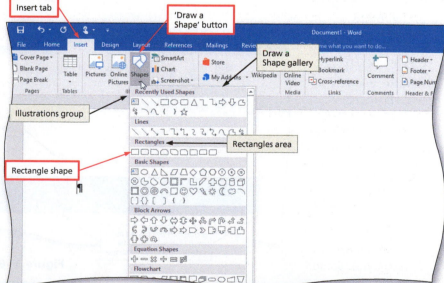

Figure 3–3

2

• Click the Rectangle shape in the Rectangles area in the Draw a Shape gallery, which removes the gallery.

Q&A What if I am using a touch screen?
The shape is inserted in the document window. Skip Steps 3 and 4, and proceed to Step 5.

• Position the pointer (a crosshair) in the approximate location for the upper-left corner of the desired shape (Figure 3–4).

Q&A What is the purpose of the crosshair pointer?
You drag the crosshair pointer from the upper-left corner to the lower-right corner to form the desired location and size of the shape.

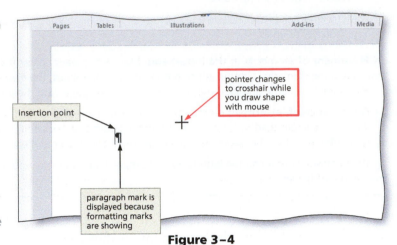

Figure 3–4

3

• Drag the mouse to the right and downward to form the boundaries of the shape, as shown in Figure 3–5. Do not release the mouse button.

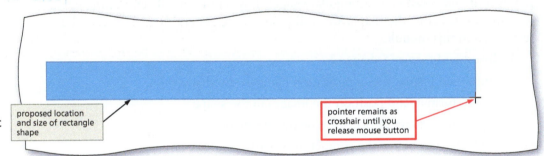

Figure 3–5

4

• Release the mouse button so that Word draws the shape according to your drawing in the document window.

5

• Verify your shape is the same approximate height and width as the one in this project by reviewing, and if necessary changing, the values in the Shape Height box and Shape Width boxes (Drawing Tools Format tab | Size group) to 0.53" and 5.7" by typing each value in the respective box and then pressing the ENTER key (Figure 3–6).

Q&A What is the purpose of the rotate handle?
When you drag an object's **rotate handle**, which is the white circle on the top of the object, Word rotates the object in the direction you drag the mouse.

What if I wanted to delete a shape and start over?
With the shape selected, you would press the DELETE key.

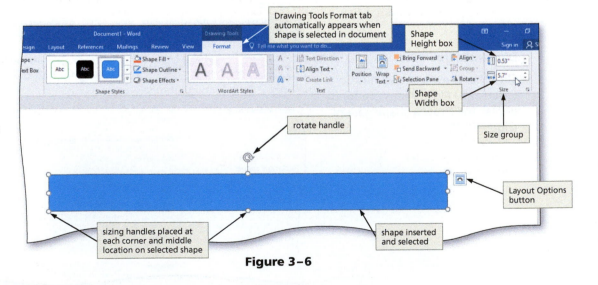

Figure 3–6

Floating versus Inline Objects

When you insert an object in a document, Word inserts it as either an inline object or a floating object. An **inline object** is an object that is part of a paragraph. With inline objects, you change the location of the object by setting paragraph options, such as centered, right-aligned, and so on. For example, when you inserted the picture of the surfer in Module 1, Word inserted it as an inline object. A **floating object**, by contrast, is an object that can be positioned at a specific location in a document or in a layer over or behind text in a document. The shape you just inserted is a floating object. You have more flexibility with floating objects because you can position a floating object anywhere on the page.

In addition to changing an object from inline to floating and vice versa, Word provides several floating options, which (along with inline) are called text wrapping options because they affect how text wraps with or around the object. Table 3–1 presents the various text wrapping options.

Table 3–1 Text Wrapping Options		
Text Wrapping Option	**Object Type**	**How It Works**
In Line with Text	Inline	Object positioned according to paragraph formatting; for example, if paragraph is centered, object will be centered with any text in the paragraph.
Square	Floating	Text wraps around object, with text forming a box around the object.
Tight	Floating	Text wraps around object, with text forming to shape of the object.
Through	Floating	Object appears at beginning, middle, or end of text. Moving object changes location of text.
Top and Bottom	Floating	Object appears above or below text. Moving object changes location of text.
Behind Text	Floating	Object appears behind text.
In Front of Text	Floating	Object appears in front of text and may cover the text.

To Change an Object's Position

1 CREATE & FORMAT LETTERHEAD WITH GRAPHICS | 2 SPECIFY LETTER FORMATS
3 INSERT TABLE | 4 FORMAT TABLE | 5 INSERT BULLETED LIST | 6 ADDRESS ENVELOPE

You can specify an object's vertical position on a page (top, middle, bottom) and its horizontal position (left, center, right). The following steps change the position of an object, specifically, the rectangle shape. *Why? You want the shape to be centered at the top of the page in the letterhead.*

1

- With the shape still selected, click the Position Object button (Drawing Tools Format tab | Arrange group) to display the Position Object gallery (Figure 3–7).

Q&A What if the shape is not still selected? Click the shape to select it.

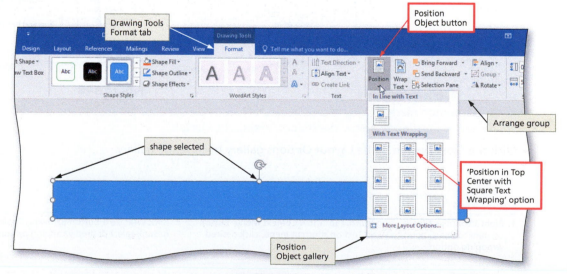

Figure 3–7

Experiment

- Point to various options in the Position Object gallery and watch the shape move to the selected position option.

2

- Click 'Position in Top Center with Square Text Wrapping' in the Position Object gallery so that the object does not cover the document and is centered at the top of the document.

Other Ways

1. Click Layout Options button attached to graphic (shown in Figure 3–8), click See more link in Layout Options gallery, click Horizontal Alignment arrow and select alignment (Layout dialog box), click Vertical Alignment arrow and select alignment, click OK button

2. Click Advanced Layout: Size Dialog Box Launcher (Drawing Tools Format tab | Size group), click Position tab (Layout dialog box), click Horizontal Alignment arrow and select alignment, click Vertical Alignment arrow and select alignment, click OK button

To Change an Object's Text Wrapping

1 CREATE & FORMAT LETTERHEAD WITH GRAPHICS | 2 SPECIFY LETTER FORMATS

3 INSERT TABLE | 4 FORMAT TABLE | 5 INSERT BULLETED LIST | 6 ADDRESS ENVELOPE

When you insert a shape in a Word document, the default text wrapping is In Front of Text, which means the object will cover any text behind it. The previous steps, which changed the shape's position, changed the text wrapping to Square. In the letterhead, you want the shape's text wrapping to be Top and Bottom. *Why? You want the letterhead above the contents of the letter when you type it, instead of covering the contents of the letter.* The following steps change an object's text wrapping.

1

- With the shape still selected, click the Layout Options button attached to the graphic to display the Layout Options gallery (Figure 3–8).

2

- Click 'Top and Bottom' in the Layout Options gallery so that the object does not cover the document text (shown in Figure 3–9).

Q&A

How can I tell that the text wrapping has changed?

Because the letter has no text, you need to look at the paragraph mark, which now is positioned below the shape instead of to its left.

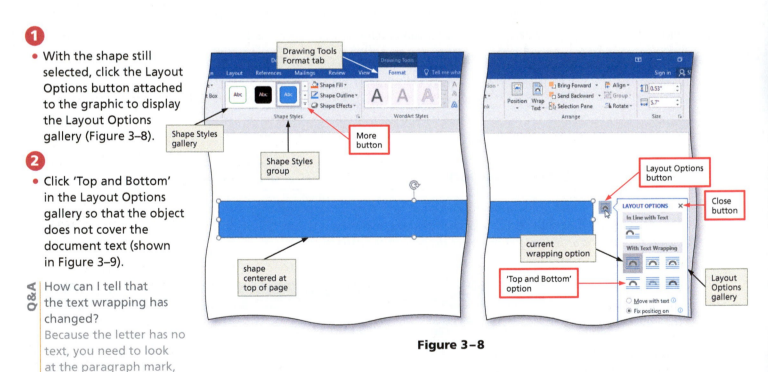

Figure 3–8

- Click the Close button in the Layout Options gallery to close the gallery.

Other Ways

1. Right-click object (or, if using touch, tap 'Show Context Menu' button on mini toolbar), point to Wrap Text on shortcut menu, click desired wrapping option

2. Click Wrap Text button (Drawing Tools Format tab | Arrange group), select desired wrapping option

To Apply a Shape Style

Why apply a shape style? *Word provides a Shape Styles gallery so that you easily can change the appearance of the shape.* The following steps apply a shape style to the rectangle shape.

1

- With the shape still selected, click the More button (shown in Figure 3–8) in the Shape Styles gallery (Drawing Tools Format tab | Shape Styles group) to expand the gallery.

Q&A What if the shape no longer is selected?

Click the shape to select it.

- Point to 'Moderate Effect - Gray-50%, Accent 3' (fourth effect in fifth row) in the Shape Styles gallery to display a live preview of that style applied to the shape in the document (Figure 3–9).

Experiment

- Point to various styles in the Shape Styles gallery and watch the style of the shape change in the document.

Figure 3–9

2

- Click 'Moderate Effect - Gray-50%, Accent 3' in the Shape Styles gallery to apply the selected style to the shape.

Other Ways
1. Right-click shape, click 'Shape Quick Styles' button on mini toolbar, select desired style   2. Click Format Shape Dialog Box Launcher (Drawing Tools Format tab | Shape Styles group), click 'Fill & Line' button (Format Shape task pane), expand Fill section, select desired colors, click Close button

To Add Text to a Shape

The following steps add text (the organization name) to a shape. *Why? In the letterhead for this module, the name is in the shape. Similarly, an individual could put his or her name in a shape on a letterhead in order to create personalized letterhead.*

1

- Right-click the shape to display a mini toolbar and/or shortcut menu (Figure 3–10).

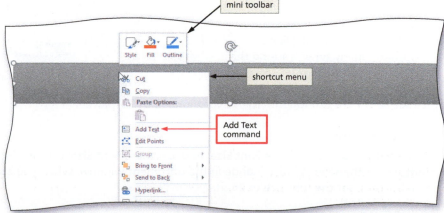

Figure 3–10

• Click Add Text on the shortcut menu to place an insertion point in the shape.

Q&A What if I am using a touch screen?
Tap the Edit Text button on the mini toolbar.

Why do the buttons on my mini toolbar differ?
If you are using a mouse in Mouse mode, the buttons on your mini toolbar will differ from those that appear when you use a touch screen in Touch mode.

• If the insertion point and paragraph mark are not centered in the shape, click the Center button (Home tab | Paragraph group) to center them.

• Type **Village of Apple Park** as the name in the shape (Figure 3–11).

If requested by your instructor, enter your name instead of the name shown in Figure 3–11.

text entered and centered

Village·of·Apple·Park¶

Figure 3–11

To Use the 'Increase Font Size' Button

1 CREATE & FORMAT LETTERHEAD WITH GRAPHICS | 2 SPECIFY LETTER FORMATS
3 INSERT TABLE | 4 FORMAT TABLE | 5 INSERT BULLETED LIST | 6 ADDRESS ENVELOPE

In previous modules, you used the Font Size arrow (Home tab | Font group) to change the font size of text. Word also provides an 'Increase Font Size' button (Home tab | Font group), which increases the font size of selected text each time you click the button. The following steps use the 'Increase Font Size' button to increase the font size of the name in the shape to 26 point. *Why?* *You want the name to be as large as possible in the shape.*

1

• Drag through the text to be formatted (in this case, the name in the shape).

2

• If necessary, display the Home tab.

• Repeatedly click the 'Increase Font Size' button (Home tab | Font group) until the Font Size box displays 26 to increase the font size of the selected text (Figure 3–12).

Q&A What if I click the 'Increase Font Size' button (Home tab | Font group) too many times, causing the font size to be too big?
Click the 'Decrease Font Size' button (Home tab | Font group) until the desired font size is displayed.

Home tab

'Increase Font Size' button

'Decrease Font Size' button

Font group

Font Size box displays 26

Village·of·Apple·Park¶

selected text changed to 26 point

Figure 3–12

Experiment

• Repeatedly click the 'Increase Font Size' and 'Decrease Font Size' buttons (Home tab | Font group) and watch the font size of the selected text change in the document window. When you are finished experimenting with these two buttons, set the font size to 26.

Other Ways

1. Press CTRL+SHIFT+>

To Bold Selected Text

To make the name stand out even more, bold it. The following steps bold the selected text.

1 With the text selected, click the Bold button (Home tab | Font group) to bold the selected text (shown in Figure 3–13).

2 Click anywhere in the text in the shape to remove the selection and place the insertion point in the shape.

To Change the Document Theme

1 CREATE & FORMAT LETTERHEAD WITH GRAPHICS | 2 SPECIFY LETTER FORMATS
3 INSERT TABLE | 4 FORMAT TABLE | 5 INSERT BULLETED LIST | 6 ADDRESS ENVELOPE

A **document theme** is a coordinated combination of colors, fonts, and effects. The current default document theme is Office, which uses Calibri and Calibri Light as its font and shades of grays and blues primarily. The following steps change the document theme to Circuit for the letter in this module. *Why? You want to use shades of reds and oranges in the letterhead because those colors are associated with energy, success, creativity, and enthusiasm.*

1

- Display the Design tab.

- Click the Themes button (Design tab | Document Formatting group) to display the Themes gallery.

- Point to Circuit in the Themes gallery to display a live preview of that theme applied to the document (Figure 3–13).

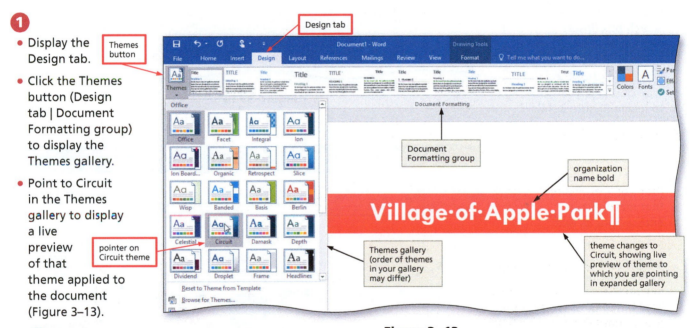

Figure 3–13

 Experiment

- Point to various themes in the Themes gallery and watch the color scheme and font set change in the document window.

2

- Click Circuit in the Themes gallery to change the document theme.

To Insert an Online Picture

1 CREATE & FORMAT LETTERHEAD WITH GRAPHICS | 2 SPECIFY LETTER FORMATS
3 INSERT TABLE | 4 FORMAT TABLE | 5 INSERT BULLETED LIST | 6 ADDRESS ENVELOPE

Files containing graphics are available from a variety of sources. In the Module 1 flyer, you inserted a digital picture taken with a camera. In this project, you insert a picture from the web. Microsoft Office applications can access a collection of royalty-free photos and animations.

The letterhead in this project contains a picture of an apple (shown in Figure 3–1). ***Why?*** *Because the name of the organization is Village of Apple Park, an apple is an appropriate image for this letterhead.* The following steps insert an online picture in the document.

1

- If necessary, click the paragraph mark below the shape to position the insertion point where you want to insert the picture.

- Display the Insert tab.

- Click the Online Pictures button (Insert tab | Illustrations group) to display the Insert Pictures dialog box.

- Type **apple** in the Search box (Insert Pictures dialog box) to specify the search text, which indicates the type of image you want to locate (Figure 3–14).

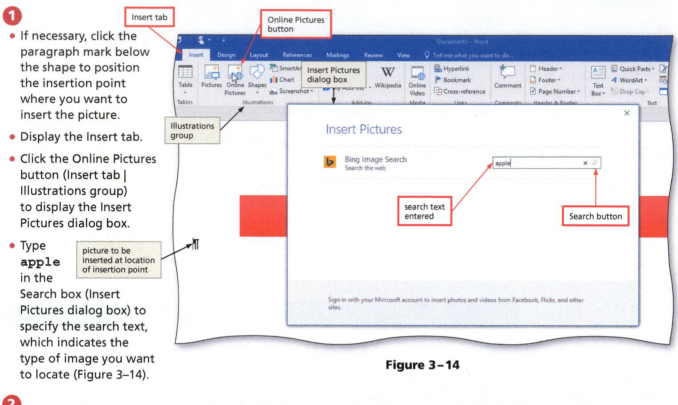

Figure 3–14

2

- Click the Search button to display a list of online pictures that matches the entered search text.

- Scroll through the list of pictures to locate the one shown in Figure 3–15, or a similar image.

Q&A

Why is my list of pictures different from Figure 3–15? The online images are continually updated.

What is Creative Commons? **Creative Commons** is a nonprofit organization that provides several standard licensing options that owners of creative works may specify when granting permission for others to use their digital content, such as the online pictures that appear in the Bing Image Search. Be sure to follow an image's guidelines when using it in a document.

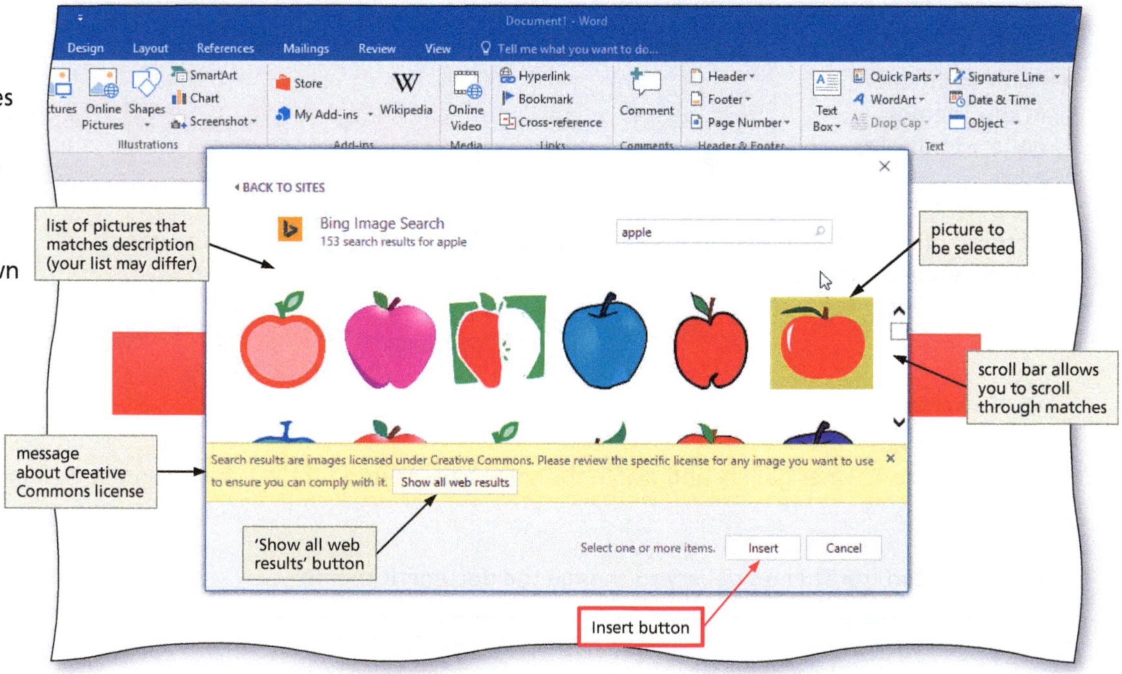

Figure 3–15

What if I cannot locate the image in Figure 3–15, and I would like to use that exact image?
The image is located in the Data Files. You can click the Cancel button and then click the From File button (Insert tab | Illustrations group), navigate to the file called apple-02.wmf in the Data Files, and then click the Insert button (Insert Picture dialog box).

- If necessary, click the 'Show all web results' button to display more images that match the search text.
- Click the desired picture to select it.
- Click the Insert button to insert the selected image in the document at the location of the insertion point. If necessary, scroll to display the image (picture) in the document window (Figure 3–16).

Figure 3–16

To Resize a Graphic to a Percent of the Original Size

1 CREATE & FORMAT LETTERHEAD WITH GRAPHICS | 2 SPECIFY LETTER FORMATS
3 INSERT TABLE | 4 FORMAT TABLE | 5 INSERT BULLETED LIST | 6 ADDRESS ENVELOPE

Instead of dragging a sizing handle to change the graphic's size, as you learned in Module 1, you can specify that the graphic be resized to a percent of its original size. In this module, the graphic is resized to 8 percent of its original size. **Why?** *The original size of the picture is too large for the letterhead.* The following steps resize a graphic to a percent of the original.

- With the graphic still selected, click the Advanced Layout: Size Dialog Box Launcher (Picture Tools Format tab | Size group) to display the Size sheet in the Layout dialog box.

Q&A What if the graphic is not selected or the Picture Tools Format tab is not on the ribbon?
Click the graphic to select it or double-click the graphic to make the Picture Tools Format tab the active tab.

- In the Scale area (Layout dialog box), double-click the current value in the Height box to select it.
- Type 8 in the Height box and then press the TAB key to display the same percent value in the Width box (Figure 3–17).

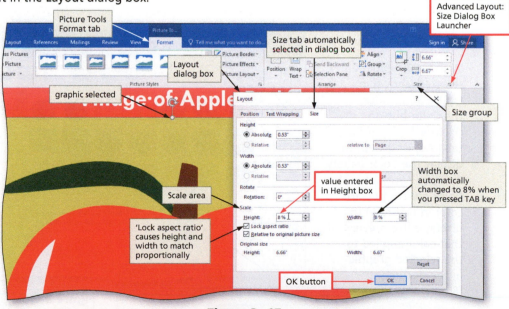

Figure 3–17

Why did Word automatically fill in the value in the Width box?
When the 'Lock aspect ratio' check box (Layout dialog box) is selected, Word automatically maintains the size proportions of the graphic.

How do I know to use 8 percent for the resized graphic?
The larger graphic consumed too much room on the page. Try various percentages to determine the size that works best in the letterhead design.

 3

- Click the OK button to close the dialog box and resize the selected graphic.
- If necessary, scroll to display the top of the document
- Verify that the Shape Height and Shape Width boxes (Picture Tools Format tab | Size group) display 0.53". If they do not, change their values to 0.53" (Figure 3–18).

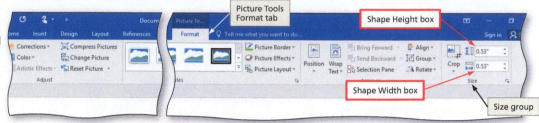

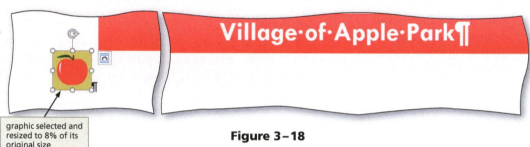

Figure 3–18

Other Ways

1. Click Layout Options button attached to graphic, click See more link in the Layout Options gallery, click Size tab (Layout dialog box), enter height and width values, click OK button

2. Right-click graphic, click 'Size and Position' on shortcut menu, enter height and width values (Layout dialog box), click OK button

To Change the Color of a Graphic

1 CREATE & FORMAT LETTERHEAD WITH GRAPHICS | 2 SPECIFY LETTER FORMATS
3 INSERT TABLE | 4 FORMAT TABLE | 5 INSERT BULLETED LIST | 6 ADDRESS ENVELOPE

In Word, you can change the color of a graphic. The apple image (graphic) currently is a bright red color. The following steps change the color of the graphic. **Why?** *Because the image in this project will be placed beside the rectangle shape, you prefer to use lighter colors.*

1

- With the graphic still selected (shown in Figure 3–18), click the Color button (Picture Tools Format tab | Adjust group) to display the Color gallery.
- Point to Washout in the Color gallery (fourth color in first row) to display a live preview of that color applied to the selected graphic in the document (Figure 3–19).

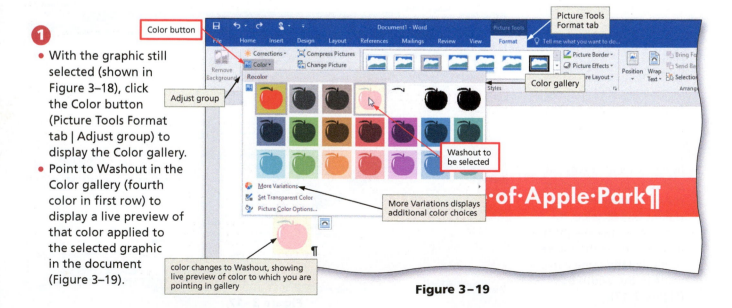

Figure 3–19

1 CREATE & FORMAT LETTERHEAD WITH GRAPHICS | 2 SPECIFY LETTER FORMATS
3 INSERT TABLE | 4 FORMAT TABLE | 5 INSERT BULLETED LIST | 6 ADDRESS ENVELOPE

🔍 **Experiment**

- Point to various colors in the Color gallery and watch the color of the graphic change in the document.

2

- Click Washout in the Color gallery to change the color of the selected graphic.

Q&A How would I change a graphic back to its original colors?
With the graphic selected, you would click No Recolor, which is the upper-left color in the Color gallery.

Other Ways

1. Click Format Shape Dialog Box Launcher (Picture Tools Format tab | Picture Styles group), click Picture button (Format Picture task pane), expand Picture Color section, select desired options

2. Right-click graphic (or, if using touch, tap 'Show Context Menu' button on mini toolbar), click Format Picture on shortcut menu (or, if using touch, tap Format Object), click Picture button (Format Picture task pane), expand Picture Color section, select desired options

---

To Set a Transparent Color in a Graphic

In Word, you can make one color in a graphic transparent; that is, you remove the color. You would make a color transparent if you wanted to remove part of a graphic or see text or colors behind a graphic. The following steps set the light green background around the apple in a transparent color. ***Why?*** *You prefer the light green color to be transparent.*

1

- With the graphic still selected, click the Color button (Picture Tools Format tab | Adjust group) to display the Color gallery (Figure 3–20).

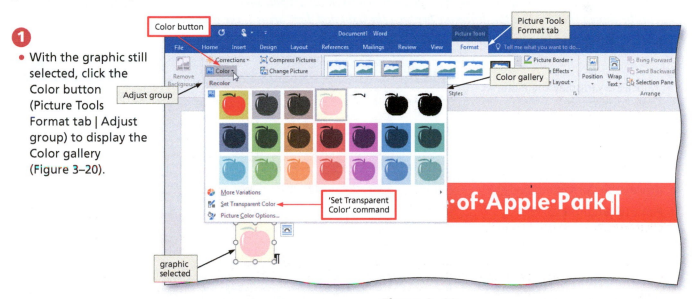

Figure 3–20

2

- Click 'Set Transparent Color' in the Color gallery to display a pen pointer in the document window.

Q&A What if I am using a touch screen?
You may need to use a stylus or mouse to perform these steps.

- Position the pen pointer in the graphic where you want to make the color transparent (Figure 3–21).

Q&A Can I make multiple colors in a graphic transparent?
No, you can make only one color transparent.

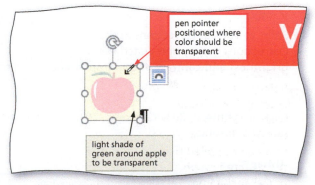

Figure 3–21

3

- Click the location in the graphic where you want the color to be transparent (Figure 3–22).

Q&A What if I make the wrong color transparent? Click the Undo button on the Quick Access Toolbar, or press CTRL+Z, and then repeat these steps.

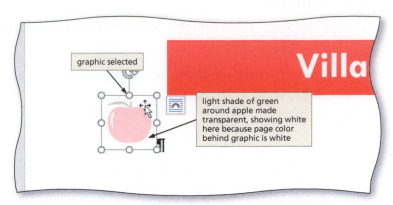

Figure 3–22

To Adjust the Brightness and Contrast of a Graphic

1 CREATE & FORMAT LETTERHEAD WITH GRAPHICS | 2 SPECIFY LETTER FORMATS
3 INSERT TABLE | 4 FORMAT TABLE | 5 INSERT BULLETED LIST | 6 ADDRESS ENVELOPE

In Word, you can adjust the brightness, or lightness, of a graphic and also the **contrast**, or the difference between the lightest and darkest areas of the graphic. The following steps decrease the brightness and contrast of the apple graphic, each by 20%. ***Why?*** *You want to darken the graphic slightly to increase its emphasis on the page and, at the same time, decrease the difference between the light and dark areas of the graphic.*

1

- If necessary, display the Picture Tools Format tab.

- With the graphic still selected (shown in Figure 3–22), click the Corrections button (Picture Tools Format tab | Adjust group) to display the Corrections gallery.

- Point to 'Brightness: -20% Contrast: -20%' (second image in second row) in the Corrections gallery to display a live preview of that correction applied to the graphic in the document (Figure 3–23).

 **Experiment**

- Point to various corrections in the Corrections gallery and watch the brightness and contrast of the graphic change in the document.

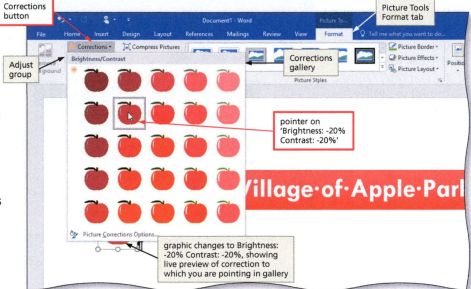

Figure 3–23

2

- Click 'Brightness: -20% Contrast: -20%' in the Corrections gallery to change the brightness and contrast of the selected graphic.

Other Ways
1. Click Format Shape Dialog Box Launcher (Picture Tools Format tab | Picture Styles group), click Picture button (Format Picture task pane), expand Picture Corrections section, select desired options   2. Right-click graphic (or, if using touch, tap 'Show Context Menu' button on mini toolbar), click Format Picture on shortcut menu (or, if using touch, tap Format Object on shortcut menu), click Picture button (Format Picture task pane), expand Picture Corrections section, select desired options

1 CREATE & FORMAT LETTERHEAD WITH GRAPHICS | 2 SPECIFY LETTER FORMATS
3 INSERT TABLE | 4 FORMAT TABLE | 5 INSERT BULLETED LIST | 6 ADDRESS ENVELOPE

To Change the Border Color on a Graphic

The apple graphic currently has no border (outline). The following steps change the border color on the graphic. **Why?** *You would like the graphic to have a lime border so that it is in the same color family as the leaf on the apple.*

1
- Click the Picture Border arrow (Picture Tools Format tab | Picture Styles group) to display the Picture Border gallery.
- Point to 'Lime, Accent 1, Darker 25%' (fifth theme color in fifth row) in the Picture Border gallery to display a live preview of that border color around the picture (Figure 3–24).

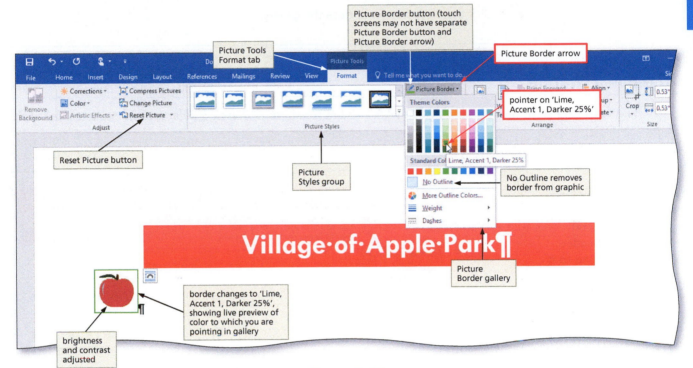

Figure 3–24

Q&A What if I click the Picture Border button by mistake?
Click the Picture Border arrow and proceed with Step 2.

Experiment

- Point to various colors in the Picture Border gallery and watch the border color on the graphic change in the document window.

2
- Click 'Lime, Accent 1, Darker 25%' in the Picture Border gallery to change the picture border color.

Q&A How would I remove a border from a graphic?
With the graphic selected, you would click No Outline in the Picture Border gallery.

Can I remove all formatting applied to a graphic and start over?
Yes. With the graphic selected, you would click the Reset Picture button (Picture Tools Format tab | Adjust group).

To Change an Object's Text Wrapping

The apple graphic is to be positioned to the left of the shape. By default, when you insert a picture, it is formatted as an inline graphic. Inline graphics cannot be moved to a precise location on a page. Recall that inline graphics are part of a paragraph and, thus, can be positioned according to paragraph formatting, such as centered or left-aligned. To move the graphic to the left of the shape, you format it as a floating object with In Front of Text wrapping. The following steps change a graphic's text wrapping.

1 If necessary, click the graphic to select it.

2 Click the Layout Options button attached to the graphic to display the Layout Options gallery.

3 Click 'In Front of Text' in the Layout Options gallery so that you can position the object on top of any item in the document, in this case, on top of the rectangular shape.

4 Click the Close button to close the gallery.

To Move a Graphic

1 CREATE & FORMAT LETTERHEAD WITH GRAPHICS | 2 SPECIFY LETTER FORMATS
3 INSERT TABLE | 4 FORMAT TABLE | 5 INSERT BULLETED LIST | 6 ADDRESS ENVELOPE

The following steps move a graphic. *Why? In this letterhead, the first apple graphic is positioned to the left of the shape.*

1

• Position the pointer in the graphic so that the pointer has a four-headed arrow attached to it (Figure 3–25).

when pointer has four-headed arrow attached to it, you can drag floating graphic to any location in document

Figure 3–25

2

• Drag the graphic to the left of the shape, as shown in Figure 3–26.

Q&A What if I moved the graphic to the wrong location?
Repeat these steps. You can drag a floating graphic to any location in a document.

Why do green lines appear on my screen as I drag a graphic?
You have alignment guides set, which help you line up graphics. To set alignment guides, click the Align Objects button (Picture Tools Format tab | Arrange group) and then click 'Use Alignment Guides'.

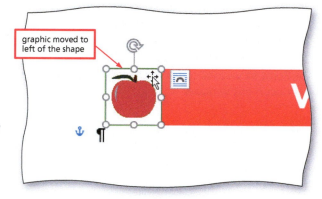

graphic moved to left of the shape

Figure 3–26

To Copy a Graphic

In this project, the same apple graphic is to be placed to the right of the shape. Instead of performing the same steps to insert and format a second identical apple graphic, you can copy the graphic to the Office Clipboard, paste the graphic from the Office Clipboard, and then move the graphic to the desired location.

You use the same steps to copy a graphic as you used in Module 2 to copy text. The following steps copy a graphic.

1 If necessary, click the graphic to select it.

2 Display the Home tab.

3 Click the Copy button, shown in Figure 3–27 (Home tab | Clipboard group), to copy the selected item to the Office Clipboard.

To Use Paste Options

1 CREATE & FORMAT LETTERHEAD WITH GRAPHICS | 2 SPECIFY LETTER FORMATS
3 INSERT TABLE | 4 FORMAT TABLE | 5 INSERT BULLETED LIST | 6 ADDRESS ENVELOPE

The following steps paste a graphic using the Paste Options gallery. **Why?** *Recall from Module 2 that you can specify the format of a pasted item using Paste Options.*

1

• Click the Paste arrow (Home tab | Clipboard group) to display the Paste gallery.

Q&A | What if I accidentally click the Paste button?
Click the Paste Options button below the graphic pasted in the document to display a Paste Options gallery.

• Point to the 'Keep Source Formatting' button in the Paste gallery to display a live preview of that paste option (Figure 3–27).

🔎 **Experiment**

• Point to the two buttons in the Paste gallery and watch the appearance of the pasted graphic change.

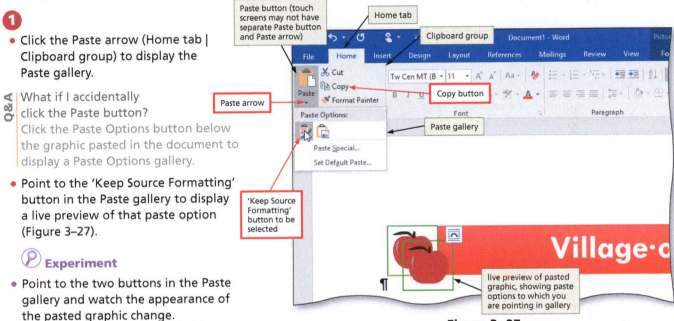

Figure 3–27

Q&A | What do the buttons in the Paste gallery mean?
The 'Keep Source Formatting' button indicates the pasted graphic should have the same formats as it did in its original location. The Picture button removes some formatting from the graphic.

Why are these paste buttons different from the ones in Module 2?
The buttons that appear in the Paste gallery differ depending on the item you are pasting. Use live preview to see how the pasted object will look in the document.

2

• Click the 'Keep Source Formatting' button in the Paste gallery to paste the object using the same formatting as the original.

To Move a Graphic

The next step is to move the second apple graphic so that it is positioned to the right of the rectangle shape. The following steps move a graphic.

If you are using a mouse, position the pointer in the graphic so that the pointer has a four-headed arrow attached to it.

 Drag the graphic to the location shown in Figure 3–28.

To Flip a Graphic

1 CREATE & FORMAT LETTERHEAD WITH GRAPHICS | 2 SPECIFY LETTER FORMATS
3 INSERT TABLE | 4 FORMAT TABLE | 5 INSERT BULLETED LIST | 6 ADDRESS ENVELOPE

The following steps flip a graphic horizontally. *Why? In this letterhead, you want the leaves on the apple graphics to point toward the edge of the paper.*

1

- If necessary, display the Picture Tools Format tab.

- With the graphic still selected, click the Rotate Objects button (Picture Tools Format tab | Arrange group) to display the Rotate Objects gallery (Figure 3–28).

🔍 **Experiment**

- Point to the various rotate options in the Rotate Options gallery and watch the picture rotate in the document window.

2

- Click Flip Horizontal in the Rotate Options gallery, so that Word flips the graphic to display its mirror image (shown in Figure 3–29).

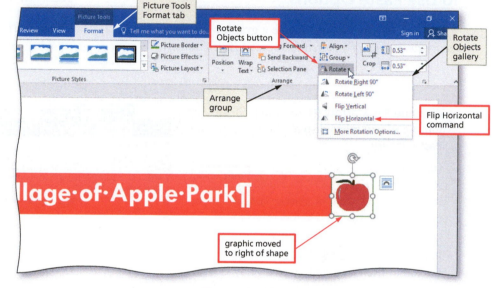

Figure 3–28

Q&A | Can I flip a graphic vertically?
Yes, you would click Flip Vertical in the Rotate Options gallery. You also can rotate a graphic clockwise or counterclockwise by clicking 'Rotate Right 90°' and 'Rotate Left 90°', respectively, in the Rotate Options gallery.

- Save the letterhead on your hard drive, OneDrive, or other storage location using the file name, Apple Park Letterhead.

Q&A | Why should I save the letterhead at this time?
You have performed many tasks while creating this letterhead and do not want to risk losing work completed thus far.

To Format and Enter Text

The contact information for the letterhead in this project is located on the line below the shape containing the name. The following steps format and then enter the mailing address in the letterhead.

1 Position the insertion point on the line below the shape containing the name.

2 If necessary, display the Home tab. Click the Center button (Home tab | Paragraph group) to center the paragraph.

3 Click the 'Increase Font Size' button (Home tab | Font group) to increase the font size to 12 point.

4 Type **15 Center Street, Horizon, MT 33568** and then press the SPACEBAR (shown in Figure 3–29).

To Insert a Symbol from the Symbol Dialog Box

Word provides a method of inserting dots and other symbols, such as letters in the Greek alphabet and mathematical characters, that are not on the keyboard. The following steps insert a dot symbol, sometimes called a bullet symbol, in the letterhead. *Why? You want a visual separator between the mailing address and phone number in the letterhead and also between the phone number and email address.*

1

- If necessary, position the insertion point as shown in Figure 3–29.

- Display the Insert tab.

- Click the 'Insert a Symbol' button (Insert tab | Symbols group) to display the Insert a Symbol gallery (Figure 3–29).

 What if the symbol I want to insert already appears in the Insert a Symbol gallery?

You can click any symbol shown in the Insert a Symbol gallery to insert it in the document.

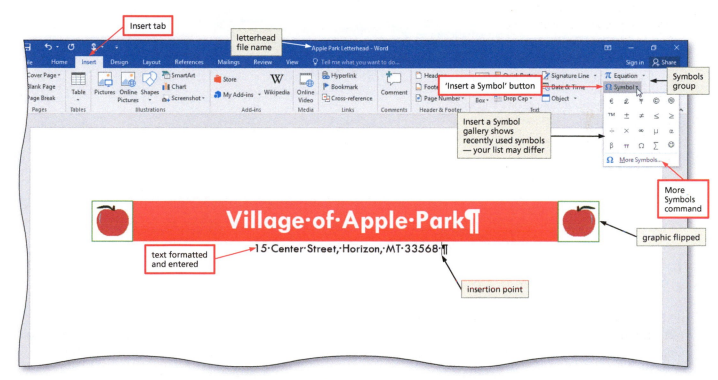

Figure 3–29

2

- Click More Symbols in the Insert a Symbol gallery to display the Symbol dialog box.
- If the font in the Font box is not (normal text), click the Font arrow (Symbol dialog box) and then scroll to and click (normal text) to select this font.
- If the subset in the Subset box is not General Punctuation, click the Subset arrow and then scroll and click General Punctuation to select this subset.
- In the list of symbols, if necessary, scroll to the dot symbol shown in Figure 3–30 and then click the symbol to select it.
- Click the Insert button (Symbol dialog box) to place the selected symbol in the document to the left of the insertion point (Figure 3–30).

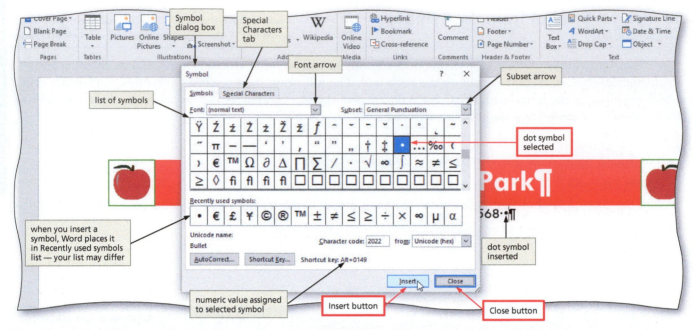

Figure 3–30

Q&A Why is the Symbol dialog box still open?
The Symbol dialog box remains open, allowing you to insert additional symbols.

3

- Click the Close button (Symbol dialog box) to close the dialog box.

To Insert a Symbol from the Insert a Symbol Gallery

1 CREATE & FORMAT LETTERHEAD WITH GRAPHICS | 2 SPECIFY LETTER FORMATS
3 INSERT TABLE | 4 FORMAT TABLE | 5 INSERT BULLETED LIST | 6 ADDRESS ENVELOPE

In the letterhead, another dot symbol separates the phone number from the email address. The following steps use the Insert a Symbol gallery to insert a dot symbol between the phone number and email address. *Why? Once you insert a symbol using the Symbol dialog box, Word adds that symbol to the Insert a Symbol gallery so that it is more readily available.*

1

- Press the SPACEBAR, type **Phone: (870) 555-4400** and then press the SPACEBAR.

2

- Click the 'Insert a Symbol' button (Insert tab | Symbols group) to display the Insert a Symbol gallery (Figure 3–31).

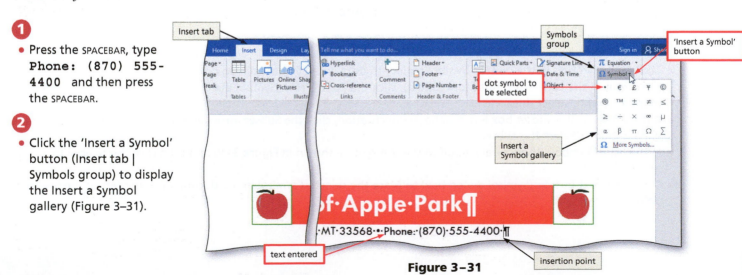

Figure 3–31

Why is the dot symbol now in the Insert a Symbol gallery?

When you insert a symbol from the Symbol dialog box, Word automatically adds the symbol to the Insert a Symbol gallery.

3

- Click the dot symbol in the Insert a Symbol gallery to insert the symbol at the location of the insertion point (shown in Figure 3–32).

To Enter Text

The following steps enter the email address in the letterhead.

1 Press the SPACEBAR.

2 Type **Email: applepark@world.com** to finish the text in the letterhead (Figure 3–32).

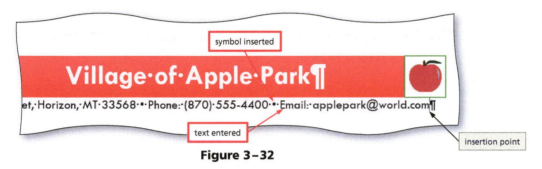

Figure 3–32

To Bottom Border a Paragraph

1 CREATE & FORMAT LETTERHEAD WITH GRAPHICS | 2 SPECIFY LETTER FORMATS
3 INSERT TABLE | 4 FORMAT TABLE | 5 INSERT BULLETED LIST | 6 ADDRESS ENVELOPE

In Word, you can draw a solid line, called a **border**, at any edge of a paragraph. That is, borders may be added above or below a paragraph, to the left or right of a paragraph, or in any combination of these sides.

The letterhead in this project has a border that extends from the left margin to the right margin immediately below the mailing address, phone, and email address information. *Why? The horizontal line separates the letterhead from the rest of the letter.* The following steps add a bottom border to a paragraph.

1

- Display the Home tab.

- With the insertion point in the paragraph to border, click the Borders arrow (Home tab | Paragraph group) to display the Borders gallery (Figure 3–33).

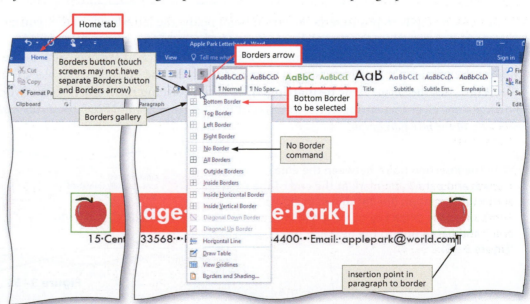

Figure 3–33

• Click Bottom Border in the Borders gallery to place a border below the paragraph containing the insertion point (Figure 3–34).

Figure 3–34

Q&A
If the face of the Borders button displays the border icon I want to use, can I click the Borders button instead of using the Borders arrow?
Yes.

How would I remove an existing border from a paragraph?
If, for some reason, you wanted to remove a border from a paragraph, you would position the insertion point in the paragraph, click the Borders arrow (Home tab | Paragraph group), and then click No Border in the Borders gallery.

Other Ways

1. Click 'Borders and Shading' button (Design tab | Page Background group), click Borders tab (Borders and Shading dialog box), select desired border options, click OK button

To Clear Formatting

1 CREATE & FORMAT LETTERHEAD WITH GRAPHICS | 2 SPECIFY LETTER FORMATS
3 INSERT TABLE | 4 FORMAT TABLE | 5 INSERT BULLETED LIST | 6 ADDRESS ENVELOPE

The next step is to position the insertion point below the letterhead, so that you can type the contents of the letter. When you press the ENTER key at the end of a paragraph containing a border, Word moves the border forward to the next paragraph. The paragraph also retains all current settings, such as the center format. Instead, you want the paragraph and characters on the new line to use the Normal style: black font with no border.

Word uses the term, **clear formatting**, to refer to returning the formats to the Normal style. The following steps clear formatting at the location of the insertion point. *Why? You do not want to retain the current formatting in the new paragraph.*

• With the insertion point between the email address and paragraph mark at the end of the contact information line (as shown in Figure 3–34), press the ENTER key to move the insertion point and paragraph to the next line (Figure 3–35).

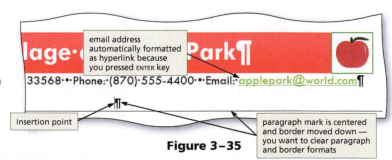

Figure 3–35

2

- Click the 'Clear All Formatting' button (Home tab | Font group) to apply the Normal style to the location of the insertion point (Figure 3–36).

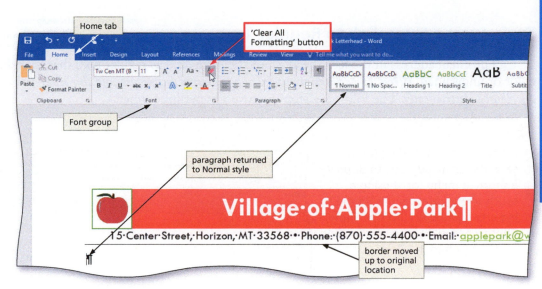

Figure 3–36

AutoFormat As You Type

As you type text in a document, Word automatically formats some of it for you. For example, when you press the ENTER key or SPACEBAR after typing an email address or web address, Word automatically formats the address as a hyperlink, that is, in a different color and underlined. In Figure 3–35, for example, Word formatted the email address as a hyperlink because you pressed the ENTER key at the end of the line. Table 3–2 outlines commonly used AutoFormat As You Type options and their results.

Table 3–2 Commonly Used AutoFormat As You Type Options		
Typed Text	**AutoFormat As You Type Feature**	**Example**
Quotation marks or apostrophes	Changes straight quotation marks or apostrophes to curly ones	"the" becomes "the"
Text, a space, one hyphen, one or no spaces, text, space	Changes the hyphen to an en dash	ages 20-45 becomes ages 20–45
Text, two hyphens, text, space	Changes the two hyphens to an em dash	Two types--yellow and red becomes Two types—yellow and red
Web or email address followed by SPACEBAR or ENTER key	Formats web or email address as a hyperlink	www.cengagebrain.com becomes www.cengagebrain.com
Number followed by a period, hyphen, right parenthesis, or greater than sign and then a space or tab followed by text	Creates a numbered list	1. Word 2. PowerPoint becomes 1. Word 2. PowerPoint
Asterisk, hyphen, or greater than sign and then a space or tab followed by text	Creates a bulleted list	* Home tab * Insert tab becomes • Home tab • Insert tab
Fraction and then a space or hyphen	Condenses the fraction entry so that it consumes one space instead of three	1/2 becomes ½
Ordinal and then a space or hyphen	Makes part of the ordinal a superscript	3rd becomes 3rd

To Convert a Hyperlink to Regular Text

The email address in the letterhead should be formatted as regular text; that is, it should not be a different color or underlined. *Why? Hyperlinks are useful only in online documents, and this letter will be printed instead of distributed electronically.* The following steps remove a hyperlink format.

- Right-click the hyperlink (in this case, the email address) to display a shortcut menu (or, if using a touch screen, press and hold the hyperlink and then tap the 'Show Context Menu' button on the mini toolbar) (Figure 3–37).

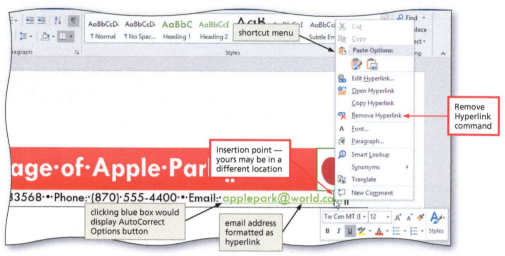

Figure 3–37

2

- Click Remove Hyperlink on the shortcut menu to remove the hyperlink format from the text.
- Position the insertion point on the paragraph mark below the border because you are finished with the letterhead (Figure 3–38).

Q&A

Could I have used the AutoCorrect Options button instead of the Remove Hyperlink command?
Yes. Alternatively, you could have pointed to the small blue box at the beginning of the hyperlink, clicked the AutoCorrect Options button, and then clicked Undo Hyperlink on the AutoCorrect Options menu.

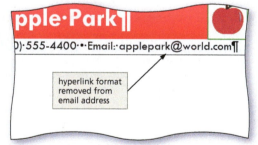

Figure 3–38

- Save the letterhead again on the same storage location with the same file name.

Other Ways
1. With insertion point in hyperlink, click 'Add a Hyperlink' button (Insert tab | Links group), click Remove Link button

Break Point: If you wish to take a break, this is a good place to do so. You can exit Word now. To resume at a later time, run Word, open the file called Apple Park Letterhead, and continue following the steps from this location forward.

Creating a Business Letter

With the letterhead for the business letter complete, the next task is to create the remainder of the content in the letter. The following sections use Word to create a business letter that contains a table and a bulleted list.

What should you consider when writing a business letter?
A finished business letter should look like a symmetrically framed picture with evenly spaced margins, all balanced below an attractive letterhead. The letter should be well written, properly formatted, logically organized, and use visuals where appropriate. The content of a letter should contain proper grammar, correct spelling, logically constructed sentences, flowing paragraphs, and sound ideas.

Be sure to include all essential elements, use proper spacing and formats, and determine which letter style to use.

- **Include all essential letter elements.** All business letters contain the same basic elements, including the date line, inside address, message, and signature block (shown in Figure 3–1 at the beginning of this module). If a business letter does not use a letterhead, then the top of the letter should include return address information in a heading.

- **Use proper spacing and formats for the contents of the letter below the letterhead.** Use a font that is easy to read, in a size between 8 and 12 point. Add emphasis with bold, italic, and bullets where appropriate, and use tables to present numeric information. Paragraphs should be single-spaced, with double-spacing between paragraphs.

- **Determine which letter style to use.** You can follow many different styles when creating business letters. A letter style specifies guidelines for the alignment and spacing of elements in the business letter.

If possible, keep the length of a business letter to one page. Be sure to proofread the finished letter carefully.

To Save a Document with a New File Name

The current open file has the name Apple Park Letterhead, which is the name of the organization letterhead. Because you want the letterhead file to remain intact so that you can reuse it, you save the document with a new file name. The following step saves a document with a new file name. For a detailed example of the procedure summarized below, refer to the Office and Windows module at the beginning of this book.

1 Save the letter on your hard drive, OneDrive, or other storage location using a new file name, Lee Vendor Letter.

1 CREATE & FORMAT LETTERHEAD WITH GRAPHICS | 2 SPECIFY LETTER FORMATS
3 INSERT TABLE | 4 FORMAT TABLE | 5 INSERT BULLETED LIST | 6 ADDRESS ENVELOPE

To Apply a Style

Recall that the Normal style in Word places 8 points of blank space after each paragraph and inserts a vertical space equal to 1.08 lines between each line of text. You will need to modify the spacing used for the paragraphs in the business letter. *Why? Business letters should use single spacing for paragraphs and double spacing between paragraphs.*

Word has many built-in, or predefined, styles that you can use to format text. The No Spacing style, for example, defines line spacing as single and does not insert any additional blank space between lines when you press the ENTER key. To apply a style to a paragraph, you first position the insertion point in the paragraph. The following step applies the No Spacing style to a paragraph.

BTW

Organizing Files and Folders
You should organize and store files in folders so that you easily can find the files later. For example, if you are taking an introductory technology class called CIS 101, a good practice would be to save all Word files in a Word folder in a CIS 101 folder. For a discussion of folders and detailed examples of creating folders, refer to the Office and Windows module at the beginning of this book.

1

- With the insertion point positioned in the paragraph to be formatted, click No Spacing in the Styles gallery (Home tab | Styles group) to apply the selected style to the current paragraph (Figure 3–39).

Q&A

Will this style be used in the rest of the document?

Yes. The paragraph formatting, which includes the style, will carry forward to subsequent paragraphs each time you press the ENTER key.

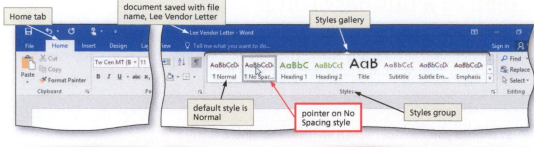

Figure 3–39

Other Ways

1. Click Styles Dialog Box Launcher (Home tab | Styles group), click desired style in Styles task pane

2. Press CTRL+SHIFT+S, click Style Name arrow in Apply Styles task pane, click desired style in list

---

CONSIDER THIS

What elements should a business letter contain?

Be sure to include all essential business letter elements, properly spaced, in your letter:

- The **date line**, which consists of the month, day, and year, is positioned two to six lines below the letterhead.

- The **inside address**, placed three to eight lines below the date line, usually contains the addressee's courtesy title plus full name, job title, business affiliation, and full geographical address.

- The **salutation**, if present, begins two lines below the last line of the inside address. If you do not know the recipient's name, avoid using the salutation "To whom it may concern" — it is impersonal. Instead, use the recipient's title in the salutation, e.g., Dear Personnel Director. In a business letter, use a colon (:) at the end of the salutation; in a personal letter, use a comma.

- The body of the letter, the **message**, begins two lines below the salutation. Within the message, paragraphs are single-spaced with one blank line between paragraphs.

- Two lines below the last line of the message, the **complimentary close** is displayed. Capitalize only the first word in a complimentary close.

- Type the **signature block** at least four blank lines below the complimentary close, allowing room for the author to sign his or her name.

CONSIDER THIS

What are the common styles of business letters?

Three common business letter styles are the block, the modified block, and the modified semi-block. Each style specifies different alignments and indentations.

- In the block letter style, all components of the letter begin flush with the left margin.

- In the modified block letter style, the date, complimentary close, and signature block are positioned approximately one-half inch to the right of center or at the right margin. All other components of the letter begin flush with the left margin.

- In the modified semi-block letter style, the date, complimentary close, and signature block are centered, positioned approximately one-half inch to the right of center or at the right margin. The first line of each paragraph in the body of the letter is indented one-half to one inch from the left margin. All other components of the letter begin flush with the left margin.

The business letter in this project follows the modified block style.

Using Tab Stops to Align Text

A **tab stop** is a location on the horizontal ruler that tells Word where to position the insertion point when you press the TAB key on the keyboard. Word, by default, places a tab stop at every one-half inch mark on the ruler. You also can set your own custom tab stops. Tab settings are a paragraph format. Thus, each time you press the ENTER key, any custom tab stops are carried forward to the next paragraph.

To move the insertion point from one tab stop to another, press the TAB key on the keyboard. When you press the TAB key, a **tab character** formatting mark appears in the empty space between the tab stops.

When you set a custom tab stop, you specify how the text will align at a tab stop. The tab marker on the ruler reflects the alignment of the characters at the location of the tab stop. Table 3–3 shows types of tab stop alignments in Word and their corresponding tab markers.

Table 3–3 Types of Tab Stop Alignments

Tab Stop Alignment	Tab Marker	Result of Pressing TAB Key	Example
Left Tab	⌊	Left-aligns text at the location of the tab stop	toolbar ruler
Center Tab	⊥	Centers text at the location of the tab stop	toolbar ruler
Right Tab	⌋	Right-aligns text at the location of the tab stop	toolbar ruler
Decimal Tab	⊥	Aligns text on decimal point at the location of the tab stop	45.72 223.75
Bar Tab	I	Aligns text at a bar character at the location of the tab stop	toolbar ruler

To Display the Ruler

One way to set custom tab stops is by using the horizontal ruler. Thus, the following steps display the ruler in the document window.

1 If the rulers are not showing, display the View tab.

2 Click the View Ruler check box (View tab | Show group) to place a check mark in the check box and display the horizontal and vertical rulers on the screen (shown in Figure 3–40).

To Set Custom Tab Stops

1 CREATE & FORMAT LETTERHEAD WITH GRAPHICS | **2 SPECIFY LETTER FORMATS**

3 INSERT TABLE | **4 FORMAT TABLE** | **5 INSERT BULLETED LIST** | **6 ADDRESS ENVELOPE**

The first required element of the business letter is the date line, which in this letter is positioned two lines below the letterhead. The date line contains the month, day, and year, and begins four inches from the left margin. **Why?** *Business letter guidelines specify to begin the date line approximately one-half inch to the right of center. Thus, you should set a custom tab stop at the 4" mark on the ruler.* The following steps set a left-aligned tab stop.

1

- With the insertion point on the paragraph mark below the border (shown in Figure 3–39), press the ENTER key so that a blank line appears above the insertion point.

- If necessary, click the tab selector at the left edge of the horizontal ruler until it displays the type of tab you wish to use, which is the Left Tab icon in this case.

- Position the pointer on the 4" mark on the ruler, which is the location of the desired custom tab stop (Figure 3–40).

Q&A

What is the purpose of the tab selector?
Before using the ruler to set a tab stop, ensure the correct tab stop icon appears in the tab selector. Each time you click the tab selector, its icon changes. The Left Tab icon is the default. For a list of the types of tab stops, see Table 3–3.

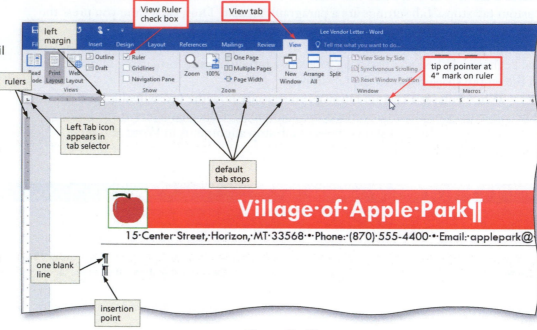

Figure 3–40

2

- Click the 4" mark on the ruler to place a tab marker at that location (Figure 3–41).

Q&A

What if I click the wrong location on the ruler?
You can move a custom tab stop by dragging the tab marker to the desired location on the ruler. Or, you can remove an existing custom tab stop by pointing to the tab marker on the ruler and then dragging the tab marker down and out of the ruler.

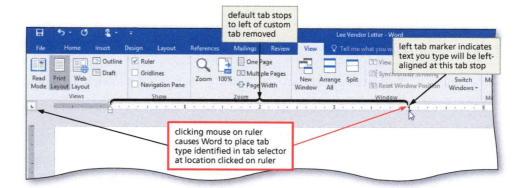

Figure 3–41

What if I am using a touch screen?
Display the Home tab, tap the Paragraph Settings Dialog Box Launcher (Home tab | Paragraph group), tap the Tabs button (Paragraph dialog box), type **4** in the Tab stop position box (Tabs dialog box), tap the Set button, and then tap the OK button to set a custom tab stop and place a corresponding tab marker on the ruler.

Other Ways

1. Click Paragraph Dialog Box Launcher (Home tab or Layout tab | Paragraph group), click Tabs button (Paragraph dialog box), type tab stop position (Tabs dialog box), click Set button, click OK button

To Insert the Current Date in a Document

The next step is to enter the current date at the 4" tab stop in the document. *Why? The date in this letter will be positioned according to the guidelines for a modified block style letter.* In Word, you can insert a computer's system date in a document. The following steps insert the current date in the letter.

- Press the TAB key to position the insertion point at the location of the tab stop in the current paragraph.
- Display the Insert tab.
- Click the 'Insert Date and Time' button (Insert tab | Text group) to display the Date and Time dialog box.
- Select the desired format (Date and Time dialog box), in this case October 2, 2017.
- If the Update automatically check box is selected, click the check box to remove the check mark (Figure 3–42).

Q&A

Why should the Update automatically check box not be selected?

In this project, the date at the top of the letter always should show today's date (for example, October 2, 2017). If, however, you wanted the date always to change to reflect the current computer date (for example, showing the date you open or print the letter), then you would place a check mark in this check box.

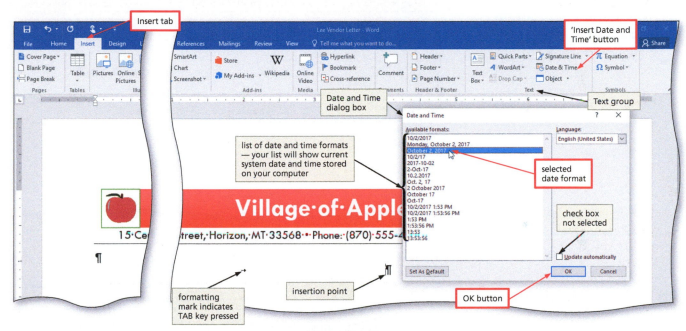

Figure 3–42

2

- Click the OK button to insert the current date at the location of the insertion point (Figure 3–43).

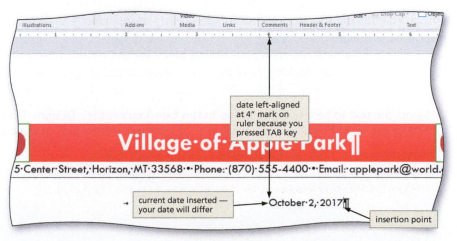

Figure 3–43

BTW

Tabs Dialog Box
You can use the Tabs dialog box to set, change the alignment of, and remove custom tab stops. To display the Tabs dialog box, click the Paragraph Settings Dialog Box Launcher (Home tab or Layout tab | Paragraph group) and then click the Tabs button (Paragraph dialog box). To set a custom tab stop, enter the desired tab position (Tabs dialog box) and then click the Set button. To change the alignment of a custom tab stop, click the tab stop position to be changed, click the new alignment, and then click the Set button. To remove an existing tab stop, click the tab stop position to be removed and then click the Clear button. To remove all tab stops, click the Clear All button in the Tabs dialog box.

To Enter the Inside Address and Salutation

The next step in composing the business letter is to type the inside address and salutation. The following steps enter this text.

1 With the insertion point at the end of the date (shown in Figure 3–43), press the ENTER key three times.

2 Type **Ms. Tamara Lee** and then press the ENTER key.

3 Type **Tam's Artistic Designs** and then press the ENTER key.

4 Type **1587 Willow Road** and then press the ENTER key.

5 Type **Juniper, MT 33522** and then press the ENTER key twice.

6 Type **Dear Ms. Lee:** to complete the inside address and salutation entries. Scroll up, if necessary (Figure 3–44).

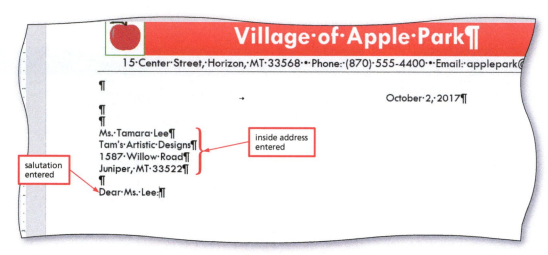

Figure 3–44

To Create a Building Block

1 CREATE & FORMAT LETTERHEAD WITH GRAPHICS | 2 SPECIFY LETTER FORMATS
3 INSERT TABLE | 4 FORMAT TABLE | 5 INSERT BULLETED LIST | 6 ADDRESS ENVELOPE

If you use the same text or graphic frequently, you can store the text or graphic as a **building block** and then insert the stored building block entry in the open document, as well as in future documents. That is, you can create the entry once as a building block and then insert the building block when you need it. In this way, you avoid entering text or graphics inconsistently or incorrectly in different locations throughout the same or multiple documents.

The following steps create a building block for the vendor business name, Tam's Artistic Designs. *Why? Later, you will insert the building block in the document instead of typing the vendor business name again.*

• Select the text to be a building block, in this case Tam's Artistic Designs. Do not select the paragraph mark at the end of the text because you do not want the paragraph to be part of the building block.

Q&A Why is the paragraph mark not part of the building block?
Select the paragraph mark only if you want to store paragraph formatting, such as indentation and line spacing, as part of the building block.

- Click the 'Explore Quick Parts' button (Insert tab | Text group) to display the Explore Quick Parts gallery (Figure 3–45).

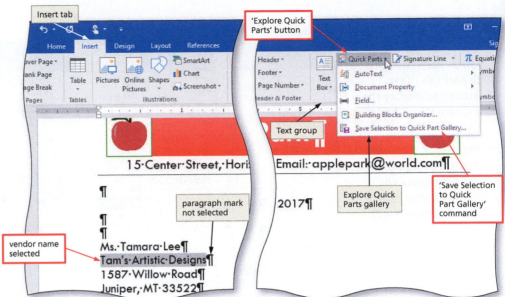

Figure 3–45

2

- Click 'Save Selection to Quick Part Gallery' in the Explore Quick Parts gallery to display the Create New Building Block dialog box.

- Type **tad** in the Name text box (Create New Building Block dialog box) to replace the proposed building block name (Tam's Artistic, in this case) with a shorter building block name (Figure 3–46).

3

- Click the OK button to store the building block entry and close the dialog box.

- If Word displays another dialog box, click the Yes button to save changes to the building blocks.

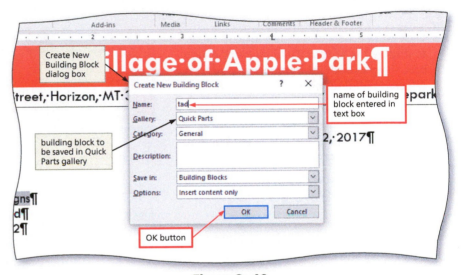

Figure 3–46

Q&A | Will this building block be available in future documents?
When you exit Word, a dialog box may appear asking if you want to save changes to the building blocks. Click the Save button if you want to use the new building block in future documents.

1 CREATE & FORMAT LETTERHEAD WITH GRAPHICS | **2 SPECIFY LETTER FORMATS**
3 INSERT TABLE | 4 FORMAT TABLE | 5 INSERT BULLETED LIST | 6 ADDRESS ENVELOPE

To Modify a Building Block

When you save a building block in the Explore Quick Parts gallery, the building block is displayed at the top of the Explore Quick Parts gallery. When you point to the building block in the Explore Quick Parts gallery, a ScreenTip displays the building block name. If you want to display more information when the user points to the building block, you can include a description in the ScreenTip.

The following steps modify a building block to include a description and change its category to AutoText. *Why? Because you want to reuse this text, you place it in the AutoText gallery, which also is accessible through the Explore Quick Parts gallery.*

- Click the 'Explore Quick Parts' button (Insert tab | Text group) to display the Explore Quick Parts gallery.

- Right-click the Tam's Artistic Design building block to display a shortcut menu (Figure 3–47).

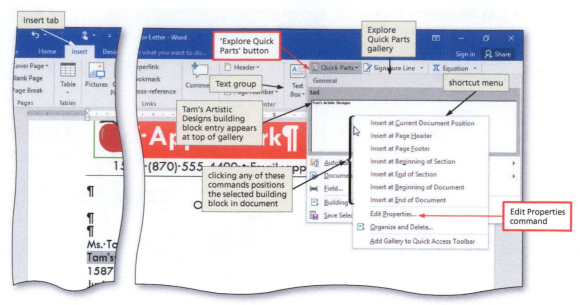

Figure 3–47

- Click Edit Properties on the shortcut menu to display the Modify Building Block dialog box, filled in with information related to the selected building block.

- Click the Gallery arrow (Modify Building Block dialog box) and then click AutoText to change the gallery in which the building block will be placed.

- Type **Event Vendor** in the Description text box (Figure 3–48).

- Click the OK button to store the building block entry and close the dialog box.

- Click the Yes button when asked if you want to redefine the building block entry.

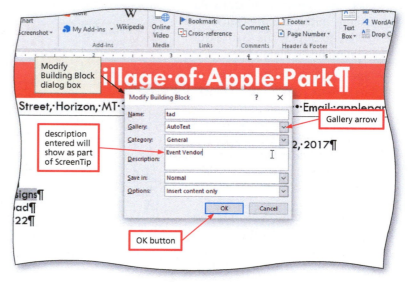

Figure 3–48

To Insert a Building Block

1 CREATE & FORMAT LETTERHEAD WITH GRAPHICS | 2 SPECIFY LETTER FORMATS
3 INSERT TABLE | 4 FORMAT TABLE | 5 INSERT BULLETED LIST | 6 ADDRESS ENVELOPE

The vendor business name, Tam's Artistic Designs, appears in the first sentence in the body of the letter. You will type the building block name, tad, and then instruct Word to replace this building block name with the stored building block entry, Tam's Artistic Designs. The following steps insert a building block. *Why? Instead of typing the name, you will insert the stored building block.*

- Click to the right of the colon in the salutation and then press the ENTER key twice to position the insertion point one blank line below the salutation.

- Type the beginning of the first sentence as follows, entering the building block name as shown: **The park district board has approved the vendor application for your business, tad** (Figure 3–49).

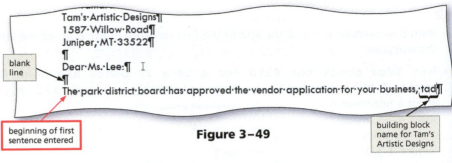

Figure 3–49

2

- Press the F3 key to instruct Word to replace the building block name (tad) with the stored building block entry (Tam's Artistic Designs).

- Press the PERIOD key (Figure 3–50).

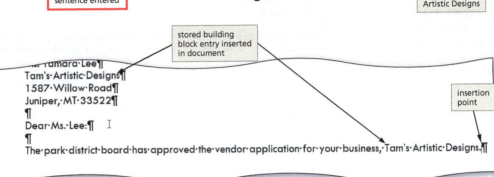

Figure 3–50

Other Ways

1. Click 'Explore Quick Parts' button (Insert tab | Text group), if necessary point to AutoText, select desired building block

2. Click 'Explore Quick Parts' button (Insert tab | Text group), click Building Blocks Organizer, select desired building block, click Insert button

Building Blocks versus AutoCorrect

In Module 2, you learned how to use the AutoCorrect feature, which enables you to insert and create AutoCorrect entries, similarly to how you created and inserted building blocks in this module. The difference between an AutoCorrect entry and a building block entry is that the AutoCorrect feature makes corrections for you automatically as soon as you press the SPACEBAR or type a punctuation mark, whereas you must instruct Word to insert a building block. That is, you enter the building block name and then press the F3 key, or click the Explore Quick Parts button and select the building block from one of the galleries or the Building Blocks Organizer.

To Insert a Nonbreaking Space

1 CREATE & FORMAT LETTERHEAD WITH GRAPHICS | **2 SPECIFY LETTER FORMATS**

3 INSERT TABLE | 4 FORMAT TABLE | 5 INSERT BULLETED LIST | 6 ADDRESS ENVELOPE

Some compound words, such as proper nouns, dates, units of time and measure, abbreviations, and geographic destinations, should not be divided at the end of a line. These words either should fit as a unit at the end of a line or be wrapped together to the next line.

Word provides two special characters to assist with this task: the nonbreaking space and the nonbreaking hyphen. A **nonbreaking space** is a special space character that prevents two words from splitting if the first word falls at the end of a line. Similarly, a **nonbreaking hyphen** is a special type of hyphen that prevents two words separated by a hyphen from splitting at the end of a line.

The following steps insert a nonbreaking space between the two words, Fall Festival. *Why? You want these two words to appear on the same physical line.*

- With the insertion point at the end of the first sentence in the body of the letter (as shown in Figure 3–50), press the SPACEBAR.

- Type **Your check for $150 for a 10 x 20 booth has been deposited, and we are excited that you will be participating in our Fall** and then press CTRL+SHIFT+SPACEBAR to insert a nonbreaking space after the entered word (Figure 3–51).

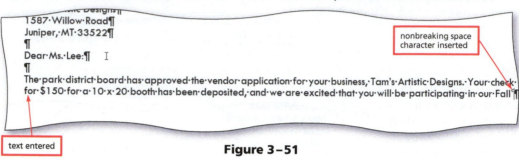

nonbreaking space character inserted

text entered

Figure 3–51

❷
- Type **Festival** and then press PERIOD key (Figure 3–52).

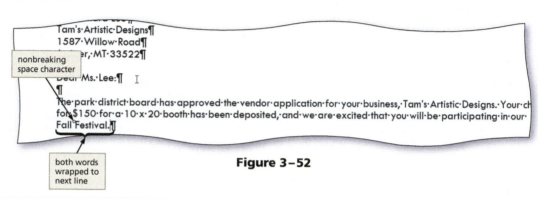

nonbreaking space character

both words wrapped to next line

Figure 3–52

Other Ways

1. Click 'Insert a Symbol' button (Insert tab | Symbols group), click More Symbols, click Special Characters tab (Symbol dialog box), click Nonbreaking Space in Character list, click Insert button, click Close button

BTW

Nonbreaking Hyphen

If you wanted to insert a nonbreaking hyphen, you would press CTRL+SHIFT+HYPHEN.

To Enter Text

The next step in creating the letter is to enter the rest of the text in the first paragraph. The following steps enter this text.

❶ Press the SPACEBAR.

❷ Type this sentence: **The table below outlines the timetable for vendors:**

❸ Press the ENTER key twice to place a blank line between paragraphs (shown in Figure 3–53).

Q&A Why does my document wrap on different words?

Differences in wordwrap may relate to the printer connected to your computer. Thus, it is possible that the same document could wordwrap differently if associated with a different printer.

❹ Save the letterhead again on the same storage location with the same file name.

Break Point: If you wish to take a break, this is a good place to do so. You can exit Word now. To resume at a later time, run Word, open the file called Lee Vendor Letter, and continue following the steps from this location forward.

Tables

The next step in composing the business letter is to place a table listing the vendor timetable (shown in Figure 3–1). A Word **table** is a collection of rows and columns. The intersection of a row and a column is called a **cell**, and cells are filled with data.

The first step in creating a table is to insert an empty table in the document. When inserting a table, you must specify the total number of rows and columns required, which is called the **dimension** of the table. The table in this project has three columns. You often do not know the total number of rows in a table. Thus, many Word users create one row initially and then add more rows as needed. In Word, the first number in a dimension is the number of columns, and the second is the number of rows. For example, in Word, a 3×1 (pronounced "three by one") table consists of three columns and one row.

To Insert an Empty Table

1 CREATE & FORMAT LETTERHEAD WITH GRAPHICS | 2 SPECIFY LETTER FORMATS

3 INSERT TABLE | 4 FORMAT TABLE | 5 INSERT BULLETED LIST | 6 ADDRESS ENVELOPE

The next step is to insert an empty table in the letter. The following steps insert a table with three columns and one row at the location of the insertion point. *Why? The first column will identify the activity, the second will identify the event dates, and the third will identify the activity times. You will start with one row and add them as needed.*

1

- Scroll the document so that you will be able to see the table in the document window.

- Display the Insert tab.

- With the insertion point positioned as shown in Figure 3–53, click the 'Add a Table' button (Insert tab | Tables group) to display the Add a Table gallery (Figure 3–53).

 Experiment

- Point to various cells on the grid to see a preview of various table dimensions in the document window.

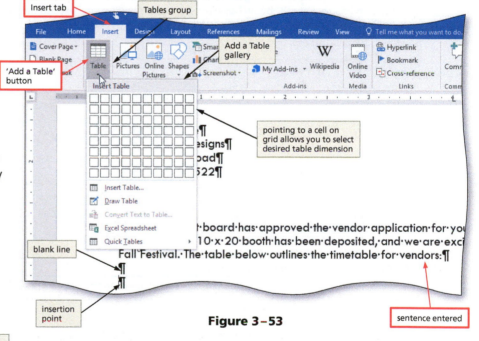

Figure 3–53

2

- Position the pointer on the cell in the first row and third column of the grid to preview the desired table dimension in the document (Figure 3–54).

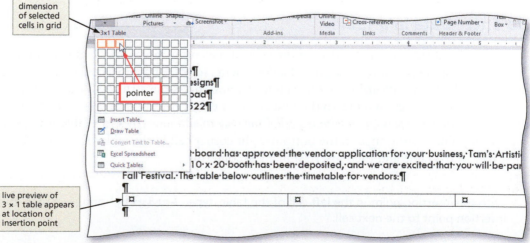

Figure 3–54

- Click the cell in the first row and third column of the grid to insert an empty table with one row and three columns in the document.

- If necessary, scroll the document so that the table is visible (Figure 3–55).

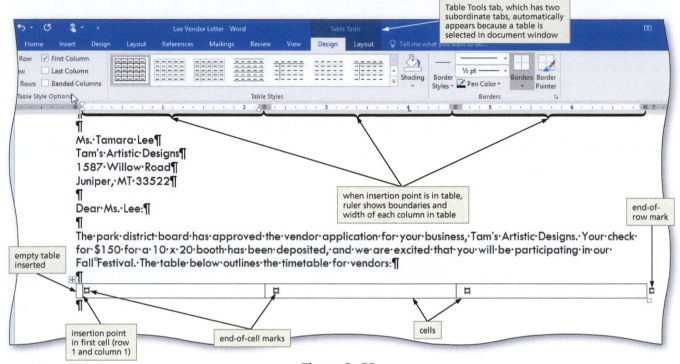

Figure 3–55

Q&A What are the small circles in the table cells?

Each table cell has an **end-of-cell mark**, which is a formatting mark that assists you with selecting and formatting cells. Similarly, each row has an **end-of-row mark**, which you can use to add columns to the right of a table. Recall that formatting marks do not print on a hard copy. The end-of-cell marks currently are left-aligned, that is, positioned at the left edge of each cell.

Other Ways

1. Click 'Add a Table' button (Insert tab | Tables group), click Insert Table in Add a Table gallery, enter number of columns and rows (Insert Table dialog box), click OK button

To Enter Data in a Table

1 CREATE & FORMAT LETTERHEAD WITH GRAPHICS | 2 SPECIFY LETTER FORMATS
3 INSERT TABLE | 4 FORMAT TABLE | 5 INSERT BULLETED LIST | 6 ADDRESS ENVELOPE

The next step is to enter data in the cells of the empty table. The data you enter in a cell wordwraps just as text wordwraps between the margins of a document. To place data in a cell, you click the cell and then type.

To advance rightward from one cell to the next, press the TAB key. When you are at the rightmost cell in a row, press the TAB key to move to the first cell in the next row; do not press the ENTER key. *Why? The ENTER key is used to begin a new paragraph within a cell.* One way to add new rows to a table is to press the TAB key when the insertion point is positioned in the bottom-right corner cell of the table. The following step enters data in the first row of the table and then inserts a blank second row.

- With the insertion point in the left cell of the table, type **Activity** and then press the TAB key to advance the insertion point to the next cell.

- Type **Event Dates** and then press the TAB key to advance the insertion point to the next cell.
- Type **Times** and then press the TAB key to add a second row at the end of the table and position the insertion point in the first column of the new row (Figure 3–56).

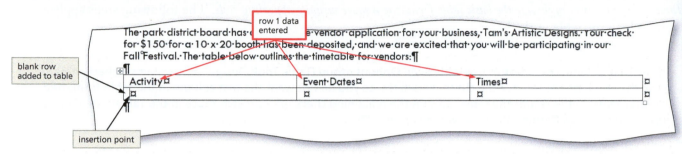

Figure 3–56

Q&A How do I edit cell contents if I make a mistake?
Click in the cell and then correct the entry.

To Enter More Data in a Table

The following steps enter the remaining data in the table.

1 Type **Booth Setup** and then press the TAB key to advance the insertion point to the next cell. Type **Friday, October 27** and then press the TAB key to advance the insertion point to the next cell. Type **5:00 to 9:00 p.m.** and then press the TAB key to add a row at the end of the table and position the insertion point in the first column of the new row.

2 In the third row, type **Booth Sales** in the first column, **Saturday, October 28** in the second column, and **9:00 a.m. to 6:00 p.m.** in the third column. Press the TAB key to position the insertion point in the first column of a new row.

3 In the fourth row, type **Booth Sales** in the first column, **Sunday, October 29** in the second column, and **9:00 a.m. to 3:00 p.m.** in the third column. Press the TAB key.

4 In the fifth row, type **Booth Takedown** in the first column, **Sunday, October 29** in the second column, and **3:00 to 7:00 p.m.** in the third column (Figure 3–57).

BTW

Tables
For simple tables, such as the one just created, Word users often select the table dimension in the Add a Table gallery to create the table. For a more complex table, such as one with a varying number of columns per row, Word has a Draw Table feature that allows users to draw a table in the document using a pencil pointer. To use this feature, click the 'Add a Table' button (Insert tab | Tables group) and then click Draw Table on the Add a Table menu.

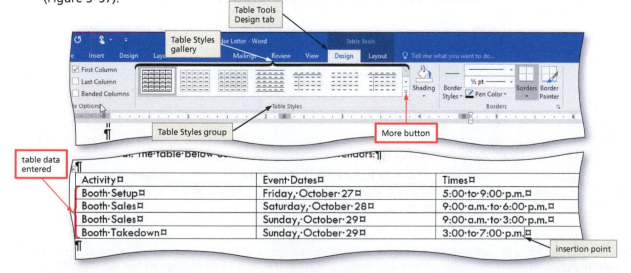

Figure 3–57

To Apply a Table Style

Word provides a gallery of more than 90 table styles, which include a variety of colors and shading. ***Why?*** *Table styles allow you to change the basic table format to a more visually appealing style.* The following steps apply a table style to the table in the letter.

- If the First Column check box in the Table Style Options group (Table Tools Design tab) contains a check mark, click the check box to remove the check mark because you do not want the first column in the table formatted differently from the rest of the table. Be sure the remaining check marks match those in the Table Style Options group (Table Tools Design tab) as shown in Figure 3–58.

Q&A

What if the Table Tools Design tab no longer is the active tab?

Click in the table and then display the Table Tools Design tab.

What do the options in the Table Style Options group mean?

When you apply table styles, if you want the top row of the table (header row), a row containing totals (total row), first column, or last column to be formatted differently, select those check boxes. If you want the rows or columns to alternate with colors, select Banded Rows or Banded Columns, respectively.

- With the insertion point in the table, click the More button in the Table Styles gallery (Table Tools Design tab | Table Styles group), shown in Figure 3–57, to expand the gallery.

- Scroll and then point to 'Grid Table 6 Colorful - Accent 3' in the Table Styles gallery to display a live preview of that style applied to the table in the document (Figure 3–58).

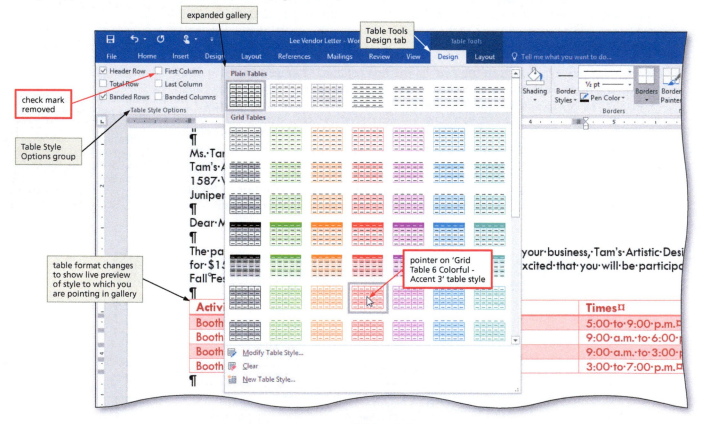

Figure 3–58

🔎 Experiment

- Point to various styles in the Table Styles gallery and watch the format of the table change in the document window.

3

- Click 'Grid Table 6 Colorful - Accent 3' in the Table Styles gallery to apply the selected style to the table. Scroll up, if necessary (Figure 3–59).

🔍 **Experiment**

- Select and remove check marks from various check boxes in the Table Style Options group and watch the format of the table change in the document window. When finished experimenting, be sure the check marks match those shown in Figure 3–58.

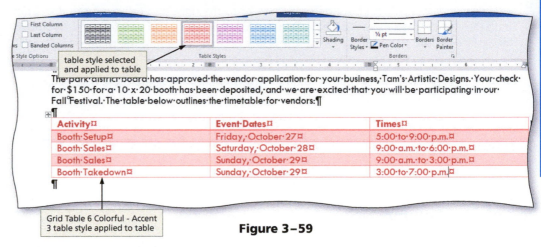

Figure 3–59

To Resize Table Columns to Fit Table Contents

1 CREATE & FORMAT LETTERHEAD WITH GRAPHICS | 2 SPECIFY LETTER FORMATS
3 INSERT TABLE | **4 FORMAT TABLE** | 5 INSERT BULLETED LIST | 6 ADDRESS ENVELOPE

The table in this project currently extends from the left margin to the right margin of the document. The following steps instruct Word to fit the width of the columns to the contents of the table automatically. **Why?** *You want each column to be only as wide as the longest entry in the table. That is, the first column must be wide enough to accommodate the words, Booth Takedown, and the second column should be only as wide as the words, Saturday, October 28, and so on.*

1

- With the insertion point in the table, display the Table Tools Layout tab.

- Click the AutoFit button (Table Tools Layout tab | Cell Size group) to display the AutoFit menu (Figure 3–60).

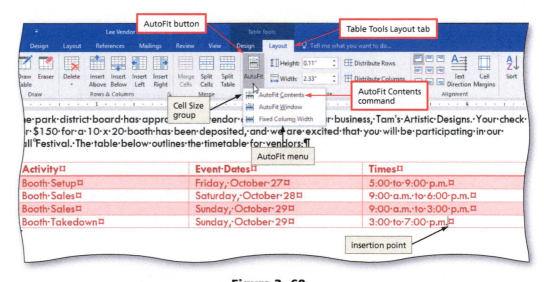

Figure 3–60

2

- Click AutoFit Contents on the AutoFit menu, so that Word automatically adjusts the widths of the columns based on the text in the table (Figure 3–61).

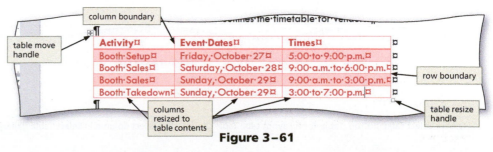

Figure 3–61

Q&A Can I resize columns manually?

Yes, you can drag a **column boundary**, the border to the right of a column, until the column is the desired width. Similarly, you can resize a row by dragging the **row boundary**, the border at the bottom of a row, until the row is the desired height. You also can resize the entire table by dragging the **table resize handle**, which is a small square that appears when you point to a corner of the table.

What causes the table move handle and table resize handle to appear and disappear from the table?

They appear whenever you position the pointer in the table.

Other Ways

1. Double-click column boundary

To Select a Column

1 CREATE & FORMAT LETTERHEAD WITH GRAPHICS | 2 SPECIFY LETTER FORMATS | 3 INSERT TABLE | 4 FORMAT TABLE | 5 INSERT BULLETED LIST | 6 ADDRESS ENVELOPE

The next task is to change the alignment of the data in cells in the third column of the table. To do this, you first must select the column. ***Why?*** *If you want to format the contents of a single cell, simply position the insertion point in the cell. To format a series of cells, you first must select them.* The following step selects a column.

1

- Position the pointer at the boundary above the column to be selected, the third column in this case, so that the pointer changes to a downward pointing arrow and then click to select the column (Figure 3–62).

Q&A What if I am using a touch screen?

Position the insertion point in the third column, tap the Select Table button (Table Tools Layout tab | Table group), and then tap Select Column on the Select Table menu.

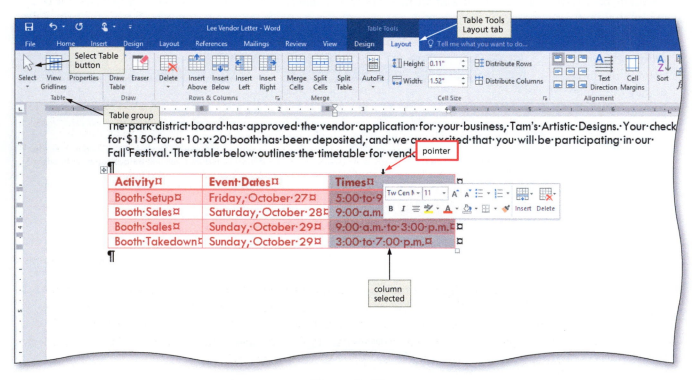

Figure 3–62

Other Ways

1. Click Select Table button (Table Tools Layout tab | Table group), click Select Column in Select Table gallery

Selecting Table Contents

When working with tables, you may need to select the contents of cells, rows, columns, or the entire table. Table 3–4 identifies ways to select various items in a table.

Table 3–4 Selecting Items in a Table	
Item to Select	**Action**
Cell	Point to left edge of cell and then click when the pointer changes to a small solid upward angled pointing arrow. Or Position insertion point in cell, click Select Table button (Table Tools Layout tab | Table group), and then click Select Cell on the Select Table menu.
Column	Point to border at top of column and then click when the pointer changes to a small solid downward-pointing arrow. Or Position insertion point in column, click Select Table button (Table Tools Layout tab | Table group), and then click Select Column on the Select Table menu.
Row	Point to the left of the row and then click when pointer changes to a right-pointing block arrow. Or Position insertion point in row, click Select Table button (Table Tools Layout tab | Table group), and then click Select Row on the Select Table menu.
Multiple cells, rows, or columns adjacent to one another	Drag through cells, rows, or columns.
Multiple cells, rows, or columns not adjacent to one another	Select first cell, row, or column (as described above) and then hold down CTRL key while selecting next cell, row, or column.
Next cell	Press TAB key.
Previous cell	Press SHIFT+TAB
Table	Point somewhere in table and then click table move handle that appears in upper-left corner of table (shown in Figure 3-63). Or Position insertion point in table, click Select Table button (Table Tools Layout tab | Table group), and then click Select Table on the Select Table menu.

BTW

Word Help
At any time while using Word, you can find answers to questions and display information about various topics through Word Help. Used properly, this form of assistance can increase your productivity and reduce your frustrations by minimizing the time you spend learning how to use Word. For instructions about Word Help and exercises that will help you gain confidence in using it, read the Office and Windows module at the beginning of this book.

To Align Data in Cells

1 CREATE & FORMAT LETTERHEAD WITH GRAPHICS | 2 SPECIFY LETTER FORMATS
3 INSERT TABLE | 4 FORMAT TABLE | 5 INSERT BULLETED LIST | 6 ADDRESS ENVELOPE

The next step is to change the alignment of the data in cells in the third column of the table. In addition to aligning text horizontally in a cell (left, center, or right), you can align it vertically within a cell (top, center, bottom). When the height of the cell is close to the same height as the text, however, differences in vertical alignment are not readily apparent, which is the case for this table. The following step centers data in cells. *Why?* *The column containing the times would look better if its contents are centered.*

1

- With the cells (column) selected, as shown in Figure 3–62, click the desired alignment, in this case the 'Align Top Center' button (Table Tools Layout tab | Alignment group) to center the contents of the selected cells (Figure 3–63).

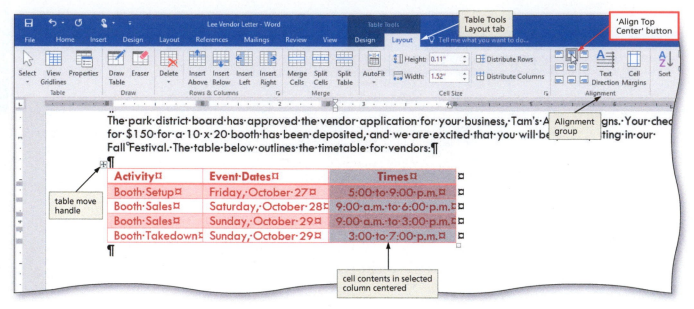

Figure 3–63

To Center a Table

1 CREATE & FORMAT LETTERHEAD WITH GRAPHICS | 2 SPECIFY LETTER FORMATS
3 INSERT TABLE | **4 FORMAT TABLE** | 5 INSERT BULLETED LIST | 6 ADDRESS ENVELOPE

When you first create a table, it is left-aligned; that is, it is flush with the left margin. In this letter, the entire table should be centered between the margins of the page. To center a table, you first select the entire table. The following steps select and center a table using the mini toolbar. ***Why?*** *Recall that you can use buttons and boxes on the mini toolbar instead of those on the ribbon.*

1

- Position the pointer in the table so that the table move handle appears (shown in Figure 3–63).

Q&A What if the table move handle does not appear?
You also can select a table by clicking the Select Table button (Table Tools Layout tab | Table group) and then clicking Select Table on the menu.

2

- Click the table move handle to select the entire table (Figure 3–64).

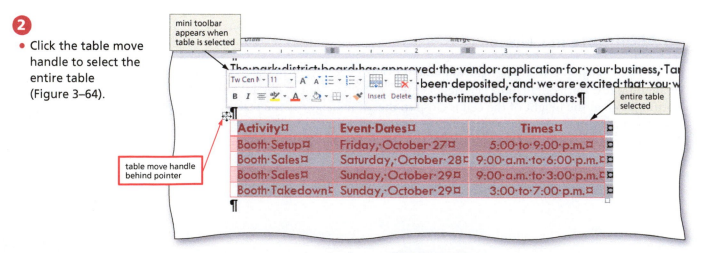

Figure 3–64

What if I am using a touch screen?
Tap the Select Table button (Table Tools Layout tab | Table group) and then tap Select Table on the Select Table menu to select the table.

- Click the Center button on the mini toolbar to center the selected table between the left and right page margins (Figure 3–65).

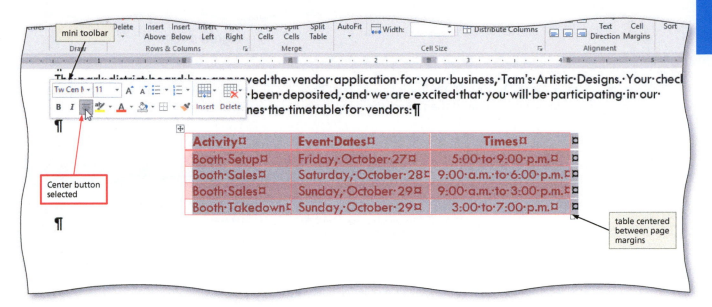

Figure 3–65

Could I have clicked the Center button on the Home tab?
Yes. If the command you want to use is not on the currently displayed tab on the ribbon and it is available on the mini toolbar, use the mini toolbar instead of switching to a different tab. This technique minimizes mouse movement.

What if I am using a touch screen?
Display the Home tab and then tap the Center button (Home tab | Paragraph group) to center the table.

To Insert a Row in a Table

1 CREATE & FORMAT LETTERHEAD WITH GRAPHICS | 2 SPECIFY LETTER FORMATS
3 INSERT TABLE | 4 FORMAT TABLE | 5 INSERT BULLETED LIST | 6 ADDRESS ENVELOPE

The next step is to insert a row at the top of the table. *Why? You want to place a title on the table.* As discussed earlier, you can insert a row at the end of a table by positioning the insertion point in the bottom-right corner cell and then pressing the TAB key. You cannot use the TAB key to insert a row at the beginning or middle of a table. Instead, you use the 'Insert Rows Above' or 'Insert Rows Below' command (Table Tools Layout tab | Rows & Columns group) or the Insert Control (shown in Figure 3–70). The following steps insert a row at the top of a table.

- Position the insertion point somewhere in the first row of the table because you want to insert a row above this row (Figure 3–66).

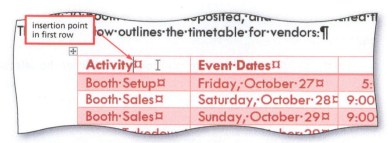

Figure 3–66

- Click the 'Insert Rows Above' button (Table Tools Layout tab | Rows & Columns group) to insert a row above the row containing the insertion point and then select the newly inserted row (Figure 3–67).

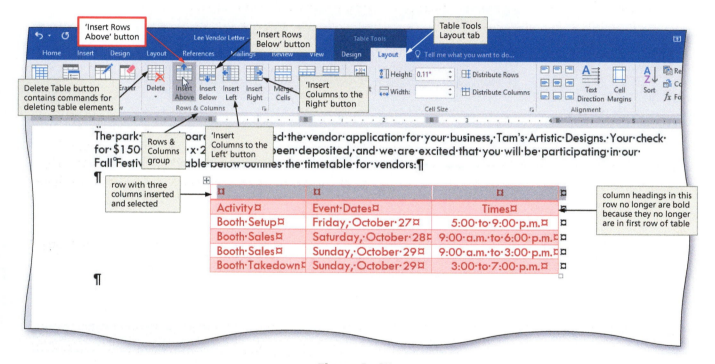

Figure 3–67

Q&A

Do I have to insert rows above the row containing the insertion point?

No. You can insert below the row containing the insertion point by clicking the 'Insert Rows Below' button (Table Tools Layout tab | Rows & Columns group).

Why did the colors in the second row change?

The table style specifies to format the header row differently, which is the first row.

Other Ways

1. Point to the left of the table and click the desired Insert Control

2. Right-click row, point to Insert on shortcut menu (or, if using touch, tap Insert Table button on mini toolbar), click desired option on Insert submenu

TO INSERT A COLUMN IN A TABLE

If you wanted to insert a column in a table, instead of inserting rows, you would perform the following steps.

1. Point above the table and then click the desired Insert Control.

or

1. Position the insertion point in the column to the left or right of where you want to insert the column.

2. Click the 'Insert Columns to the Left' button (Table Tools Layout tab | Rows & Columns group) to insert a column to the left of the current column, or click the 'Insert Columns to the Right' button (Table Tools Layout tab | Rows & Columns group) to insert a column to the right of the current column.

or

1. Right-click the table, point to Insert on the shortcut menu (or, if using touch, tap Insert Table button on the mini toolbar), and then click 'Insert Columns to the Left' or 'Insert Columns to the Right' on the Insert submenu (or, if using touch, tap Insert Left or Insert Right).

BTW

Resizing Table Columns and Rows
To change the width of a column or height of a row to an exact measurement, hold down the ALT key while dragging markers on the ruler. Or, enter values in the 'Table Column Width' or 'Table Row Height' boxes (Table Tools Layout tab | Cell Size group).

To Merge Cells

1 CREATE & FORMAT LETTERHEAD WITH GRAPHICS | 2 SPECIFY LETTER FORMATS

3 INSERT TABLE | **4 FORMAT TABLE** | 5 INSERT BULLETED LIST | 6 ADDRESS ENVELOPE

The row just inserted has one cell for each column, in this case, three cells (shown in Figure 3–67). The top row of the table, however, is to be a single cell that spans all rows. *Why?* *The top row contains the table title, which should be centered above the columns of the table.* Thus, the following steps merge the three cells into a single cell.

• With the cells to merge selected (as shown in Figure 3–67), click the Merge Cells button (Table Tools Layout tab | Merge group) to merge the selected cells into a single cell (Figure 3–68).

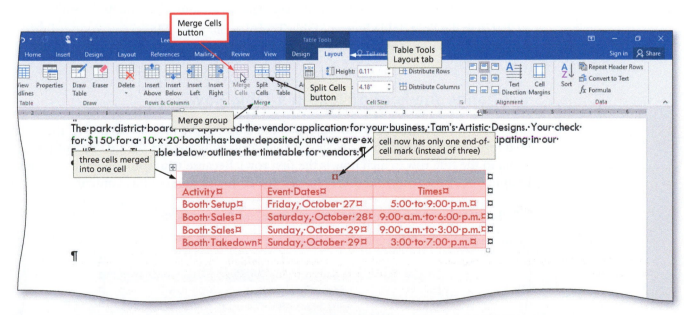

Figure 3–68

2

• Position the insertion point in the first row and then type **Vendor Timetable** as the table title (Figure 3–69).

Figure 3–69

Other Ways

1. Right-click selected cells (or, if using touch, tap 'Show Context Menu' button on mini toolbar), click Merge Cells on shortcut menu

---

To Split Table Cells

Instead of merging multiple cells into a single cell, sometimes you want to split a single cell into multiple cells. If you wanted to split cells, you would perform the following steps.

1. Position the insertion point in the cell to split.
2. Click the Split Cells button (Table Tools Layout tab | Merge group) (or, if using touch, tap 'Show Context Menu' button on mini toolbar), or right-click the cell and then click Split Cells on the shortcut menu, to display the Split Cells dialog box.
3. Enter the number of columns and rows into which you want the cell split (Split Cells dialog box).
4. Click the OK button.

To Split a Table

Instead of splitting table cells into multiple cells, sometimes you want to split a single table into multiple cells. If you wanted to split a table, you would perform the following steps.

1. Position the insertion point in the cell where you want the table to be split.
2. Click the Split Table button (Table Tools Layout tab | Merge group) to split the table into two tables at the location of the insertion point.

To Change the Font of Text in a Table Row

When you added a row to the top of the table for the title, Word moved the bold format from the column headings (which originally were in the first row of the table) to the title row (which now is the first row). Because you would like the columns headings bold also, the following steps select a table row and bold its contents.

1 Select the row containing the column headings (Figure 3–70).

Figure 3–70

2 With the text selected, click the Bold button (Home tab | Font group) to bold the selected text.

Q&A What is the symbol that appeared to the left of the table?

When you select a row or column in a table, Word displays an Insert Control. You can click the **Insert Control** to add a row or column to the table at that location.

Deleting Table Data

If you want to delete row(s) or delete column(s) from a table, position the insertion point in the row(s) or column(s) to delete, click the Delete Table button (Table Tools Layout tab | Rows & Columns group), and then click Delete Rows or Delete Columns on the Delete Table menu. Or, select the row or column to delete, right-click the selection, and then click Delete Rows or Delete Columns on the mini toolbar or shortcut menu.

To delete the contents of a cell, select the cell contents and then press the DELETE or BACKSPACE key. You also can drag and drop or cut and paste the contents of cells. To delete an entire table, select the table, click the Delete Table button (Table Tools Layout tab | Rows & Columns group), and then click Delete Table on the Delete Table menu. To delete the contents of a table and leave an empty table, you would select the table and then press the DELETE key.

To Add More Text

The table now is complete. The next step is to enter text below the table. The following steps enter text.

1 Position the insertion point on the paragraph mark below the table and then press the ENTER key.

2 Type **Please note the following vendor guidelines:** and then press the ENTER key (shown in Figure 3–71).

1 CREATE & FORMAT LETTERHEAD WITH GRAPHICS | 2 SPECIFY LETTER FORMATS
3 INSERT TABLE | 4 FORMAT TABLE | **5 INSERT BULLETED LIST** | 6 ADDRESS ENVELOPE

To Bullet a List as You Type

In Module 1, you learned how to apply bullets to existing paragraphs. If you know before you type that a list should be bulleted, you can use Word's AutoFormat As You Type feature to bullet the paragraphs as you type them (see Table 3–2 shown earlier in this module). **Why?** *The AutoFormat As You Type feature saves you time because it applies formats automatically.* The following steps add bullets to a list as you type.

1
- Press the ASTERISK key (*) as the first character on the line (Figure 3–71).

2
- Press the SPACEBAR to convert the asterisk to a bullet character.

BTW
AutoFormat Options
Before you can use them, AutoFormat options must be enabled. To check if an AutoFormat option is enabled, click File on the ribbon to open the Backstage view, click the Options tab in the Backstage view, click Proofing in the left pane (Word Options dialog box), click the AutoCorrect Options button, click the AutoFormat As You Type tab, select the appropriate check boxes, and then click the OK button in each open dialog box.

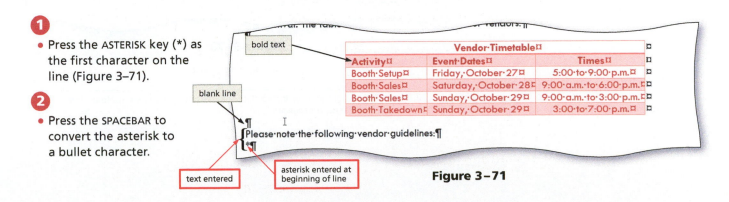

Figure 3–71

What if I did not want the asterisk converted to a bullet character?

You could undo the AutoFormat by clicking the Undo button; pressing CTRL+Z; clicking the AutoCorrect Options button that appears to the left of the bullet character as soon as you press the SPACEBAR and then clicking Undo Automatic Bullets on the AutoCorrect Options menu; or clicking the Bullets button (Home tab | Paragraph group).

3

- Type **Vendors must bring their own tables and chairs.** as the first bulleted item.

- Press the ENTER key to place another bullet character at the beginning of the next line (Figure 3–72).

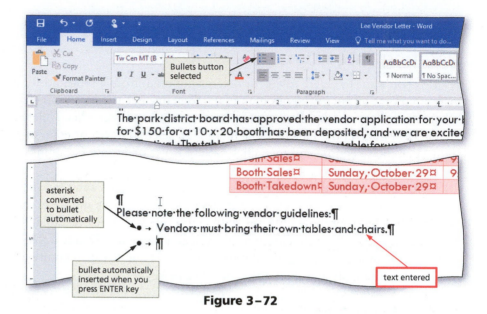

Figure 3–72

4

- Type **Vendors must supply their own electrical cords.** and then press the ENTER key.

- Type **Vendors shall comply with fire, safety, and health regulations.** and then press the ENTER key.

- Press the ENTER key to turn off automatic bullets as you type (Figure 3–73).

Why did automatic bullets stop?

When you press the ENTER key without entering any text after the automatic bullet character, Word turns off the automatic bullets feature.

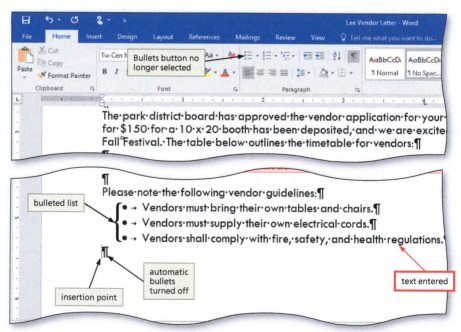

Figure 3–73

Other Ways

1. Click Bullets arrow (Home tab | Paragraph group), click desired bullet style

2. Right-click paragraph to be bulleted, click Bullets button on mini toolbar, click desired bullet style, if necessary

To Enter More Text and then Save and Print the Letter

The following steps enter the remainder of text in the letter.

1 With the insertion point positioned on the paragraph below the bulleted list, press the ENTER key and then type the paragraph shown in Figure 3–74, making certain you use the building block name, tad, to insert the organization name.

2 Press the ENTER key twice. Press the TAB key to position the insertion point at the tab stop set at the 4" mark on the ruler. Type **Sincerely,** and then press the ENTER key four times.

3 Press the TAB key to position the insertion point at the tab stop set at the 4" mark on the ruler. Type **Camden Ackerman** and then press the ENTER key.

If requested by your instructor, enter your name instead of the name stated above.

4 Press the TAB key to position the insertion point at the tab stop set at the 4" mark on the ruler. Type **Park District Events Coordinator** to finish the letter. Scroll up, if necessary (Figure 3–74).

5 Save the letter again on the same storage location with the same file name.

6 If requested by your instructor, print the letter.

BTW

Conserving Ink and Toner

If you want to conserve ink or toner, you can instruct Word to print draft quality documents by clicking File on the ribbon to open the Backstage view, clicking the Options tab in the Backstage view to display the Word Options dialog box, clicking Advanced in the left pane (Word Options dialog box), scrolling to the Print area in the right pane, placing a check mark in the 'Use draft quality' check box, and then clicking the OK button. Then, use the Backstage view to print the document as usual.

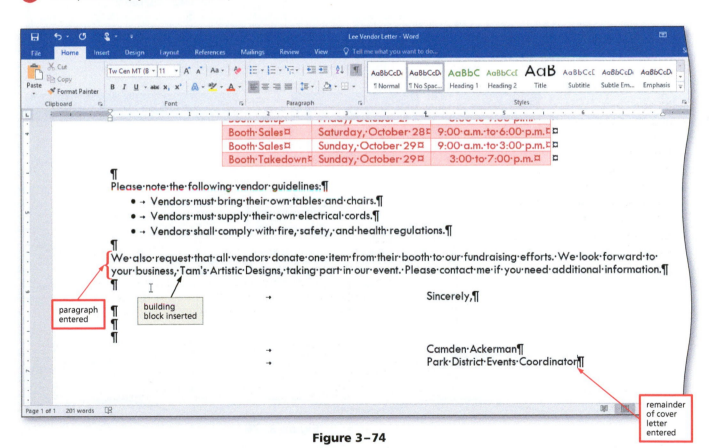

Figure 3–74

Addressing and Printing Envelopes and Mailing Labels

With Word, you can print mailing address information on an envelope or on a mailing label. Computer-printed addresses look more professional than handwritten ones.

To Address and Print an Envelope

The following steps address and print an envelope. If you are in a lab environment, check with your instructor before performing these steps. *Why? Some printers may not accommodate printing envelopes; others may stop printing until an envelope is inserted.*

1

- Scroll through the letter to display the inside address in the document window.

- Drag through the inside address to select it (Figure 3–75).

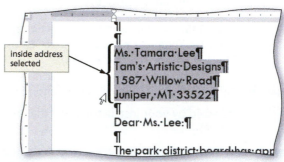

Figure 3–75

2

- Display the Mailings tab.

- Click the Create Envelopes button (Mailings tab | Create group) to display the Envelopes and Labels dialog box.

- If necessary, click the Envelopes tab (Envelopes and Labels dialog box), which automatically displays the selected delivery address in the dialog box.

- Type the return address as shown in Figure 3–76.

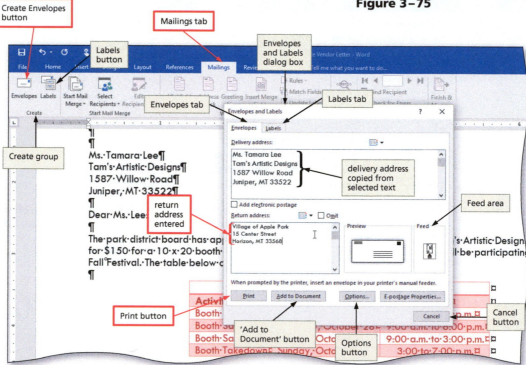

Figure 3–76

3

- Insert an envelope in your printer, as shown in the Feed area of the dialog box (your Feed area may be different depending on your printer).

- If your printer can print envelopes, click the Print button (Envelopes and Labels dialog box) to print the envelope; otherwise, click the Cancel button to close the dialog box.

- Because the project now is complete, you can exit Word.

Envelopes and Labels

Instead of printing the envelope immediately, you can add it to the document by clicking the 'Add to Document' button (Envelopes and Labels dialog box) (shown in Figure 3–76). To specify a different envelope or label type (identified by a number on the box of envelopes or labels), click the Options button (Envelopes and Labels dialog box) (shown in Figure 3–76).

Instead of printing an envelope, you can print a mailing label. To do this, click the Labels button (Mailings tab | Create group) (shown in Figure 3–76) and then type the delivery address in the Delivery address box. To print the same address on all labels on the page, select the 'Full page of the same label' option button in the Print area. Click the Print button (Envelopes and Labels dialog box) to print the label(s).

Summary

In this module, you have learned how to use Word to change margins, insert and format a shape, change text wrapping, insert and format a picture, move and copy graphics, insert symbols, add a border, clear formatting, convert a hyperlink to regular text, set and use tab stops, insert the current date, create and insert building blocks, insert and format tables, and address and print envelopes and mailing labels.

CONSIDER THIS: PLAN AHEAD

What decisions will you need to make when creating your next business letter?

Use these guidelines as you complete the assignments in this module and create your own business letters outside of this class.

1. Create a letterhead.

   a) Ensure that the letterhead contains a complete legal name, mailing address, phone number, and if applicable, fax number, email address, web address, logo, or other image.

   b) Place elements in the letterhead in a visually appealing location.

   c) Format the letterhead with appropriate fonts, font sizes, font styles, and color.

2. Compose an effective business letter.

   a) Include a date line, inside address, message, and signature block.

   b) Use proper spacing and formats for letter contents.

   c) Follow the alignment and spacing guidelines based on the letter style used (i.e., block, modified block, or modified semi-block).

   d) Ensure the message is well written, properly formatted, and logically organized.

BTW

Saving a Template

As an alternative to saving the letterhead as a Word document, you could save it as a template. To do so, click File on the ribbon to open the Backstage view, click the Export tab to display the Export gallery, click 'Change File Type', click Template in the right pane, click the Save As button, enter the template file name (Save As dialog box), if necessary select the Templates folder, and then click the Save button in the dialog box. To use the template, tap or click File on the ribbon to open the Backstage view, click the New tab to display the New gallery, click the PERSONAL tab in the New gallery, and then click the template icon or file name.

Apply Your Knowledge

Reinforce the skills and apply the concepts you learned in this module.

Working with Tabs and a Table

Note: To complete this assignment, you will be required to use the Data Files. Please contact your instructor for information about accessing the Data Files.

Instructions: Run Word. Open the document called Apply 3–1 Fall Semester Schedule Draft located on the Data Files. The document is a Word table that you are to edit and format. The revised table is shown in Figure 3–77.

Fall Semester Schedule

Class/Activity	Monday	Tuesday	Wednesday	Thursday	Friday	Saturday
ENG 101	9:30-11:00 a.m.		9:30-11:00 a.m.			
COM 110		12:30-2:00 p.m.		12:30-2:00 p.m.		
MAT 120	1:00-2:00 p.m.		1:00-2:00 p.m.		1:00-2:00 p.m.	
CHM 102	3:30-5:00 p.m.		3:30-5:00 p.m.		3:00-5:00 p.m.	
MUS 152		9:30-11:00 a.m.		9:30-11:00 a.m.		
Yoga	6:00-7:00 p.m.			3:00-4:00 p.m.		8:00-9:00 a.m.
Work		4:00-8:00 p.m.			8:00-11:00 a.m.	1:00-4:00 p.m.

Figure 3–77

Perform the following tasks:

1. Change the document theme to Organic.

2. In the line containing the table title, Fall Semester Schedule, remove the tab stop at the 1" mark on the ruler.

3. Set a centered tab at the 3" mark on the ruler. Move the centered tab stop to the 3.5" mark on the ruler.

4. Bold the characters in the title. Use the 'Increase Font Size' button to increase their font size to 14. Change their color to Red, Accent 4, Darker 25%.

5. In the table, delete the row containing the HIS 107 class.

6. In the table, delete the Sunday column.

7. Insert a column between the Monday and Wednesday columns. Fill in the column as follows:

Column Title – Tuesday

COM 110 – 12:30-2:00 p.m.

MUS 152 – 9:30-11:00 a.m.

If the column heading, Tuesday, is not bold, apply the bold format to the text in this cell.

8. Insert a new row at the bottom of the table. In the first cell of the new row, enter the word, Work, in the cell. If this cell's contents are bold, remove the bold format. Fill in the cells in the remainder of the row as follows:

Tuesday – 4:00-8:00 p.m.

Friday – 8:00-11:00 a.m.

Saturday – 1:00-4:00 p.m.

9. In the Table Style Options group (Table Tools Design tab), ensure that these check boxes have check marks: Header Row, Banded Rows, and First Column. The Total Row, Last Column, and Banded Columns check boxes should not have check marks.

10. Apply the Grid Table 5 Dark - Accent 4 style to the table.

11. Select the entire table. Click the 'Decrease Font Size' button once to decrease the font size of all characters in the table to 10 point.

12. Make all columns as wide as their contents (AutoFit Contents). Note that you may need to perform this step a couple of times to achieve the desired results.

13. Align center left all cells in the first column.

14. Align center the column headings containing the weekday names.

15. Align center right all cells containing times.

16. Center the table between the left and right margins of the page.

17. If requested by your instructor, enter your name on the line below the table.

18. Save the document using the file name, Apply 3–1 Fall Semester Schedule Modified, and submit the document (shown in Figure 3–77) in the format specified by your instructor.

19. ✺ If you wanted to add a row to the middle of the table, how would you add the row?

Extend Your Knowledge

Extend the skills you learned in this module and experiment with new skills. You may need to use Help to complete the assignment.

Working with Formulas, Graphics, Sorting, Picture Bullets, and Mailing Labels

Note: To complete this assignment, you will be required to use the Data Files. Please contact your instructor for information about accessing the Data Files.

Instructions: Run Word. Open the document called Extend 3–1 Donation Letter Draft located on the Data Files. You will use the Format Picture task pane, group objects, enter formulas in the table, change the table style, sort paragraphs, use picture bullets, move tabs, and print mailing labels.

Perform the following tasks:

1. Use Help to learn about grouping objects, entering formulas, sorting, picture bullets, and printing mailing labels.

Continued >

Extend Your Knowledge *continued*

2. Select the graphic of the globe in the hand, click the Format Shape Dialog Box Launcher (Picture Tools Format tab | Picture Styles group) to display the Format Picture task pane, and then click the Picture button in the task pane (Figure 3–78). Experiment with all the buttons in the task pane and modify the look of the graphic to your preferences.

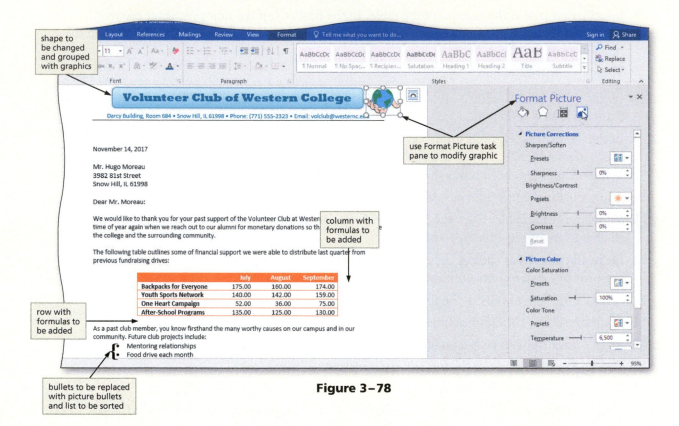

Figure 3–78

3. Select the shape around the Volunteer Club of Western College title and then use the Edit Shape button (Drawing Tools Format tab | Insert Shapes group) to change the shape to your preference. Position the globe in the hand graphic in the desired location to the right of the shape.

4. Copy and paste the modified globe in the hand graphic, flip it horizontally, and then position it on the opposite site of the shape. Group the two globe in hand graphics with the shape at the top of the letterhead. Change the text wrapping of the grouped shape to Top and Bottom.

5. Add a row to the bottom of the table. Insert the word, Total, in the first column of the new row. In the cell to contain the total for September, use the Formula dialog box to insert a formula that adds the cells in the column so that the total amount is displayed; in the dialog box, select a number format so that the total displays with dollar signs. *Hint:* Click the Formula button (Table Tools Format tab | Data group). Repeat this process for the August and July totals. Which formula did you use? Which number format?

6. Add a column to the right of the table. Insert the word, Total, as the column heading for the new column. Use the Formula dialog box to insert a formula that adds the cells each row so that the total amount is displayed. Use the same number format as you used in the previous step. Which formula did you use? What is the grand total for the quarter?

7. Position the insertion point in the table and one at a time, select and deselect each check box in the Table Style Options group. What are the functions of each check box: Header Row, Total Row, Banded Rows, First Column, Last Column, and Banded Columns? Select the check boxes you prefer for the table.

8. Sort the paragraphs in the bulleted list.

9. Change the bullets in the bulleted list to picture bullets.

10. Set a tab stop for the date line at the 4" mark on the ruler. Move the tab stops in the complimentary close and signature block from the 3.5" mark to the 4" mark on the ruler.

11. If requested by your instructor, change the name in the signature block to your name.

12. Save the revised document using the file name, Extend 3–1 Donation Letter Modified, and then submit it in the format specified by your instructor.

13. If requested by your instructor, print a single mailing label for the letter and then a full page of mailing labels, each containing the address shown in Figure 3–78.

14. ✸ Answer the questions posed in #5, #6, and #7. Why would you group objects? Which picture bullet did you use and why?

Expand Your World

Create a solution that uses cloud or web technologies by learning and investigating on your own from general guidance.

Using Google Docs to Upload and Edit Files

Notes:
- To complete this assignment, you will be required to use the Data Files. Please contact your instructor for information about accessing the Data Files.

- To complete this assignment, you will use a Google account, which you can create at no cost. If you do not have a Google account and do not want to create one, read this assignment without performing the instructions.

Instructions: You have created a letter in Word at your office and want to proofread and edit it at home. The problem is that you do not have Word at home. You do, however, have an Internet connection at home. Because you have a Google account, you upload your Word document to Google Drive so that you can view and edit it later from a computer that does not have Word installed.

Perform the following tasks:
1. In Word, open the document, Expand 3–1 Inquiry Letter in Word, from the Data Files. Look through the letter so that you are familiar with its contents and formats. If desired, print the letter so that you easily can compare it to the Google Docs converted file. Close the document.

2. Run a browser. Search for the text, google docs, using a search engine. Visit several websites to learn about Google Docs and Google Drive. Navigate to the Google website. Read about how to create files in Google Docs and upload files to Google Drive. If you do not have a Google account and you want to create one, follow the instructions to create an account. If you do not have a Google account and you do not want to create one, read the remaining instructions without performing them. If you have a Google account, sign in to your account.

3. If necessary, display Google Drive. Upload the file, Expand 3–1 Inquiry Letter in Word, to Google Drive.

Continued >

Expand Your World *continued*

4. Rename the file on Google Drive to Expand 3–1 Inquiry Letter in Google. Open the file in Google Docs (Figure 3–79). What differences do you see between the Word document and the Google Docs converted document?

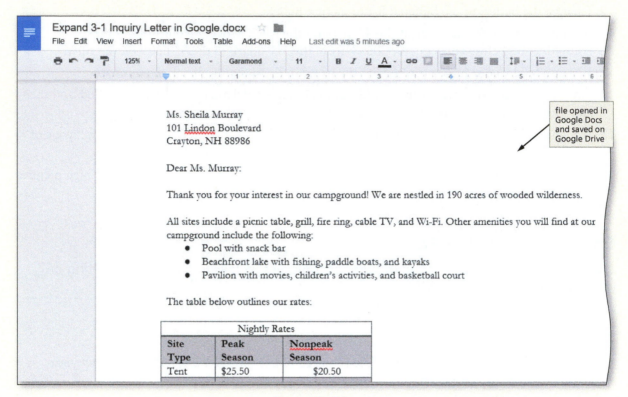

Figure 3–79

5. Fix the document in Google Docs so that it looks appealing, based on the concepts and techniques learned in this module. Add another item to the bulleted list: Fully-stocked camp store with attached laundry facilities. Add a row to the table: Pavilion, $20.00, $40.00. Insert a horizontal line below the line containing the mailing address.

6. If requested by your instructor, change the name in the signature block to your name.

7. Download the revised document to your local storage media, changing its format to Microsoft Word. Submit the document in the format requested by your instructor.

8. ✳ What is Google Drive? What is Google Docs? Answer the question posed in #4. Do you prefer using Google Docs or Word? Why?

In the Labs

Design, create, modify, and/or use a document following the guidelines, concepts, and skills presented in this module. Labs 1 and 2, which increase in difficulty, require you to create solutions based on what you learned in the module; Lab 3 requires you to apply your creative thinking and problem-solving skills to design and implement a solution.

Lab 1: **Creating a Letter with a Letterhead**

Problem: As a junior at your school, you are seeking a summer internship. One letter you prepare is shown in Figure 3–80.

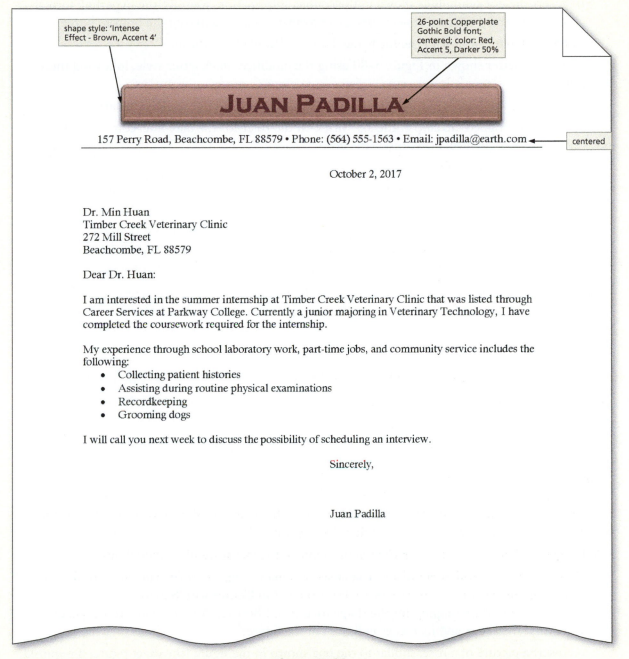

shape style: 'Intense Effect - Brown, Accent 4'

26-point Copperplate Gothic Bold font; centered; color: Red, Accent 5, Darker 50%

JUAN PADILLA

157 Perry Road, Beachcombe, FL 88579 • Phone: (564) 555-1563 • Email: jpadilla@earth.com

centered

October 2, 2017

Dr. Min Huan
Timber Creek Veterinary Clinic
272 Mill Street
Beachcombe, FL 88579

Dear Dr. Huan:

I am interested in the summer internship at Timber Creek Veterinary Clinic that was listed through Career Services at Parkway College. Currently a junior majoring in Veterinary Technology, I have completed the coursework required for the internship.

My experience through school laboratory work, part-time jobs, and community service includes the following:

- Collecting patient histories
- Assisting during routine physical examinations
- Recordkeeping
- Grooming dogs

I will call you next week to discuss the possibility of scheduling an interview.

Sincerely,

Juan Padilla

Figure 3–80

Perform the following tasks:

1. Run Word. Create a new blank document. Change the theme to Slate.

2. Create the letterhead shown at the top of Figure 3–80, following these guidelines:

   a. Insert the Rounded Same Side Corner Rectangle shape at an approximate height of 0.53" and width of 5.4". Change position of the shape to 'Position in Top Center with Square Text

Continued >

In the Labs *continued*

Wrapping'. Change the text wrapping for the shape to Top and Bottom. Add the student name, Juan Padilla, to the shape. Format the shape and its text as indicated in the figure.

b. Insert the dot symbols as shown in the contact information. Remove the hyperlink format from the email address. If necessary, clear formatting after entering the bottom border.

c. Save the letterhead with the file name, Lab 3–1 Padilla Letterhead.

3. Create the letter shown in Figure 3–80 using the modified block letter style, following these guidelines:

a. Apply the No Spacing Quick Style to the document text (below the letterhead).

b. Set a left-aligned tab stop at the 3.5" mark on the ruler for the date line, complimentary close, and signature block. Insert the current date.

c. Bullet the list as you type it.

d. If requested by your instructor, change the name in the shape and the signature block to your name.

e. Check the spelling of the letter. Save the letter with Lab 3–1 Internship Letter as the file name and then submit it in the format specified by your instructor.

4. If your instructor permits, address and print an envelope or a mailing label for the letter.

5. ✳ The letter in this assignment uses the modified block letter style. If you wanted to use the modified semi-block letter style, what changes would you make to this letter?

Lab 2: Creating a Letter with a Letterhead and Table

Note: To complete this assignment, you may be required to use the Data Files. Please contact your instructor for information about accessing the Data Files.

Problem: As the community education class coordinator, you are responsible for sending class registration confirmation letters. You prepare the letter shown in Figure 3–81.

Perform the following tasks:

1. Run Word. Create a new blank document. Change the theme to Berlin. Change the margins to 1" top and bottom and .75" left and right (Moderate).

2. Create the letterhead shown at the top of Figure 3–81, following these guidelines:

a. Insert the Horizontal Scroll shape at an approximate height of 0.74" and width of 6.32". Change the position of the shape to 'Position in Top Center with Square Text Wrapping'. Change the text wrapping for the shape to Top and Bottom. Add the name to the shape. Format the shape and its text as indicated in the figure.

b. Insert a picture of a rose, similar to the one shown in the figure (the exact figure, if required, is located in the Data Files). Resize the picture, change its text wrapping to In Front of Text, and move it to the left on the shape. Change its color tone to Temperature: 4700K. Copy the picture and move the copy of the image to the right on the shape, as shown in the figure. Flip the copied image horizontally.

c. Insert the small open diamond symbols as shown in the contact information. Remove the hyperlink format from the email address. If necessary, clear formatting after entering the bottom border.

d. Save the letterhead with the file name, Lab 3–2 Rosewood Letterhead.

3. Create the letter shown in Figure 3–81, following these guidelines:

a. Apply the No Spacing Quick Style to the document text (below the letterhead).

b. Set a left-aligned tab stop at the 4" mark on the ruler for the date line, complimentary close, and signature block. Insert the current date.

shape style: Subtle Effect - Rose, Accent 6

28-point Script MT Bold font, centered; color: Aqua, Accent 4, Darker 50%

11-point font; color: Aqua, Accent 4, Darker 50%; centered

9600 Brighton Parkway, Apollo, WY 29642 ◊ Phone: (212) 555-9600 ◊ Email: info@rosewood.net

October 16, 2017

Ms. Natalia Zajak
88 Sycamore Street
Apollo, WY 29642

Dear Ms. Zajak:

Thank you for your interest in our community education classes. We look forward to seeing you! The table below confirms the classes in which you are registered during November:

bold text

table style: Grid Table 5 Dark - Accent 4; table style options: Header Row and Banded Rows

November Class Registration Confirmation			
Class	**Date**	**Time**	**Location**
Diabetes Risk Assessment	November 6	5:00 to 6:00 p.m.	Suite 101
First Aid and CPR	November 11	9:00 a.m. to 3:00 p.m.	Suite 220
Healthy Cooking	November 14	4:00 to 5:00 p.m.	Suite 203
Basics of Meditation	November 17	11:00 a.m. to 12:30 p.m.	Suite 124

Please note the following:

- Arrive 10 minutes early for all classes.
- No outside food or drink allowed in classrooms.
- Kindly give 48-hour cancellation notice.

If you have any questions, please contact me via email at jgreen@rosewood.net or phone at 212-555-9612.

Sincerely,

Jerome Green
Community Education Class Coordinator

Figure 3–81

Continued >

In the Labs *continued*

    c. If requested by your instructor, change the name in the inside address and salutation to your name.

    d. Insert and center the table. Format the table as specified in the figure. Make all columns as wide as their contents (AutoFit Contents). Left-align the Class, Date, and Location columns. Center the Time column.

    e. Bullet the list as you type it.

    f. Convert the email address to regular text.

    g. Use nonbreaking hyphens in the phone number.

    h. Check the spelling of the letter. Save the letter with Lab 3–2 Confirmation Letter as the file name and then submit it in the format specified by your instructor.

4. If your instructor permits, address and print an envelope or a mailing label for the letter.

5. ✳ What is the purpose of the nonbreaking hyphens in this letter? Why do you think the picture in this letter used a text wrapping of In Front of Text? If the table used banded columns instead of banded rows, how would its appearance change?

Lab 3: **Consider This: Your Turn**

Create a Letter to a Potential Employer

Note: To complete this assignment, you may be required to use the Data Files. Please contact your instructor for information about accessing the Data Files.

Problem: As an intern in the career development office at your school, your boss has asked you to prepare a sample letter to a potential employer. Students seeking employment will use this letter as a reference document when creating their own letters.

Perform the following tasks:

Part 1: Using your name, mailing address, phone number, and email address, create a letterhead for the letter. Once the letterhead is designed, write the letter to this potential employer: Ms. Latisha Adams, Personnel Director, Cedar Plank Hotels, 85 College Grove Lane, P.O. Box 582, Gartner, TX 74812.

    The draft wording for the letter is as follows:

First paragraph:
    I am responding to your advertisement in the Texas Post for the Assistant Manager position. I have the credentials you are seeking and believe I can be a valuable asset to Cedar Plank Hotels.

Second paragraph:
    In May, I will be earning my bachelor's degree in Hospitality Management from Greenville College. My relevant coursework includes the following:

Below the second paragraph, insert the following table:

Restaurant management	18 hours
Nutrition	15 hours
Tourism management	12 hours
Hotel management	12 hours

Third paragraph:
In addition to my college coursework, I have the following experience:

Below the third paragraph, insert the following items as a bulleted list:
Assistant to school cafeteria director; Volunteer in Hope Mission kitchen; Developed website and Facebook page for local cafe.

Last paragraph:
I look forward to hearing from you to schedule an interview and to discuss my career opportunities at Cedar Plank Hotels.

The letter should contain a letterhead that uses a shape and picture(s); a table with an appropriate table title, column headings, and table style applied (unformatted table shown above); and a bulleted list (to present the experience). Insert nonbreaking spaces in the company name. Create a building block for the company name, edit the building block so that it has a ScreenTip, and insert the building block whenever you have to enter the company name.

Use the concepts and techniques presented in this module to create and format a letter according to a letter style, creating appropriate paragraph breaks and rewording the draft as necessary. The unformatted paragraphs in the letter are in a file called Lab 3–1 Letter Paragraphs, which is located on the Data Files. If you prefer, you can copy and paste this text into your letter instead of typing the paragraphs yourself. Use your name in the signature line in the letter. Be sure to check the spelling and grammar of the finished letter. Submit your assignment in the format specified by your instructor.

Part 2:   ✳ You made several decisions while creating the letter in this assignment: where to position elements in the letterhead, how to format elements in the letterhead, which graphics to use in the letterhead, which theme to use in the letter, which font size to use for the letter text, which table style to use, and which letter style to use. What was the rationale behind each of these decisions?

4 Creating a Document with a Title Page, Lists, Tables, and a Watermark

Objectives

You will have mastered the material in this module when you can:

- Border a paragraph
- Change paragraph indentation
- Insert and format a SmartArt graphic
- Apply character effects
- Insert a section break
- Insert a Word document in an open document
- Insert formatted headers and footers
- Sort paragraphs and tables
- Use the format painter
- Add picture bullets to a list
- Create a multilevel list
- Modify and format Word tables
- Sum columns in a table
- Create a watermark
- Change theme fonts

Introduction

During the course of your business and personal endeavors, you may want or need to provide a recommendation to a person or group of people for their consideration. You might suggest they purchase a product, such as a vehicle or books, or contract a service, such as designing their webpage or remodeling their house. Or, you might try to convince an audience to take an action, such as signing a petition, joining a club, visiting an establishment, or donating to a cause. You may be asked to request funds for a new program or activity or to promote an idea, such as a benefits package to company employees or a budget plan to upper management. To present these types of recommendations, you may find yourself writing a proposal.

A proposal generally is one of three types: sales, research, or planning. A **sales proposal** sells an idea, a product, or a service. A **research proposal** usually requests funding for a research project. A **planning proposal** offers solutions to a problem or improvement to a situation.

Project — Sales Proposal

Sales proposals describe the features and value of products and services being offered, with the intent of eliciting a positive response from the reader. Desired outcomes include the reader accepting ideas, purchasing products, contracting services, volunteering time, contributing to a cause, or taking an action. A well-written proposal can be the key to obtaining the desired results.

The project in this module follows generally accepted guidelines for writing short sales proposals and uses Word to create the sales proposal shown in Figure 4–1. The sales proposal in this module is designed to persuade readers to patronize an animal clinic. The proposal has a colorful title page to attract readers' attention. To add impact, the sales proposal has a watermark consisting of animal paw prints, positioned behind the content on each page. It also uses lists and tables to summarize and highlight important data.

In this module, you will learn how to create the sales proposal shown in Figure 4–1. The following roadmap identifies general activities you will perform as you progress through this module:

1. CREATE a TITLE PAGE for the proposal.
2. INSERT an EXISTING Word DOCUMENT in the proposal.
3. CREATE a HEADER AND FOOTER in the proposal.
4. EDIT AND FORMAT LISTS in the proposal.
5. EDIT AND FORMAT TABLES in the proposal.
6. CREATE a WATERMARK in the proposal.

To Run Word and Change Word Settings

If you are using a computer to step through the project in this module and you want your screens to match the figures in this book, you should change your screen's resolution to 1366 × 768.

The following steps run Word, display formatting marks, and change the zoom to page width.

1 Run Word and create a blank document in the Word window. If necessary, maximize the Word window.

2 If the Print Layout button on the status bar is not selected (shown in Figure 4–2), click it so that your screen is in Print Layout view.

3 If the 'Show/Hide ¶' button (Home tab | Paragraph group) is not selected already, click it to display formatting marks on the screen.

4 To display the page the same width as the document window, if necessary, click the Page Width button (View tab | Zoom group).

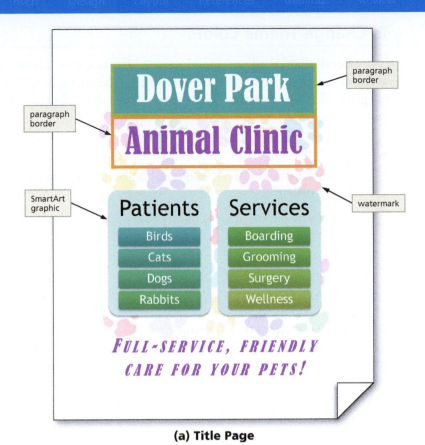

(a) Title Page

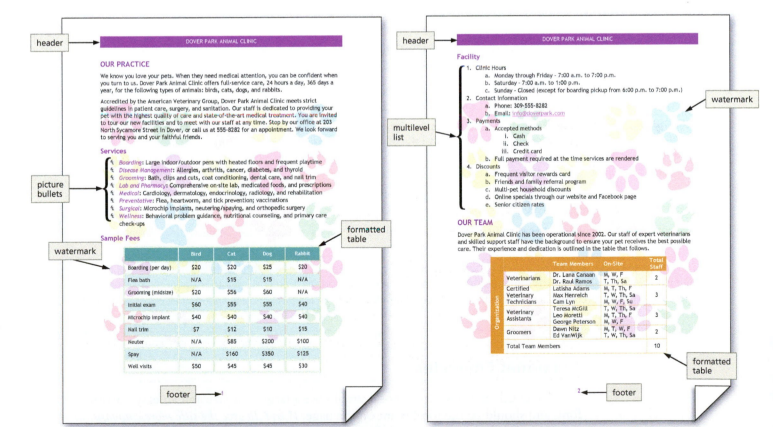

(b) First Page of Body of Proposal

(c) Second Page of Body of Proposal

Figure 4–1

To Change Theme Colors

Recall that Word provides document themes, which contain a variety of color schemes and other effects. You should select a theme that includes colors that reflect the goals of a sales proposal. This proposal uses the Celestial document theme. The following steps change the document theme.

1 Click Design on the ribbon to display the Design tab.

2 Click the Themes button (Design tab | Document Formatting group) to display the Themes gallery.

3 Click Celestial in the Themes gallery to change the document theme to the selected theme.

Creating a Title Page

A **title page** is a separate cover page that contains, at a minimum, the title of a document. For a sales proposal, the title page usually is the first page of the document. Solicited proposals often have a specific format for the title page. Guidelines for the title page of a solicited proposal may stipulate the margins, spacing, layout, and required contents, such as title, sponsor name, author name, date, etc. With an unsolicited proposal, by contrast, you can design the title page in a way that best presents its message.

CONSIDER THIS

How do you design an eye-catching title page?

The title page is the first section a reader sees on a sales proposal. Thus, it is important that the title page appropriately reflects the goal of the sales proposal. When designing the title page, consider its text and graphics.

- **Use concise, descriptive text.** The title page should contain a short, descriptive title that accurately reflects the message of the sales proposal. The title page also may include a theme or slogan. Do not place a page number on the title page.

- **Identify appropriate fonts, font sizes, and colors for the text.** Use fonts that are easy to read. Avoid using more than three different fonts because too many fonts can make the title page visually confusing. Use larger font sizes to add impact to the title page. To give the title more emphasis, its font size should be larger than any other text on the title page. Use colors that complement one another and convey the meaning of the proposal.

- **Use graphics to reinforce the goal.** Select simple graphics that clearly communicate the fundamental nature of the proposal. Possible graphics include shapes, pictures, and logos.

- **Use colors that complement text colors.** Be aware that too many graphics and colors can be distracting. Arrange graphics with the text so that the title page is attractive and uncluttered.

The title page of the sales proposal in this module (shown in Figure 4–1a) contains a colorful title that is surrounded by a border with some shading, an artistic graphic with text, a colorful slogan, and the faded paw prints image in the background. The steps in the next several sections create this title page. The faded image of the paw prints is added to all pages at the end of this module.

To Format Characters

The title in the sales proposal should use a large font size and an easy-to-read font, and should be the focal point on the page. *Why? To give the title more emphasis, its font size should be larger than any other text on the title page.* The following steps enter the title, Dover Park Animal Clinic, with the first two words centered on the first line and the second two words centered on the second line.

1 Click Home on the ribbon to display the Home tab.

2 Click the Center button (Home tab | Paragraph group) to center the paragraph that will contain the title.

3 Click the Font arrow (Home tab | Font group). Scroll to and then click 'Bernard MT Condensed' (or a similar font) in the Font gallery, so that the text you type will use the selected font.

4 Click the Font Size arrow (Home tab | Font group) and then click 72 in the Font Size gallery, so that the text you type will use the selected font size.

5 Type **Dover Park** and then press the ENTER key to enter the first line of the title.

6 Click the Font Color arrow (Home tab | Font group) and then click 'Purple, Accent 1' (fifth color, first row) in the Font Color gallery, so that the text you type will use the selected font color.

7 Type **Animal Clinic** as the second line of the title (shown in Figure 4–2).

BTW

The Ribbon and Screen Resolution
Word may change how the groups and buttons within the groups appear on the ribbon, depending on the computer or mobile device's screen resolution. Thus, your ribbon may look different from the ones in this book if you are using a screen resolution other than 1366 × 768.

To Border a Paragraph

1 CREATE TITLE PAGE | 2 INSERT EXISTING DOCUMENT | 3 CREATE HEADER & FOOTER
4 EDIT & FORMAT LISTS | 5 EDIT & FORMAT TABLES | 6 CREATE WATERMARK

If you click the Borders button (Home tab | Paragraph group), Word applies the most recently defined border, or, if one has not been defined, it applies the default border to the current paragraph. To specify a border different from the most recently defined border, you click the Borders arrow (Home tab | Paragraph group).

In this project, the first line of the title in the sales proposal (Dover Park) has a 6-point olive green border around it. *Why? You want the title to stand out more than the rest of the text on the title page.* The following steps add a border to all edges of a paragraph.

1

• Position the insertion point in the paragraph to border, in this case, the first line of the document.

• Click the Borders arrow (Home tab | Paragraph group) to display the Borders gallery (Figure 4–2).

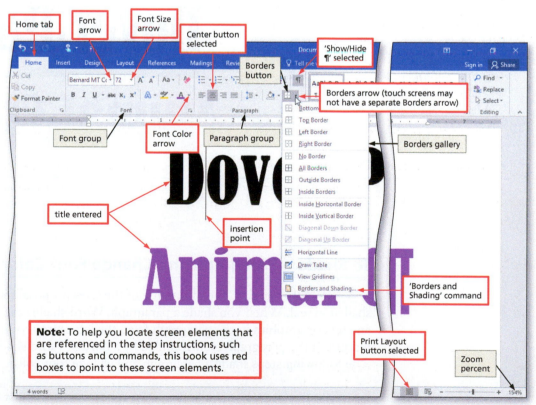

Figure 4–2

2

- Click Borders and Shading in the Borders gallery to display the Borders and Shading dialog box.
- Click Box in the Setting area (Borders and Shading dialog box), which will place a border on each edge of the current paragraph.
- Click the Color arrow and then click 'Olive Green, Accent 4' (eighth color, first row) in the Color palette to specify the border color.
- Click the Width arrow and then click 6 pt to specify the thickness of the border (Figure 4–3).

Q&A For what purpose are the buttons in the Preview area used?

They are toggles that display and remove the top, bottom, left, and right borders from the diagram in the Preview area.

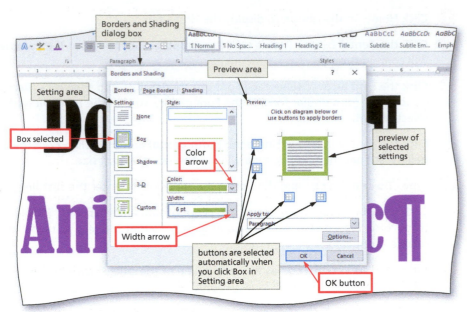

Figure 4–3

3

- Click the OK button (Borders and Shading dialog box) to place the border shown in the preview area of the dialog box around the current paragraph in the document (Figure 4–4).

Q&A How would I remove an existing border from a paragraph?

Click the Borders arrow (Home tab | Paragraph group) and then click the border in the Borders gallery that identifies the border you wish to remove, or click No Border to remove all borders.

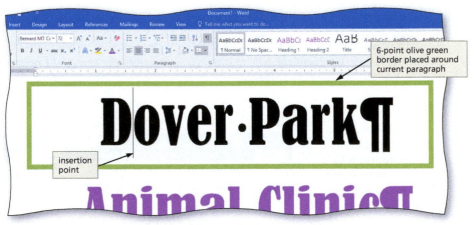

Figure 4–4

Other Ways

1. Click 'Borders and Shading' button (Design tab | Page Background group), click Borders tab (Borders and Shading dialog box), select desired border, click OK button

To Shade a Paragraph and Change Font Color

To make the first line of the title of the sales proposal more eye-catching, it is shaded in teal. When you shade a paragraph, Word shades the rectangular area behind any text or graphics in the paragraph from the left margin of the paragraph to the right margin. If the paragraph is surrounded by a border, Word shades inside the border. The following steps shade a paragraph and change font color.

1 With the insertion point in the paragraph to shade, the first line in this case (shown in Figure 4–4), click the Shading arrow (Home tab | Paragraph group) to display the Shading gallery.

2 Click 'Teal, Accent 3' (seventh color, first row) in the Shading gallery to shade the current paragraph (shown in Figure 4–5).

3 Drag through the words, Dover Park, in the first line of the title to select the text.

4 Click the Font Color arrow (Home tab | Font group) to display the Font Color gallery and then click 'White, Background 1' (first color, first row) to change the color of the selected text (shown in Figure 4–5).

To Border Another Paragraph

To make the second line of the title of the sales proposal (Animal Clinic) more eye-catching, it has a 6-point gold border around it. The following steps add a border to all edges of a paragraph.

1 Position the insertion point in the paragraph to border (in this case, the second paragraph containing the text, Animal Clinic).

2 Click the Borders arrow (Home tab | Paragraph group) to display the Borders gallery and then click 'Borders and Shading' in the Border gallery to display the Borders and Shading dialog box.

3 Click Box in the Setting area (Borders and Shading dialog box), which will place a border on each edge of the current paragraph.

4 Click the Color arrow and then click 'Gold, Accent 5' (ninth color, first row) in the Color palette to specify the border color.

5 If necessary, click the Width arrow and then click 6 pt to specify the thickness of the border.

6 Click the OK button to place the defined border shown around the current paragraph in the document (Figure 4–5).

BTW

Touch Screen Differences
The Office and Windows interfaces may vary if you are using a touch screen. For this reason, you might notice that the function or appearance of your touch screen differs slightly from this module's presentation.

Figure 4–5

To Change Spacing after a Paragraph

Currently, a small amount of blank space exists between the two paragraph borders because Word automatically places 8 points of blank space below paragraphs (shown in Figure 4–5). The following steps remove the blank space below the first paragraph.

1 Position the insertion point in the paragraph to be adjusted (in this case, the paragraph containing the text, Dover Park).

2 Display the Layout tab. Click the Spacing After down arrow (Layout tab | Paragraph group) as many times as necessary until 0 pt is displayed in the Spacing After box to remove the space below the current paragraph (shown in Figure 4–6).

Q&A What if I am using a touch screen?
Tap the Spacing After box (Layout tab | Paragraph group) and then type 0 to change the spacing below the paragraph.

To Change Left and Right Paragraph Indent

1 CREATE TITLE PAGE | 2 INSERT EXISTING DOCUMENT | 3 CREATE HEADER & FOOTER
4 EDIT & FORMAT LISTS | 5 EDIT & FORMAT TABLES | 6 CREATE WATERMARK

The borders around the first and second paragraphs and the shading in the first paragraph currently extend from the left margin to the right margin (shown in Figure 4–5). In this project, the edges of the border and shading are closer to the text in the title. **Why?** *You do not want such a large gap between the edge of the text and the border.* If you want the border and shading to start and end at a location different from the margin, you change the left and right paragraph indent.

The Increase Indent and Decrease Indent buttons (Home tab | Paragraph group) change the left indent by ½-inch, respectively. In this case, however, you cannot use these buttons because you want to change both the left and right indent. The following steps change the left and right paragraph indent.

- Be sure the insertion point is positioned in the paragraph to indent (the first paragraph, in this case). Click the Indent Left up arrow (Layout tab | Paragraph group) five times so that 0.5" is displayed in the Indent Left box because you want to adjust the paragraph left indent by this amount (or, if using touch, tap the Indent Left box (Layout tab | Paragraph group) and then type 0.5 to change the left indent).
- Click the Indent Right up arrow (Layout tab | Paragraph group) five times so that 0.5" is displayed in the Indent Right box because you want to adjust the paragraph right indent by this amount (or, if using touch, tap the Indent Right box (Layout tab | Paragraph group) and then type 0.5 to change the right indent) (Figure 4–6).

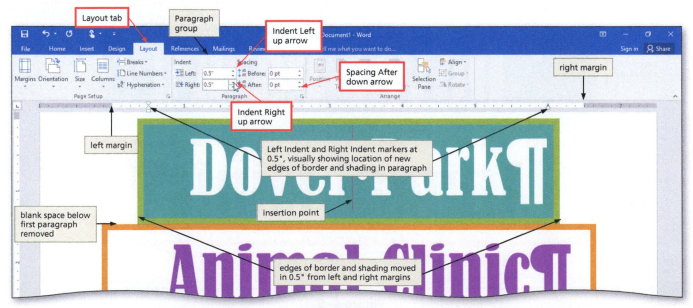

Figure 4–6

Experiment

- Repeatedly click the Indent Right and Indent Left up and down arrows (Layout tab | Paragraph group) and watch the left and right edges of the current paragraph change in the document window. When you have finished experimenting, set the left and right indent each to 0.5".

2

- Repeat Step 1 for the second paragraph, so that the paragraph containing the words, Animal Clinic, also has a left and right indent of 0.5" (shown in Figure 4–7).

Other Ways

1. Drag Left Indent and Right Indent markers on ruler	2. Click Paragraph Settings Dialog Box Launcher (Home tab | Paragraph group), click Indents and Spacing tab (Paragraph dialog box), set indentation values, click OK button	3. Right-click paragraph (or, if using touch, tap 'Show Context Menu' button on mini toolbar), click Paragraph on shortcut menu, click Indents and Spacing tab (Paragraph dialog box), set indentation values, click OK button

To Clear Formatting

The title is finished. When you press the ENTER key to advance the insertion point from the end of the second line to the beginning of the third line on the title page, the border will be carried forward to line 3, and any text you type will be a 72-point Bernard MT Condensed Purple, Accent 1 font. The paragraphs and characters on line 3 should not have the same paragraph and character formatting as line 2. Instead, they should be formatted using the Normal style. The following steps clear formatting, which applies the Normal style formats to the location of the insertion point.

1 If necessary, press the END key to position the insertion point at the end of line 2, that is, after the c in Clinic.

2 Press the ENTER key.

3 Display the Home tab. Click the 'Clear All Formatting' button (Home tab | Font group) to apply the Normal style to the location of the insertion point (Figure 4–7).

Q&A Could I have clicked Normal in the Styles gallery instead of the Clear All Formatting button?
Yes.

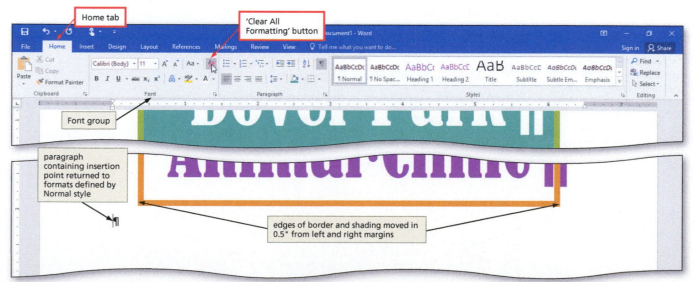

Figure 4–7

④ Save the title page on your hard drive, OneDrive, or other storage location using the file name, Animal Clinic Title Page.

Q&A Why should I save the title page at this time?
You have performed many tasks while creating this title page and do not want to risk losing work completed thus far.

SmartArt Graphics

Microsoft Office 2016 includes **SmartArt graphics**, which are visual representations of information. Many different types of SmartArt graphics are available, allowing you to choose one that illustrates your message best. Table 4–1 identifies the purpose of some of the more popular types of SmartArt graphics. Within each type, Office provides numerous layouts. For example, you can select from 40 different layouts of the list type.

Table 4–1 SmartArt Graphic Types	
Type	**Purpose**
List	Shows nonsequential or grouped blocks of information.
Process	Shows progression, timeline, or sequential steps in a process or workflow.
Cycle	Shows continuous sequence of steps or events.
Hierarchy	Illustrates organization charts, decision trees, and hierarchical relationships.
Relationship	Compares or contrasts connections between concepts.
Matrix	Shows relationships of parts to a whole.
Picture	Uses images to present a message.
Pyramid	Shows proportional or interconnected relationships with the largest component at the top or bottom.

SmartArt graphics contain shapes. You can add text or pictures to shapes, add more shapes, or delete shapes. You also can modify the appearance of a SmartArt graphic by applying styles and changing its colors. The next several sections demonstrate the following general tasks to create the SmartArt graphic on the title page in this project:

1. Insert a SmartArt graphic.
2. Delete unneeded shapes from the SmartArt graphic.
3. Add shapes to the SmartArt graphic.
4. Add text to the shapes in the SmartArt graphic.
5. Change colors of the SmartArt graphic.
6. Apply a style to the SmartArt graphic.

BTW

Resetting Graphics
If you want to remove all formats from a SmartArt graphic and start over, you would click the Reset Graphic button (SmartArt Tools Design tab | Reset group), which is shown in Figure 4–15.

To Insert a SmartArt Graphic

Below the title on the title page is a grouped list SmartArt graphic. *Why? The Grouped List SmartArt graphic allows you to place multiple lists side by side on the document, which works well for the content on this title page.* The following steps insert a SmartArt graphic centered below the title on the title page.

1

- With the insertion point on the blank paragraph below the title (shown in Figure 4–7), click the Center button (Home tab | Paragraph group) so that the inserted SmartArt graphic will be centered below the title.
- Display the Insert tab.
- Click the 'Insert a SmartArt Graphic' button (Insert tab | Illustrations group) to display the Choose a SmartArt Graphic dialog box (Figure 4–8).

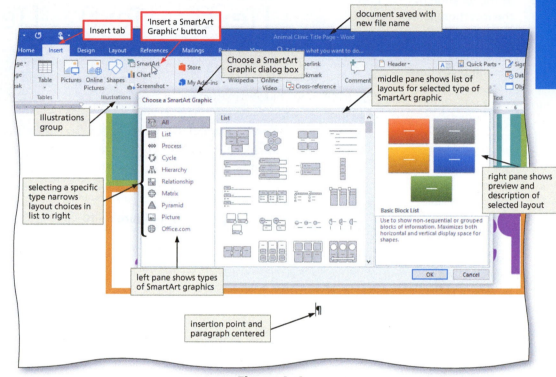

Figure 4–8

**Experiment**

- Click various SmartArt graphic types in the left pane of the dialog box and watch the related layout choices appear in the middle pane.
- Click various layouts in the list of layouts in the middle pane to see the preview and description of the layout appear in the right pane of the dialog box.

2

- Click List in the left pane (Choose a SmartArt Graphic dialog box) to display the layout choices related to the selected SmartArt graphic type.
- Click Grouped List in the middle pane, which displays a preview and description of the selected layout in the right pane (Figure 4–9).

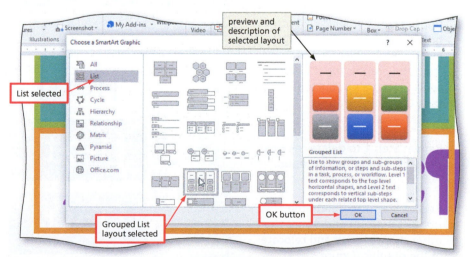

Figure 4–9

- Click the OK button to insert the selected SmartArt graphic in the document at the location of the insertion point (Figure 4–10).

Q&A

What if the Text Pane appears next to the SmartArt graphic?
Close the Text Pane by clicking its Close button or clicking the Text Pane button (SmartArt Tools Design tab | Create Graphic group).

Can I change the layout of the inserted SmartArt graphic?
Yes. Click the More button in the Layouts gallery (SmartArt Tools Design tab | Layouts group) to display the list of layouts and then select the desired layout.

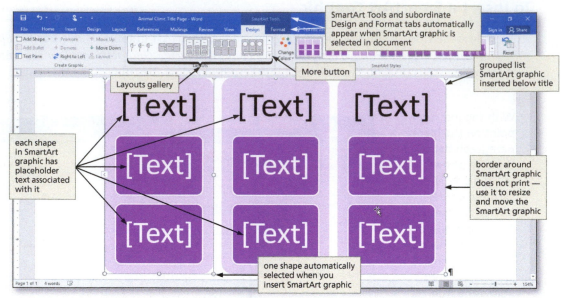

Figure 4–10

To Delete Shapes from a SmartArt Graphic

1 CREATE TITLE PAGE | 2 INSERT EXISTING DOCUMENT | 3 CREATE HEADER & FOOTER
4 EDIT & FORMAT LISTS | 5 EDIT & FORMAT TABLES | 6 CREATE WATERMARK

The Grouped List SmartArt graphic initially has three outer groups that consist of nine different shapes (shown in Figure 4–10). Notice that each shape in the SmartArt graphic initially shows **placeholder text**, which indicates where text can be typed in a shape. The next step in this project is to delete one entire group. *Why? The SmartArt graphic in this project consists of only two major groups (Patients and Services).* The following steps delete one entire group, or three shapes, in the SmartArt graphic.

- Click one of the shapes in the rightmost group in the SmartArt graphic and then press the DELETE key to delete the selected shape from the graphic (or, if using touch, tap the Cut button (Home tab | Clipboard group)).

- Repeat Step 1 to delete the next shape in the rightmost group.

- Repeat Step 1 to delete the rightmost group and notice the other shapes resize and relocate in the graphic (Figure 4–11).

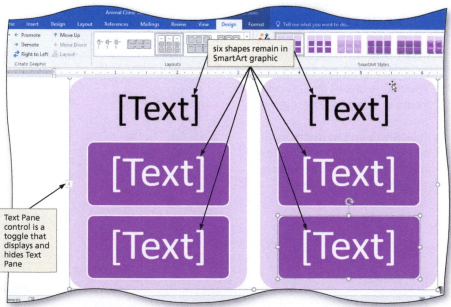

Figure 4–11

To Add Text to Shapes in a SmartArt Graphic

The placeholder text in a shape indicates where text can be typed in the shape. The following steps add text to the three shapes in the first group via their placeholder text. *Why? After entering the text in these three shapes, you will need to add two more shapes to finish the content in the group.*

- Click the top-left shape to select it and then type **Patients** to replace the placeholder text, [Text], with the entered text.

Q&A
How do I edit placeholder text if I make a mistake?
Click the placeholder text to select it and then correct the entry.

What if my typed text is longer than the shape?
The font size of the text may be adjusted or the text may wordwrap within the shape.

- Click the middle-left shape to select it and then type **Birds** as the new text.

- Click the lower-left shape to select it and then type **Cats** as the new text (Figure 4–12).

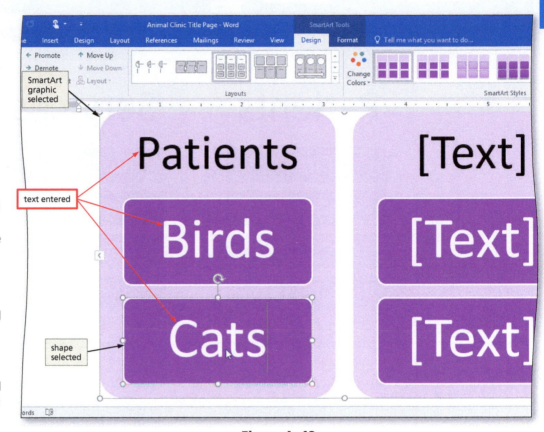

Figure 4–12

Other Ways

1. Click Text Pane control, enter text in Text Pane, close Text Pane
2. Click Text Pane button (SmartArt Tools Design tab | Create Graphic group), enter text in Text Pane, click Text Pane button again
3. Right-click shape (or, if using touch, tap Edit Text button on mini toolbar), click Exit Edit Text on shortcut menu, enter text

To Add Shapes to a SmartArt Graphic

The following steps add shapes to the SmartArt graphic. *Why? Each group in this project has four subordinate items, which means two shapes need to be added to each group.*

1

- Click the Add Shape button (SmartArt Tools Design tab | Create Graphic group) to add a shape to the SmartArt graphic (or, if using touch, tap the Add Shape button (SmartArt Tools Design tab | Create Graphic group) and then tap 'Add Shape After').

2

- Repeat Step 1 to add the final shape to the group.

3

- Click a subordinate shape on the right (one of the purple shapes) to select it.
- Repeat Steps 1 and 2 so that the same number of shapes appear on the right and left sides of the SmartArt graphic.

4

- Enter the text in the shapes as shown in Figure 4–13.

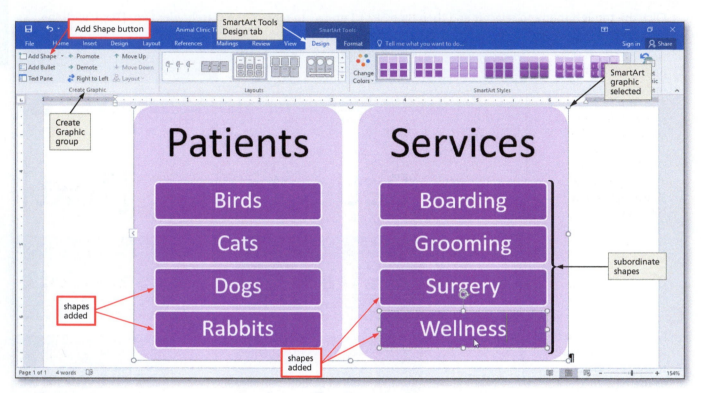

Figure 4–13

Other Ways

1. Click Add Shape arrow (SmartArt Tools Design tab), click desired shape position

2. Right-click paragraph (or, if using touch, tap 'Show Context Menu' button on mini toolbar), point to Add Shape on shortcut menu, click desired shape position

To Change Colors of a SmartArt Graphic

1 CREATE TITLE PAGE | 2 INSERT EXISTING DOCUMENT | 3 CREATE HEADER & FOOTER
4 EDIT & FORMAT LISTS | 5 EDIT & FORMAT TABLES | 6 CREATE WATERMARK

Word provides a variety of colors for a SmartArt graphic and the shapes in the graphic. In this project, the inside shapes are green, instead of purple. *Why? The current dark purple color competes with the title, so you want a softer color for the shapes.* The following steps change the colors of a SmartArt graphic.

1

- With the SmartArt graphic selected (shown in Figure 4–13), click the Change Colors button (SmartArt Tools Design tab | SmartArt Styles group) to display the Change Colors gallery.

 What if the SmartArt graphic is not selected?
Click the SmartArt graphic to select it.

- Point to 'Colorful Range - Accent Colors 3 to 4' in the Change Colors gallery to display a live preview of the selected color applied to the SmartArt graphic in the document (Figure 4–14).

 Experiment

- Point to various colors in the Change Colors gallery and watch the colors of the graphic change in the document window.

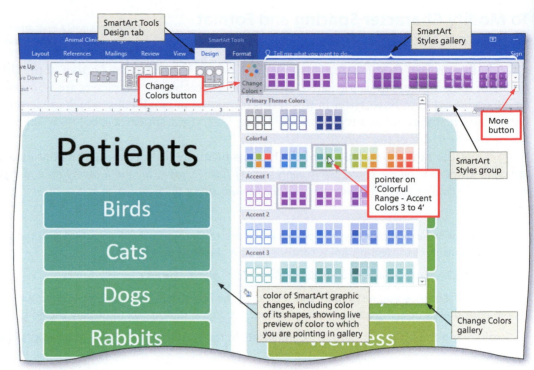

Figure 4–14

- Click 'Colorful Range - Accent Colors 3 to 4' in the Change Colors gallery to apply the selected color to the SmartArt graphic.

To Apply a SmartArt Style

1 CREATE TITLE PAGE | 2 INSERT EXISTING DOCUMENT | 3 CREATE HEADER & FOOTER
4 EDIT & FORMAT LISTS | 5 EDIT & FORMAT TABLES | 6 CREATE WATERMARK

The next step is to apply a SmartArt style to the SmartArt graphic. *Why?* *Word provides a SmartArt Styles gallery, allowing you to change the SmartArt graphic's format to a more visually appealing style.* The following steps apply a SmartArt style to a SmartArt graphic.

1

- With the SmartArt graphic still selected, click the More button in the SmartArt Styles gallery (shown in Figure 4–14) to expand the SmartArt Styles gallery.

- Point to Moderate Effect in the SmartArt Styles gallery to display a live preview of that style applied to the graphic in the document (Figure 4–15).

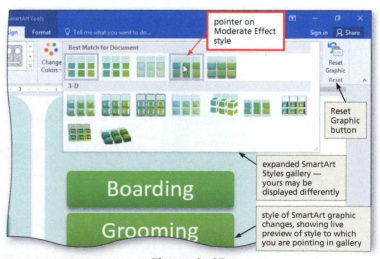

Figure 4–15

 Experiment

- Point to various SmartArt styles in the SmartArt Styles gallery and watch the style of the graphic change in the document window.

- Click Moderate Effect in the SmartArt Styles gallery to apply the selected style to the SmartArt graphic.

To Modify Character Spacing and Format Characters Using the Font Dialog Box

In this project, the next step is to enter and format the text at the bottom of the title page. This text is the theme of the proposal and is formatted so that it is noticeable. Its characters are a 36-point, italic, purple Bernard MT Condensed font. Each letter in this text is formatted in **small caps**, which are letters that look like capital letters but are not as tall as a typical capital letter. Also, you want extra space between each character so that the text spans the width of the page.

Thus, the next steps apply all of the formats mentioned above using the Font dialog box. *Why? Although you could use buttons on the Home tab to apply some of these formats, the small caps effect and expanded spacing are applied using the Font dialog box. Thus, you apply all the formats using the Font dialog box.*

- Position the insertion point on the paragraph mark to the right of the SmartArt graphic and then press the ENTER key to position the insertion point centered below the SmartArt graphic.

- Type **Full-service, friendly care for your pets!**

- Select the sentence you just typed and then click the Font Dialog Box Launcher (Home tab | Font group) to display the Font dialog box. If necessary, click the Font tab in the dialog box to display the Font sheet.

- Scroll to and then click 'Bernard MT Condensed' in the Font list (Font dialog box) to change the font of the selected text.

- Click Italic in the Font style list to italicize the selected text.

- Scroll through the Size list and then click 36 to change the font size of the selected text.

- Click the Font color arrow and then click 'Purple, Accent 1' (fifth color, first row) in the Font color palette to change the color of the selected text.

- Click the Small caps check box in the Effects area so that each character is displayed as a small capital letter (Figure 4–16).

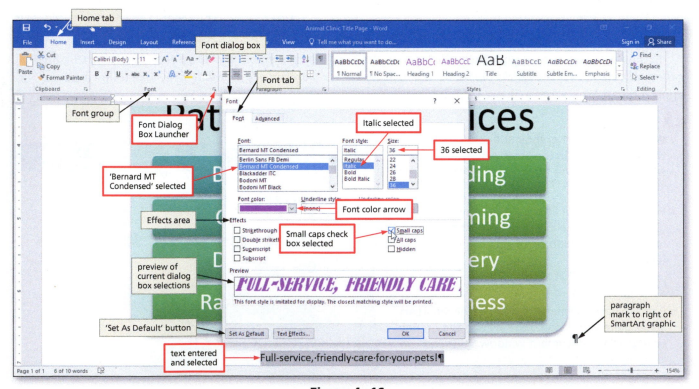

Figure 4–16

2

- Click the Advanced tab (Font dialog box) to display the Advanced sheet in the Font dialog box.
- Click the Spacing arrow and then click Expanded to increase the amount of space between characters by 1 pt, which is the default.
- Double-click the value in the Spacing By box to select it and then type   7   because you want this amount of blank space to be displayed between each character.
- Click in any box in the dialog box for the change to take effect and display a preview of the entered value in the Preview area (Figure 4–17).

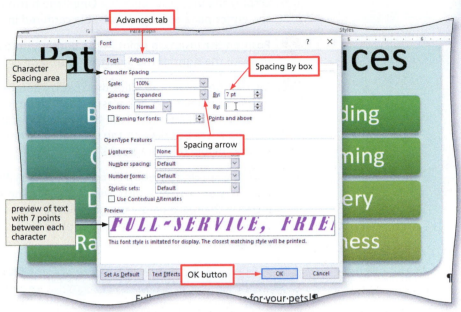

Figure 4–17

Q&A Can I click the Spacing By arrows instead of typing a value in the box?

Yes.

3

- Click the OK button to apply font changes to the selected text. If necessary, scroll so that the selected text is displayed completely in the document window.
- Click to remove the selection from the text (Figure 4–18).

Figure 4–18

Other Ways

1. Right-click selected text (or, if using touch, tap 'Show Context Menu' button on mini toolbar), click Font on shortcut menu, select formats (Font dialog box), click OK button

2. Press CTRL+D, select formats (Font dialog box), click OK button

---

To Zoom One Page, Change Spacing before and after a Paragraph, and Set Zoom Level

The final step in creating the title page is to adjust spacing above and below the SmartArt graphic. You want to see the entire page while adjusting the spacing. Thus, the following steps zoom one page, increase spacing before and after the paragraph containing the SmartArt graphic, and then set the zoom level back to page width because you will be finished with the title page.

1 Display the View tab. Click the One Page button (View tab | Zoom group) to display the entire page as large as possible centered in the document window.

2 Position the insertion point in the paragraph to adjust, in this case, on the paragraph mark to the right of the SmartArt graphic.

3 Display the Layout tab. Click the Spacing Before up arrow (Layout tab | Paragraph group) as many times as necessary until 42 pt is displayed in the Spacing Before box because you want to increase the space above the graphic (or, if using touch, tap the Spacing After box (Layout tab | Paragraph group) and then type 42 to change the spacing below the paragraph).

4 Click the Spacing After up arrow (Layout tab | Paragraph group) as many times as necessary until 30 pt is displayed in the Spacing After box because you want to increase the space below the graphic (or, if using touch, tap the Spacing After box (Layout tab | Paragraph group) and then type 30 to change the spacing below the paragraph) (Figure 4–19).

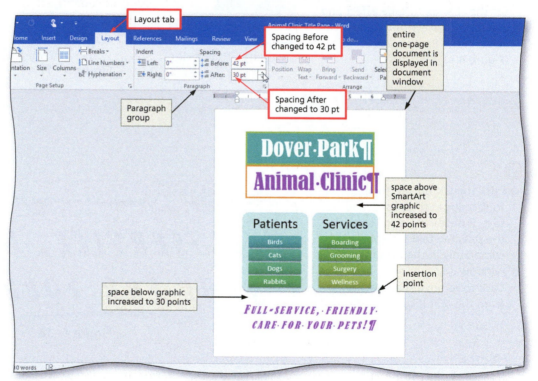

Figure 4–19

Q&A What if the document spills to two pages?
Decrease the spacing above or below the SmartArt graphic until the title page contents fit on a single page.

5 Display the View tab. Click the Page Width button (View tab | Zoom group) to change the zoom to page width.

6 Save the title page again on the same storage location with the same file name.

Break Point: If you wish to take a break, this is a good place to do so. You can exit Word now. To resume at a later time, run Word, open the file called Animal Clinic Title Page, and continue following the steps from this location forward.

Inserting an Existing Document in an Open Document

Assume you already have prepared a draft of the body of the proposal and saved it with the file name, Animal Clinic Draft. You would like the draft to be displayed on a separate page following the title page.

In the following sections, you will insert the draft of the proposal below the title page and then edit the draft by deleting a page break and applying styles.

To Save an Open Document with a New File Name

The current file name on the title bar is Animal Clinic Title Page, yet the document you will work on from this point forward in the module will contain both the title page and the body of the sales proposal. To keep the title page as a separate document called Animal Clinic Title Page, you should save the open document with a new file name. If you save the open document by using the Save button on the Quick Access Toolbar, Word will assign it the current file name. You want the open document to have a new file name. The following step saves the open document with a new file name.

 Save the title page on your hard drive, OneDrive, or other storage location using the file name, Animal Clinic Sales Proposal.

Sections

All Word documents have at least one section. A Word document can be divided into any number of sections. During the course of creating a document, you will create a new **section** if you need to change the top margin, bottom margin, page alignment, paper size, page orientation, page number position, or contents or position of headers, footers, or footnotes in just a portion of the document.

The pages in the body of the sales proposal require page formatting different from that of the title page. The title page will not have a header or footer; the next two pages will have a header and footer. When you want to change page formatting for a portion of a document, you create a new section in the document. Each section then may be formatted differently from the others. Thus, the title page formatted with no header or footer will be in one section, and the next two pages of the proposal, which will have a header and footer, will be in another section.

To Insert a Next Page Section Break

1 CREATE TITLE PAGE | **2 INSERT EXISTING DOCUMENT** | 3 CREATE HEADER & FOOTER
4 EDIT & FORMAT LISTS | 5 EDIT & FORMAT TABLES | 6 CREATE WATERMARK

When you insert a section break, you specify whether the new section should begin on a new page. *Why?* *Sometimes you want a page break to occur with a section break, as in this project. Other times, you do not want a page break to occur with a section break (which will be illustrated in a later module).* In this project, the title page is separate from the next two pages. Thus, the section break should contain a page break. The following steps insert a next page section break, which instructs Word to begin the new section on a new page in the document.

- Position the insertion point at the end of the title page (following the exclamation point), which is the location where you want to insert the next page section break.

BTW

Inserting Documents
When you insert a Word document in another Word document, the entire inserted document is placed at the location of the insertion point. If the insertion point is positioned in the middle of the open document when you insert another Word document, the open document continues after the last character of the inserted document; therefore, pay close attention to where the insertion point is positioned before inserting a document.

BTW

Section Numbers
If you want to display the current section number on the status bar, right-click the status bar to display the Customize Status Bar menu and then click Section on the Customize Status Bar menu. The section number appears at the left edge of the status bar. To remove the section number from the status bar, perform the same steps.

- Display the Layout tab. Click the 'Insert Page and Section Breaks' button (Layout tab | Page Setup group) to display the Insert Page and Section Breaks gallery (Figure 4–20).

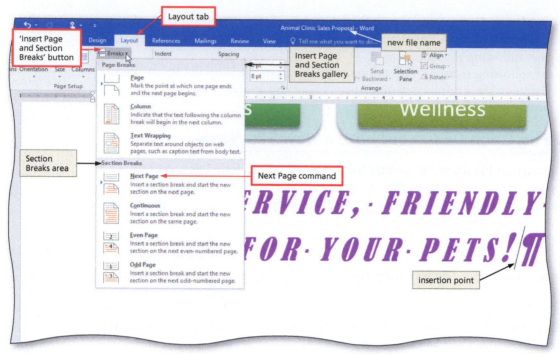

Figure 4–20

2

- Click Next Page in the Section Breaks area of the Insert Page and Section Breaks gallery to insert a next page section break in the document at the location of the insertion point. If necessary, scroll so that your screen matches Figure 4–21.

Figure 4–21

TO DELETE A SECTION BREAK

Word stores all section formatting in the section break. If you wanted to delete a section break and all associated section formatting, you would perform the following tasks.

1. Select the section break notation by dragging through it.
2. Right-click the selection to display a mini toolbar or shortcut menu and then click Cut on the mini toolbar or shortcut menu to delete the selection.

or

1. Position the insertion point immediately to the left or right of the section break notation.
2. Press the DELETE key to delete a section break to the right of the insertion point or press the BACKSPACE key to delete a section break to the left of the insertion point.

To Clear Formatting

When you create a section break, Word carries forward any formatting at the location of the insertion point to the next section. Thus, the current paragraph is formatted the same as the last line of the title page. In this project, the paragraphs and characters on the second page should be returned to the Normal style. Thus, the following step clears formatting.

1 Display the Home tab. With the insertion point positioned on the paragraph mark on the second page, click the 'Clear All Formatting' button (Home tab | Font group) to apply the Normal style to the location of the insertion point (shown in Figure 4–22).

To Insert a Word Document in an Open Document

1 CREATE TITLE PAGE | **2 INSERT EXISTING DOCUMENT** | 3 CREATE HEADER & FOOTER
4 EDIT & FORMAT LISTS | 5 EDIT & FORMAT TABLES | 6 CREATE WATERMARK

The next step is to insert the draft of the sales proposal at the top of the second page of the document. **Why?** *You will modify a draft of the body of the proposal, which is located on the Data Files. Please contact your instructor for information about accessing the Data Files.* The following steps insert an existing Word document in an open document.

1

- Be sure the insertion point is positioned on the paragraph mark at the top of page 2, which is the location where you want to insert the contents of the Word document.
- Display the Insert tab.
- Click the Object arrow (Insert tab | Text group) to display the Object menu (Figure 4–22).

Q&A What if I click the Object button by mistake?
Click the Cancel button (Object dialog box) and then repeat this step.

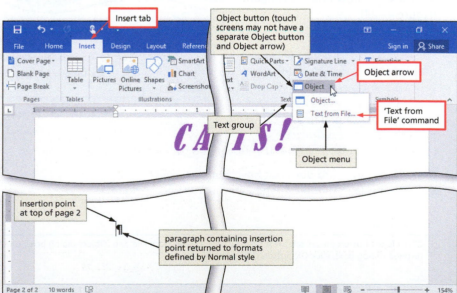

Figure 4–22

BTW

Sections
To see the formatting associated with a section, double-click the section break notation, or click the Page Setup Dialog Box Launcher (Layout tab | Page Setup group) to display the Page Setup dialog box. You can change margin settings and page orientation for a section in the Margins sheet. To change paper sizes for a section, click the Paper tab (Page Setup dialog box). The Layout tab (Page Setup dialog box) allows you to change header and footer specifications and vertical alignment for the section. To add a border to a section, click the Borders button in the Layout sheet.

2

- Click 'Text from File' on the Object menu to display the Insert File dialog box.

- Navigate to the location of the file to be inserted (in this case, the Module 04 folder in the Data Files folder in the Word folder).

- Click Animal Clinic Draft to select the file name (Figure 4–23).

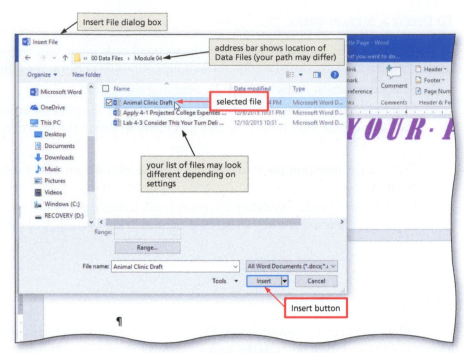

Figure 4–23

3

- Click the Insert button (Insert File dialog box) to insert the file, Animal Clinic Draft, in the open document at the location of the insertion point.

Q&A Where is the insertion point now? When you insert a file in an open document, Word positions the insertion point at the end of the inserted document.

- Press SHIFT+F5 to position the insertion point on line 1 of page 2, which was its location prior to inserting the new Word document (Figure 4–24).

Q&A What is the purpose of SHIFT+F5? The keyboard shortcut, SHIFT+F5, positions the insertion point at your last editing location. Word remembers your last three editing locations, which means you can press this keyboard shortcut repeatedly to return to one of your three most recent editing locations.

What if my keyboard does not have function keys? Scroll to display the top of page 2 in the document window.

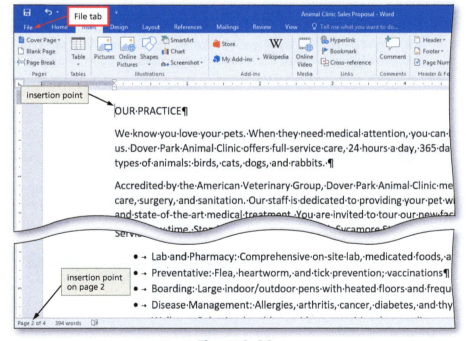

Figure 4–24

Other Ways

1. Click Object button (Insert tab | Text group), click 'Create from File' tab (Object dialog box), click Browse button, locate file, click Insert button (Browse dialog box), click OK button (Object dialog box)

To Print Specific Pages in a Document

The title page is the first page of the proposal. The body of the proposal spans the second and third pages. The following steps print a hard copy of only the body of the proposal, that is, pages 2 and 3. *Why? You would like to see the contents of the body of the proposal before you begin modifying it.*

- Click File on the ribbon to open the Backstage view and then click the Print tab in the Backstage view to display the Print gallery.
- Verify that the printer listed on the Printer Status button will print a hard copy of the document. If necessary, click the Printer Status button to display a list of available printer options and then click the desired printer to change the selected printer.
- Type **2–3** in the Pages text box in the Settings area of the Print gallery (Figure 4–25).

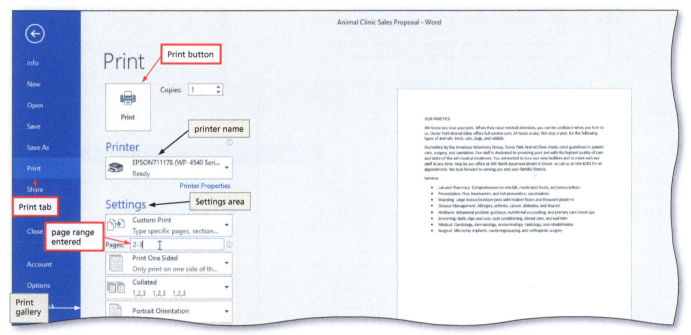

Figure 4–25

- Click the Print button to print the inserted draft of the sales proposal (Figure 4–26).

Q&A

How would I print pages from a certain point to the end of a document?
You would enter the page number followed by a dash in the Pages text box. For example, 5- will print from page 5 to the end of the document. To print up to a certain page, put the dash first (e.g., -5 will print pages 1 through 5).

Why does my document wrap on different words than Figure 4–26?
Differences in wordwrap may be related to the printer used by your computer.

Why does my screen show the document has four pages?
You may have an extra blank page at the end of the document. This blank page will be deleted later in the module.

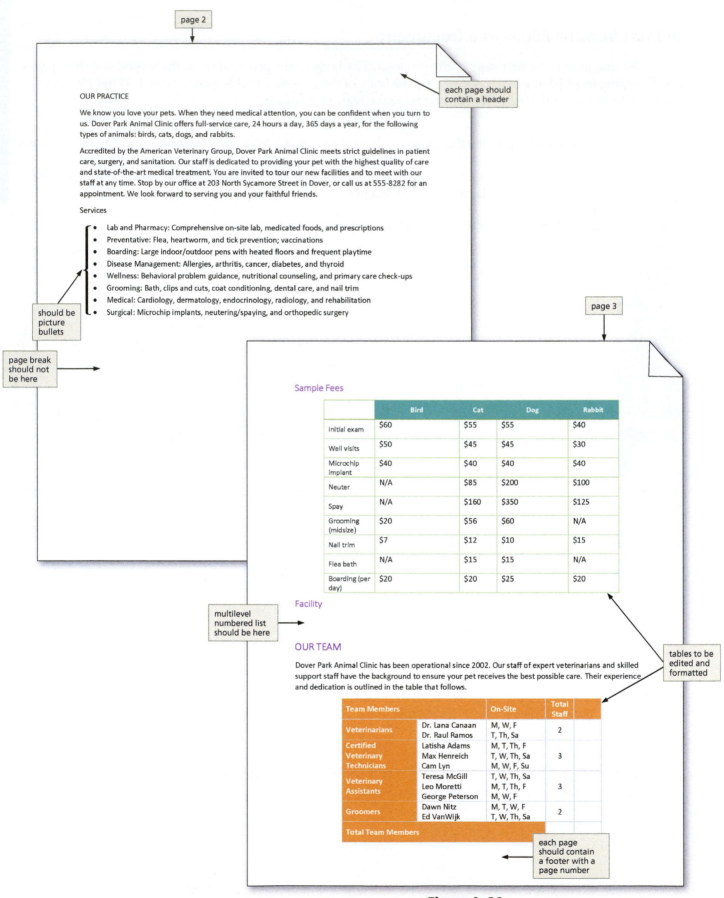

Figure 4–26

What elements should the body of a sales proposal contain?
Be sure to include basic elements in your sales proposals:

- **Include an introduction, body, and conclusion.** The introduction could contain the subject, purpose, statement of problem, need, background, or scope. The body may include costs, benefits, supporting documentation, available or required facilities, feasibility, methods, timetable, materials, or equipment. The conclusion summarizes key points or requests an action.

- **Use headers and footers.** Headers and footers help to identify every page. A page number should be in either the header or footer. If the sales proposal should become disassembled, the reader can use the page numbers in the headers or footers to determine the order and pieces of your proposal.

To Delete a Page Break

1 CREATE TITLE PAGE | 2 INSERT EXISTING DOCUMENT | 3 CREATE HEADER & FOOTER
4 EDIT & FORMAT LISTS | 5 EDIT & FORMAT TABLES | 6 CREATE WATERMARK

After reviewing the draft in Figure 4–26, you notice it contains a page break below the bulleted list. The following steps delete a page break. *Why? This page break below the bulleted list should not be in the proposal.*

 1
- Scroll to display the page break notation.
- To select the page break notation, double-click it (Figure 4–27).

2
- Press the DELETE key to remove the page break from the document.

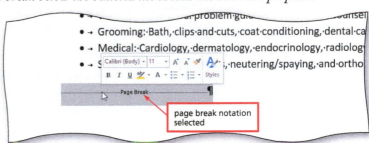

Figure 4–27

> **Other Ways**
>
> 1. With page break notation selected, click Cut button (Home tab | Clipboard group)
> 2. With page break notation selected, right-click selection and then click Cut on mini toolbar or shortcut menu
> 3. With the insertion point to the left or right of the page break notation, press DELETE or BACKSPACE, respectively

To Apply Heading Styles

Word has many built-in, or predefined, styles that you can use to format text. Three of the Styles shown in the Styles gallery in Figure 4–28 are for headings: Heading 1 for the major headings and Heading 2 and Heading 3 for minor headings. In the Animal Clinic Draft, all headings except for the first two were formatted using heading styles.

The following steps apply the Heading 1 style to the paragraph containing the text, OUR PRACTICE, and the Heading 2 style to the paragraph containing the text, Services.

1 Position the insertion point in the paragraph to be formatted to the Heading 1 style, in this case, the first line on the second page with the text, OUR PRACTICE.

2 Click Heading 1 in the Style gallery (Home tab | Styles group) to apply the selected style to the paragraph containing the insertion point.

Q&A Why did a square appear on the screen near the left edge of the paragraph formatted with the Heading 1 style?
The square is a nonprinting character, like the paragraph mark, that indicates text to its right has a special paragraph format applied to it.

3 Position the insertion point in the paragraph to be formatted to the Heading 2 style, in this case, the line above the bulleted list with the text, Services.

4 Click Heading 2 in the Style gallery (Home tab | Styles group) to apply the selected style to the paragraph containing the insertion point (Figure 4–28).

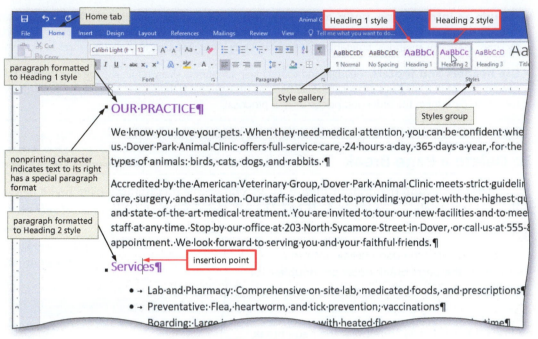

Figure 4–28

To Change Spacing before and after a Paragraph

The next step is to adjust spacing above and below the current paragraph, that is, the heading above the bulleted list. This paragraph is formatted using the Heading 2 style, which places no space above the paragraph and 8 points below the paragraph. You would like this paragraph, and all other paragraphs formatted using the Heading 2 style, to have 12 points of space above them and 6 points of space below them. Thus, the following steps adjust the spacing before and after a paragraph.

1 Display the Layout tab. Position the insertion point as shown in Figure 4–29. Click the Spacing Before up arrow (Layout tab | Paragraph group) as many times as necessary so that 12 pt is displayed in the Spacing Before box (or, if using touch, tap the Spacing Before box (Layout tab | Paragraph group) and then type **12** to change the spacing above the paragraph).

2 If necessary, click the Spacing After up arrow (Layout tab | Paragraph group) so that 6 pt is displayed in the Spacing After box (or, if using touch, tap the Spacing After box (Layout tab | Paragraph group) and then type **6** to change the spacing below the paragraph).

To Update a Style to Match a Selection

You want all paragraphs formatted in the Heading 2 style in the proposal to use this adjusted spacing. Thus, the following steps update the Heading 2 style so that this adjusted spacing is applied to all Heading 2 paragraphs in the document.

1 If necessary, position the insertion point in the paragraph containing the style to be updated.

2 Display the Home tab. Right-click Heading 2 in the Styles gallery (Home tab | Styles group) to display a shortcut menu (Figure 4–29).

3 Click 'Update Heading 2 to Match Selection' on the shortcut menu to update the Heading 2 style to reflect the settings at the location of the insertion point.

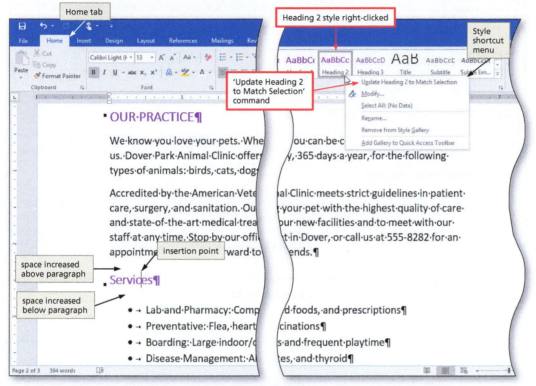

Figure 4–29

Creating Headers and Footers

A header is text that prints at the top of each page in the document. A footer is text that prints at the bottom of each page. In this proposal, you want the header and footer to appear on each page after the title page; that is, you do not want the header and footer on the title page. Recall that the title page is in a separate section from the rest of the sales proposal. Thus, the header and footer should not be in section 1, but they should be in section 2. The steps in the following sections explain how to create a header and footer in section 2 only.

To Insert a Formatted Header Different from the Previous Header

1 CREATE TITLE PAGE | 2 INSERT EXISTING DOCUMENT | 3 CREATE HEADER & FOOTER
4 EDIT & FORMAT LISTS | 5 EDIT & FORMAT TABLES | 6 CREATE WATERMARK

Word provides several built-in preformatted header designs for you to insert in documents. The following steps insert a formatted header in section 2 of the sales proposal that is different from the previous header. *Why? You do not want the header to appear on the title page, so you will instruct Word to not place the header in the previous section. Recall that the title page is in section 1 and the body of the proposal is in section 2.*

1

- Display the Insert tab. Click the 'Add a Header' button (Insert tab | Header & Footer group) and then click Edit Header in the Header gallery to switch to the header for section 2.
- If the 'Link to Previous' button (Header & Footer Tools Design tab | Navigation group) is selected, click it to deselect the button because you do not want the header in this section to be copied to the previous section (that is, the header should not be on the title page).

BTW

Headers and Footers
If a portion of a header or footer does not print, it may be in a nonprintable area. Check the printer user instructions to see how close the printer can print to the edge of the paper. Then, click the Page Setup Dialog Box Launcher (Layout tab | Page Setup group), click the Layout tab (Page Setup dialog box), adjust the From edge text box to a value that is larger than the printer's minimum margin setting, click the OK button, and then print the document again.

- Click the 'Add a Header' button (Header & Footer Tools Design tab | Header & Footer group) to display the Add a Header gallery (Figure 4–30).

⚲ Experiment

- Scroll through the list of built-in headers to see the variety of available formatted header designs.

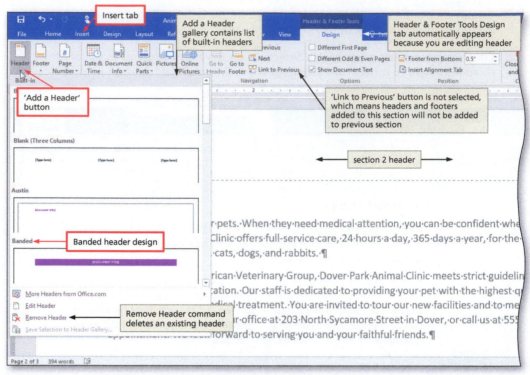

Figure 4–30

2

- If necessary, scroll to and then click the Banded header design in the Add a Header gallery to insert the formatted header in the header of section 2, which contains a content control (Figure 4–31).

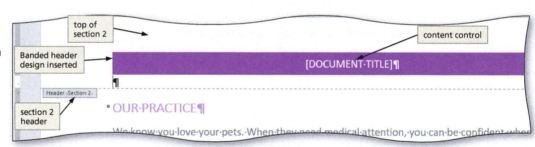

Figure 4–31

Q&A What is a content control?

A **content control** is an object that contains sample text or instructions for filling in text and graphics.

3

- Click the content control, [DOCUMENT TITLE], to select it and then type **Dover Park Animal Clinic** in the content control (Figure 4–32).

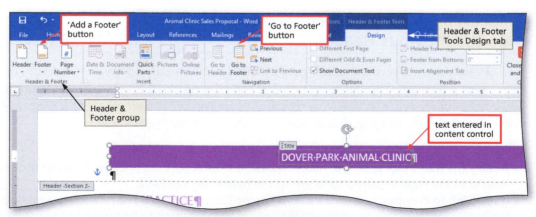

Figure 4–32

If requested by your instructor, enter your name instead of the clinic name shown in Figure 4–32.

Q&A How would I delete a header?
You would click Remove Header in the Header gallery.

Other Ways

1. Click 'Add a Header' button (Insert tab | Header & Footer group), select desired header in list

2. Click 'Explore Quick Parts' button (Insert tab | Text group), click 'Building Blocks Organizer' on Quick Parts menu, select desired header (Building Blocks Organizer dialog box), click Insert button

---

To Insert a Formatted Footer

The next step is to insert the footer. Word provides the same built-in preformatted footer designs as header designs. The footer design that corresponds to the header just inserted contains a centered page number. The following steps insert a formatted footer in section 2 of the sales proposal that corresponds to the header just inserted.

1 Click the 'Go to Footer' button (shown in Figure 4–32) (Header & Footer Tools Design tab | Navigation group) to display the footer for section 2.

2 If the 'Link to Previous' button (Header & Footer Tools Design tab | Navigation group) is selected, click it to deselect the button because you do not want the footer in this section to be copied to the previous section (that is, the footer should not be on the title page).

3 Click the 'Add a Footer' button (shown in Figure 4–32) (Header & Footer Tools Design tab | Header & Footer group) to display the Add a Footer gallery.

4 Click the Banded footer design to insert the formatted footer in the footer of section 2 (shown in Figure 4–33).

Q&A Why is the page number a 2?
The page number is 2 because, by default, Word begins numbering pages from the beginning of the document.

BTW

Page Numbers
If Word displays {PAGE} instead of the actual page number, press ALT+F9 to turn off field codes. If Word prints {PAGE} instead of the page number, open the Backstage view, click the Options tab to display the Word Options dialog box, click Advanced in the left pane (Word Options dialog box), scroll to the Print area, remove the check mark from the 'Print field codes instead of their values' check box, and then click the OK button.

To Format Page Numbers to Start at a Different Number

1 CREATE TITLE PAGE | 2 INSERT EXISTING DOCUMENT | **3 CREATE HEADER & FOOTER**
4 EDIT & FORMAT LISTS | 5 EDIT & FORMAT TABLES | 6 CREATE WATERMARK

On the page after the title page in the proposal, you want to begin numbering with a number 1, instead of a 2 as shown in Figure 4–33. **Why?** *Word begins numbering pages from the beginning of the document, and you want it to begin numbering from the first page of the body of the proposal. Thus, you need to instruct Word to begin numbering the pages in section 2 with the number 1.* The following steps format the page numbers so that they start at a different number.

1

- Click the 'Add Page Numbers' button (Header & Footer Tools Design tab | Header & Footer group) to display the Add Page Numbers menu (Figure 4–33).

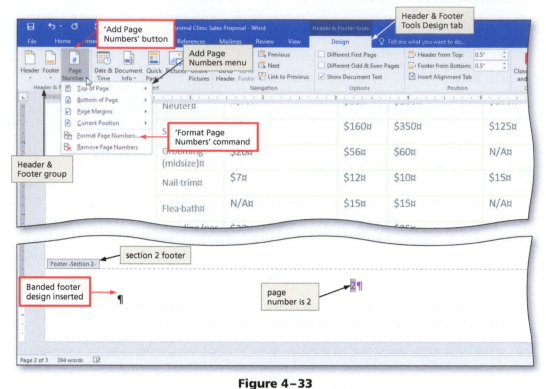

Figure 4–33

2

- Click 'Format Page Numbers' on the Add Page Numbers menu to display the Page Number Format dialog box.

- Click Start at in the Page numbering area (Page Number Format dialog box), which displays a 1 by default as the starting page number (Figure 4–34).

Q&A Can I also change the look of the page number?
Yes. Click the Number format arrow (Page Number Format dialog box) for a list of page number variations.

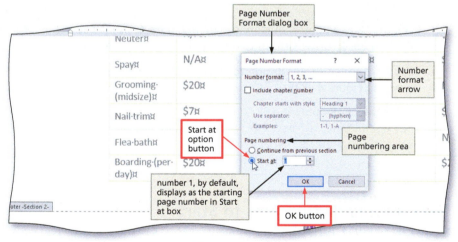

Figure 4–34

3

- Click the OK button to change the starting page number for section 2 to the number 1 (Figure 4–35).

- Click the 'Close Header and Footer' button (Header & Footer Tools Design tab | Close group) to close the header and footer.

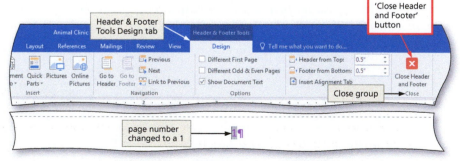

Figure 4–35

Other Ways

1. Click 'Add Page Numbers' button (Insert tab | Header & Footer group), click 'Format Page Numbers' on Add Page Numbers menu, set page formats (Page Number Format dialog box), click OK button

Editing and Formatting Lists

The finished sales proposal in this module has two lists: a bulleted list and a numbered list (shown in Figures 4–1b and 4–1c at the beginning of this module). The bulleted list is in alphabetical (sorted) order, the first word of each list item is emphasized, and the bullets are graphical instead of simple round dots. The numbered list has multiple levels for each numbered item. The following sections illustrate steps used to edit and format the lists in the proposal:

1. Sort a list of paragraphs.
2. Format text in the first list item and then copy the format to text in each of the remaining list items.
3. Customize bullets in a list of paragraphs.
4. Create a multilevel numbered list.

To Sort Paragraphs

1 CREATE TITLE PAGE | 2 INSERT EXISTING DOCUMENT | 3 CREATE HEADER & FOOTER
4 EDIT & FORMAT LISTS | 5 EDIT & FORMAT TABLES | 6 CREATE WATERMARK

The next step is to alphabetize the paragraphs in the bulleted list. *Why? It is easier for readers to locate information in lists that are in alphabetical order.* In Word, you can arrange paragraphs in alphabetic, numeric, or date order based on the first character in each paragraph. Ordering characters in this manner is called **sorting**. The following steps sort paragraphs.

- If necessary, scroll to display the paragraphs to be sorted.
- Drag through the paragraphs to be sorted, in this case, the bulleted list.
- Click the Sort button (Home tab | Paragraph group) to display the Sort Text dialog box (Figure 4–36).

&Q&A& What does ascending mean?
Ascending means to sort in alphabetic, numeric, or earliest-to-latest date order.

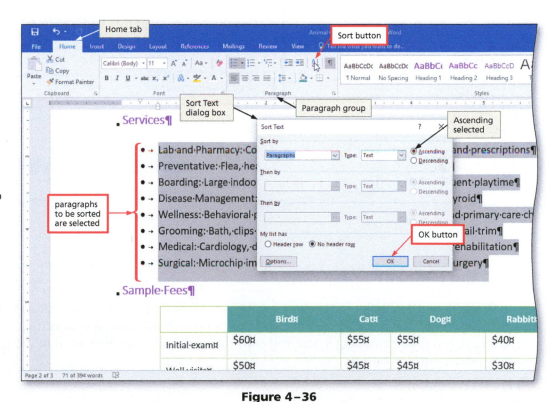

Figure 4–36

❷

- Click the OK button (Sort Text dialog box) to instruct Word to alphabetize the selected paragraphs (shown in Figure 4–37).
- Click anywhere to remove the selection from the text.

To Apply a Style Using the Mini Toolbar

The text up to the colon in each list item is to be formatted in italic with the color purple. Although you could apply formatting using buttons in the Font group on the ribbon, it is more efficient to use the Intense Emphasis style. If you use a style and decide at a later time that you want to modify the formatting, you simply modify the style and Word will apply the changes to all text formatted with that style. Thus, the following steps format text using a style.

1 Select the text to be formatted (in this case, the text, Boarding, in the first list item).

2 Click the Styles button on the mini toolbar to display the Styles gallery (Figure 4–37).

3 Click Intense Emphasis in the Styles gallery to apply the selected style to the selected text.

Q&A Could I use the Styles gallery on the Home tab instead of the mini toolbar?
Yes.

BTW

Format Painter
If you also want to copy paragraph formatting, such as alignment and line spacing, select the paragraph mark at the end of the paragraph prior to clicking the Format Painter button (Home tab | Clipboard group). If you want to copy only character formatting, such as fonts and font sizes, do not include the paragraph mark in your selected text.

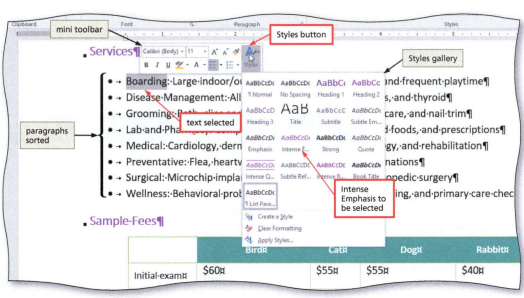

Figure 4–37

To Use the Format Painter Button

1 CREATE TITLE PAGE | 2 INSERT EXISTING DOCUMENT | 3 CREATE HEADER & FOOTER
4 EDIT & FORMAT LISTS | 5 EDIT & FORMAT TABLES | 6 CREATE WATERMARK

The first words in each of the remaining list items is to be formatted the same as the first words in the first list item. **Why?** *You would like the lists to be formatted consistently.* Instead of selecting the text in each list item one at a time and then formatting it, you will copy the format from the first word to the remaining words. The following steps copy formatting.

1

• Position the insertion point in the text that contains the formatting you wish to copy (the text, Boarding, in this case).

• Double-click the Format Painter button (Home tab | Clipboard group) to turn on the format painter.

Q&A Why double-click the Format Painter button?
To copy formats to only one other location, click the Format Painter button (Home tab | Clipboard group) once. If you want to copy formatting to multiple locations, however, double-click the Format Painter button so that the format painter remains active until you turn it off.

- Move the pointer to where you want to copy the formatting (the text, Disease Management, in this case) and notice that the format painter is active (Figure 4–38).

Q&A How can I tell if the format painter is active?
The pointer has a paintbrush attached to it when the format painter is active.

 2

- Select the text in the next list item (the text, Disease Management, in this case) to paste the copied format to the selected text.

Q&A What if the Format Painter button no longer is selected?
Repeat Step 1.

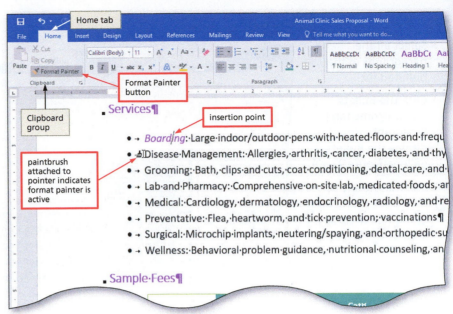

Figure 4–38

3

- Repeat Step 2 for the remaining the list items, selecting text up to the colon in Grooming, Lab and Pharmacy, Medical, Preventative, Surgical, and Wellness.
- Click the Format Painter button (Home tab | Clipboard group) to turn off the format painter (Figure 4–39).

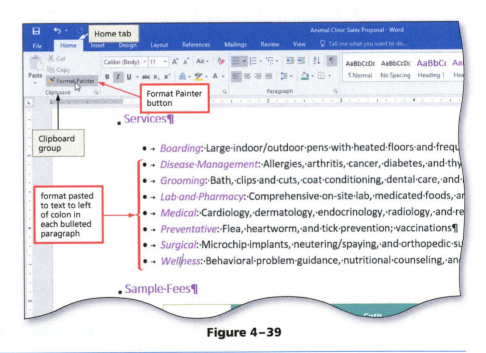

Figure 4–39

1 CREATE TITLE PAGE | 2 INSERT EXISTING DOCUMENT | 3 CREATE HEADER & FOOTER
4 EDIT & FORMAT LISTS | 5 EDIT & FORMAT TABLES | 6 CREATE WATERMARK

To Customize Bullets in a List

The bulleted list in the sales proposal draft uses default bullet characters, that is, the dot symbol. The following steps change the bullets in a list from the default to picture bullets. *Why? You want to use a more visually appealing bullet that looks like a veterinary caduceus. Word refers to graphical bullets as picture bullets.*

①

- Select all the paragraphs in the bulleted list.

- Click the Bullets arrow (Home tab | Paragraph group) to display the Bullets gallery (Figure 4–40).

Q&A

Can I select any of the bullet characters in the Bullet Library area of the Bullets gallery?
Yes, but if you prefer a different bullet character, follow the rest of these steps.

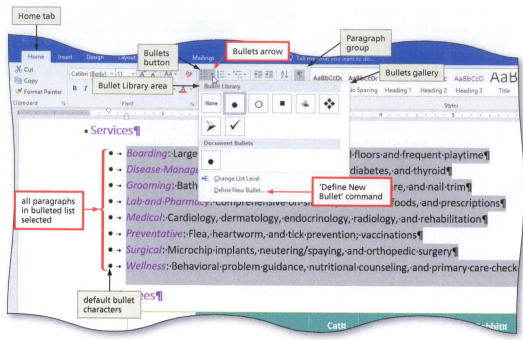

Figure 4–40

②

- Click 'Define New Bullet' in the Bullets gallery to display the Define New Bullet dialog box.

- Click the Picture button (Define New Bullet dialog box) to display the Insert Pictures dialog box.

- Type **veterinary caduceus** in the search box (Insert Pictures dialog box) and then click the Search button to display a list of pictures that matches the entered search text.

- Scroll through the list of pictures to locate the one shown in Figure 4–41, or a similar image. (If necessary, click the 'Show all web results' button to display more images that match the search text.)

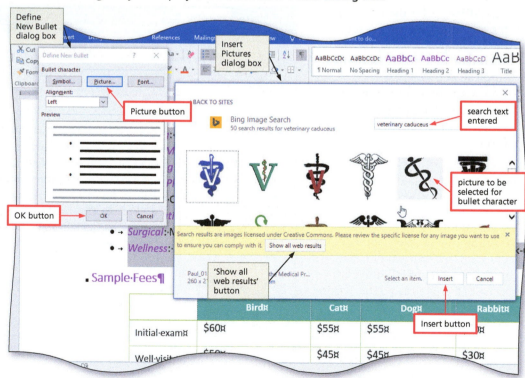

Figure 4–41

Q&A

What if I cannot locate the image in Figure 4-41, and I would like to use that exact image?
The image is located on the Data Files. You can click the Cancel button, click the 'Browse from a file' link in the Insert Pictures dialog box, navigate to the file called aesculab-stab-2400px.png in the Data Files, select the file, and then click the Insert button (Insert Picture dialog box) to show a preview of the selected picture bullet in the Define New Bullet dialog box. Proceed to Step 4.

- Click the desired picture to select it.

- Click the Insert button (Insert Pictures dialog box) to download the image, close the dialog box, and show a preview of the selected picture bullet in the Define New Bullet dialog box.

- Click the OK button (Define New Bullet dialog box) to change the bullets in the selected list to picture bullets.

- When the Word window is visible again, click in the selected list to remove the selection (Figure 4–42).

Figure 4–42

To Create a Multilevel Numbered List

1 CREATE TITLE PAGE | 2 INSERT EXISTING DOCUMENT | 3 CREATE HEADER & FOOTER
4 EDIT & FORMAT LISTS | 5 EDIT & FORMAT TABLES | 6 CREATE WATERMARK

The next step is to create a multilevel numbered list below the Facility heading on the last page of the sales proposal in this module (shown in Figure 4–1c at the beginning of this module). **Why?** *You would like to list the team members and their hours at the clinic.*

A **multilevel list** is a list that contains several levels of list items, with each lower level displaying a different numeric, alphabetic, or bullet character. In a multilevel list, the first level is displayed at the left edge of the list and subsequent levels are indented; that is, the second level is indented below the first, the third level is indented below the second level, and so on. The list is referred to as a numbered list if the first level contains numbers or letters and is referred to as a bulleted list if the first level contains a character other than a number or letter.

For the list in this project, the first level uses numbers (i.e., 1., 2., 3.), the second level uses lowercase letters (a., b., c.), and the third level uses lowercase Roman numerals (for example, i., ii., iii.). The following steps create a multilevel numbered list.

- Position the insertion point at the location for the multilevel numbered list, which in this case is the blank line below the Facility heading on the last page of the sales proposal.

- Click the Multilevel List button (Home tab | Paragraph group) to display the Multilevel List gallery (Figure 4–43).

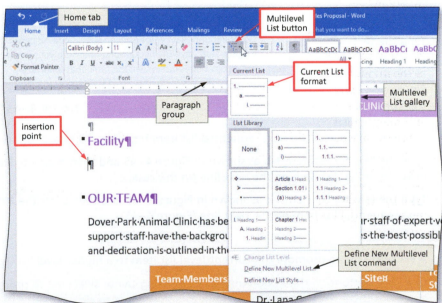

Figure 4–43

2

- Click the Current List format in the Multilevel List gallery to display the current paragraph as a multilevel list item using the current number format, which in this case is an indented 1 followed by a period.

Q&A

What if I wanted a different number format?
You would click the Multilevel List button (Home tab | Paragraph group) and then select the desired format in the Multilevel List gallery, or click Define New Multilevel List in the Multilevel List gallery (shown in Figure 4-43) to define your own format.

- Type **Clinic Hours** as a first-level list item and then press the ENTER key, which automatically places the next sequential number for the current level at the beginning of the next line (in this case, 2.) (Figure 4-44).

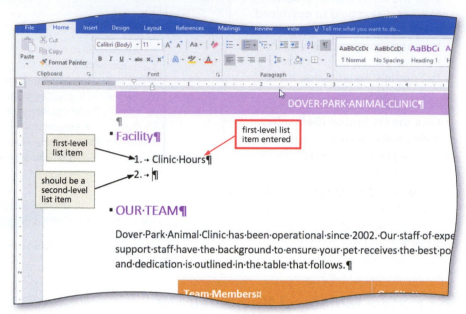

Figure 4-44

3

- Press the TAB key to demote the current list item (the 2.) to the next lower level, which is indented below the higher-level list item (in this case, converting 2. to a.).

4

- Type the text for list item 1-a as shown in Figure 4-45 and then press the ENTER key, which

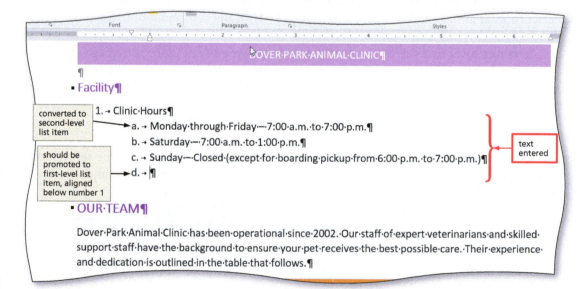

Figure 4-45

automatically places the next sequential list item for the current level on the next line (in this case, b.).

- Type the text for list item 1-b as shown in Figure 4-45 and then press the ENTER key, which automatically places the next sequential list item on the next line (in this case, c.).

- Type the text for list item 1-c as shown in Figure 4-45 and then press the ENTER key, which automatically places the next sequential list item on the next line (Figure 4-45).

5

- Press SHIFT+TAB to promote the current-level list item to a higher-level list item (in this case, converting d. to 2.).

Q&A

Can I use buttons on the ribbon instead of pressing TAB or SHIFT+TAB to promote and demote list items?
Yes. With the insertion point in the item to adjust, you can click the Increase Indent or Decrease Indent button (Home tab | Paragraph group) or right-click the list item and then click the desired command on the shortcut menu.

6

- Type **Contact Information** as a first-level list item and then press the ENTER key.

- Press the TAB key to demote the current level list item to a lower-level list item (in this case, converting 3. to a.).

- Type **Phone: 309-555-8282** and then press the ENTER key.

- Type **Email: info@ doverpark.com** and then press the ENTER key.

- Press SHIFT+TAB to promote the current-level list item to a higher-level list item (in this case, converting c. to 3.).

- Type **Payments** as a first-level list item, press the ENTER key, and then press the TAB key to demote the current-level list item to a lower-level list item (in this case, converting 4. to a.).

- Type **Accepted methods** and then press the ENTER key (Figure 4-46).

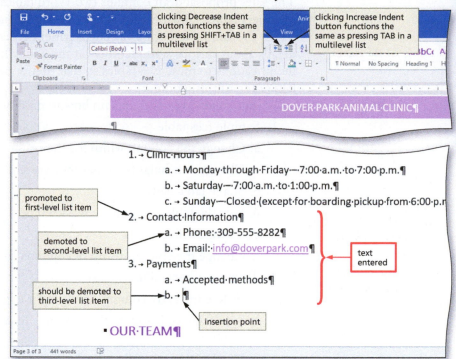

Figure 4–46

7

- Press the TAB key to demote the current-level list item to a lower-level list item (in this case, converting b. to i.).

- Type **Cash** and then press the ENTER key.

- Type **Check** and then press the ENTER key.

- Type **Credit card** and then press the ENTER key.

- Press SHIFT+TAB to promote the current-level list item to a higher-level list item (in this case, converting iii. to b.).

- Type the text for list item 3-b as shown in Figure 4–47 and then press the ENTER key.

- Press SHIFT+TAB to promote the current-level list item to a higher-level list item (in this case, converting c. to 4.).

- Finish entering the list as shown in Figure 4–47.

Figure 4–47

- Save the proposal again on the same storage location with the same file name.

Other Ways

1. Type **1.,** press SPACEBAR, type numbered list, pressing ENTER key at end of each item in list

Break Point: If you wish to take a break, this is a good place to do so. You can exit Word now. To resume at a later time, run Word, open the file called Animal Clinic Sales Proposal, and continue following the steps from this location forward.

Editing and Formatting Tables

The sales proposal draft contains two Word tables: the sample fees table and the team members table (shown earlier in the module in Figure 4–26). The sample fees table shows the sample fees for a variety of patient types, and the team members table shows details about various staff members at the clinic. In this section, you will make several modifications to these two tables so that they appear as shown in Figure 4–1 at the beginning of this module.

The following pages explain how to modify the tables in the sales proposal draft:

1. Sample fees table

    a. Change the column width for the column containing the type of services.

    b. Change row heights so that they are not so tall.

    c. Shade table cells.

    d. Sort the table contents by service type.

    e. Change cell spacing.

    f. Change the column width of columns containing costs.

2. Team members table

    a. Delete the extra column on the right edge of the table.

    b. Split table cells so that the heading, Team Members, is above the second column.

    c. Display text in a cell vertically to the left of the table.

    d. Remove cell shading from the table.

    e. Add borders to the table.

    f. Sum columns in the table.

BTW

Table Wrapping
If you want text to wrap around a table, instead of displaying above and below the table, do the following: either right-click the table and then click Table Properties on the shortcut menu, or click the Table Properties button (Table Tools Layout tab | Table group), click the Table tab (Table Properties dialog box), click Around in the Text wrapping area, and then click the OK button.

CONSIDER THIS

Why should you include visuals in a sales proposal?

Studies have shown that most people are visually oriented, preferring images to text. Use tables to clarify ideas and illustrate points. Be aware, however, that too many visuals can clutter a document.

1 CREATE TITLE PAGE | 2 INSERT EXISTING DOCUMENT | 3 CREATE HEADER & FOOTER
4 EDIT & FORMAT LISTS | **5 EDIT & FORMAT TABLES** | 6 CREATE WATERMARK

To Show Gridlines

When a table contains no borders or light borders, it may be difficult to see the individual cells in the table. Thus, the following step shows gridlines. *Why? To help identify the location of cells, you can display gridlines, which show cell outlines on the screen.* **Gridlines** are formatting marks, which means the gridlines do not print.

- Display the table to be edited in the document window (in this case, the sample fees table).
- Position the insertion point in any cell in the table.
- Display the Table Tools Layout tab.

- If gridlines are not displayed on the screen, click the 'View Table Gridlines' button (Table Tools Layout tab | Table group) to show gridlines in the table (Figure 4–48).

Q&A How do I turn off table gridlines? Click the 'View Table Gridlines' button again.

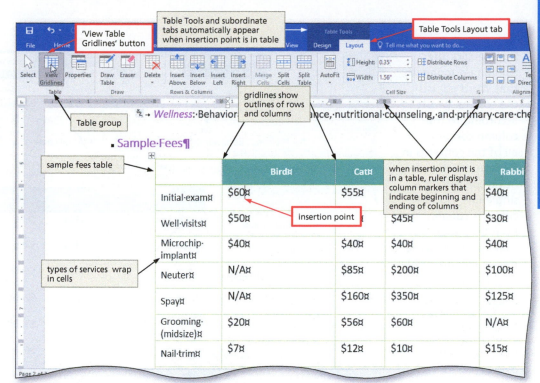

Figure 4–48

To Change Column Width

1 CREATE TITLE PAGE | 2 INSERT EXISTING DOCUMENT | 3 CREATE HEADER & FOOTER
4 EDIT & FORMAT LISTS | 5 EDIT & FORMAT TABLES | 6 CREATE WATERMARK

Notice in Figure 4–48 that the leftmost column containing the types of services is not wide enough to fit the contents; that is, some of the services wrap in the cells. Thus, you will change the column width of just this single column. *Why? In this proposal, the services should appear on a single line that is just wide enough to accommodate the types of services.*

You can change a column width by entering a specific value on the ribbon or in a dialog box, or by using a marker on the ruler or the column boundary. The following steps change column width by using a column's boundary.

1

- Position the pointer on the column boundary to the right of the column to adjust (in this case, to the right of the first column) so that the pointer changes to a double-headed arrow split by two vertical bars (Figure 4–49).

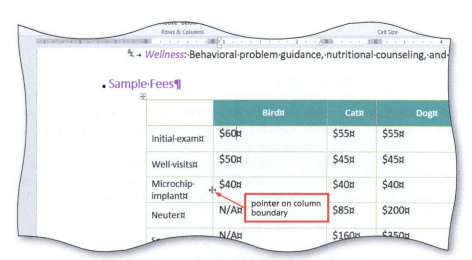

Figure 4–49

2

- Double-click the column boundary so that Word adjusts the column width according to the column contents. (If all of the contents in the column still are not displayed on a single line, double-click the column boundary again so that all contents are displayed on a single line) (Figure 4–50).

Q&A

What if I am using a touch screen? Position the insertion point in the column to adjust, tap the AutoFit button (Table Tools Layout tab | Cell Size group), and then tap AutoFit Contents on the AutoFit menu.

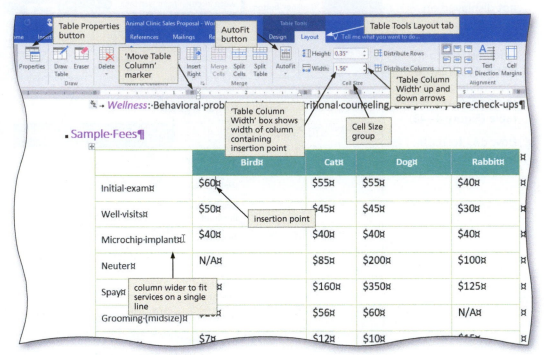

Figure 4–50

 **Experiment**

- Practice changing this column's width using other techniques: drag the 'Move Table Column' marker on the horizontal ruler to the right and then to the left. Click the 'Table Column Width' box up and down arrows (Table Tools Layout tab | Cell Size group). When you have finished experimenting, type **1.34** in the 'Table Column Width' box (Table Tools Layout tab | Cell Size group).

Other Ways

1. Drag 'Move Table Column' marker on horizontal ruler to desired width
2. Enter desired value in 'Table Column Width' box (Table Tools Layout tab | Cell Size group)
3. Click Table Properties button (Table Tools Layout tab | Table group), click Column tab (Table Properties dialog box), enter width, click OK button

To Change Row Height

The next step in this project is to narrow the height of the rows containing the services and fees. ***Why?*** *This table extends close to the bottom of the page, and you want to ensure that it does not spill onto the next page. (Note that it already may spill onto a second page.)*

You change row height in the same ways you change column width. That is, you can change row height by entering a specific value on the ribbon or in a dialog box, or by using a marker on the ruler or the row boundary. The latter two methods, however, work only for a single row at a time. The following steps change row height by entering a value on the ribbon.

1

- Select the rows to change (in this case, all the rows below the first row).

Q&A

How do I select rows?

Point to the left of the first row and then drag downward when the pointer changes to a right-pointing arrow (or, if using touch, drag through the rows).

2

- Click the 'Table Row Height' box up or down arrows (Table Tools Layout tab | Cell Size group) as many times as necessary until the box displays 0.3" to change the row height to this value (or, if using touch, enter **0.3** in the 'Table Row Height' box (Table Tools Layout tab | Cell Size group) (Figure 4–51).

- Click anywhere to remove the selection from the table.

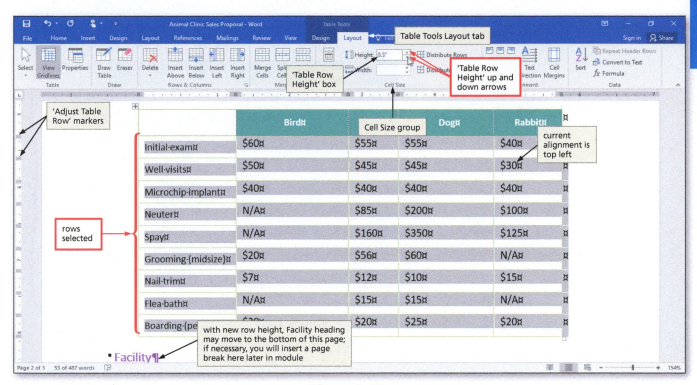

Figure 4–51

Other Ways

1. Click Table Properties button (Table Tools Layout tab | Table group), click Row tab (Table Properties dialog box), enter row height, click OK button

2. Right-click selected row (or, if using touch, tap 'Show Context Menu' button on mini toolbar), click Table Properties on shortcut menu, click Row tab, enter row height (Table Properties dialog box), click OK button

3. For a single row, drag row boundary (horizontal gridline at bottom of row in table) to desired height

4. Drag 'Adjust Table Row' marker on vertical ruler to desired height

To Align Data in Cells

The next step is to change the alignment of the data in cells that contain the dollar amounts. Recall that, in addition to aligning text horizontally in a cell (left, center, or right), you can align it vertically within a cell (top, center, or bottom). Currently, the dollar amounts have a top left alignment (shown in Figure 4–51). In this project, they should be aligned center so that they are more centered within the row height and width. The following steps change the alignment of data in cells.

1 Select the cells containing dollar amounts, as shown in Figure 4–52.

Q&A
How do I select a series of cells?
Drag through the cells.

BTW

Page Breaks and Tables

If you do not want a page break to occur in the middle of a table, position the insertion point in the table, click the Table Properties button (Table Tools Layout tab | Table group), click the Row tab (Table Properties dialog box), remove the check mark from the 'Allow row to break across pages' check box, and then click the OK button. To force a table to break across pages at a particular row, click in the row that you want to appear on the next page and then press CTRL+ENTER.

2 Click the Align Center button (Table Tools Layout tab | Alignment group) to center the contents of the selected cells (Figure 4–52).

3 Click anywhere to remove the selection from the table.

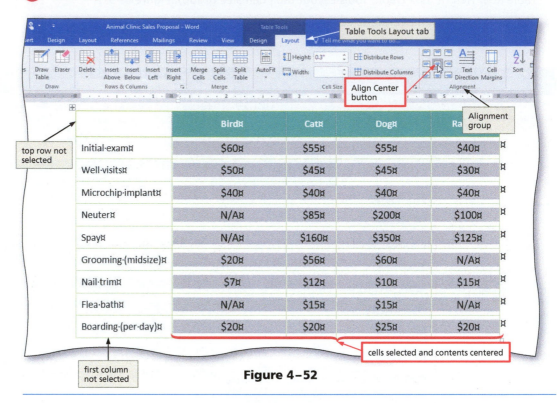

Figure 4–52

To Shade a Table Cell

In this table, the cell in the upper-left corner of the table is to be shaded teal. *Why? You want all cells in the top row shaded the same color.* The following steps shade a cell.

1
- Position the insertion point in the cell to shade (in this case, the cell in the upper-left corner of the table).

- Display the Table Tools Design tab.

- Click the Shading arrow (Table Tools Design tab | Table Styles group) to display the Shading gallery (Figure 4–53).

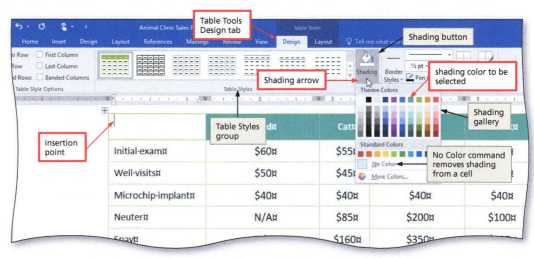

Figure 4–53

 **Experiment**

- Point to various colors in the Shading gallery and watch the shading color of the current cell change.

②

- Click 'Teal, Accent 3' (seventh color, first row) in the Shading gallery to apply the selected shading color to the current cell (shown in Figure 4-54).

Q&A How do I remove shading from a cell?
Click the Shading arrow (Table Tools Design tab | Table Styles group) and then click No Color in the Shading gallery.

To Sort a Table

1 CREATE TITLE PAGE | 2 INSERT EXISTING DOCUMENT | 3 CREATE HEADER & FOOTER
4 EDIT & FORMAT LISTS | 5 EDIT & FORMAT TABLES | 6 CREATE WATERMARK

The next task is to sort rows in the table. ***Why?*** *The services should be listed in alphabetical order.* The following steps sort rows in a table.

①

- Select the rows to be sorted (in this case, all the rows below the first row).

Q&A What if I want to sort all rows in the table?
Place the insertion point anywhere in the table instead of selecting the rows.

- Display the Table Tools Layout tab.
- Click the Sort button (Table Tools Layout tab | Data group) to display the Sort dialog box (Figure 4–54).

Q&A What is the purpose of the Then by area (Sort dialog box)?
If you have multiple values for a particular column, you can sort by columns within columns. For example, if the table had a city column and a last name column, you could sort by last names within cities.

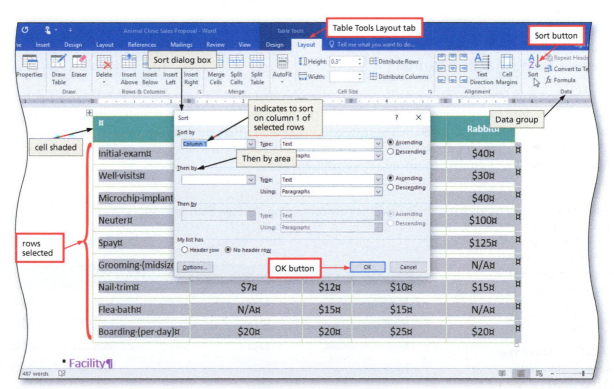

Figure 4–54

- Click the OK button (Sort dialog box) to instruct Word to alphabetize the selected rows.
- Click anywhere to remove the selection from the text (Figure 4–55).

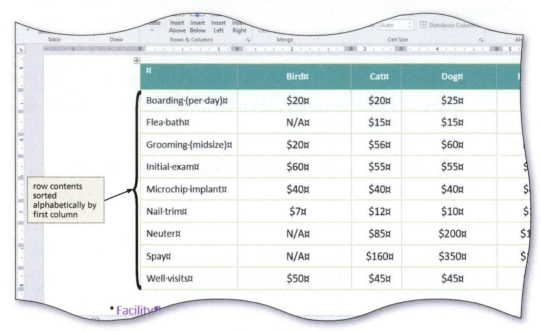

Figure 4–55

To Select Nonadjacent Items

1 CREATE TITLE PAGE | 2 INSERT EXISTING DOCUMENT | 3 CREATE HEADER & FOOTER
4 EDIT & FORMAT LISTS | **5 EDIT & FORMAT TABLES** | 6 CREATE WATERMARK

The next step is to select every other row in the table and shade it light teal. **Why?** *You feel that using shading on alternating rows will make it easier to read across individual rows.* Word provides a method of selecting nonadjacent items, which are items such as text, cells, or graphics that are not next to each other, that is, not to the immediate right, left, top, or bottom. When you select nonadjacent items, you can format all occurrences of the items at once. The following steps select nonadjacent cells.

- Select the first row to format (in this case, the row containing the Flea bath service).

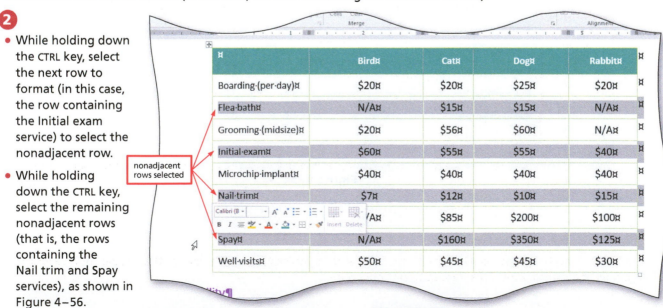

- While holding down the CTRL key, select the next row to format (in this case, the row containing the Initial exam service) to select the nonadjacent row.

- While holding down the CTRL key, select the remaining nonadjacent rows (that is, the rows containing the Nail trim and Spay services), as shown in Figure 4–56.

Figure 4–56

Q&A Do I follow the same procedure to select any nonadjacent item?
Yes. Select the first item and then hold down the CTRL key while selecting the remaining items.

What if my keyboard does not have a CTRL key?
You will need to format each row individually, one at a time.

To Shade Selected Cells

With the alternating rows selected, the next step is to shade them light teal. The following steps shade selected cells.

1 Display the Table Tools Design tab.

2 With the rows selected, click the Shading arrow (Table Tools Design tab | Table Styles group) to display the Shading gallery and then click 'Teal, Accent 3, Lighter 80%' (seventh color, second row) in the Shading gallery to shade the selected rows with the selected color.

3 Click anywhere to remove the selection from the table (Figure 4–57).

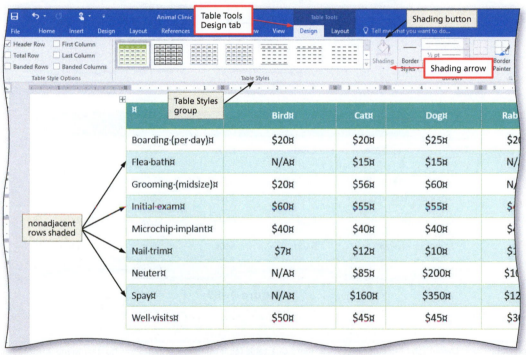

Figure 4–57

BTW

Table Headings
If a table continues on the next page, you can instruct Word to repeat the table headings at the top of the subsequent page(s) containing the table. To do this, select the first row in the table and then click the 'Repeat Header Rows' button (Table Tools Layout tab | Data group).

1 CREATE TITLE PAGE | 2 INSERT EXISTING DOCUMENT | 3 CREATE HEADER & FOOTER
4 EDIT & FORMAT LISTS | 5 EDIT & FORMAT TABLES | 6 CREATE WATERMARK

To Change Cell Spacing

The next step in formatting the sample fees table is to place a small amount of white space between every cell in the table. *Why? You feel the table would be easier to read with white space surrounding each cell.* The following steps change spacing between cells.

1

- Display the Table Tools Layout tab.
- Position the insertion point somewhere in the table and then click the Cell Margins button (Table Tools Layout tab | Alignment group) to display the Table Options dialog box.

- Place a check mark in the 'Allow spacing between cells' check box and then click the up arrow once so that 0.02" is displayed in this box, because you want to increase space between cells by this value (Figure 4–58).

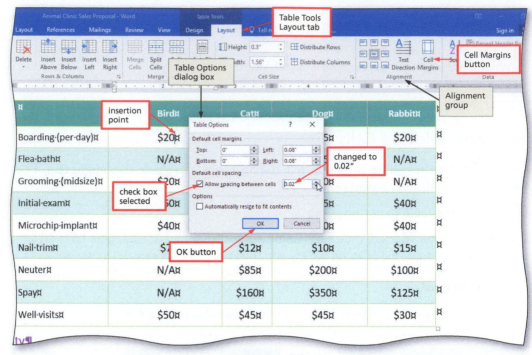

Figure 4–58

2

- Click the OK button (Table Options dialog box) to apply the cell spacing changes to the current table (Figure 4–59).

Q&A

Why are the column dividers in the first row wavy?
Gridlines are still showing, which causes a wavy appearance of the lines. When you hide gridlines later in the project, the wavy lines will disappear.

Figure 4–59

Other Ways

1. Click Table Properties button (Table Tools Layout tab | Table group), click Table tab (Table Properties dialog box), click Options button, select desired options (Table Options dialog box), click OK button in each dialog box

2. Right-click table (or, if using touch, tap 'Show Context Menu' button on mini toolbar), click Table Properties on shortcut menu, click Table tab (Table Properties dialog box), click Options button, select desired options (Table Options dialog box), click OK button in each dialog box

To Change Column Width

In reviewing the sample fees table, you notice that the columns containing the fees are different widths. Thus, the final step in formatting the sample fees table is to change the column widths because you want the columns containing the rates to all be the same width, specifically .95". The following steps change column widths by specifying a value on the ribbon.

1 Select the columns to be resized, in this case, all columns except the first.

2 Click the 'Table Column Width' box (Table Tools Layout tab | Cell Size group) to select it.

3 Type .95 in the 'Table Column Width' box and then press the ENTER key to change the width of the selected table columns (Figure 4–60).

4 Click anywhere to remove the selection from the table.

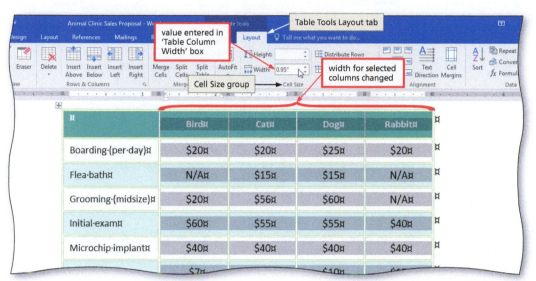

Figure 4–60

BTW

Table Columns
If you hold down the ALT key while dragging a column marker on the ruler or a column boundary in the table, the width measurements of all columns appear on the ruler as you drag the column marker or boundary.

To Page Break Manually

If the Facility heading appears at the bottom of the page below the sample fees table, insert a page break immediately to its left so that this heading appears at the top of the last page of the proposal (as shown in Figure 4–1 at the beginning of this module). The following steps insert a manual page break, if necessary.

1 If the Facility heading is not on the last page of the proposal, position the insertion point immediately to the left of the F in Facility.

2 Display the Insert tab.

3 Click the 'Insert a Page Break' button (Insert tab | Pages group) to insert a manual page break at the location of the insertion point, which will move the Facility heading to the last page of the proposal.

To Delete a Column

1 CREATE TITLE PAGE | 2 INSERT EXISTING DOCUMENT | 3 CREATE HEADER & FOOTER
4 EDIT & FORMAT LISTS | 5 EDIT & FORMAT TABLES | 6 CREATE WATERMARK

With the service fees table finished, the next task is to format the team members table. The following steps delete a column from a table. *Why? The table in the draft of the proposal contains a blank column that should be deleted.*

1
• Scroll to display the team members table in the document window.
• Position the insertion point in the column to be deleted (in this case, the rightmost column).

- Click the Delete Table button (Table Tools Layout tab | Rows & Columns group) to display the Delete Table menu (Figure 4–61).

- Click Delete Columns on the Delete Table menu to delete the column containing the insertion point (shown in Figure 4–62).

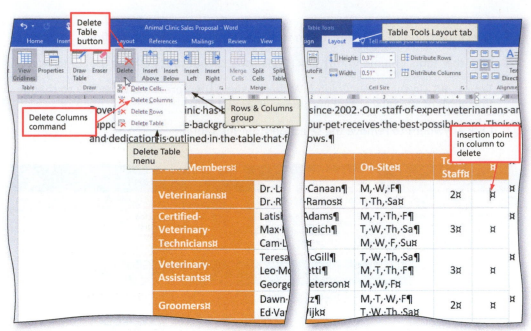

Figure 4–61

Other Ways

1. Right-click column to delete, click Delete Cells on shortcut menu, click 'Delete entire column' (Delete Cells dialog box), click OK button

2. Select column, right-click selection, click Delete Columns on shortcut menu

3. If using touch, press and hold column to delete, tap Delete Table button on mini toolbar, tap Delete Columns

---

TO DELETE A ROW

If you wanted to delete a row, you would perform the following tasks.

1. Position the insertion point in the row to be deleted; click the Delete Table button (Table Tools Layout tab | Rows & Columns group) and then click Delete Rows on the Delete Table menu.

or

2. If using touch, press and hold row to delete, tap Delete Table button on mini toolbar, tap Delete Rows.

or

3. Right-click the row to delete, click Delete Cells on the shortcut menu, click 'Delete entire row' (Delete Cells dialog box), and then click the OK button.

or

4. Select the row to be deleted, right-click the selected row, and then click Delete Rows on the shortcut menu.

To Split Cells

1 CREATE TITLE PAGE | 2 INSERT EXISTING DOCUMENT | 3 CREATE HEADER & FOOTER
4 EDIT & FORMAT LISTS | 5 EDIT & FORMAT TABLES | 6 CREATE WATERMARK

The top, left cell of the table contains the text, Team Members. In the draft of the sales proposal, this row is above the first two columns in the table (the job titles and employee name). This heading, Team Members, should be above the descriptions of the employee names, that is, above the second column. Thus, you will split the cell into two cells. **Why?** *With the cell split, you can reposition the heading, Team Members, above the second column.* The following steps split a single cell into two separate cells.

- Position the insertion point in the cell to split, in this case the top left cell as shown in Figure 4–62.
- Click the Split Cells button (Table Tools Layout tab | Merge group) to display the Split Cells dialog box (Figure 4–62).

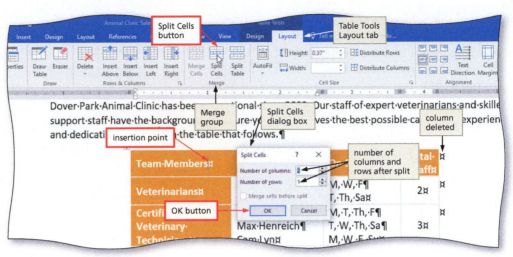

Figure 4–62

2

- Verify the number of columns and rows into which you want the cell split, in this case, 2 columns and 1 row.
- Click the OK button (Split Cells dialog box) to split the one cell into two columns (Figure 4–63).

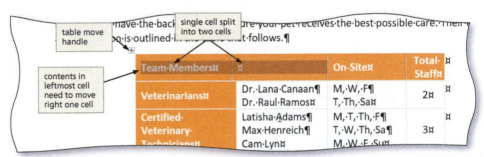

Figure 4–63

Other Ways

1. Right-click cell, click Split Cells on shortcut menu (or, if using touch, tap 'Show Context Menu' button on mini toolbar)

To Move Cell Contents

When you split a cell into two cells, Word places the contents of the original cell in the leftmost cell after the split. In this case, the contents (Team Members) should be in the right cell. Thus, the following steps move cell contents.

1 Select the cell contents to be moved (in this case, Team Members).

2 Drag the cell contents to the desired location (in this case, the second cell in the first row) (shown in Figure 4–64).

Q&A What if I cannot drag the cell contents properly?
Use the Cut and Paste commands.

1 CREATE TITLE PAGE | 2 INSERT EXISTING DOCUMENT | 3 CREATE HEADER & FOOTER
4 EDIT & FORMAT LISTS | 5 EDIT & FORMAT TABLES | 6 CREATE WATERMARK

To Move a Cell Boundary

Notice in Figure 4–64 that the cell boundary to the left of the Team Members label does not line up with the boundary to the right of the job titles. *Why not? This is because when you split a cell, Word divides the cell into evenly sized cells.* If you want the boundary to line up with other column boundaries, drag it to the desired location. The following steps move a cell boundary.

BTW

Moving Tables
If you wanted to move a table to a new location, you would click in the table to display the table move handle in the upper-left corner of the table (shown in Figure 4–63) and then drag the table move handle to move the entire table to a new location.

- Position the pointer on the cell boundary you wish to move so that the pointer changes to a double-headed arrow split by two vertical bars (Figure 4–64).

Q&A What if I cannot see the cell boundary?
Be sure that table gridlines are showing: View Table Gridlines button (Table Tools Layout tab | Table group).

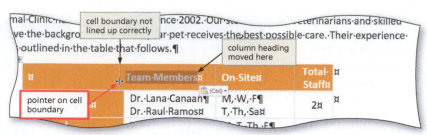

Figure 4–64

- Drag the cell boundary to the desired new location, in this case, to line up with the column boundary to its right, as shown in Figure 4–65.

Q&A What if I am using a touch screen?
Position the insertion point in the upper-left cell, tap the Table Properties button (Table Tools Layout tab | Table group), tap the Cell tab (Table Properties dialog box), type 1.27 in the Preferred width box, and then tap the OK button.

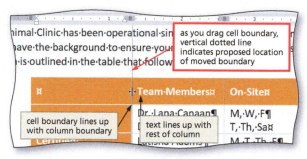

Figure 4–65

Other Ways

1. Drag 'Move Table Column' marker on horizontal ruler to desired width

To Distribute Columns

1 CREATE TITLE PAGE | 2 INSERT EXISTING DOCUMENT | 3 CREATE HEADER & FOOTER
4 EDIT & FORMAT LISTS | 5 EDIT & FORMAT TABLES | 6 CREATE WATERMARK

The next step in formatting the team members table is to make the width of the first three columns uniform, that is, the same width. The following step distributes selected columns. *Why? Instead of checking and adjusting the width of each column individually, you can make all columns uniform at the same time.*

- Select the columns to format, in this case, the three leftmost columns.
- Click the Distribute Columns button (Table Tools Layout tab | Cell Size group) to make the width of the selected columns uniform (Figure 4–66).

Q&A How would I make all columns in the table uniform?
Simply place the insertion point somewhere in the table before clicking the Distribute Columns button.

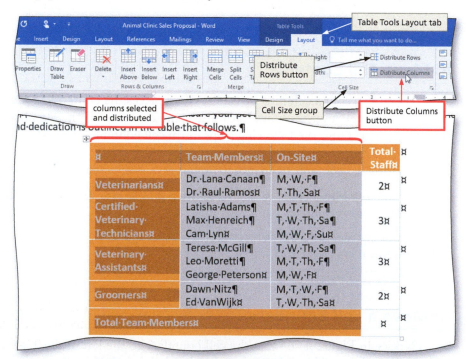

Figure 4–66

Other Ways

1. Right-click selected columns, click 'Distribute Columns Evenly' on shortcut menu (or, if using touch, tap 'Show Context Menu' button on mini toolbar)

To Distribute Rows

If you wanted to make rows the same height, you would perform the following tasks.

1. Select the rows to format.

2. Click the Distribute Rows button (Table Tools Layout tab | Cell Size group) (shown in Figure 4-66) to make the width of the selected rows uniform.

or

1. Right-click selected columns and then click 'Distribute Rows Evenly' on the shortcut menu (or, if using touch, tap the 'Show Context Menu' button on the mini toolbar).

To Insert a Column

In this project, the left edge of the team members table has a column that displays the label, Organization. Thus, the following steps insert a column at the left edge of the table.

1 Position the insertion point somewhere in the first column of the table.

2 Click the 'Insert Columns to the Left' button (Table Tools Layout tab | Rows & Columns group) to insert a column to the left of the column containing the insertion point (Figure 4-67).

3 Click anywhere in the table to remove the selection.

BTW

Draw Table

If you want to draw the boundary, rows, and columns of a table, click the 'Add a Table' button (Insert tab | Tables group) and then click Draw Table in the Add a Table gallery. Use the pencil-shaped pointer to draw the perimeter of the table and the inside rows and columns. Use the Table Eraser button (Table Tools Design tab | Draw group) to erase lines in the table. To continue drawing, click the Draw Table button (Table Tools Design tab | Draw group).

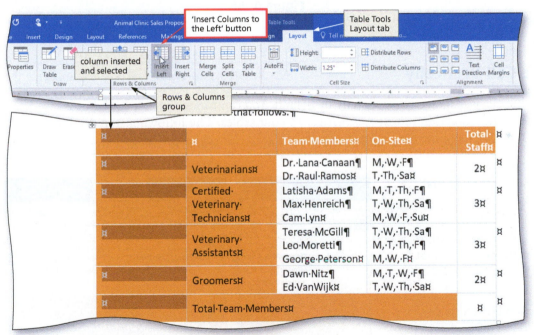

Figure 4–67

To Merge Cells and Enter Text

The label, Organization, is to be displayed vertically to the left of the bottom five rows in the table. To display this text, the five cells should be merged into a single cell. The following steps merge cells and then enter text in the merged cell.

1 Select the cells to merge, in this case, the bottom five cells in the first column of the table.

2 Click the Merge Cells button (Table Tools Layout tab | Merge group) to merge the five selected cells into one cell.

3 Type **Organization** in the merged cell.

4 If necessary, center the entered text (Figure 4–68).

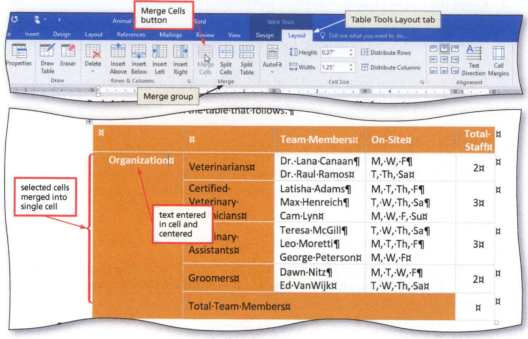

Figure 4–68

To Display Text in a Cell Vertically

1 CREATE TITLE PAGE | 2 INSERT EXISTING DOCUMENT | 3 CREATE HEADER & FOOTER
4 EDIT & FORMAT LISTS | 5 EDIT & FORMAT TABLES | 6 CREATE WATERMARK

The data you enter in cells is displayed horizontally by default. You can rotate the text so that it is displayed vertically. Changing the direction of text adds variety to your tables. The following step displays text vertically in a cell. *Why? The label, Organization, is displayed vertically at the left edge of the table.*

1

- Position the insertion point in the cell that contains the text to rotate (in this case, Organization).

- Click the Text Direction button twice (Table Tools Layout tab | Alignment group) so that the text reads from bottom to top in the cell (Figure 4–69).

Q&A | Why click the Text Direction button twice?
The first time you click the Text Direction button (Table Tools Layout tab | Alignment group), the text in the cell reads from top to bottom. The second time you click it, the text is displayed so that it reads from bottom to top (Figure 4–69). If you were to click the button a third time, the text would be displayed horizontally again.

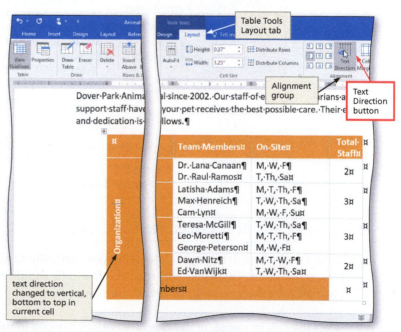

Figure 4–69

To Change Column Width

The cell containing the vertical text is too wide. Thus, the next step is to change the width of that column. The following step changes column width using the ruler.

1 Drag the column's boundary inward, as shown in Figure 4–70, to resize the column.

Q&A What if I am using a touch screen?
Position the insertion point in the column to adjust. Tap the 'Table Column Width' box (Table Tools Layout tab | Cell Size group), type `.35` as the column width, and then press the ENTER key.

Figure 4–70

To Remove Cell Shading

In this table, only the first row and first column should have shading. Thus, the following steps remove shading from table cells.

1 Select the cells that should not contain shading (in this case, all of the cells below the first row and to the right of the first column).

2 Display the Table Tools Design tab. Click the Shading arrow (Table Tools Design tab | Table Styles group) to display the Shading gallery (Figure 4–71).

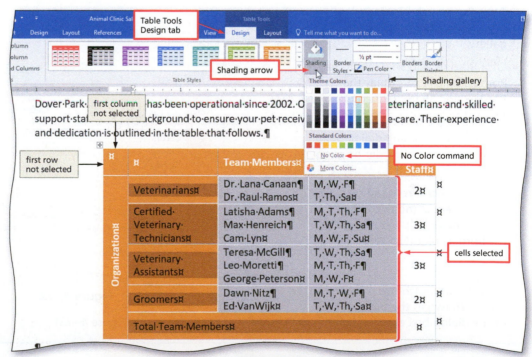

Figure 4–71

3 Click No Color in the Shading gallery to remove the shading from the selected cells (shown in Figure 4–72).

4 Click anywhere in the table to remove the selection.

To Hide Gridlines

You no longer need to see the gridlines in the table. Thus, you can hide the gridlines. The following steps hide gridlines.

1 If necessary, position the insertion point in a table cell.

2 Display the Table Tools Layout tab.

3 Click the 'View Table Gridlines' button (Table Tools Layout tab | Table group) to hide gridlines in the table on the screen.

To Border a Table

1 CREATE TITLE PAGE | 2 INSERT EXISTING DOCUMENT | 3 CREATE HEADER & FOOTER
4 EDIT & FORMAT LISTS | **5 EDIT & FORMAT TABLES** | 6 CREATE WATERMARK

The table in this project has a ½-point, gold border around all cells. The following steps change the border color in a table using the Borders and Shading dialog box. *Why? Earlier in this module when you created the title page, the border line weight was changed to 6 point. Because the table border should be ½ point, you will use the Borders and Shading dialog box to change the line weight before adding the border to the table.*

- Position the insertion point somewhere in the table.

- Display the Table Tools Design tab. Click the Borders arrow (Table Tools Design tab | Table Styles group) to display the Borders gallery.

- Click Borders and Shading in the Borders gallery to display the Borders and Shading dialog box.

- Click All in the Setting area (Borders and Shading dialog box), which will place a border on every cell in the table.

- Click the Color arrow and then click 'Gold, Accent 5' (ninth color, first row) in the Color palette to specify the border color (Figure 4–72).

2

- Click the OK button to place the border shown in the preview area of the dialog box around the table cells in the document (shown in Figure 4–73).

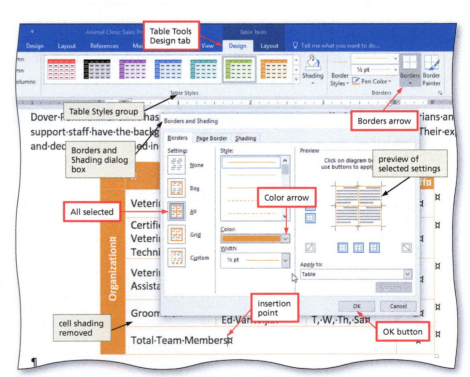

Figure 4–72

To Sum Columns in a Table

Word can calculate the totals of rows and columns. You also can specify the format for how the totals will be displayed. The following steps sum a column in the table. **Why?** *In this project, the last row should display the sum (total) of the values in the last column: Total Staff.*

1

- Position the insertion point in the cell to contain the sum (last row, Total Staff column).

2

- Display the Table Tools Layout tab.

- Click the Formula button (Table Tools Layout tab | Data group) to display the Formula dialog box (Figure 4–73).

Q&A What is the formula that shows in the Formula box, and can I change it?
Word places a default formula in the Formula box, depending on the location of the

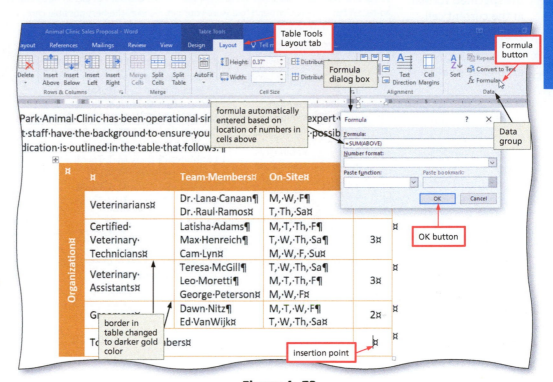

Figure 4–73

numbers in surrounding cells. In this case, because numbers are above the current cell, Word displays a formula that will add the numbers above the current cell. You can change the formula that Word proposes, or type a different formula. For example, instead of summing numbers you can multiply them.

3

- Click the Number format arrow (Formula dialog box) and then click the desired format for the result of the computation, in this case, the format with the numeral 0 (Figure 4–74).

Q&A Why select the format with the numeral 0?
You want the result to be displayed as a whole number, so you select the numeral 0. If you

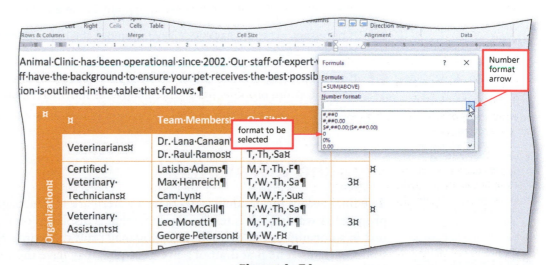

Figure 4–74

wanted the result to display with cents, you would select the format #,##0.00 (the # symbol means to display a blank if the number has a value of zero).

4

- Click the OK button (Formula dialog box) to place the sum of the numbers using the specified format in the current cell (Figure 4–75).

Q&A

Can I sum a row instead of a column?
Yes. You would position the insertion point in an empty cell at the right edge of the row before clicking the Formula button.

If I make a change to a number in a table, does Word automatically recalculate the sum?
No. You will need to update the field by right-clicking it and then clicking Update Field on the shortcut menu or by selecting the field and then pressing the F9 key.

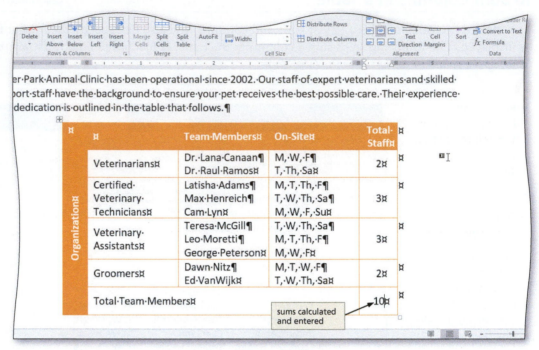

Figure 4–75

To Delete a Blank Paragraph

If you notice an extra paragraph mark below the team member table that it is causing an extra blank page in the document, you should delete the blank paragraph. If necessary, the following steps delete a blank paragraph.

1 Press CTRL+END to position the insertion point at the end of the document.

2 If necessary, press the BACKSPACE key to remove the extra blank paragraph and delete the blank page.

3 If text spills onto a fourth page, remove space above paragraphs in the sales proposal until the entire proposal fits on three pages, as shown in Figure 4–1.

BTW

Distributing a Document
Instead of printing and distributing a hard copy of a document, you can distribute the document electronically. Options include sending the document via email; posting it on cloud storage (such as OneDrive) and sharing the file with others; posting it on social media, a blog, or other website; and sharing a link associated with an online location of the document. You also can create and share a PDF or XPS image of the document, so that users can view the file in Acrobat Reader or XPS Viewer instead of in Word.

Creating a Watermark

The final task in this module is to create a watermark for the pages of the sales proposal. A **watermark** is text or a graphic that is displayed on top of or behind the text in a document. For example, a catalog may print the words, Sold Out, on top of sold-out items. The first draft of a five-year-plan may have the word, Draft, printed behind the text of the document. Some companies use their logos or other graphics as watermarks to add visual appeal to their documents.

To Zoom Multiple Pages

The following steps display multiple pages in their entirety in the document window as large as possible, so that you can see the position of the watermark as you create it.

1 Press CTRL+HOME to position the insertion point at the beginning of the document.

2 Display the View tab. Click the Multiple Pages button (View tab | Zoom group) to display all three pages in the document window as large as possible.

To Create a Watermark

1 CREATE TITLE PAGE | 2 INSERT EXISTING DOCUMENT | 3 CREATE HEADER & FOOTER
4 EDIT & FORMAT LISTS | 5 EDIT & FORMAT TABLES | 6 CREATE WATERMARK

In this project, the image of paw prints is displayed behind all content in the proposal as a watermark. *Why? The graphic adds visual appeal to the document, enticing readers to look at its contents.* The following steps create a watermark.

- Display the Design tab.

- Click the Watermark button (Design tab | Page Background group) to display the Watermark gallery (Figure 4–76).

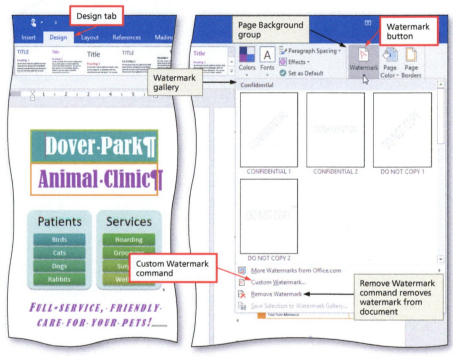

Figure 4–76

- Click Custom Watermark in the Watermark gallery to display the Printed Watermark dialog box.

- Click the Picture watermark option button to select it (Printed Watermark dialog box), which enables you to select an image for the watermark.

- Click the Select Picture button to display the Insert Pictures dialog box.

- Type **paw prints** in the Search box and then click the Search button. Click the paw prints image shown in Figure 4–1, or a similar image, and then click the Insert button to download the image and close the dialog box. (Or, you can click the 'Browse from a file' link in the Insert Pictures dialog box, navigate to the file called Colorful-Paw-Prints-Pattern-Background-2400px.png in the Data Files, select the file, and then click the Insert button (Insert Picture dialog box)).

• Click the Apply button to show a preview of the watermark on the pages in the document window (Figure 4–77).

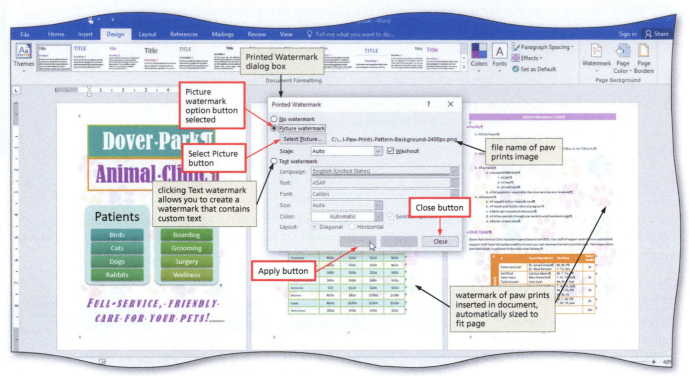

Figure 4–77

3

• Click the Close button (Printed Watermark dialog box) to close the dialog box.

Q&A How do I remove a watermark from a document?

Click the Watermark button (Design tab | Page Background group) and then click Remove Watermark in the Watermark gallery (shown in Figure 4-76).

How do I create a text watermark?

Click Text watermark in the Printed Watermark dialog box (shown in Figure 4–77), select or type the text for the watermark, select format options, and then click the OK button.

Other Ways

1. Click 'Explore Quick Parts' button (Insert tab | Text group), click 'Building Blocks Organizer' on Explore Quick Parts menu, select desired watermark (Building Blocks Organizer dialog box), click Insert button

To Change Theme Fonts

The final step in formatting this project is to change the fonts used for text in the document. *Why? With the watermark, some of the text is difficult to read. You would prefer a bolder font.* If text is entered using the headings and body text fonts, you easily can change the font in the entire document by changing the theme fonts, or font set. A **font set** defines one font for headings and another for body text. The default font set is Office, which uses the Cambria font for headings and the Calibri font for body text. In Word, you can select from more than 20 predefined, coordinated font sets to give the document's text a new look.

If you previously changed a font using buttons on the ribbon or mini toolbar, Word will not alter those when you change the font set because changes to the font set are not applied to individually changed fonts. This means the font of the title on the title page will remain as Bernard MT Condensed if you change the font set. The following steps change the theme fonts to TrebuchetMs for headings and for body text.

1

- Click the Theme Fonts button (Design tab | Document Formatting group) to display the Theme Fonts gallery (Figure 4–78).

Experiment

- Point to various font sets in the Theme Fonts gallery and watch the fonts of text in the document change.

2

- Scroll through the Theme Fonts gallery and then click TrebuchetMs in the Fonts gallery to set the document theme fonts to the selected font (shown in Figure 4-1 at the beginning of this module).

Q&A What if I want to return to the default font set?
You would click the Theme Fonts button and then click Office in the Fonts gallery.

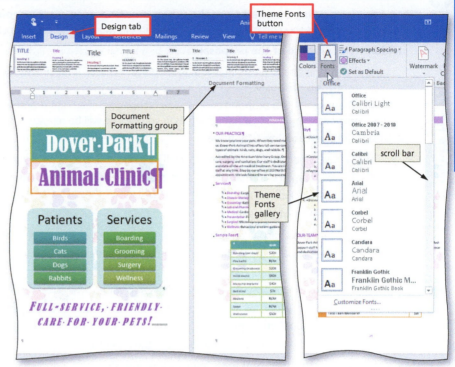

Figure 4–78

- If necessary, insert a page break before the Facility heading. Make any additional adjustments to spacing, table column widths, etc., so that your document looks like Figure 4–1 shown at the beginning of this module.

To Check Spelling, Save, Print, and Exit Word

The following steps check the spelling of the document, save and print the document, and then exit Word.

1 Display the Review tab. Click the 'Spelling & Grammar' button (Review tab | Proofing group) to begin the spelling and grammar check. Correct any misspelled words.

2 Save the sales proposal again with the same file name.

3 If requested by your instructor, print the sales proposal (shown in Figure 4–1 at the beginning of this module).

4 Exit Word.

Summary

In this module, you learned how to add a border to a paragraph, change paragraph indentation, insert and format a SmartArt graphic, apply character effects, insert a section break, insert a Word document in an open document, change theme fonts, insert formatted headers and footers, sort lists and tables, modify and format existing Word tables, sum columns in a table, insert a watermark, and change theme fonts.

BTW

Conserving Ink and Toner

If you want to conserve ink or toner, you can instruct Word to print draft quality documents by clicking File on the ribbon to open the Backstage view, clicking the Options tab in the Backstage view to display the Word Options dialog box, clicking Advanced in the left pane (Word Options dialog box), scrolling to the Print area in the right pane, placing a check mark in the 'Use draft quality' check box, and then clicking the OK button. Then, use the Backstage view to print the document as usual.

What decisions will you need to make when creating your next proposal?

Use these guidelines as you complete the assignments in this module and create your own proposals outside of this class.

1. Identify the nature of the proposal.

a) If someone else requests that you develop the proposal, it is solicited. Be sure to include all requested information in a **solicited proposal**.

b) When you write a proposal because you recognize a need, the proposal is unsolicited. With an **unsolicited proposal**, you must gather information you believe will be relevant and of interest to the intended audience.

2. Design an eye-catching title page.

a) The title page should convey the overall message of the sales proposal.

b) Use text, graphics, formats, and colors that reflect the goals of the sales proposal.

c) Be sure to include a title.

3. Compose the text of the sales proposal.

a) Sales proposals vary in length, style, and formality, but all should be designed to elicit acceptance from the reader.

b) The sales proposal should have a neat, organized appearance.

c) A successful sales proposal uses succinct wording and includes lists for textual messages.

d) Write text using active voice, instead of passive voice.

e) Assume that readers of unsolicited sales proposals have no previous knowledge about the topic.

f) Be sure the goal of the proposal is clear.

g) Establish a theme and carry it throughout the proposal.

4. Enhance the sales proposal with appropriate visuals.

a) Use visuals to add interest, clarify ideas, and illustrate points.

b) Visuals include tables, charts, and graphical images (i.e., photos, etc.).

5. Proofread and edit the proposal.

a) Carefully review the sales proposal to be sure it contains no spelling, grammar, mathematical, or other errors.

b) Check that transitions between sentences and paragraphs are smooth. Ensure that the purpose of the proposal is stated clearly.

c) Ask others to review the proposal and give you suggestions for improvements.

Apply Your Knowledge

Reinforce the skills and apply the concepts you learned in this module.

Working with a Table

Note: To complete this assignment, you will be required to use the Data Files. Please contact your instructor for information about accessing the Data Files.

Instructions: Run Word. Open the document called Apply 4–1 Projected College Expenses Draft located on the Data Files. The document contains a Word table that you are to modify. The modified table is shown in Figure 4–79.

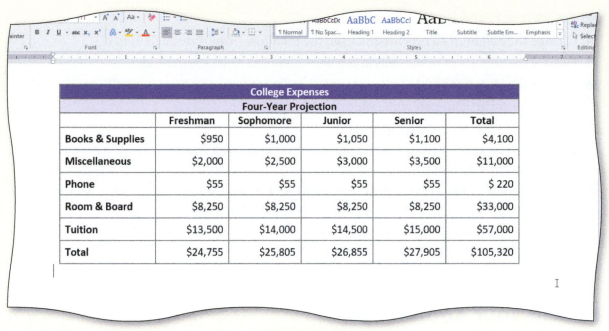

College Expenses					
Four-Year Projection					
	Freshman	Sophomore	Junior	Senior	Total
Books & Supplies	$950	$1,000	$1,050	$1,100	$4,100
Miscellaneous	$2,000	$2,500	$3,000	$3,500	$11,000
Phone	$55	$55	$55	$55	$ 220
Room & Board	$8,250	$8,250	$8,250	$8,250	$33,000
Tuition	$13,500	$14,000	$14,500	$15,000	$57,000
Total	$24,755	$25,805	$26,855	$27,905	$105,320

Figure 4–79

Perform the following tasks:

1. Show gridlines.

2. Delete the blank column between the Junior and Senior columns.

3. Use the Distribute Rows command to evenly space all the rows in the table.

4. Use the Distribute Columns command to make the Freshman, Sophomore, Junior, Senior, and Total columns evenly spaced.

5. Change the width of the Freshman, Sophomore, Junior, Senior, and Total columns to 1".

6. Use the Formula button (Table Tools Layout tab | Data group) to place totals in the bottom row for the Freshman, Sophomore, Junior, and Senior columns. The totals should be formatted to display dollar signs (no cents). *Hint:* You will need to edit the formula and remove the .00 from the end of it.

7. Use the Formula button (Table Tools Layout tab | Data group) to place totals in the right column, also formatted to display dollar signs (no cents). Start in the bottom-right cell and work your way up the column.

8. Add a row to the top of the table. Merge all cells in the first row into a single cell. Enter the title, College Expenses, as the table title. Change the alignment to Align Top Center.

9. Split the cell in the first row into two rows (one column). In the new cell below the title, enter the text, Four-Year Projection, as the subtitle.

10. Shade the first row Purple, Accent 4, Darker 25%. Change the font color of text in the first row to White, Background 1. Shade the second row Purple, Accent 4, Lighter 80%.

11. Add a 1 pt, White, Background 1, Darker 50% border to all cells in the table.

12. Hide gridlines.

13. Change the height of the row containing the year-in-college headings (row 3) to 0.1". Change the alignment of these headings to Align Top Center.

Continued >

Apply Your Knowledge *continued*

14. Change the height of all expense rows and the total row (rows 4 through 9) to 0.3".

15. Change the alignment of the cells in the first column to Align Center Left.

16. Change the alignment of the cells containing dollar amounts to Align Center Right.

17. Center the entire table across the width of the page.

18. Sort the rows containing the expenses.

19. If requested by your instructor, add your last name to the first row of the table before the words, College Expenses.

20. Save the modified file with the file name, Apply 4–1 Projected College Expenses Modified, and submit it (shown in Figure 4–79) in the format specified by your instructor.

21. ✷ Which number format did you use in the Formula dialog box in #6 in this exercise? Why do some totals have a space after the dollar sign and others do not? Which formula appeared in #7?

Extend Your Knowledge

Extend the skills you learned in this module and experiment with new skills. You may need to use Help to complete the assignment.

Using Word's Draw Table Feature

Instructions: Run Word. You will use Word's Draw Table feature to draw a table.

Perform the following tasks:

1. Use Help to learn about Draw Table and text watermarks.

2. Draw the table shown in Figure 4–80. That is, use the Draw Table button to create the blank table.

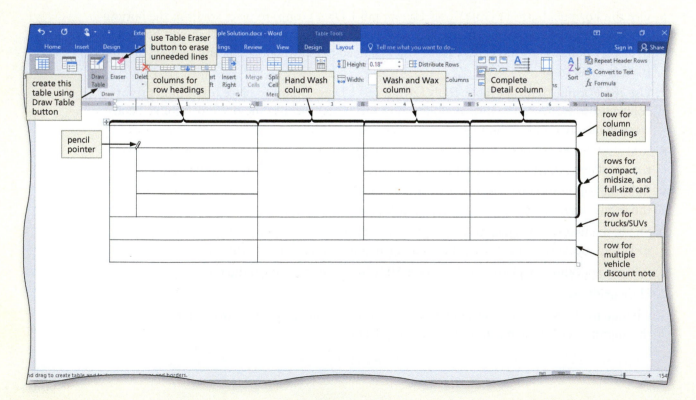

Figure 4–80

3. In the top row, enter these headings in the columns: Type of Vehicle, Hand Wash, Wash and Wax, and Complete Detail.

4. In the leftmost column of the table, enter the text, Car, so that it displays vertically in the cell.

5. In the second column of the table, enter these labels in the second, third, and fourth rows (to the right of the vertical text, Car): Compact, Midsize, and Full-size. Enter these labels in the bottom two leftmost rows: Truck/SUV and Multiple vehicle discount.

6. For the Hand Wash column, enter $50 in the cell to the right of the Compact, Midsize, and Full-size rows.

7. For the Wash and Wax column, use this data for the table: Compact – $100, Midsize - $115, Full-size - $120, and Truck/SUV - $150.

8. For the Complete Detail column, use this data for the table: Compact – $225, Midsize - $250, Full-size - $300, and Truck/SUV - $375.

9. Enter the text, $20 savings per vehicle serviced in a single month!, in the rightmost bottom row.

10. Align and shade table cells, along with any other relevant enhancements, as you deem appropriate (alignment, shading, etc.).

11. If requested by your instructor, enter your name below the table.

12. Save the revised document using the file name, Extend 4–1 Car Wash Table, and then submit it in the format specified by your instructor.

13. ✹ Which alignment and shading for the table cells did you choose and why?

Expand Your World

Create a solution that uses cloud or web technologies by learning and investigating on your own from general guidance.

Using Word Online to Create a Table

Instructions: You are using a mobile device or computer at school that does not have Word but has Internet access. To make use of time between classes, you use Word Online to create a table showing your volunteer service (Figure 4–81).

Perform the following tasks:
1. Run a browser. Search for the text, Word Online, using a search engine. Visit several websites to learn about Word Online. Navigate to the Office Online website. You will need to sign in to your OneDrive account.

2. Create a new blank Word document using Word Online. Name the document Expand 4–1 Volunteer Services. Change the zoom to page width.

3. Enter and format the table, as shown in Figure 4–81.

4. Apply a table style to the table (any style).

5. Change colors of the table to a color other than blue.

6. Remove the First Column shading (Table Tools Layout tab | Table Style Options group).

Continued >

Expand Your World *continued*

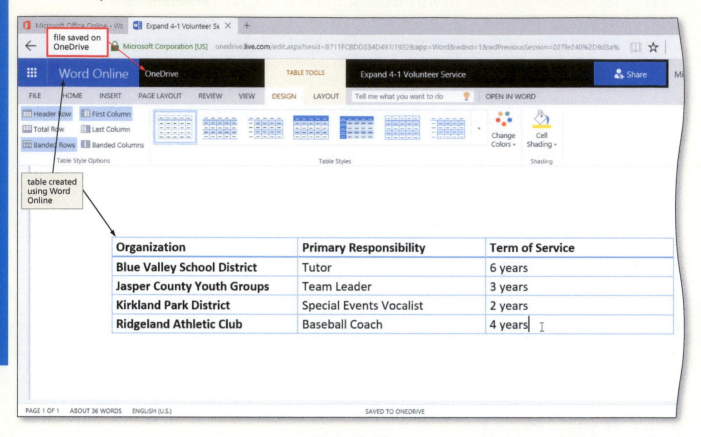

Figure 4–81

7. Narrow the width of the last column to fit the contents better and then change the cell alignment in this column to Align Top Center. How did you adjust the column width?

8. Add a row to the bottom of the table that identifies volunteer service you have performed.

9. Save the document again.

10. Submit the Expand 4–1 Volunteer Service document in the format requested by your instructor. Sign out of your OneDrive account.

11. ✺ Which table features that are covered in the module are not available in Word Online? Answer the question posed in #7.

In the Labs

Design, create, modify, and/or use a document following the guidelines, concepts, and skills presented in this module. Labs 1 and 2, which increase in difficulty, require you to create solutions based on what you learned in the module; Lab 3 requires you to apply your creative thinking and problem-solving skills to design and implement a solution.

Lab 1: **Creating a Proposal with a SmartArt Graphic, a Bulleted List, and a Table**

Note: To complete this assignment, you will be required to use the Data Files. Please contact your instructor for information about accessing the Data Files.

Problem: The owner of Java Junction has hired you to prepare a sales proposal for her coffee shop (Figure 4–82).

Perform the following tasks:

1. Change the document theme to Retrospect.

2. Change the theme fonts to the Tw Cen MT-Rockwell font set.

3. Create the title page as shown in Figure 4–82a. Be sure to do the following:

   a. Insert the SmartArt graphic, add text to it, and bold the text. Change the colors and style of the SmartArt graphic as shown. Change the spacing above the SmartArt graphic to 42 points and the spacing after the graphic to 54 points.

   b. Change the fonts, font sizes, and font colors as specified in the figure. Add the paragraph border. Indent the left and right edges of the title paragraph by 0.25 inches and the left and right edges of the paragraph below the SmartArt graphic by 0.5 inches. Expand the characters in the sentence at the bottom of the page by 7 points.

4. At the bottom of the title page, insert a next page section break. Clear formatting.

5. Create the second page of the proposal as shown in Figure 4–82b.

   a. Format the Heading 1 style as shown and update the Heading 1 style accordingly.

   b. Enter the multilevel list as shown.

   c. Create the table as shown. Border the table as specified. Distribute rows so that they are all the same height. Change the row height to 0.21 inches. Center the table between the margins. Change the first column's alignment to Align Top Left the text, and all other text in the table to Align Top Center. Shade the table cells as specified. Change cell spacing to 0.04 inches between cells.

   d. Insert the formatted footer using the Blank (Three Columns) design. The footer should appear only on the second page (section) of the proposal. Enter the footer text as shown.

   e. If requested by your instructor, change the phone number in the footer to your phone number.

6. Add a picture watermark of the coffee beans. The picture is located on the Data Files. Scale the picture to 50% in the Printed Watermark dialog box.

7. Adjust the spacing above and below paragraphs as necessary to fit all content as shown in the figure.

8. Check the spelling. Save the document with Lab 4–1 Coffee House Proposal as the file name.

9. ✸ This proposal contains a multilevel numbered list. How would you change the font size of the numbers and letters at the beginning of each list item?

Continued >

In the Labs *continued*

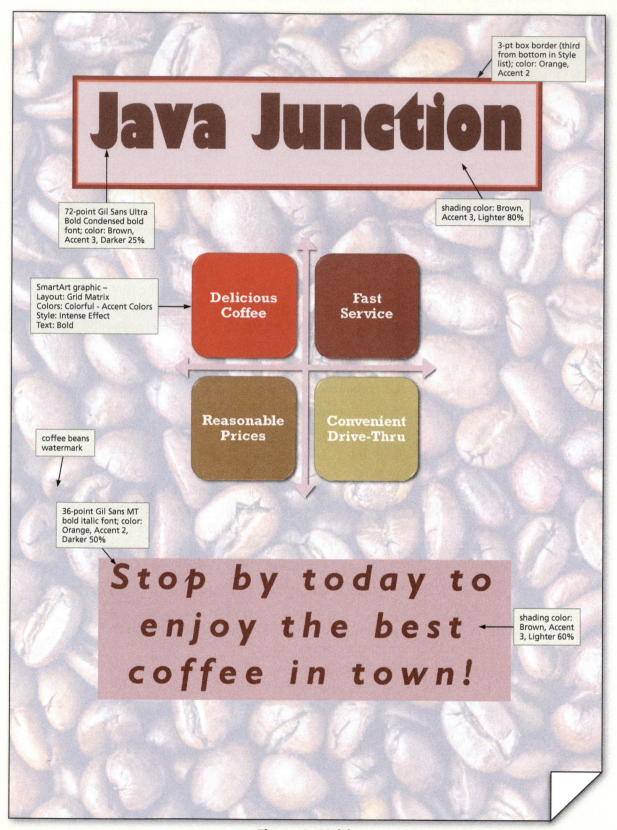

Figure 4–82 (a)

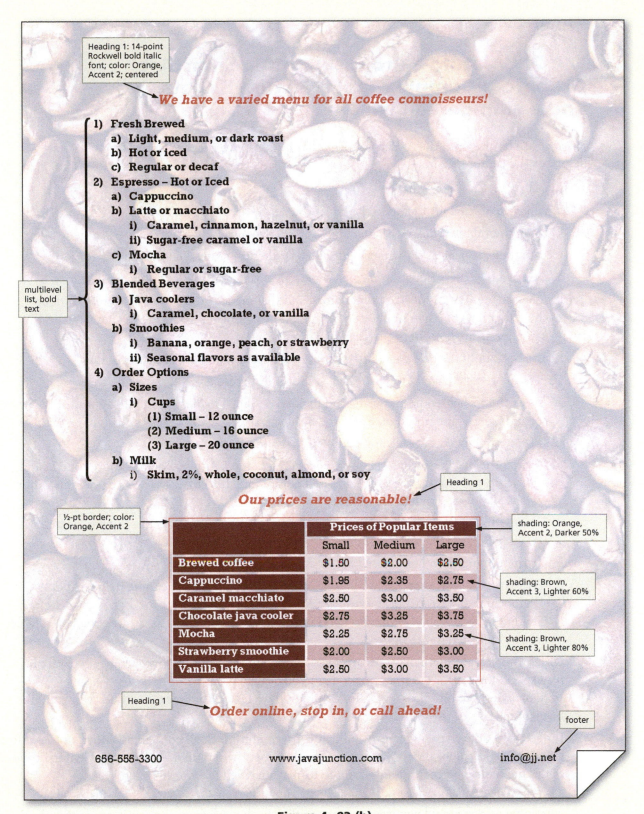

Heading 1: 14-point Rockwell bold italic font; color: Orange, Accent 2; centered

We have a varied menu for all coffee connoisseurs!

1) **Fresh Brewed**
   a) **Light, medium, or dark roast**
   b) **Hot or iced**
   c) **Regular or decaf**
2) **Espresso – Hot or Iced**
   a) **Cappuccino**
   b) **Latte or macchiato**
      i) **Caramel, cinnamon, hazelnut, or vanilla**
      ii) **Sugar-free caramel or vanilla**
   c) **Mocha**
      i) **Regular or sugar-free**
3) **Blended Beverages**
   a) **Java coolers**
      i) **Caramel, chocolate, or vanilla**
   b) **Smoothies**
      i) **Banana, orange, peach, or strawberry**
      ii) **Seasonal flavors as available**
4) **Order Options**
   a) **Sizes**
      i) **Cups**
         (1) **Small – 12 ounce**
         (2) **Medium – 16 ounce**
         (3) **Large – 20 ounce**
   b) **Milk**
      i) **Skim, 2%, whole, coconut, almond, or soy**

multilevel list, bold text

Heading 1

Our prices are reasonable!

½-pt border; color: Orange, Accent 2

shading: Orange, Accent 2, Darker 50%

shading: Brown, Accent 3, Lighter 60%

shading: Brown, Accent 3, Lighter 80%

Prices of Popular Items		
	Small	Medium	Large
Brewed coffee	$1.50	$2.00	$2.50
Cappuccino	$1.95	$2.35	$2.75
Caramel macchiato	$2.50	$3.00	$3.50
Chocolate java cooler	$2.75	$3.25	$3.75
Mocha	$2.25	$2.75	$3.25
Strawberry smoothie	$2.00	$2.50	$3.00
Vanilla latte	$2.50	$3.00	$3.50

Heading 1

Order online, stop in, or call ahead!

footer

656-555-3300   www.javajunction.com   info@jj.net

Figure 4–82 (b)

Continued >

In the Labs *continued*

Lab 2: Creating a Proposal with a SmartArt Graphic, a Complex Table, Picture Bullets, and a Numbered List

Problem: The owner of the A-Plus Tutoring has hired you to prepare a sales proposal that describes the center (Figure 4–83).

Perform the following tasks:

1. Change the document theme to the Facet theme.

2. Change the theme fonts to the Franklin Gothic font set.

3. Create the title page as shown in Figure 4–83a. Be sure to do the following:

   a. Insert the Vertical Equation SmartArt graphic, located in the Relationship category.

   b. Change the fonts, font sizes, font colors, and shading as indicated in the figure. Indent the left and right edges of the title paragraph by 0.5 inches. Expand the characters in the sentence at the bottom of the page by 7 points.

4. At the bottom of the title page, insert a next page section break. Clear formatting.

5. Create the second page of the proposal as shown in Figure 4–83b.

   a. Insert the formatted header using the Banded design. The header should appear only on the second page of the proposal. Enter the header text as shown.

   b. If requested by your instructor, add your name to the header.

   c. Format the headings using the heading styles specified. Adjust spacing before the Heading 1 style to 18 point and after to 6 point, and before the Heading 2 style to 12 point and after to 6 point. Update both heading styles.

   d. Create the bulleted list using the picture bullets shown (search for the keyword, star, or use the image on the Data Files).

   e. Create the multilevel numbered list as shown.

   f. Create the table as shown. Distribute rows so that they are all the same height (about 0.29"). Align center all text except the row headings, which should be set to Align Center Left. Center the table. Change the direction of the Weekdays heading as shown. Shade the table cells as indicated in the figure.

6. Create a text watermark of 10 occurrences of the text, A+, with each occurrence separated by a space. In the Printed Watermark dialog box, change the watermark to 48-point Verdana with a semitransparent color of Blue-Gray, Text 2, Lighter 60%. The layout should be diagonal.

7. If necessary, adjust spacing above and below paragraphs to fit all content as shown in the figure. Check the spelling of the proposal. Save the document with Lab 4–2 Tutoring Center Proposal as the file name and then submit it in the format specified by your instructor.

8. ✸ This proposal contains a text watermark, which is semitransparent by default. For what type of text would you want to remove the check mark from the semitransparent check box?

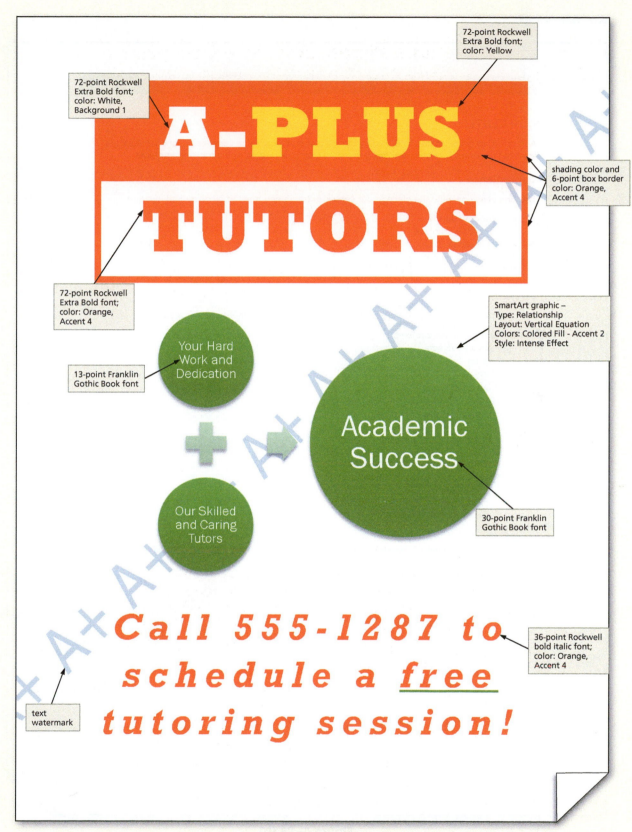

Figure 4–83 (a)

Continued >

In the Labs continued

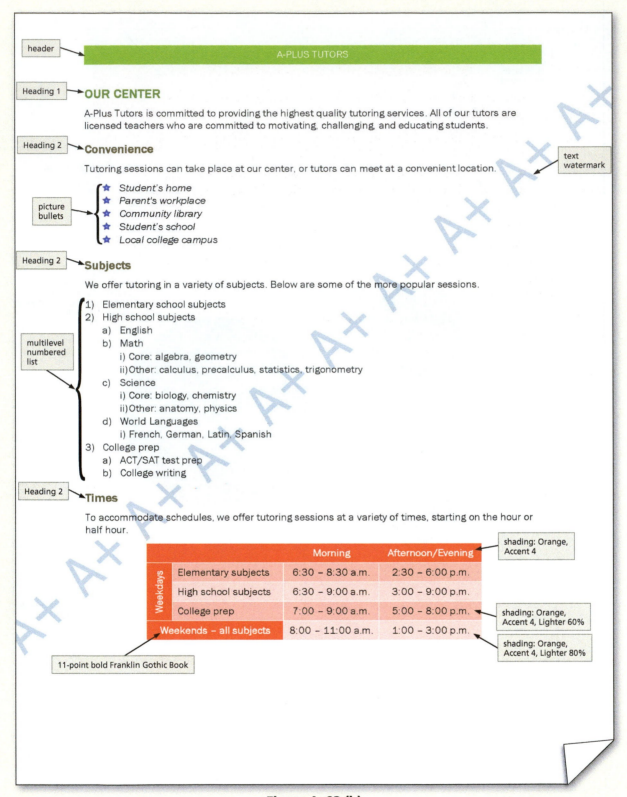

Figure 4–83 (b)

Lab 3: **Consider This: Your Turn**

Create a Proposal for a Small Business

Note: To complete this assignment, you will be required to use the Data Files. Please contact your instructor for information about accessing the Data Files.

Problem: As a part-time employee at a local deli, you have been asked to design a multipage sales proposal that can be distributed in the community.

Part 1:   The proposal should contain a title page, followed by a page of information about the deli. The title page is to contain the deli name, Deli Delicious, formatted with a border and shading. Include an appropriate SmartArt graphic that contains these words, at a minimum: fresh ingredients, reasonable prices, fast service, and dine in or carry out. Include this text on the title page: Stop by, call ahead, or order online!

The source content for the second page of the proposal is in a file called Lab 4–3 Consider This Your Turn Deli Draft. Use the concepts and techniques presented in this module to create and format the sales proposal. Include an appropriate watermark. Be sure to check the spelling and grammar of the finished document. Submit your assignment in the format specified by your instructor.

Part 2:   ✳ You made several decisions while creating the sales proposal in this assignment: how to organize and format the title page (fonts, font sizes, colors, shading, styles, etc.), which SmartArt graphic to use on the title page, and how to organize and format the tables and lists. What was the rationale behind each of these decisions? When you proofread the document, what further revisions did you make and why?

5 Using a Template to Create a Resume and Sharing a Finished Document

Objectives

You will have mastered the material in this module when you can:

- Use a template to create a document
- Change document margins
- Personalize a document template
- Indent a paragraph
- Customize theme fonts
- Create and modify a style
- Insert a building block
- Save a Word document as a PDF file and edit a PDF file

- Run the compatibility checker
- Enable others to access a document on OneDrive
- Send a Word document using email
- Save a Word document as a webpage
- Format text as a hyperlink
- Change a style set

Introduction

Some people prefer to use their own creative skills to design and compose Word documents. Using Word, for example, you can develop the content and decide the location of each item in a document. On occasion, however, you may have difficulty composing a particular type of document. To assist with the task of creating certain types of documents, such as resumes and letters, Word provides templates. A **template** is similar to a form with prewritten text; that is, Word prepares the requested document with text and/or formatting common to all documents of this nature. After Word creates a document from a template, you fill in the blanks or replace prewritten words in the document.

Once you have created a document, such as a resume, you often share it with others electronically via email, webpages, or links.

Project — Resume

At some time, you will prepare a resume to send to prospective employers. In addition to some personal information, a **resume** usually contains the applicant's educational background and job experience. Employers review many resumes for each vacant position. Thus, you should design your resume carefully so that it presents you as the best candidate for the job.

The project in this module follows generally accepted guidelines for creating resumes and uses Word to create the resume shown in Figure 5–1. The resume for Nina Tamaya Yazzie, an upcoming graduate of a journalism program, uses a Word template to present relevant information to a potential employer.

2640 Bartlett Street
Ponrolet, MI 66589
872-555-1547 (cell)
nyazzie@world.net

NINA TAMAYA YAZZIE

OBJECTIVE To obtain a full-time reporter position with a broadcasting station in the Midwest.

EDUCATION **B.A. JOURNALISM – HARTFORD COLLEGE**
December 2017, GPA 3.92/4.00

- Dean's List, every semester
- Student Publications Award, May 2017
- *Civics Journal*, 1st Place, political perspective article
- Areas of concentration:
  Broadcast reporting
  Intercultural communications
  Mass media
  Newswriting

A.A. TECHNICAL WRITING – WHEATON COMMUNITY COLLEGE
December 2015, GPA 3.94/4.00

EXPERIENCE **ASSISTANT COORDINATOR – PONROLET COMMUNITY CENTER**
August 2016 – Present

Assist in developing programs designed to increase literacy and reading skills; conduct reading programs for children; compose, proofread, and edit monthly newsletter.

MEMBERSHIPS Alpha Kappa Omega National Honor Society

Literacy Council, Ponrolet Village Board

Student Government Association, Secretary

COMMUNITY SERVICE **READING BUDDY – PONROLET PARK DISTRICT**
October 2016 – Present

Volunteer eight hours a week at the local community center in the district's Reading Buddy program, which works to develop reading skills of children in elementary school.

Figure 5–1

In this module, you will learn how to create the resume shown in Figure 5–1. The following roadmap identifies general activities you will perform as you progress through this module:

1. **CREATE** a new resume **DOCUMENT FROM** a Word **TEMPLATE**.

2. **MODIFY AND FORMAT** the resume **TEMPLATE**.

3. **SAVE** the resume **DOCUMENT IN OTHER FORMATS** so that you can share it with others.

4. **MAKE** the resume **DOCUMENT AVAILABLE ONLINE** so that others can access it.

5. **CREATE** a **WEBPAGE FROM** the resume **WORD DOCUMENT**.

6. **FORMAT** the resume **WEBPAGE**.

To Run Word and Change Word Settings

If you are using a computer to step through the project in this module and you want your screens to match the figures in this book, you should change your screen's resolution to 1366 × 768. The following steps run Word, display formatting marks, and change the zoom to page width.

1 Run Word and create a blank document in the Word window. If necessary, maximize the Word window.

2 If the Print Layout button on the status bar is not selected (shown in Figure 5–4), click it so that your screen is in Print Layout view.

3 If the 'Show/Hide ¶' button (Home tab | Paragraph group) is not selected already, click it to display formatting marks on the screen.

4 To display the page the same width as the document window, if necessary, click the Page Width button (View tab | Zoom group).

BTW
Touch Screen Differences
The Office and Windows interfaces may vary if you are using a touch screen. For this reason, you might notice that the function or appearance of your touch screen differs slightly from this module's presentation.

Using a Template to Create a Resume

Although you could compose a resume in a blank document window, this module shows how to use a template instead, where Word formats the resume with appropriate headings and spacing. You then customize the resume that the template generated by filling in blanks and by selecting and replacing text.

To Create a New Document from an Online Template

1 CREATE DOCUMENT FROM TEMPLATE | 2 MODIFY & FORMAT TEMPLATE | 3 SAVE DOCUMENT IN OTHER FORMATS
4 MAKE DOCUMENT AVAILABLE ONLINE | 5 CREATE WEBPAGE FROM WORD DOCUMENT | 6 FORMAT WEBPAGE

Word has a variety of templates available online to assist you with creating documents. Available online templates include agendas, award certificates, calendars, expense reports, greeting cards, invitations, invoices, letters, meeting minutes, memos, resumes, and statements. When you select an online template, Word downloads (or copies) it from the Office.com website to your computer or mobile device. Many of the templates use the same design or style. *Why? If you create related documents, such as a resume and a cover letter, you can use the same template design or style so that the documents complement one another.* The following steps create a resume using the Basic resume (Timeless design) template.

1

- Click File on the ribbon to open the Backstage view and then click the New tab in the Backstage view to display the New gallery, which initially lists several featured templates.

- Type **resume** in the 'Search for online templates' box and then click the Start searching button to display a list of online resume templates.

- If necessary, scroll through the list of templates to display the Basic resume (Timeless design) thumbnail (Figure 5–2).

Q&A Can I select a template from the Word start screen that appears when I initially run Word? Yes, instead of selecting Blank document from the Word start screen, you can select any of the available templates.

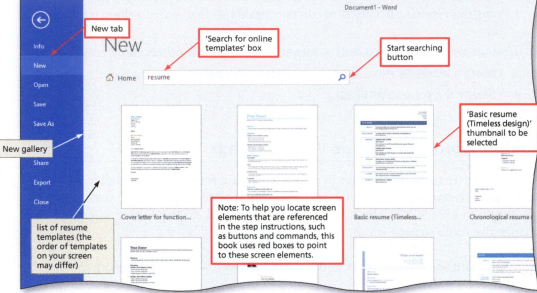

Figure 5–2

2

- Click the 'Basic resume (Timeless design)' thumbnail to select the template and display it in a preview window (Figure 5–3).

Experiment

- Click the Back and Forward buttons on the sides of the preview window to view previews of other templates. When finished, display the 'Basic resume (Timeless design)' thumbnail in the preview window.

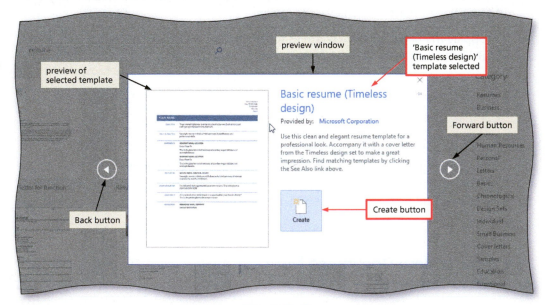

Figure 5–3

Q&A What if I cannot locate the Basic resume (Timeless design) template?
Exit the Backstage view and then proceed to the steps called To Open a Document Created from a Template that are shaded yellow and immediately follow these steps.

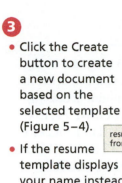

3
- Click the Create button to create a new document based on the selected template (Figure 5–4).
- If the resume template displays your name instead of the text, YOUR NAME, as shown in Figure 5–4, click the Undo button on the Quick Access Toolbar to reset the content control (content controls are discussed in the next section).

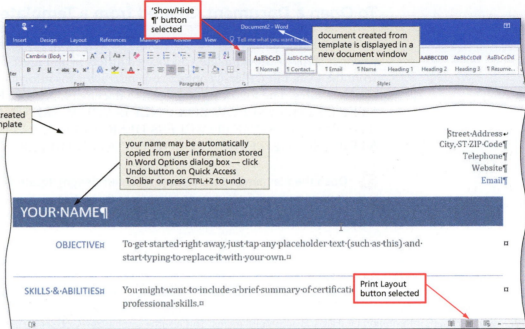

Figure 5–4

4
- If requested by your instructor, print the resume template so that you can see the entire resume created by the resume template using the Basic resume (Timeless design) (Figure 5–5).

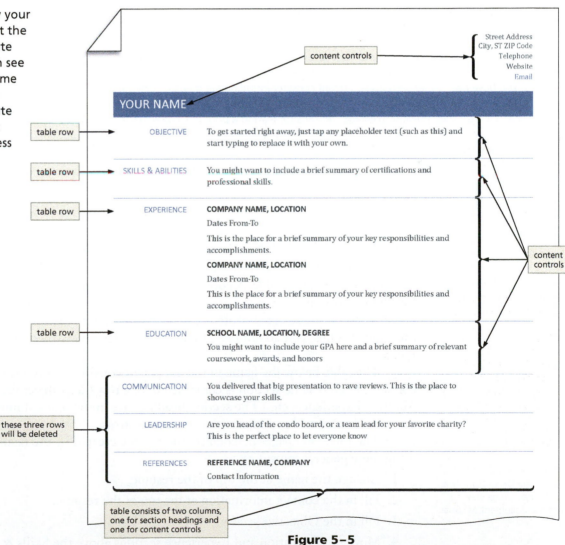

Figure 5–5

To Open a Document Created from a Template

If you are unable to locate the Basic resume (Timeless design) template in the previous steps or the template you located differs from Figure 5–5, you can open it from the Data Files. Please contact your instructor for information about accessing the Data Files. The following step opens a document. NOTE: PERFORM THE STEP IN THIS YELLOW BOX ONLY IF YOU WERE UNABLE TO LOCATE THE BASIC RESUME (TIMELESS DESIGN) TEMPLATE IN THE PREVIOUS STEPS OR THE TEMPLATE YOU LOCATED DIFFERS FROM FIGURE 5–5.

 1 Open the file named Basic resume (Timeless design), located on the Data Files, from your hard drive, OneDrive, or other storage location.

CONSIDER THIS

How do you craft a successful resume?

Two types of resumes are the chronological resume and the functional resume. A chronological resume sequences information by time, with the most recent listed first. This type of resume highlights a job seeker's job continuity and growth. A functional resume groups information by skills and accomplishments. This resume emphasizes a job seeker's experience and qualifications in specialized areas. Some resumes use a combination of the two formats. For an entry-level job search, experts recommend a chronological resume or a combination of the two types of resumes.

When creating a resume, be sure to include necessary information and present it appropriately. Keep descriptions concise, using action words and bulleted lists.

- **Include necessary information.** Your resume should include contact information, a clearly written objective, educational background, and experience. Use your legal name and mailing address, along with your phone number and email address, if you have one. Other sections you might consider including are memberships, skills, recognitions and awards, and/or community service. Do not include your Social Security number, marital status, age, height, weight, gender, physical appearance, health, citizenship, previous pay rates, reasons for leaving a prior job, current date, high-school information (if you are a college graduate), and references. Employers assume you will provide references, if asked, and this information simply clutters a resume.

- **Present your resume appropriately.** For printed resumes, use a high-quality ink-jet or laser printer to print your resume on standard letter-sized white or ivory paper. Consider using paper that contains cotton fibers for a professional look.

BTW

Conserving Ink and Toner

If you want to conserve ink or toner, you can instruct Word to print draft quality documents by clicking File on the ribbon to open the Backstage view, clicking the Options tab in the Backstage view to display the Word Options dialog box, clicking Advanced in the left pane (Word Options dialog box), scrolling to the Print area in the right pane, placing a check mark in the 'Use draft quality' check box, and then clicking the OK button. Then, use the Backstage view to print the document as usual.

Resume Template

The resume created from the template, shown in Figure 5–5, contains several content controls and a table. A **content control** is an object that contains instructions for filling in text and graphics. To select a content control, you click it. As soon as you begin typing in the selected content control, your typing replaces the instructions in the control. Thus, you do not need to delete the selected instructions before you begin typing.

The table below the name in the document consists of seven rows and two columns. Each resume section is contained in one row (i.e., Objective, Skills & Abilities, Experience, etc.) The section headings are in the first column, followed by the second column that contains the content controls.

The following pages personalize the resume created by the resume template using these general steps:

1. Change the name at the top of the resume.
2. Fill in the contact information at the top of the resume.
3. Fill in the Objective section.
4. Move the Education and Experience sections above the Skills & Abilities section.

5. Fill in the Education and Experience sections.

6. Change the Skills & Abilities heading to Memberships and fill in this section.

7. Add a row for the Community Service section and fill in this section.

8. Delete the last three unused rows.

To Change Theme Colors

Recall that Word provides document themes, which contain a variety of color schemes and other effects. This resume uses the Aspect theme colors. The following steps change the theme colors.

① Click Design on the ribbon to display the Design tab.

② Click the Themes Colors button (Design tab | Document Formatting group) to display the Theme Colors gallery.

③ Scroll to and then click Aspect in the Theme Colors gallery to change the theme colors to the selected theme.

BTW

The Ribbon and Screen Resolution
Word may change how the groups and buttons within the groups appear on the ribbon, depending on the computer or mobile device's screen resolution. Thus, your ribbon may look different from the ones in this book if you are using a screen resolution other than 1366 x 768.

To Set Custom Margins

1 CREATE DOCUMENT FROM TEMPLATE | 2 MODIFY & FORMAT TEMPLATE | 3 SAVE DOCUMENT IN OTHER FORMATS
4 MAKE DOCUMENT AVAILABLE ONLINE | 5 CREATE WEBPAGE FROM WORD DOCUMENT | 6 FORMAT WEBPAGE

The resume template selected in this project uses .75-inch top, bottom, left, and right margins. You prefer slightly wider margins for the top, left, and right edges of the resume and a smaller bottom margin. *Why? You do not want the text to run so close to the top edge and sides of the page and do not want the resume to spill to a second page.* In earlier modules, you changed the margins by selecting predefined settings in the Margins gallery. The margins you will use for the resume in this module, however, are not predefined. Thus, the next steps set custom margins.

①

• Display the Layout tab.

• Click the Adjust Margins button (Layout tab | Page Setup group) to display the Margins gallery (Figure 5–6).

 What is the difference between the Custom Margins setting and the Custom Margins command?
The Custom Margins setting applies the most recent custom margins to the current document, whereas the Custom Margins command displays the Custom Margins dialog box so that you can specify new margin settings.

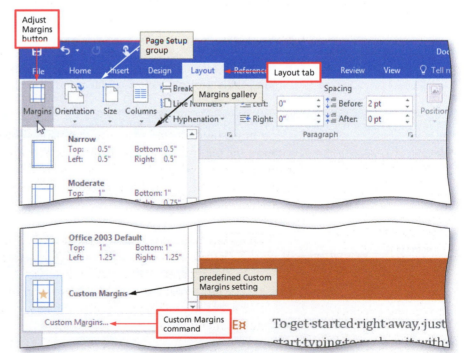

Figure 5–6

- Click Custom Margins in the Margins gallery to display the Page Setup dialog box. If necessary, click the Margins tab (Page Setup dialog box) to display the Margins sheet.

- Type **1** in the Top box to change the top margin setting and then press the TAB key to position the insertion point in the Bottom box.

- Type **.5** in the Bottom box to change the bottom margin setting and then press the TAB key to position the insertion point in the Left box.

- Type **1** in the Left box to change the left margin setting and then press the TAB key to position the insertion point in the Right box.

- Type **1** in the Right box to change the right margin setting (Figure 5–7).

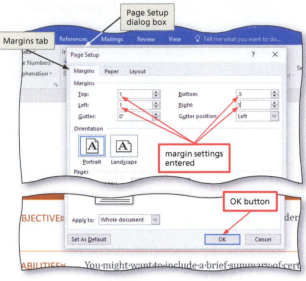

Figure 5–7

3

- Click the OK button to set the custom margins for this document.

Other Ways
1. Drag margin boundaries on ruler

To View Gridlines

When tables contain no borders, such as those in this resume, it can be difficult to see the individual cells in the table. To help identify the location of cells, you can display gridlines, which show cell outlines on the screen. The following steps show gridlines.

1 Scroll the document up, if desired. Position the insertion point in any table cell (in this case, the cell containing the Objective heading).

2 Display the Table Tools Layout tab.

3 If it is not selected already, click the 'View Table Gridlines' button (Table Tools Layout tab | Table group) to show gridlines in the table (Figure 5–8).

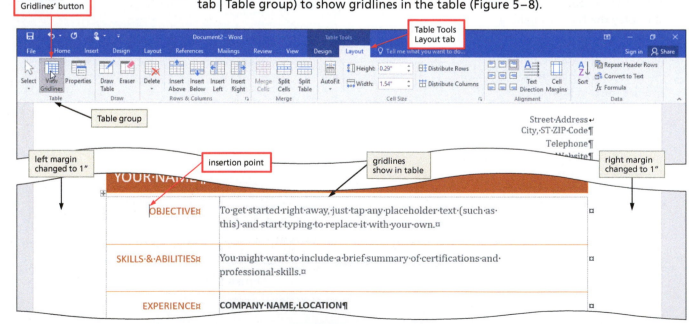

Figure 5–8

To Modify a Content Control and Replace Its Placeholder Text

1 CREATE DOCUMENT FROM TEMPLATE | 2 MODIFY & FORMAT TEMPLATE | 3 SAVE DOCUMENT IN OTHER FORMATS
4 MAKE DOCUMENT AVAILABLE ONLINE | 5 CREATE WEBPAGE FROM WORD DOCUMENT | 6 FORMAT WEBPAGE

The next step is to select the Your Name content control that the template inserted in the resume, increase its font size slightly, and replace its placeholder text with the job seeker's name. Word uses **placeholder text** to indicate where text can be typed. To replace placeholder text in a content control, you select the content control and then type.

The Your Name content control on your resume may already contain your name. *Why? Word copies the user name from the Word Options dialog box and places it in the Your Name content control. Note that if your name appears instead of the text, YOUR NAME, the following steps may execute differently.* The next steps modify a content control and replace its placeholder text.

• Click the content control to be modified (in this case, the Your Name content control) to select it.

Q&A How can I tell if a content control is selected?
The appearance of selected content controls varies. When you select some content controls, they are surrounded by a rectangle. Selected content controls also may have a name that is attached to the top, and/or a tag that is attached to its upper-left corner. You can drag a tag to move a content control from one location to another. With other content controls, the text inside the content control appears selected as shown in Figure 5–9.

• If necessary, click the content control name (in this case, the words Your Name) to select the contents of the content control (Figure 5–9).

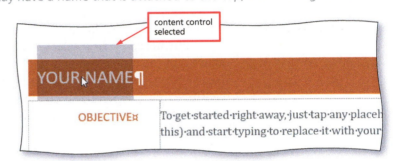

Figure 5–9

• Click the 'Increase Font Size' button (Home tab | Font group) to increase the font size of the text in the selected content control to the next font size (Figure 5–10).

Q&A What if my font size does not change?
You may need to modify the style: right-click the Name style in the Styles gallery, click Modify on the shortcut menu, change the font size to 18 (Modify Style dialog box), and then click the OK button.

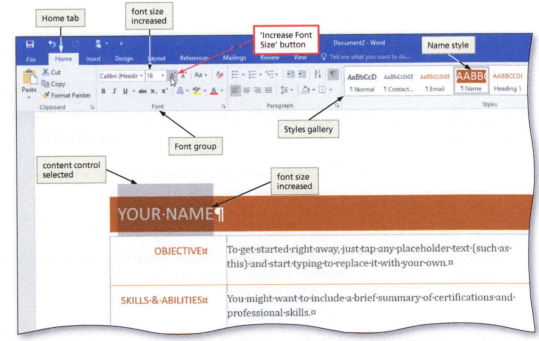

Figure 5–10

• Type **Nina Tamaya Yazzie** to replace the content control with the job seeker's name (Figure 5–11).

If requested by your instructor, enter your name instead of the job seeker's name shown in Figure 5–11.

Q&A Why does the text appear in uppercase letters even though I type in lowercase letters?
This content control includes formatting that displays the text in uppercase letters.

Figure 5–11

To Replace Placeholder Text in More Content Controls

The next step is to select the Contact Info, Telephone, and Email content controls in the upper-right corner of the resume and replace their placeholder text with personal information. Because you do not have a website, you will leave the website contact control as is and delete it in later steps. The following steps replace the placeholder text in content controls.

❶ Click the Contact Info content control to select it (Figure 5–12).

Figure 5–12

❷ Type **2640 Bartlett Street** as the street address, press the ENTER key, and then type **Ponrolet, MI 66589** as the city, state, and ZIP code.

❸ Click the Telephone content control to select it and then type **872-555-1547 (cell)** as the cell phone number.

❹ Click the Email content control to select it and then type **nyazzie@world.net** as the email address.

To Delete a Content Control

1 CREATE DOCUMENT FROM TEMPLATE | **2 MODIFY & FORMAT TEMPLATE** | 3 SAVE DOCUMENT IN OTHER FORMATS
4 MAKE DOCUMENT AVAILABLE ONLINE | 5 CREATE WEBPAGE FROM WORD DOCUMENT | 6 FORMAT WEBPAGE

The following steps delete the Website content control. *Why?* *You do not have a website.*

1

- Click the Website content control to select it.

- Right-click the selected content control to display a shortcut menu (Figure 5–13).

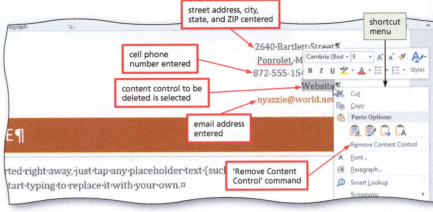

Figure 5–13

2

- Click 'Remove Content Control' on the shortcut menu to delete the selected content control, which also deletes the placeholder text contained in the content control.

- Press the DELETE key to remove the blank line between the phone number and the email address (Figure 5–14).

3

- Save the title page on your hard drive, OneDrive, or other storage location using the file name, Yazzie Resume.

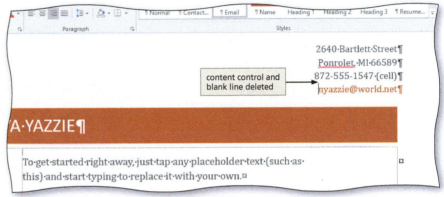

Figure 5–14

Q&A

Why should I save the resume at this time?
You have performed many tasks while creating this resume and do not want to risk losing work completed thus far.

Other Ways

1. With content control selected, click Cut button (Home tab | Clipboard group)

2. With content control selected, press CTRL+X or DELETE or BACKSPACE

To Move Table Rows

1 CREATE DOCUMENT FROM TEMPLATE | 2 MODIFY & FORMAT TEMPLATE | 3 SAVE DOCUMENT IN OTHER FORMATS
4 MAKE DOCUMENT AVAILABLE ONLINE | 5 CREATE WEBPAGE FROM WORD DOCUMENT | 6 FORMAT WEBPAGE

In the resume, you would like the Education and Experience sections immediately below the Objective section, in that order. *Why? You want to emphasize your educational background and experience.* Thus, the next step is to move rows in the resume. Each row contains a separate section in the resume. You will move the row containing the Education section below the row containing the Objective section. Then, you will move the row containing the Experience section so that it is below the moved row containing the Education section.

You use the same procedure to move table rows as to move text. That is, select the rows to move and then drag them to the desired location. The following steps use drag-and-drop editing to move table rows.

1

- Display the View tab. Click the 100% button (View tab | Zoom group) to display the resume at 100 percent zoom in the document window.

- Scroll so that the Objective, Experience, and Education sections appear in the document window at the same time.

2

- Select the row to be moved, in this case, the row containing the Education section.

- Position the pointer in the selected row, press and hold down the mouse button and then drag the insertion point to the location where the selected row is to be moved (Figure 5–15).

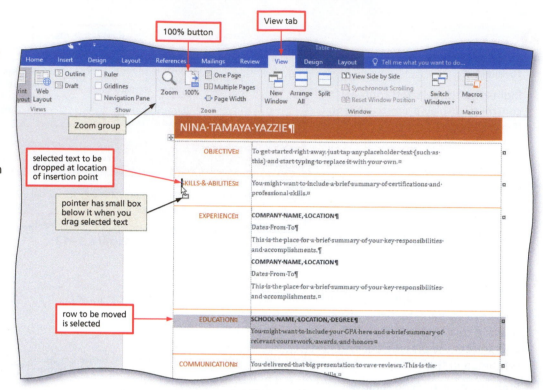

Figure 5–15

3

- Release the mouse button to move the selected row to the location of the insertion point (Figure 5–16).

Q&A What if I accidentally drag text to the wrong location?
Click the Undo button on the Quick Access Toolbar and try again.

What if I am using a touch screen?
If you have a stylus,

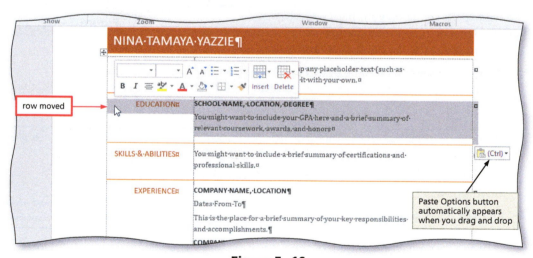

Figure 5–16

you can follow Steps 1 through 3 using the stylus. If you are using your finger, you will need to use the cut-and-paste technique: tap to position the insertion point in the row to be moved, tap the Select Table button (Table Tools Layout tab | Table group), and then tap Select Row; press the selection to display the mini toolbar and then tap the Cut button on the mini toolbar to remove the row; tap to position the insertion point at the location where you want to move the row; display the Home tab and then tap the Paste button (Home tab | Clipboard group) to place the row at the location of the insertion point.

- Repeat Steps 2 and 3 to move the row containing the Experience section so that it is positioned below the row containing the Education section (Figure 5–17).

- Click anywhere to remove the selection.

- Change the zoom to page width.

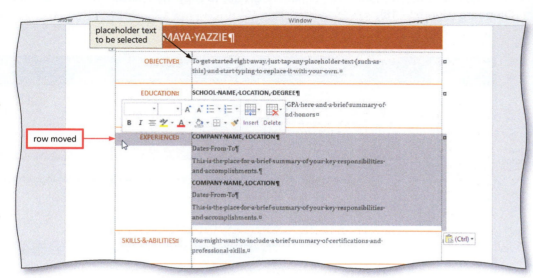

Figure 5–17

Other Ways

1. Click Cut button (Home tab | Clipboard group), click where text or object is to be pasted, click Paste button (Home tab | Clipboard group)

2. Right-click selected text, click Cut on shortcut menu or mini toolbar, right-click where text or object is to be pasted, click 'Keep Source Formatting' on shortcut menu (or, if using touch, tap Paste on mini toolbar)

3. Press CTRL+X, position insertion point where text or object is to be pasted, press CTRL+V

To Modify Text in a Content Control

The following steps select the Objective content control in the resume and then replace its placeholder text with personal information.

1 If necessary, scroll to display the Objective section of the resume in the document window.

2 In the Objective section of the resume, click the placeholder text that begins, 'To get started…', in the Objective content control (shown in Figure 5–17) to select it.

3 Type the objective: `To obtain a full-time reporter position with a broadcasting station in the Midwest.`

BTW

Insert Controls
The content controls in some templates contain an Insert Control, which allows you to duplicate text in the control. Because the template used in the module does not contain an Insert Control, you copy and paste items to duplicate them. Lab 2 in the student assignments at the end of this module uses a template that contains an Insert Control.

To Copy and Paste Items in a Table Cell

1 CREATE DOCUMENT FROM TEMPLATE | **2 MODIFY & FORMAT TEMPLATE** | 3 SAVE DOCUMENT IN OTHER FORMATS
4 MAKE DOCUMENT AVAILABLE ONLINE | 5 CREATE WEBPAGE FROM WORD DOCUMENT | 6 FORMAT WEBPAGE

In the resume, you copy the school name information in the Education section so that it appears twice in the table cell containing the Education content control. *Why? You would like to add two degrees to the resume.* The following steps copy and paste text in a cell.

1

- Select the text to be copied (in this case, all of the text in the Education content control).

- Display the Home tab.

- Click the Copy button (Home tab | Clipboard group) to copy the selected item in the table cell to the Office Clipboard (Figure 5–18).

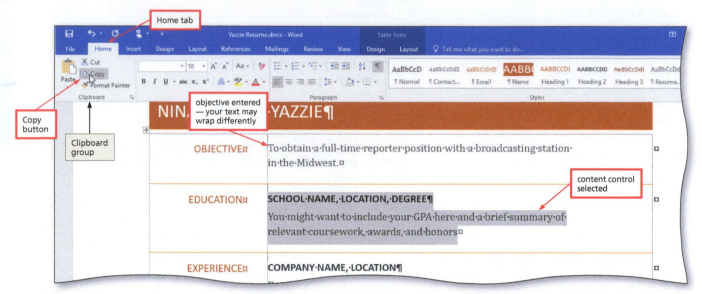

Figure 5–18

2

- Position the insertion point at the end of the text in the Education content control (that is, after the s in honors) and then press the ENTER key to place the insertion point at the location where the copied item should be pasted.

- Click the Paste button (Home tab | Clipboard group) to paste the copied item in the document at the location of the insertion point (Figure 5–19).

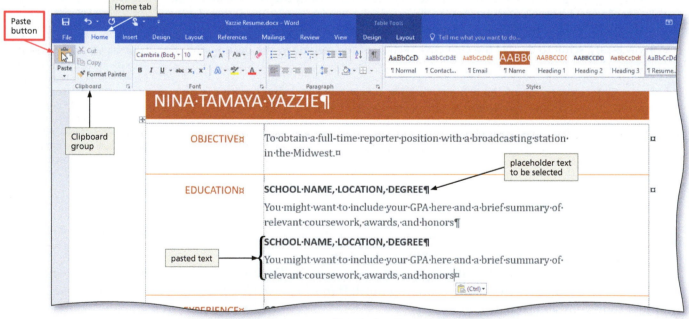

Figure 5–19

Q&A | What if I click the Paste arrow by mistake?

Click the Paste arrow again to remove the Paste menu and repeat Step 2.

Other Ways

1. Click Copy on shortcut menu (or, if using touch, tap Copy on mini toolbar), right-click where item is to be pasted, click 'Keep Source Formatting' in Paste Options area on shortcut menu (or, if using touch, tap Paste on mini toolbar)

2. Select item, press CTRL+C, position insertion point at paste location, press CTRL+V

To Replace Placeholder Text in a Content Control

The next step is to begin to enter text in the Education section of the resume. The following step replaces placeholder text.

1 In the Education section of the resume, select the placeholder text, SCHOOL NAME, LOCATION, DEGREE, in the first content control (shown in Figure 5–19) and then type **B.A. JOURNALISM - HARTFORD COLLEGE** as the degree and school name (shown in Figure 5–20).

To Use AutoComplete

1 CREATE DOCUMENT FROM TEMPLATE | **2 MODIFY & FORMAT TEMPLATE** | 3 SAVE DOCUMENT IN OTHER FORMATS
4 MAKE DOCUMENT AVAILABLE ONLINE | 5 CREATE WEBPAGE FROM WORD DOCUMENT | 6 FORMAT WEBPAGE

As you begin typing, Word may display a ScreenTip that presents a suggestion for the rest of the word or phrase you are typing. **Why?** *With its **AutoComplete** feature, Word predicts the word or phrase you are typing and displays its prediction in a ScreenTip.* If the AutoComplete prediction is correct, you can instruct Word to finish your typing with its prediction, or you can ignore Word's prediction. Word draws its AutoComplete suggestions from its dictionary and from AutoText entries you create and save in the Normal template.

The following steps use the AutoComplete feature as you type the graduation date in the Education section of the resume.

1

- In the Education section of the resume, click the placeholder text that begins, 'You might want to…', in the first content control and then type **Dece** and notice the AutoComplete ScreenTip that appears on the screen (Figure 5–20).

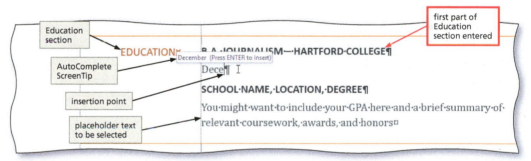

Figure 5–20

Q&A Why would my screen not display the AutoComplete ScreenTip?

Depending on previous Word entries, you may need to type more characters in order for Word to predict a particular word or phrase accurately. Or, you may need to turn on AutoComplete by clicking File on the ribbon to open the Backstage view, clicking the Options tab in the Backstage view to display the Word Options dialog box, clicking Advanced in the left pane (Word Options dialog box), placing a check mark in the 'Show AutoComplete suggestions' check box, and then clicking the OK button.

2

- Press the ENTER key to instruct Word to finish your typing with the word or phrase that appeared in the AutoComplete ScreenTip.

Q&A What if I do not want to use the text proposed in the AutoComplete ScreenTip?

Simply continue typing and the AutoComplete ScreenTip will disappear from the screen.

3

- Press the SPACEBAR. Type **2017, GPA 3.92/4.00** and then press the ENTER key (Figure 5–21).

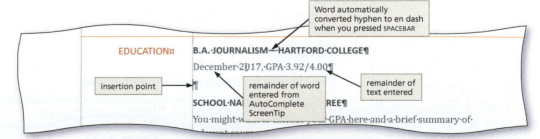

Figure 5–21

To Enter More Text

The following steps continue entering text in the Education section of the resume.

1 Type **Dean's List, every semester** and then press the ENTER key.

2 Type **Student Publications Award, May 2017** and then press the ENTER key.

3 Type **Civics Journal, 1st Place, political perspective article** and then italicize the journal title.

4 Bullet the three paragraphs just entered (Figure 5–22).

BTW
AutoFormat
Word automatically formats quotation marks, dashes, lists, fractions, ordinals, and other items, depending on your typing and settings. To check if an AutoFormat option is enabled, click File on the ribbon to open the Backstage view, click the Options tab in the Backstage view, click Proofing in the left pane (Word Options dialog box), click the AutoCorrect Options button, click the 'AutoFormat As You Type' tab (AutoCorrect dialog box), select the appropriate check boxes, and then click the OK button in each open dialog box.

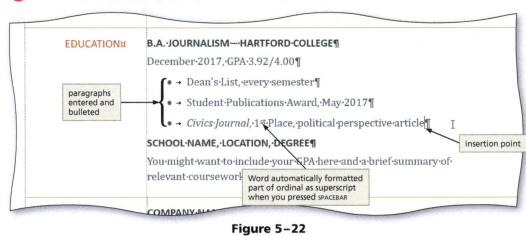

Figure 5–22

To Enter a Line Break

The next step in personalizing the resume is to enter the areas of concentration in the Education section. You want only the first line, which says, Areas of concentration:, to begin with a bullet. If you press the ENTER key on subsequent lines, Word automatically will carry forward the paragraph formatting, which includes the bullet. Thus, you will not press the ENTER key between each line. Instead, you will create a line break. *Why? A line break advances the insertion point to the beginning of the next physical line, ignoring any paragraph formatting.* The following steps enter the areas of concentration using a line break, instead of a paragraph break, between each line.

• With the insertion point positioned as shown in Figure 5–22, press the ENTER key.

• If necessary, turn off italics. Type **Areas of concentration:** and then press SHIFT+ENTER to insert a line break character and move the insertion point to the beginning of the next physical line (Figure 5–23).

Figure 5–23

2

- Type **Broadcast reporting** and then press SHIFT+ENTER.

- Type **Intercultural communications** and then press SHIFT+ENTER.

- Type **Mass media** and then press SHIFT+ENTER.

- Type **Newswriting** as the last entry. Do not press SHIFT+ENTER at the end of this line (Figure 5–24).

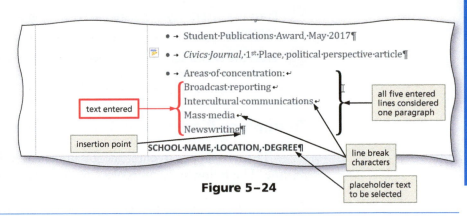

Figure 5–24

To Replace Placeholder Text in Content Controls

The next step is to enter the information for the second degree in the Education section of the resume. The following steps replace placeholder text.

1 In the Education section of the resume, select the placeholder text, SCHOOL NAME, LOCATION, DEGREE, in the second content control (shown in Figure 5–24) and then type **A.A. TECHNICAL WRITING – WHEATON COMMUNITY COLLEGE** as the degree and school name.

2 Select the placeholder text that begins, 'You might want to…', in the second content control and then type **December 2015, GPA 3.94/4.00** (Figure 5–25).

BTW

Line Break Characters
A line break character is a formatting mark that indicates a line break at the end of the line. Like paragraph marks, tab characters, and other formatting marks, line break characters do not print.

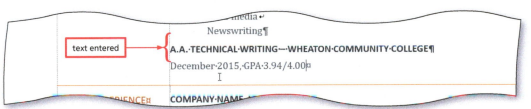

Figure 5–25

To Delete Text

The following steps delete text from the Experience content control. *Why? You have only one job experience entry for the resume.*

1 Select the text to delete (in this case, the entire second job experience entry in the Experience section) (Figure 5–26).

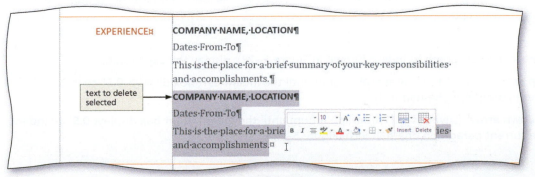

Figure 5–26

2 Press the DELETE key to delete the second job experience entry from the content control.

3 Press the BACKSPACE key to remove the blank line below the remaining item in the content control (shown in Figure 5–27).

To Replace Placeholder Text in Content Controls

The next step is to enter the job information for the Experience section of the resume. The following steps replace placeholder text.

1 In the Experience section of the resume, select the placeholder text, COMPANY NAME, LOCATION, in the content control and then type **ASSISTANT COORDINATOR – PONROLET COMMUNITY CENTER** as the job title and company name.

2 Select the placeholder text that begins 'Dates From...' in the content control and then type **August 2016 – Present** as the dates. Press the SPACEBAR so that the hyphen changes to an en dash.

3 Select the placeholder text that begins 'This is the place...' in the content control and then type this text (Figure 5–27): **Assist in developing programs designed to increase literacy and reading skills; conduct reading programs for children; compose, proofread, and edit monthly newsletter.**

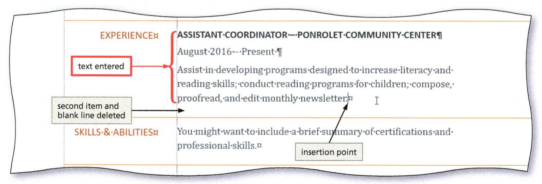

Figure 5–27

To Indent a Paragraph

1 CREATE DOCUMENT FROM TEMPLATE | **2 MODIFY & FORMAT TEMPLATE** | 3 SAVE DOCUMENT IN OTHER FORMATS
4 MAKE DOCUMENT AVAILABLE ONLINE | 5 CREATE WEBPAGE FROM WORD DOCUMENT | 6 FORMAT WEBPAGE

In the resume, the lines below the job start date and end date that contain the job responsibilities are to be indented. *Why? You believe the responsibilities would be easier to read if they are indented.* The following step indents the left and right edges of a paragraph.

- With the insertion point in the paragraph to indent (shown in Figure 5–27), display the Layout tab.

- Click the Indent Left up arrow (Layout tab | Paragraph group) until the Indent Left box displays 0.5" to indent the left margin of the current paragraph one-half inch.

- Click the Indent Right down arrow (Layout tab | Paragraph group) until the Indent Right box displays 0.5" to indent the right margin of the current paragraph one-half inch (Figure 5–28).

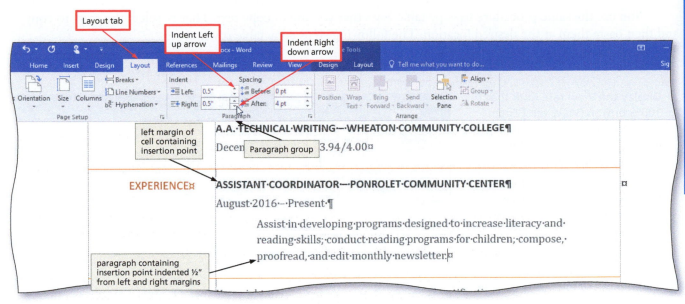

Figure 5–28

Other Ways

1. Drag Left Indent/Right Indent marker on horizontal ruler

2. For left margin, click Increase Indent button (Home tab | Paragraph group)

3. Click Paragraph Dialog Box Launcher (Home tab | Paragraph group), click Indents and Spacing tab (Paragraph dialog box), set indentation in Left/Right boxes, click OK button

4. Right-click text (or, if using touch, tap 'Show Context Menu' button on mini toolbar), click Paragraph on shortcut menu, click Indents and Spacing tab (Paragraph dialog box), set indentation in Left/Right boxes, click OK button

5. For left margin, press CTRL+M

To Replace Placeholder Text in Content Controls

The next step is to enter the membership information. You will replace the text in the Skills & Abilities section with membership information. The following steps replace placeholder text.

1 Select the text, SKILLS & ABILITIES, and then type **MEMBERSHIPS** as the new section heading.

2 In the Memberships section, select the placeholder text that begins, 'You might want…', in the content control and then type **Alpha Kappa Omega National Honor Society** and then press the ENTER key.

3 Type **Literacy Council, Ponrolet Village Board** and then press the ENTER key.

4 Type **Student Government Association, Secretary** as the final item in this section (shown in Figure 5–29).

To Copy and Paste a Table Item

1 CREATE DOCUMENT FROM TEMPLATE | **2 MODIFY & FORMAT TEMPLATE** | 3 SAVE DOCUMENT IN OTHER FORMATS
4 MAKE DOCUMENT AVAILABLE ONLINE | 5 CREATE WEBPAGE FROM WORD DOCUMENT | 6 FORMAT WEBPAGE

The next section of the resume in this module is the Community Service section, which is organized exactly like the Experience section. Thus, you copy the Experience section and paste it below the Memberships section. **Why?** *It will be easier to edit the Experience section rather than format the Community Service section from scratch.*

You use the same procedure to copy table rows that you use to copy text. That is, select the rows to copy and then paste them at the desired location. The following steps copy table rows.

- Display the View tab. Click the 100% button (View tab | Zoom group) to display the resume at 100 percent zoom in the document window.

- If necessary, scroll so that the Experience and Memberships sections appear in the document window at the same time.

- Select the row to be copied, in this case, the row containing the Experience section in the resume.

- Display the Home tab.

- Click the Copy button (Home tab | Clipboard group) to copy the selected row in the document to the Office Clipboard (Figure 5–29).

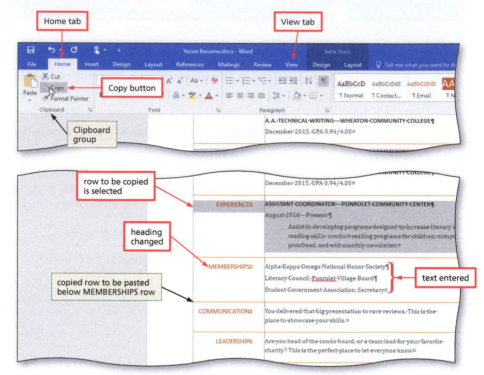

Figure 5–29

- Position the insertion point at the location where the copied row should be pasted, in this case, to the left of the M in the Memberships heading.

- Click the Paste arrow (Home tab | Clipboard group) to display the Paste gallery.

Q&A What if I click the Paste button by mistake?
Click the Undo button on the Quick Access Toolbar and then try again.

- Point to the 'Insert as New Rows' button in the Paste gallery to display a live preview of that paste option applied to the row in the table (Figure 5–30).

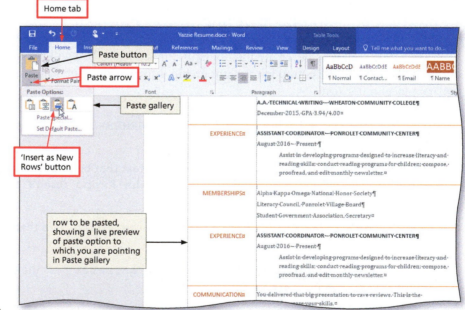

Figure 5–30

 **Experiment**

- Point to the four options in the Paste gallery and watch the format of the pasted row change in the document window.

3
- Click the 'Insert as New Rows' button in the Paste gallery to apply the selected option to the pasted table row because you want the pasted row to use the same formatting as the copied row.
- Change the zoom to page width.

Other Ways

1. Right-click selected item, click Copy on mini toolbar or shortcut menu, right-click where item is to be pasted, click desired option in Paste Options area on shortcut menu
2. Select item, press CTRL+C, position insertion point at paste location, press CTRL+V

To Delete Rows and Edit Text

Because you will not be using the last three rows of the resume template, the next step is to delete them and then enter the remainder of the text in the resume, that is, the Community Service section. The following steps delete rows and edit text.

1 If necessary, display the Table Tools Layout tab.

2 Select the last three rows of the table (Communication, Leadership, and References), which might appear on a second page, click the Delete Table button (Table Tools Layout tab | Rows & Columns group), and then click Delete Rows on the Delete Table menu.

3 Below the Memberships heading, select the text, EXPERIENCE, and then type **COMMUNITY SERVICE** as the new section heading.

4 In the Community Service section of the resume, select the text, ASSISTANT COORDINATOR, and then type **READING BUDDY** to replace the text.

5 Select the text, COMMUNITY CENTER, and then type **PARK DISTRICT** to replace the text.

6 Select the text, August, and then type **October** to replace the month.

7 Select the indented paragraph of text and then type this text (Figure 5–31):
Volunteer eight hours a week at the local community center in the district's Reading Buddy program, which works to develop reading skills of children in elementary school.

8 Save the resume again on the same storage location with the same file name.

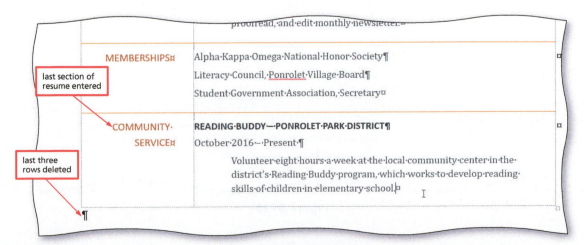

Figure 5–31

To Customize Theme Fonts

Recall that a font set defines one font for headings in a document and another font for body text. This resume currently uses the Calibri-Cambria font set, which specifies the Calibri font for the headings and the Cambria font for body text. The resume in this module creates a customized font set (theme font). *Why?* *You want the headings to use the Berlin Sans FB Demi font and the body text to use the Bookman Old Style font.* The following steps create a customized theme font set with the name, Resume Text.

- Display the Design tab.
- Click the Theme Fonts button (Design tab | Document Formatting group) to display the Theme Fonts gallery (Figure 5–32).

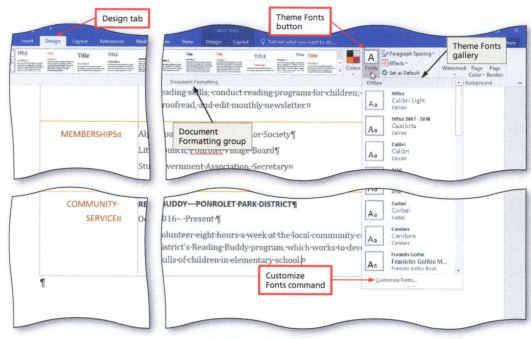

Figure 5–32

- Click Customize Fonts in the Theme Fonts gallery to display the Create New Theme Fonts dialog box.
- Click the Heading font arrow (Create New Theme Fonts dialog box); scroll to and then click 'Berlin Sans FB Demi' (or a similar font).
- Click the Body font arrow; scroll to and then click 'Bookman Old Style' (or a similar font).
- Type **Resume Text** in the Name text box as the name for the new theme font (Figure 5–33).

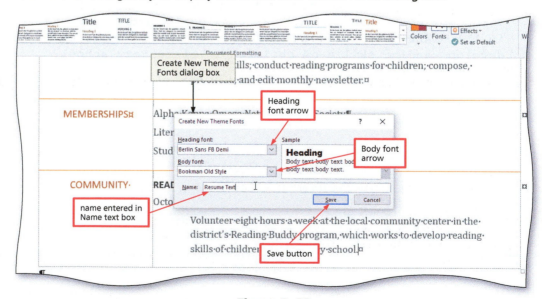

Figure 5–33

- Click the Save button (Create New Theme Fonts dialog box) to create the customized theme font with the entered name (Resume Text, in this case) and apply the new heading fonts to the current document (Figure 5–34).

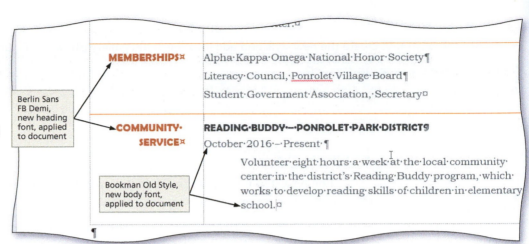

Figure 5–34

To Create a Style

1 CREATE DOCUMENT FROM TEMPLATE | 2 MODIFY & FORMAT TEMPLATE | 3 SAVE DOCUMENT IN OTHER FORMATS
4 MAKE DOCUMENT AVAILABLE ONLINE | 5 CREATE WEBPAGE FROM WORD DOCUMENT | 6 FORMAT WEBPAGE

Recall that a style is a predefined set of formats that appears in the Styles gallery. You have used styles in the Styles gallery to apply formats to text and have updated existing styles. You also can create your own styles.

The next task in this project is to create a style for the section headings in the resume. *Why? To illustrate creating a style, you will increase the font size of a section heading and save the new format as a style. Then, you will apply the newly defined style to the remaining section headings.* The following steps format text and then create a style based on the formats in the selected paragraph.

- Position the insertion point in the Memberships heading, display the Home tab, and then click the 'Increase Font Size' button (Home tab | Font group) to increase the font size of the heading.

- Click the More button (shown in Figure 5–36) in the Styles gallery (Home tab | Styles group) to expand the gallery (Figure 5–35).

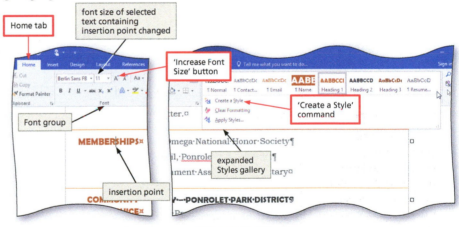

Figure 5–35

- Click 'Create a Style' in the Styles gallery to display the Create New Style from Formatting dialog box.

- Type **Resume Headings** in the Name text box (Create New Style from Formatting dialog box) (Figure 5–36).

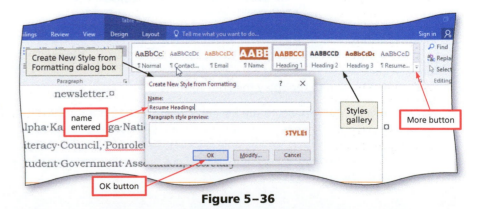

Figure 5–36

- Click the OK button to create the new style and add it to the Styles gallery (shown in Figure 5–37).

Q&A | How can I see the style just created?
If the style name does not appear in the in-ribbon Styles gallery, click the More button in the Styles gallery (Home tab | Styles group) to display the expanded Styles gallery.

To Apply a Style

The next step is to apply the style just created to the other section headings in the resume. The following step applies a style.

1. One at a time, position the insertion point in the remaining section headings (Objective, Education, Experience, and Community Service) and then click Resume Headings in the Styles gallery to apply the selected style to each heading.

To Reveal Formatting

1 CREATE DOCUMENT FROM TEMPLATE | 2 MODIFY & FORMAT TEMPLATE | 3 SAVE DOCUMENT IN OTHER FORMATS
4 MAKE DOCUMENT AVAILABLE ONLINE | 5 CREATE WEBPAGE FROM WORD DOCUMENT | 6 FORMAT WEBPAGE

Sometimes, you want to know what formats were applied to certain text items in a document. *Why? For example, you may wonder which font, font size, font color, and other effects were applied to the degree and job titles in the resume.* To display formatting applied to text, use the Reveal Formatting task pane. The following steps open and then close the Reveal Formatting task pane.

- Position the insertion point in the text for which you want to reveal formatting (in this case, the degree name in the Education section).

- Press SHIFT+F1 to open the Reveal Formatting task pane, which shows formatting applied to the location of the insertion point in (Figure 5–37).

🔎 Experiment

- Click the Font collapse button to hide the Font formats. Click the Font expand button to redisplay the Font formats.

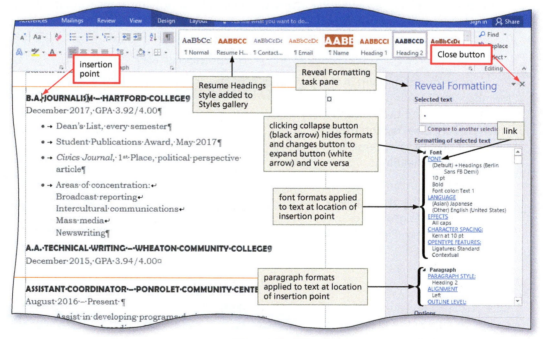

Figure 5–37

Q&A | Why do some of the formats in the Reveal Formatting task pane appear as links?
Clicking a link in the Reveal Formatting task pane displays an associated dialog box, allowing you to change the format of the current text. For example, clicking the Font link in the Reveal Formatting task pane would display the Font dialog box. If you made changes in the Font dialog box and then clicked the OK button, Word would change the format of the current text.

2

- Close the Reveal Formatting task pane by clicking its Close button.

To Modify a Style Using the Styles Dialog Box

The next step is to modify the Heading 2 style. *Why? The degree and job names in the resume currently have a different font than the other text in the resume. You prefer that all text in the resume use the same font.* Thus, the following steps modify a style.

❶

- Right-click the style name to modify in the Styles gallery (Heading 2 in this case) (Home tab | Styles group) to display a shortcut menu (Figure 5–38).

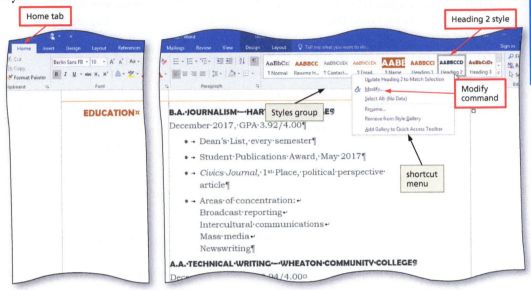

Figure 5–38

❷

- Click Modify on the shortcut menu to display the Modify Style dialog box.

- Click the Font arrow (Modify Style dialog box) and then click Bookman Old Style in the Font gallery to change the font of the current style.

- Place a check mark in the Automatically update check box so that any future changes you make to the style in the document will update the current style automatically (Figure 5–39).

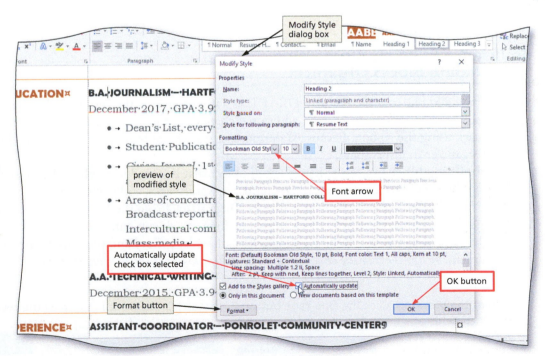

Figure 5–39

Q&A What is the purpose of the Format button in the Modify Style dialog box?

If the formatting you wish to change for the style is not available in the Modify Style dialog box, you can click the Format button and then select the desired command after you click the Format button to display a dialog box that contains additional formatting options.

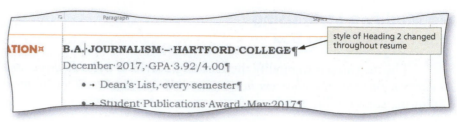

3

- Click the OK button to close the dialog box and apply the style changes to the paragraphs in the document (Figure 5–40).

- Save the resume again on the same storage location with the same file name.

Figure 5–40

- If requested by your instructor, print the finished resume (shown in Figure 5–1).

Other Ways
1. Click Styles Dialog Box Launcher (Home tab | Styles group), click arrow to right of style to modify, click Modify on menu, change settings (Modify Style dialog box), click OK button   2. Click Styles Dialog Box Launcher, click Manage Styles button, scroll to style and then select it (Manage Styles dialog box), click Modify button, change settings (Modify Style dialog box), click OK button in each dialog box

Break Point: If you wish to take a break, this is a good place to do so. You can exit Word now. To resume at a later time, run Word, open the file called Yazzie Resume, and continue following the steps from this location forward.

Sharing a Document with Others

You may want to share Word documents with others electronically, such as via email, USB flash drive, or cloud storage. To ensure that others can read and/or open the files successfully, Word provides a variety of formats and tools to assist with sharing documents. This section uses the Yazzie Resume created in this module to present a variety of these formats and tools.

To Insert a Building Block Using the Building Blocks Organizer

1 CREATE DOCUMENT FROM TEMPLATE | 2 MODIFY & FORMAT TEMPLATE | 3 **SAVE DOCUMENT IN OTHER FORMATS**
4 MAKE DOCUMENT AVAILABLE ONLINE | 5 CREATE WEBPAGE FROM WORD DOCUMENT | 6 FORMAT WEBPAGE

You would like to place the text, DRAFT, as a watermark on the resume before you share it, so that others are aware you might be making additional changes to the document. In an earlier module, you inserted a watermark using the ribbon. Because watermarks are a type of building block, you also can use the Building Blocks Organizer to insert them.

A **building block** is a reusable formatted object that is stored in a gallery. Examples of building blocks include cover pages, headers, footers, page numbers, watermarks, and text boxes. You can see a list of every available building block in the **Building Blocks Organizer**. From the Building Blocks Organizer, you can sort building blocks, change their properties, or insert them in a document.

The next steps sort the Building Blocks Organizer by gallery and then insert the Draft 1 building block in the document. **Why?** *Sorting the building blocks by gallery makes it easier to locate them.*

- Display the View tab. Click the One Page button (View tab | Zoom group) to display the resume in its entirety in the document window.

- Display the Insert tab.

- Click the 'Explore Quick Parts' button (Insert tab | Text group) to display the Explore Quick Parts menu (Figure 5–41).

Figure 5–41

2

- Click 'Building Blocks Organizer' on the Explore Quick Parts menu to display the Building Blocks Organizer dialog box.

Experiment

- Drag the scroll bars in the Building Blocks Organizer so that you can look at all the columns and rows in the dialog box.

- Click the Gallery heading (Building Blocks Organizer dialog box) in the building blocks list to sort the building blocks by gallery (Figure 5–42).

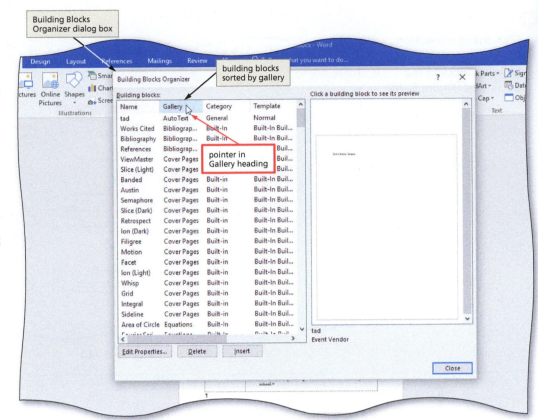

Figure 5–42

Experiment

- Click various names in the building blocks list and notice that a preview of the selected building block appears in the dialog box.

3

- Scroll through the building blocks list to the Watermarks group in the Gallery column and then click DRAFT 1 to select this building block (Figure 5–43).

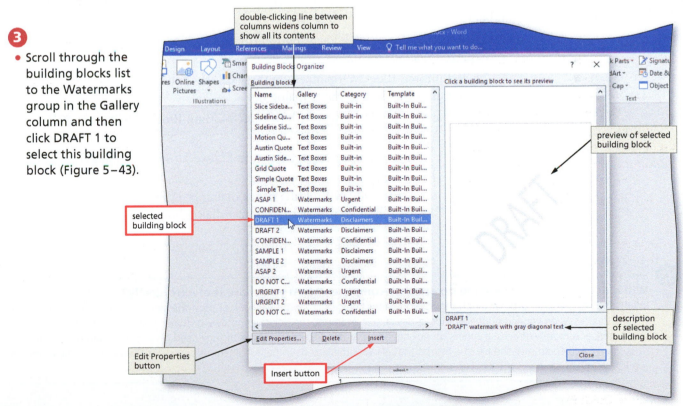

Figure 5–43

4

• Click the Insert button to insert the selected building block in the document (Figure 5–44).

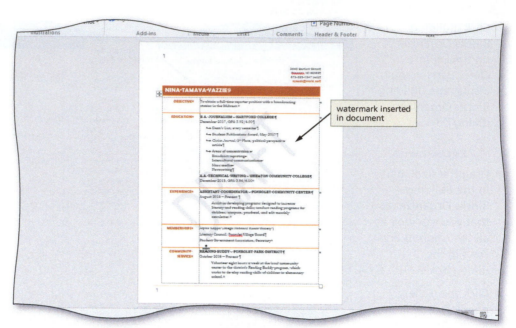

watermark inserted in document

Figure 5–44

TO EDIT PROPERTIES OF BUILDING BLOCK ELEMENTS

Properties of a building block include its name, gallery, category, description, location where it is saved, and how it is inserted in the document. If you wanted to change any of these building block properties for a particular building block, you would perform these steps.

1. Click the 'Explore Quick Parts' button (Insert tab | Text group) to display the Explore Quick Parts menu.

2. Click 'Building Blocks Organizer' on the Explore Quick Parts menu to display the Building Blocks Organizer dialog box.

3. Select the building block you wish to edit (Building Blocks Organizer dialog box).

4. Click the Edit Properties button (shown in Figure 5–43) to display the Modify Building Block dialog box.

5. Edit any property (Modify Building Block dialog box) and then click the OK button. Close the Building Blocks Organizer dialog box.

CONSIDER THIS

Will a document look the same on another computer when you share it electronically?

When sharing a Word document with others, you cannot be certain that it will look or print the same on their computers or mobile devices as on your computer or mobile device. For example, the document may wordwrap text differently on others' computers and mobile devices. If others do not need to edit the document (that is, if they need only to view and/or print the document), you could save the file in a format that allows others to view the document as you see it. Two popular such formats are PDF and XPS.

To Save a Word Document as a PDF File and View the PDF File in Adobe Reader

PDF, which stands for Portable Document Format, is a file format created by Adobe Systems that shows all elements of a printed document as an electronic image. Users can view a PDF file without the software that created the original document. Thus, the PDF format enables users to share documents with others easily. To view, navigate, and print a PDF file, you use an application called **Adobe Reader**, which can be downloaded free from Adobe's website.

When you save a Word document as a PDF file, the original Word document remains intact; that is, Word creates a copy of the file in the PDF format. The following steps save the Yazzie Resume Word document as a PDF file and then open the Yazzie Resume PDF file in Adobe Reader. *Why? You want to share the resume with others but want to ensure it looks the same on their computer or mobile device as it does on yours.*

1

- Open the Backstage view and then click the Export tab in the Backstage view to display the Export gallery.

- If necessary, click 'Create PDF/ XPS Document' in the left pane of the Export gallery to display information about creating PDF/ XPS documents in the right pane (Figure 5–45).

Q&A Why does the left pane of my Export gallery have an additional command related to creating an Adobe PDF?
Depending on your installation settings in Adobe, you may have an additional tab on your ribbon and/or additional commands in galleries, etc., related to Adobe functionality.

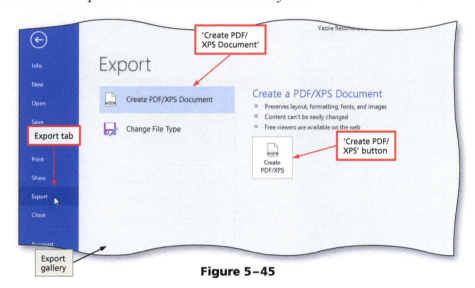

Figure 5–45

2

- Click the 'Create PDF/XPS' button in the right pane to display the Publish as PDF or XPS dialog box.

- Navigate to the desired save location (Publish as PDF or XPS dialog box).

Q&A Can the file name be the same for the Word document and the PDF file?
Yes. The file names can be the same because the file types are different: one is a Word document and the other is a PDF file.

- If necessary, click the 'Save as type' arrow and then click PDF.

- If necessary, place a check mark in the 'Open file after publishing' check box so that Word will display the resulting PDF file in Adobe Reader (Figure 5–46).

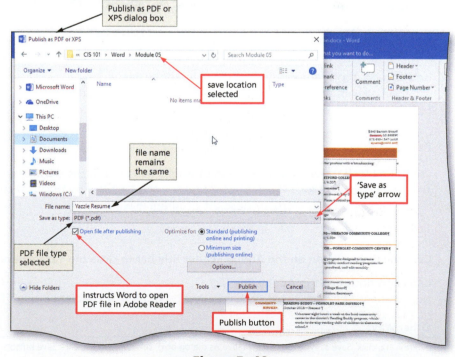

Figure 5–46

Why is my 'Open file after publishing' check box dimmed?
You do not have Adobe Reader installed on your computer. Use a search engine, such as Google, to search for the text, get adobe reader. Then, click the link in the search results to download Adobe Reader and follow the on-screen instructions to install the program. After installing Adobe Reader, repeat these steps.

3

- Click the Publish button to create the PDF file from the Word document and then, because the check box was selected, open the resulting PDF file in Adobe Reader.

- If necessary, click the Maximize button in the Adobe Reader window to maximize the window (Figure 5–47).

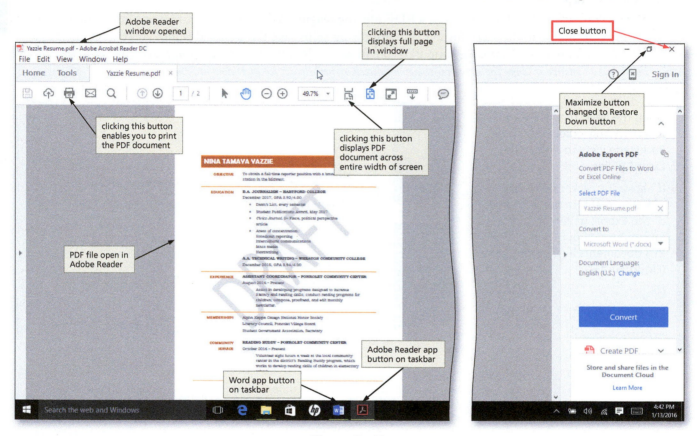

Figure 5–47

Do I have to display the resulting PDF file in Adobe Reader?
No. If you do not want to display the document in Adobe Reader, you would not place a check mark in the 'Open file after publishing' check box in the Publish as PDF or XPS dialog box (shown in Figure 5–46).

Is the Yazzie Resume Word document still open?
Yes. Word still is running with the Yazzie Resume document opened.

What if a blank screen appears instead of Adobe Reader or if the document appears in a different program?
You may not have Adobe Reader installed. Press the Start key on the keyboard to redisplay the Start screen and then navigate back to Word, or close the program in which the document opened.

4

- Click the Close button on the Adobe Reader title bar to close the Yazzie Resume.pdf file and exit Adobe Reader.

Can I edit documents in Adobe Reader?
No, you need Adobe Acrobat or some other program that enables editing of PDF files.

Other Ways

1. Press F12, click 'Save as type' box arrow (Save As dialog box), select PDF in list, click Save button

To Open a PDF File from Word

When you use Word to open a PDF file, Word converts it to an editable document. *Why? You may want to change the contents of a PDF file.* The editable PDF file that Word creates from the PDF file may appear slightly different from the PDF due to the conversion process. To illustrate this feature, the next steps open the PDF file just saved.

1

- Open the Backstage view and then click the Open tab in the Backstage view to display the Open gallery.

- Click OneDrive, This PC, or another location in the left pane that references the location of the saved PDF file, click the Browse button, and then navigate to the location of the PDF file to be opened.

- If necessary, click the File Types arrow to display a list of file types that can be opened by Word (Figure 5–48).

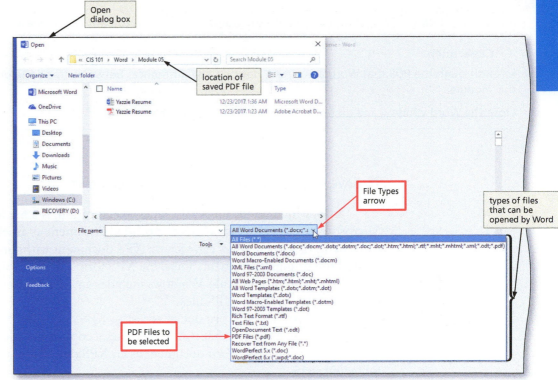

Figure 5–48

 Q&A Why does the PDF file already appear in my list?
If the file type is All Word Documents, Word displays all file types that it can open in the file list.

2

- Click PDF Files in the File Types list, so that Word displays PDF file names in the dialog box.

- Click Yazzie Resume to select the PDF file to be opened (Figure 5–49).

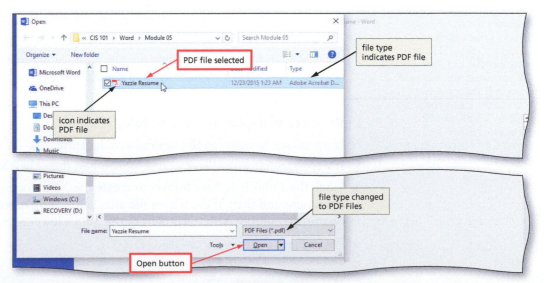

Figure 5–49

- Click the Open button (Open dialog box) to open the selected file and display the opened document in the Word window.

- If Word displays a dialog box indicating it will begin converting the document, click its OK button.

- If necessary, click the Print Layout button on the status bar to switch to Print Layout view.

 **Experiment**

- Scroll through the PDF that Word converted, noticing any differences between it and the original resume created in this module.

- Close the Word window and do not save this converted PDF file.

TO SAVE A WORD DOCUMENT AS AN XPS DOCUMENT

XPS, which stands for XML Paper Specification, is a file format created by Microsoft that shows all elements of a printed document as an electronic image. As with the PDF format, users can view an XPS document without the software that created the original document. Thus, the XPS format also enables users to share documents with others easily. Windows includes an XPS Viewer, which enables you to view, navigate, and print XPS files.

When you save a Word document as an XPS document, the original Word document remains intact; that is, Word creates a copy of the file in the XPS format. If you wanted to save a Word document as an XPS document, you would perform the following steps.

BTW

Distributing a Document

Instead of printing and distributing a hard copy of a document, you can distribute the document electronically. Options include sending the document via email; posting it on cloud storage (such as OneDrive) and sharing the file with others; posting it on social media, a blog, or other website; and sharing a link associated with an online location of the document. You also can create and share a PDF or XPS image of the document, so that users can view the file in Adobe Reader or XPS Viewer instead of in Word.

1. Open the Backstage view and then click the Export tab in the Backstage view to display the Export gallery.

2. Click 'Create PDF/XPS Document' in the left pane of the Export gallery to display information about PDF/XPS documents in the right pane and then click the 'Create PDF/XPS' button to display the Publish as PDF or XPS dialog box.

3. If necessary, navigate to the desired save location.

4. If necessary, click the 'Save as type' arrow and then click XPS Document.

5. Click the Publish or Save button to create the XPS document from the Word document and then, if the 'Open file after publishing' check box was selected, open the resulting XPS document in the XPS Viewer.

or

1. Press F12 to display the Save As dialog box.

2. If necessary, navigate to the desired save location.

3. If necessary, click the 'Save as type' arrow and then click XPS Document.

4. Click the Publish or Save button to create the XPS document from the Word document and then, if the 'Open file after publishing' check box was selected, open the resulting XPS document in the XPS Viewer.

Q&A What if I do not have an XPS Viewer?
The document will open in a browser window.

5. If necessary, exit the XPS Viewer.

To Run the Compatibility Checker

Word 2016 enables you to determine if a document is compatible (will work with) with earlier versions of Microsoft Word. **Why?** *If you would like to save a document, such as your resume, in the Word 97-2003 format so that it can be opened by users with earlier versions of Microsoft Word, you want to ensure that all of its elements (such as building blocks, content controls, and graphics) are compatible with earlier versions of Word.* The following steps run the compatibility checker.

1

- Open the Backstage view and then, if necessary, click the Info tab in the Backstage view to display the Info gallery.

- Click the 'Check for Issues' button in the Info gallery to display the Check for Issues menu (Figure 5–50).

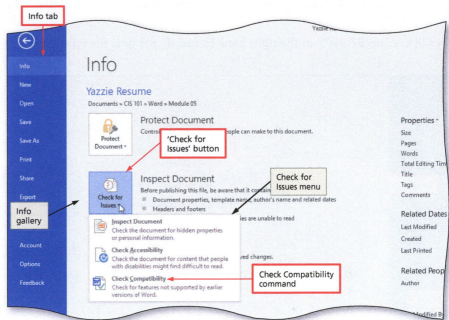

Figure 5–50

2

- Click Check Compatibility on the Check for Issues menu to display the Microsoft Word Compatibility Checker dialog box, which shows any content that may not be supported by earlier versions of Word (Figure 5–51).

3

- Click the OK button (Microsoft Word Compatibility Checker dialog box) to close the dialog box.

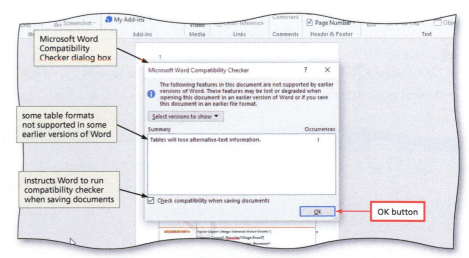

Figure 5–51

To Save a Word 2016 Document in an Earlier Word Format

If you send a document created in Word 2016 to users who have a version of Word earlier than Word 2007, they will not be able to open the Word 2016 document. **Why?** *Word 2016 saves documents in a format that is not backward compatible with versions earlier than Word 2007. Word 2016 documents have a file type of .docx, and* *versions prior to Word 2007 have a .doc file type*. To ensure that all Word users can open your Word 2016 document, you should save the document in a Word 97-2003 format. The following steps save the Word 2016 format of the Yazzie Resume document in the Word 97-2003 format.

1

- Open the Backstage view and then click the Export tab in the Backstage view to display the Export gallery.

- Click 'Change File Type' in the left pane of the Export gallery to display information in the right pane about various Word file types.

- Click 'Word 97-2003' in the right pane to specify the new file type (Figure 5–52).

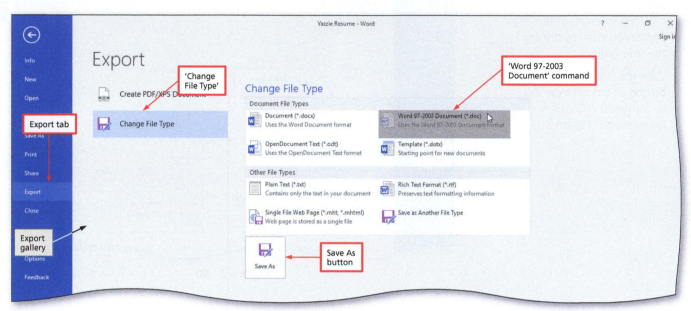

Figure 5–52

2

- Click the Save As button in the right pane to display the Save As dialog box.

- If necessary, navigate to the desired save location (Save As dialog box) (Figure 5–53).

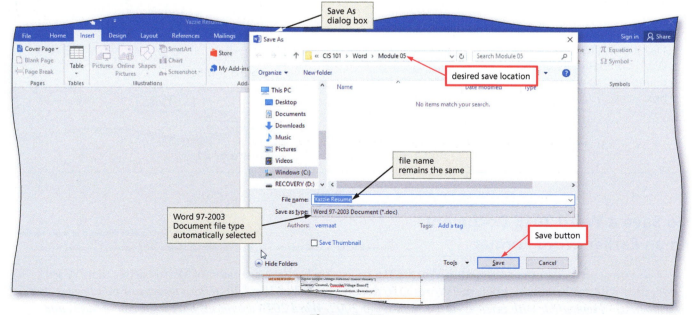

Figure 5–53

Q&A Can the file name be the same for the Word 2016 document and the Word 97-2003 document?
Yes. The file names can be the same because the file types are different: one is a Word document with a .docx extension, and the other is a Word document with a .doc extension. The next section discusses file types and extensions.

3

- Click the Save button, which may display the Microsoft Word Compatibility Checker dialog box before saving the document (Figure 5–54).

Q&A My screen did not display the Microsoft Word Compatibility Checker dialog box. Why not?
If the 'Check compatibility when saving documents' check box is not selected (as shown in Figure 5–51), Word will not check compatibility when saving a document.

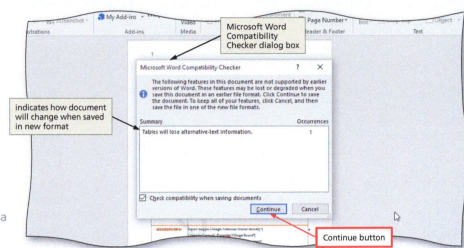

Figure 5–54

4

- If the Microsoft Word Compatibility Checker dialog box is displayed, click its Continue button to save the document on the selected drive with the current file name in the specified format (Figure 5–55).

Q&A Is the Word 2016 format of the Yazzie Resume document still open?
No. Word closed the original document (the Word 2016 format of the Yazzie Resume).

Can I use Word 2016 to open a document created in an earlier version of Word?
Yes, but you may notice that the appearance of the document differs when opened in Word 2016.

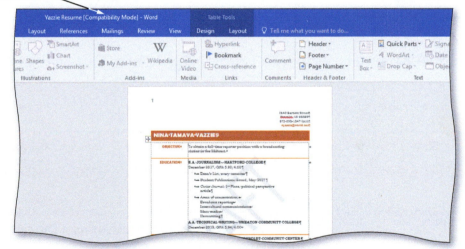

Figure 5–55

- Because you are finished with the Word 97-2003 format of the Yazzie Resume, close the document.

Other Ways

1. Press F12, click 'Save as type' arrow (Save As dialog box), select 'Word 97-2003 Document' in list, click Save button

File Types

When saving documents in Word, you can select from a variety of file types that can be opened in Word using the Export gallery in the Backstage view (shown in Figure 5–52) or by clicking the 'Save as type' arrow in the Save As dialog box. To save in these varied formats (Table 5–1), you follow the same basic steps as just illustrated.

Table 5–1 File Types

File Type	File Extension	File Explorer Image	Description
OpenDocument Text	.odt		Format used by other word processing programs, such as Google Docs and OpenOffice.org
PDF	.pdf		Portable Document Format, which can be opened in Adobe Reader
Plain Text	.txt		Format where all or most formatting is removed from the document
Rich Text Format	.rtf		Format designed to ensure file can be opened and read in many programs; some formatting may be lost to ensure compatibility
Single File Web Page	.mht		HTML (Hypertext Markup Language) format that can be opened in a browser; all elements of the webpage are saved in a single file
Web Page	.htm		HTML format that can be opened in a browser; various elements of the webpage, such as graphics, saved in separate files and folders
Word 97-2003 Document	.doc		Format used for documents created in versions of Word from Word 97 to Word 2003
Word 97-2003 Template	.dot		Format used for templates created in versions of Word from Word 97 and Word 2003
Word Document	.docx		Format used for Word 2016, Word 2013, Word 2010, or Word 2007 documents
Word Template	.dotx		Format used for Word 2016, Word 2013, Word 2010, or Word 2007 templates
XPS	.xps		XML (Extensible Markup Language) Paper Specification, which can be opened in the XPS Viewer

TO SAVE A WORD 2016 DOCUMENT AS A DIFFERENT FILE TYPE

To save a Word 2016 document as a different file type, you would follow these steps.

Note: The steps in the next several sections require that you have a Microsoft account and an Internet connection. If you do not have a Microsoft account or an Internet connection, read the steps without performing them.

1. Open the Backstage view and then click the Export tab in the Backstage view to display the Export gallery.

2. Click 'Change File Type' in the Export gallery to display information in the right pane about various file types that can be opened in Word.

3. Click the desired file type in the right pane and then click the Save As button to display the Save As dialog box.

4. Navigate to the desired save location (Save As dialog box) and then click the Save button in the dialog box.

5. If the Microsoft Word Compatibility Checker dialog box appears and you agree with the changes that will be made to the document, click the Continue button (Microsoft Word Compatibility Checker dialog box) to save the document on the selected drive with the current file name in the specified format.

To Invite Others to View or Edit a Document

If you have a OneDrive account, you can share a Word document saved on OneDrive with others through email message invitations. *Why? Invited users can click a link in an email message that displays a webpage enabling them to view or edit the document on OneDrive.* The following steps invite a user to view the Yazzie Resume document. If you do not have a Microsoft account or an Internet connection, read these steps without performing them.

1

- If necessary, run Word. Open the Word 2016 format of the Yazzie Resume and then save the Yazzie Resume on OneDrive.

- Click the Share button in the upper-right corner of the ribbon to open the Share pane (Figure 5–56).

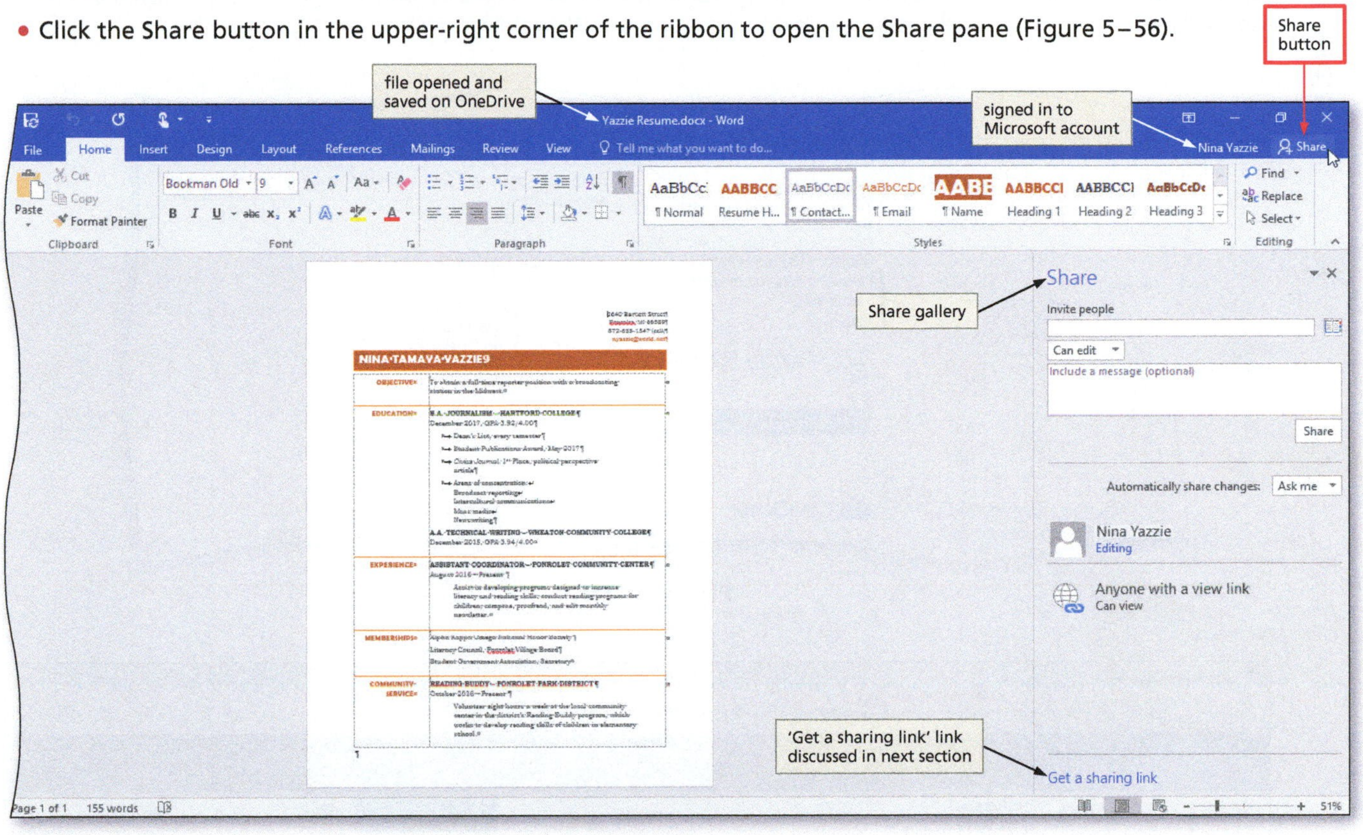

Figure 5–56

Q&A Why does my screen display a 'Save to Cloud' button in the Share pane?

The document has not been saved on OneDrive and/or you are not signed in to your Microsoft account.

2

- In the Share pane, type the email address(es) of the person(s) with whom you want to share the document, click the box arrow so that you can specify Can edit, if necessary, and then type a message to the recipient(s) (Figure 5–57).

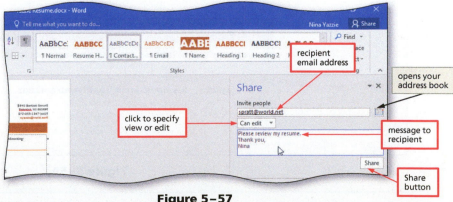

Figure 5–57

• Click the Share button in the Share pane to send the message along with a link to the document on OneDrive to the listed recipient(s).

Other Ways

1. Open Backstage view, click Share tab, click 'Share with People' in left pane in Share gallery, enter email address and message in Share pane, click Share button in Share pane

CONSIDER THIS

How does a recipient access the shared document?

The recipient receives an email message that indicates it contains a link to a shared document (Figure 5–58). When the recipient clicks the link in the email message, the document opens in Word Online on OneDrive (Figure 5–59).

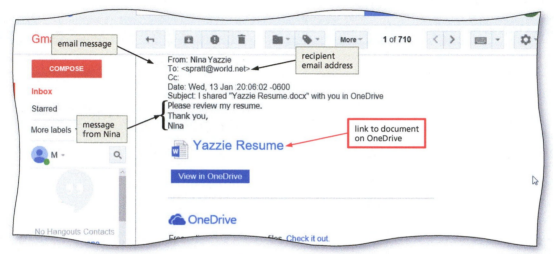

Figure 5–58

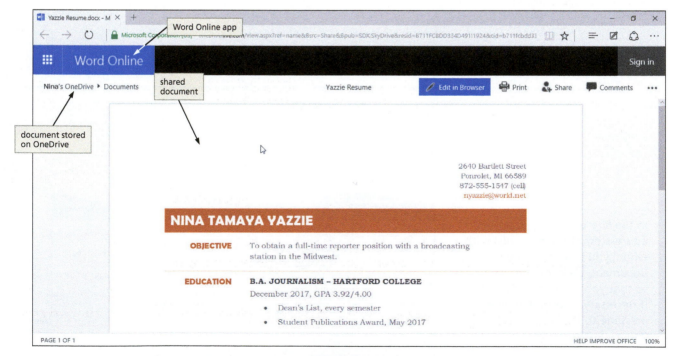

Figure 5–59

To Get a Sharing Link

Why share a link? *Instead of inviting people to view or edit a document, you can create a link to the document's location on OneDrive and then send others the link via an email message or text message, post it on a website or online social network, or communicate it via some other means.* The following steps get a sharing link. If you do not have a Microsoft account or an Internet connection, read these steps without performing them.

1

- If necessary, click Share button in the upper-right corner of the ribbon to open the Share pane and then click 'Get a sharing link' at the bottom of the Share pane (shown in Figure 5–56) to display options for obtaining a link to a document on OneDrive in the right pane (Figure 5–60).

Q&A Why does my screen display a 'Save to Cloud' button in the right pane?

The document has not been saved on OneDrive and/or you are not signed in to your Microsoft account.

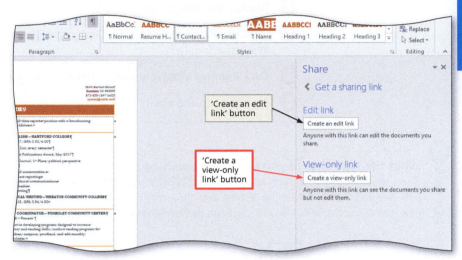

Figure 5–60

2

- Click the 'Create a view-only link' button in the Share pane to create the link associated with the file on OneDrive (Figure 5–61).

Q&A What do I do with the link?

You can copy and paste the link in an email or text message, on a webpage, or some other location.

What is the difference between a view link and an edit link?

A view link enables others to read the document but not modify it, while an edit link enables others to both view and edit the document.

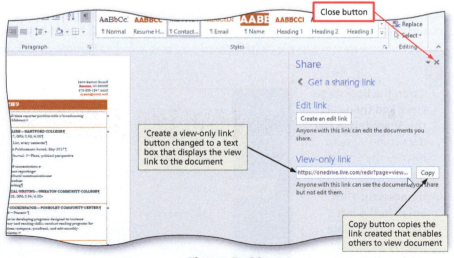

Figure 5–61

3

- Click the Close button in the upper-right corner of the Share pane to close the pane.

Other Ways

1. Open Backstage view, click Share tab, click 'Share with People' in right pane in Share gallery, enter email address and message in Share pane, click 'Get a sharing link' in Share pane

To Remove a Watermark

The following steps remove the DRAFT watermark from the resume in the document window, if it was saved with the document, because you now consider the document final and would like to distribute it to potential employers.

① If necessary, open the Yazzie Resume (Word 2016 format).

② Display the Design tab.

③ Click the Watermark button (Design tab | Page Background group) to display the Watermark gallery.

④ Click Remove Watermark in the Watermark gallery to remove the watermark.

⑤ Save the resume again with the same file name.

CONSIDER THIS

What file type should you use when emailing documents?

If you email a document, such as your resume, consider that the recipient, such as a potential employer, may not have the same software you used to create the resume and, thus, may not be able to open the file. As an alternative, you could save the file in a format, such as a PDF or XPS, that can be viewed with a reader program. Many job seekers also post their resumes on the web.

To Send a Document Using Email

1 CREATE DOCUMENT FROM TEMPLATE | 2 MODIFY & FORMAT TEMPLATE | 3 SAVE DOCUMENT IN OTHER FORMATS | 4 MAKE DOCUMENT AVAILABLE ONLINE | 5 CREATE WEBPAGE FROM WORD DOCUMENT | 6 FORMAT WEBPAGE

In Word, you can include the current document as an attachment to an email message. An attachment is a file included with an email message. The following steps send the Yazzie Resume as an email attachment, assuming you use Outlook as your default email program. *Why? When you attach an email document from within Word, it automatically uses the default email program, which is Outlook in this case.*

①

- Open the Backstage view and then click the Share tab in the Backstage view to display the Share gallery.

- If necessary, click Email in the left pane of the Share gallery to display information in the right pane about various ways to send a document via email from within Word (Figure 5–62).

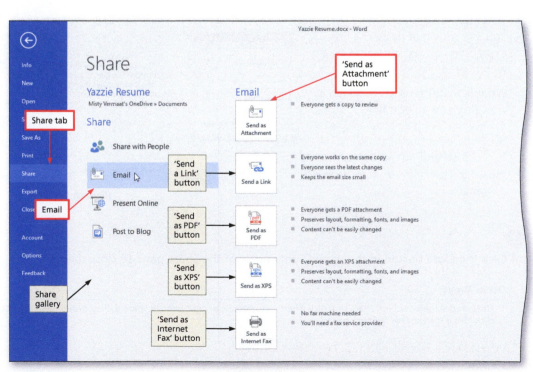

Figure 5–62

Why is my list of share options in the Share gallery shorter?
You have not saved the document previously on OneDrive.

What are the purpose of the 'Send as PDF' and 'Send as XPS' buttons?
Depending on which button you click, Word converts the current document either to the PDF or XPS format and then attaches the PDF or XPS document to the email message.

Why is my 'Send a Link' button dimmed?
You have not saved the document previously on OneDrive.

- Click the 'Send as Attachment' button to run your default email program (Outlook, in this case), which automatically attaches the active Word document to the email message.

- Fill in the To text box with the recipient's email address.

- Fill in the message text (Figure 5–63).

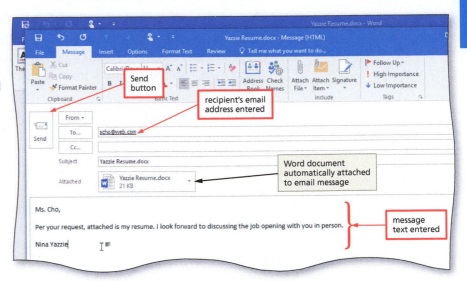

Figure 5–63

- Click the Send button to send the email message along with its attachment to the recipient named in the To text box and then close the email window.

- Because you are finished working with the Yazzie Resume on OneDrive, you can sign out of your Microsoft Account, if you wish to do so.

To Use the Document Inspector

Word includes a Document Inspector that checks a document for content you might not want to share with others, such as personal information. Before sharing a document with others, you may want to check for this type of content. If you wanted to use the Document Inspector, you would do the following:

1. Open the Backstage view and, if necessary, click the Info tab in the Backstage view to display the Info gallery.

2. Click the 'Check for Issues' button in the Info gallery to display the Check for Issues menu.

3. Click Inspect Document on the Check for Issues menu to display the Document Inspector dialog box.

4. Click the Inspect button (Document Inspector dialog box) to instruct Word to inspect the document.

5. Review the results (Document Inspector dialog box) and then click the Remove All button(s) for any item that you do not want to be saved with the document.

6. When finished removing information, click the Close button to close the dialog box.

To Customize How Word Opens Email Attachments

When a user sends you an email message that contains a Word document as an attachment, Word may display the document in Read mode. This view is designed to

BTW

Internet Fax
If you do not have a stand-alone fax machine, you can send and receive faxes in Word by clicking the 'Send as Internet Fax' button in the Backstage view (shown in Figure 5–62). To send or receive faxes using Word, you first must sign up with a fax service provider by clicking the OK button in the Microsoft Office dialog box that appears the first time you click the 'Send as Internet Fax' button, which displays an Available Fax Services webpage. You also may need to install either the Windows Fax printer driver or Windows Fax Services component on your computer. When sending a fax, Word converts the document to an image file and attaches it to an email message where you enter the recipient's fax number, name, subject, and message for the cover sheet, and then click a Send button to deliver the fax.

increase the readability and legibility of an on-screen document. Read mode, however, does not represent how the document will look when it is printed. For this reason, many users prefer working in Print Layout view to read documents. To exit Read mode, press the ESC key.

If you wanted to customize how Word opens email attachments, you would do the following.

1. Open the Backstage view and then click the Options tab in the Backstage view to display the Word Options dialog box.

2. If necessary, click General in the left pane (Word Options dialog box).

3. If you want email attachments to open in Read mode, place a check mark in the 'Open e-mail attachments and other uneditable files in reading view' check box; otherwise, remove the check mark to open email attachments in Print Layout view.

4. Click the OK button to close the dialog box.

Creating a Webpage from a Word Document

If you have created a document, such as a resume, using Word, you can save it in a format that can be opened by a browser, such as Internet Explorer. When you save a file as a webpage, Word converts the contents of the document into **HTML** (Hypertext Markup Language), which is a set of codes that browsers can interpret. Some of Word's formatting features are not supported by webpages. Thus, your webpage may look slightly different from the original Word document.

When saving a document as a webpage, Word provides you with three choices:

- The **single file web page format** saves all of the components of the webpage in a single file that has a **.mht** extension. This format is particularly useful for sending documents via email in HTML format.

- The **web page format** saves some of the components of the webpage in a folder, separate from the webpage. This format is useful if you need access to the individual components, such as images, that make up the webpage.

- The **filtered web page format** saves the file in webpage format and then reduces the size of the file by removing specific Microsoft Office formats. This format is useful if you want to speed up the time it takes to download a webpage that contains graphics, video, audio, or animations.

The webpage created in this section uses the single file web page format.

To Save a Word Document as a Webpage

1 CREATE DOCUMENT FROM TEMPLATE | 2 MODIFY & FORMAT TEMPLATE | 3 SAVE DOCUMENT IN OTHER FORMATS
4 MAKE DOCUMENT AVAILABLE ONLINE | **5 CREATE WEBPAGE FROM WORD DOCUMENT** | 6 FORMAT WEBPAGE

The following steps save the Yazzie Resume created earlier in this module as a webpage. *Why? You intend to post your resume online.*

- If necessary, open the Word 2016 format of the resume file. Open the Backstage view and then click the Export tab in the Backstage view to display the Export gallery.

- Click 'Change File Type' in the left pane of the Export gallery to display information in the right pane about various file types that are supported by Word.

- Click 'Single File Web Page' in the right pane to specify a new file type (Figure 5–64).

Q&A

What if I wanted to save the document as a web page instead of a single file web page?

You would click 'Save as Another File Type' in the Change File Type area, click the Save As button, click the 'Save as type' arrow in the Save As dialog box, and then click Web Page in the Save as type list.

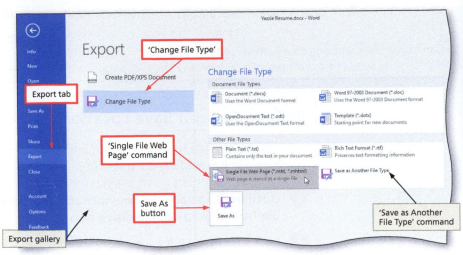

Figure 5–64

2

- Click the Save As button in the right pane to display the Save As dialog box.

- If necessary, navigate to the desired save location (Save As dialog box).

- If necessary, type **Yazzie Resume** in the File name box to change the file name.

- Click the Change Title button to display the Enter Text dialog box.

- Type **Yazzie Resume** in the Page title text box (Enter Text dialog box) (Figure 5–65).

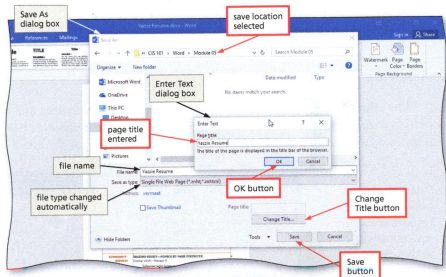

Figure 5–65

3

- Click the OK button (Enter Text dialog box) to close the dialog box.

- Click the Save button (Save As dialog box) to save the resume as a webpage and then display it in the document window in Web Layout view.

- If necessary, change the zoom to 100% (Figure 5–66).

- If the Microsoft Word Compatibility Checker dialog box appears, click its Continue button.

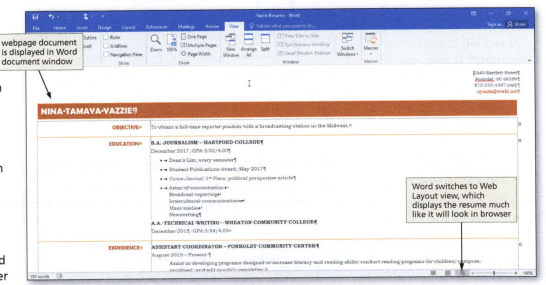

Figure 5–66

Q&A Can I switch to Web Layout view at any time by clicking the Web Layout button on the taskbar?
Yes.

Can I save the webpage to a web server?
If you have access to a web server, you can save the webpage from Word directly to the web server.

To Set a Default Save Location

If you wanted to change the default location that Word uses when it saves a document, you would do the following.

1 Open the Backstage view and then click the Options tab in the Backstage view to display the Word Options dialog box.

2 Click Save in the left pane (Word Options dialog box) to display options for saving documents in the right pane.

3 In the 'Default file location' text box, type the new desired save location.

4 Click the OK button to close the dialog box.

To Format Text as a Hyperlink

1 CREATE DOCUMENT FROM TEMPLATE | 2 MODIFY & FORMAT TEMPLATE | 3 SAVE DOCUMENT IN OTHER FORMATS
4 MAKE DOCUMENT AVAILABLE ONLINE | 5 CREATE WEBPAGE FROM WORD DOCUMENT | **6 FORMAT WEBPAGE**

The email address in the resume webpage should be formatted as a hyperlink. *Why? When webpage visitors click the hyperlink-formatted email address, you want their email program to run automatically and open an email window with the email address already filled in.* The following steps format the email address as a hyperlink.

1

- Select the email address in the resume webpage (nyazzie@world.net, in this case).

- Display the Insert tab.

- Click the 'Add a Hyperlink' button (Insert tab | Links group) to display the Insert Hyperlink dialog box (Figure 5–67).

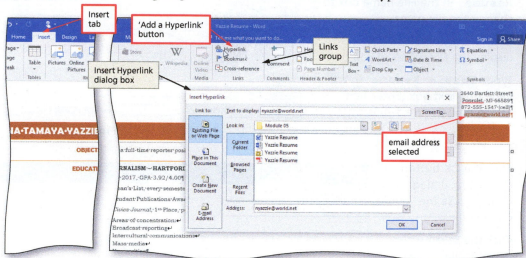

Figure 5–67

2

- Click E-mail Address in the Link to bar (Insert Hyperlink dialog box) so that the dialog box displays email address settings instead of webpage settings.

- In the E-mail address text box, type **nyazzie@world.net** to specify the email address that the browser uses when a user clicks the hyperlink.

Q&A Can I change the text that automatically appeared in the 'Text to display' text box?
Yes. Word assumes that the hyperlink text should be the same as the email address, so as soon as you enter the email address, the same text is entered in the 'Text to display' text box.

- If the email address in the 'Text to display' text box is preceded by the text, mailto:, delete this leading text because you want only the email address to appear in the document.

- Click the ScreenTip button to display the Set Hyperlink ScreenTip dialog box.

- Type **Send email message to Nina Yazzie.** in the 'ScreenTip text' text box (Set Hyperlink ScreenTip dialog box) to specify the text that will be displayed when a user points to the hyperlink (Figure 5–68).

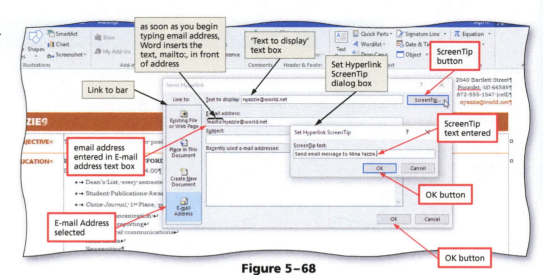

Figure 5–68

3

- Click the OK button in each dialog box to format the email address as a hyperlink (Figure 5–69).

Q&A

How do I know if the hyperlink works?
In Word, you can test the hyperlink by holding down the CTRL key while clicking the hyperlink. In this case, CTRL+clicking the email address should open an email window.

Figure 5–69

Other Ways

1. Right-click selected text, click Hyperlink on shortcut menu   2. Select text, press CTRL+K

TO EDIT A HYPERLINK

If you needed to edit a hyperlink, for example, to change its ScreenTip or its link, you would follow these steps.

1. Position the insertion point in the hyperlink.
2. Click the 'Add a Hyperlink' button (Insert tab | Links group) or press CTRL+K to display the Edit Hyperlink dialog box.

   or

1. Right-click the hyperlink to display a shortcut menu.
2. Click Edit Hyperlink on the shortcut menu to display the Edit Hyperlink dialog box.

To Change the Style Set

1 CREATE DOCUMENT FROM TEMPLATE | 2 MODIFY & FORMAT TEMPLATE | 3 SAVE DOCUMENT IN OTHER FORMATS
4 MAKE DOCUMENT AVAILABLE ONLINE | 5 CREATE WEBPAGE FROM WORD DOCUMENT | 6 FORMAT WEBPAGE

Word provides several built-in style sets to help you quickly change the look of an entire document. *Why? A style set contains formats for fonts and paragraphs.* The following steps change the style set to the Shaded style set.

1

- Display the Design tab.

- Click the More button (Design tab | Document Formatting group) (shown in Figure 5–71) to display the expanded Style Set gallery (Figure 5–70).

(🔍) **Experiment**

- Point to various style sets in the Style Set gallery and watch the font and paragraph formatting change in the document window.

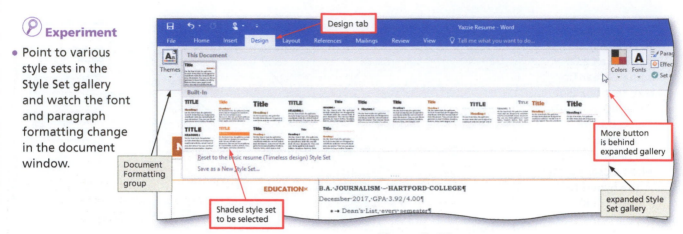

Figure 5–70

2

- Click Shaded to change the style set to the selected style set (Figure 5–71).

Q&A

Can I create my own style sets?
Yes. Modify the fonts and other formats as desired, click 'Save as a New Style Set' in the expanded Style Set gallery (shown in Figure 5–70), enter the name for the style set (Save as a New Style Set dialog box), and then click the Save button to create the custom style set. You then can access the custom style set through the Style Set gallery.

Figure 5–71

- Save the resume webpage again on the same storage location with the same file name and then exit Word.

To Test a Webpage in a Browser

1 CREATE DOCUMENT FROM TEMPLATE | 2 MODIFY & FORMAT TEMPLATE | 3 SAVE DOCUMENT IN OTHER FORMATS
4 MAKE DOCUMENT AVAILABLE ONLINE | 5 CREATE WEBPAGE FROM WORD DOCUMENT | **6 FORMAT WEBPAGE**

After creating and saving a webpage, you should test it in at least one browser. ***Why?*** *You want to be sure it looks and works the way you intended.* The following steps use File Explorer to display the resume webpage in the Microsoft Edge browser.

1

- Click the File Explorer button on the Windows taskbar to open the File Explorer window.

- Navigate to the location of the saved resume webpage file (Figure 5–72).

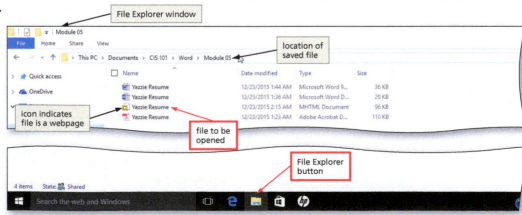

Figure 5–72

2

- Double-click the webpage file name, Yazzie Resume, to run Microsoft Edge and display the webpage file in the browser window (Figure 5–73).

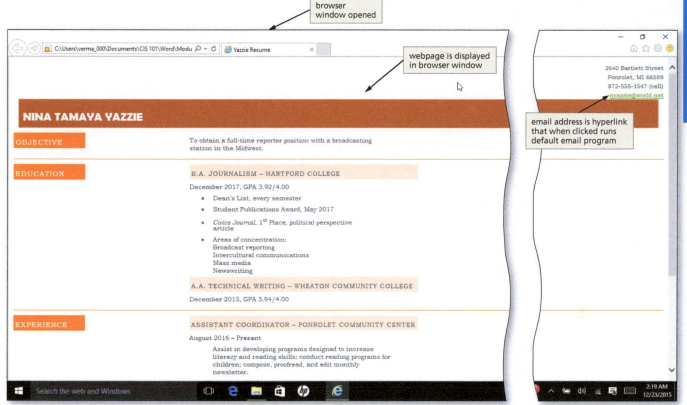

Figure 5–73

3

- With the webpage document displayed in the browser, click the email address link to run the email program with the email address displayed in the email window (Figure 5–74).

- If Microsoft Edge displays a security dialog box, click its Allow button.

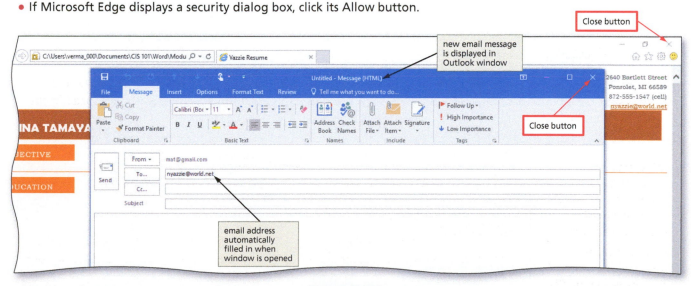

Figure 5–74

4

- Exit all running apps.

CONSIDER THIS

How do you publish a webpage?

Once you have created a webpage, you can publish it. **Publishing** is the process of making a webpage available to others on a network, such as the Internet or a company's intranet. Many Internet service providers (ISPs) offer storage space on their web servers at no cost to their subscribers.

Summary

In this module, you learned how to use a Word template to create a document, set custom margins, personalize a document template, indent a paragraph, customize theme fonts, create a style, modify a style, insert building blocks, save a Word document in a variety of formats, share a document online via OneDrive, insert a hyperlink, and change the style set.

CONSIDER THIS: PLAN AHEAD

What decisions will you need to make when creating your next resume?

Use these guidelines as you complete the assignments in this module and create your own resumes outside of this class.

1. Craft a successful resume.

    a) Include necessary information (at a minimum, your contact information, objective, educational background, and work experience).

    b) Honestly present all your positive points.

    c) Organize information appropriately.

    d) Ensure the resume is error free.

2. For electronic distribution, ensure the document is in the proper format.

    a) Save the resume in a format that can be shared with others.

    b) Ensure that others will be able to open the resume using software on their computers or mobile devices and that the look of the resume will remain intact when recipients open the resume.

3. If desired, create a resume webpage from your resume Word document.

    a) Improve the usability of the resume webpage by making your email address a link to an email program.

    b) Enhance the look of the webpage by adding, for example, a background color.

    c) Test your finished webpage document in at least one browser to be sure it looks and works as intended.

    d) Publish your resume webpage.

Apply Your Knowledge

Reinforce the skills and apply the concepts you learned in this module.

Saving a Word Document in a Variety of Formats

Note: To complete this assignment, you will be required to use the Data Files. Please contact your instructor for information about accessing the Data Files.

Instructions: Run Word. Open the document, Apply 5 – 1 Protect Your Hearing, from the Data Files. You are to save the document as a single file web page (Figure 5 – 75), a PDF document, an XPS document, and in the Word 97-2003 format.

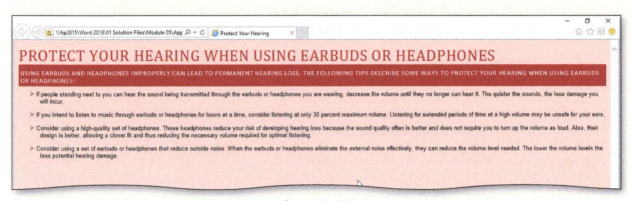

Figure 5 – 75

Perform the following tasks:

1. Save the document as a single file web page using the file name, Apply 5 – 1 Protect Your Hearing Webpage. In the Save As dialog box, click the Change Title button and change the webpage title to Protect Your Hearing. If necessary, increase the zoom percentage so that the document is readable on your screen.

2. If requested by your instructor, add another bullet point with a personal suggestion about protecting hearing when using earbuds or headphones followed by your name in parentheses.

3. Add the background color Orange, Accent 2, Lighter 80% to the webpage document.

4. Change the style set to Shaded. Save the file again.

5. Use Microsoft Edge or another browser to view the webpage (shown in Figure 5 – 75). If requested by your instructor, print the webpage. What differences do you notice between the Word document format and the single file web page format? Exit the browser and then close the webpage document in Word.

6. Open the original Apply 5 – 1 Protect Your Hearing document. If requested by your instructor, perform Step 2 again. Save the document as a PDF document and then view the PDF document in Adobe Reader. Submit the document as specified by your instructor. Exit Adobe Reader. In Word, open the PDF document just created. What differences do you notice between the Word document format and the PDF format? Close the converted PDF document without saving it.

7. If necessary, open the original Apply 5 – 1 Protect Your Hearing document. If requested by your instructor, perform Step 2 again. Save the document as an XPS Document and then view the XPS document in the XPS Viewer. Submit the document as specified by your instructor. What differences do you notice between the Word document format and the XPS format? Exit the XPS Viewer.

Continued >

Apply Your Knowledge *continued*

8. If necessary, open the original Apply 5–1 Protect Your Hearing document. Run the compatibility checker. What issue(s) were identified by the compatibility checker? Save the document in the Word 97-2003 format. Submit the document as specified by your instructor.

9. If your instructor allows, email the document saved in #8 to his or her email account.

10. ✺ Answer the questions posed in #5, #6, #7, and #8. If you wanted to email this document to others, which format would you choose and why?

Extend Your Knowledge

Extend the skills you learned in this module and experiment with new skills. You may need to use Help to complete the assignment.

Creating a Multi-File Webpage, Applying a Fill Effect and Highlights, and Inserting Screen Shots

Note: To complete this assignment, you will be required to use the Data Files. Please contact your instructor for information about accessing the Data Files.

Instructions: Run Word. Open the document called Extend 5–1 NFC Chips and Tags located on the Data Files. You will save a Word document as a multi-file webpage and format it by inserting links, adding a pattern fill effect as the background, and applying highlights to text. Then, you will create a new document that contains screen shots of the webpage and files created for the webpage.

Perform the following tasks:
1. Use Help to learn about saving as a webpage (not a single file web page), hyperlinks, pattern fill effects, text highlight color, and screen shots.

2. If requested by your instructor, add your name on a separate line at the end of the document.

3. Save the Extend 5–1 NFC Chips and Tags file in the web page format (not as a single file web page) using the file name, Extend 5–1 NFC Chips and Tags Webpage.

4. Using a browser, search for a website that lists phones with NFC technology. At the end of the document, type a line of text that directs the reader to that web address for a list of phones with NFC technology. Format the web address in the document as a hyperlink so that when a user clicks the web address, the associated webpage is displayed in the browser window.

5. Add a page color of your choice to the document. Add a pattern fill effect of your choice to the page color.

6. Apply a text highlight color of your choice to at least five words in the document.

7. Save the document again. Test the webpage by double-clicking its file name in File Explorer. Test the web address link on the webpage. Leave this window open so that you can include its screen shot in the next step.

8. Redisplay the Word window. Create a new Word document. Use Word to insert a screen shot of the webpage displaying in the File Explorer window. Below the screen shot of the webpage, insert a screen shot(s) of File Explorer that shows all the files and folders created by saving the document as a webpage. Insert callout shapes with text that points to and identifies the files and folders created by saving the document as a webpage (Figure 5–76). Save the document with the file name, Extend 5–1 NFC Chips and Tags Screen Shots.

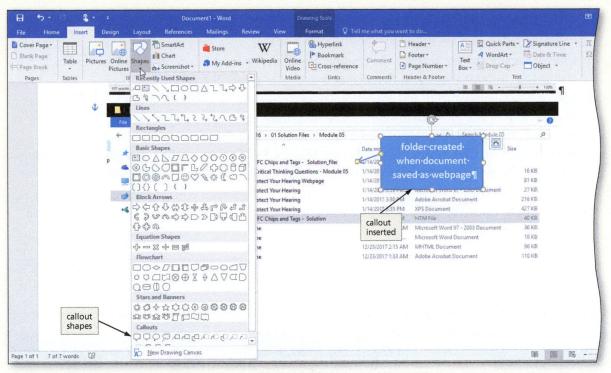

Figure 5–76

9. Close all open windows. Submit the files in the format specified by your instructor.

10. ✷ Why would you add a pattern fill effect to a background?

Expand Your World

Create a solution that uses cloud or web technologies by learning and investigating on your own from general guidance.

Sharing a Resume Online

Notes:

- You will use OneDrive and a job sharing website account, which you can create at no cost, to complete this assignment. If you do not have these accounts and do not want to create them, read this assignment without performing the instructions.

- To complete this assignment, you will be required to use the Data Files. Please contact your instructor for information about accessing the Data Files.

Instructions: You are a marketing management graduate from Mockingbird College. You have prepared a resume and are ready to share it with potential employers. You will save it on your OneDrive account, invite others to view it, get a sharing link, send it via email, and post it on a job sharing website (Figure 5–77).

Perform the following tasks:

1. In Word, open the document, Expand 5–1 Cucci Resume, from the Data Files. Look through the resume so that you are familiar with its contents and formats.

2. If requested by your instructor, change the name at the top of the resume to your name.

3. Save the resume on your OneDrive account.

Continued >

Expand Your World *continued*

4. In Word, invite at least one of your classmates to view your resume document. If requested, include your instructor in the invitation.

5. In Word, get a sharing link for the resume. Email the sharing link to at least one of your classmates. Submit the link in the format requested by your instructor.

6. Save the resume as a PDF file. Search for the text, post resume online, using a search engine. Visit several of the job search websites and determine on which one you would like to post a resume. If requested, create an account or profile, fill in the requested information, and then upload the PDF format of the resume (Figure 5–77). Submit the posting in the format requested by your instructor. Delete the posted resume from the job search website.

7. ✴ Which job search websites did you evaluate? Which one did you select to use and why? What would cause the file size of your resume to be too large to upload (post)? How can you reduce the file size?

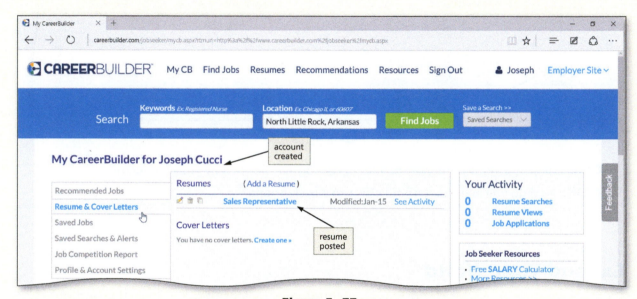

Figure 5–77

In the Labs

Design, create, modify, and/or use a document following the guidelines, concepts, and skills presented in this module. Labs 1 and 2, which increase in difficulty, require you to create solutions based on what you learned in the module; Lab 3 requires you to apply your creative thinking and problem-solving skills to design and implement a solution.

Lab 1: Creating a Resume from a Template (same template as in this module's project)

Problem: You are psychology student at Olympia State College. As graduation quickly is approaching, you prepare the resume shown in Figure 5–78 using one of Word's resume templates.

Perform the following tasks:

1. Use the Basic resume (Timeless design) template to create a resume. If you cannot locate this template or if the template you locate differs from Figure 5–5 shown at the beginning of this module, open the file called Basic resume (Timeless design) from the Data Files.

2. Change the document theme to Headlines.

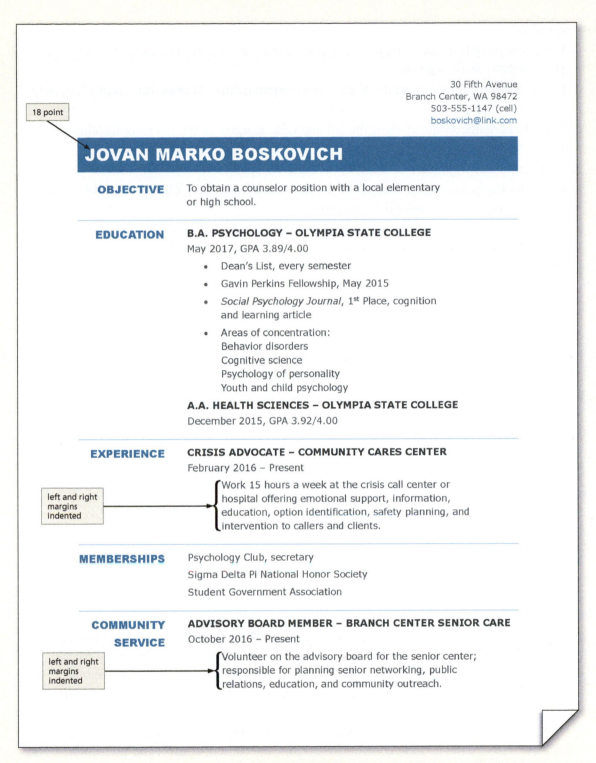

Figure 5–78

3. Personalize the resume as shown in Figure 5–78. Following are some guidelines for some sections of the resume:

a. Change the margins to 1" on the top, left, and right, and .5" on the bottom.

b. If requested by your instructor, use your own name and contact information in the content controls. Delete the line containing the Website content control.

c. Move the Education and Experience rows so that they appear as shown in Figure 5–78. Insert line breaks in the areas of concentration section of the education information.

Continued >

In the Labs *continued*

    d. Copy and paste the text in the table cell containing the Education content control so that you can enter both degrees.

    e. Delete the second item from the Experience content control because the resume lists only one job.

    f. In the Experience section, indent the left and right margins of the job responsibilities paragraphs one-half inch.

    g. Change the heading, Skill & Abilities, to Memberships.

    h. Copy the Experience section to below the Memberships section. Change the added row to show the community service information.

    i. Customize the theme fonts so that the headings are Arial Black and the body text is Verdana. Name the customized font Lab 1 Resume.

    j. Modify the Heading 2 style to the Verdana font.

    k. Delete any unused rows in the resume.

4. The entire resume should fit on a single page. If it flows to two pages, decrease spacing before and after paragraphs until the entire resume text fits on a single page.

5. Check the spelling of the resume. Save the resume with Lab 5 – 1 Boskovich Resume as the file name, and submit it in the format specified by your instructor.

6. ✳ Look through the other resume templates available. Which would work best for your resume? Why?

Lab 2: Creating a Resume from a Template (different template from this module's project)

Problem: You are a business student at Eureka Falls College. As graduation is approaching quickly, you prepare the resume shown in Figure 5 – 79 using one of Word's resume templates.

Perform the following tasks:

1. Use the Resume (color) template to create a resume. If you cannot locate this template, open the file called Resume (color) from the Data Files.

2. Change the document theme to slate. Personalize, modify, format the resume as shown in Figure 5 – 79. If requested by your instructor, use your personal information in the contact information content controls at the top of the resume. Insert and remove other content controls, as necessary, and modify placeholder in the resume as shown in the figure. Following are some guidelines for some sections of the resume:

    a. After entering text in the contact information content controls at the top of the resume template, remove the content controls (right-click the content control and then click 'Remove Content Control' on the shortcut menu so that your text remains but the content control is deleted). When you selected the contact information content controls, they appeared on the screen different from the template used in this module. How did they differ?

    b. To add the third job in the Experience section, click the bottom job experience control to select it and then click the Insert Control at the bottom right edge of the selected control. After entering the text in the content control, remove the content control so that text remains but the content control is deleted. Note that the resume template in this module's project did not contain an Insert Control. Describe the appearance of the Insert Control.

    c. Create a customized theme font set that uses Rockwell for headings and Arial for body text. Save the theme font with the name, Lab 2 Resume.

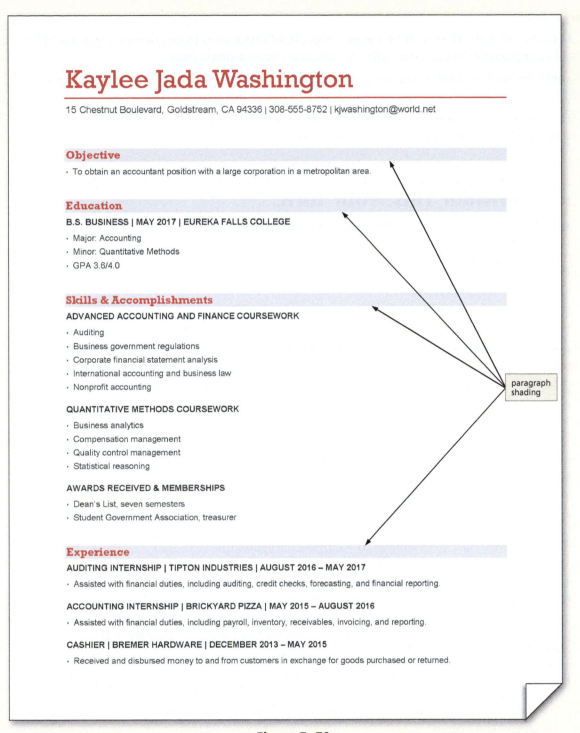

Figure 5–79

d. Modify the Section style to contain paragraph shading of Gray 80%, Text 2, Lighter 90%. Update the style so that it applies to the entire resume.

e. Increase the font size of the name to 28 point and the street address control to 10 point. Create a style called Contact Info using the format in the street address. Apply the Contact Info style to the city, state, ZIP code, phone number, and email address (the vertical bars before and after the phone number should remain at 9 point).

Continued >

In the Labs *continued*

3. The entire resume should fit on a single page. If it flows to two pages, decrease spacing before and after paragraphs until the entire resume text fits on a single page.

4. Check the spelling of the resume. Save the resume with Lab 5 – 2 Washington Resume as the file name, and submit it in the format specified by your instructor.

5. ✸ Answer the questions posed in #2a and 2b. Look through the templates available besides resumes. Which ones might you find useful? Why?

Lab 3: **Consider This: Your Turn**

Create a Calendar and an Invitation Using Templates

Problem: To help organize your appointments and important dates, you use a calendar template. While filling in the calendar, you decide to schedule a retirement party for your dad for which you will need to send out invitations.

Part 1: Browse through Word's online templates and download appropriate calendar and invitation templates and then use the text in the next two paragraphs for content. Use the concepts and techniques presented in this module to create and format the invitation and calendar. Be sure to check the spelling and grammar of the finished documents. When finished with the two documents, save them in a form suitable for electronic distribution. Decide which document would be best to create as a webpage; then, create the webpage from that document and format the webpage. Submit your assignment documents in the format specified by your instructor.

Calendar information: November 1 – Send out retirement party invitations, November 2 – Student Council meeting at 1:00 p.m. in Room 103 in Pace Hall, November 7 – Vote! It's Election Day, November 8 – Marianne's birthday, November 10 – Job Fair from noon to 4:00 p.m. in Bard Hall, November 11 – Volunteer at VFW's pancake breakfast for Veteran's Day, November 14 – My birthday!, November 15 – Grandma's birthday, November 17 – Dentist appointment at 9:00 a.m. and Photography Club luncheon at Jack's Pizza from 11:30 a.m. to 2:00 p.m., November 18 – Thanksgiving break starts, November 20 – Eye doctor appointment at 1:00 p.m., November 23 – Thanksgiving Day, November 25 – Dad's retirement party from 2:00 to 6:00 p.m. at Reimer's Restaurant, November 26 – Thanksgiving break ends, November 27 – Corporate Law term paper due by 11:59 p.m., November 28 – internship presentation at 10:00 a.m., and November 30 – capstone project due.

If the template requires, insert appropriate clip art or an image of your own. If requested by your instructor, insert a personal event in the calendar.

Invitation information: Congratulations Jeremy Winters!; Retirement Party!; Saturday, November 26, 2:00 to 6:00 p.m.; Reimer's Restaurant, 10 Chestnut Street, Mitcheltown, DE 19722; Come hungry!; Send a photo of you and Jeremy to mwinters@earth.link by November 20 for the slide show!; Hope you can join us!

If the template requires, insert appropriate clip art or an image of your own. If requested by your instructor, use your name and contact information instead of the information listed here.

Part 2: ✸ You made several decisions while creating the calendar and invitation in this assignment: which template to use, where to position elements, how to format elements, which graphic(s) to use, in which format to save the documents for electronic distribution, which document to create as a webpage, and how to format the webpage. What was the rationale behind each of these decisions?

6 Generating Form Letters, Mailing Labels, and a Directory

Objectives

You will have mastered the material in this module when you can:

- Explain the merge process
- Use the Mail Merge task pane and the Mailings tab on the ribbon
- Use a letter template as the main document for a mail merge
- Create and edit a data source
- Insert merge fields in a main document
- Use an IF field in a main document
- Merge form letters
- Select records to merge
- Sort data records
- Address and print mailing labels and envelopes
- Change page orientation
- Merge all data records to a directory
- Convert text to a table

Introduction

People are more likely to open and read a personalized letter than a letter addressed as Dear Sir, Dear Madam, or To Whom It May Concern. Creating individual personalized letters, though, can be a time-consuming task. Thus, Word provides the capability of creating a form letter, which is an easy way to generate mass mailings of personalized letters. The basic content of a group of form letters is similar. Items such as name and address, however, vary from one letter to the next. With Word, you easily can address and print mailing labels or envelopes for the form letters.

Project — Form Letters, Mailing Labels, and a Directory

Both businesses and individuals regularly use form letters to communicate with groups of people via the postal service or email. Types of form letter correspondence include announcements of sales to customers, notices of benefits to employees, invitations to the public to participate in a sweepstakes giveaway, and job application letters to potential employers.

The project in this module follows generally accepted guidelines for writing form letters and uses Word to create the form letters shown in Figure 6–1. The form letters inform potential employers of your interest in a job opening at their organization. Each form letter states the potential employer's name and address, available job position, and whether the job is at a radio or television station.

To generate form letters, such as the ones shown in Figure 6–1, you create a main document for the form letter (Figure 6–1a), create or specify a data source (Figure 6–1b), and then **merge**, or blend, the main document with the data source to generate a series of individual letters (Figure 6–1c). In Figure 6–1a, the main document represents the portion of the form letter that is repeated from one merged letter to the next. In Figure 6–1b, the data source contains the individual's and organization's name and address, available position, and type of broadcast station for various potential employers. To personalize each letter, you merge the potential employer data in the data source with the main document for the form letter, which generates or prints an individual letter for each potential employer listed in the data source.

Word provides two methods of merging documents: the Mail Merge task pane and the Mailings tab on the ribbon. The Mail Merge task pane displays a wizard, which is a step-by-step progression that guides you through the merging process. The Mailings tab provides buttons and boxes you use to merge documents. This module illustrates both techniques.

In this module, you will learn how to create the form letters shown in Figure 6–1. The following roadmap identifies general activities you will perform as you progress through this module:

1. IDENTIFY the MAIN DOCUMENT for the form letters.

2. CREATE a DATA SOURCE.

3. COMPOSE the MAIN DOCUMENT for the form letters.

4. MERGE the DATA SOURCE with the main document.

5. ADDRESS the MAILING LABELS.

6. MERGE all data records TO a DIRECTORY.

To Run Word and Change Word Settings

If you are using a computer to step through the project in this module and you want your screens to match the figures in this book, you should change your screen's resolution to 1366 × 768. The following steps run Word, display formatting marks, and change the zoom to page width.

1 Run Word and create a blank document in the Word window. If necessary, maximize the Word window.

2 If the Print Layout button on the status bar is not selected, click it so that your screen is in Print Layout view.

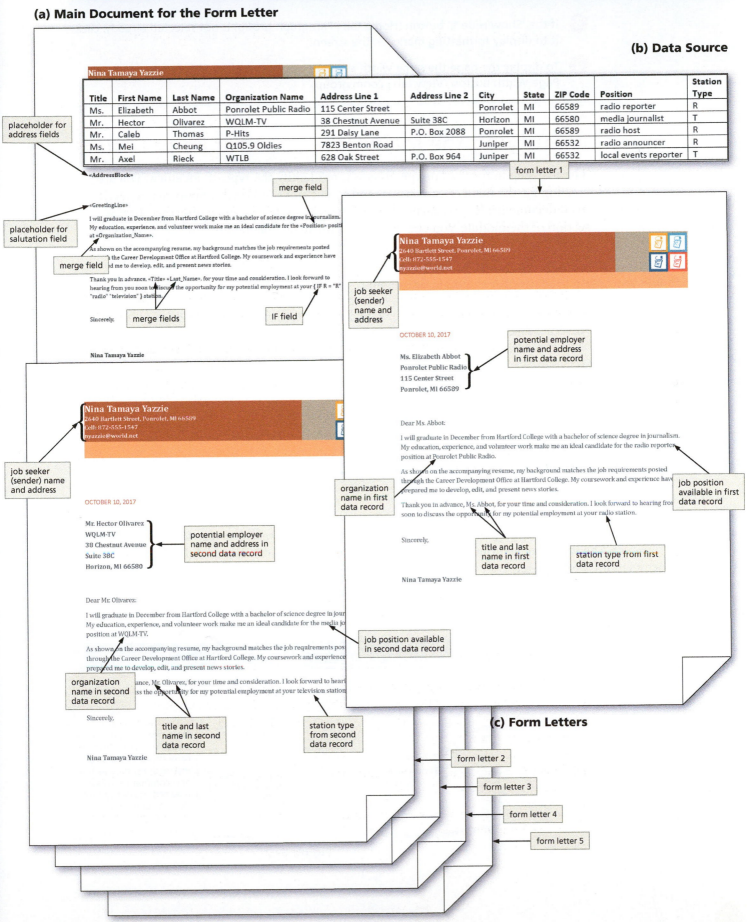

Figure 6–1

3 If the 'Show/Hide ¶' button (Home tab | Paragraph group) is not selected already, click it to display formatting marks on the screen.

4 To display the page the same width as the document window, if necessary, click the Page Width button (View tab | Zoom group).

Identifying the Main Document for Form Letters

The first step in the mail merge process is to identify the type of document you are creating for the main document. Typical installations of Word support five types of main documents: letters, email messages, envelopes, labels, and a directory. In this section of the module, you create letters as the main document. Later in this module, you will specify labels and a directory as the main document.

CONSIDER THIS

How should you create the letter for the main document?
When creating form letters, you either can type the letter for the main document from scratch in a blank document window or use a letter template. If you enter the contents of the main document from scratch, you can compose it according to the block, modified block, or semi-block letter style, formatted appropriately with business letter spacing. Alternatively, you can use a letter template to save time because Word prepares a letter with text and/or formatting common to all letters. Then, you customize the resulting letter by selecting and replacing prewritten text.

To Identify the Main Document for the Form Letter Using the Mail Merge Task Pane

1 IDENTIFY MAIN DOCUMENT | 2 CREATE DATA SOURCE | 3 COMPOSE MAIN DOCUMENT
4 MERGE DATA SOURCE | 5 ADDRESS MAILING LABELS | 6 MERGE TO DIRECTORY

This module uses a template for the main document for the form letter, where you select predefined content controls and placeholder text and replace them with personalized content, adjusting formats as necessary. *Why? You use the same style that you used with the resume in the previous module so that the two documents complement one another.* The following steps use the Mail Merge task pane to identify the Timeless letter template as the main document for a form letter.

1

• Click Mailings on the ribbon to display the Mailings tab.

• Click the 'Start Mail Merge' button (Mailings tab | Start Mail Merge group) to display the Start Mail Merge menu (Figure 6–2).

Q&A What is the function of the E-mail Messages command?
Instead of sending individual letters, you can send individual email messages using email addresses in the data source or using a Microsoft Outlook Contacts list.

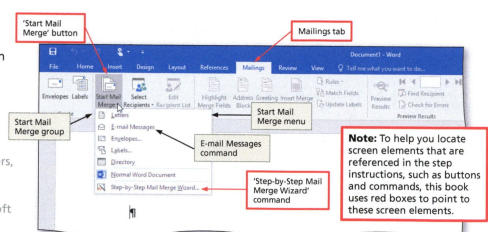

Figure 6–2

2

- Click 'Step-by-Step Mail Merge Wizard' on the Start Mail Merge menu to display Step 1 of the Mail Merge wizard in the Mail Merge task pane (Figure 6–3).

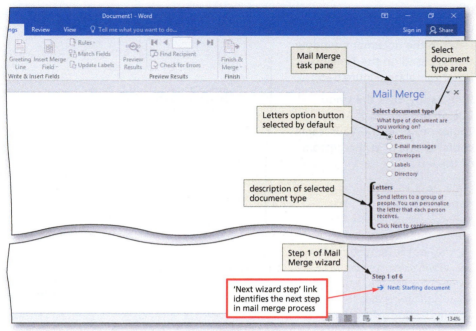

Figure 6–3

3

- Click the 'Next wizard step' link at the bottom of the Mail Merge task pane to display Step 2 of the Mail Merge wizard, which requests you select a starting document.

- Click 'Start from a template' in the Select starting document area and then click the 'Select mail merge template' link to display the Select Template dialog box.

Q&A

Why does the link name in the step differ from the name displayed in the Mail Merge task pane?

As with buttons and boxes, the text that appears on the screen may vary, depending on your screen resolution. The name that appears in the ScreenTip (when you point to the link), however, never changes. For this reason, this book uses the name that appears in the ScreenTip to identify links, buttons, boxes, and other on-screen elements.

- Click the Letters tab (Select Template dialog box) to display the Letters sheet and then click Timeless letter, which shows a preview of the selected template in the Preview area (Figure 6–4).

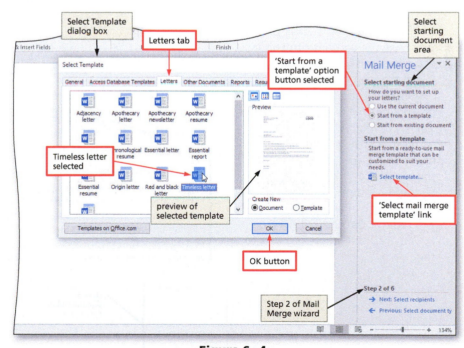

Figure 6–4

Experiment

- Click various Letter templates in the Letters sheet and watch the preview change in the right pane of the dialog box. When you are finished experimenting, click the Timeless letter template to select it.

Q&A

What if I cannot locate the Timeless letter template?

Skip the remainder of these steps and proceed to the steps called To Start a Mail Merge from an Existing Document that are shaded yellow, which immediately follow this set of steps.

4

- Click the OK button to display a letter in the document window that is based on the Timeless letter template (Figure 6–5).

- If necessary, click the Undo button on the Quick Access Toolbar to reset the Your Name content control at the bottom of the letter.

Q&A
Can I close the Mail Merge task pane?
Yes, you can close the Mail Merge task pane at any time by clicking its Close button. When you want to continue with the merge process, you repeat these steps and Word will resume the merge process at the correct step in the Mail Merge wizard.

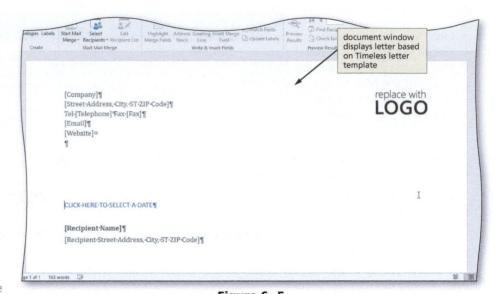

Figure 6–5

5

- Print the document shown on the screen so that you easily can see the entire letter contents (Figure 6–6).

Q&A
What are the content controls in the document?
Recall that a content control contains placeholder text and instructions for filling in areas of the document. To select a content control, click it. Later in this module, you will personalize the placeholder text and content controls. You also will remove the content controls as you are finished adding text to them.

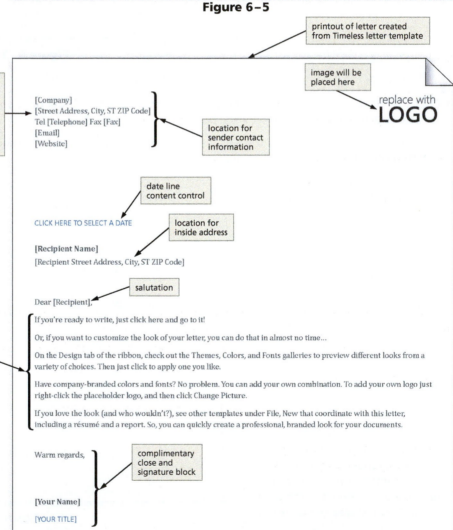

Figure 6–6

Other Ways

1. Open Backstage view, click New tab, type `letters` in 'Search for online templates' box, click Start searching button, click desired letter template, click Create button

To Start a Mail Merge from an Existing Document

If you are unable to locate the Timeless letter template in the previous steps or if your template differs from the one shown in Figure 6–6, you can open the template from the Data Files. Please contact your instructor for information about accessing the Data Files. The following steps open a document. NOTE: PERFORM THE STEPS IN THIS YELLOW BOX ONLY IF YOU WERE UNABLE TO LOCATE THE TIMELESS LETTER TEMPLATE IN THE PREVIOUS STEPS.

1. Click the 'Start from existing document' option button in the Mail Merge task pane to display options for opening a document in the task pane.

2. Click the Open button that appears in the Mail Merge task pane to display the Open dialog box.

3. Navigate to the location of the Timeless letter file to be opened. Click the Timeless letter file to select it.

4. Click the Open button (Open dialog box) to open the selected file.

To Change the User Name and Initials

If you wanted to change the user name and initials associated with your copy of Microsoft Word, you would perform the following steps.

1. Open the Backstage view and then click the Options tab to display the Word Options dialog box.

2. If necessary, click General in the left pane (Word Options dialog box).

3. Enter your name in the User name text box.

4. Enter your initials in the Initials text box.

5. Click the OK button.

BTW
Touch Screen Differences
The Office and Windows interfaces may vary if you are using a touch screen. For this reason, you might notice that the function or appearance of your touch screen differs slightly from this module's presentation.

To Change Theme Colors

Recall that Word provides document themes, which contain a variety of color schemes and other effects. This cover letter uses the Aspect theme colors to match the theme colors used in the resume. The following steps change the theme colors.

1. Click Design on the ribbon to display the Design tab.

2. Click the Theme Colors button (Design tab | Document Formatting group) to display the Theme Colors gallery.

3. Scroll to and then click Aspect in the Theme Colors gallery to change the theme colors to the selected theme.

To Enter and Format the Sender Information

The next step is to enter the sender's contact information at the top of the letter. You will use the [Company] placeholder text for the sender's name. You will delete the [Fax] and [Website] placeholder text because this sender does not have a fax or website.

Then, you will change the font size of the text. The following steps enter and format the sender information.

1 Select the placeholder text, [Company], and then type **Nina Tamaya Yazzie** as the sender name.

If requested by your instructor, enter your name instead of the job seeker's name.

2 Select the placeholder text, [Street Address, City, ST ZIP Code], and then type **2640 Bartlett Street, Ponrolet, MI 66589** as the sender's address.

3 Select the text, Tel, and then type **Cell:** as the label. Select the placeholder text, [Telephone], and then type **872-555-1547** as the sender's cell phone number.

4 Delete the Fax label and [Fax] placeholder text.

5 Select the placeholder text, [Email], and then type **nyazzie@world.net** as the sender's email address.

6 Delete the [Website] placeholder text and then press the BACKSPACE key to delete the blank line.

7 Increase the font size of the name to 14 point, and decrease the font size of the street address, cell phone, and email address to 9 point.

8 Select the name and all contact information. Bold the text (shown in Figure 6–7).

BTW

The Ribbon and Screen Resolution
Word may change how the groups and buttons within the groups appear on the ribbon, depending on the computer or mobile device's screen resolution. Thus, your ribbon may look different from the ones in this book if you are using a screen resolution other than 1366 × 768.

To Change a Picture and Format It

The current picture in the letter contains the text, replace with LOGO, which is a placeholder for a picture. The following steps change a picture.

1 Right-click the picture to be changed (in this case, the picture placeholder with the text, replace with LOGO) to display a shortcut menu (Figure 6–7).

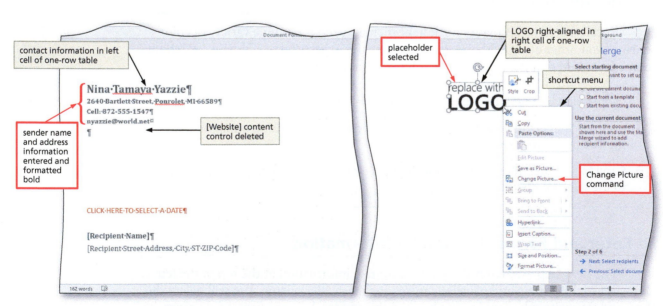

Figure 6–7

2 Click Change Picture on the shortcut menu to display the Insert Pictures dialog box.

Q&A Can I use the Change Picture button (Picture Tools Format tab | Adjust group) instead of the shortcut menu to display the Insert Pictures dialog box?
Yes.

3 Type **notepad** in the Search box (Insert Pictures dialog box) and then click the Search button to display a list of images that matches the entered search text.

4 Scroll through the list of images to locate the one shown in Figure 6–8 (or a similar image), click the image to select it, and then click the Insert button (Insert Picture dialog box) to download the image, close the dialog box, and replace the selected placeholder with the new picture file (shown in Figure 6–8).

Q&A What if I cannot locate the same image?
Click the Cancel button and then click the From File button (Insert tab | Illustrations group), navigate to the Notepad-Icons-2400px.png file on the Data Files, and then click the Insert button (Insert Picture dialog box) to insert the picture.

5 Use the Shape Height and Shape Width boxes (Picture Tools Format tab | Size group) to change the picture height to approximately .8" and width to .79".

To Shade Cells and a Shape

In the letter in this module, the left and right cells of the table containing the contact information and picture are shaded different colors. These two cells are contained in a rectangular shape, which extends below these two cells. By shading the cells in the table and the rectangular shape each a separate color, you create a letterhead with three different colors. The following steps shade table cells and a shape.

1 Position the insertion point in the contact information (upper-left cell of table). Display the Table Tools Layout tab and then, if necessary, click the 'View Table Gridlines' button (Table Tools Layout tab | Table group) to show table gridlines.

Q&A Why show table gridlines?
With table gridlines showing, the cells are easier to see.

2 Display the Table Tools Design tab. With the insertion point in the left cell, click the Shading arrow (Table Tools Design tab | Table Styles group) and then click 'Orange, Accent 1, Darker 25%' (fifth color, fifth row) to shade the current cell with the selected color.

3 Select the contact information in the left cell and change its font color to 'White, Background 1' (first color, first row).

4 Position the insertion point in the cell with the picture, click the Shading arrow (Table Tools Design tab | Table Styles group) and then click 'Tan, Background 2, Darker 25%' (third color, third row) to shade the current cell with the selected color.

5 Position the insertion point on the paragraph mark below the shaded cell to select the rectangle drawing object. Display the Drawing Tools Format tab. Click the Shape Fill arrow (Drawing Tools Format tab | Shape Styles group) to display the Shape Fill gallery (Figure 6–8) and then click 'Orange, Accent 1, Lighter 40%' (fifth color, fourth row) to shade the selected shape with the selected color.

6 Hide table gridlines.

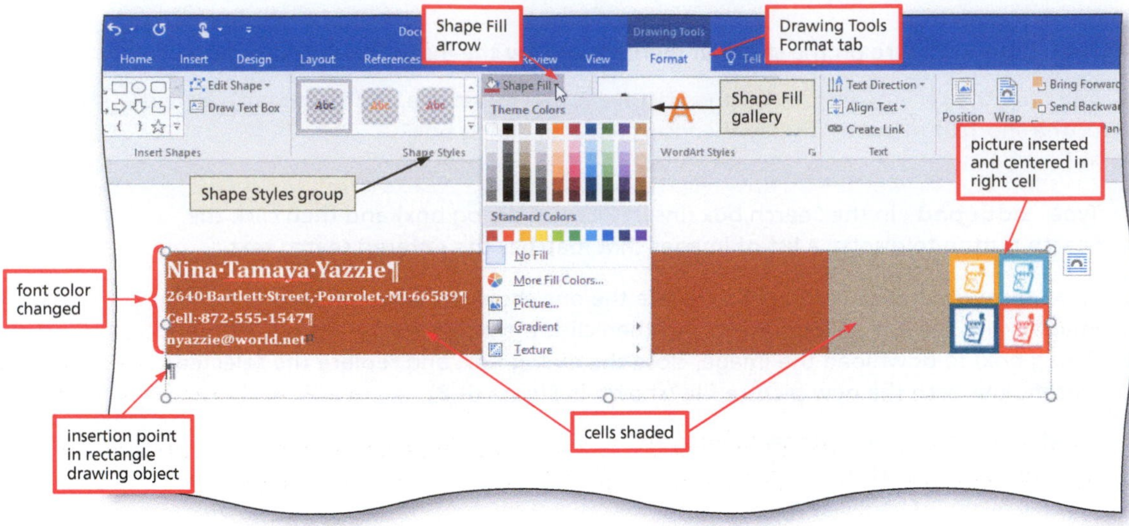

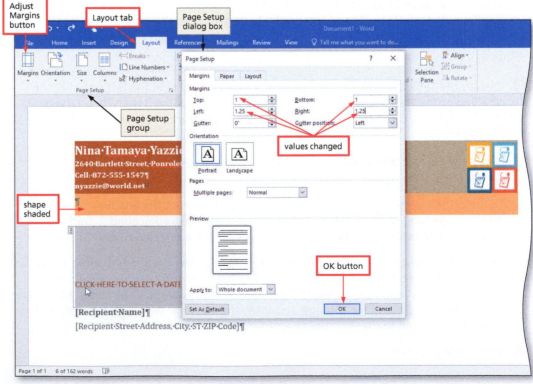

Figure 6–8

To Change Margin Settings

The Timeless letter template uses 1.9-inch top and .75-inch bottom, left, and right margins. You want the form letter to use 1-inch top and bottom margins and 1.25-inch left and right margins. The following steps change the margin settings.

1 Click the Date content control to deselect the drawing object.

2 Display the Layout tab. Click the Adjust Margins button (Layout tab | Page Setup group) to display the Margins gallery and then click Custom Margins at the bottom of the gallery to display the Page Setup dialog box.

3 Change the values in the Top, Bottom, Left, and Right boxes (Page Setup dialog box) to 1", 1", 1.25", and 1.25", respectively (Figure 6–9).

Figure 6–9

4 Click the OK button to change the margin values.

Why is the top margin unchanged?

The template specifies that the rectangle shape be positioned a certain distance from the top of the page, regardless of margin settings. The next steps change the position of the shape.

To Specify the Position of a Graphic

The next step is to change the distance between the shape and the top of the page. *Why? You want a one-inch space above the shape.* The following steps specify the position of a graphic.

1

- Click the rectangle shape to select it.

- Click the Layout Options button attached to the shape to display the Layout Options gallery (Figure 6–10).

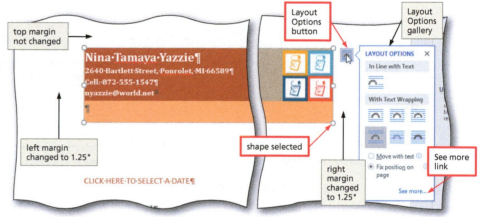

Figure 6–10

2

- Click the See more link (Layout Options gallery) to display the Position tab in the Layout dialog box.

- Click Absolute position in the Vertical area (Layout dialog box), select the value in the Absolute position box, and then type **1** to specify the distance in inches from the top of the page.

- If necessary, click the below arrow and select Page (Figure 6–11).

Q&A What is the difference between the specifications in the Horizontal and Vertical areas? Horizontal settings specify the graphic's position left to right on the page, whereas vertical settings specify the graphic's position top to bottom on the page.

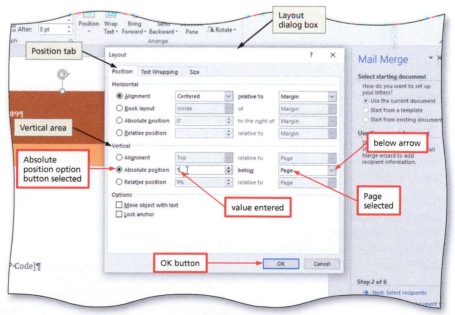

Figure 6–11

• Click the OK button to change the position of the selected graphic (Figure 6–12).

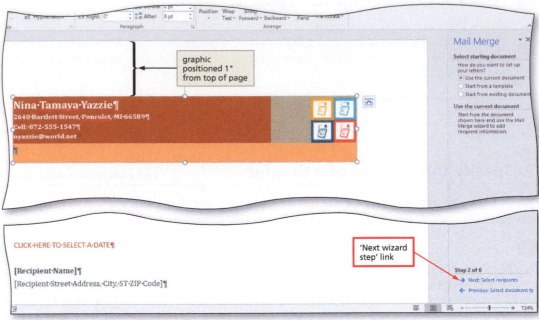

Figure 6–12

To Create a Folder while Saving

1 IDENTIFY MAIN DOCUMENT | 2 CREATE DATA SOURCE | 3 COMPOSE MAIN DOCUMENT
4 MERGE DATA SOURCE | 5 ADDRESS MAILING LABELS | 6 MERGE TO DIRECTORY

You have performed several tasks while creating this project and, thus, should save it. The following steps assume you already have created folders for storing files, for example, a CIS 101 folder (for your class) that contains a Word folder and module folders. You want to save this and all other documents created in this module in a folder called Job Hunting folder in the Word folder. The following steps create a folder during the process of saving a document. ***Why?*** *This folder does not exist, so you must create it. Rather than creating the folder in Windows, you can create folders in Word.*

• Display the Save As dialog box associated with your desired save location, type **Yazzie Cover Letter** as the file name, and navigate to the desired save location for the new folder.

• Click the 'Create a new folder' button to display a new folder icon with the name, New folder, selected in the dialog box (Figure 6–13).

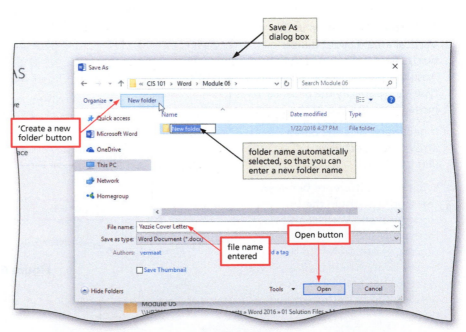

Figure 6–13

2

- Type **Job Hunting** as the new folder name and then press the ENTER key to create the new folder.

- Click the Open button to open the selected folder, in this case, the Job Hunting folder (Figure 6–14).

3

- Click the Save button (Save As dialog box) to save the current document in the selected folder on the selected drive.

Q&A Can I create a folder in any other dialog box?
Yes. Any dialog box that displays a File list, such as the Open and Insert File dialog boxes, also has the 'Create a new folder' button, allowing you to create a new folder in Word instead of using Windows for this task.

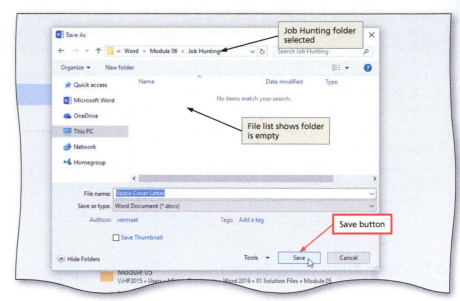

Figure 6–14

Creating a Data Source

The **data source** is a file that contains the variable, or changing, values from one merged document to the next. A data source can be an Access database table, an Outlook contacts list, or an Excel worksheet. If the necessary and properly organized data already exists in one of these Office programs, you can instruct Word to use the existing file as the data source for the mail merge. Otherwise, you can create a new data source using one of these programs.

As shown in Figure 6–15, a data source often is shown as a table that consists of a series of rows and columns. Each row is called a **record**. The first row of a data source is called the **header record** because it identifies the name of each column. Each row below the header row is called a data record. A **data record** contains the text that varies in each occurrence of the merged document. The data source for the project in this module contains five data records. In this project, each data record identifies a different potential employer. Thus, five form letters will be generated from this data source.

Each column in the data source is called a **data field**. A data field represents a group of similar data. Each data field must be identified uniquely with a name, called a **field name**. For example, Position is the name of the data field (column) that contains the available job position. In this module, the data source contains 11 data fields with the following field names: Title, First Name, Last Name, Organization Name, Address Line 1, Address Line 2, City, State, ZIP Code, Position, and Station Type.

BTW

Fields and Records
Field and record are terms that originate from the software development field. Do not be intimidated by these terms. A field is simply a column in a table, and a record is a row. Instead of as a field, some software developers identify a column of data as a variable or an attribute. All three terms (field, variable, and attribute) have the same meaning.

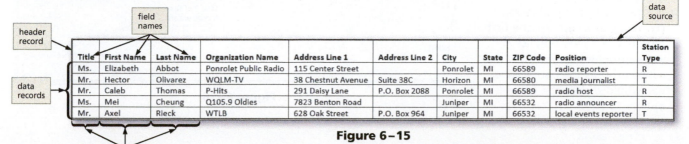

Title	First Name	Last Name	Organization Name	Address Line 1	Address Line 2	City	State	ZIP Code	Position	Station Type
Ms.	Elizabeth	Abbot	Ponrolet Public Radio	115 Center Street		Ponrolet	MI	66589	radio reporter	R
Mr.	Hector	Olivarez	WQLM-TV	38 Chestnut Avenue	Suite 38C	Horizon	MI	66580	media journalist	T
Mr.	Caleb	Thomas	P-Hits	291 Daisy Lane	P.O. Box 2088	Ponrolet	MI	66589	radio host	R
Ms.	Mei	Cheung	Q105.9 Oldies	7823 Benton Road		Juniper	MI	66532	radio announcer	R
Mr.	Axel	Rieck	WTLB	628 Oak Street	P.O. Box 964	Juniper	MI	66532	local events reporter	T

Figure 6–15

What guidelines should you follow when creating a data source?

When you create a data source, you will need to determine the fields it should contain. That is, you will need to identify the data that will vary from one merged document to the next. Following are a few important points about fields:

- For each field, you may be required to create a field name. Because data sources often contain the same fields, some programs create a list of commonly used field names that you may use.

- Field names must be unique; that is, no two field names may be the same.

- Fields may be listed in any order in the data source. That is, the order of fields has no effect on the order in which they will print in the main document.

- Organize fields so that they are flexible. For example, separate the name into individual fields: title, first name, and last name. This arrangement allows you to print a person's title, first name, and last name (e.g., Ms. Elizabeth Abbot) in the inside address but only the title and last name in the salutation (Dear Ms. Abbot).

To Create a New Data Source

1 IDENTIFY MAIN DOCUMENT | **2 CREATE DATA SOURCE** | 3 COMPOSE MAIN DOCUMENT
4 MERGE DATA SOURCE | 5 ADDRESS MAILING LABELS | 6 MERGE TO DIRECTORY

Word provides a list of 13 commonly used field names. This project uses 9 of the 13 field names supplied by Word: Title, First Name, Last Name, Company Name, Address Line 1, Address Line 2, City, State, and ZIP Code. This project does not use the other four field names supplied by Word: Country or Region, Home Phone, Work Phone, and E-mail Address. Thus, you will delete these four field names. Then, you will change the Company Name field name to Organization Name. *Why? The term, organization, better describes the potential employers in this project.* You also will add two new field names (Position and Station Type) to the data source. *Why? You want to reference the available position, as well as the station type, in the form letter.* The next steps create a new data source for a mail merge.

- Click the 'Next wizard step' link at the bottom of the Mail Merge task pane (shown in Figure 6–12) to display Step 3 of the Mail Merge wizard, which requests you select recipients.

- Click 'Type a new list' in the Select recipients area, which displays the Type a new list area.

- Click the 'Create new recipient list' link to display the New Address List dialog box (Figure 6–16).

Q&A
When would I use the other two option buttons in the Select recipients area?
If a data source already was created, you would use the first option: Use an existing list. If you wanted to use your Outlook contacts list as the data source, you would choose the second option.

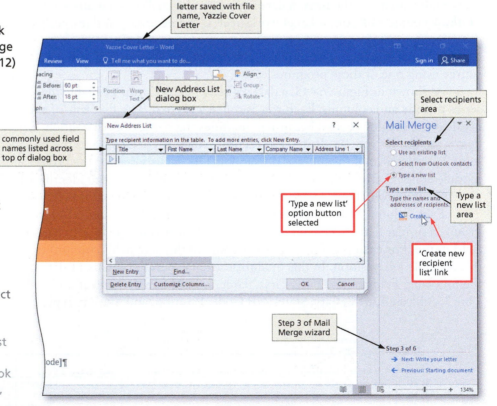

Figure 6–16

2

- Click the Customize Columns button (New Address List dialog box) to display the Customize Address List dialog box (Figure 6–17).

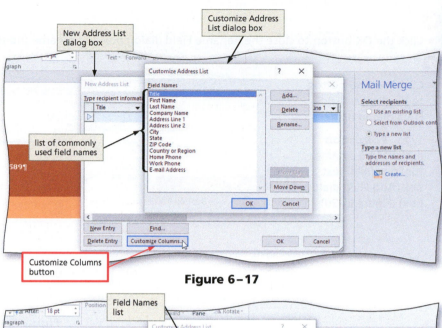

Figure 6–17

3

- Click 'Country or Region' in the Field Names list (Customize Address List dialog box) to select the field to be deleted and then click the Delete button to display a dialog box asking if you are sure you want to delete the selected field (Figure 6–18).

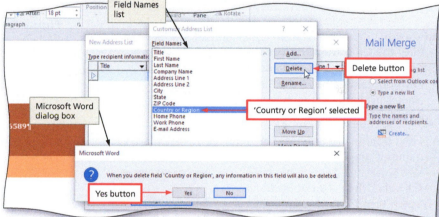

Figure 6–18

4

- Click the Yes button (Microsoft Word dialog box) to delete the field.

- Click Home Phone in the Field Names list to select the field. Click the Delete button (Customize Address List dialog box) and then click the Yes button (Microsoft Word dialog box) to delete the field.

- Use this same procedure to delete the Work Phone and E-mail Address fields.

5

- Click Company Name in the Field Names list to select the field to be renamed.

- Click the Rename button to display the Rename Field dialog box.

- Type **Organization Name** in the To text box (Rename Field dialog box) (Figure 6–19).

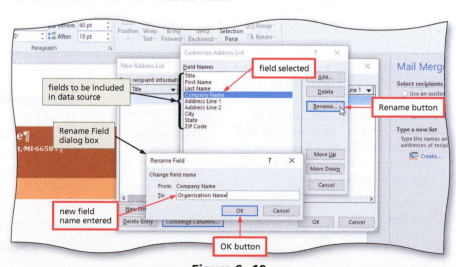

Figure 6–19

6

- Click the OK button to close the Rename Field dialog box and rename the selected field.

7

- Click the Add button to display the Add Field dialog box.

- Type **Position** in the 'Type a name for your field' text box (Add Field dialog box) (Figure 6–20).

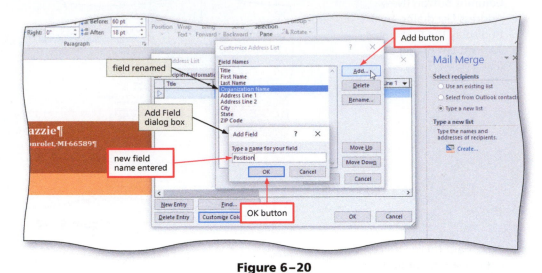

Figure 6–20

8

- Click the OK button to close the Add Field dialog box and add the Position field name to the Field Names list immediately below the selected field (Figure 6–21).

Q&A Can I change the order of the field names in the Field Names list?
Yes. Select the field name and then click the Move Up or Move Down button (Customize Address List dialog box) to move the selected field in the direction of the button name.

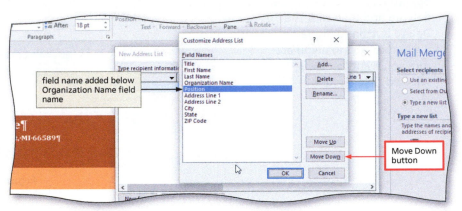

Figure 6–21

9

- With the Position field selected, click the Move Down button five times to position the selected field at the end of the Field Names list.

- Click the Add button to display the Add Field dialog box.

- Type **Station Type** (Add Field dialog box) in the 'Type a name for your field' text box and then click the OK button to close the Add Field dialog box and add the Station Type field name to the bottom of the Field Names list (Figure 6–22).

Q&A Could I add more field names to the list?
Yes. You would click the Add button for each field name you want to add.

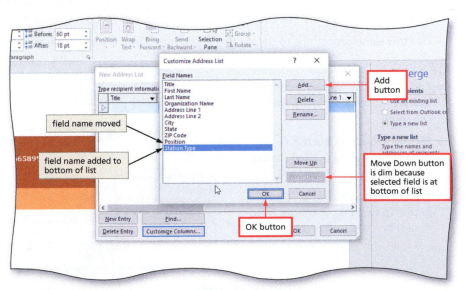

Figure 6–22

10

- Click the OK button to close the Customize Address List dialog box, which positions the insertion point in the Title text box for the first record (row) in the New Address List dialog box (Figure 6–23).

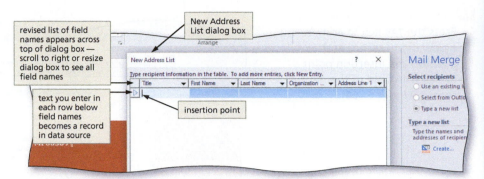

Figure 6–23

 11

- Type **Ms.** and then press the TAB key to enter the title for the first data record.

- Type **Elizabeth** and then press the TAB key to enter the first name.

- Type **Abbot** and then press the TAB key to enter the last name.

- Type **Ponrolet Public Radio** and then press the TAB key to enter the organization name.

- Type **115 Center Street** to enter the first address line (Figure 6–24).

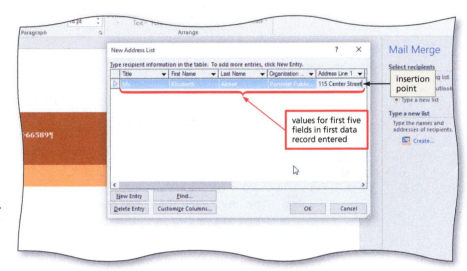

Figure 6–24

Q&A What if I notice an error in an entry?
Click the entry and then correct the error as you would in the document window.

What happened to the rest of the Organization Name entry?
It is stored in the field, but you cannot see the entire entry because it is longer than the display area.

 12

- Press the TAB key twice to leave the second address line empty.

- Type **Ponrolet** and then press the TAB key to enter the city.

- Type **MI** and then press the TAB key to enter the state code.

- Type **66589** and then press the TAB key to enter the ZIP code.

- Type **radio reporter** and then press the TAB key to enter the position.

- Type **R** to enter the code for the station type (Figure 6–25).

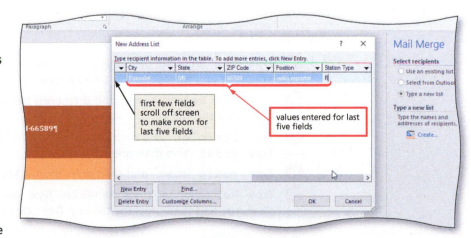

Figure 6–25

Q&A What does the R mean in the station type?
You decide to enter R for radio station and T for television station to minimize the amount of redundant typing for these records.

- Press the TAB key to add a new blank record and position the insertion point in the Title field of the new record (Figure 6–26).

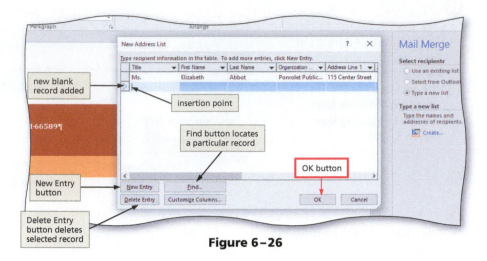

Figure 6–26

Other Ways

1. Click Select Recipients button (Mailings tab | Start Mail Merge group)

To Enter More Records

The following steps enter the remaining four records in the New Address List dialog box.

1 Type **Mr.** and then press the TAB key. Type **Hector** and then press the TAB key. Type **Olivarez** and then press the TAB key. Type **WQLM-TV** and then press the TAB key.

2 Type **38 Chestnut Avenue** and then press the TAB key. Type **Suite 38C** and then press the TAB key.

3 Type **Horizon** and then press the TAB key. Type **MI** and then press the TAB key. Type **66580** and then press the TAB key.

4 Type **media journalist** and then press the TAB key. Type **T** and then press the TAB key.

Q&A Instead of pressing the TAB key, can I click the New Entry button at the end of one row to add a new blank record?
Yes. Clicking the New Entry button at the end of a row has the same effect as pressing the TAB key.

5 Type **Mr.** and then press the TAB key. Type **Caleb** and then press the TAB key. Type **Thomas** and then press the TAB key. Type **P-Hits** and then press the TAB key.

6 Type **291 Daisy Lane** and then press the TAB key. Type **P.O. Box 2088** and then press the TAB key.

7 Type **Ponrolet** and then press the TAB key. Type **MI** and then press the TAB key. Type **66589** and then press the TAB key.

8 Type **radio host** and then press the TAB key. Type **R** and then press the TAB key.

9 Type **Ms.** and then press the TAB key. Type **Mei** and then press the TAB key. Type **Cheung** and then press the TAB key. Type **Q105.9 Oldies** and then press the TAB key.

10 Type **7823 Benton Road** and then press the TAB key twice. Type **Juniper** and then press the TAB key. Type **MI** and then press the TAB key. Type **66532** and then press the TAB key.

11 Type **radio announcer** and then press the TAB key. Type **R** and then press the TAB key.

BTW
Saving Data Sources
Word, by default, saves a data source in the My Data Sources folder on your computer or mobile device's default storage location. Likewise, when you open a data source, Word initially looks in the My Data Sources folder for the file. Because the data source files you create in Word are saved as Microsoft Access database file types, you can open and view these files in Access if you are familiar with Microsoft Access.

⑫ Type **Mr.** and then press the TAB key. Type **Axel** and then press the TAB key. Type **Rieck** and then press the TAB key. Type **WTLB** and then press the TAB key.

⑬ Type **628 Oak Street** and then press the TAB key. Type **P.O. Box 694** and then press the TAB key.

⑭ Type **Juniper** and then press the TAB key. Type **MI** and then press the TAB key. Type **66532** and then press the TAB key.

⑮ Type **local events reporter** and then press the TAB key. Type **T** and then click the OK button (shown in Figure 6–26), which displays the Save Address List dialog box (shown in Figure 6–27).

To Save a Data Source when Prompted by Word

1 IDENTIFY MAIN DOCUMENT | 2 CREATE DATA SOURCE | 3 COMPOSE MAIN DOCUMENT
4 MERGE DATA SOURCE | 5 ADDRESS MAILING LABELS | 6 MERGE TO DIRECTORY

When you click the OK button in the New Address List dialog box, Word displays the Save Address List dialog box. **Why?** *You immediately save the data source so that you do not lose any entered information.* By default, the save location is the My Data Sources folder on your computer's hard drive. In this module, you save the data source to the Job Hunting folder created earlier in this module. The following steps save the data source.

- Type **Yazzie Prospective Employers** in the File name box (Save Address List dialog box) as the name for the data source. Do not press the ENTER key after typing the file name because you do not want to close the dialog box at this time.

- Navigate to the desired save location for the data source (for example, the Job Hunting folder) (Figure 6–27).

Q&A What is a Microsoft Office Address Lists file type?

It is a Microsoft Access database file. If you are familiar with Microsoft Access, you can open the Yazzie Prospective Employers file in Access. You do not have to be familiar with Access or have

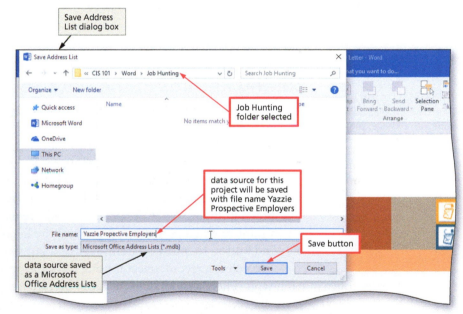

Figure 6–27

Access installed on your computer, however, to continue with this mail merge process. Word simply stores a data source as an Access table because it is an efficient method of storing a data source.

- Click the Save button (Save Address List dialog box) to save the data source in the selected folder using the entered file name and then display the Mail Merge Recipients dialog box (Figure 6–28).

Q&A What if the fields in my Mail Merge Recipients list are in a different order?

The order of fields in the Mail Merge Recipients list has no effect on the mail merge process. If Word rearranges the order, you can leave them in the revised order.

- Click the OK button to close the Mail Merge Recipients dialog box.

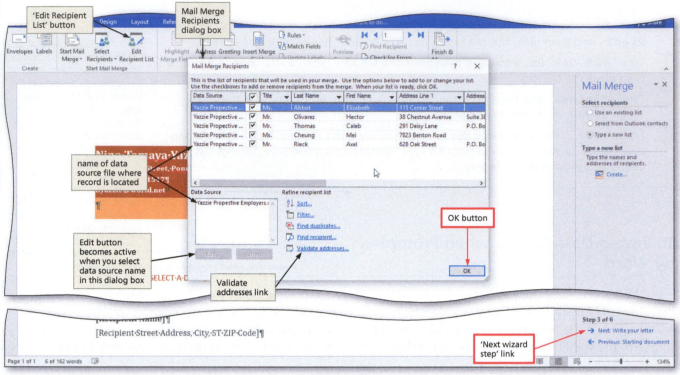

Figure 6–28

BTW

Validating Addresses
If you have installed address validation software, you can click the Validate addresses link (shown in Figure 6–28) in the Mail Merge Recipients dialog box to validate your recipients' addresses. If you have not yet installed address validation software and would like information about doing so, click the Validate addresses link in the Mail Merge Recipients dialog box and then click the Yes button in the Microsoft Word dialog box to display a related Microsoft Office webpage.

Editing Records in the Data Source

All of the data records have been entered in the data source and saved with the file name, Yazzie Prospective Employers. To add or edit data records in the data source, you would click the 'Edit Recipient List' button (Mailings tab | Start Mail Merge group) to display the Mail Merge Recipients dialog box (shown in Figure 6–28). Click the data source name in the Data Source list and then click the Edit button (Mail Merge Recipients dialog box) to display the data records in a dialog box similar to the one shown in Figure 6–26. Then, add or edit records as described in the previous steps. If you want to edit a particular record and the list of data records is long, you can click the Find button to locate an item, such as a last name, quickly in the list.

To delete a record, select it using the same procedure described in the previous paragraph. Then, click the Delete Entry button in the dialog box (shown in Figure 6–26).

Using an Existing Data Source

Instead of creating a new data source, you can use an existing Microsoft Outlook Contacts list, an Access database table, or an Excel table as a data source in a mail merge. To use an existing data source, select the appropriate option in the Select recipients area in the Mail Merge task pane or click the Select Recipients button (Mailings tab | Start Mail Merge group) and then click the desired option on the Select Recipients menu.

For a Microsoft Outlook Contacts list, click 'Select from Outlook contacts' in the Mail Merge task pane or 'Choose from Outlook Contacts' on the Select Recipients menu to display the Select Contacts dialog box. Next, select the contact folder you wish to import (Select Contacts dialog box) and then click the OK button.

For other existing data source types, such as an Access database table or an Excel worksheet, click 'Use an existing list' in the Mail Merge task pane or on the Select Recipients menu to display the Select Data Source dialog box. Next, select the file name of the data source you wish to use and then click the Open button (Select Data Source dialog box).

With Access, you can use any field in the database in the main document. (Later in this module you use an existing Access database table as the data source.) For the merge to work correctly with an Excel table, you must ensure data is arranged properly and that the table is the only element in the file. The first row of the table should contain unique field names, and the table cannot contain any blank rows.

Composing the Main Document for the Form Letters

The next step in this project is to enter and format the text and fields in the main document for the form letters (shown in Figure 6–1a at the beginning of this module). A **main document** contains the constant, or unchanging, text, punctuation, spaces, and graphics, as well as references to the data in the data source. You will follow these steps to compose the main document for the form letter.

1. Enter the date.
2. Enter the address block.
3. Enter the greeting line (salutation).
4. Enter text and insert a merge field.
5. Enter additional text and merge fields.
6. Insert an IF field.
7. Enter the remainder of the letter.
8. Merge the letters.

What guidelines should you follow when composing the main document for a form letter?

The finished main document letter should look like a symmetrically framed picture with evenly spaced margins, all balanced below an attractive letterhead or return address. The content of the main document for the form letter should contain proper grammar, correct spelling, logically constructed sentences, flowing paragraphs, and sound ideas; it also should reference the data in the data source properly.

Be sure the main document for the form letter includes all essential business letter elements. All business letters should contain a date line, inside address, message, and signature block. Many business letters contain additional items, such as a special mailing notation(s), an attention line, a salutation, a subject line, a complimentary close, reference initials, and an enclosure notation. When finished, proofread your letter carefully.

CONSIDER THIS

To Display the Next Step in the Mail Merge Wizard

The following step displays the next step in the Mail Merge wizard, which is to write the letter.

 Click the 'Next wizard step' link at the bottom of the Mail Merge task pane (shown in Figure 6–28) to display Step 4 of the Mail Merge wizard in the Mail Merge task pane (shown in Figure 6–29).

To Enter the Date

The next step is to enter the date in the letter. *Why? All business letters should contain a date, which usually is positioned below the letterhead or return address.* You can click the date content control and type the correct date, or you can click the arrow and select the date from a calendar. The following steps use the calendar to select the date.

- Click the Date content control to select it and then click its arrow to display a calendar.

- Scroll through the calendar months until the desired month appears, October 2017, in this case (Figure 6–29).

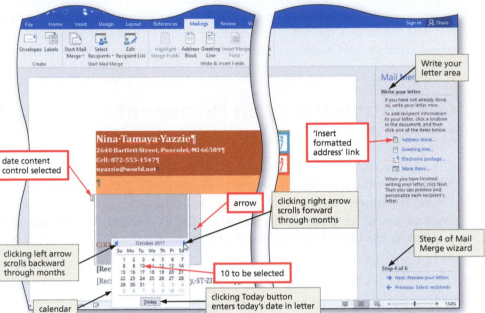

Figure 6–29

- Click 10 in the calendar to display the selected month, day, and year in the date line of the form letter (shown in Figure 6–30).

- Click outside the content control to deselect it.

- Right-click the date to display a shortcut menu and then click 'Remove Content Control' on the shortcut menu so that your text (the selected date) remains but the content control is deleted.

Q&A Why delete the content control?
You no longer need the content control because you already selected the date.

Other Ways

1. Type date in Date content control
2. Click 'Insert Date & Time' button (Insert tab | Text group)

Merge Fields

In this form letter, the inside address appears below the date line, and the salutation is placed below the inside address. The contents of the inside address and salutation are located in the data source. To link the data source to the main document, you insert the field names from the data source in the main document.

In the main document, field names linked to the data source are called **merge fields** because they merge, or combine, the main document with the contents of the data source. When a merge field is inserted in the main document, Word surrounds the field name with **merge field characters**, which are chevrons (« ») that mark the beginning and ending of a merge field. Merge field characters are not on the keyboard; therefore, you cannot type them directly in the document. Word automatically displays them when a merge field is inserted in the main document.

Most letters contain an address and salutation. For this reason, Word provides an AddressBlock merge field and a GreetingLine merge field. The **AddressBlock merge field** contains several fields related to an address: Title, First Name, Middle Name, Last Name, Suffix, Company, Street Address 1, Street Address 2, City, State, and ZIP Code. When Word uses the AddressBlock merge field, it automatically looks for any fields in the associated data source that are related to an address and then formats the address block properly when you merge the data source with the main document. For example, if your inside address does not use a middle name, suffix, or company, Word omits these items from the inside address and adjusts the spacing so that the address prints correctly.

To Insert the AddressBlock Merge Field

1 IDENTIFY MAIN DOCUMENT | 2 CREATE DATA SOURCE | 3 COMPOSE MAIN DOCUMENT
4 MERGE DATA SOURCE | 5 ADDRESS MAILING LABELS | 6 MERGE TO DIRECTORY

The default format for the AddressBlock merge field is the first name and last name on one line, followed by the street address on the next line, and then the city, state, and postal code on the next line. In this letter, you want the potential employer's title (i.e., Ms.) to appear to the left of the first name. *Why? You want to address the potential employers formally.* You also want the organization name to appear above the street address, if it does not already. The following steps insert the AddressBlock merge field in this format.

- Delete the content control that contains placeholder text for the recipient's address and then press the DELETE key to delete the blank paragraph.

- Delete the [Recipient Name] placeholder text but leave the paragraph mark; position the insertion point to the left of the paragraph mark because you will insert the AddressBlock merge field in that location.

- Click the 'Insert formatted address' link in the Mail Merge task pane (shown in Figure 6–29) to display the Insert Address Block dialog box.

- Scroll through the list of recipient name formats (Insert Address Block dialog box) and then click the format 'Mr. Joshua Randall Jr.' in this list, because that format places the title to the left of the first name and last name.

 Experiment

- Click various recipient name formats and watch the preview change in the dialog box. When finished experimenting, click 'Mr. Joshua Randall Jr.' for the format.

Q&A Why is the 'Insert company name' check box dimmed?

The data source does not have a match to the Company Name in the AddressBlock merge field so this check box will be dimmed. Recall that earlier in this project the Company Name field was renamed as Organization Name, which causes the fields to be unmatched. The next step shows how to match the fields. If the Organization Name already appears in your AddressBlock merge field, proceed to Step 4.

- Click the Match Fields button (Insert Address Block dialog box) to display the Match Fields dialog box (Figure 6–30).

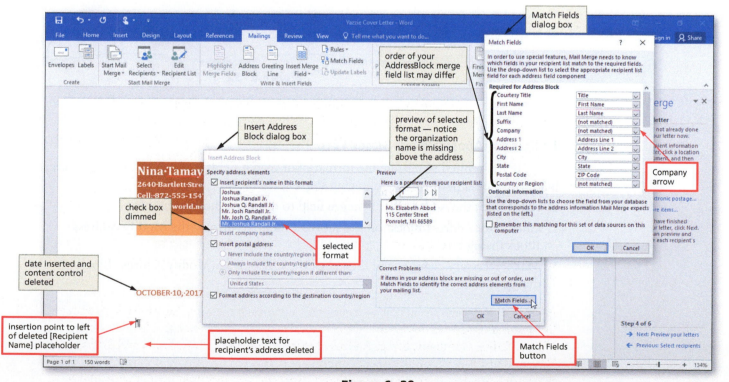

Figure 6–30

● Click the Company arrow (Match Fields dialog box) to display a list of fields in the data source and then click Organization Name to place that selected field as the match field (Figure 6–31).

● Click the OK button (Match Fields dialog box) to close the dialog box, and notice the 'Insert company name' check box no longer is dimmed (Insert Address Block dialog box) because the Company field now has a matched field in the data source.

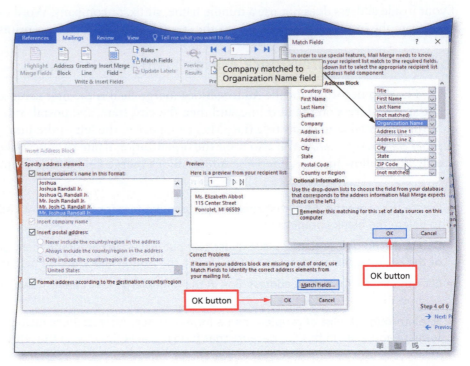

Figure 6–31

● Click the OK button (Insert Address Block dialog box) to insert the AddressBlock merge field at the location of the insertion point (Figure 6–32).

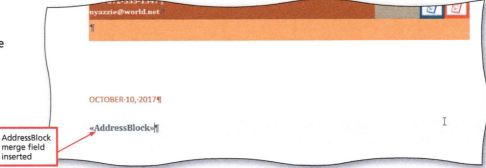

Figure 6–32

TO EDIT THE ADDRESSBLOCK MERGE FIELD

If you wanted to change the format of or match fields in the AddressBlock merge field, you would perform the following steps.

1. Right-click the AddressBlock merge field to display a shortcut menu.

2. Click 'Edit Address Block' on the shortcut menu to display the Modify Address Block dialog box.

3. Make necessary changes and then click the OK button (Modify Address Block dialog box).

To View Merged Data in the Main Document

Instead of displaying merge fields, you can display merged data. ***Why?*** *One way to see how fields, such as the AddressBlock fields, will look in the merged letter, is to view merged data.* The following step views merged data.

- Click the 'View Merged Data' button (Mailings tab | Preview Results group) to display the values in the current data record, instead of the merge fields.

- Scroll up, if necessary, to view the address fields (Figure 6–33).

Q&A
How can I tell which record is showing?
The current record number is displayed in the Preview Results group.

Why is the spacing in my address different from Figure 6–33?
You may have inserted the AddressBlock field on the line in the template that contained the recipient's address, instead of the line that contained the recipient's name. To fix the address spacing, select the entire address and then change the spacing before and after to 2 pt (Layout tab | Paragraph group).

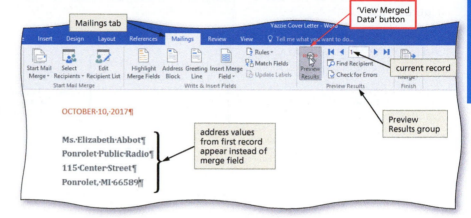

Figure 6–33

To Insert the GreetingLine Merge Field

The **GreetingLine merge field** contains text and fields related to a salutation. The default greeting for the salutation is in the format, Dear Elizabeth, followed by a comma. In this letter, you want the salutation to be followed by a colon. ***Why?*** *Business letters use a more formal salutation (Dear Ms. Abbot:) in the cover letter.* The following steps insert the GreetingLine merge field.

- Delete the word, Dear, the [Recipient] placeholder text, and the comma in the salutation but leave the paragraph mark; position the insertion point to the left of the paragraph mark because you will insert the GreetingLine merge field in that location.

- Click the 'Insert formatted salutation' link in the Mail Merge task pane to display the Insert Greeting Line dialog box.

- If necessary, click the middle arrow in the Greeting line format area (Insert Greeting Line dialog box); scroll to and then click the format, Mr. Randall, in this list because you want the title followed by the last name format.

- If necessary, click the rightmost arrow in the Greeting line format area and then click the colon (:) in the list (Figure 6–34).

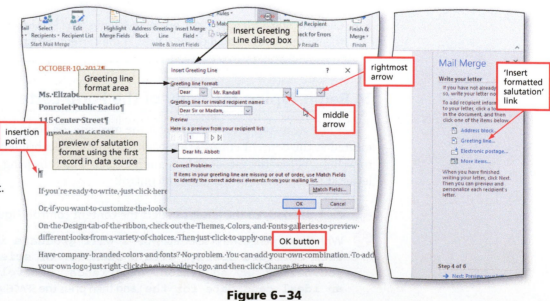

Figure 6–34

2

- Click the OK button (Insert Greeting Line dialog box) to insert the GreetingLine merge field at the location of the insertion point (Figure 6–35).

Q&A

Why are the values for the title and last name displayed instead of the merge field names? With the 'View Merged Data' button (Mailings tab | Preview Results group) still selected, the field values are displayed instead of the field names.

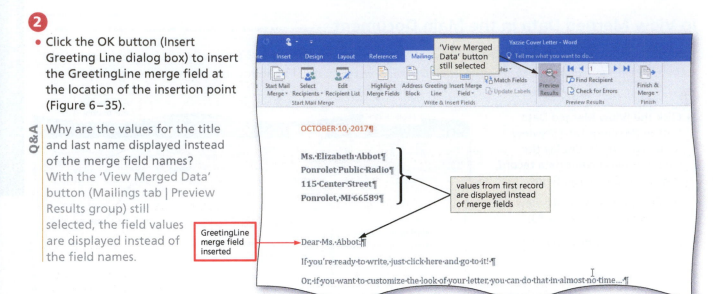

Figure 6–35

To Edit the GreetingLine Merge Field

If you wanted to change the format of or match fields in the GreetingLine merge field, you would perform the following steps.

1. Right-click the GreetingLine merge field to display a shortcut menu.
2. Click 'Edit Greeting Line' on the shortcut menu to display the Modify Greeting Line dialog box.
3. Make the necessary changes and then click the OK button (Modify Greeting Line dialog box).

To View Merge Fields in the Main Document

Because you will be entering merge fields in the document next, you wish to display the merge fields instead of the merged data. The following step views merge fields instead of merged data.

1 Click the 'View Merged Data' button (Mailings tab | Preview Results group) to display the merge fields instead of the values in the current data record (shown in Figure 6–36).

To Begin Typing the Body of the Form Letter

The next step is to begin typing the message, or body of the letter, which is located at the content control that begins with the placeholder text, If you're ready to write..., below the GreetingLine merge field. The following steps begin typing the letter at the location of the content control.

1 Click the body of the letter to select the content control (Figure 6–36).

2 With the content control selected, type `I will graduate in December from Hartford College with a bachelor of science degree in journalism. My education, experience, and volunteer work make me an ideal candidate for the` and then press the SPACEBAR (shown in Figure 6–37).

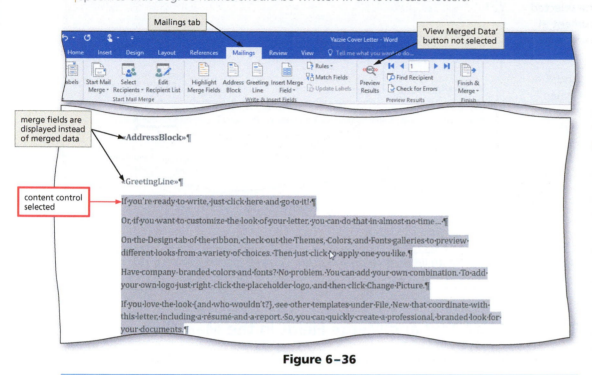

Figure 6–36

Q&A Why is the text, bachelor of science, in all lowercase letters?

This book uses the *Chicago Manual of Style* for grammar and punctuation rules, which specifies that degree names should be written in all lowercase letters.

BTW

'Insert Merge Field' Button

If you click the 'Insert Merge Field' button instead of the 'Insert Merge Field' arrow (Figure 6–37), Word displays the Insert Merge Field dialog box instead of the Insert Merge Field menu. To insert fields from the dialog box, click the field name and then click the Insert button. The dialog box remains open so that you can insert multiple fields, if necessary. When you have finished inserting fields, click the Close button in the dialog box.

To Insert a Merge Field in the Main Document

1 IDENTIFY MAIN DOCUMENT | 2 CREATE DATA SOURCE | 3 COMPOSE MAIN DOCUMENT
4 MERGE DATA SOURCE | 5 ADDRESS MAILING LABELS | 6 MERGE TO DIRECTORY

The next step is to insert the Position merge field into the main document. *Why? The first sentence in the first paragraph of the letter identifies the advertised job position, which is a merge field.* To instruct Word to use data fields from the data source, you insert merge fields in the main document for the form letter. The following steps insert a merge field at the location of the insertion point.

1

• Click the 'Insert Merge Field' arrow (Mailings tab | Write & Insert Fields group) to display the Insert Merge Field menu (Figure 6–37).

Q&A What if I accidentally click the 'Insert Merge Field' button instead of the arrow?

Click the Cancel button in the Insert Merge Field dialog box and repeat Step 1.

Why is the underscore character in some of the field names?

Word places an underscore character in place of the space in merge fields.

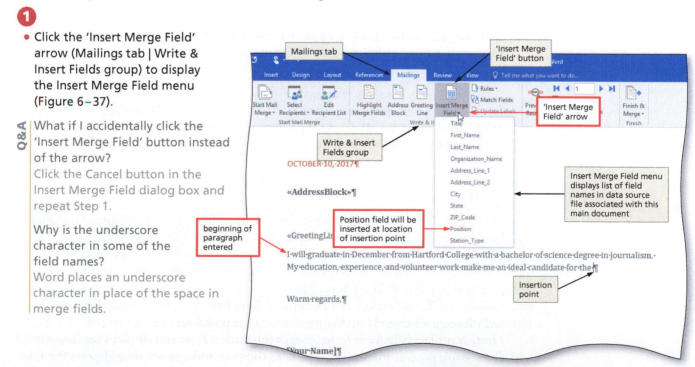

Figure 6–37

• Click Position on the Insert Merge Field menu to insert the selected merge field in the document at the location of the insertion point (Figure 6–38).

Q&A

Will the word, Position, and the chevron characters print when I merge the form letters?

No. When you merge the data source with the main document, the value in the Position field (e.g., radio reporter) will print at the location of the merge field, Position.

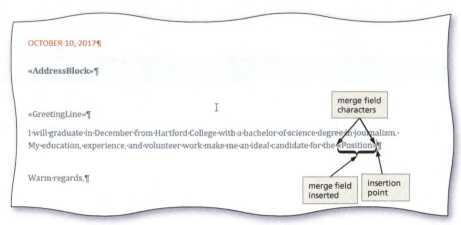

Figure 6–38

Other Ways

1. Click 'Insert Merge Field' button (Mailings tab | Write & Insert fields group), click desired field (Insert Merge Field dialog box), click Insert button, click Close button

---

BTW

Merge Fields

When you insert fields in a document, the displayed fields may be surrounded by braces instead of chevrons, and extra instructions may appear between the braces. If this occurs, then field codes have been turned on. To turn off field codes so that they are not displayed, press ALT+F9.

To Enter More Text and Merge Fields in the Main Document

The following steps enter more text and merge fields into the form letter.

1 With the insertion point at the location shown in Figure 6–38, press the SPACEBAR, type **position at** and then press the SPACEBAR again.

2 Click the 'Insert Merge Field' arrow (Mailings tab | Write & Insert Fields group) and then click Organization_Name on the Insert Merge Field menu to insert the selected merge field in the document. Press the PERIOD key.

3 Press the ENTER key. Type **As shown on the accompanying resume, my background matches the job requirements posted through the Career Development Office at Hartford College. My coursework and experience have prepared me to develop, edit, and present news stories.** and then press the ENTER key.

4 Type **Thank you in advance,** and then press the SPACEBAR. Insert the Title merge field, press the SPACEBAR, and then insert the Last Name merge field. Type **, for your time and consideration. I look forward to hearing from you soon to discuss the opportunity for my potential employment at your** and then press the SPACEBAR (shown in Figure 6–39).

IF Fields

In addition to merge fields, you can insert Word fields that are designed specifically for a mail merge. An **IF field** is an example of a Word field. One form of the IF field is called an **If...Then:** If a condition is true, then perform an action. For example, if Mary owns a house, then send her information about homeowner's insurance. Another form of the IF field is called an **If...Then...Else:** if a condition is true, then perform an action; else perform a different action. For example, if John has an email address, then send him an email message; else send him the message via the postal service.

In this project, the form letter checks the station type and displays text associated with the station type. If the station type is R, then the form letter should print the text, radio; else if the station type is T, then the form letter should print the text, television. Thus, you will use an If...Then...Else: IF the Station_Type is equal to R, then insert radio; else insert television.

The phrase that appears after the word If is called a rule, or condition. A **condition** consists of an expression, followed by a comparison operator, followed by a final expression.

Expression   The expression in a condition can be a merge field, a number, a series of characters, or a mathematical formula. Word surrounds a series of characters with quotation marks ("). To indicate an empty, or null, expression, Word places two quotation marks together ("").

Comparison Operator   The comparison operator in a condition must be one of six characters: = (equal to or matches the text), <> (not equal to or does not match text), < (less than), <= (less than or equal to), > (greater than), or >= (greater than or equal to).

If the result of a condition is true, then Word evaluates the **true text**. If the result of the condition is false, Word evaluates the **false text** if it exists. In this project, the first expression in the condition is a merge field (Station_Type); the comparison operator is equal to (=); and the second expression is the text "R". The true text is "radio". The false text is "television". The complete IF field is as follows:

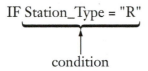

IF Station_Type = "R"   "radio"   "television"

    condition   true text   false text

BTW

IF Fields
The phrase, IF field, originates from computer programming. Do not be intimidated by the terminology. An IF field simply specifies a decision. Some software developers refer to it as an IF statement. Complex IF statements include one or more nested IF fields. A nested IF field is a second IF field inside the true or false text of the first IF field.

To Insert an IF Field in the Main Document

1 IDENTIFY MAIN DOCUMENT | 2 CREATE DATA SOURCE | **3 COMPOSE MAIN DOCUMENT**
4 MERGE DATA SOURCE | 5 ADDRESS MAILING LABELS | 6 MERGE TO DIRECTORY

The next step is to insert an IF field in the main document. **Why?** *You want to print the station type in the letter.* The following steps insert this IF field in the form letter: If the Station_Type is equal to R, then insert radio, else insert television.

• With the insertion point positioned as shown in Figure 6–39, click the Rules button (Mailings tab | Write & Insert Fields group) to display the Rules menu (Figure 6–39).

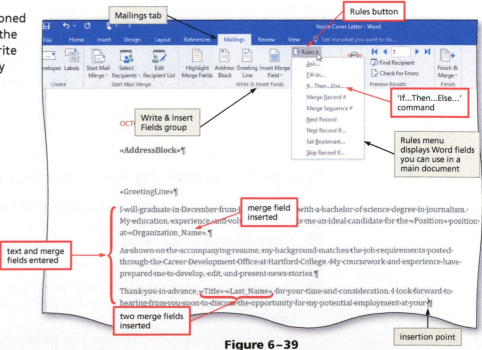

Figure 6–39

2

- Click 'If...Then...Else...' on the Rules menu to display the Insert Word Field: IF dialog box, which is where you enter the components of the IF field (Figure 6–40).

Figure 6–40

3

- Click the Field name arrow (Insert Word Field: IF dialog box) to display the list of fields in the data source.

- Scroll through the list of fields in the Field name list and then click Station_Type to select the field.

- Position the insertion point in the Compare to text box and then type **R** as the comparison text.

- Press the TAB key and then type **radio** as the true text.

- Press the TAB key and then type **television** as the false text (Figure 6–41).

Q&A Does the capitalization matter in the comparison text?

Yes. The text, R, is different from the text, r, in a comparison. Be sure to enter the text exactly as you entered it in the data source.

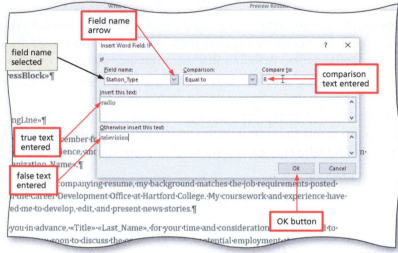

Figure 6–41

4

- Click the OK button (Insert Word Field: IF dialog box) to insert the IF field at the location of the insertion point (Figure 6–42).

Q&A Why does the main document display the text, radio, instead of the IF field instructions?

The text, radio, is displayed because the first record in the data source has a station type equal to R. Word, by default, evaluates the IF field using the current record and displays the results, called the **field results**, in the main document instead of displaying the IF field instructions. Later in the module, you will view the IF field instructions.

Figure 6–42

To Enter the Remaining Text in the Main Document

The following steps enter the remainder of the text into the form letter.

1 Press the SPACEBAR. Type **station** and then press the PERIOD key.

2 Change the closing to the word, Sincerely.

3 Change the placeholder text in the Your Name content control to Nina Tamaya Yazzie. If necessary, delete the content control so that the name remains but the content control is deleted.

If requested by your instructor, enter your name instead of the job seeker's name.

4 Delete the Your Title content control (Figure 6–43).

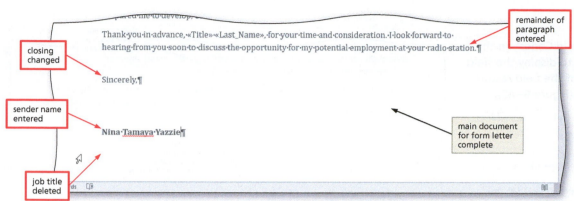

Thank·you·in·advance,·«Title»·«Last_Name»,·for·your·time·and·consideration.·I·look·forward·to·
hearing·from·you·soon·to·discuss·the·opportunity·for·my·potential·employment·at·your·radio·station.¶

Sincerely,¶

Nina·Tamaya·Yazzie¶

- **remainder of paragraph entered**
- **closing changed**
- **sender name entered**
- **job title deleted**
- **main document for form letter complete**

Figure 6–43

5 Make any additional adjustments to spacing, formats, etc., so that your main document looks like Figure 5–1 shown at the beginning of this module.

TO HIGHLIGHT MERGE FIELDS

If you wanted to highlight all the merge fields in a document so that you could identify them quickly, you would perform the following steps.

1. Click the 'Highlight Merge Fields' button (Mailings tab | Write & Insert Fields group) to highlight the merge fields in the document.

2. When finished viewing merge fields, click the 'Highlight Merge Fields' button (Mailings tab | Write & Insert Fields group) again to remove the highlight from the merge fields in the document.

BTW

Word Fields
In addition to the IF field, Word provides other fields that may be used in form letters. For example, the ASK and FILLIN fields prompt the user to enter data for each record in the data source. The SKIP RECORD IF field instructs the mail merge not to generate a form letter for a data record if a specific condition is met.

To Display a Field Code

1 IDENTIFY MAIN DOCUMENT | 2 CREATE DATA SOURCE | 3 COMPOSE MAIN DOCUMENT
4 MERGE DATA SOURCE | 5 ADDRESS MAILING LABELS | 6 MERGE TO DIRECTORY

The instructions in the IF field are not displayed in the document; instead, the field results are displayed for the current record (shown in Figure 6–42). The instructions of an IF field are called **field codes**, and the default for Word is for field codes not to be displayed. Thus, field codes do not print or show on the screen unless you turn them on. You use one procedure to show field codes on the screen and a different procedure to print them on a hard copy.

The following steps show a field code on the screen. *Why? You might want to turn on a field code to verify its accuracy or to modify it. Field codes tend to clutter the screen. Thus, most Word users turn them off after viewing them.*

1

- If necessary, scroll to display the last paragraph of the letter in the document window.

- Right-click the field results showing the text, radio, to display a shortcut menu (Figure 6–44).

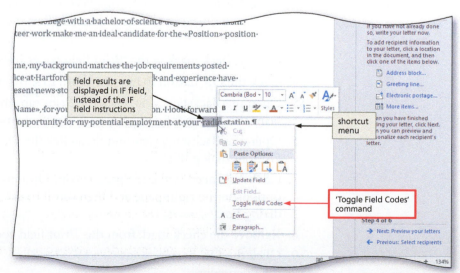

Figure 6–44

2

- Click 'Toggle Field Codes' on the shortcut menu to display the field codes instead of the field results for the IF field (Figure 6–45).

Q&A

Will displaying field codes affect the merged documents?
No. Displaying field codes has no effect on the merge process.

What if I wanted to display all field codes in a document?
You would press ALT+F9. Then, to hide all the field codes, press ALT+F9 again.

Why does the IF field turn gray?
Word, by default, shades a field in gray when the field is selected. The shading displays on the screen to help you identify fields; the shading does not print on a hard copy.

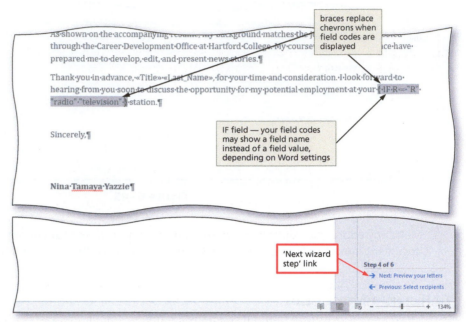

Figure 6–45

- Save the main document for the form letter again on the same storage location with the same file name.

Other Ways

1. With insertion point in field, press SHIFT+F9

BTW

Locking Fields
If you wanted to lock a field so that its field results cannot be changed, click the field and then press CTRL+F11. To subsequently unlock a field so that it may be updated, click the field and then press CTRL+SHIFT+F11.

To Print Field Codes in the Main Document

When you merge or print a document, Word automatically converts field codes that show on the screen to field results. You may want to print the field codes version of the form letter, however, so that you have a hard copy of the field codes for future reference. When you print field codes, you must remember to turn off the field codes option so that merged documents print field results instead of field codes. If you wanted to print the field codes in the main document, you would perform the following steps.

1. Open the Backstage view and then click the Options tab to display the Word Options dialog box.

2. Click Advanced in the left pane (Word Options dialog box) to display advanced options in the right pane and then scroll to the Print area in the right pane of the dialog box.

3. Place a check mark in the 'Print field codes instead of their values' check box.

4. Click the OK button to instruct Word to show field codes when the document prints.

5. Open the Backstage view, click the Print tab, and then click the Print button to print the document with all field codes showing.

6. Open the Backstage view and then click the Options tab to display the Word Options dialog box.

7. Click Advanced in the left pane (Word Options dialog box) to display advanced options in the right pane and then scroll to the Print area in the right pane of the dialog box.

8. Remove the check mark from the 'Print field codes instead of their values' check box.

9. Click the OK button to instruct Word to show field results the next time you print the document.

Opening a Main Document

You open a main document the same as you open any other Word document (i.e., clicking Open in the Backstage view). If Word displays a dialog box indicating it will run an SQL command, click the Yes button (Figure 6–46).

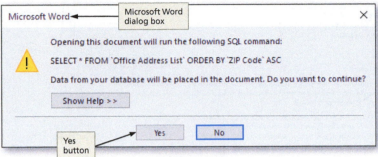

Figure 6–46

When you open a main document, Word attempts to open the associated data source file, too. If the data source is not in exactly the same location (i.e., drive and folder) as when it originally was saved, Word displays a dialog box indicating that it could not find the data source (Figure 6–47). When this occurs, click the 'Find Data Source' button to display the Open Data Source dialog box, which allows you to locate the data source file. (Word may display several dialog boxes requiring you to click an OK (or similar) button until the one shown in Figure 6–47 appears.)

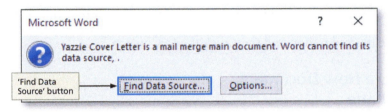

Figure 6–47

BTW

Data Source and Main Document Files
When you open a main document, if Word cannot locate the associated data source file or it does not display a dialog box with the 'Find Data Source' button, then the data source may not be associated with the main document. To associate the data source with the main document, click the Select Recipients button (Mailings tab | Start Mail Merge group), click 'Use an Existing List' on the Select Recipients menu, and then locate the data source file. When you save the main document, Word will associate the data source with the main document.

Break Point: If you wish to take a break, this is a good place to do so. You can exit Word now. To resume at a later time, run Word, open the file called Yazzie Cover Letter, and continue following the steps from this location forward.

Merging the Data Source with the Main Document to Generate Form Letters

The next step in this project is to merge the data source with the main document to generate the form letters (shown in Figure 6–1c at the beginning of this module). **Merging** is the process of combining the contents of a data source with a main document.

You can merge the form letters to a new document, which you can edit, or merge them directly to a printer. You also have the option of merging all data in a data source or merging just a portion of it. The following sections discuss various ways to merge.

To Preview the Merged Letters Using the Mail Merge Task Pane

1 IDENTIFY MAIN DOCUMENT | 2 CREATE DATA SOURCE | 3 COMPOSE MAIN DOCUMENT
4 MERGE DATA SOURCE | 5 ADDRESS MAILING LABELS | 6 MERGE TO DIRECTORY

Earlier in this module, you previewed the data in the letters using a button on the ribbon. The following step uses the Mail Merge wizard to preview the letters. *Why? The next wizard step previews the letters so that you can verify the content is accurate before performing the merge.*

• Click the 'Next wizard step' link at the bottom of the Mail Merge task pane (shown in Figure 6–45) to display Step 5 of the Mail Merge wizard in the Mail Merge task pane (Figure 6–48).

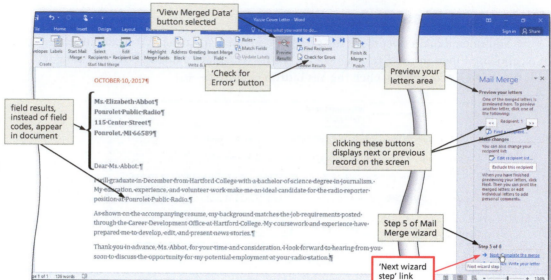

Figure 6–48

TO CHECK FOR ERRORS

Before merging documents, you can instruct Word to check for errors that might occur during the merge process. If you wanted to check for errors, you would perform the following steps.

1. Click the 'Check for Errors' button (Mailings tab | Preview Results group) (shown in Figure 6–48) or press ALT+SHIFT+K to display the Checking and Reporting Errors dialog box.

2. Select the desired option and then click the OK button.

To Merge the Form Letters to a New Document Using the Mail Merge Task Pane

1 IDENTIFY MAIN DOCUMENT | 2 CREATE DATA SOURCE | 3 COMPOSE MAIN DOCUMENT
4 MERGE DATA SOURCE | 5 ADDRESS MAILING LABELS | 6 MERGE TO DIRECTORY

With the data source and main document for the form letter complete, the next step is to merge them to generate the individual form letters. You can merge the letters to the printer or to a new document. **Why?** *If you merge the documents to a new document, you can save the merged documents in a file and then print them later, review the merged documents for accuracy and edit them as needed, or you can add personal messages to individual merged letters.* The following steps merge the form letters to a new document.

• Click the 'Next wizard step' link at the bottom of the Mail Merge task pane (shown in Figure 6–48) to display Step 6 of the Mail Merge wizard in the Mail Merge task pane.

• Click the 'Merge to new document' link in the Mail Merge task pane to display the Merge to New Document dialog box (Figure 6–49).

Q&A What if I wanted to print the merged letters immediately instead of reviewing them first in a new document window?

You would click the 'Merge to printer' link instead of the 'Merge to new document' link.

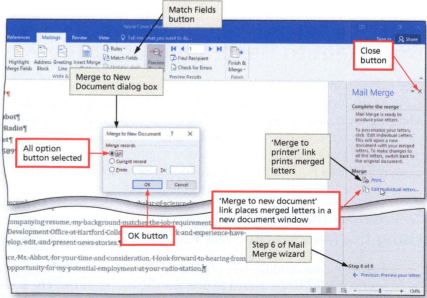

Figure 6–49

2

- If necessary, click All (Merge to New Document dialog box) so that all records in the data source are merged.

Q&A Do I have to merge all records?
No. Through this dialog box, you can merge the current record or a range of record numbers.

- Click the OK button to merge the letters to a new document, in this case, five individual letters — one for each potential employer in the data source. (If Word displays a dialog box containing a message about locked fields, click its OK button.)

- Display the View tab and then click the Multiple Pages button (View tab | Zoom group) so that you can see miniature versions of all five letters in the document window at once (Figure 6–50).

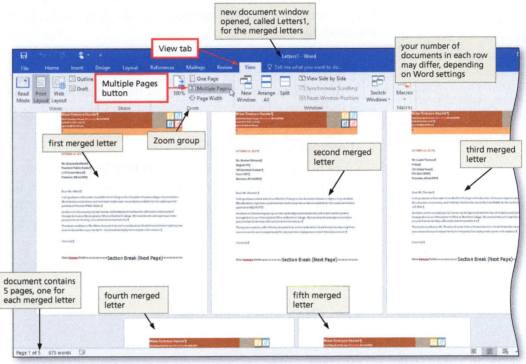

Figure 6–50

4

- Change the zoom back to page width.

Experiment

- Scroll through the merged documents so that you can read all five letters.

Q&A Why does my screen show an extra blank page at the end?
You might have a blank record in the data source, or the spacing may cause an overflow to a blank page.

Can I edit the merged letters?
Yes, you can edit the letters as you edit any other Word document. Always proofread the merged letters for accuracy before distributing them.

- Save the merged letters in the Job Hunting folder on your hard drive, OneDrive, or other storage location using the file name, Yazzie Merged Cover Letters. If requested by your instructor, print the merged letters. Close the document window containing the merged letters.

Q&A Do I have to save the document containing the merged letters?
No. You can close the document without saving it.

- Click the Close button on the Mail Merge task pane title bar (shown in Figure 6–49) because you are finished with the Mail Merge wizard.

- If necessary, click the 'View Merged Data' button to show field codes instead of merged data.

Other Ways

1. Click 'Finish & Merge' button (Mailings tab | Finish group), click 'Edit Individual Documents'

Correcting Merge Field Errors in Merged Documents

If the wrong field results appear, Word may be mapping the fields incorrectly. To view fields, click the Match Fields button (Mailings tab | Write & Insert Fields group) (shown in Figure 6–49). Then, review the fields in the list. For example, Last Name should map to the Last Name field in the data source. If it does not, click the arrow to change the name of the data source field.

If the fields are mapped incorrectly, the data in the data source may be incorrect. For a discussion about editing records in the data source, refer to that section earlier in this module.

BTW

Conserving Ink and Toner

If you want to conserve ink or toner, you can instruct Word to print draft quality documents by clicking File on the ribbon to open the Backstage view, clicking the Options tab in the Backstage view to display the Word Options dialog box, clicking Advanced in the left pane (Word Options dialog box), scrolling to the Print area in the right pane, placing a check mark in the 'Use draft quality' check box, and then clicking the OK button. Then, use the Backstage view to print the document as usual.

TO MERGE THE FORM LETTERS TO A PRINTER

If you are certain the contents of the merged letters will be correct and do not need individual editing, you can perform the following steps to merge the form letters directly to the printer.

1. If necessary, display the Mailings tab.

2. Click the 'Finish & Merge' button (Mailings tab | Finish group) and then click Print Documents on the Finish & Merge menu, or click the 'Merge to printer' link (Mail Merge task pane), to display the Merge to Printer dialog box.

3. If necessary, click All (Merge to Printer dialog box) and then click the OK button to display the Print dialog box.

4. Select desired printer settings. Click the OK button (Print dialog box) to print five separate letters, one for each potential employer in the data source, as shown in Figure 6–1c at the beginning of this module. (If Word displays a message about locked fields, click its OK button.)

To Select Records to Merge

1 IDENTIFY MAIN DOCUMENT | 2 CREATE DATA SOURCE | 3 COMPOSE MAIN DOCUMENT
4 MERGE DATA SOURCE | 5 ADDRESS MAILING LABELS | 6 MERGE TO DIRECTORY

Instead of merging all of the records in the data source, you can choose which records to merge, based on a condition you specify. The dialog box in Figure 6–49 allows you to specify by record number which records to merge. Often, though, you want to merge based on the contents of a specific field. The following steps select records for a merge. **Why?** *You want to merge just those potential employers who are television stations.*

- Click the 'Edit Recipient List' button (Mailings tab | Start Mail Merge group) to display the Mail Merge Recipients dialog box (Figure 6–51).

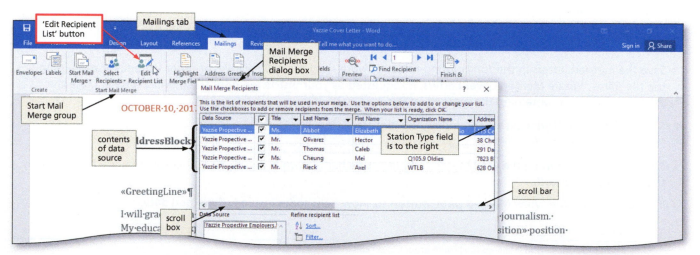

Figure 6–51

2

- Drag the scroll box to the right edge of the scroll bar (Mail Merge Recipients dialog box) so that the Station Type field appears in the dialog box.

- Click the arrow to the right of the field name, Station Type, to display sort and filter criteria for the selected field (Figure 6–52).

Q&A What are the filter criteria in the parentheses?
The (All) option clears any previously set filter criteria. The (Blanks) option selects records that contain blanks in that field, and the (Nonblanks) option selects records that do not contain blanks in that field. The (Advanced) option displays the Filter and Sort dialog box, which allows you to perform more advanced record selection operations.

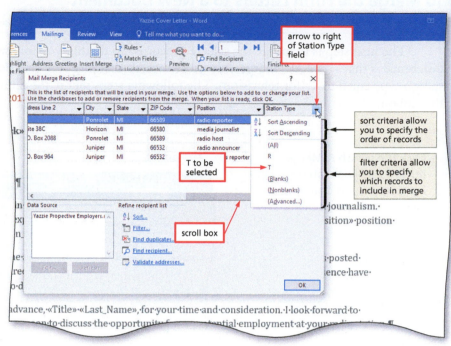

Figure 6–52

3

- Click T to reduce the number of data records displayed (Mail Merge Recipients dialog box) to two, because two potential employers are television stations (Figure 6–53).

Q&A What happened to the other three records that did not meet the criteria?
They still are part of the data source; they just are not appearing in the Mail Merge Recipients dialog box. When you clear the filter, all records will reappear.

4

- Click the OK button to close the Mail Merge Recipients dialog box.

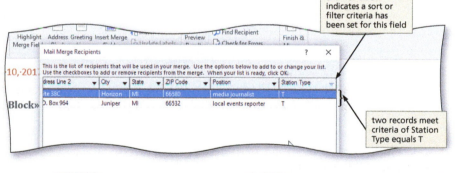

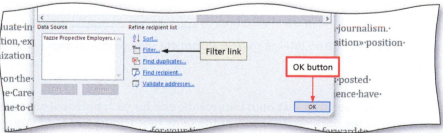

Figure 6–53

Other Ways

1. Click Filter link (Mail Merge Recipients dialog box), click Filter Records tab (Sort and Filter dialog box), enter filter criteria, click OK button

To Merge the Form Letters to a New Document Using the Ribbon

The next step is to merge the selected records. To do this, you follow the same steps described earlier. The difference is that Word will merge only those records that meet the criteria specified, that is, just those with a station type equal to T (for television). The following steps merge the filtered records to a new document using the ribbon.

1

- Click the 'Finish & Merge' button (Mailings tab | Finish group) to display the Finish & Merge menu (Figure 6–54).

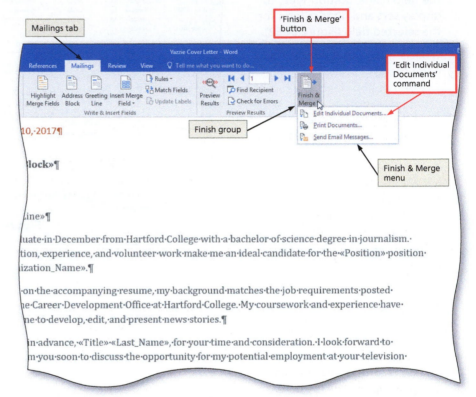

Figure 6–54

2

- Click 'Edit Individual Documents' on the Finish & Merge menu to display the Merge to New Document dialog box. If necessary, click All in the dialog box.

- Click the OK button (Merge to New Document dialog box) to display the merged documents in a new document window.

3

- Change the zoom so that both documents, one for each potential employer whose station type field equals T, appear in the document window at the same time (Figure 6–55). (If Word displays a message about locked fields, click its OK button.)

4

- Close the window. Do not save the merged documents.

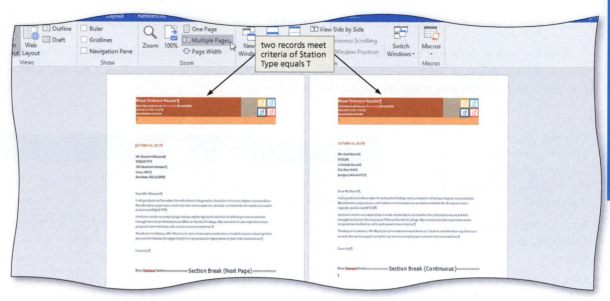

Figure 6-55

To Remove a Merge Condition

1 IDENTIFY MAIN DOCUMENT | 2 CREATE DATA SOURCE | 3 COMPOSE MAIN DOCUMENT
4 MERGE DATA SOURCE | 5 ADDRESS MAILING LABELS | 6 MERGE TO DIRECTORY

The next step is to remove the merge condition. *Why? You do not want future merges be restricted to potential employers with a station type equal to T.* The following steps remove a merge condition.

- Click the 'Edit Recipient List' button (Mailings tab | Start Mail Merge group) to display the Mail Merge Recipients dialog box.

- Click the Filter link (Mail Merge Recipients dialog box) to display the Filter and Sort dialog box.

- If necessary, click the Filter Records tab to display the Filter Records sheet (Figure 6-56).

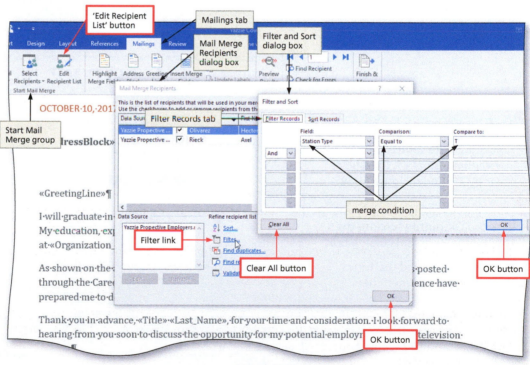

Figure 6-56

Q&A Can I specify a merge condition in this dialog box instead of using the box arrow in the Mail Merge Recipients dialog box?
Yes.

- Click the Clear All button (Filter and Sort dialog box) to remove the merge condition from the dialog box.
- Click the OK button in each of the two open dialog boxes to close the dialog boxes.

To Sort the Data Records in a Data Source

The following steps sort the data records by ZIP code. *Why? You may want the form letters printed in a certain order. For example, if you mail the form letters using the U.S. Postal Service's bulk rate mailing service, the post office requires that you sort and group the form letters by ZIP code.*

- Click the 'Edit Recipient List' button (Mailings tab | Start Mail Merge group) to display the Mail Merge Recipients dialog box.

- Scroll to the right until the ZIP Code field shows in the dialog box.

- Click the arrow to the right of the field name, ZIP Code, to display a menu of sort and filter criteria (Figure 6–57).

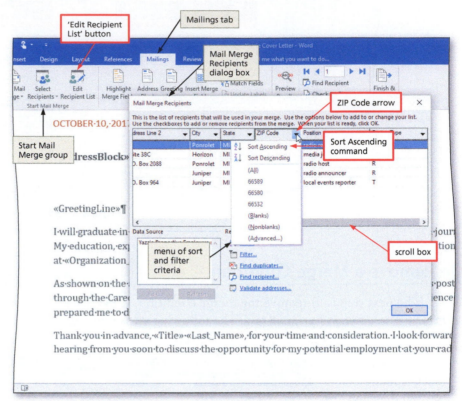

Figure 6–57

- Click Sort Ascending on the menu to sort the data source records in ascending (smallest to largest) order by ZIP Code (Figure 6–58).

- Click the OK button to close the Mail Merge Recipients dialog box.

Q&A

In what order would the form letters print if I merged them again now?

Word would merge them in ZIP code order; that is, the records with ZIP code 66532 would appear first, and the records with ZIP code 66589 would appear last.

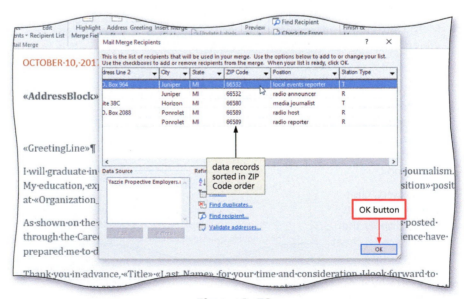

Figure 6–58

Other Ways

1. Click Sort link (Mail Merge Recipients dialog box), enter sort criteria (Sort and Filter dialog box), click OK button

To Find and Display Data

Why? *If you wanted to find a particular record in the data source and display that record's data in the main document on the screen, you can search for a field value.* The following steps find Cheung, which is a last name in the data source, and display that record's values in the form letter currently displaying on the screen.

- If necessary, click the 'View Merged Data' button (Mailings tab | Preview Results group) to show field results instead of merged fields on the screen.

- Click the Find Recipient button (Mailings tab | Preview Results group) to display the Find Entry dialog box.

- Type **Cheung** in the Find text box (Find Entry dialog box) as the search text.

- Click the Find Next button to display the record containing the entered text (Figure 6–59).

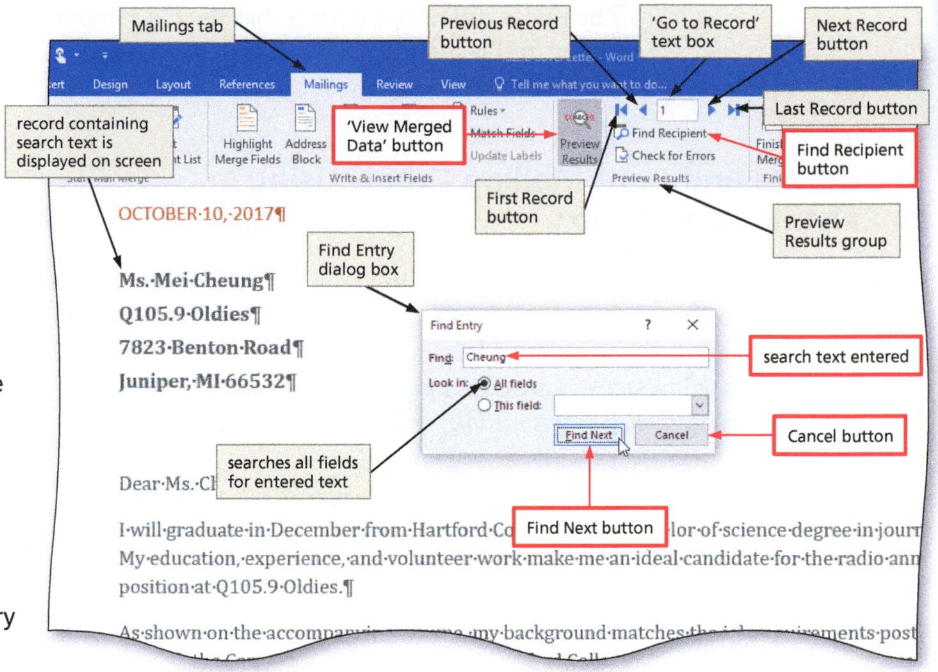

2

- Click the Cancel button (Find Entry dialog box) to close the dialog box.

- Close the open document. If a Microsoft Word dialog box is displayed, click the Save button to save the changes.

Figure 6–59

Displaying Data Source Records in the Main Document

When you are viewing merged data in the main document (shown in Figure 6–59) — that is, the 'View Merged Data' button (Mailings tab | Preview Results group) is selected — you can click buttons and boxes in the Preview Results group on the Mailings tab to display different results and values. For example, click the Last Record button to display the values from the last record in the data source, the First Record button to display the values in record one, the Next Record button to display the values in the next consecutive record number, or the Previous Record button to display the values from the previous record number. You also can display a specific record by clicking the 'Go to Record' text box, typing the record number you would like to be displayed in the main document, and then pressing the ENTER key.

BTW

Closing Main Document Files

Word always asks if you want to save changes when you close a main document, even if you just saved the document. If you are sure that no additional changes were made to the document, click the Don't Save button; otherwise, click the Save button — just to be safe.

Addressing Mailing Labels and Envelopes

Now that you have merged and printed the form letters, the next step is to print addresses on mailing labels to be affixed to envelopes for the form letters. The mailing labels will use the same data source as the form letter, Yazzie Prospective Employers. The format and content of the mailing labels will be exactly the same as the inside address in the main document for the form letter. That is, the first line will contain the title and first name followed by the last name. The second line will contain the organization name, and so on. Thus, you will use the AddressBlock merge field in the mailing labels.

You follow the same basic steps to create the main document for the mailing labels as you did to create the main document for the form letters. That is, determine the appropriate data source, create the label main document, and then merge the main document with the data source to generate the mailing labels and envelopes. The major difference here is that the data source already exists because you created it earlier in this module.

To Address and Print Mailing Labels Using an Existing Data Source

1 IDENTIFY MAIN DOCUMENT | 2 CREATE DATA SOURCE | 3 COMPOSE MAIN DOCUMENT
4 MERGE DATA SOURCE | **5 ADDRESS MAILING LABELS** | 6 MERGE TO DIRECTORY

To address mailing labels, you specify the type of labels you intend to use. Word will request the label information, including the label vendor and product number. You can obtain this information from the box of labels. For illustration purposes in addressing these labels, the label vendor is Avery and the product number is J8158. The following steps address and print mailing labels using an existing data source. *Why? You already created the data source earlier in this module, so you will use that data source.*

Note: If your printer does not have the capability of printing mailing labels, read these steps without performing them. If you are in a laboratory environment, ask your instructor if you should perform these steps or read them without performing them.

1
- Open the Backstage view. Click the New tab in the Backstage view to display the New gallery. Click the Blank document thumbnail to open a new blank document window.

- If necessary, change the zoom to page width.

- Display the Mailings tab. Click the 'Start Mail Merge' button (Mailings tab | Start Mail Merge group) and then click 'Step-by-Step Mail Merge Wizard' on the Start Mail Merge menu to display Step 1 of the Mail Merge wizard in the Mail Merge task pane.

- Click Labels in the Select document type area to specify labels as the main document type (Figure 6–60).

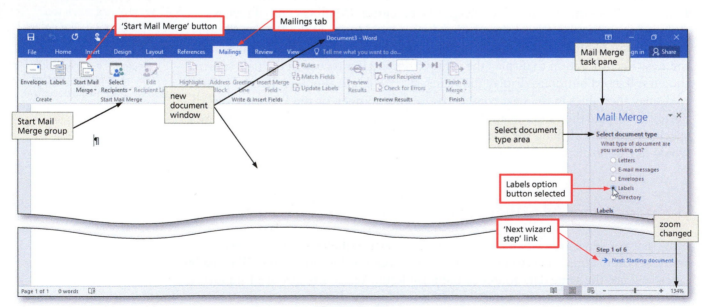

Figure 6–60

2

- Click the 'Next wizard step' link at the bottom of the Mail Merge task pane to display Step 2 of the Mail Merge wizard.

- In the Mail Merge task pane, click the 'Select label size' link to display the Label Options dialog box.

- Select the label vendor and product number (in this case, Avery A4/A5 and J8158), as shown in Figure 6–61.

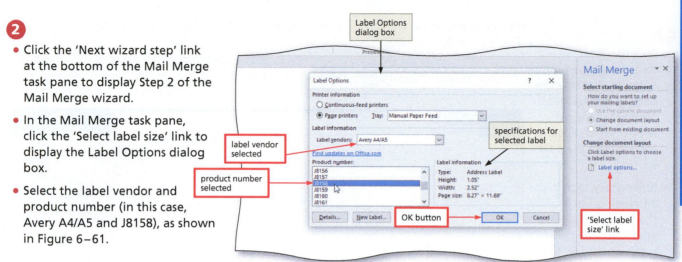

Figure 6–61

3

- Click the OK button (Label Options dialog box) to display the selected label layout as the main document (Figure 6–62).

- If gridlines are not displayed, click the 'View Table Gridlines' button (Table Tools Layout tab | Table group) to show gridlines.

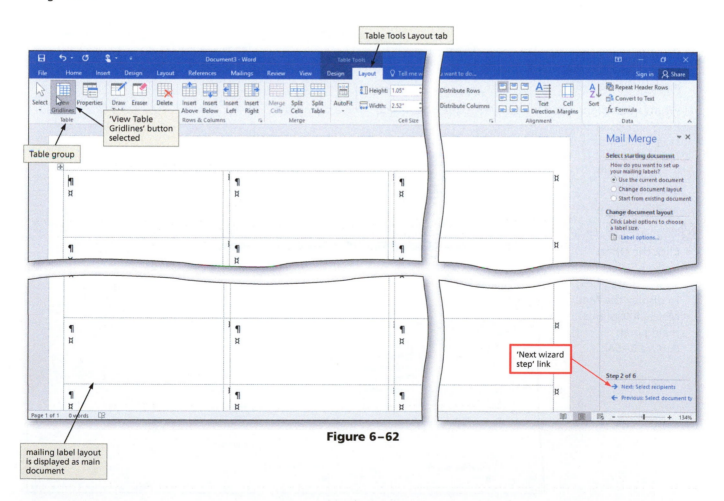

Figure 6–62

4

• Click the 'Next wizard step' link at the bottom of the Mail Merge task pane to display Step 3 of the Mail Merge wizard, which allows you to select the data source.

• If necessary, click 'Use an existing list' in the Select recipients area. Click the 'Select recipient list file' link to display the Select Data Source dialog box.

• If necessary, navigate to the location of the data source (in this case, the Job Hunting folder).

• Click the file name, Yazzie Prospective Employers, to select the data source you created earlier in the module (Figure 6–63).

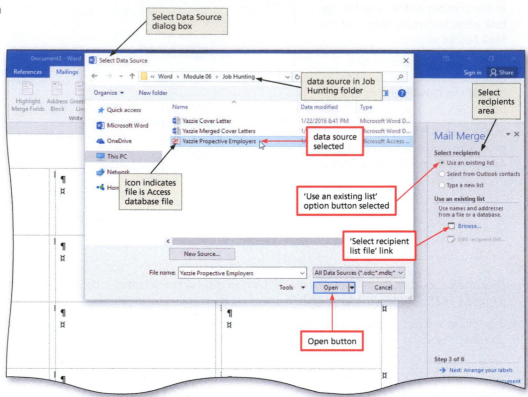

Figure 6–63

Q&A

What is the folder initially displayed in the Select Data Source dialog box?

It is the default folder for storing data source files. Word looks in that folder, by default, for an existing data source.

5

• Click the Open button (Select Data Source dialog box) to display the Mail Merge Recipients dialog box (Figure 6–64).

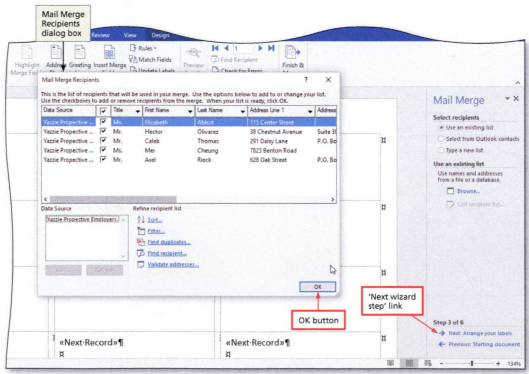

Figure 6–64

6
- Click the OK button (Mail Merge Recipients dialog box) to close the dialog box.

- At the bottom of the Mail Merge task pane, click the 'Next wizard step' link to display Step 4 of the Mail Merge wizard in the Mail Merge task pane.

- In the Mail Merge task pane, click the 'Insert formatted address' link to display the Insert Address Block dialog box (Figure 6–65).

- If necessary, match the company name to the Organization Name field by clicking the Match Fields button (Insert Address Block dialog box), clicking the Company box arrow (Match Fields dialog box), clicking Organization Name in the list, and then clicking the OK button (Match Fields dialog box).

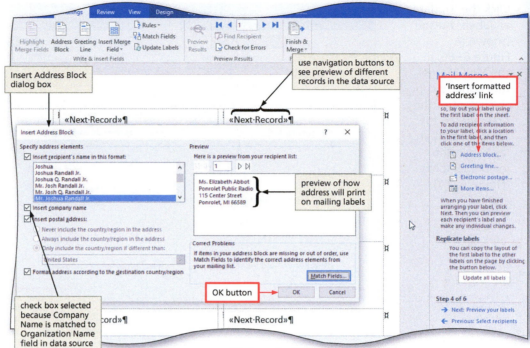

Figure 6–65

7
- Click the OK button to close the dialog box and insert the AddressBlock merge field in the first label of the main document (Figure 6–66).

Q&A Do I have to use the AddressBlock merge field?

No. You can click the Insert Merge Field button (Mailings tab | Write & Insert Fields group) and then select the preferred fields for the mailing labels, organizing the fields as desired.

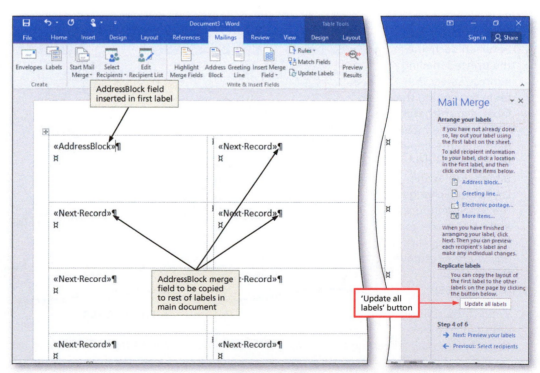

Figure 6–66

• Click the 'Update all labels' button (shown in Figure 6–66) in the Mail Merge task pane to copy the layout of the first label to the remaining label layouts in the main document (Figure 6–67).

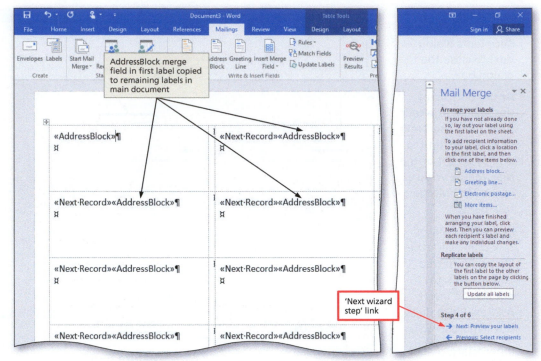

Figure 6–67

• Click the 'Next wizard step' link at the bottom of the Mail Merge task pane to display Step 5 of the Mail Merge wizard, which shows a preview of the mailing labels in the document window.

• Because you do not want a blank space between each line in the printed mailing address, select the table containing the label layout (that is, click the table move handle in the upper-left corner of the table), display the Layout tab, change the Spacing Before and After boxes to 0 pt, and then click anywhere to remove the selection (Figure 6–68).

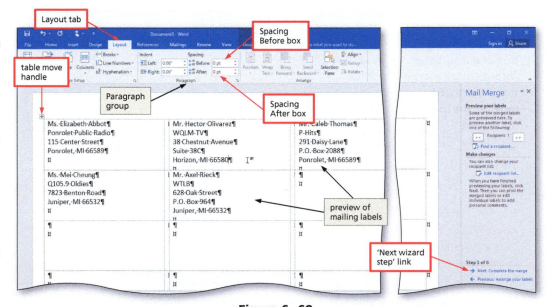

Figure 6–68

Q&A   What if the spacing does not change?

Drag through the labels and try changing the Spacing Before and After boxes to 0 again.

10

- Click the 'Next wizard step' link at the bottom of the Mail Merge task pane to display Step 6 of the Mail Merge wizard.

- Click the 'Merge to a new document' link to display the Merge to New Document dialog box.

- If necessary, click All (Merge to New Document dialog box) so that all records in the data source will be included in the merge (Figure 6–69).

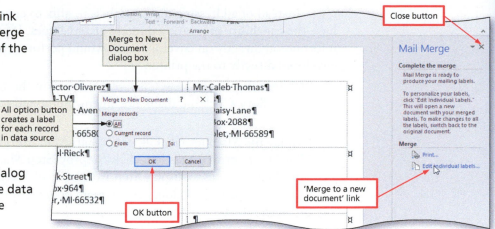

Figure 6–69

11

- If necessary, insert a sheet of blank mailing labels in the printer.

- Click the OK button (Merge to New Document dialog box) to merge the mailing labels to a new document.

- Save the merged mailing labels in the Job Hunting folder on your hard drive, OneDrive, or other storage location using the file name, Yazzie Merged Mailing Labels. If requested by your instructor, print the merged labels (Figure 6–70).

12

- Close the document window containing the merged labels.

- Click the Close button at the right edge of the Mail Merge task pane.

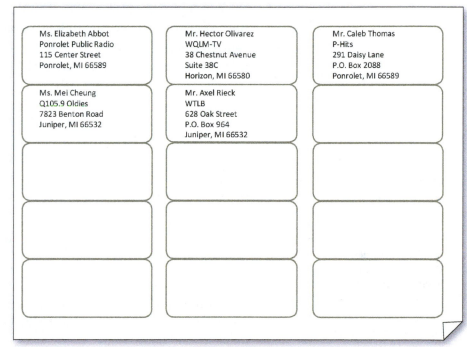

Ms. Elizabeth Abbot Ponrolet Public Radio 115 Center Street Ponrolet, MI 66589	Mr. Hector Olivarez WQLM-TV 38 Chestnut Avenue Suite 38C Horizon, MI 66580	Mr. Caleb Thomas P-Hits 291 Daisy Lane P.O. Box 2088 Ponrolet, MI 66589
Ms. Mei Cheung Q105.9 Oldies 7823 Benton Road Juniper, MI 66532	Mr. Axel Rieck WTLB 628 Oak Street P.O. Box 964 Juniper, MI 66532	

Figure 6–70

- Click the 'View Merged Data' button to show field codes instead of merged data on the labels.

- Save the mailing label main document in the Job Hunting folder on your hard drive, OneDrive, or other storage location using the file name, Yazzie Mailing Labels.

- Close the mailing label main document.

How should you position addresses on an envelope?

An envelope should contain the sender's full name and address in the upper-left corner of the envelope. It also should contain the addressee's full name and address, positioned approximately in the vertical and horizontal center of the envelope. The address can be printed directly on the envelope or on a mailing label that is affixed to the envelope.

CONSIDER THIS

To Address and Print Envelopes

Instead of addressing mailing labels to affix to envelopes, your printer may have the capability of printing directly on envelopes. If you wanted to print address information directly on envelopes, you would perform the following steps to merge the envelopes directly to the printer.

1. Open the Backstage view. Click the New tab in the Backstage view to display the New gallery. Click the Blank document thumbnail to open a new blank document window.

2. Display the Mailings tab. Click the 'Start Mail Merge' button (Mailings tab | Start Mail Merge group) and then click 'Step-by-Step Mail Merge Wizard' on the Start Mail Merge menu to display Step 1 of the Mail Merge wizard in the Mail Merge task pane. Specify envelopes as the main document type by clicking Envelopes in the Select document type area.

3. Click the 'Next wizard step' link at the bottom of the Mail Merge task pane to display Step 2 of the Mail Merge wizard. In the Mail Merge task pane, click the 'Set Envelope Options' link to display the Envelope Options dialog box.

4. Select the envelope size and then click the OK button (Envelope Options dialog box), which displays the selected envelope layout as the main document.

5. If your envelope does not have a preprinted return address, position the insertion point in the upper-left corner of the envelope layout and then type a return address.

6. Click the 'Next wizard step' link at the bottom of the Mail Merge task pane to display Step 3 of the Mail Merge wizard, which allows you to select the data source. Select an existing data source or create a new one. At the bottom of the Mail Merge task pane, click the 'Next wizard step' link to display Step 4 of the Mail Merge wizard in the Mail Merge task pane.

7. Position the insertion point in the middle of the envelope. In the Mail Merge task pane, click the 'Insert formatted address' link to display the Insert Address Block dialog box. Select desired settings and then click the OK button to close the dialog box and insert the AddressBlock merge field in the envelope layout of the main document. If necessary, match fields so that the Company is matched to the Organization_Name field.

8. Click the 'Next wizard step' link at the bottom of the Mail Merge task pane to display Step 5 of the Mail Merge wizard, which shows a preview of an envelope in the document window.

9. Click the 'Next wizard step' link at the bottom of the Mail Merge task pane to display Step 6 of the Mail Merge wizard. In the Mail Merge task pane, click the 'Merge to printer' link to display the Merge to Printer dialog box. If necessary, click All (Merge to Printer dialog box) so that all records in the data source will be included in the merge.

10. If necessary, insert blank envelopes in the printer. Click the OK button to display the Print dialog box. Click the OK button (Print dialog box) to print the addresses on the envelopes. Close the Mail Merge task pane.

BTW

AddressBlock Merge Field

Another way to insert the AddressBlock merge field in a document is to click the Address Block button (Mailings tab | Write & Insert Fields group).

Merging All Data Records to a Directory

You may want to print the data records in the data source. Recall that the data source is saved as a Microsoft Access database table. Thus, you cannot open the data source in Word. To view the data source, you click the 'Edit Recipient List' button

(Mailings tab | Start Mail Merge group), which displays the Mail Merge Recipients dialog box. This dialog box, however, does not have a Print button.

One way to print the contents of the data source is to merge all data records in the data source into a single document, called a directory. A **directory** is a listing from the contents of the data source. A directory does not merge each data record to a separate document; instead, a directory lists all records together in a single document. When you merge to a directory, the default organization of a directory places each record one after the next, similar to the look of entries in a telephone book.

To create a directory, follow the same process as for the form letters. That is, determine the appropriate data source, create the directory main document, and then merge the main document with the data source to create the directory.

The directory in this module is more organized with the rows and columns divided and field names placed above each column (shown in Figure 6–83). To accomplish this look, the following steps are required:

1. Change the page orientation from portrait to landscape, so that each record fits on a single row.

2. Create a directory layout, placing a separating character between each merge field.

3. Merge the directory to a new document, which creates a list of all records in the data source.

4. Convert the directory to a table, using the separator character as the identifier for each new column.

5. Format the table containing the directory.

6. Sort the table by organization name within city, so that it is easy to locate a particular record.

BTW

Converting Main Document Files

If you wanted to convert a mail merge main document to a regular Word document, you would open the main document, click the 'Start Mail Merge' button (Mailings tab | Start Mail Merge group), and then click 'Normal Word Document' on the Start Mail Merge menu (shown in Figure 6–72).

To Change Page Orientation

1 IDENTIFY MAIN DOCUMENT | 2 CREATE DATA SOURCE | 3 COMPOSE MAIN DOCUMENT
4 MERGE DATA SOURCE | 5 ADDRESS MAILING LABELS | **6 MERGE TO DIRECTORY**

When a document is in **portrait orientation**, the short edge of the paper is the top of the document. You can instruct Word to lay out a document in **landscape orientation**, so that the long edge of the paper is the top of the document. The following steps change the orientation of the document from portrait to landscape. *Why? You want an entire record to fit on a single line in the directory.*

1

- If necessary, create a new blank document in the Word window and change the zoom to page width.

- Display the Layout tab.

- Click the 'Change Page Orientation' button (Layout tab | Page Setup group) to display the Change Page Orientation gallery (Figure 6–71).

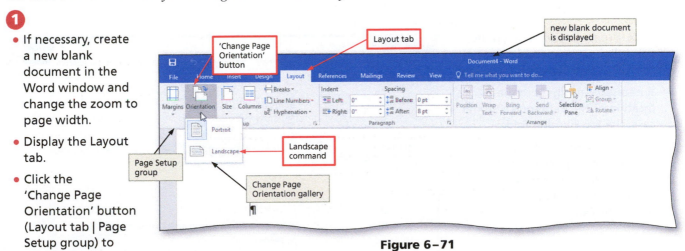

Figure 6–71

2

- Click Landscape in the Change Page Orientation gallery to change the page orientation to landscape.

- If necessary, change the zoom to page width again so that both the left and right edges of the page are visible in the document window.

To Merge to a Directory

The next steps merge the data records in the data source to a directory. *Why? You would like a listing of all records in the data source.* For illustration purposes, the following steps use the buttons on the Mailings tab rather than using the Mail Merge task pane to merge to a directory.

- Display the Mailings tab.
- Click the 'Start Mail Merge' button (Mailings tab | Start Mail Merge group) to display the Start Mail Merge menu (Figure 6–72).

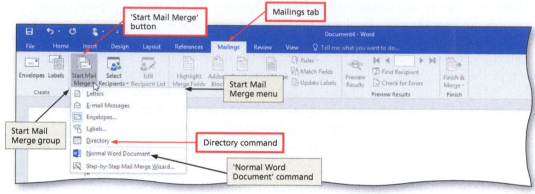

Figure 6–72

- Click Directory on the Start Mail Merge menu to select the main document type.

- Click the Select Recipients button (Mailings tab | Start Mail Merge group) to display the Select Recipients menu (Figure 6–73).

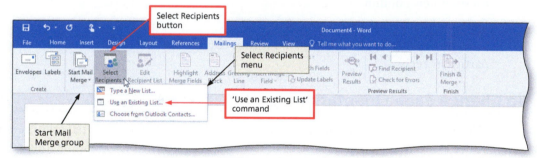

Figure 6–73

- Click 'Use an Existing List' on the Select Recipients menu to display the Select Data Source dialog box.
- If necessary, navigate to the location of the data source (in this case, the Job Hunting folder).
- Click the file name, Yazzie Prospective Employers, to select the data source you created earlier in the module (Figure 6–74).

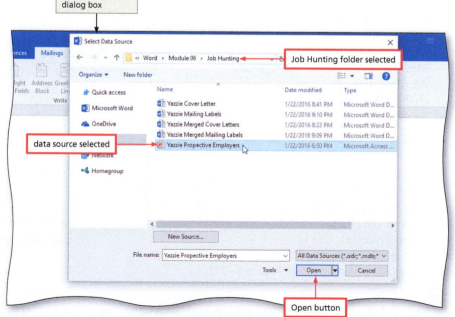

Figure 6–74

5

- Click the Open button (Select Data Source dialog box) to associate the selected data source with the current main document.

6

- Click the 'Insert Merge Field' arrow (Mailings tab | Write & Insert Fields group) to display the Insert Merge Field menu (Figure 6–75).

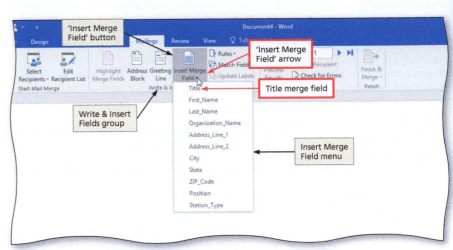

Figure 6–75

7

- Click Title on the Insert Merge Field menu to insert the selected merge field in the document.

- Press the COMMA (,) key to place a comma after the inserted merge field.

Q&A Why insert a comma after the merge field?

In the next steps, you will convert the entered merge fields to a table format with the records in rows and the fields in columns. To do this, Word divides the columns based on a character separating each field. In this case, you use the comma to separate the merge fields.

8

- Repeat Steps 6 and 7 for the First_Name, Last_Name, Organization_Name, Address_Line_1, Address_Line_2, City, State, and ZIP_Code fields on the Insert Merge Field menu, so that these fields in the data source appear in the main document separated by a comma, except do not type a comma after the last field (ZIP_Code).

Mailings tab

'Finish & Merge' button

merge fields from data source inserted in main document

'Insert Merge Field' arrow

Write & Insert Fields group

Finish group

«Title»,«First_Name»,«Last_Name»,«Organization_Name»,«Address_Line_1»,«Address_Line_2»,«City»,«State»,«ZIP_Code»¶

insertion point

comma separates each merge field

no comma after ZIP_Code field

- Press the ENTER key (Figure 6–76).

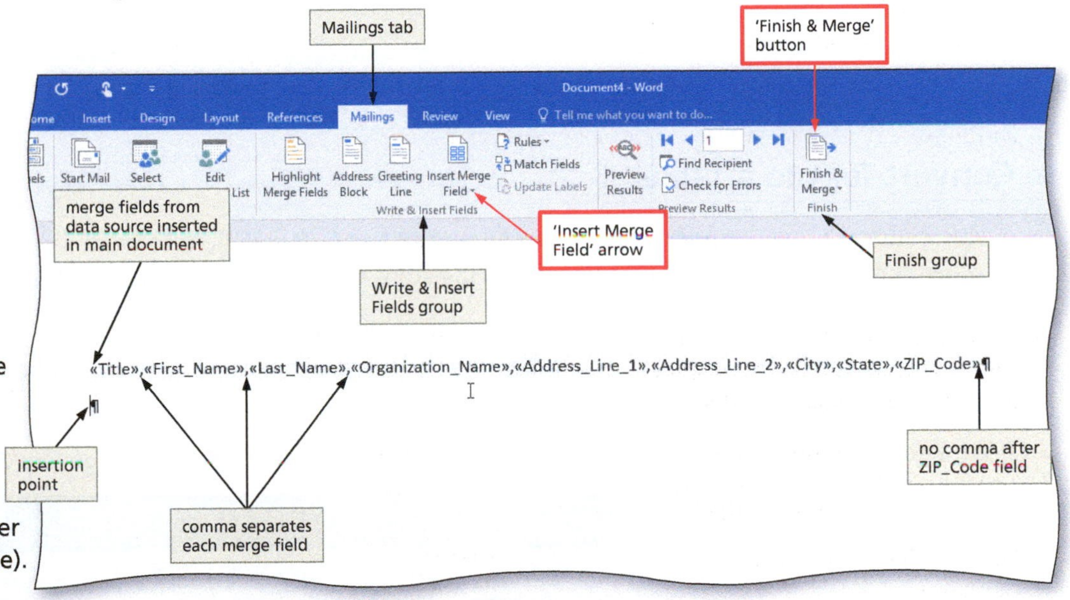

Figure 6–76

Q&A Why press the ENTER key after entering the merge fields names?

This will place the first field in each record at the beginning of a new line.

Why are the Position and Station_Type fields not included in the directory?

You just want the directory listing to show the contact information for each potential employer.

9

- Save the directory main document in the Job Hunting folder on your hard drive, OneDrive, or other storage location using the file name, Yazzie Potential Employer Directory.

To Merge to a New Document

The next step is to merge the data source and the directory main document to a new document, so that you can edit the resulting document. The following steps merge to a new document.

1. Click the 'Finish & Merge' button (Mailings tab | Finish group) to display the Finish & Merge menu.

2. Click 'Edit Individual Documents' on the Finish & Merge menu to display the Merge to New Document dialog box.

3. If necessary, click All (Merge to New Document dialog box).

4. Click the OK button to merge the data records to a directory in a new document window (Figure 6–77).

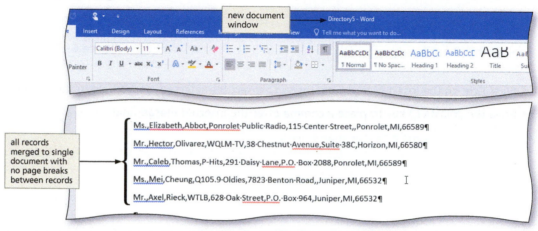

Figure 6–77

To Convert Text to a Table

1 IDENTIFY MAIN DOCUMENT | 2 CREATE DATA SOURCE | 3 COMPOSE MAIN DOCUMENT
4 MERGE DATA SOURCE | 5 ADDRESS MAILING LABELS | **6 MERGE TO DIRECTORY**

You want each data record to be in a single row and each merge field to be in a column. *Why? The directory will be easier to read if it is in table form.* The following steps convert the text containing the merge fields to a table.

- Press CTRL+A to select the entire document, because you want all document contents to be converted to a table.

- Display the Insert tab.

- Click the 'Add a Table' button (Insert tab | Tables group) to display the Add a Table gallery (Figure 6–78).

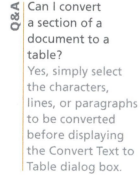
Q&A
Can I convert a section of a document to a table?
Yes, simply select the characters, lines, or paragraphs to be converted before displaying the Convert Text to Table dialog box.

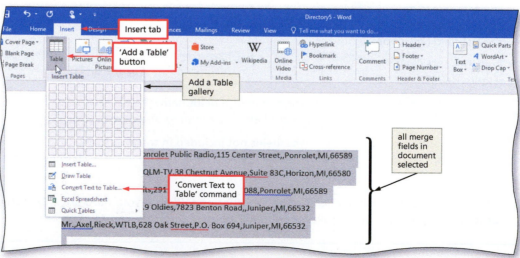

Figure 6–78

2

- Click 'Convert Text to Table' in the Add a Table gallery to display the Convert Text to Table dialog box.

- If necessary, type   9   in the 'Number of columns' box (Convert Text to Table dialog box) to specify the number of columns for the resulting table.

- Click 'AutoFit to window', which instructs Word to fit the table and its contents to the width of the window.

- If necessary, click Commas to specify the character that separates the merge fields in the document (Figure 6–79).

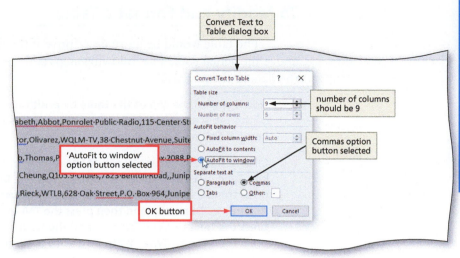

Figure 6–79

3

- Click the OK button to convert the selected text to a table and then, if necessary, click to remove the selection from the table (Figure 6–80).

Q&A Can I format the table?
Yes. You can use any of the commands on the Table Tools Design and Table Tools Layout tabs to change the look of the table.

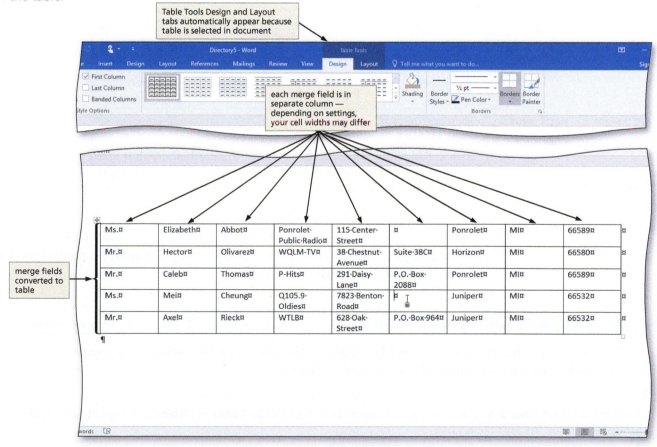

Figure 6–80

To Modify and Format a Table

The table would be more descriptive if the field names were displayed in a row above the actual data. The following steps add a row to the top of a table and format the data in the new row.

1 Add a row to the top of the table by positioning the insertion point in the first row of the table and then clicking the 'Insert Rows Above' button (Table Tools Layout tab | Rows & Columns group).

2 Click in the first (leftmost) cell of the new row. Type **Title** and then press the TAB key. Type **First Name** and then press the TAB key. Type **Last Name** and then press the TAB key. Type **Organization Name** and then press the TAB key. Type **Address Line 1** and then press the TAB key. Type **Address Line 2** and then press the TAB key. Type **City** and then press the TAB key. Type **State** and then press the TAB key. Type **ZIP Code** as the last entry in the row.

3 Bold the contents of the first row.

4 Use the AutoFit Contents command on the ribbon or the shortcut menu to make all columns as wide as their contents. If necessary, adjust individual column widths so that the table looks like Figure 6–81.

5 Center the table between the margins (Figure 6–81).

header row added and bold

Title¤	First·Name¤	Last·Name¤	Organization·Name¤	Address·Line·1¤	Address·Line·2¤	City¤	State¤	ZIP·Code¤¤
Ms.¤	Elizabeth¤	Abbot¤	Ponrolet·Public·Radio¤	115·Center·Street¤	¤	Ponrolet¤	MI¤	66589¤	¤
Mr.¤	Hector¤	Olivarez¤	WQLM-TV¤	38·Chestnut·Avenue¤	Suite·38C¤	Horizon¤	MI¤	66580¤	¤
Mr.¤	Caleb¤	Thomas¤	P-Hits¤	291·Daisy·Lane¤	P.O.·Box·2088¤	Ponrolet¤	MI¤	66589¤	¤
Ms.¤	Mei¤	Cheung¤	Q105.9·Oldies¤	7823·Benton·Road¤	¤	Juniper¤	MI¤	66532¤	¤
Mr.¤	Axel¤	Rieck¤	WTLB¤	628·Oak·Street¤	P.O.·Box·964¤	Juniper¤	MI¤	66532¤	¤

Figure 6–81

To Repeat Header Rows

If you had a table that exceeded a page in length and you wanted the header row (the first row) to appear at the top of the table on each continued page, you would perform the following steps.

1. Position the insertion point in the header row.

2. Click the 'Repeat Header Rows' button (Table Tools Layout tab | Data group) (shown in Figure 6–82) to repeat the row containing the insertion point at the top of every page on which the table continues.

To Sort a Table by Multiple Columns

1 IDENTIFY MAIN DOCUMENT | 2 CREATE DATA SOURCE | 3 COMPOSE MAIN DOCUMENT
4 MERGE DATA SOURCE | 5 ADDRESS MAILING LABELS | 6 MERGE TO DIRECTORY

The next step is to sort the table. *Why? In this project, the table records are displayed by organization name within city.* The following steps sort a table by multiple columns.

1
- With the table selected or the insertion point in the table, click the Sort button (Table Tools Layout tab | Data group) to display the Sort dialog box.
- Click the Sort by arrow (Sort dialog box); scroll to and then click City in the list.
- Click the first Then by arrow and then click Organization Name in the list.
- If necessary, click Header row so that the first row remains in its current location when the table is sorted (Figure 6–82).

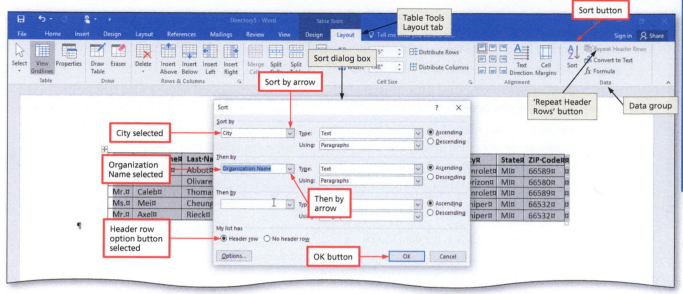

Figure 6–82

2

- Click the OK button to sort the records in the table in ascending Organization Name order within ascending City order (Figure 6–83).

- If necessary, click to deselect the table.

- Save the merged directory in the Job Hunting folder on your hard drive, OneDrive, or other storage location using the file name, Yazzie Merged Potential Employer Directory.

- If requested by your instructor, print the merged directory.

Q&A If Microsoft Access is installed on my computer, can I use that to print the data source?
As an alternative to merging to a directory and printing the results, if you are familiar with Microsoft Access and it is installed on your computer, you can open and print the data source in Access.

- **Exit Word.**

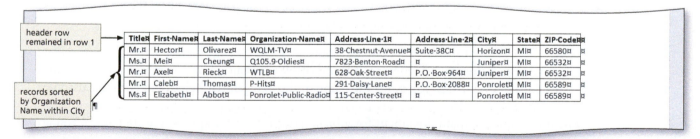

Figure 6–83

Summary

In this module, you learned how to create and print form letters, work with merge fields and an IF field, open a main document, create and edit a data source, address mailing labels and envelopes from a data source, change page orientation, merge to a directory, and convert text to a table.

STUDENT ASSIGNMENTS

CONSIDER THIS: PLAN AHEAD

What decisions will you need to make when creating your next form letter?

Use these guidelines as you complete the assignments in this module and create your own form letters outside of this class.

1. Identify the main document for the form letter.

   a) Determine whether to type the letter from scratch in a blank document window or use a letter template.

2. Create or specify the data source.

   a) Determine if the data exists already in an Access database table, an Outlook contacts list, or an Excel worksheet.

   b) If you cannot use an existing data source, create a new one using appropriate field names.

3. Compose the main document for the form letter.

   a) Ensure the letter contains all essential business letter elements and is visually appealing.

   b) Be sure the letter contains proper grammar, correct spelling, logically constructed sentences, flowing paragraphs, and sound ideas.

   c) Properly reference the data in the data source.

4. Merge the main document with the data source to create the form letters.

   a) Determine the destination for the merge (i.e., a new document, the printer, etc.).

   b) Determine which records to merge (all of them or a portion of them).

5. Determine whether to generate mailing labels or envelopes.

   a) Create or specify the data source.

   b) Ensure the mailing label or envelope contains all necessary information.

6. Create a directory of the data source.

   a) Create or specify the data source.

   b) If necessary, format the directory appropriately.

Apply Your Knowledge

Reinforce the skills and apply the concepts you learned in this module.

Editing, Printing, and Merging a Form Letter and Its Data Source

Note: To complete this assignment, you will be required to use the Data Files. Please contact your instructor for information about accessing the Data Files.

Instructions: Run Word. Open the document, Apply 6–1 Oil Change Letter Draft, from the Data Files. When you open the main document, if Word displays a dialog box about an SQL command, click the Yes button. If Word prompts for the name of the data source, select Apply 6–1 Customer List on the Data Files.

The document is a main document for a form letter for Auto Express (Figure 6–84). You are to edit the date content control and GreetingLine merge field, add a merge field, print the form letter, add a record to the data source, and merge the form letters to a file.

Perform the following tasks:

1. Edit the date content control so that it contains the date 10/30/2017.

2. Edit the GreetingLine merge field so that the salutation ends with a comma (,).

3. At the end of the last paragraph of the letter, insert the Vehicle_Type merge field between the word, your, and the exclamation point (shown in Figure 6–84).

4. Save the modified main document for the form letter with the file name, Apply 6–1 Oil Change Letter Modified.

5. Highlight the merge fields in the document. How many were highlighted? Remove the highlight from the merge fields.

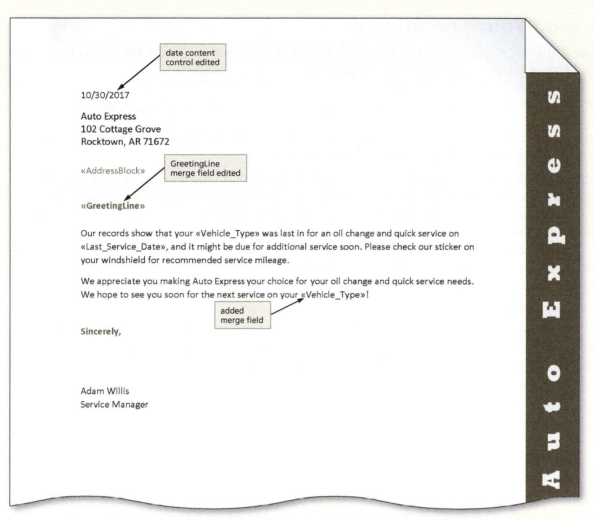

Figure 6–84

6. View merged data in the document. Use the navigation buttons in the Preview Results group to display merged data from various records in the data source. What is the last name shown in the first record? The third record? The fifth record? View merge fields (that is, turn off the view merged data).

7. Print the main document for the form letter (shown in Figure 6–84). If requested by your instructor, save the main document as a PDF.

8. If requested by your instructor, add a record to the data source that contains your personal information. Type **7/14/2016** in the Last_Service_Date field, and add the type of vehicle you own (or would like to own) in the Vehicle_Type field.

9. In the data source, change Kimberly Johnson's last name to Holloway.

10. Sort the data source by the Last Name field.

11. Save the main document for the form letter again.

12. Merge the form letters to a new document. Save the new document with the file name, Apply 6–1 Oil Change Merged Letters.

13. If requested by your instructor, merge the form letters directly to the printer.

14. Submit the saved documents in the format specified by your instructor.

15. ✳ Answer the questions posed in #5 and #6. The form letter used in this assignment was based on one of Word's online mail merge letter templates called Adjacency letter. What other online mail merge letter templates are available through Word? Which template do you like best and why?

Extend Your Knowledge

Extend the skills you learned in this module and experiment with new skills. You may need to use Help to complete the assignment.

Editing an IF Field, Inserting a Fill-In Field, and Merging Using Outlook and Access

Note: To complete this assignment, you will be required to use the Data Files. Please contact your instructor for information about accessing the Data Files.

Instructions: Run Word. Open the document called Extend 6–1 Donation Letter Draft located on the Data Files. When you open the main document, if Word displays a dialog box about an SQL command, click the Yes button. If Word prompts for the name of the data source, select Extend 6–1 Donor List on the Data Files.

The document is a main document for a form letter thanking and inviting a donor to a pancake breakfast (Figure 6–85). You will modify an IF field, and add a Fill-in field, print field codes, create envelopes for records in the data source, use an Access database file as a data source, and merge to email addresses.

Perform the following tasks:

1. Use Help to learn about mail merge, IF fields, Fill-in fields, and merging to email addresses.
2. The IF field in the draft file has the true and false text reversed. Edit the IF field so that donations greater than or equal to $25 may bring two guests and all others may bring one guest. *Hint*: Use the 'Toggle Field Codes' command on the shortcut menu (right-click the IF field code in the document window) and edit the IF field directly in the document.
3. Above the GreetingLine merge field (shown in Figure 6–85), insert a Fill-in field that asks this question: What date will you be mailing these letters? Select the Ask once check box so that the question is asked only once, instead of for each letter. When merging the letters, use a date in October of 2017. What is the purpose of the Fill-in field?
4. If requested by your instructor, add a record to the data source that contains your personal information and a donation amount of 25.
5. Save the modified letter with the file name, Extend 6–1 Donation Letter Modified.
6. Merge the letters to a new document. Save the merged letters using the file name, Extend 6–1 Donation Merged Letters. On the letter with the donation of $100, add an extra sentence of thanks at the end of the first paragraph.
7. Print the main document for the form letter. If requested by your instructor, save the main document as a PDF.
8. Print the form letter with field codes showing; that is, print it with the 'Print field codes instead of their values' check box selected in the Word Options dialog box. Be sure to deselect this check box after printing the field codes version of the letter. How does this printout differ from the one printed in #7?
9. Submit the main document and merged letters in the format specified by your instructor.
10. If your instructor requests, create envelopes for each letter in the data source. Submit the merged envelopes in the format specified by your instructor.
11. If Access is installed on your computer or mobile device, and if you are familiar with Access and your instructor requests it, create the data source included with the assignment in Access and then open the main document with the Access database file as the data source.
12. If your instructor requests, display your personal record on the screen and merge the form letter to an email message, specifying that only the current receives the message. Submit the merged email message in the format specified by your instructor.
13. ✳ Answer the questions posed in #3 and #8. If you choose to merge to email addresses, what is the purpose of the various email formats?

Figure 6–85

Expand Your World

Create a solution that uses cloud or web technologies by learning and investigating on your own from general guidance.

Exploring Add-Ins for Office Apps

Instructions: You regularly use apps on your phone and tablet to look up a variety of information. In Office apps, you can use add-ins, which essentially are apps that work with Word and the other Office apps. You would like to investigate some of the add-ins available for Word to determine which ones would be helpful for you to use.

Note: You will be required to use your Microsoft account to complete this assignment. If you do not have a Microsoft account and do not want to create one, read this assignment without performing the instructions.

Perform the following tasks:

1. Use Help to learn about Office add-ins. If necessary, sign in to your Windows account.

2. If you are not signed in already, sign in to your Microsoft Account in Word.

3. Display the Insert tab and then click the 'Insert an Add-in' button (Insert tab | Add-ins group) to display the Office Add-ins dialog box. (If a menu is displayed, click the See All link to display the Office Add-ins dialog box.) Click the Office Store button or the STORE tab (Office Add-ins dialog box) to visit the online Office Store.

4. Scroll through add-ins in the various categories (Figure 6–86). Locate a free add-in that you feel would be helpful to you while you use Word, click the Add button, and then follow the instructions to add the add-in to Word.

5. In Word, click the 'Insert an Add-in' button again to display the Office Add-ins dialog box. Click the add-in you added and then click the Insert button to use the add-in. Click the 'Insert an Add-in' arrow to see the added add-in in the list.

6. Practice using the add-in. Does the add-in work as you intended? Would you recommend the add-in to others?

7. ✺ Which add-ins, if any, were already on your computer or mobile device? Which add-in did you download and why? Answer the questions in #6.

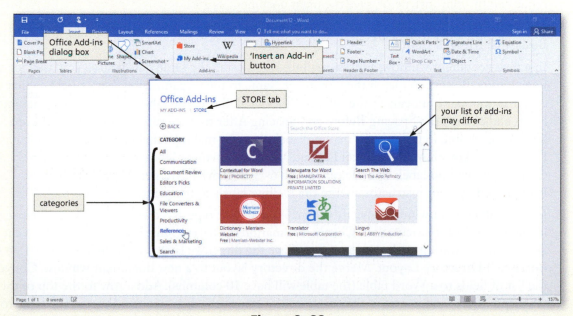

Figure 6–86

In the Labs

Design, create, modify, and/or use a document following the guidelines, concepts, and skills presented in this module. Labs 1 and 2, which increase in difficulty, require you to create solutions based on what you learned in the module; Lab 3 requires you to apply your creative thinking and problem-solving skills to design and implement a solution.

Lab 1: Creating a Form Letter Using a Template, a Data Source, Mailing Labels, and a Directory

Problem: You are graduating this May and have prepared your resume (shown in Figure 5–78 in Module 5). You decide to create a cover letter for your resume as a form letter that you will send to potential employers. The main document for the form letter is shown in Figure 6–87a.

Perform the following tasks:

1. Use the Timeless letter template to begin creating the main document for the form letter. If you cannot locate this template, open the file called Timeless letter from the Data Files. If necessary, change the document theme to Headlines (or a similar theme). Customize the theme fonts to match the resume (that is, headings Arial Black and body text Verdana). Save the main document for the form letter with the file name, Lab 6–1 Boskovich Cover Letter.

2. Type a new data source using the data shown in Figure 6–87b. Delete the field names not used and add one field name: Position. Rename the Company_Name field to Organization_Name. If requested by your instructor, add a record to the data source that contains your personal information. Save the data source with the file name, Lab 6–1 Boskovich Potential Employers.

3. Save the main document for the form letter again. Enter the text, image, merge fields, and formats as shown in the figure. Insert the AddressBlock and GreetingLine merge fields according to the sample formats shown in the figure. (Be sure to match the Company Name to the Organization_Name field so that the organization name appears in the AddressBlock field. *Hint:* Use the Insert Address Block dialog box, or click the Match Fields button (Mailings tab | Write & Insert Fields group). Change the top and bottom margins to 1 inch and the left and right margins to 1.25 inches. Specify the position of the rectangle graphic to 1 inch from the top of the page. Reduce the space above the paragraph containing the date to 36 point. If requested by your instructor, save the main document as a PDF.

4. Merge the form letters to a new document. Save the merged letters in a file called Lab 6–1 Boskovich Merged Letters.

5. In a new document window, address mailing labels using the same data source you used for the form letters. Be sure to match the Company Name to the Organization_Name field so that the organization name appears in the AddressBlock field. Select the table containing the mailing labels and change the Spacing Before and Spacing After to 0 point to remove the blank space between each line in the printed mailing label. Save the mailing label layout with the file name, Lab 6–1 Boskovich Mailing Label Layout. Merge the mailing labels to a new document. Save the merged mailing labels in a file called Lab 6–1 Boskovich Merged Mailing Labels. If requested by your instructor, merge the mailing labels to the printer.

6. In a new document window, specify the main document type as a directory. Change the page layout to landscape orientation. Change the margins to narrow. Insert all merge fields in the document, separating each with a comma. Save the directory layout with the file name, Lab 6–1 Boskovich Directory Layout. Merge the directory layout to a new document window. Convert the list of fields to a Word table (the table will have 10 columns). Add a row to the top of the table and insert field names in the empty cells. Change the font size of all text in the table to 9 point. Apply the List Table 3 - Accent 3 table style (remove formatting from the first column).

Resize the table columns so that the table looks like Figure 6–87b. Center the table. Sort the table in the directory listing by the Last Name field. Save the merged directory with the file name, Lab 6–1 Boskovich Merged Sorted Directory Listing.

7. Submit all documents in the format specified by your instructor.

8. ✳ If you did not want to use the AddressBlock and Greeting Line fields, how would you enter the address and salutation so that the letters printed the correct fields from each record?

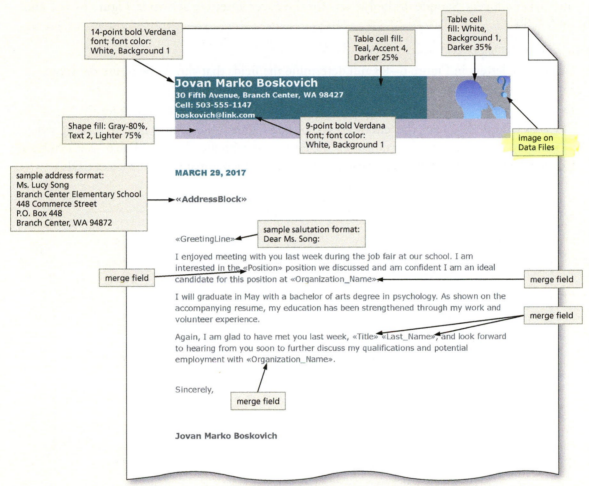

(a) Main Document for Form Letter

Figure 6–87

Title	First Name	Last Name	Organization Name	Address Line 1
Ms.	Lucy	Song	Branch Center Elementary School	448 Commerce Street
Mr.	Miguel	Arroyo	Johnston Elementary	829 Placid Boulevard
Mr.	Dashuan	Titus	Delman High School	17 South Street
Ms.	LaToya	Carrothers	Harrust High School	85 Windmill Lane
Mr.	Matthew	Mason	Squire Elementary	200 Eaton Parkway

Address Line 2	City	State	ZIP Code	Position
P.O. Box 448	Branch Center	WA	98472	counselor
	Sandfly	WA	98420	school counselor
P.O Box 17	Delman	WA	98404	high school counselor
	Harrust	WA	98496	student services counselor
	Mitcheltown	WA	98461	school counselor

(b) Data Source

Figure 6–87

Continued >

STUDENT ASSIGNMENTS

In the Labs *continued*

Lab 2: Designing a Data Source, Form Letter, and Directory from Sample Letters

Problem: You are graduating this May and have prepared your resume (shown in Figure 5–79 in Module 5). You decide to create a cover letter for your resume as a form letter that you will send to potential employers. Sample drafted letters for the cover letter are shown in Figure 6–88a and Figure 6–88b.

Perform the following tasks:

1. Review the letters in Figure 6–88 and determine the fields that should be in the data source. Write the field names on a piece of paper.

2. Do not use a template to create this form letter. In Word, create a main document for the letters using the block letter style. Create the letterhead as shown in Figure 6–88a. Apply the No Spacing style to all paragraphs. Save the main document for the form letter with the file name, Lab 6–2 Washington Cover Letter. If requested by your instructor, save the cover letter main document as a PDF.

Kaylee Jada Washington
15 Chestnut Boulevard, Goldstream, CA 94336 • Phone: 308-555-8752 • Email: kjwashington@world.com

letterhead

April 19, 2017

Ms. Lana Canaan
Morgan Industries
22 Chambers Lane
P.O. Box 22
Goldstream, CA 94336

Dear Ms. Canaan:

I am writing in response to your advertisement for the staff accountant position at Morgan Industries. I will graduate in May from Eureka Falls College with a bachelor of science degree in business, with a major in accounting and a minor in quantitative methods.

My coursework and experience make me an ideal candidate for this full-time position. As shown on my accompanying resume, I have firsthand experience with many financial duties, including payroll, inventory, receivables, invoicing, reporting, auditing, credit checks, and forecasting.

I am confident I will be a valuable asset to your staff. I look forward to the opportunity to meet with you, Ms. Canaan, to discuss my qualifications and potential employment with Morgan Industries.

Sincerely,

Kaylee Washington

(a) Sample First Letter

Figure 6–88

3. Create a data source containing five records, consisting of data from the two letters shown in Figure 6–88 and then add three more records with your own data. If requested by your instructor, add a record to the data source that contains your personal information. Save the data source with the file name, Lab 6–2 Washington Potential Employers.

4. Enter the text and merge fields into the letter. The letter requires one IF field that displays the text, full-time, if the available job position is for a full-time employee; otherwise, it displays the words, part-time, if the available job position is for a part-time employee. Merge the form letters to a new document. Save the merged letters with the file name, Lab 6–2 Washington Merged Letters. Submit the merged letters in the format specified by your instructor.

5. Merge the data source to a directory. Convert it to a Word table. Add an attractive border to the table and apply any other formatting you feel necessary. Submit the directory in the format specified by your instructor.

6. ✹ Which fields did you use in your data source?

Kaylee Jada Washington

15 Chestnut Boulevard, Goldstream, CA 94336 • Phone: 308-555-8752 • Email: kjwashington@world.com

April 19, 2017

Mr. Raul Ramos
Bartlett Insurance
104 Michigan Street
P.O. Box 104
Goldstream, CA 94336

Dear Mr. Ramos:

I am writing in response to your advertisement for the accounting analyst position at Bartlett Insurance. I will graduate in May from Eureka Falls College with a bachelor of science degree in business, with a major in accounting and a minor in quantitative methods.

My coursework and experience make me an ideal candidate for this part-time position. As shown on my accompanying resume, I have firsthand experience with many financial duties, including payroll, inventory, receivables, invoicing, reporting, auditing, credit checks, and forecasting.

I am confident I will be a valuable asset to your staff. I look forward to the opportunity to meet with you, Mr. Ramos, to discuss my qualifications and potential employment with Bartlett Insurance.

Sincerely,

Kaylee Washington

(b) Sample Second Letter
Figure 6–88

Continued >

In the Labs *continued*

Lab 3: **Consider This: Your Turn**

Create Thank You Form Letters

Problem: As owner of Pine Valley Campground, you would like to send form letters to recent guests, thanking them for their stay.

Part 1: Pine Valley Campground is located at 8754 Wilderness Lane, Harpville, KY 42194; website is www.pinevalley.com; email address is info@pinevalley.com. In the form letters, thank guests for their recent stay — identifying the starting date of their stay, the type of campsite in which they stayed, and the length of their stay. Mention you hope they enjoyed their stay and look forward to seeing them again. Also mention that they will receive a 10 percent discount on any future stays this season if they bring this letter to check-in.

Use the concepts and techniques presented in this module to create and format this form letter. Use your name and phone number in the sender information in the main document. The merge fields for the data source are shown in Table 6–1. All merge fields in the data source should be used at least once in the form letter. Merge all records and use a filter to merge just those guests who stayed at tent sites. Be sure to check the spelling and grammar of the finished documents. Create a directory of the data source records. Address and print accompanying labels or envelopes for the form letters. Submit your assignment in the format specified by your instructor.

Table 6–1

Title	First Name	Last Name	Address Line 1	Address Line 2	City	State	ZIP Code	Site Type	Reservation Date	Length of Stay
Mr.	Jonah	Weinberg	35009 Clark Street	Apt. D3	Harpville	KY	42194	tent	September 8	two nights
Ms.	Shannon	O'Malley	13292 Cherry Street		Hill City	KY	42002	full hookup	September 12	four nights
Mr.	Tyrone	Davis	908 Wilson Court	P.O. Box 77	Harpville	KY	42194	water and electric	September 7	three nights
Ms.	Louella	Drake	172 East Park Street	Apt. 132	Blackburg	KY	42392	full hookup	September 8	two nights
Ms.	Roberta	Jeffries	201 Timmons Place	Unit 20C	Horizon	KY	42509	tent	September 10	two nights

Part 2: ✺ You made several decisions while creating the form letter, data source, and directory in this assignment: whether to use a template or create the letter from scratch, wording to use, where to position text and merge fields in the letter, how to format elements, how to set up the data source, and how to format the directory. What was the rationale behind each of these decisions?

7 Creating a Newsletter with a Pull-Quote and Graphics

Objectives

You will have mastered the material in this module when you can:

- Insert and format WordArt
- Set custom tab stops
- Crop a graphic
- Rotate a graphic
- Format a document in multiple columns
- Justify a paragraph
- Hyphenate a document
- Format a character as a drop cap

- Insert a column break
- Insert and format a text box
- Copy and paste using a split window
- Balance columns
- Modify and format a SmartArt graphic
- Copy and paste using the Office Clipboard
- Add an art page border

Introduction

Professional-looking documents, such as newsletters and brochures, often are created using desktop publishing software. With desktop publishing software, you can divide a document in multiple columns, wrap text around diagrams and other graphical images, change fonts and font sizes, add color and lines, and so on, to create an attention-grabbing document. Desktop publishing software, such as Microsoft Publisher, Adobe PageMaker, or QuarkXpress, enables you to open an existing word processing document and enhance it through formatting tools not provided in your word processing software. Word, however, provides many of the formatting features that you would find in a desktop publishing program. Thus, you can use Word to create eye-catching newsletters and brochures.

Project — Newsletter

A newsletter is a publication geared for a specific audience that is created on a recurring basis, such as weekly, monthly, or quarterly. The audience may be subscribers, club members, employees, customers, patrons, students, etc.

The project in this module uses Word to produce the two-page newsletter shown in Figure 7–1. The newsletter is a monthly publication called *Security Trends*. Each issue of *Security Trends* contains a feature article and announcements. This month's feature article discusses biometrics. The feature article spans the first two columns of the first page of the newsletter and then continues on the second page. The announcements, which are located in the third column of the first page, inform subscribers about discounts and an upcoming webinar and announce the topic of the next issue's feature article.

The *Security Trends* newsletter in this module incorporates the desktop publishing features of Word. The body of each page of the newsletter is divided in three columns. A variety of fonts, font sizes, and colors add visual appeal to the document. The first page has text wrapped around a pull-quote, and the second page has text wrapped around a graphic. Horizontal and vertical lines separate distinct areas of the newsletter, including a page border around the perimeter of each page.

The project in this module involves several steps requiring you to drag and drop. If you drag to the wrong location, you may want to cancel an action. Remember that you always can click the Undo button on the Quick Access Toolbar or press CTRL+Z to cancel your most recent action.

In this module, you will learn how to create the newsletter shown in Figure 7–1. The following roadmap identifies general activities you will perform as you progress through this module:

1. **CREATE** the **NAMEPLATE FOR** the **FIRST PAGE** of the newsletter.
2. **FORMAT** the **FIRST PAGE** of the body of the newsletter.
3. **CREATE** a **PULL-QUOTE** on the first page of the newsletter.
4. **CREATE** the **NAMEPLATE FOR** the **SECOND PAGE** of the newsletter.
5. **FORMAT** the **SECOND PAGE** of the body of the newsletter.
6. **ADD** a **PAGE BORDER** to the newsletter.

Desktop Publishing Terminology

As you create professional-looking newsletters and brochures, you should be familiar with several desktop publishing terms. Figure 7–1 identifies these terms:

- A **nameplate**, or **banner**, is the portion of a newsletter that contains the title of the newsletter and usually an issue information line.
- The **issue information line** identifies the specific publication.
- A **ruling line**, usually identified by its direction as a **horizontal rule** or **vertical rule**, is a line that separates areas of the newsletter.
- A **subhead** is a heading within the body of the newsletter.
- A **pull-quote** is text that is *pulled*, or copied, from the text of the document and given graphical emphasis.

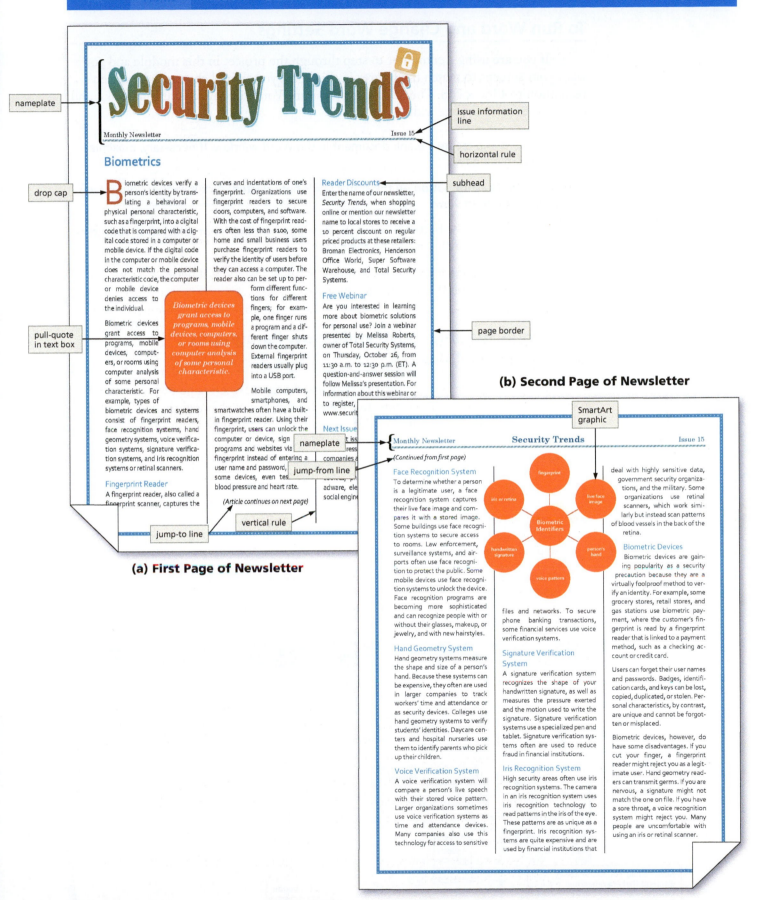

Figure 7-1

To Run Word and Change Word Settings

If you are using a computer to step through the project in this module and you want your screens to match the figures in this book, you should change your screen's resolution to 1366 × 768. The following steps run Word, display formatting marks, and change the zoom to page width.

1. Run Word and create a blank document in the Word window. If necessary, maximize the Word window.

2. If the Print Layout button on the status bar is not selected, click it so that your screen is in Print Layout view.

3. If the 'Show/Hide ¶' button (Home tab | Paragraph group) is not selected already, click it to display formatting marks on the screen.

4. To display the page the same width as the document window, if necessary, click the Page Width button (View tab | Zoom group).

BTW

The Ribbon and Screen Resolution
Word may change how the groups and buttons within the groups appear on the ribbon, depending on the computer or mobile device's screen resolution. Thus, your ribbon may look different from the ones in this book if you are using a screen resolution other than 1366 × 768.

To Change Spacing above and below Paragraphs and Margin Settings

Recall that Word is preset to use standard 8.5-by-11-inch paper, with 1-inch top, bottom, left, and right margins. In earlier modules, you changed the margins by selecting predefined settings in the Margins gallery. For the newsletter in this module, all margins (left, right, top, and bottom) are .75 inches, which is not a predefined setting in the Margins gallery. Thus, the following steps set custom margins.

1. Display the Layout tab.

2. Click the Adjust Margins button (Layout tab | Page Setup group) to display the Margins gallery and then click Custom Margins at the bottom of the Margins gallery to display the Page Setup dialog box.

3. Change each value in the Top, Bottom, Left, and Right boxes (Page Setup dialog box) to .75 (Figure 7–2).

4. Click the OK button to change the margin values.

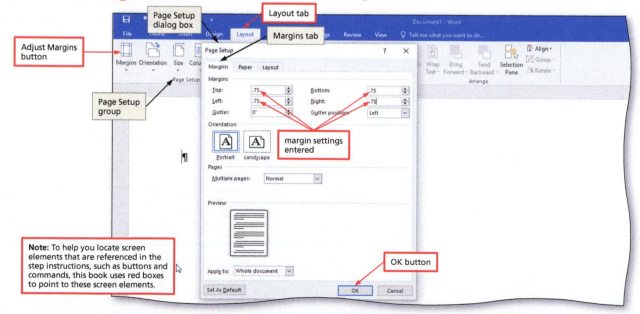

Figure 7–2

To Change Theme Colors

The newsletter in this module uses the Frame theme. The following steps change the theme to Frame.

1 Display the Design tab.

2 Click the Themes button (Design tab | Document Formatting group) and then click Frame in the Themes gallery to change the document theme.

BTW

Touch Screen Differences

The Office and Windows interfaces may vary if you are using a touch screen. For this reason, you might notice that the function or appearance of your touch screen differs slightly from this module's presentation.

Creating the Nameplate

The nameplate on the first page of this newsletter consists of the information above the multiple columns (shown in Figure 7–1a at the beginning of this module). In this project, the nameplate includes the newsletter title, Security Trends, an image of a lock, and the issue information line.

The following sections use the steps outlined below to create the nameplate for the first page of the newsletter in this module.

1. Enter and format the newsletter title using WordArt.
2. Set custom tab stops for the issue information line.
3. Enter text in the issue information line.
4. Add a horizontal rule below the issue information line.
5. Insert and format the image.

How should you design a nameplate?

A nameplate visually identifies a newsletter. It should catch the attention of readers, enticing them to read a newsletter. Usually, the nameplate is positioned horizontally across the top of the newsletter, although some nameplates are vertical. The nameplate typically consists of the title of the newsletter and the issue information line. Some also include a subtitle, a slogan, and a graphical image or logo.

Guidelines for the newsletter title and other elements in the nameplate are as follows:

- Compose a title that is short, yet conveys the contents of the newsletter. In the newsletter title, eliminate unnecessary words such as these: the, newsletter. Use a decorative font in as large a font size as possible so that the title stands out on the page.

- Other elements on the nameplate should not compete in size with the title. Use colors that complement the title. Select easy-to-read fonts.

- Arrange the elements of the nameplate so that it does not have a cluttered appearance. If necessary, use ruling lines to visually separate areas of the nameplate.

CONSIDER THIS

To Insert WordArt

1 CREATE NAMEPLATE FOR FIRST PAGE | 2 FORMAT FIRST PAGE | 3 CREATE PULL-QUOTE |
4 CREATE NAMEPLATE FOR SECOND PAGE | 5 FORMAT SECOND PAGE | 6 ADD PAGE BORDER

In Module 3, you inserted a shape drawing object in a document. Recall that a drawing object is a graphic you create using Word. Another type of drawing object, called **WordArt**, enables you to create text with special effects, such as shadowed, rotated, stretched, skewed, and wavy effects.

This project uses WordArt for the newsletter title, Security Trends. *Why? A title created with WordArt is likely to draw the reader's attention.* The following steps insert WordArt.

①

- Display the Insert tab.

- Click the Insert WordArt button (Insert tab | Text group) to display the Insert WordArt gallery (Figure 7–3).

Q&A Once I select a WordArt style, can I customize its appearance?
Yes. The next steps customize the WordArt style selected here.

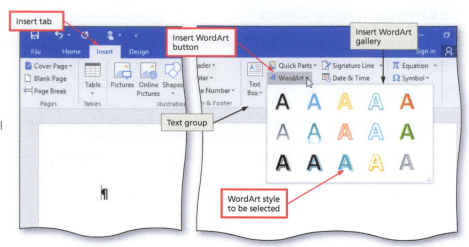

Figure 7–3

②

- Click 'Fill - Teal, Accent 1, Outline - Background 1, Hard Shadow - Accent 1' in the WordArt gallery (third WordArt style in last row) to insert a drawing object in the document that is formatted according to the selected WordArt style, which contains the placeholder text, Your text here (Figure 7–4).

③

- Type **Security Trends** to replace the selected placeholder text in the WordArt drawing object (shown in Figure 7–5).

Q&A What if my placeholder text no longer is selected?
Drag through it to select it.

How do I correct a mistake in the WordArt text?
You correct WordArt text using the same techniques you use to correct document text.

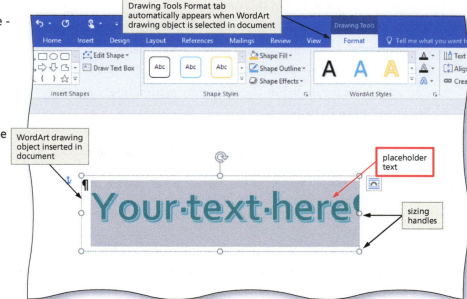

Figure 7–4

To Resize WordArt

You resize WordArt the same way you resize any other graphic. That is, you can drag its sizing handles or enter values in the Shape Height and Shape Width boxes. The next steps resize the WordArt drawing object.

① With the WordArt drawing object selected, if necessary, display the Drawing Tools Format tab.

② Change the value in the Shape Height box to 1.44 and the value in the Shape Width box to 7 (Figure 7–5).

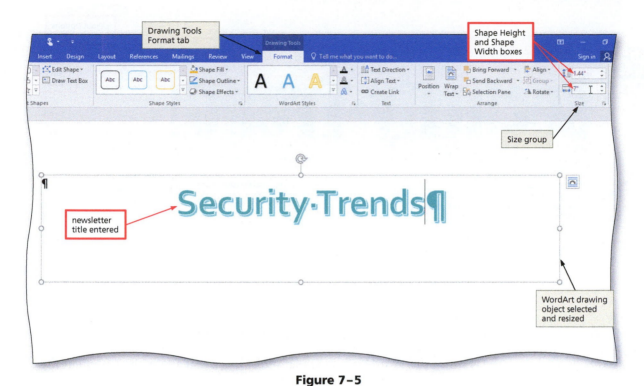

Figure 7–5

To Change the Font and Font Size of WordArt Text

You change the font and font size of WordArt text the same way you change the font and font size of any other text. That is, you select the text and then change its font and font size. The following steps change the font and font size of WordArt text.

1 Select the WordArt text, in this case, Security Trends.

2 Change the font of the selected text to Bernard MT Condensed (or a similar font).

3 Change the font size of the selected text to 72 point (shown in Figure 7–6).

BTW

Deleting WordArt
If you want to delete a WordArt drawing object, right-click it and then click Cut on the shortcut menu, or select the WordArt drawing object and then click the Cut button (Home tab | Clipboard group).

To Change an Object's Text Wrapping

When you insert a drawing object in a Word document, the default text wrapping is Square, which means text will wrap around the object in the shape of a square. Because you want the nameplate above the rest of the newsletter, you change the text wrapping for the drawing object to Top and Bottom. The following steps change a drawing object's text wrapping.

1 With the WordArt drawing object selected, click the Layout Options button that is attached to the WordArt drawing object to display the Layout Options gallery.

2 Click 'Top and Bottom' in the Layout Options gallery so that the WordArt drawing object will not cover the document text; in this case, the paragraph mark moves below the WordArt drawing object (Figure 7–6).

3 Close the Layout Options gallery.

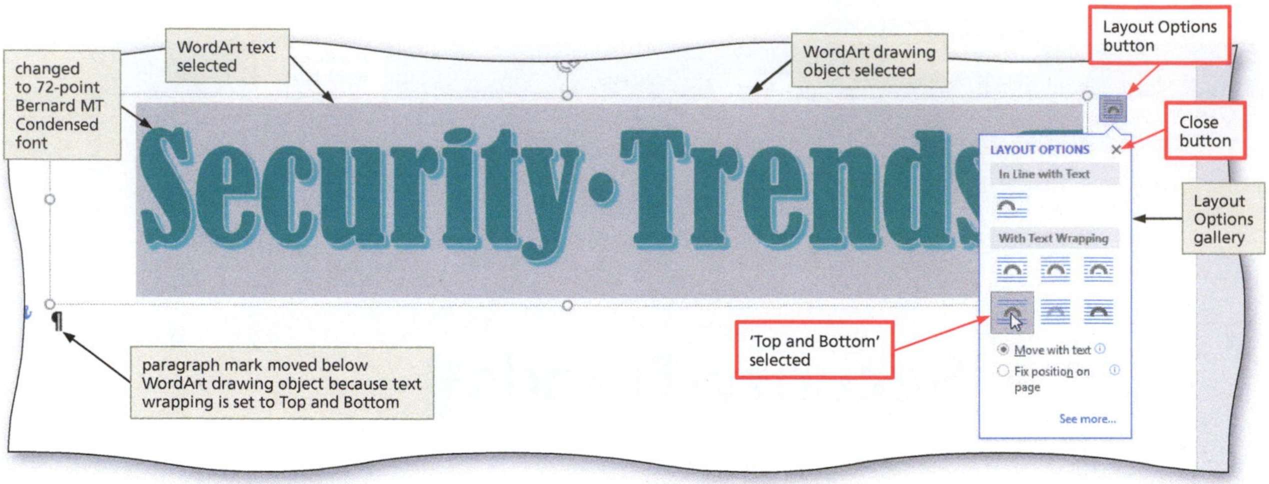

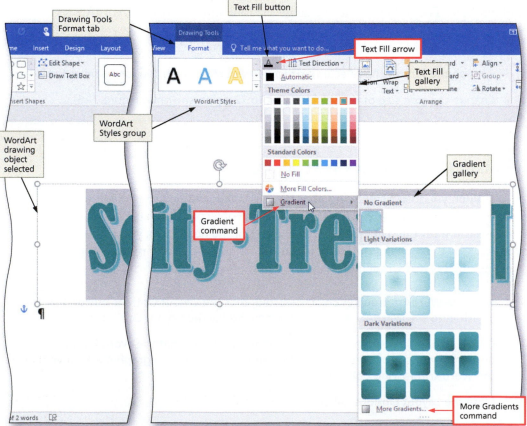

Figure 7–6

To Change the WordArt Fill Color

1 CREATE NAMEPLATE FOR FIRST PAGE | 2 FORMAT FIRST PAGE | 3 CREATE PULL-QUOTE
4 CREATE NAMEPLATE FOR SECOND PAGE | 5 FORMAT SECOND PAGE | 6 ADD PAGE BORDER

The next step is to change the color of the WordArt text so that it displays a teal and orange gradient fill color. **Gradient** means the colors blend into one another. Word includes several built-in gradient fill colors, or you can customize one for use in drawing objects. The following steps change the fill color of the WordArt drawing object to a built-in gradient fill color and then customize the selected fill color. **Why?** *Using a gradient fill color will add interest to the title.*

• With the WordArt drawing object selected, click the Text Fill arrow (Drawing Tools Format tab | WordArt Styles group) to display the Text Fill gallery.

Q&A

The Text Fill gallery did not appear. Why not?

Be sure you click the Text Fill arrow, which is to the right of the Text Fill button. If you mistakenly click the Text Fill button, Word places a default fill in the selected WordArt instead of displaying the Text Fill gallery.

• Point to Gradient in the Text Fill gallery to display the Gradient gallery (Figure 7–7).

Figure 7–7

3

- Click More Gradients in the Gradient gallery to open the Format Shape task pane. If necessary, click the Text Options tab in the Format Shape task pane and then, if necessary, click the 'Text Fill & Outline' button. If necessary, expand the Text Fill section.

- Click Gradient fill in the Text Fill section to display options related to gradient colors in the task pane (Figure 7–8).

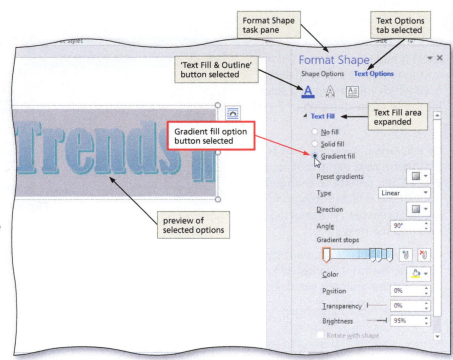

Figure 7–8

4

- Click the Preset gradients button in the Format Shape task pane to display a palette of built-in gradient fill colors (Figure 7–9).

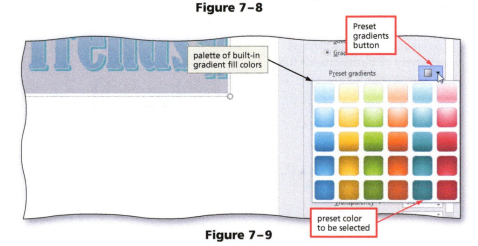

Figure 7–9

5

- Click 'Radial Gradient - Accent 5' (bottom row, fifth column) in the Preset gradients palette to select the built-in gradient color, which shows a preview in the Gradient stops area (Figure 7–10).

Q&A What is a gradient stop?
A gradient stop is the location where two colors blend. You can change the color of a stop so that Word changes the color of the blend. You also can add or delete stops, with a minimum of two stops and a maximum of ten stops per gradient fill color.

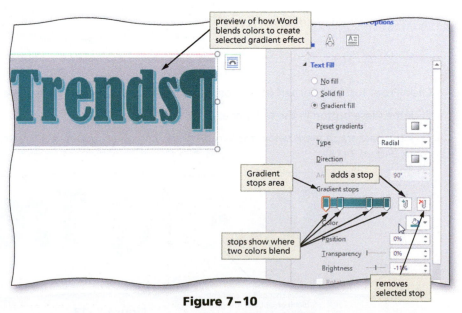

Figure 7–10

6

- Click the second gradient stop to select it and then click the Color button to display a Color palette, from which you can select a color for the selected stop (Figure 7–11).

7

- Click 'Orange, Accent 4, Darker 25%' (fifth row, eighth column) in the Color palette to change the color of the selected stop and the gradient between the selected stop and the next stop.

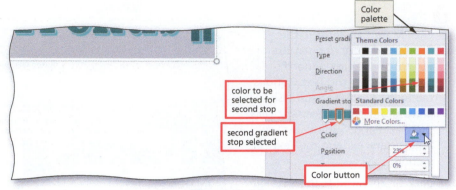

Figure 7–11

- Click the rightmost gradient stop to select it and then click the Color button to display a Color palette. Click 'Orange, Accent 4, Darker 25%' (fifth row, eighth column) in the Color palette to change the color of the selected stop and the gradient between the selected stop and the previous stop.

Q&A Can I move a gradient stop?
Yes. You can drag a stop to any location along the color bar. You also can adjust the position, brightness, and transparency of any selected stop.

8

- Click the Direction button to display a gallery that shows a variety of directions for the gradient colors (Figure 7–12).

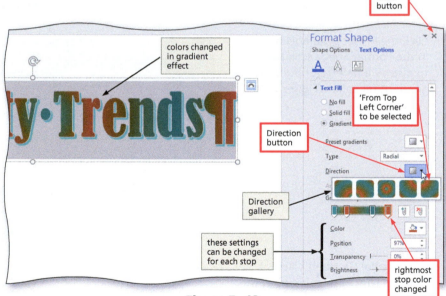

Figure 7–12

9

- Click 'From Top Left Corner' (rightmost direction) in the Direction gallery to specify the direction to blend the colors.

- Click the Close button in the task pane.

- Click the paragraph mark below the WordArt drawing object to deselect the text so that you can see its gradient fill colors (Figure 7–13).

Figure 7–13

1 CREATE NAMEPLATE FOR FIRST PAGE | 2 FORMAT FIRST PAGE | 3 CREATE PULL-QUOTE
4 CREATE NAMEPLATE FOR SECOND PAGE | 5 FORMAT SECOND PAGE | 6 ADD PAGE BORDER

To Change the WordArt Shape

Word provides a variety of shapes to make your WordArt more interesting. The following steps change the WordArt shape. *Why? The WordArt in this newsletter has a wavy appearance.*

- Click the WordArt drawing object to select it.

- If necessary, display the Drawing Tools Format tab.

- Click the Text Effects button (Drawing Tools Format tab | WordArt Styles group) to display the Text Effects gallery.

- Point to Transform in the Text Effects gallery to display the Transform gallery.

- Point to 'Double Wave 1' (third effect, fifth row in Warp area) in the Transform gallery to display a live preview of the selected transform effect applied to the selected drawing object (Figure 7–14).

Experiment

- Point to various text effects in the Transform gallery and watch the selected drawing object conform to that transform effect.

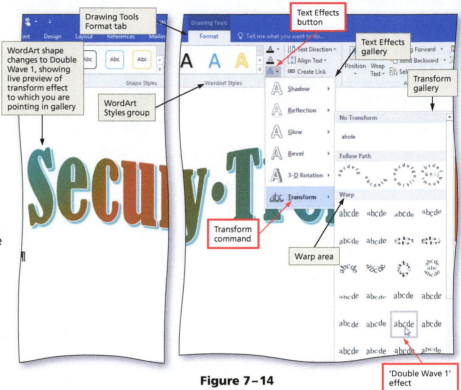

Figure 7–14

- Click 'Double Wave 1' in the Transform gallery to change the shape of the WordArt drawing object.

To Set Custom Tab Stops Using the Tabs Dialog Box

1 CREATE NAMEPLATE FOR FIRST PAGE | 2 FORMAT FIRST PAGE | 3 CREATE PULL-QUOTE
4 CREATE NAMEPLATE FOR SECOND PAGE | 5 FORMAT SECOND PAGE | 6 ADD PAGE BORDER

The issue information line in this newsletter contains the text, Monthly Newsletter, at the left margin and the issue number at the right margin (shown in Figure 7–1a at the beginning of this module). In Word, a paragraph cannot be both left-aligned and right-aligned. *Why? If you click the 'Align Text Right' button (Home tab | Paragraph group), for example, all text will be right-aligned.* To place text at the right margin of a left-aligned paragraph, you set a tab stop at the right margin.

One method of setting custom tab stops is to click the ruler at the desired location of the tab stop, which you learned in an earlier module. You cannot click, however, at the right margin location. Thus, the following steps use the Tabs dialog box to set a custom tab stop.

- If necessary, display the Home tab.

- Position the insertion point on the paragraph mark below the WordArt drawing object, which is the paragraph to be formatted with the custom tab stops.

- Click the Paragraph Settings Dialog Box Launcher to display the Paragraph dialog box (Figure 7–15).

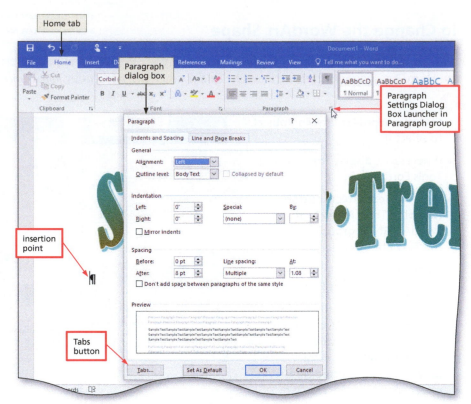

Figure 7–15

- Click the Tabs button (Paragraph dialog box) to display the Tabs dialog box.

- Type   7   in the 'Tab stop position' text box (Tabs dialog box).

- Click Right in the Alignment area to specify alignment for text at the tab stop (Figure 7–16).

- Click the Set button (Tabs dialog box) to set a right-aligned custom tab stop at the specified position.

- Click the OK button to set the defined tab stops.

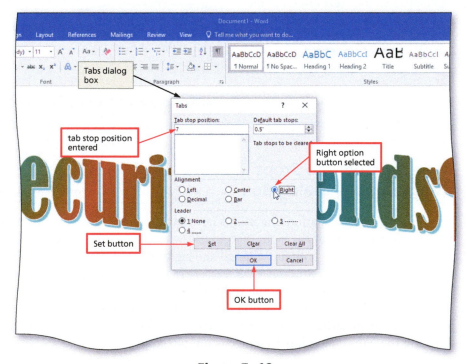

Figure 7–16

Other Ways

1. Click desired tab stop on ruler

2. Right-click paragraph (or, if using touch, tap 'Show Context Menu' button on mini toolbar), click Paragraph on shortcut menu, click Tabs button (Paragraph dialog box), enter desired settings, click OK button

To Enter Text

The following steps enter the issue information line text.

1 With the insertion point on the paragraph below the WordArt, change the font to Century Schoolbook (or a similar font) and the font size to 10 point.

2 Type **Monthly Newsletter** on line 2 of the newsletter.

If requested by your instructor, enter your name instead of the word, Monthly.

3 Press the TAB key and then type **Issue 15** to complete the issue information line (Figure 7–17).

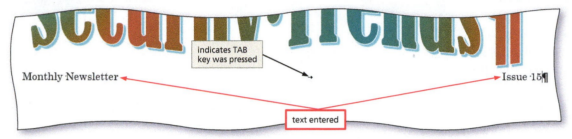

indicates TAB key was pressed

Monthly Newsletter

Issue 15¶

text entered

Figure 7–17

Q&A The nameplate does not appear to extend to the right margin. Why not?
If you have formatting marks displaying, the paragraph mark consumes space at the right margin. To see how the nameplate will print, turn off formatting marks.

To Border One Edge of a Paragraph

1 CREATE NAMEPLATE FOR FIRST PAGE | 2 FORMAT FIRST PAGE | 3 CREATE PULL-QUOTE
4 CREATE NAMEPLATE FOR SECOND PAGE | 5 FORMAT SECOND PAGE | 6 ADD PAGE BORDER

In Word, you use borders to create ruling lines. As discussed in previous modules, Word can place borders on any edge of a paragraph; that is, Word can place a border on the top, bottom, left, and right edges of a paragraph.

One method of bordering paragraphs is by clicking the desired border in the Borders gallery, which you learned in an earlier module. If you want to specify a particular border, for example, one with color, you use the Borders and Shading dialog box. The following steps use the Borders and Shading dialog box to place a border below a paragraph. ***Why?*** *In this newsletter, the issue information line has a 3-point diagonally striped teal border below it.*

1

- Click the Borders arrow (Home tab | Paragraph group) to display the Borders gallery (Figure 7–18).

Home tab

Borders arrow

Paragraph group

Borders gallery

insertion point

Issue 15¶

'Borders and Shading' command

Figure 7–18

2

- Click 'Borders and Shading' in the Borders gallery to display the Borders and Shading dialog box.

- Click Custom in the Setting area (Borders and Shading dialog box) because you are setting just a bottom border.

- Scroll through the Style list and click the style shown in Figure 7–19, which is a diagonally striped line for the border.

- Click the Color button and then click 'Teal, Accent 5, Darker 50%' (ninth column, bottom row) in the Color gallery.

- Click the Bottom Border button in the Preview area of the dialog box to show a preview of the selected border style (Figure 7–19).

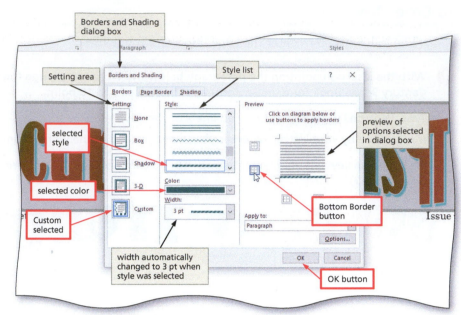

Figure 7–19

Q&A
What is the purpose of the buttons in the Preview area?
They are toggles that display and remove the top, bottom, left, and right borders from the diagram in the Preview area.

3

- Click the OK button to place the defined border on the paragraph containing the insertion point (Figure 7–20).

Figure 7–20

Q&A
How would I change an existing border?
You first remove the existing border by clicking the Borders arrow (Home tab | Paragraph group) and then clicking the border in the Borders gallery that identifies the border you wish to remove. Then, add a new border as described in these steps.

Other Ways

1. Click 'Borders and Shading' button (Design tab | Page Background group), click Borders tab (Borders and Shading dialog box), select desired border, click OK button

---

To Insert a Picture

The next steps insert an image of locks in the nameplate.

1 Display the Insert tab.

2 Click the Online Pictures button (Insert tab | Illustrations group) to display the Insert Pictures dialog box.

3 Type **locks** in the Search box (Insert Pictures dialog box) to specify the search text and then click the Search button to display a list of images that match the entered search text.

4 Scroll through the list of images to locate the one shown in Figure 7–21 (or a similar image), click the image to select it, and then click the Insert button (Insert Picture dialog box) to download the image, close the dialog box, and insert the selected image at the location of the insertion point in the document.

Q&A What if I cannot locate the same image as in Figure 7–21?
Click the Cancel button to close the dialog box and then click the From File button (Insert tab | Illustrations group) to display the Insert Picture dialog box, navigate to and select the 1383900176-2400px.png file on the Data Files, and then click the Insert button (Insert Picture dialog box) to insert the picture.

What if my inserted image is not in the same location as in Figure 7–21?
The image may be in a different location, depending on the position of the insertion point when you inserted the image. In a later section, you will move the image to a different location.

To Change the Color of a Graphic

The following steps change the color of the graphic (the locks) to a shade of gold.

1 With the graphic still selected, click the Color button (Picture Tools Format tab | Adjust group) to display the Color gallery (Figure 7–21).

2 Click 'Gold, Accent color 2 Light' (third color, bottom row) in the Recolor area in the Color gallery to change the color of the selected graphic.

Figure 7–21

To Crop a Graphic

The next step is to format the image just inserted. You would like to remove the rightmost lock from the image. **Why?** *You want just one lock to appear in the newsletter.* Word allows you to **crop**, or remove edges from, a graphic. The following steps crop a graphic.

1

- With the graphic selected, click the Crop button (Picture Tools Format tab | Size group), which places cropping handles on the image in the document.

Q&A What if I mistakenly click the Crop arrow?
Click the Crop button.

- Position the pointer on the right-middle cropping handle so that it looks like a sideways letter T (Figure 7–22).

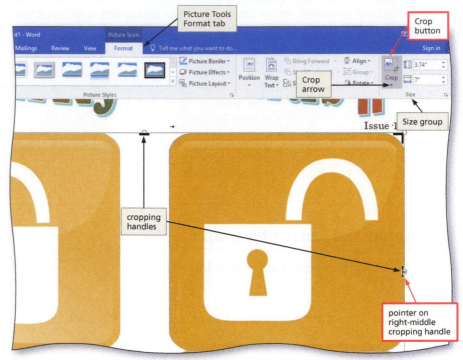

Figure 7–22

2

- Drag the right-middle cropping handle inward to the location shown in Figure 7–23 to crop the rightmost lock from the image.

3

- Click the Crop button (Picture Tools Format tab | Size group) to deactivate the cropping tool, which removes the cropping handles from the selected image.

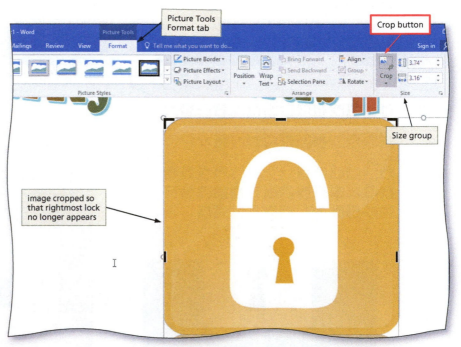

Figure 7–23

Other Ways

1. Right-click graphic, click Crop button on mini toolbar, drag cropping handles, click Crop button

To Change an Object's Text Wrapping and Size

When you insert an object (image) in a Word document, the default text wrapping is In Line with Text, which means the object is part of the current paragraph. Because you want the lock image behind the newsletter title, you change the text wrapping for the image to Behind Text. The next steps change a drawing object's text wrapping and also change its size.

1 With the lock graphic selected, click the Layout Options button attached to the graphic to display the Layout Options gallery.

2 Click Behind Text in the Layout Options gallery so that the image is positioned behind text in the document.

3 Close the Layout Options gallery.

4 Change the values in the Shape Height and Shape Width boxes (Picture Tools Format tab | Size group) to .6" and .51", respectively.

To Move a Graphic

The clip art image needs to be moved up so that the bottom of the lock is on the s in the word, Trends, in the newsletter title. The following steps move a graphic.

1 Hide formatting marks so that you can see exactly where the letter s ends.

2 Drag the graphic to the location shown in Figure 7–24.

Figure 7–24

1 CREATE NAMEPLATE FOR FIRST PAGE | **2** FORMAT FIRST PAGE | **3** CREATE PULL-QUOTE

4 CREATE NAMEPLATE FOR SECOND PAGE | **5** FORMAT SECOND PAGE | **6** ADD PAGE BORDER

To Use the Selection Task Pane

The next step is to rotate the lock image, but because it is positioned behind the text, it may be difficult to select it. The following step opens the Selection task pane. *Why? The Selection task pane enables you easily to select items on the screen that are layered behind other objects.*

1

- If necessary, click in the graphic to display the Picture Tools Format tab.

- Click the 'Display the Selection Pane' button (Picture Tools Format tab | Arrange group) to open the Selection task pane (Figure 7–25).

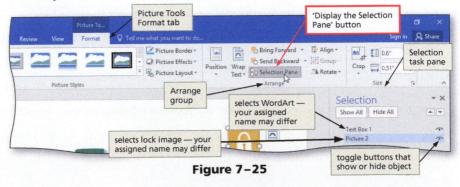

Figure 7–25

 **Experiment**

- Click Text Box 1 in the Selection task pane to select the WordArt drawing object. Click Picture 2 in the Selection task pane to select the lock image.

 What are the displayed names in the Selection task pane?

Word assigns names to each object in the document. The names displayed on your screen may differ.

To Rotate a Graphic

1 CREATE NAMEPLATE FOR FIRST PAGE | 2 FORMAT FIRST PAGE | 3 CREATE PULL-QUOTE
4 CREATE NAMEPLATE FOR SECOND PAGE | 5 FORMAT SECOND PAGE | 6 ADD PAGE BORDER

The following steps rotate a graphic. *Why? You would like the lock image angled inward a bit more.*

1

- If necessary, click Picture 2 in the Selection task pane to select the lock image.

- Position the pointer on the graphic's rotate handle (Figure 7–26).

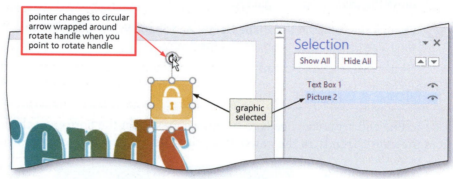

Figure 7–26

2

- Drag the rotate handle rightward and outward to rotate the graphic slightly as shown in Figure 7–27. (You may need to rotate the graphic a few times to position it in the desired location.)

 Can I drag the rotate handle in any direction?

You can drag the rotate handle clockwise or counterclockwise.

What if I am using a touch screen?

Because the rotate handle is not available on a touch screen, you enter the degree of rotation in the Size dialog box. Tap the Rotate Objects button (Picture Tools Format tab | Arrange group) to display the Rotate Objects menu, tap 'More Rotation Options' on the Rotate Objects menu to display the Size sheet in the Layout dialog box, change the Rotation value to 14, and then tap the OK button.

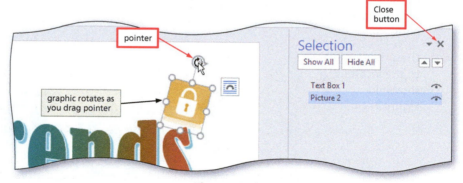

Figure 7–27

3

- Click the Close button on the Selection task pane to close the task pane.

- Click somewhere in the issue information line to deselect the graphic.

- Save the title page on your hard drive, OneDrive, or other storage location using the file name, Security Trends Newsletter.

Break Point: If you wish to take a break, this is a good place to do so. You can exit Word now. To resume at a later time, run Word, open the file called Security Trends Newsletter, and continue following the steps from this location forward.

Formatting the First Page of the Body of the Newsletter

The next step is to format the first page of the body of the newsletter. The body of the newsletter in this module is divided in three columns (shown in Figure 7–1a at the beginning of this module). The first two columns contain the feature article, and the third column contains announcements. The characters in the paragraphs are aligned on both the right and left edges — similar to newspaper columns. The first letter in the first paragraph is much larger than the rest of the characters in the paragraph. A vertical rule separates the columns. The steps in the following sections format the first page of the body of the newsletter using these desktop publishing features.

What guidelines should you follow when creating the body of a newsletter?

While content and subject matter of newsletters may vary, the procedures used to create newsletters are similar:

- **Write the body copy.** Newsletters should contain articles of interest and relevance to readers. Some share information, while others promote a product or service. Use active voice in body copy, which is more engaging than passive voice. Proofread the body copy to be sure it is error free. Check all facts for accuracy.

- **Organize body copy in columns.** Most newsletters arrange body copy in columns. The body copy in columns, often called **snaking columns** or newspaper-style columns, flows from the bottom of one column to the top of the next column.

- **Format the body copy.** Begin the feature article on the first page of the newsletter. If the article spans multiple pages, use a continuation line, called a jump or jump line, to guide the reader to the remainder of the article. The message at the end of the article on the first page of the newsletter is called a **jump-to line**, and a **jump-from line** marks the beginning of the continuation, which is usually on a subsequent page.

- **Maintain consistency.** Be consistent with placement of body copy elements in newsletter editions. If the newsletter contains announcements, for example, position them in the same location in each edition so that readers easily can find them.

- **Maximize white space.** Allow plenty of space between lines, paragraphs, and columns. Tightly packed text is difficult to read. Separate the text adequately from graphics, borders, and headings.

- **Incorporate color.** Use colors that complement those in the nameplate. Be careful not to overuse color. Restrict color below the nameplate to drop caps, subheads, graphics, and ruling lines. If you do not have a color printer, still change the colors because the colors will print in shades of black and gray, which add variety to the newsletter.

- **Select and format subheads.** Develop subheads with as few words as possible. Readers should be able to identify content of the next topic by glancing at a subhead. Subheads should be emphasized in the newsletter but should not compete with text in the nameplate. Use a larger, bold, or otherwise contrasting font for subheads so that they stand apart from the body copy. Use this same format for all subheads for consistency. Leave a space above subheads to visually separate their content from the previous topic. Be consistent with spacing above and below subheads throughout the newsletter.

- **Divide sections with vertical rules.** Use vertical rules to guide the reader through the newsletter.

- **Enhance the document with visuals.** Add energy to the newsletter and emphasis to important points with graphics, pull-quotes, and other visuals, such as drop caps, to mark beginning of an article. Use these elements sparingly, however, so that the newsletter does not have a crowded appearance. Fewer, large visuals are more effective than several smaller ones. If you use a graphic that you did not create, be sure to obtain permission to use it in the newsletter and give necessary credit to the creator of the graphic.

To Clear Formatting

The next step is to enter the title of the feature article below the horizontal rule. To do this, position the insertion point at the end of the issue information line (after the 5 in Issue 15) and then press the ENTER key. Recall that the issue information line has a bottom border. When you press the ENTER key in a bordered paragraph, Word carries forward any borders to the next paragraph. Thus, after you press the ENTER key, you should clear formatting to format the new paragraph as the Normal style. The following steps clear formatting.

1 Click at the end of line 2 (the issue information line) so that the insertion point is immediately after the 5 in Issue 15. Press the ENTER key to advance the insertion point to the next line, which also moves the border down one line.

2 If necessary, display the Home tab. Click the 'Clear All Formatting' button (Home tab | Font group) to apply the Normal style to the location of the insertion point, which in this case moves the new paragraph below the border on the issue information line.

To Format Text as a Heading Style, Modify a Heading Style, and Adjust Spacing before and after the Paragraph

Below the bottom border in the nameplate is the title of the feature article, Biometrics. The following steps apply the Heading 1 style to this paragraph, modify the style, and adjust the paragraph spacing.

1 If necessary, display formatting marks.

2 With the insertion point on the paragraph mark below the border, click Heading 1 (Home tab | Styles group) to apply the Heading 1 style to the paragraph containing the insertion point.

3 Increase the font size 20 point. Bold the paragraph. Update the Heading 1 style to reflect these changes.

4 Type **Biometrics** as the title of the feature article.

5 Display the Layout tab. Change the Spacing Before box to 18 pt and the Spacing After box to 12 pt (Figure 7–28).

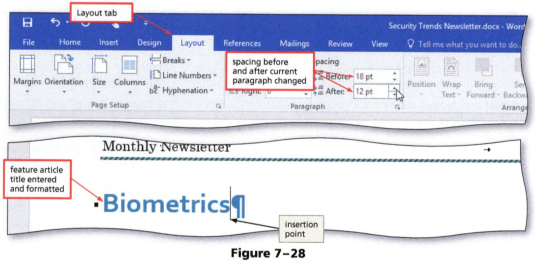

Figure 7–28

Columns

When you begin a document in Word, it has one column. You can divide a portion of a document or the entire document in multiple columns. Within each column, you can type, modify, or format text.

To divide a portion of a document in multiple columns, you use section breaks. Word requires that a new section be created each time you alter the number of columns in a document. Thus, if a document has a nameplate (one column) followed by an article of three columns followed by an article of two columns, the document would be divided in three separate sections.

Be consistent from page to page with the number of columns. Narrow columns generally are easier to read than wide ones. Columns, however, can be too narrow. A two- or three-column layout generally is appealing and offers a flexible design. Try to have between five and fifteen words per line. To do this, you may need to adjust the column width, the font size, or the leading (line spacing). Font size of text in columns should be no larger than 12 point but not so small that readers must strain to read the text.

1 CREATE NAMEPLATE FOR FIRST PAGE | 2 FORMAT FIRST PAGE | 3 CREATE PULL-QUOTE

To Insert a Continuous Section Break

4 CREATE NAMEPLATE FOR SECOND PAGE | 5 FORMAT SECOND PAGE | 6 ADD PAGE BORDER

The next step is to insert a continuous section break below the nameplate. *Why? In this module, the nameplate is one column and the body of the newsletter is three columns.* The term, continuous, means the new section should be on the same page as the previous section, which, in this case, means that the three columns of body copy will be positioned directly below the nameplate on the first page of the newsletter. The following steps insert a continuous section break.

1

- With the insertion point at the end of the feature article title (shown in Figure 7–28), press the ENTER key to position the insertion point below the article title.

- Click the 'Insert Page and Section Breaks' button (Layout tab | Page Setup group) to display the Insert Page and Section Breaks gallery (Figure 7–29).

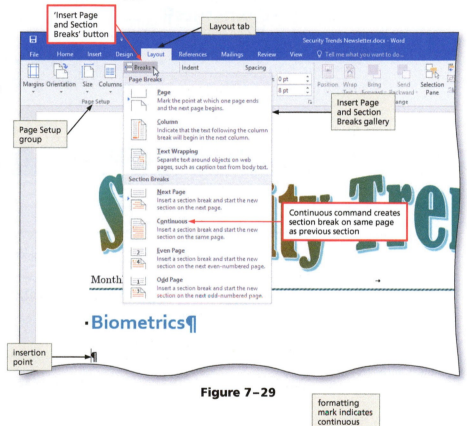

Figure 7–29

2

- Click Continuous in the Insert Page and Section Breaks gallery to insert a continuous section break above the insertion point (Figure 7–30).

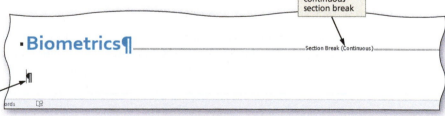

Figure 7–30

1 CREATE NAMEPLATE FOR FIRST PAGE | 2 FORMAT FIRST PAGE | 3 CREATE PULL-QUOTE

To Change the Number of Columns

4 CREATE NAMEPLATE FOR SECOND PAGE | 5 FORMAT SECOND PAGE | 6 ADD PAGE BORDER

The document now has two sections. The nameplate is in the first section, and the insertion point is in the second section. The second section should be formatted to three columns. *Why? The feature article and announcements appear in three columns that snake across the page.* Thus, the following steps format the second section in the document as three columns.

1

• Click the 'Add or Remove Columns' button (Layout tab | Page Setup group) to display the Add or Remove Columns gallery (Figure 7–31).

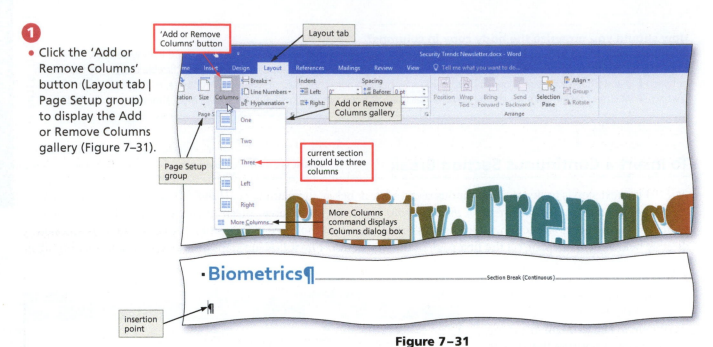

Figure 7–31

2

• Click Three in the Add or Remove Columns gallery to divide the section containing the insertion point in three evenly sized and spaced columns

• Display the View tab and then, if necessary, click the View Ruler check box so that the rulers appear on the screen (Figure 7–32).

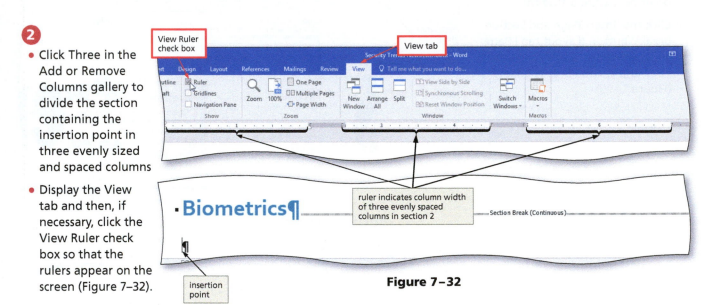

Figure 7–32

Q&A

Why display the rulers?
You want to see the column widths on the ruler.

What if I want columns of different widths?
You would click More Columns in the Add or Remove Columns gallery, which displays the Columns dialog box. In this dialog box, you can specify varying column widths and spacing.

1 CREATE NAMEPLATE FOR FIRST PAGE | 2 FORMAT FIRST PAGE | 3 CREATE PULL-QUOTE
4 CREATE NAMEPLATE FOR SECOND PAGE | 5 FORMAT SECOND PAGE | 6 ADD PAGE BORDER

To Justify a Paragraph

The following step enters the first paragraph of the feature article using justified alignment. **Why?** *The text in the paragraphs of the body of the newsletter is **justified**, which means that the left and right margins are aligned, like the edges of newspaper columns.*

- Display the Home tab.

- Click the Justify button (Home tab | Paragraph group) so that Word aligns both the left and right margins of typed text.

- Type the first paragraph of the feature article (Figure 7–33): `Biometric devices verify a person's identity by translating a behavioral or physical personal characteristic, such as a fingerprint, into a digital code that is compared with a digital code stored in a computer or mobile device. If the digital code in the computer or mobile device does not match the personal characteristic code, the computer or mobile device denies access to the individual.` and then press the ENTER key.

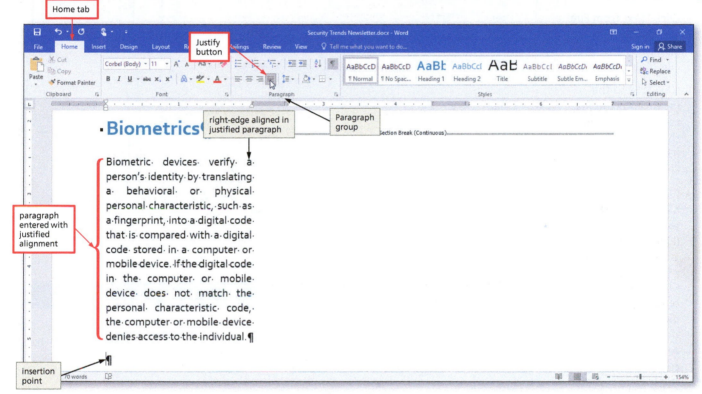

Figure 7–33

Q&A Why do some words have extra space between them?

When a paragraph is formatted to justified alignment, Word places extra space between words so that the left and right edges of the paragraph are aligned. To remedy big gaps, sometimes called rivers, you can add or rearrange words, change the column width, change the font size, and so on.

Other Ways

1. Right-click paragraph (or, if using touch, tap 'Show Context Menu' button on mini toolbar), click Paragraph on shortcut menu, click 'Indents and Spacing' tab (Paragraph dialog box), click Alignment arrow, click Justified, click OK button

2. Click Paragraph Settings Dialog Box Launcher (Home tab or Layout tab | Paragraph group), click Indents and Spacing tab (Paragraph dialog box), click Alignment arrow, click Justified, click OK button

3. Press CTRL+J

To Insert a File in a Column of the Newsletter

1 CREATE NAMEPLATE FOR FIRST PAGE | 2 FORMAT FIRST PAGE | 3 CREATE PULL-QUOTE
4 CREATE NAMEPLATE FOR SECOND PAGE | 5 FORMAT SECOND PAGE | 6 ADD PAGE BORDER

The next step is to insert a file named Biometrics Article in the newsletter. **Why?** *To save you time typing, the rest of the feature article is located on the Data Files.* Please contact your instructor for information about accessing the Data Files. The following steps insert the Biometrics Article file in a column of the newsletter.

- Display the Insert tab.

- With the insertion point positioned in the left column as shown in Figure 7–33, click the Object arrow (Insert tab | Text group) to display the Object menu.

- Click 'Text from File' on the Object menu to display the Insert File dialog box.

- Navigate to the location of the file to be inserted (in this case, the Module 07 files in the Data Files folder).

- Click the file named Biometrics Article to select the file (Figure 7–34).

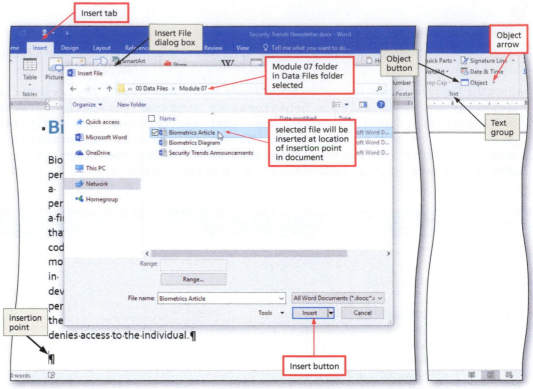

Figure 7–34

- Click the Insert button (Insert File dialog box) to insert the file, Biometrics Article, in the current document at the location of the insertion point.

- So that you can see the entire inserted article, display multiple pages on the screen by clicking the Multiple Pages button (View tab | Zoom group) (Figure 7–35).

- When you are finished viewing the document, change the zoom to page width so that the newsletter content is larger on the screen.

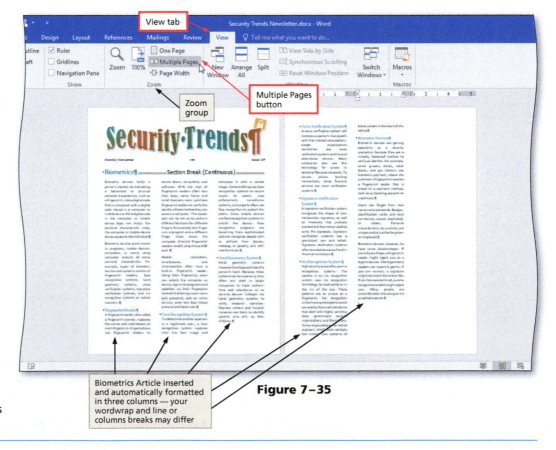

Figure 7–35

To Increase Column Width and Place a Vertical Rule between Columns

1 CREATE NAMEPLATE FOR FIRST PAGE | 2 FORMAT FIRST PAGE | 3 CREATE PULL-QUOTE
4 CREATE NAMEPLATE FOR SECOND PAGE | 5 FORMAT SECOND PAGE | 6 ADD PAGE BORDER

The columns in the newsletter currently contain many rivers. *Why? The justified alignment in the narrow column width often causes large gaps between words.* To eliminate some of the rivers, you increase the size of the columns slightly in this newsletter. In newsletters, you often see a vertical rule separating columns. Through the Columns dialog box, you can change column width and add vertical rules. The following steps increase column widths and add vertical rules between columns.

1

- Position the insertion point somewhere in the feature article text.

- Display the Layout tab.

- Click the 'Add or Remove Columns' button (Layout tab | Page Setup group) to display the Add or Remove Columns gallery (Figure 7–36).

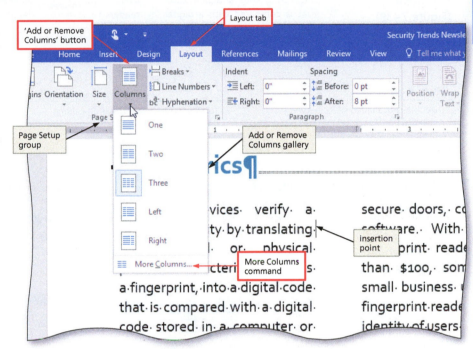

Figure 7–36

2

- Click More Columns in the Add or Remove Columns gallery to display the Columns dialog box.

- If necessary, in the Width and spacing area (Columns dialog box), click the Width up arrow until the Width box reads 2.1".

Q&A
How would I make the columns different widths?
You would remove the check mark from the 'Equal column width' check box and then set the individual column widths in the dialog box.

- Place a check mark in the Line between check box to select the check box (Figure 7–37).

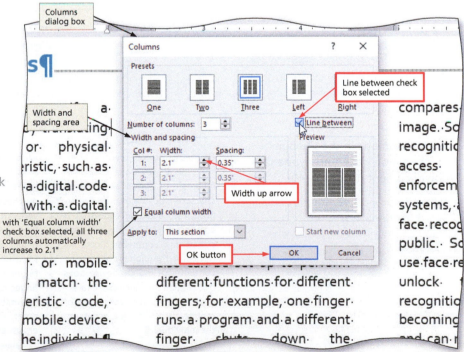

Figure 7–37

• Click the OK button to make the columns slightly wider and place a line (vertical rule) between each column in the document (Figure 7–38).

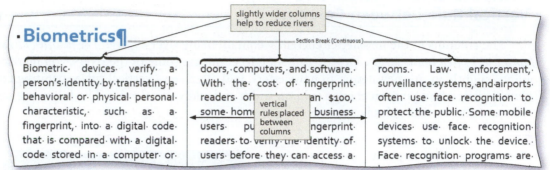

Figure 7–38

Other Ways

1. Double-click shaded space between columns on ruler, enter settings (Columns dialog box), click OK button

2. To adjust column widths, drag column boundaries on ruler

3. To insert single rule, click Borders arrow (Home tab | Paragraph group)

1 CREATE NAMEPLATE FOR FIRST PAGE | 2 FORMAT FIRST PAGE | 3 CREATE PULL-QUOTE
4 CREATE NAMEPLATE FOR SECOND PAGE | 5 FORMAT SECOND PAGE | 6 ADD PAGE BORDER

To Hyphenate a Document

The following steps turn on the hyphenation feature. *Why? To further eliminate some of the rivers in the columns of the newsletter, you turn on Word's hyphenation feature so that words with multiple syllables are hyphenated at the end of lines instead of wrapped in their entirety to the next line.*

• Click the Change Hyphenation button (Layout tab | Page Setup group) to display the Change Hyphenation gallery (Figure 7–39).

Q&A What is the difference between Automatic and Manual hyphenation?
Automatic hyphenation places hyphens wherever words can break at a syllable in the document. With manual hyphenation, Word displays a dialog box for each word it could hyphenate, enabling you to accept or reject the proposed hyphenation.

Figure 7–39

• Click Automatic in the Change Hyphenation gallery to hyphenate the document (Figure 7–40).

Q&A What if I do not want a particular word hyphenated?
You can reword text, and Word will redo the hyphenation automatically.

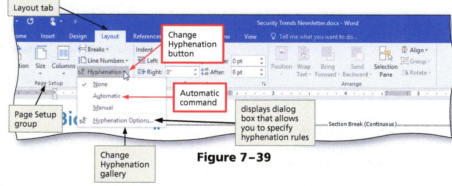

Figure 7–40

To Format a Character as a Drop Cap

The first character in the feature article in this newsletter; that is, the capital letter B, is formatted as a drop cap. **Why?** *To add interest to an article, you often see a* **drop cap***, which is a capital letter whose font size is larger than the rest of the characters in the paragraph.* In Word, the drop cap can sink into the first few lines of text, or it can extend into the left margin, which often is called a stick-up cap. In this newsletter, the paragraph text wraps around the drop cap.

The following steps create a drop cap in the first paragraph of the feature article in the newsletter.

- Position the insertion point somewhere in the first paragraph of the feature article.

- Display the Insert tab.

- Click the 'Add a Drop Cap' button (Insert tab | Text group) to display the Add a Drop Cap gallery (Figure 7–41).

Experiment

- Point to various commands in the Add a Drop Cap gallery to see a live preview of the drop cap formats in the document.

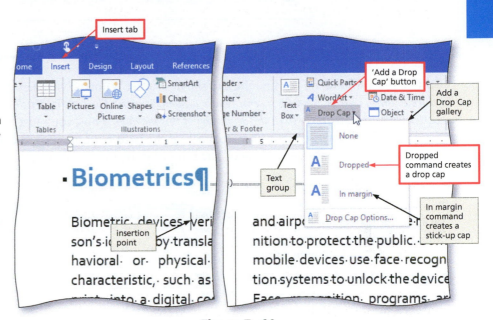

Figure 7–41

- Click Dropped in the Add a Drop Cap gallery to format the first letter in the paragraph containing the insertion point (the B in Biometric, in this case) as a drop cap and wrap subsequent text in the paragraph around the drop cap (Figure 7–42).

Q&A

What is the outline around the drop cap in the document?
When you format a letter as a drop cap, Word places a frame around it. A **frame** is a container for text that allows you to position the text anywhere on the page. Word formats a frame for the drop cap so that text wraps around it. The frame also contains a paragraph mark nonprinting character to the right of the drop cap, which may or may not be visible on your screen.

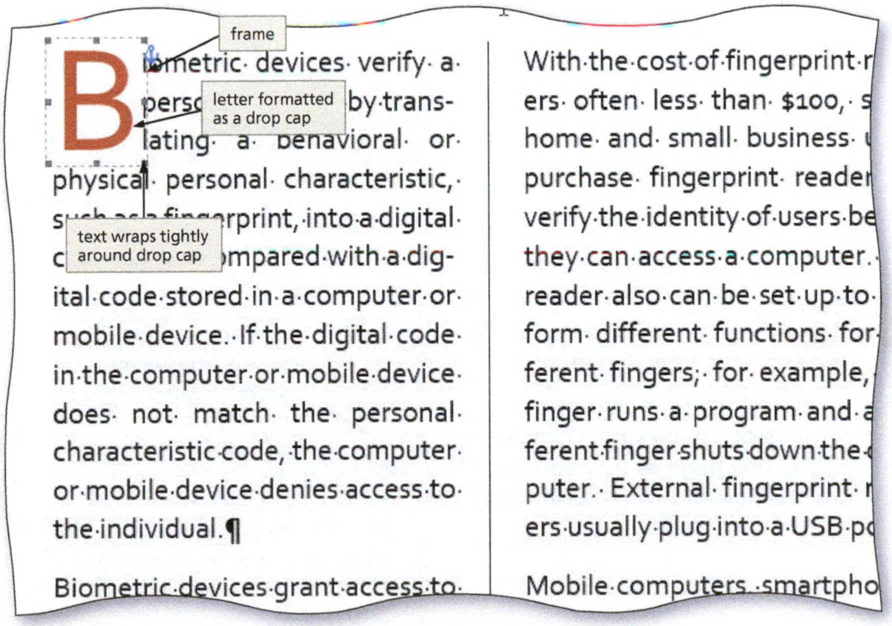

Figure 7–42

To Format the Drop Cap

The following step changes the font color of the drop cap.

1 With the drop cap selected, display the Home tab and then change the font color of the drop cap to 'Orange, Accent 4, Darker 25%' (eighth color, fifth row) in Font Color gallery (shown in Figure 7-1a at the beginning of this module).

Q&A What if my frame no longer is displayed?
Click the drop cap to select it. Then, click the blue selection rectangle to display the frame.

To Insert a Next Page Section Break

1 CREATE NAMEPLATE FOR FIRST PAGE | **2 FORMAT FIRST PAGE** | 3 CREATE PULL-QUOTE
4 CREATE NAMEPLATE FOR SECOND PAGE | 5 FORMAT SECOND PAGE | 6 ADD PAGE BORDER

The third column on the first page of the newsletter is not a continuation of the feature article. *Why not?* *The third column, instead, contains several reader announcements. The feature article continues on the second page of the newsletter (shown in Figure 7–1b at the beginning of this module).* Thus, you must insert a next page section break, which is a section break that also contains a page break, at the bottom of the second column so that the remainder of the feature article moves to the second page. The following steps insert a next page section break in the second column.

- Position the insertion point at the location for the section break, in this case, to the left of the F in the Face Recognition System heading.

- Display the Layout tab.

- Click the 'Insert Page and Section Breaks' button (Layout tab | Page Setup group) to display the Insert Page and Section Breaks gallery (Figure 7–43).

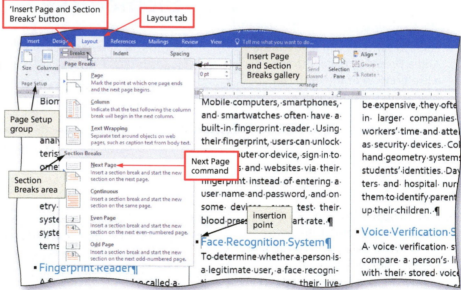

Figure 7–43

- In the Section Breaks area in the gallery, click Next Page to insert a next page section break, which positions the insertion point on the next page.

- If necessary, scroll to the bottom of the first page so that you can see the moved text (Figure 7–44).

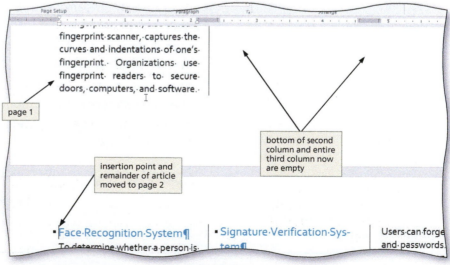

Figure 7–44

To Enter Text

The next step is to insert a jump-to line at the end of the second column, informing the reader where to look for the rest of the feature article. The following steps insert a jump-to line at the end of the text in the second column on the first page of the newsletter.

1 Scroll to display the end of the text in the second column of the first page of the newsletter and then position the insertion point to the left the paragraph mark that is to the left of the section break notation.

2 Press the ENTER key twice to insert a blank line for the jump-to text above the section break notation.

3 Press the UP ARROW key to position the insertion point on the blank line. If the blank line is formatted in the Heading 1 style, click the 'Clear All Formatting' button (Home tab | Font group) so that the entered text follows the Normal style.

4 Press CTRL+R to right align the paragraph mark. Press CTRL+I to turn on the italic format. Type **(Article continues on next page)** as the jump-to text and then press CTRL+I again to turn off the italic format.

To Insert a Column Break

1 CREATE NAMEPLATE FOR FIRST PAGE | **2 FORMAT FIRST PAGE** | 3 CREATE PULL-QUOTE
4 CREATE NAMEPLATE FOR SECOND PAGE | 5 FORMAT SECOND PAGE | 6 ADD PAGE BORDER

In the *Security Trends* newsletters, for consistency, the reader announcements always begin at the top of the third column. If you insert the Security Trends Announcements at the current location of the insertion point, however, they will begin at the bottom of the second column. **Why?** *The insertion point currently is at the bottom of the second column.*

For the reader announcements to be displayed in the third column, you insert a **column break** at the bottom of the second column, which places the insertion point at the top of the next column. Thus, the following steps insert a column break at the bottom of the second column.

1

- Position the insertion point to the left of the paragraph mark on the line containing the next page section break, which is the location where the column break should be inserted.

- If necessary, display the Layout tab.

- Click the 'Insert Page and Section Breaks' button (Layout tab | Page Setup group) to display the Insert Page and Section Breaks gallery (Figure 7–45).

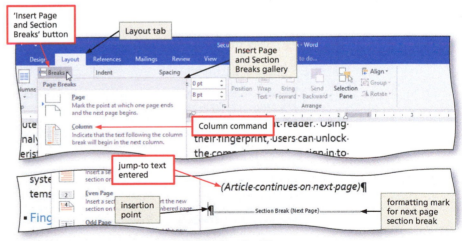

Figure 7–45

2

- Click Column in the Insert Page and Section Breaks gallery to insert a column break at the location of the insertion point and move the insertion point to the top of the next column (Figure 7–46).

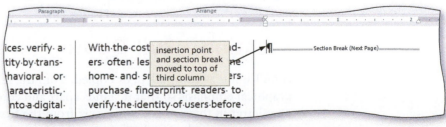

Figure 7–46

What if I wanted to remove a column break?

You would double-click it to select it and then click the Cut button (Home tab | Clipboard group) or press the DELETE key.

Other Ways

1. Press CTRL+SHIFT+ENTER

To Insert a File in a Column of the Newsletter

So that you do not have to enter the entire third column of announcements in the newsletter, the next step in the project is to insert the file named Security Trends Announcements in the third column of the newsletter. This file contains the three announcements: the first about reader discounts, the second about an upcoming webinar, and the third about the topic of the next newsletter issue.

The Security Trends Announcements file is located on the Data Files. Please contact your instructor for information about accessing the Data Files. The following steps insert a file in a column of the newsletter.

1 With the insertion point at the top of the third column, display the Insert tab.

2 Click the Object arrow (Insert tab | Text group) to display the Object menu and then click 'Text from File' on the Object menu to display the Insert File dialog box.

3 Navigate to the location of the file to be inserted (in this case, the Data Files folder).

4 Click Security Trends Announcements to select the file.

5 Click the Insert button (Insert File dialog box) to insert the file, Security Trends Announcements, in the document at the location of the insertion point.

What if text from the announcements column spills onto the second page of the newsletter?

You will format text in the announcements column so that all of its text fits in the third column of the first page.

6 Press SHIFT+F5 to return the insertion point to the last editing location, in this case, the top of the third column on the first page of the newsletter (Figure 7–47).

7 Save the newsletter again on the same storage location with the same file name.

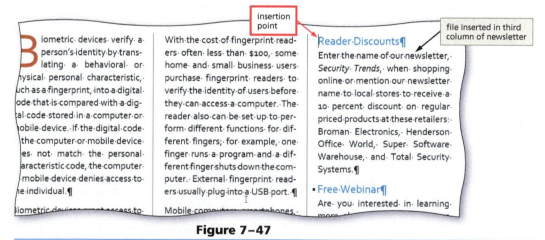

Figure 7–47

Creating a Pull-Quote

A pull-quote is text pulled, or copied, from the text of the document and given graphical emphasis so that it stands apart and commands the reader's attention. The newsletter in this project copies text from the first page of the newsletter and places it in a pull-quote, also on the first page between the first and second columns (shown in Figure 7–1a at the beginning of this module).

What guidelines should you follow when using pull-quotes?

Because of their bold emphasis, pull-quotes should be used sparingly in a newsletter. Pull-quotes are useful for breaking the monotony of long columns of text. Typically, quotation marks are used only if you are quoting someone directly. If you use quotation marks, use curly (or smart) quotation marks instead of straight quotation marks.

To create the pull-quote in this newsletter, follow this general procedure:

1. Create a **text box**, which is a container for text that allows you to position the text anywhere on the page.

2. Copy the text from the existing document to the Office Clipboard and then paste the text from the Office Clipboard to the text box.

3. Resize and format the text box.

4. Move the text box to the desired location.

1 CREATE NAMEPLATE FOR FIRST PAGE | 2 FORMAT FIRST PAGE | 3 CREATE PULL-QUOTE
4 CREATE NAMEPLATE FOR SECOND PAGE | 5 FORMAT SECOND PAGE | 6 ADD PAGE BORDER

To Insert a Text Box

The first step in creating the pull-quote is to insert a text box. A text box is like a frame; the difference is that a text box has more graphical formatting options than does a frame. The following steps insert a built-in text box. **Why?** *Word provides a variety of built-in text boxes, saving you the time of formatting the text box.*

- Click the 'Choose a Text Box' button (Insert tab | Text group) to display the Choose a Text Box gallery.

Experiment

- Scroll through the Choose a Text Box gallery to see the variety of available text box styles.

- Scroll to display Simple Quote in the Choose a Text Box gallery (Figure 7–48).

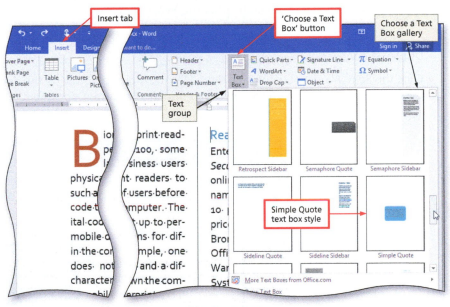

Figure 7–48

- Click Simple Quote in the Choose a Text Box gallery to insert that style of text box in the document.

- If necessary, drag the text box to the approximate location shown in Figure 7–49.

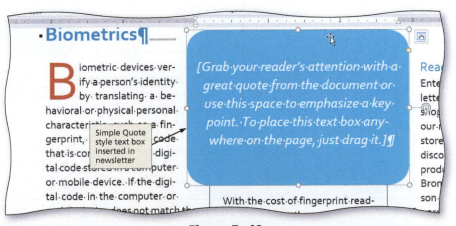

Figure 7–49

Q&A

Does my text box need to be in the exact same location as in Figure 7–49?
No. You will move the text box later.

The layout of the first page is not correct because of the text box. What do I do?
You will enter text in the text box and then position it in the correct location. At that time, the layout of the first page will be fixed.

Other Ways

1. Click 'Explore Quick Parts' button (Insert tab | Text group), click 'Building Blocks Organizer' on Explore Quick Parts menu, select desired text box name in Building blocks list, click Insert button

---

1 CREATE NAMEPLATE FOR FIRST PAGE | 2 FORMAT FIRST PAGE | 3 CREATE PULL-QUOTE
4 CREATE NAMEPLATE FOR SECOND PAGE | 5 FORMAT SECOND PAGE | 6 ADD PAGE BORDER

To Split the Window

The text that you will copy for the pull-quote is in the middle of the first page on the newsletter and the pull-quote (text box) is near the top of the first page of the newsletter. Thus, the next step is to copy the pull-quote text from the middle of the first page and then paste it in the pull-quote at the top of the first page. You would like to view the pull-quote and the text to be copied on the screen at the same time. *Why? Viewing both simultaneously will simplify the copying and pasting process.*

Word allows you to split the window in two separate panes, each containing the current document and having its own scroll bar. This enables you to scroll to and view two different portions of the same document at the same time. The following step splits the Word window.

- Display the View tab.

- Click the Split Window button (View tab | Window group) to divide the document window in two separate panes — both the upper and lower panes display the current document (Figure 7–50).

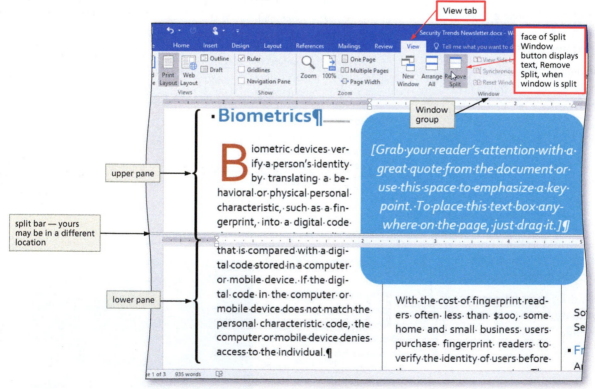

Figure 7–50

Other Ways

1. Press ALT+CTRL+S

TO ARRANGE ALL OPEN WORD DOCUMENTS ON THE SCREEN

If you have multiple Word documents open and want to view all of them at the same time on the screen, you can instruct Word to arrange all the open documents on the screen from top to bottom. If you wanted to arrange all open Word documents on the same screen, you would perform the following steps.

1. Click the Arrange All button (View tab | Window group) to display each open Word document on the screen.
2. To make one of the arranged documents fill the entire screen again, maximize the window by clicking its Maximize button or double-clicking its title bar.

To Copy and Paste Using Split Windows

1 CREATE NAMEPLATE FOR FIRST PAGE | 2 FORMAT FIRST PAGE | **3 CREATE PULL-QUOTE**
4 CREATE NAMEPLATE FOR SECOND PAGE | 5 FORMAT SECOND PAGE | 6 ADD PAGE BORDER

The following steps copy text from the middle of the first page of the newsletter to the Clipboard (the source) and then paste the text into the text box (the destination) at the top of the newsletter. *Why? The item being copied is called the **source**. The location to which you are pasting is called the **destination**.*

- In the upper pane, scroll so that all placeholder text in the text box is visible, as shown in Figure 7–51.

- In the lower pane, scroll to display the text to be copied, as shown in Figure 7–51, and then select the text to be copied: Biometric devices grant access to programs, mobile devices, computers, or rooms using computer analysis of some personal characteristic.

- Display the Home tab.

- Click the Copy button (Home tab | Clipboard group) to copy the selected text to the Clipboard (Figure 7–51).

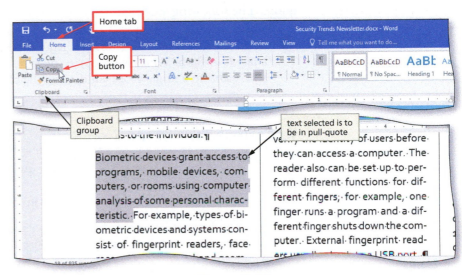

Figure 7–51

- In the upper pane, if necessary, scroll to display the text in the text box. Click the text in the text box to select it.

- Click the Paste arrow (Home tab | Clipboard group) to display the Paste menu.

Q&A What if I click the Paste button by mistake?
Click the Paste Options button to the right of the pasted text in the text box to display the Paste Options menu.

- Point to the Merge Formatting button on the Paste menu and notice the text box shows a live preview of the selected paste option (Figure 7–52).

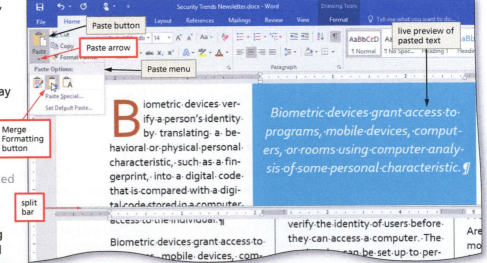

Figure 7–52

Q&A Why select the Merge Formatting button on the Paste menu?

You want the pasted text to use the formats that were in the text box (the destination) instead of the formats of the copied text (the source).

- Click the Merge Formatting button on the Paste menu to paste the copied text into the text box.

Q&A Why does a hyphen appear in the source?

Word may have hyphenated the word automatically. You will format the pull-quote text next.

Other Ways

1. Click copy on shortcut menu (or, if using touch, tap Copy on mini toolbar), right-click where item is to be pasted, click 'Keep Source Formatting' in Paste Options area on shortcut menu (or, if using touch, tap Paste on mini toolbar)

2. Select text to copy, press CTRL+C; select destination for pasted text, press CTRL+V

To Remove a Split Window

The next step is to remove the split window so that you can position the pull-quote. The following step removes a split window.

1. Double-click the split bar (shown in Figure 7–52), or click the Split Window button again (View tab | Window group), or press ALT+SHIFT+C, to remove the split window and return to a single Word window on the screen.

To Format Text in the Text Box

The next steps format text in the pull-quote.

1. If necessary, scroll to display the text box in the document window.

2. Select all the text in the text box, change its font to Century Schoolbook (or a similar font), bold the text, and change its font size to 11 point. If necessary, center this paragraph.

3. Click in the text box to deselect the text, but leave the text box selected (shown in Figure 7–53).

BTW

Rotating Text Box Text

To rotate text in a text box, select the text box, click the Text Direction button (Drawing Tools Format tab | Text group), and then click the desired direction on the Text Direction menu.

To Resize a Text Box

The next step in formatting the pull-quote is to resize the text box. You resize a text box the same way as any other object. That is, you drag its sizing handles or enter values in the height and width boxes through the Size button (Drawing Tools Format tab | Size group). The following steps resize the text box and insert line break characters.

1. Drag the sizing handles so that the pull-quote looks about the same size as Figure 7–53.

2. Verify the pull-quote dimensions in the Shape Height and Shape Width boxes (Drawing Tools Format tab | Size group) and, if necessary, change the value in the Shape Height box to 1.75 and the Shape Width box to 2.08.

Q&A What if some of the words in the text box are hyphenated?

Insert line break characters to eliminate any hyphenated words in the text box; that is, position the insertion point to the left of the first letter in the hyphenated word and then press SHIFT+ENTER to insert a line break character, which places the entire word on the next line and removes the hyphen.

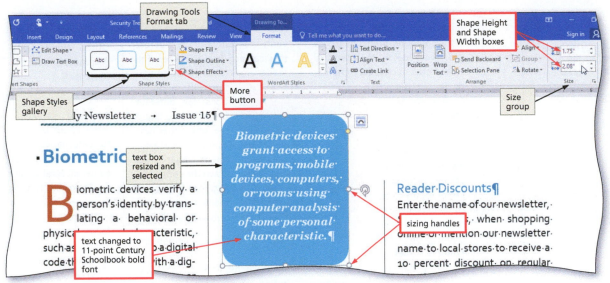

Figure 7–53

To Apply a Shape Style to a Text Box

The next step in formatting the pull-quote is to apply a shape style to the text box to coordinate its colors with the rest of the newsletter. The following steps apply a shape style to a text box.

1 With the text box still selected, click the More button (shown in Figure 7–53) in the Shape Styles gallery (Drawing Tools Format tab | Shape Styles group) to expand the gallery.

2 Point to 'Colored Fill - Orange, Accent 4' (fifth style, second row) in the Shape Styles gallery to display a live preview of that style applied to the text box (Figure 7–54).

3 Click 'Colored Fill - Orange, Accent 4' in the Shape Styles gallery to apply the selected style to the shape.

Figure 7–54

To Position a Text Box

The following steps move the text box to the desired location in the newsletter.

1 With the text box still selected, drag the text box to its new location (Figure 7–55). You may need to drag and/or resize the text box a couple of times so that it looks similar to this figure.

BTW

Moving Text Boxes
To move a text box using the keyboard, select the text box and then press the arrow keys on the keyboard. For example, each time you press the down arrow key, the selected text box moves down one line.

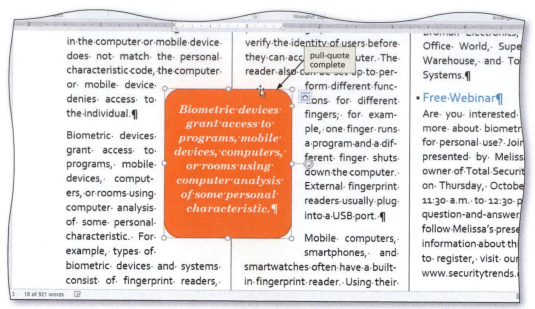

Figure 7–55

2 Click outside the text box to remove the selection.

Q&A Why does my text wrap differently around the text box?
Differences in wordwrap often relate to the printer used by your computer. Thus, your document may wordwrap around the text box differently.

3 If the jump-to line, which is supposed to appear at the bottom of the second column (shown in Figure 7–56), moved to the top of the third column, position the insertion point in the article title (Biometrics) and decrease the spacing before and after (Layout tab) until the jump-to line moves back to the bottom of the second column.

4 Save the newsletter again on the same storage location with the same file name.

Break Point: If you wish to take a break, this is a good place to do so. You can exit Word now. To resume at a later time, run Word, open the file called Security Trends Newsletter, and continue following the steps from this location forward.

Formatting the Second Page of the Newsletter

The second page of the newsletter (shown in Figure 7–1b at the beginning of this module) continues the feature article that began in the first two columns on the first page. The nameplate on the second page is less elaborate than the one on the first page of the newsletter. In addition to the text in the feature article, page two contains a graphic. The following sections format the second page of the newsletter in this project.

CONSIDER THIS

How do you create a nameplate for inner pages of a newsletter?
The top of the inner pages of a newsletter may or may not have a nameplate. If you choose to create one for your inner pages, it should not be the same as, or compete with, the one on the first page. Inner page nameplates usually contain only a portion of the nameplate from the first page of a newsletter.

To Change Column Formatting

1 CREATE NAMEPLATE FOR FIRST PAGE | 2 FORMAT FIRST PAGE | 3 CREATE PULL-QUOTE
4 CREATE NAMEPLATE FOR SECOND PAGE | 5 FORMAT SECOND PAGE | 6 ADD PAGE BORDER

The document currently is formatted in three columns. The nameplate at the top of the second page, however, should be in a single column. *Why? The nameplate should span across the top of the three columns below it.* The next step, then, is to change the number of columns at the top of the second page from three to one.

As discussed earlier in this project, Word requires a new section each time you change the number of columns in a document. Thus, you first must insert a continuous section break and then format the section to one column so that the nameplate can be entered on the second page of the newsletter. The following steps insert a continuous section break and then change the column format.

1

- If you have a blank page between the first and second pages of the newsletter, position the insertion point to the left of the paragraph mark at the end of the third column on the first page of the newsletter and then press the DELETE key as many times as necessary to delete the blank line causing the overflow.

- Position the insertion point at the upper-left corner of the second page of the newsletter (to the left of F in Face).

- Display the Layout tab.

- Click the 'Insert Page and Section Breaks' button (Layout tab | Page Setup group) to display the Insert Page and Section Breaks gallery (Figure 7–56).

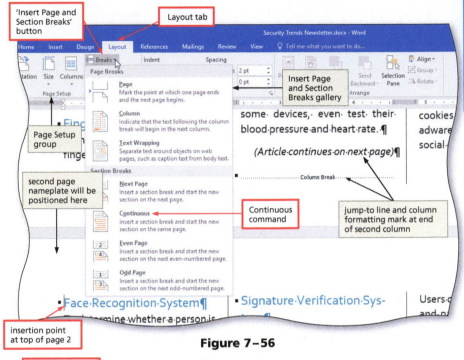

Figure 7–56

2

- Click Continuous in the Insert Page and Section Breaks gallery to insert a continuous section break above the insertion point.

- Press the UP ARROW key to position the insertion point to the left of the continuous section break just inserted.

- Click the 'Add or Remove Columns' button (Layout tab | Page Setup group) to display the Add or Remove Columns gallery (Figure 7–57).

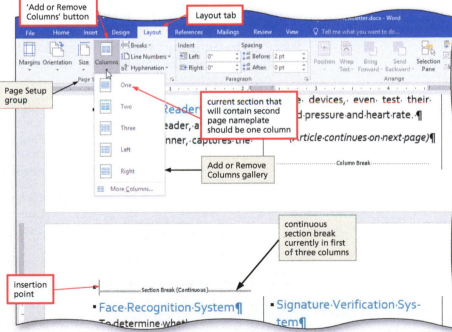

Figure 7–57

3

- Click One in the Add or Remove Columns gallery to format the current section to one column, which now is ready for the second page nameplate.

- If necessary, scroll to display the bottom of the first page and the top of the second page, so that you can see the varying columns in the newsletter (Figure 7–58).

Q&A Can I change the column format of existing text?
Yes. If you already have typed text and would like it to be formatted in a different number of columns, select the text, click the 'Add or Remove Columns' button (Layout tab | Page Setup group), and then click the number of columns desired in the Add or Remove Columns gallery. Word automatically creates a new section for the newly formatted columns.

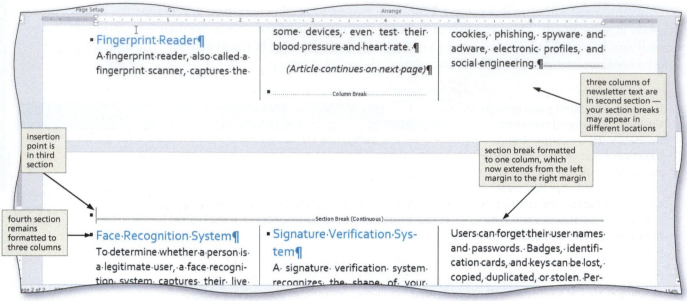

Figure 7–58

To Set Custom Tab Stops Using the Tabs Dialog Box

The nameplate on the second page of the newsletter contains the text, Monthly Newsletter, at the left margin, the newsletter title in the center, and the issue number at the right margin (shown in Figure 7–1a at the beginning of this module). To properly align the text in the center and at the right margin, you will set custom tab stops at these locations. The following steps set custom tab stops.

1 Press the ENTER key twice and then position the insertion point on the first line of the second page of the newsletter, which is the paragraph to be formatted with the custom tab stops.

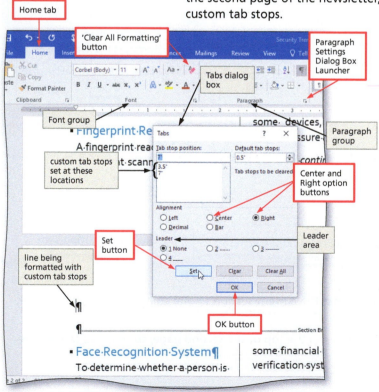

Figure 7–59

2 Display the Home tab and then click the 'Clear All Formatting' button (Home tab | Font group) to apply the Normal style to the first line on the second page of the newsletter.

3 Click the Paragraph Settings Dialog Box Launcher (Home tab | Paragraph group) to display the Paragraph dialog box and then click the Tabs button (Paragraph dialog box) to display the Tabs dialog box.

4 Type **3.5** in the Tab stop position text box (Tabs dialog box), click Center in the Alignment area to specify the tab stop alignment, and then click the Set button to set the custom tab stop.

5 Type **7** in the Tab stop position text box (Tabs dialog box), click Right in the Alignment area to specify the tab stop alignment, and then click the Set button to set the custom tab stop (Figure 7–59).

6 Click the OK button to set custom tab stops using the specified alignments.

To Format and Enter Text and Add a Border

The following steps enter the newsletter title at the top of the second page in the third section.

1 With the insertion point on the first line of the second page of the newsletter, click the Font Color arrow and then change the font color of the current text to 'Teal, Accent 5, Darker 50%' (ninth column, bottom row). Change the font to Century Schoolbook (or a similar font) and then type **Monthly Newsletter** at the left margin.

If requested by your instructor, enter your name instead of the word, Monthly.

2 Press the TAB key to advance the insertion point to the centered tab stop. Increase the font size to 14 point and then click the Bold button (Home tab | Font group) to bold the text. Type **Security Trends** at the centered tab stop.

3 Press the TAB key to advance the insertion point to the right-aligned tab stop. Reduce the font size to 11 point and then click the Bold button (Home tab | Font group) to turn off the bold format. Type **Issue 15** at the right-aligned tab stop.

4 Click the Borders button (Home tab | Paragraph group) to add a bottom border (shown in Figure 7–60).

Q&A Why is the border formatted already?
When you define a custom border, Word uses that custom border the next time you click the Borders button in the Borders gallery.

BTW

Leader Characters
Leader characters, such as a series of dots, often are used in a table of contents to precede page numbers. Four types of leader characters, which Word places in the space occupied by a tab character, are available in the Leader area of the Tabs dialog box (shown in Figure 7–59).

To Enter Text

The second page of the feature article on the second page of this newsletter begins with a jump-from line (the continued message) immediately below the nameplate. The next steps enter the jump-from line.

1 Position the insertion point on the blank line above the heading, Face Recognition System, to the left of the paragraph mark.

2 Click the 'Clear All Formatting' button (Home tab | Font group) to apply the Normal style to the location of the insertion point.

3 Press CTRL+I to turn on the italic format.

4 Type **(Continued from first page)** and then press CTRL+I to turn off the italic format (Figure 7–60).

Figure 7–60

To Balance Columns

Currently, the text on the second page of the newsletter completely fills up the first and second columns and almost fills the third column. The text in the three columns should consume the same amount of vertical space. **Why?** *Typically, the text in columns of a newsletter is balanced.* To balance columns, you insert a continuous section break at the end of the text. The following steps balance columns.

- Scroll to the bottom of the text in the third column on the second page of the newsletter and then position the insertion point at the end of the text.

- If an extra paragraph mark is below the last line of text, press the DELETE key to remove the extra paragraph mark.

- Display the Layout tab.

- Click the 'Insert Page and Section Breaks' button (Layout tab | Page Setup group) to display the Insert Page and Section Breaks gallery (Figure 7–61).

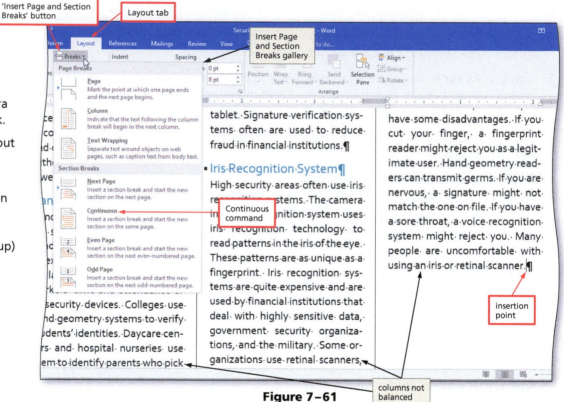

Figure 7–61

- Click Continuous in the Insert Page and Section Breaks gallery to insert a continuous section break, which balances the columns on the second page of the newsletter (Figure 7–62).

- Save the newsletter again on the same storage location with the same file name.

...because these systems be expensive, they often are used in larger companies to track workers' time and attendance or as security devices. Colleges use hand geometry systems to verify students' identities. Daycare centers and hospital nurseries use them to identify parents who pick up their children. ¶

▪ Voice Verification System¶
A voice verification system will compare a person's live speech with their stored voice pattern.

¶

▪ Iris Recognition System¶
High security areas often use iris recognition systems. The camera in an iris recognition system uses iris recognition technology to read patterns in the iris of the eye. These patterns are as unique as a fingerprint. Iris recognition systems are quite expensive and are used by financial institutions that deal with highly sensitive data, government security organizations, and the military. Some organizations use retinal scanners,

are unique and cannot be forgotten or misplaced.¶

Biometric devices, however, do have some disadvantages. If you cut your finger, a fingerprint reader might reject you as a legitimate user. Hand geometry readers can transmit germs. If you are nervous, a signature might not match the one on file. If you have a sore throat, a voice recognition system might reject you. Many people are uncomfortable with using an iris or retinal scanner.

columns balanced

Figure 7–62

Modifying and Formatting a SmartArt Graphic

Recall from Module 4 that Microsoft Office includes **SmartArt graphics**, which are visual representations of ideas. Many different types of SmartArt graphics are available, allowing you to choose one that illustrates your message best.

In this newsletter, a SmartArt graphic is positioned on the second page, at the top of the second column. Because the columns are small in the newsletter, it is best to work with a SmartArt graphic in a separate document window so that you easily can see all of its components. When finished editing the graphic, you can copy and paste it in the newsletter. You will follow these steps for the SmartArt graphic in this newsletter:

1. Open the document that contains the SmartArt graphic for the newsletter.
2. Modify the layout of the graphic.
3. Add a shape and text to the graphic.
4. Format a shape and the graphic.
5. Copy and paste the graphic in the newsletter.
6. Resize the graphic and position it in the desired location.

To Open a Document from Word

The first draft of the SmartArt graphic is in a file called Biometrics Diagram on the Data Files. Please contact your instructor for information about accessing the Data Files. The following steps open the Biometrics Diagram file.

1 Navigate to the location of the Data Files on your hard drive, OneDrive, or other storage location.

2 Open the file named Biometrics Diagram on the Data Files.

3 Click the graphic to select it and display the SmartArt Tools Design and Format tabs (Figure 7–63).

Q&A Is the *Security Trends* Newsletter file still open?
Yes. Leave it open because you will copy the modified diagram to the second page of the newsletter.

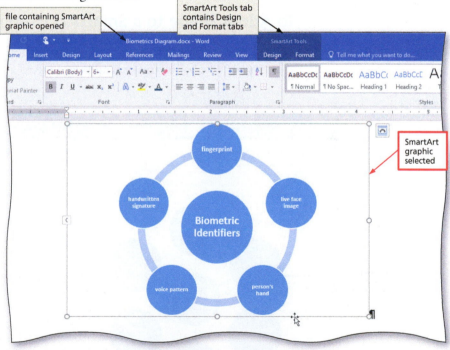

Figure 7–63

1 CREATE NAMEPLATE FOR FIRST PAGE | 2 FORMAT FIRST PAGE | 3 CREATE PULL-QUOTE
4 CREATE NAMEPLATE FOR SECOND PAGE | 5 FORMAT SECOND PAGE | 6 ADD PAGE BORDER

To Change the Layout of a SmartArt Graphic

The following step changes the layout of an existing SmartArt graphic. *Why? The SmartArt graphic currently uses the Radial Cycle layout, and this newsletter uses the Basic Radial layout.*

1

• If necessary, display the SmartArt Tools Design tab.

• Scroll through the layouts in the Layouts gallery until Basic Radial appears, if necessary, and then click Basic Radial to change the layout of the SmartArt graphic (Figure 7–64).

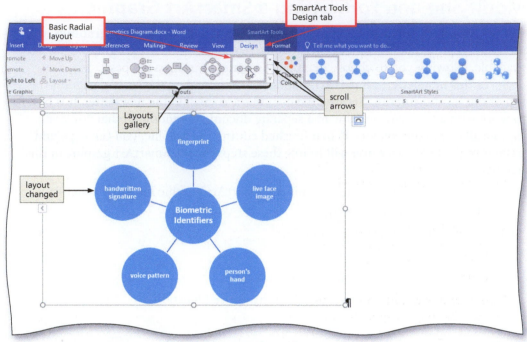

Figure 7–64

Other Ways

1. Right-click the selected graphic, click Layout button on mini toolbar and select desired layout, or click Change Layout on shortcut menu, select desired layout, click OK button

To Add a Shape to a SmartArt Graphic

The current SmartArt graphic has five perimeter shapes. This newsletter has a sixth shape. The following step adds a shape to a SmartArt graphic.

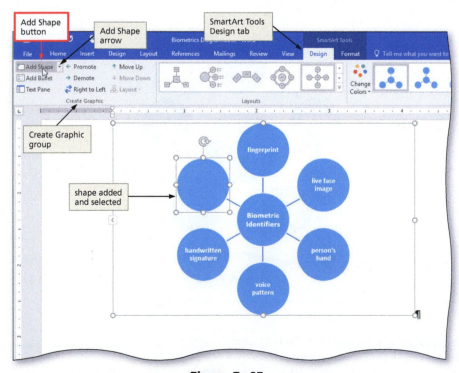

Figure 7–65

1 With the diagram selected, click the Add Shape button (SmartArt Tools Design tab | Create Graphic group) to add a shape to the SmartArt graphic (Figure 7–65).

Q&A Why did my screen display a menu instead of adding a shape?
You clicked the Add Shape arrow instead of the Add Shape button. Clicking the Add Shape button adds the shape automatically; clicking the Add Shape arrow displays a menu allowing you to specify the location of the shape.

How do I delete a shape?
Select the shape by clicking it and then press the DELETE key, or right-click the shape and then click Cut on the mini toolbar or shortcut menu.

To Add Text to a SmartArt Graphic through the Text Pane

1 CREATE NAMEPLATE FOR FIRST PAGE | 2 FORMAT FIRST PAGE | 3 CREATE PULL-QUOTE
4 CREATE NAMEPLATE FOR SECOND PAGE | 5 FORMAT SECOND PAGE | 6 ADD PAGE BORDER

In Module 4, you added text directly to the shapes in a SmartArt graphic. In this project, you enter the text through the Text Pane. *Why? Some users prefer to enter text in the Text Pane instead of in the shape.* The following steps use the Text Pane to add text to a shape.

- Click the Text Pane control, which is on the left side of the SmartArt graphic, to display the Text Pane to the left of the SmartArt graphic.

- In the Text Pane, if necessary, position the insertion point to the right of the bullet that has no text to its right.

- Type **iris or retina** as the text for the shape (Figure 7–66).

3

- Click the Close button in the Text Pane to close the Text Pane.

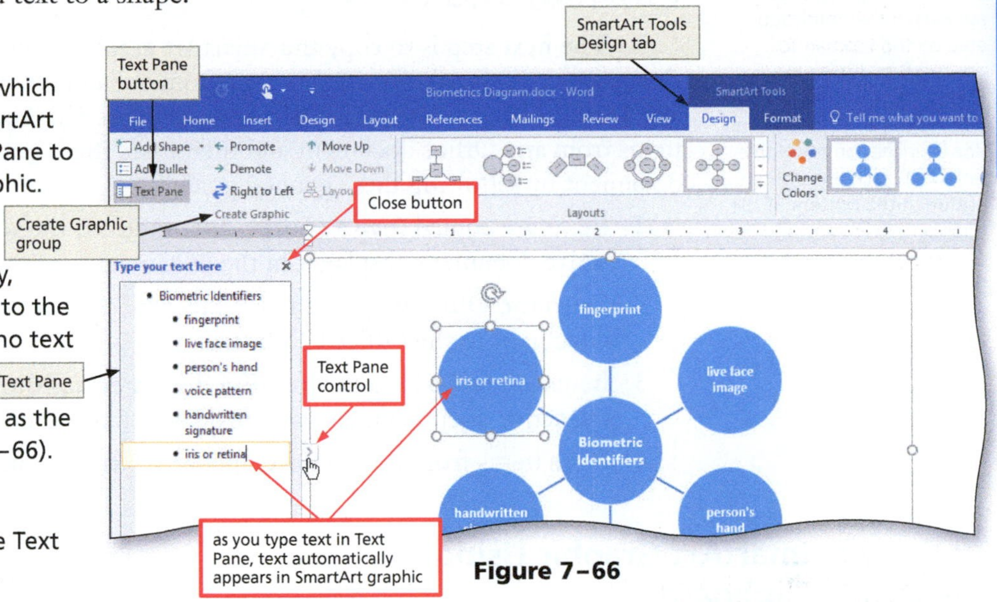

Figure 7–66

Q&A Can I instead close the Text Pane by clicking the Text Pane button (SmartArt Tools Design tab | Create Graphic group)? Yes.

- Save the file containing the SmartArt graphic with a new file name on your hard drive, OneDrive, or other storage location using Biometrics Diagram Modified as the file name.

> **Other Ways**
> 1. Click Text Pane button (SmartArt Tools Design tab | Create Graphic group)

To Format SmartArt Graphic Text

To format text in an entire SmartArt graphic, select the graphic and then apply the format. The following steps bold the text in the SmartArt graphic.

1 If necessary, click the shape just added to select it.

2 Display the Home tab. Click the Bold button (Home tab | Font group) to bold the text in the SmartArt graphic (shown in Figure 7–67).

TO MODIFY THEME EFFECTS

If you wanted to change the look of graphics, such as SmartArt graphics, you would perform the following steps to change the theme effects.

1. Click the Theme Effects button (Design tab | Document Formatting group).
2. Click the desired effect in the Theme Effects gallery.

TO SAVE CUSTOMIZED THEMES

When you modify the theme effects, theme colors, or theme fonts, you can save the modified theme for future use. If you wanted to save a customized theme, you would perform the following steps.

1. Click the Themes button (Design tab | Document Formatting group) to display the Themes gallery.

BTW

Demoting Text Pane Text

Instead of pressing the TAB key in the Text Pane, you could click the Demote Selection button (SmartArt Tools Design tab | Create Graphic group) to increase (or move to the right) the indent for a bulleted item. You also can click the Promote Selection button (SmartArt Tools Design tab | Create Graphic group) to decrease (or move to the left) the indent for a bulleted item.

BTW
Clipboard Task Pane and Icon
You can control when the Clipboard task pane appears on the Word screen and the Office Clipboard icon appears in the notification area on the taskbar. To do this, first display the Clipboard task pane by clicking the Clipboard Dialog Box Launcher on the Home tab. Next, click the Options button at the bottom of the Clipboard task pane and then click the desired option on the menu. For example, if you want to be able to open the Clipboard task pane by clicking the Office Clipboard icon on the Windows taskbar, click 'Show Office Clipboard Icon on Taskbar' on the Options menu.

2. Click 'Save Current Theme' in the Themes gallery.

3. Enter a theme name in the File name box (Save Current Theme dialog box).

4. Click the Save button to add the saved theme to the Themes gallery.

Copying and Pasting

The next step is to copy the SmartArt graphic from this document window and then paste it in the newsletter. To copy from one document and paste into another, you can use the Office Clipboard. Through the Office Clipboard, you can copy multiple items from any Office document and then paste them into the same or another Office document by following these general guidelines:

1. Items are copied *from* a **source document**. If the source document is not the active document, display it in the document window.

2. Open the Office Clipboard task pane and then copy items from the source document to the Office Clipboard.

3. Items are copied *to* a **destination document**. If the destination document is not the active document, display the destination document in the document window.

4. Paste items from the Office Clipboard to the destination document.

To Copy a SmartArt Graphic Using the Office Clipboard

1 CREATE NAMEPLATE FOR FIRST PAGE | 2 FORMAT FIRST PAGE | 3 CREATE PULL-QUOTE
4 CREATE NAMEPLATE FOR SECOND PAGE | 5 FORMAT SECOND PAGE | 6 ADD PAGE BORDER

The following step copies the SmartArt graphic to the Office Clipboard. **Why?** *Sometimes you want to copy multiple items to the Office Clipboard through the Clipboard task pane and then paste them later.*

- Click the Clipboard Dialog Box Launcher (Home tab | Clipboard group) to open the Clipboard task pane.

- If the Office Clipboard in the Clipboard task pane is not empty, click the Clear All button in the Clipboard task pane.

- With the SmartArt graphic selected in the document window, click the Copy button (Home tab | Clipboard group) to copy the selected text to the Clipboard (Figure 7–67).

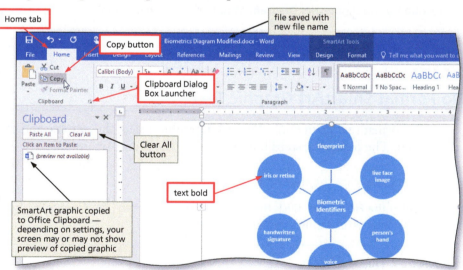

Figure 7–67

Other Ways

1. With Clipboard task pane open, right-click selected item, click Copy on mini toolbar or shortcut menu

2. With Clipboard task pane open and item to copy selected, press CTRL+C

To Switch from One Open Document to Another

1 CREATE NAMEPLATE FOR FIRST PAGE | 2 FORMAT FIRST PAGE | 3 CREATE PULL-QUOTE
4 CREATE NAMEPLATE FOR SECOND PAGE | 5 FORMAT SECOND PAGE | 6 ADD PAGE BORDER

The following steps switch from the open Biometrics Diagram Modified document (the source document) to the open Security Trends Newsletter document (the destination document). **Why?** *You want to paste the copied diagram into the newsletter document.*

1

- Point to the Word app button on the taskbar to display a live preview of the open documents or window titles of the open documents, depending on your computer's configuration (Figure 7–68).

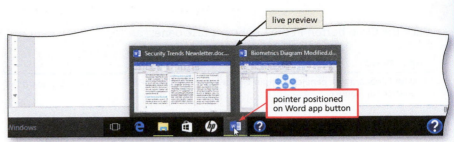

Figure 7–68

2

- Click the live preview of the Security Trends Newsletter on the Windows taskbar to display the selected document in the document window (shown in Figure 7–69).

Other Ways

1. Click Switch Windows button (View tab | Window group), click document name

2. Press ALT+TAB

---

1 CREATE NAMEPLATE FOR FIRST PAGE | 2 FORMAT FIRST PAGE | 3 CREATE PULL-QUOTE
4 CREATE NAMEPLATE FOR SECOND PAGE | 5 FORMAT SECOND PAGE | 6 ADD PAGE BORDER

To Paste from the Office Clipboard

The following steps paste from the Office Clipboard. *Why? You want to paste the copied SmartArt graphic into the destination document, in this case, the newsletter document.*

1

- Position the insertion point at the end of the first paragraph at the top of the second column on the second page of the newsletter.

- If the Clipboard task pane is not open on the screen, display the Home tab and then click the Clipboard Dialog Box Launcher (Home tab | Clipboard group) to open the Clipboard task pane.

- Click the SmartArt graphic entry in the Office Clipboard to paste it in the document at the location of the insertion point (Figure 7–69).

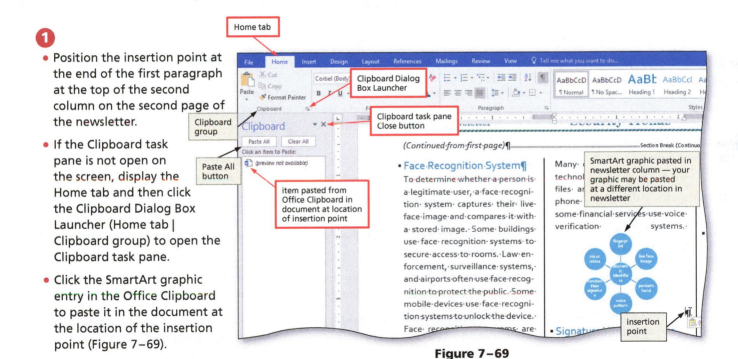

Figure 7–69

Q&A What if my pasted graphic is in a different location?
The location of your graphic may differ. You will move the graphic in the next steps.

Does the destination document have to be a different document?
No. The source and destination documents can be the same document.

What is the function of the Paste All button?
If you have multiple items on the Office Clipboard, it pastes all items in a row, without any characters between them, at the location of the insertion point or selection.

● Click the Close button in the Clipboard task pane.

Other Ways
1. With Clipboard task pane open, right-click selected item, click Paste on shortcut menu   2. With Clipboard task pane open, press CTRL+V

To Format a Graphic as Floating

The text in the newsletter should wrap tightly around the graphic; that is, the text should conform to the graphic's shape. Thus, the next step is to change the graphic from inline to floating with a wrapping style of tight. The following steps format the graphic as floating with tight wrapping.

1 Click the SmartArt graphic to select it.

2 With the SmartArt graphic selected, click the Layout Options button that is attached to the graphic to display the Layout Options gallery.

3 Click Tight in the Layout Options gallery to change the graphic from inline to floating with tight wrapping.

4 Close the Layout Options gallery.

To Format and Position the SmartArt Graphic

The next tasks are to change the color of the graphic, increase its size, and then position it at the top of the second column on the second page. The following steps format and then position the graphic.

1 With the graphic selected, click the Change Colors button (SmartArt Design tab | SmartArt Styles group) and then click 'Colored Fill - Accent 4'.

2 Drag the sizing handles outward until the graphic is approximately the same size as shown in Figure 7–70, which has a height of 3.32" and a width of 4.25". (Verify the dimensions of the graphic in the Height and Width boxes (SmartArt Tools Format tab | Size group)).

3 Drag the edge of the graphic to the location shown in Figure 7–70. You may have to drag the graphic a couple of times to position it similarly to the figure.

4 If the newsletter spills onto a third page, reduce the size of the SmartArt graphic. You may need to delete an extra paragraph mark at the end of the document, as well.

TO LAYER THE SMARTART GRAPHIC IN FRONT OF TEXT

In Word, you can layer objects on top of or behind other objects. If you wanted to layer the SmartArt graphic on top of all text, you would perform the following steps.

1. Click the SmartArt graphic to select it. Click the Bring Forward arrow (SmartArt Tools Format tab | Arrange group) to display the Bring Forward menu.

2. Click 'Bring in Front of Text' on the Bring Forward menu to position the selected object on top of all text.

BTW

Space around Graphics
The space between a graphic and the text, which sometimes is called the run-around, should be at least 1/8" and should be the same for all graphics in a document. Adjust the run-around of a selected floating graphic by doing the following: click the Wrap Text button (SmartArt Tools Format tab | Arrange group), click 'More Layout Options' on the Wrap Text menu, click the Position tab (Layout dialog box), adjust the values in the Horizontal and Vertical boxes, and then click the OK button.

1 CREATE NAMEPLATE FOR FIRST PAGE | 2 FORMAT FIRST PAGE | 3 CREATE PULL-QUOTE
4 CREATE NAMEPLATE FOR SECOND PAGE | 5 FORMAT SECOND PAGE | 6 ADD PAGE BORDER

To Edit Wrap Points in an Object

In Word, you can change how text wraps around an object, called editing wrap points. The following steps edit the wrap points in the SmartArt diagram at the top of the second page of the newsletter. *Why? You want to ensure that text starts on a complete line below the bottom of the graphic.*

1

- If necessary, click the SmartArt graphic to select it. Click the Wrap Text button (SmartArt Tools Format tab | Arrange group) to display the Wrap Text menu (Figure 7–70).

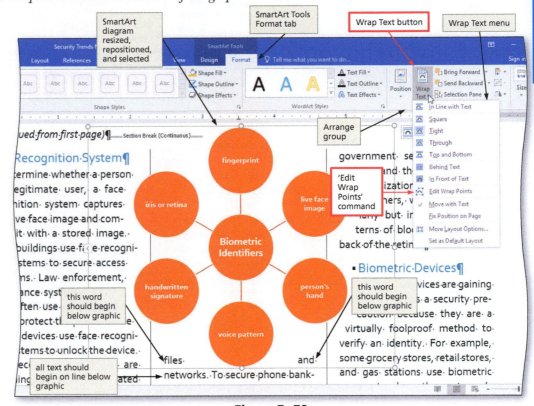

Figure 7–70

2

- Click 'Edit Wrap Points' on the Wrap Text menu to display wrap points around the graphic.

- Position the pointer on the black wrap point to the lower-left of the shape in the diagram containing the text, voice pattern, as shown in Figure 7–71, so that the pointer changes to a four-headed dot.

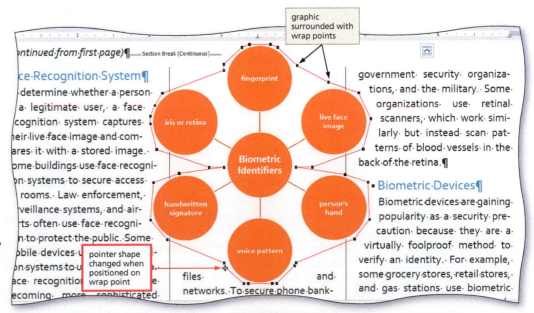

Figure 7–71

3

- Drag the black wrap point to the lower-left of the graphic as shown in Figure 7–72, so that the text (the word, files, in this case) will appear on a complete line below the shape.

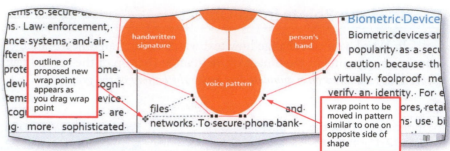
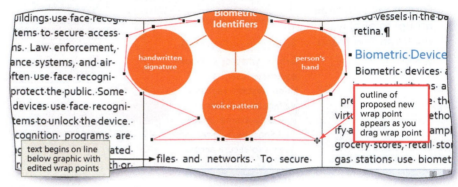

Figure 7–72

4

- Drag the black wrap point to the lower-right of the graphic as shown in Figure 7–73, so that the text begins on a complete line below the graphic.

- Click outside the graphic so that it no longer is selected.

Figure 7–73

Finishing the Newsletter

With the text and graphics in the newsletter entered and formatted, the next step is to view the newsletter as a whole and determine if it looks finished in its current state. To give the newsletter a finished appearance, you will add a border to its edges.

BTW

Distributing a Document

Instead of printing and distributing a hard copy of a document, you can distribute the document electronically. Options include sending the document via email; posting it on cloud storage (such as OneDrive) and sharing the file with others; posting it on social media, a blog, or other website; and sharing a link associated with an online location of the document. You also can create and share a PDF or XPS image of the document, so that users can view the file in Adobe Reader or XPS Viewer instead of in Word.

To Adjust Headings, Turn Off Formatting Marks, and Zoom Multiple Pages

The last step in formatting the newsletter is to place a border around its edges. First, you remove a hyphen from a heading by adding a line break. Then, you turn off formatting marks to remove the clutter from the screen, and you place both pages in the document window at once so that you can see all the page borders applied. The following steps add a line break, turn off formatting marks, and zoom multiple pages.

1 If necessary, scroll below the SmartArt graphic to display the Signature Verification System heading. To remove the hyphen in the word, System, place the insertion point to the left of the S and then press SHIFT+ENTER to create a line break and move the entire word, System, to the next line (shown in Figure 7–74).

2 If necessary, display the Home tab and then turn off formatting marks.

3 Display the View tab and then display multiple pages on the screen. You may need to increase the zoom slightly so that the borders in the nameplates appear.

To Add an Art Page Border

The following steps add a page border around the pages of the newsletter. *Why? This newsletter has a teal art border around the perimeter of each page.*

1

- Display the Design tab.

- Click the 'Borders and Shading' button (Design tab | Page Background group) to display the Borders and Shading dialog box. If necessary, click the Page Border tab.

Q&A What if I cannot select the 'Borders and Shading' button because it is dimmed?
Click somewhere in the newsletter to make the newsletter the active document and then repeat Step 1.

2

- Click Box in the Setting area (Borders and Shading dialog box) to specify a border on all four sides of the page.

- Click the Art arrow, scroll to and then click the art border shown in Figure 7–74.

- Click the Color arrow and then click 'Teal, Accent 5, Darker 50%' (bottom row, ninth column) on the palette (Figure 7–74).

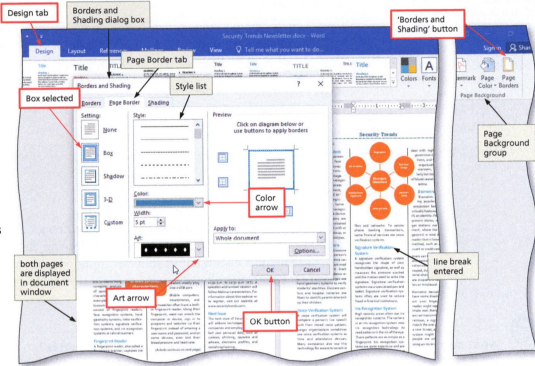

Figure 7–74

3

- Click the OK button to place the defined border on each page of the newsletter (Figure 7–75).

Figure 7–75

BTW
Conserving Ink and Toner
If you want to conserve ink or toner, you can instruct Word to print draft quality documents by clicking File on the ribbon to open the Backstage view, clicking the Options tab in the Backstage view to display the Word Options dialog box, clicking Advanced in the left pane (Word Options dialog box), scrolling to the Print area in the right pane, placing a check mark in the 'Use draft quality' check box, and then clicking the OK button. Then, use the Backstage view to print the document as usual.

To Save, Print, and Exit Word

The newsletter now is complete. You should save the document, print it, and then exit Word.

1 Save the newsletter again on the same storage location with the same file name.

2 If desired, print the newsletter (shown in Figure 7–1 at the beginning of this module).

Q&A What if an error message appears about margins?
Depending on the printer you are using, you may need to set the margins differently for this project.

What if one or more of the borders do not print?
Click the 'Borders and Shading' button (Design tab | Page Background group), click the Options button (Borders and Shading dialog box), click the Measure from arrow and click Text, change the four text boxes to 15 pt, and then click the OK button in each dialog box. Try printing the document again. If the borders still do not print, adjust the text boxes in the dialog box to a number smaller than 15 pt.

3 Exit Word, closing all open documents.

Summary

In this module, you have learned how to create a professional-looking newsletter using Word's desktop publishing features such as the following: inserting and modifying WordArt, organizing a document in columns, adding horizontal and vertical rules, inserting and formatting pull-quotes, inserting and formatting graphics, and adding an art page border.

CONSIDER THIS: PLAN AHEAD

What decisions will you need to make when creating your next newsletter?
Use these guidelines as you complete the assignments in this module and create your own newsletters outside of this class.

1. Create the nameplate.

   a) Determine the location of the nameplate.

   b) Determine content, formats, and arrangement of text and graphics.

   c) If appropriate, use ruling lines.

2. Determine content for the body of the newsletter.

   a) Write the body copy.

   b) Organize the body copy in columns.

   c) Format the body copy and subheads.

   d) Incorporate color.

   e) Divide sections with vertical rules.

   f) Enhance with visuals.

3. Bind and distribute the newsletter.

   a) Determine if newsletters should be printed, posted on bulletin boards, sent as an email message, or posted on websites.

   b) For multipage newsletters that will be printed, determine the appropriate method of binding the pages.

   c) For online newsletters, select a format that most users will be able to open.

Apply Your Knowledge

Reinforce the skills and apply the concepts you learned in this module.

Working with Desktop Publishing Elements of a Newsletter

Note: To complete this assignment, you will be required to use the Data Files. Please contact your instructor for information about accessing the Data Files.

Instructions: Run Word. Open the document named Apply 7–1 Energy Saver Newsletter Draft from the Data Files. The document contains a newsletter that you are to modify so that it appears as shown in Figure 7–76.

Perform the following tasks:

1. Change the WordArt shape to Chevron Down.

2. Turn on automatic hyphenation.

3. Change the column width of the columns in the body of the newsletter to 1.9".

4. Add a vertical rule (line) between each column.

5. Change the style of the pull-quote (text box) to 'Light 1 Outline, Colored Fill - Dark Green, Accent 3' (Drawing Tools Format tab | Shape Styles group).

6. Format the first paragraph with a drop cap.

7. Change the alignment of the paragraph containing the drop cap from left-aligned to justified.

8. Change the layout of the SmartArt graphic to Converging Radial.

9. Use the Text Pane to add the text, Building Automation, to the empty shape in the SmartArt graphic. Verify that the font size of text in the top and bottom shapes is 14 point and 11 point, respectively.

10. If necessary, move the SmartArt graphic and the pull-quote so that they are positioned similarly to the ones in Figure 7–76.

11. Change the color of the page border to Orange, Accent 5, Lighter 40%.

12. If requested by your instructor, add your name to the left of the text, Weekly Newsletter, in the issue information line.

13. If the newsletter flows to two pages, reduce the size of elements such as WordArt or pull-quote, or adjust spacing above or below paragraphs so that the newsletter fits on a single page. Make any other necessary adjustments to the newsletter.

14. Save the modified file with the file name, Apply 7–1 Energy Saver Newsletter Modified.

15. Submit the revised newsletter in the format specified by your instructor.

16. ✴ When you use hyphenation to divide words at the end of a line, what are the accepted guidelines for dividing the words? *Hint:* Use a search engine to search the text, end of line hyphenation.

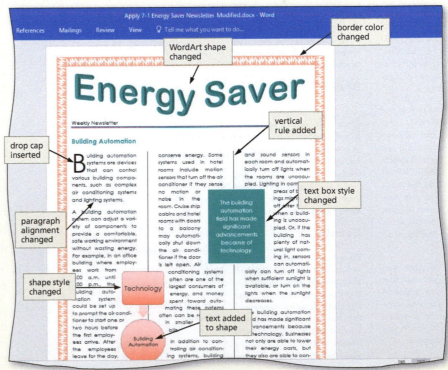

Figure 7–76

Extend Your Knowledge

Extend the skills you learned in this module and experiment with new skills. You may need to use Help to complete the assignment.

Adding Equations to a Newsletter and Enhancing a Nameplate

Note: To complete this assignment, you will be required to use the Data Files. Please contact your instructor for information about accessing the Data Files.

Instructions: Run Word. Open the document, Extend 7–1 Frosh Tips Newsletter Draft, from the Data Files. You will add equations to the newsletter, change the format of the WordArt, format the drop cap, adjust the hyphenation rules, move the page border closer to the text, clear tabs, and insert leader characters.

Perform the following tasks:

1. Use Help to learn about equations, WordArt options, borders, hyphenation, and tabs.

2. Insert the equations shown in Figure 7–77 in the newsletter in their appropriate locations. *Hint:* Use the 'Insert an Equation' arrow or 'Insert an Equation' button (Insert tab | Symbols group).

3. Change the WordArt by adding at least two WordArt style text effects. Change the color of the WordArt text outline. Change the color of the WordArt text fill color.

4. Add a shape fill color to the text box surrounding the WordArt.

5. Add a drop cap to the first paragraph in the body of the newsletter. Change the number of lines to drop from three to four lines. Change the distance from the text to 0.1".

6. Change the hyphenation rules to limit consecutive hyphens to two.

7. Change the page border so that the border is closer to the text.

8. If the newsletter flows to two pages, reduce the size of elements, such as WordArt or the pull-quote or the table, or adjust spacing above or below paragraphs so that the newsletter fits on a single page. Make any other necessary adjustments to the newsletter.

9. Clear the tabs in the issue information line in the nameplate. Use the Tabs dialog box to insert a right-aligned tab stop at the 7" mark. Fill the tab space with a leader character of your choice.

10. If requested by your instructor, change the word, Freshman, in the issue information line to your last name.

11. Submit the revised newsletter in the format specified by your instructor.

12. ✸ Which equations are predefined in Word? Which structures are available on the Equation Tools Design tab? How do you change the alignment of an equation?

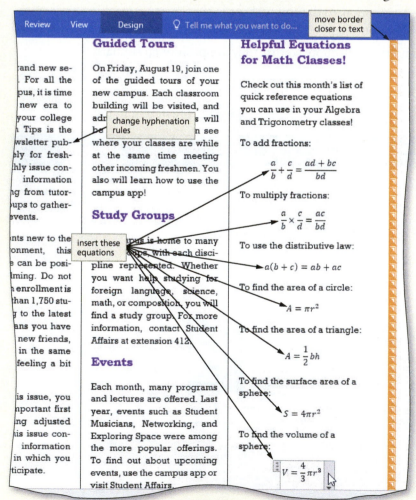

Figure 7–77

Expand Your World

Create a solution that uses cloud or web technologies by learning and investigating on your own from general guidance.

Using Windows Essentials

Instructions: You have heard that Windows Essentials includes some useful programs, so you decide to learn about it, download it, and use its programs.

Note: You may be required to use your Microsoft account to complete this assignment. If you do not have a Microsoft account and do not want to create one, read the assignment without performing the instructions.

Perform the following tasks:

1. Run a browser. Search for the text, Windows Essentials, using a search engine. Click a link to learn about Windows Essentials.

2. Navigate to the website to download Windows Essentials (Figure 7–78) and then follow the instructions to download Windows Essentials.

3. One at a time, run each program included with Windows Essentials. Browse through the features and functions of each program.

4. ❈ What programs are included with Windows Essentials? What is the purpose of each program? Which programs will you use and why?

Figure 7–78

In the Labs

Design, create, modify, and/or use a document following the guidelines, concepts, and skills presented in this module. Labs 1 and 2, which increase in difficulty, require you to create solutions based on what you learned in the module; Lab 3 requires you to apply your creative thinking and problem-solving skills to design and implement a solution.

Lab 1: Creating a Newsletter with a Pull-Quote (Text Box) and an Article on File

Note: To complete this assignment, you will be required to use the Data Files. Please contact your instructor for information about accessing the Data Files.

Problem: You are an editor of the newsletter, *Vintage Living*. The next edition is due out in one week (Figure 7–79). The text for the articles in the newsletter is in a file on the Data Files. You need to create the nameplate and the text box for the pull-quote.

Perform the following tasks:

1. Change all margins to .75 inches. Depending on your printer, you may need different margin settings. Change the theme to Retrospect.

2. Create the nameplate using the formats identified in Figure 7–79. Create the title using WordArt. Set the WordArt wrapping to 'Top and Bottom'. If necessary, drag the bottom of the WordArt up to shorten the image. Dimensions of WordArt should be approximately 1.41" x 7.06". Set a right-aligned custom tab stop at the right margin.

Continued >

In the Labs continued

3. Below the nameplate, enter the heading, Purchasing an Old House: Part 1, as shown in the figure. Format the heading using the Heading 1 style. Change the spacing above this paragraph to 24 pt and the spacing after to 12 pt.

4. Create a continuous section break below the heading, Purchasing an Old House: Part 1.

5. Format section 2 to three columns.

6. Insert the Lab 7–1 Purchasing an Old House - Part 1 Article file, which is located on the Data Files, in section 2 below the nameplate.

7. Format the newsletter according to Figure 7–79. Insert a column break before the heading, Brick and Stone. Columns should have a width of 2.1" with spacing of 0.35". Place a vertical rule between the columns.

8. If necessary, insert a continuous section break at the end of the document to balance the columns.

9. Format the subheads using the Heading 2 style.

10. Insert a text box using the Retrospect Quote built-in text box. The text for the pull-quote is in the Paint section of the article. Split the window. Use the split window to copy the text and then paste it in the text box. Remove the split window. Change the fill color (shape fill) of the text box to Brown, Accent 4. Change the font to 12-point Bookman Old Style. Resize the text box so that it is similar in size to Figure 7–79. Position the text box as shown in Figure 7–79.

11. Add the page border as shown in the figure.

12. If the document does not fit on a single page, adjust spacing above and below paragraphs.

13. If requested by your instructor, change the word, Weekly, in the issue information line to your name.

14. Save the document with Lab 7–1 Vintage Living Newsletter as the file name and then submit it in the format specified by your instructor.

15. ✹ This newsletter used a pull-quote. What other text in the newsletter could appear in the pull-quote?

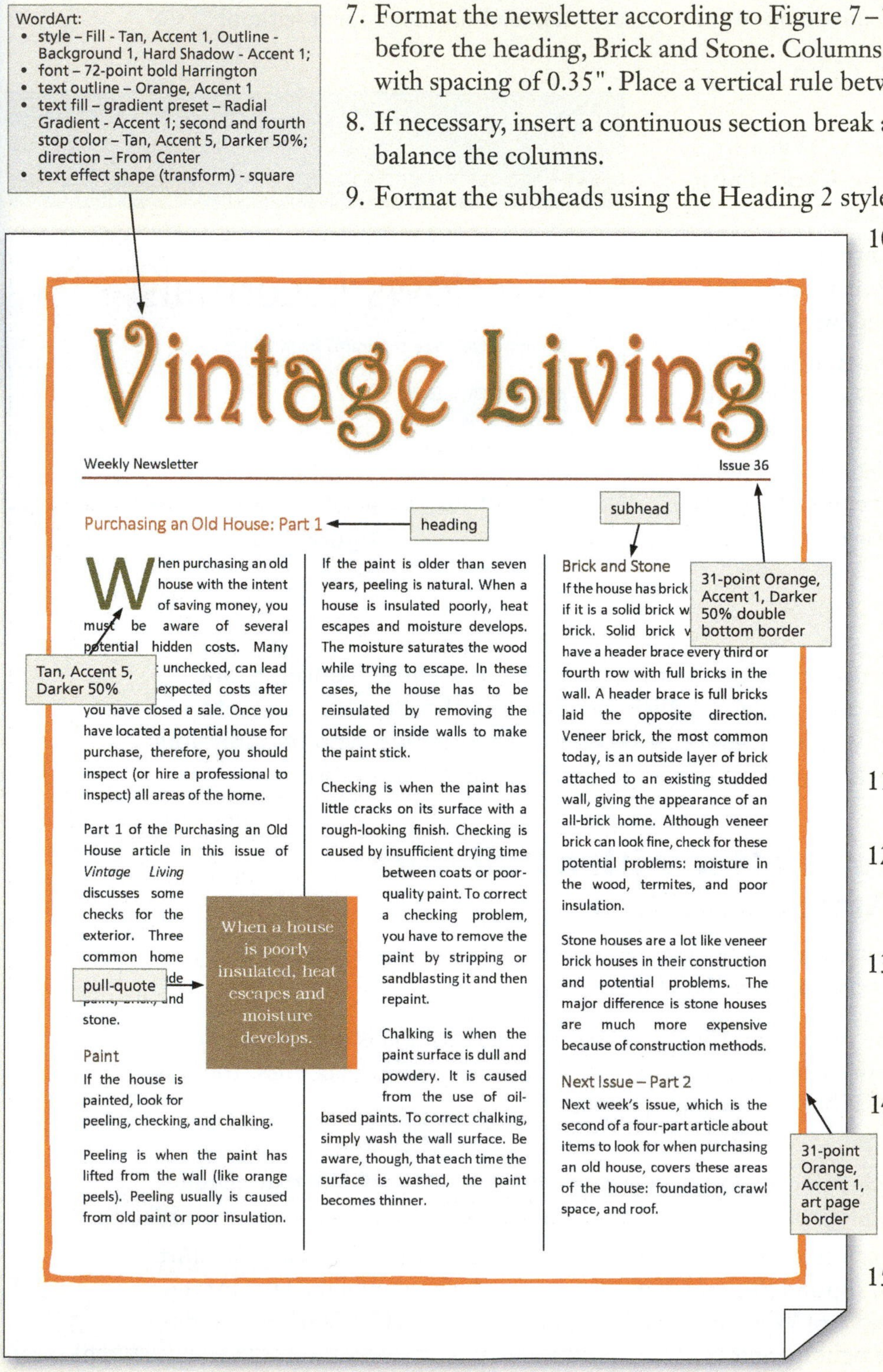

Figure 7–79

Lab 2: **Creating a Newsletter with a SmartArt Graphic and an Article on File**

Note: To complete this assignment, you will be required to use the Data Files. Please contact your instructor for information about accessing the Data Files.

Problem: You are responsible for the monthly preparation of the newsletter called *Health Check*. The next edition discusses technology-related repetitive strain injuries (Figure 7–80). This article already has been prepared and is on the Data Files. You need to create the nameplate, the SmartArt graphic, and the section at the bottom of the newsletter.

Perform the following tasks:

1. Change all margins to .75 inches. Depending on your printer, you may need different margin settings. Change the document theme to Droplet.

2. Create the nameplate using the formats identified in Figure 7–80. Create the title using WordArt. Set a right-aligned custom tab stop at the right margin. Set the WordArt wrapping to Top and Bottom. If necessary, drag the bottom of the Word Art up to shorten the image. Search for and insert an image of a check mark, similar to the one shown in the figure (the exact image is located on the Data Files). Resize and rotate the image as shown in the figure. Format the image as Behind Text and position the image as shown.

3. Below the nameplate, enter the heading, Technology-Related Repetitive Strain Injuries, as shown in the figure.

4. Create a continuous section break below the heading.

5. Format section 2 to two columns.

6. Insert the Lab 7–2 Health Risks for Technology Users Article file, which is located on the Data Files, in section 2 below the nameplate.

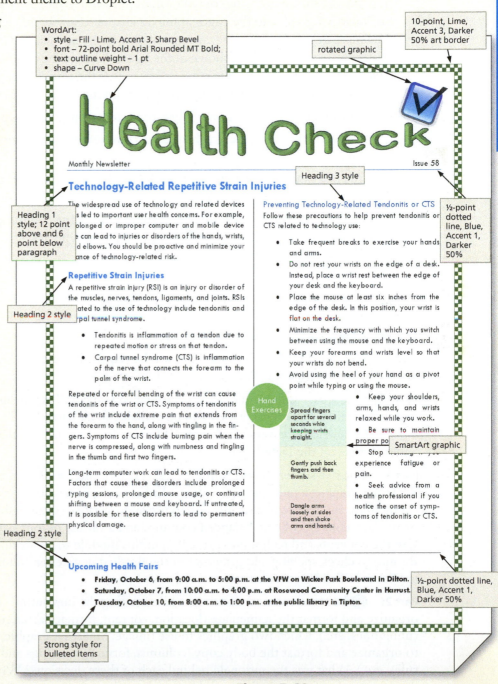

Figure 7–80

Continued >

In the Labs *continued*

7. Format the newsletter according to Figure 7–80. Columns should have a width of 3.33" with spacing of 0.35". Place a vertical rule between the columns.

8. Use Word's automatic hyphenation feature to hyphenate the document.

9. Insert a continuous section break at the end of the last bulleted item in the second column to balance the columns.

10. In the next section, change the number of columns from two to one. Enter the text shown at the bottom of the newsletter.

11. Add the page border as shown in the figure.

12. Open a new document window and create the SmartArt graphic shown in Figure 7–80. Use the Stacked List layout. Because this newsletter has only one list, delete the shapes for the second list. Add the text shown in the figure (you will need to add shapes to this list). Resize the border of the SmartArt graphic to the edges of the list shapes. Use the Office Clipboard to copy and paste the SmartArt graphic from the current window to the newsletter. Change the wrapping to tight. Resize the pasted graphic as shown in the figure. Change the colors to Colorful Range - Accent Colors 3 to 4. Edit wrap points as necessary so that the text wrapping is similar to the figure. Note that your graphic may look slightly different from the figure due to variations in the shape size.

13. If the document does not fit on a single page, adjust spacing above and below paragraphs.

14. If requested by your instructor, change the community center name from Rosewood to your last name.

15. Save the newsletter using Lab 7–2 Health Check Newsletter as the file name and submit it in the format specified by your instructor.

16. ✸ How many sections are in this newsletter? How many columns are in each section? If you wanted to add a second page to this newsletter, what type of section break would appear at the end of the first page?

Lab 3: **Consider This: Your Turn**

Create a Newsletter about ATM Safety

Note: To complete this assignment, you will be required to use the Data Files. Please contact your instructor for information about accessing the Data Files.

Problem: As a part-time employee at a local bank, you have been assigned the task of creating a newsletter called *Bank News*, which will be available to all patrons. The article in Issue 28 of the *Bank News* newsletter covers ATM safety. The text for the article is in a file called Lab 7–3 ATM Safety Article on the Data Files.

Part 1: The newsletter should contain at least two of these graphical elements: an image, a SmartArt graphic, a pull-quote, or a table. Enhance the newsletter with a drop cap, WordArt, color, ruling lines, and a page border. Be sure to use appropriate desktop publishing elements, including a nameplate, columns of text, balanced columns, and a variety of font sizes, font colors, and shading. Use the concepts and techniques presented in this module to create and format the newsletter. Be sure to check spelling and grammar of the finished newsletter. Submit your assignment in the format specified by your instructor.

Part 2: ✸ You made several decisions while creating the newsletter in this assignment: how to organize and format the nameplate (location, content, formats, arrangement of text and graphics, ruling lines, etc.), which two graphics to use (image, SmartArt graphic, text box, or table), and how to organize and format the body copy (columns, formats, headings and subheads, color, vertical rules, etc.). What was the rationale behind each of these decisions? When you proofread the document, what further revisions did you make and why?

8 Using Document Collaboration, Integration, and Charting Tools

Objectives

You will have mastered the material in this module when you can:

- Insert, edit, view, and delete comments
- Track changes
- Review tracked changes
- Compare documents
- Combine documents
- Link an Excel worksheet to a Word document
- Break a link

- Create a chart in Word
- Format a Word chart
- View and scroll through side-by-side documents
- Create a new document for a blog post
- Insert a quick table
- Publish a blog post

Introduction

Word provides the capability for users to work with other users, or **collaborate**, on a document. For example, you can show edits made to a document so that others can review the edits. You also can merge edits from multiple users or compare two documents to determine the differences between them.

From Word, you can interact with other programs and incorporate the data and objects from those programs in a Word document. For example, you can link an Excel worksheet in a Word document or publish a blog post from Word. You also can use the charting features of Microsoft Office 2016 in Word.

Project — Memo with Chart

A memo is an informal document that businesses use to correspond with others. Memos often are internal to an organization, for example, to employees or coworkers.

The project in this module uses Word to produce the memo shown in Figure 8–1. First, you open an existing document that contains the memo and the Word table. Next, you insert comments and edit the document, showing the changes so that other users can review the changes. The changes appear on the screen with options that allow the author of the document to accept or reject the changes and delete the comments. Then, you chart the Word table using charting features available in several Microsoft Office applications. In this module, you also learn how to link an Excel worksheet to a Word document and create a document for a blog post.

INTEROFFICE MEMORANDUM

TO:	ALL EMPLOEES
FROM:	TIMO PEREZ
SUBJECT:	QUARTERLY REVENUE COMPARISON
DATE:	OCTOBER 20, 2017

Revenue figures for the third quarter have been compiled. I would like to thank everyone for helping our fitness center realize an increase in revenue during the third quarter. Below are a table and chart that show a revenue comparison for the last two quarters. In the next few days, you will see a post on our blog, indicating upcoming dates associated with our appreciation events.

Second and Third Quarter Revenue Comparison

Word table

Revenue Category	Third Quarter	Second Quarter
Athletic Instruction	$4,689.25	$4,140.25
Guest Admission Fees	$987.32	$897.65
Membership Fees	$31,975.99	$28,676.47
Merchandise Sales	$9,547.22	$8,569.14
Personal Training Services	$9,876.32	$8,762.77
Snack Bar	$6,842.75	$6,157.50
Supplement Sales	$3,021.22	$2,729.42

chart created from Word table

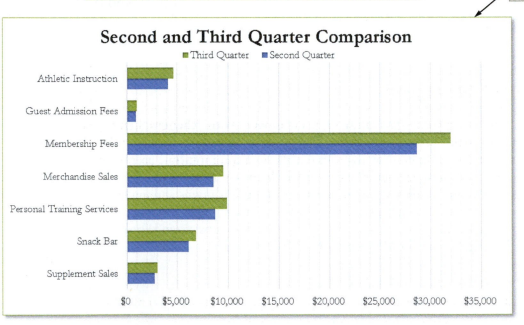

Second and Third Quarter Comparison
■ Third Quarter ■ Second Quarter

Figure 8–1

In this module, you will learn how to create the document shown in Figure 8–1. The following roadmap identifies general activities you will perform as you progress through this module:

1. **INSERT COMMENTS AND TRACK CHANGES** in the memo with the table.

2. **REVIEW** the **COMMENTS AND TRACKED CHANGES**.

3. **LINK** an **EXCEL WORKSHEET TO** a **WORD DOCUMENT**.

4. **CHART** a **WORD TABLE** using Word's Chart Tools tab.

5. **CREATE AND PUBLISH** a **BLOG POST**.

To Run Word and Change Word Settings

If you are using a computer to step through the project in this module and you want your screens to match the figures in this book, you should change your screen's resolution to 1366 × 768. The following steps run Word, display formatting marks, and change the zoom to page width.

1 Run Word and create a blank document in the Word window. If necessary, maximize the Word window.

2 If the Print Layout button on the status bar is not selected, click it so that your screen is in Print Layout view.

3 If the 'Show/Hide ¶' button (Home tab | Paragraph group) is not selected already, click it to display formatting marks on the screen.

4 To display the page the same width as the document window, if necessary, click the Page Width button (View tab | Zoom group).

Reviewing a Document

Word provides many tools that allow users to collaborate on a document. One set of collaboration tools within Word allows you to track changes in a document and review the changes. That is, one computer user can create a document and another user(s) can make changes and insert comments in the same document. Those changes then appear on the screen with options that allow the originator (author) to accept or reject the changes and delete the comments. With another collaboration tool, you can compare and/or merge two or more documents to determine the differences between them.

To illustrate Word collaboration tools, this section follows these general steps:

1. Open a document to be reviewed.

2. Insert comments in the document for the originator (author).

3. Track changes in the document.

4. View and delete the comments.

5. Accept and reject the tracked changes. For illustration purposes, you assume the role of originator (author) of the document in this step.

6. Compare the reviewed document to the original to view the differences.

7. Combine the original document with the reviewed document and with another reviewer's suggestions.

To Open a Document and Save It with a New File Name

Assume your coworker has created a draft of a memo and is sending it to you for review. The file, called Fitness Center Revenue Comparison Memo Draft, is located on the Data Files. Please contact your instructor for information about accessing the Data Files. To preserve the original memo, you save the open document with a new file name. The following steps save an open document with a new file name.

 1 Navigate to the location of the Data Files on your hard drive, OneDrive, or other storage location.

2 Open the file Fitness Center Revenue Comparison Memo Draft.

If requested by your instructor, change the name Timo Perez at the top of the memo to your name.

3 Navigate to the desired save location on your hard drive, OneDrive, or other storage location.

4 Save the file just opened on your hard drive, OneDrive, or other storage location using Fitness Center Revenue Comparison Memo with Comments and Tracked Changes as the file name.

To Insert a Comment

1 INSERT COMMENTS & TRACK CHANGES | **2 REVIEW COMMENTS & TRACKED CHANGES**
3 LINK EXCEL WORKSHEET TO WORD DOCUMENT | **4 CHART WORD TABLE** | **5 CREATE & PUBLISH BLOG POST**

Reviewers often use comments to communicate suggestions, tips, and other messages to the author of a document. A **comment** is a note inserted in a document. Comments do not affect the text of the document.

After reading through the memo, you have two comments for the originator (author) of the document. The following steps insert a comment in the document. **Why?** *You insert a comment that requests that the author insert a graph in the document.*

1

• Position the insertion point at the location where the comment should be located (in this case, in the third sentence of the memo immediately to the left of the t in the word, table).

• Display the Review tab.

• If the 'Display for Review' box (Review tab | Tracking group) does not show All Markup, click the 'Display for Review' arrow (Review tab | Tracking group) and then click All Markup on the Display for Review menu to instruct Word to display the document with all proposed edits shown as markup (Figure 8–2).

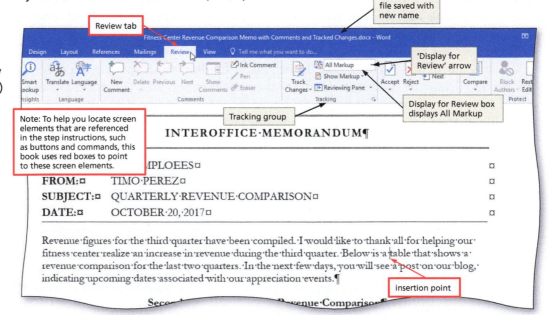

Figure 8–2

What are the other Display for Review options?

If you click the 'Display for Review' arrow, several options appear. Simple Markup means Word incorporates proposed changes in the document and places a vertical line near the margin of the line containing the proposed change or a comment balloon at the location of a user comment. All Markup means that all proposed changes are highlighted and all comments appear in full. No Markup shows the proposed edits as part of the final document, instead of as markup. Original shows the document before changes.

2

- Click the 'Insert a Comment' button (Review tab | Comments group) to display a comment balloon in the markup area in the document window and place comment marks around the commented text in the document window.

- Change the zoom so that the entire document and markup area are visible in the document window (Figure 8–3).

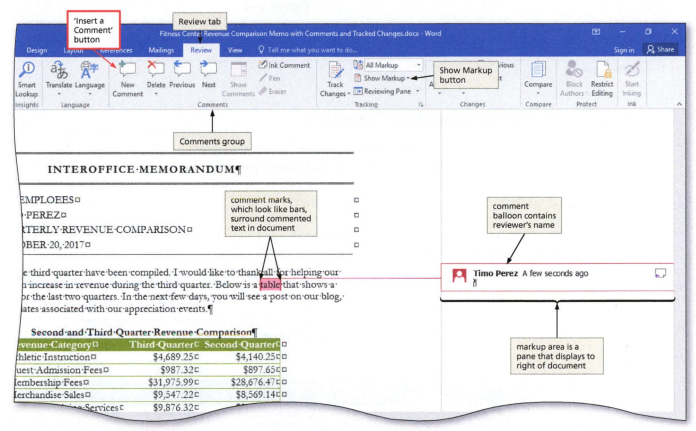

Figure 8–3

What if the markup area does not appear with the comment balloon?

The balloons setting has been turned off. Click the Show Markup button (Review tab | Tracking group) and then, if a check mark does not appear to the left of Comments on the Show Markup menu, click Comments. If comments still do not appear, click the Show Markup button again, point to Balloons on the Show Markup menu, and then click 'Show Only Comments and Formatting in Balloons' on the Balloons submenu, which is the default setting.

Why do comment marks surround selected text?

A comment is associated with text. If you do not select text on which you wish to comment, Word automatically selects the text to the right or left of the insertion point for the comment.

3

- In the comment balloon, type the following comment text: **Add a graph of the data below the table.**

- If necessary, scroll to the right so that the entire comment is visible on the screen (Figure 8–4).

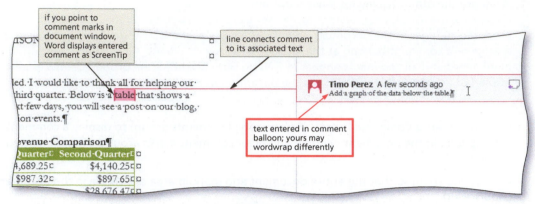

Figure 8–4

Other Ways

1. Press CTRL+ALT+M

To Insert Another Comment

BTW
Touch Screen Differences
The Office and Windows interfaces may vary if you are using a touch screen. For this reason, you might notice that the function or appearance of your touch screen differs slightly from this module's presentation.

The second comment you want to insert in the document is to request that the blog post also contain a calendar. Because you want the comment associated with several words, you select the text before inserting the comment. The following steps insert another comment in the document.

1 Select the text where the comment should be located (in this case, the text, post on our blog, in the last sentence of the memo).

2 Click the 'Insert a Comment' button (Review tab | Comments group) to display another comment balloon in the markup area in the document window.

3 In the new comment balloon, type the following comment text: **Suggest posting a calendar on the blog.** (Figure 8–5).

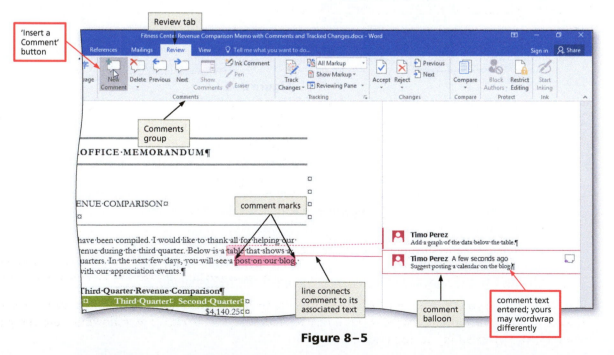

Figure 8–5

TO CHANGE REVIEWER INFORMATION

Word uses predefined settings for the reviewer's initials and/or name that appears in the document window, the comment balloon, and the Reviewing task pane. If the reviewer's name or initials are not correct, you would change them by performing the following steps.

1a. Click the Change Tracking Options Dialog Box Launcher (Review tab | Tracking group) to display the Track Changes Options dialog box. Click the 'Change User Name' button (Track Changes Options dialog box) to display the Word Options dialog box.

or

1b. Open the Backstage view and then click the Options tab to display the Word Options dialog box. If necessary, click General in the left pane.

2. Enter the correct name in the User name text box (Word Options dialog box), and enter the correct initials in the Initials text box.

3. Click the OK button to change the reviewer information. If necessary, click the OK button in the Track Changes Options dialog box.

To Edit a Comment in a Comment Balloon

You modify comments in a comment balloon by clicking inside the comment balloon and editing the same way you edit text in the document window. In this project, you change the word, graph, to the word, chart, in the first comment. The following steps edit a comment in a balloon.

1 Click the first comment balloon to select it.

Q&A How can I tell if a comment is selected?
A selected comment appears surrounded by a rectangle and contains a Reply button to the right of the comment.

2 Position the insertion point at the location of the text to edit (in this case, to the left of the g in graph in the first comment) (Figure 8–6).

3 Replace the word, graph, with the word, chart, to edit the comment (shown in Figure 8–7).

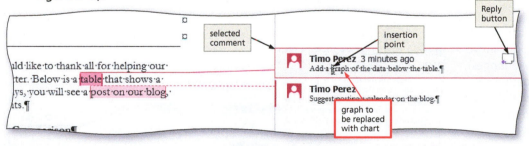

Figure 8–6

To Reply to a Comment

1 INSERT COMMENTS & TRACK CHANGES | 2 REVIEW COMMENTS & TRACKED CHANGES
3 LINK EXCEL WORKSHEET TO WORD DOCUMENT | 4 CHART WORD TABLE | 5 CREATE & PUBLISH BLOG POST

Sometimes, you want to reply to an existing comment. *Why? You may want to respond to a question by another reviewer or provide additional information to a previous comment you inserted.* The following steps reply to the first comment you inserted in the document.

● If necessary, click the comment to which you wish to reply so that the comment is selected (in this case, the first comment).

2

● Click the Reply button in the selected comment to display a reply comment for the selected comment.

3

● In the new indented comment, type the following comment text: **Suggest using horizontal bars to plot the categories.** (Figure 8–7).

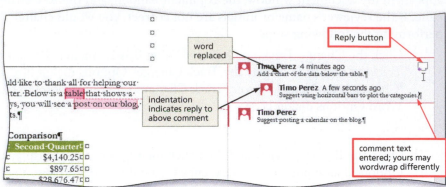

Figure 8–7

Other Ways

1. Click 'Insert a Comment' button (Review tab | Comments group)   2. Press CTRL+ALT+M

To Customize the Status Bar

1 INSERT COMMENTS & TRACK CHANGES | 2 REVIEW COMMENTS & TRACKED CHANGES
3 LINK EXCEL WORKSHEET TO WORD DOCUMENT | 4 CHART WORD TABLE | 5 CREATE & PUBLISH BLOG POST

You can customize the items that appear on the status bar. Recall that the status bar presents information about a document, the progress of current tasks, the status of certain commands and keys, and controls for viewing. Some indicators and buttons appear and disappear as you type text or perform certain commands. Others remain on the status bar at all times.

The following steps customize the status bar to show the Track Changes indicator. **Why?** *The Track Changes indicator does not appear by default on the status bar.*

● If the status bar does not show a desired item (in this case, the Track Changes indicator), right-click anywhere on the status bar to display the Customize Status Bar menu.

2

● Click the item on the Customize Status Bar menu that you want to show (in this case, Track Changes) to place a check mark beside the item, which also immediately may show as an indicator on the status bar (Figure 8–8).

Q&A

Can I show or hide any of the items listed on the Customize Status Bar menu?

Yes, click the item to display or remove its check mark.

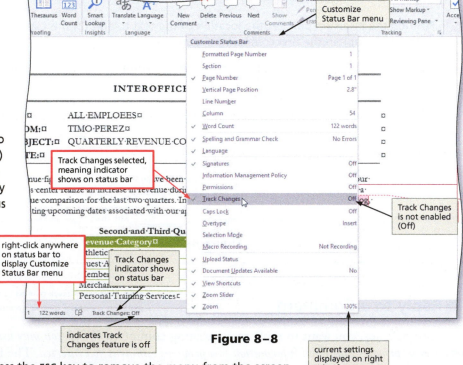

Figure 8–8

3

● Click anywhere outside of the Customize Status Bar menu or press the ESC key to remove the menu from the screen.

To Enable Tracked Changes

When you edit a document that has the track changes feature enabled, Word marks all text or graphics that you insert, delete, or modify and refers to the revisions as **markups** or **revision marks**. An author can identify the changes a reviewer has made by looking at the markups in a document. The author also has the ability to accept or reject any change that a reviewer has made to a document.

The following step enables tracked changes. *Why? To track changes in a document, you must enable (turn on) the track changes feature.*

- If the Track Changes indicator on the status bar shows that the track changes feature is off, click the Track Changes indicator on the status bar to enable the track changes feature (Figure 8–9).

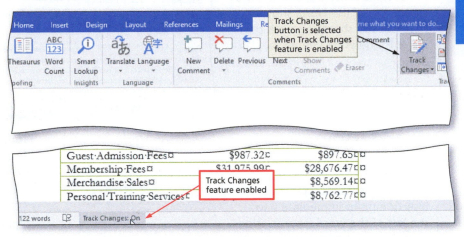

Figure 8–9

Other Ways

1. Click Track Changes button (Review tab | Tracking group)
2. Click Track Changes arrow (Review tab | Tracking group), click Track Changes
3. Press CTRL+SHIFT+E

To Track Changes

You have four suggested changes for the current document:

1. Insert the words, and chart, after the word, table, in the third sentence so that it reads: ... a table and chart that ...

2. Delete the letter, s, at the end of the word, shows.

3. Insert the word, upcoming, before the word, appreciation, in the last sentence so that it reads: ... our upcoming appreciation events.

4. Change the word, all, to the word, everyone, in the first sentence so that it reads: ... thank everyone for....

The following steps track these changes as you enter them in the document. *Why? You want edits you make to the document to show so that others can review the edits.*

- Position the insertion point immediately to the left of the word, that, in the third sentence of the memo to position the insertion point at the location for the tracked change.

- Type **and chart** and then press the SPACEBAR to insert the typed text as a tracked change (Figure 8–10).

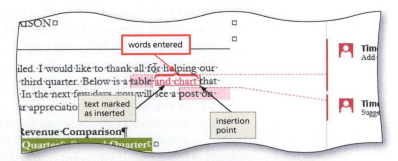

Figure 8–10

Why is the inserted text in color and underlined?

When the track changes feature is enabled, Word marks (signals) all text inserts by underlining them and changing their color, and marks all deletions by striking through them and changing their color.

When I scroll left, I see a vertical bar in the margin. What is the bar?

The bar is called a changed line (shown in Figure 8–16), which indicates a tracked change is on the line to the right of the bar.

2

• In the same sentence, delete the s at the end of the word, shows (so that it reads, show), to mark the letter for deletion (Figure 8–11).

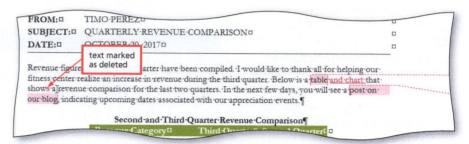

Figure 8–11

3

• In the next sentence, position the insertion point immediately to the left of the word, appreciation. Type **upcoming** and then press the SPACEBAR to insert the typed text as a tracked change.

• In the second sentence, double-click the word, all, to select it.

• Type **everyone** as the replacement text, which tracks a deletion and an insertion change (Figure 8–12).

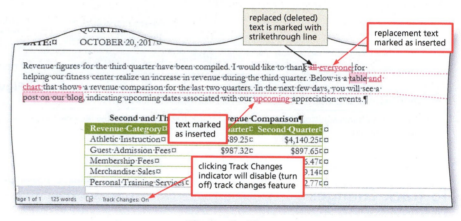

Figure 8–12

Can I see the name of the person who tracked a change?

You can point to a tracked change in the document window; Word then will display a ScreenTip that identifies the reviewer's name and the type of change made by that reviewer.

TO CHANGE HOW MARKUPS AND COMMENTS ARE DISPLAYED

The tracked changes entered in the previous steps appeared inline instead of in markup balloons. Inline means that the inserts are underlined and the deletions are shown as strikethroughs. The default Word setting displays comments and formatting changes in balloons and all other changes inline. If you wanted all changes and comments to appear in balloons or all changes and comments to appear inline, you would perform the following steps.

1. Click the Show Markup button (Review tab | Tracking group) to display the Show Markup menu and then point to Balloons on the Show Markup menu.

2. If you want all revisions and comments to appear in balloons, click 'Show Revisions in Balloons' on the Balloons submenu. If you want all revisions and comments to appear inline, click 'Show All Revisions Inline' on the Balloons submenu. If you want to use the default Word setting, click 'Show Only Comments and Formatting in Balloons' on the Balloons submenu.

To Disable Tracked Changes

When you have finished tracking changes, you should disable (turn off) the track changes feature so that Word stops marking your revisions. You follow the same steps to disable tracked changes as you did to enable them; that is, the indicator or button or keyboard shortcut functions as a toggle, turning the track changes feature on or off each time the command is issued. The following step disables tracked changes.

1 To turn the track changes feature off, click the Track Changes indicator on the status bar (shown in Figure 8–12), or click the Track Changes button (Review tab | Tracking group), or press CTRL+SHIFT+E.

To Use the Reviewing Task Pane

1 INSERT COMMENTS & TRACK CHANGES | 2 REVIEW COMMENTS & TRACKED CHANGES
3 LINK EXCEL WORKSHEET TO WORD DOCUMENT | 4 CHART WORD TABLE | 5 CREATE & PUBLISH BLOG POST

Word provides a Reviewing task pane that can be displayed either at the left edge (vertically) or the bottom (horizontally) of the screen. ***Why?*** *As an alternative to reading through tracked changes in the document window and comment balloons in the markup area, some users prefer to view tracked changes and comments in the Reviewing task pane.* The following steps display the Reviewing task pane on the screen.

1
- Click the Reviewing Pane arrow (Review tab | Tracking group) to display the Reviewing Pane menu (Figure 8–13).

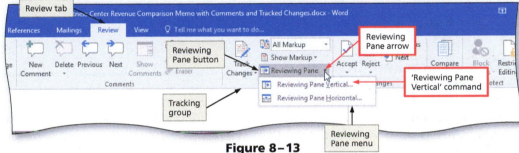

2
- Click 'Reviewing Pane Vertical' on the Reviewing Pane menu to display the Reviewing task pane on the left side of the Word window.

Figure 8–13

◄ | What if I click the Reviewing Pane button instead of the button arrow?
Q&A | Word displays the Reviewing task pane in its most recent location, that is, either vertically on the left side of the screen or horizontally on the bottom of the screen.

3
- Click the Show Markup button (Review tab | Tracking group) to display the Show Markup menu.
- Point to Balloons on the Show Markup menu to display the Balloons submenu (Figure 8–14).

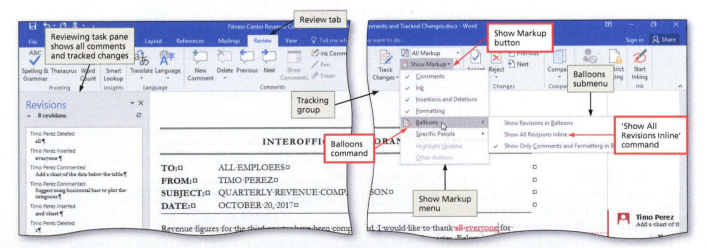

Figure 8–14

Q&A Why display the Balloons submenu?

Because the Reviewing task pane shows all comments, you do not need the markup area to display comment balloons. Thus, you will display all revisions inline.

4

• Click 'Show All Revisions Inline' on the Balloons submenu to remove the markup area from the Word window and place all markups inline (Figure 8–15).

Q&A Can I edit revisions in the Reviewing task pane?

Yes. Simply click in the Reviewing task pane and edit the text the same way you edit in the document window.

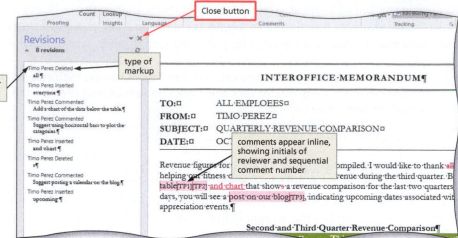

5

• Click the Close button in the Reviewing task pane to close the task pane.

Figure 8–15

Q&A Can I also click the Reviewing Pane button on the ribbon to close the task pane?

Yes.

To Display Tracked Changes and Comments as Simple Markup

1 INSERT COMMENTS & TRACK CHANGES | 2 REVIEW COMMENTS & TRACKED CHANGES
3 LINK EXCEL WORKSHEET TO WORD DOCUMENT | 4 CHART WORD TABLE | 5 CREATE & PUBLISH BLOG POST

Word provides a Simple Markup option instead of the All Markup option for viewing tracked changes and comments. *Why? Some users feel the All Markup option clutters the screen and prefer the cleaner look of the Simple Markup option.* The following step displays tracked changes using the Simple Markup option.

1

• Click the 'Display for Review' arrow (Review tab | Tracking group) to display the Display for Review menu.

• Click Simple Markup on the Display for Review menu to show a simple markup instead of all markups in the document window (Figure 8–16).

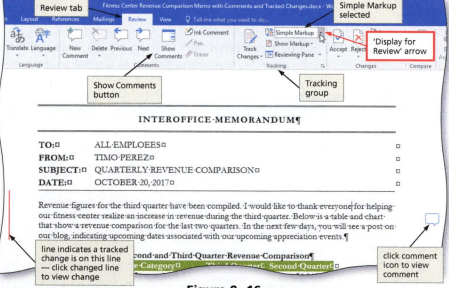

Q&A What if the comments appear in the markup area instead of as icons in the document?

Be sure the Show Comments button (Review tab | Comments group) is not selected. When the Show Comments button is selected, the comments appear in the markup area to the right of the document.

 Experiment

• Click the comment icon to display the comments. Click the comment icon again to hide the comments.

Click one of the changed lines to display the tracked changes. Click one of the changed lines to hide the tracked changes.

Figure 8–16

To Show All Markup

You prefer to show all markup where comments appear in the markup area and have tracked changes visible in the document window. The following steps show all markup and comments in balloons.

1 Click the 'Display for Review' arrow (Review tab | Tracking group) and then click All Markup on the Display for Review menu to instruct Word to display the document with all proposed edits shown as markup.

2 Click the Show Markup button (Review tab | Tracking group) to display the Show Markup menu, point to Balloons on the Show Markup menu, and then click 'Show Only Comments and Formatting in Balloons', so that the markup area reappears with the comment balloons.

3 Save the memo again on the same storage location with the same file name.

TO PRINT MARKUPS

When you print a document with comments and tracked changes, Word chooses the zoom percentage and page orientation that will best show the comments on the printed document. You can print the document with its markups, which looks similar to how the Word window shows the markups on the screen, or you can print just the list of the markups. If you wanted to print markups, you would perform the following steps.

1. Open the Backstage view and then click the Print tab in the Backstage view to display the Print gallery.
2. Click the first button in the Settings area to display a list of options specifying what you can print. To print the document with the markups, if necessary, place a check mark to the left of Print Markup. To print just the markups (without printing the document), click 'List of Markup' in the Document Info area.
3. Click the Print button.

Reviewing Tracked Changes and Comments

After tracking changes and entering comments in a document, you send the document to the originator for his or her review. For demonstration purposes in this module, you assume the role of originator and review the tracked changes and comments in the document.

To do this, be sure the markups are displayed on the screen. Click the Show Markup button (Review tab | Tracking group) and verify that the Comments, 'Insertions and Deletions', and Formatting check boxes each contain a check mark. Ensure the 'Display for Review' box (Review tab | Tracking group) shows All Markup; if it does not, click the 'Display for Review' arrow (Review tab | Tracking group) and then click All Markup on the Display for Review menu. This option shows the final document with tracked changes.

If you wanted to see how a document would look if you accepted all the changes, without actually accepting them, click the 'Display for Review' arrow (Review tab | Tracking group) and then click No Markup on the Display for Review menu. If you print this view of the document, it will print how the document will look if you accept all the changes. If you wanted to see how the document looked before any changes were made, click the 'Display for Review' arrow (Review tab | Tracking group) and then click Original on the Display for Review menu. When you have finished reviewing the various options, if necessary, click the 'Display for Review' arrow (Review tab | Tracking group) and then click All Markup on the Display for Review menu.

To View Comments

The next step is to read the comments in the marked-up document using the Review tab. *Why? You could scroll through the document and read each comment that appears in the markup area, but you might overlook one or more comments using this technique. Thus, it is more efficient to use the Review tab.* The following step views comments in the document.

- Position the insertion point at the beginning of the document, so that Word begins searching for comments from the top of the document.

- Click the Next Comment button (Review tab | Comments group), which causes Word to locate and select the first comment in the document (Figure 8–17).

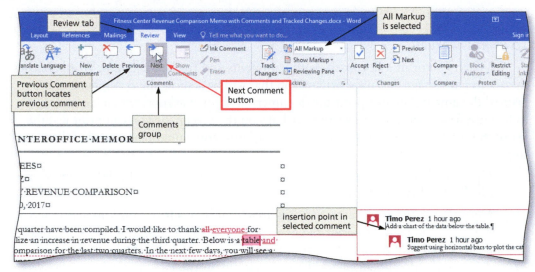

Figure 8–17

To Delete a Comment

The following step deletes a comment. *Why? You have read the comment and want to remove it from the document.*

- Click the Delete Comment button (Review tab | Comments group) to remove the comment balloon from the markup area (Figure 8–18).

Q&A | What if I accidentally click the Delete Comment arrow?
Click Delete on the Delete Comment menu.

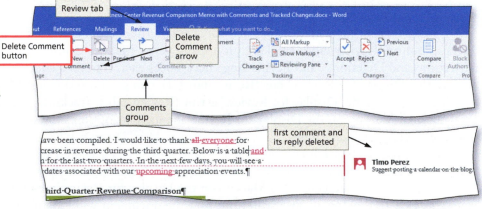

Figure 8–18

Other Ways

1. Right-click comment (or, if using touch, tap 'Show Context Menu' button on mini toolbar), click Delete Comment on shortcut menu

TO MARK COMMENTS AS DONE

Instead of deleting comments, some users prefer to leave them in the document but mark them as done. When you mark a comment as done, it changes color. If you wanted to mark a comment as done, you would perform the following steps.

1. Right-click the comment to display a shortcut menu.
2. Click 'Mark Comment Done' on the shortcut menu.

To Delete All Comments

1 INSERT COMMENTS & TRACK CHANGES | 2 REVIEW COMMENTS & TRACKED CHANGES
3 LINK EXCEL WORKSHEET TO WORD DOCUMENT | 4 CHART WORD TABLE | 5 CREATE & PUBLISH BLOG POST

The following steps delete all comments at once. *Why? Assume you now want to delete all the comments in the document at once because you have read them all.*

1

- Click the Delete Comment arrow (Review tab | Comments group) to display the Delete Comment menu (Figure 8–19).

2

- Click 'Delete All Comments in Document' on the Delete Comment menu to remove all comments from the document, which also closes the markup area (shown in Figure 8–20).

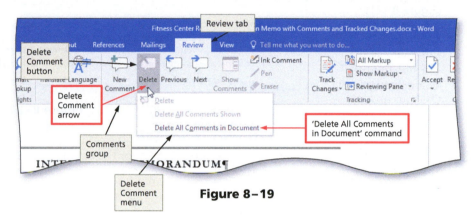

Figure 8–19

To Review Tracked Changes

1 INSERT COMMENTS & TRACK CHANGES | 2 REVIEW COMMENTS & TRACKED CHANGES
3 LINK EXCEL WORKSHEET TO WORD DOCUMENT | 4 CHART WORD TABLE | 5 CREATE & PUBLISH BLOG POST

The next step is to review the tracked changes in the marked-up document using the Review tab. *Why? As with the comments, you could scroll through the document and point to each markup to read it, but you might overlook one or more changes using this technique. A more efficient method is to use the Review tab to review the changes one at a time, deciding whether to accept, modify, or delete each change.* The following steps review the changes in the document.

1

- Position the insertion point at the beginning of the document, so that Word begins the review of tracked changes from the top of the document.

- Click the Next Change button (Review tab | Changes group), which causes Word to locate and select the first markup in the document (in this case, the deleted word, all) (Figure 8–20).

Q&A

What if my document also had contained comments?

When you click the Next Change button (Review tab | Changes group), Word locates the next tracked change or comment, whichever appears first.

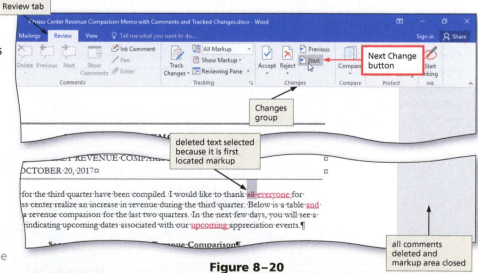

Figure 8–20

2

- Because you agree with this change, click the 'Accept and Move to Next' button (Review tab | Changes group) to accept the deletion of the word, all, and instruct Word to locate and select the next markup (in this case, the inserted word, everyone) (Figure 8–21).

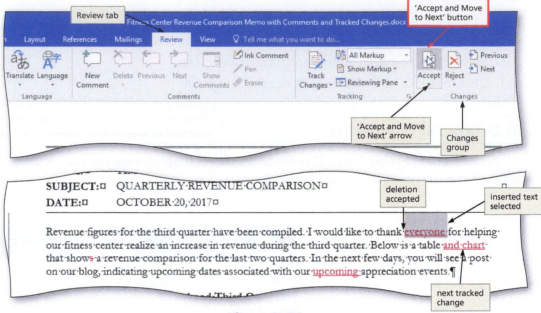

Figure 8–21

What if I accidentally click the 'Accept and Move to Next' arrow (Review tab | Changes group)? Click 'Accept and Move to Next' on the Accept and Move to Next menu.

What if I wanted to accept the change but not search for the next tracked change? You would click the 'Accept and Move to Next' arrow and then click 'Accept This Change' on the Accept and Move to Next menu.

3

- Click the 'Accept and Move to Next' button (Review tab | Changes group) to accept the insertion of the word, everyone, and instruct Word to locate and select the next markup (in this case, the inserted words, and chart).

- Click the 'Accept and Move to Next' button (Review tab | Changes group) to accept the insertion of the words, and chart, and instruct Word to locate and select the next markup (in this case, the deleted letter s).

- Click the 'Accept and Move to Next' button (Review tab | Changes group) to accept the deletion of the letter s, and instruct Word to locate and select the next markup (in this case, the inserted word, upcoming) (Figure 8–22).

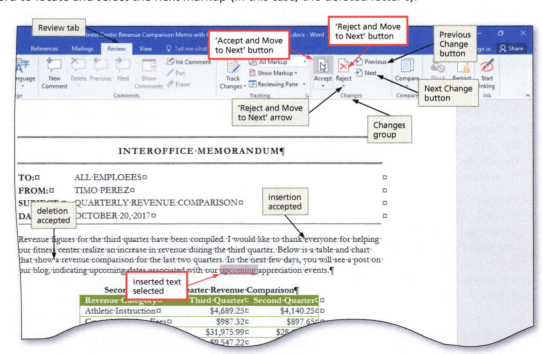

Figure 8–22

4

- Because you do not agree with this change, click the 'Reject and Move to Next' button (Review tab | Changes group) to reject the marked deletion, and instruct Word to locate and select the next markup.

Q&A

What if I accidentally click the 'Reject and Move to Next' arrow (Review tab | Changes group)?
Click 'Reject and Move to Next' on the Reject and Move to Next menu.

What if I wanted to reject the change but not search for the next tracked change?
You would click the 'Reject and Move to Next' arrow (Review tab | Changes group) and then click Reject Change on the Reject and Move to Next menu.

What if I did not want to accept or reject a change but wanted to locate the next tracked change?
You would click the Next Change button (Review tab | Changes group) to locate the next tracked change or comment. Likewise, to locate the previous tracked change or comment, you would click the Previous Change button (Review tab | Changes group).

5

- Click the OK button in the dialog box that appears, which indicates the document contains no more comments or tracked changes.

- Save the reviewed file on your hard drive, OneDrive, or other storage location using Fitness Center Revenue Comparison Memo Reviewed as the file name.

Other Ways

1. Right-click comment or tracked change (or, if using touch, tap 'Show Context Menu' button on mini toolbar), click desired command on shortcut menu

To Accept or Reject All Tracked Changes

If you wanted to accept or reject all tracked changes in a document at once, you would perform the following step.

1. To accept all tracked changes, click the 'Accept and Move to Next' arrow (Review tab | Changes group) to display the Accept and Move to Next menu and then click 'Accept All Changes' on the menu to accept all changes in the document and continue tracking changes or click 'Accept All Changes and Stop Tracking' to accept all changes in the document and stop tracking changes.

   or

1. To reject all tracked changes, click the 'Reject and Move to Next' arrow (Review tab | Changes group) to display the Reject and Move to Next menu and then click 'Reject All Changes' on the menu to reject all changes in the document and continue tracking changes or click 'Reject All Changes and Stop Tracking' to reject all changes in the document and stop tracking changes.

Changing Tracking Options

If you wanted to change the color and markings reviewers use for tracked changes and comments or change how balloons are displayed, use the Advanced Track Changes Options dialog box (Figure 8–23). To display the Advanced Track Changes Options dialog box, click the Change Tracking Options Dialog Box Launcher (Review tab | Tracking group) and then click the Advanced Options button (Track Changes Options dialog box).

BTW

Document Inspector
If you wanted to ensure that all comments were removed from a document, you could use the document inspector. Open the Backstage view, display the Info gallery, click the 'Check for Issues' button, and then click Inspect Document. Place a check mark in the 'Comments, Revisions, Versions, and Annotations' check box and then click the Inspect button (Document Inspector dialog box). If any comments are located, click the Remove All button.

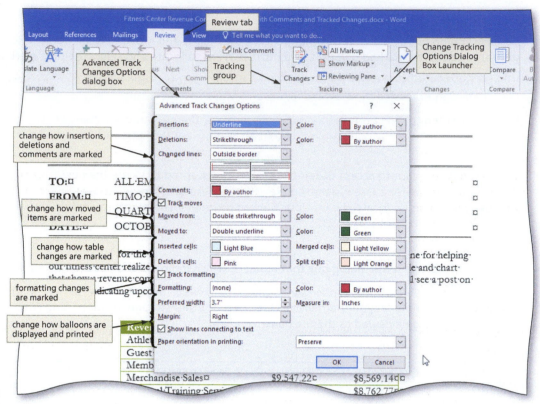

Figure 8–23

To Compare Documents

1 INSERT COMMENTS & TRACK CHANGES | 2 REVIEW COMMENTS & TRACKED CHANGES

3 LINK EXCEL WORKSHEET TO WORD DOCUMENT | 4 CHART WORD TABLE | 5 CREATE & PUBLISH BLOG POST

With Word, you can compare two documents to each other. *Why? Comparing documents allows you easily to identify any differences between two files because Word displays the differences between the documents as tracked changes for your review. By comparing files, you can verify that two separate files have the same or different content. If no tracked changes are found, then the two documents are identical.*

Assume you want to compare the original Fitness Center Revenue Comparison Memo Draft document with the Fitness Center Revenue Comparison Memo Reviewed document so that you can identify the changes made to the document. The following steps compare two documents.

1

- If necessary, display the Review tab.

- Click the Compare button (Review tab | Compare group) to display the Compare menu (Figure 8–24).

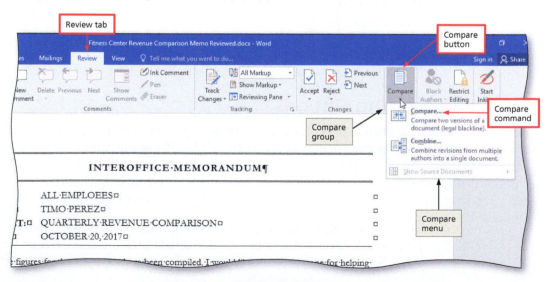

Figure 8–24

2

- Click Compare on the Compare menu to display the Compare Documents dialog box.

- Click the Original document arrow (Compare Documents dialog box) and then click the file, Fitness Center Revenue Comparison Memo Draft, in the Original document list to select the first file to compare and place the file name in the Original document box.

Q&A What if the file is not in the Original document list?
Click the Open button to the right of the Original document arrow, locate the file, and then click the Open button (Open dialog box).

- Click the Revised document arrow (Compare Documents dialog box) and then click the file, Fitness Center Revenue Comparison Memo Reviewed, in the Revised document list to select the second file to compare and place the file name in the Revised document box. If necessary, change the name in the 'Label changes with' box to Timo Perez.

Q&A What if the file is not in the Revised document list?
Click the Open button to the right of the Revised document arrow, locate the file, and then click the Open button (Open dialog box).

- If a More button appears in the dialog box, click it to expand the dialog box, which changes the More button to a Less button.

- If necessary, in the Show changes in area, click New document so that tracked changes are marked in a new document. Ensure that all your settings in the expanded dialog box (below the Less button) match those in Figure 8–25.

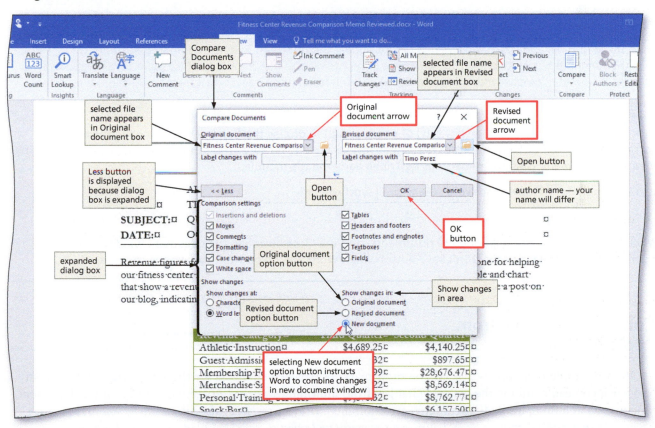

Figure 8–25

3

- Click the OK button to open a new document window and display the differences between the two documents as tracked changes in a new document window; if the Reviewing task pane appears on the screen, click its Close button (Figure 8–26). Note that, depending on settings, your compare results may differ from Figure 8–26.

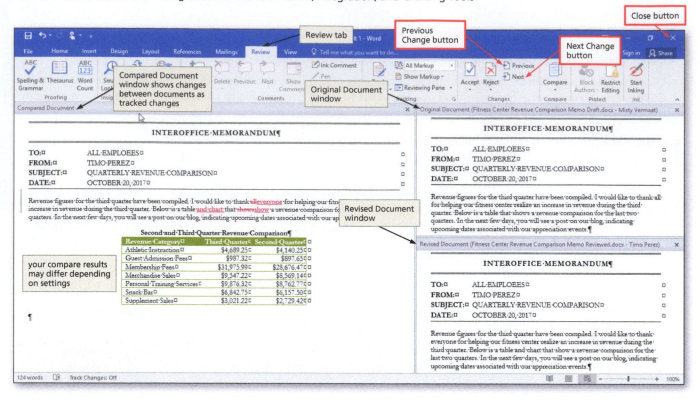

Figure 8–26

Q&A
What if the original and source documents do not appear on the screen with the compared document?

Click the Compare button (Review tab | Compare group) to display the Compare menu, point to 'Show Source Documents' on the Compare menu, and then click Show Both on the Show Source Documents submenu.

Experiment

• Click the Next Change button (Review tab | Changes group) to display the first tracked change in the compared document. Continue clicking the Next Change or Previous Change buttons. You can accept or reject changes in the compared document using the same steps described earlier in the module.

• Scroll through the windows and watch them scroll synchronously.

4

• When you have finished comparing the documents, click the Close button in the document window (shown in Figure 8–26) and then click the Don't Save button when Word asks if you want to save the compare results.

To Combine Revisions from Multiple Authors

1 INSERT COMMENTS & TRACK CHANGES | 2 REVIEW COMMENTS & TRACKED CHANGES
3 LINK EXCEL WORKSHEET TO WORD DOCUMENT | 4 CHART WORD TABLE | 5 CREATE & PUBLISH BLOG POST

Often, multiple reviewers will send you their markups (tracked changes) for the same original document. Using Word, you can combine the tracked changes from multiple reviewers' documents into a single document, two documents at a time, until all documents are combined. *Why? Combining documents allows you to review all markups from a single document, from which you can accept and reject changes and read comments. Each reviewer's markups are shaded in a different color to help you visually differentiate among multiple reviewers' markups.*

Assume you want to combine the original Fitness Center Revenue Comparison Memo Draft document with the Fitness Center Revenue Comparison Memo with Comments and Tracked Changes document and also with a document called Fitness Center Revenue Comparison Memo Reviewed by W Evans. The file by W Evans identifies another grammar error in the memo. The following steps combine these three documents, two at a time.

1
- Click the Compare button (Review tab | Compare group) to display the Compare menu (Figure 8–27).

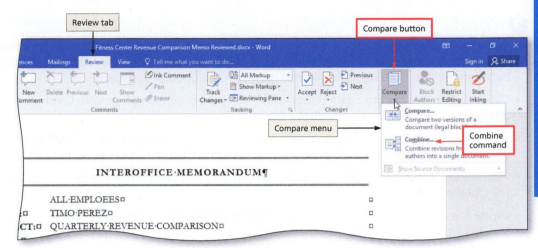

Figure 8–27

2
- Click Combine on the Compare menu to display the Combine Documents dialog box.

- Click the Original document arrow (Combine Documents dialog box) and then click the file, Fitness Center Revenue Comparison Memo Draft, in the Original document list to select the first file to combine and place the file name in the Original document box.

Q&A What if the file is not in the Original document list?
Click the Open button to the right of the Original document arrow, locate the file, and then click the Open button (Open dialog box).

- Click the Revised document arrow (Combine Documents dialog box) and then click the file, Fitness Center Revenue Comparison Memo with Comments and Tracked Changes, in the Revised document list to select the second file to combine and place the file name in the Revised document box.

Q&A What if the file is not in the Revised document list?
Click the Open button to the right of the Revised document arrow, locate the file, and then click the Open button (Open dialog box).

- If a More button appears in the dialog box, click it to expand the dialog box, which changes the More button to a Less button.

- In the Show changes in area, if necessary, click Original document so that tracked changes are marked in the original document (Fitness Center Revenue Comparison Memo Draft). Ensure that all your settings in the expanded dialog box (below the Less button) match those in Figure 8–28.

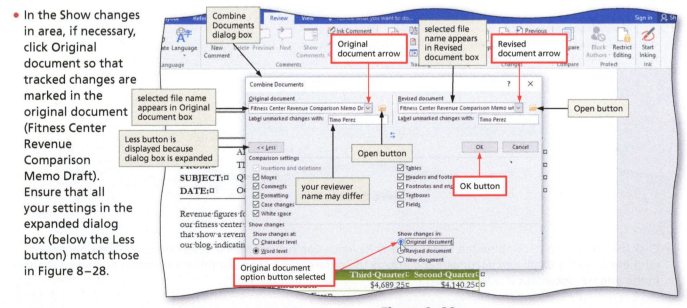

Figure 8–28

- Click the OK button to combine the Fitness Center Revenue Comparison Memo Draft document with the Fitness Center Revenue Comparison Memo with Comments and Tracked Changes document and display the differences between the two documents as tracked changes in the original document.

- Click the Compare button again (Review tab | Compare group) and then click Combine on the Compare menu to display the Combine Documents dialog box.

- Locate and display the file name, Fitness Center Revenue Comparison Memo Draft, in the Original document text box (Combine Documents dialog box) to select the first file and place the file name in the Original document box.

- Click the Open button to the right of the Revised document box arrow (Combine Documents dialog box) to display the Open dialog box.

- Locate the file name, Fitness Center Revenue Comparison Memo Reviewed by W Evans, in the Data Files and then click the Open button (Open dialog box) to display the selected file name in the Revised document box (Combine Documents dialog box).

- If a More button appears in the Combine Documents dialog box, click it to expand the dialog box.

- If necessary, in the 'Show changes in' area, click Original document so that tracked changes are marked in the original document (Fitness Center Revenue Comparison Memo Draft). Ensure that all your settings in the expanded dialog box (below the Less button) match those in Figure 8–29.

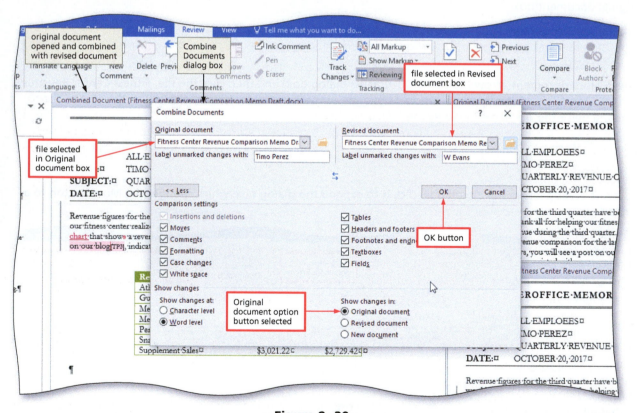

Figure 8–29

- Click the OK button to combine the Fitness Center Revenue Comparison Memo Reviewed by W Evans document with the currently combined document and display the differences among the three documents as tracked changes in the original document (Figure 8–30).

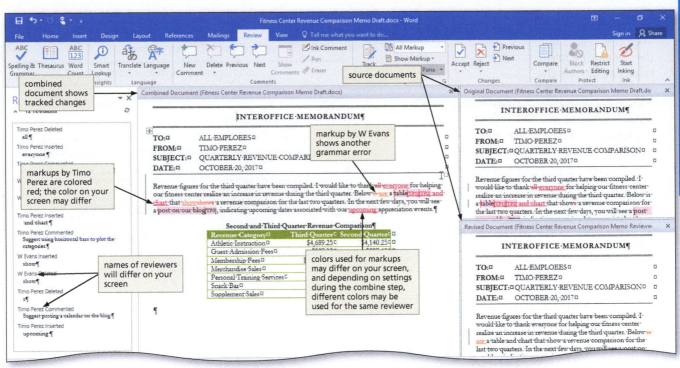

Figure 8–30

Q&A What if my screen does not display the original and source documents?
Click the Compare button (Review tab | Compare group) to display the Compare menu, point to 'Show Source Documents' on the Compare menu, and then click Show Both on the Show Source Documents submenu.

🔎 Experiment

- Click the Next Change button (Review tab | Changes group) to display the first tracked change in the combined document. Continue clicking the Next Change or Previous Change buttons. You can accept or reject changes in the combined document using the same steps described earlier in the module.

To Show Tracked Changes and Comments by a Single Reviewer

1 INSERT COMMENTS & TRACK CHANGES | 2 REVIEW COMMENTS & TRACKED CHANGES

3 LINK EXCEL WORKSHEET TO WORD DOCUMENT | 4 CHART WORD TABLE | 5 CREATE & PUBLISH BLOG POST

Why? *Instead of looking through a document for a particular reviewer's markups, you can show markups by reviewer.* The following steps show the markups by the reviewer named W Evans.

1
- Click the Show Markup button (Review tab | Tracking group) to display the Show Markup menu and then point to Specific People on the Show Markup menu to display the Specific People submenu (Figure 8–31).

Q&A What if my Specific People submenu differs?
Your submenu may have additional, different, or duplicate reviewer names or colors, depending on your Word settings.

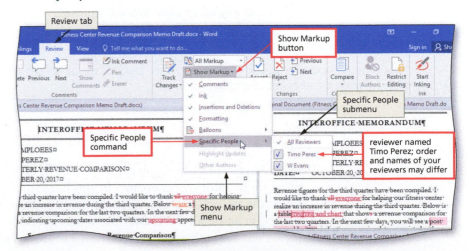

Figure 8–31

2

- Click Timo Perez on the Specific People submenu to hide the selected reviewer's markups and leave other markups on the screen (Figure 8–32).

Q&A

Are the Timo Perez reviewer markups deleted?

No. They are hidden from view.

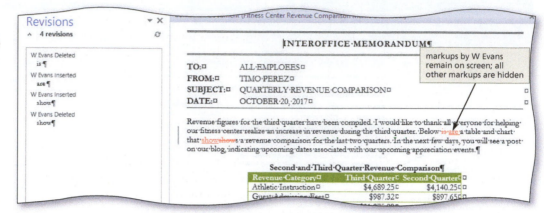

Figure 8–32

**Experiment**

- Practice hiding and showing reviewer markups in this document.

3

- Redisplay all reviewer comments by clicking the Show Markup button (Review tab | Tracking group), pointing to Specific People, and then clicking All Reviewers on the Specific People submenu.

BTW

Locating Comments by Reviewer
You can find a comment from a specific reviewer through the Go To dialog box. Click the Find arrow (Home tab | Editing group) and then click Go To or press CTRL+G to display the Go To sheet in the Find and Replace dialog box. Click Comment in the Go to what list (Find and Replace dialog box). Select the reviewer whose comments you wish to find and then click the Next button.

To Customize the Status Bar and Close the Document

You are finished working with tracked changes in this module. The following steps remove the Track Changes indicator from the status bar and close the combined document without saving it.

1 Right-click anywhere on the status bar to display the Customize Status Bar menu.

2 Remove the check mark to the left of Track Changes on the Customize Status Bar menu, which removes the Track Changes indicator from the status bar.

3 Click anywhere outside of the Customize Status Bar menu, or press the ESCAPE key, to remove the Customize Status Bar menu from the screen.

4 Close the Word window containing the combined document. When Word displays the dialog box, click the Don't Save button.

5 Close any other open Word documents.

Break Point: If you wish to take a break, this is a good place to do so. You can exit Word now. To resume at a later time, run Word and continue following the steps from this location forward.

Linking an Excel Worksheet to a Word Document

With Microsoft Office, you can copy part or all of a document created in one Office program to a document created in another Office program. The item being copied is called the **object**. For example, you could copy an Excel worksheet (the object) that is located in an Excel workbook (the source file) to a Word document (the destination file). That is, an object is copied from a source to a destination.

You can use one of three techniques to copy objects from one program to another: copy and paste, embed, or link.

- **Copy and paste**: When you copy an object and then paste it, the object becomes part of the destination document. You edit a pasted object using editing features of the destination program. For example, when you select an Excel worksheet in an Excel workbook, click the Copy button (Home tab | Clipboard group) in Excel, and then click the Paste button (Home tab | Clipboard group) in Word, the Excel worksheet becomes a Word table.

- **Embed:** When you embed an object, like a pasted object, it becomes part of the destination document. The difference between an embedded object and a pasted object is that you edit the contents of an embedded object using the editing features of the source program. The embedded object, however, contains static data; that is, any changes made to the object in the source program are not reflected in the destination document. If you embed an Excel worksheet in a Word document, the Excel worksheet remains as an Excel worksheet in the Word document. When you edit the Excel worksheet from within the Word document, you will use Excel editing features.

- **Link:** A linked object, by contrast, does not become a part of the destination document even though it appears to be a part of it. Rather, a connection is established between the source and destination documents so that when you open the destination document, the linked object appears as part of it. When you edit a linked object, the source program runs and opens the source document that contains the linked object. For example, when you edit a linked worksheet, Excel runs and displays the Excel workbook that contains the worksheet; you then edit the worksheet in Excel. Unlike an embedded object, if you open the Excel workbook that contains the Excel worksheet and then edit the Excel worksheet, the linked object will be updated in the Word document, too.

How do I determine which method to use: copy/paste, embed, or link?

- If you simply want to use the object's data and have no desire to use the object in the source program, then copy and paste the object.

- If you want to use the object in the source program but you want the object's data to remain static if it changes in the source file, then embed the object.

- If you want to ensure that the most current version of the object appears in the destination file, then link the object. If the source file is large, such as a video clip or a sound clip, link the object to keep the size of the destination file smaller.

CONSIDER THIS

The steps in this section show how to link an Excel worksheet (the object), which is located in an Excel workbook (the source file), to a Word document (the destination file). The Word document is similar to the same memo used in the previous section, except that all grammar errors are fixed and it does not contain the table. To link the worksheet to the memo, you will follow these general steps:

1. Run Excel and open the Excel workbook that contains the object (worksheet) you want to link to the Word document.

2. Select the object (worksheet) in Excel and then copy the selected object to the Clipboard.

3. Switch to Word and then link the copied object to the Word document.

Note: The steps in this section assume you have Microsoft Excel 2016 installed on your computer. If you do not have Excel 2016, read the steps in this section without performing them.

To Open a Word Document, Run Excel, and Open an Excel Workbook

The first step in this section is to open the memo that is to contain the link to the Excel worksheet object. The memo file, named Fund-Raising Memo without Table, is located on the Data Files. The Excel worksheet to be linked to the memo is in an Excel workbook called Fitness Center Revenue Comparison in Excel, which also is located on the Data Files. Please contact your instructor for information about accessing the Data Files. The following steps open a Word document, run Excel, and open an Excel workbook. (Do not exit Word or close the open Word document during these steps.)

1 In Word, open the file called Fitness Center Revenue Comparison Memo without Table located on the Data Files.

2 Run Excel and open a blank workbook.

3 In Excel, open the file called Fitness Center Revenue Comparison on the Data Files.

BTW

Linked Objects
When you open a document that contains linked objects, Word displays a dialog box asking if you want to update the Word document with data from the linked file. Click the Yes button only if you are certain the linked file is from a trusted source; that is, you should be confident that the source file does not contain a virus or other potentially harmful program before you instruct Word to link the source file to the destination document.

Excel Basics

The Excel window contains a rectangular grid that consists of columns and rows. A column letter above the grid identifies each column. A row number on the left side of the grid identifies each row. The intersection of each column and row is a cell. A cell is referred to by its unique address, which is the coordinates of the intersection of a column and a row. To identify a cell, specify the column letter first, followed by the row number. For example, cell reference A1 refers to the cell located at the intersection of column A and row 1 (Figure 8–33).

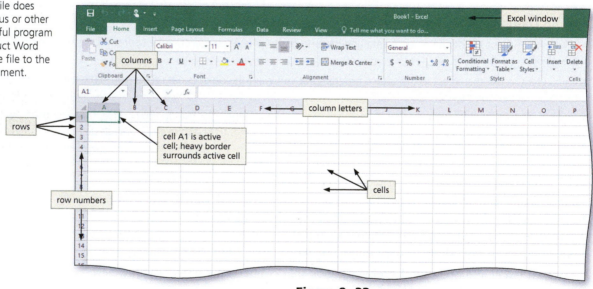

Figure 8–33

To Link an Excel Worksheet to a Word Document

1 INSERT COMMENTS & TRACK CHANGES | 2 REVIEW COMMENTS & TRACKED CHANGES
3 LINK EXCEL WORKSHEET TO WORD DOCUMENT | 4 CHART WORD TABLE | 5 CREATE & PUBLISH BLOG POST

The following steps link an Excel worksheet to a Word document. **Why?** *You want to copy the Excel worksheet to the Clipboard and then link the Excel worksheet to the Word document.*

1

- In the Excel window, drag through the cells in the range A1 through C8 to select them.

- In the Excel window, click the Copy button (Home tab | Clipboard group) to copy the selected cells to the Clipboard (Figure 8–34).

Q&A What if I click the Copy arrow by mistake?
Click Copy on the Copy menu.

What is the dotted line around the selected cells?
Excel surrounds copied cells with a moving marquee to help you visually identify the copied cells.

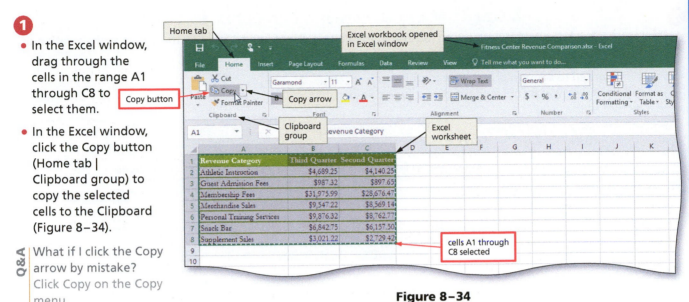

Figure 8–34

2

- Click the Word app button on the taskbar to switch to Word and display the open document in the Word window.

- Position the insertion point on the paragraph mark below the table title.

- In Word, click the Paste arrow (Home tab | Clipboard group) to display the Paste gallery.

Q&A What if I accidentally click the Paste button instead of the Paste arrow?
Click the Undo button on the Quick Access Toolbar and then click the Paste arrow.

- Point to the 'Link & Keep Source Formatting' button in the Paste gallery to display a live preview of that paste option (Figure 8–35).

Experiment

- Point to the various buttons in the Paste gallery to display a live preview of each paste option.

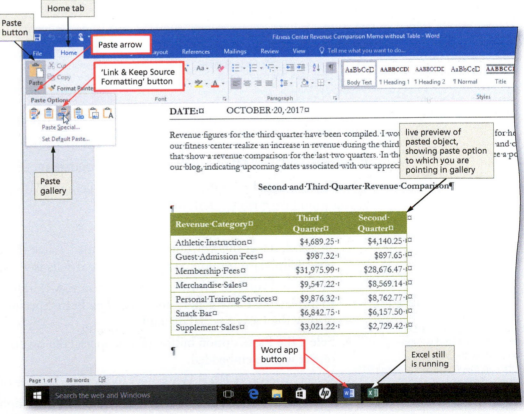

Figure 8–35

- Click the 'Link & Keep Source Formatting' button in the Paste gallery to paste and link the object at the location of the insertion point in the document.

Q&A What if I wanted to copy an object instead of link it?

To copy an object, you would click the 'Keep Source Formatting' button in the Paste gallery. To convert the object to a picture so that you can use tools on Word's Picture Tools Format tab to format it, you would click the Picture button in the Paste gallery.

- Select and then center the linked Excel table using the same technique you use to select and center a Word table.

- Resize the linked Excel table until the table is approximately the same size as Figure 8–36.

DATE: OCTOBER 20, 2017

Revenue figures for the third quarter have been compiled. I would like to thank everyone for helping our fitness center realize an increase in revenue during the third quarter. Below are a table and chart that show a revenue comparison for the last two quarters. In the next few days, you will see a post on our blog, indicating upcoming dates associated with our appreciation events.

Second and Third Quarter Revenue Comparison

Excel worksheet inserted, linked, and centered in Word document

Revenue Category	Third Quarter	Second Quarter
Athletic Instruction	$4,689.25	$4,140.25
Guest Admission Fees	$987.32	$897.65
Membership Fees	$31,975.99	$28,676.47
Merchandise Sales	$9,547.22	$8,569.14
Personal Training Services	$9,876.32	$8,762.77
Snack Bar	$6,842.75	$6,157.50
Supplement Sales	$3,021.22	$2,729.42

Figure 8–36

Q&A What if I wanted to delete the linked worksheet?

You would select the linked worksheet and then press the DELETE key.

Other Ways

1. Click Paste arrow (Home tab | Clipboard group), click Paste Special, click Paste link (Paste Special dialog box), click 'Microsoft Excel Worksheet Object' in As list, click OK button

2. To link an entire source file, click Object button (Insert tab | Text group), click Create from File tab (Object dialog box), locate file, click 'Link to file' check box, click OK button

---

BTW

Editing Embedded Objects

If you wanted to edit an embedded object in the Word document, you would double-click the object to display the source program's interface in the destination program. For example, double-clicking an embedded Excel worksheet in a Word document displays the Excel ribbon in the Word window. To redisplay the Word ribbon in the Word window, double-click outside of the embedded object.

TO EMBED AN EXCEL WORKSHEET IN A WORD DOCUMENT

If you wanted to embed an Excel worksheet in a Word document, instead of link it, you would perform the following steps.

1. Run Excel.

2. In Excel, select the worksheet cells to embed. Click the Copy button (Home tab | Clipboard group) to copy the selected cells to the Clipboard.

3. Switch to Word. In Word, click the Paste arrow (Home tab | Clipboard group) to display the Paste gallery and then click Paste Special in the Paste gallery to display the Paste Special dialog box.

4. Select the Paste option button (Paste Special dialog box), which indicates the object will be embedded.

5. Select 'Microsoft Excel Worksheet Object' as the type of object to embed.

6. Click the OK button to embed the contents of the Clipboard in the Word document at the location of the insertion point.

To Edit a Linked Object

At a later time, you may find it necessary to change the data in the Excel worksheet. Any changes you make to the Excel worksheet while in Excel will be reflected in the Excel worksheet in the Word document because the objects are linked to the Word document. If you wanted to edit a linked object, such as an Excel worksheet, you would perform these steps.

1. In the Word document, right-click the linked Excel worksheet, point to 'Linked Worksheet Object' on the shortcut menu, and then click Edit Link on the Linked Worksheet Object submenu to run Excel and open the source file that contains the linked worksheet.

2. In Excel, make changes to the Excel worksheet.

3. Click the Save button on the Quick Access Toolbar to save the changes.

4. Exit Excel.

5. If necessary, redisplay the Word window.

6. If necessary, to update the worksheet with the edited Excel data, click the Excel worksheet in the Word document and then press the F9 key, or right-click the linked object and then click Update Link on the shortcut menu to update the linked object with the revisions made to the source file.

BTW

Opening Word Documents with Links
When you open a document that contains a linked object, Word attempts to locate the source file associated with the link. If Word cannot find the source file, open the Backstage view, display the Info tab, then click 'Edit Links to Files' in the Related Documents area at the bottom of the right pane to display the Links dialog box. Next, select the appropriate source file in the list (Links dialog box), click the Change Source button, locate the source file, and then click the OK button.

To Break a Link

1 INSERT COMMENTS & TRACK CHANGES | 2 REVIEW COMMENTS & TRACKED CHANGES

3 LINK EXCEL WORKSHEET TO WORD DOCUMENT | 4 CHART WORD TABLE | 5 CREATE & PUBLISH BLOG POST

Why? *You can convert a linked or embedded object to a Word object by breaking the link. That is, you break the connection between the source file and the destination file.* When you break a linked object, such as an Excel worksheet, the linked object becomes a Word object, a Word table in this case. The following steps break the link to the Excel worksheet.

- Right-click the linked object (the linked Excel worksheet, in this case) to display a shortcut menu.

- Point to 'Linked Worksheet Object' on the shortcut menu to display the Linked Worksheet Object submenu (Figure 8–37).

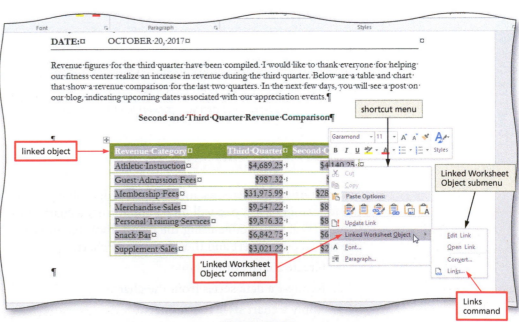

Figure 8–37

● Click Links on the Linked Worksheet Object submenu to display the Links dialog box.

● If necessary, click the source file listed in the dialog box to select it (Links dialog box).

● Click the Break Link button, which displays a dialog box asking if you are sure you want to break the selected links (Figure 8–38).

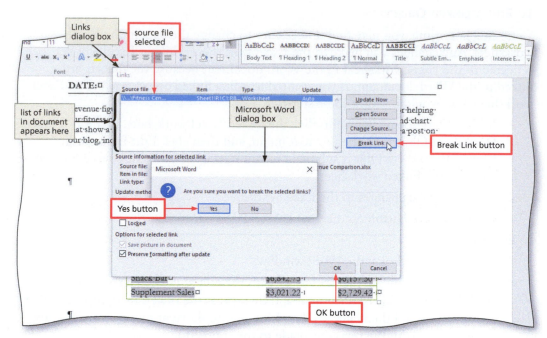

Figure 8–38

● Click the Yes button in the dialog box to remove the source file from the list (break the link).

Q&A

How can I verify the link is broken?

Right-click the table in the Word document to display a shortcut menu. If the shortcut menu does not contain a 'Linked Worksheet Object' command, a link does not exist for the object. Or, when you double-click the table, Excel should not open an associated workbook.

● Close the Word document without saving it.

● Exit Excel without saving changes to the workbook.

Other Ways

1. Select link, press CTRL+SHIFT+F9

CONSIDER THIS

Why would I break a link?

If you share a Word document that contains a linked object, such as an Excel worksheet, users will be asked by Word if they want to update the links when they open the Word document. If users are unfamiliar with links, they will not know how to answer the question. Further, if they do not have the source program, such as Excel, they may not be able to open the Word document. When sharing documents, it is recommended you convert links to a regular Word object; that is, break the link.

Charting a Word Table

Several Office applications, including Word, enable you to create charts from data. In the following pages, you will insert and format a chart of the Fitness Center Revenue Comparison Word table using the Chart Tools tab in Word. You will follow these general steps to insert and then format the chart:

1. Create a chart of the table.
2. Remove a data series from the chart.
3. Apply a chart style to the chart.
4. Change the colors of the chart.
5. Add a chart element.
6. Edit a chart element.

7. Format chart elements.

8. Add an outline to the chart.

To Open a Document

The next step is to open the Fitness Center Revenue Comparison Memo file that contains the final wording so that you can create a chart of its Word table. This file, called Fitness Center Revenue Comparison Memo with Table, is located on the Data Files. Please contact your instructor for information about accessing the Data Files. The following step opens a document.

 Navigate to the Data Files and then open the file called Fitness Center Revenue Comparison Memo with Table.

To Chart a Table

1 INSERT COMMENTS & TRACK CHANGES | 2 REVIEW COMMENTS & TRACKED CHANGES
3 LINK EXCEL WORKSHEET TO WORD DOCUMENT | 4 CHART WORD TABLE | 5 CREATE & PUBLISH BLOG POST

The following steps insert a default chart and then copy the data to be charted from the Word table in the Word document to a chart spreadsheet. *Why? To chart a table, you fill in or copy the data into a chart spreadsheet that automatically opens after you insert the chart.*

- Center the paragraph mark below the table so that the inserted chart will be centered. Leave the insertion point on this paragraph mark because the chart will be inserted at the location of the insertion point.

- Display the Insert tab.

- Click the 'Add a Chart' button (Insert tab | Illustrations group) to display the Insert Chart dialog box.

- Click Bar in the left pane (Insert Chart dialog box) to display the available types of bar charts in the right pane.

Experiment

- Click the various types of charts in the left pane and watch the subtypes appear in the right pane. When finished experimenting, click Bar in the left pane.

- If necessary, click Clustered Bar in the right pane to select the chart type (Figure 8–39).

Experiment

- Click the various types of bar charts in the right pane and watch the graphic change in the right pane. When finished experimenting, click Clustered Bar in the right pane.

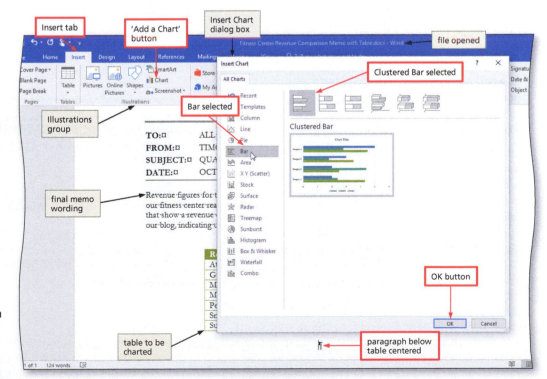

Figure 8–39

2

- Click the OK button so that Word creates a default clustered bar chart in the Word document at the location of the insertion point (Figure 8–40).

Q&A What are the requirements for the format of a table that can be charted? The chart spreadsheet window shows the layout for the selected chart type. In this case, the categories are in the rows and the series are in the columns. Notice the categories appear in the chart in reverse order.

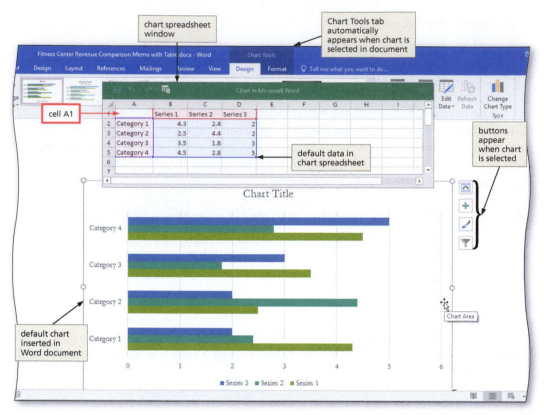

Figure 8–40

3

- In the Word document, select the table to be charted. (If necessary, drag the chart spreadsheet window or scroll in the document window so that the table is visible.)
- Click the Copy button (Home tab | Clipboard group) to copy the selected table to the Clipboard (Figure 8–41).

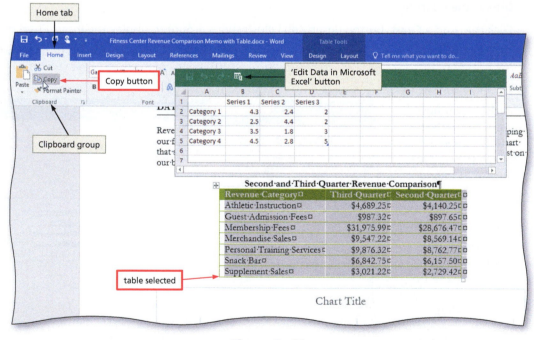

Figure 8–41

Q&A Instead of copying table data to the chart spreadsheet, could I type the data directly into the spreadsheet?

Yes. If the chart spreadsheet window does not appear, click the Edit Data arrow (Chart Tools Design tab | Data group) and then click Edit Data on the menu. You also can click the 'Edit Data in Microsoft Excel' button to use Excel to enter the data (if Excel is installed on your computer), or click the Edit Data arrow (Chart Tools Design tab | Data group) and then click 'Edit Data in Excel' on the Edit Data menu.

- In the chart spreadsheet window, click the Select All button (upper-left corner of worksheet) to select the entire worksheet.

- Right-click the selected worksheet to display a mini toolbar or shortcut menu (Figure 8–42).

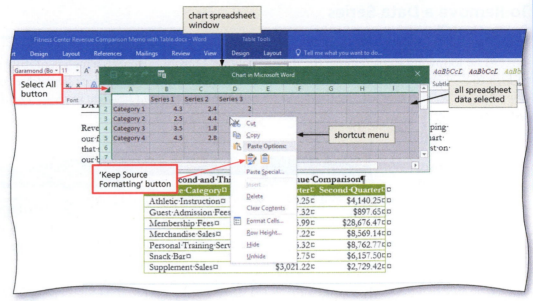

Figure 8–42

5

- Click the 'Keep Source Formatting' button on the shortcut menu to paste the contents of the Clipboard starting in the upper-left corner of the worksheet.

- When Word displays a dialog box indicating that the pasted contents are a different size from the selection, click the OK button.

Q&A | Why did Word display this dialog box?
The source table contains three columns, and the target worksheet has four columns. In the next section, you will delete the fourth column from the chart spreadsheet.

- Resize the chart worksheet window by dragging its window edges, move it by dragging its title bar, and resize the columns by dragging the borders of the column headings so the worksheet window appears as shown in Figure 8–43. Notice that the chart in the Word window automatically changes to reflect the new data in the chart worksheet (Figure 8–43).

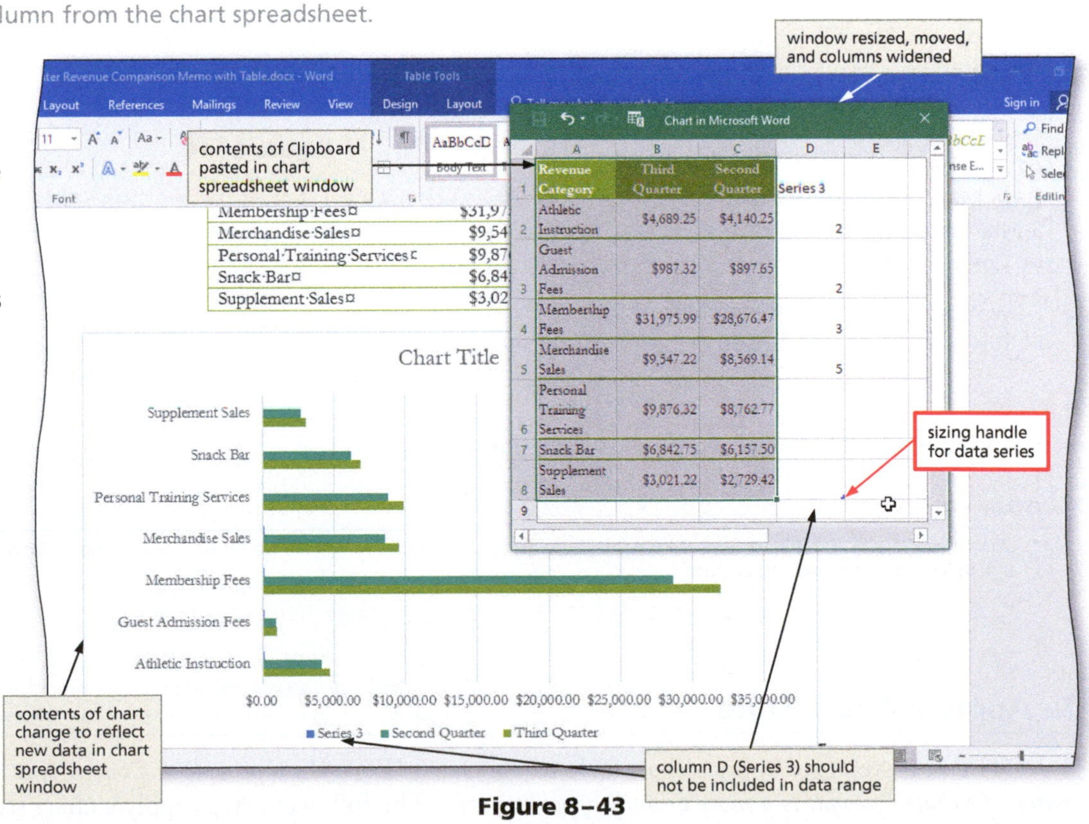

Q&A | Why did some of the cells have the # symbol in them before I resized the columns?
Excel places a # symbol in cells whose value is too wide to fit in a cell.

Figure 8–43

To Remove a Data Series from the Chart

The following steps remove the data in column D from the chart, which is plotted as Series 3 (shown in Figure 8–43). *Why? By default, Word selects the first four columns in the chart spreadsheet window. The chart in this project covers only the first three columns: the revenue categories and two data series — Third Quarter and Second Quarter.*

● Ensure the chart is selected in the Word document and then drag the sizing handle in cell D8 of the chart spreadsheet leftward so that the selection ends at cell C8; that is, the selection should encompass cells A1 through C8 (Figure 8–44).

Q&A

How would I add a data series?

Add a column of data to the chart spreadsheet. Drag the sizing handle outward to include the series, or you could click the Select Data button (Chart Tools Design tab | Data group), click the Add button (Select Data Source dialog box), click the Select Range button (Edit Series dialog box), drag through the data range in the worksheet, and then click the OK button.

How would I add or remove data categories?

Follow the same steps to add or remove data series, except work with spreadsheet rows instead of columns.

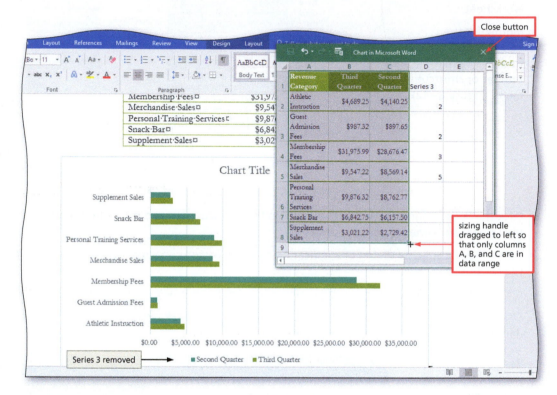

Figure 8–44

● Close the chart spreadsheet window by clicking its Close button.

Other Ways

1. Click Select Data button (Chart Tools Design tab | Data group), click series to remove (Select Data Source dialog box), click Remove button, click OK button

To Apply a Chart Style

The next step is to apply a chart style to the chart. *Why? Word provides a Chart Styles gallery, allowing you to change the chart's format to a more visually appealing style.* The following steps apply a chart style to a chart.

1

- Display the Chart Tools Design tab.

- If necessary, click the chart to select it.

- Point to Style 5 in the Chart Styles gallery (Chart Tools Design tab | Chart Styles group) to display a live preview of that style applied to the graphic in the document (Figure 8–45).

🔍 **Experiment**

- Point to various styles in the Chart Styles gallery and watch the style of the chart change in the document window.

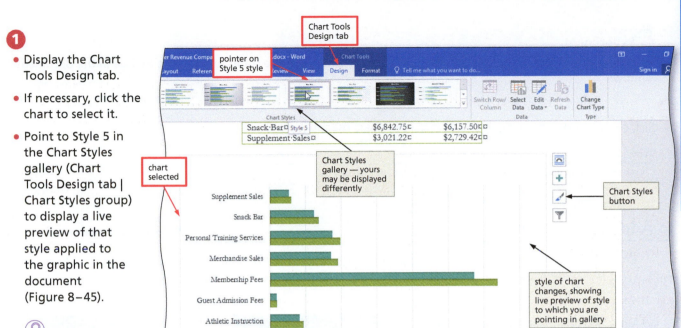

Figure 8–45

2

- Click Style 5 in the Chart Styles gallery (Chart Tools Design tab | Chart Styles group) to apply the selected style to the chart.

Other Ways

1. Click Chart Styles button attached to chart, click Style tab, click desired style

To Change Colors of a Chart

1 INSERT COMMENTS & TRACK CHANGES | 2 REVIEW COMMENTS & TRACKED CHANGES

3 LINK EXCEL WORKSHEET TO WORD DOCUMENT | **4 CHART WORD TABLE** | 5 CREATE & PUBLISH BLOG POST

The following steps change the colors of the chart. *Why? Word provides a predefined variety of colors for charts. You select one that best matches the colors already used in the letter.*

1

- With the chart selected, click the 'Chart Quick Colors' button (Chart Tools Design tab | Chart Styles group) to display the Chart Quick Colors gallery.

Q&A What if the chart is not selected? Click the chart to select it.

- Point to Color 2 in the Chart Quick Colors gallery to display a live preview of the selected color applied to the chart in the document (Figure 8–46).

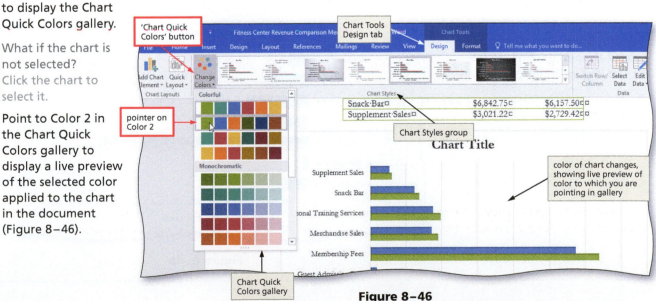

Figure 8–46

Experiment

- Point to various colors in the Chart Quick Colors gallery and watch the colors of the chart change in the document window.

2

- Click Color 2 in the Chart Quick Colors gallery to apply the selected color to the chart.

Other Ways

1. Click Chart Styles button attached to chart, click Color tab, click desired style

To Add a Chart Element

1 INSERT COMMENTS & TRACK CHANGES | 2 REVIEW COMMENTS & TRACKED CHANGES
3 LINK EXCEL WORKSHEET TO WORD DOCUMENT | **4 CHART WORD TABLE** | 5 CREATE & PUBLISH BLOG POST

The following steps add minor vertical gridlines to the chart. *Why? You want to add more vertical lines to the chart so that it is easier to see the dollar values associated with each bar length.*

1

- With the chart selected, click the 'Add Chart Element' button (Chart Tools Design tab | Chart Layouts group) to display the Add Chart Element gallery and then point to Gridlines to display the Gridlines submenu (Figure 8–47).

Experiment

- Point to various elements in the Add Chart Element gallery so that you can see the other types of elements you can add to a chart. When finished, point to Gridlines.

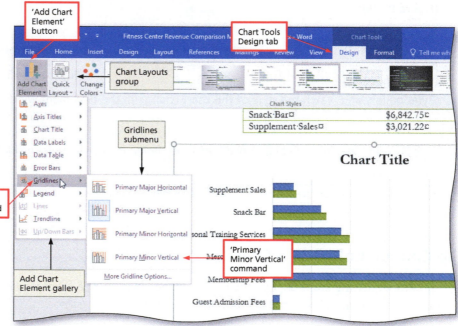

Figure 8–47

2

- Click 'Primary Minor Vertical' on the Gridline submenu to add vertical minor gridlines to the chart (Figure 8–48).

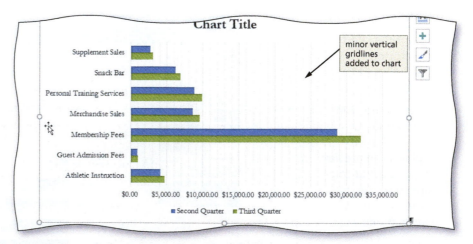

Figure 8–48

To Select a Chart Element and Edit It

The following steps change the chart title. **Why?** *You want to change the title from the default to a more meaningful name.*

- Display the Chart Tools Format tab.

- With the chart selected, click the Chart Elements arrow (Chart Tools Format tab | Current Selection group) to display the Chart Elements list (Figure 8–49).

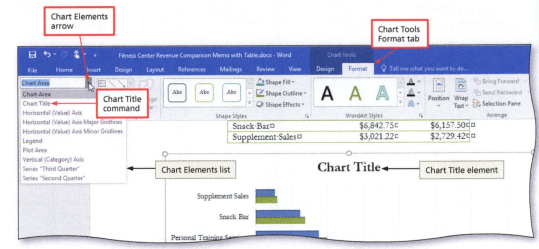

Figure 8–49

- Click Chart Title in the Chart Elements list to select the chart's title.

- Type `Second and Third Quarter Comparison` as the new title (Figure 8–50).

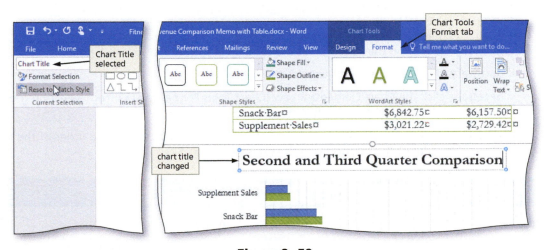

Figure 8–50

Other Ways

1. Click chart element in chart to select element

To Format Chart Elements

Currently, the category names on the vertical axis are in reverse order of the row labels in the table; that is, category names are in alphabetical order from bottom to top and the row labels in the table are in alphabetical order from top to bottom. Also, the numbers across the bottom display with two decimal places following the dollar values. The following steps format axis elements. **Why?** *You want the categories to display in the same order as the table, the numbers to display as whole numbers, and the legend to appear at the top of the chart.*

- If necessary, select the chart by clicking it.

- With the chart selected, click the Chart Elements arrow (Chart Tools Format tab | Current Selection group) to display the Chart Elements list and then click 'Vertical (Category) Axis'.

- Click the Chart Elements button attached to the right of the chart to display the CHART ELEMENTS gallery.

- Point to and then click the Axes arrow in the CHART ELEMENTS gallery to display the Axes fly-out menu (Figure 8–51).

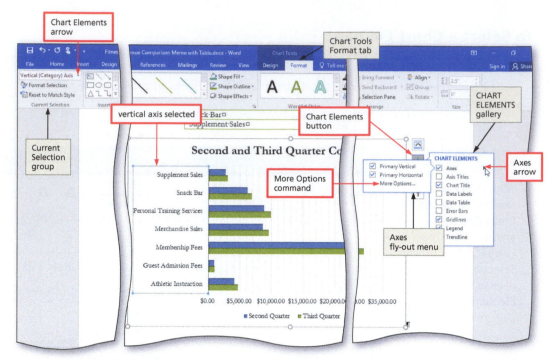

Figure 8–51

2

- Click More Options on the Axes fly-out menu to open the Format Axis task pane.

- If necessary, click Axis Options to expand the section.

- If necessary, click the Chart Elements arrow (Chart Tools Format tab | Current Selection group) to display the Chart Elements list and then click 'Vertical (Category) Axis'.

- Place a check mark in the 'Categories in reverse order' check box so that the order of the categories in the chart matches the order of the categories in the table (Figure 8–52).

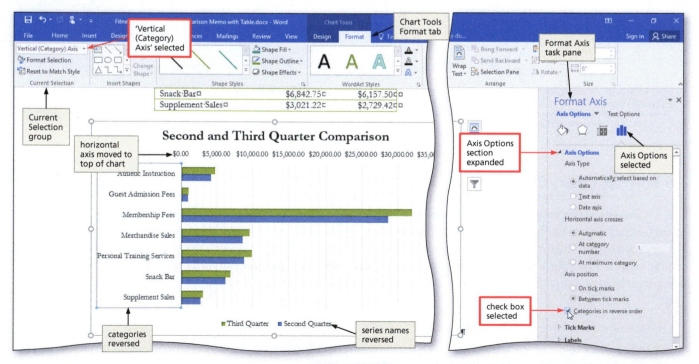

Figure 8–52

Why did the horizontal axis move from the bottom of the chart to the top?

When you reverse the categories, the horizontal axis automatically moves from the bottom of the chart to the top of the chart. Notice that the series names below the chart also are reversed.

- With the chart selected, click the Chart Elements arrow (Chart Tools Format tab | Current Selection group) to display the Chart Elements list and then click 'Horizontal (Value) Axis'.

- If necessary, click Labels and click Number at the bottom of the Format Axis task pane to expand these two sections in the task pane.

- If necessary, scroll the task pane to display the entire Labels and Number sections.

- In the Labels section, click the Label Position arrow and then click High to move the axis to the bottom of the chart.

- In the Number section, change the value in the Decimal places text box to 0 (the number zero) and then press the ENTER key (Figure 8–53).

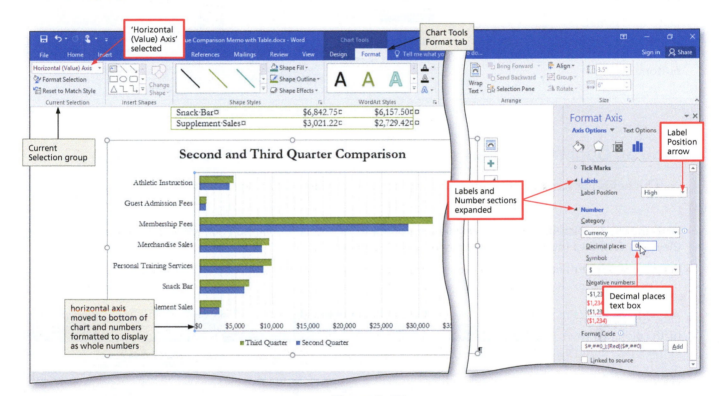

Figure 8–53

- With the chart selected, click the Chart Elements arrow (Chart Tools Format tab | Current Selection group) to display the Chart Elements list and then click Legend.

What happened to the Format Axis task pane?

It now is the Format Legend task pane. The task pane title and options change, depending on the element you are using or formatting.

- If necessary, click Legend Options to expand the section in the Format Legend task pane.

- Click Top to select the option button.

- Remove the check mark from the 'Show the legend without overlapping the chart' check box so that the legend drops down into the chart a bit (Figure 8–54).

5

- Drag the legend up slightly so that it rests on top of the vertical lines in the chart.

- Close the Format Legend task pane by clicking its close button.

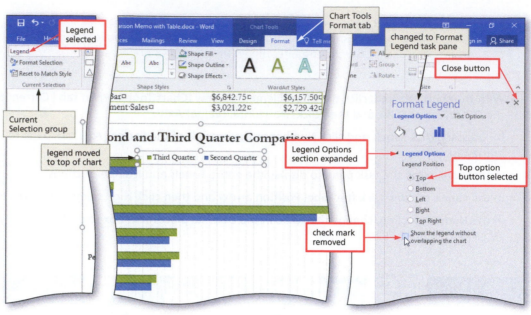

Figure 8–54

To Add an Outline to a Chart

1 INSERT COMMENTS & TRACK CHANGES | 2 REVIEW COMMENTS & TRACKED CHANGES | 3 LINK EXCEL WORKSHEET TO WORD DOCUMENT | 4 CHART WORD TABLE | 5 CREATE & PUBLISH BLOG POST

The following steps add an outline to the chart with a shadow. **Why?** *You want a border surrounding the chart.*

1

- With the chart selected, click the Chart Elements arrow (Chart Tools Format tab | Current Selection group) to display the Chart Elements list and then, if necessary, click Chart Area.

- Click the Shape Outline arrow (Chart Tools Format tab | Shape Styles group) to display the Shape Outline gallery.

2

- Click 'Green, Accent 1' (fifth color, first row) in the Shape Outline gallery to change the outline color.

- Click the Shape Outline arrow (Chart Tools Format tab | Shape Styles group) again and then point to Weight in the Shape Outline gallery to display the Weight gallery (Figure 8–55).

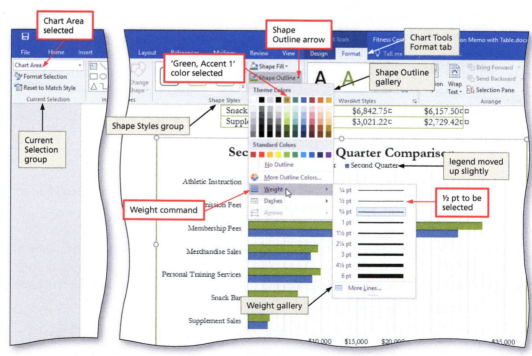

Figure 8–55

- Click ½ pt in the Weight gallery to apply the selected weight to the outline.

- Click the Shape Effects button (Chart Tools Format tab | Shape Styles group) and then point to Shadow in the Shape Effects gallery to display the Shadow gallery (Figure 8–56).

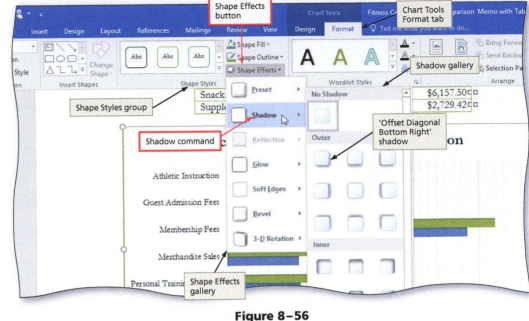

Figure 8–56

- Click 'Offset Diagonal Bottom Right' in the Shadow gallery to apply the selected shadow to the outline.

- Save the modified memo on your hard drive, OneDrive, or other storage location using Fitness Center Revenue Comparison Memo with Table and Clustered Chart as the file name.

To Change a Chart Type

1 INSERT COMMENTS & TRACK CHANGES | 2 REVIEW COMMENTS & TRACKED CHANGES
3 LINK EXCEL WORKSHEET TO WORD DOCUMENT | 4 CHART WORD TABLE | 5 CREATE & PUBLISH BLOG POST

The following steps change the chart type. **Why?** *After reviewing the document, you would like to see how the chart looks as a 3-D clustered bar chart.*

- Display the Chart Tools Design tab.

- Click the 'Change Chart Type' button (Chart Tools Design tab | Type group) to display the Change Chart Type dialog box.

- Click '3-D Clustered Bar' (Change Chart Type dialog box) in the right pane to change the chart type (Figure 8–57).

Experiment

- Point to the chart preview in the dialog box to see in more detail how the chart will look in the document.

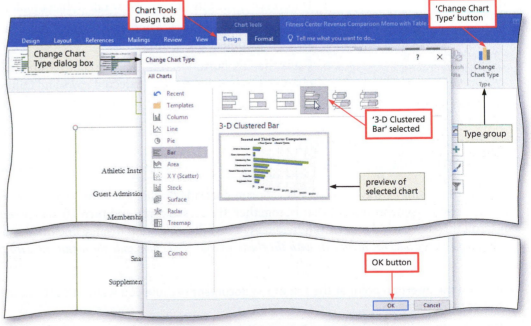

Figure 8–57

2

- Click the OK button to change the chart type (Figure 8–58).

- Save the revised memo on your hard drive, OneDrive, or other storage location using Fitness Center Revenue Comparison Memo with Table and 3-D Clustered Chart as the file name.

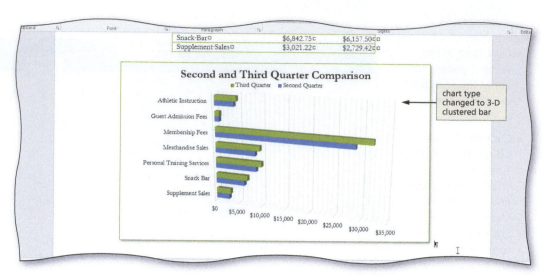

Figure 8–58

BTW

Conserving Ink and Toner

If you want to conserve ink or toner, you can instruct Word to print draft quality documents by clicking File on the ribbon to open the Backstage view, clicking the Options tab in the Backstage view to display the Word Options dialog box, clicking Advanced in the left pane (Word Options dialog box), scrolling to the Print area in the right pane, placing a check mark in the 'Use draft quality' check box, and then clicking the OK button. Then, use the Backstage view to print the document as usual.

TO CHART A WORD TABLE USING MICROSOFT GRAPH

In previous versions of Word, you charted Word tables using an embedded program called Microsoft Graph, or simply Graph. When working with the chart, Graph has its own menus and commands because it is a program embedded in Word. Using Graph commands, you can modify the appearance of the chart after you create it. If you wanted to create a chart using the legacy Graph program, you would perform these steps.

1. Select the rows and columns or table to be charted.

2. Display the Insert tab.

3. Click the Object button (Insert tab | Text group) to display the Object dialog box.

4. If necessary, click the Create New tab (Object dialog box).

5. Scroll to and then select 'Microsoft Graph Chart' in the Object type list to specify the object being inserted.

6. Click the OK button to run the Microsoft Graph program, which creates a chart of the selected table or selected rows and columns.

To View and Scroll through Documents Side by Side

1 INSERT COMMENTS & TRACK CHANGES | 2 REVIEW COMMENTS & TRACKED CHANGES
3 LINK EXCEL WORKSHEET TO WORD DOCUMENT | 4 CHART WORD TABLE | 5 CREATE & PUBLISH BLOG POST

Word provides a way to display two documents side by side, each in a separate window. By default, the two documents scroll synchronously, that is, together. If necessary, you can turn off synchronous scrolling so that you can scroll through each document individually. The following steps display documents side by side. *Why? You would like to see the how the document with the clustered chart looks alongside the document with the 3-D clustered bar chart.*

- Position the insertion point at the top of the document because you want to begin viewing side by side from the top of the documents.

- Open the file called Fitness Center Revenue Comparison Memo with Table and Clustered Chart so that both documents are open in Word.

- Display the View tab (Figure 8–59).

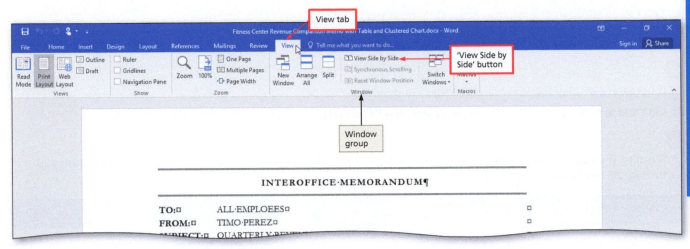

Figure 8–59

2

- Click the 'View Side by Side' button (View tab | Window group) to display each open window side by side (Figure 8–60).

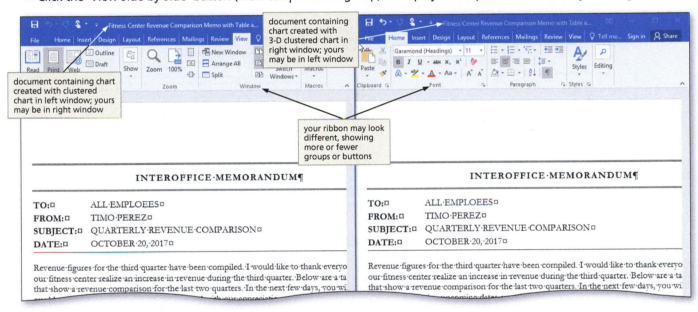

Figure 8–60

3

- If necessary, adjust the zoom to fit the memo contents in each window.

- Scroll to the bottom of one of the windows and notice how both windows (documents) scroll together (Figure 8–61).

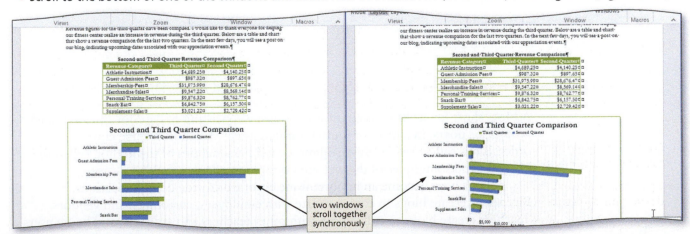

Figure 8–61

Can I scroll through one window separately from the other?

By default, synchronous scrolling is active when you display windows side by side. If you want to scroll separately through the windows, simply turn off synchronous scrolling.

4

- If necessary, display the View tab (in either window).
- Click the Synchronous Scrolling button (View tab | Window group) to turn off synchronous scrolling.

5

- Scroll to the top of the window on the right and notice that the window on the left does not scroll because you turned off synchronous scrolling (Figure 8–62).

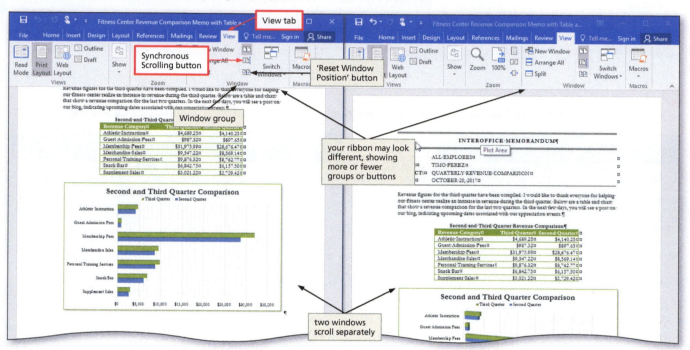

Figure 8–62

What is the purpose of the 'Reset Window Position' button?

It repositions the side-by-side windows so that each consumes the same amount of screen space.

6

- In either window, click the 'View Side by Side' button (View tab | Window group) to turn off side-by-side viewing and display each window in the full screen.
- Close each open Word document, saving them if prompted.

Break Point: If you wish to take a break, this is a good place to do so. You can exit Word now. To resume at a later time, run Word and continue following the steps from this location forward

Creating a Blog Post

A **blog**, short for **weblog**, is an informal website consisting of date- or time-stamped articles, or **posts**, in a diary or journal format, usually listed in reverse chronological order. Blogs reflect the interests, opinions, and personalities of the author, called the **blogger**, and sometimes of the website visitors as well.

Blogs have become an important means of worldwide communications. Businesses create blogs to communicate with employees, customers, and vendors. Teachers create blogs to collaborate with other teachers and students, and home users create blogs to share aspects of their personal life with family, friends, and others.

This section of the module creates a blog post and then publishes it to a registered blog account at WordPress, which is a blogging service on the web. The blog relays current events for the Yellville Fitness Center employees. This specific blog post is a communication about the upcoming events.

What should you consider when creating and posting on a blog?

When creating a blog post, you should follow these general guidelines:

1. **Create a blog account on the web.** Many websites exist that allow users to set up a blog free or for a fee. Blogging services that work with Word 2016 include Blogger, SharePoint blog, Telligent Community, TypePad, and WordPress. For illustration purposes in this module, a free blog account was created at WordPress.com.

2. **Register your blog account in Word.** Before you can use Word to publish a blog post, you must register your blog account in Word. This step establishes a connection between Word and your blog account. The first time you create a new blog post, Word will ask if you want to register a blog account. You can click the Register Later button if you want to learn how to create a blog post without registering a blog account.

3. **Create a blog post.** Use Word to enter the text and any graphics in your blog post. Some blogging services accept graphics directly from a Word blog post. Others require that you use a picture hosting service to store pictures you use in a blog post.

4. **Publish a blog post.** When you publish a blog post, the blog post in the Word document is copied to your account at the blogging service. Once the post is published, it appears at the top of the blog webpage. You may need to click the Refresh button in the browser window to display the new post.

TO REGISTER A BLOG ACCOUNT

Once you set up a blog account with a blog provider, you must register it in Word so that you can publish your Word post on the blog account. If you wanted to register a blog account, with WordPress for example, you would perform the following steps.

1. Click the Manage Accounts button (Blog Post tab | Blog group) to display the Blog Accounts dialog box.

2. Click the New button (Blog Accounts dialog box) to display the New Blog Account dialog box.

3. Click the Blog arrow (New Blog Account dialog box) to display a list of blog providers and then select your provider in the list.

4. Click the Next button to display the New [Provider] Account dialog box (i.e., a New WordPress Account dialog box would appear if you selected WordPress as the provider).

5. In the Blog Post URL text box, replace the <Enter your blog URL here> text with the web address for your blog account. (Note that your dialog box may differ, depending on the provider you select.)

Q&A What is a URL?

A URL (Uniform Resource Locator), often called a web address, is the unique address for a webpage. For example, the web address for a WordPress blog account might be smith.wordpress.com; in that case, the complete blog post URL would read as http://smith.wordpress.com/xhlrpc.php in the text box.

6. In the Enter account information area, enter the user name and password you use to access your blog account.

Q&A Should I click the Remember Password check box?

If you do not select this check box, Word will prompt you for a password each time you publish to the blog account.

7. If your blog provider does not allow pictures to be stored, click the Picture Options button, select the correct option for storing your posted pictures, and then click the OK button (Picture Options dialog box).

8. Click the OK button to register the blog account.

9. When Word displays a dialog box indicating the account registration was successful, click the OK button.

To Create a Blank Document for a Blog Post

1 INSERT COMMENTS & TRACK CHANGES | 2 REVIEW COMMENTS & TRACKED CHANGES
3 LINK EXCEL WORKSHEET TO WORD DOCUMENT | 4 CHART WORD TABLE | 5 CREATE & PUBLISH BLOG POST

The following steps create a new blank Word document for a blog post. *Why? Word provides a blog post template you can use to create a blank blog post document.*

- Open the Backstage view.

- Click the New tab in the Backstage view to display the New gallery.

- Click the Blog post thumbnail to select the template and display it in a preview window (Figure 8–63).

Figure 8–63

2

- Click the Create button in the preview window to create a new document based on the selected template (Figure 8–64). If necessary, adjust the zoom so that the text is readable on the screen.

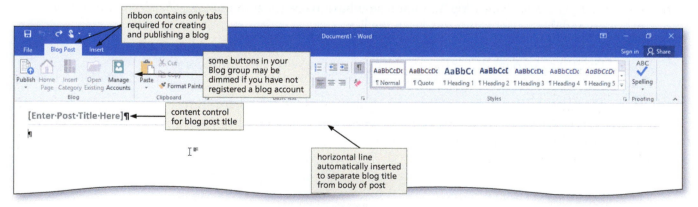

Figure 8–64

Q&A

What if a Register a Blog Account dialog box appears?

Click the Register Later button to skip the registration process at this time. Or, if you have a blog account, you can click the Register Now button and follow the instructions to register your account.

Why did the ribbon change?

When creating a blog post, the ribbon in Word changes to display only the tabs required to create and publish a blog post.

To Enter Text

The next step is to enter the blog post title and text in the blog post. The following steps enter text in the blog post.

1 Click the 'Enter Post Title Here' content control and then type `Appreciation Events` as the blog title.

2 Position the insertion point below the horizontal line and then type these two lines of text, pressing the ENTER key at end of each sentence (Figure 8–65):

`Thank you to everyone for helping our fitness center realize an increase in revenue during the third quarter!`

`See the following calendar for key dates, including appreciation events!`

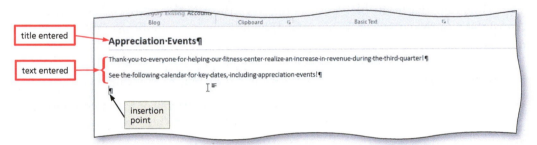

Figure 8–65

Q&A Can I format text in the blog post?
Yes, you can use the Basic Text and other groups on the ribbon to format the post. You also can check spelling using the Proofing group.

To Insert a Quick Table

1 INSERT COMMENTS & TRACK CHANGES | 2 REVIEW COMMENTS & TRACKED CHANGES
3 LINK EXCEL WORKSHEET TO WORD DOCUMENT | 4 CHART WORD TABLE | 5 CREATE & PUBLISH BLOG POST

Word provides several quick tables, which are preformatted table styles that you can customize. Calendar formats are one type of quick table. The following steps insert a calendar in the blog. **Why?** *You will post the upcoming key dates in the calendar.*

1

- Display the Insert tab.

- With the insertion point positioned as shown in Figure 8–65, click the 'Add a Table' button (Insert tab | Tables group) to display the Add a Table gallery.

- Point to Quick Tables in the Add a Table gallery to display the Quick Tables gallery (Figure 8–66).

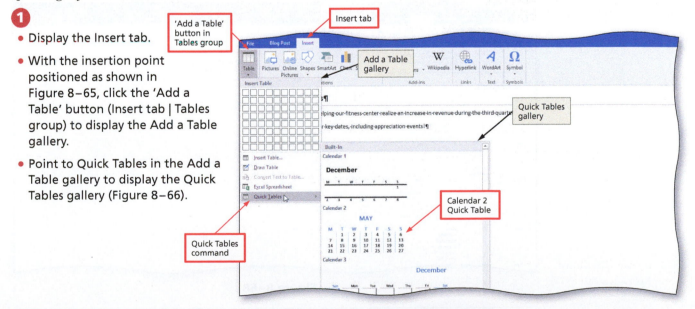

Figure 8–66

2

- Click Calendar 2 in the Quick Tables gallery to insert the selected Quick Table in the document at the location of the insertion point (Figure 8–67).

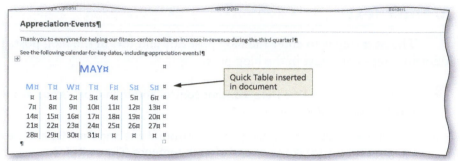

Figure 8–67

To Edit and Format a Table

The calendar in the blog post should show the month of November with a first day of the month starting on Wednesday. The following steps edit the table and apply a quick style.

1 Change the month in the first cell of the table from May to November.

2 Edit the contents of the cells in the table so that the first day of the month starts on a Wednesday and the 30 (the last day of the month) is on a Thursday.

3 Enter the text in the appropriate cells for November 1, 7, 16, and 22, as shown in Figure 8–68.

4 If necessary, display the Table Tools Design tab.

5 Remove the check mark from the First Column check box (Table Tools Design tab | Table Style Options group) because you do not want the first column in the table formatted differently.

6 Apply the 'Grid Table 1 Light - Accent 6' table style to the table.

7 If necessary, left-align the heading and resize the table column widths to 1".

8 Make any other necessary adjustments so that the table appears as shown in Figure 8–68.

9 Save the blog on your hard drive, OneDrive, or other storage location using Fitness Center Blog as the file name.

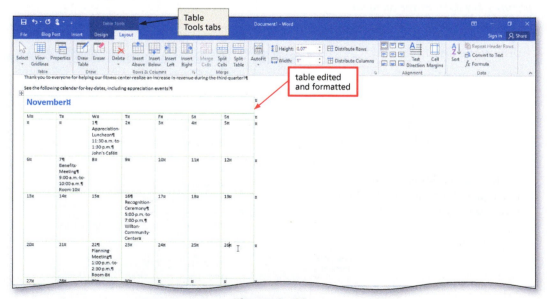

Figure 8–68

Note: If you have not registered a blog account, read the next series of steps without performing them.

To Publish a Blog Post

The following step publishes the blog post. **Why?** *Publishing the blog post places the post at the top of the webpage associated with this blog account.*

- Display the Blog Post tab.
- Click the Publish button (Blog Post tab | Blog group), which causes Word to display a brief message that it is contacting the blog provider and then display a message on the screen that the post was published (Figure 8–69).

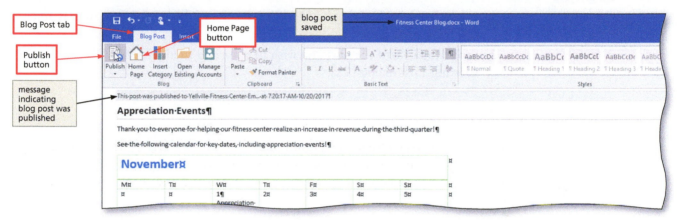

Figure 8–69

To Display a Blog Webpage in a Browser Window

The following steps display the current blog account's webpage in a browser window. **Why?** *You can view a blog account associated with Word if you want to verify a post was successful.*

- Click the Home Page button (Blog Post tab | Blog group) (shown in Figure 8–69), which runs the default browser (Microsoft Edge, in this case) and displays the webpage associated with the registered blog account in the browser window. You may need to click the Refresh button in your browser window to display the most current webpage contents (Figure 8–70).

Figure 8–70

Q&A What if the wrong webpage is displayed?
You may have multiple blog accounts registered with Word. To select a different blog account registered with Word, switch back to Word, click the Manage Accounts button (Blog Post tab | Blog group), click the desired account (Blog Accounts dialog box), and then click the Close button. Then, repeat Step 1.

2

- Exit both the browser and Word.

BTW
Deleting Blog Posts
If you want to delete a blog post from your blog account, sign in to your blog account and then follow the instructions from your blog provider to delete a post from your blog.

To Open an Existing Blog Post

If you wanted to open an existing blog post to modify or view it in Word, you would perform the following steps.

1. Click the Open Existing button (Blog Post tab | Blog group) to display the Open Existing Post dialog box.
2. Select the title of the post you wish to open and then click the OK button (Open Existing Post dialog box).

Summary

In this module, you have learned how to insert comments, track changes, review tracked changes, compare documents and combine documents, link or embed an Excel worksheet to a Word document, chart a table and format the chart, and create and publish a blog post.

CONSIDER THIS: PLAN AHEAD

What decisions will you need to make when creating documents to share or publish?
Use these guidelines as you complete the assignments in this module and create your own shared documents outside of this class.

1. If sharing documents, be certain received files and copied objects are virus free.

a) Do not open files created by others until you are certain they do not contain a virus or other malicious program (malware).

b) Use an antivirus program to verify that any files you use are free of viruses and other potentially harmful programs.

2. If necessary, determine how to copy an object.

a) Your intended use of the Word document will help determine the best method for copying the object: copy and paste, embed, or link.

3. Enhance a document with appropriate visuals.

a) Use visuals to add interest, clarify ideas, and illustrate points. Visuals include tables, charts, and graphical images (i.e., pictures).

4. If desired, post communications on a blog.

Apply Your Knowledge

Reinforce the skills and apply the concepts you learned in this module.

Working with Comments and Tracked Changes

Note: To complete this assignment, you will be required to use the Data Files. Please contact your instructor for information about accessing the Data Files.

Instructions: Run Word. Open the file named Apply 8–1 Social Engineering Draft from the Data Files. The document includes two paragraphs of text that contain tracked changes and comments. You are to insert additional tracked changes and comments, accept and reject tracked changes, and delete comments.

Perform the following tasks:

1. If necessary, customize the status bar so that it displays the Track Changes indicator.

2. Enable (turn on) tracked changes.

3. If requested by your instructor, change the user name and initials so that your name and initials are displayed in the tracked changes and comments.

4. Use the Review tab to navigate to the first comment. Follow the instruction in the comment. Be sure tracked changes are on when you add the required text to the document.

5. When you have finished making the change, reply to the comment with a new comment that includes a message stating you completed the requested task. Mark the comment as done. How does a comment marked as done differ from the other comments? What color are the WU markups? What color are your markups?

6. Insert the following comment for the word, naivety, at the end of the first sentence in the first paragraph: Is this word spelled correctly?

7. With tracked changes on, change the word, that, in the fourth sentence to the word, who.

8. Reply to the comment entered in Step 6 to add this sentence: Be sure to look it up in the dictionary or a dictionary app.

9. Navigate to the remaining comments and read through each one.

10. Print the document with tracked changes.

11. Print only the tracked changes.

12. Save the document with the file name, Apply 8–1 Social Engineering Reviewed (Figure 8–71).

13. Show only your tracked changes in the document. Show all users' tracked changes in the document.

14. Reject the insertion of the words, that are, in the last sentence in the first paragraph.

15. If necessary, delete the comment that begins with the words, Reject the tracked change….

16. Insert the word, social, as a tracked change at the beginning of the second paragraph as instructed in the comment.

17. Accept all the remaining edits in the document.

18. Delete all the remaining comments.

19. Disable (turn off) tracked changes. Remove the Track Changes indicator from the status bar.

20. If requested by your instructor, add your name on a line below the bulleted list.

21. Save the modified file with the file name, Apply 8–1 Social Engineering Final. Submit the documents in the format specified by your instructor.

22. ✳ Answer the questions posed in #5. How would you change the color of your tracked changes?

Figure 8–71

Extend Your Knowledge

Extend the skills you learned in this module and experiment with new skills. You may need to use Help to complete the assignment.

Using Microsoft Graph to Create a Chart

Note: To complete this assignment, you will be required to use the Data Files. Please contact your instructor for information about accessing the Data Files.

Instructions: Run Word. Open the file named Extend 8–1 Workshop Registrations Memo Draft from the Data Files. You will use Microsoft Graph to chart the table in the memo.

Perform the following tasks:

1. Search the web to learn about Microsoft Graph. What is Microsoft Graph?

2. Select the table in the memo to be charted and then insert a Microsoft Graph chart (Figure 8–72) (refer to the section in this module titled To Chart a Word Table Using Microsoft Graph). Close the Datasheet window.

3. Click Help on the menu bar in the Graph window and then click 'Microsoft Graph Help' to open the Graph Help window. Browse through the help information to learn how to use Graph.

4. Click the By Column button on the Standard toolbar to plot the data by column instead of by row. What text appears along the horizontal axis now?

5. Move the legend to the bottom of the chart.

6. Change the chart type to a bar chart.

7. Display the categories on the category axis in reverse order, leaving the value axis at the bottom. *Hint*: Select the Scale tab in Format Axis dialog box and then place check marks in all three check boxes. If necessary, also change the number of tick marks between items to show all classes.

8. Resize the table so that workshop titles appear on a single line.

9. Change the color of the chart area.

10. Change the color of the series named Registrations, which changes the color of the bars.

11. If they are not displayed already, display value axis major gridlines.

12. Center the chart below the table.

13. If requested by your instructor, change the name at the top of the memo to your name.

14. Save the modified file with the file name, Apply 8–1 Workshop Registrations Memo Final. Submit the document in the format specified by your instructor.

15. ✹ Answer the question posed in #4. Do you prefer using Microsoft Graph or the Chart Tools tab to create a chart in Word? Why?

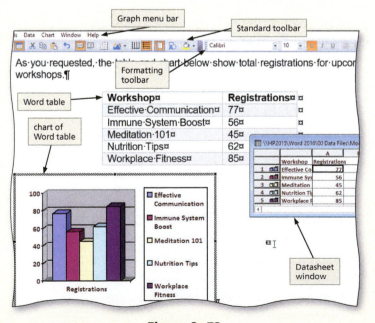

Figure 8–72

Expand Your World

Create a solution that uses cloud or web technologies by learning and investigating on your own from general guidance.

Creating a Blog Account Using a Blogger Service

Instructions: You would like to create a blog account so that you can use Word for blog posts. You research a variety of blogging services and select one for use.

Note: You will use a blog account, many of which you can create at no cost, to complete this assignment. If you do not want to create a blog account, read this assignment without performing the instructions.

Perform the following tasks:

1. Run a browser. Research these blogging services: Blogger, SharePoint blog, Telligent Community, TypePad, and WordPress.

2. Navigate to the blogger service with which you want to set up an account and then follow the instructions to set up an account.

3. Set up your blog in the blogger service.

4. In Word, register your blog account (refer to the section in this module titled To Register a Blog Account).

5. Create a blog post in Word and then publish your blog post to your account.

6. ✳ Which blogger service did you select and why? Would you recommend this blogger service? Why or why not?

In the Labs

Design, create, modify, and/or use a document following the guidelines, concepts, and skills presented in this module. Labs 1 and 2, which increase in difficulty, require you to create solutions based on what you learned in the module; Lab 3 requires you to apply your creative thinking and problem-solving skills to design and implement a solution.

Lab 1: Creating a Memo with an Excel Table and Chart

Note: To complete this assignment, you will be required to use the Data Files. Please contact your instructor for information about accessing the Data Files.

Problem: Your supervisor has asked you to prepare a memo that contains an Excel table and a chart comparing current and projected subscriber enrollments. (*Note:* If you do not have Excel on your computer, create the table using Word instead of importing it from Excel.) You prepare the document shown in Figure 8–73.

Perform the following tasks:

1. Use the Memo (elegant) template to create a new memo and then enter all text in the memo, as shown in the figure. (If you cannot locate this template, open the file called Memo (elegant) from the Data Files.) Delete the row containing the cc in the header. Remove the first line indent from the paragraphs below the header. *Hint*: Use the Paragraph Settings Dialog Box Launcher.

2. Run Excel and open the Lab 8–1 Subscriber Breakdown in Excel workbook, which is located on the Data Files. Below the paragraph in the memo, link the worksheet in the Lab 8–1

Continued >

In the Labs *continued*

Subscriber Breakdown in Excel workbook to the Word memo. (If you do not have Excel on your computer, create the table in Word.)

3. Break the link between the Excel table in the Word document and the Excel worksheet in the Excel workbook. Center the table. If necessary, resize the table so that it looks like the one in Figure 8–73.

4. Insert a line with markers chart, centered below the table.

   a. Copy the rows from the table to the chart spreadsheet window. Remove the Series 3 data series from the chart spreadsheet.

   b. Apply the Style 11 chart style to the chart.

   c. Change the colors to Color 3.

   d. Add a vertical axis title, NUMBER OF SUBSCRIBERS. *Hint:* Use the Chart Elements gallery.

   e. Change the chart title to SUBSCRIBER PROJECTIONS.

   f. Move the legend so that it appears in the upper-right portion of the chart. Remove the check mark from the 'Show the legend without overlapping the chart' check box. If necessary, position the legend as shown in the figure.

   g. Format the vertical axis so that its minimum value (starting point) is 5000 and the maximum is 100000. Add primary major horizontal gridlines to the chart.

   h. Add an "Inside Left Shadow" effect to the chart.

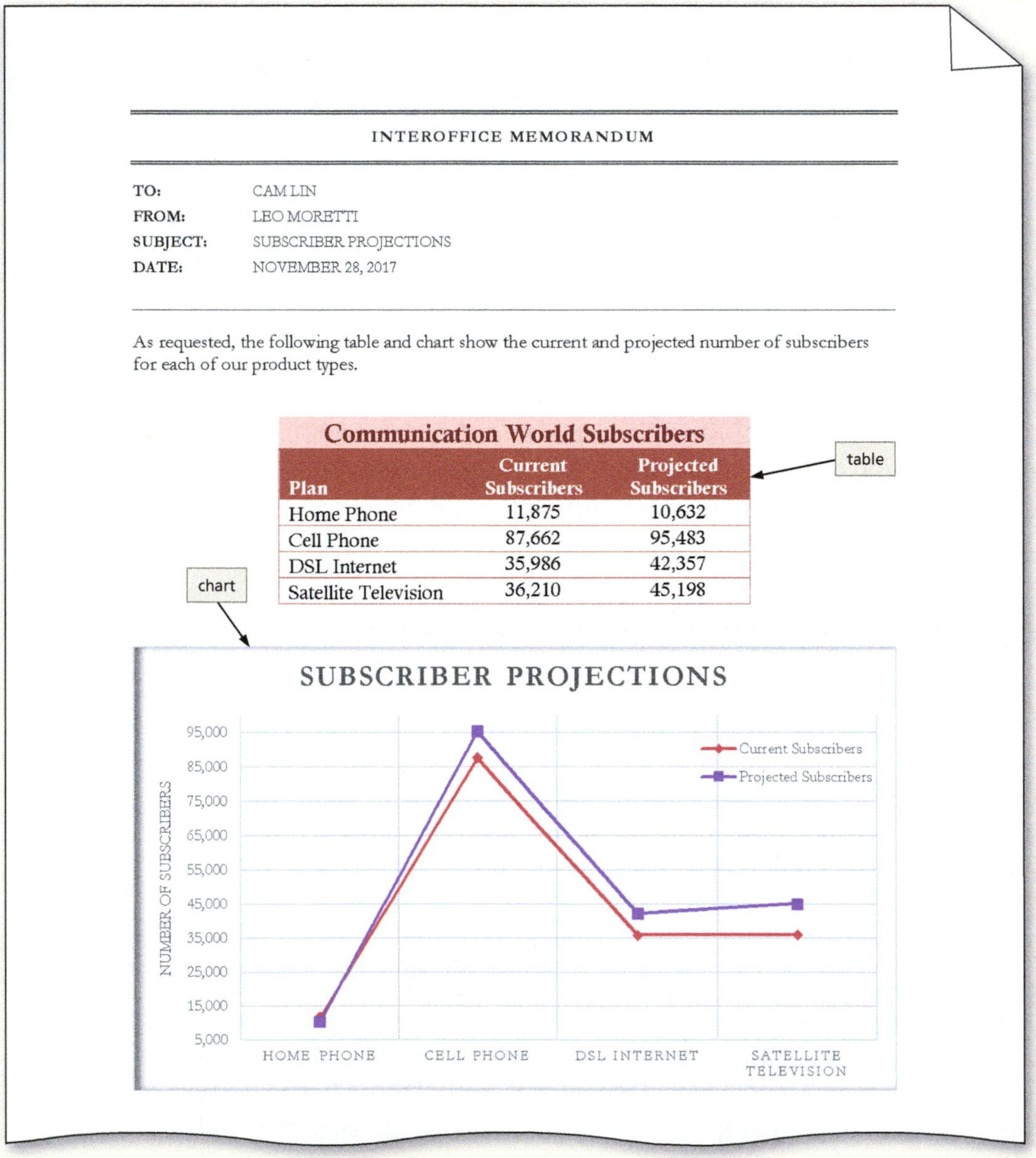

INTEROFFICE MEMORANDUM

TO:	CAM LIN
FROM:	LEO MORETTI
SUBJECT:	SUBSCRIBER PROJECTIONS
DATE:	NOVEMBER 28, 2017

As requested, the following table and chart show the current and projected number of subscribers for each of our product types.

Communication World Subscribers

Plan	Current Subscribers	Projected Subscribers
Home Phone	11,875	10,632
Cell Phone	87,662	95,483
DSL Internet	35,986	42,357
Satellite Television	36,210	45,198

table

chart

SUBSCRIBER PROJECTIONS

Figure 8–73

5. Adjust spacing above and below paragraphs as necessary so that all of the memo contents fit on a single page.

6. If requested by your instructor, change the name at the top of the memo from Leo Moretti to your name.

7. Save the document with Lab 8–1 Subscriber Projections as the file name and then submit it in the format specified by your instructor.

8. ✸ This lab instructed you to remove the first line indent from the paragraphs in the memo. Why do you think this was requested?

Lab 2: **Working with Comments and Tracked Changes**

Note: To complete this assignment, you will be required to use the Data Files. Please contact your instructor for information about accessing the Data Files.

Problem: Your supervisor has asked you to prepare a draft of a document, showing all tracked changes and comments. You mark up the document shown in Figure 8–74.

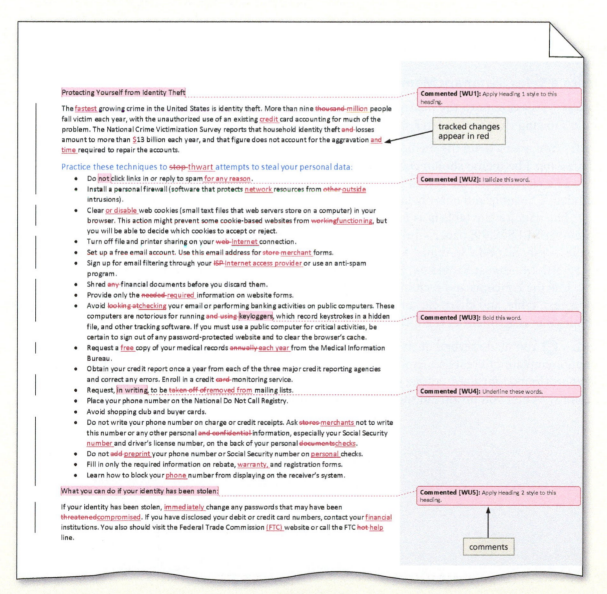

Figure 8–74

Continued >

In the Labs *continued*

Perform the following tasks:

1. Open the file named Lab 8–2 Preventing Identity Theft Draft from the Data Files.

2. Insert the comments and track all changes shown in Figure 8–74.

3. Save the document with the file name, Lab 8–2 Preventing Identity Theft Draft with Markups.

4. Make the changes indicated in the comments and then delete the comments in the document.

5. Accept all tracked changes in the document.

6. Save the document with the file name, Lab 8–2 Preventing Identity Theft Final.

7. Compare the Lab 8–2 Preventing Identity Theft Draft file (original document) with the Lab 8–2 Preventing Identity Theft Final file (revised document). Save the compare result with the file name, Lab 8–2 Preventing Identity Theft Compared.

8. Close all windows and then open the Lab 8–2 Preventing Identity Theft Compared file. Print the document with markups. Use the Review tab to review each change. Close the document without saving.

9. ✺ How could you determine if two documents contained the same content?

Lab 3: **Consider This: Your Turn**

Create a Sales Summary Memo with a Table and Chart

Problem: As assistant to the manager of an office supply store, you have been asked to create a memo showing the third quarter sales figures by category.

Part 1: You are to write the memo to Carlos Mendez with a subject of Third Quarter Sales. Use today's date. The memo should contain a table and chart as specified below.

The wording for the text in the memo is as follows: Third quarter sales figures have been compiled. The table and chart below show sales by category for the third quarter.

The data for the table is as follows: technology – July $15,210.10, August $13,298.11, September $14,879.99; paper – July $3,546.29, August $4,687.19, September $4,983.21; office supplies – July $2,688.23, August $3,021.25, September $2,234.66; and breakroom supplies – July $5,302.14, August $5,843.54, September $6,001.03. Create a chart of all table data.

Use the concepts and techniques presented in this module to create and format the memo and its text, table, and chart. Be sure to check the spelling and grammar of the finished memo. Submit your assignment in the format specified by your instructor.

Part 2: ✺ You made several decisions while creating the memo in this assignment: whether to use a memo template or create a memo from scratch, and how to organize and format the memo, table, and chart (fonts, font sizes, colors, shading, styles, etc.). What was the rationale behind each of these decisions? When you proofread the document, what further revisions did you make and why?

9 | Creating a Reference Document with a Table of Contents and an Index

Objectives

You will have mastered the material in this module when you can:

- Insert a screenshot
- Add and modify a caption
- Create a cross-reference
- Insert and link text boxes
- Compress pictures
- Work in Outline view
- Work with a master document and subdocuments

- Insert a cover page
- Create and modify a table of contents
- Use the Navigation Pane
- Create and update a table of figures
- Build, modify, and update an index
- Create alternating footers
- Add bookmarks

Introduction

During the course of your academic studies and professional activities, you may find it necessary to compose a document that is many pages or even hundreds of pages in length. When composing a long document, you must ensure that the document is organized so that a reader easily can locate material in that document. Sometimes a document of this nature is called a **reference document**.

Project — Reference Document

A **reference document** is any multipage document organized so that users easily can locate material and navigate through the document. Examples of reference documents include user guides, term papers, pamphlets, manuals, proposals, and plans.

The project in this module uses Word to produce the reference document shown in Figure 9–1. This reference document, titled *Using Microsoft Word 2016*, is a

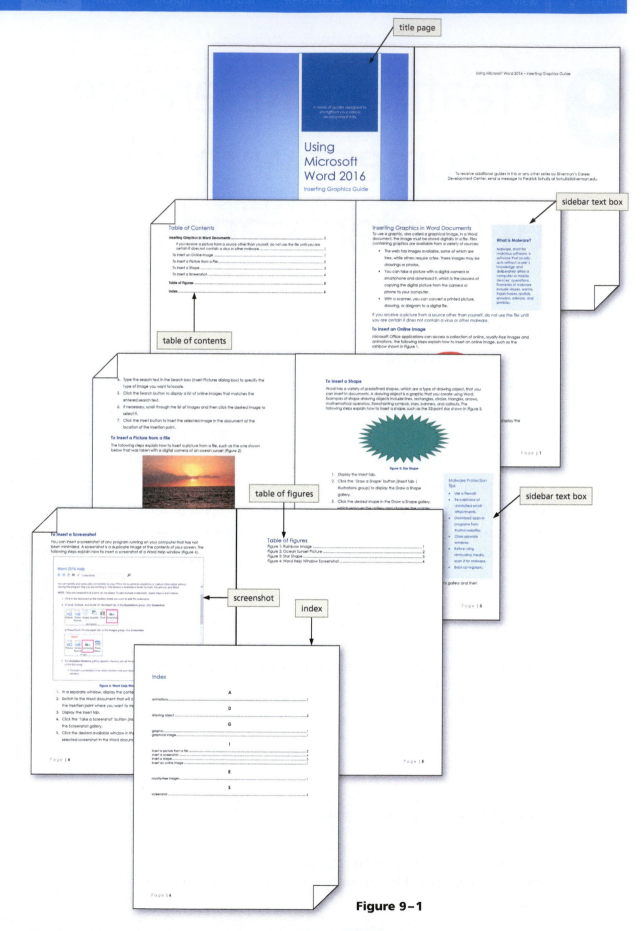

Figure 9–1

multipage guide that is distributed by Silverman College to students and staff. Notice that the inner margin between facing pages has extra space to allow duplicated copies of the document to be bound (i.e., stapled or fastened in some manner) — without the binding covering the words.

The *Using Microsoft Word 2016* reference document begins with a title page designed to entice the target audience to open the document and read it. Next is the copyright page, followed by the table of contents. The document then describes how to insert four types of graphics in a Word document: online image, picture from a file, shape, and screenshot. The end of this reference document has a table of figures and an index to assist readers in locating information contained within the document. A miniature version of the *Using Microsoft Word 2016* reference document is shown in Figure 9–1.

The section of the *Using Microsoft Word 2016* reference document that is titled Inserting Graphics in Word Documents is a draft document that you will modify. The draft document is located on the Data Files. Please contact your instructor for information about accessing the Data Files. After editing content in the draft document, you will incorporate a final version in the reference document.

In this module, you will learn how to create the document shown in Figure 9–1. The following roadmap identifies general activities you will perform as you progress through this module:

1. **MODIFY** a draft of a **REFERENCE DOCUMENT**.
2. **CREATE** a **MASTER DOCUMENT** for the reference document.
3. **ORGANIZE** the **REFERENCE DOCUMENT**.

To Run Word and Change Word Settings

If you are using a computer to step through the project in this module and you want your screens to match the figures in this book, you should change your screen's resolution to 1366 × 768. The following steps run Word, display formatting marks, and change the zoom to page width.

1 Run Word and create a blank document in the Word window. If necessary, maximize the Word window.

2 If the Print Layout button on the status bar is not selected, click it so that your screen is in Print Layout view.

3 To display the page the same width as the document window, if necessary, click the Page Width button (View tab | Zoom group).

BTW

The Ribbon and Screen Resolution
Word may change how the groups and buttons within the groups appear on the ribbon, depending on the computer's screen resolution. Thus, your ribbon may look different from the ones in this book if you are using a screen resolution other than 1366 x 768.

Preparing a Document to Be Included in a Reference Document

Before including the Inserting Graphics Draft document in a longer document, you will make several modifications to the document:

1. Insert a screenshot.
2. Add captions to the images in the document.
3. Insert references to the figures in the text.
4. Mark an index entry.

5. Insert text boxes that contain information about malware.

6. Compress the pictures.

7. Change the bullet symbol.

The following pages outline these changes.

CONSIDER THIS

How should you prepare a document to be included in a longer document?

Ensure that reference elements in a document, such as captions and index entries, are formatted properly and entered consistently.

• **Captions:** A **caption** is text that appears outside of an illustration, usually below it. If the illustration is identified with a number, the caption may include the word, Figure, along with the illustration number (i.e., Figure 1). In the caption, separate the figure number from the text of the figure by a space or punctuation mark, such as a period or colon (Figure 1: Rainbow Image).

• **Index Entries:** If your document will include an index, read through the document and mark any terms or headings that you want to appear in the index. Include any term that the reader may want to locate quickly. Omit figures from index entries if the document will have a table of figures; otherwise, include figures in the index if appropriate.

BTW

Protected View

To keep your computer safe from potentially dangerous files, Word may automatically open certain files in a restricted mode, called Protected View. To see the Protected View settings, click File on the ribbon to open the Backstage view, click the Options tab to display the Word Options dialog box, click Trust Center in the left pane (Word Options dialog box), click the 'Trust Center Settings' button in the right pane to display the Trust Center dialog box, and then click Protected View in the left pane to show the current Protected View settings.

To Open a Document and Save It with a New File Name

The draft document that you will insert in the reference document is named Inserting Graphics Draft. The draft document is located on the Data Files. Please contact your instructor for information about accessing the Data Files. To preserve the contents of the original draft, you save it with a new file name. The following steps open the draft file and then save it with a new file name.

1 Navigate to the location of the Data Files on your hard drive, OneDrive, or other storage location.

2 Open the file named Inserting Graphics Draft.

3 Navigate to the desired save location on your hard drive, OneDrive, or other storage location.

4 Save the file just opened on your hard drive, OneDrive, or other storage location using Inserting Graphics Final as the file name.

5 If the 'Show/Hide ¶' button (Home tab | Paragraph group) is selected, click it to hide formatting marks.

Q&A What if some formatting marks still appear after clicking the 'Show/Hide ¶' button? Open the Backstage view, click the Options tab to display the Word Options dialog box, click Display in the left pane (Word Options dialog box), remove the check mark from the Hidden text check box, and then click the OK button.

6 Display the View tab and then click the Multiple Pages button (View tab | Zoom group) so that you can see all three pages of the document at once (Figure 9–2).

7 When you have finished viewing the document, click the Page Width button (View tab | Zoom group) to display the document as wide as possible in the document window.

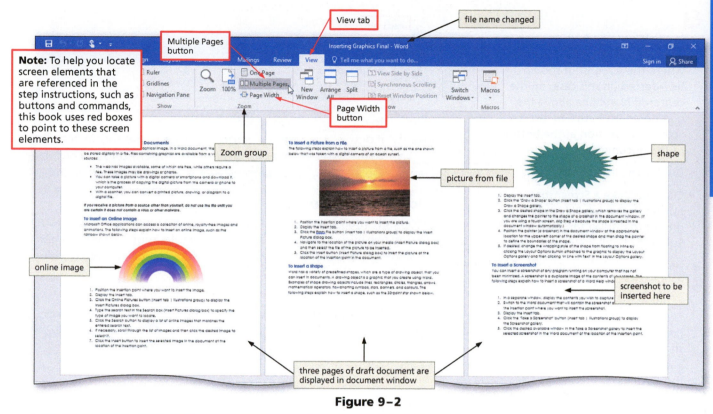

Figure 9–2

To Insert a Screenshot

A **screenshot** is a duplicate image of the contents of your computer or mobile device's screen. The current document is missing a screenshot of a Word Help window. To insert a screenshot, you first must display the screen for which you want a screenshot in a window on your computer or mobile device. *Why? From within Word, you can insert a screenshot of any app running on your computer, provided the app has not been minimized.* The following steps insert a screenshot in a document.

1

- Display the contents you want to capture in a screenshot (in this case, type **screenshots** in the 'Tell me what you want to do' text box, click 'Get Help on "screenshots"' on the menu to open a Word 2016 Help window, and then click the 'Insert a screenshot or clipping - Office Support' link to display the associated Help information. If necessary, scroll through, reposition and resize the Word Help window so that it matches Figure 9–3.

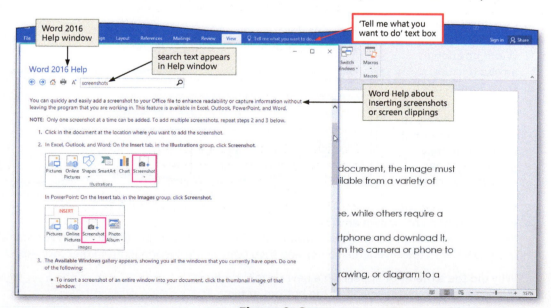

Figure 9–3

- In the Word window, position the insertion point in the document where the screenshot should be inserted (in this case, on the centered blank line above the numbered list in the To Insert a Screenshot section at the bottom of the document).
- Display the Insert tab.
- Click the 'Take a Screenshot' button (Insert tab | Illustrations group) to display the Take a Screenshot gallery (Figure 9–4).

What is a screen clipping?
A screen clipping is a section of a window. When you select Screen Clipping in the Take a Screenshot gallery, the window turns opaque so that you can drag through the part of the window to be included in the document.

Why does my Take a Screenshot gallery show more windows?
You have additional programs running on your desktop, and their windows are not minimized.

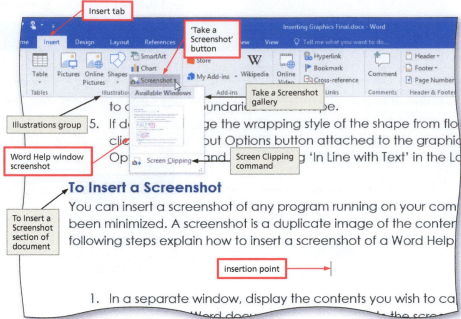

Figure 9–4

- Click the Word Help window screenshot in the Take a Screenshot gallery to insert the selected screenshot in the Word document at the location of the insertion point.
- Click the Shape Height and Shape Width box down arrows (Picture Tools Format tab | Size group) as many times as necessary to resize the screenshot to approximately 5.1" tall by 6.28" wide (Figure 9–5).

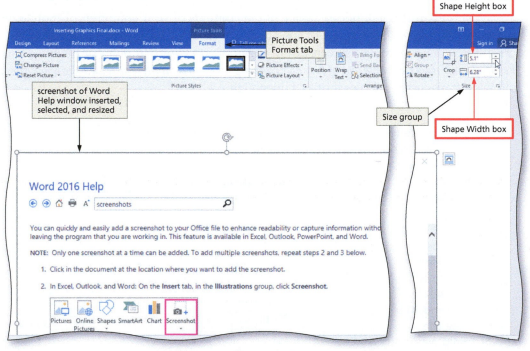

Figure 9–5

Why can I not set the exact measurements shown above?
You may need to click the Advanced Layout: Size Dialog Box Launcher (Picture Tools Format tab | Size group) to display the Size sheet in the Layout dialog box and then remove the checkmark from the 'Lock aspect ratio' check box.

Why did the screenshot appear on a new page?
The screenshot is too tall to fit at the bottom of page 3.

To Add a Caption

In Word, you can add a caption to an equation, a figure, and a table. If you move, delete, or add captions in a document, Word renumbers remaining captions in the document automatically. In this reference document, the captions contain the word, Figure, followed by the figure number, a colon, and a figure description. The following steps add a caption to a graphic, specifically, the screenshot. *Why? The current document contains four images: an image from an online source, a picture from a file, a shape, and a screenshot. All of these images should have captions.*

- If the screenshot is not selected already, click it to select the graphic for which you want a caption.
- Display the References tab.
- Click the Insert Caption button (References tab | Captions group) to display the Caption dialog box with a figure number automatically assigned to the selected graphic (Figure 9–6).

Q&A
Why is the figure number a 1?
No other captions have been assigned in this document yet. When you insert a new caption, or move or delete items containing captions, Word automatically updates caption numbers throughout the document.

What if the Caption text box has the label Table or Equation instead of Figure? Click the Label arrow (Caption dialog box) and then click Figure in the Label list.

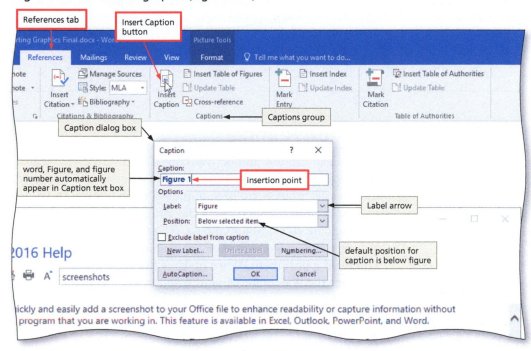

Figure 9–6

- Press the COLON key (:) and then press the SPACEBAR in the Caption text box (Caption dialog box) to place separating characters between the figure number and description.

- Type **Help Window Screenshot** as the figure description (Figure 9–7).

Q&A
Can I change the format of the caption number?
Yes, click the Numbering button (Caption dialog box), adjust the format as desired, and then click the OK button.

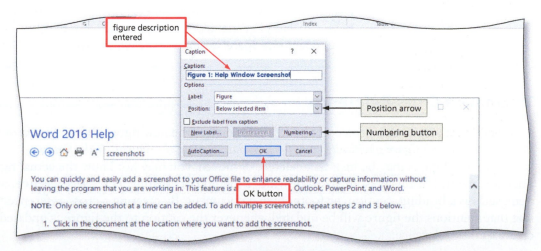

Figure 9–7

3

- Click the OK button to insert the caption below the selected graphic.
- If necessary, scroll to display the caption in the document window (Figure 9–8).

Q&A

How do I change the position of a caption?

Click the Position arrow (Caption dialog box) and then select the desired position of the caption.

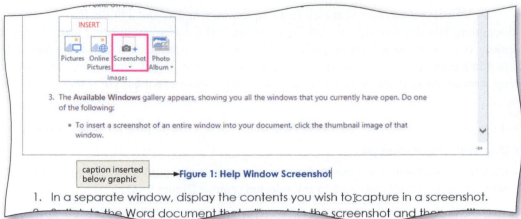

Figure 9–8

Caption Numbers

Each caption number contains a field. In Word, recall that a **field** is a placeholder for data that can change in a document. Examples of fields you have used in previous projects are page numbers, merge fields, IF fields, and the current date. You update caption numbers using the same technique used to update any other field. That is, to update all caption numbers, select the entire document and then press the F9 key, or right-click the field and then click Update Field on the shortcut menu. When you print a document, Word updates the caption numbers automatically, regardless of whether the document window displays the updated caption numbers.

To Hide White Space

White space is the space displayed in the margins at the top and bottom of pages (including any headers and footers) and also space between pages. To make it easier to see the text in this document as you scroll through it, the following step hides white space.

1 Position the pointer in the document window in the space between the pages or below the last page in the document and then double-click when the pointer changes to a 'Hide White Space' button to hide white space.

To Create a Cross-Reference

1 MODIFY REFERENCE DOCUMENT | 2 CREATE MASTER DOCUMENT | 3 ORGANIZE REFERENCE DOCUMENT

The next step in this project is to add a reference to the new figure. *Why? In reference documents, the text should reference each figure specifically and, if appropriate, explain the contents of the figure.*

Because figures may be inserted, deleted, or moved, you may not know the actual figure number in the final document. For this reason, Word provides a method of creating a **cross-reference**, which is a link to an item, such as a heading, caption, or footnote in a document. By creating a cross-reference to the caption, the text that mentions the figure will be updated whenever the caption to the figure is updated. The following steps create a cross-reference.

1

- At the end of the last sentence below the To Insert a Screenshot heading, position the insertion point to the left of the period, press the SPACEBAR, and then press the LEFT PARENTHESIS (( ) key.

- Display the Insert tab.

- Click the 'Insert Cross-reference' button (Insert tab | Links group) to display the Cross-reference dialog box (Figure 9–9).

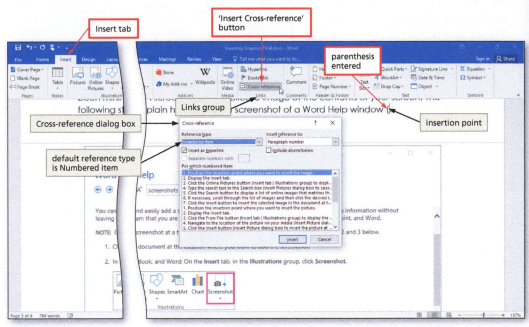

Figure 9–9

2

- Click the Reference type arrow (Cross-reference dialog box) to display the Reference type list; scroll to and then click Figure, which displays a list of figures from the document in the For which caption list (which, at this point, is only one figure).

- If necessary, click 'Figure 1: Help Window Screenshot' in the For which caption list to select the caption to reference.

- Click the 'Insert reference to' arrow and then click 'Only label and number' to instruct Word that the cross-reference in the document should list just the label, Figure, followed by the figure number (Figure 9–10).

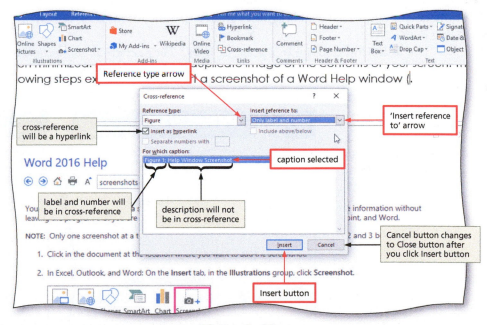

Figure 9–10

3

- Click the Insert button to insert the cross-reference in the document at the location of the insertion point.

What if my cross-reference is shaded in gray?

The cross-reference is a field. Depending on your Word settings, fields may appear shaded in gray to help you identify them on the screen.

4

- Click the Close button (Cross-reference dialog box).

- Press the RIGHT PARENTHESIS ( )) key to close off the cross-reference (Figure 9–11).

Q&A

How do I update a cross-reference if a caption is added, deleted, or moved?

In many cases, Word automatically updates a cross-reference in a document if the item to which it refers changes. To update a cross-reference manually, select the cross-reference and then press the F9 key, or right-click the cross-reference and then click Update Field on the shortcut menu.

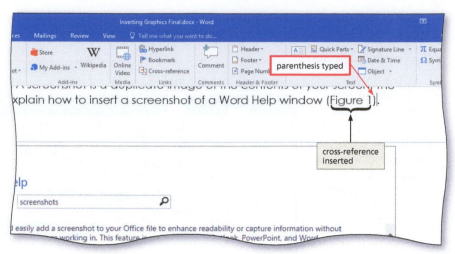

Figure 9–11

Other Ways

1. Click 'Insert Cross-reference' button (References tab | Captions group)

To Go to an Object

1 MODIFY REFERENCE DOCUMENT | 2 CREATE MASTER DOCUMENT | 3 ORGANIZE REFERENCE DOCUMENT

Often, you would like to bring a certain page, graphic, or other part of a document into view in the document window. Although you could scroll through the document to find a desired page, graphic, or part of the document, Word enables you to go to a specific location via the Go To sheet in the Find and Replace dialog box.

The following steps go to a graphic. *Why? The next step in this module is to add a caption to another graphic in the document, so you want to display the graphic in the document window.*

1

- Display the Home tab.

- Click the Find arrow (Home tab | Editing group) to display the Find menu (Figure 9–12).

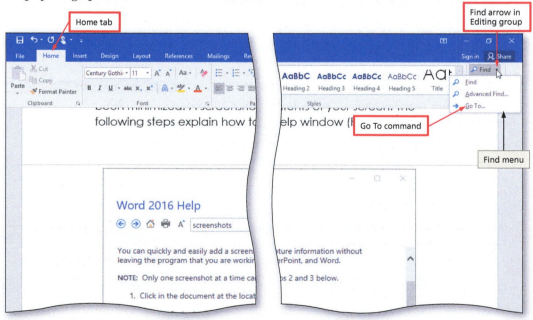

Figure 9–12

- Click Go To on the Find menu to display the Find and Replace dialog box.

- Scroll through the Go to what list and then click Graphic to select it.

- Click the Previous button to display the previous graphic in the document window (which is the star shape, in this case) (Figure 9–13).

- Click Close button to close the dialog box.

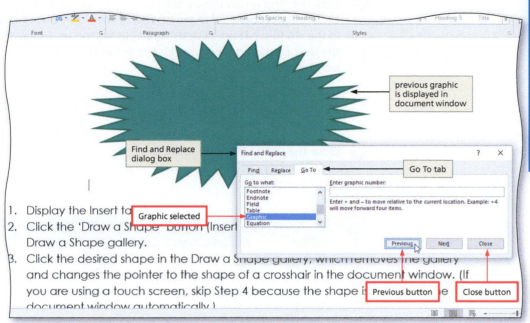

Figure 9–13

Other Ways

1. Press CTRL+G

To Add Captions and Create Cross-References

The previous steps added a caption to the screenshot graphic and then created a cross-reference to that caption. The following steps add captions to the remaining three graphics in the document (that is, the star shape, the picture, and the online image).

1 Click the star shape to select the graphic for which you want to add a caption.

2 Click the Insert Caption button (References tab | Captions group) to display the Caption dialog box with a figure number automatically assigned to the selected graphic.

3 Press the COLON (:) key and then press the SPACEBAR in the Caption text box (Caption dialog box) to place separating characters between the figure number and description.

4 Type **Star Shape** as the figure description and then click the OK button to insert the caption below the selected graphic.

5 At the end of the last sentence above the graphic, change the word, below, to the word, in, and then press the SPACEBAR.

6 Click the 'Insert Cross-reference' button (Insert or References tab | Links or Captions group) to display the Cross-reference dialog box, if necessary, click 'Figure 1: Star Shape' in the For which caption list to select the caption to reference, click the Insert button to insert the cross-reference at the location of the insertion point, and then click the Close button in the Cross-reference dialog box.

Q&A Why did I not need to change the settings for the reference type and reference to in the dialog box?
Word retains the previous settings in the dialog box.

BTW

Touch Screen Differences
The Office and Windows interfaces may vary if you are using a touch screen. For this reason, you might notice that the function or appearance of your touch screen differs slightly from this module's presentation.

7 Click the Find arrow (Home tab | Editing group) to display the Find menu and then click Go To on the Find menu to display the Go To dialog box. With Graphic selected in the Go to what list, click the Previous button to display the previous graphic in the document window (which is the ocean sunset picture in this case). Click the Close button to close the dialog box.

8 Repeat Steps 1 through 7 to add the caption, Ocean Sunset Picture, to the picture of the ocean sunset and the caption, Rainbow Image, to the image of the rainbow. Also add a cross-reference at the end of the sentences above each image (Figure 9–14).

9 Close the Cross-reference dialog box.

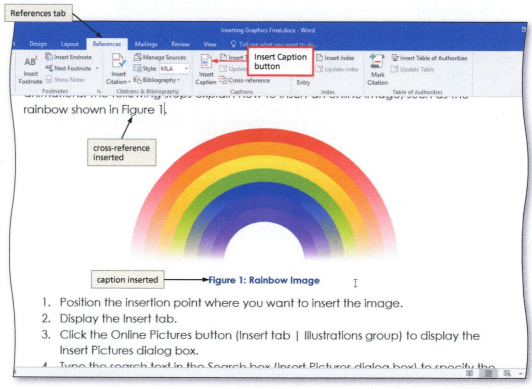

Figure 9–14

To Mark an Index Entry

1 MODIFY REFERENCE DOCUMENT | 2 CREATE MASTER DOCUMENT | 3 ORGANIZE REFERENCE DOCUMENT

The last page of the reference document in this project is an index, which lists important terms discussed in the document along with each term's corresponding page number. For Word to generate the index, you first must mark any text you wish to appear in the index. **Why?** *When you mark an index entry, Word creates a field that it uses to build the index.* Index entry fields are hidden and are displayed on the screen only when you show formatting marks, that is, when the 'Show/Hide ¶' button (Home tab | Paragraph group) is selected.

In this document, you want the word, animations, in the first sentence below the To Insert an Online Image heading to be marked as an index entry. The following steps mark an index entry.

①

- Select the text you wish to appear in the index (the word, animations, in the first sentence of the document in this case).

- Click the Mark Entry button (References tab | Index group) to display the Mark Index Entry dialog box (Figure 9–15).

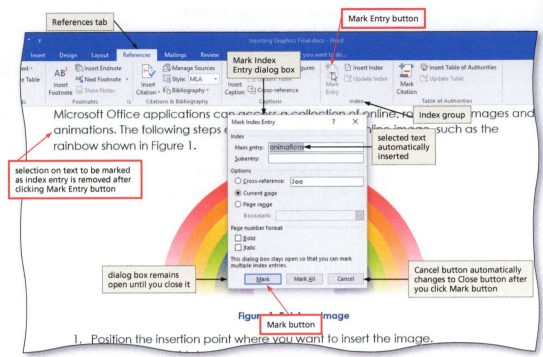

Figure 9–15

②

- Click the Mark button (Mark Index Entry dialog box) to mark the selected text in the document as an index entry.

Q&A Why do formatting marks now appear on the screen?
When you mark an index entry, Word automatically shows formatting marks (if they are not showing already) so that you can see the index entry field. Notice that the marked index entry begins with the letters, XE.

- Click the Close button in the Mark Index Entry dialog box to close the dialog box (Figure 9–16).

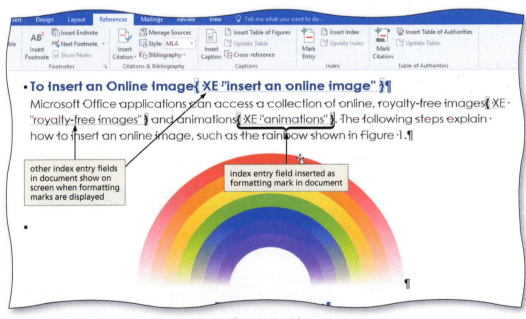

Figure 9–16

Q&A How could I see all index entries marked in a document?
With formatting marks displaying, you could scroll through the document, scanning for all occurrences of XE, or you could use the Navigation Pane (that is, place a check mark in the 'Open the Navigation Pane' check box (View tab | Show group)) to find all occurrences of XE.

Other Ways

1. Select text, press ALT+SHIFT+X

TO MARK MULTIPLE INDEX ENTRIES

Word leaves the Mark Index Entry dialog box open until you close it, which allows you to mark multiple index entries without having to reopen the dialog box repeatedly. To mark multiple index entries, you would perform the following steps.

1. With the Mark Index Entry dialog box displayed, click in the document window; scroll to and then select the next index entry.
2. If necessary, click the Main entry text box (Mark Index Entry dialog box) to display the selected text in the Main entry text box.
3. Click the Mark button.
4. Repeat Steps 1 through 3 for all entries. When finished, click the Close button in the Mark Index Entry dialog box.

To Hide Formatting Marks

To remove the clutter of index entry fields from the document, you should hide formatting marks. The following step hides formatting marks.

1 If the 'Show/Hide ¶' button (Home tab | Paragraph group) is selected, click it to hide formatting marks.

Q&A What if the index entries still appear after clicking the 'Show/Hide ¶' button?
Open the Backstage view, click the Options tab to display the Word Options dialog box, click Display in the left pane (Word Options dialog box), remove the check mark from the Hidden text check box, and then click the OK button.

To Change Paragraph Spacing in a Document

1 MODIFY REFERENCE DOCUMENT | 2 CREATE MASTER DOCUMENT | 3 ORGANIZE REFERENCE DOCUMENT

In Word, you easily can expand or condense the amount of space between lines in all paragraphs in a document. The following steps expand paragraph spacing. **Why?** *You feel the document text would be easier to read if the paragraphs were more open.*

1

- Display the Design tab.
- Click the Paragraph Spacing button (Design tab | Document Formatting group) to display the Paragraph Spacing gallery (Figure 9–17).

Experiment

- Point to various spacing commands in the Paragraph Spacing gallery and watch the paragraphs conform to that spacing.

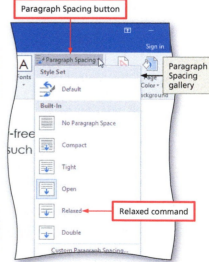

Figure 9–17

2

- Click Relaxed in the Paragraph Spacing gallery to expand the spacing of paragraphs in the document.

To Show White Space

For the remainder of creating this project, you would like to see headers, footers, and margins. Thus, you should show white space. The following step shows white space.

 Position the pointer in the document window on the page break and then double-click when the pointer changes to a 'Show White Space' button to show white space.

To Insert a Sidebar Text Box

1 MODIFY REFERENCE DOCUMENT | 2 CREATE MASTER DOCUMENT | 3 ORGANIZE REFERENCE DOCUMENT

A **sidebar text box** is a text box that runs across the top or bottom of a page or along the right or left edge of a page. The following steps insert a built-in sidebar text box. **Why?** *Sidebar text boxes take up less space on the page than text boxes positioned in the middle of the page.*

- Be sure the insertion point is near the top of page 1 of the document, as shown in Figure 9–18.

Q&A Does the insertion point need to be at the top of the page?
The insertion point should be close to where you want to insert the text box.

- Display the Insert tab.

- Click the 'Choose a Text Box' button (Insert tab | Text group) to display the Choose a Text Box gallery.

🔎 Experiment

- Scroll through the Choose a Text Box gallery to see the variety of available text box styles.

- Scroll to display Grid Sidebar in the Choose a Text Box gallery (Figure 9–18).

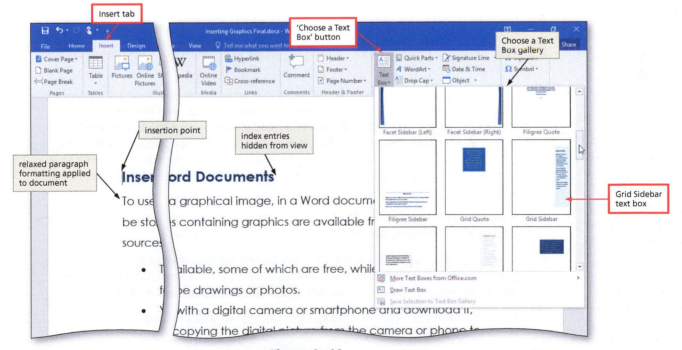

Figure 9–18

2

- Click Grid Sidebar in the Choose a Text Box gallery to insert that text box style in the document (Figure 9–19).

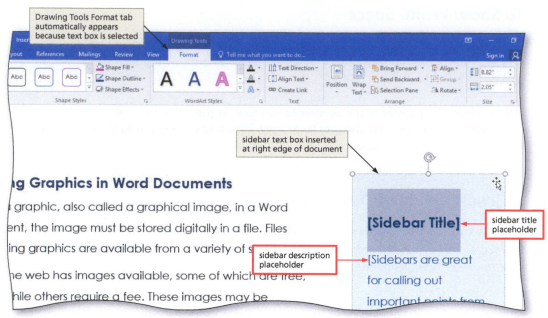

Figure 9–19

Other Ways

1. Click 'Explore Quick Parts' button (Insert tab | Text group), click 'Building Blocks Organizer' on Explore Quick Parts menu, select desired text box name in Building blocks list, click Insert button

To Enter and Format Text in the Sidebar Text Box

The next step is to enter the text in the sidebar text box. The following steps enter text in the text box.

1 If necessary, click the sidebar title placeholder in the text box to select it.

2 Type **What Is Malware?** and then change the font size of the entered text to 12 point.

3 Click the sidebar description placeholder and then type the following paragraph: **Malware, short for malicious software, is software that usually acts without a user's knowledge and deliberately alters a computer or mobile device's operations. Examples of malware include viruses, worms, trojan horses, rootkits, spyware, adware, and zombies.** Change the font size of the entered text to 10 point.

4 Press the ENTER key. Change the font size to 12 point. Type **Malware Protection Tips** and then press the ENTER key.

5 Change the font size to 10 point. Click the Bullets button (Home tab | Paragraph group) to bullet the list. Click the Decrease Indent button (Home tab | Paragraph group) to move the bullet symbol left one-half inch. Type **Use a firewall.**

6 Press the ENTER key. Type **Be suspicious of unsolicited email attachments.**

7 Press the ENTER key. Type **Download apps or programs from trusted websites.**

8 Press the ENTER key. Type `Close spyware windows.`

9 Press the ENTER key. Type `Before using removable media, scan it for malware.` If necessary, drag the bottom of the text box down to make it longer so that all of the entered text is visible.

10 Press the ENTER key. Type `Back up regularly.`

11 Click the One Page button (View tab | Zoom group) so that you can see all of the entered text at once (Figure 9–20).

12 Change the zoom to page width.

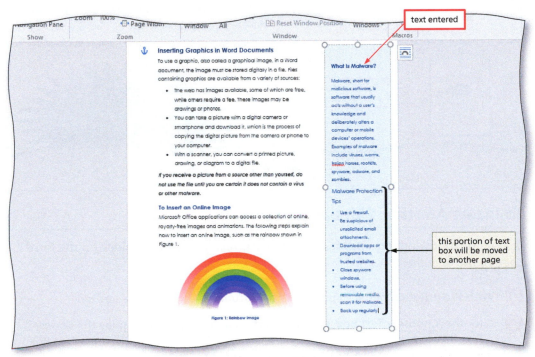

Figure 9–20

To Use the Navigation Pane to Go to a Page

Instead of one long text box, this project splits the text box across the top of two pages, specifically, the first and third pages of this document. The following steps use the Navigation Pane to display page 3 in the document window so that you can insert another text box on that page.

1 If necessary, display the View tab. Place a check mark in the 'Open the Navigation Pane' check box (View tab | Show group) to open the Navigation Pane at the left edge of the Word window.

2 Click the Pages tab in the Navigation Pane to display thumbnail images of the pages in the document.

3 Scroll to and then click the thumbnail of the third page in the Navigation Pane to display the top of the selected page in the top of the document window (Figure 9–21).

4 Leave the Navigation Pane open for use in the next several steps.

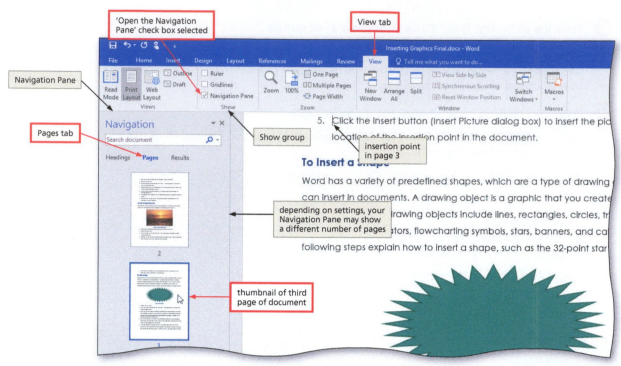

Figure 9-21

BTW

Deleting Building Blocks

To delete an existing building block, click the 'Explore Quick Parts' button (Insert tab | Text group) to display the Explore Quick Parts menu, click 'Building Blocks Organizer' on the Explore Quick Parts menu to display the Building Blocks Organizer dialog box, select the building block to delete (Building Blocks Organizer dialog box), click the Delete button, click the Yes button in the dialog box that appears, and then close the Building Blocks Organizer dialog box.

To Insert Another Sidebar Text Box

The following steps insert a Grid Sidebar text box building block on the third page in the document.

1 With the insertion point on page 3 in the document, display the Insert tab.

2 Click the 'Choose a Text Box' button (Insert tab | Text group) to display the Choose a Text Box gallery and then locate and select Grid Sidebar in the Choose a Text Box gallery to insert that text box style in the document.

3 Press the DELETE key four times to delete the current contents from the text box (Figure 9-22).

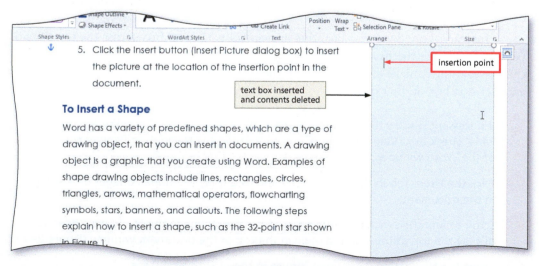

Figure 9-22

To Link Text Boxes

1 MODIFY REFERENCE DOCUMENT | 2 CREATE MASTER DOCUMENT | 3 ORGANIZE REFERENCE DOCUMENT

Word allows you to link two separate text boxes. ***Why?*** *You can flow text from one text box into the other.* To link text boxes, the second text box must be empty, which is why you deleted the contents of the text box in the previous steps. The following steps link text boxes.

- Click the thumbnail of the first page in the Navigation Pane to display the top of the selected page in the document window.

- Click the text box on the first page to select it.

- If necessary, display the Drawing Tools Format tab.

- Click the Create Link button (Drawing Tools Format tab | Text group), which changes the pointer to the shape of a cup.

- Move the pointer in the document window to see its new shape (Figure 9–23).

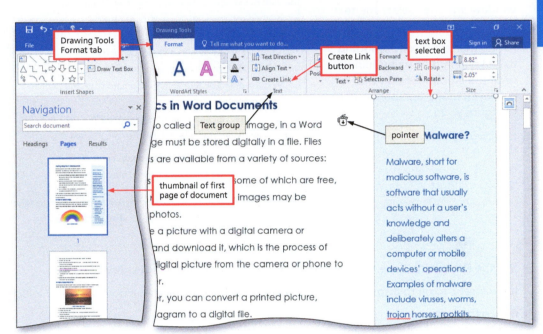

Figure 9–23

- Scroll through the document to display the second text box, which is located on the third page, in the document window.

Q&A

Can I use the Navigation Pane to go to the second text box?

No. If you click in the Navigation Pane, the link process will stop and the pointer will return to its default shape.

- Position the pointer in the empty text box, so that the pointer shape changes to a pouring cup (Figure 9–24).

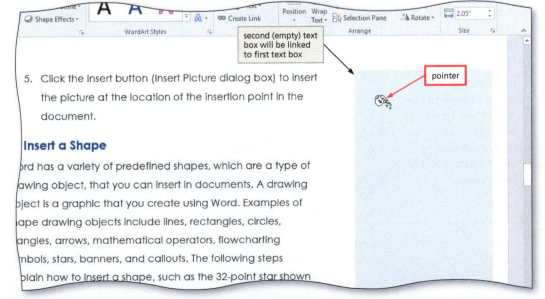

Figure 9–24

3

- Click the empty text box to link it to the first text box (or, if using a touch screen, you will need to use a stylus to tap the empty text box).

- If necessary, scroll to display the first text box in the document window and then select the text box.

- Resize the text box by dragging its bottom-middle sizing handle until the amount of text that is displayed in the text box is similar to Figure 9–25.

Q&A How would I remove a link?
Select the text box in which you created the link and then click the Break Link button (Drawing Tools Format tab | Text group).

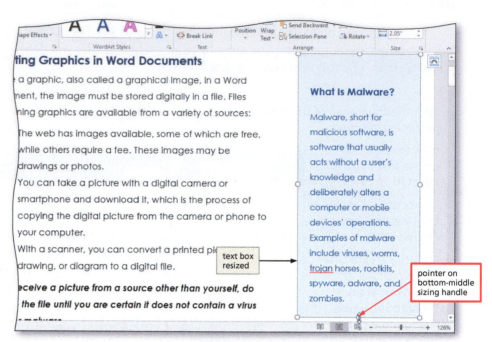

Figure 9–25

4

- Use the Navigation Pane to display the third page in the document window.

- If necessary, scroll to display the second text box in the document window and then select the text box.

- Resize the text box by dragging its bottom-middle sizing handle until the amount of text that is displayed in the text box is similar to Figure 9–26.

- Drag the entire text box to position it as shown in Figure 9–26.

- If necessary, insert a page break to the left of the To Insert a Shape heading so that the heading begins at the top of third page.

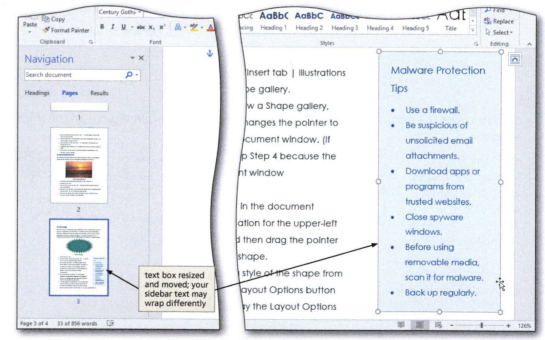

Figure 9–26

To Compress Pictures

If you plan to use email to send a Word document that contains pictures or graphics or post it for downloading, you may want to reduce its file size to speed up file transmission time. ***Why?*** *Pictures and other graphics in Word documents can increase the size of these files.* In Word, you can compress pictures, which reduces the size of the Word document. Compressing the pictures in Word does not cause any loss in their original quality. The following steps compress pictures in a document.

1
- Click a picture in the document to select it, such as the ocean sunset, and then display the Picture Tools Format tab.

- Click the Compress Pictures button (Picture Tools Format tab | Adjust group) to display the Compress Pictures dialog box.

- If the 'Apply only to this picture' check box (Compress Pictures dialog box) contains a check mark, remove the check mark so that all pictures in the document are compressed.

- If necessary, click 'Print (220 ppi): excellent quality on most printers and screens' in the Target output area to specify how images should be compressed (Figure 9–27).

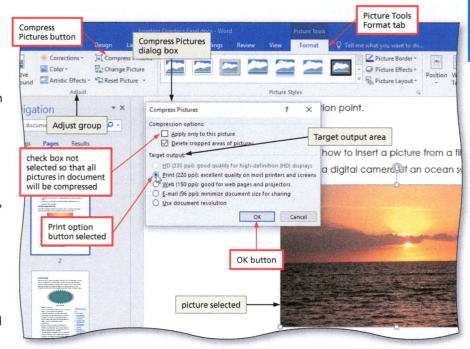

Figure 9–27

2
- Click the OK button to compress all pictures in the document.

Q&A Can I compress a single picture?
Yes. Select the picture and then place a check mark in the 'Apply only to this picture' check box (Compress Pictures dialog box).

> **Other Ways**
>
> 1. Click the Tools button in Save As dialog box, click Compress Pictures on Tools menu, select options (Compress Pictures dialog box), click OK button

TO SAVE PICTURES IN OTHER FORMATS

You can save any graphic in a document as a picture file for use in other documents or apps. If you wanted to save a graphic in a Word document, you would perform the following steps.

1. Right-click the graphic to display a shortcut menu.
2. Click 'Save as Picture' on the shortcut menu to display the File Save dialog box.
3. Navigate to the location you want to save the graphic.

BTW

Compressing Pictures
Selecting a lower ppi (pixels per inch) in the Target output area (Compress Picture dialog box) creates a smaller document file, but also lowers the quality of the images.

4. Click the 'Save as type' arrow (File Save dialog box) and then select the graphic type for the saved graphic.

5. Click the Save button (File Save dialog box) to save the graphic in the specified location using the specified graphic type.

To Change the Symbol Format in a Bulleted List

1 MODIFY REFERENCE DOCUMENT | 2 CREATE MASTER DOCUMENT | 3 ORGANIZE REFERENCE DOCUMENT

The following steps change the symbol in a bulleted list. **Why?** *The project in this module uses a square bullet symbol for the bulleted list instead of the default round bullet symbol.* Word provides several predefined bullet symbols for use in bulleted lists.

1

• Navigate to the first page and then select the bulleted list for which you want to change the bullet symbol (in this case, the three bulleted paragraphs on the first page).

• Click the Bullets arrow (Home tab | Paragraph group) to display the Bullets gallery (Figure 9–28).

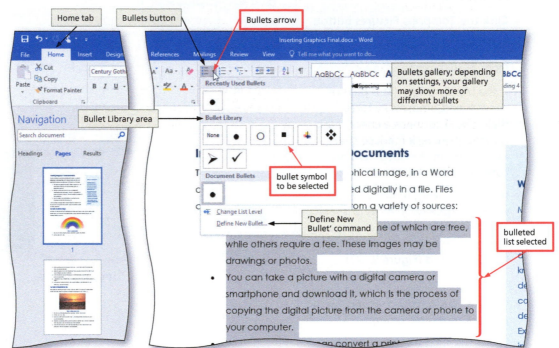

Figure 9–28

2

• Click the desired bullet symbol in the Bullet Library area to change the bullet symbol on the selected bulleted list (Figure 9–29).

Can I select any bullet symbol in the Bullet Library area?
Yes. You also can click 'Define New Bullet' in the Bullets gallery if the bullet symbol you desire is not shown in the Bullet Library area.

To use a graphic, also called a graphical image, in a Word document, the image must be stored digitally in a file. Files containing graphics are available from a variety of sources:

bullet symbol changed

• The web has images available, some of which are free, while others require a fee. These images may be drawings or photos.

• You can take a picture with a digital camera or smartphone and download it, which is the process of copying the digital picture from the camera or phone to your computer.

• With a scanner, you can convert a printed picture, drawing, or diagram to a digital file.

What Is Malw

Malware, short f malicious softwo software that usu acts without a us knowledge and deliberately alte computer or mo devices' operat Examples of ma include viruses, trojan horses, ro

Figure 9–29

3

• Click anywhere to remove the selection from the text.

• Save the document again on the same storage location with the same file name.

To Close Open Panes, Documents, and Windows

The following steps close the open Word document and the Word Help window.

1 Close the Navigation Pane.

2 Close the open document (leave Word running).

3 If necessary, display the Word Help window and close it.

TO RECOVER UNSAVED DOCUMENTS (DRAFT VERSIONS)

If you accidently exit Word without saving a document, you may be able to recover the unsaved document, called a **draft version**, in Word. If you wanted to recover an unsaved document, you would perform these steps.

1. Run Word and create a blank document in the Word window.
2. Open the Backstage view and then, if necessary, click the Open tab to display the Open gallery. Scroll to the bottom of the Recent Documents list. Click the 'Recover Unsaved Documents' button to display an Open dialog box that lists unsaved files retained by Word.

    or

    Open the Backstage view and then, if necessary, click the Info tab to display the Info gallery. Click the Manage Document button to display the Manage Document menu. Click 'Recover Unsaved Documents' on the Manage Document menu to display an Open dialog box that lists unsaved files retained by Word.
3. Select the file to recover and then click the Open button to display the unsaved file in the Word window.
4. To save the document, click the Save As button on the Message Bar.

TO DELETE ALL UNSAVED DOCUMENTS (DRAFT VERSIONS)

If you wanted to delete all unsaved documents, you would perform these steps.

1. Run Word and create a blank document in the Word window.
2. Open the Backstage view and then, if necessary, click the Info tab to display the Info gallery.
3. Click the Manage Document button to display the Manage Document menu.
4. If available, click 'Delete All Unsaved Documents' on the Manage Document menu.
5. When Word displays a dialog box asking if you are sure you want to delete all copies of unsaved files, click the Yes button to delete all unsaved documents.

BTW

Bullets
You can select from a variety of other bullet symbols or change the font attributes of a bullet by clicking 'Define New Bullet' in the Bullets gallery and then clicking the Symbol button or Font button in the Define New Bullet dialog box. You also can change the level of a bullet by clicking 'Change List Level' in the Bullets gallery.

BTW

Distributing a Document
Instead of printing and distributing a hard copy of a document, you can distribute the document electronically. Options include sending the document via email; posting it on cloud storage (such as OneDrive) and sharing the file with others; posting it on social media, a blog, or other website; and sharing a link associated with an online location of the document. You also can create and share a PDF or XPS image of the document, so that users can view the file in Adobe Reader or XPS Viewer instead of in Word.

Break Point: If you wish to take a break, this is a good place to do so. You can exit Word now. To resume at a later time, run Word and continue following the steps from this location forward.

BTW
Master Documents
Master documents can be used when multiple people prepare different sections of a document or when a document contains separate elements, such as the modules in a book. If multiple people in a network need to work on the same document simultaneously, each person can work on a section (subdocument); all subdocuments can be stored together collectively in a master document on the network server.

Working with a Master Document

When you are creating a document that includes other files, you may want to create a master document to organize the documents. A **master document** is simply a document that contains links to one or more other documents, each of which is called a **subdocument**. In addition to subdocuments, a master document can contain its own text and graphics.

In this project, the master document file is named Using Microsoft Word 2016 - Inserting Graphics Guide. This master document file contains a link to one subdocument: Inserting Graphics Final. The master document also contains other items: a title page, a copyright page, a table of contents, a table of figures, and an index. The following sections create this master document and insert the necessary elements in the document to create the finished Using Microsoft Word 2016 – Inserting Graphics Guide document.

To Change the Document Theme

The first step in creating this master document is to change its document theme to Slice. The following steps change the document theme.

1 If necessary, run Word and create a new blank document.

2 Click Design on the ribbon to display the Design tab.

3 Click the Themes button (Design tab | Document Formatting group) to display the Themes gallery.

4 Click Slice in the Themes gallery to change the document theme to the selected theme.

Outlines

To create a master document, Word must be in Outline view. You then enter the headings of the document as an outline using Word's built-in heading styles. In an outline, the major heading is displayed at the left margin with each subordinate, or lower-level, heading indented. In Word, the built-in Heading 1 style is displayed at the left margin in Outline view. Heading 2 style is indented below Heading 1 style, Heading 3 style is indented further, and so on. (Outline view works similarly to multilevel lists.)

You do not want to use a built-in heading style for the paragraphs of text within the document, because when you create a table of contents, Word places all lines formatted using the built-in heading styles in the table of contents. Thus, the text below each heading is formatted using the Body Text style.

Each heading should print at the top of a new page. Because you might want to format the pages within a heading differently from those pages in other headings, you insert next page section breaks between each heading.

To Switch to Outline View

The following steps switch to Outline view. *Why? To create a master document, Word must be in Outline view.*

- Display the View tab (Figure 9–30).

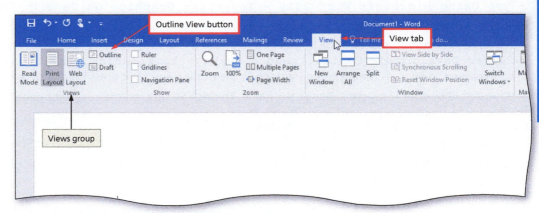

Figure 9–30

- Click the Outline View button (View tab | Views group), which displays the Outlining tab on the ribbon and switches to Outline view.

- Be sure the 'Show Text Formatting' check box is selected and the 'Show First Line Only' check box is not selected (Outlining tab | Outline Tools group) (Figure 9–31).

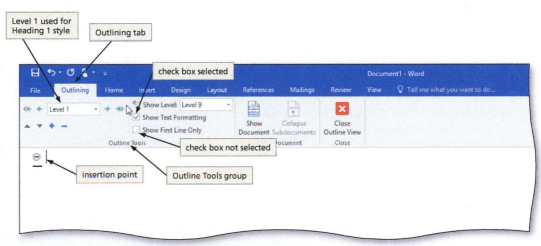

Figure 9–31

To Add Entries in Outline View

The Using Microsoft Word 2016 – Inserting Graphics Guide document contains these three major headings: Inserting Graphics in Word Documents, Table of Figures, and Index. The heading, Inserting Graphics in Word Documents, is not entered in the outline. *Why not? It is part of the subdocument inserted in the master document.*

The first page of the outline (the copyright page) does not contain a heading; instead it contains three paragraphs of body text, which you enter directly in the outline. The Inserting Graphics in Word Documents content is inserted from the subdocument. You will instruct Word to create the content for the Table of Figures and Index later in this module. The following steps create an outline that contains headings and body text to be used in the master document.

- Click the 'Demote to Body Text' button (Outlining tab | Outline Tools group), so that you can enter the paragraphs of text for the copyright page.

- Type **Using Microsoft Word 2016 – Inserting Graphics Guide** as the first paragraph in the outline and then press the ENTER key.

- Type **To receive additional guides in this or any other series by Silverman's Career Development Center, send a message to Fredrick Schultz at fschultz@ silverman.edu.** as the second paragraph in the outline and then press the ENTER key.

  If requested by your instructor, change the name, Fredrick Schultz, on the copyright page to your name.

Q&A Why is only my first line of text in the paragraph displayed?
Remove the check mark from the 'Show First Line Only' check box (Outlining tab | Outline Tools group).

- Right-click the hyperlink (in this case, the email address) to display a shortcut menu and then click Remove Hyperlink on the shortcut menu.

- Click the third Body Text style bullet and then type **Copyright 2017** as the third paragraph and then press the ENTER key.

- Click the 'Promote to Heading 1' button (Outlining tab | Outline Tools group) because you are finished entering body text and will enter the remaining headings in the outline next (Figure 9–32).

Q&A Could I press SHIFT+TAB instead of clicking the 'Promote to Heading 1' button?
Yes.

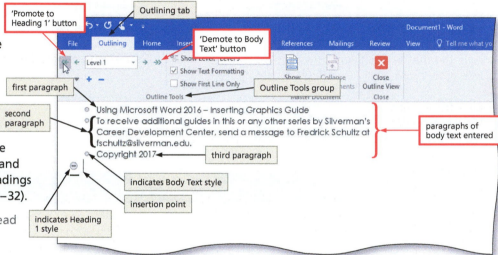

Figure 9–32

- Display the Layout tab.

- Click the 'Insert Page and Section Breaks' button (Layout tab | Page Setup group) and then click Next Page in the Section Breaks area in the Insert Page and Section Breaks gallery because you want to enter a next page section break before the next heading.

- Type **Table of Figures** and then press the ENTER key.

- Repeat Step 2.

- Type **Index** as the last entry (Figure 9–33).

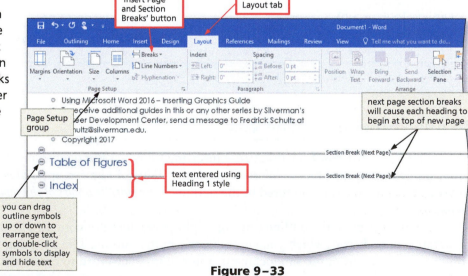

Figure 9–33

Q&A Why do the outline symbols contain a minus sign?
The minus sign means the outline level does not have any subordinate levels. If an outline symbol contains a plus sign, it means the outline level has subordinate levels.

To Show First Line Only

Users often instruct Word to display just the first line of each paragraph of body text. ***Why?*** *When only the first line of each paragraph is displayed, the outline often is more readable.* The following step displays only the first line of body text paragraphs.

- Display the Outlining tab.

- Place a check mark in the 'Show First Line Only' check box (Outlining tab | Outline Tools group), so that Word displays only the first line of each paragraph (Figure 9–34).

Q&A How would I redisplay all lines of the paragraphs of body text?
Remove the check mark from the 'Show First Line Only' check box (Outlining tab | Outline Tools group).

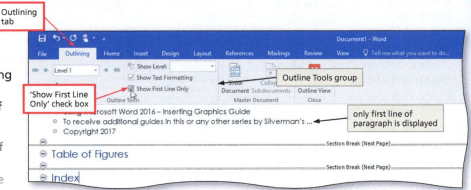

Figure 9–34

- Save this master document on your hard drive, OneDrive, or other storage location using the file name, Using Microsoft Word 2016 - Inserting Graphics Guide.

Other Ways

1. Press CTRL+SHIFT+L

To Insert a Subdocument

The next step is to insert a subdocument in the master document. The subdocument to be inserted is the Inserting Graphics Final file, which you created earlier in the module. Word places the first line of text in the subdocument at the first heading level in the master document. ***Why?*** *The first line in the subdocument was defined using the Heading 1 style.* The following steps insert a subdocument in a master document.

- Display the Home tab. If formatting marks do not appear, click the 'Show/Hide ¶' button (Home tab | Paragraph group).

- Position the insertion point where you want to insert the subdocument (on the section break above the Table of Figures heading).

- Display the Outlining tab. Click the Show Document button (Outlining tab | Master Document group) so that all commands in the Master Document group appear.

- Click the Insert Subdocument button (Outlining tab | Master Document group) to display the Insert Subdocument dialog box.

- Locate and select the Inserting Graphics Final file (Insert Subdocument dialog box) (Figure 9–35).

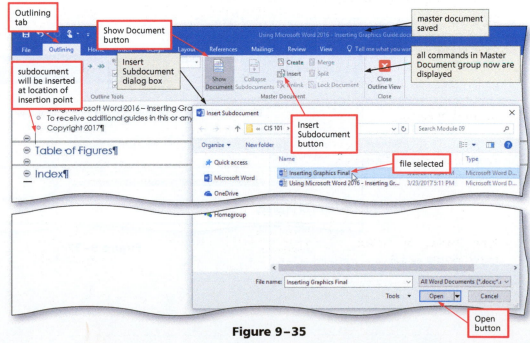

Figure 9–35

2

- Click the Open button (Insert Subdocument dialog box) to insert the selected file as a subdocument.
- If Word displays a dialog box about styles, click the 'No to All' button.
- Press CTRL+HOME to position the insertion point at the top of the document (Figure 9–36).

Figure 9–36

BTW

Locked Subdocuments

If a lock icon is displayed next to a subdocument's name, either the master document is collapsed or the subdocument is locked. If the master document is collapsed, simply click the Expand Subdocuments button (Outlining tab | Master Document group). If the subdocument is locked, you will be able to display the contents of the subdocument but will not be able to modify it.

Master Documents and Subdocuments

When you open the master document, the subdocuments initially are collapsed; that is, they are displayed as hyperlinks (Figure 9–37). To work with the contents of a master document after you open it, switch to Outline view and then expand the subdocuments by clicking the Expand Subdocuments button (Outlining tab | Master Document group).

You can open a subdocument in a separate document window and modify it. To open a collapsed subdocument, click the hyperlink. To open an expanded subdocument, double-click the subdocument icon to the left of the document heading (shown in Figure 9–37).

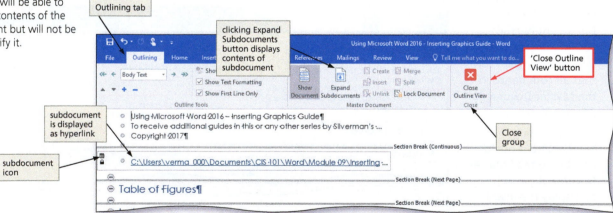

Figure 9–37

If, for some reason, you wanted to remove a subdocument from a master document, you would expand the subdocuments, click the subdocument icon to the left of the subdocument's first heading, and then press the DELETE key. Although Word removes the subdocument from the master document, the subdocument file remains on the storage media.

Occasionally, you may want to convert a subdocument to part of the master document — breaking the connection between the text in the master document and the subdocument. To do this, expand the subdocuments, click the subdocument icon, and then click the Remove Subdocument button (Outlining tab | Master Document group).

To Hide Formatting Marks

To remove the clutter of index entry fields from the document, you should hide formatting marks. The following step hides formatting marks.

1 Display the Home tab. If the 'Show/Hide ¶' button (Home tab | Paragraph group) is selected, click it to hide formatting marks.

To Exit Outline View

1 MODIFY REFERENCE DOCUMENT | **2 CREATE MASTER DOCUMENT** | **3 ORGANIZE REFERENCE DOCUMENT**

The following step exits Outline View. **Why?** *You are finished organizing the master document.*

1

- Display the Outlining tab.

- Click the 'Close Outline View' button (shown in Figure 9–37) (Outlining tab | Close group) to redisplay the document in Print Layout view, which selects the Print Layout button on the status bar.

- If necessary, press CTRL+HOME to display the top of the document (Figure 9–38).

Experiment

- Scroll through the document to familiarize yourself with the sections. When finished, display the top of the subdocument in the document window.

- Save the document again on the same storage location with the same file name.

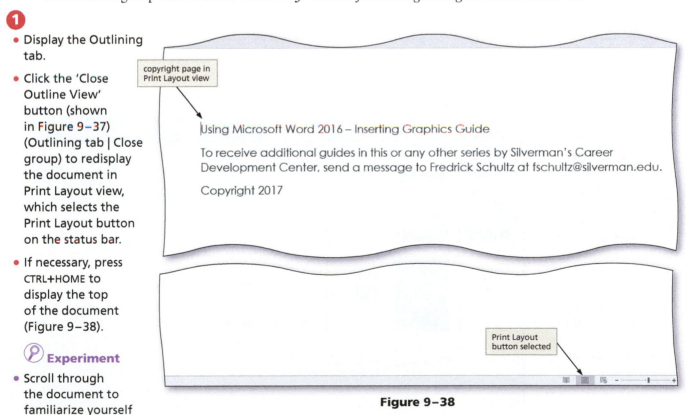

copyright page in Print Layout view

Using Microsoft Word 2016 – Inserting Graphics Guide

To receive additional guides in this or any other series by Silverman's Career Development Center, send a message to Fredrick Schultz at fschultz@silverman.edu.

Copyright 2017

Print Layout button selected

Figure 9–38

Organizing a Reference Document

Reference documents are organized and formatted so that users easily can navigate through and read the document. The reference document in this module includes the following elements: a copyright page, a title page, a table of contents, a table of figures, an index, alternating footers, and a gutter margin. This section illustrates the tasks required to include these elements.

CONSIDER THIS

What elements are common to reference documents?

Reference documents often include a title page, a table of contents, a table of figures or list of tables (if one exists), and an index.

- **Title Page.** A title page should contain, at a minimum, the title of the document. Some also contain the author, a subtitle, an edition or volume number, and the date written.

- **Table of Contents.** The table of contents should list the title (heading) of each chapter or section and the starting page number of the chapter or section. You may use a leader character, such as a dot or hyphen, to fill the space between the heading and the page number. Sections preceding the table of contents are not listed in it — list only material that follows the table of contents.

- **Table of Figures or List of Tables.** If you have multiple figures or tables in a document, consider identifying all of them in a table of figures or a list of tables. The format of the table of figures or list of tables should match the table of contents.

- **Index.** The index usually is set in two columns or one column. The index can contain any item a reader might want to look up, such as a heading or a key term. If the document does not have a table of figures or list of tables, also include figures and tables in the index.

To Insert a Cover Page

1 MODIFY REFERENCE DOCUMENT | 2 CREATE MASTER DOCUMENT | **3 ORGANIZE REFERENCE DOCUMENT**

Word has many predefined cover page formats that you can use for the title page in a document. The following steps insert a cover page. **Why?** *The reference document in this module includes a title page.*

1

- Display the Insert tab.

- Click the 'Add a Cover Page' button (Insert tab | Pages group) to display the Add a Cover Page gallery (Figure 9–39).

 **Experiment**

- Scroll through the Add a Cover Page gallery to see the variety of available predefined cover pages.

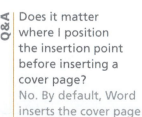 Does it matter where I position the insertion point before inserting a cover page?

No. By default, Word inserts the cover page as the first page in a document.

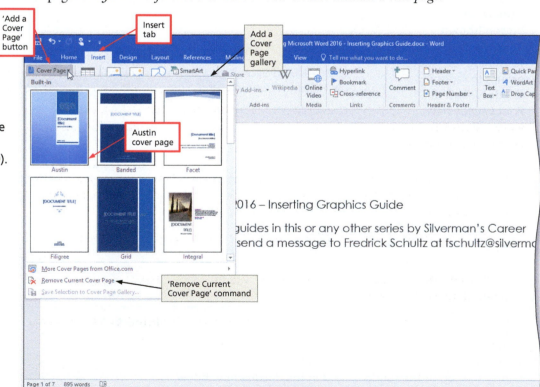

Figure 9–39

2

- Click Austin in the Add a Cover Page gallery to insert the selected cover page as the first page in the current document.

- Display the View tab. Click the One Page button (View tab | Zoom group) to display the entire cover page in the document window (Figure 9–40).

Q&A Does the cover page have to be the first page?
No. You can right-click the desired cover page and then click the desired location on the submenu.

How would I delete a cover page?
You would click the 'Add a Cover Page' button (Insert tab | Pages group) and then click 'Remove Current Cover Page' in the Add a Cover Page gallery (shown in Figure 9–39).

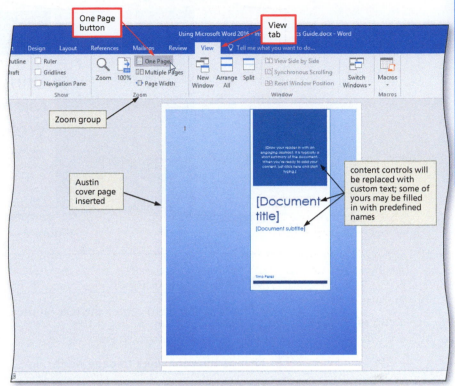

Figure 9–40

Other Ways

1. Click 'Explore Quick Parts' button (Insert tab | Text group), click 'Building Blocks Organizer', select desired cover page building block (Building Blocks Organizer dialog box), click Insert button, click Close button

To Enter Text in Content Controls

The next step is to select content controls on the cover page and replace their instructions or text with the title page information. Keep in mind that the content controls present suggested text. Depending on settings on your computer or mobile device, some content controls already may contain customized text, which you will change. You can enter any appropriate text in any content control. The following steps enter title page text on the cover page.

1 Click the content control that begins with the instruction, [Draw your reader in with an engaging abstract...] and then type **A series of guides designed to strengthen your career development skills.**

2 Click the [Document title] content control and then type **Using Microsoft Word 2016** as the title.

3 Click the [Document subtitle] content control and then type **Inserting Graphics Guide** as the subtitle.

4 Click the author content control and then type **Fredrick Schultz** as the name (Figure 9–41).

Q&A Why is my author content control filled in?
Depending on settings, your content control already may display an author name.

If requested by your instructor, change the name, Fredrick Schultz, to your name.

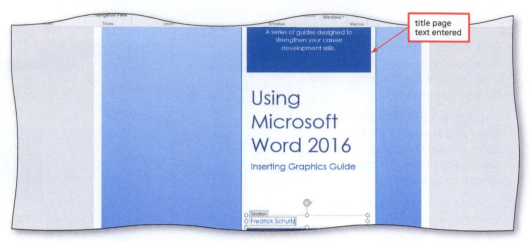

Figure 9–41

To Center Text

The next step is to center the text on the copyright page. The following steps center text.

1 Change the zoom back to page width.

2 Scroll to display the copyright page text in the document window.

3 Select the text on the copyright page and then center it.

4 Deselect the text.

To Insert a Continuous Section Break and Change the Margins in the Section

The margins on the copyright page are wider than the rest of the document. To change margins for a page, the page must be in a separate section. The next steps insert a continuous section break and then change the margins.

1 Position the insertion point at the location for the section break, in this case, to the left U in Using on the copyright page.

2 Display the Layout tab. Click the 'Insert Page and Section Breaks' button (Layout tab | Page Setup group) to display the Insert Page and Section Breaks gallery.

3 Click Continuous in the Insert Page and Section Breaks gallery to insert a continuous section break to the left of the insertion point.

4 Click the Adjust Margins button (Layout tab | Page Setup group) to display the Adjust Margins gallery and then click Wide in the Adjust Margins gallery to change the margins on the copyright page to the selected settings (Figure 9–42).

Figure 9–42

To Adjust Vertical Alignment on a Page

You can instruct Word to center the contents of a page vertically using one of two options: place an equal amount of space above and below the text on the page, or evenly space each paragraph between the top and bottom margins. The following steps vertically center text on a page. *Why? The copyright page in this project evenly spaces each paragraph on a page between the top and bottom margins, which is called justified vertical alignment.*

- Click the Page Setup Dialog Box Launcher (Layout tab | Page Setup group) to display the Page Setup dialog box.
- Click the Layout tab (Page Setup dialog box) to display the Layout sheet.
- Click the Vertical alignment arrow and then click Justified (Figure 9–43).

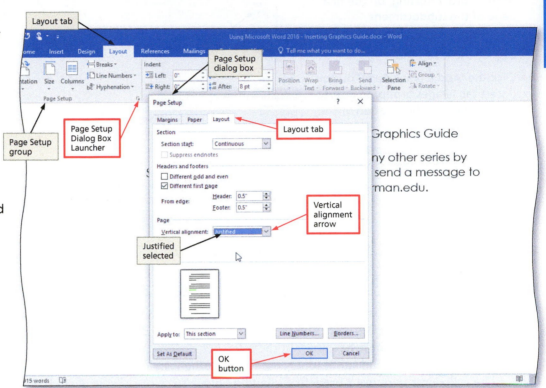

Figure 9–43

- Click the OK button to justify the text in the current section.
- To see the entire justified page, display the View tab and then click the One Page button (View tab | Zoom group) (Figure 9–44).

- Change the zoom back to page width.

Q&A What are the other vertical alignments?

Top, the default, aligns contents starting at the top margin on the page. Center places all contents centered vertically on the page, and Bottom places contents at the bottom of the page.

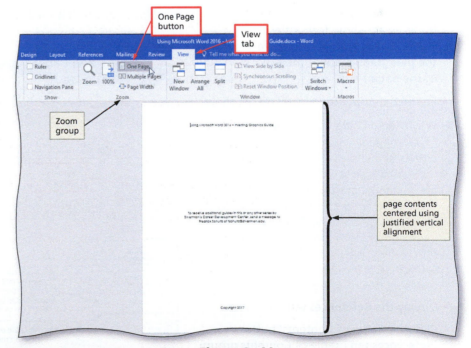

Figure 9–44

To Insert a Blank Page

The following step inserts a blank page. *Why? In the reference document in this module, the table of contents is on a page between the copyright page and the first page of the subdocument.*

- Position the insertion point to the left of the word, Inserting, on the first page of the subdocument (as shown in Figure 9–45).

- Display the Insert tab.

- Click the 'Add a Blank Page' button (Insert tab | Pages group) to insert a blank page at the location of the insertion point.

- If necessary, scroll to display the blank page in the document window (Figure 9–45).

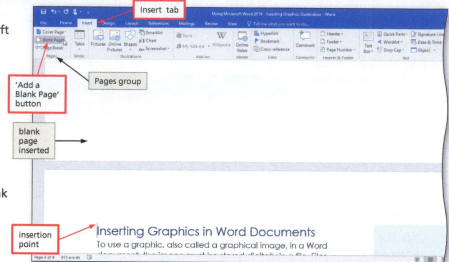

Figure 9–45

To Create a Table of Contents

A table of contents lists all headings in a document and their associated page numbers. When you use Word's built-in heading styles (for example, Heading 1, Heading 2, and so on), you can instruct Word to create a table of contents from these headings. In the reference document in this module, the heading of each section uses the Heading 1 style, and subheadings use the Heading 2 style.

The following steps use a predefined building block to create a table of contents. *Why? Using Word's predefined table of contents formats can be more efficient than creating a table of contents from scratch.*

- Position the insertion point at the top of the blank page 3, which is the location for the table of contents. (If necessary, show formatting marks so that you easily can see the paragraph mark at the top of the page.)

- Ensure that formatting marks do not show.

Q&A

Why should I hide formatting marks? Formatting marks, especially those for index entries, sometimes can cause wrapping to occur on the screen that will be different from how the printed document will wrap. These differences could cause a heading to move to the next page. To ensure that the page references in the table of contents reflect the printed pages, be sure that formatting marks are hidden when you create a table of contents.

- Display the References tab.

- Click the 'Table of Contents' button (References tab | Table of Contents group) to display the Table of Contents gallery (Figure 9–46).

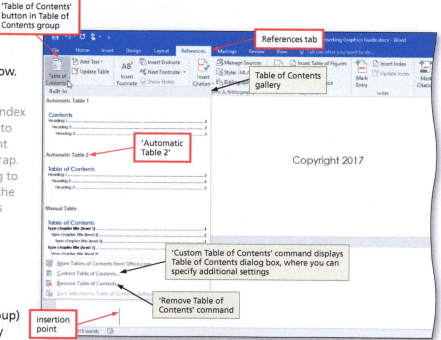

Figure 9–46

2

- Click 'Automatic Table 2' in the Table of Contents gallery to insert the table of contents at the location of the insertion point (Figure 9–47). If necessary, scroll to see the table of contents.

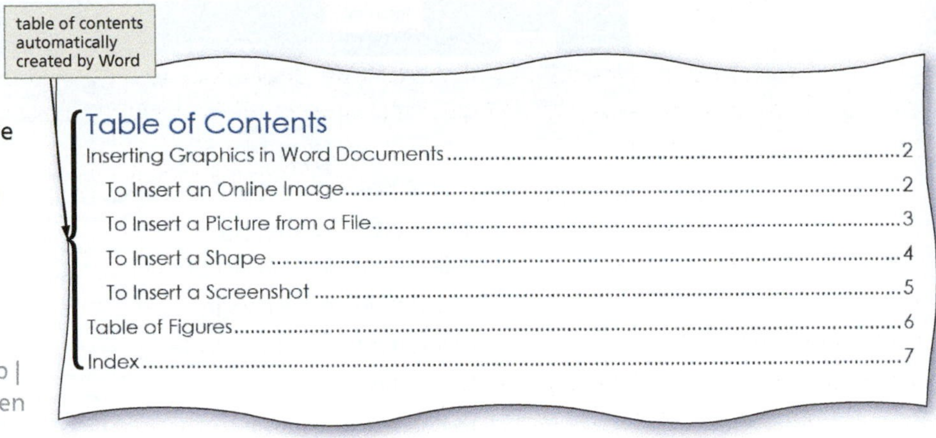

Q&A

How would I delete a table of contents?
You would click the 'Table of Contents' button (References tab | Table of Contents group) and then click 'Remove Table of Contents' in the Table of Contents gallery (shown in Figure 9-46).

table of contents automatically created by Word

Table of Contents

Figure 9–47

Other Ways

1. Click 'Table of Contents' button (References tab | Table of Contents group), click 'Custom Table of Contents', select table of contents options (Table of Contents dialog box), click OK button

2. Click 'Explore Quick Parts' button (Insert tab | Text group), click 'Building Blocks Organizer', select desired table of contents building block (Building Blocks Organizer dialog box), click Insert button, click Close button

To Insert a Continuous Section Break and Change the Starting Page Number in the Section

The table of contents should not be the starting page number; instead, the subdocument should be the starting page number in the document. To change the starting page number, the page must be in a separate section. The following steps insert a continuous section break and then change the starting page number for the table of contents.

1 Position the insertion point at the location for the section break, in this case, to the left of I in Inserting Graphics in Word Documents on page 4 of the document.

2 Display the Layout tab. Click the 'Insert Page and Section Breaks' button (Layout tab | Page Setup group) to display the Insert Page and Section Breaks gallery.

3 Click Continuous in the Insert Page and Section Breaks gallery to insert a continuous section break to the left of the insertion point.

4 Position the insertion point in the table of contents.

5 Display the Insert tab. Click the 'Add Page Numbers' button (Insert tab | Header & Footer group) to display the Add Page Numbers menu and then click 'Format Page Numbers' on the Add Page Numbers menu to display the Page Number Format dialog box.

6 Click the Start at down arrow (Page Number Format dialog box) until 0 is displayed in the Start at box (Figure 9–48).

7 Click the OK button to change the starting page for the current section.

BTW

Advanced Layout Options
You can adjust Word's advanced layout options by clicking File on the ribbon to open the Backstage View, clicking the Options tab in the Backstage View to display the Word Options dialog box, clicking Advanced in the left pane (Word Options dialog box), scrolling to the Layout options for area in the right pane, placing a check mark in the desired settings, and then clicking the OK button.

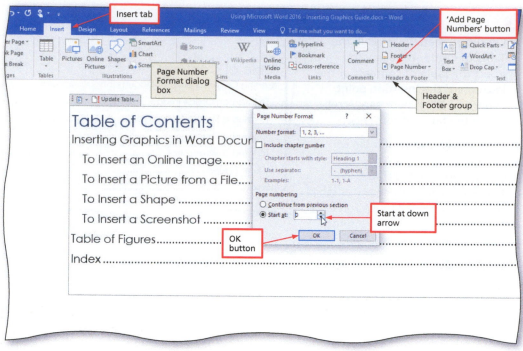

Figure 9–48

To Update Page Numbers in a Table of Contents

1 MODIFY REFERENCE DOCUMENT | 2 CREATE MASTER DOCUMENT | 3 ORGANIZE REFERENCE DOCUMENT

When you change a document, you should update the associated table of contents. The following steps update the page numbers in the table of contents. **Why?** *The starting page number change will affect the page numbers in the table of contents.*

- If necessary, click the table of contents to select it.

Q&A Why does the ScreenTip say 'CTRL+Click to follow link'?
Each entry in the table of contents is a link. If you hold down the CTRL key while clicking an entry in the table of contents, Word will display the associated heading in the document window.

- Click the Update Table button that is attached to the table of contents to display the Update Table of Contents dialog box.

- Ensure the 'Update page numbers only' option button is selected because you want to update only the page numbers in the table of contents (Figure 9–49).

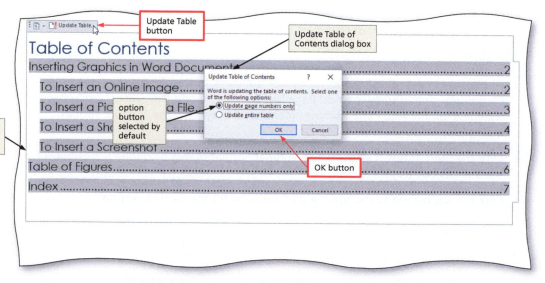

Figure 9–49

3

- Click the OK button (Update Table of Contents dialog box) to update the page numbers in the table of contents.

- Click outside the table of contents to remove the selection from the table (Figure 9–50).

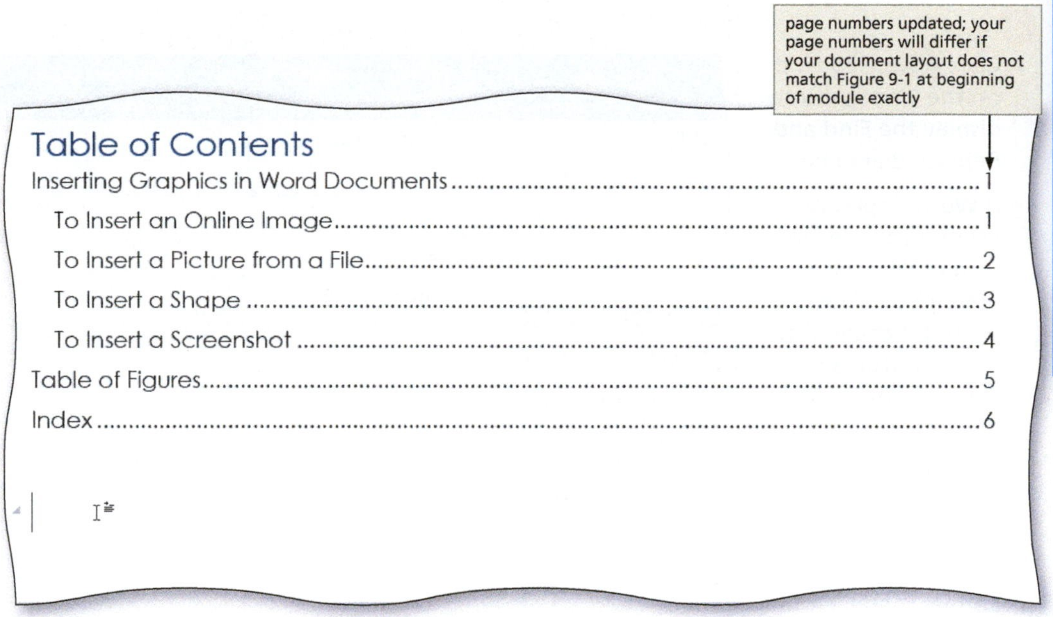

page numbers updated; your page numbers will differ if your document layout does not match Figure 9-1 at beginning of module exactly

Table of Contents

Figure 9–50

Other Ways

1. Select table, click Update Table button (References tab | Table of Contents group)

2. Select table, press F9 key

To Find a Format

1 MODIFY REFERENCE DOCUMENT | 2 CREATE MASTER DOCUMENT | **3 ORGANIZE REFERENCE DOCUMENT**

The subdocument contains a sentence of text formatted as bold italic. To find this text in the document, you could scroll through the document until it is displayed on the screen. A more efficient way is to find the bold, italic format using the Find and Replace dialog box. The following steps find a format. ***Why? You want to add the text to the table of contents.***

1

- If necessary, display the Home tab.

- Click the Find arrow (Home tab | Editing group) to display the Find menu (Figure 9–51).

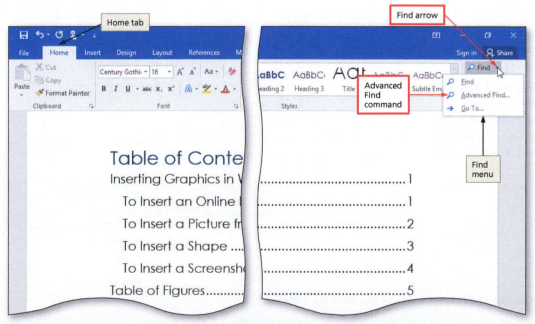

Figure 9–51

2

- Click Advanced Find on the Find menu to display the Find and Replace dialog box.

- If Word displays a More button in the Find and Replace dialog box, click it so that it changes to a Less button and expands the dialog box.

- Click the Format button (Find and Replace dialog box) to display the Format menu (Figure 9–52).

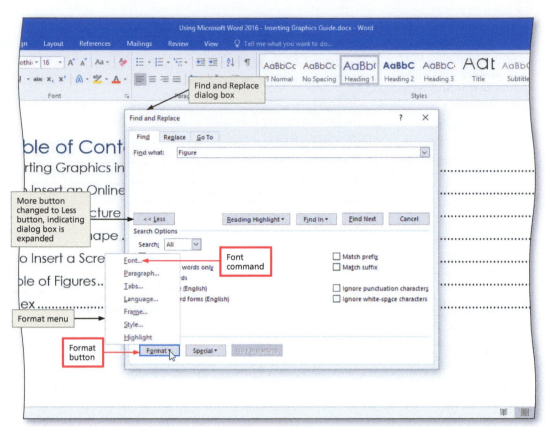

Figure 9–52

3

- Click Font on the Format menu to display the Find Font dialog box. If necessary, click the Font tab (Find Font dialog box) to display the Font sheet.

- Click Bold Italic in the Font style list because that is the format you want to find (Figure 9–53).

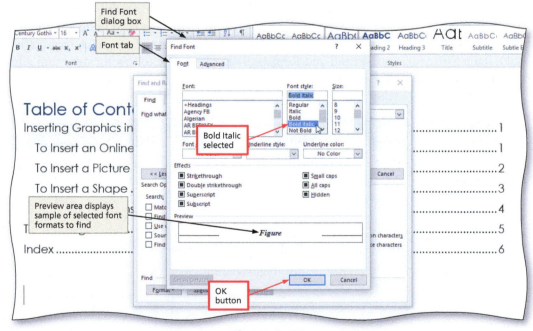

Figure 9–53

4

- Click the OK button to close the Find Font dialog box.

- Be sure no text is in the Find what text box (or click the Find what arrow and then click [Formatting Only]).

- Be sure all check boxes in the Search Options area are cleared.

- When the Find and Replace dialog box is active again, click its Find Next button to locate and highlight in the document the first occurrence of the specified format (Figure 9–54).

Q&A
How do I remove a find format?
You would click the No Formatting button in the Find and Replace dialog box.

 5

- Click the Cancel button (Find and Replace dialog box) because the located occurrence is the one you wanted to find.

Q&A
Can I search for (find) special characters, such as page breaks?
Yes. To find special characters, you would click the Special button in the Find and Replace dialog box.

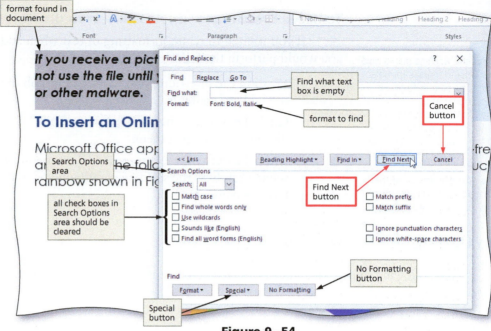

Figure 9–54

Other Ways

1. Press CTRL+F

To Format Text as a Heading

The following steps format a paragraph of text as a Heading 3 style. Occasionally, you may want to add a paragraph of text, which normally is not formatted using a heading style, to a table of contents. One way to add the text is to format it as a heading style.

1. With the formatted paragraph still selected (shown in Figure 9–54), if necessary, display the Home tab.

2. Click Heading 3 in the Styles gallery to apply the selected style to the current paragraph in the document. Click outside the paragraph to deselect it (Figure 9–55).

3. If necessary, drag the bottom of the sidebar text box up so that it ends after the word 'zombies'.

BTW

Find and Replace
The expanded Find and Replace dialog box allows you to specify how Word locates search text. For example, selecting the Match case check box instructs Word to find the text exactly as you typed it, and selecting the 'Find whole words only' check box instructs Word to ignore text that contains the search text (i.e., the word, then, contains the word, the). If you select the Use wildcard check box, you can use wildcard characters in a search. For example, with this check box selected, the search text of *ing would search for all words that end with the characters, ing.

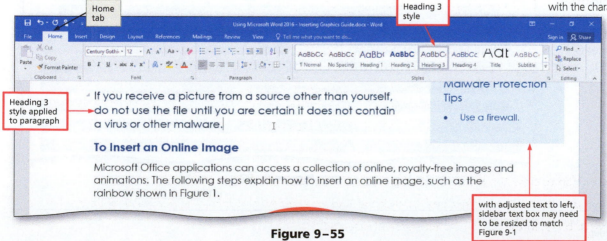

Figure 9–55

BTW

Replace Formats
You can click the Replace tab (Find and Replace dialog box) to find and replace formats. Enter the format to find in the Find what text box and then follow the same steps to enter the format to replace in the Replace with text box. Next, click the Replace or Replace All button to replace the next occurrence of the format or all occurrences of the format in the document.

TO RETAIN FORMATTING WHEN ADDING TEXT TO THE TABLE OF CONTENTS

If you wanted to retain formatting of text when adding it to the table of contents, you would perform the following steps.

1. Position the insertion point in the paragraph of text that you want to add to the table of contents.
2. Click the Add Text button (References tab | Table of Contents group) to display the Add Text menu.
3. Click the desired level on the Add Text menu, which adds the format of the selected style to the selected paragraph and adds the paragraph of text to the table of contents.

To Update the Entire Table of Contents

1 MODIFY REFERENCE DOCUMENT | 2 CREATE MASTER DOCUMENT | **3 ORGANIZE REFERENCE DOCUMENT**

The following steps update the entire table of contents. *Why? The text changed to the Heading 3 style should appear in the table of contents.*

- Display the table of contents in the document window.
- Click the table of contents to select it.
- Click the Update Table button that is attached to the table of contents to display the Update Table of Contents dialog box.
- Click the 'Update entire table' option button (Update Table of Contents dialog box) because you want to update the entire table of contents (Figure 9–56).

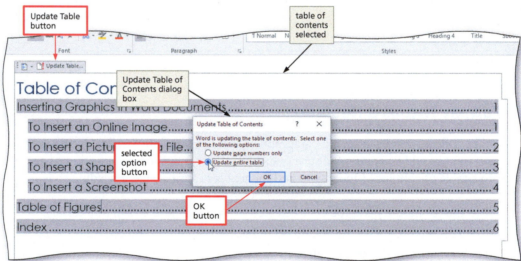

Figure 9–56

- Click the OK button (Update Table of Contents dialog box) to update the entire table of contents (Figure 9–57).

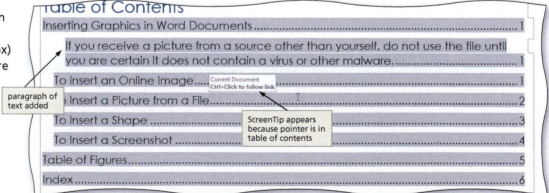

Figure 9–57

Other Ways

1. Select table, click Update Table button (References tab | Table of Contents group)

2. Select table, press F9 key

To Change the Format of a Table of Contents

You can change the format of the table of contents to any of the predefined table of contents styles or to custom settings. The following steps change the table of contents format. *Why? In this table of contents, you specify the format, page number alignment, and tab leader character.*

1
- Display the References tab.

- Click the 'Table of Contents' button (References tab | Table of Contents group) to display the Table of Contents gallery (Figure 9–58).

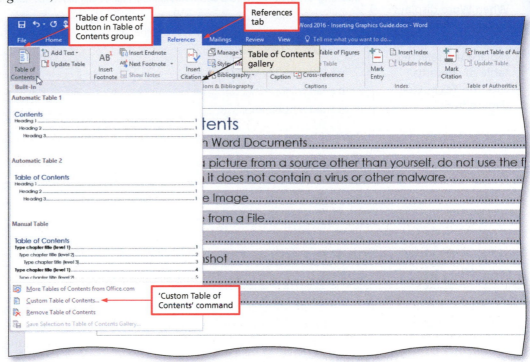

Figure 9–58

2
- Click 'Custom Table of Contents' in the Table of Contents gallery to display the Table of Contents dialog box.

- Click the Formats arrow (Table of Contents dialog box) and then click Simple to change the format style for the table of contents.

- Place a check mark in the 'Right align page numbers' check box so that the page numbers appear at the right margin in the table of contents.

- If necessary, click the Tab leader arrow and then click the first leader type in the list so that the selected leader characters appear between the heading name and the page numbers in the table of contents (Figure 9–59).

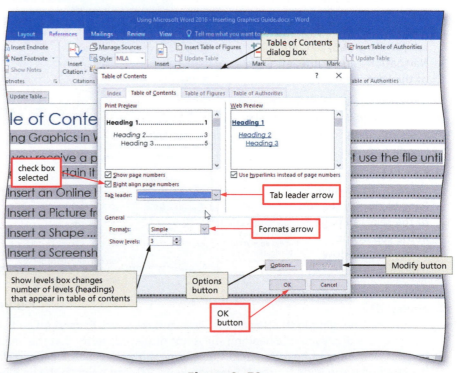

Figure 9–59

- Click the OK button to modify the table of contents according to the specified settings. When Word displays a dialog box asking if you want to replace the selected table of contents, click the Yes button (Figure 9–60).

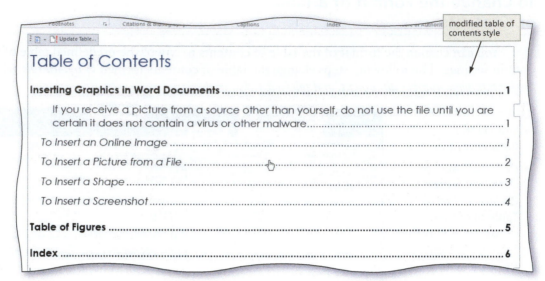

Figure 9–60

To Use the Navigation Pane to Go to a Heading in a Document

1 MODIFY REFERENCE DOCUMENT | 2 CREATE MASTER DOCUMENT | **3 ORGANIZE REFERENCE DOCUMENT**

When you use Word's built-in heading styles in a document, you can use the Navigation Pane to go to headings in a document quickly. *Why? When you click a heading in the Navigation Pane, Word displays the page associated with that heading in the document window.* The following step uses the Navigation Pane to display an associated heading in the document window.

- Display the View tab. Place a check mark in the 'Open the Navigation Pane' check box (View tab | Show group) to open the Navigation Pane at the left edge of the Word window.

- If necessary, click the Headings tab in the Navigation Pane to display the text that is formatted using Heading styles.

- Click the Table of Figures heading in the Navigation Pane to display the top of the selected page in the top of the document window (Figure 9–61).

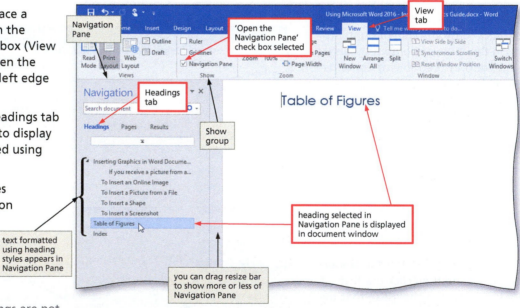

Figure 9–61

Q&A

What if all of the headings are not displayed?

Right-click a heading in the Navigation Pane and then click Expand All on the shortcut menu to ensure that all headings are displayed. If a heading still is not displayed, verify that the heading is formatted with a heading style. To display or hide subheadings below a heading in the Navigation Pane, click the triangle to the left of the heading. If a heading is too wide for the Navigation Pane, you can point to the heading to display a ScreenTip that shows the complete title.

To Create a Table of Figures

1 MODIFY REFERENCE DOCUMENT | 2 CREATE MASTER DOCUMENT | **3 ORGANIZE REFERENCE DOCUMENT**

The following steps create a table of figures. *Why?* *At the end of the reference document is a table of figures, which lists all figures and their corresponding page numbers. Word generates this table of figures from the captions in the document.*

- Ensure that formatting marks are not displayed.

- Position the insertion point at the end of the Table of Figures heading and then press the ENTER key, so that the insertion point is on the line below the heading.

- Display the References tab.

- Click the 'Table of Figures Dialog' button (References tab | Captions group) to display the Table of Figures dialog box.

- Be sure that all settings in your dialog box match those in Figure 9–62.

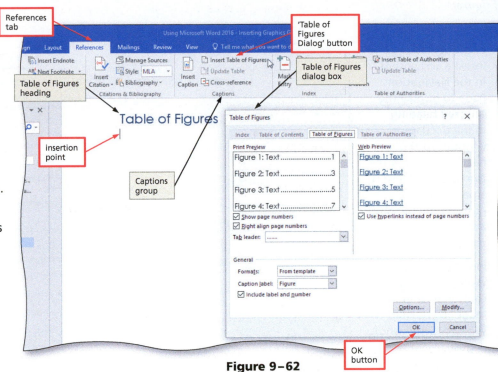

Figure 9–62

2
- Click the OK button (Table of Figures dialog box) to create a table of figures at the location of the insertion point (Figure 9–63).

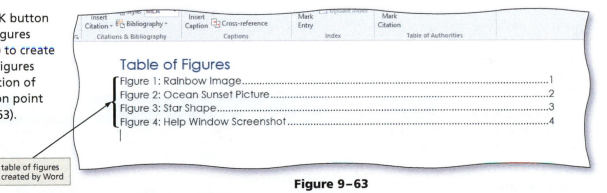

Table of Figures

Figure 1: Rainbow Image..1
Figure 2: Ocean Sunset Picture..2
Figure 3: Star Shape..3
Figure 4: Help Window Screenshot...4

Figure 9–63

TO CHANGE THE FORMAT OF THE TABLE OF FIGURES

If you wanted to change the format of the table of figures, you would perform the following steps.

1. Click the table of figures to select it.

2. Click the 'Table of Figures Dialog' button (References tab | Captions group) to display the Table of Figures dialog box.

3. Change settings in the dialog box as desired.

4. Click the OK button (Table of Figures dialog box) to apply the changed settings.

5. Click the OK button when Word asks if you want to replace the selected table of figures.

BTW

Table of Contents Styles
If you wanted to change the level associated with each style used in a table of contents, click the Options button in the Table of Contents dialog box (shown in Figure 9–59), enter the desired level number in the text box beside the appropriate heading or other styled item, and then click the OK button. To change the formatting associated with a style, click the Modify button in the Table of Contents dialog box.

To Edit a Caption and Update the Table of Figures

The following steps change the Figure 4 caption and then update the table of figures. **Why?** *When you modify captions in a document or move illustrations to a different location in the document, you will have to update the table of figures.*

- Click the heading, To Insert a Screenshot, in the Navigation Pane to display the selected heading in the document window. (If this heading is not at the top of page 7, insert a page break to position the heading at the top of a new page.)

- Insert the text, Word, in the Figure 4 caption so that it reads: Word Help Window Screenshot (Figure 9–64).

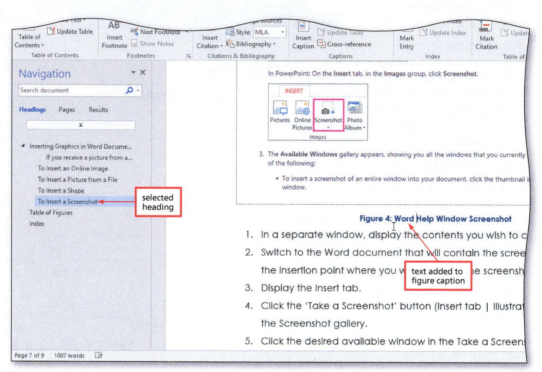

Figure 9–64

- Click the heading, Table of Figures, in the Navigation Pane to display the Table of Figures heading in the document window.

- Click the table of figures to select it.

- Click the 'Update Table of Figures' button (References tab | Captions group) to display the Update Table of Figures dialog box.

- Click 'Update entire table' (Update Table of Figures dialog box), so that Word updates the contents of the entire table of figures instead of updating only the page numbers (Figure 9–65).

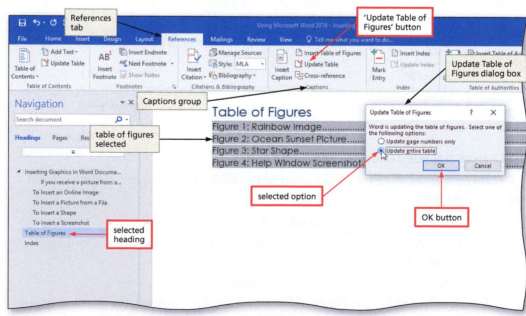

Figure 9–65

3

- Click the OK button to update the table of figures and then click outside the table to deselect it (Figure 9–66).

Are the entries in the table of figures links? Yes. As with the table of contents, you can CTRL+click any entry in the table of figures and Word will display the associated figure in the document window.

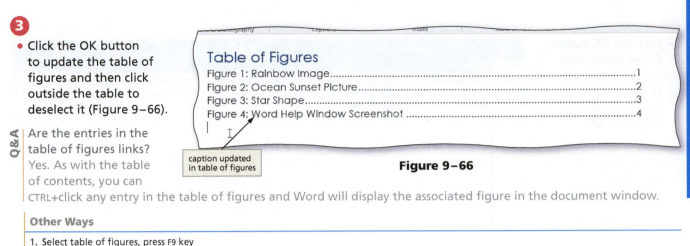

Table of Figures

Figure 1: Rainbow Image..1
Figure 2: Ocean Sunset Picture..2
Figure 3: Star Shape...3
Figure 4: Word Help Window Screenshot 4

caption updated in table of figures

Figure 9–66

Other Ways

1. Select table of figures, press F9 key

To Build an Index

1 MODIFY REFERENCE DOCUMENT | 2 CREATE MASTER DOCUMENT | **3 ORGANIZE REFERENCE DOCUMENT**

The reference document in this module ends with an index. Earlier, this module showed how to mark index entries. **Why?** *For Word to generate the index, you first must mark any text you wish to appear in the index.*

Once all index entries are marked, Word can build the index from the index entry fields in the document. Recall that index entry fields begin with XE, which appears on the screen when formatting marks are displayed. When index entry fields show on the screen, the document's pagination probably will be altered because of the extra text in the index entries. Thus, be sure to hide formatting marks before building an index. The following steps build an index.

1

- Click the heading, Index, in the Navigation Pane to display the Index heading in the document window.

- Click to the right of the Index heading and then press the ENTER key, so that the insertion point is on the line below the heading.

- Ensure that formatting marks are not displayed.

- Click the Insert Index button (References tab | Index group) to display the Index dialog box.

- If necessary, click the Formats arrow in the dialog box and then click Classic in the Formats list to change the index format.

- Place a check mark in the 'Right align page numbers' check box.

- Click the Tab leader arrow and then click the first leader character in the list to specify the leader character to be displayed between the index entry and the page number.

- Click the Columns down arrow until the number of columns is 1 to change the number of columns in the index (Figure 9–67).

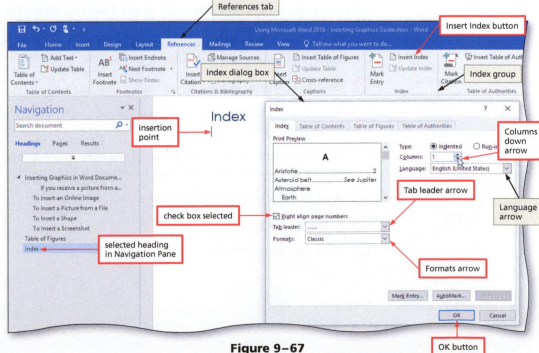

Figure 9–67

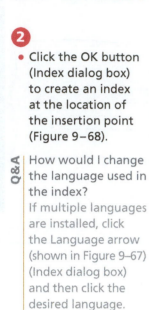

2

- Click the OK button (Index dialog box) to create an index at the location of the insertion point (Figure 9–68).

Q&A How would I change the language used in the index?
If multiple languages are installed, click the Language arrow (shown in Figure 9–67) (Index dialog box) and then click the desired language.

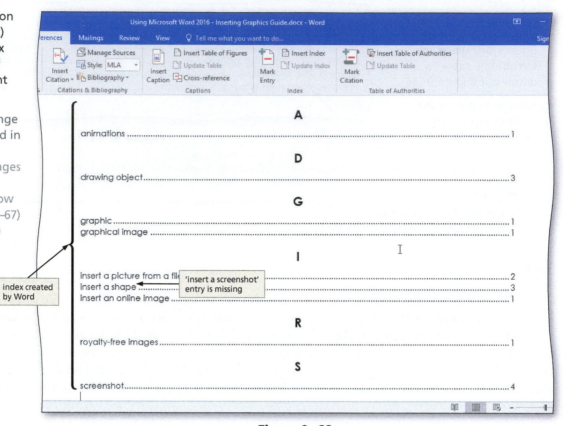

Figure 9–68

BTW

Index Files
Instead of marking index entries in a document, you can create a concordance file that contains all index entries you wish to mark. A concordance file contains two columns: the first column identifies the text in the document you want Word to mark as an index entry, and the second column lists the index entries to be generated from the text in the first column. To mark entries in the concordance file, click the AutoMark button in the Index and Tables dialog box.

To Mark Another Index Entry

Notice in Figure 9–68 that the 'insert a screenshot' index entry is missing. The following steps mark an index entry in the Insert a Screenshot section.

1 Click the heading, To Insert a Screenshot, in the Navigation Pane to display the selected heading in the document window.

2 Select the words, Insert a Screenshot, in the heading.

3 Click the Mark Entry button (References tab | Index group) to display the Mark Index Entry dialog box.

4 Type `insert a screenshot` in the Main entry text box (Mark Index Entry dialog box) so that the entry is all lowercase (Figure 9–69).

5 Click the Mark button to mark the entry.

6 Close the dialog box.

7 Hide formatting marks.

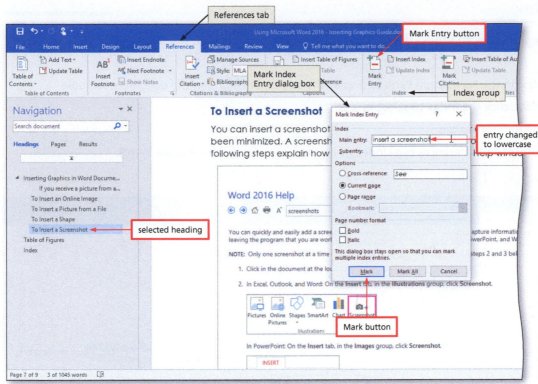

Figure 9–69

BTW
Navigation Pane
You can drag any heading in the Navigation Pane to reorganize document content. For example, you could drag the To Insert a Screenshot heading upward in the Navigation Pane so that its content appears earlier in the document.

TO EDIT AN INDEX ENTRY

At some time, you may want to change an index entry after you have marked it. For example, you may forget to lowercase the entry for the headings. If you wanted to change an index entry, you would perform the following steps.

1. Display formatting marks.
2. Locate the XE field for the index entry you wish to change (i.e., { XE "Insert a Screenshot" }).
3. Change the text inside the quotation marks (i.e., { XE "insert a screenshot" }).
4. Update the index as described in the steps in the upcoming steps titled To Update an Index.

TO DELETE AN INDEX ENTRY

If you wanted to delete an index entry, you would perform the following steps.

1. Display formatting marks.
2. Select the XE field for the index entry you wish to delete (i.e., { XE "insert a screenshot" }).
3. Press the DELETE key.
4. Update the index as described in the steps in the next set of steps.

BTW
Field Codes
If your index, table of contents, or table of figures displays odd characters inside curly braces ({ }), then Word is displaying field codes instead of field results. Press ALT+F9 to display the index or table correctly.

To Update an Index

The following step updates an index. *Why? After marking a new index entry, you must update the index.*

- Click the heading, Index, in the Navigation Pane to display the selected heading in the document window.
- In the document window, click the index to select it.
- If necessary, display the References tab.
- Click the Update Index button (References tab | Index group) to update the index (Figure 9–70).

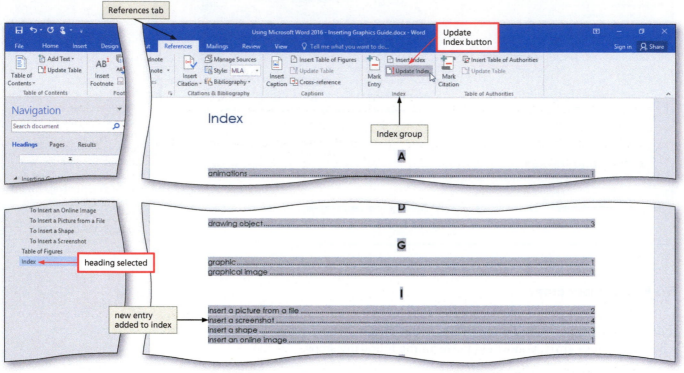

Figure 9–70

Other Ways

1. Select index, press F9 key

TO CHANGE THE FORMAT OF THE INDEX

If you wanted to change the format of the index, you would perform the following steps.

1. Click the index to select it.

2. Click the Insert Index button (References tab | Index group) to display the Index dialog box.

3. Change settings in the dialog box as desired. If you want to modify the style used for the index, click the Modify button.

4. Click the OK button (Index dialog box) to apply the changed settings.

5. Click the OK button when Word asks if you want to replace the selected index.

To Delete an Entire Index

If you wanted to delete an index, you would perform the following steps.

1. Click the index to select it.
2. Press SHIFT+F9 to display field codes.
3. Drag through the entire field code, including the braces, and then press the DELETE key.

Table of Authorities

In addition to creating an index, table of figures, and table of contents, you can use Word to create a table of authorities. Legal documents often include a **table of authorities** to list references to cases, rules, statutes, etc. To create a table of authorities, mark the citations first and then build the table of authorities.

The procedures for marking citations, editing citations, creating the table of authorities, changing the format of the table of authorities, and updating the table of authorities are the same as those for indexes. The only difference is you use the buttons in the Table of Authorities group on the References tab instead of the buttons in the Index group.

BTW

Table of Authorities
See the Supplementary Word Tasks section in Module 11 for additional instructions related to creating a table of authorities.

To Create Alternating Footers Using a Footer Building Block

1 MODIFY REFERENCE DOCUMENT | 2 CREATE MASTER DOCUMENT | 3 ORGANIZE REFERENCE DOCUMENT

The *Using Microsoft Word 2016* document is designed so that it can be duplicated back-to-back. That is, the document prints on nine separate pages. When it is duplicated, however, pages are printed on opposite sides of the same sheet of paper. ***Why?*** *Back-to-back duplicating saves resources because it enables the nine-page document to use only five sheets of paper.*

In many books and documents that have facing pages, the page number is always on the same side of the page — often on the outside edge. In Word, you accomplish this task by specifying one type of header or footer for even-numbered pages and another type of header or footer for odd-numbered pages. The following steps create alternating footers beginning on the fourth page of the document (the beginning of the subdocument).

1
- If necessary, hide formatting marks.
- Use the Navigation Pane to display the page with the heading, Inserting Graphics in Word Documents.
- Display the Insert tab.
- Click the 'Add a Footer' button (Insert tab | Header & Footer group) and then click Edit Footer to display the footer area.
- Be sure the 'Link to Previous' button (Header & Footer Tools Design tab | Navigation group) is not selected.
- Place a check mark in the 'Different Odd & Even Pages' check box (Header & Footer Tools Design tab | Options group), so that you can enter a different footer for odd and even pages.
- If necessary, click the Show Next button (Header & Footer Tools Design tab | Navigation group) to display the desired footer page (in this case, the Odd Page Footer -Section 4-).

- Click the 'Insert Alignment Tab' button (Header & Footer Tools Design tab | Position group) to display the Alignment Tab dialog box.

- Click Right (Alignment Tab dialog box) because you want to place a right-aligned tab stop in the footer (Figure 9–71).

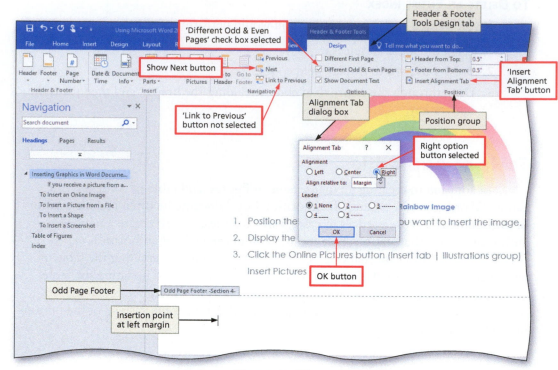

Figure 9–71

- Click the OK button to align the paragraph and insertion point in the footer at the right margin.

- Click the 'Add Page Numbers' button (Header & Footer Tools Design tab | Header & Footer group) to display the Add Page Numbers gallery.

- Point to Current Position in the Add Page Numbers gallery to display the Current Position gallery (Figure 9–72).

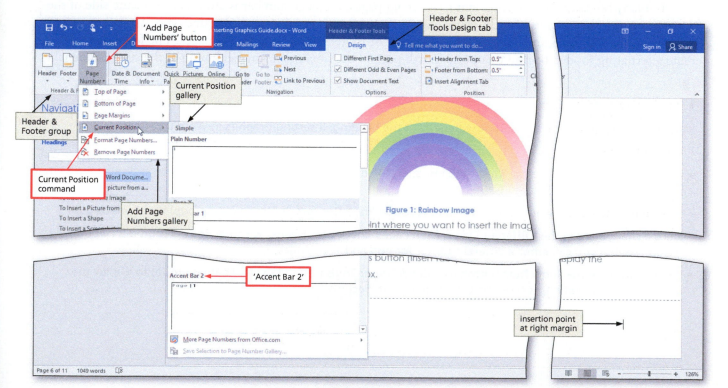

Figure 9–72

4

- Click 'Accent Bar 2' in the Current Position gallery to insert the selected page number in the footer (Figure 9–73).

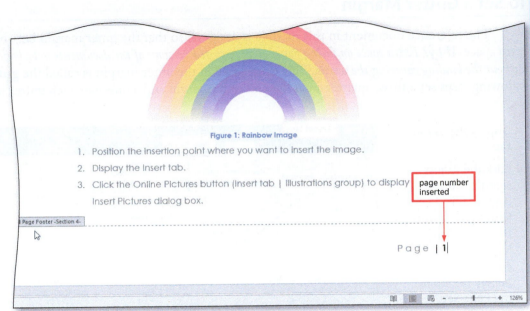

Figure 1: Rainbow Image

1. Position the insertion point where you want to insert the image.
2. Display the Insert tab.
3. Click the Online Pictures button (Insert tab | Illustrations group) to display Insert Pictures dialog box.

page number inserted

Page | 1

Figure 9–73

5

- Click the Show Next button (Header & Footer Tools Design tab | Navigation group) to display the next footer, in this case, Even Page Footer -Section 4-.

- Be sure the 'Link to Previous' button (Header & Footer Tools Design tab | Navigation group) is not selected.

- Click the 'Add Page Numbers' button (Header & Footer Tools Design tab | Header & Footer group) to display the Add Page Numbers gallery.

- Point to Current Position in the Add Page Numbers gallery to display the Current Position gallery and the click 'Accent Bar 2' in the Current Position gallery to insert the selected page number in the footer (Figure 9–74).

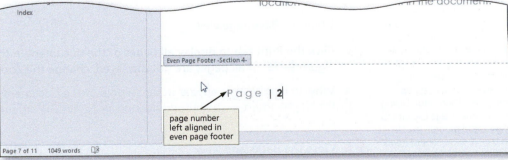
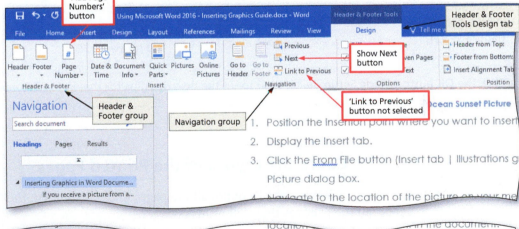

'Add Page Numbers' button

Header & Footer Tools Design tab

Show Next button

'Link to Previous' button not selected

Header & Footer group

Navigation group

Even Page Footer -Section 4-

Page | 2

page number left aligned in even page footer

Figure 9–74

Q&A Can I create alternating headers?
Yes. Follow the same basic procedure, except insert a header building block or header text.

To Set a Gutter Margin

The reference document in this module is designed so that the inner margin between facing pages has extra space. *Why? Extra space on facing pages allows printed versions of the documents to be bound (such as stapled) — without the binding covering the words.* This extra space in the inner margin is called the **gutter margin**. The following steps set a three-quarter-inch left and right margin and a one-half-inch gutter margin.

- Display the Layout tab.

- Click the Adjust Margins button (Layout tab | Page Setup group) and then click Custom Margins in the Adjust Margins gallery to display the Page Setup dialog box.

- Type .75 in the Left box, .75 in the Right box, and .5 in the Gutter box (Page Setup dialog box).

- Click the Apply to arrow and then click Whole document (Figure 9–75).

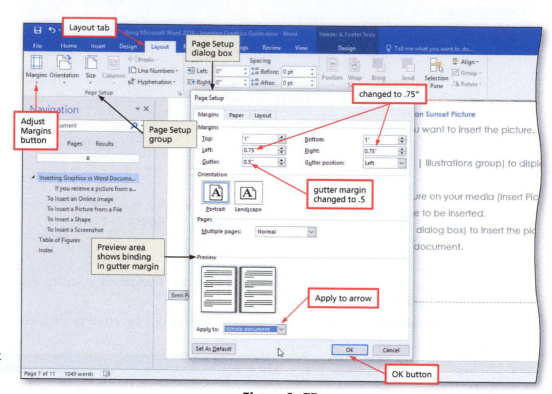

Figure 9–75

- Click the OK button (Page Setup dialog box) to set the new margins for the entire document.

BTW

Header and Footer Margins

If you want the margins of the header or footer to be different from the default of one-half inch, you would adjust the margin in the 'Header Position from Top' or 'Footer Position from Bottom' boxes (Header & Footer Tools Design tab | Position group) or in the Layout sheet of the Page Setup dialog box through the Page Setup Dialog Box Launcher (Page Layout tab | Page Setup group). You also can specify alignment of items in the header or footer by clicking the 'Insert Alignment Tab' button (Header & Footer Tools Design tab | Position group) and then clicking the desired alignment in the Alignment Tab dialog box.

To Check the Layout of the Printed Pages

To view the layout of all the pages in the document, the following steps display all the pages as they will print.

① Open the Backstage view.

② Click the Print tab to display all pages of the document in the right pane, as shown in Figure 9–76. (If all pages are not displayed, change the Zoom level to 10%.)

Q&A Why do blank pages appear in the middle of the document?
When you insert even and odd headers or footers, Word may add pages to fill the gaps.

③ Close the Backstage view.

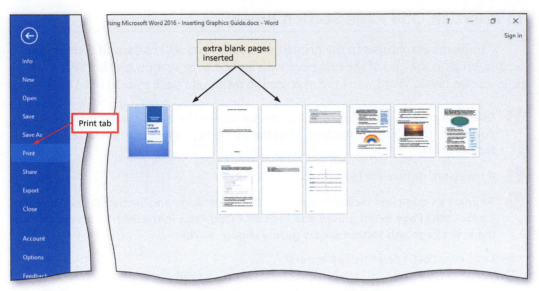

Figure 9–76

BTW

Set Print Scaling
If you wanted to ensure a document prints on a certain paper size, you can scale the document by opening the Backstage view, clicking the Print tab to display the Print gallery, clicking the bottom option in the Settings area (Print gallery), pointing to 'Scale to Paper Size', and then clicking the desired paper size before printing the document.

To Switch to Draft View

1 MODIFY REFERENCE DOCUMENT | 2 CREATE MASTER DOCUMENT | 3 ORGANIZE REFERENCE DOCUMENT

To adjust the blank pages automatically inserted in the printed document by Word, you change the continuous section break at the top of the document to an odd page section break. The following step switches to Draft view. **Why?** *Section breaks are easy to see in Draft view.*

1

• Display the View tab. Click the Draft View button (View tab | Views group) to switch to Draft view.

• Scroll to the top of the document and notice how different the document looks in Draft view (Figure 9–77).

 Q&A What happened to the graphics, footers, and other items?

They do not appear in Draft view because Draft view is designed to make editing text in a document easier.

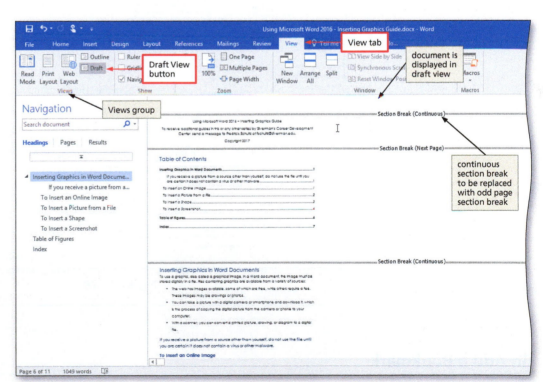

Figure 9–77

BTW
Different First Page
If you wanted only the first page of a document to have a different header or footer, you could place a check mark in the 'Different First Page' check box (Header & Footer Tools Design tab | Options group). Doing so instructs Word to create a first page header or first page footer that can contain content that differs from the rest of the headers or footers.

To Insert an Odd Page Section Break

To fix the extra pages in the printed document, you will replace the continuous section break at the end of the title page with an odd page section break. With an odd page section break, Word starts the next section on an odd page instead of an even page.

1 Select the continuous section break at the bottom of the title page (or top of the document in Draft view) and then press the DELETE key to delete the selected section break.

2 If necessary, display the Layout tab.

3 To insert an odd page section break, click the 'Insert Page and Section Breaks' button (Layout tab | Page Setup group) and then click Odd Page in the Section Breaks area in the Insert Page and Section Breaks gallery (Figure 9–78).

Q&A Can I insert even page section breaks?
Yes. To instruct Word to start the next section on an even page, click Even Page in the Insert Page and Section Breaks gallery.

4 Click the Print Layout button on the status bar to switch to Print Layout view.

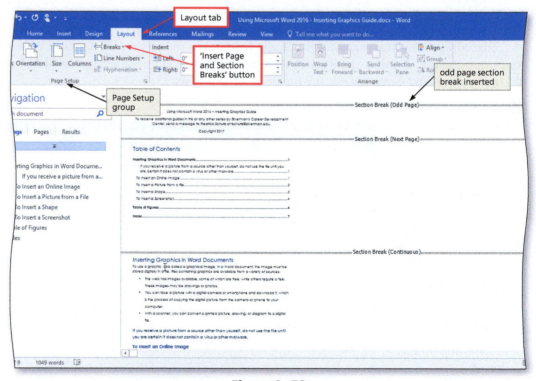

Figure 9–78

To Add a Bookmark

1 MODIFY REFERENCE DOCUMENT | 2 CREATE MASTER DOCUMENT | 3 ORGANIZE REFERENCE DOCUMENT

A **bookmark** is an item in a document that you name for future reference. The following steps add bookmarks. *Why? Bookmarks assist users in navigating through a document online. For example, you could bookmark the headings in the document, so that users easily could jump to these areas of the document.*

- Use the Navigation Pane to display the To Insert an Online Image heading in the document window and then select the heading in the document.
- Display the Insert tab.
- Click the 'Insert a Bookmark' button (Insert tab | Links group) to display the Bookmark dialog box.
- Type **OnlineImage** in the Bookmark name text box (Figure 9–79).

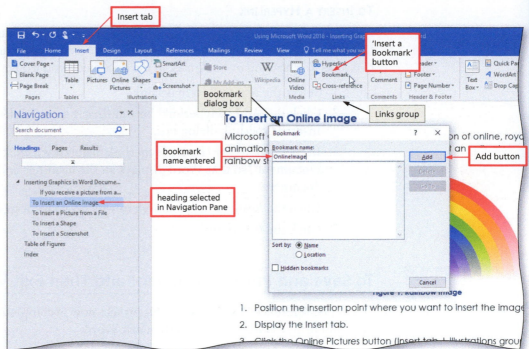

Figure 9–79

What are the rules for bookmark names?
Bookmark names can contain only letters, numbers, and the underscore character (_). They also must begin with a letter and cannot contain spaces.

- Click the Add button (Bookmark dialog box) to add the bookmark name to the list of existing bookmarks in the document.

- Repeat Steps 1 and 2 for these headings in the document: To Insert a Picture from a File, To Insert a Shape, and To Insert a Screenshot (use bookmark names PictureFromFile, Shape, and Screenshot).

TO GO TO A BOOKMARK

Once you have added bookmarks, you can jump to them. If you wanted to go to a bookmark, you would perform the following steps.

1. Click the 'Insert a Bookmark' button (Insert tab | Links group) to display the Bookmark dialog box (shown in Figure 9–79).
2. Click the bookmark name in the Bookmark name list (Bookmark dialog box) and then click the Go To button.

or

1. Press the F5 key to display the Go To sheet in the Find and Replace dialog box.
2. Click Bookmark in the list (Find and Replace dialog box), select the bookmark name, and then click the Go To button.

BTW

Link to Graphic
If you wanted to link a graphic in a document to a webpage, you would click the 'Add a Hyperlink' button (Insert tab | Links group), enter the web address in the Address text box (Insert Hyperlink dialog box), and then click the OK button. To display the webpage associated with the graphic, tap or CTRL+click the graphic.

TO INSERT A HYPERLINK

Instead of or in addition to bookmarks in online documents, you can insert hyperlinks that link one part of a document to another. If you wanted to insert a hyperlink that links to a heading or bookmark in the document, you would follow these steps.

1. Select the text to be a hyperlink.
2. Click the 'Add a Hyperlink' button (Insert tab | Links group) to display the Insert Hyperlink dialog box.
3. In the Link to bar (Insert Hyperlink dialog box), click 'Place in This Document', so that Word displays all the headings and bookmarks in the document.
4. Click the heading or bookmark to which you want to link.
5. Click the OK button.

To Save and Print a Document and Then Exit Word

The reference document for this project now is complete. The following steps save and print the document and then exit Word.

1 Save the document again on the same storage location with the same file name.

2 If requested by your instructor, print the finished document (shown in Figure 9–1 at the beginning of this module).

3 Save the document as a PDF file and submit the PDF in the format requested by your instructor.

4 Exit Word.

Summary

In this module, you have learned how to insert a screenshot, add captions, create cross-references, insert a sidebar text box, link text boxes, compress pictures, use Outline view, work with master documents and subdocuments, and create a table of contents, a table of figures, and an index.

BTW

Conserving Ink and Toner

If you want to conserve ink or toner, you can instruct Word to print draft quality documents by clicking File on the ribbon to open the Backstage view, clicking the Options tab to display the Word Options dialog box, clicking Advanced in the left pane (Word Options dialog box), scrolling to the Print area in the right pane, placing a check mark in the 'Use draft quality' check box, and then clicking the OK button. Then, use the Backstage view to print the document as usual.

CONSIDER THIS: PLAN AHEAD

What decisions will you need to make when creating reference documents?

Use these guidelines as you complete the assignments in this module and create your own reference documents outside of this class.

1. Prepare a document to be included in a longer document.

   a) If a document contains multiple illustrations (figures), each figure should have a caption and be referenced from within the text.

   b) All terms in the document that should be included in the index should be marked as an index entry.

2. Include elements common to a reference document, such as a title page, a table of contents, and an index.

   a) The title page entices passersby to take a copy of the document.

   b) A table of contents at the beginning of the document and an index at the end helps a reader locate topics within the document.

   c) If a document contains several illustrations, you also should include a table of figures.

3. Prepare the document for distribution, including page numbers, gutter margins for binding, bookmarks, and hyperlinks as appropriate.

Apply Your Knowledge

Reinforce the skills and apply the concepts you learned in this module.

Working with Outline View

Note: To complete this assignment, you will be required to use the Data Files. Please contact your instructor for information about accessing the Data Files.

Instructions: Run Word. Open the document, Apply 9-1 Communications Outline Draft, from the Data Files. The document is an outline for a paper. You are to modify the outline in Outline view. The final outline is shown in Figure 9–80.

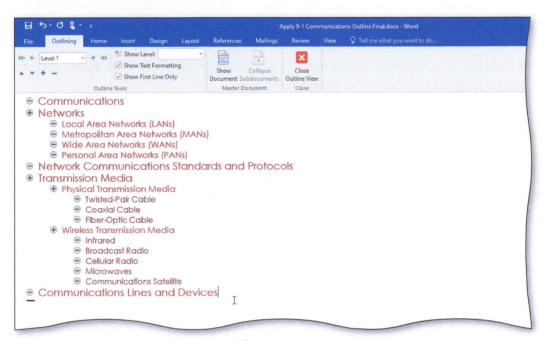

Figure 9–80

Perform the following tasks:

1. If necessary, switch to Outline view.

2. Move the item on the fourth line, Communications, up four lines so that it is at the top of the outline.

3. Promote the item, PANs, so that it is Level 2 instead of Level 3.

4. In the Physical Transmission Media section, move the item, Coaxial Cable, down one line.

5. Practice collapsing and expanding by collapsing the Physical Transmission Media item and then expanding the Physical Transmission Media item.

6. Change the word, Links, in the Communications Links and Devices item to the word, Lines, so that it reads: Communications Lines and Devices.

7. Promote the item, Communications Lines and Devices, to Heading 1 (Level 1).

8. Demote the five items in the outline below the item, Wireless Transmission Media (Infrared, Broadcast Radio, Cellular Radio, Microwaves, and Communications Satellite) so that they are Level 3 instead of Level 2.

9. Insert an item, called Metropolitan Area Networks (MANs), as a Level 2 item below the Local Area Networks (LANs) item.

10. Delete the item called Monitoring Network Traffic.

Continued >

Apply Your Knowledge *continued*

11. Remove the check mark in the 'Show Text Formatting' check box (Outlining tab | Outline Tools group). Place the check mark in the check box again. What is the purpose of this check box?

12. Close Outline View. How does the document differ when displayed in Print Layout view?

13. If requested by your instructor, add your name at the end of the first line of the outline. Save the modified file with the new file name, Apply 9-1 Communications Outline Final. Submit the document in the format specified by your instructor.

14. ✳ Answer the questions posed in #11 and #12. What are two different ways to expand and collapse items in an outline, to move items up and down an outline, and to demote and promote items in an outline?

Extend Your Knowledge

Extend the skills you learned in this module and experiment with new skills. You may need to use Help to complete the assignment.

Working with Screenshots

Note: To complete this assignment, you will be required to use the Data Files. Please contact your instructor for information about accessing the Data Files.

Instructions: Run Word. Open the document, Extend 9-1 Word 2016 Screenshots Draft, from the Data Files. You will insert a screenshot and a screen clipping in the document.

Perform the following tasks:
1. Use Help to expand your knowledge about screenshots, screen clippings, saving images, and print scaling.

2. Change the page from portrait to landscape orientation. Change the margins to Narrow.

3. From Word, create a blank document so that you have two separate Word windows open. Switch to the Word window with the Extend 9-1 Word 2016 Screenshots Draft file open. Insert a screenshot, centered on the blank line below the first paragraph. If necessary, crop the bottom of the screenshot so that it ends at the status bar.

4. Insert a screen clipping of the ribbon, centered on the blank line below the second paragraph.

5. Save the Word screenshot as a JPEG file with the name, Extend 9-1 Word 2016 Screenshot.

6. Save the screen clipping of the ribbon as a JPEG file with the file name, Extend 9-1 Word 2016 Ribbon Screen Clipping.

7. Add a border, shadow, or glow effect to the screenshot and the screen clipping.

8. Add these callouts to the screenshot: Quick Access Toolbar, ribbon, status bar. Change the callout lines to arrows. Format the callouts as necessary for readability.

9. Add these callouts to the screen clipping: tab, group, button. Change the callout lines to arrows. Format the callouts as necessary for readability (Figure 9–81).

10. Print the document so that it fits on a single page; that is, make sure it is scaled to the paper size.

11. Locate the saved JPEG files and then double-click them. In what program did they open?

12. If requested by your instructor, add a text box to the Word screen with your name in it. Save the modified file with the new file name, Extend 9-1 Word Screenshots Final. Submit the documents in the format specified by your instructor.

13. ✳ Answer the question posed in #11. How did you print the document so that it fits on a single page? What changes could you make to the document so that it all fits on a single page when you view it on the screen?

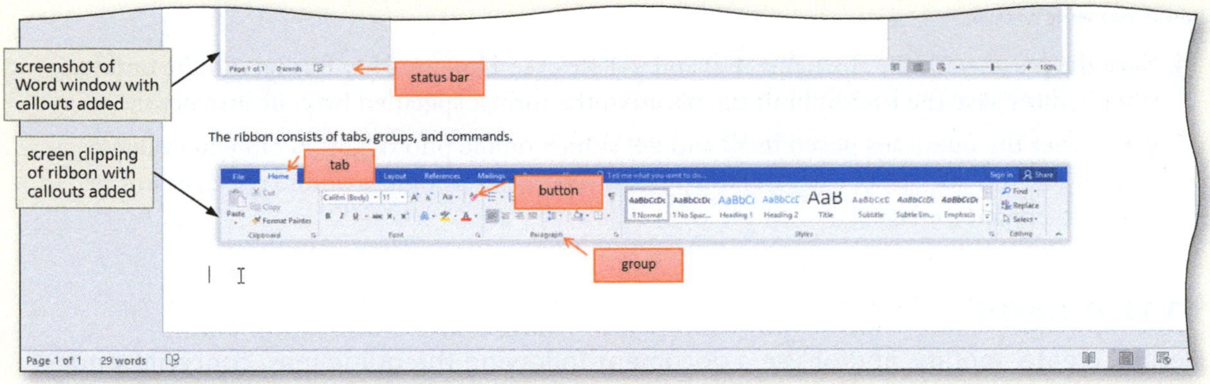

screenshot of Word window with callouts added
status bar
screen clipping of ribbon with callouts added
The ribbon consists of tabs, groups, and commands.
tab
button
group
Page 1 of 1 29 words

Figure 9–81

Expand Your World

Create a solution that uses cloud or web technologies by learning and investigating on your own from general guidance.

Using an Online Photo Editor

Note: To complete this assignment, you will be required to use the Data Files. Please contact your instructor for information about accessing the Data Files.

Instructions: Assume you have a digital photo that you want to edit before including it in a Word document.

Perform the following tasks:

1. Run a browser. Search for the text, online photo editor, using a search engine. Visit several of the online photo editors and determine which you would like to use to edit a photo. Navigate to the desired online photo editor.
2. In the photo editor, open the image called Dog.JPG from the Data Files (Figure 9–82). Use the photo editor to enhance the image. Apply at least five enhancements. Which enhancements did you apply?
3. If requested by your instructor, add your name as a text element to the photo.

fotor®
EDIT
COLLAGE
NEW
DESIGN
Like
1.1M
BASIC EDITS
Open
CROP
ROTATE
BASIC
FINE-TUNE
COLOR
CURVES
RESIZE
HDR
Allowing you to capture highlights, shadows and striking details of your photos!
16%
1868 X 2376
1:1

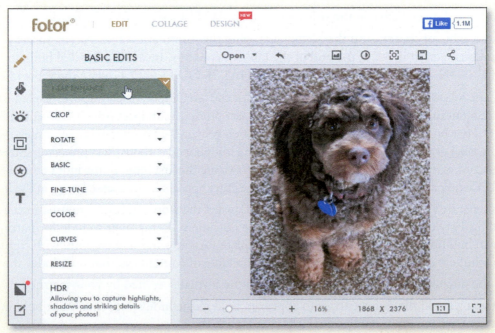

Figure 9–82

Continued >

Expand Your World *continued*

4. Save the photo with the file name, Expand 9-1 Revised Dog. In what format did the online photo editor save the file? Submit the photo in the format specified by your instructor.

5. ✸ Answer the questions posed in #2 and #4. Which online photo editors did you evaluate? Which one did you select to use, and why? Do you prefer using the online photo editor or Word to enhance images?

In the Labs

Design, create, modify, and/or use a document following the guidelines, concepts, and skills presented in this module. Labs 1 and 2, which increase in difficulty, require you to create solutions based on what you learned in the module; Lab 3 requires you to apply your creative thinking and problem-solving skills to design and implement a solution.

Lab 1: Creating a Reference Document with a Cover Page, a Table of Contents, and an Index

Note: To complete this assignment, you will be required to use the Data Files. Please contact your instructor for information about accessing the Data Files.

Problem: As a part-time assistant in the Technology Center at Baxter County Library, you have been asked to prepare a guide briefly describing types of output. A miniature version of this document is shown in Figure 9–83. A draft of the body of the document is on the Data Files.

Perform the following tasks:

1. Open the document, Lab 9-1 Output Draft, from the Data Files. Save the document with a new file name, Lab 9-1 Output Final.

2. Create a title page by inserting the Ion (Dark) style cover page. Use the following information on the title page: year - 2017; title – Learning Technology; subtitle – Output; author – Technology Center; company name - Baxter County Library; company address - 10 Center Street, Baxter, UT 20189.

3. If requested by your instructor, use your name as the author instead of Technology Center.

4. Insert a blank page between the title page and the WHAT IS OUTPUT? heading.

5. Create a table of contents on the blank page using the Automatic Table 1 style. Insert a continuous section break at the end of the table of contents. Insert the Banded built-in footer starting on the page with the section titled WHAT IS OUTPUT? Update the table of contents.

6. Mark the following terms in the document as index entries: Output, display device, display, flat-panel display, monitor, liquid crystal display, printer, impact printer, nonimpact printer, ink-jet printer, photo printer, laser printer, all-in-one printer, multifunction printer, 3-D printer, thermal printer, mobile printer, label printer, plotter, large-format printer, Headphones, earbuds, data projector, interactive whiteboard, force feedback, and tactile output. Lowercase the first letter in the index entries for the words, Output and Headphones, so that the entire entry appears in lowercase letters in the index.

7. On a separate page at the end of the document, insert the word, Index, formatted in the Heading 1 style and then build an index for the document. Remember to hide formatting marks prior to building the index. Use the From template format using one column, with right-aligned page numbers and leader characters. Update the table of contents so that it includes the index.

8. Save the document again and then submit it in the format specified by your instructor.

9. ✸ If you wanted the index entries to appear in bold in the index but remain not bold in the document, what steps would you take to accomplish this?

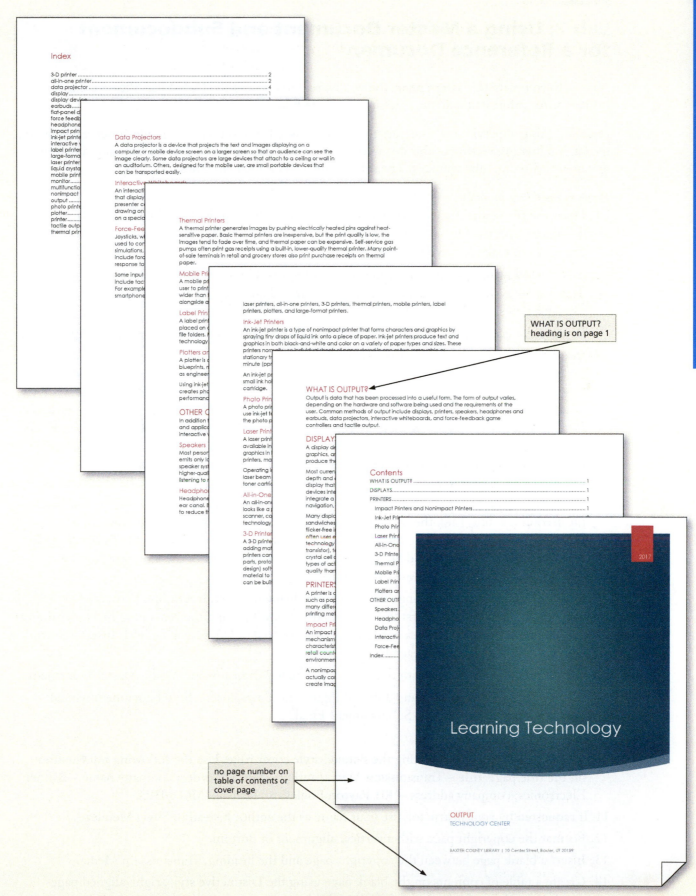

Figure 9–83

Continued >

In the Labs *continued*

Lab 2: Using a Master Document and Subdocument for a Reference Document

Note: To complete this assignment, you will be required to use the Data Files. Please contact your instructor for information about accessing the Data Files.

Problem: Your supervisor at your part-time job has asked you to prepare a guide about transmission media. A miniature version of this document is shown in Figure 9–84. The document is a master document with one subdocument. The subdocument is on the Data Files.

Perform the following tasks:

1. Open the file named Lab 9-2 Transmission Media Draft from the Data Files. Save the document with the file name, Lab 9-2 Transmission Media Subdocument Final, so that any changes you make are saved in a new file.

2. Add the following captions to the figures: first figure – Figure 1: Transfer Rates for Physical Transmission Media Used in LANs; second figure – Figure 2: Wireless Transmission Media Transfer Rates; third figure – Figure 3: Communication Satellites.

3. Replace the occurrences of XX in the document with cross-references to the figure captions.

4. Insert a Retrospect Sidebar text box on the first page. Enter this text in the text box: **What is bandwidth?** Select the description placeholder and then type: **Bandwidth is the amount of data that can travel over transmission media. Higher bandwidths can transmit more data.** Press the ENTER key. Type: **What is a GPS?** Press the ENTER key. Type: **A GPS (global positioning system) is a navigation system that consists of one or more earth-based receivers that accept and analyze signals sent by satellites in order to determine the receiver's geographic location.** Format the second question the same as the first.

5. On the last page, insert another Retrospect Sidebar text box and then delete the contents of the second text box. Link the two text boxes together. Resize each text box so that each one contains just one question and answer. Move the first text box to the top of the first page and the second text box to the middle of the second page to the right of the Communications Satellite heading. Save and close the document.

6. Create a new document. Change the document theme to Facet. In Outline View, type **Copyright 2017** as the first line formatted as Body Text, and the remaining lines containing the Table of Figures and Index headings, each formatted as Heading 1/Level 1. Insert a next page section break between each line.

7. Save the master document with the file name, Lab 9-2 Transmission Media Master Document.

8. Between the Copyright line and Table of Figures headings, insert the subdocument named Lab 9-2 Transmission Media Subdocument Final.

9. Switch to Print Layout view.

10. Create a cover page by inserting the Banded style cover page. Use the following information on the title page: title – Transmission Media; author – Silvia Mendez; company name – Banner Electronics; company address – 403 Payton Boulevard, Hanson, MO 30393.

11. If requested by your instructor, use your name as the author instead of Silvia Mendez.

12. Format the copyright page with a vertical alignment of Bottom.

13. Insert a blank page between the copyright page and the heading, Transmission Media.

14. Create a table of contents on the blank page using the Distinctive style, right-aligned page numbers, and dots for leader characters.

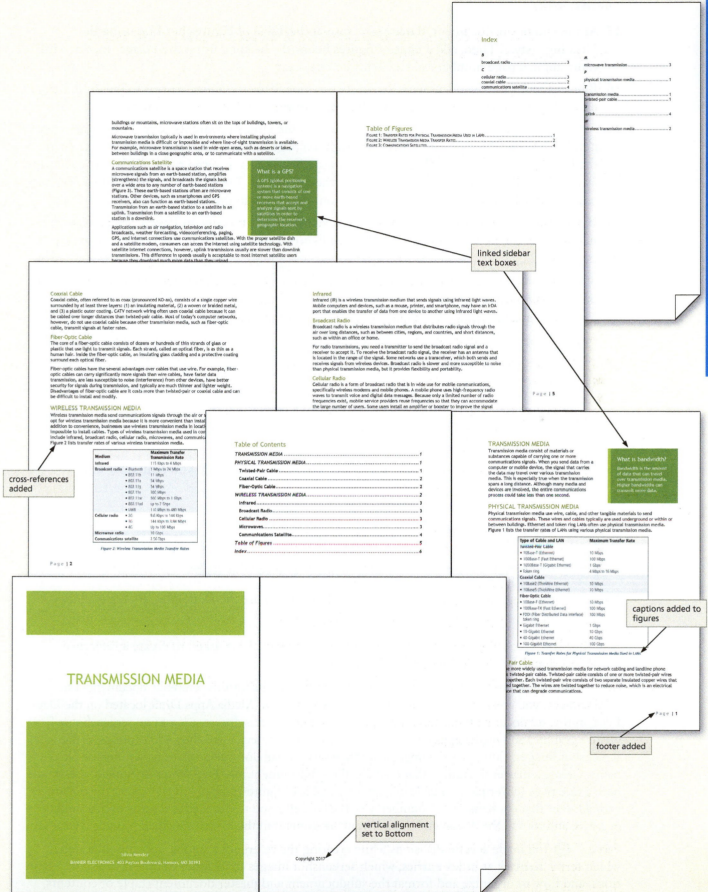

Figure 9–84

Continued >

In the Labs *continued*

15. At the end of the document, if necessary, format the Table of Figures heading using the Heading 1 style. Then, add a table of figures below the heading using the Formal format with right-aligned page numbers and a tab leader character.

16. Build an index for the document. Remember to hide formatting marks prior to building the index. Use the Formal format in two columns with right-aligned page numbers.

17. Insert a continuous section break at the bottom of the table of contents page. Format the page number on the table of contents page to begin on page 0. Beginning on the fourth page (with the heading, Transmission Media), create alternating footers. Insert a right tab for the even page footer. Align left the odd page footer. Insert the Accent Bar 2 page number style. The cover page, copyright page, or table of contents should not contain the footer.

18. If necessary, resize Figure 1 so that the Twisted-Pair Cable text fits on Page 1, resize Figure 2 so that it fits at the bottom of page 2, and resize Figure 3 so that it fits at the bottom of page 4.

19. From the copyright page forward, set the left and right margins to .75" and set a gutter margin of .5". You may need to fix extra pages inserted by replacing next page section breaks with odd or even page section breaks.

20. Insert a bookmark for each Heading 1 and Heading 2 in the document.

21. Compress the pictures in the document.

22. Update the table of contents, table of figures, and index.

23. Make any additional adjustments so that the document looks like Figure 9–84.

24. Save the document again. Also save the document as a PDF file. Submit the Word documents or the PDF file in the format specified by your instructor. If requested by your instructor, print the document back to back.

25. ✳ If you added a figure in the Broadcast Radio section, how would you renumber the remaining figures in the document?

Lab 3: **Consider This: Your Turn**

Create a Reference Document about Graphics and Media Apps

Note: To complete this assignment, you will be required to use the Data Files. Please contact your instructor for information about accessing the Data Files.

Problem: In your Introduction to Computers class, you have been asked to create a reference document that discusses various graphics and media apps.

Part 1: You decide to use master documents and subdocuments for this reference document. The subdocument you created is a file named Lab 9-3 Graphics and Media Apps Draft located on the Data Files. In this subdocument, mark at least 10 terms as index entries. Insert at least two screenshots of various graphics and media apps on your computer or mobile device and then add captions to the screenshot images. Compress the images and then save the subdocument file using a different file name. Create a master document that contains the subdocument file. The master document also should have a title page (cover page), a table of contents, a table of figures, and an index. Format the document with a footer that contains a page number. Use the concepts and techniques presented in this module to organize and format the document. Submit your assignment in the format specified by your instructor.

Part 2: ✳ You made several decisions while creating the reference document in this assignment: which terms to mark as index entries, which screenshot images to include, what text to use for captions, and how to organize and format the subdocument and master document (table of contents, table of figures, index, gutter margins, etc.). What was the rationale behind each of these decisions? When you proofread the document, what further revisions did you make and why?

10 | Creating a Template for an Online Form

Objectives

You will have mastered the material in this module when you can:

- Save a document as a template
- Change paper size
- Change page color
- Insert a borderless table in a form
- Show the Developer tab
- Insert plain text, drop-down list, check box, rich text, combo box, and date picker content controls
- Edit placeholder text

- Change properties of content controls
- Insert and format a rectangle shape
- Customize a theme
- Protect a form
- Open a new document based on a template
- Fill in a form

Introduction

During your personal and professional life, you undoubtedly have filled in countless forms. Whether a federal tax form, a time card, a job application, an order, a deposit slip, a request, or a survey, a form is designed to collect information. In the past, forms were printed; that is, you received the form on a piece of paper, filled it in with a pen or pencil, and then returned it manually. With an **online form**, you use a computer or mobile device to access, fill in, and then return the form. In Word, you easily can create an online form for electronic distribution; you also can fill in that same form using Word.

Project — Online Form

Today, people are concerned with using resources efficiently. To minimize paper waste, protect the environment, enhance office efficiency, and improve access to data, many businesses have moved toward a paperless office. Thus, online forms have replaced many paper forms. You access online forms on a website, on your company's intranet, or from your inbox if you receive the form via email.

The project in this module uses Word to produce the online form shown in Figure 10–1. Ellie's Coffee Stop is a coffeehouse interested in customer feedback. Instead of sending a survey via the postal service, Ellie's Coffee Stop will send the

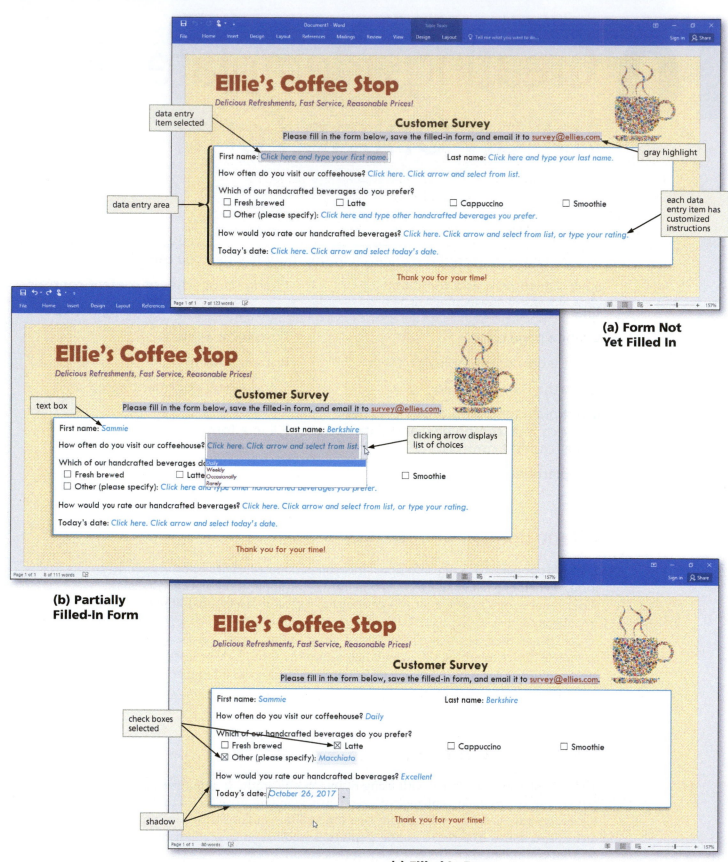

(a) Form Not Yet Filled In

(b) Partially Filled-In Form

(c) Filled-In Form

Figure 10–1

survey via email to customers for whom it has email addresses. Upon receipt of the online form (a survey), the customer fills in the form, saves it, and then sends it back via email to Ellie's Coffee Stop.

Figure 10–1a shows how the form is displayed on a user's screen initially, Figure 10–1b shows the form partially filled in by one user, and Figure 10–1c shows how this user filled in the entire form.

The data entry area of the form contains three text boxes (named First Name, Last Name, and Other Beverages), one drop-down list box (named Frequency of Visits), five check boxes (named Fresh Brewed, Latte, Cappuccino, Smoothie, and Other Beverages), a combination text box/drop-down list box (named Beverage Rating), and a date picker (named Today's Date).

The form is designed so that it fits completely within a Word window that is set at a page width zoom and has the ribbon collapsed, which reduces the chance a user will have to scroll the window while filling in the form. The data entry area of the form is enclosed by a rectangle that has a shadow on its left and bottom edges. The line of text above the data entry area is covered with the color gray, giving it the look of text that has been marked with a gray highlighter pen.

In this module, you will learn how to create the form shown in Figure 10–1. The following roadmap identifies general activities you will perform as you progress through this module:

1. SAVE a DOCUMENT as a TEMPLATE.

2. SET FORM FORMATS FOR the TEMPLATE.

3. ENTER TEXT, GRAPHICS, AND CONTENT CONTROLS in the form.

4. PROTECT the FORM.

5. USE the FORM.

To Run Word and Change Word Settings

If you are using a computer to step through the project in this module and you want your screens to match the figures in this book, you should change your screen's resolution to 1366 × 768. The following steps run Word, display formatting marks, and change the zoom to page width.

1 Run Word and create a blank document in the Word window. If necessary, maximize the Word window.

2 If the Print Layout button on the status bar is not selected, click it so that your screen is in Print Layout view.

3 To display the page the same width as the document window, if necessary, click the Page Width button (View tab | Zoom group).

4 If the 'Show/Hide ¶' button (Home tab | Paragraph group) is not selected already, click it to display formatting marks on the screen.

5 If the rulers are displayed on the screen, click the View Ruler check box (View tab | Show group) to remove the rulers from the Word window.

Saving a Document as a Template

A **template** is a file that contains the definition of the appearance of a Word document, including items such as default font, font size, margin settings, and line spacing; available styles; and even placement of text. Every Word document you create is based on a template. When you select the Blank document thumbnail on the Word start screen or in the New gallery of the Backstage view, Word creates a document based on the Normal template. Word also provides other templates for more specific types of documents, such as memos, letters, and resumes, some of which you have used in previous modules. Creating a document based on these templates can improve your productivity because Word has defined much of the document's appearance for you.

In this module, you create an online form. If you create and save an online form as a Word document, users will be required to open that Word document to display the form on the screen. Next, they will fill in the form. Then, to preserve the content of the original form, they will have to save the form with a new file name. If they accidentally click the Save button on the Quick Access Toolbar during the process of filling in the form, Word will replace the original blank form with a filled-in form.

If you create and save the online form as a template instead, users will open a new document window that is based on that template. This displays the form on the screen as a brand new Word document; that is, the document does not have a file name. Thus, the user fills in the form and then clicks the Save button on the Quick Access Toolbar to save his or her filled-in form. By creating a Word template for the form, instead of a Word document, the original template for the form remains intact when the user clicks the Save button.

BTW

The Ribbon and Screen Resolution
Word may change how the groups and buttons within the groups appear on the ribbon, depending on the computer's screen resolution. Thus, your ribbon may look different from the ones in this book if you are using a screen resolution other than 1366 x 768.

To Save a Document as a Template

1 SAVE DOCUMENT TEMPLATE | 2 SET FORM FORMATS FOR TEMPLATE
3 ENTER TEXT, GRAPHICS, & CONTENT CONTROLS | 4 PROTECT FORM | 5 USE FORM

The following steps save a new blank document as a template. **Why?** *The template will be used to create the online form shown in Figure 10–1.*

- With a new blank document in the Word window, open the Backstage view and then click the Export tab in the left pane of the Backstage view to display the Export gallery.

- Click 'Change File Type' in the Export gallery to display information in the right pane about various file types that can be opened in Word.

- Click Template in the right pane to specify the file type for the current document (Figure 10–2).

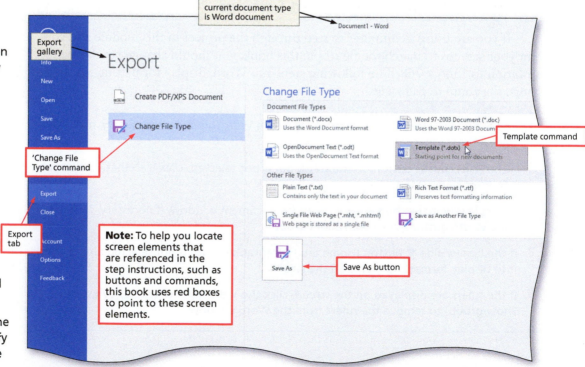

Figure 10–2

2

- Click the Save As button to display the Save As dialog box with the file type automatically changed to Word Template.

Q&A How does Word differentiate between a saved Word template and a saved Word document?
Files typically have a file name and a file extension. The file extension identifies the file type. The source program often assigns a file type to a file. A Word document has an extension of .docx, whereas a Word template has an extension of .dotx. Thus, a file named July Report.docx is a Word document, and a file named Fitness Form.dotx is a Word template.

- Type **Coffeehouse Customer Survey** in the File name box to change the file name and then navigate to the desired save location (Figure 10–3).

Q&A Why is my save location the Custom Office Templates folder?
The default save location for your templates may be the Custom Office Templates folder. If you are using a home computer, you can save your template in that folder. If you are using a public computer, you should change the save location to your local storage location.

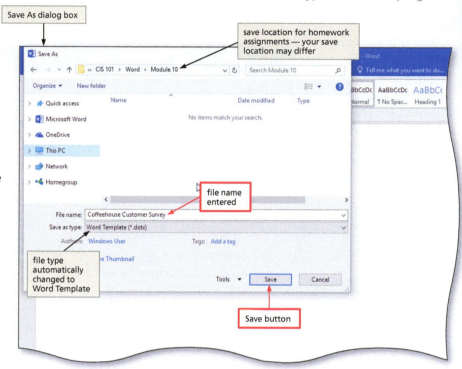

Figure 10–3

3

- Click the Save button (Save As dialog box) to save the document as a Word template with the entered file name in the specified location.

Other Ways

1. Press F12, change document type to Word Template

2. Open Backstage view, click Save As, change document type to Word Template

Changing Document Settings

To enhance the look of the form, you change several default settings in Word:

1. Display the page as wide as possible in the document window to maximize the amount of space for text and graphics on the form, called page width zoom.
2. Change the size of the paper so that it fits completely within the document window.
3. Adjust the margins so that as much text as possible will fit in the document.
4. Change the document theme to Headlines and the theme fonts to the Tw Cen MT font set.
5. Change the page color to a shade of gold with a pattern.

The first item was completed earlier in the module. The following sections make the remaining changes to the document.

BTW

Touch Screen Differences
The Office and Windows interfaces may vary if you are using a touch screen. For this reason, you might notice that the function or appearance of your touch screen differs slightly from this module's presentation.

To Change Paper Size

For the online form in this module, all edges of the page appear in the document window. Currently, only the top, left, and right edges are displayed in the document window. The following steps change paper size. *Why? To display all edges of the document in the document window in the current resolution, change the height of the paper from 11 inches to 4 inches.*

1

- Display the Layout tab.

- Click the 'Choose Page Size' button (Layout tab | Page Setup group) to display the Choose Page Size gallery (Figure 10–4).

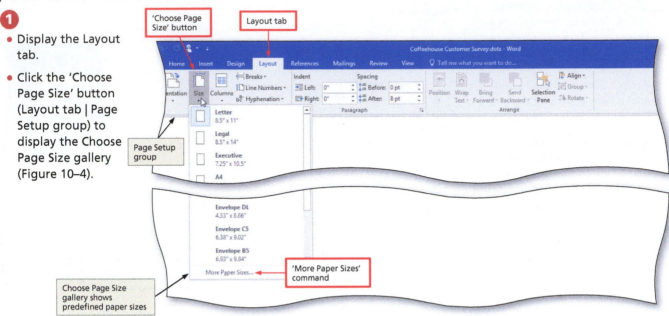

Figure 10–4

2

- Click 'More Paper Sizes' in the Choose Page Size gallery to display the Paper sheet in the Page Setup dialog box.

- In the Height box (Page Setup dialog box), type **4** as the new height (Figure 10–5).

3

- Click the OK button to change the paper size to the entered measurements, which, in this case, are 8.5 inches wide by 4 inches tall.

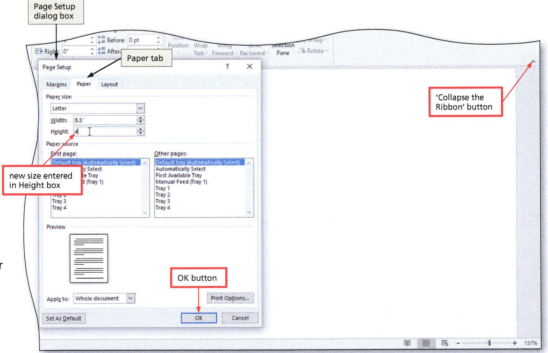

Figure 10–5

To Collapse the Ribbon

To display more of a document or other item in the Word window, you can collapse the ribbon, which hides the groups on the ribbon and displays only the main tabs. For the online form to fit entirely in the Word window, you collapse the ribbon. The following step collapses the ribbon so that you can see how the form fits in the document window.

1 Click the 'Collapse the Ribbon' button on the ribbon (shown in Figure 10–5) to collapse the ribbon (Figure 10–6).

Q&A What happened to the 'Collapse the Ribbon' button?
The 'Pin the ribbon' button replaces the 'Collapse the Ribbon' button when the ribbon is collapsed. You will see the 'Pin the ribbon' button only when you expand a ribbon by clicking a tab.

What if the height of my document does not match the figure?
You may need to show white space. To do this, position the pointer above the top of the page below the ribbon and then double-click when the pointer changes to a 'Show White Space' button (or, if using touch, double-tap below the page). Or, your screen resolution may be different; if so, you may need to adjust the page height or width values.

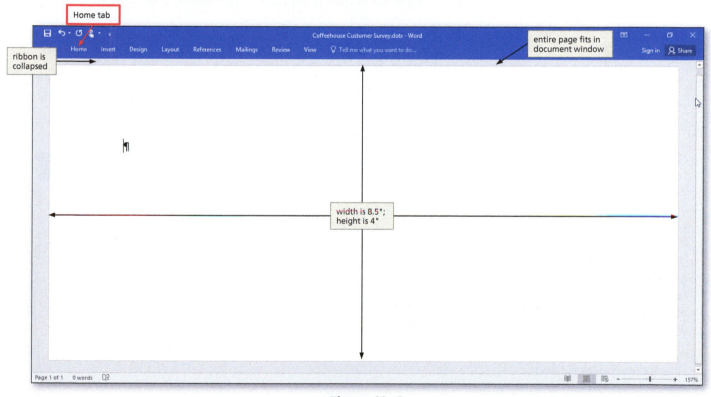

Figure 10–6

To Expand the Ribbon

After you verify that the entire form will fit in the document window, you should expand the ribbon so that you can see the groups while creating the online form. The following steps expand the ribbon.

1 Click Home on the collapsed ribbon to expand the Home tab.

2 Click the 'Pin the ribbon' button on the expanded Home tab to restore the ribbon.

To Set Custom Margins

Recall that Word is preset to use 1-inch top, bottom, left, and right margins. To maximize the space for the contents of the form, this module sets the left and right margins to .5 inches, the top margin to .25 inches, and the bottom margin to 0 inches. The following steps set custom margins.

1 Display the Layout tab. Click the Adjust Margins button (Layout tab | Page Setup group) to display the Adjust Margins gallery.

2 Click Custom Margins in the Adjust Margins gallery to display the Margins sheet in the Page Setup dialog box.

3 Type .25 in the Top box (Page Setup dialog box) to change the top margin setting.

4 Type 0 (zero) in the Bottom box to change the bottom margin setting.

Q&A | Why set the bottom margin to zero?
This allows you to place form contents at the bottom of the page, if necessary.

5 Type .5 in the Left box to change the left margin setting.

6 Type .5 in the Right box to change the right margin setting (Figure 10–7).

7 Click the OK button to set the custom margins for this document.

Q&A | What if Word displays a dialog box indicating margins are outside the printable area?
Click the Ignore button because this is an online form that is not intended for printing.

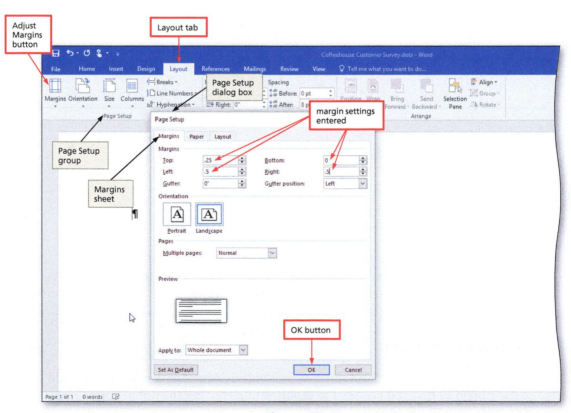

Figure 10–7

To Change the Document Theme and Theme Fonts

The following steps change the document theme colors to Headlines and the theme fonts to Tw Cen MT.

1 Display the Design tab. Click the Themes button (Design tab | Document Formatting group) and then click Headlines in the Themes gallery to change the document theme.

2 Click the Theme Fonts button (Design tab | Document Formatting group) and then scroll through the Theme Fonts gallery to display the Tw Cen MT font set (Figure 10–8).

3 Click 'Tw Cen MT' in the Theme Fonts gallery to change the font set.

BTW

Set a Theme as the Default
If you wanted to change the default theme, you would select the theme you want to be the default theme, or select the color scheme, font set, and theme effects you would like to use as the default. Then, click the 'Set as Default' button (Design tab | Document Formatting group), which uses the current settings as the new default.

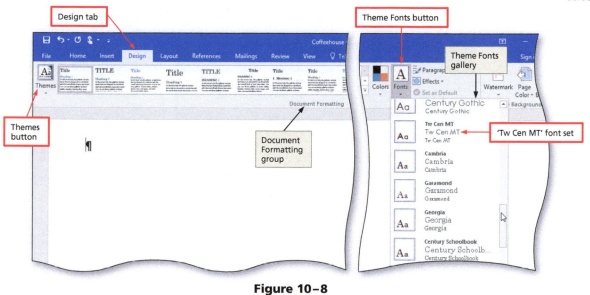

Figure 10–8

To Add a Page Color

1 SAVE DOCUMENT TEMPLATE | **2 SET FORM FORMATS FOR TEMPLATE**
3 ENTER TEXT, GRAPHICS, & CONTENT CONTROLS | 4 PROTECT FORM | 5 USE FORM

The following steps change the page color. *Why? This online form uses a shade of gold for the page color (background color) so that the form is more visually appealing.*

1

- Click the Page Color button (Design tab | Page Background group) to display the Page Color gallery.

- Point to 'Gold, Accent 3' (seventh color in the first row) in the Page Color gallery to display a live preview of the selected background color (Figure 10–9).

Experiment

- Point to various colors in the Page Color gallery and watch the page color change in the document window.

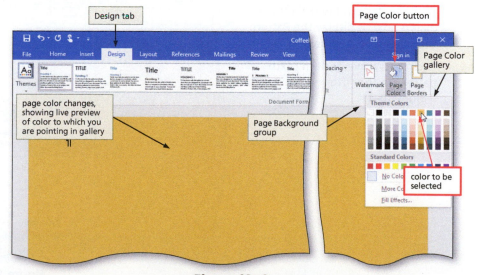

Figure 10–9

- Click 'Gold, Accent 3' to change the page color to the selected color.

Q&A Do page colors print?
When you change the page color, it appears only on the screen. Changing the page color does not affect a printed document.

To Add a Pattern Fill Effect to a Page Color

1 SAVE DOCUMENT TEMPLATE | **2 SET FORM FORMATS FOR TEMPLATE**
3 ENTER TEXT, GRAPHICS, & CONTENT CONTROLS | 4 PROTECT FORM | 5 USE FORM

When you changed the page color in the previous steps, Word placed a solid color on the screen. The following steps add a pattern to the page color. *Why? For this online form, the solid background color is a little too bold. To soften the color, you can add a pattern to it.*

- Click the Page Color button (Design tab | Page Background group) to display the Page Color gallery (Figure 10–10).

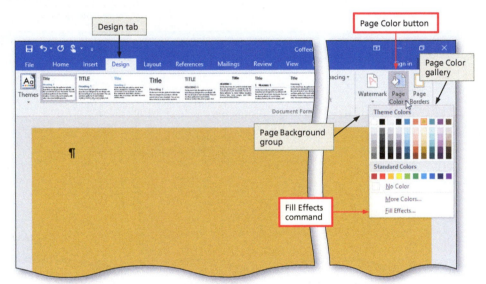

Figure 10–10

- Click Fill Effects in the Page Color gallery to display the Fill Effects dialog box.

- Click the Pattern tab (Fill Effects dialog box) to display the Pattern sheet in the dialog box.

- Click the Weave pattern (sixth pattern in the fifth row) to select it (Figure 10–11).

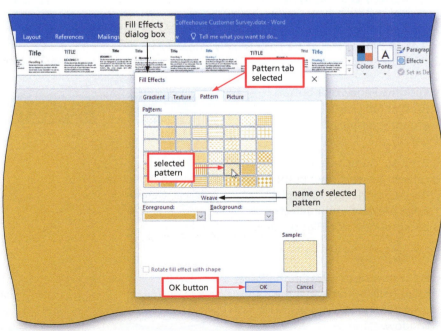

Figure 10–11

- Click the OK button to add the selected pattern to the current page color (Figure 10–12).

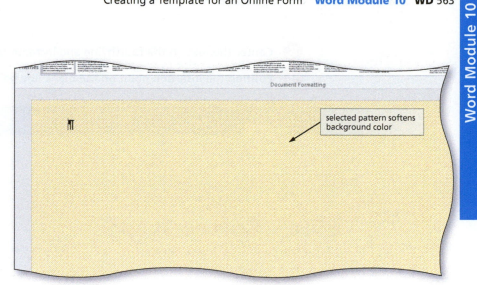

selected pattern softens background color

Figure 10–12

Enter Content in the Online Form

The next step in creating the online form in this module is to enter the text, graphics, and content controls in the document. The following sections describe this process.

To Enter and Format Text

The following steps enter the text at the top of the online form.

1 Type **Ellie's Coffee Stop** and then press the ENTER key.

2 Type **Delicious Refreshments, Fast Service, Reasonable Prices!** and then press the ENTER key.

3 Type **Customer Survey** and then press the ENTER key.

4 Type **Please fill in the form below, save the filled-in form, and email it to survey@ellies.com.** and then press the ENTER key.

If requested by your instructor, change the name, ellies, in the email address to your name.

Q&A Why did the email address change color?
In this document theme, the color for a hyperlink is a shade of aqua. When you pressed the ENTER key, Word automatically formatted the hyperlink in this color. Later in this module, you will change the color of the hyperlink.

5 Format the characters on the first line to 28-point Berlin Sans FB Demi font with the color of Orange, Accent 2, Darker 50% and then remove space after the paragraph (spacing after should be 0 pt).

6 Format the characters on the second line to italic with the color of Purple, Accent 5, Darker 25%.

7 Format the characters on the third line to 16-point bold font with the color of Brown, Accent 6, Darker 50% and center the text on the line. Remove space before and after this paragraph (spacing before and after should be 0 pt).

8 Center the text on the fourth line and increase the spacing after this line to 12 point.

9 Position the insertion point on the blank line below the text (Figure 10–13).

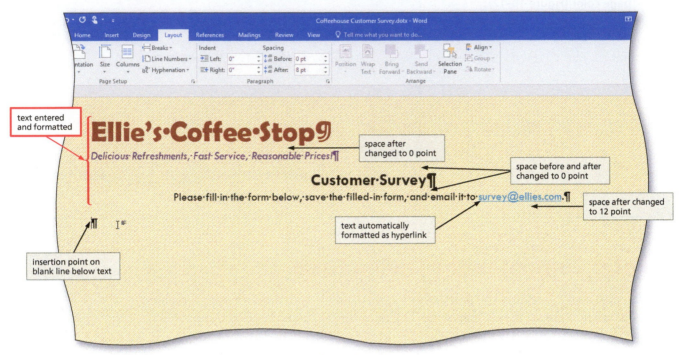

Figure 10–13

To Insert an Image and Scale It

The next step is to insert an image of a coffee cup in the form. Because the graphic's original size is too large, you will reduce its size. The following steps insert and scale a graphic.

1 Display the Insert tab. Click the Online Pictures button (Insert tab | Illustrations group) to display the Insert Pictures dialog box.

2 Type **coffee cup** in the Search box (Insert Pictures dialog box) and then click the Search button to display a list of images that matches the entered search text.

3 Click the coffee cup image that matches the one in Figure 10–14 (or a similar image) and then click the Insert button to download the image, close the dialog box, and insert the graphic in the document at the location of the insertion point.

Q&A What if I cannot locate the same image?
Click the Cancel button and then close the Insert Pictures dialog box. Click the From File button (Insert tab | Illustrations group) to display the Insert Picture dialog box, navigate to the Colorful-Coffee-Circles-6-2400px.png file on the Data Files (Insert Picture dialog box), and click the Insert button to insert the picture.

4 With the graphic still selected, use the Shape Height and Shape Width boxes (Picture Tools Format tab | Size group) to change the graphic height to approximately 1.3" and width to 1.03", respectively (shown in Figure 10–14).

Q&A What if the Picture Tools Format tab is not the active tab on my ribbon?
Double-click the graphic, or click the Picture Tools Format tab on the ribbon.

To Format a Graphic's Text Wrapping

Word inserted the coffee cup image as an inline graphic, that is, as part of the current paragraph. In this online form, the graphic should be positioned to the right of the company name (shown in Figure 10–1 at the beginning of this module). Thus, the graphic should be a floating graphic instead of an inline graphic. The text in the online form should not wrap around the graphic. Thus, the graphic should float in front of the text. The following steps change the graphic's text wrapping to In Front of Text.

1 With the graphic selected, click the Layout Options button attached to the graphic to display the LAYOUT OPTIONS gallery (Figure 10–14).

2 Click 'In Front of Text' in the LAYOUT OPTIONS gallery to change the graphic from inline to floating with the selected wrapping style.

3 Click the Close button in the LAYOUT OPTIONS gallery to close the gallery.

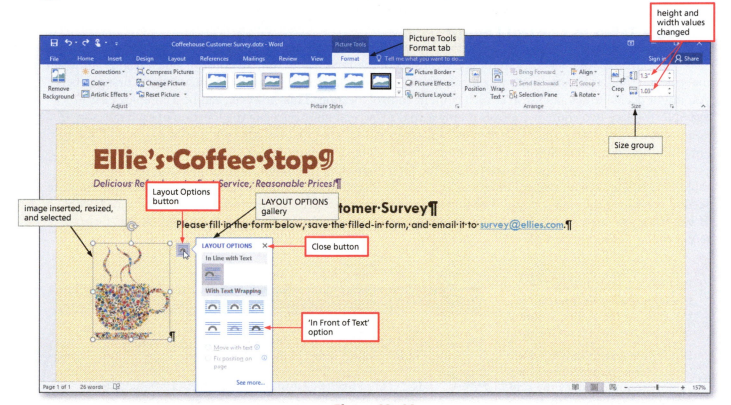

Figure 10–14

To Move a Graphic

The final step associated with the graphic is to move it so that it is positioned on the right side of the online form. The following steps move a graphic.

1 If necessary, scroll to display the top of the form in the document window.

2 Drag the graphic to the location shown in Figure 10–15.

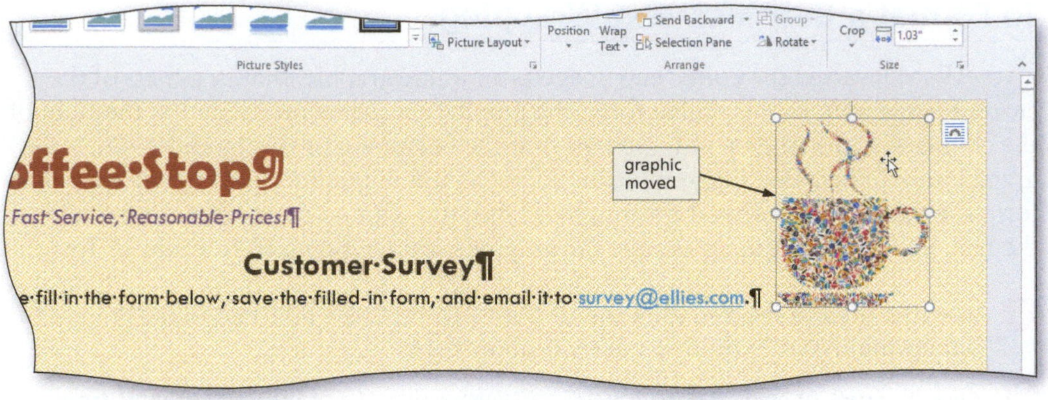

Figure 10–15

To Use a Table to Control Layout

The first line of data entry in the form consists of the First Name content control, which begins at the left margin, and the Last Name content control, which begins at the center point of the same line. At first glance, you might decide to set a tab stop at each content control location. This, however, can be a complex task. For example, to place two content controls evenly across a row, you must calculate the location of each tab stop. If you insert a 2 × 1 table instead, Word automatically calculates the size of two evenly spaced columns. Thus, to enter multiple content controls on a single line, insert a table to control layout.

In this online form, the line containing the First Name and Last Name content controls will be a 2 × 1 table, that is, a table with two columns and one row. By inserting a 2 × 1 table, Word automatically positions the second column at the center point. The following steps insert a 2 × 1 table in the form and remove its border. *Why? When you insert a table, Word automatically surrounds it with a border. Because you are using the tables solely to control layout, you do not want the table borders visible.*

1

• Position the insertion point where the table should be inserted, in this case, on the blank paragraph mark below the text on the form.

• Display the Insert tab. Click the 'Add a Table' button (Insert tab | Tables group) to display the Add a Table gallery (Figure 10–16).

Figure 10–16

2

• Click the cell in the first row and second column of the grid to insert an empty 2 × 1 table at the location of the insertion point.

• Select the table.

Q&A How do I select a table?
Point somewhere in the table and then click the table move handle that appears in the upper-left corner of the table (or, if using touch, tap the Select Table button (Table Tools Layout tab | Table group) and then tap Select Table on the Select Table menu).

- If necessary, display the Table Tools Design tab.

- Click the Borders arrow (Table Tools Design tab | Borders group) to display the Borders gallery (Figure 10–17).

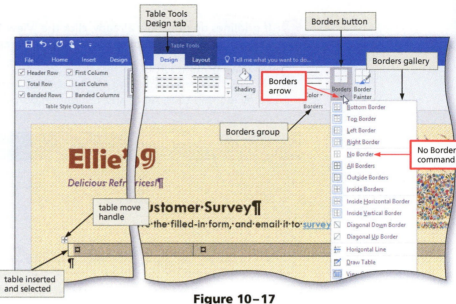

Figure 10–17

3
- Click No Border in the Borders gallery to remove the borders from the table.

4
- Click the first cell of the table to remove the selection (Figure 10–18).

Q&A My screen does not display the end-of-cell marks. Why not?
Display formatting marks by clicking the 'Show/Hide ¶' button (Home tab | Paragraph group).

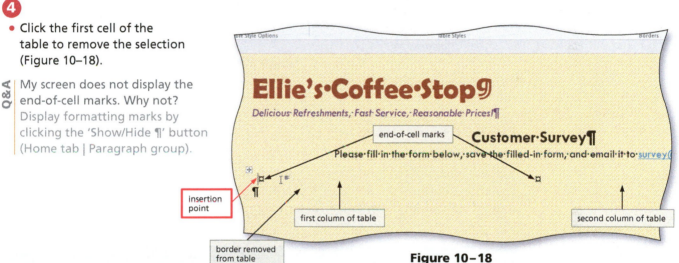

Figure 10–18

Other Ways

1. Click 'Add a Table' button (Insert tab | Tables group), click Insert Table in Add a Table gallery, enter number of columns and rows, click OK button (Insert Table dialog box)

To Show Table Gridlines

When you remove the borders from a table, you no longer can see the individual cells in the table. To help identify the location of cells, you can display **gridlines**, which show cell outlines on the screen. The following steps show gridlines.

1 If necessary, position the insertion point in a table cell.

2 Display the Table Tools Layout tab.

③ If gridlines do not show already, click the 'View Table Gridlines' button (Table Tools Layout tab | Table group) to show table gridlines on the screen (Figure 10–19).

Q&A

Do table gridlines print?

No. Gridlines are formatting marks that show only on the screen. Gridlines help users easily identify cells, rows, and columns in borderless tables.

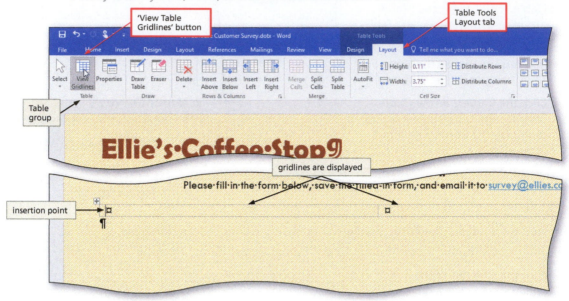

Figure 10–19

Content Controls

To add data entry fields in a Word form, you insert content controls. Word includes nine different content controls you can insert in your online forms. Table 10–1 outlines the use of each of these controls. The following sections insert content controls in the online form for the project in this module.

Table 10–1 Content Controls

Type	Icon	Use
Building Block Gallery		User selects a built-in building block from the gallery.
Check Box		User selects or deselects a check box.
Combo Box		User types text entry or selects one item from a list of choices.
Date Picker		User interacts with a calendar to select a date or types a date in the placeholder.
Drop-Down List		User selects one item from a list of choices.
Picture		User inserts a drawing, a shape, a picture, image, or a SmartArt graphic.
Plain Text	Aa	User enters text, which may not be formatted.
Repeating Section		Users can instruct Word to create a duplicate of the content control.
Rich Text	Aa	User enters text and, if desired, may format the entered text.

How do you determine the correct content control to use for each data entry field?

For each data entry field, decide which content control best maps to the type of data the field will contain. The field specifications for the fields in this module's online form are listed below:

• The First Name, Last Name, and Other Beverages data entry fields will contain text. The first two will be plain text content controls and the last will be a rich text content control.

• The Frequency of Visits data entry field must contain one of these four values: Daily, Weekly, Occasionally, Rarely. This field will be a drop-down list content control.

• The Fresh Brewed, Latte, Cappuccino, Smoothie, and Other Beverage data entry fields will be check boxes that the user can select or deselect.

• The Beverage Rating data entry field can contain one of these four values: Excellent, Good, Fair, and Poor. In addition, users should be able to enter their own value in this data entry field if none of these four values is applicable. A combo box content control will be used for this field.

• The Today's Date data entry field should contain only a valid date value. Thus, this field will be a date picker content control.

To Show the Developer Tab

1 SAVE DOCUMENT TEMPLATE | 2 SET FORM FORMATS FOR TEMPLATE
3 ENTER TEXT, GRAPHICS, & CONTENT CONTROLS | 4 PROTECT FORM | 5 USE FORM

To create a form in Word, you use buttons on the Developer tab. The following steps display the Developer tab on the ribbon. *Why? Because it allows you to perform more advanced tasks not required by everyday Word users, the Developer tab does not appear on the ribbon by default.*

• Open the Backstage view (Figure 10–20).

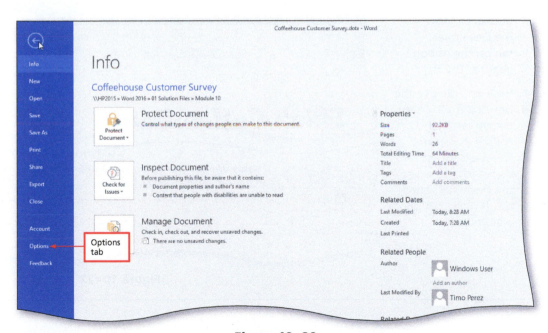

Figure 10–20

2

- Click the Options tab in the left pane of the Backstage view to display the Word Options dialog box.

- Click Customize Ribbon in the left pane (Word Options dialog box) to display associated options in the right pane.

- Place a check mark in the Developer check box in the Main Tabs list (Figure 10–21).

Q&A What are the plus symbols to the left of each tab name?

Clicking the plus symbol expands to show the groups.

Can I show or hide any tab in this list?

Yes. Place a check mark in the check box to show the tab, or remove the check mark to hide the tab.

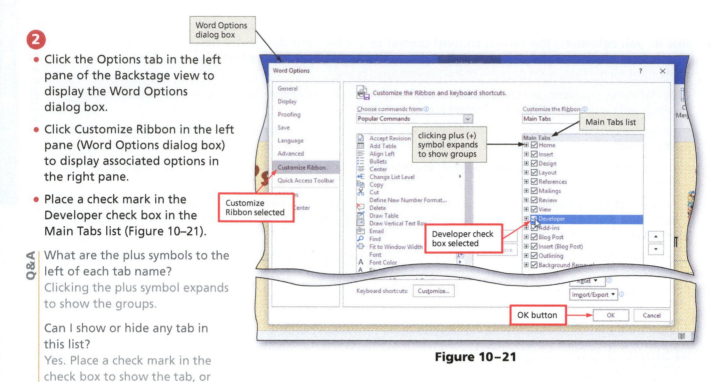

Figure 10–21

3

- Click the OK button to show the Developer tab on the ribbon (Figure 10–22).

Q&A How do I remove the Developer tab from the ribbon?

Follow these same steps, except remove the check mark from the Developer check box (Word Options dialog box).

Figure 10–22

To Insert a Plain Text Content Control

1 SAVE DOCUMENT TEMPLATE | 2 SET FORM FORMATS FOR TEMPLATE
3 ENTER TEXT, GRAPHICS, & CONTENT CONTROLS | 4 PROTECT FORM | 5 USE FORM

The first item that a user enters in the Customer Survey is his or her first name. Because the first name entry contains text that the user should not format, this online form uses a plain text content control for the First Name data entry field. The following steps enter the label, First name:, followed by a plain text content control. *Why?* *The label, First name:, is displayed to the left of the plain text content control. To improve readability, a colon or some other character often separates a label from the content control.*

- With the insertion point in the first cell of the table as shown in Figure 10–22, type **First name:** as the label for the content control.
- Press the SPACEBAR (Figure 10–23).

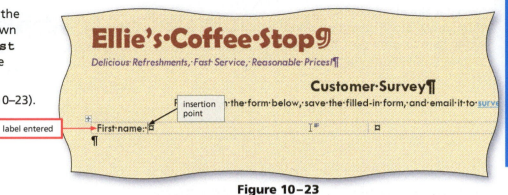

Figure 10–23

- Display the Developer tab.
- Click the 'Plain Text Content Control' button (Developer tab | Controls group) to insert a plain text content control at the location of the insertion point (Figure 10–24).

Q&A Is the plain text content control similar to the content controls that I have used in templates installed with Word, such as in the letter, memo, and resume templates? Yes. The content controls you insert through the Developer tab have the same functionality as the content controls in the templates installed with Word.

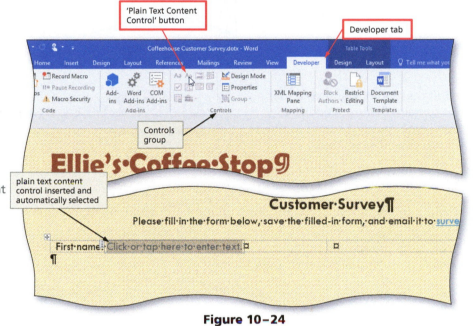

Figure 10–24

To Edit Placeholder Text

1 SAVE DOCUMENT TEMPLATE | 2 SET FORM FORMATS FOR TEMPLATE
3 ENTER TEXT, GRAPHICS, & CONTENT CONTROLS | 4 PROTECT FORM | 5 USE FORM

A content control displays **placeholder text,** which instructs the user how to enter values in the content control. The default placeholder text for a plain text content control is the instruction, Click or tap here to enter text. The following steps edit the placeholder text for the plain text content control just entered. *Why? You can change the wording in the placeholder text so that it is more instructional or applicable to the current form.*

- With the plain text content control selected (shown in Figure 10–24), click the Design Mode button (Developer tab | Controls group) to turn on Design mode, which displays tags at the beginning and ending of the placeholder text (Figure 10–25).

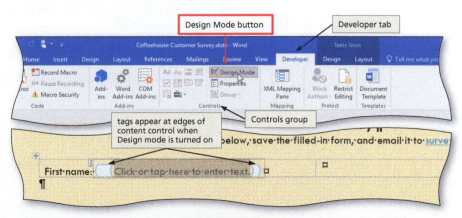

Figure 10–25

• Even if it already is selected, drag through the placeholder text, Click or tap here to enter text., because you want to edit the instruction (Figure 10–26).

Figure 10–26

• Edit the placeholder text so that it contains the text, Click here and type your first name., as the instruction (Figure 10–27).

Q&A What if the placeholder text wraps to the next line?

Because of the tags at each edge of the placeholder text, the entered text may wrap in the table cell. Once you turn off Design mode, the placeholder text should fit on a single line. If it does not, you can adjust the font size of the placeholder text to fit.

Figure 10–27

• Click the Design Mode button (Developer tab | Controls group) to turn off Design mode (Figure 10–28).

Q&A What if I notice an error in the placeholder text?

Follow these steps to turn on Design mode, correct the error, and then turn off Design mode.

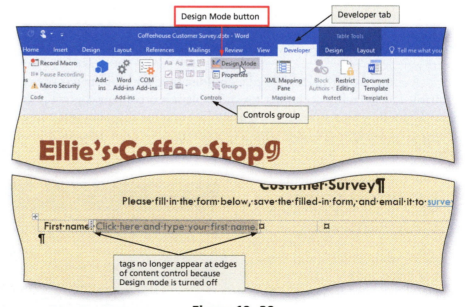

Figure 10–28

To Change the Properties of a Plain Text Content Control

You can change a variety of properties to customize content controls. The following steps change the properties of a plain text content control. *Why? In this form, you assign a tag name to a content control for later identification. You also apply a style to the content control to define how text will look as a user types data or makes selections, and you lock the content control so that a user cannot delete the content control during the data entry process.*

1

• With the content control selected, click the Control Properties button (Developer tab | Controls group) to display the Content Control Properties dialog box (Figure 10–29).

Q&A How do I know the content control is selected?
A selected content control is surrounded by an outline. It also may be shaded.

Figure 10–29

2

• Type **First Name** in the Tag text box (Content Control Properties dialog box).

• Place a check mark in the 'Use a style to format text typed into the empty control' check box so that the Style box becomes active.

• Click the Style arrow to display the Style list (Figure 10–30).

Q&A Why leave the Title text box empty?
When you click a content control in a preexisting Word template, the content control may display an identifier in its top-left corner. For templates that you create, you can instruct Word to display this identifier, called the Title, by changing the properties of the content control. In this form, you do not want the identifier to appear.

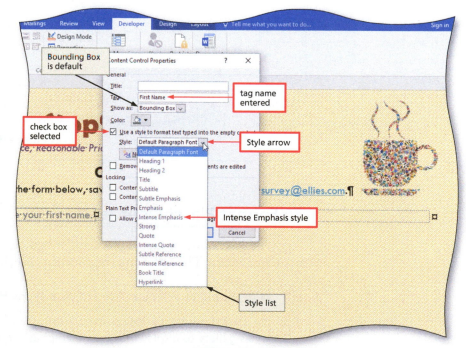

Figure 10–30

What is a bounding box?
A bounding box is a rectangle that surrounds the content control on the form. You can show content controls with a bounding box, with tags, or with no visible markings.

3

- Click Intense Emphasis to select the style for the content control.

- Place a check mark in the 'Content control cannot be deleted' check box so that the user cannot delete the content control (Figure 10–31).

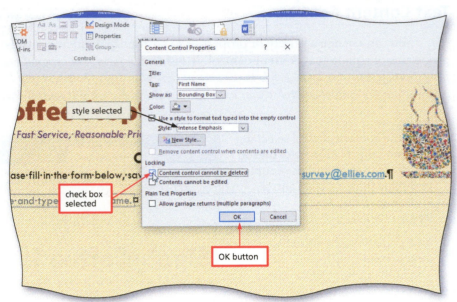

Figure 10–31

4

- Click the OK button to assign the modified properties to the content control (Figure 10–32).

Q&A

Why is the placeholder text not formatted to the selected style, Intense Emphasis, in this case? When you apply a style to a content control, as described in these steps, the style is applied to the text the user types during the data entry process. To change the appearance of the placeholder text, apply a style using the Home tab as described in the next steps.

Figure 10–32

To Format Placeholder Text

In this online form, the placeholder text has the same style applied to it as the content control. The following steps format placeholder text.

1 With the placeholder text selected, display the Home tab.

2 Click the Styles gallery down arrow (Home tab | Styles group) to scroll through the Styles gallery to display the Intense Emphasis style or click the More button (Home tab | Styles group).

3 Click Intense Emphasis in the Styles gallery (even if it is selected already) to apply the selected style to the selected placeholder text (Figure 10–33).

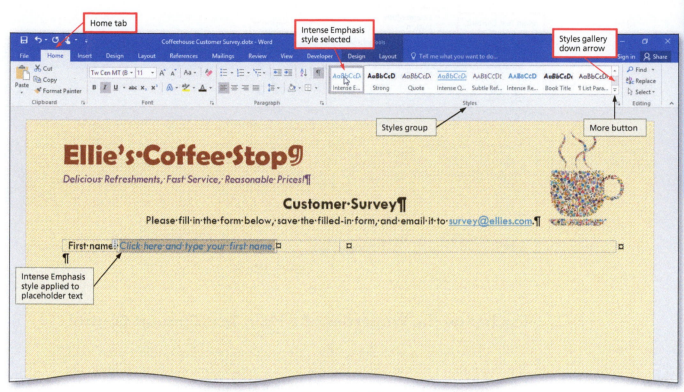

Figure 10-33

To Insert Another Plain Text Content Control and Edit Its Placeholder Text

The second item that a user enters in the Customer Survey is his or her last name. The steps for entering the last name content control are similar to those for the first name, because the last name also is a plain text content control. The following steps enter the label, Last Name:, and then insert a plain text content control and edit its placeholder text.

1 Position the insertion point in the second cell (column) in the table.

2 With the insertion point in the second cell of the table, type **Last name:** as the label for the content control and then press the SPACEBAR.

3 Display the Developer tab. Click the 'Plain Text Content Control' button (Developer tab | Controls group) to insert a plain text content control at the location of the insertion point.

4 With the plain text content control selected, click the Design Mode button (Developer tab | Controls group) to turn on Design mode (Figure 10–34).

5 Select the placeholder text to be changed.

6 Edit the placeholder text so that it contains the text, Click here and type your last name., as the instruction.

7 Click the Design Mode button (Developer tab | Controls group) to turn off Design mode.

BTW

Deleting Content Controls
To delete a content control, right-click it and then click 'Remove Content Control' on the shortcut menu.

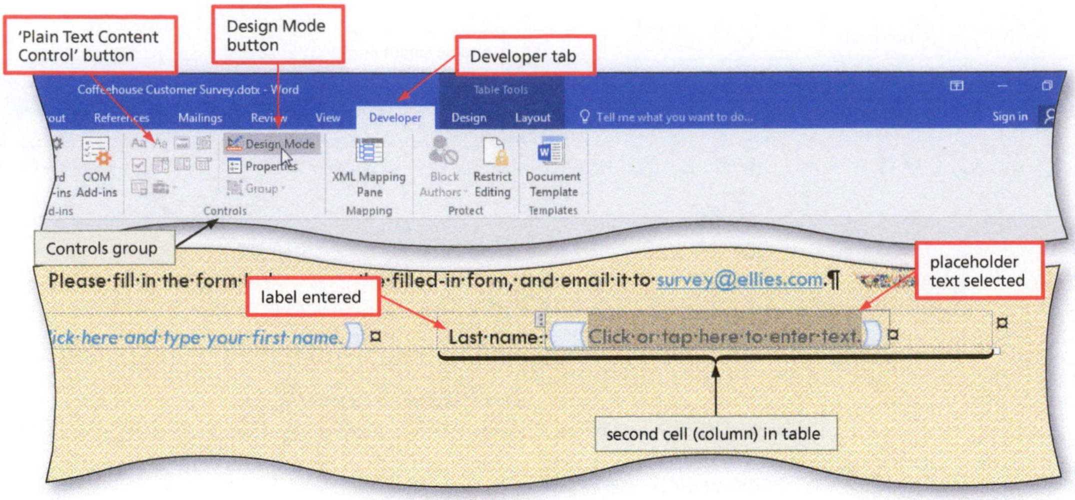

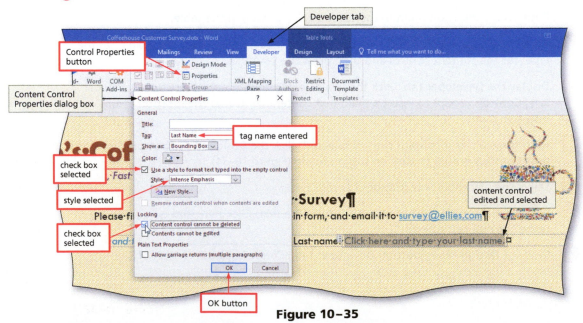

Figure 10–34

To Change the Properties of a Plain Text Content Control

The next step is to change the title, style, and locking properties of the Last Name content control, just as you did for the First Name content control. The following steps change properties of a plain text content control.

1 With the content control selected, click the Control Properties button (Developer tab | Controls group) to display the Content Control Properties dialog box.

2 Type **Last Name** in the Tag text box (Content Control Properties dialog box).

3 Place a check mark in the 'Use a style to format text typed into the empty control' check box to activate the Style box.

4 Click the Style arrow and then select Intense Emphasis in the list to specify the style for the content control.

5 Place a check mark in the 'Content control cannot be deleted' check box (Figure 10–35).

6 Click the OK button to assign the properties to the content control.

Figure 10–35

To Format Placeholder Text

As with the placeholder text for the first name, the placeholder text for the last name should use the Intense Emphasis style. The following steps format placeholder text.

1 With the last name placeholder text selected, display the Home tab.

2 Locate and select the Intense Emphasis style in the Styles gallery (Home tab | Styles group) to apply the selected style to the selected placeholder text.

To Increase Space before a Paragraph

The next step in creating this online form is to increase space before a paragraph so that the space below the table is consistent with the space between other elements on the form. The following steps increase space before a paragraph.

1 Position the insertion point on the blank line below the table.

2 Display the Layout tab.

3 Change the value in the Spacing Before box (Layout tab | Paragraph group) to 8 pt to increase the space between the table and the paragraph (shown in Figure 10–36).

To Insert a Drop-Down List Content Control

1 SAVE DOCUMENT TEMPLATE | 2 SET FORM FORMATS FOR TEMPLATE
3 ENTER TEXT, GRAPHICS, & CONTENT CONTROLS | 4 PROTECT FORM | 5 USE FORM

In the online form in this module, the user selects from one of these four choices for the Frequency of Visits content control: Daily, Weekly, Occasionally, or Rarely. The following steps insert a drop-down list content control. ***Why?*** *To present a set of choices to a user in the form of a drop-down list, from which the user selects one, insert a drop-down list content control. To view the set of choices, the user clicks the arrow at the right edge of the content control.*

- With the insertion point positioned on the blank paragraph mark below the First Name content control, using either the ruler or the Layout tab, change the left indent to 0.06" so that the entered text aligns with the text immediately above it (that is, the F in First).

- Type **How often do you visit our coffeehouse?** and then press the SPACEBAR.

2

- Display the Developer tab.

- Click the 'Drop-Down List Content Control' button (Developer tab | Controls group) to insert a drop-down list content control at the location of the insertion point (Figure 10–36).

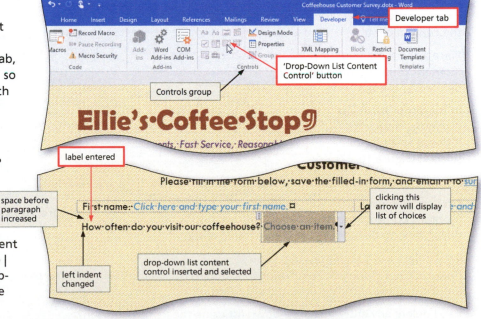

Figure 10–36

To Edit Placeholder Text

The following steps edit the placeholder text for the drop-down list content control.

1 If necessary, display the Developer tab. With the drop-down list content control selected, click the Design Mode button (Developer tab | Controls group) to turn on Design mode.

2 Edit the placeholder text so that it contains this instruction, which contains two separate sentences: Click here. Click arrow and select from list.

3 Click the Design Mode button (Developer tab | Controls group) to turn off Design mode.

To Change the Properties of a Drop-Down List Content Control

1 SAVE DOCUMENT TEMPLATE | 2 SET FORM FORMATS FOR TEMPLATE
3 ENTER TEXT, GRAPHICS, & CONTENT CONTROLS | 4 PROTECT FORM | 5 USE FORM

The following steps change the properties of a drop-down list content control. *Why? In addition to identifying a tag, selecting a style, and locking the drop-down list content control, you can specify the choices that will be displayed when a user clicks the arrow to the right of the content control.*

1

- With the drop-down list content control selected, click the Control Properties button (Developer tab | Controls group) to display the Content Control Properties dialog box.

- Type **Frequency of Visits** in the Tag text box (Content Control Properties dialog box).

- Place a check mark in the 'Use a style to format text typed into the empty control' check box to activate the Style box.

- Click the Style arrow and then select Intense Emphasis in the list to specify the style for the content control.

- Place a check mark in the 'Content control cannot be deleted' check box.

- In the Drop-Down List Properties area, click 'Choose an item.' to select it (Figure 10–37).

2

- Click the Remove button (Content Control Properties dialog box) to delete the 'Choose an item.' entry.

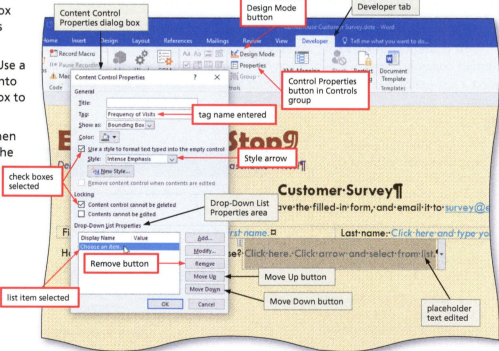

Figure 10–37

Q&A Why delete the 'Choose an item.' entry?
If you leave it in the list, it will appear as the first item in the list when the user clicks the content control arrow. You do not want it in the list, so you delete it.

Can I delete any entry in a drop-down list using the Remove button?
Yes, select the entry in this dialog box and then click the Remove button. You also can rearrange the order of entries in a list by selecting the entry and then clicking the Move Up or Move Down buttons.

3

- Click the Add button to display the Add Choice dialog box.

- Type **Daily** in the Display Name text box (Add Choice dialog box), and notice that Word automatically enters the same text in the Value text box (Figure 10–38).

Q&A What is the difference between a display name and a value?
Often, they are the same, which is why when you type the display name, Word automatically enters the same text in the Value text box. Sometimes, however, you may want to store a shorter or different value. If the display name is long, entering shorter values makes it easier for separate programs to analyze and interpret entered data.

Figure 10–38

4

- Click the OK button (Add Choice dialog box) to add the entered display name and value to the list of choices in the Drop-Down List Properties area (Content Control Properties dialog box).

5

- Click the Add button to display the Add Choice dialog box.

- Type **Weekly** in the Display Name text box.

- Click the OK button to add the entry to the list.

- Click the Add button to display the Add Choice dialog box.

- Type **Occasionally** in the Display Name text box.

- Click the OK button to add the entry to the list.

- Click the Add button to display the Add Choice dialog box.

- Type **Rarely** in the Display Name text box.

- Click the OK button to add the entry to the list (Figure 10–39).

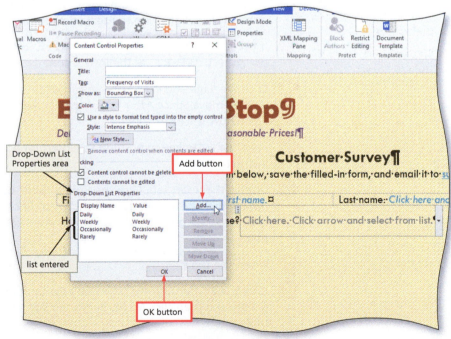

Figure 10–39

6

- Click the OK button (Content Control Properties dialog box) to change the content control properties.

Q&A What if I want to change an entry in the drop-down list?
You would select the drop-down list content control, click the Control Properties button (Developer tab | Controls group) to display the Content Control Properties dialog box, select the entry to change, click the Modify button, adjust the entry, and then click the OK button.

To Format Placeholder Text

As with the previous placeholder text, the placeholder text for the Frequency of Visits content control should use the Intense Emphasis style. The following steps format placeholder text.

1 With the Frequency of Visits placeholder text selected, display the Home tab.

2 Locate and select the Intense Emphasis style in the Styles gallery (Home tab | Styles group) to apply the selected style to the selected placeholder text.

3 Press the END key to position the insertion point at the end of the current line and then press the ENTER key to position the insertion point below the Frequency of Visits content control. If necessary, turn off italics.

To Enter Text and Use a Table to Control Layout

The next step is to enter the user instructions for the check box content controls and insert a 4 × 1 borderless table so that four evenly spaced check boxes can be displayed horizontally below the check box instructions. The following steps enter text and insert a borderless table.

1 With the insertion point positioned on the paragraph below the Frequency of Visits content control, click Normal in the Styles gallery (Home tab | Styles group) to format the current paragraph to the Normal style.

2 Using either the ruler or the Layout tab, change the left indent to 0.06" so that the entered text aligns with the text immediately above it (that is, the H in How).

3 If necessary, turn off italics. Type **Which of our handcrafted beverages do you prefer?** as the instruction.

4 Click the 'Line and Paragraph Spacing' button (Home tab | Paragraph group) and then click 'Remove Space After Paragraph' so that the check boxes will appear one physical line below the instructions.

5 Press the ENTER key to position the insertion point on the line below the check box instructions.

6 Display the Insert tab. Click the 'Add a Table' button (Insert tab | Tables group) to display the Add a Table gallery and then click the cell in the first row and fourth column of the grid to insert an empty 4 × 1 table at the location of the insertion point.

7 Select the table.

8 Click the Borders arrow (Table Tools Design tab | Borders group) to display the Borders gallery and then click No Border in the Borders gallery to remove the borders from the table.

9 Click the first cell of the table to remove the selection (shown in Figure 10–40).

To Insert a Check Box Content Control

The following step inserts the first check box content control. *Why? In the online form in this module, the user can select up to five check boxes: Fresh brewed, Latte, Cappuccino, Smoothie, and Other.*

1

- Position the insertion point at the location for the check box content control, in this case, the leftmost cell in the 4 × 1 table.

- Display the Developer tab.

- Click the 'Check Box Content Control' button (Developer tab | Controls group) to insert a check box content control at the location of the insertion point (Figure 10–40).

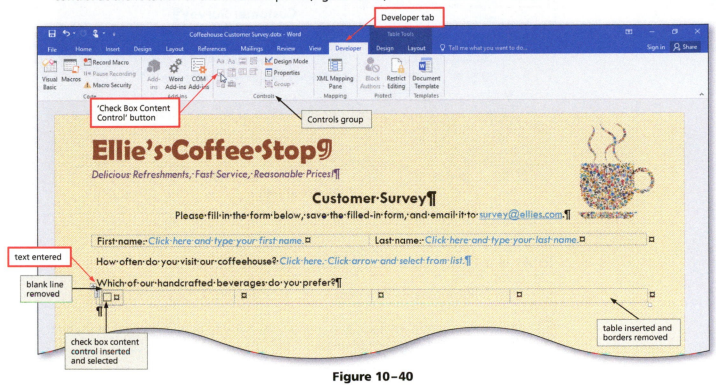

Figure 10–40

To Change the Properties of a Check Box Content Control

The next step is to change the title and locking properties of the content control. The following steps change properties of a check box content control.

1 With the content control selected, click the Control Properties button (Developer tab | Controls group) to display the Content Control Properties dialog box.

2 Type **Fresh Brewed** in the Tag text box (Content Control Properties dialog box).

3 Click the Show as arrow and then select None in the list, because you do not want a border surrounding the check box content control.

4 Place a check mark in the 'Content control cannot be deleted' check box (Figure 10–41).

5 Click the OK button to assign the properties to the selected content control.

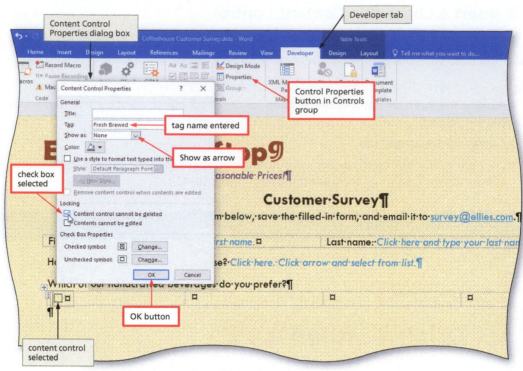

Figure 10–41

To Add a Label to a Check Box Content Control

The following steps add a label to the right of a check box content control.

1 With content control selected, press the END key twice to position the insertion point after the inserted check box content control.

2 Press the SPACEBAR and then type `Fresh brewed` as the check box label (Figure 10–42).

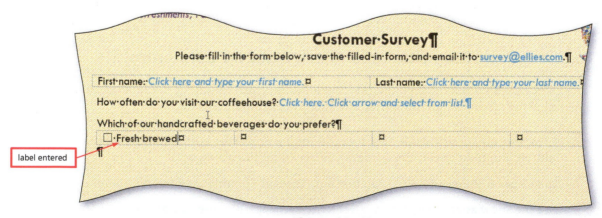

Figure 10–42

To Insert Additional Check Box Content Controls

The following steps insert the remaining check box content controls and their labels.

1 Press the TAB key to position the insertion point in the next cell, which is the location for the next check box content control.

2 Click the 'Check Box Content Control' button (Developer tab | Controls group) to insert a check box content control at the location of the insertion point.

3 With the content control selected, click the Control Properties button (Developer tab | Controls group) to display the Content Control Properties dialog box.

4 Type **Latte** in the Tag text box (Content Control Properties dialog box).

5 Click the Show as arrow and then select None in the list because you do not want a border surrounding the check box content control.

6 Place a check mark in the 'Content control cannot be deleted' check box and then click the OK button to assign the properties to the selected content control.

7 With content control selected, press the END key twice to position the insertion point after the inserted check box content control.

8 Press the SPACEBAR and then type **Latte** as the check box label.

9 Repeat Steps 1 through 8 for the Cappuccino and Smoothie check box content controls.

10 Position the insertion point on the blank line below the 4 × 1 table and then repeat Steps 1 through 8 for the Other Beverage check box content control, which has the label, Other (please specify):, followed by the SPACEBAR. If necessary, using either the ruler or the Layout tab, change the left indent so that check box above is aligned with the check box below (Figure 10–43).

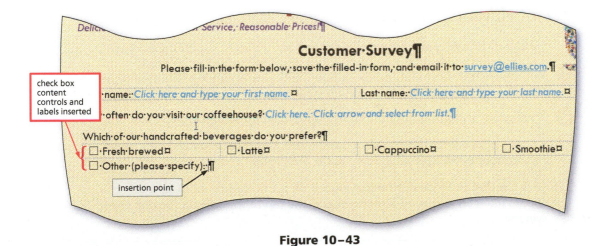

Figure 10–43

To Insert a Rich Text Content Control

The next step is to insert the content control that enables users to type in any other beverages they prefer. The difference between a plain text and rich text content control is that the users can format text as they enter it in the rich text content control. The following step inserts a rich text content control. *Why? Because you want to allow users to format the text they enter in the Other Beverage content control, you use the rich text content control.*

- If necessary, position the insertion point at the location for the rich text content control (shown in Figure 10–43).

- If necessary, display the Developer tab.

- Click the 'Rich Text Content Control' button (Developer tab | Controls group) to insert a rich text content control at the location of the insertion point (Figure 10–44).

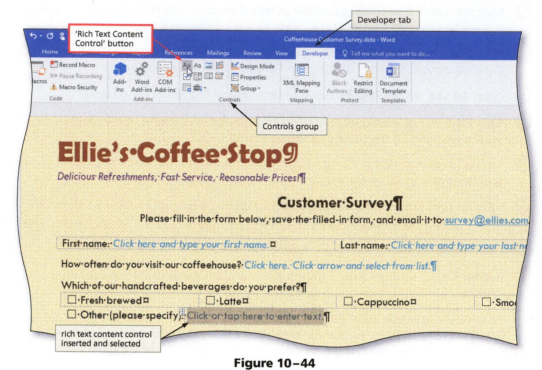

Figure 10–44

To Edit Placeholder Text

The following steps edit placeholder text for the rich text content control.

1 With the rich text content control selected, click the Design Mode button (Developer tab | Controls group) to turn on Design mode.

2 If necessary, scroll to display the content control in the document window.

3 Edit the placeholder text so that it contains the text, Click here and type other handcrafted beverages you prefer., as the instruction.

4 Click the Design Mode button (Developer tab | Controls group) to turn off Design mode. If necessary, scroll to display the top of the form in the document window.

To Change the Properties of a Rich Text Content Control

In the online form in this module, you change the same three properties for the rich text content control as for the plain text content control. That is, you enter a tag name, specify the style, and lock the content control. The following steps change the properties of the rich text content control.

1 With the content control selected, click the Control Properties button (Developer tab | Controls group) to display the Content Control Properties dialog box.

2 Type **Other Beverages** in the Tag text box (Content Control Properties dialog box).

3 Place a check mark in the 'Use a style to format text typed into the empty control' check box to activate the Style box.

4 Click the Style arrow and then select Intense Emphasis in the list to specify the style for the content control.

5 Place a check mark in the 'Content control cannot be deleted' check box (Figure 10–45).

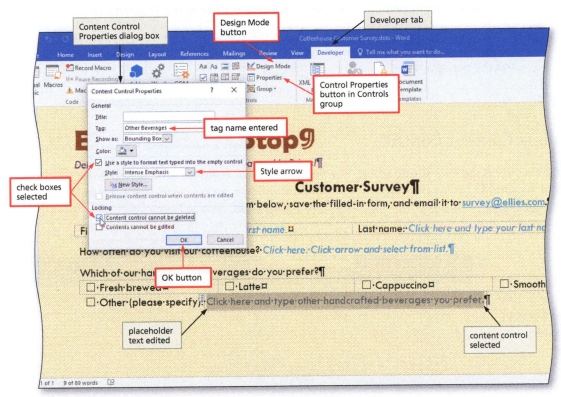

Figure 10–45

6 Click the OK button to assign the properties to the content control.

To Format Placeholder Text and Add Space before a Paragraph

The placeholder text for the Other Beverage text entry should use the Intense Emphasis style, and the space below the check boxes should be consistent with the space between other elements on the form. The next steps format placeholder text and increase space before a paragraph.

1 With the Other Beverage placeholder text selected, display the Home tab.

2 Locate and select the Intense Emphasis style in the Styles gallery (Home tab | Styles group) to apply the selected style to the selected placeholder text.

3 Press the END key to position the insertion point on the paragraph mark after the Other Beverage content control and then press the ENTER key to position the insertion point below the Other Beverage content control.

4 If necessary, display the Home tab. With the insertion point positioned on the paragraph below the Other Beverage content control, click Normal in the Styles gallery (Home tab | Styles group) to format the current paragraph to the Normal style.

5 Using either the ruler or the Layout tab, change the left indent to 0.06" so that the entered text aligns with the text two lines above it (that is, the W in Which).

6 Display the Layout tab. Change the value in the Spacing Before box (Layout tab | Paragraph group) to 8 pt to increase the space between the Other Beverage check box and the paragraph.

To Insert a Combo Box Content Control

1 SAVE DOCUMENT TEMPLATE | 2 SET FORM FORMATS FOR TEMPLATE
3 ENTER TEXT, GRAPHICS, & CONTENT CONTROLS | 4 PROTECT FORM | 5 USE FORM

In Word, a combo box content control allows a user to type text or select from a list. The following steps insert a combo box content control. *Why? In the online form in this module, users can type their own entry in the Beverage Rating content control or select from one of these four choices: Excellent, Good, Fair, or Poor.*

1

- With the insertion point positioned on the blank paragraph mark, type **How would you rate our handcrafted beverages?** and then press the SPACEBAR.

2

- Display the Developer tab.

- Click the 'Combo Box Content Control' button (Developer tab | Controls group) to insert a combo box content control at the location of the insertion point (Figure 10–46).

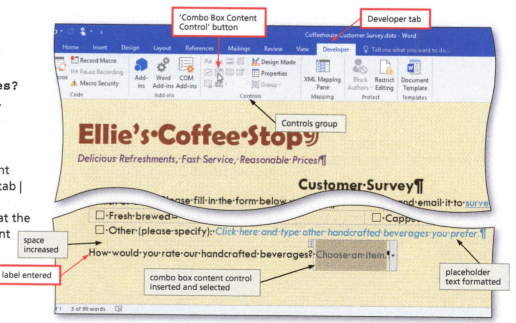

Figure 10–46

To Edit Placeholder Text

The following steps edit the placeholder text for the combo box content control.

1 With the combo box content control selected, click the Design Mode button (Developer tab | Controls group) to turn on Design mode.

2 If necessary, scroll to page 2 to display the combo box content control.

Q&A What if the content control moves to another page?

Because Design mode displays tags, the content controls and placeholder text are not displayed in their proper positions on the screen. When you turn off Design mode, the content controls will return to their original locations and the extra page should disappear.

3 Edit the placeholder text so that it contains this instruction, which contains two sentences (Figure 10–47): Click here. Click arrow and select from list, or type your rating.

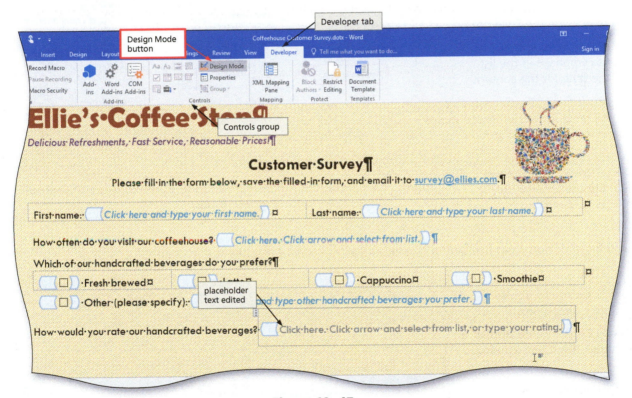

Figure 10–47

4 Click the Design Mode button (Developer tab | Controls group) to turn off Design mode.

To Change the Properties of a Combo Box Content Control

You follow similar steps to enter the list for a combo box content control as you do for the drop-down list content control. The following steps change the properties of a combo box content control. *Why?* You enter the *tag name, specify the style for typed text, and enter the choices for the drop-down list.*

- With the content control selected, click the Control Properties button (Developer tab | Controls group) to display the Content Control Properties dialog box.

- Type **Beverage Rating** in the Tag text box (Content Control Properties dialog box).

- Place a check mark in the 'Use a style to format text typed into the empty control' check box to activate the Style box.

- Click the Style arrow and then select Intense Emphasis in the list to specify the style for the content control.

- Place a check mark in the 'Content control cannot be deleted' check box.

- In the Drop-Down List Properties area, click 'Choose an item.' to select it (Figure 10–48).

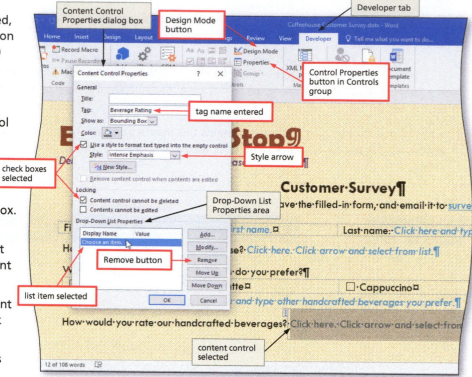

Figure 10–48

- Click the Remove button (Content Control Properties dialog box) to delete the selected entry.

- Click the Add button to display the Add Choice dialog box.

- Type **Excellent** in the Display Name text box (Add Choice dialog box).

- Click the OK button to add the entered display name to the list of choices in the Drop-Down List Properties area (Content Control Properties dialog box).

- Click the Add button and add **Good** to the list.

- Click the Add button and add **Fair** to the list.

- Click the Add button and add **Poor** to the list (Figure 10–49).

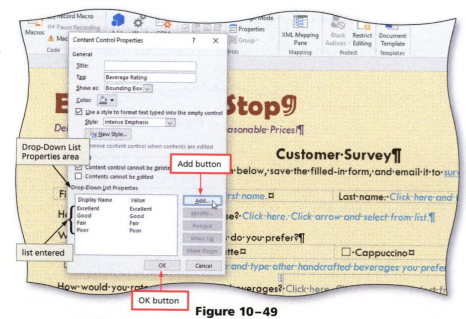

Figure 10–49

4

- Click the OK button (Content Control Properties dialog box) to change the content control properties.

Q&A | How do I make adjustments to entries in the list?
Follow the same procedures as you use to make adjustments to entries in a drop-down list content control.

To Format Placeholder Text

As with the previous placeholder text, the placeholder text for the Beverage Rating should use the Intense Emphasis style. The following steps format placeholder text.

1 With the Beverage Rating placeholder text selected, display the Home tab.

2 Locate and select the Intense Emphasis style in the Styles gallery (Home tab | Styles group) to apply the selected style to the selected placeholder text.

3 Press the END key to position the insertion point at the end of the current line and then press the ENTER key to position the insertion point below the Beverage Rating content control.

4 Click Normal in the Styles list (Home tab | Styles group) to format the current paragraph to the Normal style.

5 Using either the ruler or the Layout tab, change the left indent to 0.06" so that the entered text aligns with the text above it (that is, the H in How).

To Insert a Date Picker Content Control

1 SAVE DOCUMENT TEMPLATE | 2 SET FORM FORMATS FOR TEMPLATE
3 ENTER TEXT, GRAPHICS, & CONTENT CONTROLS | 4 PROTECT FORM | 5 USE FORM

To assist users with entering dates, Word provides a date picker content control, which displays a calendar when the user clicks the arrow to the right of the content control. Users also can enter a date directly in the content control without using the calendar. The following steps enter the label, Today's date:, and a date picker content control. *Why? The last item that users enter in the Coffeehouse Customer Survey is today's date.*

1

- With the insertion point below the Beverage Rating content control, type **Today's date:** as the label for the content control and then press the SPACEBAR.

2

- Display the Developer tab.

- Click the 'Date Picker Content Control' button (Developer tab | Controls group) to insert a date picker content control at the location of the insertion point (Figure 10–50).

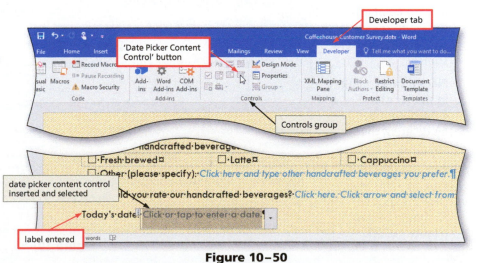

Figure 10–50

To Edit Placeholder Text

The following steps edit the placeholder text for the date picker content control.

1 With the date picker content control selected, click the Design Mode button (Developer tab | Controls group) to turn on Design mode.

2 If necessary, scroll to display the date picker content control.

3 Edit the placeholder text so that it contains this instruction, which contains two sentences: Click here. Click arrow and select today's date.

4 Click the Design Mode button (Developer tab | Controls group) to turn off Design mode.

5 If necessary, scroll to display the top of the form in the document window.

To Change the Properties of a Date Picker Content Control

1 SAVE DOCUMENT TEMPLATE | 2 SET FORM FORMATS FOR TEMPLATE

3 ENTER TEXT, GRAPHICS, & CONTENT CONTROLS | 4 PROTECT FORM | 5 USE FORM

The following steps change the properties of a date picker content control. *Why? In addition to identifying a tag name for a date picker content control, specifying a style, and locking the control, you will specify how the date will be displayed when the user selects it from the calendar.*

- With the content control selected, click the Control Properties button (Developer tab | Controls group) to display the Content Control Properties dialog box.

- Type **Today's Date** in the Tag text box.

- Place a check mark in the 'Use a style to format text typed into the empty control' check box to activate the Style box.

- Click the Style arrow and then select Intense Emphasis in the list to specify the style for the content control.

- Place a check mark in the 'Content control cannot be deleted' check box.

- In the Display the date like this area, click the desired format in the list (Figure 10–51).

Figure 10–51

2

- Click the OK button to change the content control properties.

To Format Placeholder Text

As with the previous placeholder text, the placeholder text for today's date should use the Intense Emphasis style. The following steps format placeholder text.

1 With the today's date placeholder text selected, display the Home tab.

2 Locate and select the Intense Emphasis style in the Styles gallery (Home tab | Styles group) to apply the selected style to the selected placeholder text.

3 Press the END key to position the insertion point at the end of the current line and then press the ENTER key to position the insertion point below the Today's Date content control.

4 Click Normal in the Styles gallery (Home tab | Styles group) to format the current paragraph to the Normal style.

To Enter and Format Text

The following steps enter and format the line of text at the bottom of the online form.

1 Be sure the insertion point is on the line below the Today's Date content control.

2 Center the paragraph mark.

3 Format the text to be typed with the color of Orange, Accent 2, Darker 50%.

4 Type **Thank you for your time!**

5 Change the space before the paragraph to 18 point (Figure 10–52).

6 If the text flows to a second page, reduce spacing before paragraphs in the form so that all lines fit on a single page.

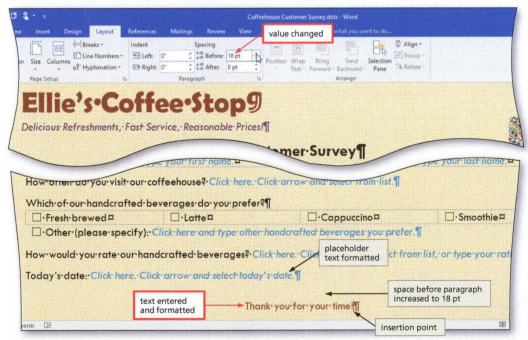

Figure 10–52

To Hide Gridlines and Formatting Marks

Because you are finished with the tables in this form and will not enter any additional tables, you will hide the gridlines. You also are finished with entering and formatting text on the screen. To make the form easier to view, you hide the formatting marks, which can clutter the screen. The following steps hide gridlines and formatting marks.

1 If necessary, position the insertion point in a table cell.

2 Display the Table Tools Layout tab. If gridlines are showing, click the 'View Table Gridlines' button (Table Tools Layout tab | Table group) to hide table gridlines.

3 Display the Home tab. If the 'Show/Hide ¶' button (Home tab | Paragraph group) is selected, click it to remove formatting marks from the screen.

4 Save the template again on the same storage location with the same file name.

Break Point: If you wish to take a break, this is a good place to do so. You can exit Word now. To resume at a later time, run Word, open the file called Coffeehouse Customer Survey, and continue following the steps from this location forward.

To Draw a Rectangle

1 SAVE DOCUMENT TEMPLATE | 2 SET FORM FORMATS FOR TEMPLATE
3 ENTER TEXT, GRAPHICS, & CONTENT CONTROLS | 4 PROTECT FORM | 5 USE FORM

The next step is to emphasize the data entry area of the form. The data entry area includes all the content controls in which a user enters data. The following steps draw a rectangle around the data entry area, and subsequent steps format the rectangle. *Why? To call attention to the data entry area of the form, this module places a rectangle around the data entry area, changes the style of the rectangle, and then adds a shadow to the rectangle.*

1
- Position the insertion point on the last line in the document (shown in Figure 10–52).
- Display the Insert tab.
- Click the 'Draw a Shape' button (Insert tab | Illustrations group) to display the Draw a Shape gallery (Figure 10–53).

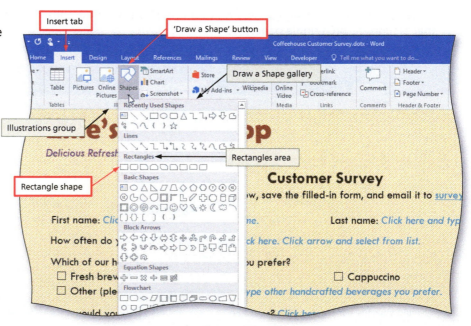

Figure 10–53

2

- Click the Rectangle shape in the Rectangles area of the Draw a Shape gallery, which removes the gallery and changes the pointer to the shape of a crosshair in the document window.

What if I am using a touch screen? Proceed to Step 5 because the shape is inserted in the document window after you tap the rectangle shape in the Draw a Shape gallery.

- Position the pointer (a crosshair) in the approximate location for the upper-left corner of the desired shape (Figure 10–54).

Figure 10–54

3

- Drag the pointer downward and rightward to form a rectangle around the data entry area, as shown in Figure 10–55.

Figure 10–55

4

- Release the mouse button to draw the rectangle shape on top of the data entry area (Figure 10–56).

What happened to all the text in the data entry area? When you draw a shape in a document, Word initially places the shape in front of, or on top of, any text in the same area. You can change the stacking order of the shape so that it is displayed behind the text. Thus, the next steps move the shape behind the text.

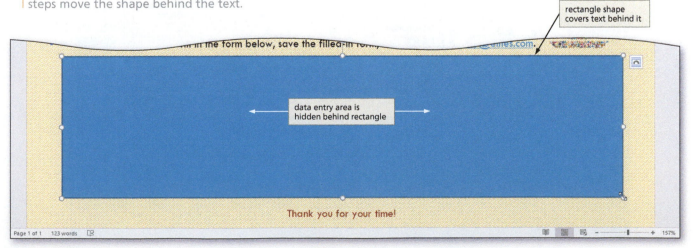

Figure 10–56

- If necessary, change the values in the Shape Height and Shape Width boxes (Drawing Tools Format tab | Size group) to 1.95" and 7.58" (shown in Figure 10–59).

To Send a Graphic behind Text

The following steps send a graphic behind text. **Why?** *You want the rectangle shape graphic to be positioned behind the data entry area text, so that you can see the text in the data entry area along with the shape.*

- If necessary, display the Drawing Tools Format tab.

- With the rectangle shape selected, click the Layout Options button attached to the graphic to display the LAYOUT OPTIONS gallery (Figure 10–57).

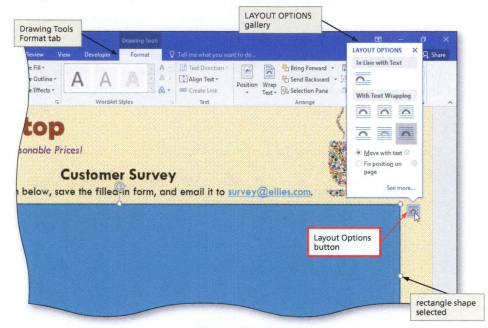

Figure 10–57

- Click Behind Text in the LAYOUT OPTIONS gallery to position the rectangle shape behind the text (Figure 10–58).

Q&A What if I want a shape to cover text?
You would click 'In Front of Text' in the LAYOUT OPTIONS gallery.

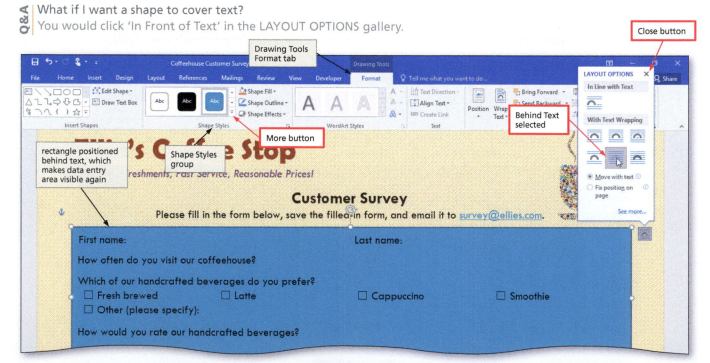

Figure 10–58

3

• Click the Close button in the LAYOUT OPTIONS gallery to close the gallery.

Other Ways

1. Click Wrap Text button (Drawing Tools Format tab | Arrange group), click desired option

2. Right-click object (or, if using touch, tap 'Show Context Menu' button on mini toolbar), point to Wrap Text on shortcut menu, click desired option

---

To Apply a Shape Style

The next step is to apply a shape style to the rectangle, so that the text in the data entry area is easier to read. The following steps apply a style to the rectangle shape.

1 With the shape still selected, click the More button in the Shape Styles gallery (Drawing Tools Format tab | Shape Styles group) (shown in Figure 10–58) to expand the Shape Styles gallery.

2 Point to 'Colored Outline - Aqua, Accent 1' in the Shape Styles gallery (second effect in first row) to display a live preview of that style applied to the rectangle shape in the form (Figure 10–59).

3 Click 'Colored Outline - Aqua, Accent 1' in the Shape Styles gallery to apply the selected style to the selected shape.

BTW

Formatting Shapes
Like other drawing objects or pictures, shapes can be formatted or have styles applied. You can change the fill in a shape by clicking the Shape Fill arrow (Drawing Tools Format tab | Shape Styles group), add an outline or border to a shape by clicking the Shape Outline arrow (Drawing Tools Format tab | Shape Styles group), and apply an effect (such as shadow or 3-D effects) by clicking the Shape Effects arrow (Drawing Tools Format tab | Shape Styles group).

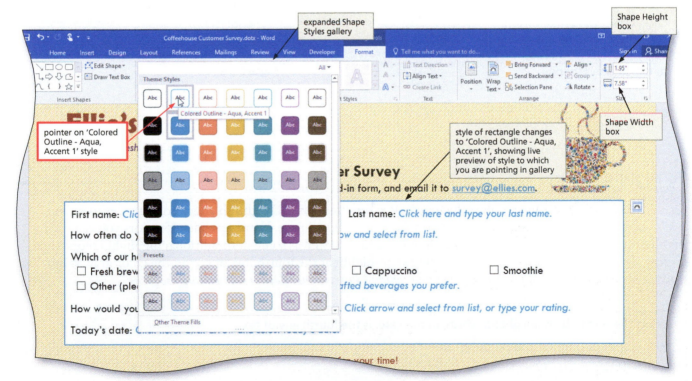

Figure 10–59

To Add a Shadow to a Shape

The following steps add a shadow to the rectangle shape. *Why? To further offset the data entry area of the form, this online form has a shadow on the outside bottom and left edges of the rectangle shape.*

1

● With the shape still selected, click the Shape Effects button (Drawing Tools Format tab | Shape Styles group) to display the Shape Effects menu.

2

● Point to Shadow on the Shape Effects menu to display the Shadow gallery.

● Point to 'Offset Diagonal Bottom Left' in the Outer area in the Shadow gallery to display a live preview of that shadow effect applied to the selected shape in the document (Figure 10–60).

🔍 **Experiment**

● Point to various shadows in the Shadow gallery and watch the shadow on the selected shape change.

3

● Click 'Offset Diagonal Bottom Left' in the Shadow gallery to apply the selected shadow to the selected shape.

Figure 10–60

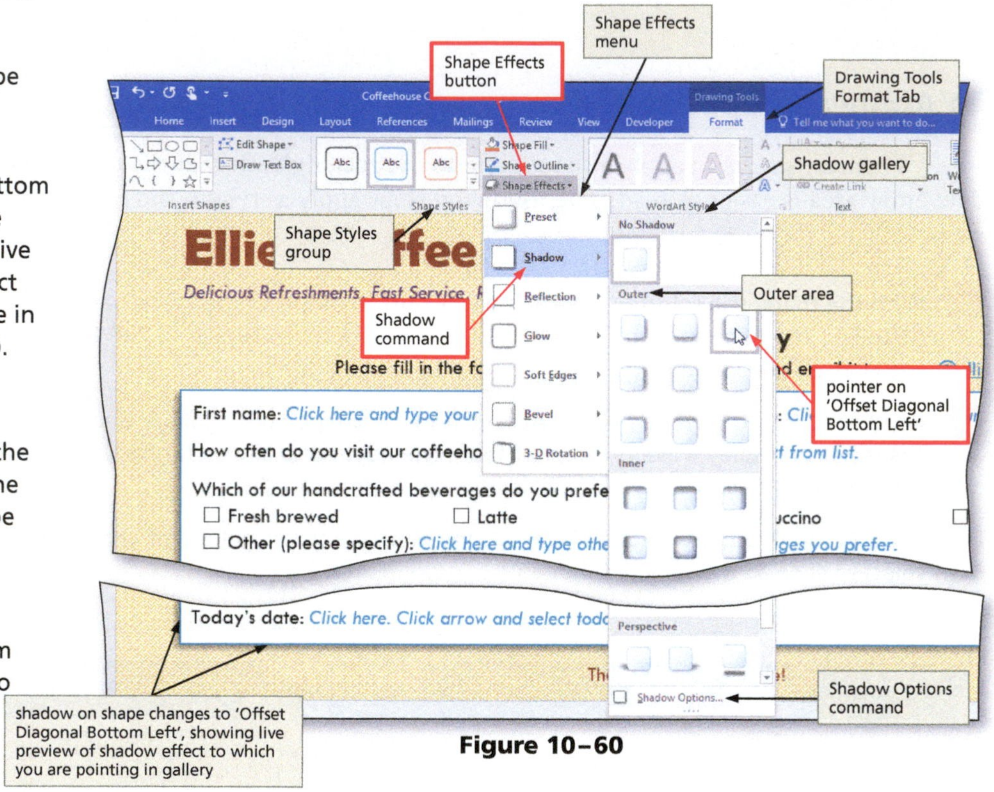

Q&A | Can I change the color of a shadow?
Yes. Click Shadow Options (shown in Figure 10–60) in the Shadow gallery.

To Highlight Text

To emphasize text in an online document, you can highlight it. **Highlighting** alerts a reader to online text's importance, much like a highlighter pen does on a printed page. Word provides 15 colors you can use to highlight text, including the traditional yellow and green, as well as some nontraditional highlight colors, such as gray, dark blue, and dark red. The following steps highlight the fourth line of text in the color gray. *Why? You want to emphasize the line of text on the form that contains instructions related to completing the form.*

1

● Select the text to be highlighted, which, in this case, is the fourth line of text.

Q&A | Why is the selection taller than usual?
Earlier in this project you increased the space after this paragraph. The selection includes this vertical space.

● If necessary, display the Home tab.

● Click the 'Text Highlight Color' arrow (Home tab | Font group) to display the Text Highlight Color gallery.

Q&A | The Text Highlight Color gallery did not appear. Why not?
You clicked the 'Text Highlight Color' button instead of the 'Text Highlight Color' arrow. Click the Undo button on the Quick Access Toolbar and then repeat Step 1.

What if the icon on the 'Text Highlight Color' button already displays the color I want to use?
You can click the 'Text Highlight Color' button instead of the arrow.

- Point to Gray-25% in the Text Highlight Color gallery to display a live preview of this highlight color applied to the selected text (Figure 10–61).

🔍 **Experiment**

- Point to various colors in the Text Highlight Color gallery and watch the highlight color on the selected text change.

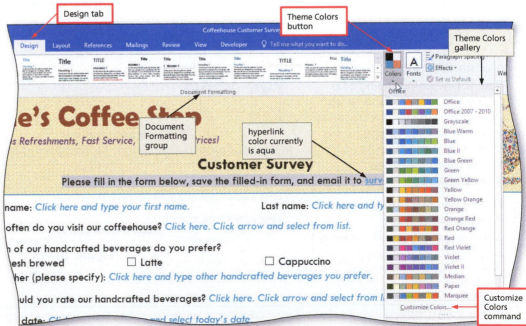

Figure 10–61

- Click Gray-25% in the Text Highlight Color gallery to highlight the selected text in the selected highlight color.

Q&A How would I remove a highlight from text?
Select the highlighted text, click the 'Text Highlight Color' arrow, and then click No Color in the Text Highlight Color gallery.

Other Ways

1. Click 'Text Highlight Color' arrow (Home tab | Font group), select desired color, select text to be highlighted in document, select any additional text to be highlighted, click 'Text Highlight Color' button to turn off highlighting

To Customize a Theme Color and Save It with a New Theme Name

1 SAVE DOCUMENT TEMPLATE | 2 SET FORM FORMATS FOR TEMPLATE
3 ENTER TEXT, GRAPHICS, & CONTENT CONTROLS | 4 PROTECT FORM | 5 USE FORM

The final step in formatting the online form in this module is to change the color of the hyperlink. A document theme has 12 predefined colors for various on-screen objects, including text, backgrounds, and hyperlinks. You can change any of the theme colors. The following steps customize the Headlines theme, changing its designated theme color for hyperlinks. *Why? You would like the hyperlink to be dark orange, to match other text on the form.*

1

- Display the Design tab.

- Click the Theme Colors button (Design tab | Document Formatting group) to display the Theme Colors gallery (Figure 10–62).

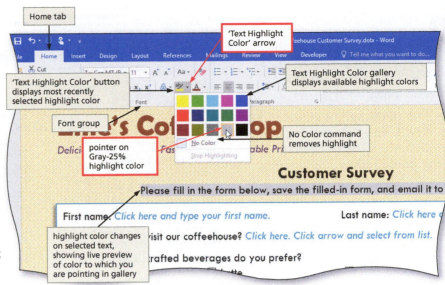

Figure 10–62

2

- Click **Customize Colors** in the Theme Colors gallery to display the Create New Theme Colors dialog box.

- Click the **Hyperlink** button (Create New Theme Colors dialog box) to display the Theme Colors gallery (Figure 10–63).

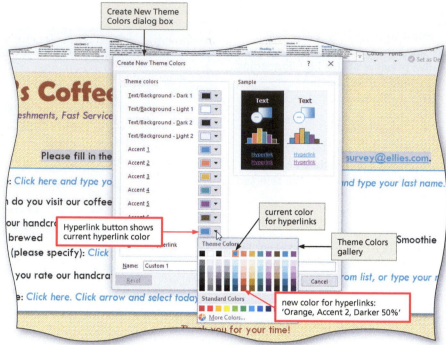

Figure 10–63

3

- Click 'Orange, Accent 2, Darker 50%' in the Hyperlink column (sixth color in bottom row) as the new hyperlink color.

- Type **Coffeehouse Customer Survey** in the Name text box (Figure 10–64).

Q&A What if I wanted to reset all the original theme colors?
You would click the Reset button (Create New Theme Colors dialog box) before Clicking the Save button.

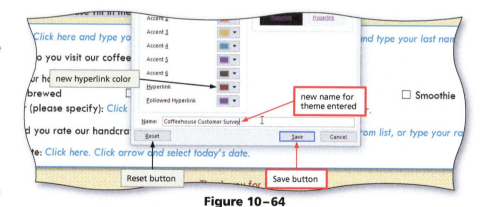

Figure 10–64

4

- Click the **Save** button (Create New Theme Colors dialog box) to save the modified theme with the name, Coffeehouse Customer Survey, which will be positioned at the top of the Theme Colors gallery for future access (Figure 10–65).

Q&A What if I do not enter a name for the modified theme?
Word assigns a name that begins with the letters, Custom, followed by a number (i.e., Custom8).

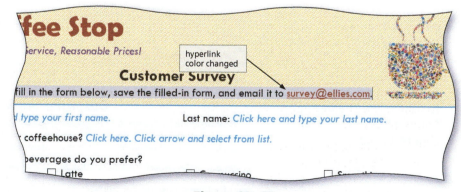

Figure 10–65

Other Ways

1. Make changes to theme colors, fonts, and/or effects; click Themes button (Design tab | Document Formatting group), click 'Save Current Theme' in Themes gallery

To Protect a Form

When you **protect a form**, you are allowing users to enter data only in designated areas — specifically, the content controls. The following steps protect the online form. *Why? To prevent unwanted changes and edits to the form, it is crucial that you protect a form before making it available to users.*

- Display the Developer tab.

- Click the Restrict Editing button (Developer tab | Protect group) to open the Restrict Editing task pane (Figure 10–66).

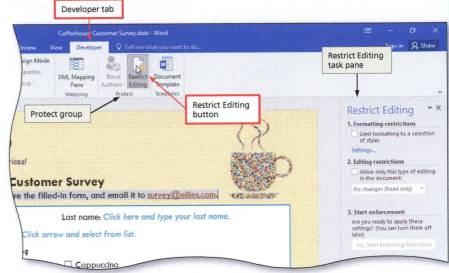

Figure 10–66

- In the Editing restrictions area, place a check mark in the 'Allow only this type of editing in the document' check box and then click its arrow to display a list of the types of allowed restrictions (Figure 10–67).

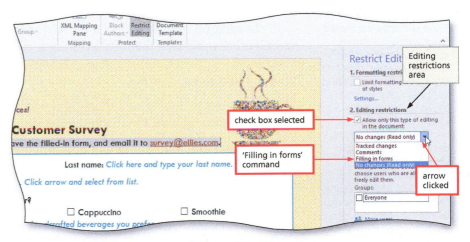

Figure 10–67

- Click 'Filling in forms' in the list to instruct Word that the only editing allowed in this document is to the content controls.

- In the Start enforcement area, click the 'Yes, Start Enforcing Protection' button, which displays the Start Enforcing Protection dialog box (Figure 10–68).

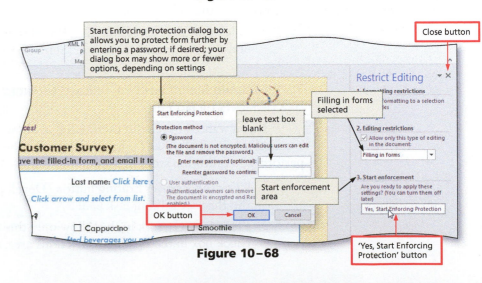

Figure 10–68

4

- Click the OK button (Start Enforcing Protection dialog box) to protect the document without a password.

Q&A

What if I enter a password?

If you enter a password, only a user who knows the password will be able to unprotect the document.

- Close the Restrict Editing task pane to show the protected form (Figure 10–69).

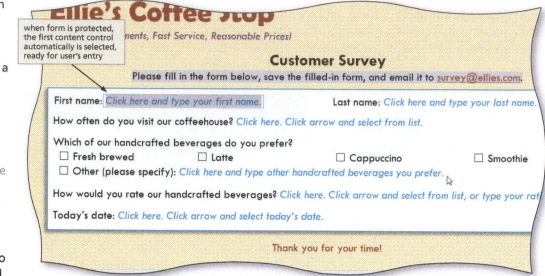

Figure 10–69

Other Ways

1. Open Backstage view, click Info tab, click Protect Document button, click Restrict Editing on Protect Document menu

BTW

Highlighter
If you click the 'Text Highlight Color' button (Home tab | Font group) without first selecting any text, the highlighter remains active until you turn it off. This allows you to continue selecting text that you want to be highlighted. To deactivate the highlighter, click the 'Text Highlight Color' button (Home tab | Font group) again, click the 'Text Highlight Color' arrow (Home tab | Font group) and then click Stop Highlighting on the Text Highlight Color menu, or press the ESC key.

Protecting Documents

In addition to protecting a form so that it only can be filled in, Word provides several other options in the Restrict Editing task pane.

TO SET FORMATTING RESTRICTIONS

If you wanted to restrict users from making certain types of formatting changes to a document, you would perform the following steps.

1. Click the Restrict Editing button (Developer tab | Protect group) to display the Restrict Editing task pane.

2. Place a check mark in the 'Limit formatting to a selection of styles' check box in the Formatting restrictions area.

3. Click the Settings link and then select the types of formatting you want to allow (Formatting Restrictions dialog box).

4. Click the OK button.

5. Click the 'Yes, Start Enforcing Protection' button, enter a password if desired, and then click the OK button (Start Enforcing Protection dialog box).

TO SET EDITING RESTRICTIONS TO TRACKED CHANGES OR COMMENTS OR NO EDITS

If you wanted to restrict users' edits to allow only tracked changes, allow only comments, or not allow any edits (that is, make the document read only), you would perform the following steps.

1. Click the Restrict Editing button (Developer tab | Protect group) to display the Restrict Editing task pane.

2. Place a check mark in the 'Allow only this type of editing in the document' check box in the Editing restrictions area, click the arrow, and then click the

desired option — that is, Tracked changes, Comments, or No changes (Read only) — to specify the types of edits allowed in the document.

3. Click the 'Yes, Start Enforcing Protection' button, enter a password if desired, and then click the OK button (Start Enforcing Protection dialog box).

To Hide the Developer Tab

You are finished using the commands on the Developer tab. Thus, the following steps hide the Developer tab from the ribbon.

1 Open the Backstage view and then click the Options tab in the left pane of the Backstage view to display the Word Options dialog box.

2 Click Customize Ribbon in the left pane (Word Options dialog box).

3 Remove the check mark from the Developer check box in the Main Tabs list.

4 Click the OK button to hide the Developer tab from the ribbon.

To Hide the Ruler, Collapse the Ribbon, Save the Template, and Exit Word

If the ruler is displayed on the screen, you want to hide it. You also want to collapse the ribbon so that when you test the form in the next steps, the ribbon is collapsed. Finally, the online form template for this project now is complete, so you can save the template again and exit Word. The following steps perform these tasks.

1 If the ruler is displayed on the screen, remove the check mark from the View Ruler check box (View tab | Show group).

2 Click the 'Collapse the Ribbon' button on the ribbon (shown in Figure 10–5 earlier in this module) to collapse the ribbon.

3 Save the template again on the same storage location with the same file name.

4 Exit Word.

Working with an Online Form

When you create a template, you use the Open tab in the Backstage view to open the template so that you can modify it. After you have created a template, you then can make it available to users. Users do not open templates with the Open command in Word. Instead, a user creates a new Word document that is *based* on the template, which means the title bar displays the default file name, Document1 (or a similar name) rather than the template name. When Word creates a new document that is based on a template, the document window contains any text and formatting associated with the template. If a user accesses a letter template, for example, Word displays the contents of a basic letter in a new document window.

BTW

Password-Protecting Documents
You can save documents with a password to keep unauthorized users from accessing files. To do this, type the password in the Start Enforcing Protection dialog box (shown in Figure 10–68); or open the Backstage view, click Save As, display the Save As dialog box, click the Tools button (Save As dialog box), click General Options on the Tools menu, type the password in the appropriate text box (General Options dialog box), type the password again (Confirm Password dialog box), and then click the OK button and Save button (Save As dialog box). As you type a password in the text box, Word displays a series of dots instead of the actual characters so that others cannot see your password as you type it.

Be sure to keep the password confidential. Choose a password that is easy to remember and that no one can guess. Do not use any part of your first or last name, Social Security number, birthday, and so on. Use a password that is at least six characters long, and if possible, use a mixture of numbers and letters.

To Use File Explorer to Create a New Document That Is Based on a Template

When you save a template on storage media, as instructed earlier in this module, a user can create a new document that is based on the template through File Explorer. *Why? This allows the user to work with a new document instead of risking the chance of altering the original template.* The following steps create a new Word document that is based on the Coffeehouse Customer Survey template.

1

- Click the File Explorer button on the Windows taskbar to open a File Explorer window.

- Navigate to the location of the saved template (Figure 10–70).

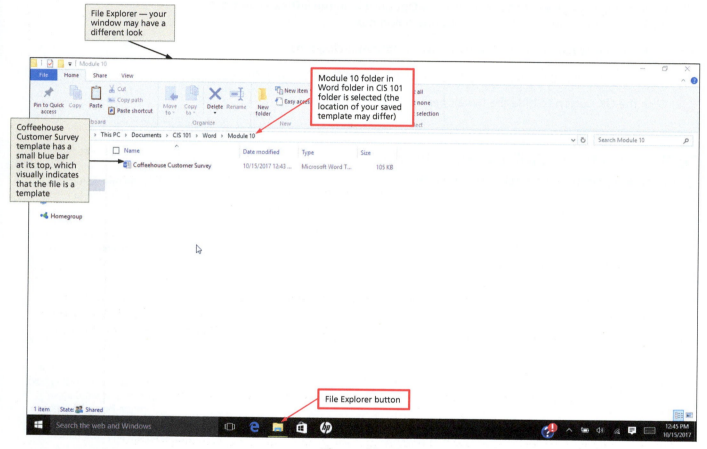

Figure 10–70

2

- Double-click the Coffeehouse Customer Survey file in the File Explorer window, which runs Word and creates a new document that is based on the contents of the selected template (Figure 10–71).

Q&A

Why did my background page color disappear?

If the background page color does not appear, open the Backstage view, click the Options tab to display the Word Options dialog box, click Advanced in the left pane (Word Options dialog box), scroll to the Show document content section, place a check mark in the 'Show background colors and images in Print Layout view' check box, and then click the OK button.

Why does my ribbon show only three tabs: File, Tools, and View?

Your screen is in Read mode. Click the View tab and then click Edit Document to switch to Print Layout view.

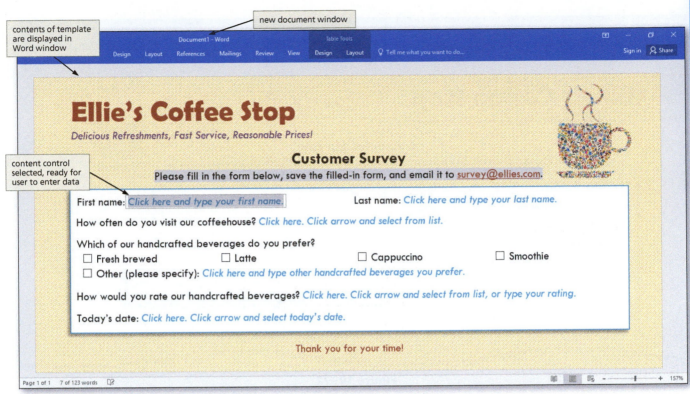

Figure 10–71

1 SAVE DOCUMENT TEMPLATE | 2 SET FORM FORMATS FOR TEMPLATE
3 ENTER TEXT, GRAPHICS, & CONTENT CONTROLS | 4 PROTECT FORM | 5 USE FORM

To Fill In a Form and Save It

The next step is to enter data in the form. To advance from one content control to the next, a user can click the content control or press the TAB key. To move to a previous content control, a user can click it or press SHIFT+TAB. The following steps fill in the Coffeehouse Customer Survey form. **Why?** *You want to test the form to be sure it works as you intended.*

1

- With the First Name content control selected, type **Sammie** and then press the TAB key.

- Type **Berkshire** in the Last Name content control.

  If requested by your instructor, use your first and last name instead of the name, Sammie Berkshire.

- Press the TAB key to select the Frequency of Visits content control and then click its arrow to display the list of choices (shown in Figure 10–1b at the beginning of this module).

- Click Weekly in the list.

- Click the Latte and Other Beverage check boxes to select them.

- Type **Macchiato** in the Other Beverage content control.

- Click the Beverage Rating content control and then click its arrow to display the list of choices (Figure 10–72).

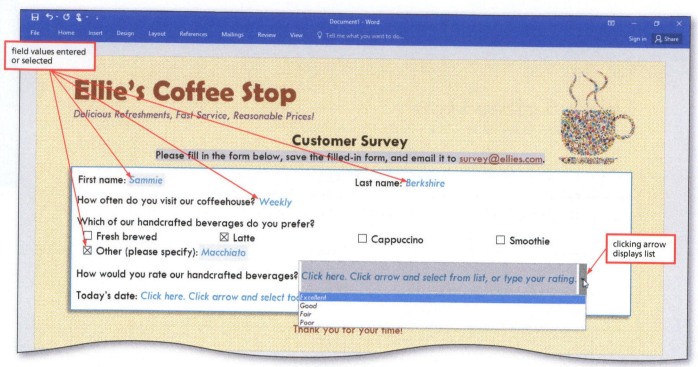

Figure 10–72

2

- Select Excellent in the list.

- Click the Today's Date content control and then click its arrow to display a calendar (Figure 10–73).

3

- Click October 26, 2017 in the calendar to complete the data entry (shown in Figure 10–1c at the beginning of this module).

4

- Save the file on your storage location with the file name, Berkshire Survey. If Word asks if you want to also save changes to the document template, click the No button.

  If requested by your instructor, use your last name in the file name instead of the name, Berkshire.

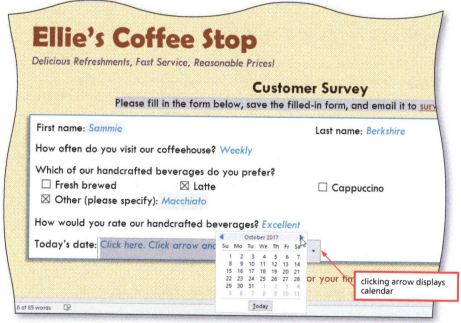

Figure 10–73

Q&A

Can I print the form?

You can print the document as you print any other document. Keep in mind, however, that the colors used were designed for viewing online. Thus, different color schemes would have been selected if the form had been designed for a printout.

- Exit Word. (If Word asks if you want to save the modified styles, click the Don't Save button.)

- If the File Explorer window still is open, close it.

Working with Templates

If you want to modify the template, open it by clicking the Open tab in the Backstage view, clicking the template name, and then clicking the Open button in the dialog box. Then, you must **unprotect the form** by clicking the Restrict Editing button (Developer tab | Protect group) and then clicking the Stop Protection button in the Restrict Editing task pane.

When you created the template in this module, you saved it on your local storage location. In environments other than an academic setting, you would not save the template on your own storage location; instead, you would save the file in the Custom Office Templates folder. When you save a template in the Custom Office Templates folder, you can locate the template by opening the Backstage view, clicking the New tab to display the New gallery, and then clicking the PERSONAL tab in the New gallery, which displays the template in the New gallery (Figure 10–74).

BTW

Protected Documents
If you open an existing form that has been protected, Word will not allow you to modify the form's appearance until you unprotect it. To unprotect a form (or any protected document), open the Restrict Formatting and Editing task pane by clicking the Restrict Editing button (Developer tab | Protect group) or opening the Backstage view, displaying the Info gallery, clicking the Protect Document button, and clicking Restrict Editing on the Protect Document menu. Then, click the Stop Protection button in the Restrict Editing task pane and close the task pane. If a document has been protected with a password, you will be asked to enter the password when you attempt to unprotect the document.

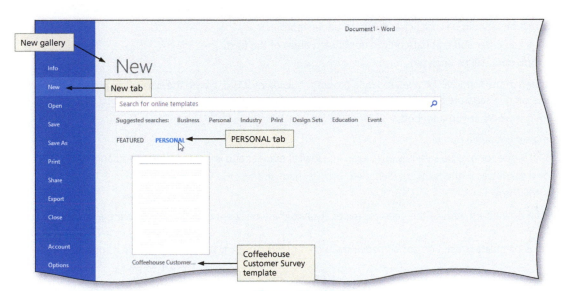

Figure 10–74

BTW

Linking a Form to a Database
If you want to use or analyze the data that a user enters into a form in an Access database or an Excel worksheet, you could save the form data in a comma-delimited text file. This file separates each data item with a comma and places quotation marks around text data items. Then, you can use Access or Excel to import the comma-delimited text file for use in the respective program. To save form data, open the Backstage view, click Save As in the Backstage view, and then display the Save As dialog box. Click the Tools button (Save As dialog box) and then click Save Options on the Tools menu to display the Word Options dialog box. Click Advanced in the left pane (Word Options dialog box), scroll to the Preserve fidelity when sharing this document area in the right pane, place a check mark in the 'Save form data as delimited text file' check box, and then click the OK button. Next, be sure the file type is Plain Text (Save As dialog box) and then click the Save button to save the file as a comma-delimited text file. You can import the resulting comma-delimited file in an Access database or an Excel worksheet. To convert successfully, you should use the legacy controls (i.e., text form field, check box form field, etc.), which are available through the Legacy Tools button (Developer tab | Controls group). To use Word 2016 content controls, use the 'XML Mapping Pane' button (Developer tab | Mapping group) and refer to the Supplementary Word Tasks section in Module 11 for instructions about working with XML.

Summary

In this module, you have learned how to create an online form. Topics covered included saving a document as a template, changing paper size, using a table to control layout, showing the Developer tab, inserting content controls, editing placeholder text, changing properties of content controls, and protecting a form.

What decisions will you need to make when creating online forms?

Use these guidelines as you complete the assignments in this module and create your own online forms outside of this class.

1. Design the form.

    a) To minimize the time spent creating a form while using a computer or mobile device, consider sketching the form on a piece of paper first.

    b) Design a well-thought-out draft of the form — being sure to include all essential form elements, including the form's title, text and graphics, data entry fields, and data entry instructions.

2. For each data entry field, determine its field type and/or list of possible values that it can contain.

3. Save the form as a template, instead of as a Word document, to simplify the data entry process for users of the form.

4. Create a functional and visually appealing form.

    a) Use colors that complement one another.

    b) Draw the user's attention to important sections.

    c) Arrange data entry fields in logical groups on the form and in an order that users would expect.

    d) Data entry instructions should be succinct and easy to understand.

    e) Ensure that users can enter and edit data only in designated areas of the form.

5. Determine how the form data will be analyzed.

    a) If the data entered in the form will be analyzed by a program outside of Word, create the data entry fields so that the entries are stored in separate fields that can be shared with other programs.

6. Test the form, ensuring it works as you intended.

    a) Fill in the form as if you are a user.

    b) Ask others to fill in the form to be sure it is organized in a logical manner and is easy to understand and complete.

    c) If any errors or weaknesses in the form are identified, correct them and test the form again.

7. Publish or distribute the form.

    a) Not only does an online form reduce the need for paper, it saves the time spent making copies of the form and distributing it.

    b) When the form is complete, post it on social media, the web, or your company's intranet, or email it to targeted recipients.

Apply Your Knowledge

Reinforce the skills and apply the concepts you learned in this module.

Filling In an Online Form

Note: To complete this assignment, you will be required to use the Data Files. Please contact your instructor for information about accessing the Data Files.

Instructions: In this assignment, you access a template through File Explorer. The template is located on the Data Files. The template contains an online form (Figure 10–75). You are to fill in the form.

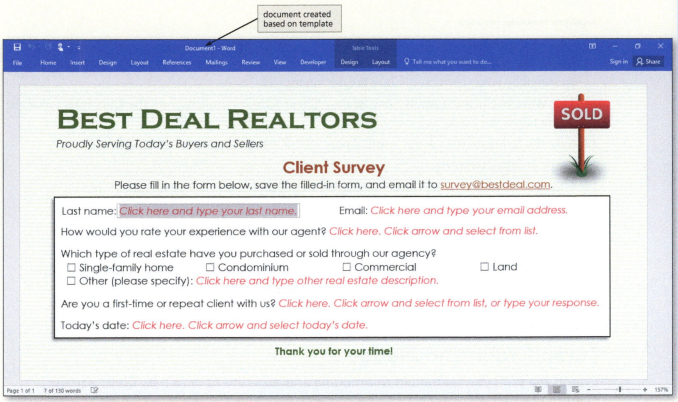

document created
based on template

Figure 10–75

Perform the following tasks:

1. Run File Explorer. Double-click the Apply 10-1 Realtor Client Survey template in File Explorer to create a new document based on the template.

2. When Word displays a new document based on the template, if necessary, collapse the ribbon, hide formatting marks, and change the zoom to page width. Your screen should look like Figure 10–75 and display Document1 on the title bar instead of the file name.

3. With the Last Name content control selected, type **Janda** as the last name, or if requested by your instructor, enter your last name.

4. Click the Email content control selected, type **janda@world.net** or, if requested by your instructor, enter your email address.

5. Click the Agent Rating content control and then click its arrow. Click Excellent in the list.

6. Click the Land check box to select it.

7. Click the Other check box. If necessary, click the Other text box and then type **Multi-family home** in the text box.

8. Click the Client Type content control to select it. Click the Client Type arrow and then review the list. Press the ESC key because none of these choices answers the question. Type **Repeat buyer and seller** as the response.

9. Click the Today's Date content control and then click the arrow to display a calendar. If necessary, scroll to display the calendar for November 2017. Click 'November 2, 2017', (or today's date, if requested by your instructor) in the calendar.

Continued >

Apply Your Knowledge *continued*

10. Save the modified file with a new file name, Apply 10-1 Janda Survey (or, if requested by your instructor, replace the name, Janda, with your last name). Submit the document in the format specified by your instructor. Close the document.

11. Use Word to open the Apply 10-1 Realtor Client Survey template from the Data Files (click the Open tab in the Backstage view).

12. Save the template with a new name, Apply 10-1 Realtor Client Survey Modified.

13. Unprotect the template.

14. Change the Today's Date content control to the format d-MMM-yy (i.e., 12-Nov-17).

15. Protect the modified template.

16. Save the modified template. Submit the revised template in the format specified by your instructor.

17. ✳ In this form, what are the options in the Agent Rating and Client Type lists? What items might you add to the Client Type list? How would you add those items?

Extend Your Knowledge

Extend the skills you learned in this module and experiment with new skills. You may need to use Help to complete the assignment.

Working with Picture Content Controls, Grouping Objects, Themes, and Passwords

Note: To complete this assignment, you will be required to use the Data Files. Please contact your instructor for information about accessing the Data Files.

Instructions: Run Word. Open the document, Extend 10-1 Contest Entry Form Draft, from the Data Files. You will add a picture content control in a text box and then format the text box, group the graphical images, change the text highlight color, change the shadow color, change the shape fill effect to a texture, change theme colors, reset theme colors, save a modified theme, and protect a form with a password.

Perform the following tasks:

1. Use Help to review and expand your knowledge about these topics: picture content controls, text boxes, grouping objects, shadows, shape fill effects, changing theme colors, and protecting forms with passwords.

2. Add a simple text box to the empty space in the right side of the data entry area. Remove space after the paragraph. Resize the text box so that it fits completely in the data entry area.

3. In the text box, type the label, Recipe Photo:, and then below the label, insert a picture content control. Resize the picture content control so that it fits in the text box and then center both the picture and label in the text box (Figure 10–76). Remove the border from the text box.

4. Change the fill effect in the rectangle shape to a texture of your choice. If necessary, change the font color or style of text in the data entry area so that it is readable on the texture.

5. Group the three graphics at the top of the form together. Move the grouped graphics. Return them to their original location.

6. Change the text highlight color of the third line of text to a color other than yellow. If necessary, change the text color so that you can read the text in the new highlight color.

7. Add a shadow to the rectangle and then change the color of the shadow on the rectangle to a color other than the default.

8. Customize the theme colors for Accent 3 (Customize Colors command in Theme Colors gallery). Reset the theme colors before closing the dialog box. Customize the theme colors for Accent 1 and Hyperlink. Customize theme colors for other items as desired. Save the modified theme colors.

9. Make any necessary formatting changes to the form.

10. If requested by your instructor, change the email address to your email address.

11. Protect the form using the word, fun, as the password.

12. Save the revised document with the file name, Extend 10-1 Contest Entry Form Modified.

13. Test the form. When filling in the form, use your own recipe photo or the picture called Beef Stew on the Data Files for the picture content control. Submit the online form in the format specified by your instructor.

14. ✺ Which texture did you select and why? What is the advantage of grouping graphics? Besides changing the color of the shadow, what other shadow settings can you adjust?

Figure 10–76

STUDENT ASSIGNMENTS

Expand Your World

Create a solution that uses cloud or web technologies by learning and investigating on your own from general guidance.

Inserting Online Videos

Note: To complete this assignment, you will be required to use the Data Files. Please contact your instructor for information about accessing the Data Files.

Instructions: You have created an online form for a pool opening and would like to add to the form an online video that shows a pool being vacuumed.

Perform the following tasks:

1. Use Help to learn about inserting online videos.
2. Open the document named Expand 10-1 Pool Opening Form Draft from the Data Files.
3. If requested by your instructor, replace Junior's in the company name with your first name.
4. Display the Insert tab and then click the Online Video button (Insert tab | Media group) to display the Insert Video dialog box (Figure 10–77). Type **pool vacuuming** in the one of the search boxes to display a list of videos that match your search criteria.
5. Scroll through the list of videos, clicking several to see their name, length, and source. Click the View Larger button in the lower-right corner of the video so that you can watch the video. Select an appropriate video and then click the Insert button to insert it on the form. Change the layout to In Front of Text, position the video on the right side of the data entry form, and resize the video border if necessary.

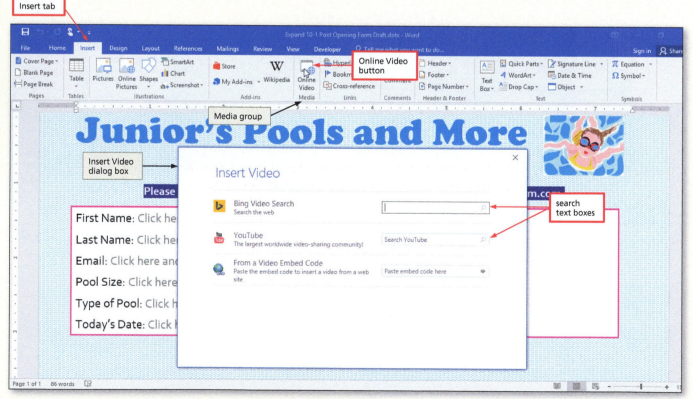

Figure 10–77

6. Protect the form. Save the form again and then submit it in the format specified by your instructor.

7. Access the template through File Explorer. Test the video.

8. ✳ What options are available in the search results dialog box while you are watching a video? What are some of the sources for the videos in the dialog box? Which video did you insert in the form, and why? How do you play the video inserted on the form? Does the video play where you inserted it on the form? If not, where does it play?

In the Labs

Design, create, modify, and/or use a document following the guidelines, concepts, and skills presented in this module. Labs 1 and 2, which increase in difficulty, require you to create solutions based on what you learned in the module; Lab 3 requires you to apply your creative thinking and problem-solving skills to design and implement a solution.

Lab 1: Creating an Online Form with Plain Text and Drop-Down List Content Controls

Problem: Your aunt owns Dee's Dog Grooming and has asked you to prepare an online survey, shown in Figure 10–78.

Perform the following tasks:

1. Save a blank document as a template, called Lab 10-1 Dog Grooming Request Form, for the online form.

2. If necessary, change the view to page width.

3. Change the paper size to a width of 8.5 inches and a height of 4 inches.

4. Change the margins as follows: top – 0.25", bottom – 0", left – 0.5", and right – 0.5".

5. Change the document theme to Celestial.

6. Change the page color to Dark Blue, Text 2, Lighter 60%. Change the fill effect to the 30% pattern.

7. Enter and format the company name, message, and form title as shown in Figure 10–78 (or with similar fonts). If requested by your instructor, change the business name from Dee's to your first name. Insert the image shown (or a similar image) using the term, dog bath, as the search text (the exact image is located on the Data Files). Change the wrapping style of the graphics to In Front of Text. If necessary, resize the graphic and position it in the location shown.

8. Enter the instructions above the data entry area and highlight the line in Gray-50%.

9. Customize the colors so that the hyperlink color is Blue, Accent 2, Darker 50%. Save the modified theme.

STUDENT ASSIGNMENTS

In the Labs continued

11-point italic Calibri font with a color of Blue, Accent 2, Darker 50%, 8 pt spacing after

28-point Gil Sans Ultra Bold font with a color of Purple, Accent 1, Darker 50%, 0 pt spacing after

16-point bold Calibri font with a color of Gold, Accent 5, Darker 50%, 0 pt spacing after

11-point bold Calibri font with a color of Black, Text 1, 12 pt spacing after

body text font

11-point Calibri font with a color of with a color of Blue, Accent 2, Darker 50%, 12 pt spacing before

Figure 10–78

10. In the data entry area, enter the labels as shown in Figure 10–78 and the content controls as follows: First Name, Last Name, Email, Dog Name, and Dog Breed are plain text content controls. Dog Weight is a drop-down list content control with these choices: Less than 10 pounds, 10 to 25 pounds, 26 to 45 pounds, 46 to 65 pounds, More than 65 pounds. Grooming Type is a combo box content control with these choices: Bath and brush; Bath and haircut; Bath and shed treatment; Bath, shed treatment, and haircut. Preferred Time is a combo box content control with these choices: Weekday mornings, Weekday afternoons, Weekend mornings, Weekend afternoons.

11. Format the placeholder text to the Intense Emphasis style. Edit the placeholder text of all content controls to match Figure 10–78. Change the properties of the content controls so that each contains a tag name, uses the Intense Emphasis style, and has locking set so that the content control cannot be deleted.

12. Enter the line below the data entry area as shown in Figure 10–78.

13. Adjust spacing above and below paragraphs as necessary so that all contents fit on a single screen.

14. Draw a rectangle around the data entry area and send it behind the text. Change the shape style of the rectangle to Colored Outline - Gold, Accent 5. Apply the Offset Diagonal Bottom Left shadow to the rectangle.

15. Protect the form.

16. Save the form again and then submit it in the format specified by your instructor.

17. Access the template through File Explorer. Fill in the form using personal data and then submit the filled-in form in the format specified by your instructor.

18. ✳ If the dog groomer wanted the owner's middle name on the same line as the first and last names, how would you evenly space the three items across the line?

Lab 2: Creating an Online Form with Plain Text, Drop-Down List, Combo Box, Rich Text, Check Box, and Date Picker Content Controls

Problem: You work part-time for Antwon's DJ Service. Your supervisor has asked you to prepare a customer survey (Figure 10–79).

Perform the following tasks:

1. Save a blank document as a template for the online form and name it Lab 10-2 DJ Customer Survey.

2. If necessary, change the view to page width.

3. Change the paper size to a width of 8.5 inches and a height of 4 inches.

4. Change the margins as follows: top – 0.25", bottom – 0", left – 0.5", and right – 0.5".

5. Change the document theme to Berlin.

6. Change the page color to Brown, Accent 1. Change the fill effect to the dotted diamond pattern.

7. Enter and format the company name, business tag line, and form title as shown in Figure 10–79 (or with similar fonts). If requested by your instructor, change the business name from Antwon's to your first name. Insert the image using the text, music note, as the search text (the exact image is located on the Data Files). Change the wrapping style of the graphic to In Front of Text. If necessary, resize the graphic and move it to the location shown.

8. Enter the instructions above the data entry area and highlight the line Dark Yellow.

9. In the data entry area, enter the labels as shown in Figure 10–79 and the content controls as follows: First Name and Last Name are plain text content controls. Event Type is a combo box content control with these choices: Birthday, Corporate, Fundraiser, Graduation, Prom, Reunion, Wedding. Event Date is a date picker content control. Ballads, Country, Dance, Ethnic, Hip-Hop, Jazz, Oldies, Rock, and Other Genre are check boxes. Other Genre is a rich text content control. Rating is a drop-down list content control with these choices: Excellent, Good, Fair, Poor.

10. Format the placeholder text to Intense Emphasis. Edit the placeholder text of all content controls to match Figure 10–79. Change the properties of the content controls so that each contains a tag name, uses the Intense Emphasis style, and has locking specified so that the content control cannot be deleted.

11. Customize the colors so that the hyperlink color is White, Hyperlink. Save the modified theme.

12. Enter the line below the data entry area as shown in Figure 10–79.

Continued >

STUDENT ASSIGNMENTS

In the Labs continued

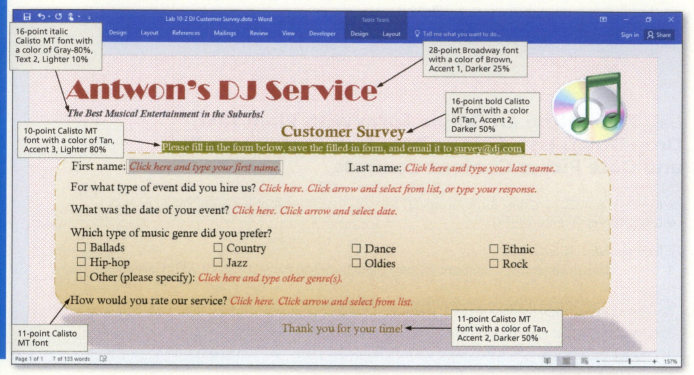

16-point italic Calisto MT font with a color of Gray-80%, Text 2, Lighter 10%

28-point Broadway font with a color of Brown, Accent 1, Darker 25%

16-point bold Calisto MT font with a color of Tan, Accent 2, Darker 50%

Antwon's DJ Service

The Best Musical Entertainment in the Suburbs!

10-point Calisto MT font with a color of Tan, Accent 3, Lighter 80%

Customer Survey

Please fill in the form below, save the filled-in form, and email it to survey@dj.com

First name: *Click here and type your first name.*   Last name: *Click here and type your last name.*

For what type of event did you hire us? *Click here. Click arrow and select from list, or type your response.*

What was the date of your event? *Click here. Click arrow and select date.*

Which type of music genre did you prefer?

☐ Ballads   ☐ Country   ☐ Dance   ☐ Ethnic
☐ Hip-hop   ☐ Jazz   ☐ Oldies   ☐ Rock
☐ Other (please specify): *Click here and type other genre(s).*

How would you rate our service? *Click here. Click arrow and select from list.*

11-point Calisto MT font

Thank you for your time!

11-point Calisto MT font with a color of Tan, Accent 2, Darker 50%

Page 1 of 1   7 of 133 words

Figure 10–79

13. Change the color of labels in the data entry area as shown in the figure.

14. Adjust spacing above and below paragraphs as necessary so that all contents fit on the screen.

15. Draw a Rounded Rectangle around the data entry area. Change the shape style of the rectangle to Subtle Effect - Tan, Accent 2. Change the shape outline to Long Dash Dot. Add a Perspective Diagonal Lower Right shadow.

16. Protect the form.

17. Save the form again and then submit it in the format specified by your instructor.

18. Access the template through File Explorer. Fill in the form using personal data and submit the filled-in form in the format specified by your instructor.

19. ✳ What other question might a DJ service ask its customers? If you were to add this question to the form, how would you fit it so that the form still displays in its entirety on a single page?

Lab 3: Consider This: Your Turn

Create an Online Form for a Deli

Problem: As a part-time employee at your local deli, you have been asked to create an online customer survey.

Part 1:   Create a template that contains the deli name (Rick's Deli), the deli's tag line (Fresh Ingredients Everyday!), and an appropriate image. The third line should have the text, Customer Survey. The fourth line should be highlighted and should read: Please fill in the form below, save the filled-in form, and then email it to survey@ricksdeli.com. The data entry area should contain the following. First Name and Last Name are plain text content controls within a table.

A combo box content control with the label, How do you usually place your order?, has these choices: Counter, Phone, Online, Text. The following instruction should appear above these check boxes: What foods do you like at our deli (check all that apply)?; the check boxes are Sandwiches, Soups, Salads, Sides, Desserts, and Other. A rich text content control has the label, Other (please specify), where customers can enter their own response. A drop-down list content control with the label, How would you rate our food?, has these choices: Excellent, Good, Fair, and Poor. A rich text content control has the label, Would you like to see any items added to our menu?, where customers can enter their own response. A date picker content control with the label, What date were you last in our deli? On the last line, include the text: Thank you for your business!

Use the concepts and techniques presented in this module to create and format the online form. Use meaningful placeholder text for all content controls. (For example, the placeholder text for the First Name plain text content control could be as follows: Click here and type your first name.) Draw a rectangle around the data entry area of the form. Add a shadow to the rectangle. Apply a style to the placeholder text. Assign names, styles, and locking to each content control. Protect the form, test it, and submit it in the format specified by your instructor.

Part 2: You made several decisions while creating the online form in this assignment: placeholder text to use, graphics to use, and how to organize and format the online form (fonts, font sizes, styles, colors, etc.). What was the rationale behind each of these decisions? When you proofread and tested the online form, what further revisions did you make, and why?

11 | Enhancing an Online Form and Using Macros

Objectives

You will have mastered the material in this module when you can:

- Unprotect a document
- Specify macro settings
- Convert a table to text
- Insert and edit a field
- Create a character style
- Apply and modify fill effects
- Change a shape

- Remove a background from a graphic
- Apply an artistic effect to a graphic
- Insert and format a text box
- Group objects
- Record and execute a macro
- Customize the Quick Access Toolbar
- Edit a macro's VBA code

Introduction

Word provides many tools that allow you to improve the appearance, functionality, and security of your documents. This module discusses tools used to perform the following tasks:

- Modify text and content controls.
- Enhance with color, shapes, effects, and graphics.
- Automate a series of tasks with a macro.

Project — Online Form Revised

This module uses Word to improve the visual appearance of and add macros to the online form created in Module 10, producing the online form shown in Figure 11–1a. This project begins with the Coffeehouse Customer Survey online form created in Module 10. Thus, you will need the online form template created in Module 10 to complete this project. (If you did not create the template, see your instructor for a copy.)

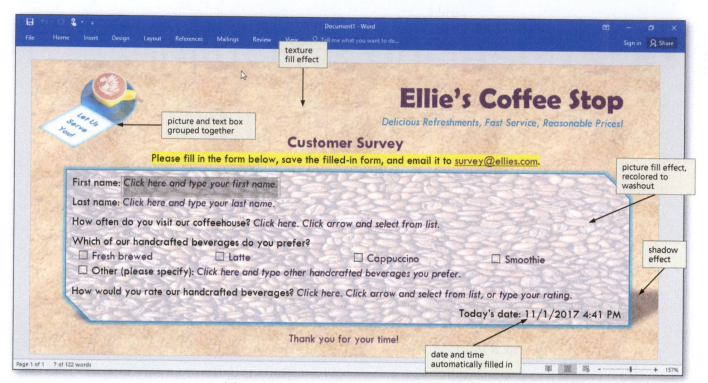

(a) Modified and Enhanced Online Form

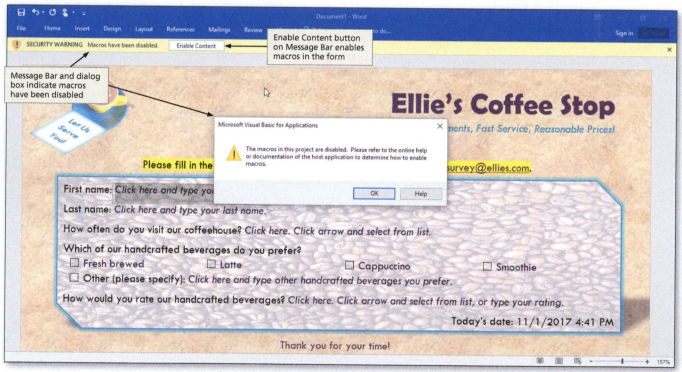

(b) Macros in Online Form Generate Security Warning

Figure 11–1

This project modifies the fonts and font colors of the text in the Coffeehouse Customer Survey online form and enhances the contents of the form to include a texture fill effect, a picture fill effect, and a text box and picture grouped together. The date in the form automatically displays the computer or mobile device's system date, instead of requiring the user to enter the date.

This form also includes macros to automate tasks. A **macro** is a set of commands and instructions grouped together to allow a user to accomplish a task automatically. One macro allows the user to hide formatting marks and the ruler by pressing a keyboard shortcut (sometimes called a shortcut key) or clicking a button on the Quick Access Toolbar. Another macro specifies how the form is displayed initially on a user's Word screen. As shown in Figure 11–1b, when a document contains macros, Word may generate a security warning. If you are sure the macros are from a trusted source and free of viruses, then enable the content. Otherwise, do not enable the content, which protects your computer from potentially harmful viruses or other malicious software.

In this module, you will learn how to create the form shown in Figure 11–1. The following roadmap identifies general activities you will perform as you progress through this module:

1. SAVE a DOCUMENT AS a MACRO-ENABLED TEMPLATE.

2. MODIFY the TEXT AND FORM CONTENT CONTROLS.

3. ENHANCE the FORM'S VISUAL APPEAL.

4. CREATE MACROS TO AUTOMATE TASKS in the form.

To Run Word and Change Word Settings

If you are using a computer to step through the project in this module and you want your screens to match the figures in this book, you should change your screen's resolution to 1366 × 768. The following steps run Word, hide formatting marks, and change the zoom to page width.

1 Run Word and create a blank document in the Word window. If necessary, maximize the Word window.

2 If the Print Layout button on the status bar is not selected, click it so that your screen is in Print Layout view.

3 If the 'Show/Hide ¶' button (Home tab | Paragraph group) is selected, click it to hide formatting marks because you will not use them in this project.

4 If the rulers are displayed on the screen, click the View Ruler check box (View tab | Show group) to remove the rulers from the Word window because you will not use the rulers in this project.

5 If the edges of the page do not extend to the edge of the document window, display the View tab and then click the Page Width button (View tab | Zoom group).

BTW

The Ribbon and Screen Resolution
Word may change how the groups and buttons within the groups appear on the ribbon, depending on the computer's screen resolution. Thus, your ribbon may look different from the ones in this book if you are using a screen resolution other than 1366 x 768.

To Save a Macro-Enabled Template

1 SAVE DOCUMENT AS MACRO-ENABLED TEMPLATE | 2 MODIFY TEXT & FORM CONTENT CONTROLS
3 ENHANCE FORM'S VISUAL APPEAL | 4 CREATE MACROS TO AUTOMATE TASKS

The project in this module contains macros. Thus, the first step in this module is to open the Coffeehouse Customer Survey template created in Module 10 (see your instructor for a copy if you did not create the template) and then save the template as a macro-enabled template. *Why?* *To provide added security to templates, a basic Word template cannot store macros. Word instead provides a specific type of template, called a* **macro-enabled template***, in which you can store macros.*

- Open the template named Coffeehouse Customer Survey created in Module 10.

- Open the Backstage view, click the Save As tab to display the Save As gallery, navigate to the desired save location, and display the Save As dialog box.

- Type `Coffeehouse Customer Survey Modified` in the File name text box (Save As dialog box) to change the file name.

- Click the 'Save as type' arrow to display the list of available file types and then click 'Word Macro-Enabled Template' in the list to change the file type (Figure 11–2).

- Click the Save button (Save As dialog box) to save the file using the entered file name as a macro-enabled template.

Q&A

How does Word differentiate between a Word template and a Word macro-enabled template?

A Word template has an extension of .dotx, whereas a Word macro-enabled template has an extension of .dotm. Also, the icon for a macro-enabled template contains an exclamation point.

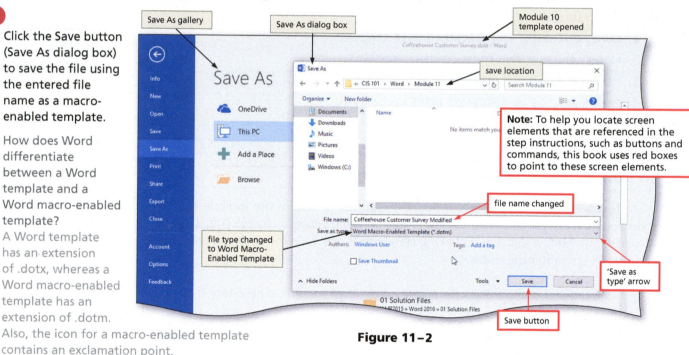

Figure 11–2

BTW

Macro-Enabled Documents

The previous set of steps showed how to create a macro-enabled template. If you wanted to create a macro-enabled document, you would click the 'Save as type' arrow (Save As dialog box), click 'Word Macro-Enabled Document', and then click the Save button.

To Show the Developer Tab

Many of the tasks you will perform in this module use commands on the Developer tab. Thus, the following steps show the Developer tab on the ribbon.

1 Open the Backstage view and then click the Options tab in the left pane of the Backstage view to display the Word Options dialog box.

2 Click Customize Ribbon in the left pane (Word Options dialog box) to display associated options in the right pane.

3 If it is not selected already, place a check mark in the Developer check box in the Main Tabs list.

4 Click the OK button to show the Developer tab on the ribbon.

To Unprotect a Document

The Coffeehouse Customer Survey Modified template is protected. Recall that Module 10 showed how to protect a form so that users could enter data only in designated areas, specifically, the content controls. The following steps unprotect a document. *Why? Before this form can be modified, it must be unprotected. Later in this project, after you have completed the modifications, you will protect it again.*

1

• Display the Developer tab.

• Click the Restrict Editing button (Developer tab | Protect group) to open the Restrict Editing task pane (Figure 11–3).

2

• Click the Stop Protection button in the Restrict Editing task pane to unprotect the form.

• Click the Close button in the Restrict Editing task pane to close the task pane.

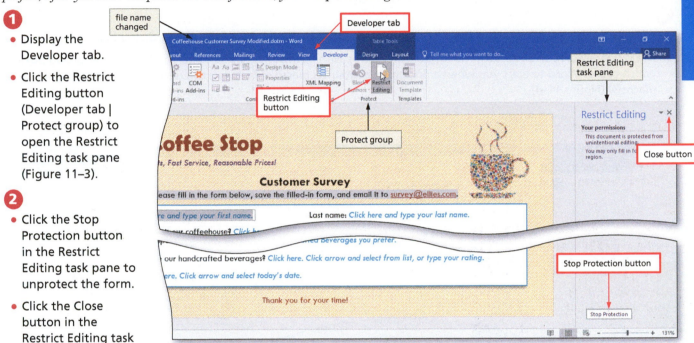

Figure 11–3

Other Ways

1. Click File on ribbon, if necessary, click Info tab in Backstage view, click Protect Document button, click Restrict Editing on Protect Document menu, click Stop Protection button in Restrict Editing task pane

---

CONSIDER THIS

How do you protect a computer from macro viruses?

A **computer virus** is a type of malicious software, or malware, which is a potentially damaging computer program that affects, or infects, a computer or mobile device negatively by altering the way the computer or mobile device works, usually without the user's knowledge or permission. Millions of known viruses and other malicious programs exist. The increased use of networks, the Internet, and email has accelerated the spread of computer viruses and other malicious programs.

• To combat these threats, most computer users run an **antivirus program** that searches for viruses and other malware and destroys the malicious programs before they infect a computer or mobile device. Macros are known carriers of viruses and other malware. For this reason, you can specify a macro setting in Word to reduce the chance your computer or mobile device will be infected with a macro virus. These macro settings allow you to enable or disable macros. An **enabled macro** is a macro that Word will execute, and a **disabled macro** is a macro that is unavailable to Word.

• As shown in Figure 11–1b at the beginning of this module, you can instruct Word to display a security warning on a Message Bar if it opens a document that contains a macro(s). If you are confident of the source (author) of the document and macros, enable the macros. If you are uncertain about the reliability of the source of the document and macros, then do not enable the macros.

To Specify Macro Settings in Word

Why? *When you open the online form in this module, you want the macros enabled. At the same time, your computer or mobile device should be protected from potentially harmful macros. Thus, you will specify a macro setting that allows you to enable macros each time you open this module's online form or any document that contains a macro from an unknown source.* The following steps specify macro settings.

- Click the Macro Security button (Developer tab | Code group) to display the Trust Center dialog box.

- If it is not selected already, click the 'Disable all macros with notification' option button (Trust Center dialog box), which causes Word to alert you when a document contains a macro so that you can decide whether to enable the macro(s) (Figure 11–4).

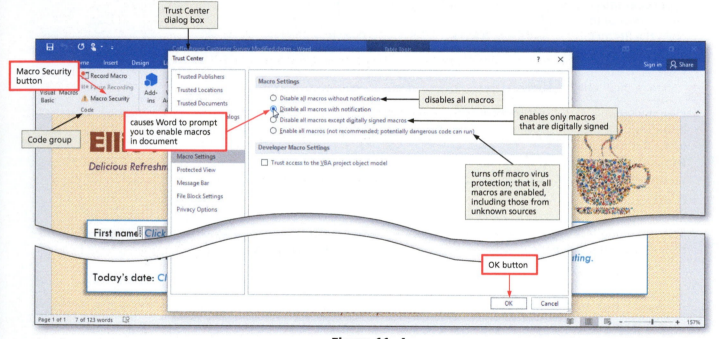

Figure 11–4

- Click the OK button to close the dialog box.

Other Ways

1. Click File on ribbon, click Options tab in Backstage view, click Trust Center in left pane (Word Options dialog box), click 'Trust Center Settings' button in right pane, if necessary, click Macro Settings in left pane (Trust Center dialog box), select desired setting, click OK button in each dialog box

Modifying Text and Form Content Controls

The form created in Module 10 is enhanced in this module by performing these steps:

1. Delete the current image.
2. Change the fonts, colors, and alignments of the first four lines of text and the last line.
3. Convert the 2 × 1 table containing the First Name and Last Name content controls to text so that each of these content controls is on a separate line.
4. Delete the date picker content control and replace it with a date field.
5. Modify the color of the hyperlink and the first row of check box labels.

The following pages apply these changes to the form.

To Delete a Graphic, Format Text, and Change Paragraph Alignment

The online form in this module contains a different image. It also has different formats for the company name, business tag line, form name, form instructions, date line, and thank you line. The following steps delete the image, format text, and change paragraph alignment.

1 Click the coffee cup image to select it and then press the DELETE key to delete the selected image.

2 Change the color of the first line of text, Ellie's Coffee Stop, third line of text, Customer Survey, and the last line of text, Thank you for your time!, to 'Purple, Accent 5, Darker 25%' (ninth color in fifth row).

3 Change the color of the business tag line to Aqua, Accent 1 (fifth color in first row).

4 Right-align the first and second lines of text (company name and business tag line).

5 Change the highlight color on the fourth line of text to Yellow.

6 Right-align the line of text containing the Today's date content control.

7 If necessary, widen the text box surrounding the data entry area to include the entire date placeholder (Figure 11–5).

If requested by your instructor, change the name, ellies, in the email address to your name.

BTW

Saving and Resetting Themes
If you have changed the color scheme and font set and want to save this combination for future use, save it as a new theme by clicking the Themes button (Design tab | Themes group), clicking 'Save Current Theme' in the Themes gallery, entering a theme name in the File name box (Save Current Theme dialog box), and then clicking the Save button. If you want to reset the theme template to the default, you would click the Themes button (Design tab | Themes group) and then click 'Reset to Theme from Template' in the Themes gallery.

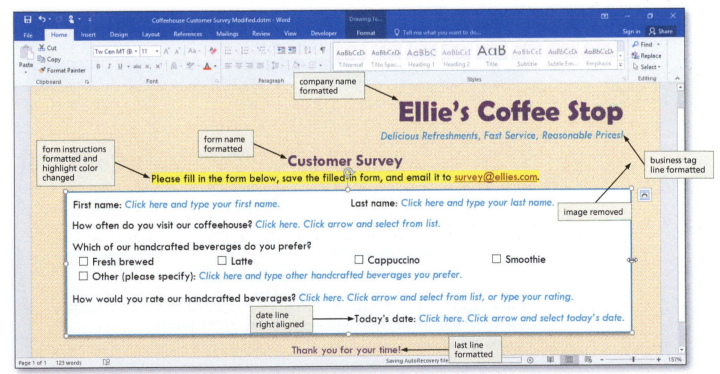

Figure 11–5

BTW
Document Properties
If you wanted to insert document properties into a document, you would click the 'Explore Quick Parts' button (Insert tab | Text group) to display the Explore Quick Parts menu, Point to Document Property on the Explore Quick Parts menu, and then click the property you want to insert on the Document Property menu. To create custom document properties for a document, open the Backstage view, if necessary, click the Info tab to display the Info gallery, click the Properties button in the far right pane to display the Properties menu, click Advanced Properties on the Properties menu to display the Document Properties dialog box, click the Custom tab (Document Properties dialog box) to display the Custom sheet, enter the name of the new property in the Name text box, select its type and value in the dialog box, click the Add button to add the property to the document, and then click the OK button to close the dialog box.

To Change the Properties of a Plain Text Content Control

In this online form, the First Name and Last Name content controls are on separate lines. In Module 10, you selected the 'Content control cannot be deleted' check box in the Content Control Properties dialog box so that users could not delete the content control accidentally while filling in the form. With this check box selected, however, you cannot move a content control from one location to another on the form. Thus, the following steps change the locking properties of the First Name and Last Name content controls so that you can rearrange them.

1 Display the Developer tab.

2 Click the First Name content control to select it.

3 Click the Control Properties button (Developer tab | Controls group) to display the Content Control Properties dialog box.

4 Remove the check mark from the 'Content control cannot be deleted' check box (Content Control Properties dialog box) (Figure 11–6).

5 Click the OK button to assign the modified properties to the content control.

6 Click the Last Name content control to select it and then click the Control Properties button (Developer tab | Controls group) to display the Content Control Properties dialog box.

7 Remove the check mark from the 'Content control cannot be deleted' check box (Content Control Properties dialog box) and then click the OK button to assign the modified properties to the content control.

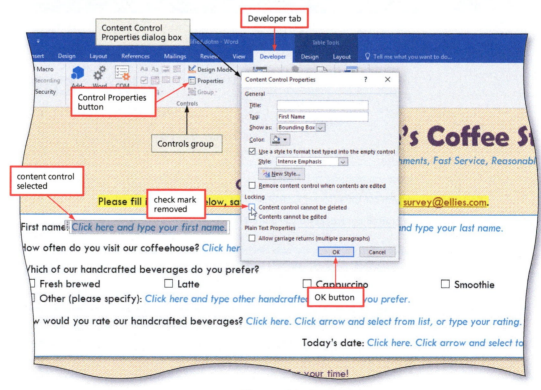

Figure 11–6

To Convert a Table to Text

The First Name and Last Name content controls currently are in a 2 × 1 table. The following steps convert the table to regular text, placing a paragraph break at the location of the second column. *Why? In this online form, these content controls are on separate lines, one below the other. That is, they are not in a table.*

- Position the insertion point somewhere in the table.

- Display the Table Tools Layout tab.

- Click the 'Convert to Text' button (Table Tools Layout tab | Data group) to display the Convert Table To Text dialog box.

- Click Paragraph marks (Convert Table To Text dialog box), which will place a paragraph mark at the location of each new column in the table (Figure 11–7).

- Click the OK button to convert the table to text, separating each column with the specified character, a paragraph mark in this case.

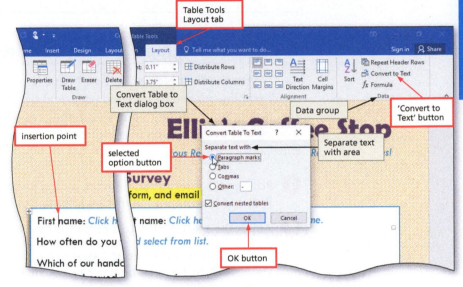

Figure 11–7

Q&A Why did the Last Name content control move below the First Name content control?

The Separate text with area (Convert Table To Text dialog box) controls how the table is converted to text. The Paragraph marks setting converts each column in the table to a line of text below the previous line. The Tabs setting places a tab character where each column was located, and the Commas setting places a comma where each column was located.

- With the First Name and Last Name lines selected, using either the ruler or the Layout tab, change the left indent to 0.06" so that the text aligns with the text immediately below it (that is, the H in How), as shown in Figure 11–8.

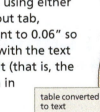

- Click anywhere to remove the selection from the text.

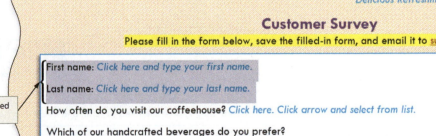

Figure 11–8

To Change the Properties of a Plain Text Content Control

You are finished moving the First Name and Last Name content controls. The following steps reset the locking properties of these content controls.

1 Display the Developer tab.

2 Click the First Name content control to select it and then click the Control Properties button (Developer tab | Controls group) to display the Content Control Properties dialog box.

3 Place a check mark in the 'Content control cannot be deleted' check box (Content Control Properties dialog box) and then click the OK button to assign the modified properties to the content control.

4 Repeat Steps 2 and 3 for the Last Name content control.

To Adjust Paragraph Spacing and Resize the Rectangle Shape

With the First Name and Last Name content controls on separate lines, the thank you line moved to a second page, and the rectangle outline in the data entry area now is too short to accommodate the text. The following steps adjust paragraph spacing and extend the rectangle shape downward so that it surrounds the entire data entry area.

1 Position the insertion point in the second line of text on the form (the business tag line) and then adjust the spacing after to 6 pt (Layout tab | Paragraph group).

2 Adjust the spacing after to 6 pt for the First Name and Last Name lines.

3 Adjust the spacing before and after to 6 pt for the line that begins, How often do you visit..., and the line that begins, How would you rate...

4 Adjust the spacing before to 12 pt for the thank you line.

5 Scroll to display the entire form in the document window. If necessary, reduce spacing after other paragraphs so that the entire form fits in a single document window.

6 Click the rectangle shape to select it.

7 Position the pointer on the bottom-middle sizing handle of the rectangle shape.

8 Drag the bottom-middle sizing handle downward so that the shape includes the bottom content control, in this case, the Today's Date content control (Figure 11–9). If necessary, resize the other edges of the shape to fit the text.

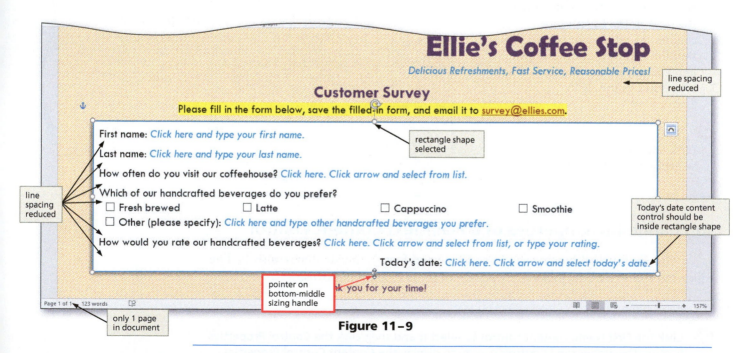

Figure 11–9

To Change the Properties of a Date Picker Content Control

In this online form, instead of the user entering the current date, the computer or mobile device's system date will be filled in automatically by Word. Thus, the Today's Date content control is not needed and can be deleted. To delete the content control, you first will need to remove the check mark from the 'Content control cannot be deleted' check box in the Content Control Properties dialog box. The following steps change the locking properties of the Today's Date content control and then delete the content control.

1 Display the Developer tab.

2 Click the Today's Date content control to select it.

3 Click the Control Properties button (Developer tab | Controls group) to display the Content Control Properties dialog box.

4 Remove the check mark from the 'Content control cannot be deleted' check box (Content Control Properties dialog box) (Figure 11–10).

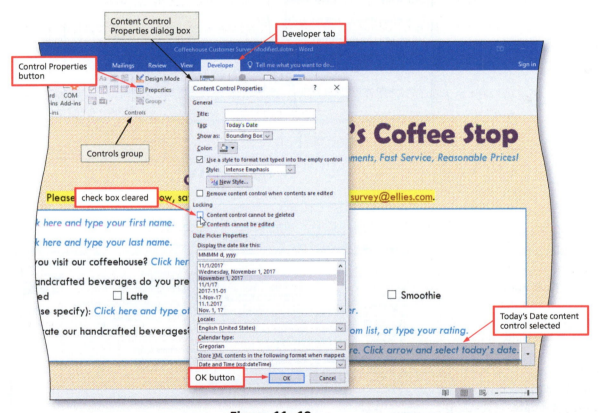

Figure 11–10

5 Click the OK button to assign the modified properties to the content control.

6 Right-click the Today's Date content control to display a shortcut menu and then click 'Remove Content Control' on the shortcut menu to delete the selected content control.

To Insert a Date Field

The following steps insert the date and time as a field in the form at the location of the insertion point. *Why? The current date and time is a field so that the form automatically displays the current date and time. Recall that a field is a set of codes that instructs Word to perform a certain action.*

- Display the Insert tab.

- With the insertion point positioned as shown in Figure 11–11, which is the location for the date and time, click the 'Explore Quick Parts' button (Insert tab | Text group) to display the Explore Quick Parts menu.

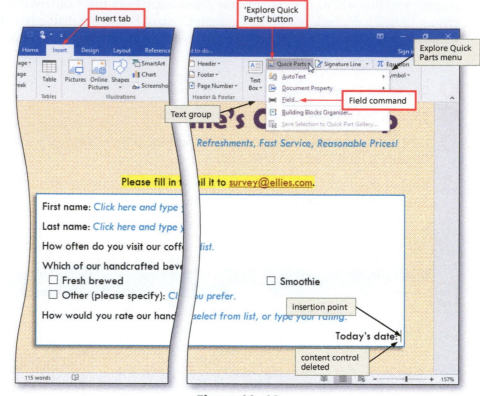

Figure 11–11

- Click Field on the Explore Quick Parts menu to display the Field dialog box.

- Scroll through the Field names list (Field dialog box) and then click Date, which displays the Date formats list in the Field properties area.

- Click the date in the format of 11/1/2017 1:29:14 PM in the Date formats list to select a date format — your date and time will differ (Figure 11–12).

What controls the date that appears?

Your current computer or mobile device date appears in this dialog box. The format for the selected date shows in the Date formats box. In this case, the format for the selected date is M/d/yyyy h:mm:ss am/pm, which displays the date as month/day/year hours:minutes:seconds AM/PM.

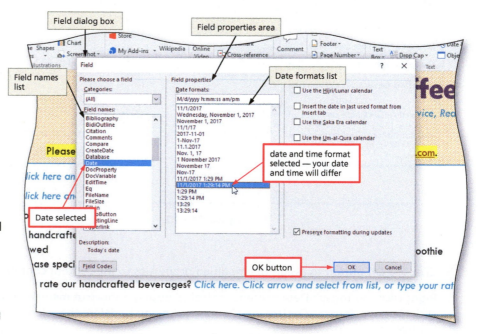

Figure 11–12

- Click the OK button to insert the current date and time at the location of the insertion point (Figure 11–13).

Q&A How do I delete a field?
Select it and then press the DELETE key or click the Cut button (Home tab | Clipboard group), or right-click the field and then click Cut on the shortcut menu or mini toolbar.

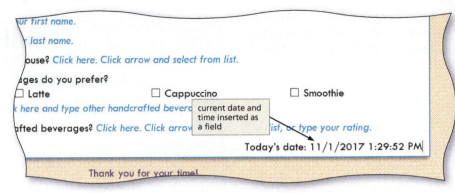

Figure 11–13

Other Ways

1. Click 'Insert Date and Time' button (Insert tab | Text group), select date format (Date and Time dialog box), place check mark in Update automatically check box, click OK button

To Edit a Field

1 SAVE DOCUMENT AS MACRO-ENABLED TEMPLATE | **2 MODIFY TEXT & FORM CONTENT CONTROLS**

3 ENHANCE FORM'S VISUAL APPEAL | 4 CREATE MACROS TO AUTOMATE TASKS

The following steps edit the field. *Why? After you see the date and time in the form, you decide not to include the seconds in the time. That is, you want just the hours and minutes to be displayed.*

- Right-click the date field to display a shortcut menu (Figure 11–14).

Figure 11–14

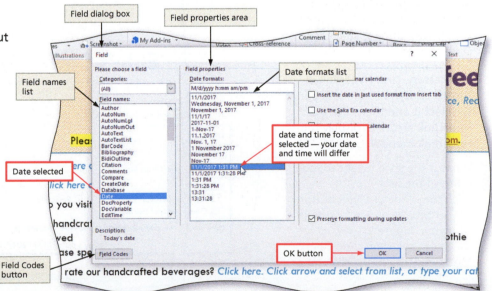

- Click Edit Field on the shortcut menu to display the Field dialog box.

- If necessary, scroll through the Field names list (Field dialog box) and then click Date to display the Date formats list in the Field properties area.

- Select the desired date format, in this case 11/1/2017 1:31 PM (Figure 11–15).

Figure 11–15

3

- Click the OK button to insert the edited field at the location of the insertion point (Figure 11–16).

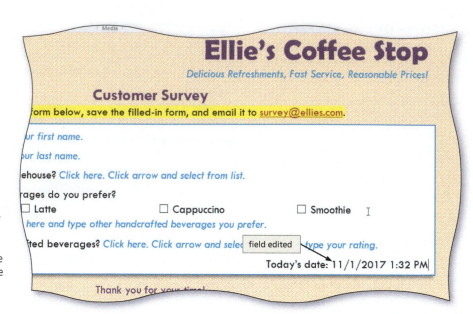

Figure 11–16

To Modify a Style Using the Styles Task Pane

1 SAVE DOCUMENT AS MACRO-ENABLED TEMPLATE | 2 MODIFY TEXT & FORM CONTENT CONTROLS
3 ENHANCE FORM'S VISUAL APPEAL | 4 CREATE MACROS TO AUTOMATE TASKS

The new text highlight color of the form instructions makes it difficult to see the hyperlink. In this online form, the hyperlink should be the same color as the company name so that the hyperlink is noticeable. The following steps modify a style using the Styles task pane. *Why? The Hyperlink style is not in the Styles gallery. To modify a style that is not in the Styles gallery, you can use the Styles task pane.*

1

- Position the insertion point in the hyperlink in the form.

- Display the Home tab.

- Click the Styles Dialog Box Launcher (Home tab | Styles group) to open the Styles task pane.

- If necessary, click Hyperlink in the list of styles in the task pane to select it and then click the Hyperlink arrow to display the Hyperlink menu (Figure 11–17).

Q&A

What if the style I want to modify is not in the list?
Click the Manage Styles button at the bottom of the task pane (shown in Figure 11–18), locate the style, and then click the Modify button in the dialog box.

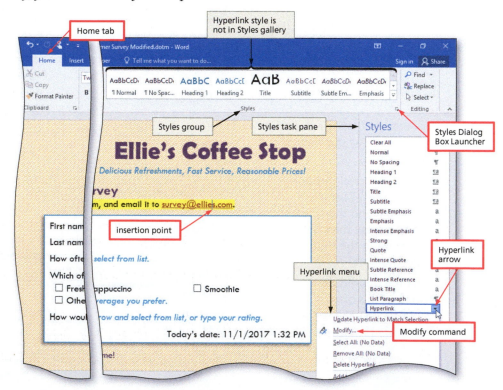

Figure 11–17

2
- Click Modify on the Hyperlink menu to display the Modify Style dialog box.

- Click the Font Color arrow (Modify Style dialog box) to display the Font Color gallery (Figure 11–18).

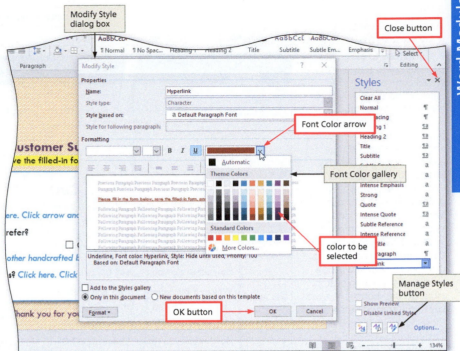

Figure 11–18

3
- Click 'Purple, Accent 5, Darker 25%' (ninth color in fifth row) as the new hyperlink color.

- Click the OK button to close the dialog box. Close the Styles task pane (Figure 11–19).

Figure 11–19

To Modify a Style

In this online form, the placeholder text is to be one shade darker than the company name. Currently, the placeholder text is formatted using the Intense Emphasis style, which uses a shade of aqua as the font color. Thus, the following steps modify the color of the Intense Emphasis style to the darkest shade of purple.

1 Scroll through the Styles gallery (Home tab | Styles group) to locate the Intense Emphasis style.

2 Right-click Intense Emphasis in the Styles gallery to display a shortcut menu and then click Modify on the shortcut menu to display the Modify Style dialog box.

3 Click the Font Color arrow (Modify Style dialog box) to display the Font Color gallery (Figure 11–20).

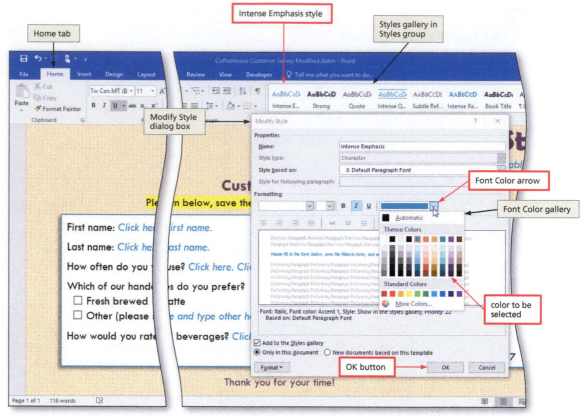

Figure 11–20

④ Click 'Purple, Accent 5, Darker 50%' (ninth color in last row) as the new color.

⑤ Click the OK button to change the color of the style, which automatically changes the
color of every item formatted using this style in the document.

TO MODIFY THE DEFAULT FONT SETTINGS

You can change the default font so that the current document and all future
documents use the new font settings. That is, if you exit Word, restart the computer
or mobile device, and run Word again, documents you create will use the new default
font. If you wanted to change the default font from 11-point Calibri to another font,
font style, font size, font color, and/or font effects, you would perform the following
steps.

1. Click the Font Dialog Box Launcher (Home tab | Font group) to display the
   Font dialog box.

2. Make desired changes to the font settings in the Font dialog box.

3. Click the 'Set As Default' button to change the default settings to those specified
   in Step 2.

4. When the Microsoft Word dialog box is displayed, select the desired option
   button and then click the OK button.

To Reset the Default Font Settings

To change the font settings back to the default, you would follow the steps in the previous section, using the default font settings when performing Step 2. If you do not remember the default settings, you would perform the following steps to restore the original Normal style settings.

1. Exit Word.

2. Use File Explorer to locate the Normal.dotm file (be sure that hidden files and folders are displayed and include system and hidden files in your search), which is the file that contains default font and other settings.

3. Rename the Normal.dotm file to oldnormal.dotm file so that the Normal.dotm file no longer exists.

4. Run Word, which will recreate a Normal.dotm file using the original default settings.

To Create a Character Style

1 SAVE DOCUMENT AS MACRO-ENABLED TEMPLATE | 2 MODIFY TEXT & FORM CONTENT CONTROLS

3 ENHANCE FORM'S VISUAL APPEAL | 4 CREATE MACROS TO AUTOMATE TASKS

In this online form, the first row of check box labels are to be the same color as the placeholder text. The following steps create a character style called Check Box Labels. *Why? Although you could select each of the check box labels and then format them, a more efficient technique is to create a character style.* If you decide to modify the formats of the check box labels at a later time, you simply change the formats assigned to the style to automatically change all characters in the document based on that style.

1

- Position the insertion point in one of the check box labels.

- Click the Styles Dialog Box Launcher (Home tab | Styles group) to open the Styles task pane.

- Click the Manage Styles button in the Styles task pane to display the Manage Styles dialog box (Figure 11–21).

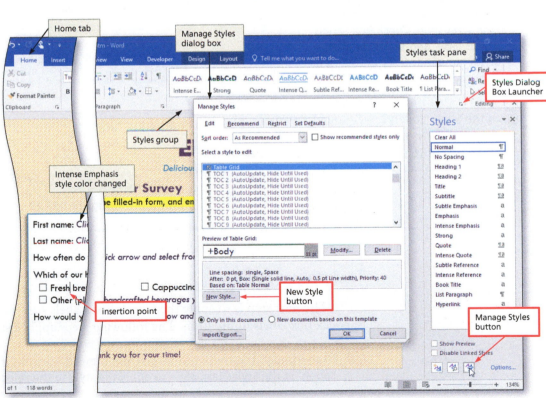

Figure 11–21

2

- Click the New Style button (Manage Styles dialog box) to display the Create New Style from Formatting dialog box.

- Type **Check Box Labels** in the Name text box (Create New Style from Formatting dialog box) as the name of the new style.

- Click the Style type arrow and then click Character so that the new style does not contain any paragraph formats.

- Click the Font Color arrow to display the Font Color gallery and then click 'Purple, Accent 5, Darker 50%' (ninth color in last row) as the new color (Figure 11–22).

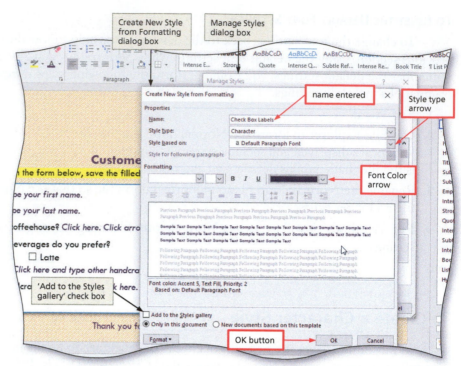

Figure 11–22

3

- Click the OK button in each open dialog box to create the new character style, Check Box Labels in this case, and insert the new style name in the Styles task pane (Figure 11–23).

Q&A

What if I wanted the style added to the Styles gallery?

You would place a check mark in the 'Add to the Styles gallery' check box (Create New Style from Formatting dialog box), shown in Figure 11–22.

Figure 11–23

To Apply a Style

The next step is to apply the Check Box Labels style just created to the first row of check box labels in the form. The following steps apply a style.

1 Drag through the check box label, Fresh brewed, to select it and then click 'Check Box Labels' in the Styles task pane to apply the style to the selected text.

2 Repeat Step 1 for these check box labels (Figure 11–24): Latte, Cappuccino, and Smoothie.

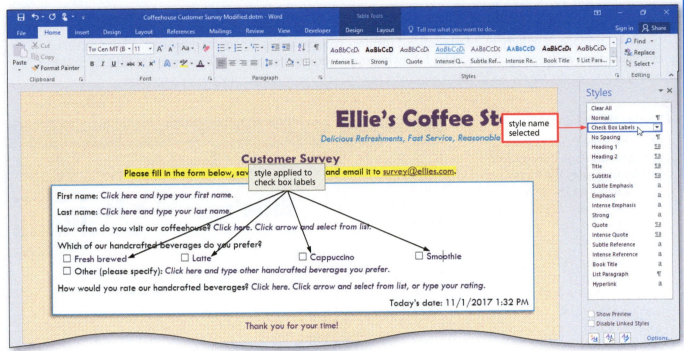

Figure 11–24

BTW

Saving Templates
When you save a template
that contains building blocks,
the building blocks are
available to all users who
access the template.

Q&A
Do I have to drag through one word labels to apply a style?
No. You simply can position the insertion point in the word before clicking the desired
style to apply.

③ Close the Styles task pane.

④ If necessary, click anywhere to remove the selection from the check box label.

⑤ Save the template again on the same storage location with the same file name.

Break Point: If you wish to take a break, this is a good place to do so. You can exit Word now. To resume at a later time, run
Word, open the file called Coffeehouse Customer Survey Modified, and continue following the steps from this location forward.

Enhancing with Color, Shapes, Effects, and Graphics

You will enhance the form created in Module 10 by performing these steps:

1. Apply a texture fill effect for the page color.
2. Change the appearance of the shape.
3. Change the color of a shadow on the shape.
4. Fill a shape with a picture.
5. Insert a picture, remove its background, and apply an artistic effect.
6. Insert and format a text box.
7. Group the picture and the text box together.

The following pages apply these changes to the form.

To Use a Fill Effect for the Page Color

Word provides a gallery of 24 predefined textures you can use as a page background. These textures resemble various wallpaper patterns. The following steps change the page color to a texture fill effect. *Why? Instead of a simple color for the background page color, this online form uses a texture for the page color.*

1

• Display the Design tab.

• Click the Page Color button (Design tab | Page Background group) to display the Page Color gallery (Figure 11–25).

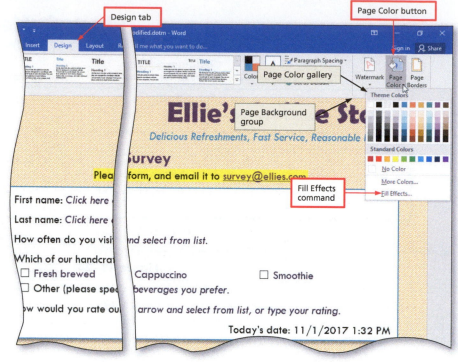

Figure 11–25

2

• Click Fill Effects in the Page Color gallery to display the Fill Effects dialog box.

• Click the Texture tab (Fill Effects dialog box) to display the Texture sheet.

• Scroll to, if necessary, and then click the Stationery texture in the Texture gallery to select the texture (Figure 11–26).

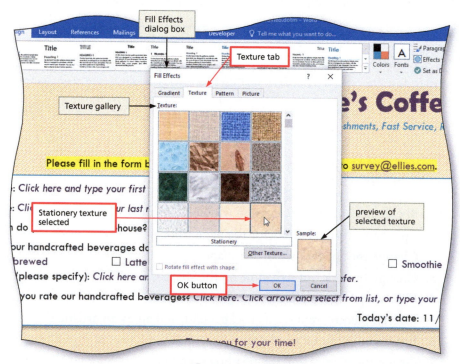

Figure 11–26

3

- Click the OK button to apply the selected texture as the page color in the document (Figure 11–27).

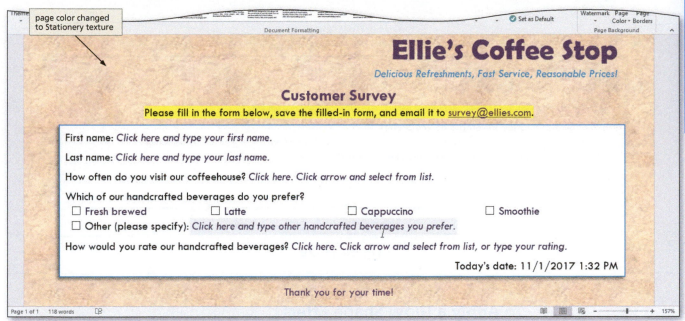

Figure 11–27

How would I remove a texture page color?

You would click the Page Color button (Design tab | Page Background group) and then click No Color in the Page Color gallery.

To Change a Shape

1 SAVE DOCUMENT AS MACRO-ENABLED TEMPLATE | 2 MODIFY TEXT & FORM CONTENT CONTROLS
3 ENHANCE FORM'S VISUAL APPEAL | 4 CREATE MACROS TO AUTOMATE TASKS

The following steps change a shape. *Why? This online form uses a variation of the standard rectangle shape.*

1

- Click the rectangle shape to select it.

- Display the Drawing Tools Format tab.

- Click the Edit Shape button (Drawing Tools Format tab | Insert Shapes group) to display the Edit Shape menu.

- Point to Change Shape on the Edit Shape menu to display the Change Shape gallery (Figure 11–28).

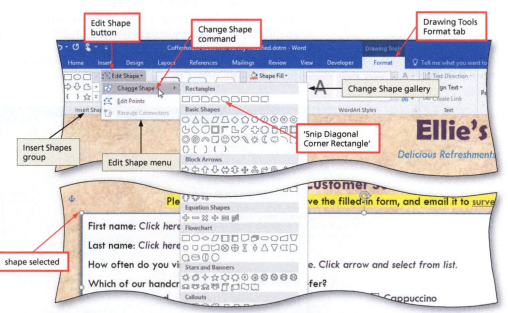

Figure 11–28

2

● Click 'Snip Diagonal Corner Rectangle' in the Rectangles area in the Change Shape gallery to change the selected shape (Figure 11–29).

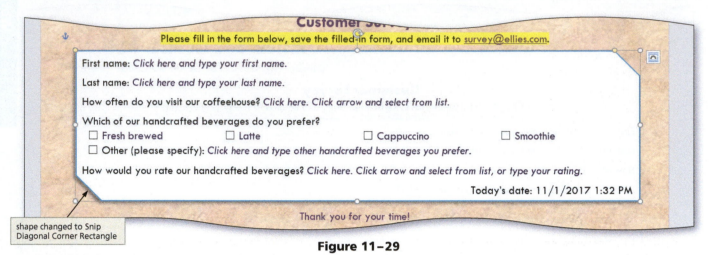

shape changed to Snip Diagonal Corner Rectangle

Figure 11–29

To Apply a Glow Shape Effect

The next step is to apply a glow effect to the rectangle shape. You can apply the same effects to shapes as to pictures. That is, you can apply shadows, reflections, glows, soft edges, bevels, and 3-D rotations to pictures and shapes. The following steps apply a shape effect.

1 With the rectangle shape selected, click the Shape Effects button (Drawing Tools Format tab | Shape Styles group) to display the Shape Effects menu.

2 Point to Glow on the Shape Effects menu to display the Glow gallery.

3 Point to 'Aqua, 5 pt glow, Accent color 1' in the Glow Variations area (first glow in first row) to display a live preview of the selected glow effect applied to the selected shape in the document window (Figure 11–30).

4 Click 'Aqua, 5 pt glow, Accent color 1' in the Glow gallery (first glow in first row) to apply the shape effect to the selected shape.

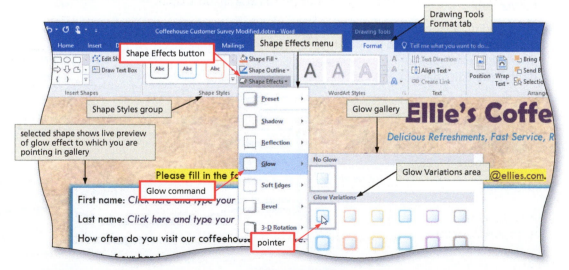

Figure 11–30

To Apply a Shadow Shape Effect

The following steps apply a shadow effect and change its color. *Why? The rectangle in this online form has a shadow with a similar color to the placeholder text.*

1

- With the rectangle shape still selected, click the Shape Effects button (Drawing Tools Format tab | Shape Styles group) again to display the Shape Effects menu.

- Point to Shadow on the Shape Effects menu to display the Shadow gallery.

- Point to 'Perspective Diagonal Upper Right' in the Perspective area at the bottom of the Shadow gallery to display a live preview of that shadow applied to the shape in the document (Figure 11–31).

 **Experiment**

- Point to various shadows in the Shadow gallery and watch the shadow on the selected shape change.

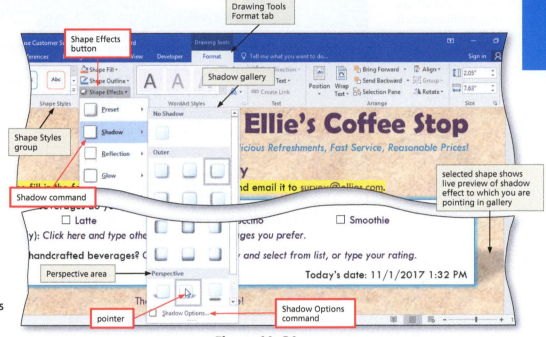

Figure 11–31

2

- Click 'Perspective Diagonal Upper Right' in the Shadow gallery to apply the selected shadow to the selected shape.

- Click the Shape Effects button (Drawing Tools Format tab | Shape Styles group) again to display the Shape Effects menu.

- Point to Shadow in the Shape Effects menu to display the Shadow gallery.

- Click Shadow Options in the Shadow gallery to open the Format Shape task pane.

- Click the Shadow Color button (Format Shape task pane) and then click 'Purple, Accent 5, Darker 50%' (ninth color in last row) in the Shadow Color gallery to change the shadow color.

- Click the Transparency down arrow as many times as necessary until the Transparency box displays 60% to change the amount of transparency in the shadow (Figure 11–32).

3

- Click the Close button to close the Format Shape task pane.

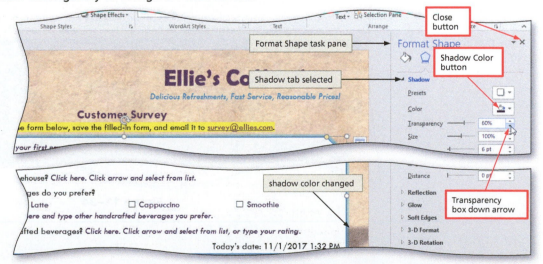

Figure 11–32

To Fill a Shape with a Picture

The following steps fill a shape with a picture. **Why?** *The rectangle in this online form contains a picture of coffee beans. The picture, called Coffee Beans, is located on the Data Files. Please contact your instructor for information about accessing the Data Files.*

1

- With the rectangle shape still selected, click the Shape Fill arrow (Drawing Tools Format tab | Shape Styles group) to display the Shape Fill gallery (Figure 11–33).

Q&A
My Shape Fill gallery did not appear. Why not?
You clicked the Shape Fill button instead of the Shape Fill arrow. Repeat Step 1.

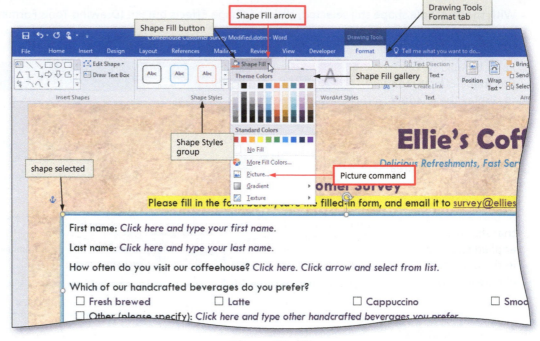

Figure 11–33

2

- Click Picture in the Shape Fill gallery to display the Insert Pictures dialog box.

- Click the Browse button (Insert Pictures dialog box) to display the Insert Picture dialog box. Locate and then select the file called Coffee Beans (Insert Picture dialog box).

- Click the Insert button (Insert Picture dialog box) to fill the rectangle shape with the picture (Figure 11–34).

Figure 11–34

To Change the Color of a Picture

The text in the rectangle shape is difficult to read because the picture just inserted is too dark. You can experiment with adjusting the brightness, contrast, and color of a picture so that the text is readable. In this project, the color is changed to the washout setting so that the text is easier to read. The following steps change the color of the picture to washout.

1 Display the Picture Tools Format tab.

2 With the rectangle shape still selected, click the Color button (Picture Tools Format tab | Adjust group) to display the Color gallery.

3 Point to Washout in the Recolor area in the Color gallery to display a live preview of the selected color applied to the selected picture (Figure 11–35).

4 Click Washout in the Color gallery to apply the selected color to the selected picture.

Figure 11–35

To Insert, Change Wrapping Style, and Resize a Picture

The top of the online form in this module contains a picture of a coffee cup on a saucer with a spoon on the saucer. The picture, called Coffee Cup, is located on the Data Files. Please contact your instructor for information about accessing the Data Files.

You will change the wrapping style of the inserted picture so that it can be positioned in front of the text. Because the graphic's original size is too large, you also will resize it. The following steps insert a picture, change its wrapping style, and resize it.

1 Position the insertion point in a location near where the picture will be inserted, in this case, near the top of the online form.

2 Display the Insert tab. Click the From File button (Insert tab | Illustrations group) to display the Insert Picture dialog box.

3 Locate and then click the file called Coffee Cup (Insert Picture dialog box) to select the file.

BTW

Drawing Canvas
Some users prefer inserting graphics on a drawing canvas, which is a rectangular boundary between a shape and the rest of the document; it also is a container that helps you resize and arrange shapes on the page. To insert a drawing canvas, click the 'Draw a Shape' button (Insert tab | Illustrations group) and then click 'New Drawing Canvas' in the Draw a Shape gallery. You can use the Drawing Tools Format tab to insert objects in the drawing canvas or format the appearance of the drawing canvas.

④ Click the Insert button to insert the picture at the location of the insertion point.

⑤ With the picture selected, click the Wrap Text button (Picture Tools Format tab | Arrange group) and then click 'In Front of Text' so that the graphic can be positioned on top of text.

⑥ Change the value in the Shape Height box (Picture Tools Format tab | Size group) to 1" and the value in the Shape Width box (Picture Tools Format tab | Size group) to 1.78".

⑦ If necessary, scroll to display the online form in the document window (Figure 11–36).

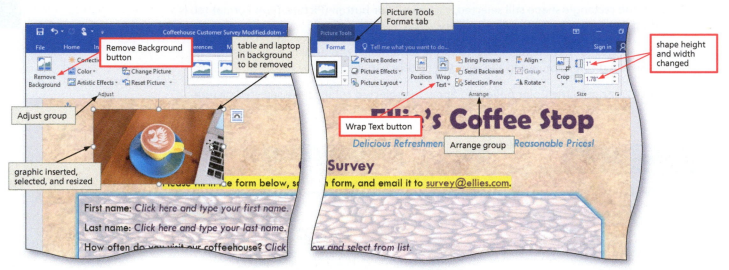

Figure 11–36

To Remove a Background

In Word, you can remove a background from a picture. The following steps remove a background. *Why? You remove the table and laptop in the background from the picture of the coffee cup.*

① • With the coffee cup picture selected, click the Remove Background button (Picture Tools Format tab | Adjust group) (shown in Figure 11–36), to display the Background Removal tab and show the proposed area to be deleted in purple (Figure 11–37).

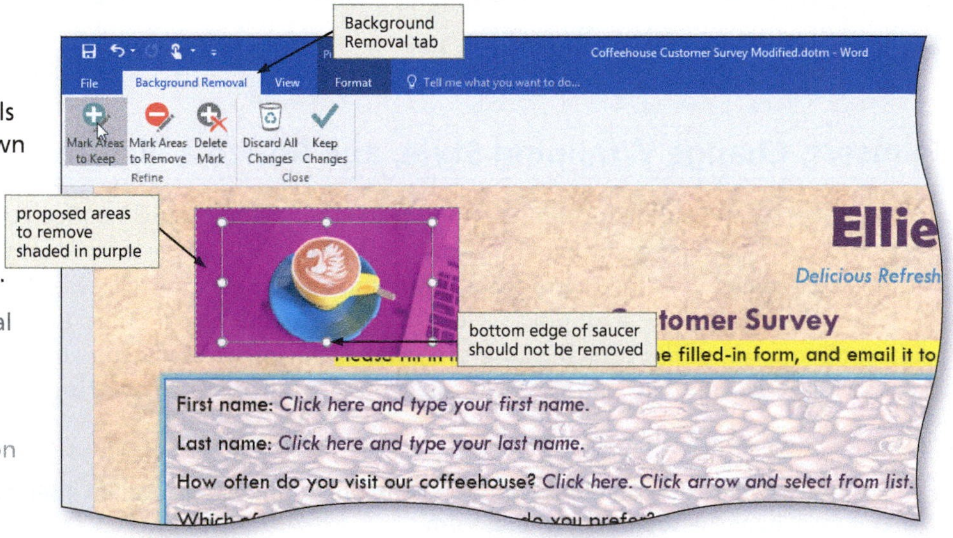

Q&A What is the Background Removal tab?
You can draw around areas to keep or areas to remove by clicking the respective buttons on the Background Removal tab. If you mistakenly mark too much, use the Delete Mark button. You also can drag the proposed rectangle to adjust the proposed removal area. When finished marking, click the 'Close Background Removal and Keep Changes' button, or to start over, click the 'Close Background Removal and Discard Changes' button.

Figure 11–37

2

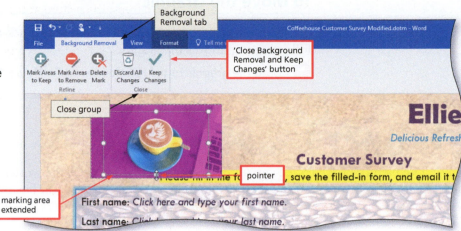

- Drag the proposed marking lines downward slightly, as shown in Figure 11–38, so that the entire saucer shows and the entire table and laptop in the background is shaded purple. If necessary, drag the marking lines a few times.

Figure 11–38

3

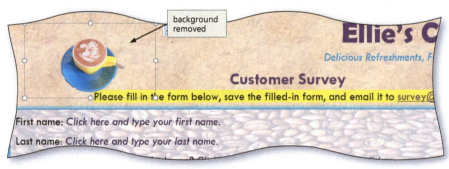

- Click the 'Close Background Removal and Keep Changes' button (Background Removal tab | Close group) to remove the area shaded purple to close the Background Removal tab (Figure 11–39).

Figure 11–39

To Apply an Artistic Effect

1 SAVE DOCUMENT AS MACRO-ENABLED TEMPLATE | 2 MODIFY TEXT & FORM CONTENT CONTROLS
3 ENHANCE FORM'S VISUAL APPEAL | 4 CREATE MACROS TO AUTOMATE TASKS

Word provides several different artistic effects, such as blur, line drawing, and paint brush, that alter the appearance of a picture. The following steps apply an artistic effect to the picture. **Why?** *You want to soften the look of the picture a bit.*

1

- With the picture still selected, click the Artistic Effects button (Picture Tools Format tab | Adjust group) to display the Artistic Effects gallery.

- Point to Crisscross Etching (third effect in fourth row) in the Artistic Effects gallery to display a live preview of the effect applied to the selected picture in the document window (Figure 11–40).

2

- Click Crisscross Etching in the Artistic Effects gallery to apply the selected effect to the selected picture.

Figure 11–40

To Move the Graphic

In this project, the graphic is to be positioned on the left edge of the form. The following step moves the graphic.

1 Drag the graphic to the location shown in Figure 11–41.

To Draw a Text Box

1 SAVE DOCUMENT AS MACRO-ENABLED TEMPLATE | 2 MODIFY TEXT & FORM CONTENT CONTROLS
3 ENHANCE FORM'S VISUAL APPEAL | 4 CREATE MACROS TO AUTOMATE TASKS

The picture of the coffee cup in this form has a text box with the words, Let Us Serve You!, positioned near the lower-left corner of the saucer. The following steps draw a text box. **Why?** *The first step in creating the text box is to draw its perimeter. You draw a text box using the same procedure as you do to draw a shape.*

1

- Position the insertion point somewhere in the top of the online form.
- Display the Insert tab.
- Click the 'Choose a Text Box' button (Insert tab | Text group) to display the Choose a Text Box gallery (Figure 11–41).

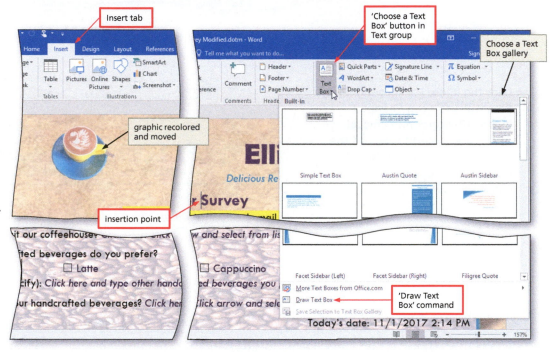

Figure 11–41

2

- Click 'Draw Text Box' in the Text Box gallery, which removes the gallery and changes the shape of the pointer to a crosshair.

- Drag the pointer to the right and downward to form the boundaries of the text box, as shown in Figure 11–42.

Q&A
What if I am using a touch screen?
A text box is inserted in the document window. Proceed to Step 4.

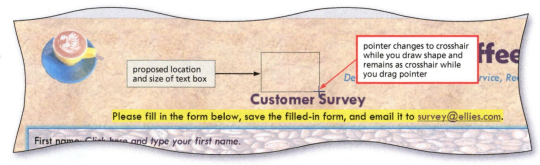

Figure 11–42

3

- Release the mouse button so that Word draws the text box according to your drawing in the document window.

4

- Verify your shape is the same approximate height and width as the one in this project by changing the values in the Shape Height and Shape Width boxes (Drawing Tools Format tab | Size group) to 0.68" and 0.8", respectively (Figure 11–43).

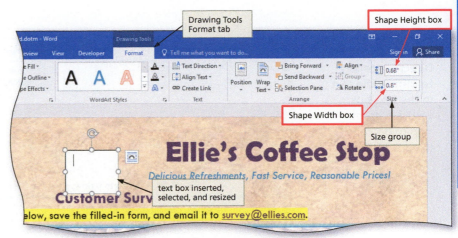

Figure 11–43

To Add Text to a Text Box and Format the Text

The next step is to add the phrase, Let Us Serve You!, centered in the text box using a text effect. You add text to a text box using the same procedure you do when adding text to a shape. The following steps add text to a text box.

1 Display the Home tab. With the text box selected, click the Center button (Home tab | Paragraph group) so that the text you enter is centered in the text box.

2 With the text box selected, click the 'Text Effects and Typography' button (Home tab | Font group) and then click 'Fill - Aqua, Accent 1, Shadow' (second effect in first row) in the Text Effects gallery to specify the format for the text in the text box.

3 If your insertion point is not positioned in the text box (shape), right-click the shape to display a shortcut menu and the mini toolbar and then click Edit Text on the shortcut menu or mini toolbar to place an insertion point centered in the text box.

4 Type **Let Us Serve You!** as the text for the text box (shown in Figure 11–44). (If necessary, adjust the height of the text box to fit the text.)

To Change Text Direction in a Text Box

1 SAVE DOCUMENT AS MACRO-ENABLED TEMPLATE | 2 MODIFY TEXT & FORM CONTENT CONTROLS
3 ENHANCE FORM'S VISUAL APPEAL | 4 CREATE MACROS TO AUTOMATE TASKS

The following steps change text direction in a text box. **Why?** *The direction of the text in the text box should be vertical instead of horizontal.*

1

- Display the Drawing Tools Format tab.

- With the shape still selected, click the Text Direction button (Drawing Tools Format tab | Text group) to display the Text Direction gallery (Figure 11–44).

Q&A What if my text box no longer is selected?
Click the text box to select it.

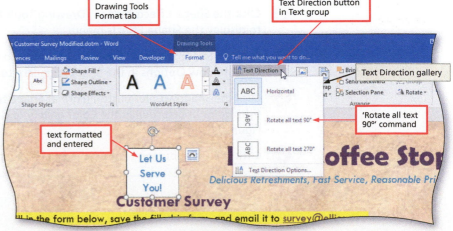

Figure 11–44

2

• Click 'Rotate all text 90°' in the Text Direction gallery to display the text in the text box vertically from top to bottom (Figure 11–45).

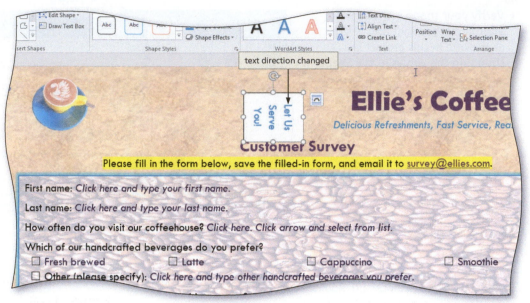

Figure 11–45

Other Ways

1. Right-click text box, click Format Shape on shortcut menu, click Text Options tab (Format Shape task pane), click Layout & Properties button, expand Text Box section, click Text direction box, select desired direction, click Close button

To Apply a Shadow Shape Effect to a Text Box

The text box in this online form has an inside shadow that is in the same color as the business tag line. The following steps apply a shadow effect and change its color.

1 Move the text box to the left so that it is visible when you change the shadows and colors.

2 With the text box still selected, click the Shape Effects button (Drawing Tools Format tab | Shape Styles group) to display the Shape Effects menu.

3 Point to Shadow in the Shape Effects menu to display the Shadow gallery and then click Inside Center in the Inner area of the Shadow gallery to apply the selected shadow to the selected shape.

4 Click the Shape Effects button (Drawing Tools Format tab | Shape Styles group) again to display the Shape Effects menu.

5 Point to Shadow in the Shape Effects menu to display the Shadow gallery and then click Shadow Options in the Shadow gallery to display the Format Shape task pane.

6 Click the Shadow Color button (Format Shape task pane) and then click 'Aqua, Accent 1' (fifth color in first row) in the Color gallery to change the shadow color (shown in Figure 11–46).

7 Click the Close button to close the Format Shape task pane.

To Change a Shape Outline of a Text Box

You change an outline on a text box (shape) using the same procedure as you do with a picture. The following steps remove the shape outline on the text box. **Why?** *The text box in this form has no outline.*

- With the text box still selected, click the Shape Outline arrow (Drawing Tools Format tab | Shape Styles group) to display the Shape Outline gallery (Figure 11–46).

Q&A The Shape Outline gallery did not display. Why not?
You clicked the Shape Outline button instead of the Shape Outline arrow. Repeat Step 1.

 **Experiment**

- Point to various colors in the Shape Outline gallery and watch the color of the outline on the text box change in the document.

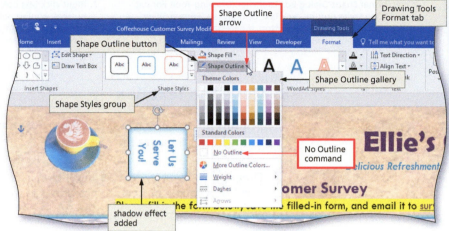

Figure 11–46

- Click No Outline in the Shape Outline gallery to remove the outline from the selected shape.

Other Ways

1. Click Format Shape Dialog Box Launcher (Drawing Tools Format tab | Shape Styles group); expand Line section (Format Shape task pane); click No line to remove line, or click Solid line, click Outline color button, and select desired color to change line color; click Close button

2. Right-click text box (or, if using touch, tap 'Show Context Menu' button on mini toolbar), click Format Shape on shortcut menu, expand Line section (Format Shape task pane), click No line to remove line, or click Solid line, click Outline color button, and select desired color to change line color; click Close button

---

To Apply a 3-D Effect to a Text Box

Word provides 3-D effects for shapes (such as text boxes) that are similar to those it provides for pictures. The following steps apply a 3-D rotation effect to a text box. **Why?** *In this form, the text box is rotated using a 3-D rotation effect.*

- With the text box selected, click the Shape Effects button (Drawing Tools Format tab | Shape Styles group) to display the Shape Effects gallery.

- Point to '3-D Rotation' in the Shape Effects gallery to display the 3-D Rotation gallery.

- Point to 'Isometric Top Up' in the Parallel area (third rotation in first row) to display a live preview of the selected 3-D effect applied to the text box in the document window (Figure 11–47).

 **Experiment**

- Point to various 3-D rotation effects in the 3-D Rotation gallery and watch the text box change in the document window.

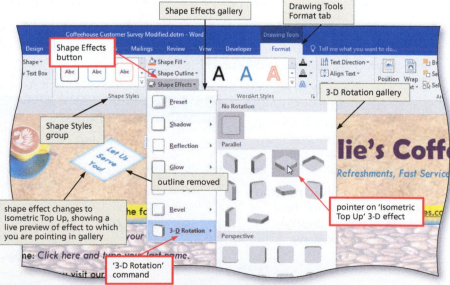

Figure 11–47

2

- Click 'Isometric Top Up' in the 3-D Rotation gallery to apply the selected 3-D effect.

Other Ways
1. Click Format Shape Dialog Box Launcher (Drawing Tools Format tab | Shape Styles group), click Text Options tab (Format Shape task pane), click Text Effects button, if necessary expand 3-D Rotation Section, select desired options, click Close button	2. Right-click text box (or, if using touch, tap 'Show Context Menu' button on mini toolbar), click Format Shape on shortcut menu, click Text Options tab (Format Shape task pane), click Text Effects button, if necessary expand 3-D Rotation Section, select desired options, click Close button

To Move the Text Box

In this project, the text box is to be positioned near the lower-left of the graphic. The following step moves the text box.

1 Drag the text box to the location shown in Figure 11–48. (You may need to drag the text box a couple of times to position it as shown in the figure.)

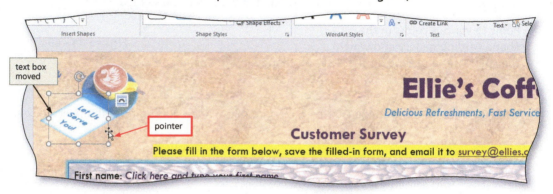

Figure 11–48

To Group Objects

1 SAVE DOCUMENT AS MACRO-ENABLED TEMPLATE | 2 MODIFY TEXT & FORM CONTENT CONTROLS
3 ENHANCE FORM'S VISUAL APPEAL | 4 CREATE MACROS TO AUTOMATE TASKS

When you have multiple graphics, such as pictures, shapes, and text boxes, positioned on a page, you can group them so that they are a single graphic instead of separate graphics. The following steps group the coffee cup graphic and the text box together. *Why? Grouping the graphics makes it easier to move them because they all move together as a single graphic.*

1

- With the text box selected, hold down the CTRL key while clicking the coffee cup picture (that is, CTRL+click), so that both graphics are selected at the same time.

Q&A What if I had more than two graphics that I wanted to group? For each subsequent graphic to select, CTRL+click the graphic, which enables you to select multiple objects at the same time.

- Click the Group Objects button (Drawing Tools Format tab | Arrange group) to display the Group Objects menu (Figure 11–49).

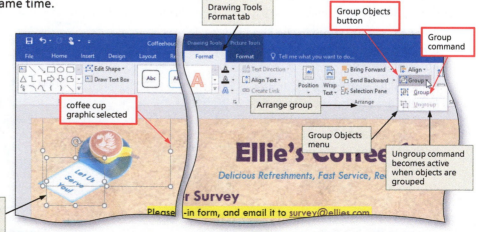

Figure 11–49

2

- Click Group on the Group Objects menu to group the selected objects into a single selected object (Figure 11–50).

Q&A What if I wanted to ungroup grouped objects?
Select the object to ungroup, click the Group Objects button (Drawing Tools Format tab | Arrange group), and then click Ungroup on the Group Objects menu.

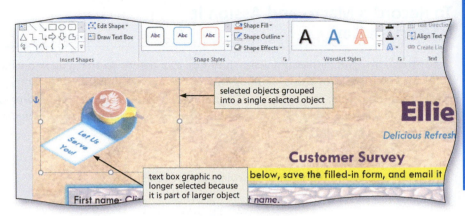

Figure 11–50

3

- Click outside of the graphic to position the insertion point in the document and deselect the graphic.

- Save the template again on the same storage location with the same file name.

> **Break Point:** If you wish to take a break, this is a good place to do so. You can exit Word now. To resume at a later time, run Word, open the file called Coffeehouse Customer Survey Modified, and continue following the steps from this location forward.

Using a Macro to Automate a Task

A **macro** consists of a series of Word commands or instructions that are grouped together as a single command. This single command is a convenient way to automate a difficult or lengthy task. Macros often are used to simplify formatting or editing activities, to combine multiple commands into a single command, or to select an option in a dialog box using a shortcut key.

To create a macro, you can use the macro recorder or the Visual Basic Editor. With the macro recorder, Word generates the VBA instructions associated with the macro automatically as you perform actions in Word. If you wanted to write the VBA instructions yourself, you would use the Visual Basic Editor. This module uses the macro recorder to create a macro and the Visual Basic Editor to modify it.

The **macro recorder** creates a macro based on a series of actions you perform while the macro recorder is recording. The macro recorder is similar to a video camera: after you start the macro recorder, it records all actions you perform while working in a document and stops recording when you stop the macro recorder. To record a macro, you follow this sequence of steps:

1. Start the macro recorder and specify options about the macro.

2. Execute the actions you want recorded.

3. Stop the macro recorder.

After you record a macro, you can execute the macro, or play it, any time you want to perform the same set of actions.

BTW

Naming Macros
If you give a new macro the same name as an existing built-in command in Microsoft Word, the new macro's actions will replace the existing actions. Thus, you should be careful not to assign a macro a name reserved for automatic macros (see Table 11–1 later in this module) or after any Word commands. To view a list of built-in macros in Word, click the View Macros button (View tab | Macros group) to display the Macros dialog box. Click the Macros in arrow and then click Word commands.

To Record a Macro and Assign It a Shortcut Key

In Word, you can assign a shortcut key to a macro so that you can execute the macro by pressing the shortcut key instead of using a dialog box to execute it. The following steps record a macro that hides formatting marks and the rulers; the macro is assigned the shortcut key, ALT+H. *Why? Assume you find that you are repeatedly hiding the formatting marks and rulers while designing the online form. To simplify this task, the macro in this project hides these screen elements.*

- Display formatting marks and the rulers on the screen.

- Display the Developer tab.

- Click the Record Macro button (Developer tab | Code group) to display the Record Macro dialog box.

- Type **HideScreenElements** in the Macro name text box (Record Macro dialog box).

Q&A Do I have to name a macro?
If you do not enter a name for the macro, Word assigns a default name. Macro names can be up to 255 characters in length and can contain only numbers, letters, and the underscore character. A macro name cannot contain spaces or other punctuation.

- Click the 'Store macro in' arrow and then click 'Documents Based On Coffeehouse Customer Survey Modified'.

Q&A What is the difference between storing a macro with the document template versus the Normal template?
Macros saved in the Normal template are available to all future documents; macros saved with the document template are available only with a document based on the template.

- In the Description text box, type this sentence (Figure 11–51): **Hide formatting marks and the rulers.**

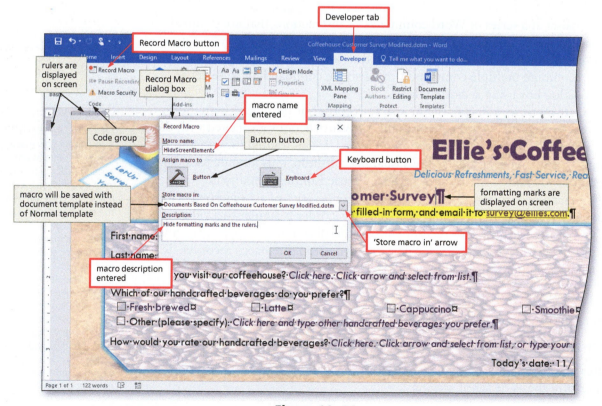

Figure 11–51

2

- Click the Keyboard button to display the Customize Keyboard dialog box.

- Press ALT+H to display the characters, Alt+H, in the 'Press new shortcut key' text box (Customize Keyboard dialog box) (Figure 11–52).

Q&A Can I type the letters in the shortcut key (ALT+H) in the text box instead of pressing them?
No. Although typing the letters places them in the text box, the shortcut key is valid only if you press the shortcut key combination itself.

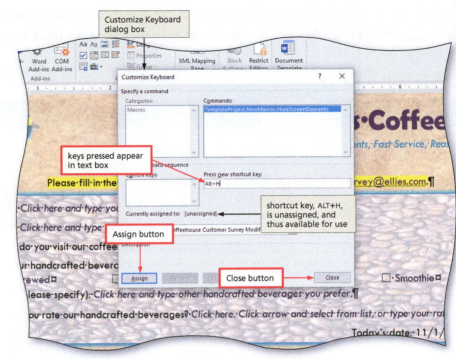

Figure 11–52

3

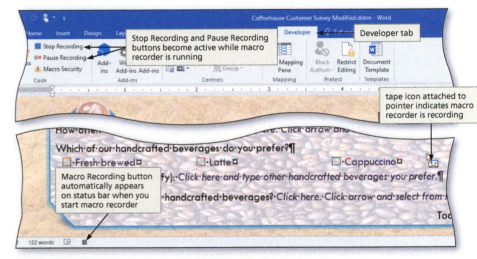

- Click the Assign button (Customize Keyboard dialog box) to assign the shortcut key, ALT+H, to the macro named HideScreenElements.

- Click the Close button (Customize Keyboard dialog box), which closes the dialog box, displays a Macro Recording button on the status bar, and starts the macro recorder (Figure 11–53).

Q&A How do I record the macro?
While the macro recorder is running, any action you perform in Word will be part of the macro — until you stop or pause the macro.

Figure 11–53

What is the purpose of the Pause Recording button (Developer tab | Code group)?
If, while recording a macro, you want to perform some actions that should not be part of the macro, click the Pause Recording button to suspend the macro recorder. The Pause Recording button changes to a Resume Recorder button that you click when you want to continue recording.

4

- Display the Home tab.

Q&A What happened to the tape icon?
While recording a macro, the tape icon might disappear from the pointer when the pointer is in a menu, on the ribbon, or in a dialog box.

- Click the 'Show/Hide ¶' button (Home tab | Paragraph group) to hide formatting marks.
- Display the View tab. Remove the check mark from the View Ruler check box (View tab | Show group) to hide the rulers (Figure 11–54).

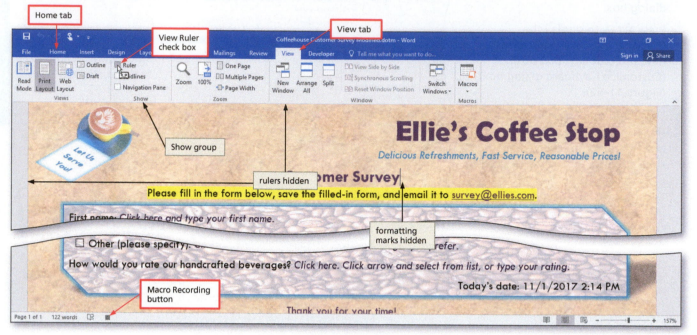

Figure 11–54

- Click the Macro Recording button on the status bar to turn off the macro recorder, that is, to stop recording actions you perform in Word.

Q&A What if I made a mistake while recording the macro?

Delete the macro and record it again. To delete a macro, click the View Macros button (Developer tab | Code group), select the macro name in the list (Macros dialog box), click the Delete button, and then click the Yes button.

What if I wanted to assign the macro to a button instead of a shortcut key?

You would click the Button button in the Record Macro dialog box (shown in Figure 11–51) and then follow Steps 4 and 5 in this section.

Other Ways

1. Click View Macros arrow (View tab | Macros group), click Record Macro on View Macros menu
2. Press ALT+F8, click Create button (Macros dialog box)

To Run a Macro

BTW

Running Macros
You can run a macro by clicking the View Macros button (Developer tab | Code group or View tab | Macros group) or by pressing ALT+F8 to display the Macros dialog box, selecting the macro name in the list, and then clicking the Run button (Macros dialog box).

The next step is to execute, or run, the macro to ensure that it works. Recall that this macro hides formatting marks and the rulers, which means you must be sure the formatting marks and rulers are displayed on the screen before running the macro. Because you created a shortcut key for the macro in this project, the following steps show formatting marks and the rulers so that you can run the HideScreenElements macro using the shortcut key, ALT+H.

1. Display formatting marks on the screen.

2. Display rulers on the screen.

3. Press ALT+H, which causes Word to perform the instructions stored in the HideScreenElements macro, that is, to hide formatting marks and rulers.

To Add a Command and a Macro as Buttons on the Quick Access Toolbar

Word allows you to add buttons to and delete buttons from the Quick Access Toolbar. You also can assign a command, such as a macro, to a button on the Quick Access Toolbar. The following steps add an existing command to the Quick Access Toolbar and assign a macro to a new button on the Quick Access Toolbar. *Why? This module shows how to add the New File command to the Quick Access Toolbar and also shows how to create a button for the HideScreenElements macro so that instead of pressing the shortcut keys, you can click the button to hide formatting marks and the rulers.*

1

- Click the 'Customize Quick Access Toolbar' button on the Quick Access Toolbar to display the Customize Quick Access Toolbar menu (Figure 11–55).

Q&A

What happens if I click the commands listed on the Customize Quick Access Toolbar menu?
If the command does not have a check mark beside it and you click it, Word places the button associated with the command on the Quick Access Toolbar. If the command has a check mark beside it and you click (deselect) it, Word removes the command from the Quick Access Toolbar.

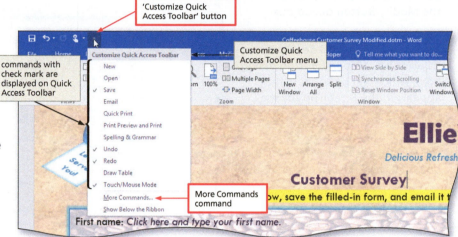

Figure 11–55

2

- Click More Commands on the Customize Quick Access Toolbar menu to display the Word Options dialog box with Quick Access Toolbar selected in the left pane.

- Scroll through the list of popular commands (Word Options dialog box) and then click New File to select the command.

- Click the Add button to add the selected command (New File, in this case) to the Customize Quick Access Toolbar list (Figure 11–56).

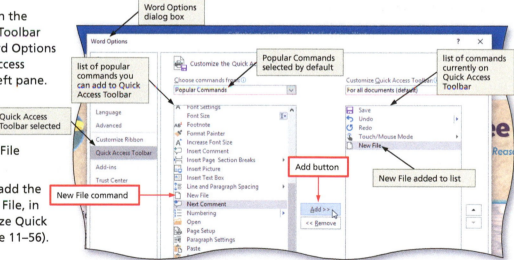

Figure 11–56

3

- Click the 'Choose commands from' arrow to display a list of categories of commands (Figure 11–57).

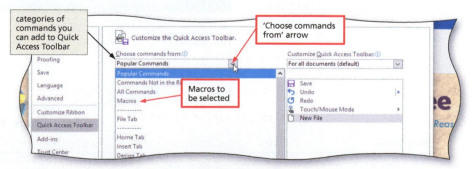

Figure 11–57

- Click Macros in the Choose commands from list to display the macro in this document.
- If necessary, click the macro to select it.
- Click the Add button (Word Options dialog box) to display the selected macro in the Customize Quick Access Toolbar list.
- Click the Modify button to display the Modify Button dialog box.
- Change the name in the Display name text box to **Hide Screen Elements** (Modify Button dialog box), which will be the text that appears in the ScreenTip for the button.
- In the list of symbols, click the screen icon as the new face for the button (Figure 11–58).

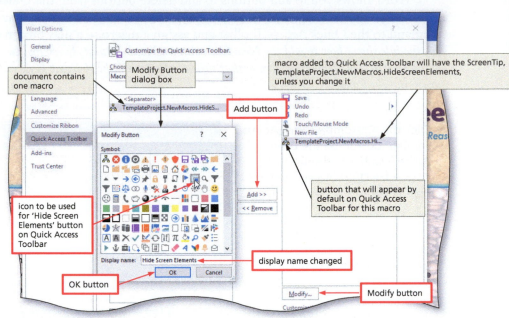

Figure 11–58

- Click the OK button (Modify Button dialog box) to change the button characteristics in the Customize Quick Access Toolbar list (Figure 11–59).

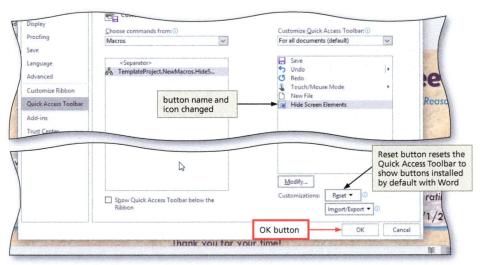

Figure 11–59

- Click the OK button (Word Options dialog box) to add the buttons to the Quick Access Toolbar (Figure 11–60).

Figure 11–60

Other Ways

1. Right-click Quick Access Toolbar, click 'Customize Quick Access Toolbar' on shortcut menu

To Use the New Buttons on the Quick Access Toolbar

The next step is to test the new buttons on the Quick Access Toolbar, that is, the New button and the 'Hide Screen Elements' button, which will execute, or run, the macro that hides formatting marks and the rulers. The following steps use buttons on the Quick Access Toolbar.

1 Click the New button on the Quick Access Toolbar to display a new blank document window. Close the new blank document window.

2 Display formatting marks on the screen.

3 Display rulers on the screen.

4 Click the 'Hide Screen Elements' button on the Quick Access Toolbar, which causes Word to perform the instructions stored in the HideScreenElements macro, that is, to hide formatting marks and the rulers.

To Delete Buttons from the Quick Access Toolbar

1 SAVE DOCUMENT AS MACRO-ENABLED TEMPLATE | 2 MODIFY TEXT & FORM CONTENT CONTROLS
3 ENHANCE FORM'S VISUAL APPEAL | **4 CREATE MACROS TO AUTOMATE TASKS**

The following steps delete the New button and the 'Hide Screen Elements' button from the Quick Access Toolbar. **Why?** *If you no longer plan to use a button on the Quick Access Toolbar, you can delete it.*

1
- Right-click the button to be deleted from the Quick Access Toolbar, in this case the 'Hide Screen Elements' button, to display a shortcut menu (Figure 11–61).

2
- Click 'Remove from Quick Access Toolbar' on the shortcut menu to remove the button from the Quick Access Toolbar.

3
- Repeat Steps 1 and 2 for the New File button on the Quick Access Toolbar.

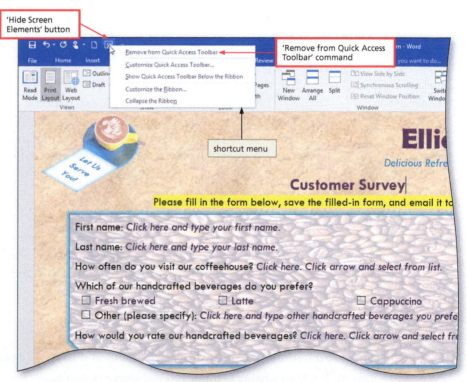

Figure 11–61

To Delete a Macro

If you wanted to delete a macro, you would perform the following steps.

1. Click the View Macros button (Developer tab | Code group) to display the Macros dialog box.
2. Click the macro to delete and then click the Delete button (Macros dialog box) to display a dialog box asking if you are sure you want to delete the macro. Click the Yes button in the dialog box.
3. Close the Macros dialog box.

Automatic Macros

The previous section showed how to create a macro, assign it a unique name (HideScreenElements) and a shortcut key, and then add a button that executes the macro on the Quick Access Toolbar. This section creates an **automatic macro**, which is a macro that executes automatically when a certain event occurs. Word has five prenamed automatic macros. Table 11–1 lists the name and function of these automatic macros.

Table 11–1 Automatic Macros

Macro Name	Event That Causes Macro to Run
AutoClose	Closing a document that contains the macro
AutoExec	Running Word
AutoExit	Exiting Word
AutoNew	Creating a new document based on a template that contains the macro
AutoOpen	Opening a document that contains the macro

The automatic macro you choose depends on when you want certain actions to occur. In this module, when a user creates a new Word document that is based on the Coffeehouse Customer Survey Modified template, you want to be sure that the zoom is set to page width. Thus, the AutoNew automatic macro is used in this online form.

To Create an Automatic Macro

1 SAVE DOCUMENT AS MACRO-ENABLED TEMPLATE | 2 MODIFY TEXT & FORM CONTENT CONTROLS
3 ENHANCE FORM'S VISUAL APPEAL | **4 CREATE MACROS TO AUTOMATE TASKS**

The following steps use the macro recorder to create an AutoNew macro. *Why? The online form in this module is displayed properly when the zoom is set to page width. Thus, you will record the steps to zoom to page width in the AutoNew macro.*

- Display the Developer tab.
- Click the Record Macro button (Developer tab | Code group) to display the Record Macro dialog box.
- Type **AutoNew** in the Macro name text box (Record Macro dialog box).
- Click the 'Store macro in' arrow and then click 'Documents Based On Coffeehouse Customer Survey Modified'.
- In the Description text box, type this sentence (Figure 11–62): **Specifies how the form initially is displayed.**

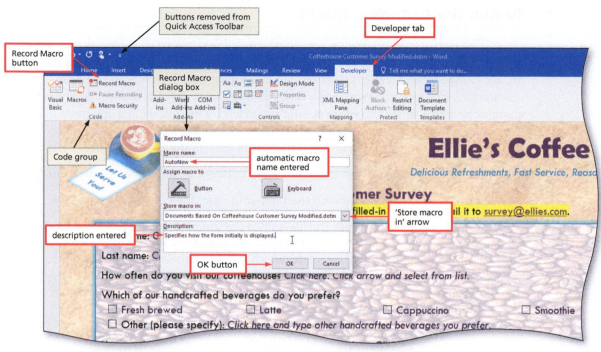

Figure 11–62

2

- Click the OK button to close the Record Macro dialog box and start the macro recorder.
- Display the View tab.
- Click the Page Width button (View tab | Zoom group) to zoom page width (Figure 11–63).

3

- Click the Macro Recording button on the status bar to turn off the macro recorder, that is, stop recording actions you perform in Word.

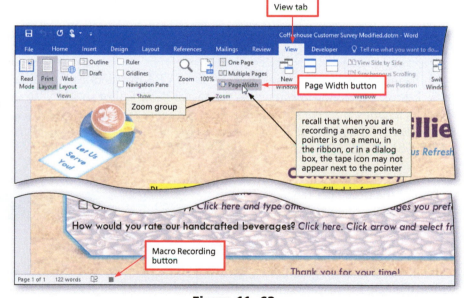

Figure 11–63

Q&A How do I test an automatic macro?

Activate the event that causes the macro to execute. For example, the AutoNew macro runs whenever you create a new Word document that is based on the template.

To Run the AutoNew Macro

The next step is to execute, or run, the AutoNew macro to ensure that it works. To run the AutoNew macro, you need to create a new Word document that is based on the Coffeehouse Customer Survey Modified template. This macro contains instructions to zoom page width. To verify that the macro works as intended, you will change the zoom to 100% before testing the macro. The following steps run a macro.

1 Use the Zoom Out button on the status bar to change the zoom to 100%.

2 Save the template with the same file name, Coffeehouse Customer Survey Modified.

3 Click the File Explorer button on the taskbar to open the File Explorer window.

4 Locate and then double-click the file named Coffeehouse Customer Survey Modified to display a new document window that is based on the contents of the Coffeehouse Customer Survey Modified template, which should be zoomed to page width as shown in Figure 11–1a at the beginning of this module. (If Word displays a dialog box about disabling macros, click its OK button. If the Message Bar displays a security warning, click the Enable Content button.)

5 Close the new document that displays the form in the Word window. Click the Don't Save button when Word asks if you want to save the changes to the new document.

6 Close the File Explorer window.

7 Change the zoom back to page width.

BTW

VBA

VBA includes many more statements than those presented in this module. You may need a background in programming if you plan to write VBA code instructions in macros you develop and if the VBA code instructions are beyond the scope of those instructions presented in this module.

To Edit a Macro's VBA Code

1 SAVE DOCUMENT AS MACRO-ENABLED TEMPLATE | 2 MODIFY TEXT & FORM CONTENT CONTROLS
3 ENHANCE FORM'S VISUAL APPEAL | 4 CREATE MACROS TO AUTOMATE TASKS

As mentioned earlier, a macro consists of VBA instructions. To edit a recorded macro, you use the Visual Basic Editor. The following steps use the Visual Basic Editor to add VBA instructions to the AutoNew macro. *Why? In addition to zooming page width when the online form is displayed in a new document window, you would like to be sure that the Developer tab is hidden and the ribbon is collapsed. These steps are designed to show the basic composition of a VBA procedure and illustrate the power of VBA code statements.*

1

- Display the Developer tab.

- Click the View Macros button (Developer tab | Code group) to display the Macros dialog box.

- If necessary, select the macro to be edited, in this case, AutoNew (Figure 11–64).

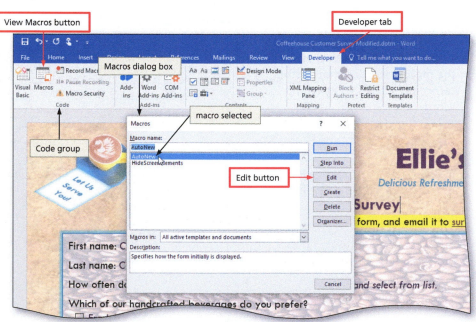

Figure 11–64

2

- Click the Edit button (Macros dialog box) to run the Visual Basic Editor and display the VBA code for the AutoNew macro in the Code window — your screen may look different depending on previous Visual Basic Editor settings (Figure 11–65).

Q&A

What if the Code window does not appear in the Visual Basic Editor?
In the Visual Basic Editor, click View on the menu bar and then click Code. If it still does not appear and you are in a network environment, this feature may be disabled for some users.

What are the lines of text (instructions) in the Code window?
The named set of instructions associated with a macro is called a **procedure**. It is this set of instructions — beginning with the word, Sub, and continuing sequentially to the line with the words, End Sub — that executes when you run the macro. The instructions within a procedure are called **code statements**.

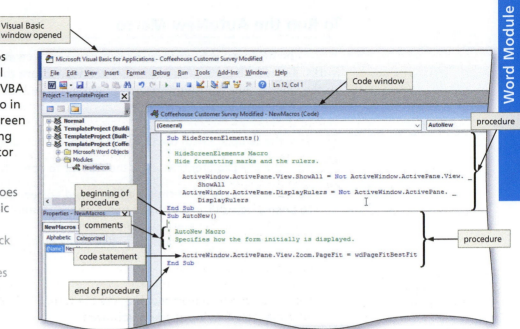

Figure 11–65

3

- Position the insertion point at the end of the second-to-last line in the AutoNew macro and then press the ENTER key to insert a blank line for a new code statement.

- On a single line, type `Options.ShowDevTools = False` and then press the ENTER key, which enters the VBA code statement that hides the Developer tab.

Q&A

What are the lists that appear in the Visual Basic Editor as I enter code statements?
The lists present valid statement elements to assist you with entering code statements. Because they are beyond the scope of this module, ignore them.

- On a single line, type `If Application.CommandBars.Item("Ribbon").Height > 100 Then` and then press the ENTER key, which enters the beginning VBA if statement that determines whether to collapse the ribbon.

- On a single line, press the TAB key, type `ActiveWindow.ToggleRibbon` and then press the ENTER key, which enters the beginning VBA code statement that collapses the ribbon.

- On a single line, press SHIFT+TAB and then type `End If` to enter the ending VBA code statement that determines whether to collapse the ribbon (Figure 11–66).

4

- Click the Close button on the right edge of the Microsoft Visual Basic window title bar.

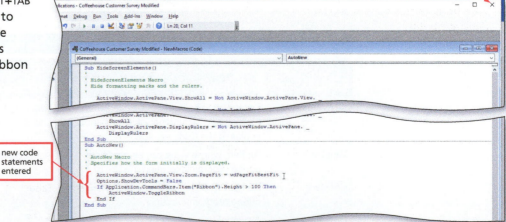

Figure 11–66

To Run the AutoNew Macro

The next step is to execute, or run, the AutoNew macro again to ensure that it works. To be sure the macro works as intended, ensure the Developer tab is displayed on the ribbon. The AutoNew macro should hide the Developer tab. The following steps run the automatic macro.

1 Save the template with the same file name, Coffeehouse Customer Survey Modified.

2 Click the File Explorer button on the taskbar to open the File Explorer window.

3 Locate and then double-click the file named Coffeehouse Customer Survey Modified to open a new document that is based on the contents of the Coffeehouse Customer Survey Modified template, which should be zoomed to page width and display no Developer tab. (If Word displays a dialog box about disabling macros, click its OK button. If the Message Bar displays a security warning, click the Enable Content button.)

4 Close the new document that displays the form in the Word window. Click the Don't Save button when Word asks if you want to save the changes to the new document.

5 Close the File Explorer window.

VBA

As shown in the previous steps, a VBA procedure begins with a Sub statement and ends with an End Sub statement. The Sub statement is followed by the name of the procedure, which is the macro name (AutoNew). The parentheses following the macro name in the Sub statement are required. They indicate that arguments can be passed from one procedure to another. Passing arguments is beyond the scope of this module, but the parentheses still are required. The End Sub statement signifies the end of the procedure and returns control to Word.

Comments often are added to a procedure to help you remember the purpose of the macro and its code statements at a later date. Comments begin with an apostrophe (') and appear in green in the Code window. The macro recorder, for example, placed four comment lines below the Sub statement. These comments display the name of the macro and its description, as entered in the Record Macro dialog box. Comments have no effect on the execution of a procedure; they simply provide information about the procedure, such as its name and description, to the Developer of the macro.

For readability, code statement lines are indented four spaces. Table 11–2 explains the function of each element of a code statement.

Table 11–2 Elements of a Code Statement		
Code Statement		
Element	**Definition**	**Examples**
Keyword	Recognized by Visual Basic as part of its programming language; keywords appear in blue in the Code window	Sub End Sub
Variable	An item whose value can be modified during program execution	ActiveWindow.ActivePane.View.Zoom.PageFit
Constant	An item whose value remains unchanged during program execution	False
Operator	A symbol that indicates a specific action	=

To Protect a Form Using the Backstage View and Exit Word

You now are finished enhancing the online form and adding macros to it. Because the last macro hid the Developer tab on the ribbon, you will use the Backstage view to protect the form. The following steps use the Backstage view to protect the online form so that users are restricted to entering data only in content controls.

1 Open the Backstage view and then, if necessary, display the Info gallery.

2 Click the Protect Document button to display the Protect Document menu.

3 Click Restrict Editing on the Protect Document menu to open the Restrict Editing task pane.

4 In the Editing restrictions area, if necessary, place a check mark in the 'Allow only this type of editing in the document' check box, click its arrow, and then select 'Filling in forms' in the list.

5 Click the 'Yes, Start Enforcing Protection' button and then click the OK button (Start Enforcing Protection dialog box) to protect the document without a password.

6 Close the Restrict Editing task pane.

7 Save the template again on the same storage location with the same file name.

8 Exit Word.

9 If the File Explorer window still is open, close it.

Supplementary Word Tasks

If you plan to take the certification exam, you should be familiar with the skills in the following sections.

Adding a Digital Signature to a Document

Some users attach a **digital signature** to a document to verify its authenticity. A digital signature is an electronic, encrypted, and secure stamp of authentication on a document. This signature confirms that the file originated from the signer (file creator) and that it has not been altered.

A digital signature references a digital certificate. A **digital certificate** is an attachment to a file, macro project, email message, or other digital content that vouches for its authenticity, provides secure encryption, or supplies a verifiable signature. Many users who receive online forms enable the macros based on whether they are digitally signed by a developer on the user's list of trusted sources. You can obtain a digital certificate from a commercial certification authority or from your network administrator.

Once a digital signature is added, the document becomes a read-only document, which means that modifications cannot be made to it. Thus, you should create a digital signature only when the document is final. In Word, you can add two types of digital signatures to a document: (1) an invisible digital signature or (2) a signature line.

TO ADD AN INVISIBLE DIGITAL SIGNATURE TO A DOCUMENT

An invisible digital signature does not appear as a tangible signature in the document. If the status bar displays a Signatures button, the document has an invisible digital signature. If you wanted to add an invisible digital signature to a document, you would perform the following steps.

1. Open the Backstage view and then, if necessary, display the Info gallery.

2. Click the Protect Document button to display the Protect Document menu and then click 'Add a Digital Signature' on the Protect Document menu to display the Sign dialog box. (If a dialog box appears indicating you need a digital ID, click the Yes button and then follow the on-screen instructions. If a dialog box about signature services appears, click its OK button.)

3. Type the purpose of the digital signature in the Purpose for signing this document text box.

4. Click the Sign button to add the digital signature, show the Signatures button on the status bar, and display Marked as Final on a Message Bar.

Q&A How can I view or remove the digital signatures in a document?
Open the Backstage view, if necessary, display the Info tab, and then click the View Signatures button to display the Signatures task pane. To remove a digital signature, click the arrow beside the signature name, click Remove Signature on the menu, and then click the Yes button in the dialog box.

TO ADD A SIGNATURE LINE TO A DOCUMENT

A **digital signature line**, which resembles a printed signature placeholder, allows a recipient of the electronic file to type a signature, include an image of his or her signature, or write a signature using the ink feature on a mobile computer or device. Digital signature lines enable organizations to use paperless methods of obtaining signatures on official documents, such as contracts. If you wanted to add a digital signature line to a document, you would perform the following steps.

1. Position the insertion point at the location for the digital signature.

2. Display the Insert tab. Click the 'Add a Signature Line' button (Insert tab | Text group) to display the Signature Setup dialog box. (If a dialog box appears about signature services, click its OK button.)

3. Type the name of the person who should sign the document in the appropriate text box.

4. If available, type the signer's title and email address in the appropriate text boxes.

5. Place a checkmark in the 'Allow the signer to add comments in the Sign dialog' check box so that the recipient can send a response back to you.

6. Click the OK button (Signature Setup dialog box) to insert a signature line in the document at the location of the insertion point.

Q&A How does a recipient insert his or her digital signature?
When the recipient opens the document, a Message Bar appears that contains a View Signatures button. The recipient can click the View Signatures button to display the Signatures task pane, click the requested signature arrow, and then click Sign on the menu (or double-click the signature line in the document) to display a dialog box that the recipient then completes.

BTW

Lock Tracking
If you wanted to require a password to turn off tracked changes, you would click the Track Changes button (Review tab | Tracking group), click Lock Tracking on the Track Changes menu, enter the password in each text box, and then click the OK button. To enter the password to turn off tracked changes, follow the same steps, entering the password when prompted.

Copying and Renaming Styles and Macros

If you have created a style or macro in one document or template, you can copy the style or a macro to another so that you can use it in a second document or template.

TO COPY A STYLE FROM ONE TEMPLATE OR DOCUMENT TO ANOTHER

If you wanted to copy a style from one template or document to another, you would perform the following steps.

1. Open the document or template into which you want to copy the style.

2. If necessary, click the Styles Dialog Box Launcher (Home tab | Styles group) to open the Styles task pane, click the Manage Styles button at the bottom of the Styles task pane to display the Manage Styles dialog box, and then click the Import/Export button (Manage Styles dialog box) to display Styles sheet in the Organizer dialog box. Or, click the Document Template button (Developer tab | Templates group) to display the Templates and Add-ins dialog box, click the Organizer button (Templates and Add-ins dialog box) to display the Organizer dialog box, and then, if necessary, click the Styles tab to display the Styles sheet in the dialog box. Notice that the left side of the dialog box displays the style names in the currently open document or template.

3. Click the Close File button (Organizer dialog box) to clear the right side of the dialog box.

Q&A | What happened to the Close File button?
It changed to an Open File button.

4. Click the Open File button (Organizer dialog box) and then locate the file that contains the style you wish to copy. Notice that the styles in the located document or template appear on the right side of the dialog box.

5. On the ride side of the dialog box, select the style you wish to copy and then click the Copy button to copy the selected style to the document or template on the left. You can continue to copy as many styles as necessary.

6. When finished copying styles, click the Close button to close the dialog box.

TO RENAME A STYLE

If you wanted to rename a style, you would perform the following steps.

1. Open the document or template that contains the style to rename.

2. If necessary, click the Styles Dialog Box Launcher (Home tab | Styles group) to display the Styles task pane, click the Manage Styles button at the bottom of the Styles task pane to display the Manage Styles dialog box, and then click the Import/Export button (Manage Styles dialog box) to display the Styles sheet in the Organizer dialog box. Or, click the Document Template button (Developer tab | Templates group) to display the Templates and Add-ins dialog box, click the Organizer button (Templates and Add-ins dialog box) to display the Organizer dialog box, and then, if necessary, click the Styles tab to display the Styles sheet in the dialog box. Notice that the left side of the dialog box displays the style names in the currently open document or template.

BTW

Building Blocks
If you wanted to make building blocks available in other documents and templates, instead of just the current document or template, you would save them in the Normal.dotm file instead of the Building Blocks.dotx file. To do this, click the 'Explore Quick Parts' button (Insert tab | Text group), click Building Blocks Organizer on the Explore Quick Parts menu, click the building block for which you want to change the save location, click the Edit Properties button (Building Blocks Organizer dialog box), click the Save in button (Modify Building Block dialog box), select Normal in the list, click the OK button (Modify Building Block dialog box), and then click the Close button (Building Blocks Organizer dialog box).

3. Select the style you wish to rename and then click the Rename button (Organizer dialog box) to display the Rename dialog box.

4. Type the new name of the style in the text box and then click the OK button (Rename dialog box).

Q&A Can I delete styles too?
Yes, click the Delete button (Organizer dialog box) to delete any selected styles.

5. When finished renaming styles, click the Close button (Organizer dialog box) to close the dialog box.

TO COPY A MACRO FROM ONE TEMPLATE OR DOCUMENT TO ANOTHER

If you wanted to copy a macro from one template or document to another, you would perform the following steps.

1. Open the document or template into which you want to copy the macro.

2. If necessary, click the View Macros button (Developer tab | Code group or View tab | Macros group) to display the Macros dialog box, click the Organizer button (Macros dialog box) to display Macro Project Items sheet in the Organizer dialog box. Or, click the Document Template button (Developer tab | Templates group) to display the Templates and Add-ins dialog box, click the Organizer button (Templates and Add-ins dialog box) to display the Organizer dialog box, and then, if necessary, click the Macro Project Items tab to display the Macro Project Items sheet in the dialog box. Notice that the left side of the dialog box displays the macro names in the currently open document or template.

3. Click the Close File button (Organizer dialog box) to clear the right side of the dialog box.

Q&A What happened to the Close File button?
It changed to an Open File button.

4. Click the Open File button (Organizer dialog box) and then locate the file that contains the macro you wish to copy. Notice that the macros in the located document or template appear on the right side of the dialog box.

5. On the ride side of the dialog box, select the macro you wish to copy and then click the Copy button to copy the selected macro to the document or template on the left. You can continue to copy as many macros as necessary.

6. When finished copying macros, click the Close button (Organizer dialog box) to close the dialog box.

TO RENAME A MACRO

If you wanted to rename a macro, you would perform the following steps.

1. Open the document that contains the macro to rename.

2. If necessary, click the View Macros button (Developer tab | Code group or View tab | Macros group) to display the Macros dialog box and then click the Organizer button (Macros dialog box) to display Macro Project Items sheet in the Organizer dialog box. Or, click the Document Template button (Developer tab | Templates group) to display the Templates and Add-ins dialog box, click the

Organizer button (Templates and Add-ins dialog box) to display the Organizer dialog box, and then, if necessary, click the Macro Project Items tab to display the Macro Project Items sheet in the dialog box. Notice that the left side of the dialog box displays the macro names in the currently open document or template.

3. Select the macro you wish to rename and then click the Rename button (Organizer dialog box) to display the Rename dialog box.

4. Type the new name of the macro in the text box and then click the OK button (Rename dialog box).

Q&A Can I delete macros, too?
Yes, click the Delete button (Organizer dialog box) to delete any selected macros.

5. When finished renaming macros, click the Close button to close the dialog box.

Preparing a Document for Internationalization

Word provides internationalization features you can use when creating documents and templates. Use of features should be determined based on the intended audience of the document or template. By default, Word uses formatting consistent with the country or region selected when installing Windows. In addition to inserting symbols, such as those for currency, and using date and time formats that are recognized internationally or in other countries, you can set the language used for proofing tools and other language preferences.

TO SET THE LANGUAGE FOR PROOFING TOOLS

If you wanted to change the language that Word uses to proof documents or templates, you would perform the following steps.

1. Click the Language button (Review tab | Language group) to display the Language menu.

2. Click 'Set Proofing Language' on the Language menu to display the Language dialog box. (If you want to set this language as the default, click the 'Set As Default' button.)

3. Select the desired language to use for proofing tools and then click the OK button.

TO SET LANGUAGE PREFERENCES

If you wanted to change the language that Word uses for editing, display, Help, and ScreenTips, you would perform the following steps.

1. Click the Language button (Review tab | Language group) to display the Language menu and then click Language Preferences on the Language menu to display the language settings in the Word Options dialog box. Or, open the Backstage view, click the Options tab in the left pane to display the Word Options dialog box, and then click Language in the left pane (Word Options dialog box) to display the language settings.

2. Select preferences for the editing language, display language, and Help language, and then click the OK button.

BTW

Advanced Paragraph Options
A widow is when the last line of a paragraph appears by itself at the top of a page, and an orphan is when the first line of a paragraph appears by itself at the bottom of a page. To prevent widows and orphans, click the Paragraph Settings Dialog Box Launcher (Home tab | Paragraph group), click the Line and Page Breaks tab (Paragraph dialog box), place a check mark in the 'Widow/Orphan control' check box, and then click the OK button. Similarly, you can select the 'Keep with next' check box to keep selected paragraphs together, the 'Keep lines together' check box to keep selected lines together, and the 'Page break before' check box to insert a page break before the selected paragraph.

BTW
Removing Metadata
If you wanted to remove document metadata, such as personal information and comments, you would do the following with the document open in a document window: open the Backstage view, if necessary, click the Info tab in the Backstage view to display the Info gallery, click the 'Check for Issues' button in the Info gallery to display the Check for Issues menu, click Inspect Document on the Check for Issues menu to display the Document Inspector dialog box, click the Inspect button (Document Inspector dialog box) to instruct Word to inspect the document, review the results (Document Inspector dialog box), and then click the Remove All button(s) for any item that you do not want to be saved with the document. When you have finished removing information, click the Close button to close the dialog box.

Enhancing a Document's Accessibility

Word provides several options for enhancing the accessibility of documents for individuals who have difficulty reading. Some previously discussed tasks you can perform to assist users include increasing zoom and font size, customizing the ribbon, ensuring tab/reading order in tables is logical, and using Read mode. You also can use the accessibility checker to locate and address problematic issues, and you can add alternative text to graphics and tables.

TO USE THE ACCESSIBILITY CHECKER

The accessibility checker scans a document and identifies issues that could affect a person's ability to read the content. Once identified, you can address each individual issue in the document. If you wanted to check accessibility of a document, you would perform the following steps.

1. Open the Backstage view and then, if necessary, display the Info gallery.
2. Click the 'Check for Issues' button to display the Check for Issues menu.
3. Click Check Accessibility on the Check for Issues menu, which scans the document and then displays accessibility issues in the Accessibility Checker task pane.
4. Address the errors and warnings in the Accessibility Checker task pane and then close the task pane.

TO ADD ALTERNATIVE TEXT TO GRAPHICS

For users who have difficulty seeing images on the screen, you can include **alternate text**, also called **alt text**, to your graphics so that these users can see or hear the alternate text when working with your document. Graphics you can add alt text to include pictures, shapes, text boxes, SmartArt graphics, and charts. If you wanted to add alternative text to graphics, you would perform the following steps.

1. Click the Format Shape Dialog Box Launcher (Picture Tools Format tab | Picture Styles group or Drawing Tools Format tab or SmartArt Tools Format tab or Chart Tools Format tab | Shape Styles group); right-click the object and then click Format Picture, Format Shape, Format Object, or Format Chart Area on the shortcut menu to open the Format Picture, Format Shape, or Format Chart Area task pane.
2. Click the 'Layout & Properties' button (Format Picture, Format Shape, or Format Chart Area task pane) and then, if necessary, expand the Alt Text section.
3. Type a brief title and then type a narrative description of the picture in the respective text boxes.
4. Close the task pane.

TO ADD ALTERNATIVE TEXT TO TABLES

For users who have difficulty seeing tables on the screen, you can include alternative text to your tables so that these users can see or hear the alternative text when working with your document. If you wanted to add alternative text to a table, sometimes called a table title, you would perform the following steps.

1. Click the Table Properties button (Table Tools Layout tab | Table group), or right-click the table and then click Table Properties on the shortcut menu to display the Table Properties dialog box.

2. Click the Alt Text tab (Table Properties dialog box) to display the Alt Text sheet.

3. Type a brief title and then type a narrative description of the table in the respective text boxes.

4. Click the OK button to close the dialog box.

Table of Authorities

Legal documents often include a **table of authorities** to list references to cases, rules, statutes, etc., along with the page number(s) on which the references appear. To create a table of authorities, mark the citations first and then build the table of authorities. The procedures for marking citations, editing citations, creating the table of authorities, changing the format of the table of authorities, and updating the table of authorities are the same as those for indexes. The only difference is that you use the buttons in the Table of Authorities group on the References tab instead of the buttons in the Index group.

TO MARK A CITATION

If you wanted to mark a citation, creating a citation entry, you would perform the following steps.

1. Select the long, full citation that you wish to appear in the table of authorities (for example, State v. Smith 220 J.3d 167 (UT, 1997)).

2. Click the Mark Citation button (References tab | Table of Authorities group) or press ALT+SHIFT+I to display the Mark Citation dialog box.

3. If necessary, click the Category arrow (Mark Citation dialog box) and then select a new category type.

4. If desired, enter a short version of the citation in the Short citation text box.

5. Click the Mark button to mark the selected text in the document as citation.

Q&A Why do formatting marks now appear on the screen?
When you mark a citation, Word automatically shows formatting marks (if they are not showing already) so that you can see the citation field. The citation entry begins with the letters, TA.

6. Click the Close button in the Mark Citation dialog box.

Q&A How could I see all marked citation entries in a document?
With formatting marks displaying, you could scroll through the document, scanning for all occurrences of TA, or you could use the Navigation Pane (that is, place a check mark in the 'Open the Navigation Pane' check box (View tab | Show group)) to find all occurrences of TA.

BTW
Working with Lists
In a numbered list, if you wanted to restart numbering, you would click the Numbering arrow, click 'Set Numbering Value' in the Numbering Library gallery to display the Set Numbering Value dialog box, click 'Start new list' (Set Numbering Value dialog box), and then click the OK button. To continue list numbering in a subsequent list, you would click 'Continue from previous list' in the Set Numbering Value dialog box. You also can specify a starting number in a list by entering the value in the 'Set value to' box (Set Numbering Value dialog box).

BTW
Line Numbers
If you wanted to insert line numbers in a document, click the 'Show Line Numbers' button (Layout tab | Page Setup group) and then click the desired line number setting on the Show Line Numbers menu.

To Mark Multiple Citations

Word leaves the Mark Citation dialog box open until you close it, which allows you to mark multiple citations without having to redisplay the dialog box repeatedly. To mark multiple citations, you would perform the following steps.

1. With the Mark Citation dialog box displayed, click in the document window; scroll to and then select the next citation.
2. If necessary, click the Selected text text box (Mark Citation dialog box) to display the selected text in the Selected text text box.
3. Click the Mark button.
4. Repeat Steps 1 through 3 for all citations you wish to mark. When finished, click the Close button in the dialog box.

To Edit a Citation Entry

At some time, you may want to change a citation entry after you have marked it. For example, you may need to change the case of a letter. If you wanted to change a citation entry, you would perform the following steps.

1. Display formatting marks.
2. Locate the TA field for the citation entry you wish to change.
3. Change the text inside the quotation marks.
4. Update the table of authorities as described in the steps at the end of this section.

To Delete a Citation Entry

If you wanted to delete a citation entry, you would perform the following steps.

1. Display formatting marks.
2. Select the TA field for the citation entry you wish to delete.
3. Press the DELETE key, or click the Cut button (Home tab | Clipboard group), or right-click the field and then click Cut on the mini toolbar or shortcut menu.
4. Update the table of authorities as described in the steps at the end of this section.

To Build a Table of Authorities

Once all citations are marked, Word can build a table of authorities from the citation entries in the document. Recall that citation entries begin with TA, and they appear on the screen when formatting marks are displayed. When citation entries show on the screen, the document's pagination probably will be altered because of the extra text in the citation entries. Thus, be sure to hide formatting marks before building a table of authorities. To build a table of authorities, you would perform the following steps.

1. Position the insertion point at the location for the table of authorities.
2. Ensure that formatting marks are not displayed.

3. Click the 'Insert Table of Authorities' button (References tab | Table of Authorities group) to display the Table of Authorities dialog box.

4. If necessary, select the category to appear in the table of authorities by clicking the desired option in the Category list, or leave the default selection of All so that all categories will be displayed in the table of authorities.

5. If necessary, click the Formats arrow (Table of Authorities dialog box) and then select the desired format for the table of authorities.

6. If necessary, click the Tab leader arrow and then select the desired leader character in the list to specify the leader character to be displayed between the marked citation and the page number.

7. If you wish to display the word, passim, instead of page numbers for citations with more than four page references, select the Use passim check box.

Q&A What does the word, passim, mean?
Here and there.

8. Click the OK button (Table of Authorities dialog box) to create a table of authorities using the specified settings at the location of the insertion point.

TO UPDATE A TABLE OF AUTHORITIES

If you add, delete, or modify citation entries, you must update the table of authorities to display the new or modified citation entries. If you wanted to update a table of authorities, you would perform the following steps.

1. In the document window, click the table of authorities to select it.

2. Click the 'Update Table of Authorities' button (References tab | Table of Authorities group) or press the F9 key to update the table of authorities.

TO CHANGE THE FORMAT OF THE TABLE OF AUTHORITIES

If you wanted to change the format of the table of authorities, you would perform the following steps.

1. Click the table of authorities to select it.

2. Click the 'Insert Table of Authorities' button (References tab | Table of Authorities group) to display the Table of Authorities dialog box.

3. Change settings in the dialog box as desired. To change the style of headings, alignment, etc., click the Formats arrow and then click From template; next, click the Modify button to display the Style dialog box, make necessary changes, and then click the OK button (Style dialog box).

4. Click the OK button (Table of Authorities dialog box) to apply the changed settings.

5. Click the OK button when Word asks if you want to replace the selected category of the table of authorities.

To Delete a Table of Authorities

If you wanted to delete a table of authorities, you would perform the following steps.

1. Click the table of authorities to select it.
2. Press SHIFT+F9 to display field codes.
3. Drag through the entire field code, including the braces, and then press the DELETE key, or click the Cut button (Home tab | Clipboard group), or right-click the field and then click Cut on the mini toolbar or shortcut menu.

Working with XML

You can convert an online form to the XML format so that the data in the form can be shared with other programs, such as Microsoft Access. XML is a popular format for structuring data, which allows the data to be reused and shared. **XML**, which stands for Extensible Markup Language, is a language used to encapsulate data and a description of the data in a single text file, the **XML file**. XML uses **tags** to describe data items. Each data item is called an **element**. Businesses often create standard XML file layouts and tags to describe commonly used types of data.

In Word, you can save a file in a default XML format, in which Word parses the document into individual components that can be used by other programs. Or, you can identify specific sections of the document as XML elements; the elements then can be used in other programs, such as Access. This feature may not be available in all versions of Word.

To Save a Document in the Default XML Format

If you wanted to save a document in the XML format, you would perform the following steps.

1. Open the file to be saved in the XML format (for example, a form containing content controls).
2. Open the Backstage view and then click Save As to display the Save As gallery.
3. Navigate to the desired save location and then display the Save As dialog box.
4. Click the 'Save as type' arrow (Save As dialog box), click 'Word XML Document' in the list, and then click the Save button to save the template as an XML document.

Q&A How can I identify an XML document?

XML documents typically have an .xml extension.

To Attach a Schema File

To identify sections of a document as XML elements, you first attach an XML schema to the document, usually one that contains content controls. An **XML schema** is a special type of XML file that describes the layout of elements in other XML files. Word users typically do not create XML schema files. Software developers or other technical personnel create an XML schema file and provide it to Word users. XML schema files, often simply called **schema files**, usually have an extension of .xsd. Once the schema is attached, you can use the XML Mapping Pane (Developer tab |

Mapping group) to insert controls from the schema into the document. If you wanted to attach a schema file to a document, such as an online form, you would perform the following steps.

1. Open the file to which you wish to attach the schema, such as an online form that contains content controls.

2. Open the Backstage view and then use the Save As command to save the file with a new file name, to preserve the contents of the original file.

3. Click the Document Template button (Developer tab | Templates group) to display the Templates and Add-ins dialog box.

4. Click the XML Schema tab (Templates and Add-ins dialog box) to display the XML Schema sheet and then click the Add Schema button to display the Add Schema dialog box.

5. Locate and select the schema file (Add Schema dialog box) and then click the Open button to display the Schema Settings dialog box.

6. Enter the URI and alias in the appropriate text boxes (Schema Settings dialog box) and then click the OK button to add the schema to the Schema Library and to add the namespace alias to the list of available schemas in the XML Schema sheet (Templates and Add-ins dialog box).

Q&A

What is a URI and an alias?

Word uses the URI, also called a **namespace**, to refer to the schema. Because these names are difficult to remember, you can define a namespace alias. In a setting outside of an academic environment, a computer administrator would provide you with the appropriate namespace entry.

7. If necessary, place a check mark in the desired schema's check box.

8. Click the OK button, which causes Word to attach the selected schema to the open document and open the XML Structure task pane in the Word window.

TO DELETE A SCHEMA FROM THE SCHEMA LIBRARY

To delete a schema from a document, you would remove the check mark from the schema name's check box in the XML Schema sheet in the Templates and Add-ins dialog box. If you wanted to delete a schema altogether from the Schema Library, you would do the following.

1. Click the Document Template button (Developer tab | Templates group) to display the Templates and Add-ins dialog box.

2. Click the XML Schema tab (Templates and Add-ins dialog box) to display the XML Schema sheet and then click the Schema Library button to display the Schema Library dialog box.

3. Click the schema you want to delete in the Select a schema list (Schema Library dialog box) and then click the Delete Schema button.

4. When Word displays the Schema Library dialog box asking if you are sure you wish to delete the schema, click the Yes button.

5. Click the OK button (Schema Library dialog box) and then click the Cancel button (Templates and Add-ins dialog box).

BTW

Opening Files
In addition to current and previous versions of Word documents and templates, XML and PDF files, and webpage files, all discussed previously, you can open a variety of other types of documents through the Open dialog box, including rich text format, text files, OpenDocument text, WordPerfect files, and Works files. To open these documents, open the Backstage view, click the Open tab to display the Open gallery, click the Browse button to display the Open dialog box, click the file type arrow (Open dialog box), click the desired file type to open, locate the file, and then click the Open button to open the file and display its contents in a Word window. Through the Save dialog box, you can save these open files in their native format or save them as a Word document or template.

Summary

In this module, you learned how to enhance the look of text and graphics and automate a series of tasks with a macro. You also learned about several supplementary tasks that you should know if you plan to take the certification exam.

What decisions will you need to make when creating macro-enabled and enhanced online forms?

Use these guidelines as you complete the assignments in this module and create your own online forms outside of this class.

1. Save the form to be modified as a macro-enabled template, if you plan to include macros in the template for the form.

2. Enhance the visual appeal of a form.

   a) Arrange data entry fields in logical groups on the form and in an order that users would expect.

   b) Draw the user's attention to important sections.

   c) Use colors and images that complement one another.

3. Add macros to automate tasks.

   a) Record macros, if possible.

   b) If you are familiar with computer programming, write VBA code to extend capabilities of recorded macros.

4. Determine how the form data will be analyzed.

   a) If the data entered in the form will be analyzed by a program outside of Word, create the data entry fields so that the entries are stored in a format that can be shared with other programs.

Apply Your Knowledge

Reinforce the skills and apply the concepts you learned in this module.

Working with Graphics, Shapes, and Fields

Note: To complete this assignment, you will be required to use the Data Files. Please contact your instructor for information about accessing the Data Files.

Instructions: Run Word. Open the template, Apply 11-1 Realtor Client Survey, from the Data Files. In this assignment, you add an artistic effect to pictures, group images, change a shape, use a texture fill effect, and insert a date field (Figure 11–67).

Perform the following tasks:

1. Unprotect the template.
2. Apply the Glow Diffused artistic effect to the sale sign image (the image to the right in the Data File). Change the color saturation of the same image (the sale sign) to 400%. Apply the following glow effect to the SOLD stamp image: Orange, 5 pt glow, Accent color 2. *Hint:* Picture Effects button (Picture Tools Format tab | Picture Styles group).
3. Move the SOLD stamp image on top of the sale sign image as shown in Figure 11–67. Group the two sale sign and SOLD stamp images together. Move the grouped images down so that the base of the sign post is even with the instruction line.
4. Change the page color to the Recycled paper texture fill effect.
5. Change the shape around the data entry area from Rectangle to Snip Single Corner Rectangle.

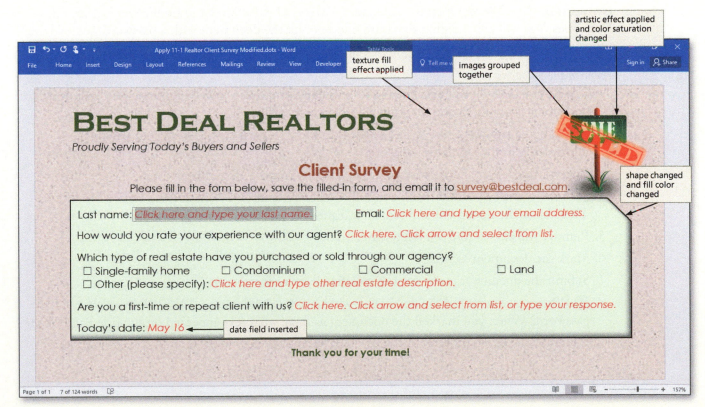

Figure 11–67

Continued >

Apply Your Knowledge *continued*

6. Change the fill color of the rectangle shape to Lime, Accent 4, Lighter 80%.

7. Apply the Inside Diagonal Bottom Right shadow to the rectangle shape.

8. Display the Developer tab. Change the properties of the date picker content control so that its contents can be deleted and then delete the content control. Insert a date field after the Today's Date: label in the format month day (i.e., September 13). Change the format of the displayed date field to Intense Emphasis. Hide the Developer tab.

9. If requested by your instructor, change the email address on the form to your email address.

10. Protect the form. Save the modified form using the file name, Apply 11-1 Realtor Client Survey Modified. Submit the revised template in the format specified by your instructor.

11. ✳ If you wanted to change the picture on the form, you could delete the current pictures and then insert new ones, or you could use the Change Picture button (Picture Tools Format tab | Adjust group). Which technique would you use and why?

Extend Your Knowledge

Extend the skills you learned in this module and experiment with new skills. You may need to use Help to complete the assignment.

Working with Document Security

Note: To complete this assignment, you will be required to use the Data Files. Please contact your instructor for information about accessing the Data Files.

Instructions: Run Word. Open the document, Extend 11-1 Billing Issue Letter Draft, from the Data Files. You will add a digital signature line, encrypt the document with a password, remove the password, and mark the document as final.

Perform the following tasks:

1. Use Help to review and expand your knowledge about these topics: signature lines, passwords, document encryption, and marking the document as final.

2. Add a digital signature line to end of the document (Figure 11–68). Use your personal information in the signature line.

3. Encrypt the document. Be sure to use a password you will remember.

4. Save the revised document with a new file name, Extend 11-1 Billing Issue Letter Modified. Then, close the document and reopen it. Enter the password when prompted.

5. Remove the password from the document.

6. Mark the document as final.

7. Submit the document in the format specified by your instructor.

8. ✳ When you encrypted the document, what password did you use? Why did you choose that password? When you marked the document as final, what text appeared on the title bar? What text appeared in the Message Bar? What appeared on the status bar?

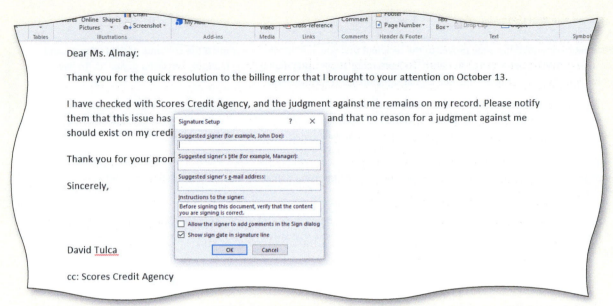

Figure 11–68

Expand Your World

Create a solution that uses cloud or web technologies by learning and investigating on your own from general guidance.

Obtaining Digital IDs

Instructions: You are interested in obtaining a digital ID so that you can digitally sign your documents in Word. You plan to research various digital ID services to determine the one best suited to your needs.

Perform the following tasks:
1. Run Word. Open the Backstage view and then, if necessary, display the Info tab. Click the Protect Document button and then click 'Add a Digital Signature' on the Protect Document menu.

2. When Word displays the Get a Digital ID dialog box, click the Yes button, which runs a browser and displays an Office Help window with a list of services that issue digital IDs (Figure 11–69).

3. Click the link beside each service to learn more about each one.

4. Use a search engine to read reviews about these services.

5. Compose a Word document comparing and contrasting the digital ID services suggested by Microsoft. Be sure to cite your sources. In your report, recommend the service you feel best suits your needs.

6. ✳ Which digital ID services did you evaluate? When you read the reviews, were there other services not listed on the Office website? If so, what were their names? Which digital ID service would you recommend? Why?

Continued >

Expand Your World *continued*

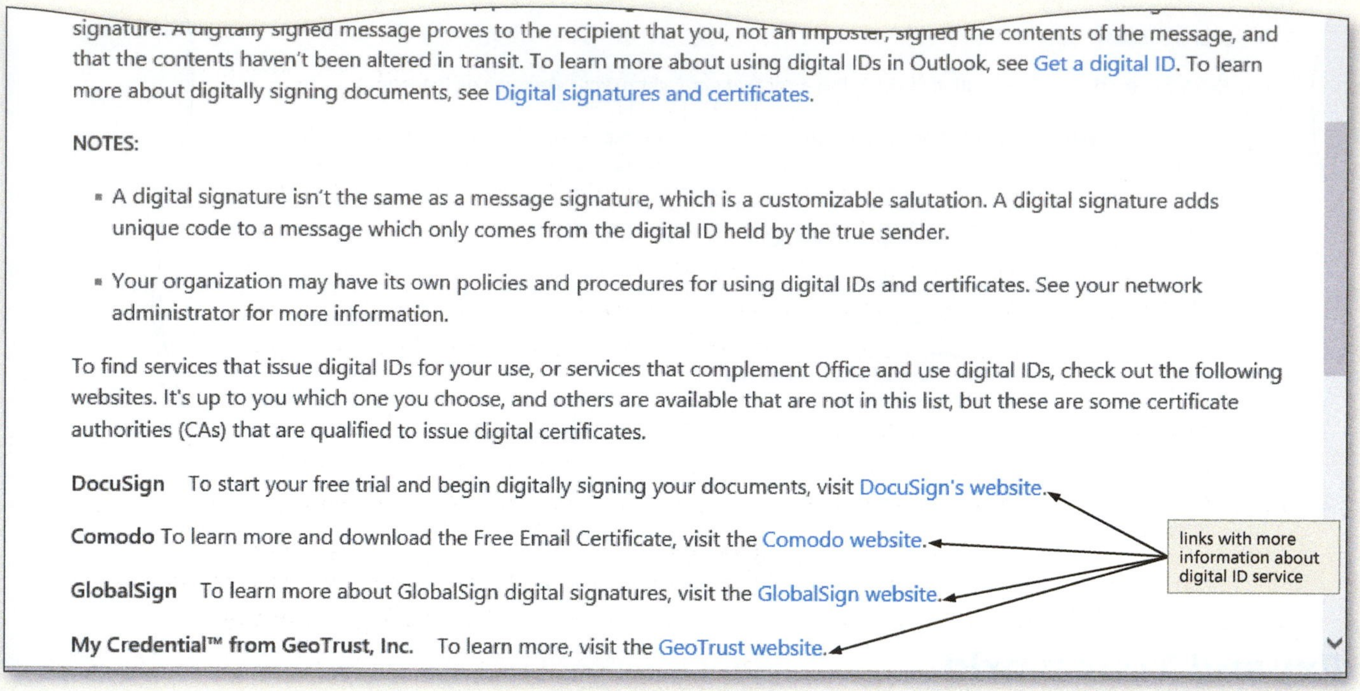

signature. A digitally signed message proves to the recipient that you, not an imposter, signed the contents of the message, and that the contents haven't been altered in transit. To learn more about using digital IDs in Outlook, see Get a digital ID. To learn more about digitally signing documents, see Digital signatures and certificates.

NOTES:

- A digital signature isn't the same as a message signature, which is a customizable salutation. A digital signature adds unique code to a message which only comes from the digital ID held by the true sender.

- Your organization may have its own policies and procedures for using digital IDs and certificates. See your network administrator for more information.

To find services that issue digital IDs for your use, or services that complement Office and use digital IDs, check out the following websites. It's up to you which one you choose, and others are available that are not in this list, but these are some certificate authorities (CAs) that are qualified to issue digital certificates.

DocuSign To start your free trial and begin digitally signing your documents, visit DocuSign's website.

Comodo To learn more and download the Free Email Certificate, visit the Comodo website.

GlobalSign To learn more about GlobalSign digital signatures, visit the GlobalSign website.

My Credential™ from GeoTrust, Inc. To learn more, visit the GeoTrust website.

links with more information about digital ID service

Figure 11–69

In the Labs

Design, create, modify, and/or use a document following the guidelines, concepts, and skills presented in this module. Labs 1 and 2, which increase in difficulty, require you to create solutions based on what you learned in the module; Lab 3 requires you to apply your creative thinking and problem-solving skills to design and implement a solution.

Lab 1: Enhancing the Graphics, Shapes, and Text Boxes on an Online Form

Problem: You created the Dee's Dog Grooming online form shown in Figure 10–78 in the Student Assignments for Module 10. Your aunt has asked you to change the form's appearance and add a text box. You modify the form so that it looks like the one shown in Figure 11–70.

Perform the following tasks:

1. Open the template called Lab 10-1 Dog Grooming Request Form that you created in the Lab 1 Student Assignment in Module 10. Save the template with a new file name of Lab 11-1 Dog Grooming Request Form Modified. If you did not complete the lab in Module 10, see your instructor for a copy. Unprotect the template.

2. Use the Water droplets texture fill effect for the page color.

3. Modify the formats of the company name, business tag line, form title, user instruction, and thank you lines as shown in Figure 11–70 (or with similar fonts). If requested by your instructor, change the first word in the business name from Dee's to your first name.

4. Use the picture fill effect to place a picture in the rectangle shape. Use the picture called Paw-Prints-Heart from the Data Files. Change the color of the picture in the rectangle to Washout.

5. Create a character style, with the name Data Entry Labels, for all labels in the data entry that starts with the current format and uses 11-point bold Calibri font, and a color of Gold, Accent 5.

6. Change the shape of the rectangle to Snip and Round Single Corner Rectangle. If necessary, change the shape outline color (border) to Gold, Accent 5, Darker 50%.

7. Apply the Offset Right shadow effect to the rectangle shape. Change the shadow color to Gold, Accent 5, Darker 25%. Change the transparency of the shadow to 20%.

8. Modify the Intense Emphasis style to the color Purple, Accent 1, Darker 25% and apply the bold and italic formats.

9. Change the image on the right to the picture called Dog from the Data Files. Resize the image as shown. Remove the background, as shown in the figure. Change the Color Tone to Temperature: 11200 K. Save the modified image with the file name, Dog Modified.

10. Draw a text box that is approximately 0.5" × 1.1" that contains the text, Your Dog Will Love Us!, centered in the text box. Apply the Colored Outline - Gold, Accent 5 shape style to the text box. Apply the Off Axis 2 Left 3-D rotation to the text box. Add an Offset Diagonal Bottom Right shadow to this text box. Position the text box as shown in the figure.

11. Adjust spacing above and below paragraphs as necessary so that all contents fit on a single screen. Protect the form. Save the form again and submit it in the format specified by your instructor.

12. Access the template through File Explorer. Fill in the form using personal data and submit the filled-in form in the format specified by your instructor.

13. ✸ What is the advantage of creating a style for the data entry labels?

Figure 11–70

Continued >

In the Labs continued

Lab 2: Enhancing the Look of an Online Form and Adding Macros to the Form

Problem: You created the Antwon's DJ Service online form shown in Figure 10–79 in the Student Assignments in Module 10. Your supervisor has asked you to change the form's appearance, add a field, and add some macros. You modify the form so that it looks like the one shown in Figure 11–71.

Perform the following tasks:

1. Open the template called Lab 10-2 DJ Customer Survey that you created in Lab 2 of Module 10. Save the template as a macro-enabled template with a new file name of Lab 11-2 DJ Customer Survey Modified. If you did not complete the lab in Module 10, see your instructor for a copy. Unprotect the template.

2. Change the document theme to Circuit.

3. Use the Newsprint texture fill effect for the page color.

4. Change the fill color in the rectangle shape to Red, Accent 3, Lighter 80%. Change the shape outline to small dots. Change the outline color to Red, Accent 3, Darker 25%. Change the shape shadow to Inside Center.

5. Modify the formats of the company name, business tag line, form title, user instruction, and thank you line as shown in Figure 11–71 (or with similar fonts).

6. Convert the table to text for the 2 × 1 table containing the First Name and Last Name content controls. Change the left indent to 0.06" on these two lines.

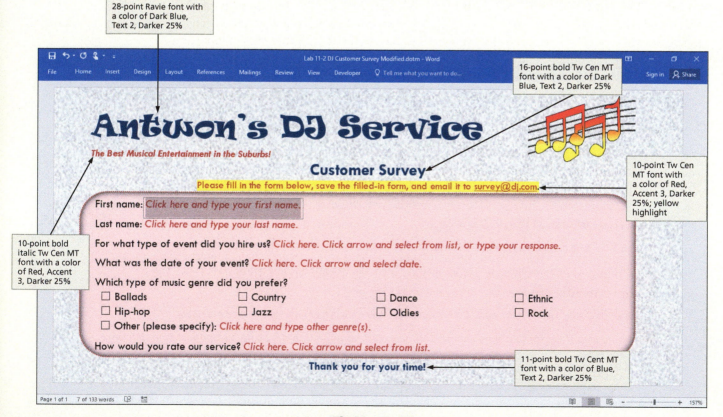

Figure 11–71

7. Modify the Intense Emphasis style to Red, Accent 3, Darker 25%.

8. Adjust spacing above and below paragraphs as necessary so that all contents fit on a single screen. If necessary, adjust the rectangle so that it covers the entire data entry area.

9. Change the current image to the one shown in the figure (or a similar image). The image in the figure is called Music-Notes on the Data Files. Resize the image and position it as shown.

10. Record a macro that hides the formatting marks and the rulers. Name it HideScreenElements. Store it in Documents Based On Lab 11-2 DJ Customer Survey Modified template. Assign it the shortcut key, ALT+H. Run the macro to test it.

11. Add a button to the Quick Access Toolbar for the macro created in Step 10. Test the button and then delete the button from the Quick Access Toolbar.

12. Create an automatic macro called AutoNew using the macro recorder. Store it in Documents Based On Lab 11-2 DJ Customer Survey Modified template. The macro should change the view to page width.

13. Edit the AutoNew macro so that it also hides the Developer tab and the ribbon.

14. Protect the form. Save the form again and submit it in the format specified by your instructor.

15. Access the template through File Explorer. Fill in the form and submit the filled-in form in the format specified by your instructor.

16. ✹ If a recorded macro does not work as intended when you test it, how would you fix it?

Lab 3: Consider This: Your Turn

Modify an Online Form for a Deli

Problem: You created the deli customer survey online form that was defined in the Lab 3: Consider This: Your Turn assignment in Module 10. Your supervisor was pleased with the initial design. You and your supervisor, however, believe the form can be improved by enhancing its appearance.

Part 1: Make the following modifications to the deli customer survey form that you created in Module 10. (If you did not complete the lab in Module 10, see your instructor for a copy.) Change the font and color of the deli name, tag line, and form title; change the page color to a texture; change the highlight color; and change the font and color of the last line. Change the rectangle shape around the data entry area. In the rectangle, add a picture fill effect using an image of a submarine sandwich (one is available on the Data Files for use, if desired) and recolor it as necessary. Change the color of the shadow in the rectangle. Delete the existing image on the form, replace it with an image of vegetables (one is available on the Data Files for use, if desired), and apply an artistic effect to the image. Draw a text box with the text, Mmm…Mmm…Good!, and apply a 3-D effect to the text box.

Specify the appropriate macro security level. Record a macro that hides screen elements and then assign the macro to a button on the Quick Access Toolbar. Record another macro for a task you would like to automate. Add another button to the Quick Access Toolbar for any Word command not on the ribbon.

Use the concepts and techniques presented in this module to modify the online form. Be sure to save it as a macro-enabled template. Protect the form, test it, and submit it in the format specified by your instructor.

Part 2: ✹ You made several decisions while creating the online form in this assignment: formats to use (i.e., fonts, font sizes, colors, styles, etc.), graphics to use, which task to automate, and which button to add to the Quick Access Toolbar. What was the rationale behind each of these decisions? When you proofread and tested the online form, what further revisions did you make, and why?

Index

Note: **Boldfaced** page numbers indicate key terms

3-D effects, online form revised, WD 647